Frommer's®

Hawaii

Here's what the critics say about Frommer's:

"Amazingly easy to use. Very portable, very complete."
—*Booklist*

◆

"The only mainstream guide to list specific prices. The Walter Cronkite of guidebooks—with all that implies."
—*Travel & Leisure*

◆

"Complete, concise, and filled with useful information."
—*New York Daily News*

◆

"Hotel information is close to encyclopedic."
—*Des Moines Sunday Register*

Other Great Guides for Your Trip:

Hawaii from $60 a Day

Frommer's Maui

Frommer's Honolulu, Waikiki & Oahu

The Complete Idiot's Guide to Hawaii

Frommer's® 99

Hawaii

by Jeanette Foster & Jocelyn Fujii

MACMILLAN • USA

ABOUT THE AUTHORS

A resident of the Big Island, **Jeanette Foster** has skied the slopes of Mauna Kea—during a Fourth of July ski meet, no less—and scuba dived with manta rays off the Kona Coast. A prolific writer widely published in travel, sports, and adventure magazines, she's also a contributing editor to *Hawaii* magazine.

Kauai-born **Jocelyn Fujii**, a resident of Honolulu, is one of Hawaii's leading journalists. She has authored *Under the Hula Moon: Living in Hawaii* and *The Best of Hawaii*, as well as articles for the *New York Times*, *National Geographic Traveler*, *Islands*, *Condé Nast Traveler*, *Travel Holiday*, and other national and international publications.

In addition to this guide, Jeanette and Jocelyn also co-authored *Frommer's Hawaii from $60 a Day*; *Frommer's Honolulu, Waikiki & Oahu*; and *Frommer's Maui*.

Find us online at **www.frommers.com**

MACMILLAN TRAVEL

A Simon & Schuster Macmillan Company
1633 Broadway
New York, NY 10019

Copyright © 1998 by Simon & Schuster, Inc.
Maps copyright © 1998 by Simon & Schuster, Inc.

ISBN 0-02-862243-X
ISSN 1090-3180

Editor: Cheryl Farr
Thanks to Lisa Renaud and Leslie Shen
Production Editor: Chrisy Wagner
Photo Editor: Richard Fox
Design by Michele Laseau
Digital Cartography by Peter Bogary, Roberta Stockwell, and Ortelius Design
Front cover photo: Makena Beach, Maui

SPECIAL SALES

Bulk purchases (10+ copies) of Frommer's and selected Macmillan travel guides are available to corporations, organizations, mail-order catalogs, institutions, and charities at special discounts, and can be customized to suit individual needs. For more information write to Special Sales, Macmillan General Reference, 1633 Broadway, New York, NY 10019.

Manufactured in the United States of America

Contents

List of Maps

AN INVITATION TO THE READER

In researching this book, we discovered many wonderful places—hotels, restaurants, shops, and more. We're sure you'll find others. Please tell us about them, so we can share the information with your fellow travelers in upcoming editions. If you were disappointed with a recommendation, we'd love to know that, too. Please write to:

Frommer's Hawaii '99
Macmillan Travel
1633 Broadway
New York, NY 10019

AN ADDITIONAL NOTE

Please be advised that travel information is subject to change at any time—and this is especially true of prices. We therefore suggest that you write or call ahead for confirmation when making your travel plans. The authors, editors, and publisher cannot be held responsible for the experiences of readers while traveling. Your safety is important to us, however, so we encourage you to stay alert and be aware of your surroundings. Keep a close eye on cameras, purses, and wallets, all favorite targets of thieves and pickpockets.

WHAT THE SYMBOLS MEAN

✪ Frommer's Favorites

Hotels, restaurants, attractions, and entertainment you should not miss.

The following abbreviations are used for credit cards:

AE	American Express	EURO	Eurocard
CB	Carte Blanche	JCB	Japan Credit Bank
DC	Diners Club	MC	MasterCard
DISC	Discover	V	Visa

FIND FROMMER'S ONLINE

Arthur Frommer's Outspoken Encyclopedia of Travel (**www.frommers.com**) offers more than 6,000 pages of up-to-the-minute travel information—including the latest bargains and candid, personal articles updated daily by Arthur Frommer himself. No other Web site offers such comprehensive and timely coverage of the world of travel.

Hotel Tax Update

Just as this book went to press, the Governer of Hawaii signed into law an increase in hotel occupancy tax from 6% to 7.25%. All hotel stays that begin on or after January 1, 1999 will be taxed at 11.41% (7.25% plus 4.16% in sales and general exise tax).

The Best of Hawaii

Hawaii is an exceptional place. The islands brim with superlatives, from America's best beaches to world-class resorts, and there's more than enough to see and do here to keep you busy for a lifetime, let alone a short vacation. It can be bewildering to plan your trip with so many options vying for your attention. To make your task easier, we've chosen what we believe to be the very best that Hawaii has to offer—the places and experiences you won't want to miss.

1 The Best Beaches

- **Lanikai Beach** (Oahu): Too gorgeous to be real, this stretch along the Windward Coast is one of Hawaii's postcard-perfect beaches—a mile of golden sand as soft as powdered sugar bordering translucent turquoise waters. The year-round swimming-pool-calm waters are excellent for swimming, snorkeling, and kayaking. To complete the picture are two tiny offshore islands that function not only as scenic backdrops but also as bird sanctuaries. See chapter 5.

- **Hapuna Beach** (Big Island): This half-mile-long crescent regularly wins kudos in the world's top travel magazines as the most beautiful beach in Hawaii—and some even consider it one of the most beautiful beaches in the whole world. One look, and you'll see why: perfect cream-colored sand slopes down to crystal-clear water that's great for swimming, snorkeling, and bodysurfing in summer; come winter, waves thunder in like stampeding wild horses. Great facilities for picnicking and camping, and plenty of parking for a day at the beach. See chapter 6.

- **Kapalua Beach** (Maui): On an island of many great beaches, this one takes the prize. A golden crescent with swaying palms protected from strong winds and currents by two outstretched lava-rock promontories, Kapalua has calm waters that are perfect for snorkeling, swimming, and kayaking. Even though it borders the Kapalua Bay Hotel, the beach is long enough for everyone to enjoy. Facilities include showers, rest rooms, and lifeguards. See chapter 7.

- **Papohaku Beach** (Molokai): One of Hawaii's longest beaches, this gold-sand beach stretches on for some 3 miles, and it's about as wide as a football field. Offshore, the ocean churns mightily in winter, but the waves lie down in summer, making the calm waters inviting for swimming. Papohaku is also great for picnics, beach walks, and sunset watching. See chapter 8.

- **Hulopoe Beach** (Lanai): This golden, palm-fringed beach off the south coast of Lanai gently slopes down to the azure waters of a Marine Life Conservation District, where clouds of tropical fish flourish and spinner dolphins come to play. A tide pool in the lava rocks defines one side of the bay, while the other is lorded over by the Manele Bay Hotel, sitting prominently on the hill above. Offshore, you'll find good swimming, snorkeling, and diving; onshore, there's a full complement of beach facilities, from rest rooms to camping areas. See chapter 9.

- **Haena Beach** (Kauai): Backed by verdant Bali Ha'i–like cliffs, this curvaceous beach has starred as Paradise in many a movie. It's easy to see why Hollywood loves this North Shore beach, with its grainy golden sand and translucent turquoise waters. Summer months bring calm waters for swimming and snorkeling, while winter brings mighty waves for surfers. There are plenty of facilities on hand, including picnic tables, rest rooms, and showers. See chapter 10.

2 The Best Island Experiences

- **Go to the Beach:** A beach is a beach is a beach, right? Not in Hawaii. With 132 islets, shoals, and reefs and a general coastline of 750 miles, Hawaii has beaches in all different sizes, shapes, and colors, from white to black; the variety on the six major islands is astonishing. You could go to a different beach every day for years and still not see them all. For the best of a spectacular bunch, see "The Best Beaches," above, as well as the "Beaches" sections in chapters 5 through 10.

- **Take the Plunge:** Don mask, fin, and snorkel and explore the magical world beneath the surface, where you'll find exotic corals and kaleidoscopic clouds of tropical fish; a sea turtle may even come over to check you out. Can't swim? That's no excuse—take one of the many submarine tours offered by **Atlantis Submarines** (☎ **888/REAL-SUB**), from Oahu, the Big Island, and Maui. See chapters 5, 6, and 7.

- **Meet Local Folks:** If you go to Hawaii and only see people like those you see back home, you might as well stay home. Extend yourself, leave the resorts and tourist quarters, go out and meet the locals, learn about Hawaii and its people. Just smile and say "Owzit?"—which means "How is it?" "It's good," is the usual response— and you'll usually make a new friend. Hawaii is remarkably cosmopolitan; every ethnic group in the world seems to be here. It's delightful to discover the varieties of food, culture, language, and customs. See the individual island chapters for suggestions on where to start making friends.

- **Watch for Whales:** If you happen to be in Hawaii during humpback-whale season—roughly December to April—when Hawaii's most impressive visitors return to winter in the offshore waters, don't miss the opportunity to see these gentle giants. A host of boats—from small inflatables to high-tech, high-speed sailing catamarans—offer a range of whale-watching cruises on every island. One of our favorites is along the Big Island's Kona Coast, where **Capt. Dan McSweeney's Year-Round Whale-Watching Adventure** (☎ **808/322-0028**) takes you right to the whales year-round, since pilot, sperm, false killer, melon-headed, pygmy killer, and beaked whales call Hawaii home even when humpbacks aren't in residence. A whale researcher for more than 20 years, Capt. Dan frequently drops an underwater microphone or video camera into the depths so you can listen to whale songs and maybe actually see what's going on. See "Hitting the Water" in chapters 5, 6, 7, and 10.

- **Experience a Turning Point in America's History—the Bombing of Pearl Harbor** (Oahu): The United States could turn its back on World War II no longer after that fateful day—December 7, 1941, the day that Japanese warplanes bombed Pearl Harbor. Standing on the deck of the USS *Arizona* Memorial, which stands as an eternal tomb for the 1,177 sailors and Marines trapped below when the battleship sank in just 9 minutes, is a moving experience you'll never forget. Admission is absolutely free. See chapter 5.

- **Creeping Up to the Ooze** (Big Island): Kilauea volcano has been adding land to the Big Island continuously since 1983. If conditions are right, you can walk up to the red-hot lava and watch it ooze along, or you can stand at the shoreline and watch with awe as 2,000° molten fire pours into the ocean. Or take to the air in a helicopter and see the Volcano Goddess's work from above. See chapter 6.

- **Big-Game Fishing off the Kona Coast** (Big Island): Don't pass up the opportunity to go try your luck in the sportfishing capital of the world, where 1,000-pound marlin are taken from the seas just about every month of the year. Not looking to set a world record? Kona's charter-boat captains specialize in conservation and will be glad to "tag and release" any fish you angle, letting it go so someone else can have the fun of fighting a big-game fish tomorrow. See chapter 6.

- **Greet the Rising Sun from atop Haleakala** (Maui): Bundle up in warm clothing, fill a thermos full of hot java, and drive up to the summit to watch the sky turn from inky black to muted charcoal as a small sliver of orange color forms on the horizon. There's something about standing at 10,000 feet, breathing in the rarefied air and watching the first rays of light streak across the sky, that makes it a mystical experience of the first magnitude. See chapter 7.

- **Take a Day Trip to Lanai** (Maui): If you'd like to visit Lanai, but you only have a day to spare, consider taking a day trip there. **Trilogy Excursions** (☎ 800/874-2666 or 808/661-4743) offers a day-long sailing, snorkeling, and whale-watching adventure; they're the only outfitter with rights to Hulupoe Beach, and the trip includes a minivan tour of the little isle (pop. 3,500). Or take **Expedition's Lahaina/Lanai Passenger Ferry** (☎ 808/661-3756) from Maui to Lanai and rent a four-wheel-drive Land Rover from **Red Rover** (☎ 808/565-7722) for a day of backcountry exploring and beach fun. See chapter 9.

- **Ride a Mule to Kalaupapa** (Molokai): Even if you have only 1 day to spend on Molokai, spend it on a mule. The trek from "topside" Molokai to Kalaupapa National Historic Park, Father Damien's world-famous leper colony, with **Molokai Mule Ride** (☎ 800/567-7550 or 808/567-6088) is a once-in-a-lifetime adventure. The cliffs are taller than 300-story skyscrapers—but Buzzy Sproat's sure-footed mules go up and down the narrow 2.9-mile trail daily, rain or shine, without ever losing a rider or mount on 26 switchbacks. Even if you can't afford to mule or heli-copter in, don't pass up the opportunity to see this hauntingly beautiful peninsula. It takes nothing more than a pair of hiking boots, a permit (available at the trail-head), and some grit to hike down the trail. The views are breathtaking; You'll see the world's highest sea cliffs and waterfalls plunging thousands of feet into the ocean. See chapter 8.

- **Fly Over the Na Pali Coast** (Kauai): Streaking low over razor-thin cliffs, fluttering past sparkling waterfalls and down into the canyons and valleys of the fabled Na Pali Coast—it's like flying in your dreams, except there's too much beauty to absorb, and it all goes by in a rush. You'll never want to stop flying over this spectacular, surreal landscape. This is the only way to see the dazzling beauty of Kauai. See chapter 10.

3   The Best of Natural Hawaii

Mother Nature pulled out all the stops when she went to work on these islands. Simply put, this is Hawaii at its finest.

- **Volcanoes:** The entire island chain is made of volcanoes; don't miss the opportunity to see one. On Maui, **Haleakala National Park** provides a bird's-eye view into a long-dormant volcanic crater; on Oahu, the entire family can hike to the top of the ancient volcano, world-famous **Diamond Head.** At the other end of the spectrum is fire-breathing Kilauea at **Hawaii Volcanoes National Park,** on the Big Island, where you can creep right up to the ooze for an up-close-and-personal experience with the red-hot lava. See chapters 5, 6, and 7.

- **Waterfalls:** Rushing waterfalls thundering downward into sparkling freshwater pools—they're some of Hawaii's most beautiful natural wonders. If you're on the Big Island, stop by **Rainbow Falls** in Hilo, or spectacular 442-foot **Akaka Falls,** just outside the city. On Maui, the Road to Hana offers numerous viewing opportunities; at the end of the road, you'll find **Oheo Gulch** (also known as the Seven Sacred Pools), some of the most dramatic and accessible waterfalls on the islands. While you're on Oahu, check out the awe-inspiring **Sacred Falls,** which end in a deep, boulder-strewn pool. Kauai is abundant with waterfalls, especially along the North Shore and in the Wailua area, where you'll find 40-foot **Opaekaa Falls,** probably the best-looking drive-up waterfall on Kauai; with scenic mountain peaks in the background and a restored Hawaiian village on the nearby river banks, it's what the tourist-bureau folks call an "eye-popping" photo op. See chapters 5, 6, 7, and 10.

- **Gardens:** The islands radiate with sweet-smelling flowers. For a glimpse at the full breadth and beauty of Hawaii's spectacular range of tropical flora, we suggest spending an afternoon at one of Hawaii's lush gardens. On Oahu, **Foster Garden** is a leafy oasis amid the high-rises of downtown Honolulu, showcasing 24 native Hawaiian trees and the last stand of several rare trees, including an East African whose white flowers bloom only at night. On the Big Island, **Liliuokalani Gardens,** the largest formal Japanese garden this side of Tokyo, resembles a postcard from the Orient with bonsai, carp ponds, pagodas, and even a moon gate bridge. Hawaii's exotic flora is also on display at Maui's **Kula Botanical Garden,** where you can take a leisurely self-guided stroll through more than 700 native and exotic plants, including orchids, proteas, and bromeliads. On lush Kauai, the **National Tropical Botanical Gardens** has an extraordinary collection of tropical fruit and spice trees, rare Hawaiian plants, and hundreds of varieties of flowers; nearby **Allerton Gardens,** the site of Queen Emma's royal home in the 1860s, is known for its formal gardens, which illustrate a delicious kind of colonial decadence. See chapters 5, 6, 7, and 10.

- **Marine Life Conservation Areas:** These Neptunian worlds possess a sensual kind of serenity that's unmatched in the world above the waves. Nine underwater parks are spread across Hawaii, most notably **Waikiki Beach** and **Hanauma Bay,** on Oahu; the Big Island's **Kealakekua Bay; Molokini,** just off the coast of Maui; and Lanai's **Manele and Hulopoe bays.** Be sure to take some snorkel gear to at least one of these wonderful places while you're in the islands. See chapters 5, 6, 7, and 9.

- **Garden of the Gods** (Lanai): Out on Lanai's North Shore lies the ultimate rock garden: a rugged, barren, beautiful place full of rocks strewn by volcanic forces and shaped by the elements into an infinite variety of shapes and colors: brilliant reds, oranges, ochres, yellows. Scientists have numerous explanations for how these boulders got here and their seemingly random placement with phrases like "ongoing post-erosional event" or "plain and simple badlands." However, the ancient Hawaiians considered this desolate, windswept place an entirely supernatural phenomenon. Natural badlands or mystical garden? Take a four-wheel-drive trip out here and decide for yourself. See chapter 9.

- **The Grand Canyon of the Pacific—Waimea Canyon** (Kauai): This valley, known for its reddish lava beds, reminds everyone who sees it of Arizona's Grand Canyon. Kauai's version is bursting with ever-changing color, just like its namesake, but it's smaller—only a mile wide, 3,567 feet deep, and 12 miles long. All this grandeur was caused by a massive earthquake, which sent all the streams flowing into a single river, which then carved this picturesque canyon—quite an astonishing bit of erosion. You can stop by the road and look at it, hike down in it, or swoop through it in a helicopter. See chapter 10.

4 The Best of Underwater Hawaii

A whole different Hawaii greets anyone with a face mask, snorkel, and fins. Under the sea, you'll find its clouds of brilliant tropical fish, lumbering green sea turtles, quick-moving game fish, slack-jawed moray eels, and prehistoric-looking corals. It's a kaleidoscope of color and wonder

- **Hanauma Bay** (Oahu): It can get crowded, but for clear, warm, calm waters, an abundance of fish that are so friendly they'll swim right up to your face mask, a beautiful setting, and easy access, there's no place like Hanauma Bay. Just wade in waist-deep and look down to see more than 50 species of reef and inshore fish common to Hawaiian waters. Snorkelers hug the safe, shallow inner bay—it's really like swimming in an outdoor aquarium. Serious divers shoot "the slot," a passage through the reef, to enter Witch's Brew, a turbulent cove. See chapter 5.
- **Kahaluu Beach** (Big Island): The calm, shallow waters of Kahaluu are a perfect place to get to know the wonders of the underwater world. This area is great for beginner snorkelers or people who are unsure of their swimming abilities and want the comfort of being able to stand up at any time. The sunlight through the shallow waters casts a dazzling spotlight on the colorful sea life and coral formations. If you listen closely, you can actually hear the parrot fish feeding. See chapter 6.
- **Kealakekua Bay** (Big Island): Mile-wide Kealakekua Bay, at the foot of massive U-shaped sea cliffs, is rich with marine life and snorkelers. And history: A white obelisk marks that spot where, in 1778, the great British navigator Capt. James Cook, who charted most of the Pacific, was killed by Hawaiians. The bay itself is a marine sanctuary that teems with schools of polychromatic tropical fish. See chapter 6.
- **Molokini** (Maui): Like a crescent moon that fell from the sky, the parenthetical islet of Molokini serves on its shallow concave side as a sheltering backstop against sea currents for tiny tropical fish, and on the opposite side as a deep-water cliff inhabited by spiny lobsters, moray eels, and white-tipped sharks. Neo-snorkelers report to the concave side, experienced scuba divers the other. Either way, the clear water and abundant marine life make this islet off the Makena Coast one of Hawaii's most popular dive spots. See chapter 7.
- **Kee Beach** (Kauai): Where the road ends on the North Shore, you'll find a dandy little reddish-gold-sand beach almost too beautiful to be real (don't be surprised if it looks familiar—it was featured in *The Thornbirds*) that fringes a reef-protected cove at the foot of fluted volcanic cliffs. Swimming and snorkeling are safe inside the reef, where long-nosed butterfly fish flitter about and schools of *taape* (bluestripe snapper) swarm over the coral. See chapter 10.

5 The Best Golf Courses

- **Mauna Kea's Beach and Hapuna Courses** (Big Island; ☎ **808/882-7222** for Beach Course, ☎ **808/882-1111** for Hapuna Course): Our on the Kohala Coast, the Mauna Kea Beach Course is everyone's old favorite. One of the first fields of play to be carved out of the black lava, the dramatic, always-challenging, par-72, 18-hole championship course is still one of Hawaii's top three. The new Arnold Palmer/Ed Seay–designed Hapuna Course rests in the rolling foothills above Hapuna Beach Prince Hotel and provides a memorable and scenic links-style golf experience and one of the best views of this unusual coast. See chapter 6.

- **Mauna Lani Resort Courses** (Big Island; ☎ **808/885-6655**): Longtime host of the Senior Skins game, Mauna Lani's two resort courses, North and South, feature a combination of oceanfront and interior lava-lined holes; both combine wonderful scenery with strategic championship-level golf. See chapter 6.

- **Kapalua Resort Courses** (Maui; ☎ **808/669-8044**): Kapalua is probably the best nationally known golf resort in Hawaii, thanks to the Lincoln/Mercury Kapalua International, played here each November. The Bay and Village courses are vintage Arnold Palmer designs, while the new Plantation Course is a strong Ben Crenshaw/Bill Coore design. All are located on Maui's windswept northwestern shore, at the rolling foothills of Puu Kukui, the summit of the West Maui Mountains. See chapter 7.

- **Wailea Resort Courses** (Maui; ☎ **808/879-2966**): On Maui's sun-baked South Shore stands Wailea Resort, *the* hotspot for golf in the islands, where three resort courses complement a string of beachfront hotels. The Blue Course is an Arthur Jack Snyder design, while Robert Trent Jones, Jr., is the mastermind behind the Emerald and Gold courses; all three boast outstanding views of the Pacific and the mid-Hawaiian Islands. See chapter 7.

- **The Lanai Courses** (Lanai; ☎ **808/565-GOLF**): For quality and seclusion, nothing in Hawaii can touch Lanai's two resort offerings: The Ted Robinson and Greg Norman–designed **The Experience at Koele** and the **The Challenge at Manele,** a wonderful Jack Nicklaus effort with ocean views from every hole, both rate among Hawaii's best courses. Both are tremendous fun to play, with the Experience featuring a par-4 8th hole that drops some 150 yards from one cliff side to another over a Pacific inlet—one of the most stunning holes in Hawaii. See chapter 9.

- **Poipu Bay Resort Golf Course** (Kauai; ☎ **808/742-8711**): On Kauai's flat, dry South Shore is a Robert Trent Jones, Jr.–designed course that skirts along dramatic cliffs above the Pacific. The 210-acre links-style course, host to the PGA Tour's Grand Slam of Golf, runs along sheer ocean cliffs and the sandy beach of Keoneloa Bay and offers azure ocean views at every hole. This course boasts some scenically spectacular holes and is a lot of fun to play. Whales, monk seals, and green sea turtles are often seen along the shore, and a flock of native Hawaiian nene geese frequents the course's lakes. See chapter 10.

- **Princeville Golf Club** (Kauai; ☎ **808/826-3580** for Makai Course, ☎ **808/826-5000** for Prince Course): You'll find 45 of the best tropical holes of golf in the world here—all the work of Robert Trent Jones, Jr.—ranging along green bluffs below sharp mountain peaks and offering stunning views in every direction. One of the top three courses in Hawaii, the 18-hole Prince provides a round of golf few ever forget; it winds along 390 acres of scenic table land bisected by tropical jungles, waterfalls, streams, and ravines. The 27-hole championship Makai Course, a favorite tournament spot, is playable for all levels of golfers. See chapter 10.

6 The Best Ways to Immerse Yourself in Hawaiian Culture

- **Experience the Hula:** For just about as long as we can remember, the Eastman Kodak Company has been hosting the **Kodak Hula Show** every Tuesday, Wednesday, and Thursday at the Waikiki Band Shell at Oahu's Kapiolani Park. It's really more '50s nostalgia than ancient culture, but it's a good bit of fun any way you slice it. Some 1,500 people flock to the shows, which are absolutely free. For a more authentic hula experience, check out the **Bishop Museum,** which has excellent performances on weekdays, or head to the Halekulani's **House Without a Key** at sunset to watch the enchanting Kanoelehua Miller dance beautiful hula under a century-old kiawe tree. The first week after Easter brings Hawaii's biggest and most prestigious hula extravaganza, the **Merrie Monarch Hula Festival,** to Hilo on the Big Island; tickets sell out by January 30, so reserve early. In May, there's the **Molokai Ka Hula Pikai,** held at Molokai's Papohaku Beach Park, a wonderful day-long festival that celebrates the birth of the hula on the island where it was born. See chapter 5 and "Hawaii Calendar of Events" in chapter 3.

- **Watch the Ancient Hawaiian Sport of Canoe Paddling** (Oahu): From February to September, on weekday evenings and weekend days, hundreds of canoe paddlers gather at Ala Wai Canal and practice the Hawaiian sport of canoe paddling. Find a comfortable spot at Ala Wai Park, next to the canal, and watch this ancient sport come to life. See chapter 5.

- **Attend a Hawaiian-Language Church Service** (Oahu): **Kawaiahao Church** (☎ **808/522-1333**) is the Westminster Abbey of Hawaii; the vestibule is lined with portraits of the Hawaiian monarchy, many of whom where crowned in this very building. The coral church is a perfect setting in which to experience an all-Hawaiian service, held every Sunday at 10:30am, complete with Hawaiian song. Admission is free; let your conscience be your guide as to a donation. See chapter 5.

- **Buy a Lei in Chinatown** (Oahu): There's actually a host of cultural sights and experiences to be had in Honolulu's Chinatown. Wander through this several-square-block area with its jumble of exotic shops offering herbs, Chinese groceries, and acupuncture services. Before you leave, be sure to check out the lei sellers on Maunakea Street (near North Hotel Street), where Hawaii's finest leis go for as little as $2.50. See chapter 5.

- **Visit Ancient Hawaii's Most Sacred Temple** (Big Island): On the Kohala Coast, where King Kamehameha the Great was born, stands Hawaii's oldest, largest, and most sacred religious site: the 1,500-year-old Mookini Heiau, used by kings to pray and offer human sacrifices. The massive three-story stone temple, dedicated to Ku, the Hawaiian god of war, was erected in A.D. 480. Each stone is said to have been passed hand-to-hand from Pololu Valley, 14 miles away, by 18,000 men who worked from sunset to sunrise. Go in late afternoon when the setting sun strikes the lava-rock walls and creates a primal mood. See chapter 6.

- **Hunt for Petroglyphs** (Big Island): Archaeologists are still unsure who made these ancient rock carvings—the majority of which are found in the 233-acre Puako Petroglyph Archaeological District, near Mauna Lani Resort, on the Kohala Coast—or why. The best time to hunt for intricate depictions of ancient life is either early in

The Welcoming Lei

Nothing makes you feel more welcome, or more like you're in paradise, than a lei. The stunning tropical beauty of the delicate garland, the deliciously sweet fragrance of the blossoms, the sensual way they curl softly around your neck . . . there's no doubt about it: Getting leid in Hawaii is a sensuous experience.

Leis are much more than just a decorative necklace of flowers; they're also one of the nicest ways to say hello, goodbye, congratulations, I salute you, my sympathies are with you, or I love you. The custom of lei-giving can be traced back to Hawaii's very roots; according to chants, the first lei was given by Hiiaka, the sister of the volcano goddess Pelé, who presented Pelé with a lei of lehua blossoms on a beach in Puna.

During ancient times, leis given to *alii* (high-ranking chiefs) were accompanied by a bow, since it was *kapu* (forbidden) for a commoner to raise his arms higher than the king's head. The presentation of a kiss with a lei didn't come about until World War II; it's generally attributed to an entertainer who kissed an officer on a dare then quickly presented him with her lei, saying it was an old Hawaiian custom. It wasn't then, but it sure caught on fast.

Lei-making is a tropical art form. All leis are fashioned by hand in a variety of traditional patterns; some leis are sewn with hundreds of tiny blooms or shells, or bits of ferns and leaves. Some are twisted, some braided, some strung; all are presented with love. Every island has its own lei of the land, so to speak—a special flower lei. On Oahu, the choice is *ilima*, a small orange flower. Big Islanders prefer the *lehua*, a large, delicate red puff. Maui likes the *lokelani*, a small rose. On Kauai, it's the *mokihana*, a fragrant green vine and berry. Molokai prefers the *kukui*, the white blossom of a candlenut tree. And Lanai's lei is made of *kaunaoa*, a bright yellow moss, while Niihau utilizes its abundant seashells to make leis that were once prized by royalty and are now worth a small fortune.

Leis are available at all of the islands' airports. Other places to get wonderful, inexpensive leis are the half-dozen lei shops on **Maunakea Street** in Honolulu's Chinatown, and **Greene Acres Leis**, off Kaimininani Drive in the Kona Palisades subdivision, across from the Kona International Airport (☎ **808/329-2399**), on the Big Island. If you plan ahead, you can also arrange to have a lei-greeter meet you and your travel party as you deplane. Reliable companies that can great you at Honolulu International Airport on Oahu, Kahului Airport on Maui, Kona Airport on the Big Island, and Lihue Airport on Kauai include **Greeters of Hawaii** (☎ 800/366-8559 or 808/836-0161), **Hawaii Greeting Service of Hawaii** (☎ 800/736-5665 or 808/834-7667), **Kamaaina Leis, Flowers & Greeters** (☎ 800/367-5183 or 808/836-3246), and **Aloha Lei Greeters** (☎ 800/367-5255 or 808/951-9990), who can meet you at all airports except Kauai.

Leis are the perfect symbol for the islands: They're given in the moment, their fragrance and beauty are enjoyed in the moment, and when they fade, their spirit of aloha lives on. Welcome to Hawaii!

- **Explore Puuhonua O Honaunau National Historical Park** (Big Island): This sacred site on the South Kona Coast was once a place of refuge and a revered place of rejuvenation. You can walk the same consecrated grounds where priests once clearly. See chapter 6. the morning or late afternoon, when the angle of the sun lets you see the forms

conducted holy ceremonies and glimpse the ancient way of life in precontact Hawaii in the re-created 180-acre village. See chapter 6.

- **Visit the Most Hawaiian Isle:** A time capsule of old Hawaii on the eve of the 21st century, Molokai allows you to experience real Hawaiian life in its most unsullied form. The island's people have woven the cultural values of ancient times into modern life. In addition to this rich community, you'll find the magnificent natural wonders it so cherishes: Hawaii's highest waterfall and greatest collection of fishponds; the world's tallest sea cliffs; plus sand dunes, coral reefs, rain forests, and empty, gloriously empty beaches—pretty much the same Molokai their ancestors saw generations ago. See chapter 8.

7 The Best Luxury Hotels & Resorts

- **Halekulani** (Oahu; ☎ **800/367-2343**): None finer in all Hawaii—and it's in Waikiki! An oasis of calm amid the buzz, this beach hotel is Oahu's only AAA Five Diamond luxury resort. When price is no object, this is really the only place to stay. Even if you don't stay here, pop by for a sunset mai tai to hear Sonny Kamehele sing the old hapa-haole tunes of the 1930s and 1940s while a lovely hula dancer sways to the music. See chapter 5.

- **Kahala Mandarin Oriental Hawaii** (Oahu; ☎ **800/367-2525**): This palatial oceanside resort is a hotel for the 21st century—but one with the grace and elegance of a softer, gentler time, when all of Hawaii moved at a more leisurely pace. Its Old Hawaii spirit is accented with pan-Asian touches and all the conveniences you could wish for, including a fabulously secluded beach. And the location, 10 minutes from Waikiki in the quiet residential community of Kahala, rounds out the get-away-from-it-all vibe and keeps everything close at hand at the same time—perfect. See chapter 5.

- **Kona Village Resort** (Big Island; ☎ **800/367-5290**): This is the best place to stay in Hawaii if you seek excellent service in a vintage Polynesian village-style resort. On 82 coastal acres of palms and tropical flowers stands this absolutely peaceful, eclectic Polynesian village, with thatched huts and various styles of Pacific architecture clustered by the big blue ocean. The authenticity and isolation of this oasis combine to revive wounded urban souls who swing in hammocks, splash like children in the bay, actually smile when spoken to, and move slowly with the calm and grace that comes from great leisure. Trade winds rustle the palms, gentle waves lap ashore. Why anyone ever leaves is a wonder. See chapter 6.

- **Four Seasons Resort Hualalai at Historic Kaupulehu** (Big Island; ☎ **800/334-3443**): Outdoor showers, private pools, unimpeded ocean views, excellent food, and a new 18-hole championship golf course—what more can any mortal want? At this new low-impact, high-ticket hideaway under the dormant Hualalai volcano, Four Seasons ups the ante with its residential resort of two-story bungalows clustered around five seaside swimming pools on a black lagoon. If you decide to stay here forever, there are oceanfront condos for sale, too, starting at $1.2 million. See chapter 6.

- **Ritz-Carlton, Kapalua** (Maui; ☎ **800/262-8440**): With location, style, and loads of hospitality, this is the best Ritz anywhere. On the coast below the picturesque West Maui Mountains, this breezy grand hotel overlooks the Pacific and Molokai across the channel. The natural setting, on an old coastal pineapple plantation, is a picture of tranquility. The service is legendary; the golf courses daunting; and the nearby beaches perfect for snorkeling, diving, and just relaxing. See chapter 7.

- **Four Seasons Resort Maui at Wailea** (Maui; ☎ 800/334-MAUI): This is the ultimate beach hotel for latter-day royals, with excellent cuisine, spacious rooms, gracious service, and Wailea Beach, one of Maui's best gold-sand beaches, out the front door. Every room has at least a partial ocean view from a private lanai. The luxury suites are as big as some Honolulu condos and full of marble and deluxe appointments. And since Four Seasons lured Chef George Mavrothalassitis away from the Halekulani, the cuisine has improved 150%. See chapter 7.

- **The Lodge at Koele** (Lanai; ☎ 800/321-4666): For old-world luxury in an old pineapple plantation town, come to the Lodge. There's nothing else like it in Hawaii: an extravagant inland hotel set amid a misty grove of pines far from any beach; it's like visiting Emile DeBeque's rubber plantation house in the Hollywood film classic *South Pacific*. With giant stone fireplaces, stuffed furniture, and lavish chintz rooms, the decor is reminiscent of an English country lodge, with the same sense of serenity that comes with that kind of rural atmosphere. If sun, sand, and surf don't top your list of requirements, this sophisticated retreat is the perfect choice. And you can always catch the free shuttle down to Manele Bay for a dip with the spinner dolphins. See chapter 9.

- **Hyatt Regency Resort and Spa** (Kauai; ☎ 800/233-1234): This art-deco beach hotel recalls Hawaii in the 1920s—before the crash—when gentlemen arrived in blue blazers and ladies in summer frocks, and they came to the islands to learn to surf and play the ukulele. Its architecture and location, on the sunny side of Kauai, make this the island's best holiday hotel. The golden beach is a bit too rough for swimming, but the saltwater swimming pool is the biggest on the island. There's an old-fashioned reading room by the sea with club chairs, billiards, and a bar well stocked with cognac and port; and Tidepools, a thatched-roof seafood restaurant, is a nice touch. Golf, horseback riding, and the shops of Koloa, a boutique plantation town, are nearby diversions. See chapter 10.

- **Princeville Hotel** (Kauai; ☎ 800/826-4400): Set in one of the most remarkable locations in the world, between the crystal-blue waters of Hanalei Bay and steepled, Bali Ha'i-like mountains, this palace of green marble and sparkling chandeliers recalls Hawaii's monarchy period of the 19th century. This grand hotel steps down the side of a cliff, so you arrive on the ninth floor and go down to the beach. Opulent rooms with magnificent views and all the activities of Princeville and Hanalei make this resort the sort of thing dreams are made of. See chapter 10.

8 The Best Moderately Priced Places to Stay

- **Doubletree Alana Waikiki** (Oahu; ☎ 800/367-6070): Located within walking distance of Waikiki Beach is this welcome oasis, with beautiful, comfortable rooms and the kind of prompt service that you usually only get at twice the price (rack rates start at $135). The elegant lobby features original Picasso ceramics, the Café Picasso restaurant offers superb Pacific Rim cuisine, and like most of the Doubletree hotels, you get a freshly baked chocolate-chip cookie every night. See chapter 5.

- **Santa's By the Sea** (Oahu; ☎ 800/262-9912): Setting, price ($99 a night), and style make this a must-stay if you plan to see Oahu's North Shore. The impeccable one-bedroom units with finely crafted woodwork and bay windows comprise one of the few North Shore B&Bs right on the beach—and not just any beach, but the famous Banzai Pipeline. You can go from your bed to the sand in less than 30 seconds. The perfect spot to watch the sun rise over the Pacific. See chapter 5.

- **Kona Tiki Hotel** (Big Island; ☎ 808/329-1425): It's hard to believe that places like this still exist. Right on the ocean, away from the hustle and bustle of downtown Kailua-Kona, is one of the hottest budget deals in Hawaii: tastefully decorated rooms with private lanais overlooking the ocean, starting at just $58 a night! Although it's called a hotel, this small, family-run operation is more like a large B&B, with plenty of friendly conversation around the pool at the morning continental breakfast buffet. See chapter 6.

- **Waipio Wayside B&B Inn** (Big Island; ☎ 800/833-8849): Jackie Horne renovated this 1938 Hamakua sugar supervisor's home—nestled among fruit trees and surrounded with sweet-smelling ginger, fragile orchids, and blooming birds of paradise—and transformed it into a gracious bed-and-breakfast. Just minutes from the Waipio Valley Lookout and Honokaa village, this comfy five-bedroom house abounds with thoughtful touches, such as a help-yourself–tea-and-cookies bar with 26 different kinds of tea. Jackie's friendly hospitality and excellent gourmet breakfasts really round out the experience. Rooms start at $70 for two. See chapter 6.

- **The Napili Bay** (Maui; ☎ 888/661-7200): One of Maui's best-kept secrets (until now, that is) is this intimate two-story condo complex, located right on half-mile-long white-sand Napili Beach. The beach here is so beautiful that people staying at the much more expensive resort down the street frequently haul all their stuff here to set up for the day. The compact studio apartments, which have everything you need, start at just $58—unbelievable! See chapter 7.

- **Makena Landing** (Maui; ☎ 808/879-6286): This oceanfront bed-and-breakfast has one of the most fabulous locations in Hawaii. The view is incredible; the sunsets are to die for; some of the best swimming, snorkeling, diving, and shoreline fishing is within walking distance; and the hosts are the nicest people you'll ever meet. Once you settle in, you may not want to leave—and at just $95 for a double, you can afford to stay awhile. See chapter 7.

- **Paniolo Hale** (Molokai; ☎ 800/367-2984): This is far and away Molokai's most charming lodging, and probably its best value. The two-story Old Hawaii ranch-house design is airy and homey, with oak floors and walls of folding glass doors that open to huge screened verandas. The whole place overlooks the Kaluakoi Golf Course, a green barrier that separates these condos (which start at $95 for two) from the rest of Kaluakoi Resort. See chapter 8.

- **Puunana/Paunalu Beachfront Cottages** (Molokai; ☎ 800/637-0861): Each of these green-and-white plantation-style cottages sits on its own secluded beach—you'll feel like you're on your own island. Impeccable decor, a magical setting, and reasonable rates ($100 for two) make these five-star cottages a must-stay. See chapter 8.

- **Hotel Lanai** (Lanai; ☎ 800/321-4666): Lanai's only budget lodging is a simple, down-home plantation-era relic that has recently been Laura Ashley–ized. The Hotel Lanai is homey, funky, and fun—and, best of all, a real bargain (starting at $95 for two) compared to its ritzy neighbors. See chapter 9.

- **Hanalei Colony Resort** (Kauai; ☎ 800/628-3004): The only North Shore resort right on the beach, these old-style two-story condos attract a loyal following of devoted beach lovers. What brings them back year after year? It's the location, ambiance, and staff, always friendly and caring. The roar of the surf and scent of the reef will haunt you long after you leave this small, appealing resort, where low-season rates start at $115. See chapter 10.

- **Waimea Plantation Cottages** (Kauai; ☎ 808/338-1625): This vintage village of 47 turn-of-the-century plantation houses, each fully restored and bearing the name of the family who once called it home, sits under a coconut palm grove at the beach on Kauai's Western Shore. There's a cottage here for just about everyone, from honeymooning couples to relatives at family reunions. Rates begin at $160. See chapter 10.

9   The Best Places to Stay with Kids

- **Royal Kuhio** (Oahu; ☎ **808/538-7145**): Families take note: This is one of the best deals in Waikiki. Just two blocks from world-famous Waikiki Beach, this high-rise condo features apartments with full kitchens, separate bedrooms, a living area with TV, and a private lanai—all for as little as $95. Lots of onsite extras, ranging from a pool to volleyball and basketball courts and a putting green, round out the family-friendly appeal. Hot tip: Ask for a corner unit, as they're the nicest. See chapter 5.

- **Ihilani Resort & Spa** (Oahu; ☎ **800/626-4446**): This sybaritic resort on Oahu's virgin leeward coast is a haven of relaxation and tropical fun for travelers of all ages. The year-round Keiki Beachcomber Club offers a wide variety of outdoor adventures and indoor learning activities, from kite-flying and tide-pool exploration to Hawaiian cultural activities like lei-making and hula dancing. The resort is so intent on pleasing the entire family that the kids even have their own clubhouse, with a Computer Learning Center (complete with SEGA Genesis, CD-ROM, and Super Nintendo), a 125-gallon fish tank, an evening lounge for teen parties, and much more. See chapter 5.

- **Kona Village Resort** (Big Island; ☎ **800/367-5290**): This is a parent's dream: custom-designed programs to entertain your kids, from tots to teenagers, from dawn to well after dusk, all at no charge. There's even a dinner seating for children, so mom and dad can enjoy an intimate dinner for two later in the evening. See chapter 6.

- **Guest House at Volcano** (Big Island: ☎ **808/967-7775**): If you're planning to visit Hawaii Volcanoes National Park, here's the place to stay with the kids. A mother herself, Bonnie Gooddell has completely child-proofed her house and installed a basketball hoop in the driveway, a swing set in the backyard, and a truck-load of toys on her large outside porch. You and the kids can make yourself right at home in Bonnie's freestanding, two-story guest cottage, which comes outfitted with everything down to extra wool socks for cold nights. And at $60 for two plus $10 for each of the kids, it's easy on the family budget. See chapter 6.

- **Four Seasons Resort Maui at Wailea** (Maui; ☎ **800/334-MAUI**): The most kid-friendly hotel on Maui not only offers a complimentary kids' program year-round and an every-day activities center (9am to 5pm daily), but also makes the keikis feel welcome with such extras as complimentary milk and cookies on their first day and children's menus at all resort restaurants and from room service. See chapter 7.

- **Koa Resort** (Maui: ☎ **800/541-3060**): The spacious, privately owned one-, two-, and three-bedroom units just across the street from the ocean start at just $85. They come fully equipped with everything you'll need, including plenty of room for your family to stretch out and get comfortable. Extras like a swimming pool, hot tub, two tennis courts, and an 18-hole putting green make this an extra-good value. See chapter 7.

- **Great Molokai Ranch Trail** (Molokai: ☎ **800/254-8871**): The Paniolo Camp at Molokai Ranch elevates camping to a new level with its comfortable, almost luxurious bungalow tents (called "*tentalows*"). The all-inclusive prices include three all-you-can-eat meals and snacks every day, plus two activities (there are lots to choose from, which special activities for the kids), transportation (including airport pickup), and daily maid service (when was the last time you got *that* at camp?). See chapter 8.

- **Hyatt Regency Kauai Resort & Spa** (Kauai; ☎ **800/233-1234**): In addition to the Camp Hyatt program (for kids ages 3 to 12), it's the collection of swimming pools—freshwater and salt, with slides, waterfalls, and secret lagoons—that makes this oceanfront Hyatt a real kids' paradise. During the summer months and the holiday season, there's "Rock Hyatt," a cool activity room for teens to gather and play electronic games. Summertime also boasts Family Fun Theatre Nights, when the whole family can enjoy a showing of one of the more than 400 movies filmed on Kauai. See chapter 10.

- **Kauai Coconut Beach Resort** (Kauai; ☎ **800/22-ALOHA**): This Coconut Coast resort has an excellent deal for families: Not only do kids 17 and under stay free, but those 11 and younger eat free when dining with a grown-up. It's situated on 10½ acres fronting Waipouli Beach, right next door to the Coconut Marketplace, so kids have plenty of room to play. See chapter 10.

10 The Best Hawaii-Style Culinary Experiences

- **Tropical Fruit:** The best thing about the coming of spring in Hawaii is the reappearance of gardenias and **mangoes.** Hayden mangoes are universally loved for their plump, juicy flesh and brilliant skins—and for their abundance—but **white piries,** with their resinous flavor and fine, fiberless flesh, are the queen of tropical fruit; this rare and ambrosial variety can be found in Oahu's Chinatown markets or at roadside fruit stands in rural Oahu. Papaya lovers, take note: **Kahuku papayas**—firm, fleshy, dark orange, and so juicy they sometimes squirt—are the ones to watch for on menus and in markets; check out the roadside stands in Kahuku and Oahu, and at supermarkets, which carry them when available. White, acid-free, extra-sweet, and grown on Kauai and the Big Island, **Sugarloaf pineapples** are the new rage in pineapples. Hilo is the town for **litchis** (also known as *lychees*) during the summer months, but Honolulu's Chinatown markets carry them, too. Decidedly Hawaiian are **Ka'u oranges,** grown in the volcanic soil of the southern Big Island and available during the winter months; don't be fooled by their brown, ugly skin—they're juicy, thin-skinned, and sweet as honey. The **Paradise Produce Company** (Oahu; ☎ **808/533-2125**), near Chinatown, features a dizzying assortment of local fruits and vegetables in spring and summer; local litchis—usually available in late summer and rarely sold in supermarkets—are worth the hunt. For other great hunting grounds, see the shopping sections of chapters 5 through 10.

- **Noodles:** Ramen, udon, saimin, pho, pasta, chow mein—they're all noodles, and we love noodles. Hawaii is the epicenter of ethnic noodle stands and houses, with many recommendable choices, all of them inexpensive. **Jimbo's** (Oahu; ☎ 808/947-2211), a neighborhood staple, is tops for freshly made udon with generous toppings and a homemade broth of utter finesse. **Hanaki** (Oahu; ☎ 808/955-1347) is a close second, with its simmering earthen pots of shiitake mushrooms with udon noodles. In the Ala Moana Center's Makai Court, **Tsuruya Noodles** (Oahu; ☎ 808/946-7214) is no more than a corner stall, but fans line up for its buckwheat Tenzaru with light-as-air shrimp tempura. On the neighbor islands, noodlemania prevails at **Hamura's Saimin Stand** (Kauai; ☎ 808/245-3271), where saimin and teriyaki sticks have replaced hamburgers and pizza as the late-night, comfort-food tradition, Hilo's **Nori's Saimin & Snacks** (Big Island; ☎ 808/935-9133) is this charming town's secret for consummate saimin of every stripe. Teriyaki beef sticks, a tasty, true-blue broth, and noodles cooked to perfection are Nori's trademark. And of course, **Oodles of Noodles** (Big Island; ☎ 808/329-9222) remains the epitome of noodle heaven. See chapters 5, 6, and 10.

- **Hawaiian Food:** The **Parc Cafe** (Oahu; ☎ **808/921-7272**) is always filled with local diners on Wednesday, the day its Hawaiian buffet is spread out on several tables. It shows that a culinary tradition can retain its integrity even when a touch of glamour is added. The Hawaiian lunch is universally pleasing: taro au gratin, laulau, squid luau (with fresh tomatoes and tons of taro leaves), fresh fish, haupia (coconut pudding), and dozens of salad selections. See chapter 5.

- **Plate Lunches:** For seasoned plate lunchers who favor the traditional "two scoop rice" lunches weighted with carbohydrates and hefty meats, **Zippy's** (17 locations throughout Oahu; call ☎ 808/955-6622 for the one nearest you) is a household word. Chili (both meaty and meatless) comes cheap and good at Zippy's as well, and the saimin scores high at most locations. Other Oahu plate-lunch spots we love: **Old Waialae Road** (☎ 808/951-7779), **Kakaako Kitchen** (☎ 808/596-7488), **I ♥ Country Cafe** (☎ 808/596-8108), **Well Bento** (☎ 808/941-5261; excellent vegetarian, macrobiotic, fish, and free-range chicken dishes), and **Yama's Fish Market** (☎ 808/941-9994). Each operation puts its own imprint on this local ritual, be it gourmet greens and Molokai potatoes (Old Waialae Road), home-style pot roast (Kakaako Kitchen), or baked ahi (Yama's). On the neighbor islands, **Pauwela Cafe** (Maui; ☎ 808/575-9242) serves gourmet feasts from a tiny kitchen, including the best smoked-turkey sandwich in the world. On Kauai, **Pono Market** (☎ 808/822-4581) and **Fish Express** (Lihue, ☎ 808/245-9918) are at the top of the plate-lunch pyramid. See chapters 5, 7, and 10.

- **Hawaii Regional Cuisine:** Hawaii has become a culinary destination thanks to Hawaii Regional Cuisine and its covey of creative chefs. It's a festival of flavors, fresh ingredients, and abundant seasonal harvests borne of volcanic soil and ideal weather. There are reputable restaurants serving Hawaii Regional Cuisine on all the islands except Molokai. For the best of the bunch, see "The Best Restaurants," below.

- **Shave Ice:** Like surfing, shave ice is synonymous with Haleiwa, the North Shore town where **Matsumoto Shave Ice** (Oahu; ☎ 808/637-4827) and neighboring **Aoki's** (no phone) serve mounds of icy treats to long, thirsty lines of takers. Hot weather causes shave-ice sales to skyrocket, and we know why: They're tasty and refreshing, and when topped with tropical fruit flavors over ice cream and azuki beans, they're a cultural phenomenon akin to rubber slippers and bentos. If you happen to be in Hanapepe on Kauai, **Jo-Jo's Clubhouse** (☎ 808/338-0056) is the hot spot for this cool treat, offering 52 flavors of shave ice, from lilikoi to mango to the classic strawberry. See chapters 5 and 10.

- **Other Mighty Morsels:** Isolated marvels throughout these islands include the biscotti-like poi sticks at **Mark Twain Square** (Big Island; ☎ 808/929-7550), far superior to plain biscotti and the consummate accompaniment to the several Kona coffees of highest esteem (all based on the Big Island, of course): **Rooster Farms** (☎ 808/328-9173), **Bong Brothers** (☎ 808/328-9289), **Holualoa Kona Coffee Company** (☎ 808/322-9937), and **Waimea Coffee Company** (☎ 808/885-4472). Serious coffee drinkers reach for these labels and take home the coffee beans still warm from the roaster. The buttery, chocolate-dipped shortbread cookies of **Big Island Candies** (Big Island; ☎ 808/935-8890) are the ultimate island cookies, worth every calorie and every dollar, individually wrapped for a life on the road and addictive to the final crumb. If you're traveling through Waimea, don't miss **Cook's Discoveries** (Big Island; ☎ 808/885-3633), where superlatives never end—the best cookies, preserves, books, vinegars, poi, and many other marvelous taste treats, as well as Hawaiian gift items. From Kauai, Hanapepe town's venerable **Taro Ko Chips** (☎ 808/335-5586) are the crunchy snack neighbor islanders drive long miles to find, then cart home in hand-carried bundles. Finally, whether it's take-out stuffed oysters, grilled vegetables, caviar, or fresh portobellos you're after, Honolulu's **Strawberry Connection of Hawaii** (Oahu; ☎ 808/842-0278) will reward your search; it's paradise for foodies, chefs, aspiring chefs, and those in pursuit of the best in Hawaii food products. See chapters 5, 6, and 10.

11 The Best Restaurants

- **Akasaka** (Oahu; ☎ **808/942-4466**): The spicy tuna handroll, hamachi sushi, clam miso soup, and sizzling tofu and scallops are among life's greatest pleasures. The tiny sushi bar with its petite tatami room is hidden among the shadowy night clubs of Honolulu's Kona Street—off the beaten track, yet always jumping with regulars. See chapter 5.

- **Alan Wong's Restaurant** (Oahu; ☎ **808/949-2526**): Master strokes at this shrine of Hawaii Regional Cuisine: crispy ahi lumpia; warm California rolls made with salmon roe, wasabi, and Kona lobster instead of rice; and ginger-crusted fresh onaga. Opihi shooters and "day boat" scallops in season are a must, grilled lamb chops a perennial. The menu changes daily, but the flavors never lose their sizzle. See chapter 5.

- **Cliquo** (Oahu; ☎ **808/377-8854**): Behold the perfect French bistro, with commendable decor, service, and ambiance, and a wonderfully executed menu of Gallic splendors. Expect excellent opakapaka, filet mignon, and a prix fixe menu worth its weight in gold—all worth the drive to this neck of suburbia, about 15 minutes east of Waikiki. See chapter 5.

- **Hawaii Seafood Paradise** (Oahu; ☎ **808/946-4514**): Nine kinds of roast duck, including a peerless Peking, are reason enough to come here. But the sizzling platters, seafood fried rice, spicy prawn soup, and kung pao scallops take Cantonese/Szechwan to new heights. A few Thai dishes spice up the menu. See chapter 5.

- **Kahala Moon Cafe** (Oahu; ☎ **808/732-7777**): The grilled lamb chops with caramelized onions are the way to go, and the lemongrass crème brûlée and mango bread pudding are the guiltless finale. Or feast on sautéed salmon, sizzling shrimp, tender tenderloin, and melt-in-your-mouth scallops in a windowless but pleasing room. See chapter 5.

- **Sam Choy's Breakfast, Lunch & Crab** (Oahu; ☎ **808/545-7979**): Roll up your sleeves, put on that bib, and tuck into the best king crab you've ever tasted at this silly, happy dining room. Local specialties at breakfast and lunch and a seafood menu unique to Honolulu draw throngs, and you'll be happy you're one of them. It's difficult to get a seat in the elevated sampan in the middle of the room, but there's plenty of elbow room everywhere else. See chapter 5.

- **Roy's Restaurant** (Oahu; ☎ **808/396-7697**): The pioneer of Hawaii Regional Cuisine still reigns at his busy, noisy flagship Hawaii Kai dining room with the trademark open kitchen. Roy's deft way with local ingredients, nostalgic ethnic preparations, and fresh fish makes his menu, which changes daily, a novel experience every time. With its airy, windowed dining room looking out over a lagoon and golf course. With its airy, windowed dining room looking out over a lagoon and golf course. **Roy's Waikoloa Bar & Grill** (Big Island; ☎ **808/885-4321**) has the best view and ambiance in Roy's Hawaii chain. When combined with the peerless quality of the Big Island's produce and seafood, and the chef's mastery in using them, Roy's Waikoloa has natural advantages that rank it a definite best. See chapters 5 and 6.

- **Maha's Café** (Big Island; ☎ **808/885-0693**): A closet-sized kitchen can yield surprising results. In an A-frame house built in 1852, Harriet-Ann Namahaokalani (Maha) Schutte serves up great home cooking with fresh local ingredients, including taro from Waipio Valley, locally made feta cheese, and homemade liilikoi salsa. See chapter 6.

- **Seaside Restaurant** (Big Island; ☎ **808/935-8825**): Open since 1946, this Hilo restaurant has improved with time yet has lost none of its local flavor. Go before dark so you can see the surrounding ponds where the Nakagawa family raises trout, catfish, mullet, and *aholehole*, the silvery mountain bass devoured by local fish lovers. They'll catch your dinner and serve it perfectly prepared. Dine on the deck if you can, and if opakapaka steamed in ti leaf is available, it's not to be missed. See chapter 6.

- **David Paul's Lahaina Grill** (Maui; ☎ **808/667-5117**): Survey after survey points to David Paul's as the apex of Maui dining—and it's not even on the ocean. David Paul Johnson is a culinary wizard whose tequila shrimp, lobster-gazpacho martini, Kona lobster crab cakes, and endless innovations are top Maui attractions. His newly opened restaurant at the foot of Diamond Head, **David Paul's Diamond Head Grill** (Oahu; ☎ **808/667-5117**) shows early promise of success. See chapters 5 and 7.

- **Seasons** (Maui; ☎ **808/874-8000**): Maui's most elegant restaurant is not all show. Chef de Cuisine George Mavrothalassitis marries the traditions of his native Provence with the best and freshest of Maui: onaga baked in a Hawaiian salt crust, baked *kumu* (goatfish) with watercress and wild mushrooms, and seared yellowtail tuna with upcountry tomato relish. By the time the warm fig tart with Armagnac rolls around to your oceanside table, Maui has become Nirvana. Fresh, exquisite, and cutting-edge brilliant are the qualities of Mavrothalassitis' menu, a celebration of Maui's best. See chapter 7.

- **A Pacific Cafe Kauai** (Kauai; ☎ **808/822-0013**): The first restaurant Jean-Marie Josselin opened in his burgeoning culinary empire is still the best, although **A Pacific Cafe Maui** (Maui; ☎ **808/879-0069**) comes close. The signature items (tiger-eye sushi, garlic-crisped mahi-mahi) are staples statewide, but it's the way he uses Kauai produce and seafood that gives this dining room the edge. See chapters 7 and 10.

12 The Best Shops & Galleries

- **The Contemporary Museum** and **Honolulu Academy of Arts** (Oahu): Architectural and cultural wonders, a legacy of the same kamaaina family, the Contemporary Museum and the Honolulu Academy of Arts both house peerless collections in garden settings. For Asian, American, and European masters, go to the Academy; for a look at some of America's most significant art since 1940 (and the prettiest forest drive in Honolulu), TCM is the only game in town. For those who want to buy as well as browse, both museums have stellar shops: The **Academy Shop** (☎ **808/523-8703**) features ethnic and contemporary gift items representing the arts-and-crafts traditions of the world, from basketry and beadwork to ikats and saris. At the **Contemporary Museum Gift Shop** (☎ **808/523-3447**), everything is art: The avant-garde jewelry, stationery, books, and gift items are brilliant, spirited, and functional—and the neon granny glasses from France are high chic. See chapter 5.

- **Avanti Fashion** (Oahu; ☎ **808/926-6886**): Avanti aloha shirts and sportswear, in authentic prints from the 1930s and 1940s reproduced on silk, elevate tropical garb from high kick to high chic. Casual, comfortable, easy-care, and light as a cloud, the silks look vintage but cost a fraction of collectibles' prices. The nostalgic treasures are available at many stores statewide, but the best bets are at the two Avanti retail stores in Waikiki. See chapter 5.

- **Native Books & Beautiful Things** (Oahu; ☎ **808/599-5511**): Hawaii is the content and the context in this shop of books, crafts, and gift items made by Island artists and crafters. Musical instruments, calabashes, jewelry, leu, books, fabrics, clothing, home accessories, jams and jellies—they're all high quality and made in Hawaii. See chapter 5.

- **Nohea Gallery** (Oahu; ☎ **808/596-0074**): This recently renovated gallery features works by some of the finest artists and crafters of Hawaii. From handcrafted fine jewelry to hair accessories, two-dimensional art, handblown glass, ceramics, and chests of curly koa, the works are stunning. See chapter 5.

- **Silk Winds** (Oahu; ☎ **808/735-6599**): Cricket cages and one-of-a-kind bamboo calligraphy wristrests are among the Asian treasures you'll find here. Mahjong tiles, jade and porcelain, Buddhas, and beads beckon from the mysterious corners of this antiques store for everyone, from casual to serious collectors. See chapter 5.

- **Silver Moon Emporium** (Oahu; ☎ **808/637-7710**): Women love this Haleiwa shop and its sister store, **Bella Luna**, the former sleek and chic, the latter chockablock with riotous tropical color. Bevies of shoppers from California, New York, France, and Japan, not to mention Hilo and Honolulu, have been known to leave with their car trunks full and their wardrobe issues resolved. See chapter 5.

- **Hula Heaven** (Big Island; ☎ **808/329-7885**): You'll turn giddy at Hula Heaven, *the* spot for collectors of Hawaiiana. Aloha shirts, hula-girl lamps, vintage ukuleles, one-of-a-kind 1940s textiles, Don Blanding dinnerware, the passionate expertise of the owners—it's a lifestyle, a celebration of nostalgia. See chapter 6.

- **Sig Zane Designs** (Big Island; ☎ **808/935-7077**): A Sig Zane fabric design is culturally meaningful, visually striking, and uniquely identifiable. There are those who wear Sig Zane shirts and muumuus, lounge on Sig Zane cushions and upholstery, sleep under Sig Zane bedspreads, and pad around the house in Sig Zane slippers. Lauhala mats and accessories, handcrafted koa books by a third-generation Vatican bookbinder, calabashes, jewelry, and the inspired line of authentic Sig Zane Hawaiian wear make Sig's the best stop in Hilo. See chapter 6.

- **Volcano Art Center** (Big Island; ☎ **808/967-8222**): I love its creaky wooden floors, the smoky scent in the air, the rolling mists, and the art. Thriving in an 1877 building, the art center offers art education, programs and performances, and wondrous works in all media, featuring the most prominent artists on the island. See chapter 6.

- **Ola's** (Maui; ☎ **808/573-1334**): With its beach-glass counters and concrete floors, Ola's sprouted suddenly in Makawao, and everybody noticed. Everything here—the lamps, vases, blown glass, strumsticks, and jewelry—even Bella's at Ola's handmade chocolates—is a work of art. See chapter 7.

- **The Mercantile** (Maui; ☎ **808/572-1407**): Down the block from Ola's, The Mercantile is off-the-charts stylish, too. You'll find flaxseed eye pillows and scented neck pillows, Italian lamps, all-cotton–down sofas, dinnerware, Kiehl's shampoo, and vetiver soaps from Provence—a place of pampering, extravagant and delicious. See chapter 7.

- **Hui No'eau Visual Arts Center** (Maui; ☎ **808/572-6560**): Upcountry in Makawao, in a 1917 Mediterranean manse on a 9-acre estate, this arts hui is part gallery; part exhibition space; part gift shop, classes, and demonstration center, and every inch a paean to beauty. See chapter 7.

- **Hana Coast Gallery** (Maui): The long and winding road leads to the Hotel Hana-Maui, where the works in the Hana Coast Gallery reflect a deep commitment to Hawaii's cultural art. Native Hawaiian artists and the master crafts of Hawaii have a presence and integrity unlike in any other gallery on the islands. See chapter 7.

- **Robert Hamada's Studio** (Kauai): Wood turner Robert Hamada works in his studio at the foot of the Sleeping Giant, quietly producing museum-quality works with unique textures and grains. His skill, his lathe, and more than 60 years of experience bring luminous life to the kou, milo, kauila, camphor, mango, and native woods he logs himself. See chapter 10.

- **Ola's** (Kauai; ☎ **808/826-6937**): Pay attention to the display spaces as well as what's displayed here. Look for Doug Britt's paintings, vanities, armoires, desks, lamps, and bookshelves scattered unobtrusively among the fine American crafts. The hand-painted candlesticks, Lundberg studio glass, one-of-a-kind tableware, and unique gift items are top-drawer, but it's Britt's works, made of found objects, that you'll remember. See chapter 10.

- **Yellowfish Trading Company** (Kauai; ☎ **808/826-1227**): Surprise yourself at Yellowfish Trading Company, where vintage bark cloth and that one-of-a-kind 1940s rattan sofa are among owner Gritt Benton's short-lived pleasures. The collectibles—1940s vases, '50s lunch boxes, '30s lampshades, antique silk piano shawls—move quickly. See chapter 10.

13 The Best Spots for Sunset Cocktails

- **Duke's Canoe Club** at the Outrigger Waikiki (Oahu; ☎ **808/923-0711**): It's crowded in the evening, but who can resist Hawaiian music while your bare toes wiggle in the sand? Come in from the beach or the street—it's always a party at Duke's. Entertainment here is tops, and it reaches a crescendo at sunset. See chapter 5.

- **House Without a Key** at the Halekulani (Oahu; ☎ **808/923-2311**): Oahu's quintessential sunset oasis claims several notable elements: It's outdoors on the ocean, with a view of Diamond Head, plus great hula and steel-guitar music—and the best mai tais on the island. Even jaded residents are unable to resist the lure of House Without a Key, a favorite spot for sendoffs, reunions, and everyday gorgeous sunsets. See chapter 5.

- **Mai Tai Bar** at the Royal Hawaiian (Oahu; ☎ **808/923-7311**): This bar without walls is perched a few feet from the sand, with views of the South Shore and the Waianae Mountains. Surfers and paddlers ride the waves while Diamond Head acquires a golden sunset halo. This is one of the most pleasing views of Waikiki Beach; sip a mighty mai tai while Carmen and Keith Haugen serenade you. See chapter 5.

- **Sunset Lanai Lounge** at the New Otani Kaimana Beach Hotel (Oahu; ☎ **808/923-5555**): The hau tree shaded Robert Louis Stevenson as he wrote poems to Princess Kaiulani; today it frames the ocean view from the Sunset Lanai Lounge, next to the Hau Tree Lanai restaurant. Sunset Lanai Lounge is the favorite watering hole of Diamond Head–area beachgoers who love Sans Souci beach, the ocean view, the consummate mai tais, and the live music during weekend sunset hours. See chapter 5.

- **Jameson's** (Oahu; ☎ **808/637-6272**): The mai tais here are dubbed the best in surf city, and the view, though not perfect, isn't hurting either. Across the street from the harbor, this open-air roadside oasis is a happy stop for North Shore wave-watchers and sunset-savvy sightseers. See chapter 5.

- **Huggo's** (Big Island; ☎ **808/329-1493**): Its proximity to the ocean and its location—toward the southern end of Kailua town, right on a coral beach—make Huggo's a magnet at sunset. With its open sides, the best view of Kailua's coastline, and long list of appetizers, you can't lose at Huggo's. See chapter 6.

- **Beach Tree Bar and Grill** at the Four Seasons Resort Hualalai (Big Island; ☎ **808/325-8000**): The thatched bar on the beach seats only a handful, but the restaurant will accept the overflow. This is the finest sunset perch in North Kona: it offers consummate people-watching, waterbirds strutting by, tasty drinks, and the gorgeous ocean. The open-air restaurant with Hawaiian music and hula dancing at sunset also serves excellent fare. See chapter 6.

- **Kimo's** (Maui; ☎ **808/661-4811**): An oceanfront dining room and deck, upstairs dining, and happy-hour libations draw a fun-loving Lahaina crowd. Nosh on sashimi or nachos and take in the views of Lanai and Molokai from this West Maui institution. See chapter 7.

- **Hula Grill** (Maui; ☎ **808/667-6636**): Sit outdoors at the Barefoot Bar, order drinks and gourmet appetizers, and marvel at the wonders of West Maui, where the sun sets slowly and Lanai looks like a giant whale offshore. It's simply magical. See chapter 7.

2

Getting to Know the Hawaiian Islands

by Jeanette Foster

The wealth is measured as in Polynesia not by what you have but by how you feel, then Hawaii may be the richest spot on earth.

Indeed, there's no place quite like this handful of sun-drenched mid-Pacific islands, so remote from any continent yet visited by nearly seven million guests a year. They come from the far corners of the globe seeking relaxation under the tropic sun and leave feeling good inside and out.

That's the nature of Hawaii's overwhelming beauty and almost perfect climate: It makes people feel fulfilled and restored. Those who live here have an inherent sense of well-being and personal connection, which they readily share with strangers through their famous form of hospitality known as "Aloha."

In Hawaii, *aloha* means hello, good-bye, and I love you. With 25 different ethnic groups living in rare harmony on the islands, it's more than a popular expression. It's also a public law. It's on bumper stickers that proclaim "Live Aloha." It makes Hawaii a gentle, kind place where a shaka sign precedes a handshake, where total strangers return your smile, and where old friends meet with a kiss.

Yes, the mythical Hawaii of South Seas literature and Hollywood films really does exist. Here, you'll find palm-fringed blue lagoons, Green-Mansion-like rain forests, hidden gardens, singing waterfalls, wild rivers running through rugged canyons, and smoking yet snow-capped volcanoes soaring 2 miles into the sky. And beaches—gold, red, black, and even green sands caressed by an endless surf are just as you imagined they would be. The possibilities for adventure—and relaxation—are endless.

Each of the six main islands is separate and distinct, larger than life and infinitely complex, as anyone who ventures here soon discovers. There's far too much to see and do on any 2-week vacation, which is why so many people return to the Aloha State year after year.

1 Hawaii Yesterday & Today

Paddling outrigger canoes, the first ancestors of today's Hawaiians followed the stars and birds across a trackless sea to Hawaii, which they called "the land of raging fire." Those first settlers were part of the great Polynesian migration that settled the vast triangle of islands stretching from New Zealand in the southwest to Easter Island in the east to Hawaii in the north. No one is sure when they arrived in Hawaii from Tahiti and the Marquesas Islands, some 2,500 miles to the south, but a dog-bone fish hook found at the southernmost tip of the Big Island has been carbon-dated to A.D. 700.

An entire Hawaiian culture arose over the next 1,500 years. The settlers built temples, fishponds, and aqueducts to irrigate taro plantations. Sailors became farmers and fishermen. Each island was a separate kingdom. The alii (high-ranking chiefs) created a caste system and established taboos. High priests asked the gods Lono and Ku for divine guidance. Ritual human sacrifices were common.

THE "FATAL CATASTROPHE" No ancient Hawaiian ever imagined a *haole* (a white person; literally, one with "no breath") would ever appear on "a floating island." But then one day in 1779, just such a white-skinned person sailed into Waimea Bay on Kauai, where he was welcomed as the god Lono.

The man was 50-year-old Capt. James Cook, already famous in Britain for "discovering" much of the South Pacific. Now on his third great voyage of exploration, Cook had set sail from Tahiti northward across uncharted waters to find the mythical Northwest Passage purportedly linking the Pacific and Atlantic oceans. On his way, Cook stumbled upon the Hawaiian Islands quite by chance. He named them the Sandwich Islands, for the Earl of Sandwich, first lord of the admiralty, who bankrolled the expedition.

Overnight, Stone-Age Hawaii entered the age of iron. Gifts were presented and trade established: nails for fresh water, pigs, and the affections of Hawaiian women. The sailors brought syphilis, measles, and other diseases to which the Hawaiians had no natural immunity, thereby unwittingly wreaking havoc on the native population.

After an unsuccessful attempt to find the Northwest Passage, Cook returned to Kealakekua Bay on the Big Island, where a fight broke out over guns, and the great navigator was killed by a blow to the head. After this "fatal catastrophe," the British survivors sailed home. But Hawaii was now on the sea charts. French, Russian, American, and other traders on the fur route between Canada's Hudson Bay Company and China anchored in Hawaii to get fresh water. More trade—and more disastrous liaisons—ensued.

Two more sea captains left indelible marks on the islands: The first was American John Kendrick, who in 1791 filled his ship with sandalwood and sailed to China. By 1825, Hawaii's sandalwood forests were gone, enabling invasive plants to take charge. The second was Englishman George Vancouver, who in 1793 left cows and sheep, which nibbled the islands to the high-tide line. King Kamehameha I sent to Mexico and Spain for cowboys to round up the wild cattle, thus beginning the islands' *paniolo* tradition.

The tightly woven Hawaiian society, enforced by royalty and religious edicts, began to unravel after the death in 1819 of King Kamehameha I, who had used guns seized

Impressions

We continued to see birds every day . . . sometimes in greater numbers than at others; and between the latitude of 10 and 11, we saw several turtle. All these are looked up as signs of the vicinity of land; we however saw none till daybreak in the Morning of the 18th when an Island was discovered . . .

—Capt. James Cook, *Journal* entry of Friday, Jan. 2, 1778

from a British ship to unite the islands under his rule. His successor, Queen Kaahumanu, abolished the old taboos, thus opening the door for religion of another form.

STAYING TO DO WELL In April of 1820, God-fearing missionaries arrived from New England bent on converting the pagans. "Can these be human beings?" exclaimed their leader, the Rev. Hiram Bingham, upon first glance of "the almost naked savages" whose "appearance of destitution, degradation, and barbarism" he found "appalling."

Intent on instilling their brand of rock-ribbed Christianity on the islands, the missionaries clothed the natives, banned them from dancing the hula, and nearly dismantled their ancient culture. They tried to keep the whalers and sailors out of the bawdy houses, where a flood of whiskey quenched fleet-size thirsts and the virtue of native women was never safe. They taught reading and writing, created the 12-letter Hawaiian alphabet, started a letter press, and began writing the islands' history, until then only an oral account in half-remembered chants.

Children of the missionaries became the islands' business leaders and politicians. They married Hawaiians and stayed on in the islands, causing one wag to remark that the missionaries "came to do good and stayed to do well." In 1848 King Kamehameha III proclaimed the Great Mahele (division), which enabled commoners and eventually foreigners to own crown land. In two generations, more than 80% of all private land was in haole hands. Sugar planters imported waves of immigrants to work the fields as contract laborers. The first Chinese came in 1852, followed by 7,000 Japanese in 1885 and the Portuguese in 1878.

King David Kalakaua was elected to the throne in 1874. This popular "Merrie Monarch" built Iolani Place in 1882, threw extravagant parties, and restored the hula and other native arts to grace. For this, he was much loved. He also gave Pearl Harbor to the United States; it became the westernmost bastion of the U.S. Navy—and the bull's-eye of the infamous Japanese air raid on the sleepy Sunday morning of December 7, 1941.

In 1891, King Kalakaua visited chilly San Francisco, caught a cold, and died in the royal suite of the Sheraton Palace. His sister, Queen Liliuokalani, assumed the throne.

A SAD FAREWELL On January 17, 1893, a group of American sugar planters and missionary descendants, with the support of gun-toting U.S. marines, imprisoned Queen Liliuokalani in her own palace, where she penned the sadly lyric *Aloha Oe*, Hawaii's song of farewell. The monarchy was dead.

A new republic was established, controlled by Sanford Dole, a powerful sugarcane planter. In 1898, Hawaii became an American territory ruled by Dole, and his fellow sugarcane planters became the Big Five, a cartel that controlled banking, shipping, hardware, and every other facet of economic life on the islands.

Oahu's central Ewa Plain soon filled with row crops. The Dole family planted pineapple on its vast acreage. Planters imported more contract laborers from Puerto Rico (1900), Korea (1903), and the Philippines (1907 to 1931). Most of the new immigrants stayed on to establish families and become a part of the islands. Meanwhile, the native Hawaiians became a landless minority.

For a half-century, sugar was king, generously subsidized by the U.S. federal government. The sugar planters dominated the territory's economy, shaped its social fabric, and kept the islands in a colonial-plantation era with bosses and field hands. But the workers eventually struck for higher wages and improved working conditions; the planters were unable to compete with cheap third-world labor costs, and their market share was shrinking. Hawaii's lush fields of sugar and pineapple gradually went to seed, and the plantation era ended.

THE TOURISTS ARRIVE Tourism proper began in the 1860s. Kilauea volcano became the world's prime attraction for adventure travelers, who rode on horseback 29 miles from Hilo to peer into the boiling hellfire. In 1865, a grass version of Volcano House was built on the Halemaumau Crater rim to shelter them; it was Hawaii's first tourist hotel. But tourism really got off the ground with the demise of the plantation era, and it has shaped the islands' history in ways that sugarcane and pineapples never did.

In 1901, W. C. Peacock built the elegant beaux-arts Moana Hotel on Waikiki Beach, and W. C. Weedon convinced Honolulu businessmen to bankroll his plan to advertise Hawaii in San Francisco. Armed with a stereopticon and tinted photos of Waikiki, Weedon sailed off in 1902 for 6 months of lecture tours to introduce "those remarkable people and the beautiful lands of Hawaii." He drew packed houses. A tourism-promotion bureau was formed in 1903, and about 2,000 visitors came to Hawaii that year.

Steamships were Hawaii's tourism lifeline. It took four and a half days to sail from San Francisco to Honolulu. Streamers, leis, and pomp welcomed each Matson Liner at downtown's Aloha Tower. Well-heeled visitors brought trunks, servants, even their Rolls, and stayed for months. Hawaii amused the idle rich with personal tours, floral parades, and shows spotlighting that naughty dance, the hula.

Beginning in 1935 and running for the next 40 years, Webley Edwards' weekly live radio show, "Hawaii Calls," planted the sounds of Waikiki—surf, sliding steel guitar, sweet Hawaiian harmonies, drum beats—in the hearts of millions of listeners in America, Australia, and Canada.

In 1936, visitors could fly to Honolulu on the *Hawaii Clipper*, a seven-passenger Pan American Martin M-130 flying boat, for $360 one way. The flight took 21 hours, 33 minutes. Modern tourism was born, with five flying boats providing daily service between San Francisco and Honolulu. The 1941 visitor count was a brisk 31,846 through December 6.

BOMBS AWAY! On December 7, 1941, Japanese Zeros came out of the rising sun to bomb American warships based at Pearl Harbor. It was the "day of infamy" that plunged the United States into World War II and gave the nation its revenge-laced battle cry, "Remember Pearl Harbor!"

The aftermath of the attack brought immediate changes to the islands. Martial law was declared, stripping the Big Five cartel of their absolute power in a single day. Feared to be spies, Japanese-Americans were interned in Hawaii as well as in California. Hawaii was "blacked out" at night, Waikiki Beach was strung with barbed wire, and Aloha Tower was painted in camouflage. Only young men bound for the Pacific came to Hawaii during the war years. Some came back to graves in a cemetery called Punchbowl.

The postwar years saw the beginnings of Hawaii's faux culture. Harry Yee invented the Blue Hawaii cocktail and dropped in a tiny Japanese parasol. Vic Bergeron created the mai tai, a rum and fresh-lime-juice drink, and opened Trader Vic's, America's first theme restaurant that featured the art, decor, and food of Polynesia. Arthur Godfrey picked up a ukulele and began singing *hapa-haole* tunes on early TV shows. Burt Lancaster and Deborah Kerr made love in the surf at Hanauma Bay in 1954's *From Here to Eternity*. In 1955, Henry J. Kaiser built the Hilton Hawaiian Village, and the 11-story high-rise Princess Kaiulani Hotel opened on a site where the real princess once played. Hawaii greeted 109,000 visitors that year.

STATEHOOD In 1959, Hawaii became the last star on the Stars and Stripes, the 50th of the United States. That year also saw the arrival of the first jet airliners, which

❓ Did You Know?

- The aloha shirt Montgomery Clift wore in his final scene in *From Here to Eternity* is worth $3,500 today.
- Honolulu is second only to San Francisco in restaurant spending—but the locals' favorite meat is Spam.
- There haven't been any billboards in Hawaii since 1926.
- Although capital of the 50th state, Honolulu is closer to Tokyo than to Washington, D.C.
- Strong trade winds during heavy rains cause waterfalls to go *up* the dramatic cliffs of Oahu's Eastern Koolau Mountains instead of down.
- The Big Island's 13,796-foot Mauna Kea volcano often wears a crown of snow between December and March—which makes Hawaii the only place in the world where you can ski and snorkel on the same day. One year, a late snow allowed a ski meet to be held on the Fourth of July.
- Buffaloes imported from Wyoming roam the Hanalei River Valley on Kauai. Some end up in Hanalei and Kapaa restaurants as buffalo burgers.

brought 250,000 tourists to the fledgling state. The personal touch that had defined aloha gave way to the sheer force of numbers. Waikiki's room count virtually doubled in 2 years, from 16,000 in 1969 to 31,000 units in 1971, and more followed before city fathers finally clamped a growth lid on the world's most famous resort. By 1980, annual arrivals had reached four million.

In the early 1980s, the Japanese government decided its citizens should travel overseas, and out they went. Waikiki was one of their favorite destinations, and they brought lots of yen to spend. Their effect on sales in Hawaii was phenomenal: European boutiques opened stores in Honolulu, and duty-free shoppers became the main supporter of Honolulu International Airport. Japanese investors competed for the chance to own or build part of Hawaii. Hotels sold so fast and at such unbelievable prices that heads began to spin with dollar signs.

In 1986, Hawaii's visitor count passed five million. Two years later, it went over six million. Expensive fantasy megaresorts bloomed on the neighbor islands like giant artificial flowers, swelling the luxury market with ever swankier accommodations.

The highest visitor count ever recorded hit 6.9 million in 1990, but the bubble burst in early 1991 with the Gulf War and worldwide recessions. In 1992, Hurricane Iniki devastated Kauai, which is only now staggering back onto its feet. Airfare wars sent Americans to Mexico and the Caribbean. Overbuilt with luxury hotels, Hawaii slashed its room rates, giving middle-class consumers access to high-end digs at affordable prices—a trend that continues as Hawaii struggles to stay atop the tourism heap.

A CULTURAL RENAISSANCE A conch shell sounds, a young man in a bright feather cape chants as torchlight flickers at sunset on Waikiki Beach, and hula dancers begin telling their graceful centuries-old stories by hand. It's a cultural scene out of the past come to life once again—for Hawaii is enjoying a renaissance of hula, chant, and other aspects of its ancient culture. In fact, it's rare to visit the islands these days and not see the real hula danced in traditional costumes.

Once banned by missionaries and then almost forgotten in the rush to embrace America's consumer-based ideals, the hula is a movement of its own today. And a major event: The Merrie Monarch Festival, in honor of King David Kalakaua, attracts an annual crowd of 20,000 to Hilo, on the Big Island, for a week of ancient and modern hula competition and celebration.

The biggest, longest, and most elaborate celebrations of Hawaiian culture are the Aloha Festivals, which encompass more than 500 cultural events from August to October throughout the state, including a reenactment of the ancient ceremony when the king was crowned and received by the royal court. "Our goal is to teach and share our culture," says Gloriann Akau, who manages the Big Island's Aloha Festivals. "In 1946, after the war, Hawaiians needed an identity. We were lost and needed to regroup. When we started to celebrate our culture, we began to feel proud. We have a wonderful culture that had been buried for a number of years. This brought it out again. Self esteem is more important than making a lot of money."

In 1985, native Hawaiian educator, author, and *kupuna* George Kanahele started integrating Hawaiian values into hotels like the Big Island's Mauna Lani and Maui's Kaanapali Beach Hotel. (A *kupuna* is an elder with leadership qualities who requires great respect; Kanahele is a *kupuna* with a Ph.D. from Cornell.) "You have the responsibility to preserve and enhance the Hawaiian culture, not because it's going to make money for you, but because it's the right thing to do," Kanahele told the Hawaii Hotel Association. "Ultimately, the only thing unique about Hawaii is its Hawaiianess. Hawaiianess is our competitive edge."

From general managers to maids, resort employees went through 16 hours of Hawaiian cultural training. They held focus groups to discuss the meaning of *aloha*—the Hawaiian concept of unremitting love. They applied aloha to their work and to their lives. The Kaanapali Beach Hotel was first to instill Hawaiian ways in the hotel staff, followed by the Outrigger hotel chain, one of the biggest in Hawaii. In the last couple of years, many others have joined the movement and instituted Hawaiian programs. No longer content with teaching hula as a joke, resorts now employ a real *kumu hula* (hula teacher) to instruct visitors and have a *kupuna* take guests on treks to visit *heiau* (Hawaiian temples), and ancient petroglyph sites.

THE QUESTION OF SOVEREIGNTY

The cultural renaissance has also made its way into politics. Under the banner of sovereignty, many *kanaka maoli*—or native people, as they call themselves—are demanding restoration of rights taken away more than a century ago when the U.S. overthrew the Hawaiian monarchy and claimed the islands. Their demands were not lost on President Bill Clinton, who was picketed at a Democratic political fundraiser at Waikiki Beach in July 1993. Four months later, Clinton signed a law in which the U.S. Congress "apologizes to Native Hawaiians on behalf of the people of the United States for the overthrow of the Kingdom of Hawaii on January 17, 1893, with the participation of agents and citizens of the United States, and deprivation of the rights of Native Hawaiians to self-determination."

While that could be construed to mean a return to the way things were in Hawaii a century ago, with kings and queens and a royal court, not even neo-nationalists are convinced that's possible. First, the Hawaiians themselves must decide if they want sovereignty, since each of the 30 identifiable sovereignty organizations (and more than 100 splinter groups) has a different view of self-determination, ranging from total independence to nation-within-a-nation status, similar to that of American Indians. In 1993, the Hawaii State Legislature created a 20-member Hawaiian Sovereignty Advisory Commission made up of native Hawaiians to "determine the will of the native Hawaiian people." The commission plans to pose the sovereignty question in a referendum open to anyone with Hawaiian blood who is over 18 years of age wherever they live, including those in jail or prison. Currently, there are an estimated 250,000 Hawaiians on the islands and elsewhere.

ON TO THE 21ST CENTURY America's only island state is emerging as the cultural center and meeting place of the Pacific Rim, with an international cast of characters playing key roles.

Even busy Waikiki Beach is cleaning up its act, replacing time-share vendors with flower lei stands and offering authentic chant and hula in traditional costumes at sunset nightly. No longer a place of tacky T-shirts and souvenir stands, it's evolving into the shopping capital of the Pacific, where people fly in to browse designer boutiques like Cartier, Dunhill, Ferragamo, and Bugatti. Adding to the state's international importance is a spanking-new $214 million Hawaii Convention Center at the gateway to Waikiki. And old and new are combining to create a level of style and service that's both unique and pervasive: Outside urban Honolulu, the islands are transitioning from rural plantation communities to full-blown tourist destinations in their own right, each with its own distinct personality and appeal.

As the sun sets on the 20th century, other tropical islands are closing in on the 50th state's position as the world's premier beach destination. But this isn't just another pretty place in the sun: Its draw continues to be that undeniable quality ingrained in local culture and lifestyle—the quick smiles to strangers, the feeling of family, the automatic extension of courtesy and brotherly love. It's the aloha spirit—and you'll find it nowhere else on the planet but on this singular fleet of islands called Hawaii.

2 Life & Language

Plantations brought so many different people to Hawaii that the state is now a rainbow of ethnic groups. No one group is a majority; everyone's a minority. Living here are Caucasians, African-Americans, American Indians, Eskimos, Japanese, Chinese, Filipinos, Koreans, Tahitians, Vietnamese, Hawaiians, Samoans, Tongans, and other Asian and Pacific islanders. Add a few Canadians, Dutch, English, French, Germans, Irish, Italians, Portuguese, Scottish, Puerto Ricans, and Spaniards.

More than a century ago, William Somerset Maugham noted about Hawaii that "All these strange people live close to each other, with different languages and different thoughts; they believe in different gods and they have different values; two passions alone they share: love and hunger."

More recently, noted travel journalist Jan Morris said of Hawaii's population: "Half the world's races seem to be represented and interbred here, and between them they have created an improbable microcosm of human society as a whole."

In combination, it's a remarkable potpourri. Nearly everyone, I have noticed, retains an element of the traditions of their homeland. Some Japanese-Americans of Hawaii, even after three and four generations removed from the homeland, are more traditional than the Japanese of Tokyo. And the same is true of many Chinese, Korean, Filipinos, and the rest of the 25 or so ethnic groups that make Hawaii a kind of living museum of various Asian and Pacific cultures.

THE HAWAIIAN LANGUAGE

Almost everyone here speaks English, so except for pronouncing the names of places, you should have no trouble communicating in Hawaii. Many folks in Hawaii now speak Hawaiian as well, for the ancient language is making a comeback. Everybody who visits Hawaii, in fact, will soon hear the words *aloha* and *mahalo* (thank you). If you just arrived, you're a *malihini*. Someone who's been here a long time is a *kamaaina*. When you finish a job or your meal, you are *pau* (over). On Friday, it's *pau hana*, work over. You put *pupus* in your mouth (that's Hawaii's version of hors d'oeuvres) when you go *pau hana*.

The Hawaiian alphabet, created by the New England missionaries, has only 12 letters: the five regular vowels (a, e, i, o, and u) and seven consonants (h, k, l, m, n, p, and w). The vowels are pronounced in the Roman fashion, that is, *ah*, *ay*, *ee*, *oh*, and *oo* (as in "too")—not *ay*, *ee*, *eye*, *oh*, and *you*, as in English. For example, *huhu* is pronounced *who-who*. Almost all vowels are sounded separately, although some are pronounced together, as in Kalakaua: *Kah-lah-cow-ah*.

WHAT *HAOLE* MEANS When Hawaiians first saw Western visitors, they called the pale-skinned, frail men *haole*, because they looked so out of breath. In Hawaiian, *ha* means *breath*, and *ole* means an absence of what precedes it. In other words, a lifeless-looking person. Today, the term *haole* is generally a synonym for Caucasian or foreigner and is used casually without intending to cause any disrespect. However, if uttered by an angry stranger who adds certain adjectives like stupid or dumb, the term haole can be construed a mild racial slur.

SOME HAWAIIAN WORDS Here are some basic Hawaiian words that you'll often hear in Hawaii and see throughout this book. For a more complete list of Hawaiian words, point your Internet browser to **www.volcanoalley.com/lang.html**.

akamai smart
alii Hawaiian royalty
aloha greeting or farewell
halau school
hale house or building
heiau Hawaiian temple or place of worship
hui club, assembly
kahuna priest or expert
kamaaina old-timer
kapa tapa, bark cloth
kapu taboo, forbidden
keiki child
lanai porch or veranda
lomilomi massage
mahalo thank you
makai a direction, toward the sea
malihini stranger, newcomer
mana spirit power
mauka a direction, toward the mountains
muumuu loose-fitting gown or dress
nene official state bird, a goose
ono delicious
pali cliff
wiki quick

PIDGIN: 'EH FO'REAL, BRAH

If you venture beyond the tourist areas, you might hear another local tongue: Pidgin English. A conglomeration of slang and words from the Hawaiian language, pidgin developed as a method sugar planters used to communicate with their Chinese laborers in the 1800s. Today it's used by people who grew up in Hawaii to talk with their peers.

"Broke da mouth" (tastes really good) is the favorite pidgin phrase and one you might hear. You could be invited to hear an elder "talk story" (relating myths and memories), or to enjoy local treats like "shave ice" (a tropical snow cone) and "crack seed" (highly seasoned preserved fruit). But since pidgin is really the province of the locals, your visit to Hawaii is likely to pass without you hearing much pidgin at all.

3   A Taste of Hawaii

by Jocelyn Fujii

THE NEW GUARD: HAWAII REGIONAL CUISINE

Since the mid-1980s, when *Hawaii Regional Cuisine* (HRC) ignited a culinary revolution, Hawaii has elevated its standing on the global epicurean map to bona-fide star status. Fresh ideas and sophisticated menus have made the islands a culinary destination applauded and emulated nationwide. (In a tip of the toque to island tradition, "ahi"—a word ubiquitous in Hawaii—has replaced "tuna" on many chic New York menus.) And options have proliferated at all levels of the local dining spectrum: Waves of new Asian residents have planted the food traditions of their homelands in the fertile soil of Hawaii, resulting in unforgettable taste treats true to their Thai, Vietnamese, Japanese, Chinese, and Indo-Pacific roots. Like the peoples of Hawaii, traditions are mixed and matched, as well—and when combined with the bountiful, fresh harvests from sea and land for which Hawaii is known, these ethnic and culinary traditions take on renewed vigor and a cross-cultural, uniquely Hawaiian quality.

This is good news for the eager palate. The best of East and West abounds on the islands. From the very haute to the informal neighborhood gathering place, from the totally eclectic to the purely Japanese to the multi-ethnic plate lunch, dining in Hawaii is one great culinary joy ride.

Expect to encounter Indonesian *sates*, Chinese stir-fries, Polynesian *imu*-baked foods, and guava-smoked meats in sophisticated presentations in the finest dining rooms in the state. If there's pasta or risotto or rack of lamb on the menu, it could be *nori* (red algae) linguine with *opihi* (limpet sauce), or risotto with local seafood served in taro cups, or a rack of lamb in Cabernet and *hoisin sauce* (fermented soybean, garlic, and spices) or with macadamia nuts and coconut. Watch for ponzu sauce, too; it's lemony and zesty, much more flavorful than the soy sauce it resembles, and a welcome new staple on local menus.

While in Hawaii, you'll encounter many labels that embrace the fundamentals of HRC and the sophistication, informality, and nostalgia it encompasses. Euro-Asian, Pacific Rim, Indo-Pacific, Pacific Edge, Euro-Pacific, Fusion cuisine, Hapa cuisine—by whatever name, Hawaii Regional Cuisine has evolved as Hawaii's singular cooking style, what some say is this country's current gastronomic, as well as geographic, frontier. It highlights the fresh seafood and produce of Hawaii's rich waters and volcanic soil, the cultural traditions of Hawaii's ethnic groups, and the skills of well-trained chefs—such as Roy Yamaguchi (Roy's on Oahu, Maui, and Kauai), Peter Merriman (Merriman's on the Big Island and Hula Grill on Maui), George Mavrothalassitis (Four Seasons Resort Wailea), Alan Wong (Alan Wong's Restaurant on Oahu), and Jean-Marie Josselin (A Pacific Cafe on Kauai, Maui, and Oahu)—who broke ranks with their European predecessors to forge new ground in the 50th state. Some of Hawaii's most prominent chefs, such as David Paul (David Paul's Lahaina Grill and the new David Paul's Diamond Head Grill), were not original HRC members but have forged ahead to form their own strong culinary identities.

Fresh ingredients are foremost, and farmers and fishermen work together to provide steady supplies of just-harvested seafood, seaweed, fern shoots, vine-ripened tomatoes, goat cheese, lamb, herbs, taros, gourmet lettuces, and countless harvests from land and sea that wind up in myriad forms on ever-changing menus, prepared in Asian and

Western culinary styles. Exotic fruits introduced by recent Southeast Asian emigrants, such as sapodilla, soursop, and rambutan, are beginning to appear regularly in China-town markets. Aquacultured seafood, from seaweed to salmon to lobster, is a staple on many menus. Additionally, fresh-fruit salsas and sauces—mango, litchi, papaya, pineapple, guava—ginger-sesame-wasabi flavorings, corn cakes with sake sauces, tamarind and fish sauces, coconut-chile accents, tropical-fruit vinaigrettes, and other local and newly arrived seasonings from Southeast Asia and the Pacific impart unique qualities to the preparations.

Here's a sampling of what you can expect to find on a Hawaii regional menu: seared Hawaiian fish with lilikoi shrimp butter; taro-crab cakes; tiger shrimp in *sake-uni* (sea urchin) beurre blanc; Pahoa corn cakes; Molokai sweet-potato or breadfruit vichys-soise; Ka'u orange sauce and Kahua Ranch lamb; fern shoots from Waipio Valley; Maui onion soup and Hawaiian bouillabaisse, with fresh snapper, Kona crab, and fresh aquacultured shrimp; blackened ahi summer rolls; herb-crusted onaga; and gourmet Waimanalo greens, picked that day. With menus that often change daily and the possibili-ties for once-in-a-lifetime dining adventures are more available than ever in Hawaii.

PLATE LUNCHES & MORE: LOCAL FOOD

At the other end of the spectrum is the cuisine of the hoi polloi, the vast and endearing world of "local food." By that, we mean plate lunches and poke, shave ice and saimin, bento lunches and manapua—cultural hybrids all.

Reflecting a polyglot population of many styles and ethnicities, Hawaii's idiosyn-cratic dining scene is eminently inclusive. Consider Surfer Chic: Barefoot in the sand, in a swimsuit, you chow down on a plate lunch ordered from a lunch wagon, con-sisting of fried mahi-mahi, "two scoops rice," macaroni salad, and a few leaves of green, typically julienned cabbage. (Generally, teriyaki beef and shoyu chicken are options.) Heavy gravy is often the condiment of choice, accompanied by a soft drink in a paper cup. Like *saimin*—the local version of noodles in broth topped with scram-bled eggs, green onions, and sometimes, pork—the plate lunch is Hawaii's version of high camp.

Because this is Hawaii, at least a few licks of *poi*—the Hawaiian staple of cooked, pounded taros—and the other examples of indigenous cuisine are de rigueur, if not at a corny luau, then at least in a Hawaiian plate lunch. The native samplers include foods from before and after Western contact, such as *lau lau* (pork, chicken, or fish steamed in ti leaves), *kalua* pork (pork cooked in a Polynesian underground oven known here as an *imu*), *lomi* salmon (salted salmon with tomatoes and green onions), chicken long rice, squid *luau* (octopus cooked in coconut milk and taro tops), *poke* (cubed, raw fish seasoned with onions and seaweed and the occasional sprinkling of roasted *kukui* nuts), *haupia* (creamy coconut pudding), and *kulolo* (a steamed pudding of coconut, brown sugar, and taros).

Bento, another popular choice for the dine-and-dash set, is also available throughout Hawaii. The compact, boxed assortment of picnic fare usually consists of neatly arranged sections of rice, pickled vegetables, and fried chicken, beef, or pork. Increas-ingly, however, the bento is becoming more streamlined and health-conscious, as in macrobiotic bento lunches or vegetarian brown-rice bentos. A derivative of the modest lunch box for Japanese immigrants who once labored in the sugar and pineapple fields, bentos are dispensed ubiquitously throughout Hawaii, from department stores like Daiei and Shirokiya (bento bonanzas) to corner delis and supermarkets.

Also from the plantations come *manapua*, a bready, doughy round with tasty fill-ings of sweetened pork or sweet beans. In the old days, the Chinese "manapua man"

Ahi, Ono & Opakapaka: A Hawaiian Seafood Primer

The fresh seafood in Hawaii has been described as the best in the world. In the pivotal book *The New Cuisine of Hawaii*, by Janice Wald Henderson, acclaimed chef Nobuyuki Matsuhisa (chef-owner of Matsuhisa in Beverly Hills and Nobu in Manhattan and London) writes, "As a chef who specializes in fresh seafood, I am in awe of the quality of Hawaii's fish; it is unparalleled anywhere else in the world." And why not? Without a doubt, the islands' surrounding waters, the waters of the remote northwestern Hawaiian Islands, and a growing aquaculture industry are fertile grounds for this most important of Hawaii's food resources.

The reputable restaurants in Hawaii buy fresh fish daily at predawn auctions or from local fishermen. Some chefs even spear-fish their ingredients themselves. "Still wiggling" is the ultimate term for freshness in Hawaii. The fish can then be grilled over *kiawe* (mesquite) or prepared in innumerable ways.

Although most menus include the Western description for the fresh fish used, most often, the local nomenclature is listed, turning dinner for the uninitiated into a confusing, quasi-foreign experience. To help familiarize you with the menu language of Hawaii, here's a basic glossary of Island fish:

ahi yellowfin or bigeye tuna, important for its use in sashimi and poke at sushi bars and in Hawaii Regional Cuisine

aku skipjack tuna, heavily used by local families in home cooking and poke

ehu red snapper, delicate and sumptuous, yet lesser known than opakapaka (see below)

hapupupu grouper, a sea bass whose use is expanding from ethnic to non-ethnic restaurants

hebi spearfish, mildly flavored and frequently featured as the "catch of the day" in upscale restaurants

TASTY TREATS: SHAVE ICE & MALASSADAS

For dessert or a snack, particularly on Oahu's North Shore, the prevailing choice is shave ice, the island version of a snow cone. At places like Matsumoto Store in Haleiwa, particularly on hot, humid days, long lines of shave-ice lovers gather for their rainbow-colored cones heaped with finely shave ice and topped with sweet, tropical syrups. (The sweet-sour li hing mui flavor is a current rage.) The fast-melting mounds requiring prompt, efficient consumption are quite the local summer ritual for sweet tooths. Aficionados order shave ice with ice cream and sweetened azuki beans plopped in the middle.

You may also encounter *malassadas*, Portuguese versions of doughnuts, and if you do, it's best to eat them immediately. A leftover malassada has all the appeal of a heavy, lumpen, cold doughnut. When fresh and hot, however, as at school carnivals (where

would make his rounds with bamboo containers balanced on a rod over his shoulders. Today, you'll find white or whole-wheat manapua containing chicken, vegetables, curry, and other savory fillings.

The dainter Chinese delicacy, dim sum, is made of translucent wrappers filled with fresh seafood, pork hash, and vegetables, served for breakfast and lunch in Chinatown restaurants. The Hong Kong-style dumplings are ordered fresh and hot from bamboo steamers from invariably brusque servers who move their carts from table to table. Much like hailing a taxi in Manhattan, you have to be quick and loud for dim sum.

kajiki Pacific blue marlin, also called *au*, with a firm flesh and high fat content that make it a plausible substitute for tuna in some raw fish dishes and as a grilled item on menus

kumu goatfish, a luxury item on Chinese and upscale menus, served en papillote or steamed whole, Oriental style, with sesame oil, scallions, ginger, and garlic

mahi-mahi dolphin fish (the game fish, not the mammal) or dorado, a classic sweet, white-fleshed fish requiring vigilance among purists, because it is often disguised as fresh when it's actually "fresh-frozen"—a big difference

monchong bigscale or sickle pomfret, an exotic, tasty fish, scarce but gaining a higher profile on Hawaiian Island menus

nairagi striped marlin, also called *au*; good as sashimi and in poke, and often substituted for ahi in raw-fish products

onaga ruby snapper, a luxury fish, versatile, moist, and flaky; top-of-the-line

ono wahoo, firmer and drier than the snappers, often served grilled and in sandwiches

opah moonfish, rich and fatty, and versatile—cooked, raw, smoked, and broiled

opakapaka pink snapper, light, flaky, and luxurious, suited for sashimi, poaching, sautéeing, and baking; the best-known upscale fish

papio jack trevally, light, firm, and flavorful, and favored in island cookery

shutome broadbill swordfish, of beef-like texture and rich flavor

tombo albacore tuna, with a high fat content, suitable for grilling and sautéeing

uhu parrot fish, most often encountered steamed, Chinese style

uku gray snapper of clear, pale-pink flesh, delicately flavored and moist

ulua large jack trevally, firm-fleshed and versatile

they attract the longest lines) or at bakeries and roadside stands (such as Agnes Portuguese Bake Shop in Kailua, Oahu), the sugary, yeasty doughnut-without-a-hole is enjoyed by many as one of the enduring legacies of the Portuguese in Hawaii.

4 The Natural World: An Environmental Guide to the Islands

Born of violent volcanic eruptions from deep beneath the ocean's surface, the first Hawaiian islands emerged about 70 million years ago—more than 200 million years after the major continental land masses had been formed. Two thousand miles from the nearest continent, Mother Nature's fury began to carve beauty from barren rock. Untiring volcanoes spewed forth curtains of fire that cooled into stone. Severe tropical storms, some with hurricane-force winds, battered and blasted the cooling lava rock into a series of shapes. Ferocious earthquakes flattened, shattered, and reshaped the islands into precipitous valleys, jagged cliffs, and recumbent flatlands. Monstrous surf and gigantic tidal waves rearranged and polished the lands above and below the reaches of the tide.

It took millions upon millions of years for nature to chisel the familiar form of Diamond Head on Oahu, to form Maui's majestic peak of Haleakala, to create the waterfalls of Molokai's northern side, to shape the reefs of Hulopoe Bay on Lanai, and to establish the lush rain forests of the Big Island. The result is an island chain like no other on the planet—a tropical dream of a landscape, rich in unique flora and fauna, surrounded by a vibrant underwater world that will haunt you forever.

THE ISLAND LANDSCAPES

Each of the six main islands has its own particular climate and topography.

OAHU Home to Honolulu, Oahu is the third-largest island in Hawaii (behind the Big Island and Maui.) It's also the most urban, with a population of nearly 900,000. Oahu is defined by two mountain ranges: the Waianae Ridge in the west, and the jagged Koolaus in the east, which form a backdrop for Honolulu. The mountain ranges divide the island into three different environments. The windward side is lush with greenery, ferns, tropical plants, and waterfalls. On the other side, the area between the Waianae Range and the ocean is drier, with sparse vegetation, little rainfall, and an arid landscape. Between the two mountain ranges lies the central Ewa Valley; it's moderate in temperature and vibrant with tropical plants, agricultural fields, and trees.

HAWAII, THE BIG ISLAND By far the largest island at some 4,034 square miles (and still growing), the Big Island is twice the size of all the other Hawaiian islands combined. It's home to every type of climate zone existing in Hawaii. It's not uncommon for there to be 12 feet of snow on the two largest mountain peaks, 13,796-foot Mauna Kea and 13,680-foot Mauna Loa. These mountains are the tallest in the state; what's more, when measured from their true base on the ocean floor, they reach 32,000 feet, making them the tallest mountains in the world. At 4,077 feet, Kilauea Volcano has been continuously erupting since January 3, 1983, and has added more than 600 acres of new land to the Big Island since then. Just a few miles from the barely cooled barren lava lies a pristine rain forest, while on the southern end, there's an arid desert. The rest of the island contains tropical terrain; white-, black-, and even green-sand beaches; windswept grasslands; and productive farming and ranching areas growing tropical fruits, macadamia nuts, coffee, and ornamental flowers.

MAUI When two volcanoes—Mauna Kahalawai, a 5,277-foot ancient volcano in the West Maui Mountains, and 10,000-foot Haleakala—flowed together a million or so years ago, the event created a "Valley Isle" with a range of climates from arid desert to tropical rain forest. This 728-square-mile island is the only place in the world where you can drive from sea level to 10,000 feet in just 38 miles, passing from tropical beaches through sugar and pineapple plantations and rolling grassy hills up past the timber line to the lunar-like surface of the top of Haleakala. In addition to 33 miles of public beaches on the south and western shores, Maui is home to the arid lands of Kihei, the swampy bogs of the West Maui Mountains, the rain forest of Hana, and the desert of Kaupo.

MOLOKAI Roughly the shape and size of Manhattan, Molokai is 37 miles long and 10 miles wide, with a "thumb" protruding out of the North Shore. The North Shore begins on the west, with miles of white-sand beaches that fringe a desert-like landscape. The thumb—the Kalaupapa Peninsula—is cut off by a fence of cliffs, some 2,000 feet tall, that line the remainder of the North Side. Molokai can be divided into two areas: the dry west end; and the rainy, tropical east and north ends, where the high point is Mount Kamakou, at 4,970 feet.

LANAI This small, kidney bean-shaped island—only 13 miles wide by 17 miles long—rises out of the ocean like the shell of a turtle, with cliffs on the west side that rise to a high point of 3,370 feet. Lanai slopes down to sea level on the east and south sides. The only town, Lanai City, sits in the clouds at 1,600 feet. The island's peak is covered with Norfolk pines and is usually shrouded in clouds, while the arid beaches survive on minimal rainfall. One area in particular stands out: the Garden of the Gods, just 7 miles from Lanai City, where oddly strewn boulders lie in the amber- and ocher-colored dirt and bizarre stone formations dot the landscape. The ancient Hawaiians formed romantic legends explaining this enigma, but modern-day scientists still debate its origins.

KAUAI   This compact island, 25 miles long by 33 miles wide, has Mt. Waialeale, the island's highest point at nearly 5,000 feet and the earth's wettest spot, with more than 400 inches of rain annually. Just west of Mt. Waialeale is the barren landscape of Waimea Canyon, dubbed "the Grand Canyon of the Pacific"—the result of the once 10,000-foot-tall Olokele shield volcano, which collapsed and formed a *caldera* (crater) some 3,600 feet deep and 14 miles across. Peaks and craters aren't Kauai's only distinctive landscape features, though, for miles of white-sand beaches rim most of the island, with majestic 2,700-foot cliffs—the spectacular Na Pali Coast—completing the circle. Lush tropical jungle inhabits the north side of the island, while balmy, palm tree–lined beaches are located in the south.

THE FLORA OF THE ISLANDS

Hawaii radiates with sweet-smelling flowers, lush vegetation, and exotic plant life.

FLOWERS

AFRICAN TULIP TREES   Even at a long distance, you can see the flaming red flowers on these large trees, which can grow to be more than 50 feet tall. Children in Hawaii love them because the buds hold water—they use them as water pistols.

ANGEL'S TRUMPET   This is a small tree that can grow up to 20 feet tall, with an abundance of large (up to 10 inches in diameter) pendants—white or pink flowers that resemble, well, trumpets. The Hawaiians call them *nana-honua*, which means "earth gazing." The flowers, which bloom continually from early spring to late fall, have a musky scent. However, beware: All parts of the plant are poisonous and contain a strong narcotic.

ANTHURIUMS   One of Hawaii's most popular cut flowers, anthuriums originally came from the tropical Americas and the Caribbean islands. There are more than 550 species, but the most popular are the heart-shaped red, orange, pink, white, and even purple flowers with tail-like spathes. Look for the heart-shaped green leaves in shaded areas. Anthuriums are very prolific on the Big Island. These exotic plants have no scent but will last several weeks as cut flowers.

BIRDS OF PARADISE   These natives of Africa have become something of a trademark of Hawaii. They're easily recognizable by the orange and blue flowers nestled in gray-green bracts, looking somewhat like birds in flight.

BOUGAINVILLEA   Originally from Brazil, these colorful, tissue-thin bracts ranging in color from majestic purple to fiery orange hide tiny white flowers. A good place to spot them is on the Big Island along the Queen Kaahumanu Highway stretching from Kona Airport to Kailua-Kona.

BROMELIADS   The pineapple plant is the best-known bromeliad; native to tropical South America and the islands of the Caribbean, there are more than 1,400 species. "Bromes," as they're affectionately called, are generally spiky plants ranging in size from a few inches to several feet in diameter. They're popular not only for their unusual foliage but also for their strange and wonderful flowers, which range from colorful spikes to delicate blossoms resembling orchids. Used widely in landscaping and interior decoration, especially in resort areas, bromeliads are found on every island.

COFFEE   Hawaii is the only U.S. state that commercially produces coffee. Coffee is an evergreen shrub with shiny, waxy, dark-green, pointed leaves. The flower is a small, fragrant white blossom that develops into half-inch berries that turn bright red when ripe. Look for coffee at elevations above 1,500 feet on the Kona side of the Big Island, where it has been cultivated for more than 100 years, and on large coffee plantations on Kauai, Molokai, and Maui.

GINGER   Some of the most fragrant flowers in Hawaii are white and yellow ginger. Usually found in clumps and growing 4 to 7 feet tall in areas blessed by rain, these sweet-smelling, 3-inch-wide flowers are composed of three dainty petal-like stamens and three long, thin petals. Both white and yellow ginger is so prolific that many people assume it is native to Hawaii; actually, it was introduced in the 19th century from the Indonesia-Malaysia area. Look for white and yellow ginger from late spring to fall. If you see it on the side of the road, stop and pick a few blossoms—your car will be filled with a divine fragrance for the rest of the day. The only downside is that, once picked, ginger lives only briefly.

Other members of the ginger family frequently seen in Hawaii (there are some 700 species) include red, shell, and torch ginger. Red ginger consists of tall, green stalks with foot-long red "flower heads." The red "petals" are actually bracts; 1-inch-long white flowers are protected by the bracts and can be seen if you look down into the red head. Red ginger, which does not share the heavenly smell of white ginger, lasts a week or longer when cut. Look for red ginger from spring through late fall. Cool, wet mountain forests are ideal conditions for shell ginger; natives of India and Burma, these plants, with their pearly white, clam shell–like blossoms, bloom from spring to fall.

Perhaps the most exotic ginger is the red or pink torch ginger. Cultivated in Malaysia as seasoning (the young flower shoots are used in curries), torch ginger rises directly out of the ground; the flower stalks, which are about 5 to 8 inches in length, resemble the fire of a lighted torch. This is one of the few types of ginger that can bloom year-round.

HELICONIA   Some 80 species of the colorful heliconia family came to Hawaii from the Caribbean and Central and South America. The bright yellow-, red-, green-, and orange-colored bracts overlap and appear to unfold like origami birds. The most obvious heliconia to spot is the lobster claw, which resembles a string of boiled crustacean pincers—the brilliant crimson bracts alternate on the stem. Another prolific heliconia is the parrot's beak; growing to about hip height, it's composed of bright-orange flower bracts with black tips, not unlike the beak of a parrot. Look for parrot's beaks in the spring and summer.

HIBISCUS   One variety of this year-round blossom, the yellow hibiscus, is the official state flower. The 4- to 6-inch hibiscus flowers come in a range of colors, from lily white to lipstick red. The flowers resemble crepe paper, with stamens and pistils protruding spire-like from the center. Hibiscus hedges can grow up to 15 feet tall. Once plucked, the flowers wither quickly.

JACARANDA   Beginning around March and sometimes lasting until early May, these huge, lacy-leaved trees metamorphose into large clusters of spectacular lavender-blue sprays. The bell-shaped flowers drop quickly, leaving a majestic purple carpet beneath the tree.

The Hawaiian Islands

HAWAII (The Big Island)

Hawaii Volcanoes Nat'l Park
Mauna Loa ▲
Kilauea Iki Crater
Mauna Kea ▲
Hilo ✈
Waimea
Kailua-Kona ✈

Alenuihaha Channel

KAHOOLAWE

MAUI
Haleakala National Park
Hana
Kihei ▲
Kahului ✈
Lahaina
Kaanapali

LANAI
Lanai City ✈

MOLOKAI
Kaunakakai ✈

OAHU
HONOLULU
Waikiki ✈
Kailua
Makaha
Laie
Haleiwa

Kauai Channel

KAUAI
Princeville
Hanalei
Lihue ✈
Poipu

NIIHAU

PACIFIC OCEAN

PACIFIC OCEAN

0   31 mi
0   50 km

1-0701

NIGHT-BLOOMING CEREUS Look along rock walls for this spectacular night-blooming flower. Originally from Central America, this vine-like member of the cactus family has green scalloped edges and produces foot-long white flowers that open as darkness falls and wither as the sun rises. The plant also bears a red fruit that's edible.

ORCHIDS To many minds, nothing says Hawaii more than orchid. The orchid family is the largest in the entire plant kingdom. The most widely grown orchid—and the major source of flowers for leis and garnish for tropical libations—are the vanda orchids. The vandas used in the commercial-flower industry in Hawaii are generally lavender or white, but they grow in a rainbow of colors, shapes, and sizes. The orchids used for corsages are the large, delicate cattleya; the ones used in floral arrangements—you'll probably see them in your hotel lobby—are usually dendrobiums. When you're on the Big Island, don't pass up a chance to wander through the numerous orchid farms around Hilo.

PLUMERIA Also known as *frangipani*, this sweet-smelling, five-petal flower, found in clusters on trees, is the most popular choice of lei makers. The Singapore plumeria has five creamy-white petals, with a touch of yellow in the center. Another popular variety, ruba—with flowers from soft pink to flaming red—is also used in leis. When picking plumeria, be careful of the sap from the flower, as it's poisonous and can stain clothes.

PROTEA Originally from South Africa, this unusual oversized plant comes in more than 40 different varieties. Proteas are shrubs that bloom into a range of flower types. Different species range from those resembling pincushions to a species that looks just like a bouquet of feathers. Proteas are long-lasting cut flowers; once dried, they will last for years.

TREES & PLANTS

In addition to these trees and plants, Hawaii abounds with fruit-bearing papaya, banana, litchi, and mango trees. For more on these wonderful edibles, see "Tropical Fruits" on page 13.

BREADFRUIT A large tree—more than 60 feet tall—with broad, sculpted, dark-green leaves, the famous breadfruit produces a round, head-size green fruit that is a staple in the diets of all Polynesians. When roasted or baked, the whitish-yellow meat tastes somewhat like a sweet potato.

MACADAMIA A transplant from Australia, macadamia nuts have become a commercial crop in recent decades in Hawaii, especially on the Big Island and Maui. The large trees—up to 60 feet tall—bear a hard-shelled nut encased in a leathery husk, which splits open and dries when ripe.

BANYAN Among the world's largest trees, banyans are tropical Indian fig trees that have branches which grow out and away from the trunk, forming descending roots that grow down to the ground to feed and form additional trunks, making the tree very stable during tropical storms. The banyan in the courtyard next to the old Court House in Lahaina, on Maui, is an excellent example of a spreading banyan—it covers two-thirds of an acre.

MONKEYPOD The monkeypod is one of Hawaii's most majestic trees; it grows more than 80 feet tall and 100 feet across. Seen near older homes and in parks, the leaves of the monkeypod drop in February and March. The wood is a favorite of wood-working artisans.

SILVERSWORD   This very uncommon and unusual plant is seen only on the Big Island and in the Haleakala Crater on Maui. Once a year, this rare relative of the sunflower family blooms between July and September. Resembling more of a pine cone than a sunflower, the silversword in bloom is a fountain of red-petaled, daisy-like flowers that turn silver soon after blooming.

PANDANUS (HALA)   Called *hala* by Hawaiians, pandanus is native to Polynesia. Thanks to its thick trunk, stilt-like supporting roots, and crown of long, sword-like leaves, the hala tree is easy to recognize. In what is quickly becoming a dying art, Hawaiians weave the *lau* (leaves) of the hala into hats, baskets, mats, bags, and the like.

TARO   Around pools, streams, and in neatly planted fields, you'll see these green heart-shaped leaves, whose dense roots are a Polynesian staple. The ancient Hawaiians pounded the roots into poi. Originally from Sri Lanka, taros are not only a food crop, but are also grown for ornamental reasons.

MARIJUANA   This not-so-rare-and-unusual plant—called *pakalolo*, or "crazy weed," in Hawaiian—is grown throughout the islands. You probably won't see it as you drive along the roads, but if you go hiking, you may glimpse the feathery green leaves with tight clusters of buds. Despite years of police efforts to eradicate the plant, the illegal industry continues. Don't be tempted to pick a few buds, as the purveyors of this nefarious industry don't take kindly to poaching.

THE FAUNA OF THE ISLAND

When the first Polynesians arrived in Hawaii between A.D. 500 and A.D. 800, scientists say they found some 67 *varieties* of endemic Hawaiian birds, a third of which are now believed to be extinct. What's even more astonishing is what they didn't find—there were no reptiles, amphibians, mosquitoes, lice, fleas, or even a cockroach.

MAMMALS

There were only two endemic mammals: the hoary bat and the monk seal. The **hoary bat** must have accidentally flown to Hawaii earlier from either North or South America. It still can be seen during its early evening forays, especially around the Kilauea Crater on the Big Island.

The **Hawaiian monk seal**, a relative of warm-water seals found in the Caribbean and the Mediterranean, was nearly slaughtered into extinction for its skin and oil during the 19th century. These seals have recently experienced a minor population explosion, forcing the relocation of some males from their protected homes in the islets north of the main islands. Periodically, these endangered marine mammals turn up at various beaches throughout the state. They're protected under federal law by the Marine Mammals Protection Act. If you're fortunate enough to see a monk seal, just look; don't disturb one of Hawaii's living treasures.

The first Polynesians brought a few animals from home: dogs, pigs, and chickens (all were for eating), as well as rats (stowaways). All four species are still found in the Hawaiian wild today.

BIRDS

More species of native birds have become extinct in Hawaii in the last 200 years than anywhere else on the planet. Of 67 native species, 23 are extinct and 30 are endangered. Even the Hawaiian crow, **alala**, is threatened.

The **aeo**, or Hawaiian stilt, a 16-inch-long bird with a black head; black coat; white underside; and long, pink legs, can be found in protected wetlands like the Kanaha Wild Life Sanctuary on Maui (where it shares its natural habitat with the Hawaiian coot), the Kealia Pond on Maui, and the Hanalei National Wildlife Refuge on Kauai, which is also home to the Hawaiian duck. Other areas in which you can see protected birds are the Kipuku Puaulu (Bird Park) and the Ola Rain Forest, both in Hawaii Volcanoes National Park on the Big Island, and at Goat Island bird refuge off Oahu, where you can see wedge-tailed shearwaters nesting.

Another great birding venue is the 4,345-acre Kokee Wilderness Forest on Kauai. Various native birds that have been spotted include some of the 22 species of the native honey creepers, whose songs fill the forest. Frequently seen are the **apapane** (a red bird with black wings and a curved black bill), **iiwi** (another red bird with black wings but with orange legs and a salmon-colored bill), **amakihi** (a plain olive-green bird with a long, straight bill), and **anianiau** (a tiny-yellow bird with a thin, curved bill). Also in the forest is the **elepaio**, a small, gray flycatcher with an orange breast and an erect tail. A curious fellow, the elepaio comes out to investigate any unusual whistles. The most common native bird at Kokee—and the most easily seen—is the **moa**, or red jungle fowl, a chicken brought to Hawaii by the Polynesians.

To get a good glimpse of the seabirds that frequent Hawaii, drive to Kilauea Point on Kauai's North Shore. Here, you can easily spot **red-** and **white-footed boobies**, **wedge-tailed shearwaters, frigate birds, red-tailed tropic birds,** and the **Laysan albatross.**

Endemic to the islands, the **nene** is Hawaii's state bird. It's being brought back from the brink of extinction through captive breeding and by strenuous protection laws. A relative of the Canadian goose, the nene stands about 2 feet high and has a black head and yellow cheek, a buff neck with deep furrows, a grayish-brown body, and clawed feet. It gets its name from its nasal, two-syllable call, "nay-nay." The approximately 500 nenes in existence can be seen in only three locations: at Haleakala National Park on Maui, at Mauna Kea State Park bird sanctuary, and on the slopes of Mauna Kea on the Big Island.

The Hawaiian short-eared owl, the **pueo,** which grows to between 12 and 17 inches, can be seen at dawn and dusk on Kauai, Maui, and the Big Island, when the black-billed, brown-and-white bird goes hunting for rodents. Pueos are highly regarded by Hawaiians; according to legend, spotting a pueo is a good omen.

OTHER LAND FAUNA

GECKOS   These harmless, soft-skinned, insect-eating lizards come equipped with suction pads on their feet that enable them to climb walls and windows so that they can reach tasty insects like mosquitoes and cockroaches. You'll see them on windows outside a lighted room at night or hear their cheerful chirp.

MONGOOSES   The mongoose was a mistake in Hawaii. It was brought here in the 19th century to counteract the ever-growing rat problem. Rats are nocturnal creatures, sleeping during the day and wandering out at night; mongooses, however, are day creatures. Instead of getting rid of the rat problem, the mongooses eat bird eggs, contributing to the deterioration of the native bird population.

SNAKES   Hawaii has but one tiny earthworm-like snake. On the island of Guam, the brown tree snake has obliterated most of the bird population. Officials in Hawaii are well aware of this danger and are committed to preventing snakes from entering the state.

SEALIFE

Approximately 680 species of fish are known to inhabit the waters around the Hawaiian Islands. Of those, approximately 450 species stay close to the reef and inshore areas.

CORAL

The reefs surrounding Hawaii are made up of various coral and algae. The living corals grow through sunlight that feeds a specialized algae, which in turn allows the development of the coral's calcareous skeleton. It takes thousands of years for reefs to develop. The reef attracts and supports fish and crustaceans, which use it for food, habitat, mating, and raising their young. Mother Nature can cause the destruction of the reef with a strong storm or large waves, but humans—through a seemingly unimportant act such as touching the coral—have proven even more destructive to the fragile reefs.

The corals most frequently seen in Hawaii are hard, rock-like formations named for their familiar shapes: antler, cauliflower, finger, plate, and razor coral. Wire coral looks just like its name—a randomly bent wire growing straight out of the reef. Some coral appears soft, such as tube coral; it can be found in the ceilings of caves. Black coral, which resembles winter-bare trees or shrubs, is found at depths of more than 100 feet.

REEF FISH

Of the approximately 450 reef fish, about 27 percent are native to Hawaii and are found nowhere else in the world. Over the millions of years of gestation of the islands, as they were born from the erupting volcanoes, ocean currents—mainly from Southeast Asia—carried the larvae of thousands of marine animals and plants to Hawaii's reef; of those, approximately 100 species not only adapted, but thrived. Some species are much bigger and more plentiful than their Pacific cousins, and many developed unique characteristics. Some, like the lemon or milletseed butterfly fish, are not only particular to Hawaii but are also unique within their larger, worldwide family in their specialized schooling and feeding behaviors. Another surprising thing about Hawaii endemically is how common some of the native fish are: You can see the saddleback wrasse, for example, on virtually any snorkeling excursion or dive in Hawaiian waters. Some of the reef fish you might spot while you're underwater follow:

ANGEL FISH Often mistaken for butterfly fish, angel fish can be distinguished by the spine, located low on the gill plate. Angel fish are very shy; several species live in colonies close to coral for protection.

BLENNIES Small, elongated fish, blennies range from 2 to 10 inches, with the majority in the 3- to 4-inch range. Blennies are so small that they can live in tide pools; you might have a hard time spotting one.

BUTTERFLY FISH Some of the most colorful of the reef fish, butterfly fish are usually seen in pairs (scientists believe they mate for life) and appear to spend most of their day feeding. There are 22 species of butterfly fish, of which three (bluestripe, lemon or milletseed, and multiband or pebbled butterfly fish) are endemic. Most butterfly fish have a dark band through the eye and a spot near the tail resembling an eye, meant to confuse their predators (moray eels love to lunch on them).

EELS Moray and conger eels are the common eels seen in Hawaii. Morays are usually docile unless provoked, or if there's food or an injured fish around. Unfortunately, some morays have been fed by divers and—being intelligent creatures—associate divers with food; thus, they can become aggressive. But most morays like to keep to themselves, hidden in their hole or crevice. While morays may look menacing, conger eels look downright happy, with big lips and pectoral fins (situated so that they look like big ears) that give them the appearance of a perpetually smiling face. Conger eels have crushing teeth so they can feed on crustaceans; in fact, since they're sloppy eaters, they usually live with shrimp and crabs who feed off the crumbs they leave.

PARROT FISH One of the largest and most colorful of the reef fish, parrot fish can grow up to 40 inches long. Parrot fish are easy to spot—their front teeth are fused together, protruding like buck teeth and resembling a parrot's beak. These unique teeth allow them to feed by scraping algae from rocks and coral. The rocks and coral pass through the parrot fish's system, resulting in fine sand. In fact, most of the white sand found in Hawaii is parrot-fish waste; one large parrot fish can produce a ton of sand a year. Native parrot fish species include yellowbar, regal, and spectacled.

SCORPION FISH This is a family of what scientists call "ambush predators." They hide under camouflaged exteriors and ambush their prey when they come along. Several sport a venomous dorsal spine. These fish don't have a gas bladder, so when they stop swimming, they sink—that's why you usually find them "resting" on ledges and on the ocean bottom. Although they're not aggressive, an inattentive snorkeler or diver could feel the effects of those venomous spines—so be very careful where you put your hands and feet in the water.

SURGEONFISH Sometimes called *tang*, surgeonfish get their name from the scalpel-like spines located on each side of their bodies near the base of their tails. Some surgeonfish have a rigid spine, while others have the ability to fold their spine against their body until it's needed for defense purposes. Some surgeonfish, like the brightly colored yellow tang, are boldly colored; others are adorned in more conservative shades of gray, brown, or black. The only endemic surgeonfish—and the most abundant in Hawaiian waters—is the convict tang, a pale white fish with vertical black stripes (like a convict's uniform).

WRASSE This is a very diverse family of fish, ranging in size from 2 to 15 inches. Several wrasse are brilliantly colored and change their colors through aging and sexual dimorphism (sex changing). Wrasse have the ability to change gender from female (when young) to male with maturation. Several types of wrasse are endemic to Hawaii: the Hawaiian cleaner, shortnose, belted, and gray (or old woman).

GAME FISH

Hawaii is known around the globe as *the* place for big-game fish—marlin, swordfish, and tuna—but its waters are also great for catching other offshore fish like mahi-mahi, rainbow runner, and wahoo; coastal fish like barracuda and scad; bottom fish such as snappers, sea bass, and amberjack; and inshore fish like trevally, bonefish, and others.

BILLFISH There are six different kinds of billfish found in the offshore waters around the islands: Pacific blue marlin, black marlin, sailfish, broadbill swordfish, striped marlin, and shortbill spearfish. Hawaii billfish range in size from the 20-pound shortbill spearfish and striped marlin to the 1,805-pound Pacific blue marlin, the largest marlin ever caught on rod and reel anywhere in the world.

TUNA Tuna ranges in size from small (a pound or less) mackerel tuna used as bait (Hawaiians call them *oioi*) to 250-pound yellowfin ahi tuna. Other local species of tuna are bigeye, albacore, kawakawa, and skipjack.

OTHER OFFSHORE FISH Some of the best fish for eating are also found in offshore waters: mahi-mahis (also known as *dolphin fish* or *dorado*), in the 20- to 70-pound range; rainbow runners, from 15 to 30 pounds; and wahoo (*ono*), from 15 to 80 pounds. Shoreline fishermen are always on the lookout for trevallies (the state record for a giant trevally is 191 lb.), bonefish, ladyfish, threadfin, leatherfish, and goatfish. Bottom fishermen pursue a range of snappers—red, pink, gray, and others—as well as sea bass (the state record is a whopping 563 lb.) and amberjack, which weigh up to 100 pounds.

WHALES

HUMPBACKS   The most popular visitors to Hawaii come every year, beginning in November and staying until the springtime (April or so) when they return to their summer home in Alaska. Humpback whales—some as big as a city bus and weighing many tons—migrate to the warm, protected Hawaiian waters in the winter to mate and calve. On every island, you can take winter whale-watching cruises that will let you observe these magnificent leviathans close up, or you can spot their signature spouts of water from shore as they expel water in the distance. Humpbacks grow to up to 45 feet long, so when they *breach* (propel their entire body out of the water) or even wave a fluke, you can see it for miles.

OTHER WHALES   Humpbacks are among the biggest whales found in Hawaiian waters, but other whales—like pilot, sperm, false killer, melon-headed, pygmy killer, and beaked—can be seen year-round, especially in the calm waters off the Big Island's Kona Coast. These whales usually travel in pods of 20 to 40 animals and are very social, interacting with each other on the surface.

SHARKS

Yes, Virginia, there *are* sharks in Hawaii, but more than likely, you won't see a shark unless you specifically go looking for one. The ancient Hawaiians had a great respect for sharks and believed that some sharks were reincarnated relatives who had returned to assist them.

About 40 different species of sharks inhabit the waters surrounding Hawaii, ranging from the totally harmless whale shark—at 60 feet, the world's largest fish—which has no teeth and is so docile that it frequently lets divers ride on its back, to the not-so-docile, infamous—and extremely uncommon—great white shark. The most common sharks seen in Hawaii are white-tip reef sharks, gray reef sharks (about 5 feet long), and black-tip reef sharks (about 6 feet long).

HAWAII'S ECOSYSTEM PROBLEMS

Officials at Hawaii Volcanoes National Park on the Big Island saw a potential problem a few decades ago with people taking a few rocks home with them as "souvenirs." To prevent this problem from escalating, the park rangers created a legend that the fiery volcano goddess, Pelé, did not like people taking anything (rocks, chunks of lava) from her home, and bad luck would befall anyone disobeying her wishes. There used to be a display case in the park's visitor center filled with letters from people who had taken rocks from the volcano, relating stories of all the bad luck that followed. Most of the letters begged Pelé's forgiveness and instructed the rangers to please return the rock to the exact location that was its original home.

Unfortunately, Hawaii's other ecosystem problems can't be handled as easily.

MARINE LIFE   Hawaii's beautiful and abundant marine life has attracted so many visitors that they threaten to overwhelm it. A great example of this overenthusiasm is Oahu's **Hanauma Bay.** Crowds flock to this beautiful bay, a marine preserve that features calm, protected swimming and snorkeling areas loaded with tropical reef fish. It was such a perfect spot that too many people flocked here, forcing government officials to charge an admission fee and limit the number of people that can enter the bay at any one time. Commercial tour operators have been restricted entirely in an effort to balance the people-to-fish ratio.

Another marine life conservation area that suffers from overuse is **Molokini,** a small crater off the coast of Maui. In the 1970s, residents made the area a conservation district in order to protect the unique aquarium-like atmosphere of the waters inside the arms of the crater. Unfortunately, once it was protected, everyone wanted to go there just to see what was worth special protection. Twenty years ago, one or two small six-passenger boats made the trip once a day to Molokini; today, it is not uncommon to sight 20 or more boats, each carrying 20 to 49 passengers, moored inside the tiny crater. One tour operator has claimed that, on some days, it's so crowded that you can actually see a slick of suntan oil floating on the surface of the water.

Hawaii's **reefs** have faced increasing impact over the years as well. Runoff of soil and chemicals from construction, agriculture, erosion, and even heavy storms can blanket and choke a reef, which needs sunlight to survive. In addition, the intrusion of foreign elements—caused by things such as breaks in sewage lines—can cause problems to Hawaii's reef. Human contact with the reef can also upset the ecosystem. Coral, the basis of the reef system, is very fragile; snorkelers and divers grabbing onto it can break off pieces that took decades to form. Feeding the fish can also upset the balance of the ecosystem (not to mention upsetting the digestive systems of the fish). One glass-bottom boat operator reported that he fed an eel for years, considering it his "pet" eel. One day, the eel decided that he wanted more than just the food being offered and bit the diver's fingers. Divers and snorkelers report that in areas where the fish are fed, the fish have become more aggressive; clouds of reef fish—normally shy—surround divers, demanding food.

FLORA One of Hawaii's most fragile environments is the rain forest. Any intrusion—from hikers carrying seeds in on their shoes to the rooting of wild boars—can upset the delicate balance in these complete ecosystems. In recent years, development has moved closer and closer to the rain forest. On the Big Island, people have protested the invasion of bulldozers and the drilling of geothermal wells in the Wao Kele O Puna rain forest for years, claiming that the damage done is irreparable.

FAUNA The biggest impact on the fauna in Hawaii is the decimation of native birds by feral animals that have destroyed the bird's habitats, and by mongooses that have eaten the birds' eggs and young. Government officials are vigilant about snakes because of the potential damage tree snakes can do to the remaining birdlife.

3

Planning a Trip to Hawaii

by Jeanette Foster

Hawaii has so many places to explore, things to do, sights to see—it can be bewildering to plan your trip with so much vying for your attention. Where to start? That's where we come in. In the pages that follow, we've compiled everything you need to know to plan your ideal trip to Hawaii: airlines, seasons, a calendar of events, how to make camping reservations, and much more (even how to get married on the islands).

The first thing to do is to **decide where you want to go.** You may stare at a map of Hawaii, looking at the six major islands—Oahu, the Big Island of Hawaii, Maui, Molokai, Lanai, and Kauai—and wonder how to choose. Each island is distinct from the others and has its own personality, which we've tried to capture in the chapters that follow. Peruse each chapter to see which islands fit the profile and offer the activities that you're looking for.

We strongly recommend that you **limit your island-hopping to one island per week.** If you decide to go to more than one in a week, be warned: You could spend much of your precious vacation time in airports, waiting to board your flights and waiting for your luggage to arrive, and checking in and out of hotels. Not much fun!

Our second trip is to **fly direct to the island of your choice if you can;** doing so can save you a 2-hour layover in Honolulu and another plane ride. Oahu, the Big Island, Maui, and Kauai all receive direct flights from the mainland now; if you're heading to Molokai or Lanai, you'll have to connect through Honolulu.

Lastly, remember that **the process of planning can be part of the excitement** of your trip. So, in addition to reading this guide, we suggest that you spend some time either on the Internet looking at sites (we've included Web site addresses throughout this book) or calling and writing for brochures. We fully believe that searching out the best deals and planning your dream vacation to Hawaii should be half the fun.

1 Visitor Information & Money

VISITOR INFORMATION

For information about traveling in Hawaii, contact the **Hawaii Visitors and Convention Bureau (HVCB)**, Suite 801, Waikiki

Business Plaza, 2270 Kalakaua Ave., Honolulu, HI 96815 (☎ **800/GO-HAWAII** or 808/923-1811; www.gohawaii.com). Among other things, the bureau publishes the helpful *Accommodations and Car Rental Guide* and supplies free brochures, maps, and the *Islands of Aloha* magazine, the official HVCB magazine.

The HVCB also has a U.S. mainland office at 180 Montgomery St., Suite 2360, San Francisco, CA 94104 (☎ **800/353-5846**). All other HVCB offices on the mainland have been closed due to budget constraints.

If you want information about working and living in Hawaii, contact **The Chamber of Commerce of Hawaii,** 1132 Bishop St., Suite 200, Honolulu, HI 96815 (☎ **808/545-4300**).

INFORMATION ON HAWAII'S PARKS

NATIONAL PARKS   Hawaii has two national parks—one on the Big Island of Hawaii and one on Maui—as well as a number of other nationally administered parks. The following offices can supply you with hiking and camping information:

- On **The Big Island: Hawaii Volcanoes National Park,** P.O. Box 52, Hawaii National Park, HI 96718 (☎ 808/985-6000; www.nps.gov/havo); **Puuhonua O Honaunau National Historical Park,** P.O. Box 129, Honaunau, HI 96726 (☎ 808/328-2326; www.nps.gov/puho); **Puukohola Heiau National Historic Site,** P.O. Box 44340, Kawaihae, HI 96743 (☎ 808/882-7218; www.nps.gov/puhe); and **Kaloko-Honokohau National Historical Park,** 72-4786 Kanalani St., Kailua-Kona, HI 96740 (☎ 808/329-6881; www.nps.gov/kaho).

- On **Maui: Haleakala National Park,** P.O. Box 369, Makawao, HI 96768 (☎ 808/572-9306; www.nps.gov/hale).

- On **Molokai: Kalaupapa National Historical Park,** P.O. Box 2222, Kalaupapa, HI 96742 (☎ 808/567-6802; www.nps.gov/kala).

STATE PARKS   To find out more about Hawaii's state parks, contact the **Hawaii State Department of Land and Natural Resources,** 1151 Punchbowl St., no. 130, Honolulu, HI 96813 (☎ **808/587-0300;** www.hawaii.gov). It can provide you with information on hiking and camping at any of Hawaii's state parks and will send you free topographic trail maps on request.

HAWAII ON THE NET

Here are some useful links to Hawaii:

- **Hawaii Visitors & Convention Bureau:** www.gohawaii.com
- **Hawaii State Vacation Planner:** www.hshawaii.com
- **Planet Hawaii:** www.planet-hawaii.com/travel
- Oahu's **Waikiki Visitors Association:** www.gohonolulu.com
- The Big Island's **Kona-Kohala Resort Association:** www.plant-hawaii.com/kohala-coast
- **Maui Visitors Bureau:** www.visitmaui.com
- **Maui information:** www.maui.net
- Maui's **Kaanapali Beach Resort Association:** www.maui.net/kbra
- **Molokai information:** www.molokai.com
- **Kauai Visitor Information:** kauai-hawaii.com
- Kauai's **Poipu Beach Resort Association:** www.poipu-beach.com
- **Hawaii Yellow Pages:** www.surfhi.com
- **Weather information:** www.weather.com/weather/us/states/Hawaii.html *or* www.cnn.com/WEATHER/cities/us.hawaii.html

- **Backpacking information:** www.backpackers-hawaii.com

For national and state parks links, see "Information on Hawaii's Parks," above.

MONEY

Hawaii pioneered the use of automatic teller machines (ATMs) more than two decades ago, and now they're everywhere except on Lanai. You'll find them at most banks, in supermarkets, at Long's Drug stores, at Honolulu International Airport, and in some resorts and shopping centers, like Ala Moana Center and Aloha Tower Market Place on Oahu and Whaler's Village in Kaanapali, Maui. It's actually cheaper and faster to get cash from an ATM than to fuss with traveler's checks; and credit cards are accepted just about everywhere. To find the ATM location nearest you, call ☎ **800/424-7787** for the **Cirrus** network or ☎ **800/843-7587** for the **Plus** system. You can also locate Cirrus ATMs on the Web at **www.mastercard.com** and Plus ATMs at **www.visa.com**.

While the United States dollar is the coin of the realm in Hawaii, you can easily exchange most major foreign currencies (see "Money" in chapter 4).

2 When to Go

The majority of visitors don't come to Hawaii when the weather's best in the islands; rather, they come when it's at its worst everywhere else. Thus, the **high season**—when prices are up and resorts are booked to capacity—is generally from mid-December through March or mid-April. The last 2 weeks of December in particular is the prime time for travel to Hawaii; if you're planning a holiday trip, make your reservations as early as possible, expect to travel with holiday crowds, and expect to pay top dollar for accommodations and airfare.

The **off-seasons,** when the best bargain rates are available and the islands less crowded, are spring (from mid-April to mid-June) and fall (from September to mid-December)—a paradox, since these are the best seasons to be in Hawaii, in terms of reliably great weather. If you're looking to save money, or if you just want to avoid the crowds, this is the time to visit. Hotel rates tend to be significantly lower during these off-seasons. Airfares also tend to be lower—again, sometimes substantially—and good packages and special deals are often available.

Note: If you plan to come to Hawaii between the last week in April and mid-May, be sure you book your accommodations, interisland air reservations, and car rental in advance. In Japan, the last week of April is called **Golden Week,** because three Japanese holidays take place one after the other. Waikiki is especially busy with Japanese tourists during this time, but the neighbor islands have seen dramatic increases in recent years.

Due to the large number of families traveling in **summer** (June through August), you won't get the fantastic bargains of spring and fall. However, you'll still do much better on packages, airfare, and accommodations than you will in the winter months.

CLIMATE

Since Hawaii lies at the edge of the tropical zone, it technically has only two seasons, both of them warm. There's a dry season that corresponds to **summer,** while the rainy season generally runs during the **winter** from November to March. It rains every day somewhere in the islands anytime of the year, but the rainy season can cause "gray" weather and spoil your tanning opportunities. Fortunately, it seldom rains in one spot for more than 3 days straight.

The **year-round temperature** usually varies no more than 15°F. At the beach, the average daytime high in summer is 85°F (29.4°C), while the average daytime high in

Travel Tip

Your best bets for total year-round sun are **Waikiki Beach** and the **Ko Olina** (southwest) coast of Oahu, the Big Island's **Kona-Kohala Coast**, the South (**Kihei-Wailea**) and West (**Lahaina-Kapalua**) Maui coasts, and **Poipu Beach** and the southwest coast of Kauai.

winter is 78°F (25.6°C); nighttime lows are usually about 10° cooler. But how warm it is on any given day really depends on *where* you are on the island.

The islands are like ships in that each has leeward sides and windward sides. The **leeward** sides (the west and south) are usually hot and dry, while the **windward** sides (east and north) are generally cooler and moist. When you want arid, sun-baked, desert-like weather, go leeward. When you want lush, often wet, jungle-like weather, go windward.

Hawaii is also full of **microclimates**, thanks to its interior valleys, coastal plains, and mountain peaks. Kauai's Mt. Waialeale on Kauai is the wettest spot on earth, yet Waimea Canyon, just a few miles away, is almost a desert. On the Big Island, Hilo is the wettest city in the nation, with 180 inches of rainfall a year, while at Puako, only 60 miles away, it rains less than 6 inches a year. If you travel into the mountains, it can change from summer to winter in a matter of hours, since it's cooler the higher up you go. So if the weather doesn't suit you, just go to the other side of the island—or head into the hills.

On rare occasions, the weather can be disastrous, like when Hurricane Iniki crushed Kauai in September 1992 with 225-mile-an-hour winds. Tsunamis, huge tidal waves caused by far-off earthquakes, have swept Hilo and the South Shore of Oahu. But those are extreme exceptions. Mostly, one day follows another here in glorious, sunny procession, each quite like the other.

HOLIDAYS

When Hawaii observes holidays, especially those over a long weekend, travel between the islands increases, interisland airline seats are fully booked, rental cars are at a premium, and hotels and restaurants are busier than at other times.

Federal, state, and county government offices are closed on all federal holidays: January 1 (New Year's Day), the third Monday in January (Martin Luther King, Jr. Day), the third Monday in February (Presidents' Day, Washington's Birthday), the last Monday in May (Memorial Day), July 4 (Independence Day), the first Monday in September (Labor Day), the second Monday in October (Columbus Day), November 11 (Veteran's Day), the fourth Thursday in November (Thanksgiving Day), and December 25 (Christmas).

State and county offices also are closed on local holidays, including Prince Kuhio Day (March 26), honoring the birthday of Hawaii's first delegate to the U.S. Congress; King Kamehameha Day (June 11), a statewide holiday commemorating Kamehameha the Great, who united the islands and ruled from 1795 to 1819; and Admissions Day (the third Friday in August), which honors the admittance of Hawaii as the 50th state on August 21, 1959.

Other special days celebrated in Hawaii by many people but which involve no closing of federal, state, and county offices are the Chinese New Year (in January or February), Girls' Day (March 3), Buddha's Birthday (April 8), Father Damien's Day (April 15), Boys' Day (May 5), Samoan Flag Day (in August), Aloha Week (in September or October), and Pearl Harbor Day (December 7).

HAWAII CALENDAR OF EVENTS

Please note that, as with any schedule of upcoming events, the following information is subject to change; always confirm the details before you plan your schedule around an event. For a complete and up-to-date list of events throughout the islands, point your Internet browser to **www.hawaiian.net/~mahalo/calendar/current.html**.

January

- **Morey World Body Boarding Championship,** Banzai Pipeline, North Shore, Oahu. Competition is determined by the best wave selection and maneuvers on the wave. Call ☎ **808/396-2326.** Early January.

- **PGA Kapalua Mercedes Championship,** Kapalua Resort, Maui. Top PGA golfers compete for $1 million. Weekend after New Year's. Call ☎ **808/669-0244** for this year's date and ticket information.

- **Hula Bowl Football All-Star Classic,** War Memorial Stadium, Maui. An annual all-star football classic featuring America's top college players. Second week in January; ticket orders start being processed on April 1 for next January's game. Call ☎ **808/947-4141.**

- **Celebration of Whales,** Four Seasons Resort Wailea, Maui. Experts host discussions, whale-watching excursions, entertainment, social functions, and art exhibits. Call ☎ **808/847-8000.** Last weekend in January.

- **Narcissus Festival,** Honolulu, Oahu. Around the Chinese New Year, this cultural festival includes a queen pageant, cooking demonstrations, and a cultural fair. January or February, depending on the Chinese New Year. Call ☎ **808/953-3181.**

- **Senior Skins Tournament,** Mauna Lani Resort, Kohala, Big Island. Longtime golfing greats participate in this four-man tournament for $500,000 in prize money. Call ☎ **808/885-6655.**

- ✪ **Ka Molokai Makahiki,** Kaunakakai Town Baseball Park, Mitchell Pauole Center, Kaunakakai, Molokai. Makahiki, a traditional time of peace in ancient Hawaii, is re-created with performances by Hawaiian music groups and hula halau, ancient Hawaiian games, a sporting competition, and Hawaiian crafts and food. A wonderful chance to experience the Hawaii of yesteryear. Late January. Call ☎ **800/800-6367** or 808/553-3876.

- **Ala Wai Challenge,** Ala Wai Park, Waikiki, Oahu. This all-day event features ancient Hawaiian games, like *ulu maika* (bowling a round stone through pegs), *oo ihe* (spear-throwing at an upright target), *huki kaula* (tug of war), and a quarter-mile outrigger canoe race. This is a great place to hear Hawaiian music. Call ☎ **808/923-1802.**

- **MasterCard Championship,** Jack Nicklaus Signature Course, Four Seasons Resort Hualalai, Kona, Big Island. Formerly known as the Tournament of Champions, this is the season-opening competition for the elite groups of champions who qualified for a berth by winning a Senior PGA Tour event. The 54-hole competition features a $1 million purse. Call ☎ **808/325-8000.**

February

- **Annual Mauna Kea Ski Meet,** Big Island. Host Dick Tillson invites intrepid skiers to open competition in men's and women's parallel slalom on the highest peak in the Pacific. First weekend in February. Call ☎ **808/943-6643.**

- **NFL Pro Bowl Battle of the Gridiron,** Ihilani Resort and Spa, Oahu. Kicking off the NFL Pro Bowl, a position and skills-oriented challenge between the best of the best in the National Football League. First Saturday in February. Call ☎ **808/521-4322.**

- **NFL Pro Bowl,** Aloha Stadium, Honolulu, Oahu. The National Football League's best pro players square off in this annual gridiron all-star game. First Sunday in February. Call ☎ **808/486-9300.**

- ✪ **Buffalo's Big Board Classic,** Makaha Beach, Oahu. A traditional Hawaiian surfing, longboarding, and canoe-surfing contest. First two weeks in February. Call ☎ **808/951-7877.**

- **United Airlines Hawaiian Open,** Waialae Country Club, Oahu. A $1.2 million PGA golf event featuring some of the game's top pros. Second week in February. Call ☎ **808/526-1232.**

- **The Great Aloha Run,** Oahu. Thousands run 8¼ miles from Aloha Tower to Aloha Stadium. Always held on Presidents' Day (third Monday in February). Call ☎ **808/528-7388.**

- ✪ **Waimea Town Celebration,** Waimea, Kauai. An annual party on Kauai's west side celebrating the Hawaiian and multi-ethnic history of the town where Capt. Cook first landed. This is the island's biggest two-day event, drawing some 10,000 people. Top Hawaiian entertainers, sporting events, rodeo, and lots of food are on tap during the weekend celebration. Call ☎ **808/338-9957.**

- **Sand Castle Building Contest,** Kailua Beach Park, Oahu. Students from the University of Hawaii School of Architecture compete against professional architects to see who can build the best, most unusual, and most outrageous sand sculpture. Call ☎ **808/956-7225** for this year's date.

- ✪ **Punahou School Carnival,** Punahou School, Honolulu. Everything you can imagine in a school carnival, from high-speed rides to homemade jellies, all benefiting scholarship funds for Hawaii's most prestigious high school. Call ☎ **808/944-5753.**

March

- **Hawaii Challenge International Sportkite Championship,** Kapiolani Park, Oahu. The longest-running sportkite competition in the world attracts the top kite pilots around the globe. First weekend in March. The next weekend is the **International Kite Festival,** on Oahu's Sandy Beach. Here, more than 130 competitors participate in events such as a kite ballet to Taiko drumming and the world's largest kite flying. Call ☎ **808/735-9059.**

- **Annual Merchant Street St. Patrick's Day Block Party,** Merchant Street between Nuuanu Avenue and Bethel Street, Honolulu, Oahu. Everybody's Irish for one evening a year, even in Hawaii, as everybody turns out in downtown Honolulu to celebrate St. Patty's day with live entertainment, food, and drinks. March 17. Call ☎ **808/734-6900.**

- **St. Patrick's Day Parade,** Kaanapali Parkway, Kaanapali Resort, Maui. Everyone becomes Irish for a day when this hometown parade makes it way through the Kaanapali Resort area. March 17. Call ☎ **808/661-3271.**

- **Maui Marathon,** Kahului to Kaanapali, Maui. For nearly three decades, runners have lined up at the Maui Mall before daybreak and headed off for Kaanapali, some 26.2 miles across the island. Sunday in mid-March. Call ☎ **808/871-6441.**

- **Kona Brewer's Festival,** King Kamehameha's Kona Beach Hotel Luau Grounds, Kailua-Kona, Big Island. This annual event features microbreweries from around the world, with beer-tasting, food, and entertainment. Mid-March. Call ☎ **808/936-2009.**

- **Molokai Hawaiian Paniolo Heritage Rodeo,** Molokai Rodeo Arena, Maunaloa, Molokai. Molokai's cowboys celebrate Hawaii's *paniolo* (cowboy) heritage. Call ☎ **808/552-2681** for this year's date.

- **Prince Kuhio Celebrations,** on all islands. Various festivals throughout the state celebrate the birth of Jonah Kuhio Kalanianaole, born March 26, 1871. He might have been Hawaii's next king, except that the Hawaiian monarchy was overthrown, and Hawaii was annexed to the United States. He was elected to Congress in 1902. Kauai, the island where Prince Kuhio was born, has a huge celebration in Lihue; call ☎ **808/245-3971.** Molokai also has a day-long event; call ☎ **808/553-5215.**

✪ **Annual Ritz-Carlton, Kapalua Celebration of the Arts,** Ritz-Carlton Kapalua, Maui. Contemporary and traditional artists give free hands-on lessons. End of March or early April. Call ☎ **808/669-6200.**

April

- **Annual Easter Sunrise Service,** National Cemetery of the Pacific, Punchbowl Crater, Honolulu, Oahu. For a century, people have gathered at this famous cemetery for Easter sunrise services. Call ☎ **808/293-9788** or 808/538-0068.

✪ **Merrie Monarch Hula Festival,** Hilo, Big Island. Hawaii's biggest hula festival features three nights of modern (*auana*) and ancient (*kahiko*) dance competition in honor of King David Kalakaua, the "Merrie Monarch" who revived the dance. Usually the week after Easter. Tickets sell out by January 30, so reserve early. Call ☎ **808/935-9168.**

- **Hawaiian Quilt Show,** Wailoa Center, Hilo, Big Island. Quilters offer workshops and classes and display traditional quilts. From first Saturday in April to end of month. Call ☎ **808/933-4360.**

- **Buddha Day,** Lahaina Jodo Mission, Lahaina, Maui. Around April 6 each year, this historic mission holds a flower festival pageant honoring the birth of Buddha. Call ☎ **808/661-4303.**

- **Hawaiian Slack Key Concert,** Honolulu Academy of Arts, Honolulu, Oahu. A great opportunity to listen to this traditional form of music. Usually mid-April. Call ☎ **808/532-8701.**

- **Hawaii Professional Rodeo,** Town and Country Stables, Waimanalo, Oahu. This fundraising event for Habilitat, a long-term substance-abuse program, has a weekend of rodeo competition with the best *paniolos* (cowboys) in Hawaii, plus bullfighting clowns, outdoor barbecue, and live country music and dancing. Call ☎ **808/235-3691.**

✪ **Honolulu International Bed Race Festival,** Honolulu, Oahu. This popular fundraising event allows visitors a minitaste of Honolulu with food booths sponsored by local restaurants, live entertainment, a *keiki* (children's) carnival with games and rides, and a race through the streets of Honolulu with runners pushing beds to raise money for local charities. Mid-April. Call ☎ **808/735-6092** or 808/696-2424.

- **Da Kine Pro Am Windsurfing Competition,** Hookipa Beach Park, Maui. The top competitors from around the globe flock to this world-famous windsurfing beach for this annual competition. Mid-April. Call ☎ **808/575-9264.**

✪ **Maui County Agricultural Trade Show and Sampling,** Ulupalakua Ranch and Tedeschi Winery, Ulupalakua, Maui. The name may be long and cumbersome, but this event is hot, hot, hot. Local product exhibits and sampling, food booths, and live entertainment. Call ☎ **808/242-6989** for this year's schedule.

May

✪ **Annual Lei Day Celebrations,** various locations on all islands. May Day is Lei Day in Hawaii, celebrated with lei-making contests, pageantry, arts and crafts, and a Brothers Cazimero concert at the Waikiki Shell. May 1. Call ☎ **808/924-8934** or

808/524-0722 for Oahu events (☎ 808/597-1888 for info on the Brothers Caz show); ☎ 808/322-3441, ext. 218, for Big Island events; ☎ 808/667-9175 for Maui events; and ☎ 808/245-6931 for Kauai events.

✪ **World Fire-Knife Dance Championships and Samoan Festival,** Polynesian Cultural Center, Laie, Oahu. Junior and adult fire-knife dancers from around the world converge on the Center in the most amazing performance you'll ever see. Authentic Samoan food and cultural festivities round out the fun. Mid-May. Call ☎ 808/293-3333.

✪ **Molokai Ka Hula Piko,** Papohaku Beach Park, Kaluakoi, Molokai. A day-long celebration of the birth of hula on the island where it was born, featuring performances by hula halau, musicians, and singers from across Hawaii. Hawaiian crafts, including quilting, woodworking, featherwork, and deer-horn scrimshaw, are demonstrated. Hawaiian food, including Molokai specialties, also is available. Call ☎ 800/800-6367 or 808/553-3876.

• **Memorial Day,** National Memorial Cemetery of the Pacific, Punchbowl, Honolulu, Oahu. The Armed Forces have a ceremony recognizing those who died for their country. Call ☎ 808/566-1430.

• **Outrigger Canoe Season,** all islands. From May to September, nearly every weekend, canoe paddlers across the state participate in outrigger canoe races. Call ☎ 808/961-5797 for this year's schedule of events.

June

✪ **King Kamehameha Celebration,** statewide. It's a state holiday with a massive floral parade, *hoolaulea* (party), and much more. First weekend in June. Call ☎ 808/586-0333 for **Oahu** events, ☎ 808/329-1603 for **Big Island** events, ☎ 808/667-9175 for **Maui** events, ☎ 808/552-2791 for **Molokai** events, and ☎ 808/245-3971 for **Kauai** events.

• **AT&T Dragon Boat Festival,** Ala Moana Beach, Honolulu, Oahu. Teams from throughout Asia race. Mid-June. Call ☎ 808/734-6900.

• **King Kamehameha Hula Competition,** Neal Blaisdell Center, Honolulu, Oahu. One of the top hula competitions, with dancers from as far away as Japan. Third weekend in June. Call ☎ 808/536-1015.

✪ **Taste of Honolulu,** Civic Center Grounds, Honolulu, Oahu. Benefiting the Easter Seals campaign, Hawaii's premier outdoor food festival features tastings from 30 restaurants. Entertainment, beer- and winetasting; cooking demos, gourmet marketplace, and children's activities. End of June. Call ☎ 808/536-1015.

• **Cowhorse Classic,** Molokai Rodeo Arena, Maunaloa, Molokai. The island's cowboys celebrate Hawaii's paniolo heritage. Usually late June. Call ☎ 808/552-2791.

July

• **Pineapple Festival,** Lanai City, Lanai. Some of Hawaii's best musicians participate in Lanai's liveliest event, celebrating the golden fruit with everything from fishing tournaments to pineapple cooking contests, food and craft booths, water activities, and demonstrations by well-known chefs. Call ☎ 808/565-7600 for this year's date.

• **Fourth of July Fireworks,** Desiderio and Sills Field, Schofield Barracks, Oahu. A day-long celebration with entertainment, food, and games that ends with a spectacular fireworks show. Free. July 4. Call ☎ 808/665-0143.

✪ **Turtle Independence Day,** Mauna Lani Resort and Bungalows, Kohala Coast, Big Island. Scores of endangered green sea turtles, which have been raised in captivity, race down to the sea each year when they're released from the historic fishponds at Mauna Lani. July 4. Call ☎ 808/885-6622.

- **Parker Ranch Rodeo**, Waimea, Big Island. Hot rodeo competition in the heart of cowboy country. Call **808/885-7311** for this year's date.

- **Makawao Parade and Rodeo**, Makawao, Maui. This annual parade and rodeo event has been taking place in this upcountry cowboy town for generations. Call ☎ **808/572-9565** or 808/572-2076 for this year's date.

- ✪ **Hoolaulea O Ke Kai—A Molokai Sea Fest**, Kaunakakai, Molokai. Canoe races, windsurfing competition, Hawaiian music, and food are offered at this day-long celebration of the sea. Call ☎ **800/800-6367**, 800/553-0404 (interisland), or 808/553-3876 for this year's date and schedule.

- **Hawaii International Jazz Festival**, Sheraton Waikiki, Honolulu, Oahu. Evening concerts and daily jam sessions plus scholarship giveaways, the University of Southern California jazz band, and many popular jazz and blues artists. Mid-July. Call ☎ **808/941-9974.**

- ✪ **Kapalua Wine Symposium**, Kapalua, Maui. Famous wine and food experts and oenophiles gather at the Ritz-Carlton and Kapalua Bay hotels for formal tastings, panel discussions, and to sample new releases. Call ☎ **800/669-0244** for this year's dates and schedule.

- **Prince Lot Hula Festival**, Moanalua Gardens, Honolulu, Oahu. Authentic ancient and modern hula, as well as demonstrations and arts and crafts. A good alternative to April's much more well-known (and much more crowded) Merrie Monarch Hula Festival. Third Sunday in July. Call ☎ **808/839-5334.**

- **Ukulele Festival**, Kapiolani Bandstand, Honolulu, Oahu. This annual event features 400 children and special guest stars. End of July. Call ☎ **808/732-3739.**

- **Crater Rim Run and Marathon**, Hawaii Volcanoes National Park, Big Island. In late July, some 1,000 runners from around the globe line up to compete in races over uneven lava terrain, up the walls of volcanic craters, and through lush rain forests for the 5-, 10- and 26.2-mile races. Call ☎ **808/982-7783.**

August

- **Hawaii State Fair**, Aloha Stadium, Honolulu, Oahu. The annual state fair is a great one: includes Hawaii agricultural products (including orchids) displays, education and cultural exhibits, entertainment, and local-style food. Early August. Call ☎ **808/531-3531.**

- **Queen Liliuokalani Keiki Hula Competition**, Neal Blaisdell Center, Honolulu, Oahu. More than 500 *keiki* (children) representing 22 *halau* (troupes) from the islands compete in this dancefest. The event is broadcast live on KITV-TV. Early August. Call ☎ **808/521-6905.**

- **Annual Hawaiian International Billfish Tournament**, Kailua-Kona, Big Island. One of the world's most prestigious billfish tournaments, the HIBT attracts teams from around the globe that compete to catch the largest fish. Based on the new moon. Call ☎ **808/326-7820.**

- ✪ **Earth Maui**, Kapalua Resort, Kapalua, Maui. A week-long series of events to encourage appreciation of Maui's natural environment, plus hiking and snorkeling trips. Call ☎ **800/527-2582** for this year's schedule of events.

- **Admissions Day**, all islands. Hawaii became the 50th state on August 21, 1959, so the state takes a holiday (all state-related facilities are closed) on the third Friday in August.

- **Molokai Museum and Cultural Center Annual Music Festival**, Meyer Sugar Mill and Museum Grounds, Kalae, Molokai. An outdoor music festival featuring top Hawaiian musicians. Saturday following Admissions Day. Call ☎ **808/567-6436.**

- **Cuisines of the Sun**, Mauna Lani Bay Hotel and Bungalows, Kohala Coast, Big Island. Chefs from all the world's sunny climates prepare a host of dishes during this

5-day eating and drinking extravaganza. Call ☎ 800/367-2323 or 808/885-6622 for this year's schedule.

September

✪ **Hawaiian Slack-Key Guitar Festival,** Oahu. Five-hour festival held annually at different locations on Oahu, presenting the best of Hawaii's slack-key guitar players. Call ☎ 808/239-4336 for date and ticket information.

✪ **Aloha Festivals,** various locations statewide. Parades and other events celebrate Hawaiian culture and friendliness throughout the state. Call ☎ 808/852-7690, 808/545-1771, or 808/885-8086 for a schedule of events.

✪ **Great Molokai Mule Drag and Hoolaulea,** Kaunakakai, Molokai. As part of the Aloha Festivals celebration on Molokai, the local residents honor the importance of the mule to the island's heritage with a mule race (which is sometimes a mule-dragging contest) down the main street of Kaunakakai. Call ☎ 800/800-6367 or 808/553-3876.

✪ **Queen Liliuokalani Long Distance Outrigger Canoe Races,** Kailua Pier to Honaunau and back. Some 2,500 paddlers from all over Hawaii, the U.S. mainland, Canada, and the Pacific vie in the world's longest canoe event. Labor Day weekend. Call ☎ 808/329-0833.

• **Outrigger Hotels Hawaiian Oceanfest,** various Oahu locations. This two-week celebration of ocean sports includes the Hawaiian International Ocean Challenge, featuring teams of the world's best professional lifeguards; Outrigger Waikiki Kings Race, an ocean iron-man race; Diamond Head Wahine Windsurfing Classic, the only all-women professional windsurfing competition; and Diamond Head Biathlon, a run/swim event. Great competitors, serious competition, a variety of evening events, and more. Second through last week in September; winds up with the Armed Forces Family Festival on the last Sunday in September. Call ☎ 808/521-4322.

✪ **Sam Choy Poke Recipe Contest,** Hapuna Beach Prince Hotel and Mauna Kea Beach Resort, Kohala Coast, Big Island. Top chefs from across Hawaii and the U.S. mainland as well as local amateurs compete in making a Hawaiian delicacy *poke* (pronounces po-KAY): chopped raw fish mixed with seaweed and spices. Yum-yum! Here's your chance to sample poke at its best. Call ☎ 808/885-8086 for this year's schedule.

• **Run to the Sun,** Paia to Haleakala, Maui. The world's top ultra-marathoners make the journey from sea level to the top of 10,000-foot Haleakala, some 37 miles. Usually early September. Call ☎ 808/871-6441.

• **Kauai Mokihana Festival,** Waimea and Lihue, Kauai. A week-long series of events focusing on Hawaiian music and dance. Call ☎ 808/882-0426.

• **A Taste of Lahaina,** Lahaina Civic Center, Maui. Some 20,000 people show up to sample 35 signature entrées of Maui's premier chefs during the weekend-long festival, which includes cooking demonstrations, winetastings and live entertainment. Usually mid-September. Call ☎ 808/667-9175 or 808/572-5071, or e-mail acton@maui.net.

October

• **Makahiki Festival,** Waimea Valley, Oahu. Hawaiian games, crafts, music, and food, all in a tremendous natural setting. The Hula Kahiko Competition is a major highlight. First weekend in October. Call ☎ 808/638-8511.

• **Maui County Fair,** War Memorial Complex, Wailuku, Maui. The oldest county fair in Hawaii features a parade, amusement rides, live entertainment, and exhibits. Early October. Call ☎ 808/875-0457.

- **Emalani Festival**, Kokee State Park, Kauai. This festival honors Her Majesty Queen Emma, an inveterate gardener and Hawaii's first environmental queen, who made a forest trek to Kokee with 100 friends in 1871. Call ☎ **808/335-9975.**

- **Winter Baseball**, islandwide. The season starts in early October and runs through mid-December, as the four teams compete: the West Oahu CaneFires, who play at Hans L'Orange Park in Waipahu; the Maui Stingrays, who play at Iron Maehara Baseball Stadium in Wailuku; the Honolulu Sharks, who play at University of Hawaii's Rainbow Stadium, in Honolulu; and the Hilo Stars, who play at Dr. Francis Wong Stadium in Hilo, on the Big Island. Call ☎ **808/973-7247** for this year's schedule and ticket information.

- **Hawaii International Rugby Tournament**, Kapiolani Park, Waikiki, Oahu. Teams from around the world gather to compete in this exciting tournament. The event has a division for all players, including Masters, Social, Championship, seven-side, nine-side, and touch. Second week in October. Call ☎ **808/926-5641.**

- **Molokai Hoe**, Molokai to Oahu. The season's biggest canoe race, this men's 40.8-mile outrigger contest crosses the channel from Molokai to finish at Fort DeRussy Beach in Waikiki. Mid-October. Call ☎ **808/261-6615.**

- ✪ **Ironman Triathlon World Championship**, Kailua-Kona, Big Island. Some 1,500-plus world-class athletes run (26.2 miles), swim (2.4 miles), and bike (112 miles) on the Kona-Kohala Coast of the Big Island of Hawaii. Spectators can watch the action along the route for free. The best place to see the 7am start is along the sea-wall on Alii Drive, facing Kailua Bay; get there before 5:30am to get a seat. The best vantage point for watching the bike-and-run portion is along Alii Drive (which will be closed to traffic; park on a side street and walk down to Alii Drive). To watch the finishers come in, line up along Alii Drive from Holualoa Street to the finish at Palani Road/Alii Drive; the first finisher can come as early as 2:30pm, and the course closes at midnight. Call ☎ **808/329-0063** for more information.

- ✪ **Aloha Classic World Wavesailing Championship**, Hookipa Beach, Maui. The top windsurfers in the world gather for this final event in the Pro Boardsailing World Tour. If you're on Maui, don't miss it—it's spectacular to watch. Call ☎ **808/575-9151.**

- ✪ **Halloween in Lahaina**, Maui. There's Carnival in Rio, Mardi Gras in New Orleans, and Halloween in Lahaina. Come to this giant costume party (some 20,000 people show up) on the streets of Lahaina; Front Street is closed off for the party. It'll be the greatest memory of your trip. Call ☎ **808/667-9175.**

November

- **Hawaii International Film Festival**, various locations in Honolulu, Oahu. A cinema festival with a cross-cultural spin featuring filmmakers from Asia, the Pacific Islands, and the U.S. First two weeks in November. Call ☎ **808/528-FILM,** or point your browser to www.hiff.org.

- **World Invitational Hula Festival**, Waikiki Shell, Oahu. Competitors from all over the world dance for the prizes. Early to mid-November. Call ☎ **808/486-3185.**

- ✪ **Annual Kona Coffee Cultural Festival**, Kailua-Kona, Big Island. Celebrates the harvest of coffee with a bean-picking contest, lei contests, song and dance, and the Miss Kona Coffee pageant. Call ☎ **808/326-7820** for this year's schedule.

- ✪ **Triple Crown of Surfing**, North Shore, Oahu. The world's top professional surfers compete in three events for a total of $250,000 in prize money. Mid-November to mid-December. Call ☎ **808/638-5024.**

- **Molokai Ranch Rodeo and Great Molokai Stew Cookoff**, Molokai Rodeo Arena, Maunaloa, Molokai. The island's cowboys celebrate Hawaii's paniolo heritage. Usu-ally mid-November. Call ☎ **800/800-6367** or 808/552-2681.

- **Winter Wine Escape,** Hapuna Beach Prince Hotel, Mauna Kea Resort, Kohala Coast, Big Island. Wine-tasting and food samplings during this weekend culinary treat. Call ☎ **808/880-1111** for this year's schedule.

December

- **Honolulu Marathon,** Honolulu, Oahu. One of the largest marathons in the world with more than 30,000 competitors. Early December. Call ☎ **808/734-7200;** www.honolulumarathon.org.

- **Festival of Trees,** Honolulu, Oahu. Downtown display of one-of-a-kind decorated trees, wreaths, and decorations to benefit Queen's Medical Center. The lighting takes place the first or second week of the month. Call ☎ **808/547-4780.**

- **Festival of Lights,** islandwide. On Oahu, the mayor throws the switch to light up the 40-foot tall Norfolk pine and other trees in front of Honolulu Hale; on Maui, marching bands, floats, and Santa roll down Lahaina's Front Street in an annual parade; on Molokai, there's a host of activities in Kaunakakai; on Kauai, the lighting ceremony takes place in front of the former county building on Rice Street, Lihue. Early December. Call ☎ **808/547-4397** on Oahu; 808/667-9175 on Maui; 808/567-6361 on Molokai; and 808/828-0014 on Kauai.

- **Aloha Bowl,** Aloha Stadium, Honolulu, Oahu. The winner of the PAC 10 will play the winner of the Big 12 in this nationally televised collegiate football classic. Christmas Day. Call ☎ **808/947-4141;** www.alohagames.com.

- **Rainbow Classic,** University of Hawaii, Manoa Valley, Oahu. Eight of the best NCAA basketball teams compete at the Special Events Arena. Week after Christmas. Call ☎ **808/956-6501.**

⭐ **First Night,** Honolulu; Maui Arts and Cultural Center; and Kailua-Kona, Big Island. Hawaii's largest festival of arts and entertainment takes place on three different islands. For 12 hours, musicians, dancers, actors, jugglers, magicians, and mimes perform, food is available, and fireworks bring in the New Year. Alcohol-free. December 31. Call ☎ **808/532-3131** on Oahu; 808/326-7820 on the Big Island; and 808/242-7469 on Maui.

3   What to Pack

Hawaii is very informal. Shorts, T-shirts, and tennis shoes will get you by at most restaurants and attractions; a casual dress or a polo shirt and khakis is fine even in the most expensive places. Dinner jackets are required only in some of the fine dining rooms of a very few ultra-exclusive resorts—such as the Halekulani on Oahu, the Big Island's Mauna Kea Beach Hotel, and the Lodge at Koele on Lanai—and they'll cordially provide you with a jacket if you don't bring your own. And aloha wear—the tropical print clothing you'll see everybody wearing throughout the islands, locals and visitors alike—is acceptable everywhere, so you may want to plan on buying an aloha shirt or a *muumuu* (a Hawaiian-style dress) while you're in the islands.

So bring T-shirts, shorts, long pants, a couple of bathing suits, a long-sleeve coverup (to throw on at the beach when you've had enough sun for the day), tennis shoes, rubber water shoes or flip-flops, hiking boots, and several pairs of good socks if you plan on hiking.

The tropical sun poses the greatest threat to anyone who ventures out to the great outdoors, so be sure to bring **sun protection:** a good pair of sunglasses, plenty of strong sunscreen, a light hat (like a baseball cap or a sun visor), binoculars (if you have them), and a canteen or water bottle if you'll be hiking—you'll easily dehydrate on the trail in the tropical heat, so figure on carrying two liters of water per day on any hike.

Campers should bring water-purification tablets or devices. Also see "Staying Healthy: Protecting Yourself Against Natural Hazards," below.

Don't bother with overstuffing your suitcase with two whole weeks' worth of shorts and T-shirts, especially if you're going to have to drag it to multiple islands. Almost all of Hawaii's hotels and resorts—even the high-end ones—have **laundry facilities.** If your accommodation doesn't have a washer and dryer or laundry service, there will likely be a Laundromat nearby. The only exception to this is Hana on Maui; the tiny town at the end of the Hana Road has no 'mat, so either check with the place you're staying beforehand, or do a load of laundry before you arrive.

One last thing: **It really can get cold in Hawaii.** If you plan to see the sunrise from the top of Maui's Haleakala Crater, venture into the Big Island's Hawaii Volcanoes National Park, or spend time in Kokee State Park on Kauai, bring a warm jacket; 40°F upcountry temperatures, even in summer when it's 80°F at the beach, are not uncommon. It's always a good idea to bring at least a windbreaker, a sweater, or a light jacket. And be sure to **toss some rain gear** into your suitcase if you'll be in Hawaii from November to March.

4 The Active Vacation Planner

If all you want from the islands is a fabulous beach to lie on and a perfectly mixed mai tai, then we have what you're looking for—some of the most spectacular beaches (not to mention the best mai tais) in the world. But Hawaii's wealth of natural wonders is hard to resist; the year-round tropical climate and spectacular scenery tend to inspire even the most committed desk jockeys and couch potatoes to get outside and explore.

PREPARING FOR YOUR ACTIVE VACATION

If you have your own snorkel gear or other watersports equipment, by all means, bring it if you can. However, if you don't have it, don't fret; everything you'll need is available for rent in the islands. We discussed all kinds of places to rent or buy gear in the island chapters later in this book.

SETTING OUT ON YOUR OWN VS. USING AN OUTFITTER   There are two ways to go: Plan all the details before you go and schlep your gear 2,500 miles across the Pacific, or go with an outfitter or a guide and let them worry about the details.

Experienced outdoors enthusiasts may follow their nose to coastal campgrounds or even trek to the 13,796-foot-high summit of Mauna Loa on their own. But in Hawaii it's often preferable to go with a local guide, who's familiar with the local conditions at both sea level and summit peaks, knows the land and its flora and fauna in detail, and has all the gear you'll need. It's also good to go with a guide if time is an issue. If you really want to see native birds, for instance, an experienced guide will take you directly to the best areas for sightings. And many forests and valleys in the interior of the islands are either on private property or in wilderness preserves that are accessible only on guided tours. If you go with a guide, plan on spending at least $100 a day per person; we've recommended the best local outfitters and tour-guide operators on each island in the chapters that follow.

But if you have the time, already own the gear, and love doing the research and planning, try exploring on your own. Each island chapter discusses the best spots to set out on your own, from the best offshore snorkel and dive spots to great day-long hikes, as well as the federal, state, and county agencies that can help you with hikes on public property; we also list references for spotting birds, plants, and sea life. We recommend that you always use the resources available and inquire about weather, trail or surf conditions, water availability, and other conditions before you take off on your adventure.

For hikers, a great alternative to hiring a private guide are the guided hikes offered by the **Nature Conservancy of Hawaii**, 1116 Smith St., Honolulu, HI 96817 (☎ 808/537-4508 on Oahu; 808/573-4147 on Maui; 808/553-5236 or 808/524-0779 on Molokai), and the **Hawaii Chapter of the Sierra Club**, P.O. Box 2577, Honolulu, HI 96803 (☎ 808/538-6616 on Oahu; 808/573-4147 on Maui). Both organizations offer guided hikes on preserves and special places during the year, as well as 1-day to week-long work trips to restore habitats and trails and to root out invasive plants like banana poka, New Zealand flax, non-native gorse, and wild ginger. It might not sound like a dream vacation to everyone, but it's a chance to see the "real" Hawaii—including wilderness areas that are ordinarily off-limits.

All Nature Conservancy hikes are free. However, you must reserve a spot for yourself, and a deposit is required for guided hikes to ensure that you'll show up; your deposit is refunded once you do. The hikes are generally offered once a month on Maui, Molokai, and Lanai (call the Oahu office for reservations), and twice a month on Oahu. There's also no charge for the trips to restore habitats. Write for a schedule of guided hikes and other programs.

The Sierra Club offers weekly hikes on Oahu and Maui. Hikes are lead by certified Sierra Club volunteers and are classified as easy, moderate, or strenuous. These half-day or all-day affairs cost $1 for Sierra Club members and $3 for nonmembers (bring exact change). For a copy of its newsletter listing all outings and trail-repair work, send $2 to the address above.

Local ecotourism opportunities are also discussed in each island chapter. For more information, contact the **Hawaii Ecotourism Association**, P.O. Box 61435, Honolulu, HI 96839 (☎ **808/956-2866;** fax 808/956-2858; planet-hawaii.com/hea; e-mail hea@aloha.net).

OUTDOOR ETIQUETTE Act locally, think globally, and carry out what you carry in. Find a rubbish container for all your litter (including cigarette butts; it's *very* bad form to throw them out of your car window). Observe *kapu* (taboo) and no trespassing signs. Don't climb on ancient Hawaiian heiau (temple) walls and temples or

Travel Tip

If you're planning on traveling to several islands and would like to rent snorkel gear on one island and keep it with you for your whole trip, try **Snorkel Bob's** (www.snorkelbob.com). Snorkel Bob lets you rent snorkels, masks, fins, boogie boards, life jackets, and wet suits on any one island and return it on another. The basic set of snorkel gear is $2.50 a day, or $9 a week—a very good deal. The best gear is $6.50 a day, or $29 a day, or $39 a week. If you're nearsighted and you need a prescription mask, it's $9 a day, or $39 a week. You can find Snorkel Bob's on **Oahu** at 702 Kapahulu Ave. (at Date Street), Honolulu (☎ 808/735-7944); on **Maui** at 161 Lahainaluna Rd. (between Front and Wainee streets), in Lahaina (☎ 808/661-4421), at Napili Village, 5425-C Lower Honapiliani Hwy., Napili (☎ 808/669-9603), and in South Maui in Kihei Market Place, 34 Keala St., just off S. Kihei Road (☎ 808/879-7449); on the **Big Island** at 75-5744 Alii Dr. (next to Huggo's and the Royal Kona Resort), and Kailua-Kona (☎ 808/329-0770); and on **Kauai** at 4-734 Kuhio Hwy. (just north of Coconut Plantation Marketplace), in Kapaa (☎ 808/823-9433), and in Koloa at 3236 Poipu Rd., near Poipu Beach (☎ 808/742-2206).

carry home rocks, all of which belong to the Hawaiian Volcano Goddess Pelé. Some say it's just a silly superstition or coincidence, but each year, the National and State Park Services get boxes of lava rocks in the mail sent back to Hawaii by visitors who've experienced unusually bad luck.

ACTIVITIES FROM A TO Z

Here's a brief rundown of the many outdoor activities available in Hawaii. For our recommendations on the best places to go, the best shops for renting equipment, and the best outfitters to use, see the individual island chapters later in this book.

BIRDING   Many of Hawaii's tropical birds are found nowhere else on earth. There are curved-bill honeycreepers, black-winged red birds, and the rare o'o, whose yellow feathers Hawaiians once plucked to make royal capes.

When you go birding, take along *A Field Guide to the Birds of Hawaii and the Tropical Pacific*, by H. Douglas Pratt, Phillip L. Bruner, and Delwyn G. Berett (Princeton University Press, 1987). It belongs in the hands of every birder who comes to Hawaii. For binoculars, most birders prefer a Leitz 10×40, easily adjustable and clear from 10 feet to infinity; they're powerful but expensive, about $800. If you go birding with a local guide, they'll usually provide a good pair for you to use; you can also rent binoculars from **Rental Warehouse** (see box below) and at other gear-rental locations throughout the islands.

Kauai and Molokai, in particular, are great places to go birding in Hawaii. On Kauai, large colonies of seabirds nest at Kilauea National Wildlife Refuge and along the Na Pali Coast. The lush rain forest of Molokai's Kamakou Preserve is home to the Molokai Thrush and Molokai Creeper, which live only on this 30-mile-long island. For details on in Hawaii, including where to go, what birds you'll see, and which outfitters will take you, see "Birding" in chapters 6 and 10, and the discussion of the Kamakou Preserve under "Seeing the Sights" in chapter 8.

BOATING   Almost every type of nautical experience is available in the islands. You can go to sea on old-fashioned Polynesian outrigger canoes, high-tech kayaks, fast-moving catamarans, inflatable rubber Zodiacs, smooth moving SWATH vessels that promise not to make you seasick, gaff-rigged schooners, America's Cup racing sloops, Kona charter fishing boats, ferries, booze-cruise barges, snorkel and dive boats, submarines, and even an interisland cruise ship. You'll find details on all these seafaring experiences throughout the individual island chapters.

No matter which vessel and type you choose, be sure to see the Hawaiian islands from offshore if you can afford it. It's easy to combine multiple activities into one cruise: Lots of snorkel boats double as sightseeing cruises and, in winter, whale-watching cruises. The main harbors for visitor activities are Kewalo Basin, Oahu; Honokohau, Kailua-Kona, and Kawaihae on the Big Island of Hawaii; Lahaina and Maaalea, Maui; Nawiliwili and Port Allen, Kauai; and Kaunakakai, Molokai.

BODY BOARDING (BOOGIE BOARDING) & BODYSURFING   Bodysurfing—riding the waves without a board, becoming one with the rolling water—is a way of life in Hawaii. Some bodysurfers just rely on their outstretched hands (or hands at their sides) to ride the waves; others use hand boards (flat, paddle-like gloves). For additional maneuverability, try a boogie- or body board (also known as *belly boards* or *paipo boards*). These 3-foot-long vehicles, which support the upper part of your body, are easy to carry and very maneuverable in the water. Both bodysurfing and body boarding require a pair of open-heeled swim fins to help propel you through the water. Both kinds of wave riding are very popular in the islands, because the equipment is inexpensive, easy to carry, and both sports can be practiced in the small, gentle waves. See the individual island chapters for details on where to rent boards and where to go.

CAMPING Hawaii's year-round balmy, tropical climate makes camping a breeze. Hawaii does have a wet season (some call it winter), and a dry season, which corresponds to the mainland's summer, but tropical campers should always be ready for rain. It rains every day somewhere in the islands, and mosquitoes are abundant when the air is still. If you're heading to the top of Hawaii's volcanoes, you'll need your goose-down mummy bag. If you plan on camping on the beach, bring your mosquito net and rain poncho. Cary a good mosquito repellent, and be prepared to deal with contaminated water (purify it by boiling, filtration, or iodine tablets) and the tropical sun (protect yourself with sunscreen, a hat, and a long-sleeved shirt). Also be sure to check out "Staying Healthy: Protecting Yourself Against Natural Hazards," later in this chapter, for hiking and camping tips.

Otherwise, camping is ideal in the islands, with many established campgrounds at beach parks, including Kauai's Anini Beach, Oahu's Malaekahana Beach, Maui's Waianapanapa Beach, and the Big Island's Hapuna Beach. Campgrounds also are open in the interior at Maui's Haleakala National Park and Hawaii Volcanoes National Park on the Big Island of Hawaii. Camping also is permitted at Kalalau Beach on Kauai's Na Pali Coast and in the cool uplands of Kokee State Park. See "Beaches" and "Hiking & Camping" in the individual island chapters for the best places to camp in the islands. For details on who to contact for regulations and information on camping in any of Hawaii's national or state parks, see "Visitor Information," earlier in this chapter.

Hawaiian Trail and Mountain Club, P.O. Box 2238, Honolulu, HI 96804, offers an information packet on hiking and camping throughout the Hawaiian Islands. Send $1.25 and a legal-size, self-addressed, stamped envelope for information. Another good source of information is the *Hiking/Camping Information Packet,* available from **Hawaii Geographic Maps and Books,** 49 S. Hotel St., Honolulu, HI 96813 (☎ **808/538-3952),** for $7 (postage included).

GOLF Nowhere else on earth can you tee off to whale spouts, putt under rainbows, or play around a live volcano. Hawaii has some of the world's top-rated golf courses. If it all sounds like paradise, be forewarned: Each course features hellish natural hazards like razor-sharp lava, gusty trade winds, an occasional wild pig, and the tropical heat. And greens fees tend to be very expensive on the islands. Still, golfers flock here from around the world and love every minute of it. See the individual island chapters for coverage of the best resort courses worth splurging on (with details, where applicable, on money-saving twilight rates), as well as the best budget and municipal courses.

A few tips on golfing in Hawaii: There's generally wind—10 to 30 m.p.h. is not unusual between 10am and 2pm—so play two to three clubs up or down to

---

Be sure to see the section "Staying Healthy: Protecting Yourself Against Natural Hazards," below, before setting out on any adventure. It includes useful information on hiking, camping, and ocean safety. Even if you just plan to lie on the beach, be sure to check out the box "Don't Get Burned: Smart Tanning Tips" on page 66 to learn how to protect yourself against the sun's harmful rays—a must for *everyone* in Hawaii.

Impressions

Thousands have daily lined the wharves to witness the carpenter, Mr. Dibble, in his novel suit of India-rubber with a glass helmet disappear beneath the surface of the water.

—1840 Honolulu newspaper article

compensate. Bring extra balls: the rough is thicker, water hazards are everywhere, and the wind wreaks havoc with your game. On the greens, your putt will *always* break toward the ocean. Hit deeper and more aggressively in the sand, because the type of sand used on most Hawaii courses is firmer and more compact (lighter sand would blow away in the constant wind). And bring a camera—you'll kick yourself if you don't capture those spectacular views.

HIKING   Hiking in Hawaii is a breathtaking experience full of natural drama, extraordinary vistas, and great outdoor encounters. Hawaii has hundreds of miles of hiking trails, and the reward at the end of the trail may be a hidden beach, a private waterfall, an Eden-like valley, or a stunning view. However, rock climbers are, sadly, out of luck: Most of Hawaii's volcanic cliffs are too steep and too brittle to scale.

Hawaiian Trail and Mountain Club, P.O. Box 2238, Honolulu, HI 96804, offers an information packet on hiking and camping in Hawaii; to receive a copy, send $1.25 and a self-addressed, stamped, legal-size envelope. **Hawaii Geographic Maps and Books,** 49 S. Hotel St., Honolulu, HI 96813 (☎ 808/538-3952), offers a *Hiking/Camping Information Packet* for $7. Also note that the **Hawaii State Department of Land and Natural Resources,** 1151 Punchbowl, St., no. 130, Honolulu, HI 96813 (☎ 808/587-0300; www.hawaii.gov), will send you free topographical trail maps.

The Nature Conservancy of Hawaii (☎ 808/537-4508 on Oahu; ☎ 808/572-7849 on Maui; ☎ 808/553-5236 or 808/524-0779 on Molokai) and the **Hawaii Chapter of the Sierra Club,** P.O. Box 2577, Honolulu, HI 96803 (☎ 808/538-6616), both offer guided hikes on preserves and special places during the year. Also see the individual island chapters for complete details on the best hikes for all ability levels.

Before you set out on the trail, see "Staying Healthy: Protecting Yourself Against Natural Hazards," later in this chapter, for tips on hiking safety, as well as "What to Pack," earlier in this chapter.

HORSEBACK RIDING   One of the best ways to really see Hawaii is on horseback; almost all the islands offer riding opportunities for just about every age and level of experience. You can ride into Maui's Haleakala Crater, along Kauai's Mahaulepu Beach, or into Oahu's remote windward valleys on Kualoa Ranch; or, you can gallop across the wide-open spaces of the Big Island's Parker Ranch, one of the largest privately owned ranches in the United States. See the individual island chapters for details. Be sure to bring a pair of long jeans and close-toed shoes to wear on your ride.

KAYAKING   Hawaii is one of the world's most popular destinations for ocean kayaking. Beginners can paddle across a tropical lagoon to two uninhabited islets off Lanikai Beach on Oahu, while more experienced kayakers can take on Kauai's awesome Na Pali Coast. Experts time their kayak expeditions to fall in the summer to take advantage of the usually flat conditions on the North Shore of Molokai, where the sea cliffs are the steepest on earth and the remote valleys can be reached only by sea. See "Hitting the Water" in chapters 6 through 10 for local outfitters and tour guides.

Using Activities Desks to Book Your Island Fun

If you want to go out with an outfitter or guide—especially if you're interested in an activity that requires an outfitter or guide, such as horseback riding, whale watching, or sportfishing—and you'd like to save some money, you might want to consider booking your activity through a discount activities center or activities desk. These agents—whose sole business it is to act as a clearinghouse for activities, much like a consolidator functions as a discount clearinghouse for airline tickets—can often get you a better price than you'd get by booking an activity directly with the outfitter.

Discount activities centers will, in effect, split their commission with you, giving themselves a smaller commission to get your business—and passing, on average, a 10% discount on to you. And not only will they save you money, but good activities centers should also be able to help you find, say, the snorkel cruise that's right for you, or the luau that's most suitable for both you *and* the kids. But it's in the activities agent's best interest to sign you up with outfitters from which they earn the most commission; some agents have no qualms about booking you into any activity if it means an extra buck for them. If an agent tries to push a particular outfitter or activity too hard, be skeptical. Conversely, they'll try to steer you away from outfitters who don't offer big commissions. For example, Trilogy, the company that offers Maui's most popular snorkel cruises to Lanai (and the only one with rights to land at Lanai's Hulupoe Beach), offers only minimum commissions to agents and does not allow agents to offer any discounts at all. As a result, most activities desks you speak to on Maui will automatically try to steer you away from Trilogy if you say you want to book with it.

Another important word of warning: Be careful to stay away from those activities centers offering discounts as fronts for timeshare sales presentations. Using a free snorkel cruise or luau tickets as bait, they'll suck you into a 90-minute presentation—and try to get you to buy into a Hawaii timeshare in the process. Not only will they try to sell you a big white elephant you never wanted in the first place, but—since their business is timeshares, not activities—they're not going to be as interested or as knowledgeable about which activities might be right for you. These shady deals seem to be particularly rampant on Maui. Just do yourself a favor and avoid them altogether.

SCUBA DIVING In 1840, when Mr. Dibble dove to inspect the hull of the USS *Porpoise*, whose copper bottom "he found somewhat out of repair," he could hardly imagine his pioneering underwater adventure in Hawaii would be followed by thousands of pleasure seekers.

Some people come to the islands solely to take the plunge in the tropical Pacific and explore the underwater world. You can see the great variety of tropical marine life (more than 100 endemic species found nowhere else on the planet), explore sea caves, and swim with sea turtles and monk seals in the clear, tropical water of Hawaii, one of the world's top-10 dive destinations.

If you dive, **go early in the morning.** Trade winds often make rough up the seas in the afternoon, especially on Maui, so most dive operators schedule early-morning dives that end at noon, and take the rest of the day off.

If you're not certified, **take classes before you come to Hawaii** so you don't "waste" time learning and can dive right in. Unsure about scuba diving? Take an introductory

Our favorite islandwide discount activities house is the **Activity Warehouse** (☎ **800/923-4004**; www.travelhawaii.com). Activity Warehouse deals in such volume that it's able to offer discounts of up to 50% on all kinds of activities (although most discounts are in the 10 to 20% range), with lots of operators to choose from. Activity Warehouse has offices on every island: On **Oahu**, call ☎ 808/923-2700; on the **Big Island**, call ☎ 808/334-1155; and on **Maui**, call ☎ 808/667-4000 in Kihei or ☎ 808/667-4000 in Lahaina. We don't recommend using the Kauai branch, however; if you want to book **Kauai** activities, call the 800 number above before you arrive on the island. You'll see Activity Warehouse ads in many local publications. All in all, we've found them to be helpful and not too sales-y. While Activity Warehouse does represent timeshares, we've never once had anyone pitch us in all the times we've used them; they seem to be committed to activities as their main business. And this was the only activities center on Maui that didn't try to book us on a different Lanai excursion when we said we wanted to book Trilogy's trip. The Lahaina, Maui location also functions as the **Rental Warehouse,** which can rent you all kinds of equipment, from snorkel sets and beach chairs to golf clubs and kayaks, at big discounts.

There are also a number of very reliable local activities centers on each of the neighbor islands. On **Maui**, your best bet is **Tom Barefoot's Cashback Tours,** at Dolphin Shopping Center, 2395 S. Kihei Rd., Kihei (☎ 808/879-4100), and at 834 Front St., Lahaina (☎ 808/661-8889). Tom offers a 10% discount on all tours, activities, and adventures when you pay in cash or with traveler's checks. If you pay with a credit card or personal check, he'll give you a 7% discount. The two showrooms are loaded with pictures and maps of all the activities they book. We found Tom's to be very reliable and honest. On the **Big Island,** check out the **Activity Connection,** in the King Kamehameha Mall, on Kuakini Hwy. (behind the King Kamehameha Hotel), Kailua-Kona (☎ 808/329-1038); they offer up to 15% off on various island activities. On Kauai, call **The Fun Lady,** 4746 Kuhio Hwy, Kapaa (☎ 808/822-7759). Chris doesn't offer discounts, but she's great for one-stop shopping.

dive; most operators offer no-experience-necessary dives, ranging from $70 to $95. You can learn from this glimpse into the sea world whether diving is for you.

If you dive on your own, order the *Dive Hawaii Guide,* which describes 44 locations on a chart created by Dive Hawaii and the University of Hawaii Sea Grant. Send $2 to **UH/SGES,** Attention: Dive Guide, 1000 Pope Rd., MSB 226, Honolulu, HI 96822.

Tip: Scuba diving is one of those activities that may be worth the extra bucks to go with a good dive operator. Check the island chapters under "Scuba Diving" for the dive operators that'll give you the most for your money.

SNORKELING   Snorkeling is the main attraction in Hawaii—and almost anyone can do it. To enjoy Hawaii's underwater world, all you need is a mask, a snorkel, fins, and some basic swimming skills. It's like a dream, floating over underwater worlds through colorful clouds of tropical fish. In many places, all you have to do is wade into the water and look down.

If you've never snorkeled before, most resorts and excursion boats offer snorkeling equipment and lessons. However, you won't really need lessons; it's plenty easy to figure out for yourself, especially once you're at the beach—everybody around you will be doing it.

While everyone heads for Oahu's Hanauma Bay—the perfect spot for first-timers—other favorite snorkel spots include Kee Beach on Kauai, Kahaluu Beach on the Big Island, Hulopoe Bay on Lanai, and Kapalua Bay on Maui. Although snorkeling is excellent on all the islands, the Big Island, with its recent lava formations and abrupt drop-offs, offers some spectacular snorkeling opportunities. Some of the best snorkel spots in the islands—notably, the Big Island's Kealakekua Bay and Molokini Crater just off Maui—are accessible only by boat; for tips on the islands' best snorkel boats, see "Boating" under "Hitting the Water" in chapters 5, 6, 7, and 10.

If you don't have your own, you can rent gear from dozens of dive shops and activity booths, discussed in the individual island chapters. The best deals, though, are at **Snorkel Bob's**; not only do you get mask, fins, and snorkel for as little as $9 a week, but you get a net bag, a snorkel map, fish food (although it's really not cool to feed the fish in the wild; you never know what might show up for lunch), no-fog goop for your mask (although spitting in it works just as well), and a fish-identification card. Prices go up for prescription masks and high-end gear. For Snorkel Bob's locations throughout the islands, see "Preparing for Your Active Vacation," above. We also recommend other good gear-rental places in the individual island chapters.

Some snorkel tips: Always snorkel with a buddy. Look up every once in a while to see where you are, how far offshore you are, and if there's any boat traffic. Don't touch anything; not only can you damage coral, but camouflaged fish and shells with poisonous spines may surprise you. Always check with a dive shop or lifeguards or others on the beach about the area in which you plan to snorkel: Are there any dangerous conditions you should know about? What are the current surf, tide, and weather conditions?

SPORTFISHING The largest blue marlin ever captured on rod and reel anywhere on the planet was landed on a charter boat operated by Capt. Cornelius Choy off Oahu. The monster weighed in at 1,805 pounds!

Big-game fishing at its best is found off the Big Island of Hawaii at Kailua-Kona, where the deep blue water offshore yields trophy marlin year-round. You can also try for spearfish; swordfish; various tuna; mahi-mahis (dorados); rainbow runners; wahoo; barracuda; trevallies; bonefish; and various snappers, groupers, and other bottom fish. Each island offers deep-sea boat charters for good-eating fish like tuna, wahoo, and mahi-mahis, and visiting anglers currently need no license.

Charter fishing boats range both in size—from small 24-foot open skiffs to luxurious 50-foot-plus yachts—and in price—from about $100 per person to "share" a boat with other anglers for a half-day to $900 a day to book an entire luxury sportfishing yacht on an exclusive basis. Shop around. Prices vary widely according to the boat, the crowd, and the captain. Also, many boat captains tag and release marlin, or keep the fish for themselves (sorry, that's Hawaii style). If you want to eat your mahi-mahi for dinner or have your marlin mounted, tell the captain before you go.

See the individual island chapters for details.

Money-saving tip: Try contacting the charter boat captain directly and bargaining. Many charter captains pay a 20 to 30% commission to charter-booking agencies and may be willing to give you a discount if you book direct.

SURFING The ancient Hawaiian sport of *hee nalu* (which translates as "wave sliding") is probably the sport most people picture in their mind's eye when they think of Hawaii. Believe it or not, you too can be doing some wave sliding—just sign up at any one of the numerous surfing schools located throughout the islands; see "Surfing" in chapters 5, 6, 7, and 10. On world-famous Waikiki Beach, you can just head over to one of the surf stands that line the sand; these guys say that they can get anybody up and standing on a board. If you're already a big kahuna in surfing, check the same listings for the best deals on rental equipment and the best places to hang 10.

TENNIS   With Hawaii's great weather, tennis is a popular sport in the islands. Each island chapter lists details on free municipal courts as well as the best deals on private courts. The etiquette at the free county courts is to play only 45 minutes if someone is waiting for the court. If no one's around, the court is yours as long as you want it.

WATER-SKIING   The wind on your face, your feet gliding over the surface, a spray of water at your back—there's nothing that can compare to water-skiing. There are two places in Hawaii that provide boat, equipment, and lessons: In the calm waters of Koko Marina on Oahu (see chapter 5), and along the Wailua River on Kauai's Coconut Coast (see chapter 10).

WHALE WATCHING   Every winter, pods of Pacific humpback whales make the 3,000-mile swim from the chilly waters of Alaska to bask in Hawaii's summery shallows, fluking, spy hopping, spouting, and having an all-around swell time. About 1,500 to 3,000 humpback whales appear in Hawaii waters each year.

Humpbacks are one of the world's oldest, most impressive inhabitants: Adults grow to be about 45 feet long and weigh a hefty 40 tons; when they splash, it looks as if a 747's hit the drink. Humpbacks are officially an endangered species; in 1992, the waters around Maui, Molokai, and Lanai were designated as a Humpback Whale National Marine Sanctuary. Despite the world's newfound ecological awareness, humpbacks and their habitats and food resources are still under threat from whalers and pollution.

The season's first whale is usually spotted in November, but the best time to see humpback whales in Hawaii is between January and April from any island. Just look out to sea. Each island also offers a variety of whale-watching cruises, which will bring you up close and personal with the mammoth mammals; see the individual island chapters for details.

Money-saving tip: Book a snorkeling/sailing cruise during the winter whale-watching months, and get three activities for the price of one. It's well worth the money.

WINDSURFING   Maui is Hawaii's top windsurfing destination. World-class windsurfers head for Hookipa Beach, where the wind roars through Maui's isthmus and creates some of the best windsurfing in the world. Funky Paia, a derelict sugar town saved from extinction by surfers, is the world capital of big-wave board sailing. Along the Hana Highway, there are lookouts where you can watch the pros flip off the lip of 10-foot waves and gain "hang time" in the air. Others, especially beginners, set their sails for Oahu's Kailua Bay, home of world-champ windsurfer Robbie Naish, or Kauai's Anini Beach, where gentle onshore breezes make learning this sport a snap. See the individual island chapters for outfitters and local instructors.

5 Staying Healthy: Protecting Yourself Against Natural Hazards

Hawaii is one of the healthiest places in the world to visit. People who live here have a longer life expectancy than anywhere else in the U.S. (74 years for men and over 79 years for women). However, there are some hazards that you should be aware of so that, in the unlikely event that you encounter them, you can take the necessary steps to prevent them from blooming into full-scale problems.

ON LAND

As in any tropical climate, there are lots of bugs in Hawaii. Most of them won't harm you; however, three insects—mosquitoes, centipedes, and scorpions—do sting and may cause anything from mild annoyance to severe swelling and pain.

MOSQUITOES   There's not much you can do about mosquitoes (which are not native, but arrived in Hawaii as larvae stowed away in the water barrels on the ship *Wellington* in 1826 when it anchored in Lahaina), except to apply commercial repellent to keep them off you, burn mosquito punk or citronella candles to keep them out of your area, or apply sting-stopping ointments (which you can pick up at any drugstore) after they have stung you to stop the itching and swelling. Most bites disappear within anywhere from a few hours to a few days.

CENTIPEDES   These segmented insects with a jillion legs come in two varieties: 6- to 8-inch-long brown ones, and the smaller 2- to 3-inch-long blue guys, which really pack a wallop with their sting. Centipedes are generally found in damp, wet places, like under wood piles or compost heaps; wearing closed-toe shoes can help prevent stings if you happen to accidentally unearth one. If stung, the reaction can range from something similar to a mild bee sting to severe pain; apply ice at once to prevent swelling and pain. See a doctor if the pain is extreme or if you experience swelling, nausea, or any other severe reaction.

SCORPIONS   Rarely seen, scorpions are found in arid, warm regions; their stings can be serious. Campers in dry areas should always check their boots before putting them on, and shake out sleeping bags and bed rolls. Symptoms of a scorpion sting include shortness of breath, hives, swelling, and nausea. In the unlikely event that you're stung, apply diluted household ammonia and cold compresses to the area of the sting and seek medical help immediately.

HIKING SAFETY

In addition to taking the appropriate precautions regarding Hawaii's bug population (above), hikers should let someone know where they're heading, when they're going, and when they plan to return; too many hikers are lost in Hawaii because they don't let others know their basic plans.

Always check weather conditions with the **National Weather Service** (☎ 808/ **973-4381** on Oahu; see individual island chapters for local weather information) before you go. Hike with a pal, never alone. Wear hiking boots, a sun hat, clothes to protect you from the sun and from getting scratches, and high-SPF sunscreen on all exposed areas of skin. Take water. Stay on the trail. Watch your step. It's easy to slip off precipitous trails and into steep canyons with often disastrous, even fatal results. Incapacitated hikers are often plucked to safety by Fire and Rescue squads, who must use helicopters to gain access to remote sites. Many experienced hikers and boaters today pack a cell phone in case of emergency; just dial ☎ **911**.

VOG

The volcanic haze dubbed *vog* is caused by gases released when molten lava—from the continuous eruption of Kilauea volcano on the Big Island—pours into the ocean. This hazy air, which looks like urban smog, limits viewing from scenic vistas and wreaks havoc with photographers trying to get clear panoramic shots. Some people claim that long-term exposure to vog even causes bronchial ailments, but it's highly unlikely to cause you any harm in the course of your visit.

There actually is a "vog" season in Hawaii: the fall and winter months, when the trade winds that blow the fumes out to sea die down. The vog is felt not only on the Big Island but as far away as Maui and Oahu.

One more word of caution: If you plan to visit the Big Island's Hawaii Volcanoes National Park and you're pregnant or have heart or breathing problems, you might want to think twice about it. You're cautioned to avoid exposure to the sulfuric fumes that are ever-present in and around the park's calderas.

OCEAN SAFETY

Because most people coming to Hawaii are unfamiliar with the ocean environment, they're unaware of the natural hazards it holds. But with just a few precautions, your ocean experience can be a safe and happy one. An excellent book to get is *All Stings Considered: First Aid and Medical Treatment of Hawaii's Marine Injuries* (University of Hawaii Press, 1997), by Craig Thomas (an emergency-medicine doctor) and Susan Scott (a registered nurse). These avid water people have put together *the* authoritative book on first aid for Hawaii's marine injuries.

Note that sharks are not a big problem in Hawaii; in fact, they're so infrequent that locals look forward to seeing them. Since records have been kept, starting in 1779, there have been only about 100 shark attacks in Hawaii, of which 40% have been fatal. The biggest number of attacks occurred after someone fell into the ocean from the shore or from a boat; in these cases, the sharks probably attacked after the person was dead. But general rules for avoiding sharks are: Don't swim at sunrise, sunset, or where the water is murky due to stream runoff—sharks may mistake you for one of their usual meals. And don't swim where there are bloody fish in the water (sharks become aggressive around blood).

SEASICKNESS   The waters in Hawaii can range from calm as glass (off the Kona Coast on the Big Island) to downright frightening (in storm conditions), and they usually fall somewhere in between. In general, expect rougher conditions in winter than in summer.

Some 90% of the population tends toward seasickness. If you've never been out on a boat, or if you've been seasick in the past, you might want to take the following suggestions:

- The day before you go out on the boat, avoid alcohol; caffeine; citrus and other acidic juices; and greasy, spicy, or hard-to-digest foods.
- Get a good night's sleep the night before.
- Take or use whatever seasickness prevention works for best you—medication, an acupressure wristband, gingerroot tea or capsules, or any combination—*before* you board; once you set sail, it's generally too late.
- While you're on the boat, stay as low and as near the center of the boat as possible. Avoid the fumes (especially if it's a diesel boat); stay out in the fresh air and watch the horizon. Do not read.
- If you start to feel queasy, drink clear fluids like water, and eat something bland, such as a soda cracker.

STINGS   The most commons stings in Hawaii come from jellyfish, particularly Portuguese man-of-war and box jellyfish. Since the poisons they inject are very different, you need to treat each sting differently.

Portuguese Man-of-War   A bluish-purple floating bubble with a long tail, the Portuguese man-of-war causes some 6,500 stings a year on Oahu alone. Stings are painful

Don't Get Burned: Smart Tanning Tips

For years, the best souvenir to bring back from Hawaii was a golden tan—especially in mid-winter. Oh, the look of green-eyed envy from your friends as your bronzed glow silently told the world that you'd just returned from Hawaii! Tanning just ain't what it use to be. Nowadays, it can kill you—especially if, in your quest for a tan, you burn instead.

Strong words, but supported by reality: Hawaii's Caucasian population has the highest incidence of deadly skin cancer, malignant melanoma, than anywhere else in the U.S. But none of us are safe from the sun's harmful rays: People of all skin types and races can burn when exposed to the sun too long.

To ensure that your vacation won't be ruined by a painful, throbbing sunburn (especially in your first few days in the islands), here are some helpful tips on how to tan safely and painlessly:

Wear a strong sunscreen at all times. Use a sunscreen with a sun-protection factor (SPF) of 15 or higher; people with a light complexion should use 30. The SPF rating works this way: A fair-skinned person, without any sun protection, can burn in 10 minutes in the sun; a sunscreen with an SPF of 30 will give its wearer 10 minutes of protection from the sun (the time before you burn) times 30 (the SPF), or 300 minutes (5 hours) of protection.

Apply sunscreen as soon as you get out of the shower in the morning and at least 30 minutes before you're exposed to the sun.

And use lots of it. Margaret Tucker, chief of genetic epidemiology at the National Cancer Institute, says "a little dab will not do ya." You need 1 tablespoon of lotion per limb; slather it on and rub it in. No matter what the box says—even if the sunscreen is waterproof—reapply it every 2 hours and immediately after swimming.

Read the labels. To avoid developing allergies to sunscreens, New York University dermatologist Robert Friedman suggests avoiding any sunscreens that contain *para-amino benzoic acid* (PABA). The American Academy of Dermatology suggests looking for sunscreens with zinc oxide, talc, or titanium dioxide, because these elements reduce the risk of developing skin allergies.

Also wear a hat and sunglasses. The hat should have a minimum 4-inchwide brim (all the way around, to cover not only your face but also the sensitive back of your neck). Make sure your sunglasses have UV filters to protect your corneas from getting sunburned and to prevent cataracts. To avoid the irritation of sunscreen dripping into your eyes, use a waxy sunscreen stick (available just about everywhere in Hawaii) to draw half-circles above your eyebrows.

and a nuisance but rarely harmful; fewer than one in a thousand requires medical treatment. The best prevention is to watch for these floating bubbles as you snorkel (look for the hanging tentacles below the surface). Get out of the water if anyone near you spots these jellyfish.

Reactions to stings range from mild burning and reddening to severe welts and blisters. *All Stings Considered* recommends the following treatment: First, pick off any visible tentacles with a gloved hand, a stick, or anything handy; then rinse the sting with salt or fresh water, and apply ice to prevent swelling and to help control pain. Hawaii folklore advises using vinegar, meat tenderizer, baking soda, papain, or alcohol, or even urinating on the wound. Studies have shown that these remedies may actually cause further damage. Most Portuguese man-of-war stings will disappear by

Don't rely on a T-shirt for protection. Believe it or not, that T-shirt you put over your bathing suit only has an SPF of 6. Either wear special UV-protective clothing, or lather on a high-SPF sunscreen.

Avoid being in the sun between 9am and 3pm. Seek the shade during these peak hours. Remember that a beach umbrella is not enough protection from the sun's harmful UV rays; in fact, with the reflection from the water, the sand, and even the sidewalk, some 85% of the ultraviolet rays are still bombarding you.

Protect children from the sun, and keep infants out of the sun altogether. Infants under 6 months should not be in the sun at all. Older babies need zinc oxide to protect their fragile skin, and children should be slathered with sunscreen every hour. The burns children get today predict what their future will be with skin cancer tomorrow.

If you start to turn red, **get out of the sun.** Contrary to popular belief, you don't have to turn red to tan; if your skin is red, it's burned, and that's serious. The redness from a burn may not show until 2 to 8 hours after you get out of the sun, and the full force of that burn may not appear for 24 to 36 hours. During that time, you can look forward to pain, itching, and peeling. The best **remedy** for a sunburn is to get out of the sun immediately and stay out of the sun until all the redness is gone. Aloe vera (straight from the plant or from a commercial preparation), cool compresses, cold baths, and anesthetic benzocaine may also help with the pain of sunburn.

Often, people go to tanning salons to prepare for a trip to the tropics. Laying this kind of base tan "will give you some protection, but the tropical sun is too intense, and you should still use sunscreen and a visor when in the sun in Hawaii," Dr. Craig Thomas, author of *All Stings Considered*, tells me. "However, I don't recommend using a tanning salon for a 'base coat,' because fair-skinned people don't do well with ultraviolet radiation from the sun *or* the tanning salon—your skin will pay the price with aging or skin cancer. The risk of melanoma is even worse with intermittent sun exposure than it is with long-term exposure; the worst thing you can do is to go to the tropics once a year for 10 years and get burned."

If you have decided to get a head start on your tan by using a "self-tanning" lotion that dyes your skin a darker shade, remember that this will not protect you from the sun, either. You'll still need to generously apply a high-SPF sunscreen before you head out.

themselves within 15 to 20 minutes if you do nothing at all to treat them. Still, be sure to see a doctor if pain persists or a rash or other symptoms develop.

Box Jellyfish These transparent, square-shaped bell jellyfish are nearly impossible to see in the water. Fortunately, they seem to follow a monthly cycle: 8 to 10 days after the full moon, they appear in the waters on the leeward side of each island and hang around for about 3 days. Also, they seem to sting more in the morning hours, when they're on or near the surface. The best prevention is to get out of the water.

Stings range from no visible marks to red, hive-like welts, blisters, and pain (a burning sensation) lasting from 10 minutes to 8 hours. *All Stings Considered* recommends the following treatment: First, pour regular household vinegar on the sting; this may not relieve the pain, but it will stop additional burning. Do not rub the area. Pick off any vinegar-soaked tentacles with a stick. For pain, apply an ice pack. Seek additional medical treatment if you experience shortness of breath, weakness, palpitations, muscle cramps, or any other severe symptoms. Again, ignore any folk remedies. Most box jellyfish stings disappear by themselves without any treatment.

PUNCTURES   Most sea-related punctures come from stepping on or brushing against the needle-like spines of sea urchins (known locally as *wana*). Be careful when you're in the water; don't put your foot down (even if you have booties or fins on) if you can't clearly see the bottom. Waves can push you into *wana* in a surge zone in shallow water (the wana's spines can even puncture a wet suit).

A sea-urchin sting can result in burning, aching, swelling, and discoloration (black or purple) around the area where the spines entered your skin. The best thing to do is to pull any protruding spines out. The body will absorb the spines within 24 hours to 3 weeks, or the remainder of the spines will work themselves out. Again, contrary to popular wisdom, do not urinate or pour vinegar on the embedded spines—this will not help.

CUTS   All cuts obtained in the marine environment must be taken seriously, because the high level of bacteria present can quickly cause the cut to become infected. The most common cuts are from coral. Contrary to popular belief, coral cannot grow inside your body. However, bacteria can—and very often does—grow inside a cut. The best way to prevent cuts is to wear a wet suit, gloves, and reef shoes. Never, under any circumstances, should you touch a coral head; not only can you get cut, but you can also damage a living organism that took decades to grow.

The symptoms of a coral cut can range from a slight scratch to severe welts and blisters. *All Stings Considered* recommends gently pulling the edges of the skin open and removing any embedded coral or grains of sand with tweezers, or rinsing well with fresh water. Next, scrub the cut well with fresh water. Never use ocean water to clean a cut. If the wound is bleeding, press a clean cloth against the wound until it stops. If bleeding continues, or the edges of the injury are jagged or gaping, seek medical treatment.

6 Getting Married in the Islands

Whatever your dreams and your budget, Hawaii is a great place for a wedding. Not only does the whole place exude romance and natural beauty, but after the ceremony, you're already on your honeymoon. And the members of your wedding party will most likely be delighted, since you've given them the perfect excuse for their own island vacation.

Just being in these spectacular islands takes the pressure down a notch or two and promotes a feeling of celebration. Many couples who were married long ago come to Hawaii to renew their vows, enjoy a second honeymoon, and rediscover the loving spirit that brought them together the first time.

It happens every day of the year in the islands, where more than 20,000 marriages are performed annually, mostly on Oahu. Nearly half (44.6%) of couples married here are from somewhere else. This booming business has spawned more than 70 companies that can help you organize a long-distance event and stage an unforgettable wedding, Hawaiian style or your style. However, you can also plan your own island wedding, even from afar, and not spend a fortune doing it.

THE PAPERWORK

The state of Hawaii has some very minimal procedures for obtaining a marriage license. The first thing you should do is contact the **Honolulu Marriage License**

Office, State Department of Health Building, 1250 Punchbowl St., Honolulu, HI 96813 (☎ **808/586-4545;** www.hawaii.gov), which is open Monday through Friday from 8am to 4pm. They'll mail you their brochure, *Getting Married,* and direct you to the marriage-licensing agent closest to where you'll be staying in Hawaii.

When you get to Hawaii, the prospective bride and groom must go together to the marriage-licensing agent to get a license. A license costs $25 and is good for 30 days. If you don't have the ceremony within the time allotted, you'll have to pay another $25 for another license. The only requirements for a marriage license are that both parties are 15 years of age or older (couples 15 to 17 years old must have proof of age, written consent of both parents, and written approval of the judge of the family court) and that they are not more closely related than first cousins. That's it.

Contrary to some reports from the media, gay couples cannot marry in Hawaii. Although the state courts ruled a few years ago that the state of Hawaii had to show a compelling reason why the state won't issue a marriage license to gay couples, the issue is still being decided in the courts and will be brought before Hawaii's voters in November 1998. Until the issue is decided, the state will not issue marriage licenses to same-sex couples.

PLANNING THE WEDDING

DOING IT YOURSELF

The marriage-licensing agents, which range from employees of the governor's satellite office in Kona to private individuals, are usually friendly, helpful people who can steer you to a nondenominational minister or marriage performer who's licensed by the state of Hawaii to perform the ceremony. These marriage performers are great sources of information for budget weddings. They usually know great places to have the ceremony for free or a nominal fee.

If you don't want to use a wedding planner (see below), but you want to make arrangements before you arrive in Hawaii, our best advice is to get a copy of the daily newspapers on the island where you want to have the wedding. People willing and qualified to conduct weddings advertise in the classifieds. They're great sources of information, as they know the best places to have the ceremony and can recommend caterers, florists, and everything else you'll need. If you want to have your wedding on the Kona/Waimea side of the Big Island, get *West Hawaii Today,* P.O. Box 789, Kailua-Kona, HI 96745 (☎ 808/329-9311); for the Hilo/Puna side, try the *Hawaii Tribune Herald,* P.O. Box 767, Hilo, HI 96720 (☎ 808/935-6621). On Maui, get the *Maui News,* P.O. Box 550, Wailuku, HI 96793 (☎ 808/244-7691). On Kauai, try the *Garden Isle,* 3137 Kuhio Hwy., Lihue, HI 96766 (☎ 808/245-3681), or the *Kauai Times,* 3133B Oihana St., Lihue HI 96766 (☎ 808/245-8825). And on Oahu, check out the *Honolulu Advertiser,* P.O. Box 3110, Honolulu, HI 96802 (☎ 808/525-8000); the *Honolulu Star Bulletin,* P.O. Box 3080, Honolulu, HI 96802 (☎ 808/525-8000); and *MidWeek,* 45-525 Luluku Rd., Kaneohe, HI 96744 (☎ 808/235-5881).

USING A WEDDING PLANNER

Wedding planners—many of whom are marriage-licensing agents as well—can arrange everything for you, from a small, private, outdoor affair to a full-blown formal ceremony in a tropical setting. They charge anywhere from $450 to a small fortune—it all depends on what you want. On the Big Island, contact **Paradise Weddings Hawaii,** P.O. Box 383433, Waikoloa, HI 96738 (☎ 800/428-5844 or 808/883-9067); on Maui, contact **A Wedding Made in Paradise,** P.O. Box 986, Kihei, HI 96753 (☎ 800/453-3440 or 808/879-3444); on Kauai, try **Coconut Coast Weddings & Honeymoons,** P.O. Box 1657, Hanalei, HI 96716 (☎ 800/585-5595 or 808/826-5557); on Oahu, contact **Aloha Wedding Planners,** 1860 Ala Moana Blvd., Suite 115, Honolulu, HI 96815 (☎ 800/288-8309 or 808/943-2711). The Hawaii Visitors and Convention Bureau (see "Visitor Information & Money," above) can provide contact information for other wedding coordinators.

7 Tips for Travelers with Special Needs

FOR TRAVELERS WITH DISABILITIES

Travelers with disabilities are made to feel very welcome in Hawaii. There are more than 2,000 ramped curbs in Oahu alone, hotels are usually equipped with wheelchair-accessible rooms, and tour companies provide many special services. **The Commission on Persons with Disabilities,** 919 Ala Moana Blvd., Suite 101, Honolulu, HI 96814 (☎ **808/586-8121**), and the **Hawaii Center for Independent Living,** 414 Kauwili St., Suite 102, Honolulu, HI 96817 (☎ **808/522-5400;** fax 808/586-8129; www.hawaii.gov/health/cpd_indx.htm; e-mail cpdpp@aloha.net), can provide information and send you a copy of the *Aloha Guide to Accessibility* ($15).

A World of Options, a 658-page book of resources for travelers with disabilities, covers everything from biking trips to scuba outfitters. It costs $45 and is available from **Mobility International USA,** P.O. Box 10767, Eugene, OR 97440 (☎ **541/343-1284,** voice and TDD; www.miusa.org).

For details on wheelchair transportation and tours around the island of Oahu, see "Getting Around" in chapter 5.

For travelers with disabilities who wish to do their own driving, hand-controlled cars can be rented from **Avis** (☎ **800/331-1212**) and **Hertz** (☎ **800/654-3131**). The number of hand-controlled cars in Hawaii is limited, so be sure to book well in advance—at least a week.

Hawaii recognizes other state's windshield placards indicating that the driver of the car is disabled. These can be used to park in specially marked handicap parking spaces, so be sure to bring yours with you.

Vision-impaired travelers who use a seeing-eye dog can now travel to Hawaii without the hassle of quarantine. A recent court decision ruled that visitors with seeing-eye dogs only need to present documentation that the dog has had rabies shots and that it is a trained seeing-eye dog, and the dog can bypass quarantine. Previously, all dogs and cats in Hawaii had to spend 4 months in quarantine, since Hawaii is rabies-free (quarantine has been reduced to 1 month, seeing-eye dogs exempted). For more information, contact the **Animal Quarantine Facility** (☎ **808/483-7171;** www.hawaii.gov).

FOR SENIORS

Discounts for seniors are available at almost all of Hawaii's major attractions, and occasionally at hotels and restaurants. When making hotel reservations, always ask about these discounts. Members of the **American Association of Retired Persons (AARP),** 601 E St. NW, Washington, D.C. 20049 (☎ **800/424-3410** or 202

Travel Tip

If you're looking for a travel agent that offers tours or can plan trips for travelers with disabilities, point your Internet browser to **www.access-able.com.** You'll also find relay and voice numbers for hotels, airlines, and car-rental companies on this user-friendly site, as well as links to accessible accommodations, attractions, transportation, and tours; local medical resources and equipment repairers; and more.

Travel Tip

Discounts for seniors are available at almost all of Hawaii's major attractions, and occasionally at hotels and restaurants. The Outrigger hotel chain, for instance, offers travelers age 50 and older a 20% discount off regular published rates—and an additional 5% off if you're a member of AARP! So, when making reservations or buying tickets, always ask. And always carry identification with proof of your age—it can really pay off.

434-2277), are usually eligible for such discounts; AARP also puts together organized tour packages at moderate rates through the AARP Travel Service. The **National Council of Senior Citizens,** 8403 Coolesville Dr., Suite 1200, Silver Spring, MD 20910 (☎ **301/578-8800**), is a not-for-profit advocacy organization with a travel program and a 24-hour emergency alert service, which entitles members ($29.95 to join) to hotel, condominium, and car-rental discounts and has an alert service for accident, injury, or illness.

If you're 62 or older and plan to visit Hawaii's national parks, you can save sightseeing dollars by picking up a **Golden Age Passport** from any national park, recreation area, or monument. This lifetime pass has a one-time fee of $10 and provides free admission to all the parks in the system, plus a 50% savings on camping and recreation fees. You can pick one up at any park entrance; be sure to have proof of your age with you.

FOR GAYS & LESBIANS

Known for its acceptance of all groups, Hawaii welcomes gays and lesbians just as it does any other group. The number of gay- or lesbian-specific accommodations on the islands is limited, but most accommodations greet gay and lesbian visitors like any other travelers—with aloha.

To get a sense of the local gay and lesbian community, contact Lifestyle Publishing, Inc., publishers of the monthly magazine *Island Lifestyle,* P.O. Box 11840, Honolulu, HI 96828 (☎ **808/737-6400;** fax 808/735-8825; www.islandlifestyle.com; e-mail editor@islandlifestyle.com). The gay and lesbian magazine presents alternative news, arts, entertainment, and happenings in Hawaii; to have a copy sent to you, enclose $5.

The **Gay and Lesbian Community Center,** 1566 Wilder Ave., Honolulu, HI 96822 (☎ **808/951-7000;** fax 808/951-7240; open Monday to Friday noon to 5pm), is a referral service for nearly every kind of gay-related service you can think of. Another Oahu-based referral service is the **Gay Community Director** (☎ **808/ 532-9000**), which can refer you to all kinds of gay-friendly places and services, from hotels to doctors to support groups; the line can also tell you where to pick up gay-oriented publications on Maui. Contact the **Bisexual/Transgender/Gay/Lesbian Community Bulletin Board** (☎ **808/823-6248**) for information on Kauai's gay community and related events.

For the latest information on the gay-marriage issue in Hawaii, contact the **Hawaii Marriage Project** (☎ **808/532-9000;** www.xq.com/hermp/).

TRAVEL AGENCIES Pacific Ocean Holidays, P.O. Box 88245, Honolulu, HI 96830 (☎ **800/735-6600** or 808/923-2400; gayhawaii.com), offers vacation packages that feature gay-owned and gay-friendly lodgings. They also publish the *Pocket Guide to Hawaii: A Guide for Gay Visitors & Kamaaina,* a list of gay-owned and gay-friendly businesses throughout the islands. Send $5 for a copy (mail order only; no phone orders, please), or access the online version on their Web site; you can even book your entire Hawaii vacation online.

FOR FAMILIES

Hawaii is paradise for children: beaches to run on, water to splash in, unusual sights to see, and a host of new foods to taste. Be sure to check out the boxes in each island chapter for kid-friendly places to stay and tips on island activities that are great for the whole family.

The larger hotels and resorts have supervised programs for children and can refer you to qualified baby-sitters. You can also contact **People Attentive to Children (PATCH)**, which can refer you to baby-sitters who have taken their training courses on childcare. On Oahu, dial ☎ 808/839-1791; on the **Big Island**, call ☎ 808/322-7101 on the Kona side of the island, or ☎ 808/934-0831 in Hilo; on **Maui**, dial ☎ 808/242-9232; and on **Kauai**, call ☎ 808/246-0622.

Baby's Away (ares.csd.net/~babyaway) rents cribs, strollers, highchairs, playpens, infant seats, and the like on **Maui** (☎ 800/942-9030 or 808/875-9030), the **Big Island** (☎ 800/931-9030 or 808/329-7475), and **Kauai** (☎ 800/996-9030 or 808/245-6259). Give them a call, and they'll deliver whatever you need to wherever you're staying and pick it up when you're done. On **Oahu**, call **Dyans Rentals** (☎ 808/591-8207).

Note that by state law, hotels that offer supervised activity programs can accept only children ages 5 to 12.

8 Getting There & Getting Around

For additional advice on getting around the Hawaiian Islands, see "Getting Around" in the individual island chapters.

ARRIVING IN THE ISLANDS

All major American and many international carriers fly to Honolulu International Airport. Some also fly direct to Kailua-Kona, on the Big Island; Kahului; Maui; and Lihue, Kauai.

United Airlines (☎ 800/225-5825; www.ual.com) offers the most frequent service from the U.S. mainland, but **American Airlines** (☎ 800/433-7300; www.americanair.com), **Continental Airlines** (☎ 800/231-0856), **Delta Airlines** (☎ 800/221-1212; www.delta-air.com), **Hawaiian Airlines** (☎ 800/367-5320; www.hawaiianair.com), **Northwest Airlines** (☎ 800/225-2525; www.nwa.com), and **TWA** (☎ 800/221-2000; ww2.twa.com) all have regular flights. In addition to flying to Honolulu, United flies nonstop from Los Angeles and San Francisco to the Big Island, Maui, and Kauai. American flies a "through flight" from Dallas or Los Angeles to Maui, with a stopover (but no plane change) in Honolulu. Both Delta and Hawaiian fly nonstop to both Honolulu and Maui. TWA flies nonstop from its St. Louis hub to Honolulu. In June 1998, Continental started offering the only daily nonstops to Honolulu from the New York area.

For information on airlines serving Hawaii from other than the U.S. mainland, see chapter 4, "For Foreign Visitors."

For details on navigating Hawaii's airports, see "Arriving" under "Orientation" in each of the island chapters that follow.

AGRICULTURAL SCREENING AT THE AIRPORTS   At Honolulu International and the neighbor-island airports, baggage and passengers bound for the mainland and other countries must be screened by agricultural officials before boarding.

This takes a little time but isn't a problem unless you happen to be carrying a football-sized local avocado home to Aunt Emma. Officials will confiscate fresh avocados, bananas, mangoes, and many other kinds of local produce in the name of fruit-fly control. Pineapples, coconuts, and papayas inspected and certified for export, boxed flowers, leis without seeds, and processed foods (macadamia nuts, coffee, jams, dried fruit, and the like) will pass. Call federal or state agricultural officials before leaving for the airport if you're not sure about your trophy.

INTERISLAND FLIGHTS

Don't expect to jump a ferry between any of the Hawaiian islands. Today, everyone island-hops by plane. In fact, almost every 20 minutes of every day from just before sunrise to well after sunset (usually around 8pm), a plane takes off or lands at Honolulu International Airport on the interisland shuttle service. If you miss a flight, don't worry; they're like buses—another one will be along real soon.

Aloha Airlines (☎ 800/367-5250 or 808/484-1111; www.alohaair.com) is the state's largest provider of interisland air transport service. It offers 180 regularly scheduled daily jet flights throughout Hawaii, using an all-jet fleet of Boeing 737 aircraft. Aloha's sibling company, **Island Air** (☎ 800/323-3345 or 808/484-2222), operates deHavilland DASH-8 and DASH-6 turboprop aircraft and serves Hawaii's small interisland airports on Maui, Molokai, and Lanai.

Hawaiian Airlines (☎ 800/367-5320 or 808/835-3700; www.hawaiianair.com; e-mail webmaster@hawaiianair.com), Hawaii's first interisland airline (which also flies daily to Hawaii from the West Coast, see above), has carried more than 100 million passengers to and around the state. It's one of the world's safest airlines, never having had a fatal incident since it started flying in 1929.

For details on making interisland connections at Honolulu International Airport, see "Arriving" under "Orientation" in chapter 5.

MULTI-ISLAND PASSES   At press time, the standard interisland fare on both interisland carriers was $86. However, both airlines offer multiple-flight deals that you might want to consider.

Aloha Airlines   Nonresidents of Hawaii can purchase Aloha's **Visitor Seven-Day Island Pass**. For just $315 per person, including tax, you get unlimited travel on Aloha and Island Air for 7 consecutive days; Aloha also offers a 1-month version for $999.

If you're traveling for more than a week but less than a month, you can buy a **Coupon Book** for $309, which contains six blank tickets that you can use—for yourself or any other traveler—any time within 1 year of purchase. This is probably the best deal going if you're island-hopping two or three times in the course of your stay.

Hawaiian Airlines   Hawaiian offers a variety of discounts based on the number of flights you're taking and the number of passengers flying. The **Hawaiian Island Pass** gives you unlimited interisland flights for $299 per person for 5 consecutive days, $349 for 7 days, $369 for 10 days, and $409 for 2 weeks.

Because Hawaiian Airlines also flies to and from the mainland U.S., you may also be able to apply your transpacific flight toward discounts on your interisland travel; be sure to inquire when booking.

CAR RENTALS

Hawaii (with the exception of the island of Lanai) has some of the lowest car-rental rates in the country. The average nondiscounted, unlimited-mileage rate for a 1-day rental for an intermediate-sized car in Honolulu was $39 in 1997; that's the fourth lowest rate in the country, compared with the national average of $53.50 a day.

Travel Deals for Net Surfers

It's possible to get some great deals on airfare, hotels, and car rentals via the Internet. So go grab your mouse and start surfing before you hit the real waves in Hawaii—you could save a bundle on your trip. The Web sites we've highlighted below are worth checking out, especially since all services are free (but don't forget that time is money when you're online).

Microsoft Expedia (www.expedia.com) The best part of this multipurpose travel site is the Fare Tracker: You fill out a form on the screen indicating that you're interested in cheap flights to Hawaii from your hometown, and, once a week, they e-mail you the best airfare deals. The site's Travel Agent will all steer you to bargains on hotels and car rentals, and you can book everything, including flights, right online. This site is even useful once you're booked: Before you go, log on to Expedia for oodles of up-to-date travel information, including weather reports and foreign exchange rates.

Preview Travel (www.reservations.com and www.vacations.com) Another useful travel site, Reservations.com has a Best Fare Finder, which will search the Apollo computer reservations system for the three lowest fares for any route on any days of the year. Say you want to go from Chicago to Honolulu and back between December 6 and 13: Just fill out the form on the screen with times, dates, and destinations, and within minutes, Preview will show you the best deals. If you find an airfare you like, you can book your ticket right online—you can even reserve hotels and car rentals on this site. If you're in the preplanning stage, head to Preview's Vacations.com site, where you can check out the latest package deals for Hawaii and other destinations around the world by clicking on "Hot Deals."

Travelocity (www.travelocity.com) This is one of the best travel sites out there. In addition to its Personal Fare Watcher, which notifies you via e-mail of the lowest airfares for up to five different destinations, Travelocity will track the three lowest fares for any routes on any dates in minutes. You can book a flight right then and there, and if you need a rental car or hotel, Travelocity will find you the best deal via the SABRE computer reservations system (a huge database used by travel agents worldwide). Click on "Last Minute Deals" for the latest travel bargains, including a link to **H.O.T. Coupons (www.hotcoupons.com)**, where you can print out coupons for travel in the U.S. and Canada, including Hawaii.

All major rental-car agencies are represented at Honolulu International Airport and most neighbor-island airports, including **Alamo** (☎ 800/327-9633; www.goalamo.com), **Avis** (☎ 800/321-3712; www.avis.com), **Budget** (☎ 800/935-6878; www.budgetrentacar.com), **Dollar** (☎ 800/800-4000; www.dollarcar.com), **Enterprise** (☎ 800/325-8007; www.pickenterprise.com), **Hertz** (☎ 800/654-3011; www.hertz.com), **National** (☎ 800/227-7368; www.nationalcar.com), and **Thrifty** (☎ 800/367-2277; www.thrifty.com). It's almost always cheaper to rent a car at the airport than in Waikiki or through your hotel (unless there's one already included in your package deal).

Rental cars are usually at a premium on Kauai, Molokai, and Lanai and may be sold out on the neighbor islands on holiday weekends, so be sure to book well ahead.

Airlines of the Web (www.itn.net/airlines) This new site may be the most comprehensive Internet airline information source to date. Among its many features are links to virtually every airline in the world; Internet-only airfare deals posted on one easy-to-scan page; and a terrific fare finder and online reservations service. A unique feature is ITN's Low Fare Ticker, which allows you to monitor fares around the clock—particularly useful during fare wars. Fare Mail will notify you via e-mail when a flight you're interested in dips below your personal price threshold.

Trip.Com (www.thetrip.com) This site is really geared toward the business traveler, but vacationers-to-be can also use Trip.Com's valuable fare-finding engine, which will e-mail you every week with the best city-to-city airfare deals on your selected route or routes.

E-Savers Programs Several major airlines, most of which service the Hawaiian islands, offer a free e-mail service known as **E-Savers**, via which they'll send you their best bargain airfares on a weekly basis. Here's how it works: Once a week (usually Wednesday), subscribers receive a list of discounted flights to and from various destinations, both international and domestic. Now here's the catch: These fares are available only if you leave the next Saturday (or sometimes Friday night) and return on the following Monday or Tuesday. It's really a service for the spontaneously inclined and travelers looking for a quick getaway (for Hawaii, that usually means travelers from the West Coast). But the fares are cheap, so it's worth taking a look. If you have a preference for certain airlines (in other words, the ones you fly most frequently), sign up with them first. Another caveat: You get frequent-flier miles if you purchase one of these fares, but you can't use miles to buy the ticket.

Here's a list of airlines and their Web sites, where you can not only get on the e-mailing lists but also book flights directly:

- **American Airlines:** www.americanair.com
- **Continental Airlines:** www.flycontinental.com
- **Northwest Airlines:** www.nwa.com
- **TWA:** www.twa.com
- **US Airways:** www.usairways.com

Epicurious Travel (travel.epicurious.com), another good travel site, allows you to sign up for all these airline e-mail lists at once.

To rent a car in Hawaii, you must be at least 25 years of age and have a valid driver's license and a credit card. Your valid home-state license will be recognized here.

MULTI-ISLAND DEALS If you're going to visit multiple islands, it's usually easiest—and cheapest—to book with one company and carry your contract through on each island for your entire stay; you just drop off your car on the island you're leaving, and there will be one waiting for you on the next island with the same company. By booking your cars this way, as one interisland rental, you can usually take advantage of weekly rates that you'd be excluded from if you treated each rental separately. Both **Avis** (☎ 800/321-3712; www.avis.com) and **Hertz** (☎ 800/654-3011; www.hertz.com) can do this for you; inquire about interisland rental arrangements when booking.

INSURANCE Hawaii is a no-fault state, which means that if you don't have collision-damage insurance, you are required to pay for all damages before you leave the state, whether or not the accident was your fault. Your personal car insurance may provide rental-car coverage; read your policy or call your insurer before you leave home. Bring your insurance identification card if you decline the optional insurance, which usually costs from $12 to $20 a day. Obtain the name of your company's local claim representative before you go. Some credit-card companies also provide collision-damage insurance for their customers; check with yours before you rent.

DRIVING LAWS When you're behind the wheel in Hawaii, make sure you obey the following rules: State law mandates that all passengers in a car must wear a **seat belt**, and all infants must be strapped in car seats. The fine is quite stiff and is enforced with vigilance, so buckle up—you'll pay a $50 fine if you don't. **Pedestrians** always have the right of way; even if they're not in the crosswalk. You can turn **right on red** from the right lane after a full and complete stop, unless there's a sign forbidding you to do so.

ROADMAPS The fold-out map at the back of this book should get you around all the islands.

The best and most detailed roadmaps are published by *This Week Magazine*, a free visitor publication available on Oahu, Big Island, Maui, and Kauai. For island maps, check out the University of Hawaii Press island maps. Updated periodically, they include a detailed network of island roads, large-scale insets of towns, historical and contemporary points of interest, parks, beaches, and hiking trails. They cost about $3 each, or about $15 for a complete set. If you can't find them in a bookstore near you, write to **University of Hawaii Press**, 2840 Kolowalu St., Honolulu, HI 96822.

If you seek topographical maps of the Hawaiian Islands, go to the **Hawaii Geographic Society**, 49 S. Hotel St., Honolulu, HI 95813, or write to them at P.O. Box 1698, Honolulu, HI 96806 (☎ **808/546-3952;** fax 808/536-5999).

9 Tips on Accommodations

Hawaii offers all kinds of accommodations, from simple rooms in resorted plantation homes and quaint cottages on the beach to luxurious ocean-view condo units and opulent suites in beachfront resorts. Each has their plusses and minuses—so before you book, make sure you know what you are getting into. Below, we discuss the various accommodation options available in Hawaii; how to get the best possible rate, when you should consider using a booking agency; and what to do if your dream accommodation turns into a nightmare.

TYPES OF ACCOMMODATIONS

HOTELS In Hawaii, "hotel" can indicate a wide range of options, from few or no on-site amenities to enough extras to call it a miniresort. Generally a hotel offers daily maid service and has a restaurant, on-site laundry facilities, a swimming pool, and a sundries/convenience—type shop (rather than the shopping arcades that most resorts have these days). Top hotels also have activities desks, concierge and valet service, room service (though it may be limited), business centers, an airport shuttle, a bar and/or lounge, and maybe a few more shops. The advantage of staying in a hotel is privacy and convenience; the disadvantage is generally noise: either thin walls between rooms or loud music from a lobby lounge late into the night.

Hotels are often a short walk from the beach rather than beachfront (although some, like the Sheraton Moana Surfrider and the New Otani in Waikiki, are right on

What to Do If Your Dream Hotel Turns Out to Be a Nightmare

Don't panic! Even if you've booked into a small B&B and you absolutely hate both of the bedrooms once you show up, usually the host wants to make you happy and may even get on the phone and book you at another place that will suit you better. Hotels, resorts, and condominiums are generally easier to deal with, since they have numerous units to offer and can probably satisfy your complaints by moving you to another room.

Here are some tips on how to complain if you're unhappy with your room:

- Find out beforehand exactly what the accommodation is offering you: the cost, the minimum stay, the included amenities. Ask if there's any penalty fee for leaving early. Read the small print in the contract—especially the information on cancellation fees.

- Discuss ahead of time with the B&B, vacation rental, condominium agent, or booking agency what their cancellation policy is if the accommodation doesn't meet your expectations. Get this policy in writing (so there are no misunderstandings later).

- When you arrive, if the room you're given doesn't meet your expectations, notify the front desk, rental agent, or booking agency immediately.

- Approach the management in a calm, reasonable manner. Voice your complaint clearly and suggest a solution. Be reasonable and be willing to compromise. Do not make threats or leave. If you leave, it may be harder to get your deposit returned.

- If all else fails, when you get home, write your credit-card company or any association the accommodation may be a member of (such as the Hawaii Visitors and Convention Bureau, a resort association, or an island association). In the letter, state the name of the accommodation, the name you registered under, the date of the complaint, the exact nature of the complaint, and why the issue was not resolved to your satisfaction. And be sure to let us know if you have a problem with a place we recommended in this book!

the sand). Since they come with fewer amenities than full-fledged resorts, hotels tend to be cheaper, though not always.

RESORTS In Hawaii, a resort offers everything a hotel offers and more. What you get varies from property to property, of course, but expect facilities, services, and amenities such as direct beach access, with beach cabanas and chairs; pools (often more than one) and a Jacuzzi; a spa and fitness center; restaurants, bars, and lounges; a 24-hour front desk; concierge, valet, and bell services; room service (often around the clock); an activities desk; tennis and golf (some of the world's best courses are at Hawaii resorts); ocean activities; a business center; kid's programs; and more.

The advantages of a resort are that you have everything you could possibly want in the way of services and things to do; the disadvantage is that the price generally reflects this. Don't be misled by a name—just because a place is called "ABC Resort" doesn't mean it actually *is* a resort. Make sure you're getting what you pay for.

CONDOS The roominess and convenience of a condo—which is usually a fully equipped, multiple-bedroom apartment—makes this a great choice for families. Condominium properties in Hawaii are generally several apartments set in either a single high-rise or a cluster of low-rise units. Condos generally have amenities such as some maid service (ranging from daily to weekly; it may or may not be included in your rate, so be sure to ask), a swimming pool, laundry facilities (either in your unit or in a central location), and an on-site front desk or a live-in property manager. The advantages of a condo are privacy, space, and convenience—which usually include full kitchen facilities, a washer and dryer, a private phone, and more. The downsides are the standard lack of an on-site restaurant and the density of the units (versus the privacy of a single-unit vacation rental).

Condos vary in price according to size, location, and amenities. Many of them are located on or near the beach, and they tend to be clustered in resort areas. While there are some very high-end condos, most tend to be quite affordable, especially if you're traveling in a group that's large enough to require more than one bedroom.

BED-AND-BREAKFASTS

Hawaii has a wide range of places that call themselves B&Bs: Everything from a traditional B&B—several bedrooms (which may or may not share a bathroom) in a home, with breakfast served in the morning—to what is essentially a vacation rental on an owner's property that comes with fixings for you to make your own breakfast. Make sure that the B&B you're booking matches your own mental picture. Would you prefer conversation around a big dining-room table as you eat a hearty breakfast, or just a muffin and juice to enjoy in your own private place? Laundry facilities and a private phone are not always available at B&Bs. We've reviewed lots of wonderful B&Bs in the island chapters that follow. If you have to share a bathroom, we've spelled it out in the listings; otherwise, you can assume that you will have a private bath.

The advantage of a traditional B&B is its individual style and congenial atmosphere. B&Bs are great places to meet other visitors to Hawaii, and the host is generally very happy to act as your own private concierge, giving you tips on where to go and what to do. In addition, they're usually an affordable way to go (though fancier ones can run $150 or more a night). The disadvantages are lack of privacy, usually a set time for breakfast, few amenities, generally no maid service, and the fact that you'll have to share the quarters beyond your bedroom with others. In addition, B&B owners usually require a minimum stay of 2 or 3 nights, and it's often a drive to the beach.

VACATION RENTALS

This is another great choice for families and for long-term stays. "Vacation rental" usually means that there will be no one on the property where you're staying. The actual accommodation can range from an apartment in a condominium building to a two-room cottage on the beach to an entire fully-equipped house. Generally, vacation rentals are the kind of places you can settle into and make yourself at home for awhile: They have kitchen facilities (which can be either a complete kitchen or a just a kitchenette with microwave, refrigerator, burners, and coffeemaker), on-site laundry facilities, and phone; some also come outfitted with such extras as TV, VCR, and stereo. The advantages of a vacation rental are complete privacy, your own kitchen (which can save you money on meals), and lots of conveniences. The disadvantages are a lack of an on-site property manager and generally no maid service; often, a minimum stay is required (sometimes as much as a week). If you book a vacation rental, be sure that you have a 24-hour contact so that when the toilet won't flush or you can't figure out how to turn on the air conditioning, you have someone to call.

BARGAINING ON PRICES

Like the price of a car, accommodation rates can sometimes be bargained down, but it depends on the place. In general, each type of accommodation allows a different amount of latitude in bargaining on their rack (or published) rates.

The best bargaining can be had at **hotels** and **resorts**. Hotels and resorts regularly pay travel agents as much as 30% of the rate they're getting for sending clients their way; if business is slow, some hotels may give you the benefit of at least part of this commission if you book directly instead of going through an airline or travel agent. Most also have *kamaaina* or "local" rates for islanders, which they may extend to visitors during slow periods. It never hurts to ask politely for a discounted or local rate; there is also a host of special rates available for the military, seniors, members of the travel industry, families, corporate travelers, and long-term stays. Ask about package deals, where for the same price as a room, you can get a car rental or free breakfast. Hotels and resorts have packages for everyone: golfers, tennis players, families, honeymooners, and more (for more on these, see "Money-Saving Package Deals," below). We've found that it's worth the extra few cents to make a local call to the hotel; sometimes the local reservations person knows about package deals that the 800 operators are unaware of. If all else fails, try to get the hotel or resort to upgrade you to a better room for the same price as a budget room, or wave the extra fees for children or the parking fee. Persistence and asking politely can pay off.

Bed-and-breakfasts are the hardest to bargain on price. Sometimes you can be successful in bargaining down the minimum stay, or you may be able to negotiate a discount if you're staying a week or longer. But generally, a B&B owner has only a few rooms and has already priced the property at a competitive rate; expect to pay what's asked.

You have somewhat more leeway to negotiate on **vacation rentals** and **condos**. In addition to asking for a discount on a multinight stay, also ask if they can throw in a rental car to sweeten the deal; believe it or not, they often will.

USING A BOOKING AGENCY VS. DOING IT YOURSELF

Sometimes you can save money by making your arrangements yourself—not only can you bargain on the phone, but some accommodations may be willing to pass on a percentage of the commission they would normally have to pay a travel agent or a booking agency.

However, if you don't have the time or money to call several places to make sure that they offer the amenities you'd like and to bargain for a price you're comfortable with, then you might consider a booking agency. The time they spend on your behalf may well be worth any fees you'll have to pay.

The top reservations service in the state is ✪ **Hawaii's Best Bed & Breakfasts**, P.O. Box 563, Kamuela, HI 96743 (☎ **800/262-9912** or 808/885-4550; fax 808/885-0559; www.bestbnb.com). They'll charge you $15 to book the first two locations, and $5 for each additional location. Barbara and Susan Campbell personally select the traditional homestays, cottages, and inns throughout the islands that they represent, based on each one's hospitality, distinctive charm, and attention to detail. Other great statewide booking agents are **Bed & Breakfast Hawaii**, P.O. Box 449, Kapaa, HI 96746 (☎ **800/733-1632** or 808/822-7771; fax 808/822-2723), offering a range of accommodations from vacation homes to B&Bs, starting at $65 a night; and **Ann and Bob Babson**, 3371 Keha Dr., Kihei, HI 96753 (☎ **800/824-6409** or 808/874-1166; fax 808/879-7906; www.maui.net/~babson), who can steer you in the right direction for both accommodations and car rentals. Not only do they personally inspect the units they recommend, but the Babsons are impeccably honest and dedicated to matching you up with the place that's right for you.

For vacation rentals, contact **Hawaii Beachfront Vacation Homes** (☎ **808/247-3637** or 808/235-2644; www.hotspots.hawaii.com/beachrent.html). **Hawaii Condo Exchange** (☎ 800/442-0404; wwte.com/condos) acts as a consolidator for condo and vacation-rental properties.

10 Money-Saving Package Deals

Booking an all-inclusive travel package that includes some combination of airfare, accommodations, rental car, meals, airport and baggage transfers, sightseeing, and more is, more often than not, the most cost-effective way to travel to Hawaii. You can sometimes save so much money by buying all the pieces of your trip through a package agent that your transpacific airfare ends up, in effect, being free.

The best place to start looking for a package deal is in the travel section of your local Sunday newspaper. Also check the ads in the back of such national travel magazines as *Travel & Leisure*, *National Geographic Traveler*, and *Condé Nast Traveler*. **Liberty Travel** (many locations; check your local directory, since there's not a central tollfree number), for instance, is one of the biggest packagers in the Northeast, usually boasts a full-page ad in Sunday papers. You won't get much in the way of service, but you will get a good deal. At press time, Liberty was offering a 7-day/6-night package to Hawaii with accommodations at the Sheraton Moana Surfrider on Waikiki Beach for $1,029 per person, double occupancy, including round-trip airfare from New York City, all airport transfers, a double room (hotel tax included), a flower-lei greeting, and some sightseeing—not a bad deal, considering that the Moana's cheapest room officially goes for $250 a night, and round-trip airfare is at least $650 or $700 each and can run as high as $800. Of course, package prices are always in flux, but this should give you an idea of how well you can do if you book your trip as a package. **American Express Travel** (☎ 800/AXP-6898; www.americanexpress.com/travel) can also book you a well-priced Hawaiian vacation; they also advertise in many Sunday travel sections.

Hawaii is such an ideal destination for vacation packages that some packagers book Hawaiian vacations as the majority of their business. **Pleasant Hawaiian Holidays** (☎ 800/2-HAWAII or 800/242-9244; www.pleasantholidays.com or www.2hawaii. com) is, by far, the biggest and most comprehensive packager to Hawaii; they offer an extensive, high-quality collection of 50 condos and hotels in every price range. **Sunscapes** (☎ 800/229-8376 or 425/643-1620; www.sunscapes.com) sells only Hawaii vacations, concentrating on budget and moderately priced hotels and condos.

Other reliable packages include the airlines themselves, which often package their flights together with accommodations. **United Vacations** (☎ 800/328-6877; www.unitedvacations.com) is by far the most comprehensive airline packager to Hawaii, offering great air-inclusive and land-only deals on a surprisingly wide selection of accommodations throughout the islands. Other airlines offering good-value packages to the islands are **American Airlines Vacations** (☎ 800/321-2121; www.2travel.com/americanair/hawaii.html), **Continental Airlines Vacations** (☎ 800/634-5555 or 800/301-3800; www.coolvacations.com), **Delta Dream Vacations** (☎ 800/872-7786; www.leisureweb.com/DELTA), and **TWA Getaway Vacations** (☎ 800/GETAWAY or 800/438-2929; www.twa.com/html/vacation/tourvac.

Package-Buying Tip

For one-stop shopping on the Web, go to **www.vacationpackager.com**, a Web-search engine that can link you up with many different package-tour operators that can help you plan a custom-tailored trip to Hawaii; be sure to look under both "Hawaii" and "Hawaiian Islands." Or point your browser to **www.2travel.com/2where/hawaii/index.html**, which takes you directly to a page with links to all the big-name packagers offering package tours to Hawaii.

html). If you're traveling to the islands from Canada, ask your travel agent about package deals through **Air Canada Vacations** (☎ 800/776-3000; www.aircanada.ca).

GREAT PACKAGE DEALS AT HAWAII'S TOP HOTEL CHAINS

Hawaii's three major hotel chains have a host of packages that will save you big bucks on accommodations.

With some 28 properties in Hawaii, including 20 in Waikiki, **Outrigger** (☎ **800/OUTRIGGER;** fax 800/622-4852, www.outrigger.com) offers excellent affordable accommodations, all with consistently dependable, clean, and well-appointed rooms. The chain's price structure is based entirely on location, room size, and amenities. You'll be comfortable at any of the chain's outposts: The small rooms at the budget Outriggers are just as tastefully decorated as the larger, more expensive Outrigger rooms right on the beach. Outrigger's empire also includes good-value condominiums and resorts on the neighbor islands. Package deals include discounted rates for spring and fall stays, a car package, discounts for multinight stays, family plans, cut rates for seniors, and even packages for scuba divers (2 days of two-tank boat dives and a 3-night stay starts at $311 per person, double occupancy).

The **Aston** chain (☎ **800/92-ASTON;** fax 808/922-8785; www.aston-hotels.com), which celebrated 50 years in Hawaii in 1998, has some 29 hotels, condominiums, and resort properties scattered throughout the islands: They range dramatically in price and style, from the luxurious Maui Aston Wailea Resort to Oahu's bargain-priced Aston Waikiki Beachside Hotel to the historic Waimea Plantation Cottages on Kauai to beachside condominiums at Kona-by-the-Sea on the Big Island. Aston offers package deals galore, including family packages; discounted senior rates; car, golf, and shopping packages; and multinight stay deals, including a wonderful Island Hopper deal, where you can hop from island to island and get 25% off on 7 nights or more at Aston properties.

Marc Resorts Hawaii (☎ **800/535-0085;** fax 800/633-5085; www.marcresorts. com) has 22 properties on every island but Lanai, ranging from Honolulu's Manoa Valley Inn, a quaint restored bed-and-breakfast, to Molokai Shores, an affordable condominium property on Molokai. They offer packages for seniors, multinight stays, honeymooners, and golfers, as well as corporate discounts and car-rental deals.

FAST FACTS: The Hawaiian Islands

AAA   Hawaii's only American Automobile Association (AAA) office is at 590 Queen St., Honolulu (☎ 808/528-2600). Please note that AAA service is available only on the island of Oahu, and not on the other islands. Some car-rental agencies now provide automobile-club-type services, so you should inquire about their availability when you rent your car.

American Express   For 24-hour traveler's check refunds and purchase information, call ☎ 800/221-7282. For local offices, see "Fast Facts" sections in the individual island chapters.

Area Code   All the Hawaiian Islands are in the **808** area code. Note that if you're calling one island from another, you'll have to dial 1-808 first, and you'll be billed at long-distance rates (which can be more expensive than calling the mainland).

Electricity   Like the rest of the United States, Hawaii's electric power is 110 volts, 60 cycles.

Emergencies   Dial ☎ 911 for police, fire, or ambulance.

Legal Aid   Call the **Legal Aid Society of Hawaii**, 1108 Nuuanu Ave., Honolulu HI 96817 (☎ **808/536-4302**).

Liquor Laws The legal drinking age in Hawaii is 21. Bars are allowed to stay open daily until 2am; places with cabaret licenses are able to keep the booze flowing until 4am. Grocery and convenience stores are allowed to sell beer, wine, and liquor 7 days a week.

Newspapers The *Honolulu Advertiser* and the *Honolulu Star Bulletin* are circulated statewide. Other weekly newspapers on Oahu include the *Honolulu Weekly* and *Pacific Business News*. Neighbor-island newspapers are published daily on Maui (*Maui News*), Kauai (*Garden Island* and *Kauai Times*), and the Big Island (*West Hawaii Today* and *Hawaii Tribune Herald*); Molokai has two weeklies.

Safety Although Hawaii is generally a safe tourist destination, visitors have been crime victims, so stay alert. The most common crime against tourists is rental car break-ins. Never leave any valuables in your car, not even in your trunk. Thieves can be in and out of your trunk faster than you can open it with your own keys. Especially be leery of high-risk areas, such as beaches and resort areas. Also, never carry large amounts of cash in Waikiki and other tourist zones. Stay in well-lighted areas after dark. Don't hike on deserted trails alone.

Smoking It's against the law to smoke in public buildings, including airports, grocery stores, retail shops, movie theaters, banks, and all government buildings and facilities. Hotels have nonsmoking rooms available, restaurants have nonsmoking sections, and car-rental agencies have nonsmoking cars. Most bed-and-breakfasts prohibit smoking inside their buildings.

Taxes Hawaii's sales tax is 4%. Hotel-occupancy tax is 6%, and hoteliers are allowed by the state to tack on an additional .0016669% excise tax. Thus, expect taxes of about 10.17% to be added to every hotel bill.

Time Hawaii Standard Time is in effect year-round. Hawaii is 2 hours behind Pacific Standard Time and 5 hours behind Eastern Standard Time. In other words, when it's noon in Hawaii, it's 2pm in California and 5pm in New York during Standard Time on the mainland. There's no daylight-saving time here, so when daylight-saving time is in effect on the mainland, Hawaii is 3 hours behind the West Coast and 6 hours behind the East Coast—so in the summer, when it's noon in Hawaii, it's 3pm in California during daylight-saving time and 6pm in New York.

Hawaii is east of the International Date Line, putting it in the same day as the U.S. mainland and Canada and a day behind Australia, New Zealand, and Asia.

For the exact **local time**, call ☎ **808/245-0212.**

4

For Foreign Visitors

by Jeanette Foster

The pervasiveness of American culture around the world may make you feel that you know the USA pretty well, but leaving your own country for the States—especially the unique island state of Hawaii—still requires an additional degree of planning.

1 Preparing for Your Trip

ENTRY REQUIREMENTS

Immigration laws are a hot political issue these days; the following requirements may have changed somewhat by the time you plan your trip. Check at any U.S. embassy or consulate for current information and requirements.

DOCUMENT REGULATIONS   Canadian citizens may enter the United States without visas; they need only proof of residence.

The U.S. State Department has a **Visa Waiver Pilot Program** allowing citizens of certain countries to enter the United States without a visa for stays of up to 90 days. At press time, these included Andorra, Australia, Austria, Belgium, Brunei, Denmark, Finland, France, Germany, Iceland, Ireland, Italy, Japan, Liechtenstein, Luxembourg, Monaco, the Netherlands, New Zealand, Norway, San Marino, Spain, Sweden, Switzerland, and the United Kingdom. Citizens of these countries need only a valid passport and a round-trip air or cruise ticket in their possession upon arrival. If they first enter the United States, they may then visit Mexico, Canada, Bermuda, and/or the Caribbean islands and return to the United States without needing a visa. Further information is available from any U.S. embassy or consulate.

Citizens of all other countries must have (1) a valid **passport** with an expiration date at least 6 months later than the scheduled end of their visit to the United States, and (2) a **tourist visa**, which may be obtained without charge from the nearest U.S. consulate.

To obtain a visa, you must submit a completed application form (either in person or by mail) with a 1½-inch-square photo, and you must demonstrate binding ties to a residence abroad. Usually, you can obtain a visa at once or within 24 hours, but it may take longer during the summer rush from June to August. If you cannot go in person, contact the nearest U.S. embassy or consulate for directions on applying by mail. Your travel agent or airline office may also be able to provide you with visa applications and instructions. The U.S.

consulate or embassy that issues your visa will determine whether you will be issued a multiple- or single-entry visa and any restrictions regarding the length of your stay.

U.K. citizens can obtain up-to-date passport and visa information by calling the **U.S. Embassy Visa Information Line** at ☎ 0891/200-290 or the **London Passport Office** at ☎ 0990/210-410 (for recorded information).

Foreign driver's licenses are recognized in Hawaii, although you may want to get an international driver's license if your home license is not written in English.

MEDICAL REQUIREMENTS Inoculations are not needed to enter the United States unless you are coming from or have stopped over in areas known to be suffering from epidemics, particularly cholera or yellow fever.

If you have a disease requiring treatment with medications containing narcotics or requiring a syringe, carry a valid signed prescription from your physician to allay suspicions that you are smuggling drugs.

CUSTOMS REQUIREMENTS Every adult visitor may bring in the following free of duty: 1 liter of wine or hard liquor, 200 cigarettes or 100 cigars (but no cigars from Cuba) or 3 pounds of smoking tobacco, and $100 worth of gifts. These exemptions are offered to travelers who spend at least 72 hours in the United States and who have not claimed them within the preceding 6 months. It is altogether forbidden to bring into the country foodstuffs (particularly cheese, fruit, cooked meats, and canned goods) and plants (vegetables, seeds, tropical plants, and so on). Foreign tourists may bring in or take out up to $10,000 in U.S. or foreign currency with no formalities; larger sums must be declared to customs on entering or leaving.

In addition, you cannot bring fresh fruits and vegetables into Hawaii, even if you're coming from the U.S. mainland and have no need to clear customs. Every passenger is asked shortly before landing to sign a certificate declaring that he or she does not have fresh fruits and vegetables in their possession. The form also asks questions for the Hawaii Visitors and Convention Bureau about your visit, such as how long you plan to stay, which island or islands you will visit, and how many times you have been to Hawaii.

INSURANCE The U.S. has no nationwide health system, and the cost of medical care in Hawaii is extremely high. Accordingly, we strongly advise you to secure health-insurance coverage before setting out.

You may want to take out a comprehensive travel policy that covers (for a relatively low premium) sickness or injury costs (medical, surgical, and hospital); loss or theft of your baggage; trip-cancellation costs; guarantee of bail in case you are arrested; and costs of accident, repatriation, or death. Such packages (for example, "Europe Assistance" in Europe) are sold by automobile clubs at attractive rates, as well as by insurance **companies and travel agencies.** U.K. travelers might call the **Association of British Insurers (**☎ 0171/600-3333**),** which gives advice by phone and publishes the free *Holiday Insurance*, a guide to policy provisions and prices.

MONEY

CURRENCY The American monetary system has a decimal base: 1 U.S. **dollar** ($1) = 100 **cents** (100¢). Dollar bills commonly come in $1 ("a buck"), $5, $10, $20,

$50, and $100 denominations (the last two are not welcome when paying for small purchases and are not accepted in taxis or movie theaters).

There are six denominations of coins: 1¢ (one cent, or a "penny"), 5¢ (five cents, or a "nickel"), 10¢ (10 cents, or a "dime"), 25¢ (25 cents, or a "quarter"), 50¢ (50 cents, or a "half-dollar"), and the rare $1 piece.

EXCHANGING CURRENCY Exchanging foreign currency for U.S. dollars can be painless in Hawaii. Generally, the best rates of exchange are available through the bank: Most major banks in Hawaii will exchange your foreign currency for U.S. dollars. In downtown Honolulu, you also can get reliable currency service at **Thomas Cook Currency,** Bishop Trust Building, 1000 Bishop St., Ground Level, facing King Street (☎ **808/523-1321**). In Waikiki, go to **A1 Foreign Exchange,** which has offices in the Royal Hawaiian Shopping Center, 2259 Kalakaua Ave., and in the Hyatt Regency Waikiki Tower, 2424 Kalakaua Ave. (☎ **808/922-3327**); or to **Monyx International,** 307 Royal Hawaiian Ave. (☎ **808/923-6626**). There also are currency services at **Honolulu International Airport.** Most of the major hotels also offer currency-exchange services, but generally the rate of exchange is not as good as what you'll get at a bank.

TRAVELER'S CHECKS It's actually cheaper and faster to get cash at an *automatic teller machine* (ATM) than to fuss with traveler's checks. As noted in "Visitor Information & Money" in chapter 3, Hawaii has ATMs almost everywhere. If you do bring traveler's checks, they are denominated in U.S. dollars and are readily accepted at most hotels, restaurants, and large stores. Do not bring traveler's checks denominated in any currency other than U.S. dollars.

CREDIT CARDS The method of payment most widely used is the credit card: Visa (BarclayCard in Britain), MasterCard (EuroCard in Europe, Access in Britain, Chargex in Canada), American Express, Diners Club, Discover, and Carte Blanche. You can save yourself trouble by using "plastic money" rather than cash or traveler's checks in most hotels, restaurants, and retail stores (a growing number of food and liquor stores now accept credit cards). You must have a credit card to rent a car in Hawaii.

SAFETY

GENERAL While tourist areas are generally safe, crime is on the increase everywhere in the United States, and Hawaii—especially Waikiki—is no exception. Visitors should always stay alert. It's wise to ask the island tourist office if you're in doubt about which neighborhoods are safe. Avoid deserted areas, especially at night. Don't go into any city park at night unless there's an event that attracts crowds—for example, the Waikiki Shell concerts in Kapiolani Park. Generally speaking, you can feel safe in areas where there are many people and open establishments.

Avoid carrying valuables with you on the street, and don't display expensive cameras or electronic equipment. Hold onto your pocketbook, and place your billfold in an inside pocket. In theaters, restaurants, and other public places, keep your possessions in sight.

Recently, there have been a series of purse-snatching incidents on Oahu. Thieves in slow-moving cars or on foot have snatched handbags from female pedestrians (in some instances, dragging women who refuse to let go of their pocketbooks down the street). The Honolulu police department advises women to carry their purses on the shoulder away from the street or, better yet, to wear the strap across the chest instead of on one shoulder. Women with clutch bags should hold their bags close to their chest.

Remember also that hotels are open to the public and, in a large hotel, security may not be able to screen everyone entering. Always lock your room door—don't assume that once inside your hotel, you are automatically safe and no longer need to be aware of your surroundings.

DRIVING Safety while driving is particularly important. Question your rental agency about personal safety, or ask for a brochure of traveler safety tips when you pick up your car. Obtain written directions or a map with the route marked in red from the agency showing you how to get to your destination.

Recently, more crime has involved burglary of tourist rental cars in hotel-parking structures and at beach parking lots. Park in well-lighted and well-traveled areas if possible. If you leave your rental car unlocked and empty of your valuables, you are probably safer than locking your car with valuables in plain view. Never leave any packages or valuables in sight. If someone attempts to rob you or steal your car, do not try to resist the thief/carjacker—report the incident to the police department immediately.

For more information on driving rules and getting around by car in Hawaii, see "Getting There & Getting Around" in chapter 3.

2 Getting to & Around the United States

Airlines serving Hawaii from other than the U.S. mainland include **Air Canada** (☎ 800/776-3000; www.aircanada.ca); **Canadian Airlines** (☎ 800/426-7000; www.cdnair.ca); **Canada 3000** (☎ 888/CAN-3000; www.canada3000.com); **Air New Zealand** (☎ 0800/737-000 in Auckland, 64-3/379-5200 in Christchurch, 800/926-7255 in the U.S.), which runs 40 flights per week between Auckland and Hawaii; **Qantas** (☎ 008/177-767 in Australia, 800/227-4500 in the U.S.), which flies between Sydney and Honolulu daily (plus additional flights 4 days a week); **Japan Air Lines** (☎ 03/5489-1111 in Tokyo, 800/525-3663 in the U.S.); **All Nippon Airways (ANA;** ☎ 03/5489-1212 in Tokyo, 800/235-9262 in the U.S.); **China Airlines** (☎ 02/715-1212 in Taipei, 800/227-5118 in the U.S.); **Garuda Indonesian** (☎ 251-2235 in Jakarta, 800/342-7832 in the U.S.); **Korean Airlines** (☎ 02/656-2000 in Seoul, 800/223-1155 on the East Coast, 800/421-8200 on the West Coast, 800/438-5000 from Hawaii); and **Philippine Airlines** (☎ 631/816-6691 in Manila, 800/435-9725 in the U.S.).

Travelers coming from Europe can take advantage of the **APEX (Advance Purchase Excursion)** fares offered by all major U.S. and European carriers. Aside from these, attractive values are offered by **Icelandair** (☎ **354/5050-100** in Reykjavik, 0171/388-5599 in London, 800/223-5500 in the U.S.; www.icelandair.is) on flights from Luxembourg to New York and by **Virgin Atlantic Airways** (☎ 0293/747-747 in Britain, 800/862-8621 in the U.S.; www.fly.virgin.com) from London to New York/Newark. You can then catch a connecting domestic flight to Honolulu.

Some large American airlines—such as **TWA, American Airlines, Northwest, United,** and **Delta**—offer travelers on transatlantic or transpacific flights special discount tickets under the name **Visit USA,** allowing travel between any U.S. destinations at reduced rates. They're not on sale in the United States and must, therefore, be purchased before you leave your foreign point of departure. This system is the best, easiest, and fastest way to see the United States at a low cost. You should obtain information well in advance from your travel agent or the office of the airline concerned, since the conditions attached to these discount tickets can change without advance notice.

The visitor arriving by air should cultivate patience and resignation before setting foot on U.S. soil. Getting through immigration control may take as long as 2 hours

Money-Saving Tip

The ETN (European Travel Network) operates a Web site offering discounts on international airfares to the United States, as well as on accommodations, car rentals, and tours; point your Internet browser to **www.discount-tickets.com**.

on some days, especially summer weekends. Add the time it takes to clear customs, and you'll see that you should make a very generous allowance for delay in planning connections between international and domestic flights—an average of 2 to 3 hours at least.

For further information about travel to Hawaii, see "Getting There & Getting Around" in chapter 3.

FAST FACTS: For the Foreign Traveler

Automobile Organizations   Auto clubs will supply maps, suggested routes, guidebooks, accident and bail-bond insurance, and emergency road service. The major auto club in the United States, with 955 offices nationwide, is the **American Automobile Association** (AAA; often called "triple A"). Members of some foreign auto clubs have reciprocal arrangements with the AAA and enjoy its services at no charge. If you belong to an auto club, inquire about AAA reciprocity before you leave. The AAA can provide you with an **International Driving Permit** validating your foreign license. You may be able to join the AAA even if you are not a member of a reciprocal club. To inquire, call ☎ **800/336-4357.**

Hawaii's only local AAA office is at 590 Queen St., Honolulu (☎ **808/528-2600**). Please note that AAA service is available only on the island of Oahu. Some car-rental agencies now provide automobile club-type services, so you should inquire about their availability when you rent your car.

Business Hours   See "Fast Facts: The Hawaiian Islands" in chapter 3.

Climate   See "When to Go" in chapter 3.

Electricity   Hawaii, like the U.S mainland and Canada, uses 110–120 volts, 60 cycles, compared to the 220–240 volts, 50 cycles used in most of Europe and in other areas of the world, including Australia and New Zealand. In addition to a 100-volt transformer, small appliances of non-American manufacture, such as hair dryers or shavers, will require a plug adapter with two flat, parallel pins.

Embassies & Consulates   All embassies are located in the national capital, Washington, D.C. Some consulates are located in major cities, and most nations have a mission to the United Nations in New York City. Listed here are the embassies and some consulates of the major English-speaking countries. Travelers from other countries can obtain telephone numbers for their embassies and consulates by calling directory information for Washington, D.C. (☎ **202/555-1212**).

The embassy of **Australia** is at 1601 Massachusetts Ave. NW, Washington, D.C. 20036 (☎ **202/797-3000**). There is also an Australian consulate in Hawaii at 1000 Bishop St., Penthouse Suite, Honolulu, HI 96813 (☎ **808/524-5050**).

The embassy of **Canada** is at 501 Pennsylvania Ave. NW, Washington, D.C. 20001 (☎ **202/682-1740**). Canadian consulates are also at 1251 Avenue of the Americas, New York, NY 10020 (☎ **212/768-2400**), and at 550 South Hope St., 9th floor, Los Angeles, CA 90071 (☎ **213/346-2700**).

The embassy of the **Republic of Ireland** is at 2234 Massachusetts Ave. NW, Washington, D.C. 20008 (☎ **202/462-3939**). There's a consulate office in San Francisco at 44 Montgomery St., Suite 3830, San Francisco, CA 94104 (☎ **415/392-4214**).

The embassy of **New Zealand** is at 37 Observatory Circle NW, Washington, D.C. 20008 (☎ **202/328-4800**). The only New Zealand consulate in the United States is at 12400 Wilshire Blvd., Los Angeles, CA 90025 (☎ **310/207-1605**).

The embassy of the **United Kingdom** is at 3100 Massachusetts Ave. NW, Washington, D.C. 20008 (☎ **202/462-1340**). British consulates are at 845 Third Ave., New York, NY 10022 (☎ **212/745-0200**), and 11766 Wilshire Blvd., Suite 400, Los Angeles, CA 90025 (☎ **310/477-3322**).

The embassy of **Japan** is at 2520 Massachusetts Ave. NW, Washington, D.C. 20008 (☎ **202/939-6700**). The consulate general of Japan is located at 1742 Nuuanu Ave., Honolulu, HI 96817 (☎ **808/536-2226**). There are several other consulates, including one in New York at 299 Park Ave., New York, NY 10171 (☎ **212/371-8222**).

Emergencies   Call ☎ **911** to report a fire, call the police, or get an ambulance.

Gasoline (Petrol)   One U.S. gallon equals 3.8 liters, while 1.2 U.S. gallons equals 1 Imperial gallon. You'll notice there are several grades (and price levels) of gasoline available at most gas stations. And you'll also notice that their names change from company to company. The ones with the highest octane are the most expensive, but most rental cars take the least expensive "regular" gas, with an octane rating of 87.

Holidays   See "When to Go" in chapter 3.

Languages   English is the official language. Major Hawaii hotels may have multilingual employees, and most Honolulu and Waikiki shops have multilingual staffs who speak English, Japanese, Korean, and several dialects of the Philipines. Unless your language is very obscure, they can usually supply a translator on request. See "Life & Language" in chapter 2 for information about the Hawaiian language.

Legal Aid   The ordinary tourist will probably never become involved with the American legal system. If you are pulled over for a minor infraction (for example, driving faster than the speed limit), never attempt to pay the fine directly to a police officer; you may wind up arrested on the much more serious charge of attempted bribery. Pay fines by mail or directly into the hands of the clerk of the court. If accused of a more serious offense, it's wise to say and do nothing before consulting a lawyer (you have a right to both remain silent and to consult an attorney under the U.S. Constitution). Under U.S. law, an arrested person is allowed one telephone call to a party of his or her choice; call your embassy or consulate.

Mail   Mailboxes are generally found at intersections, are blue with a blue-and-white eagle logo, and carry the inscription "U.S. Postal Service." If your mail is addressed to a U.S. destination, don't forget to add the five-figure postal code, or zip code, after the two-letter abbreviation of the state to which the mail is addressed. The abbreviation for Hawaii is HI.

International airmail rates are 60¢ for half-ounce letters (40¢ for letters going to Mexico and 46¢ for letters to Canada) and 50¢ for postcards (35¢ to Mexico and 40¢ to Canada). All domestic first-class mail goes from Hawaii to the U.S. mainland by air.

Taxes The United States has no VAT (value-added tax) or other indirect taxes at a national level. Every state, and each city in it, has the right to levy its own local tax on all purchases, including hotel and restaurant checks, airline tickets, and so on. In Hawaii, sales tax is 4%; there's also a 6% hotel-room tax, so the total tax on your hotel bill will be 10%.

Telephone & Fax The telephone system in the United States is run by private corporations, so rates, particularly for long-distance service and operator-assisted calls, can vary widely—especially on calls made from public telephones. Local calls—that is, calls to other locations on the island you're on—made from public phones in Hawaii cost 25¢. The international-country code is 1, just as it is for the rest of the United States and Canada.

Generally, hotel surcharges on long-distance and local calls are astronomical. You are usually better off using a **public pay telephone**, which you will find clearly marked in most public buildings and private establishments as well as on the street.

Most **long-distance and international calls** can be dialed directly from any phone. For calls to Canada and other parts of the United States, dial 1, followed by the area code and the seven-digit number. For international calls, dial 011, followed by the country code, city code, and telephone number of the person you wish to call.

In Hawaii, interisland phone calls are considered long-distance and often areas costly as calling the U.S. mainland.

For **reversed-charge or collect calls,** and for **person-to-person calls,** dial 0 (zero, not the letter "O"), followed by the area code and number you want; an operator will then come on the line, and you should specify that you are calling collect, person-to-person, or both. If your operator-assisted call is international, ask for the overseas operator.

Note that all phone numbers with the area code 800 or 888 are toll-free.

For **local directory assistance** ("information"), dial 411; for **long-distance information,** dial 1, then the appropriate area code and 555-1212.

Fax facilities are widely available and can be found in most hotels and many other establishments. Try **Mail Boxes, Etc.** (check the local Yellow Pages) or any photocopying shop.

Telephone Directory There are two kinds of telephone directories in the United States. The general directory is the so-called *White Pages,* in which private and business subscribers are listed in alphabetical order. The inside front cover lists the emergency numbers for police, fire, and ambulance, and other vital numbers (like the Coast Guard, poison-control center, crime-victims hotline, and so on). The first few pages are devoted to community-service numbers, including a guide to long-distance and international calling, complete with country codes and area codes.

The second directory, printed on yellow paper (hence its name, *Yellow Pages*), lists all local services, businesses, and industries by type of activity, with an index at the back. The listings cover not only such obvious items as automobile repairs by make of car, or drugstores (pharmacies), often by geographical location; but also restaurants by type of cuisine and geographical location, bookstores by special subject and/or language, places of worship by religious denomination, and other information that the tourist might otherwise not readily find. The Yellow Pages also include city plans or detailed maps, often showing postal zip codes and public-transportation routes.

Time   See "Fast Facts: The Hawaiian Islands" in chapter 3.

Tipping   It's part of the American way of life to tip, on the principle that you must expect to pay for any service you get. Many personnel receive little direct salary and must depend on tips for their income. In fact, the U.S. government imposes income taxes on service personnel based on an estimate of how much they should have earned in tips relative to their employer's total receipts. In other words, they may have to pay taxes on a tip you didn't give them!

Here are some rules of thumb:

In **hotels**, tip bellhops at least $1 per piece of luggage ($2 to $3 if you have a lot of luggage), and tip the chamber staff $1 per person, per day. Tip the doorman or concierge only if he or she has provided you with some specific service (for example, calling a cab for you or obtaining difficult-to-get theater tickets). Tip the valet parking attendant $1 every time you get your car.

In **restaurants, bars, and nightclubs,** tip service staff 15 to 20% of the check, tip bartenders 10 to 15%, tip checkroom attendants $1 per garment, and tip valet-parking attendants $1 per vehicle. Tip the doorman only if you were provided with some specific service (such as calling a cab for you). Tipping is not expected in cafeterias and fast-food restaurants.

Tip **cab drivers** 15% of the fare.

As for **other service personnel,** tip skycaps at airports at least $1 per piece ($2 to $3 if you have a lot of luggage), and tip hairdressers and barbers 15 to 20%. Tipping ushers at movies and theaters and gas-station attendants is not expected.

Toilets   Foreign visitors often complain that public toilets are hard to find in most U.S. cities. True, there are none on the streets, but visitors can usually find one in a bar, fast-food outlet, restaurant, hotel, museum, department store, or service station—and it will probably be clean (although the last-mentioned sometimes leaves much to be desired). Note, however, a growing practice in some restaurants and bars of displaying a notice that "toilets are for the use of patrons only." You can ignore this sign, or better yet, avoid arguments by paying for a cup of coffee or soft drink, which will qualify you as a patron. The cleanliness of toilets at parks and beaches is more open to question. Some public places are equipped with pay toilets, which require you to insert one or more coins into a slot on the door before it will open.

5

Oahu, the Gathering Place

A wise Hawaiian *kupuna* once told me that the islands are like children—that each is special yet different, that each is to be loved for its individual qualities. One thing's for sure: You will never find another island like Oahu, the commercial and population center of Hawaii.

It's astounding to spend hours flying across the barren blue of the Pacific and then to suddenly see below you the whites and pastels of Honolulu, the most remote big city on earth, a 26-mile-long metropolis of some 850,000 souls living in the middle of nowhere. Once on its streets, you'll find bright city lights, five-star restaurants, nearly all-night nightclubs, world-class shopping, great art and architecture, and grand old hotels.

Nine out of ten visitors to Hawaii—some five million a year—stop on Oahu, and most of them end up along the canyon-like streets of Waikiki, Honolulu's famous hotel district and its most densely populated neighborhood. Some days, it seems like the entire world is sunning itself on Waikiki's famous beach. Beyond Waikiki, Honolulu is clean and easy to enjoy. The city is coming of age just in time for the 21st century: The old port town has built a brand-new convention center and is reshaping its waterfront, altering its skyline, opening new world-class hotels, and all the while trying to preserve its historic roots and revive its Polynesian heritage.

Out in the country, Oahu can be as down-home as a slack-key guitar. That's where you'll find a big blue sky, perfect waves, empty beaches, rainbows and waterfalls, sweet tropical flowers, and fiery Pacific sunsets. In fact, nowhere else within 60 minutes of a major American city can you snorkel in a crystal-clear lagoon, climb an old volcano, surf monster waves, kayak to a desert isle, picnic on a sandbar, soar in a glider over tide pools, skin dive over a sunken airplane, bicycle through a rain forest, golf a championship course, or sail into the setting sun.

And weather-wise, no other Hawaiian island has it as nice as Oahu. The Big Island is hotter, Kauai is wetter, Maui has more wind, Molokai and Lanai are drier. But Oahu enjoys a kind of perpetual late spring, with light trade winds and 82°F days almost year-round. In fact, the climate is supposed to be the best on the planet. Once you have that, the rest is easy.

Kaena

Makaha

Waianae
Pokai Bay
Beach Park

Maili

Nanakuli

93

Ko Olina

Makakilo

Oneula Beach

Kapolei

Ewa

Ewa Beach

Farrington Hwy.

H1

Waipahu

750

99

Mililani

H2

Pearl
City

Pearl

Wahiawa

Schofield Barracks

**LEEWARD OAHU
(WAIANAE COAST)**

Waianae Range

Farrington Hwy.

Dillingham
Airfield

930

Mokuleia

Waialua

Haleiwa

803

99

Kamehameha Hwy.

Kawailoa

83

Waimea Bay Beach Park

Sunset Beach

THE NORTH SHORE

**CENTRAL
(EWA)**

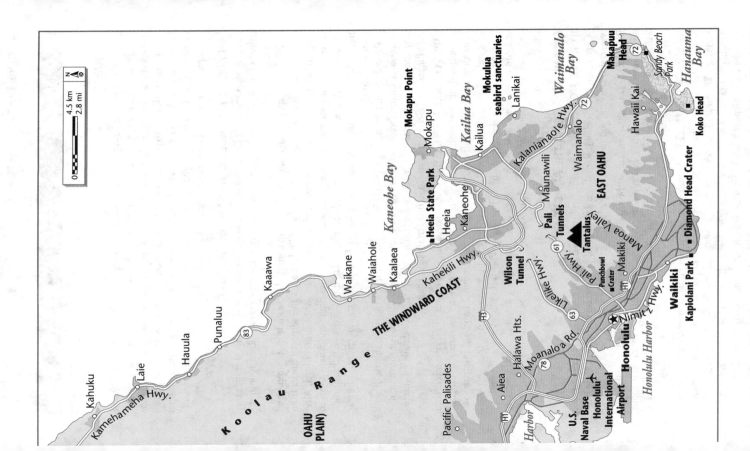

by Jeanette Foster

ARRIVING

Honolulu is your gateway to the Hawaiian Islands; even though more and more transpacific flights are going directly to the neighbor islands these days, chances are still good that no matter which islands you're visiting, you'll come to Oahu first. **Honolulu International Airport** sits on the South Shore of Oahu, west of downtown Honolulu and Waikiki near Pearl Harbor. Many major American and international carriers fly to Honolulu from the mainland; see "Getting There & Getting Around" in chapter 3 for a list of carriers and their tollfree numbers.

LANDING AT HONOLULU INTERNATIONAL AIRPORT

Landing at Honolulu is like arriving in a foreign country full of strangers from every corner of the world. On any given day, it's probably the most cosmopolitan spot in the Pacific.

While the airport is large and constantly expanding, the layout is quite simple and easy to grasp. You can walk or take the **Wiki-Wiki Bus**, a free airport shuttle, from your arrival gate to the main terminal and baggage claim, on the ground level. After collecting your bags, unless you're getting on an interisland flight immediately, exit to the palm-lined street, where uniformed attendants flag down taxis, Waikiki shuttles, and rental-car vans; they can also direct you to TheBus (for transportation information, see below).

Passengers connecting to neighbor-island flights take the Wiki-Wiki shuttle or walk to the large interisland terminal serving Aloha and Hawaiian Airlines or the more distant commuter terminal, which serves the smaller Island Air. (For details on interisland flights, see "Getting There & Getting Around" in chapter 3.)

TIPS TO MAKE LIFE EASIER   When departing the islands or making interisland connections, allow yourself plenty of time—at least 45 minutes for interisland flights, more than an hour's lead for mainland flights, and around 2 hours for international. Like most major airports, Honolulu sprawls over a huge area—larger than you want to sprint around in the tropical heat. The Wiki-Wiki Bus links the various terminals and connects distant gates with baggage areas, but it's not automated and therefore only somewhat more "wiki-wiki" than walking. Allow time to fit the island-style schedule.

GETTING TO & FROM THE AIRPORT

BY RENTAL CAR   All major rental companies have cars available at the airport (see "Getting Around," below). Rental-agency vans will pick you up curbside outside baggage claim and take you to their off-site lot.

BY TAXI   Taxis are abundant at the airport; an attendant will be happy to flag one down for you. Taxi fare from Honolulu International to downtown Honolulu is about $16, about $23 to Waikiki. If you need to call a taxi, see "Getting Around," below, for a list of cab companies.

BY AIRPORT SHUTTLE   Shuttle vans operate 24 hours a day every day of the year between the airport and all 350 hotels and condos in Waikiki. **Trans-Hawaiian Services** (☎ 800/533-8765 or 808/566-7000; fax 808/566-7580; e-mail sales@ transhawaiian.com; www.transhawaiian.com) serves the airport with passenger vans, with the name **Airport Waikiki Express Shuttle** on the side, every 20 to 30 minutes, depending on traffic; it's $8 one-way to Waikiki, $13 round-trip. No reservation is necessary (but be sure to book ahead for hotel pickup for a departing flight). You can pick up the shuttle at street level outside baggage claim; look for attendants in red shirts that say "Shuttle Vehicle." You can board with two pieces of luggage and a carryon at no extra charge; surfboards and bicycles are prohibited for safety reasons. Backpacks are okay. Tips are welcome. For advance purchase of group or family tickets, call the number above.

BY BUS **TheBus** nos. 19 and 20 (Waikiki Beach and Hotels) run from the airport to downtown Honolulu and Waikiki. The first bus from Waikiki to the airport is at 4:50am on weekdays and 5:25am on weekends; the last bus departs the airport for Waikiki at 11:45pm on weekdays, 11:25pm on weekends. There are two bus stops on the main terminal's upper level; a third is on the second level of the interisland terminal. You can board TheBus with a carryon or small suitcase, as long as it fits under the seat and doesn't disrupt other passengers; otherwise, you'll have to take a shuttle or taxi. The approximate travel time to Waikiki is an hour. The one-way fare is $1, 50¢ for students, exact change only. For more information on TheBus, see "Getting Around," below.

VISITOR INFORMATION

The **Hawaii Visitors and Convention Bureau,** 2270 Kalakaua Ave., 7th floor, Honolulu, HI 96815 (☎ **808/923-1811;** www.gohawaii.com), supplies free brochures, maps, accommodation guides, and *Islands of Aloha,* the official HVCB magazine. The **Oahu Visitors Association,** 1001 Bishop St, Pauahi Tower, Suite 47, Honolulu, HI 96813 (☎ **800/OAHU-678,** 888/GO-HONOLULU, or 808/524-0722) distributes a free 64-page visitors booklet.

A number of free publications, such as *This Week Oahu,* are packed with money-saving coupons and good regional maps; look for them on racks at the airport and around town.

THE REGIONS IN BRIEF

HONOLULU

America's 11th largest city looks like any other big metropolitan center with tall buildings. In fact, some cynics refer to it as "Los Angeles West." But within Honolulu's metes and bounds, you'll find rain forests, deep canyons, valleys and waterfalls, a nearly mile-high mountain range, coral reefs, and gold-sand beaches. The city proper—where most of Honolulu's 850,000 residents live—is approximately 12 miles wide and 26 miles long, running east-west roughly between Diamond Head and Pearl Harbor (you'll see Pearl Harbor from the left side of your airplane on your final approach into Honolulu International). The city folds over seven hills laced by seven streams that run to Mamala Bay.

A plethora of neighborhoods surround the central area, which range from quiet suburbs of Hawaii Kai to the old kamaaina neighborhoods like Manoa. These neighborhoods are generally quieter than Waikiki, more residential, yet within minutes of beaches, shopping, and all the activities Oahu has to offer.

Waikiki

Some say Waikiki is past its prime and that everybody goes to Maui now. If it has fallen out of popularity, you couldn't prove it by me. Waikiki is the very incarnation of Yogi Berra's comment about Toots Shor's famous New York restaurant: "Nobody goes there anymore. It's too crowded."

When King Kalakaua played in Waikiki, it was "a hamlet of plain cottages . . . its excitements caused by the activity of insect tribes and the occasional fall of a coconut." The Merrie Monarch, who gave his name to Waikiki's main street, would love the

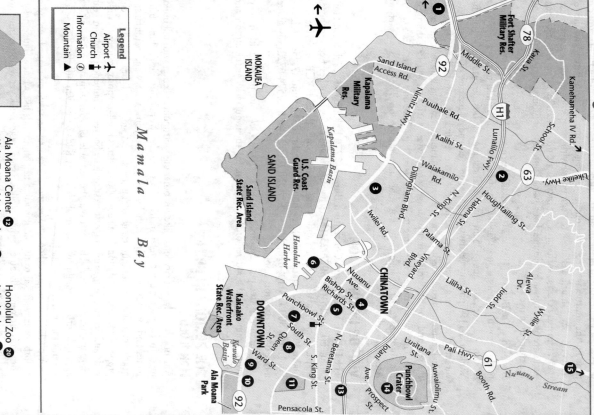

1-0741

Legend

Airport ✈
Church ⛪
Information ⓘ
Mountain ▲

OAHU
Honolulu

Mamala Bay

MOKAUEA ISLAND

Sand Island Access Rd.

Kapalama Military Res.

Kapalama Basin

SAND ISLAND

Sand Island State Rec. Area

U.S. Coast Guard Res.

Fort Shafter Military Res.

78
Kaua St.
Kamehameha IV Rd.
School St.
Likelike Hwy.
63
H1
92
Middle St.
Lunalilo Fwy.
Puuhale Rd.
Kalihi St.
Waiakamilo Rd.
Dillingham Blvd.
N. King St.
Halona St.
Houghtailing St.
Nimitz Hwy.
Palama St.
Vineyard Blvd.
Liliha St.
Alewa Dr.
Wyllie St.
Nuuanu Stream
Pali Hwy.
Booth Rd.
61
Lusitana St.
Auwaiolimu St.
Iolani Ave.
Prospect St.
Punchbowl Crater
Lunatia St.
N. Beretania St.
S. King St.
S. Beretania St.

CHINATOWN

DOWNTOWN

Nuuanu Ave.
Bishop St.
Richards St.
Punchbowl St.
South St.
Queen St.
Ward St.
Pensacola St.

Iwilei Rd.

Honolulu Harbor

Kakaako Waterfront State Rec. Area

Kewalo Basin

Ala Moana Park

92

❶ ❷ ❸ ❹ ❺ ❻ ❼ ❽ ❾ ❿ ⓫ ⓬ ⓭ ⓮ ⓯

Ala Moana Center ⓬
Aloha Tower Marketplace ❻
Bishop Museum ❷
The Contemporary Museum ⓰
Dole Cannery Square ❸
Hawaii State Legistlature ❹
Honolulu Academy of Arts ⓭

Honolulu Zoo ⓴
Iolani Palace ❺
Kodak Hula Show at the
  Waikiki Band Shell ❺
Lyon Arboretum ㉑
Mission Houses Museum ⓳
National Memorial Cemetery
  of the Pacific ⓮

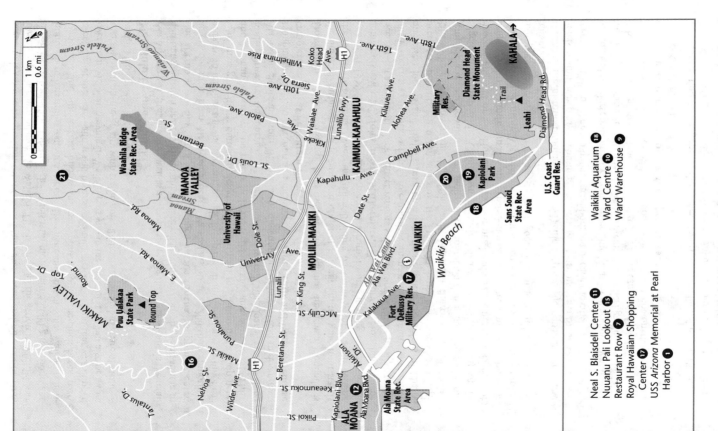

Neal S. Blaisdell Center 🕚
Nuuanu Pali Lookout 🕔
Restaurant Row 🟡
Royal Hawaiian Shopping
  Center 🕖
USS *Arizona* Memorial at Pearl
  Harbor ❶

Waikiki Aquarium 🔞
Ward Centre 🔟
Ward Warehouse 🟡

Puu Ualakaa State Park
Round Top

MAKIKI VALLEY

MANOA VALLEY

Waahila Ridge State Rec. Area

University of Hawaii

MOILIILI-MAKIKI

KAIMUKI-KAPAHULU

Ala Wai Canal
Ala Wai Blvd.

WAIKIKI

ALA MOANA

Ala Moana State Rec. Area

Fort DeRussy Military Res.

Waikiki Beach

Sans Souci State Rec. Area

U.S. Coast Guard Res.

Kapiolani Park

Diamond Head State Monument

Leahi

KAHALA

Puklei Stream
Waiomao Stream
Palolo Stream
Manoa Stream

lay. Some five million tourists visit Oahu every year, and nine out of 10 of them choose accommodations in Waikiki. This is where all the action is. Waikiki is an urban beach backed by 175 high-rise hotels with more than 33,000 guest rooms and hundreds of bars and restaurants, all in a 1½-square-mile beach zone. Waikiki is honeymooners and sun seekers, bikinis and bare buns, a round-the-clock beach party every day of the year—and it's all because of a thin crescent of sand that was shipped over from Molokai. Staying in Waikiki puts you in the heart of it all, but also be aware that this is an on-the-go city with traffic noise 24 hours a day and its share of crime— and it's almost always crowded.

Honolulu Beyond Waikiki

Ala Moana A great beach as well as a famous shopping mall, Ala Moana is the retail and transportation heart of Honolulu, a place where you can both shop and suntan in one afternoon. All bus routes lead to the open air **Ala Moana Shopping Center,** across the street from **Ala Moana Beach Park.** This 50-acre, 200-shop emporium attracts 56 million customers a year; people fly up here from Tahiti just to buy their Christmas gifts. Every European designer from Armani to Vuitton has a shop here, and Neiman-Marcus will open here in 1998. It's Honolulu's answer to Beverly Hills' Rodeo Drive. For our purposes, the neighborhood we call "Ala Moana" extends along Ala Moana Boulevard from Waikiki in the direction of Diamond Head to downtown Honolulu in the Ewa direction and includes the **Ward Centre** and **Ward Warehouse** complexes as well as **Restaurant Row.**

Downtown A tiny cluster of high-rises west of Waikiki, downtown Honolulu is the financial, business, and government center of Hawaii. On the waterfront stands the iconic 1926 Aloha Tower, the tallest building on Oahu when Hawaii became a state in 1959 and now the centerpiece of a harborfront shopping and restaurant complex known as **Aloha Tower Marketplace.** The history of Honolulu can be seen in just a few short blocks: Street vendors sell papayas from trucks on skyscraper-lined concrete canyons, where professional women wear muumuus and carry briefcases; joggers and BMWs rush by a lacy palace where champions of liberty overthrew Hawaii's last queen and stole the kingdom; burly bus drivers sport fragrant white ginger flowers on their dashboards, Methodist churches look like Asian temples, and businessmen wear aloha shirts to billion-dollar meetings. On the edge of downtown is the **Chinatown Historic District,** the oldest Chinatown in America and still one of Honolulu's liveliest neighborhoods, a nonstop pageant of people, sights, sounds, smells, and tastes—not all Chinese, now that Southeast Asians, including many Vietnamese, share the old storefronts. Go on Saturday morning when everyone shops here for fresh goods like gingerroot, fern fronds, and hogsheads.

Among the historic buildings and Pan-Pacific corporate headquarters are a few hotels, mainly geared toward business travelers. Most visitors prefer the sun and excitement or Waikiki or choose a quieter neighborhood outside the city.

Manoa Valley First inhabited by white settlers, the Moana Valley above Waikiki still has vintage *kamaaina* homes, one of Hawaii's premiere botanical gardens in the Lyon Arboretum, ever-gushing Manoa Falls, and the 320-acre campus of the University of Hawaii, where 50,000 students hit the books when they're not on the beach and scholars develop solutions to third-world problems at the East-West Center, a major Pacific-Rim think tank.

To the East: Kahala Except for the estates of world-class millionaires and the luxurious Kahala Mandarin Oriental Hotel (with Hoku's, its outstanding beachfront restaurant), there's not much out this way that's of interest to visitors.

EAST OAHU

Beyond Kahala lies East Honolulu and suburban bedroom communities like Aina Haina, Niu Valley, and Hawaii Kai, among others, all linked by Kalanianaole Highway and each chockablock with homes, condos, fast-food joints, and shopping malls. It looks like Southern California on a good day. The only reasons you're likely to find yourself out here: if you're having dinner at **Roy's**, the original and still-outstanding Hawaii Regional restaurant, in Hawaii Kai; if you're bound for **Hanauma Bay** for some snorkeling or heading to **Sandy Beach** to watch daredevil surfers risk their necks; or if you're just looking to enjoy the natural splendor of the lovely coastline, which might include a hike to **Makapuu Lighthouse.**

THE WINDWARD COAST

On the opposite side of the island from Waikiki, the windward side is where the trade winds blow cooling breezes over gorgeous beaches; rain squalls inspire lush, tropical vegetation; and miles of subdivisions dot the landscape. Numerous bed-and-breakfasts, ranging from oceanfront estates to tiny cottages on quiet residential streets, abound; vacations here are filled with enjoying ocean activities and exploring the surrounding areas. It's a quick 15-minute drive into Waikiki.

Kailua The biggest little beach town in Hawaii, Kailua sits at the foot of the sheer green Koolau Mountains, on a great bay with two of Hawaii's best beaches. The town itself is a funky low-rise cluster of time-worn shops and homes. Instead of hotels, Kailua became the B&B capital of Hawaii; it's an affordable alternative to Waikiki, with rooms and vacation rentals from $45 a day and up. With the prevailing trade winds whipping up a cooling breeze, Kailua attracts windsurfers from around the world.

Kaneohe Helter-skelter suburbia sprawls around the edges of Kaneohe, one of the most scenic bays in all the Pacific and a handful of B&Bs dotting the edge. After you clear the trafficky maze of town, Oahu returns to its more natural state. This great bay beckons you to get out on it; you can depart from Heeia Boat Harbor on snorkel or fishing charters and visit Ahu a Laka a, the sandbar that appears and disappears in the middle of the bay. From there, you'll have a panoramic view of the Koolau Range.

Kualoa/Laie The upper northeast shore is one of the most sacred spots on Oahu; an early Hawaiian landing spot where even kings dipped their sails, the cliffs hold ancient burial sites, and ghosts still march in the night. Sheer cliffs stab this sea coast fringed by coral reef, and old fishponds are tucked along the two-lane coast road that weaves around beautiful Kahana Bay and by empty gold-sand beaches in towns with too many vowels, like Kaaawa. Thousands "explore" the South Pacific at the Polynesian Cultural Center, in Laie, a Mormon settlement with its own Tabernacle Choir of sweet Samoan harmony.

THE NORTH SHORE

Here's the Hawaii of Hollywood—giant waves, surfers galore, tropical jungles, waterfalls, and mysterious Hawaiian temples. If you're looking for a quieter vacation, closer to nature, filled with swimming, snorkeling, diving, surfing, or just plain hanging out on some of the world's most beautiful beaches, the North Shore is your place; the artsy little beach town of **Haleiwa** and the surrounding shoreline seem a world away from Waikiki. The North Shore boasts good restaurants, shopping, and cultural activities—but here they come with the quiet of country living. Bed-and-breakfasts are the most common accommodations, but there's one first-class hotel and some vacation rentals as well. But be forewarned: It's a long trip—nearly an hour's drive—to Honolulu and Waikiki.

Finding Your Way Around, Oahu Style

Local residents give directions a bit differently than what mainlanders are used to. Seldom will you hear east, west, north, and south; instead, islanders refer to directions as either **makai** (MA-kae), meaning toward the sea, or **mauka** (MOW-kah), toward the mountains. In Honolulu, people use **Diamond Head** as a direction meaning to the east (in the direction of the world-famous crater called Diamond Head), and **Ewa** as a direction meaning to the west (in the direction of the town called Ewa, on the other side of Pearl Harbor).

So if you ask a local for directions, this is what you're likely to hear: "Drive two blocks makai (toward the sea), then turn Diamond Head (east) at the stop light. Go one block, and turn mauka (toward the mountains). It's on the Ewa (western) side of the street."

2 Getting Around

by Jeanette Foster

CENTRAL OAHU: THE EWA PLAIN

Flanked by the Koolau and Waianae mountain ranges, the hot, sun-baked Ewa Plain runs up and down the center of Oahu. Once covered with the sandalwood forests (hacked down for the China trade) and later the sugarcane and pineapple backbone of Hawaii, Ewa today sports a new crop: suburban houses stretching to the sea. But let your eye wander west to the Waianae Range and Mount Kaala, at 4,020 feet, the highest summit on Oahu: Up there in the misty rain forest, native birds thrive in the hummocky bog. In 1914, the U.S. Army pitched a tent camp on the plain; author James Jones would later call **Schofield Barracks** "the most beautiful army post in the world." Hollywood filmed Jones's *From Here to Eternity* here, thus launching crooner Frank Sinatra on his comeback.

LEEWARD OAHU: THE WAIANAE COAST

The West Coast of Oahu is a hot and dry place of naturally dramatic beauty: white-sand beaches bordering the deep blue ocean, steep verdant green cliffs, and miles of Mother Nature's wildness. Except the luxurious Ihilani Resort and Spa in the Ko Olina Resort, you'll find virtually no tourist services out here. The funky West Coast villages of Nanakuli, Waianae, and Makaha are the last stands of native Hawaiians. This side of Oahu is seldom visited except by surfers bound for **Yokohama Bay** and anyone else who wants to see needle-nose **Kaena Point** (the island's westernmost outpost) and a coastal wilderness park under a 768-foot peak named for the endangered Hawaiian owl.

BY CAR Oahu residents own 600,000 registered vehicles, but they have only 1,500 miles of mostly two-lane roads. That's 400 cars for every mile, a fact that becomes abundantly clear during morning and evening rush hours. You can avoid the gridlock by driving between 9am and 3pm or after 6pm.

Car Rentals All the major car-rental firms have agencies on Oahu, at the airport, and in Waikiki. For a complete list, as well as tips on insurance and driving rules, see "Car Rentals" under "Getting There & Getting Around" in chapter 3.

BY BUS One of the best deals anywhere, **TheBus** will take you around the whole island for $1. In fact, more than 260,000 people daily use the system's 68 lines and 4,000 bus stops. TheBus goes almost everywhere almost all the time. The most popular route is no. 8, which shuttles people between Waikiki and Ala Moana Center every 10 minutes or so (the ride is 15 to 20 min.); the no. 19 (Airport/Hickam), no. 20 (Airport/Halawa Gate), no. 47 (Waipahu), and no. 58 (Waikiki/Ala Moana) also cover the same stretch. Waikiki service begins daily at 5am and runs until midnight; buses run about every 15 minutes during the day and every 30 minutes in the evening. The Circle Island–North Shore route is no. 52 (Wahaiwa/Circle Island); it leaves from Ala Moana Shopping Center every 30 minutes and takes about 4½ hours to circle the island. The Circle Island–South Shore route is no. 55 (Kaneohe/Circle Island) and also leaves Ala Moana every half-hour; it takes about 3 to 4½ hours to circle the island. *Warning:* Some visitors waiting for a bus along the North Shore have been attacked and robbed in broad daylight recently. You might want to consider renting a car to visit the North Shore.

You can buy a **Visitors Pass** for $10 at any ABC store in Waikiki (ABC stores are literally everywhere in Waikiki). It's good for unlimited rides for 4 days.

For more information on routes and schedules, call **TheBus** at ☎ **808/848-5555,** 808/296-1818 for recorded information, or check out their Web site at **www.thebus.org,** which provides timetables and maps for all routes, plus directions to many local attractions and a list of upcoming events (taking TheBus is sometimes easier than parking).

BY TROLLEY It's fun to ride the 34-seat, open-air, motorized **Waikiki Trolley** (☎ **800/824-8804** or 808/596-2199), which looks like a San Francisco cable car. It loops around Waikiki and downtown Honolulu, stopping every 40 minutes at 12 key places: Hilton Hawaiian Village, Iolani Palace, Wo Fat's in Chinatown, the State Capitol, King Kamehameha's Statue, the Mission House Museum, Aloha Tower, Honolulu Academy of Arts, Hawaii Maritime Museum, Ward Centre, Fisherman's Wharf, and Restaurant Row. A 1-day pass—which costs $17 for adults, $5 for children under 12—allows you to jump on and off all day long. Five-day passes cost $30 for adults, $10 for children under 12.

BY TAXI Oahu's major cab companies offer islandwide, 24-hour, radio-dispatched service, with multilingual drivers and air-conditioned cars, limos, vans, and vehicles equipped with wheelchair lifts. Fares are standard for all taxi firms; from the airport, expect to pay about $23 (plus tip) to Waikiki, about $16.50 to downtown, about $35 to Kailua, about $35 to Hawaii Kai, and about $75 to the North Shore. Try **Aloha State Cab** (☎ 808/847-3566), **Charley's Taxi & Tours** (☎ 808/531-1333), **City Taxi** (☎ 808/524-2121), **Royal Taxi & Tour** (☎ 808/944-5513), **Sida Taxi & Tours** (☎ 808/836-0011), **Star Taxi** (☎ 808/942-7827), or **TheCab** (☎ 808/422-2222). **Coast Taxi** (☎ 808/261-3755) serves Windward Oahu; **Hawaii Kai Hui/Koko Head Taxi** (☎ 808/396-6633) serves East Honolulu/Southeast Oahu.

WHEELCHAIR TRANSPORTATION Handicabs of the Pacific, P.O. Box 22428, Honolulu, HI 96822 (☎ **808/524-3866;** fax 808/523-6056), offers wheelchair taxi services and tours. Serving Oahu since 1973, Handicabs has air-conditioned vehicles that are specially equipped with ramps and wheelchair lockdowns. They offer a range of taxi services (airport pickup to Waikiki hotels is $35 one-way, transportation within Waikiki is $16 one way), as well as complete tours (including a Honolulu city tour, a Circle the Island tour, a Pearl Harbor cruise and tour, and a sunset dinner sail and tour) for wheelchair-bound travelers.

FAST FACTS: Oahu

American Express The Honolulu office is at 1440 Kapiolani Blvd., Suite 104 (☎ 808/946-7741) and is open Monday to Friday 8am to 5pm. There's also an

1-0704

Fare $1 per ride, 50 cents for children 5–17; children under 5 ride free.

Exact change only; children under 5 ride free.

A Visitor Pass is available for $10 at any ABC Store in Waikiki. It's good for unlimited rides for four consecutive days.

Express and shuttle routes not shown.

Common Bus Routes:

Ala Moana Shopping Center: Take bus #19 & #20 AIRPORT. Return via #19 WAIKIKI, or cross Ala Moana Blvd. for #20.

Bishop Museum: Take #2 SCHOOL STREET get off at Kapalama St., cross School St., walk down Bernice St. Return to School St. and take #2 WAIKIKI.

Byodo-In Temple: Take bus #2 to Hotel-Alakea St., (TRF) to #55 KANEOHE-KAHALUU. Get off at Valley of the Temple cemetery. Also #19 and #20 AIRPORT to King-Alakea St. (TRF) on Alakea St. to #55 KANEOHE-KAHALUU.

Circle Island: Take a Bus to ALA MOANA CENTER (TRF) to #52 WAHIAWA CIRCLE ISLAND or #55 KANEOHE CIRCLE ISLAND. This is a four-hour bus ride.

Chinatown or Downtown: Take any #2 bus going out of Waikiki, to Hotel St. Return take #2 WAIKIKI on Hotel St., or #19 or #20 on King St.

The Contemporary Museum & Punchbowl (National Cemetery of the Pacific): Take #2 bus (TRF) at Alapai St. to #15 MAKIKI-PACIFIC HGTS. Return, take #15 and get off at King St. area (TRF) #2 WAIKIKI.

Diamond Head Crater: #22 HAWAII KAI-SEA LIFE PARK to the crater. Take a flashlight. Return to the same area and take #22 WAIKIKI.

Dole Plantation: Take bus to ALA MOANA CENTER (TRF) to #52 WAHIAWA CIRCLE ISLAND.

Foster Botanic Gardens: Take #2 bus to Hotel-Riviera St. Walk to Vineyard Blvd. Return to Hotel St. Take #2 WAIKIKI, or take #4 NUUANU and get off at Nuuanu-Vineyard. Cross Nuuanu Ave. and walk one block to the gardens.

Aloha Tower Marketplace & Hawaii Maritime Center: Take #19-#20 AIRPORT and get off at Alakea-Ala Moana. Cross the Street to the Aloha Tower.

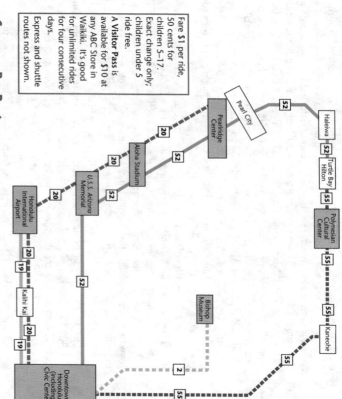

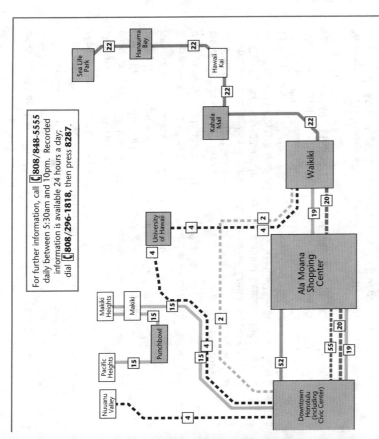

Honolulu Zoo: Take any bus on Kuhio Ave. going DIAMOND HEAD direction to Kapahulu Ave.

Iolani Palace: also **State Capitol, Honolulu Hale, Kawaihao Church, Mission Houses, Queen's Hospital, King Kamehameha Statue, State Judiciary Bldg.,** take any #2 bus and get off at Punchbowl and Beretania St. Walk to King St. Return #2 WAIKIKI on King St.

Kahala Mall: #22 HAWAII KAI–SEA LIFE PARK to Kilauea Ave. Return #22 WAIKIKI.

Kodak Hula Show: (Tues–Thurs 10AM) Free. Take #19 or #20 WAIKIKI or #2 KAPIOLANI PARK to Kapiolani Park. Walk to the Waikiki Shell.

Pearl Harbor (Arizona Memorial): Open Daily 8AM to 3PM. Free. Take #20 AIRPORT. Get off across from Memorial, or take a bus to Ala Moana Center (TRF) to #52.

Polynesian Cultural Center: Take a bus to ALA MOANA CENTER (TRF) to #55 KANEOHE CIRCLE ISLAND. Bus ride takes two hours one way. PCC opens at 12:30PM. Closed on Sundays.

Queen Emma's Summer Home: Take #4 NUUANU and it will take you there, or board a bus to ALA MOANA CENTER (TRF) to #55 KANEOHE.

Sea Life Park: #22 HAWAII KAI–SEA LIFE PARK. #22 will stop at Hanauma Bay enroute to the park.

University of Hawaii: Take #4 NUUANU. The bus will go to the University enroute to Nuuanu.

Waimea Valley & Adventure Park: Take a bus to ALA MOANA CENTER (TRF) to #52 WAHIAWA CIRCLE ISLAND or #55 KANEOHE CIRCLE ISLAND.

For further information, call ☎808/848-5555 daily between 5:30am and 10pm. Recorded information is available 24 hours a day; dial ☎808/296-1818, then press **8287**.

office at **Hilton Hawaiian Village,** 2005 Kalia Rd. (☎ 808/951-0644), and one at the **Hyatt Regency Waikiki,** 2424 Kalakaua Ave. (☎ **808/926-5441**); both offer financial services daily from 8am to 8pm.

Dentists If you need dental attention while you're on Oahu, contact the **Hawaii Dental Association** (☎ **808/536-2135**).

Doctors **Straub Doctors on Call,** 2222 Kalakaua Ave. (at Lewers St.), Honolulu, HI 96815 (☎ **808/971-6000**), can dispatch a van if you need help getting to the main clinic, or to any of their additional clinics at the Royal Hawaiian Hotel, Hyatt Regency Waikiki, Hawaiian Regent Hotel, Hilton Hawaiian Village, Kahala Mandarin Oriental, and Ihilani Resort and Spa.

Emergencies Call ☎ **911** for police, fire, and ambulance. The **Poison Control Center** is at 1319 Punahou St. (☎ **808/941-4411**).

Hospitals Hospitals offering 24-hour emergency care include **Queens Medical Center,** 1301 Punchbowl St. (☎ 808/538-9011); **Kuakini Medical Center,** 347 Kuakini St. (☎ 808/536-2236); **Straub Clinic and Hospital,** 888 S. King St. (☎ 808/522-4000); **Moanalua Medical Center,** 3288 Moanalua Rd. (☎ 808/834-5333); **Kapiolani Medical Center for Women and Children,** 1319 Punahou St. (☎ 808/973-8511); and **Kapiolani Medical Center at Pali Momi,** 98-1079 Moanalua Rd. (☎ 808/486-6000). In Central Oahu is **Wahiawa General Hospital,** 128 Lehua St. (☎ 808/621-8411). On the windward side is **Castle Medical Center,** 640 Ulukahiki St., Kailua (☎ 808/263-5500).

Newspapers The *Honolulu Advertiser* and *Honolulu Star-Bulletin* are Oahu's daily papers. *Midweek, Pacific Business News,* and *Honolulu Weekly* are weekly papers. *Honolulu Weekly,* available free at restaurants, clubs, shops, and newspaper racks around Oahu, is the best source for what's going on around town.

Post Office To find the location nearest you, call ☎ **808/423-3990.** The downtown location is in the old U.S. Post Office, Customs, and Court House Building (referred to as the "old Federal Building") at 335 Merchant St. (across from Iolani Palace and next to the Kamehameha Statue; Bus: 2). Other branch offices include the Waikiki Post Office, 330 Saratoga Ave. (Diamond Head side of Fort DeRussy; Bus: 19 or 20), and in the Ala Moana Shopping Center (Bus: 8, 19, or 20).

Weather Reports For National Weather Service recorded forecasts for Honolulu, call ☎ **808/973-4380;** for elsewhere on the island, call ☎ **808/973-4381.** For marine reports, call ☎ **808/973-4382.** For surf reports, call ☎ **808/973-4383.**

3 Accommodations

by Jeanette Foster

Before you reach for the phone to book a place to stay, consider when you'll be visiting. The high season, when hotels are full and rates are at their highest, is mid-December to March. The secondary high season, when rates are high but rooms are somewhat easier to come by, is June to September. The low seasons—when you can expect fewer tourists and better deals—are April to June and September to mid-December. For more on Hawaii's travel seasons, see "When to Go" in chapter 3. No matter when you travel, you can often get the best rate at many of Waikiki's hotels by booking a package; for details, see "Money-Saving Package Deals" in chapter 3.

Also remember that hotel and room taxes of 10.17% will be added to your hotel bill. And don't forget about parking charges—in Waikiki, they can quickly add up.

BED-&-BREAKFAST RESERVATIONS AGENCIES

For a more intimate experience, try staying in a B&B. Accommodations on Oahu calling themselves bed-and-breakfasts vary from a room in a house (sometimes with a shared bath) to a vacation rental in a private cottage. Breakfast can be anything from coffee, pastries, and fruit to a home-cooked gourmet meal with just-caught fresh fish. Due to space limitations, we could only include a handful of Oahu's best B&Bs below; for a wider selection, check out *Frommer's Honolulu, Waikiki & Oahu*. Or call one of the statewide booking agencies we recommend on page 79.

AIRPORT HOTELS

If you have a late-night flight, a long layover between flights, a delayed flight, or a long period of time between your noon check-out and your flight, consider the services of the **Honolulu Airport Mini-Hotel** (☎ **808/ 836-3044;** fax 808/834-8986). It's the perfect answer to a traveler's dilemma: The clean, comfortable single rooms come with nothing more than a bed, a nightstand, and a private shower. They provide a wake-up call if you need it, there's always coffee brewing to get you going, and if you have something that needs refrigeration (medication or flowers to bring home), the management is happy to help out. Rates are $33 for 8 hours (additional hours $5 each); you can rent showers only for $8.25. There are only 17 rooms, so book in advance. The hotel does not provide transportation to the terminal, but it's just a short walk away.

Good all-night airport choices are the **Best Western–The Plaza Hotel** (☎ **800/800-4683** or 808/836-3636; www.bestwestern.com/thisco/bw/12008/ -b.html), where rooms start at $104; and **Holiday Inn Airport** (☎ **800/800-3477** or 808/833-0661; www.holiday-inn.com), with rooms from $102. Both have free airport shuttle service.

WAIKIKI
EWA WAIKIKI

All the hotels listed below are located between Ala Wai Boulevard and the Ala Wai Yacht Harbor, and between Ala Wai Terrace in the Ewa direction (or western side of Waikiki) and Olohana Street and Fort DeRussy Park in the Diamond Head direction (or eastern side of Waikiki).

Very Expensive

Hawaii Prince Hotel. 100 Holomoana St. (just across Ala Wai Canal Bridge, on the ocean side of Ala Moana Blvd.), Honolulu, HI 96815. ☎ **800/321-OAHU** or 808/965-1111. Fax 808/946-0811. 521 units. A/C TV TEL. $240–$390 double; from $500 suite. Extra person $40; children 17 or under stay free using existing bedding. Valet parking $12, self-parking $8. Bus: 19 or 20.

The first hotel at the entrance to Waikiki is this striking $150 million, twin–33-story modern structure, which opened in April 1990. The high-ceilinged lobby is a mass of pink Italian marble with English slate accents; a grand piano sits in the midst of the raised seating area, where high tea is served every afternoon; a glass-encased elevator with views of all of Honolulu whisks you up to your room.

All the rooms face the Ala Wai Yacht Harbor, with floor-to-ceiling sliding-glass windows that let you enjoy the view. Just renovated in 1997, the comfortably appointed rooms are basically all the same, with in-room safes and hair dryers in the bathroom—but the higher the floor, the higher the price.

Waikiki Accommodations

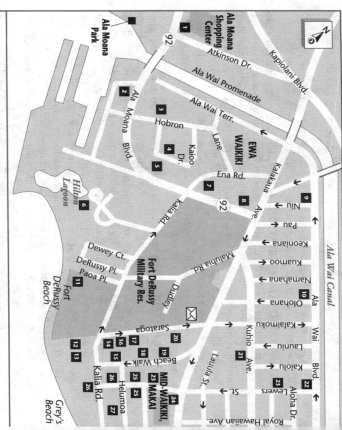

Accommodation	No.
Ala Moana Hotel	1
Aloha Punawai	20
Aston at the Waikiki Banyan	46
Aston at the Waikiki Shore Apartments	12
Aston Waikiki Beachside Hotel	42
The Breakers	18
Coconut Plaza	22
Colony Surf	49
Coral Reef Hotel	33
Diamond Head Bed & Breakfast	50
Doubletree Alana Waikiki	8
Hale Koa Hotel	11
Hale Pua Nui Hotel	15
Halekulani	26
Hawaii Prince Hotel	2
Hawaiiana Hotel	19
Hawaiian Monarch	9
Hilton Hawaiian Village	6
Holiday Inn—Waikiki	5
Holiday Surf Apartments	38
Hotel Honolulu	21
Hyatt Regency Waikiki	37
Ilima Hotel	41
Inn on the Park	7
Kai Aloha Apartment Hotel	17

1-0705

Set by Japanese standards, the level of service is impeccable: no detail is ignored, no request too small. The location is perfect for shopping—Ala Moana Center is just a 10-minute walk away, and Waikiki's beaches are just a 5-minute walk away (both are also accessible via the hotel's own shuttle bus). In addition, the Prince has its own 27-hole golf club in Ewa Beach (with shuttle service to the greens, of course).

Dining/Diversions: The Prince Court, located on the third floor overlooking the harbor, offers casual bistro-like fare (see complete review under "Dining," below). Hakone Japanese Restaurant serves traditional cuisine prepared by master chefs, while casual Japanese dining is available at Takanawa Sushi Bar and Restaurant. The outdoor Promenade Deck is the place for cafe-style dining and tropical drinks.

Amenities: Nightly turndown service (they not only leave a bedtime sweet, but also a small booklet of short stories), concierge desk, room service, complimentary newspaper, baby-sitting services, hot towels (*oshibori*) upon arrival, fitness room, full-service beauty shop. Guests on the Hokulea Floor get such extras as a snack-filled

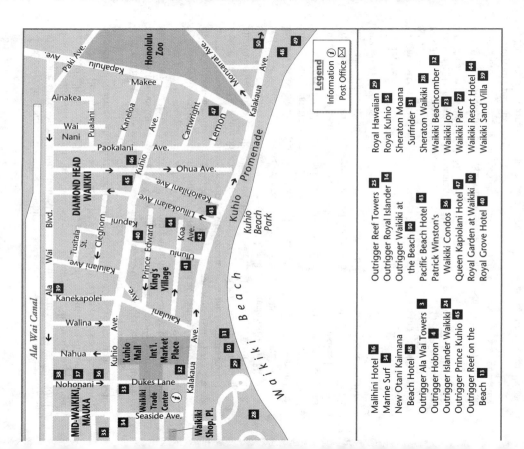

welcome basket, a coffeemaker, tea service, a toothbrush and razor, logo bathrobes, and a CD player for an additional $40 a night. A business floor can handle any business request, from computers to secretarial services.

Expensive

✪ **Hilton Hawaiian Village.** 2005 Kalia Rd. (at Ala Moana Blvd.), Honolulu, HI 96815. ☎ **800-HILTONS** or 808/949-4321. Fax 808/947-7898. www.hilton.com. 2,910 units. A/C MINIBAR TV TEL. $189–$335 double; $219–$365 Alii Tower double; from $415 suite. Extra person $30; children 18 and under stay free. AE, CB, DISC, ER, JCB, MC, V. Valet parking $12, self-parking $9. Bus: 19 or 20.

This is Waikiki's biggest resort—so big it even has its own post office. It includes nearly 3,000 rooms spread over 20 acres with tropical gardens dotted with exotic wildlife (flamingoes, peacocks, even tropical penguins!), award-winning restaurants, 100 different shops, a secluded lagoon, three swimming pools, two minigolf courses, and a gorgeous stretch of Waikiki Beach.

Like everything else in the village—which really is a mini-city unto itself—there's a wide choice of accommodations housed in four towers—Rainbow, Tapa, Diamond Head, and Alii—that range from simply lovely to ultradeluxe. All the rooms are large and beautifully furnished; if you can afford it, we highly recommend the ones in the Alii Tower. Located right on the ocean, the 348 amenity-laden rooms and suites offer all the royal treatment that the name implies, including in-room registration, an exclusive health club and swimming pool, and the full attention of a multilingual staff. Each room has a fully stocked refreshment center, in-room coffee services, no fewer than three phones (one of which is PC-compatible), and even a mini-TV on the bathroom vanity. But if you go with one of the more affordable towers, you'll still be happy. A great place to stay with the kids.

Dining/Diversions: Both the Golden Dragon (excellent Cantonese and Szechwan cuisine in exquisite Asian-style surroundings) and the romantic Bali By the Sea (see complete review under "Dining," below), with ocean views and gourmet cuisine, are named among Honolulu's best restaurants year after year. Other restaurants among the multitude include a couple of casual cafes (one with a "fitness-first" menu), a steak-and-seafood joint, a sushi bar, and a branch of Benihana. Illusionist John Hirokawa and "The Magic of Polynesia" are featured at the Hilton Dome. There are also a handful of bars and lounges—including the beachfront Hau Tree Bar—many featuring nightly entertainment.

Amenities: Multilingual concierge; same-day laundry; in-room fax and computer hookups in many rooms; year-round children's program (one of Waikiki's best); free fitness classes, Hawaiiana instruction, and walking tours for adults; on-site Atlantis Submarine rides; in-room massage; room service. Business center, fitness center, three pools, tons of shops.

Moderate

✪ **Doubletree Alana Waikiki.** 1956 Ala Moana Blvd. (on the Ewa side, between Ena Rd. and Kalakaua Ave.), Honolulu, HI 96815. ☎ **800/367-6070** or 808/941-7275. Fax 808/949-0996. www.doubletreehotels.com. 313 units. TV TEL. **$135–$215** double, from $250 suite. Extra person $25; children 18 or younger stay free. AE, CB, DC, DISC, JCB, MC, V. Parking **$7.** Bus: 19 or 20.

In 1997, the Doubletree chain (known for giving guests a freshly baked chocolate-chip cookie every night) took charge of this boutique hotel, a welcome oasis of beauty, comfort, and prompt service.

The elegant second-floor lobby and other public areas feature original Picasso ceramics and other works of art; the interior designer decided to give the rooms a more homey feel than you usually find in hotel rooms, with soft pastels dominating the palate. The result is comfortable rooms that are so inviting, you may want to curl up with a good book—if it weren't for the fact that Waikiki Beach was just a walk away. Amenities include two queen beds, two-line telephones, voice mail, computer-fax outlets, flashlights (great for that hike up Diamond Head), and coffee/tea makers. The bathrooms are compact yet outfitted with everything you need, including a phone.

A good percentage of the guests are business travelers who expect top-drawer service, and the Alana Waikiki delivers. The staff is attentive to details and willing to go to any length to make you happy. Want the New York Times delivered to your room? No problem. Need secretarial help? Within minutes, it's available. Two restaurants offer superb Pacific-Rim cuisine, and full hotel amenities range from concierge and room service to a well-outfitted business center, a fitness center with sauna and massage (in-room massage service also available), a 24-hour reading room with international newspapers and magazines, and a heated pool.

Hawaiian Monarch. 444 Niu St. (at Ala Wai Blvd.), Honolulu, HI 96815. ☎ 800/535-0085 or 808/922-9700. Fax 800/633-5085 or 808/922-2421. www.marcresorts.com. E-mail marc@aloha.net. 241 units. A/C TV TEL. High season $109–$119 double; low season $98–$109 double, $119–$131 double studio suite with kitchenette; low season $98–$109 double, $119–$131 double studio suite. Extra person $15. AE, CB, DC, DISC, JCB, MC, V. Parking $6. Bus: 19 or 20.

This part-hotel, part-condo high-rise just across the street from the Ala Wai Canal offers tropically decorated doubles outfitted with refrigerators, coffeemakers, and in-room safes. If you want more complete kitchen facilities, go for one of the suites, which have kitchenettes with a hot plate/oven and toaster. The cheapest doubles have either two twin beds or a queen; fans of king beds will have to pay a bit more for a deluxe room. The location allows easy access in and out of Waikiki by car, and the beach is just a 10-minute walk away, but there's a huge sundeck (the largest in Waikiki, they claim) and a pool if you just don't want to leave. Also on the property is a sports bar, a restaurant, and shopping. *Hot tip:* Request a room facing the Ala Wai Canal for the best view.

Holiday Inn—Waikiki. 1830 Ala Moana Blvd. (between Hobron Lane and Kalia Rd.), Honolulu, HI 96815. ☎ 888/9WAIKIKI or 808/955-1111. Fax 808/947-1799. www.holiday-inn.com. 199 units. A/C TV TEL. $110–$130 double. Extra person $15; children 19 and under stay for free using existing bedding. AE, CB, DC, DISC, JCB, MC, V. Parking $6. Bus: 19 or 20.

Holiday Inn—with its dependable quality, amenities, and service—spent some $6 million to totally renovate the aging former Hawaii Dynasty Hotel. Just two blocks from the beach, two blocks from Ala Moana Shopping Center, and a 7-minute walk from the Convention Center, it's well-placed for anyone's vacation. All the rooms, which have a modern Japanese look, come with either a king or two double beds plus TV, voice mail, computer jacks, coffeemaker with complimentary coffee, safe, and fridge. The property sits back from the street, so noise is at a minimum. The staff is unbelievably friendly (much, much more so than at the Airport Holiday Inn).

✪ **Royal Garden at Waikiki.** 440 Olohana St. (between Kuhio Ave. and Ala Wai Blvd.). ☎ 800/367-5666 or 808/943-0202. Fax 808/946-8777. 220 units. A/C TV TEL. $130–$180 double, $325 one-bedroom double, $600 two-bedroom double (sleeps up to 4). Packages galore. Extra person $25, children under 12 stay free. AE, DC, DISC, JCB, MV, V. Parking $7. Bus: 19 or 20.

Deals, deals, deals—that's what you'll find at this elegant boutique hotel, tucked away on a quiet, tree-lined side street. There's a deal for everyone: room/car packages start at $135 (that's a $130 standard room, plus a car for only $5 extra); a family plan gives you a second room at half the rack rate; and the Young-at-Heart Package allows seniors to book rooms starting at $91 (plus a 10% discount at Royal Garden restaurants). You won't believe what you get for your money: The 25-story hotel has a lobby filled with European marble and chandeliers, and plush rooms featuring a pantry kitchenette (refrigerator, wet bar, coffeemaker), sitting area, marble bath, lots of closet space, and a lanai; voice mail and computer/fax hookups are welcome amenities. Facilities include two restaurants—Cascada, serving country-French cuisine, and Shizu, serving Japanese specialties—Cascada, two freshwater pools (one with cascading waterfall), two Jacuzzis, two saunas, and a fitness center. There's also complimentary shuttle service to Kapiolani Park, Ala Moana Shopping Center, Royal Hawaiian Shopping Center, and Duty Free Shoppers. The beach is a few blocks away, but at these prices, it's worth the hike.

Inexpensive

Inn on the Park. 1920 Ala Moana Blvd. (at Kalia Rd.), Honolulu, HI 96815. ☎ 800/367-5004 or 808/946-8355. Fax 800/477-2329 or 808/946-4839. 238 units. A/C TV TEL.

Built in 1979, this well-located hotel is just across the street from Fort DeRussy and a couple of blocks from the beach. The rooms are minuscule, so don't expect to squeeze more than two in; families might want to look elsewhere or rent two rooms. Even the lanais are small—there's barely room for a chair. Most rooms have refrigerators; the studios have kitchenettes with cooktop, toaster, and coffeemaker. The 5th-floor pool has a grand view of Fort DeRussy and the Waikiki skyline. Among the shops in the lobby is a moped rental shop, for those wanting to explore Oahu on a motorized two-wheeler; there's also an Italian restaurant. If you don't mind the size of the rooms—you're in Hawaii, so how much time are you going to spend in your room, anyway?—the price here can't be beat.

MID-WAIKIKI, MAKAI

All the hotels listed below are between Kalakaua Avenue and the ocean, and between Fort DeRussy in the Ewa direction and Kaiulani Street in the Diamond Head direction.

Very Expensive

⭐🚭 **Halekulani.** 2199 Kalia Rd. (at the ocean end of Lewers St.), Honolulu, HI 96815. ☎ **800/367-2343** or 808/923-2311. Fax 808/926-8004. www.halekulani.com. 456 units. A/C MINIBAR TV TEL. $295–$520 double, from $700 suite. Heaven on Waikiki package for 2—with chilled champagne and flowers on arrival and an intimate in-room breakfast—is $1,539 for 3 nights, $3,159 for 7 nights. Heavenly Summer Program gets you a 2nd room for $295 no matter what the cost of your 1st room (for U.S. and Canadian residents only). Extra person $125; 1 child under 17 stays free using existing bedding; maximum 3 people per room. AE, CB, DC, JCB, MC, V. Parking $10. Bus: 19 or 20.

For the ultimate heavenly Hawaii vacation, this is the place. In fact, Halekulani translates as "House Befitting Heaven"—an apt description of this luxury resort, which is spread over five acres of prime Waikiki beachfront in five buildings interconnected by open courtyards and lush, tropical gardens. The elegant atmosphere envelops you as soon as you step into the terrazzo and wood-lined lobby, where you are immediately greeted and escorted to your rooms, where registration is handled in comfort and privacy.

There are so many things that set this luxury hotel apart from the others, the most important being the rooms: about 90% face the ocean, and they're big (averaging 620 square feet or so) with a separate sitting area and a large, furnished lanai. The bathroom features a deep-soaking tub, a separate glassed-in shower, and a marble basin. Other luxuries include a refrigerator, three phones, a safe, and luxurious bathrobes.

Dining/Diversions: Facilities are superb; Indo-Pacific **Orchids;** the oceanside main dining room; the award-winning neoclassic French **La Mer** (see "Dining" below for complete reviews); and ⭐ **House Without a Key,** surely one of the world's most romantic spots for sunset cocktails, light meals, and Hawaiian entertainment.

Amenities: Twice-daily maid and turndown service, complimentary daily newspaper, and complimentary local phone calls. Concierge desk, business and secretarial services, fitness room, running sessions and aerobic workouts, in-room massage, magnificent oceanside swimming pool, and easy access to a superb stretch of Waikiki Beach.

Royal Hawaiian. 2259 Kalakaua Ave. (at Royal Hawaiian Ave., on the ocean side of the Royal Hawaiian Shopping Center), Honolulu, HI 96815. ☎ **800/325-3535** or 808/923-7311. Fax

High season $95–$110 double, $120 deluxe studio with kitchenette; low season $85–$100 double, $110 deluxe studio with kitchenette. Extra person $17. AE, CB, DC, JCB, MC, V. Parking $8. Bus: 19 or 20.

808/924-7098. www.sheraton.com. 527 units. A/C MINIBAR TV TEL. $290–$540 double, from $475 suite. Extra person $50. Ask about Sheraton's Sure Saver rates, which could mean as much as 32% in savings. The Celebration package includes a bottle of pink champagne, a romantic dinner for 2 (that can be served in the privacy of your room), a pass on the Waikiki Trolley, a commemorative farewell gift, and your 5th night free. AE, MC, V. Valet parking $18, self-parking at Sheraton Waikiki $9. Bus: 19 or 20.

A shocking-pink oasis hidden away among blooming gardens in the concrete jungle that is Waikiki, the Royal Hawaiian is known around the world as a symbol of luxury. Built by Matson steamship lines and inspired by popular silent-screen star Rudolph Valentino (*The Sheik*), the Spanish-Moorish "Pink Palace" opened on February 1, 1927, on the same spot that Queen Kaahumanu had her summer palace—one of the best stretches of Waikiki Beach.

Entry into the hotel is past the lush gardens, with their spectacular banyan tree, into the black terrazzo-marble lobby, which features hand-woven pink carpets and giant floral arrangements. Every guest room is enchanting, but our hearts were won over by those in the Historic Wing, which feature carved wooden doors, four-poster canopy beds, flowered wallpaper, and period furniture. But even if you stay in one of the more modern rooms, you'll find that historic touches abound, from a traditional lei greeting and freshly baked banana bread (made from the hotel's original 1927 recipe) upon arrival to Hawaiian craft displays—Hawaiian quilts, leis, weaving, and more—by local artists every Monday, Wednesday, and Friday.

Dining/Diversions: There are two dining rooms to choose from (the Surf Room is known for its elaborate seafood buffets), plus the casual Beach Club, which features an oceanfront patio that's a great place to start your day. The ✪ **Mai Tai Bar** is one of the most popular places in Waikiki for the namesake drink, which is reputed to have originated here. The Royal Hawaiian Luau, done in the grand style, is held on Monday nights.

Amenities: 24-hour room service, daily newspaper, multilingual concierge desk, 24-hour medical service, baby-sitting, valet service, business center, hospitality suite for early arrivals and late check-outs, shops, salon, freshwater pool, beach accessories from deck chairs to umbrellas, preferential tee-off times at Makaha Resort and Golf Club.

✪ **Sheraton Moana Surfrider.** 2365 Kalakaua Ave. (ocean side of the street, across from Kaulani St.), Honolulu, HI 96815. ☎ **800/325-3535** or 808/922-3111. Fax 808/923-0308. www.sheraton.com. 835 units. A/C MINIBAR TV TEL. $250–$485 deluxe ocean view in Tower and Diamond Wings. Extra person and rollaway bed $40; children under 18 stay free using existing bedding. Inquire about Sure Saver rates, which could mean as much as 32% in savings. AE, CB, DC, MC, V. Parking $10. Bus: 19 or 20.

Step back in time to old Hawaii at Waikiki's first hotel, originally built in 1901. Considered an innovation in the travel industry, the Moana featured a private bath and a telephone in each guest room—an unheard of luxury at the turn of the century. The first guests thought the rooms were a bit "pricey" ($1.50 a night), but worth it. The prices may have gone up since then, but yesteryear lives on at this grand hotel: Entry is through the original colonial porte-cochere, past the highly polished front porch dotted with rocking chairs, and into the perfectly restored lobby with detailed millwork and intricate plasterwork; the female employees even wear traditional Victorian-era muumuus. At check-in, you'll be greeted with a lei, a glass of fruit juice, and a welcoming smile. This is a hotel not only with class, but with charm; time seems to slow down here, and the aloha spirit that pervades the place is infectious.

The hotel, which is listed in the National Register of Historic Places, consists of three wings: the original (and totally restored) Banyan Wing, the Diamond Wing, and the Tower Wing. It's hard to get a bad room here: The majority of the rooms have

A Room for Everyone in Waikiki: The Outrigger Dynasty

The largest hotel chain in Waikiki, Outrigger offers excellent accommodations across the board. All of their 20 Waikiki properties feature dependable, clean, well-appointed rooms, ranging from luxury oceanfront suites to smaller, no-thrills budget hotels that offer great deals for frugal travelers. The chain's price structure is based entirely on location, room size, and amenities; you'll be comfortable at any of their outposts—the small rooms in the budget Outriggers are just as tastefully decorated as the larger, more expensive Outriggers on the beach.

In addition to the flagship **Outrigger Waikiki** on the beach (see complete review below), here are our picks for the best of this reliable chain:

The other Outrigger on the beach is the **Outrigger Reef on the Beach**, next door to the luxurious Halekulani on Kalia Road in the heart of Waikiki. Rooms start at $150—unheard of for this stretch of Waikiki Beach; this place is an incredible bargain.

At the Ewa end of Waikiki, our two favorite Outriggers are the **Outrigger Ala Wai Towers** (on Ala Moana Boulevard between Hobron Lane and the Ala Wai Canal) and the **Outrigger Hobron** (on Hobron Lane, just off Ala Moana Boulevard). Both are conveniently located to the new Hawaii Convention Center as well as shopping (Ala Moana Center is just a block away) and the beach. Of the two, the Ala Wai Towers has more to offer, including breathtaking views; rooms with kitchenettes starting at just $85. The Hobron is more of a budget hotel, with smaller rooms starting at $70—but you'll still get plenty of bang for your buck.

In mid-Waikiki, one of the best deals is the **Outrigger Royal Islander** (at Kalia and Saratoga roads). This is about as close as you can get to the beach and still pay budget prices (doubles start at $75): Waikiki Beach is just across the street, through the beach-access walkway. The only caveat is the rooms are small (three would be a crowd), and this property shares some services (pool and parking) with a nearby Outrigger—but at these prices, this is definitely a find.

ocean views, and they all come with such amenities as refrigerators, irons and ironing boards, hair dryers, bedside controls, plush robes, safes, and voice mail. But we're especially taken with the Banyan Wing rooms; what they lack in size and amenities—they're on the smallish side and don't have lanais—they make up for in style; even the fixtures in the smallish bathrooms are modern-day replicas of 19th-century hardware.

Dining/Diversions: There are five restaurants, ranging from casual to fine dining; the Banyan Veranda is the setting for breakfast, Sunday brunch, high tea, and afternoon cocktails. The Beach Bar and a poolside snack bar are in the oceanfront courtyard that's centered around a hundred-year-old banyan tree, where there's live music in the evenings.

Amenities: 24-hour room service; concierge; free seasonal children's program featuring on-site activities and excursions to the Honolulu Zoo and the Waikiki Aquarium. Prime stretch of beach with lifeguard right out front; beach chairs, towels, and service provided. Daily activities include Hawaiian arts and crafts, such as coconut-palm weaving and Hawaiian quilting. Beach, fitness center, and freshwater pool. Be sure to visit the Historical Room, where a variety of memorabilia is on display, from turn-of-the-century antiques to a 1945 New Year's Day dinner menu advertising a four-course meal for $1.50.

Our two favorites on nearby Lewers Street (a small, busy street lined with restaurants, shopping, and nightlife within a 5-minute walk. Families might want to consider the Reef Towers, where studio units start at $135 for four and one-bedroom units are $145 for four; both units are large enough to spread out in and come with kitchenettes to save you money on eating out. The Islander Waikiki is located closer to shopping on the corner of Lewers and Kalakaua (the Royal Hawaiian Shopping Center is just across the street); it was completely renovated in 1997 (new Berber carpets, Italian tile entryways, and artwork from Hawaiian artists on the walls) but is still moderately priced—rooms start at just $115.

At the Diamond Head end of Waikiki, the **Outrigger Prince Kuhio** (Kuhio and Liliuokalani) is our pick. Also renovated in '97, this 37-story luxury Outrigger (rooms from $135 up) has a great central location: in the heart of Waikiki's shopping district, just a few blocks from Waikiki Beach and the Honolulu Zoo. Two restaurants, great Hawaiian entertainment nightly, room service, and a business center make this Outrigger the perfect choice for travelers with champagne tastes and beer budgets.

Package deals include discounted rates for spring and fall stays, a free rental car when you book at rack rates, the seventh night free when you book at rack rates for six, family plans (children 17 years and younger stay free in parents' room as long as they use the existing bedding), good deals for seniors (20% off, 25% off for AARP members), and even packages for scuba divers (2 days of two-tank boat dives and a 3-night stay starts at $311 per person, double). To ask about current offerings and make reservations at any of these or other Outrigger properties throughout the islands, just contact **Outrigger** at ☎ **800/OUTRIGGER** or 808/942-7722. Fax 800/622-4852 or 808/943-7272; www.outrigger.com; e-mail reservations@outrigger.com.

Expensive

Aston at the Waikiki Shore Apartments. 2161 Kalia Rd. (on the ocean at Saratoga Rd., across the street from Fort DeRussy), Honolulu, HI 96815. ☎ **800/367-2353** or 808/926-4733. Fax 808/922-2902. www.aston-hotels.com. 76 apts. A/C TV TEL. $160–$180 studio double, $230–$260 one-bedroom apt. (sleeps up to 4) $320–$545 two-bedroom apt. (up to 6). Ask about Island Hopper rates, which give you 20–30% off rates if you stay at Aston properties for 7 or more consecutive nights. AE, CB, DC, DISC, JCB, MC, V. Limited parking $7. Bus: 19 or 20.

As soon as you arrive, you'll see why everyone wants to stay here: The panoramic vista of the entire shoreline from Diamond Head to Honolulu is spectacular. The apartments—which are privately owned and decorated and then rented out through Aston—range in size from studio to two-bedroom. Each has a fully equipped kitchen, a big lanai, a spacious sitting area, washer/dryer, and those fabulous views. There are full-time residents who live in this complex, so it tends to be quiet, and entry to the units is through a locked gate and keyed elevators, so security is tight. The building sits on an excellent beach, close to restaurants and shopping. As you might expect, reservations are hard to get; book *way* in advance.

Amenities: Daily maid service, a few on-site shops, and plenty of assistance from the front desk give this condominium stay all the benefits of hotel service.

ℹ Great Places to Stay with the Kids

If you're traveling with the kids, you'll be welcomed with open arms by many of Oahu's resorts, condos, and B&Bs. Here are our favorites:

Halekulani (see p. 110)   If you're visiting between early June and mid-August or at Christmastime (December 18–30) and you're looking for a little luxury for you and the kids, consider the Halekulani, possibly our favorite hotel in the islands. It has a wonderful complimentary supervised program for children ages 6 to 11; the only charges are for lunch and admission to activities. Daily programs include crafts, games, sightseeing, and excursions. Another plus is the Heavenly Summer Program, which allows you to pay $295 for a second room, no matter what the cost of the first one (available to U.S. and Canadian residents only).

Hilton Hawaiian Village (see p. 107)   The Rainbow Express is Hilton's year-round daily program of activities for children ages 5 to 12. The program offers a wide range of educational and fun activities, ranging from Hawaiian arts and crafts to environmental nature walks and wildlife feedings to shell hunting and fishing, and much more. Everything about this hotel is kid-friendly, from the wildlife parading the grounds to the submarine dives offered just out front; a great place to stay with the kids.

Ilima Hotel (see p. 121)   This hotel was designed with families in mind. The units are large, and all have full-sized kitchens. Although there's no formal supervised children's program, you'll find free HBO, Disney Channel, and Super Nintendo video games in each room, and the coin-operated laundry is a big help to Mom and Dad. The beach and the International Market Place are both just a short walk away, and TheBus stops just outside. Very popular with neighbor-island families.

Outrigger Reef Towers (see p. 113)   This affordable hotel offers something for everyone, including nightlife for Mom and Dad and baby-sitting for the kids. Just 1½ blocks from the beach, the Outrigger Reef Towers also has a good-sized swimming pool on-site. The larger rooms come with kitchenettes, which let you save on food by preparing some meals for yourself.

Royal Kuhio (see p. 120)   If you have active kids, this is the place for you. The 7th-floor recreation area has volleyball courts, billiards, basketball courts, shuffleboard, an exercise room, even a putting green. Located just across the street from the International Market Place and two blocks from the beach, the Royal

★ **Outrigger Waikiki at the Beach.** 2335 Kalakaua Ave. (on the ocean, between the Royal Hawaiian Shopping Center and the Sheraton Moana Surfrider), Honolulu, HI 96815. ☎ **800/OUTRIGGER** or 808/923-0711. Fax 800/622-4852. www. outrigger.com. E-mail reservations@outrigger.com. 530 units. A/C TV TEL. $160–$350 double; $215–$530 Voyager Club rooms and suites; $500–$530 suite. Seniors 50 and older get 20% discount, AARP members 25% discount, free rental car when booking at rack rates; ask about other package deals. Extra person $25; children 17 and under stay free using existing bedding. AE, CB, DC, DISC, JCB, MC, V. Parking $10. Bus: 19 or 20.

The same value and quality that we've come to expect in every Outrigger is definitely in evidence here, only multiplied by a factor of 10. Even the standard rooms in this 16-story oceanfront hotel are large and comfortable, and $160 a day on Waikiki Beach is definitely a deal (even if it doesn't get you an ocean-view room). And the prime

Kuhio features one-bedroom apartments with sofa sleepers in the living room and full kitchens. Rates allow up to four people in a unit and will sleep five for an extra charge of $15 for a rollaway or crib.

Sheraton Waikiki Hotel (*see p. 116*) During the summer (from mid-June to mid-August), the Keiki Aloha Sunshine Club offers activities for children ages 5 to 12. On arrival, your kids are greeted with a complimentary candy lei; they can then go boogie boarding, kite-flying, catamaran sailing, compete in a photo contest, watch nightly movies, and more.

Kahala Mandarin Oriental Hawaii (*see p. 129*) The Keiki Club is the year-round activity program for kids ages 5 to 12. Your youngsters will have a blast dancing the hula, making leis, designing sand sculptures, putting on puppet shows, learning to strum a ukulele, making shell art and fish prints, listening to Hawaiian folk tales and legends, playing Hawaiian games, and much, much more.

Rodeway Inn Hukilau Resort (*see p. 133*) Children are more than welcome here—in fact, there's no charge for kids under 18 to stay with you at this two-story, plantation-style North Shore hotel. Within walking distance of the Polynesian Cultural Center, the Rodeway is set up for families, with features like free continental breakfast, pool, and laundry. To top it all off, a terrific white-sand beach is just across the street.

Turtle Bay Hilton Golf and Tennis Resort (*see p. 132*) This North Shore resort offers a year-round program for children ages 5 to 12 years. The Turtle Keiki Program offers such activities as Hawaiian-style arts and crafts, coconut painting, sand sculpturing, swimming, movies, storytelling, and a host of other fun activities to keep the kids busy while you relax.

Ihilani Resort & Spa (*see p. 134*) The Keiki Beachcomber Club, for children 4 to 12, is available every day of the year. Outdoor activities include kite-flying, tide-pool exploration, snorkeling, golf, tennis, swimming, aerobics, and international games like les boules (similar to bocce ball), Indian kickball, and tinikling (a bamboo dance from the Philippines); Hawaiian cultural activities feature lei-making and hula dancing. There's a state-of-the-art Computer Learning Center (complete with SEGA Genesis, CD-ROM, and Super Nintendo) and so many other activities that you're unlikely to even see the kids until you're ready to get on the plane to go home.

beachfront location and loads of facilities help to make this one of the chain's most attractive properties.

White columns dominate the airy atmosphere of the second-floor lobby, which is outfitted with tropical plants, rattan furniture, and big, bold artwork. The newly renovated rooms are big and comfortable, all with huge closets, roomy bathrooms, and plenty of amenities (refrigerator, iron, hair dryer, safe, coffeemaker), plus a spacious lanai; the price is entirely dependent on the view. Rooms on the top four floors are part of the Voyager Club, where guests have the use of the private lounge serving continental breakfast and complimentary pupus in the evening.

Dining/Diversions: The beachfront **Duke's Canoe Club** serves great island-style seafood and steaks, complemented by Hawaiian entertainment and an extended menu of tropical cocktails (see complete review under "Dining," below); Monterey Bay

Canners and Chuck's Steakhouse are both popular places for seafood and steaks. Other choices include a *Cheers*-like pub and deli, a casual healthy-foods place, and a snack shop on the beach. The talented Society of Seven singers perform in the showroom.

Amenities: Room service (7am to 9:45pm), concierge, ATM, coin-op laundry, salon, lots of shops, Doctors on Call medical clinic, business center, hospitality room for early check-ins and late check-outs. An 800-square-foot fitness center, beautifully landscaped pool area with Jacuzzi, easy access to a prime stretch of Waikiki Beach.

Sheraton Waikiki. 2255 Kalakaua Ave. (at Royal Hawaiian Ave., on the ocean side of the Royal Hawaiian Shopping Center and west of the Royal Hawaiian), Honolulu, HI 96815. ☎ **800/325-3535** or 808/922-4422. Fax 808/923-8785. 1,982 units. A/C MINIBAR TV TEL. $150 Sheraton Manor Hotel double, $240–$430 Waikiki double, from $600 suite. Extra person $40. Ask about Sheraton's Sure Saver rates, which can mean as much as 32% in savings. AE, CB, DC, DISC, JCB, MC, V. Valet parking $13, self-parking $9. Bus: 19 or 20.

The Sheraton chain owns a substantial portion of Waikiki, with three hotels on the beach (the Royal Hawaiian, the Moana Surfrider, and this one) and one across the street (the Princess Kaiulani). This is by far the biggest of the four—1,852 rooms spread over two 30-story towers. This place is big, big, big—the bank of 11 elevators gives you a feel for the sheer size of the place. The lobby is immense and filled with shops, travel desks, and people. Not surprisingly, this hotel hosts numerous conventions; if you're not comfortable with crowds and conventioneers, book elsewhere. However, size has its advantage: The Sheraton has everything from free kids' programs to historical walks for mom and dad.

It's hard to get a bad room here. There's a saying on the Waikiki strip that lots of hotels have great views of the Sheraton, but Sheraton guests have views of the beach and Diamond Head all to themselves; a whopping 1,200 rooms have some sort of ocean view, and 650 rooms overlook Diamond Head. The rooms are large, with big lanais to take in those magnificent views; other amenities include minibars (if you want to store your own food and drinks, call housekeeping to clear it out), safes, and coffeemakers.

For the budget-conscious, the Sheraton Manor Hotel occupies a separate adjacent wing and offers all the services and beachfront of the main hotel. The views aren't the best—overlooking the porte cochere—and the air-conditioned rooms are small (two people, max) and modestly appointed (no lanai).

Dining/Diversions: Restaurants range from the open-air Ocean Terrace for casual buffet meals to the glamorous Hanohano Room for gourmet dining in a spectacular setting (take the glass elevator just for the view). There's a nightclub for dancing, drinks, and entertainment, and the pool area features snack counters and a bar.

Amenities: Sheraton is the "king" of amenities, with 24-hour room service, concierge, coin-operated laundry, 20 shops, multilingual staff, business center, fitness center, and two freshwater pools—including one of the biggest and sunniest pools along the Waikiki beachfront. Free kids' programs that include a candy lei on arrival, plus activities ranging from catamaran sailing to nightly movies; activities for those over 12 include free cooking demonstrations, Hawaiian arts and crafts, complimentary fun runs, aerobics classes, and a historic walk of Waikiki. You "play and charge" at Waikiki's other Sheraton hotels as well as at the Makaha Golf Club's golf and tennis facilities.

★ **Waikiki Parc.** 2233 Helumoa Rd. (at Lewers St.), Honolulu, HI 96815. ☎ **800/422-0450** or 808/921-7272. Fax 808/923-1336. www.waikikiparchotel.com. 298 units. A/C MINIBAR TV TEL. $170–$255 double. Extra person $30; children 14 and under stay free. Ask about room/car, bed-and-breakfast, and 50%-off second-room packages. AE, CB, DC, JCB, MC, V. Valet parking $9. Bus: 19 or 20.

Terrifically located just 100 yards from the beach, this hotel is for people who want the elegance, grace, and style of the Halekulani but just can't quite afford their rates. Tucked just behind the Halekulani and owned and operated by the same company, the Waikiki Parc offers beautifully appointed rooms at affordable prices. The compact guest rooms all have lanais with ocean, mountain, or city views; ceramic-tile floors with plush carpeting; and a conversation area with a writing desk and rattan couch and chair. Nice extras include a refrigerator, minibar, two phones, a safe, and adjustable floor-to-ceiling shutters for those who want to sleep in.

The Parc features the same level of service that has made the Halekulani famous. On a recent visit, we asked room service for a few items that were not exactly on the menu; they not only happily complied, but the manager checked back later to make sure we got what we wanted. We requested an out-of-town newspaper one day; the bellman said he would deliver it to our room every day, no problem. We called the valet desk and asked directions to get to an out-of-the-way location; when we picked up our car, the valet desk handed us a map with the route highlighted in yellow.

Dining/Diversions: Two excellent restaurants: With its garden-terrace atmosphere, the Parc Cafe serves fabulous buffet-style meals featuring island specialties (see complete review under "Dining" below), while Kacho, one of Hawaii's few Kyoto-style restaurants, is a charming oasis for devotees of sushi and Japanese seafood dishes.

Amenities: Concierge desk, twice-daily maid service, secretarial and other business services, wheelchair accessibility to all public areas, room service. Freshwater pool on the eighth-floor recreation deck, a great stretch of Waikiki Beach nearby.

Moderate

✪ **Hawaiiana Hotel.** 260 Beach Walk (near Kalakaua Ave.), Honolulu, HI 96815. ☎ **800/535-0085** or 808/923-3811. Fax 808/926-5728. www.marcresorts.com. E-mail marc@aloha.net. 95 units (some with shower only). A/C TV TEL. High season $139–$239 double; low season $119–$219 double. Extra person $15. AE, DC, DISC, JCB, MC, V. Parking $8. Bus: 19 or 20.

"The spirit of old Hawaii"—the hotel's slogan says it all. The lush tropical flowers and carved tiki at the entrance on tiny Beach Walk set the tone for this intimate low-rise hotel. From the moment you arrive, you'll be embraced by aloha spirit: At check-in, you'll be given a pineapple; every morning, complimentary Kona coffee and tropical juice are served poolside; and at checkout, flower leis are presented to female guests as a fragrant reminder of their time at the Hawaiiana. The concrete hollow-tiled rooms feature a kitchenette (small refrigerator, two-burner hot plate, toaster oven, and coffeemaker), two beds (a double and a single), TV, phone, and a view of the gardens and swimming pool. The staff provides complimentary use of the washers and dryers. Hawaiian entertainment is featured every week. The hotel is about a block from the beach and within walking distance of Waikiki shopping and nightlife.

Inexpensive

Aloha Punawai. 305 Saratoga Rd. (across from Ft. DeRussy and the Waikiki Post Office, between Kalia Rd. and Kalakaua Ave.), Honolulu, HI 96815. ☎ **808/923-5211.** Fax 808/622-4688. 18 units (studios have showers only). TV. **$53–$75** studio double, $73–$110 one-bedroom double (sleeps up to 5). Extra person $10; children under 15 stay free. 3-night minimum; discounts for week-long (or longer) stays. MC, V. Parking $7. Bus: 19 or 20.

Here's one of Waikiki's best-kept secrets: A low-profile, family-operated (since 1959) apartment hotel just two blocks from the beach and within walking distance of most Waikiki attractions. Aloha Punawai has some of the lowest prices in Waikiki (if you stay a week, prices drop even more). And the location is great, just across the street from Fort DeRussy Park and two blocks to Gray's Beach—the same great beach facing the luxury Halekulani and Sheraton Waikiki hotels. The apartments have a mishmash of furniture and come with complete kitchens, private bath, lanai, and TV. Don't expect the Ritz (or any interior decoration, for that matter)—just clean accommodations in a great location. Towels and linen are provided, and a coin-operated washer and dryer are on the property. The phone wiring has been installed and is ready for service; you have to pay for hookup.

The Breakers, 250 Beach Walk (between Kalakaua Ave. and Kalia Rd.), Honolulu, HI 96815. ☎ **800/426-0494** or 808/923-3181. Fax 808/923-7174. E-mail tmcd@aloha.net. www.breakers-hawaii.com. 64 units (with shower only). A/C TV TEL. $91-$97 double. Extra person $8. AE, DC, MC, V. Limited free parking; $6-$8 across the street. Bus: 19 or 20.

A little gem in the midst of high-rise Waikiki, The Breakers is full of old-fashioned Hawaiian aloha—and it's only steps from fabulous Waikiki Beach. This two-story hotel has a friendly staff and a loyal following, with more than 70% returning for another stay. Its six buildings are set around a pool and a tropical garden blooming with brilliant red and yellow hibiscus; wooden jalousies and shoji doors further the tropical ambiance. The tastefully decorated, slightly oversized rooms come with a lanai and a kitchenette with two-burner stove, toaster oven, and fridge. The poolside bar and grill serves cocktails and heavy pupus. Every Wednesday and Friday, you're invited to a formal Japanese tea ceremony from 10am to noon.

Hale Pua Nui Hotel. 228 Beach Walk (across from Helumoa St.), Honolulu, HI 96815. ☎ **808/923-9693.** Fax 808/923-9678. E-mail halepua@aloha.net. 22 units (baths have showers only). TV TEL. High season $57 double; low season $45 double. 3-night minimum. MC, V. Parking $5. Bus: 19 or 20.

This four-story studio-apartment complex is a real find for budget travelers. Don't expect the luxury of the Halekulani—or even the modern look of a budget Outrigger. Built motel-style (with a series of doors down an outside hallway), Hale Pua Nui features clean, older units at 1970s prices. The large studios have seen better days—the furniture's worn, and the carpet is showing its age—but the bargain rates make up for the lack of luxury. The one-room units have two single beds, a TV, a small table, a kitchenette (small refrigerator, oven, stove, and toaster), and a phone. The Beach Walk location puts you just 1½ blocks from the beach, 1½ blocks from a bus stop, and within walking distance of restaurants, nightclubs, and other Waikiki activities.

Kai Aloha Apartment Hotel. 235 Saratoga Rd. (across from Ft. DeRussy and Waikiki Post Office, between Kalakaua Ave. and Kalia Rd.), Honolulu, HI 96815. ☎ **808/923-6723.** Fax 808/922-7592. 18 units. A/C TV TEL. $65-$70 studio double, $73-$76 one-bedroom double, $85-$90 one-bedroom for 3, $95-$100 one-bedroom for 4, $110-$115 one-bedroom for 5. 3-night minimum. AE, DC, JCB, MC, V. Parking $8. Bus: 19 or 20.

If you want to experience what Waikiki was like 25 or 30 years ago, stay here. This small, Hawaiian-style apartment hotel just a block from the beach reminds us of the low-key hotels that used to line the blocks of Waikiki in the good old days. It offers one-bedroom apartments and studios, both furnished in modest rattan and colorful island prints. The one-bedrooms have either a queen bed or two twins in the bedroom, and the living room is outfitted with a couch and two additional twins (Hawaiian houses of 30 years ago all had extra beds in the living room, called *punee,* for guests to sleep on), plus a dining table, TV, and phone with voice mail; the room is even large enough to accommodate a roll-away bed for a fifth person. The kitchens have a ¾-size refrigerator, full oven, and everything you need to cook up meals for a big family. Glass jalousies take advantage of the cooling trade winds, but there's also an air conditioner for the very hot days. The studios have two twin beds, a kitchenette with a two-burner hot plate and a small refrigerator, a balcony, a Plexiglas roof in the bathroom (the forerunner of the skylight), TV, phone with voice mail, and a screen

In case you want to see the world.

At American Express, we're here to make your journey a smooth one. So we have over 1,700 travel service locations in over 120 countries ready to help. What else would you expect from the world's largest travel agency?

do more

In case you want to be welcomed there.

We're here to see that you're always welcomed at establishments everywhere. That's why millions of people carry the American Express® Card—for peace of mind, confidence, and security, around the world or just around the corner.

do more

American Express Cards

In case you're
running low,

We're here to help with more than 118,000 Express Cash
locations around the world. In order to enroll, just call
American Express before you start your vacation.

Express
Cash

do more

And just in case,

We're here with American Express® Travelers Cheques and Cheques *for Two*® They're the safest way to carry money on your vacation and the surest way to get a refund, practically anywhere, anytime.

Another way we help you....

do more

Travelers Cheques

door for ventilation. The units aren't exactly designer showrooms, but they do have a homey, comfortable feeling—and you're sure to forgive the lack of aesthetics when you're presented with the bill. A large deck on the second floor is a great place to sip early-morning coffee or watch the sun sink into the Pacific.

Malihini Hotel. 217 Saratoga Rd. (across from Ft. DeRussy, near Kalia Rd.), Honolulu, HI 96815. ☎ **808/923-9644.** 28 studios (some with shower only), 10 units (studios have shower only). TEL. $45–$85 double. Extra person $2–$5. 3-night minimum Dec–Apr. No credit cards. Parking $7–$10. Bus: 19 or 20.

The promotional literature for this two-story hotel describes it as a "small, plain hotel with no extra frills, just a place to stay in an excellent location." That just about sums it up. The location is excellent: a half-block from the beach(!), with shopping and restaurants (including McDonald's) just around the corner. A solid lava wall blocks out the noise of busy Saratoga Road—as soon as you enter the brick courtyard, with its red picnic tables and brick barbecue, the only sounds you'll hear are the chirps of the hotel's parakeets. Three types of units are available: compact studios, lanai studios, and one-bedroom apartments. The compact studios have either twin beds or a king, plus a shower and a kitchenette (small refrigerator, oven, four-burner stove, and toaster); the lanai studios are larger and have their own lanai or garden patio that allows cross-ventilation from the trade winds. The one-bedrooms, which can sleep up to five, have a full bath, additional twin beds in the living room, and a full kitchen. The decor isn't fancy—linoleum floors, well-used furniture, and just the basics. But hey, for $45 a night, you'll get more than your money's worth here.

MID-WAIKIKI, MAUKA

These mid-Waikiki hotels, on the mountain side of Kalakaua Avenue, are a little farther away from the beach than those listed above. They're all between Kalakaua Avenue and Ala Wai Boulevard, and between Kalaimoku Street in the Ewa direction and Kaiulani Street in the Diamond Head direction.

Moderate

✪ **Coconut Plaza.** 450 Lewers St. (at Ala Wai Blvd.), Honolulu, HI 96815. ☎ **800/882-9696** or 808/923-8828. Fax 808/923-3473. 80 units. A/C TV TEL. $110 double, $130–$160 double with kitchenette, $225 suite with kitchenette. Rates include continental breakfast. Extra person $12. AE, DC, DISC, JCB, MC, V. Parking $9. Bus: 19 or 20.

This small hotel is an island of integrity in a sea of tourist schlock. Calling itself a "studio apartment boutique hotel," the Coconut Plaza offers a few perks that are rare in Waikiki: complimentary continental breakfast and the kind of personalized service that only a small hotel can offer. The recently renovated hotel has a tropical-plantation feel, with big, airy rooms, terra-cotta tile, and lots of greenery. The island-style rooms have been redone in rattan and earth tones; all have a private lanai; TV; ceramic-tile bath, and daily maid service. The majority of the rooms have kitchenettes—with minifridge, microwave, countertop range, coffeemaker, and cooking utensils—and most have views of the Ala Wai Canal and the mountains. There's an outdoor pool, a sundeck, exercise equipment, and a tour desk on the property; Ala Wai Golf Course is just across the canal, and the beach is four blocks away.

Coral Reef Hotel. 2299 Kuhio Ave. (at Duke's Lane), Honolulu, HI 96815. ☎ **800/92-ASTON** or 808/922-1262. Fax 808/922-5048 or 808/922-8785. www.aston-hotels.com. 247 units. A/C TV TEL. $100–$135 double, $115–$150 junior suite, $130–$165 one-bedroom suite (sleeps up to 4). Ask about Island Hopper rates, which give you 20–30% off if you stay at Aston properties for 7 or more consecutive nights. Extra person $18. AE, CB, DC, DISC, JCB, MC, V. Limited parking $10. Bus: 19 or 20.

If you're looking for a roomy, medium-priced hotel and don't mind a brisk walk to the beach, this 15-story Aston-operated hotel may be the one for you. It was built in 1969, when Waikiki was a totally different place, but was totally renovated in 1995–96. The rooms were brought into the '90s, both in decor and amenities—they now offer a small refrigerator, a small lanai, TV, and phone. Rates are based on views: The higher up you go, the better the view—and the higher the price. Facilities include a pool, cocktail lounge, two restaurants, sundry shops, and travel desk. Located one block from the International Market Place and Kuhio Mall and three blocks from the beach, the Coral Reef has a good central location. The only problem is that Kuhio Avenue is very busy, and very noisy, both day and night.

⭐ **Royal Kuhio.** 2240 Kuhio Ave. (between Royal Hawaiian Ave. and Seaside Ave.), c/o Paradise Mgmt., 50 S. Beretania St., Suite C207, Honolulu, HI 96813. ☎ **800/367-5205** or 808/538-7145. Fax 808/533-4621. 389 units. A/C TV TEL. $95–$120 apt for 4. Extra person $15. MC, V. Free parking. Bus: 19 or 20.

Families take note: This is one of the best deals in Waikiki. All the units in this high-rise condo are privately owned, and some are owner-occupied. Paradise Management is just one of several companies handling apartments here, but their units—and their rates—are among the best. All have full kitchens, separate bedrooms, living area with TV and phones, and lanai. Since each unit is individually owned, they're all decorated and furnished differently. The complex has a pool, exercise room, sauna, self-service Laundromat, sundeck, volleyball, billiards, basketball court, shuffleboard, and putting green. It's two blocks to Waikiki Beach, and everything else Waikiki has to offer is within walking distance. *Hot tips:* Ask for a corner unit (they're the nicest); and if you plan to go in February, be sure to book a year in advance (it's the condo's busiest month).

Waikiki Beachcomber. 2300 Kalakaua Ave. (at Duke's Lane), Honolulu, HI 96815. ☎ **800/622-4646** or 808/923-4646. Fax 808/923-4889. dps.net/~beachcomber. E-mail beach@dps.net. 500 units. A/C TV TEL. High season $160–$205 double, $295 suite; low season $150–$195 double, $285 suite. Room/car packages from $119.95. Extra person $18. 2-night minimum for packages. AE, DC, JCB, MC, V. Parking $6. Bus: 19 or 20.

The room/car package makes this stylish Waikiki hotel a real deal. One of its main plusses is the great location: a block from Waikiki Beach, just across the street from the upscale Royal Hawaiian Shopping Center, and next door to bargain shopping at the International Market Place. All 500 rooms were upgraded in 1996 with Berber carpets, new beds, TV armoires (which also created more drawer space), contemporary furniture, handheld showers, convenient hot pots for making coffee or tea, and a state-of-the-art voice-messaging system.

The Beachcomber is Waikiki's only hotel with its own rooftop vegetable farm—yes, a farm in Waikiki. This urban hydroponic project has been so successful that it's now a two-level, 3,000-square-foot garden growing a variety of lettuces, gourmet cucumbers, cherry tomatoes, and a host of herbs. Want to sample the goods? The hotel's Hibiscus Cafe features the hydroponic produce.

Yet another reason to stay at this conveniently located hotel: It's the home of the legendary Don "Tiny Bubbles" Ho Show.

⭐ **Waikiki Joy.** 320 Lewers St. (at Kuhio Ave.), Honolulu, HI 96815. ☎ **800/92-ASTON** or 808/923-2300. Fax 808/924-4010. www.aston-hotels.com. 194 units. A/C TV TEL. $160–$170 double, $180–$195 club suite, $215–$230 junior suite with kitchen (sleeps up to 4), $265–$280 one-bedroom executive suite with kitchen (up to 3). Rates include continental breakfast. Extra person $18. Ask about the Island Hopper rates, which give you 20–30% off if you stay 7 or more consecutive nights with Aston. AE, CB, DC, DISC, JCB, MC, V. Parking $10. Bus: 19 or 20.

This is one hotel that truly deserves its name. An oasis right in the heart of busy Waikiki, this hidden jewel offers not only outstanding personal service but also a Bose entertainment system and a Jacuzzi in every room! The Italian marble-accented open-air lobby and the tropical veranda—with swimming pool, sauna, and furnished deck—set the scene for the beautifully decorated guest rooms. The doubles, decorated in soft pastels, have a marble entry, a refrigerator, a safe, and a lanai wide enough for you to sit and enjoy the views. The suites are even more luxurious: Club suites have either a king bed or two doubles, a refrigerator, microwave, coffeemaker, and wet bar. Executive suites have two double beds and a kitchen with a microwave and full refrigerator; the executive king suites add a separate living room and bedroom. Every room comes with voice mail, as well as fax and modem hookups. Still, there are a couple of downsides you should be aware of: The beach is four or five blocks away (a 10- to 15-minute walk), and there's a sandwich/coffee shop on site, but the food's nothing to brag about, and the fact that they allow smoking in the tiny restaurant makes for a very unappetizing atmosphere.

Inexpensive

Outrigger Surf. 2280 Kuhio Ave. (at Nohonani St.), Honolulu, HI 96815. ☎ **800/OUTRIGGER** or 808/922-5777. Fax 800/622-4852 or 808/921-3677. www.outrigger.com. 251 rms (with showers only). A/C TV TEL. $80–$100 double with kitchenette; $125 triple studio with kitchenette. Extra person $15. AE, DC, DISC, JCB, MC, V. Parking $8. TheBus: 19 or 20.

The Outrigger chain makes sure that it has a hotel to suit every budget and every need; this one has kitchenettes—with a two-burner stove, oven, refrigerator, coffeemaker, and cooking utensils—in every room. The hotel was extensively renovated in 1995, and the rooms were outfitted with new bedspreads, chairs, refurbished furniture, new TVs, and new fridges. The Surf is centrally located, across the street from the Kuhio Mall and 2 blocks from the beach. Restaurants and nightlife are also within walking distance, and there's a pool, a steak house, and an activity desk on-site.

✪ **Ilima Hotel.** 445 Nohonani St. (at Ala Wai Blvd.), Honolulu, HI 96815. ☎ **800/801-9366** or 808/923-1877. Fax 808/924-8371. www.pete.com/ilima. E-mail mail@ilima.com. 99 units. A/C TV TEL. $86–$127 double; $132–$166 one-bedroom (sleeps up to 3); $175–$229 two-bedroom (up to 4); $267–$279 three-bedroom (up to 6). Extra person $8. Discounts available for seniors. AE, CB, DC, DISC, JCB, MC, V. Limited free parking, $8 across the street. Bus: 19 or 20.

The Teruya Brothers, owners of Hawaii's Times Supermarket, wanted to offer comfortable accommodations that Hawaii residents could afford, and they've succeeded. One of Hawaii's small, well-located condo-style hotels, the 17-story pale pink Ilima (named for the native orange flower used in royal leis) offers value for your money: Rooms are huge, the location (near the International Marketplace and the Royal Hawaiian Shopping Center, two blocks to Waikiki Beach) is great, and prices are low. A tasteful koa-wood lobby lined with works by Hawaiian artists greets you upon arrival. There's a 24-hour front desk, daily maid service, free local phone calls (a nice plus), and a full kitchen in every unit; all the couches fold out into beds, making this a particularly good deal for families. Some of the beds are waveless waterbeds. There's a heated pool, three sundecks, a dry sauna, and an Italian restaurant on-site. Sorry, there's no ocean view—what you get is great value instead.

Marine Surf. 364 Seaside Ave. (at Kuhio Ave.), Honolulu, HI 96815. ☎ **888/456-SURF** or 808/923-0277. Fax 808/926-5915. 110 units. A/C TV TEL. $80–$103 double; $150–$175 one-bedroom penthouse suite. Extra person $10. CB, DC, DISC, MC, V. Parking $5. Bus: 19 or 20.

Located in the heart of Waikiki, this high-rise is part privately owned condo units and part spacious studio apartments—only the studios are available for rent. Each one has a complete kitchen (refrigerator, stove/oven, toaster, coffeepot, and utensils), phone, two extralong double beds, TV, and a small lanai. The price difference depends on the view. *Hot tip:* The best views are from floors 17 to 22 ($90 in the summer and fall, $95 midsummer, and $103 in the winter). Located just a half-block from Kuhio Mall and the International Market Place, the hotel is just about 1½ blocks from the beach. Facilities include tour desk, pool, coin-operated laundry on every floor, and an Italian restaurant.

⭐ **Patrick Winston's Waikiki Condos.** 417 Nohonani St. (between Kuhio Ave. and Ala Wai Blvd.), Honolulu, HI 96815. ☎ **800/545-1948** or 808/924-3332. Fax 808/924-3332. E-mail winston@global-aloha.com. 11 one-bedroom apts. (with shower only). A/C TV TEL. High season $85–$119 double; low season $65–$99 double. Extra person $10. 4-night minimum. AE, DC, DISC, MC, V. Parking $7. Bus: 19 or 20.

For a luxurious experience with a hefty dose of old-fashioned aloha, we recommend Patrick Winston's rentals. When this five-story condominium hotel was built in 1981, Winston bought one unit; he has since acquired 10 more, spent some $200,000 on refurbishment, and put his elegant suites on the market at budget prices. Located on a quiet side street, Winston's units are actually a hotel within a hotel: He owns, runs, cleans, renovates, and services all his units himself—and he makes sure no guest leaves unhappy. Staying here is like having a personal concierge; he'll even give you a wakeup call. He wants to make sure that his guests enjoy Hawaii, and he's got lots of terrific tips on where to eat, where to shop, and how to get the most for your money. We get lots of glowing letters from readers telling us how much they loved both Patrick and the accommodations.

Patrick has three types of units available: one-bedroom suites, ground-floor junior business suites, and corporate business suites. All have sofabeds, separate bedrooms, lanais with breakfast table and chairs, air-conditioning and ceiling fans, TV (VCRs available on request), phone, and full kitchens; most have a washer and dryer. All are individually decorated, from the Blue Hawaiian suite (done in all blues) to the Mount Fuji suite (done in Asian style). There's an on-site cocktail lounge and a tropical courtyard with a pool. Waikiki Beach is just two blocks away, shopping is just a half-block away, and restaurants are within a 5- to 10-minute walk.

Warning: make sure that you ask for Patrick Winston's units, or the front desk at the Hawaiian King Hotel may put you in one of their units, which may not be quiet as elegant (or as inexpensive) at Patrick's units.

DIAMOND HEAD WAIKIKI

You'll find all these hotels between Ala Wai Boulevard and the ocean, and between Kaiulani Street (one block Diamond Head from the International Marketplace) in the Ewa direction and world-famous Diamond Head itself.

Expensive

✪ **Aston Waikiki Beachside Hotel.** 2452 Kalakaua Ave. (between Uluniu and Liliuokalani aves.), Honolulu, HI 96815. ☎ **800/922-7866** or 808/931-2100. Fax 808/922-2129. www.aston-hotels.com. 79 units. A/C TV TEL. $180–$320 double, $295–$375 junior suite. Rates includes continental breakfast. No more than 2 adults per room. Seniors 50 and older get 25% off rates and 7th night free, depending on availability. Ask about the Island Hopper rates, which give you 20–30% off if you stay 7 or more consecutive nights with Aston. AE, CB, DC, DISC, JCB, MC, V. Parking $10 at nearby hotel. Bus: 19 or 20.

This luxury boutique hotel is right across the street from Waikiki Beach. There's a feeling of elegance and charm throughout this intimate place: You step off busy Kalakaua Avenue into a marble-filled lobby with classical music wafting in the background, sprays of flowers everywhere, and a soothing Italian fountain. The staff is attentive to every detail. The rooms are tiny but tastefully decorated with works of art and antiques (including hand-painted Oriental screens and 18th-century furniture). Each has its own air-conditioning system, refrigerator, complimentary safe, complimentary daily newspaper, and two phones.

Dining/Diversions: There's no on-site restaurant, but a complimentary continental breakfast is served daily in the lobby. On Saturday and Sunday, a high-tea service, on antique china, is presented in the lobby and courtyard.

Amenities: Concierge, twice-daily maid service, morning newspaper, same-day laundry and dry cleaning.

Colony Surf. 2885 Kalakaua Ave. (on the ocean side between the Waikiki Aquarium and Outrigger Canoe Club), Honolulu, HI 96815. ☎ **888/924-SURF** or 808/924-3111. Fax 808/923-2249. 75 units (with shower only). A/C TV TEL. West Building (all units with full kitchens) $175–$240 studio, $285–$425 ocean-view studio; East Building $225–$275 double, from $425 suite. Rates include complimentary breakfast. AE, DC, DISC, JCB, MC, V. Free parking. Bus: 19 or 20.

This elegant, two-building condominium, fronting its own white-sand beach in the quieter Diamond Head section of town, has been totally renovated. The West Building is the Colony Surf condominium, where rental units are mixed with full-time residential studio apartments. The units are all large (1,000 square feet); studios come complete with a kitchen and double beds or one giant king bed, large bathrooms, and views of Waikiki or Diamond Head that are worth every penny you'll pay. The East Building is back off the beach with rooms of about 500 square feet; each has a small refrigerator, coffeemaker, hair dryer, safe, and views of Diamond Head.

If you're craving peace and quiet, away from the crowds of Waikiki but close enough (about a 10-minute walk) to enjoy the shops and restaurants, this is a perfect location. The surrounding buildings are mainly residential condos; Kapiolani Park is across the street, and the Waikiki Aquarium is just a few steps away. Both buildings have access to the small, private beach in front of the Colony Surf (great swimming here); complimentary beach chairs and towels are provided.

Dining/Diversions: Chef David Paul Johnson has brought his award-winning American cuisine from Maui to the East Building, where David Paul's Diamond Head Grill opened in March 1998 (see complete review under "Dining," below). For award-winning French cuisine in an elegant oceanfront setting, Michel's Restaurant is in the West Building.

Amenities: Daily complimentary breakfast, CD player and Hawaiian music CDs, daily newspaper, complimentary overnight shoe shine, daily maid service, complimentary beach equipment.

Hyatt Regency Waikiki. 2424 Kalakaua Ave. (at Kaiulani St., across the street from the beach), Honolulu, HI 96815. ☎ **800/233-1234** or 808/923-1234. Fax 808/923-7839. www.hyatt.com. E-mail hnw@pixi.com. 1,241 units. A/C MINIBAR TV TEL. $215–$375 double, $375–$450 Regency Club double, from $550 suite. Extra person $25 ($45 Regency Club); children under 19 stay free using existing bedding. AE, CB, DC, DISC, JCB, MC, V. Valet parking $10; self-parking $8. Bus: 19 or 20.

This is one of Waikiki's biggest hotels, a $100-million project sporting two 40-story towers and covering nearly an entire city block, just across the street from the Diamond Head end of Waikiki Beach. Some will find this Goliath of a hotel to be too big and impersonal, some may love the location, and some will get lost just trying to find the registration desk. The second-floor lobby is huge, decorated in koa and wrapped around an atrium that rises *40 floors* up from the ground level, and filled with the squawks of parrots and cigarette smoke (Hyatt allows smoking in the lobby, and it can get pretty cloudy in there at times).

The guest rooms are roomy, and a $10-million investment refurbished them in 1996. Every room has a coffeemaker, but the coffee isn't free—even though you are paying a minimum of $215 a night, expect to pay $3 extra per package of coffee. Other amenities such as hair dryers, bathrobes, irons and ironing boards, are complimentary. The deluxe ocean-view rooms overlooking Waikiki Beach are fabulous but can be noisy (traffic on Kalakaua is constant). For a few dollars more (well, actually more than a few dollars), you can upgrade to the Regency Club floors, where the rooms are nicer (and the coffee is free); the club entitles you to an expedited check-in and entry to the Regency Club—which serves complimentary continental breakfast, pupus in the afternoon, and concierge service all day—and a private rooftop sundeck and Jacuzzi.

Dining/Diversions: Four restaurants and five cocktail lounges, including an indoor-outdoor grill overlooking the ocean; a Japanese restaurant; a steak-and-seafood house; Harry's Bar, featuring Hawaiian and Polynesian entertainment; Ciao Mein for creative Chinese and Italian cuisine served family-style (for a complete review, see "Dining," below); the Texas Rock 'N Roll Sushi Bar, a combination of country western/rock club serving Tex Mex cuisine and sushi; and an elegant poolside bar.

Amenities: Multilingual concierge, business services (including typing, personal-computer rental, stock news, notary public), baby-sitting, Camp Hyatt program for kids, room service (6am–11pm), valet service, travel desks (airline-ticket counter, American Express, Budget, Hertz), doctor's office, bank, more than 60 shops. World-famous Waikiki is directly across the street, but you can also swim and sun at the third-floor pool.

Moderate

Aston at the Waikiki Banyan. 201 Ohua Ave. (on mountain side, at Kuhio Ave.), Honolulu, HI 96815. ☎ **800/922-7866** or 808/922-0555. Fax 808/922-8785. www.aston-hotels.com. 307 one-bedroom apts. A/C TV TEL. $145–$205 double. Seniors 50 and older get 25% and 7th night free, depending on availability; ask about Island Hopper rates that give you 20–30% off if you stay at Aston properties for 7 or more consecutive nights. Extra person $18. AE, CB, DC, DISC, JCB, MC, V. Parking $5. Bus: 19 or 20.

The one-bedrooms here combined the homey comforts of a condo apartment with the amenities of a hotel: daily maid service, bell service, front desk, coin-op laundry, a sundry store, and much more, including an enormous sixth-floor recreation deck complete with pool, tennis court, sauna, barbecue areas, snack bar, and a children's play area—a great boon for families. Your first introduction to this two-tower, 38-story complex is through the open-air lobby with impressive lacquer artwork, hand-carved and hand-painted in Hong Kong. The units have full kitchens (refrigerator, oven, microwave, rice cooker, toaster, coffeemaker, and utensils), a comfortably furnished living room (with sofabed), and a separate bedroom with two double beds or a king; the bedroom is separated from the living room by sliding doors, which can be opened to make the apartment one big unit. The one we stayed in had an old-fashioned air conditioner in the wall, but it did the job, and we could control the temperature. The apartments open out to a fairly good-sized lanai with chairs and a small table; there's a partial ocean view, with some buildings blocking the way.

✪ **Diamond Head Bed & Breakfast.** Noela Dr. (at Paki Ave., off Diamond Head Rd.), Honolulu. c/o Hawaii's Best Bed & Breakfasts, P.O. Box 563, Kamuela, HI 96743.

☎ **800/262-9912** or 808/885-4550. Fax 808/885-0559. www.bestbnb.com. E-mail bestbnb@aloha.net. 3 units. TV TEL. $100 double, $125 suite. Rates include large breakfast. Extra person $25. 2-night minimum. DISC. Free parking. Bus: 2.

Hostess Joanne and her longtime housekeeper Sumiko offer a quiet, relaxing place to stay on the far side of Kapiolani Park, away from the hustle and bustle of Waikiki. Staying here is like venturing back in time to about 50 years ago, when *kamaaina* (native-born) families built huge houses with airy rooms opening outward, via sliding wood-screen doors, to big lanais and tropical gardens. The house is filled with family heirlooms and Joanne's artwork. One room features the beyond-king-size carved koa bed that once belonged to Princess Ruth, a member of Hawaii's royal family; you'll feel like royalty sleeping in it. Other conveniences in the large room include a refrigerator, a TV, a bathroom (big enough to dance in) with an old-fashioned tub, and a large lanai facing Diamond Head. The other room in the house has two double koa beds, a lanai overlooking Waikiki through sweet-smelling plumeria trees, a TV, a fridge, and another large bathroom. A separate building houses the antique-filled Grandpa's Apartment, featuring a separate bedroom, a TV, phone, refrigerator, and a view of Diamond Head from the bed.

New Otani Kaimana Beach Hotel. 2863 Kalakaua Ave. (ocean side of the street just Diamond Head of the Waikiki Aquarium, across from Kapiolani Park), Honolulu, HI 96815. ☎ **800/35-OTANI** or 808/923-1555. Fax 808/922-9404. www.kaimana.com. E-mail kaimana@pixi.net. 124 units. A/C MINIBAR TV TEL. $115–$260 double; $180–$620 suite. Extra person $15. AE, CB, DC, DISC, JCB, MC, V. Parking $6. Bus: 19 or 20.

This is one of Waikiki's best-kept secrets: a boutique hotel nestled right on a lovely stretch of beach, at the foot of Diamond Head, with Kapiolani Park just across the street. Robert Louis Stevenson's description of the beach fronting the hotel, Sans Souci, holds true today: "If anyone desires lovely scenery, pure air, clear sea water, good food, and heavenly sunsets, I recommend him cordially to the Sans Souci."

The hotel has two buildings: On the Waikiki side, the rooms open to an atrium courtyard, and on the Diamond Head side, they feature kitchenettes. The Waikiki-side rooms are tiny but tastefully decorated in pale pastels, and they open out to large lanais with ocean and park views. Since the hotel overlooks Kapiolani Park, guests have easy access to activities such as golf, tennis, kite-flying, jogging, and bicycling; kayaking and snorkeling are available at the beach. The hotel also arranges for visitors to climb to the top of Diamond Head. The airy lobby opens onto the alfresco Hau Tree Lanai restaurant, a delightful beachfront restaurant that's one of the most romantic spots in Hawaii, set under the same banyan tree that sheltered Robert Louis Stevenson a century ago (see "Dining" below for a complete review). Miyako Restaurant offers gourmet Japanese dining with an ocean view. The beachfront ✪ **Sunset Lanai Lounge** is great for cocktails.

This is a nice hotel, but I had a couple of complaints when I stayed here: The air conditioner was positioned right over the bed, so you either had frigid air blowing on you all night or nothing, and the check-out staff at the front desk was not only slow but extremely unhelpful—and we've received a few letters from our readers with the very same complaints.

Queen Kapiolani Hotel. 150 Kapahulu Ave. (at Cartwright St., across from Kapiolani Park), Honolulu, HI 96815. ☎ **800/367-5004** or 808/922-1941. Fax 808/596-0518 or 808/922-2694. 315 units. A/C TV TEL. $107–$160 double, $157–$175 studio double with kitchenette, $250–$305 one-bedroom suite with kitchenette (sleeps up to 4). Extra person $17; children 18 and younger stay free using existing bedding. AE, CB, DC, DISC, JCB, MC, V. Parking $7. Bus: 19 or 20.

Named for Queen Kapiolani (1834–99), the wife of Hawaii's last king, David Kalakaua (1836–91), this hotel harkens back to the days of the Hawaiian monarchs. The 19th-century flavor of the hotel reflects those grand days with 10-foot chandeliers in the main dining room and a full-size portrait of the queen in the lobby. The plush decor, however, doesn't extend up to the budget rooms, which are quite small; you'll have a view of the shoreline through louvered windows, a small refrigerator, coffeemaker, phone, and TV. But the location is great: just across the street from Kapiolani Park, a half-block to the beach, and within walking distance of the Honolulu Zoo, the Waikiki Aquarium, and the activities of Waikiki. A large swimming pool and sundeck are on the third floor.

Waikiki Resort Hotel. 2460 Koa Ave. (at Liliuokalani Ave.), Honolulu, HI 96815. ☎ **800/367-5116** or 808/922-4911. Fax 808/922-9468. 296 units. A/C TV TEL. **$105–$145** double; **$145–$155** double with kitchenette, **$315–$470** penthouse suite. Excellent package deals, including room-and-breakfast buffet for **$115–$125** and room/car package for **$115–$125**; room/car/breakfast packages are **$125–$135**. Extra person **$15**; children under 17 stay free using existing bedding. AE, DISC, JCB, MC, V. Parking $5. Bus: 19 or 20.

On a quiet street one block from the beach is this 19-story hotel, offering quality rooms at budget prices. Owned by Korean Air, the recently renovated hotel has a huge marble lobby dominated by a stained-glass mural of the ocean. The rooms are decorated with tropical textiles and come with refrigerators, lanais, safes, a TV, and either two double beds or a king. The higher the floor, the better the view—and the more expensive the room, of course. If you're on a budget, consider getting a room with a kitchenette, which will save you money on food; these are also the corner units, which have great views.

Ilima Cafe features a breakfast buffet and lunch and dinner daily, while the Camellia Restaurant is one of Waikiki's few Korean restaurants. There are also two lounges: one at poolside, and one featuring dancing nightly. Other amenities include a freshwater pool, sundry and gift shops, an activities desk, laundry, and free transportation to the airport upon departure. Front-desk personnel are fluent in English, Korean, and Japanese.

Inexpensive

Royal Grove Hotel. 151 Uluniu Ave. (between Prince Edward and Kuhio aves.), Honolulu, HI 96815. ☎ **808/923-7691.** Fax 808/922-7508. 85 units. A/C TV TEL. **$42.50** double (no A/C), **$75** one-bedroom (no A/C); **$57** standard double, **$75** standard one-bedroom, **$75** deluxe double, **$85** deluxe condo double. Extra person $10. AE, DC, MC, V. Parking **$4–$6.50** a day. Bus: 19 or 20.

You can't miss the Royal Grove—it's bright pink. Among Waikiki's canyons of corporate-owned high-rises, it's also a rarity in another way: The Royal Grove is a small, family-owned hotel. What you get here is old-fashioned aloha in old-fashioned, cozy accommodations. For years, *Frommer's* readers have written us about the aloha spirit of the Fong family: They love the potluck dinners and get-togethers the Fongs have organized so their guests can get to know one another. And you can't do better for the price—this has to be *the* bargain of Waikiki. For $42.50 (about the same price a couple would pay to stay in a private room at the hostel in Waikiki) you get a clean room in the older Mauka Wing, with a double bed or two twins, TV, and a kitchenette with refrigerator and stove. We suggest that you spend a few dollars more and go for an air-conditioned room ($57) to help down out the street noise. Even the most expensive room, a one-bedroom suite with three beds, A/C, kitchenette, TV, and lanai, at $85, is half the price of similar accommodations elsewhere.

The hotel is built around a courtyard pool, but the beach is just a 3-minute walk away. All of Waikiki's attractions are within walking distance, including the Honolulu

Zoo, Kapiolani Park, and Waikiki Aquarium. There's a coin-operated laundry and a tour desk on-site. *Hot tip:* Book seven nights or more from April to November, and get a discount on the already low rates.

Waikiki Sand Villa. 2375 Ala Wai Blvd.(entrance is on Kanekapolei Ave.), Honolulu, HI 96815. ☎ **800/247-1903** or 808/922-4744. Fax 808/923-2541. www.planet-hawaii.com/sand. E-mail wsv@aloha.net. 232 units. A/C TV TEL. $70–$114 double, $129–$144 studio with kitchenette. Rates include continental breakfast served poolside every morning. Extra person $15; children under 12 stay free using existing bedding. AE, CB, DC, DISC, JCB, MC, V. Parking $5. Bus: 19 or 20.

Budget travelers should take note of this place. This very affordable hotel is located on the quieter side of Waikiki across the street from the Ala Wai Canal. The 10-story tower has medium-sized rooms, most with a double bed plus a single bed (convenient for families), lanai, refrigerator, and safe, while the three-story Pualeilani building features studio apartments with kitchenettes (refrigerator, stove, and microwave) situated adjacent to the 70-foot pool, which has its own island in the middle and an adjoining whirlpool spa. Another plus for families is the Nintendo system in every room (available at $6.20 an hour). Other facilities include laundry, a hospitality room for late checkout (complete with showers), and a luggage-storage area. A scuba-diving operation is also on the premises.

HONOLULU BEYOND WAIKIKI
ALA MOANA

Ala Moana Hotel. 410 Atkinson Dr. (at Kona St., next to Ala Moana Center), Honolulu, HI 96814. ☎ **800/367-6025** or 808/955-4811. Fax 808/944-2974. www.alamoanahotel.com. E-mail martyamh@gte.net. 1,169 units. A/C TV TEL. $115–$195 double, from $230 suite. Extra person $20; children under 18 stay free. AE, CB, DC, DISC, JCB, MC, V. Valet parking $12, self-parking $8. Bus: 19 or 20.

This hotel is big—1,169 rooms on 36 floors make it feel like a metropolis. Its proximity to Waikiki, the downtown financial and business district, the new convention center, and Hawaii's largest mall, Ala Moana Shopping Center, makes it a popular spot for out-of-state visitors and locals alike. Lots of Asian tourists choose the Ala Moana Hotel, probably because the management does an excellent job of making sure the foreign guests feel welcome by providing a bilingual staff and translators. Shoppers, mostly from neighboring islands, also make up a good percentage of the guests (especially in December). The rooms vary in size according to price: The cheaper rooms are on the smaller side, but all come with two double beds, refrigerator, safe, phones with voice mail, and computer jacks. As a full-service hotel, the Ala Moana offers everything: concierge, room service, valet, laundry, valet parking, a sundeck and pool, games room, and more. With four restaurants, a nightclub, and a Polynesian revue on-site, some guests rarely venture off-property.

Pagoda Hotel. 1525 Rycroft St. (between Keeaumoku and Kaheka sts.), Honolulu, HI 96814. ☎ **800/367-6060** or 808/923-4511. Fax 808/922-8061. 361 units. A/C TV TEL. $85–$95 double, $110 one-bedroom double (sleeps up to 4), $135 one-bedroom double (up to 6), $135 two-bedroom double (up to 5). Extra person $15. AE, DC, DISC, MC, V. Parking $3. Bus: 5 or 6.

This is where local residents from neighbor islands stay when they come to Honolulu. Close to shopping and downtown, the Pagoda has been serving Hawaii's island community for decades. All rooms have a full bath, TV, air-conditioning, phone, and refrigerator; the studios and one and two bedrooms also have kitchenettes. The property features two swimming pools, shops, self-service or valet laundry, and three different restaurants. There's easy access to Waikiki via TheBus—the nearest stop is just a half-block away.

DOWNTOWN

⭐ **Aston at Executive Centre Hotel.** 1088 Bishop St. (at S. Hotel St.), Honolulu, HI 96813. ☎ **800/949-EXEC** or 808/539-3000. Fax 808/523-1088. pr.hula.net/exec_centre. 114 all-suite units. A/C MINIBAR TV TEL. $145–$160 suite, $185–$200 executive suite. Rates include continental breakfast, local calls, and newspaper. Extra person $18; children under 17 stay free. AE, CB, DC, DISC, JCB, MC, V. Parking $10. Bus: 1, 2, 3, 9, 12.

Located in the heart of downtown, this is the perfect hotel for the business traveler. Not only is it close to the business and financial center of Honolulu, but the staff goes out of its way to make sure that every need is met; there's even a 24-hour staffed business center.

The rooms occupy the top 10 floors of a 40-story multiuse, glass-walled tower; each room boasts unobstructed views of the city, the mountains, or the Honolulu Harbor. Each is large enough to qualify as a minisuite, with three phones (with private voice mail), safe, whirlpool bath, hair dryer, iron and ironing board, and coffeemaker. The executive suites feature full kitchens, washer/dryer, and VCR. All guests awaken to a complimentary breakfast and the local newspaper outside their door. Free local phone calls make this hotel a huge plus for the business traveler.

Dining/Diversions: Andrew's Restaurant, which moved from Ward Center to this downtown location, offers breakfast, lunch, and dinner.

Amenities: Concierge, coin-op laundry, same-day laundry and dry-cleaning. The Business Services Center provides a full range of office and secretarial services: personal and laptop computers with a variety of word-processing programs, printers, copy machines, typewriters, and more. A 20-meter outdoor pool and jacuzzi with sundeck; 24-hour fitness center with free weights, aerobic equipment, men's and women's saunas. Small- to medium-sized rooms for business meetings and gatherings, plus two corporate-style boardrooms.

MANOA VALLEY

Bed & Breakfast Manoa & Hillside Cottage. 2651 Terrace Dr. (at Manoa Rd.), Honolulu, HI 96822. ☎ **808/988-6333.** Fax 808/988-5240. E-mail mgm@aloha.net 3 rms (some with shared shower), 1 cottage. TV TEL. $70 double, including breakfast; $120 cottage double, $140 cottage triple. Extra person $10 ($15 in cottage). 3-night minimum. No credit cards. Free parking. Bus: 5.

Hosts Geoffrey Paterson, an architect originally from England, and Maureen McDonough, a writer and native of New Zealand, share their gorgeous home on the hills of Manoa, located 15 minutes from the airport and a 10-minute drive from Waikiki. The rooms, which have either a king or a queen bed, are located upstairs; each has its own TV, radio, and phone, but only one room has a private bath. Breakfast is served on the huge deck that overlooks Manoa Valley, with Diamond Head and Waikiki in the distance. The downstairs cottage (which doesn't include breakfast in the rates) features an indoor-outdoor living room with the same great views and can actually sleep as many as seven people.

⭐ **Manoa Valley Inn.** 2001 Vancouver Dr. (at University Ave.), Honolulu, HI 96822. ☎ **800/535-0085** or 808/947-6019. Fax 808/633-5085 or 808/946-6168. www.marcresorts.com. E-mail marc@marcresorts.com. 8 units (3 with shared bath). TV TEL. $99–$120 double with shared bath, $140–$190 double with private bath (shower only). Rates include continental breakfast and evening wine. Children 14 and older preferred. Inquire about packages. AE, DC, JCB, MC, V. Free parking. Bus: 4 or 6.

It's completely off the tourist trail and far from the beach, but that doesn't stop travelers from heading to this historic 1915 Carpenter Gothic home, on a quiet residential street near the University of Hawaii. This eight-room Manoa landmark—it's on the National Register of Historic Places—offers a glimpse into the lifestyles of the rich and famous in early Honolulu.

Those who prefer to avoid resorts find the eclectically furnished inn refreshing. Each room has its own unique decor, and each has been named for a prominent figure in Hawaii's history: The John Guild Suite, for instance, has a turn-of-the-century parlor with antiques and old-fashioned rose wallpaper; the adjoining bedroom has a king-sized koa bed, and the bath features an old-style tub as well as a separate modern shower. The three top-floor rooms share a full bath, and the others have private baths. All have phones, and some have safes.

A genteel ambiance pervades the place. Guests regularly gather in the parlor to listen to the Victrola or play the nickelodeon. There's also a billiard room with an antique billiard table, a piano in the living room, and croquet set up in the backyard. As the sun sets, complimentary wine and cheese are served on the quiet veranda.

TO THE EAST: KAHALA

✪ **Kahala Mandarin Oriental Hawaii.** 5000 Kahala Ave. (at Kealaolu Ave.), Honolulu, HI 96816. ☎ **800/367-2525** or 808/739-8888. Fax 808/739-8800. www.mandarin-oriental.com. E-mail mohnl@aol.com. 402 units. A/C MINIBAR TV TEL. $295–$650 double, from $590 suite. Extra person $80; children 17 and under stay free. AE, CB, DC, DISC, JCB, MC, V. Parking $12.

Since 1964, when Conrad Hilton first opened it as a place to relax far from the crowds of Waikiki, the Kahala has always been rated one of Hawaii's premiere hotels; a venerable who's who of celebrities have stayed here, including every president since Richard Nixon. Now owned by the Mandarin Oriental chain, renowned for its excellent service, and with $75 million in renovations (completed in March 1996), this grande dame of hotels has reached a new level. It retains the traditional feeling of an earlier time in Hawaii—which defined the Kahala for a generation—accenting it with exotic Asian touches; the result is a resort hotel for the 21st century, but with the grace and elegance of a softer, gentler time. And the location offers a similarly wonderful compromise: Situated in one of Oahu's most prestigious residential areas, the Kahala offers the peace and serenity of a neighbor-island vacation, but with the conveniences of Waikiki just a 10-minute drive away.

All the guest rooms have been totally remodeled with 19th-century mahogany reproductions, teak parquet floors with hand-loomed Tibetan rugs, overstuffed chairs, canopy beds covered with soft throw pillows, and artwork by local artists adorning the grass-cloth-covered walls. Views from the floor-to-ceiling sliding glass doors are of the ocean, Diamond Head, and Koko Head. Some of the more modern conveniences in the rooms include two-line phones, computer and fax connections, 27-inch TV, and Super Nintendo. The large bathrooms include vintage fixtures, a freestanding glass shower, a large soaking tub, "his" and "hers" dressing areas, plush bathrobes and slippers, a hair dryer, and an illuminated makeup mirror.

Dining/Diversions: Hoku's, the main dining room, has a new multilevel layout so that every table has an ocean view and features Pacific and European cuisine (see "Dining" below for a complete review). Plumeria Beach Cafe serves both creative and traditional cuisine in a casual, open-air setting; their specialty is Sunday brunch. There's also a poolside snack bar, an oceanfront bar, and a lobby lounge with nightly entertainment.

Amenities: The lush, tropical grounds include an 800-foot crescent-shaped beach, a swimming pool, and a 26,000-square-foot lagoon, home to two bottle-nosed dolphins, sea turtles, and tropical fish. 24-hour room service, valet and self-parking, nightly turndown, in-room safe, fax and modem connections, baby-sitting, concierge, foreign exchange facilities, Hawaiian cultural program, massage, multilingual personnel, business center, shops, banquet and meeting rooms, and shuttle service to Waikiki and major shopping centers. Free scuba lessons in pool; daily dolphin-education talks by a trainer from Sea Life Park; fitness center with steam rooms, dry sauna, Jacuzzis, weight room, Stairmasters, treadmills; Kahala Keiki Club for kids.

THE WINDWARD COAST

KAILUA

Pat O'Malley of **Pat's Kailua Beach Properties,** 204 S. Kalaheo Ave., Kailua, HI 96734 (☎ **808/261-1653** or 808/262-4126; fax 808/261-0893; e-mail pats@aloha.net), books a wide range of houses and cottages on or near Kailua Beach. Rates start at $65 a day for a studio cottage near the beach and go up to $400 per day for a multimillion-dollar home right on the sand. All units are fully furnished, with everything from cooking utensils to telephone and TV, even washer and dryers.

Moderate

⭐ **Ingrid's.** Pauku St. (across from Enchanted Lakes School), Kailua. c/o Hawaii's Best Bed & Breakfasts, P.O. Box 563, Kamuela, HI 96743. ☎ **800/262-9912** or 808/885-4550. Fax 808/885-0559. www.bestbnb.com. E-mail bestbnb@aloha.net. 1 apt. TV TEL. **$110** double. Rate includes continental breakfast. Extra person **$15.** 2-night minimum. DISC. Free parking. Bus: 52, 55, or 56.

Ingrid has impeccable taste. Upstairs, past the Japanese garden and through a private entrance, is the cute one-bedroom apartment that she keeps immaculate. Decorated in modern Japanese style, this place is straight out of a magazine: The pristine white walls and cabinets are accented with such dramatic touches as black tile on the counter top, black-and-white shoji doors, and a black Oriental screen behind a king bed dressed in white quilts and red, red, red throw pillows. The tiled bathroom is done in complementary gray and has a luxurious soaking tub. The kitchenette includes a dishwasher, refrigerator, microwave, and coffeemaker. A huge tiled deck extends out from the apartment, and a small alcove is off the bedroom for a third person or a reading area. Fresh flowers are everywhere.

Inexpensive

Lanikai Bed & Breakfast. 1277 Mokulua Dr. (between Onekea and Aala drs. in Lanikai), Kailua, HI 96734. ☎ **800/258-7895** or 808/261-1059. Fax 808/262-2181. www.lanikaibb.com. E-mail hi4rent@aloha.net. 2 units. TV TEL. **$70** studio double, **$90** apt double. Rates include breakfast items in refrigerator. Extra person **$10-$20.** 3-night minimum. MC, V. Free parking. Bus: 52, 55, or 56.

This old-time bed-and-breakfast, a *kamaaina* (native-born) home that reflects the Hawaii of yesteryear, is now into its second generation: For years, Mahina and Homer Maxey ran this large, comfortable, island-style residence; today, their son, Rick, and his wife, Nini, are the hosts. The recently renovated 1,000-square-foot upstairs apartment is decorated in old Hawaii bungalow-style. With a king bed in the bedroom, separate den, large living/dining room, big bathroom, and all the modern conveniences—TV, VCR, and kitchenette—plus oversized windows to let you enjoy wonderful views, it easily accommodates four. Or, you can follow the ginger- and ti-lined path to a 540-square-foot honeymooner's delight, with queen bed and sitting area with TV, VCR, and kitchenette. Rick and Nini carry on the family tradition of hospitality by stocking the units with breakfast fixings (muffins, juice, fruit, coffee, tea) and all the beach equipment you'll need (towels, mats, chairs, coolers, water jugs). Picture-perfect white-sand Lanikai Beach access is across the street, bus routes are close by, and a 2½-mile biking-walking loop is just outside.

Schrader's Windward Marine Resort. 47-039 Lihikai Dr. (off Kamehameha Hwy.), Kaneohe, HI 96744. ☎ **800/735-5711** or 808/239-5711. Fax 808/239-6658. www.hawaiiscene.com/schrader. 20 units. A/C TV TEL. $50–$117 one-bedroom double, $70–$170 two-bedroom for 4, $190–$307 three-bedroom for 6. Rates include continental breakfast. Extra person $7.50. 2-night minimum. AE, DC, DISC, JCB, MC, V. Free parking. Bus: 52, 55, or 56.

This older cottage-style motel is nestled in a tranquil, tropical setting on Kaneohe Bay, only a 30-minute drive from Waikiki. Despite the name, the ambiance here is more motel than resort, but Schrader's offers a good alternative for families. Cottages have kitchenettes with refrigerator and microwave, TV, and phones. Prices are based on the views; depending on how much you're willing to pay, you can look out over Kahuluu fish pond, the Koolau Mountains, or Kaneohe Bay. Lots of watersports are available at an additional cost. *Hot tip:* When booking, ask for a unit with a lanai; that way, you'll end up with at least a partial view of the bay.

Sharon's Serenity. 127 Kakahiaka St. (at Mahelani St.), Kailua, HI 96734. ☎ **800/914-2271**, 808/263-3634, or 808/262-5621. www.imall.com/stores/serenity. 2 units. TV TEL. $60–$75 double. Rates include continental breakfast. Extra person $10. 3-night minimum. No credit cards. Free parking. Bus: 52, 55, 56, or 57.

This place is serenity to the max. Hostess Sharon Price has a warm, welcoming attitude that makes you feel right at home. And what a home it is—a huge living area with three large couches, a giant kitchen, and two guest rooms to chose from: one with pool view and a king bed as well as a twin, the other more romantic, with a queen bed. Out beyond the pool, deck, and grassy lawn runs a slow-moving water canal, framed by the greens of the Mid-Pacific Golf Course and the lush Koolau Range in the distance. Kailua Beach is just a couple of blocks away, but the atmosphere is so relaxing here that sometimes guests want to just stay home. Sharon has an adorably chubby Bichon Frise who loves everyone, plus two indoor-outdoor cats.

✪ **Sheffield House.** 131 Kuulei Rd. (at Kalaheo Dr.), Kailua, HI 96734. ☎/Fax **808/262-0721.** www.poi.net/~sheffieldhouse. E-mail sheffieldhouse@poi.net. 2 units. TV. $55 double (with shower only), $80 double apt. Rates include continental breakfast. Extra person $10. 3-night minimum. No credit cards. Free parking. Bus: 52, 55, or 56.

Unlike at many other B&Bs, children are welcome here. Architect Paul Sheffield and his landscape-architect wife, Rachel, have three kids who aren't shy about making new friends and including younger guests in their fun. The yard is set up for children: jungle gym, swing set, toys for children, and a tire swing. The Sheffields have two units, a one-bedroom and a studio (which is fully wheelchair-accessible), each with a private entry through elaborately landscaped tropical gardens. Both are equipped with a refrigerator, microwave, toaster oven, and coffeemaker.

KANEOHE

Inexpensive

A 5-Star Bed & Breakfast. 44-491 Kaneohe Bay Dr. (on the ocean side, by Kaneohe Yacht Club), Kaneohe, HI 96744. ☎ **800/235-5214** or 808/235-8235. Fax 808/667-9795. 3 units (2 with shared bath). TV. $75–$85 double. Rates include continental breakfast. 3-night minimum. No credit cards. Free parking. Bus: 52, 55, or 56.

An interior decorator has definitely molded this luxury house: Parquet floors, Japanese shoji doors, and creamy-white furniture give this waterfront home a tropical-Asian feel. Two bedrooms (one with twin beds and one with a queen) share a gorgeous marble bathroom, with a marble shower, that looks out onto a tropical garden. The master suite (with its less-extravagant private bath) has a view of the swimming pool, the Koolau Range, and the nearby yacht club. The rooms sit back off the street and are generally pretty quiet. A large pool with cabana is the featured entertainment. Shopping and restaurants are nearby, and Waikiki and Honolulu are just a 20- to 30-minute drive away.

Alii Bluffs Windward Bed & Breakfast. 46-251 Ilikii St. (off Kamehameha Hwy.), Kaneohe, HI 96744. ☎/Fax **800/235-1151** or 808/235-1124. 2 units. **$55–$65** double. Rates include continental breakfast. 3-night minimum. No credit cards. Free parking. Bus: 52, 55, or 56.

Realtor Donald Munro and artist L. de Chambs, who moved here from New York, have been welcoming travelers from around the globe into their home for a decade. Located on a quiet residential street, this traditional B&B is filled with antiques and collectibles as well as de Chambs's original art. The guest wing has two rooms, one with a double bed and adjacent bath, the other with two extralong twins and a bath across the hall. The yard blooms with tropical plants, and the view of Kaneohe Bay from the pool area is breathtaking. Lots of extras make this B&B stand out from the crowd, including daily maid service, a large breakfast served on the poolside lanai, afternoon tea, and hair dryers and sewing kits in the bathroom—they'll even lend you anything you need for the beach.

✪ **Hulakai Hale.** 44-002 Hulakai Pl. (off Kaneohe Bay Dr.), Kaneohe, HI 96744. ☎ **808/235-6754.** 2 units. TV. $60–$65 double. Rates include full breakfast. Extra person $25. 3-night minimum. No credit cards. Free parking. Bus: 52, 55, or 56.

Hulakai Hale ("house of the dancing waters") sits right on Kaneohe Bay, with picture-postcard views in every direction: the view from the pool deck of the bay and the yacht club next door is worth the price alone. You could lounge around the pool all day in the comfortable deck chairs and be happy just watching the birds soar overhead or the billowing sails dance in the wind. Located at the end of a private road, the house is well away from traffic but just minutes from the restaurants and shops of Kaneohe. Each of the two well-furnished units has a small fridge, microwave, coffeemaker, full bath, and a private entrance and comes stocked with beachmats, towels, and cooler; one has a king bed, the other a queen. Breakfast (tropical juice, fresh fruit, a variety of breads, cereal, coffee, and tea) is served every morning on the pool deck or in the formal dining area. Hosts Ditty and Tom Pico have a wonderful sense of humor and do everything they can to make sure you have the time of your life.

THE NORTH SHORE

Team Real Estate, 66-134 Kamehameha Hwy., Suite 1, Haleiwa, HI 96712 (☎ **800/982-8602** or 808/637-3507; fax 808/637-8881; www.teamrealestate.com), manages vacation rentals on the North Shore. Their units range from affordable cottages to oceanfront homes, at rates ranging from $95 to $250 per night. A minimum stay of 1 week is required for some properties, but shorter stays are available.

Expensive

✪ **Turtle Bay Hilton Golf and Tennis Resort.** P.O. Box 187, (Kuilima Dr., off Kamehameha Hwy. [Hwy. 83]) Kahuku, HI 96731. ☎ **800/HILTONS** or 808/293-8811. Fax 808/293-1286. www.hilton.com. 485 units. A/C TV TEL. **$180–$240** double, **$285–$600** cabana, from $400 suite. Extra person $25; children stay free. AE, CB, DC, DISC, ER, JCB, MC, V. Parking $5, $9 valet. Bus: 52 or 55.

An hour's drive from Waikiki and eons away from that tourist mecca is this luxurious oceanfront resort in a country setting. Sitting on 808 acres, this is a resort loaded with activities: 27 holes of golf, 10 tennis courts, and 5 miles of shoreline lined with secluded white-sand coves. The resort was built on Kalaeokaunu Point ("point of the altar"), where ancient Hawaiians built a small altar to the fish gods. Its remains are now at the Bishop Museum, but it is easy to see why the Hawaiians considered this holy ground. Next to the point is Kuilima Cove, one of the safest swimming beaches on the North Shore, thanks to the large reef offshore.

The feeling of old Hawaii is carried through to the guest rooms, which are decorated in Polynesian décor, a private lanai, all the amenities, and a great ocean view.

Dining/Diversions: The Palm Terrace is known for fabulous buffets. Sunday champagne brunch at the Sea Tide Room is a favorite. The Cove, which features continental and local cuisine, is best known for its excellent wine list. There's live entertainment nightly at the Bay View Lounge, while the Hang Ten Lounge is the place for poolside or sunset cocktails.

Amenities: Room service, concierge, many shops (including a branch of Liberty House), daily craft demonstrations, a children's program, sightseeing programs, and guided nature and Hawaiian reef walks. Ocean-view, championship 27-hole golf course, 10 Plexipave-court tennis complex, horseback riding, fitness center, idyllic beach, two pools, snorkeling, scuba diving, windsurfing.

Inexpensive

Ke Iki Hale. 59-579 Ke Iki Rd. (off Kamehameha Hwy.), Haleiwa, HI 96712. ☎ **800/ 377-4030** or 808/638-8229. Fax 808/638-8229. 19 units. $85 double. 2-night minimum. AE, MC, V. Free parking. Bus: 52 or 55.

The North Shore doesn't have many places for visitors to stay; this is a good choice for those who enjoy the beach. This collection of rustic one- and two-bedroom duplex cottages has a divine location: snuggled on 1½ acres, with its own 200-foot stretch of beach between two legendary surf spots: Waimea Bay and Banzai Pipeline. The winter waves are rough stuff; we regular folks can only venture in to swim in the flat summer seas. But there's a large lava reef nearby with tide pools to explore, and on the other side, Shark's Cove, a relatively protected snorkeling area. Ke Iki Hale is not for everyone, though. The furnishings are modest but clean, homey, and comfortable; kitchens, barbecues, hammocks, and laundry facilities provide some of the comforts of home. The one-bedrooms have two single beds in the living room, two beds in the separate bedroom, and a full kitchen. Nearby are tennis courts and a jogging path. The downside is that the units are subject to constant salt spray, which adds to their very evident deterioration. And none have a TV or phones (there's a pay phone in the parking lot). *Hot tip:* Don't stay in one of the noisy streetside units; instead, spring for one closer to the water.

Ke Iki Hale. 59-579 Ke Iki Rd. (off Kamehameha Hwy.), Haleiwa, HI 96712. ☎ **800/ 377-4030** or 808/638-8229. Fax 808/638-8229. 19 units. $132–$174 one- or two-bedroom double. Extra person $15. 2-night minimum. AE, MC, V. Free parking. Bus: 52 or 55.

Rodeway Inn Hukilau Resort. 55-109 Laniloa St. (off Kamehameha Hwy., near the Polynesian Cultural Center), Laie, HI 96762. ☎ **800/526-4562** or 808/293-9282. Fax 808/293-8115. E-mail rodeway@aloha.net. 48 units. A/C TV TEL. $69–$99 double. Rates include continental breakfast. Extra person $10; children under 18 stay free. AE, DISC, JCB, MC, V. Free parking. Bus: 52 or 55.

If you plan to see the Polynesian Cultural Center, you might want to stay at this Rodeway, which is within walking distance. The two-story, plantation-style hotel is a small, intimate property, also within walking distance of Brigham Young University Hawaii and the Mormon Temple. The rooms are standard, with two double beds, TV, phone, A/C, fridge, coffeemaker on request, and full bath. A continental breakfast with bagels, muffins, fresh fruit, juice, and coffee is included in the price. Access to a secluded white-sand beach is just across the street. Other amenities include a pool and sundeck, self-service Laundromat, tour desk, and free local calls.

⭐ **Santa's By the Sea.** Ke Waena Rd. (off Kamehameha Hwy.), Haleiwa, c/o Hawaii's Best Bed & Breakfasts, P.O. Box 563, Kamuela, HI 96743. ☎ **800/262-9912** or 808/885-4550. Fax 808/885-0559. E-mail bestbnb@aloha.net. 1 apt (with shower only). TV TEL. $99 double. Rate includes breakfast items in refrigerator. Extra person $5. 2-night minimum. Free parking. Bus: 52 or 55.

This certainly must be where Santa Claus comes to vacation, and for good reason: St. Nick knows a bargain when he sees it. The location, price, and style make this place a must-stay if you plan to see the North Shore. It's one of the few North-Shore B&Bs right on the beach—and not just any beach, but the famous Banzai Pipeline. You can go from your bed to the sand in less than 30 seconds to watch the sun rise over the Pacific. Hosts Gary and Cyndie renovated this vacation hideaway into an impeccable one-bedroom unit with finely crafted woodwork, bay windows, and a collection of unique Santa figurines and one-of-a-kind Christmas items that Cyndie has assembled over the years; it may sound schlocky, but somehow it gives the apartment a country charm. Honeymooners take note: There's lots of privacy here. The unit has its own entrance; a living room with TV, VCR, and stereo; and a full kitchen with everything a cook would need and an adjacent dining room. Fruit, cereal, bread, coffee, tea, and juice are provided on the first morning to get you started.

⭐ **Thomsen's Bed & Breakfast.** 59-420 Kamehameha Hwy. (6 miles from Haleiwa, near Ehukai Beach) Haleiwa, HI 96712. ☎ **808/638-7947.** Fax 808/638-7694. 1 studio (with shower only). TV TEL. $65 double. Rate includes fruit bowl on arrival. Extra person $5. 3-night minimum. No credit cards. Free parking. Bus: 52 or 55.

Thomsen's is one of the great values of the North Shore. On a 1-acre lot in the country, you'll find this quaint studio upstairs above the garage. The airy one-room apartment has a king bed (which can be made into two twins), dining area, kitchenette (with large refrigerator), wicker furniture (including a sleeper sofa), and TV, plus its own private entrance and big deck with views of the majestic Koolau Range. Washer and dryer are available for your use. Located just across the street from the world-famous Banzai Pipeline, Thomsen's has an outdoor shower to wash off the sand when you return from the beach.

LEEWARD OAHU: THE WAIANAE COAST

⭐ **Ihilani Resort & Spa.** At Ko Olina Resort, 92-1001 Olani St., Kapolei, HI 96707. ☎ **800/626-4446** or 808/679-0070. Fax 808/679-0080. 429 units. A/C MINIBAR TV TEL. $285–$575 double, from $800 suite. Extra person $35. Children under 18 free using existing bedding. AE, CB, DC, JCB, MC, V. Free parking. No bus service. Take H-1 west toward Pearl City/Ewa Beach; stay on H-1 until it becomes Hwy. 93 (Farrington Hwy.); look for the exit sign for Ihilani Resort; exit road is Alinui Dr., which goes into the Ko Olina Resort; turn right on Olani Pl.

In December 1993, some 17 miles and 25 minutes west of Honolulu Airport—and worlds away from the tourist scene of Waikiki—the first hotel in the 640-acre Ko Olina Resort community opened to much speculation. It's so far from Waikiki and Honolulu, critics charged, who would want go all the way out there? Lots of people, it turns out; the Ihilani has been well-booked ever since. Located in the quiet of Oahu's West (leeward) Coast, Ihilani ("heavenly splendor") is nestled between the Pacific Ocean and the first of four manmade beach lagoons. Featuring a luxury spa and fitness center, plus tennis and golf at Ko Olina, it's a haven of relaxation and well-being.

Rising some 15 stories along the virgin coastline, it's hard to get a bad room here—some 85% of guest rooms enjoy lagoon or ocean views. The luxuriously appointed rooms are larger than most (680 square feet) and come with huge lanais outfitted with very comfortable, cushioned teak furniture (chaise lounge, chairs, and table). The rooms feature a state-of-the-art comfort control-system panel (to operate the ceiling fans, air-conditioning, lights, and so on) built into the three phones, CD player, minibar, and in-room safe. Luxurious marble bathrooms have deep-soaking tubs, separate glass-enclosed showers, hair dryers, yukata robes, and many more amenities.

Dining/Diversions: Extraordinary cuisine, using the freshest ingredients from neighboring farms and waters, is found in all three Ihilani restaurants. The jewel in the crown is Azul, an intimate terrace overlooking the ocean serving Mediterranean-inspired cuisine. There's open-air dining on light, tropical fare at an informal poolside restaurant; and a low-fat, low-calorie menu is served at the Spa Cafe. Talented island artists provide entertainment and music to dance by in the resort's two lounges.

Amenities: Concierge, 24-hour room service, daily newspaper, business services, transportation to Waikiki and Ala Moana Shopping Center. Keiki Beachcomber Club is a year-round program for toddlers to teens, housed in its own ground-floor facility, with a wide variety of outdoor adventures and indoor learning activities, including a Computer Learning Center, a 125-gallon fish tank, an evening lounge for teen-themed parties, and more. Championship 18-hole Ko Olina Golf Course, designed by Ted Robinson and recognized as one of Hawaii's premier courses; a tennis club with pro shop; shopping arcade; 3-mile coastal fitness trail; two pools; and a stretch of four white-sand beaches for ocean activities.

The world-class Ihilani Spa offers just about everything to enhance your health, fitness, and well-being, including hydrotherapies such as thalassic treatments, Swiss showers, Grand Jets, Vichy showers, and Roman pools. Shiatsu, Swedish, and Hawaiian Lomi Lomi massages are offered, as well as herbal bodywraps. Complete fitness and relaxation programs can be custom designed. For us, the spa alone is reason enough to come here.

4 Dining

by Jocelyn Fujii

Honolulu's dining scene falls into several categories: Waikiki restaurants, chef-owned glamour restaurants, neighborhood eateries, fast-food joints, ethnic restaurants, and restaurants and food courts in shopping malls. In all these categories, Oahu is generously endowed.

Chefs once trained and celebrated in Hawaii's top resorts are moving into their own spheres beyond hotel properties and walk-in traffic, creating their own destinations and loyal clienteles who are willing to find them in unexpected neighborhoods and urban niches. Chefs such as Alan Wong, Jean-Marie Josselin, Sam Choy, and Roy Yamaguchi are worth renting a car to find, but so are Oahu's many great plate-lunch palaces for casual dining on the run.

WHAT'S NEW & NOTEWORTHY As usual, some restaurants have lost their luster or disappeared altogether, while a few newcomers have added a welcome sizzle to Honolulu's dining options. **Palomino**—large, sleek, gleaming, and hip—is the current downtown rave, and ✪ **Sam Choy's Breakfast, Lunch & Crab** is the happiest dining room around. **David Paul's Diamond Head Grill**, open since February 1998, elicits thunderous applause as the fabled Maui chef brings his vast talents to Oahu for the first time. If his new 160-seat dining room delivers the same quality of excellence as his Lahaina Grill, it will be a bright star in Honolulu's culinary scene. Alan Wong continues his reign as Honolulu's most acclaimed chef, but long waits (and a tiny waiting area) at his popular eatery have caused quite a stir among isgruntled diners. Let's hope that changes!

GREAT CHAINS It's hard to spend more than $6 at the **Ba-le Sandwich Shops,** whose French and Vietnamese specialties such as *pho* (the noodle soup that's a national ritual in Vietnam), croissants as good as the espresso, and wonderful taro/tapioca desserts have won an islandwide following. Hard work, low prices, and delectable offerings have made them a roaring success. Branches are in Ala Moana Center (☎ **808/944-4752**); at 333 Ward Ave. (☎ **808/591-0935**); in Kahala Mall, 4211 Waialae Ave. (☎ **808/735-6889**); in Manoa Marketplace, 2855 E. Manoa Rd. (☎ **808/988-1407**); and in Chinatown at 150 N. King St. (☎ **808/521-3973**). *Tip:* The Manoa Marketplace branch now serves a terrific selection of Thai dishes in an enlarged dining area, making it as much a restaurant as a place for take-out food.

The high-profile **Boston's North End Pizza Bakery** chain has an enthusiastic following among pizza lovers, and not just because it boasts "Hawaii's largest slice." Boston's reasonable prices and hefty sizes (19 in. and 3 lb.) add extra value, and fans swear by the sauces and toppings. You'll find branches in the Kaimuki section of Honolulu at 3506 Waialae Ave. (☎ **808/734-1945**); on the Windward side of the island in Kailua at 29 Hoolai St. (☎ **808/263-7757**); and in Kaneohe at 45-568 Kamehameha Hwy. (☎ **808/235-7756**).

In Waikiki, the local **Hard Rock Cafe** resides at 1837 Kapiolani Blvd. (☎ **808/955-7383**), while **Planet Hollywood Honolulu** is nearby at 2155 Kalakaua Ave. (☎ **808/924-7877**). At the Ala Moana end of Waikiki, **Red Lobster** (☎ **808/955-5656**) is crustacean central, a bustling family-style seafood haven at 1765 Ala Moana Blvd., in the same building as the new **Outback Steakhouse** (☎ **808/951-6274**), a Roy Yamaguchi/Ed Wary/Shep Gordon partnership. On downtown's Restaurant Row, beef eaters can chow down at **Ruth's Chris Steak House,** 500 Ala Moana Blvd. (☎ **808/599-3860**.) In Kahala Mall, you can taste the intriguing toppings offered by the local branch of **California Pizza Kitchen,** 4211 Waialae Ave. (☎ **808/737-9446**).

WAIKIKI
Very Expensive

Ball By the Sea. In Hilton Hawaiian Village, 2005 Kalia Rd. ☎ **808/941-2254.** Reservations recommended. Main courses $25–$30; prix fixe $39.50. AE, CB, DC, DISC, JCB, MC, V. Mon–Fri 7–9am and 11am–1pm, Mon–Sat 6–10pm. CONTINENTAL/PACIFIC RIM.

This is one of Waikiki's most memorable oceanfront dining rooms—pale and full of light, with a white grand piano at the entrance and sweeping views of the ocean. Some diners call it stuffy; others, supremely elegant. The menu includes lunchtime offerings that score high on the culinary scale: taro and crab cakes with green papaya salad; gourmet burgers and sandwiches; and, for extravagant lunchers without time or waistline considerations, herb-crusted lamb and an ample selection of seafood and pasta dishes. Dinner inches upward in scale and extravagance, with a lavish escargot strudel and Hawaiian lobster tartar to start, followed by broiled mahi-mahi, vanilla-curry sautéed prawns, thyme-infused rack of lamb, and macadamia-cilantro opakakapa with purple sweet potato and kaffir lime sauce headlining the impressive entrees. The substantial, sophisticated menu and elegant food presentation make Bali a plausible choice for foodies of all stripes.

David Paul's Diamond Head Grill. At the Colony Surf Hotel, 2885 Kalakaua Ave., 2nd floor. ☎ **808/922-3734.** Reservations recommended. Main courses $11–$14 at lunch, $22–$30 at dinner. AE, DC, DISC, JCB, MC, V. Mon–Fri 11:30am–2:30pm, daily 5:30–10pm. NEW AMERICAN.

Having established his Lahaina restaurant as Maui's best, David Paul made a leap to Oahu and created a dining room to match his reveting cuisine. At the marble

Waikiki Dining

1 Orchids
2 Prince Court
3 Outback Steakhouse
3 Red Lobster
3 Saranto's Top of the I
5 Singha Thai Cuisine
6 Parc Cafe
9 Planet Hollywood

14 Duke's Canoe Club
18 Hard Rock Cafe
18 Hau Tree Lanai
16 Hy's Steak House
4 Hawaii Seafood Paradise
11 La Mer
18 Miyako Japanese Restaurant
7 Nick's Fishmarket

19 David Paul's Diamond Head Grill
15 Ciao Mein
3 Cha Cha Cha
8 Caffelatte
6 Bali by the Sea
10 Arancino
7 Acqua

Legend
ⓘ Information
✉ Post Office

OAHU
Honolulu
Waikiki

Ala Wai Canal

DIAMOND HEAD WAIKIKI
MID-WAIKIKI, MAKAI
EWA WAIKIKI

Honolulu Zoo
Kuhio Beach Park
Waikiki Beach
Grey's Beach
Fort DeRussy Beach
Hilton Lagoon
Fort DeRussy Military Res.
Ala Moana Park
Ala Moana Shopping Center

Kapiolani Blvd
Paki Ave.
Kapahulu Ave.
Monsarrat Ave.
Kalakaua Ave.
Kuhio Ave.
Ala Wai Blvd.
Lemon
Cartwright
Makee
Kaneloa
Kealohilani Ave.
Paokalani
Ohua Ave.
Liliuokalani Ave.
Kaiulani Ave.
Kanekapolei
Walina
Nahua
Nohonani
Seaside Ave.
Royal Hawaiian Ave.
Lewers
Kaiolu
Launiu
Kalaimoku
Olohana
Namahana
Kuamoo
Keoniana
Pau
Niu
Ena Rd.
Hobron
Kaiolu Dr.
Kalia Rd.
Saratoga
Dudley
Beach Walk
Helumoa
Kuhio Promenade
Ala Moana Blvd.
Ala Wai Promenade

Int'l. Market Place
King's Village
Dukes Lane
Waikiki Trade Center
Waikiki Shop. Pl.
Prince Edward

1-0706

entryway, a serpentine martini bar and baby grand piano beckon to the left; to the right, a glass-enclosed private dining room holds a table for 10 for the chef's arranged-in-advance degustation dinners. At center front is the main dining room, with large windows looking out over Kapiolani Park and the flanks of Diamond Head. Glossy lava-colored pillars suggest volcanic cuisine, and for the most part, the chef lives up to the metaphor. The dishes are elegant and true: the Caesar salads redolent with garlic and anchovy, the lobster-mushroom lasagne understated and exquisite. With only three entrees at lunch, one is tempted to return for dinner, where the pleasures of David Paul's tequila shrimp, Kona-coffee-roasted rack of lamb, and towering napoleon of lobster, hamachi, and unagi are the bright stars on a menu that sparkles. Let's hope the kinks in service get smoothed out.

✪ **La Mer.** In the Halekulani, 2199 Kalia Rd. ☎ **808/923-2311.** Reservations recommended. Jackets required for men. Main courses $36–$46; prix fixe $85–$105. AE, CB, DC, JCB, MC, V. Daily 6–10pm. NEOCLASSIC FRENCH.

Honolulu's most elegant, sumptuous, and expensive dining takes place in this second-floor, open-sided oceanside room with views of Diamond Head and the sunset between palm fronds. Southern French influences meld seamlessly with the fresh island ingredients that La Mer has always celebrated. The impressive offerings of Michelin-award-winning chef Yves Garnier include a flawless foie gras steeped in sauternes and layered with black truffles; filet of kumu in rosemary salt crust, a La Mer staple at $43; and the veal chop sautéed with chanterelle mushrooms and baby vegetables, at $46 the most expensive item on the menu. Garnier has put his own signature on the rich legacy left by George Mavrothalassitis, who created a bouillabaisse unparalleled in Hawaii. Other temptations: the *onaga* fillet, cooked crisp on the skin, and the Hawaiian salt-crusted version, a La Mer signature. They're sublime, as are the Gallic splendors of the cheese tray, served with walnut bread. Desserts, including the Symphony of La Mer (almond tart, crème brûlée, mousse of three chocolates) are not to be ignored. Frightfully expensive though it is, La Mer is in a class of its own in Honolulu.

Miyako Japanese Restaurant. In New Otani Kaimana Beach Hotel, 2863 Kalakaua Ave. ☎ **808/923-4739.** Reservations recommended. Main courses $30–$40. AE, DC, DISC, JCB, MC, V. Daily 6pm to closing. JAPANESE.

Ikebana arrangements accent the dining room, and servers in gorgeous kimonos bustle to bring you brisk, courteous service. The food presentation is flawless: lacquer trays, precious sake cups, esthetically arranged morsels reminiscent of imperial dining in Kyoto. Offerings include make-your-own hand-sushi rolls (temaki) from a tray of vegetables, mountain yam, crab, king clam, sashimi, nori, and salmon roe; prearranged kaiseki dinners ($60); and several combinations of tempura, sashimi, shrimp, fresh lobster, soup, and pickled vegetables. This is a pretty room on the 2nd floor of the hotel, with the Waikiki skyline glittering in the distance.

Nick's Fishmarket. In Waikiki Gateway Hotel, 2070 Kalakaua Ave. ☎ **808/955-6333.** Reservations recommended. Main courses $20.95–$44.95; complete dinners $27.95–$55.95. AE, CB, DC, DISC, JCB, MC, V. Sun–Thurs 5:30–10pm, cafe menu 5:30pm–midnight; Fri–Sat 5:30–11pm, cafe menu 5:30pm–midnight. SEAFOOD.

With its extensive menu and lobster specialties, Nick's will always be the restaurant for seafood lovers with upscale tastes. A perennial award-winner, Nick's has a new Kalakaua Room with windows for Waikiki people-watching and a menu that remains one of Honolulu's finest examples of Neptunian muscle. Appetizers range from Beluga caviar to escargot, ahi tartar and salmon carpaccio, and blackened sashimi. Whether Alaskan king crab or roast chicken, filet mignon or rack of lamb, or one of the impressive lobster combinations ($32.50 to $66.95 for a 2-pound Maine lobster), the entrees are familiar, yet anything but boring. Fresh fish, Nick's trademark, comes grilled, seared, and sautéed in a medley of preparations ranging from green peppercorn to Oriental ginger. A keiki menu appeals to families, and the late-night entertainment with live music makes Nick's a magnet for the after-dinner crowd, too (see "Oahu After Dark," below).

Orchids. In the Halekulani, 2199 Kalia Rd. ☎ **808/923-2311.** Reservations recommended. Dinner main courses $27.50–$39.50; prix fixe $44.50 and $61. AE, CB, DC, JCB, MC, V. Daily 7:30–11am, 11:30am–2pm, and 6–10pm. INDO-PACIFIC.

The stunning oceanside ambiance of this Honolulu landmark hasn't changed, but its menu has. After several culinary incarnations, it's now an Indo-Pacific room featuring curries and tandoori specialties. So, while viewing Diamond Head over crisp, blindingly white linens or flickering candlelight, you can sample evening lavishments such as steamed Oriental-style onaga and wok-fried Maine lobster. At lunch, savory curries and pastas (penne with sautéed jumbo shrimp, $17.50, is a favorite) headline a menu that goes from the extravagantly minimalist yellowfin tuna salad ($17) to a $13 club sandwich and $17 beef curry. Thankfully, the superlative ambiance and service endow Orchids with a kind of immortality, keeping old-timers returning through changes in chefs and menu.

Prince Court. In Hawaii Prince Hotel, 100 Holomoana St. ☎ **808/956-1111.** Reservations recommended. Main courses $18–$38; prix fixe $32, $45, $60. AE, CB, JCB, MC, V. Daily 6–10:30am and 6–9:30pm, Mon–Fri 11:30am–2pm, Sun brunch 11am–1pm. HAWAII REGIONAL.

The gorgeous harbor view is a plus any time of the day or night, particularly at sunset, or on Friday nights when fireworks light up the skies from Waikiki shores. Diners can sample a lavish seafood buffet Friday and Saturday nights, or order off an à la carte menu appealing to lovers of seafood and steak. To complement its lighter Hawaii Regional menu, Prince Court offers stunningly simple grilled and roasted meats: rack of lamb, prime rib of beef, and a perfectly done, buttery-tender New York steak with fresh shiitake mushrooms and fresh rosemary. Lighter fare includes a melt-in-your-mouth ahi carpaccio, crab-crusted opakapaka, and a selection of salads highlighting locally grown produce. Although the menu changes monthly, the favorites remain.

Expensive

Acqua. In Hawaiian Regent Hotel, 2552 Kalakaua Ave. ☎ **808/924-0123.** Reservations recommended. Main courses $11.95–$29.95; specials can be more. Sunset special, a 3-course dinner from 5:30–6:30pm nightly, $24.95. AE, DC, DISC, JCB, MC, V. Sun–Thurs 6–9:30pm, Fri–Sat 6–10:30pm. MEDITERRANEAN/PACIFIC.

Acqua's cross-cultural touches and innovative menu make it a worthy and enjoyable stop, a good way to ward off taste-bud atrophy with the latest in culinary seductions. We like the way chef Mariano Lalica uses taro (as in clam, taro, and corn chowder, and in garlic taro mashed potatoes); Hawaiian hearts of palm; guava barbecue sauce; and local traditions such as steamed seafood lau-lau (fish, lobster, prawns, scallops, crab, taro, and spinach) in sophisticated, sybaritic ways. Acqua has won several competitions, among them the Best of Taste of Honolulu in 1996 for their guava barbecued prawns. The soups, salads, and appetizers—such as wild mushrooms gratinee, guava barbecued baby-back ribs, and seafood martini of blackened sashimi—are as distinctive as the entrees, making Acqua the perfect place for quality grazing. At $24.95, the Acqua Sunset dinner is a top value: Choose from among five appetizers; chicken, rib eye, paella, or rock shrimp risotto entrées; and a staggering selection of gourmet desserts. The dining is casual, around an open kitchen, and the

Thursday-through-Saturday evening live entertainment has featured some prominent names in island music.

Caffelatte. 339 Saratoga Rd. ☎ **808/924-1414.** Reservations recommended. Prix fixe $35. MC, V. Wed-Mon 6:30-10pm. NORTHERN ITALIAN.

Owner/chef Laura Prosepio makes everything from scratch and to order; you wouldn't catch her near a microwave oven. As a result, you won't find a better bruschetta, pasta carbonara, marinara, or risotto in Honolulu. Thanks to her generations-old recipes and long hours of simmering soups and sauces, the menu is built on solidly good, uncompromising basics. The prix-fixe-only dinner consists of appetizer or salad, soup (usually fish, lentil, or vegetable, and always good), and the entree, which could be a porcini risotto, or homemade ravioli, or any of the five veal selections (for an additional $5). While fans swear by the food quality, prices could wind up being a bit steep for pasta in a dining room this casual.

Hau Tree Lanai. In New Otani Kaimana Beach Hotel, 2863 Kalakaua Ave. ☎ **808/921-7066.** Reservations recommended. Main courses $19-$32.50. AE, CB, DC, DISC, JCB, MC, V. Mon-Sat 7-11am, 11:30am-2pm, and 5:30-9pm; Sun 7-11:30am, noon-2pm, and 5:30-9pm. Late lunch in the open-air bar, daily 2-4pm. PACIFIC RIM.

Its unparalleled outdoor setting and earnest menu have made the Hau Tree a popular informal dining spot. The centerpiece of this terrace on the sand is an ancient hau tree that provides shade and charm for diners, most of whom are busy observing the diverse parade of beachgoing bodies at Sans Souci Beach. The view of the ocean, the sunset, the Waianae Mountains, and the historic architecture of the saltwater pool called the Natatorium is blindingly beautiful and as much a part of the dining experience as the food itself. Breakfast here is a must: salmon Florentine, served on spinach and a fresh-baked scone; poi pancakes and Belgian waffles; eggs Benedict; and the Hawaiian platter of miniature poi pancakes, eggs, and three different kinds of Island sausages. Lunchtime attractions include house-cured Atlantic salmon and an assortment of burgers, sandwiches, salads, and specialties such as fresh seared garlic ahi and barbecued chicken. At dinner, choose from among 10 different appetizers and entrees of fresh moonfish, red snapper, opakapaka, ahi, and meats (ginger-steamed chicken breast, sesame crusted hoisin rack of lamb).

Hy's Steak House. 2440 Kuhio Ave. ☎ **808/922-5555.** Reservations recommended. Main courses $15.50-$36. AE, CB, DC, DISC, MC, V. Daily 6-10pm. AMERICAN.

Call it old-fashioned or call it a survivor, but there's no denying that Hy's has demonstrated admirable staying power. This dark and clubby steakhouse still scores high among carnivores and even offers a grilled vegetable platter for carniphobes, a relief for the arteries among the Chateaubriand, beef Wellington, shrimp scampi, and other fruits de mer and terre. "The Only" is its classic best, a New York strip steak kiawe-grilled and served with a mysterious signature sauce. Garlic lovers sweat by the Garlic Steak Diane, a richly endowed rib eye with sliced mushrooms. For an appetizer, you can order Thai-style scallops, buttery escargots, or wonderful salads; an excellent Caesar, warm spinach, and seafood-and-avocado. Hy's is a great choice for steak lovers with bottomless pocketbooks or for those tiring of Hawaii Regional Cuisine.

Sarento's Top of the I. In Ilikai Hotel Nikko Waikiki, 1777 Ala Moana Blvd. ☎ **808/949-3811.** Reservations recommended. Main courses $16-$41. AE, JCB, MC, V. Sun-Thurs 5:30-10:30pm, Fri-Sat 5:30-11pm. ITALIAN.

The ride up in the glass elevator is an event in itself, but Sarento's is not all show. Diners rave about the romantic view of the city, the stellar Caesar salad, a frutti de mare that's rich but engaging, and the sautéed scallops with porcini mushrooms and butter. Pizza, particularly the shrimp-pesto version, is also a success. On the lighter side, the smoked salmon Italiano is a safe bet with a judicious sprinkling of olive oil and cracked pepper, as is the crisp, cold appetizer platter of salmon, bruschetta, artichokes, and roasted peppers.

Moderate

Arancino. 255 Beach Walk. ☎ **808/923-5557.** Main courses $6.50–$14.50. AE, JCB, MC, V. Daily 11:30am–2:30pm and 5–10pm. ITALIAN.

When jaded Honolulu residents venture into Waikiki for dinner, it had better be good. And for the price, Arancino is worth the hunt. Here's what you'll find: a cheerful cafe of Monet-yellow walls and tile floors, respectable pastas, fabulous red-pepper salsa and rock-salt focaccia, we-try-harder service, and reasonable prices. The shredded-radicchio risotto (risotto changes daily) for $8.50 is notable; the steamed mussels, $5.50, come seasoned assertively; the gorgonzola-asparagus pizza, $7.50, is unconventional and zesty; and heaven forbid, you should miss out on the $14.50 lobster linguine if it's on the menu. Arancino is frequently filled, and its intimate, convivial atmosphere of fairy lights on potted trees, Italian posters, and dangling strands of garlic make it all the more enjoyable.

Ciao Mein. In Hyatt Regency Waikiki, 2424 Kalakaua Ave. ☎ **808/923-2426.** Reservations recommended. Main courses $6–$20; prix fixe $24–$33. AE, CB, DC, DISC, JCB, MC, V. Daily 6–10pm. ITALIAN/CHINESE.

The cross-cultural connection seemed gimmicky at first, but Ciao Mein has pulled it off in a large, pleasing dining room with efficient service, surprisingly good Chinese food (especially for a hotel restaurant), and award-winning menu items that make this a haven for noodle lovers. If you're feeling extravagant, the honey-walnut shrimp, with snap peas and honey-glazed walnuts, is worth every penny of its $21.50 price. The crisp fried noodles with chicken and lobster make up a dish hailed by fans, and few Honolulu festival-goers will forget the spicy wok-fried Szechwan eggplant ($6.75) that won accolades and helped put Ciao Mein on Honolulu's culinary map. Sweet tooths, take note: The celebrated tiramisu lives up to its reputation.

❂ **Duke's Canoe Club.** 2335 Kalakaua Ave., Outrigger Waikiki Hotel. ☎ **808/922-2268.** Reservations recommended for dinner. Main courses $15.95–$23. AE, DC, MC, V. Daily 7am–1am. STEAK/SEAFOOD.

This is what dining in Waikiki should be. Named after fabled surfer Duke Kahanamoku, this casual, upbeat oceanfront hotspot buzzes with diners and Hawaiian music lovers throughout the day, some of them wandering in from the beach, where they overheard slack-key guitar riffs that were too good to resist. Open-air dining gives a front-row view to the sunset. The dinner fare is steak and seafood, with high marks for the prime rib, macadamia-crab wontons, and several preparations on the daily catch. Open for breakfast, lunch, and dinner, Duke's is also loved for its barefoot bar with topnotch Island entertainment and its kamaaina, Island-style ambiance: koa-lined walls, lauhala ceilings, and Hawaiian memorabilia accenting the interior. The Concerts on the Beach series (Fri–Sun 4–6pm) features topnotch Island entertainers such as Brother Noland, Kapena, and the Lilikoi Sisters, who stroll tableside every night.

❂ **Hawaii Seafood Paradise.** 1830 Ala Moana Blvd. ☎ **808/946-4514.** Reservations recommended. Main courses $7–$32. AE, JCB, DC, MC, V. Daily 6:30am–3am. CHINESE/SEAFOOD.

You can dine as simply or as lavishly as you choose in this quirky, unpretentious restaurant that serves nine kinds of roast duck (I'd stake my life on the Peking duck); peerless shrimp fried rice; many selections of chicken, noodles, and seafood; sizzling platters; an impressive selection of abalone and clam dishes; and "hot pot" casseroles

1-0703

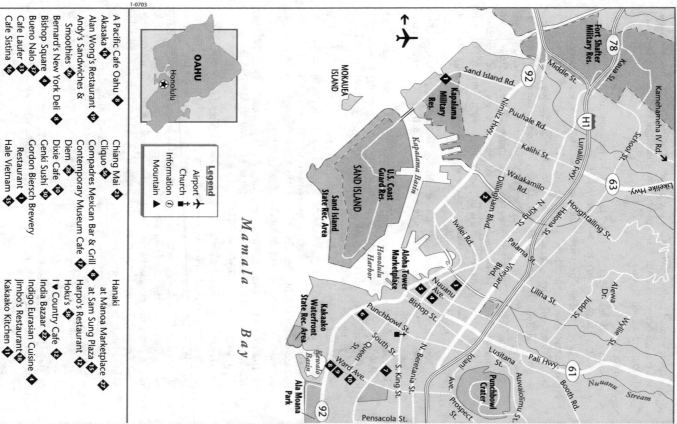

OAHU

Honolulu

MOKAUEA ISLAND

Legend
- ✈ Airport
- ■ + Church
- ✈ Information
- ▲ Mountain

A Pacific Cafe Oahu 🔶8
Akasaka 🔶14
Alan Wong's Restaurant 🔶12
Andy's Sandwiches & Smoothies 🔶26
Bernard's New York Deli 🔶6
Bishop Square 🔶
Bueno Nalo 🔶4
Cafe Laufer 🔶33
Cafe Sistina 🔶16

Chiang Mai 🔶23
Cliquo 🔶36
Compadres Mexican Bar & Grill 🔶8
Contemporary Museum Cafe 🔶17
Diem 🔶28
Dixie Cafe 🔶10
Genki Sushi 🔶30
Gordon Biersch Brewery Restaurant 🔶1
Hale Vietnam 🔶35

Hanaki at Manoa Marketplace 🔶27
Harpo's Restaurant at Sam Sung Plaza 🔶15
Hoku's 🔶38
I ♥ Country Cafe 🔶12
India Bazaar 🔶22
Indigo Eurasian Cuisine 🔶2
Jimbo's Restaurant 🔶18
Kakaako Kitchen 🔶17

Mamala Bay

Fort Shafter Military Res.
Kapalama Military Res.
SAND ISLAND
Sand Island State Rec. Area
U.S. Coast Guard Res.
Kapalama Basin
Honolulu Harbor
Aloha Tower Marketplace
Kakaako Waterfront State Rec. Area
Kewalo Basin
Ala Moana Park
Punchbowl Crater
Nuuanu Stream

Sand Island Rd.
Kamehameha IV Rd.
Kaua St.
Middle St.
Puuhale Rd.
Nimitz Hwy.
Kalihi St.
Lunalilo Hwy.
School St.
Likelike Hwy.
Waiakamilo Rd.
Dillingham Blvd.
Houghtailing St.
N. King St.
Iwilei Rd.
Palama St.
Vineyard Blvd.
Liliha St.
Alewa Dr.
Nuuanu Ave.
Bishop St.
Punchbowl St.
South St.
Queen St.
Ward Ave.
S. King St.
N. Beretania St.
Iolani Ave.
Lusitana St.
Pali Hwy.
Auwaiolimu St.
Booth Rd.
Prospect St.
Pensacola St.
Judd St.
Wyllie St.
Halona St.

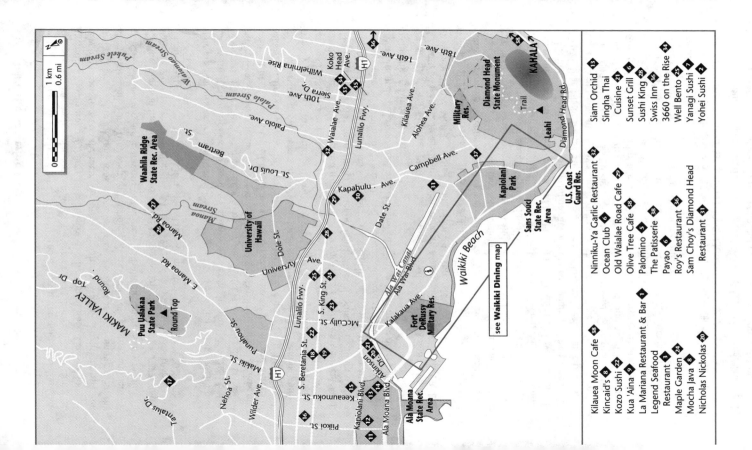

N

1 km
0.6 mi
0

Puele Stream

Waiomao Stream

Koko Head Ave.

Wilhelmina Rise

Sierra Dr.

10th Ave.

Palolo Stream

Waialae Ave.

Lunalilo Fwy.

Kilauea Ave.

Alohea Ave.

16th Ave.

18th Ave.

H1

KAHALA

Diamond Head State Monument

Trail

Military Res.

Leahi

Diamond Head Rd.

Waahila Ridge State Rec. Area

Bertram St.

St. Louis Dr.

Campbell Ave.

Kapahulu Ave.

Date St.

Manoa Stream

Manoa Rd.

University of Hawaii

Kapiolani Park

Kapiolani Blvd.

U.S. Coast Guard Res.

Sans Souci State Rec. Area

Waikiki Beach

Dole St.

University Ave.

E. Manoa Rd.

Round Top Dr.

MAKIKI VALLEY

Puu Ualakaa State Park

Round Top

Ala Wai Canal

Ala Wai Blvd.

Lunalilo Fwy.

S. King St.

S. Beretania St.

Punahou St.

Makiki St.

Wilder Ave.

Nehoa St.

Tantalus Dr.

McCully St.

Atkinson Dr.

Kalakaua Ave.

Fort DeRussy Military Res.

Kapiolani Blvd.

Keeaumoku St.

Ala Moana Blvd.

Piikoi St.

Ala Moana State Rec. Area

H1

see Waikiki Dining map

Kilauea Moon Cafe **48**
Kincaid's **8**
Kozo Sushi **22**
Kua 'Aina **9**
La Mariana Restaurant & Bar **1**
Legend Seafood Restaurant **3**
Maple Garden **24**
Mocha Java **8**
Nicholas Nickolas **20**

Ninniku-Ya Garlic Restaurant **42**
Ocean Club **6**
Old Waialae Road Cafe **29**
Olive Tree Cafe **38**
Palomino **5**
The Patisserie **6**
Payao **6**
Roy's Restaurant **46**
Sam Choy's Diamond Head Restaurant **47**

Siam Orchid **13**
Singha Thai Cuisine **21**
Sunset Grill **28**
Sushi King **46**
Swiss Inn **43**
3660 on the Rise **45**
Well Bento **7**
Yanagi Sushi **2**
Yohei Sushi

143

with everything from lamb to lobster and fish. Top quality in the more than 200 Cantonese and Szechwan selections make this a mecca for Chinese-food aficionados, including those speaking their native dialects—a sure sign of good Chinese food. A few of the best items on the menu are written in Chinese with no English translation, so don't be afraid to ask questions. There are Thai selections as well, among them the spicy, delectable Tom Yum soup with whole prawns, a hint of coconut, and lemongrass—rich but irresistible and one of the great finds on the Chinese-only menu.

✪ **Parc Cafe.** In the Waikiki Parc Hotel, 2233 Helumoa Rd. ☎ **808/921-7272.** Reservations recommended. Buffets $11.50–$22.50. Mon–Sat 6:30–10am and 11:30am–2pm; Sun 6:30–9:30am and 11am–2pm (brunch); daily 5:30–9:30pm. BUFFETS/BRUNCH.

The Halekulani's sister hotel has made a name for itself as Honolulu's top spot for buffets, with food and prices so good it has won over even the most dedicated buffet bashers. Regulars flock to the dining room for the Wednesday and Friday Hawaiian buffet—at $16.50, the finest such spread around: lau-lau, lomi salmon, kalua pig, steamed fresh catch, mashed Molokai potatoes, Kauai taro au gratin, and dozens of salads. Chafing dishes notwithstanding, this is gourmet fare using fresh, fine ingredients. A carving station serves up rotisserie duck and prime rib. The seafood soup is reliably good, and the squid luau, with coconut milk, taro tops, and a brilliant smattering of tomatoes, is arguably the best in Hawaii. Otherwise, there are breakfast and luncheon buffets (the latter featuring salads, sandwiches, pasta, and rotisserie chicken). The prime rib and seafood dinner buffet on Friday through Sunday evenings is also a roaring success: sashimi, poke, and oysters on the half shell; a wok station and fresh catch; a carving station for prime rib and rotisserie chicken; the cafe's famous salads, from Oriental chicken to duck and charbroiled eggplant; and many other selections, including smashing desserts.

⭐ **Singha Thai Cuisine.** 1910 Ala Moana Blvd. (at the Ala Moana end of Waikiki). ☎ **808/941-2898.** Reservations recommended. Main courses $11–$27. AE, CB, DC, DISC, JCB, MC, V. Mon–Fri 11am–11pm, nightly 4–11pm. THAI.

The Royal Thai dancers arch their graceful, boneless fingers nightly in classical Thai dance on the small center stage, but you may be too busy tucking into your Thai chili fresh fish or blackened ahi summer rolls to notice. Indeed, the flavors and sights are rich here; imaginative combination dinners and the use of local organic ingredients are among the special touches of this Thai-Hawaiian fusion restaurant. Complete dinners for two to five cover many tastes and are an ideal way for the uninitiated to sample this cuisine, as well as the elements of Hawaii Regional Cuisine that have had considerable influence on the chef. Some highlights of a diverse menu: local fresh catch with Thai chili and light black-bean sauce; red, green, yellow, and vegetarian curries; ginseng chicken soup; and many seafood dishes. Such extensive use of fresh fish (mahimahi, ono, ahi, opakapaka, onaga, and uku) in traditional Thai preparations is unusual for a Thai restaurant. Curry puffs (shrimp, pork, and vegetables in puff pastry), chicken and shrimp sate, fresh ahi tempura (very Japanese), blackened ahi summer rolls (very Hawaii Regional), and naked squid salad are among the many curiosities of the menu that have received acceptance. The entertainment and indoor-outdoor dining add to this first-class dining experience.

Inexpensive

Cha Cha Cha. 342 Seaside Ave. ☎ **808/395-7797.** Complete dinners $7–$9. MC, V. Mon–Fri 11:30am–11:30pm, Sat–Sun 4–11:30pm. MEXICAN/CARIBBEAN.

Two happy hours! What a cheerful place. With live music daily, heroic margaritas and beer for $2 during the twice-daily happy hours (4 to 6pm, 9 to 11pm), 99¢ pupus on

Monday and Tuesday, and an all-around lovable menu, we should all cha cha cha to this Waikiki treasure. Nothing wimpy about the flavors here; the lime, coconut, and Caribbean spices make Cha Cha more than plain ol' Mex, adding zing to the fresh fish and shrimp ceviche, the jerk-chicken breast, and the shrimp and fish stew in lime broth. Tacos, tamales, quesadillas, wraps and "unwraps" (served in crisp red tortilla shells on a bed of warm black beans) are the general categories, but don't miss the specials. Blackened swordfish, curried fresh grilled vegetables, blackened fish tacos, and homemade desserts (including a creamy toasted coconut custard you won't want to miss) make this one of Waikiki's enduring delights.

HONOLULU BEYOND WAIKIKI
ALA MOANA
Expensive

✪ **A Pacific Cafe Oahu.** At Ward Centre, 1200 Ala Moana Blvd. ☎ **808/593-0035.** Reservations recommended. Lunch $8–$14, 3-course lunch special $12.95, dinner main courses $16.50–$26.75; prix fixe $34.50. AE, DC, DISC, MC, V. Mon–Fri 11:30am–2pm, Sun–Thurs 5:30–9pm, Fri–Sat 5:30–10pm. HAWAII REGIONAL.

Chef-owner Jean-Marie Josselin is renowned for his excellent appetizers (firecracker salmon rolls, tiger-eye ahi sushi tempura, ahi carpaccio) and his seasoned hand with Island produce and seafood. Great for lunch or dinner, this Ward Centre success story keeps a creative edge with its signature sesame- and garlic-crisped mahi-mahi, his staple statewide; Pacific salmon crisped with a nori seasoning (furikake), served with a scrumptious griddled rice cake; seared opah with an herb crust; and a number of notable pizzas, salads, pastas, and grilled fish and meats. The large, split-level room with its underwater motif has its own appetizer bar and excellent servers, a seamless match for the cuisine.

Nicholas Nickolas. In Ala Moana Hotel, 410 Atkinson Dr. ☎ **808/955-4466.** Reservations recommended. Main courses $19–$42. AE, CB, DC, DISC, MC, V. Sun–Thurs 5:30–10:30pm, Fri–Sat 5:30–11:30pm; live music Sun–Thurs 9pm–1am, Fri–Sat 10pm–2:30am; late-night menu Sun–Thurs until 12:30am, Fri–Sat until 1:30am. A collared shirt, slacks, and shoes required for men. AMERICAN/CONTINENTAL/SEAFOOD.

Take the express elevator to the 36th floor, where the circular dining room reveals the city in its mountain-to-sea splendor. The menu is spare and to the point, strong on appetizers and seafood: crab cakes (a best-seller), the signature Cajun-seared ahi, clams casino, and ahi spring rolls in hot mango and garlic sauce. Beluga caviar goes for $75 for the luxury minded, sashimi for much less. Blackened onaga has always been a house specialty, seared in Cajun spices and baked. The herb-infused mahi-mahi à la Lexi is another Nicholas Nickolas notable, and for the undecided, the seafood mixed grill or surf-and-turf à la Nick. Meat lovers are not neglected: rack of lamb; New York steak; and veal, pork, and chicken round out the menu.

You'll dine at tables along the edge of the dining room or at cozy booths along the interior, and when dinner's over, the dancing begins. There's live music nightly from 9pm, Friday and Saturday from 10pm. Ask about the appetizer menu, available daily from 5pm to 2:30pm.

Moderate

✪ **Akasaka.** 1646B Kona St. ☎ **808/942-4466.** Reservations recommended. Main courses $10–$19. AE, DC, DISC, MC, V. Mon–Sat 11am–2:30am and 5pm–2am. JAPANESE.

Cozy, busy, casual, and occasionally smoky, with a tiny tatami room for small groups, Akasaka wins high marks for sushi, sizzling tofu and scallops, miso-clam soup, and the overall quality and integrity of its Japanese cuisine. The zesty, spicy tuna hand-roll (temaki) is the best in town, and many claim the California roll with flying fish roe, and hamachi also occupy the top of the sushi heap. During soft-shell crab season, lovers of these spiny delicacies can order them in sushi—a novel, tasty treat. Fresh ingredients at the sushi bar make this a good bet for top-notch Japanese, and lunch and dinner specials can help ease the bite of the bill. Although Akasaka could be listed as expensive, we include it here because ordering noodles and à la carte items can lessen the cost considerably.

Cafe Sistina. 1314 S. King St. ☎ **808/596-0061.** Reservations recommended for dinner. Main courses $12–$15. AE, DC, MC, V. Mon–Fri 11am–2pm; daily 5:30–10:30pm. NORTHERN ITALIAN.

Chef/owner Sergio Mitrotti displays his multiple talents on the walls, where his Sistine Chapel redux amuses and delights in an otherwise industrially stylized room. Word is that his abundant culinary talents have multiplied with time and his frequent visits to Italy. Frutti de mare, linguine puttanesca, and smoked-salmon fettuccine are among the staples on his tried-and-true menu, but keep a keen eye on the specials; that's where Sergio really flexes his culinary muscle. Roasted red peppers, shrimp with black squid-ink pasta, many kinds of made-to-order risotto, and a host of authentic Italian dishes are among the people-pleasers that he makes himself and a smoked salmon ravioli with sweet chili sauce and radicchio. Habitúes know about Sergio's second special menu, a well-known secret and his own private passion.

Compadres Mexican Bar & Grill. At Ward Centre, 1200 Ala Moana Blvd. ☎ **808/591-8307.** Reservations recommended. Main courses $8–$13. DC, JCB, MC, V. Mon–Thurs 11am–11pm, Fri–Sat 11am–midnight, Sun 11am–10pm; bar Sun–Thurs 12:30pm–1am, Fri–Sat 1:30pm–2am.

Cigar smoke notwithstanding, Compadres makes the best margaritas in town, served in a festive atmosphere with one wall of glass windows looking out toward Ala Moana Park. Tequila festivals, Cinco de Mayo, fund-raisers, live entertainment on Thursdays and Fridays, and every excuse for a party make this place an all-around good deal. Oh yes, the food—from chimichangas to enchilada platters to the simple pleasures of guacamole and salsa, a tip of the sombrero to Compadres. Huevos rancheros are a must any time of the day, and the locally smoked "lomi lomi" salmon in a large spinach tortilla is a local twist to a south-of-the-border classic. Eight different types of enchiladas; steak, chicken, and fish combination plates; fajitas; carnitas; and notable nachos are among the major attractions at this festive eatery, where the back-bar margarita (Gold tequila, Grand Marnier, fresh lime, sweet-and-sour, orange juice) is a libation of great renown.

Dixie Cafe. 404 Ward Ave. ☎ **808/596-8359.** Reservations accepted for groups of 8 or more. Sandwiches and entrees $6–$20. AE, DC, JCB, MC, V. Mon–Thurs 11am–11pm, Fri 7am–10pm, Sat 11am–midnight, Sun 3–11pm. AMERICAN.

Popcorn, jeans-clad furniture, video games, a TV bar, and a lusty, noisy atmosphere—that's Dixie Grill, the busiest (and perhaps noisiest) spot on Ward Avenue. There are tables outdoors (with a view of Sports Authority) and indoors in a high-decibel, quirky ambiance that matches the all-American menu of ribs, burgers, sandwiches, and a "mess 'o crabs," a medley of three kinds of crab for $19.95.

Hanaki. Sam Sung Plaza no. 101, 655 Keeaumoku St. ☎ **808/955-1347;** Manoa Marketplace, 2752 Woodlawn Dr. ☎ 808/988-1551. Reservations recommended for groups. Main courses $5.25–$14; Kaiseki $17.50–$20. AE, JCB, MC, V. Daily 11am–2pm, 5–10pm. JAPANESE.

Noodleheads love Hanaki for its nabeyaki, udon, and other slurpy specialties, all steaming in savory broths with various accompaniments of fresh vegetables, shiitake, shrimp tempura, and chicken. At lunch, the inexpensive bentos move quickly, and at dinner, the sushi bar at the new Manoa location is the best deal in town. Hanaki's recent expansion (enlarging the Keeaumoku Street location, opening in Manoa Marketplace) has met with resounding approval—try getting in on a Friday night. The reckless order fried gyoza (dumplings); we love the shiitake mushroom udon and the shiitake donburi, with the tasty black mushrooms and eggs served over hot rice. Tempura udon (with shrimp and vegetables aesthetically arranged over the thick, steaming noodles) and the teishoku (combination) dinners are deceptively elegant for a modest eatery without tablecloths.

Kincaid's. In Ward Warehouse, 1050 Ala Moana Blvd. ☎ **808/591-2005.** Reservations recommended. Lunch **$8.95–$15.95;** dinner main courses $10–$30. AE, DC, JCB, MC, V. Daily 11am–10pm (later for pupus). SEAFOOD.

Kincaid's is always winning surveys for one thing or another—best place for a business lunch, best seafood restaurant—because it manages to please wide-ranging tastes and pocketbooks. Brisk service, a pleasing harbor view, and an extensive seafood menu keep the large dining room full. Great fresh-fish sandwiches, seafood chowders and French onion soups, kiawe-grilled salmon with thyme butter, fresh mahi-mahi with key-lime butter, herbed chicken breast, and garlic prawns are among Kincaid's highlights. Steaks are big here too, and so is the mushroom garden burger, but we love the romaine-and-blue-cheese salad and the devil-may-care Dungeness crab and artichoke sandwich—open-faced, rich, and fabulous. You might want to save room for the signature dessert, the original burnt creme—sinfully rich and custardy, with a glazed sugar topping. Kincaid's is also a popular happy-hour rendezvous, with inexpensive beer and appetizers (sautéed mushrooms, potatoes stuffed with cheese and spinach, sashimi) that may carry the evening. On Friday and Saturday from 9:30pm to 12:30am, live local entertainment adds to the festivity.

Inexpensive

Bernard's New York Deli. At Ward Centre, 1200 Ala Moana Blvd. ☎ **808/594-3353.** Mini plate lunches $6; most items under $9. AE, CB, DC, DISC, JCB, MC, V. Daily 8am–10pm. DELI.

From *New Yorker* magazines on the racks to Fifth Avenue signs and Little Italy posters on the wall, Bernard's is all-out New York—bagels, attitude, and all. Now featuring Brooklyn beer exclusively, the deli boasts "New York's finest smoked nova lox," hot pastrami, Italian subs, kippered salmon salad, potato pancakes, blintzes, cold borscht with sour cream, all-beef kosher knockwurst, Hebrew National hot dogs, and tangy Hebrew National mustards. Mini-plate lunch selections include several bests and "wursts" on a menu that grows by the week.

Harpo's Restaurant. In Ala Moana Plaza, 451 Piikoi St. ☎ **808/591-0040.** Other locations throughout the city. Reservations not accepted. Pizzas $18.50–$28 for large; pasta $6.50–$10. MC, V. Daily 10:30am–10pm. PIZZA.

This place is for those who love thick-crust pan pizzas that can feed a family without breaking the bank. Two of the six Oahu locations (this one and the one at 477 Kapahulu Ave.) have tables and a full menu of sandwiches, pasta, and pizza, including at least 14 varieties of toppings, among them Thai chicken, grilled eggplant, artichoke pesto, the Gourmet (everything from homemade Italian sausage to pepperoni and olives), and prosciutto tomato. Pizza by the slice goes for $1.85—a hunger-buster for diners in a rush.

I ♥ Country Cafe. In Ala Moana Plaza, 451 Piikoi St. ☎ **808/596-8108.** Main courses $5–$8.50. MC, V. Mon–Sat 10:30am–9pm, Sun 10:30am–8pm. INTERNATIONAL.

Give yourself time to peruse the lengthy list of specials posted on the menu board, as well as the prodigious printed menu. Stand in line at the counter, place your order and pay, and find a Formica-topped table; or, wait about 10 minutes for your takeout order to appear in a Styrofoam plate heaped with salad and other accompaniments. This is a beehive with a mind-boggling selection that includes nine types of cheese steaks (including vegetarian tofu), garlic mahi-mahi, Cajun meat loaf, Thai curries, various stir-fries, shoyu chicken, and a long list of other choices spanning many cultures and tastes. Take a good look at the diners and notice that the menu appeals equally to bodybuilders and hedonists. Favorites include the vegetarian or eggplant lasagna, oven-roasted chicken Dijon, and Cajun-style ahi.

Kakaako Kitchen. 1216 Waimanu St. ☎ **808/596-7488.** Main courses $5.75–$8.50. Mon–Sat 6:30am–2pm. No credit cards. GOURMET PLATE LUNCHES.

Island-style chicken linguine is the headliner in this industrial-style kitchen (with art by local artists) near Ala Moana Center, where the owners of 3660 On the Rise, a popular Kaimuki restaurant (see below), have turned their attentions to elevating the local tradition called a plate lunch. Vegetarian specials, homemade tofu burgers, home-style pot roast, fresh catch, grilled marinated mahi-mahi sandwich on taro roll, burgers, ahi steak, and "mixed plate" with two entrees are becoming the lunches of choice among office workers in the area. At breakfast, omelets, scones, and fried rice fly out of the open kitchen. Although much of the business is takeout, there are tables for casual dining in a high-ceilinged, warehouse-like room.

Kua Aina. 1116 Auahi St. ☎ **808/591-9133.** Sandwiches $3.50–$5.70. No credit cards. Daily 10:30am–9pm. AMERICAN.

The ultimate sandwich shop, for years a North Shore fixture, has come to the Ward Center area (near Borders and Starbucks), and the result is dizzying. Phone in your order if you can. During lunch and dinner hours, long lines wait patiently for their famous burgers and sandwiches: mahi-mahi with ortega and cheese (a legend); grilled eggplant and peppers; roast turkey; tuna-avocado; roast beef and avocado; and about a dozen other selections on Kaiser roll, multigrain wheat, or rye breads. Because there are few tables and a small counter space, and there are more diners than space, takeout is a good idea.

Mocha Java. At Ward Centre, 1200 Ala Moana Blvd. ☎ **808/591-9023.** Most items under $7.95. MC, V. Mon–Sat 8am–9pm, Sun 8am–4pm. COFFEEHOUSE/CREPERIE.

This tiny café is a Honolulu staple with legions of loyal followers who love the spinach-lemon crepes and the eight types of veggie burgers, as well as the Java Jolt double espresso and light-and-tasty tofu scramble. Light, wholesome fare is the order of the day: breakfast crepes and omelets; fresh fruit smoothies; homemade soups; and many other choices. The eclectic menu includes stir-fries, Mexican salads and burritos, curried crepes—nothing fancy, but you'll want to return.

Siam Orchid. 1517 Kapiolani Blvd. ☎ **808/955-6161.** Reservations recommended. Main courses $7–$13. AE, JCB, DC, DISC, MC, V. Mon–Sat 11am–2pm, daily 5:30–9:30pm; Thai buffet Sat–Sun 11am–2pm. THAI.

A Honolulu favorite for more than 12 years, Siam Orchid recently moved to a larger, more visible location, and fans happily followed. Just around the corner from its previous location and still a stone's throw from Ala Moana Center, the restaurant still serves its tasty-beyond-belief Tom Yum spicy shrimp soup; fiery Thai garlic shrimp; and a panang vegetable curry with tofu, one of a dozen great offerings for vegetarians. Noodle lovers may consider the Pad Thai fried noodles with shrimp, while curry lovers will be pleased with the extensive selection of chicken, beef, pork, shrimp, and vegetables in the rich, nutty panang sauce or in traditional red, green, and yellow versions. For $11.95, the buffet lunch offers a generous sampling of this popular cuisine.

ALOHA TOWER MARKETPLACE

Gordon Biersch Brewery Restaurant. In Aloha Tower Marketplace, 1 Aloha Tower Dr. ☎ **808/599-4877.** Reservations recommended. Main courses $8–$20. AE, CB, DC, DISC, JCB, MC, V. Sun–Wed 11am–10pm, Thurs–Sat 11am–11pm. NEW AMERICAN/PACIFIC RIM.

German-style lagers brewed on the premises, including the new Pilsner, would be enough of a draw, but the food is the main attraction at Honolulu's liveliest after-work rendezvous. The lanai bar and the brewery bar—open until 1am—are the brightest spots in the marketplace, always teeming with downtown types who think that suds are swell as they nosh on potstickers, grilled steaks, baby-back ribs, chicken pizza, garlic fries, and any number of American classics with deft cross-cultural touches. Live music on weekends is an additional draw.

DOWNTOWN

Downtowners love the informal walk-in cafes lining one side of attractive **Bishop Square**, at 1001 Bishop St. (at King Street), in the middle of the business district, where free entertainment is offered every Friday during lunch hour. The popular **Che Pasta** is a stalwart of the square, chic enough for business meetings and not too formal (or expensive) for a spontaneous rendezvous over pasta and minestrone soup. Some operations open for breakfast and lunch, others for lunch, but most of them close when the business offices empty.

Note: Keep in mind that **Restaurant Row,** which features several hot new restaurants, offers free validated parking in the evenings.

Indigo Eurasian Cuisine. 1211 Nuuanu Ave. ☎ **808/521-2900.** Reservations recommended. Lunch $5.50–$16.50, main dishes $10.25–$18.50 at dinner. AE, DC, DISC, JCB, MC, V. Tues–Fri 11:30am–2pm, 5:30–9:30pm; Sat 5:30–9:30pm; for theater events, half-hour earlier to accommodate theatergoers. EURASIAN.

Hardwood floors, red brick, wicker, high ceilings, and an overall feeling of informal luxe give Indigo a stylish edge. Dine indoors or in a garden setting on choices that include potstickers, Buddhist bao buns, lemongrass chicken brochettes, thousand-loved crab cakes, tandoori chicken breast, miso grilled salmon, vegetable tarts, Asian-style noodles, shiitake-mushroom dumplings, curried lamb brochettes, lilikoi-glazed baby-back ribs, and a host of offerings from east and west, including Indigo's twist on pizza, "pizzettas" with Asian-influenced toppings.

✪ **Legend Seafood Restaurant.** In Chinese Cultural Plaza, 100 N. Beretania St. ☎ **808/532-1868.** Reservations recommended. Most items under $15. AE, DC, JCB, MC, V. Mon, Tues, Thurs, Fri 10:30am–2pm, 5:30–10pm; Sat–Sun 8am–2pm, 5:30–10pm. DIM SUM/SEAFOOD.

It's like dining in Hong Kong here, with a Chinese-speaking clientele poring over Chinese newspapers and the clatter of chopsticks punctuating conversations. Excellent dim sum comes in bamboo steamers that beckon from carts. Although you must often wave madly to catch the server's eye and then point to what you want, the system doesn't deter fans from returning. Among our favorites: deep-fried taro puffs and prawn dumplings; shrimp dim sum; vegetable dumplings; and the open-faced seafood with shiitake, scallops, and a tofu product called *aburage*. Dim sum is only served at lunch, but at dinner, the seafood shines.

Ocean Club. In Restaurant Row, 500 Ala Moana Blvd. ☎ **808/526-9888.** Reservations recommended. No T-shirts or beachwear allowed, and the minimum age is 23. All items $5–$9 ($2–$5 at happy hour). AE, DISC, MC, V. Tues–Thurs 4:30pm–2am, Fri 4:30pm–3am, Sat 6pm–3am. SEAFOOD.

Ocean Club could be listed as a restaurant or a night club, but we list it here because it's so much more than a drinks-only joint. Brilliant and masterfully executed, Ocean Club is a sleek, chic magnet that has redefined happy hour with its extended hours of slashed prices, excellent appetizers-only seafood menu, and ultra-cool ambiance of fake mahi-mahi and frosted glass dangling from the ceiling in a quasi-fifties-retro mood. Galvanized steel counters, mahogany bars lined with shoyu bottles, linoleum tile floors, and oddly attractive pillars resembling pahu (Hawaiian drums) are a wonderfully eclectic mix. Add deejays in bowling shirts and cat-eyed eyeglasses playing the Kingston Trio, and you get the picture. The menu of appetizers lives up to its "ultimate cocktail hour" claim, especially from 4:30–8pm nightly, when great seafood is slashed to half-price and the upbeat mood starts spiraling. A happy-hour sampling: huge lobster claws for under $5; a toothsome spinach and artichoke dip for even less, served with tortilla chips, salsa, and sour cream; Pacific crab dip; ahi tacos for less than $3; fresh ahi poke for less than $2; fresh, good-quality sashimi for less than $4; oyster, shrimp, or crab shooters; and new menu hits marinated teriyaki top sirloin, buffalo wings, and spring rolls ($2.95 before 8pm, $5.95 after).

Palomino. In Harbor Court Building, 66 Queen St. ☎ **808/528-2400.** Reservations recommended. Main dishes $6.95–$26.95. AE, DC, DISC, MC, V. Mon–Fri 11am–2:30pm, Sun–Thurs 5–10pm, Fri–Sat 5–11pm. MEDITERRANEAN.

Palomino came galloping in and took Honolulu by storm. Now *the* downtown hotspot, it offers splendid harbor views, stunning architecture, art at every turn, conscientious service, and good food that's also affordable. It's huge but always full (including the separate bar and lounge, Honolulu's liveliest spot), with a cheerful open kitchen festooned with dangling strands of peppers and garlic. From the kitchen stream kiawe-grilled fish and meats; spit-roasted pork, chicken, and duck; pastas and salads; and pizzas with such lavishments as caramelized onion and spinach. We love the herb-crusted mahi-mahi and shrimp wrapped in grape leaves; others swear by the cedar-plank roasted salmon. Roasted garlic, zesty dips for the focaccia, and a devastating dessert called Caffe Affogato (white-chocolate ice cream, espresso, and whipped cream) add up to heaps of dining enjoyment.

Payao. In Restaurant Row, 500 Ala Moana Blvd. ☎ **808/521-3511.** Lunch special $8, dinner main courses $7–$13. AE, DC, DISC, JCB, MC, V. Mon–Sat 11am–2pm, daily 5–10pm. THAI.

With its few tables indoors and 30 seats in open-air terrace-style dining, Payao brings a pleasant new option to Restaurant Row. The owners of Chiang Mai restaurant (see below) opened their uptown version with their familiar Thai specialties, among them green chicken curry rich with coconut milk and tangy spices; Tom Yum soups (chicken, shrimp, fish, and seafood combo); peanut-rich satay chicken; and stir-fried eggplant redolent with basil and garlic. Payao's Thai noodle dishes (curried, in black-bean sauce, and with vegetables) are a good bet, as are the popular lemongrass chicken and new specials, panang filet and tamarind chicken.

Sunset Grill. Restaurant Row, 500 Ala Moana Blvd. ☎ **808/521-4409.** Reservations recommended for dinner. Main courses $8–$26. AE, DC, DISC, MC, V. Mon–Thurs 11am–11pm, Fri–Sat 11am–midnight, Sun 5–10pm. SAN FRANCISCO–STYLE BISTRO CUISINE.

When *Wine Spectator* granted its "Award of Excellence" to Sunset Grill recently, it highlighted only one feature of this diner-friendly eatery in Restaurant Row. Rare vintages, a strong selection of wines by the glass, a pleasing, light-filled room, and chef Marcia Cades' (she's an honors graduate of the Culinary Institute of America) impressive menu of homemade pastas, fish, meats, appetizers, and homemade desserts are among the offerings. Count on crisp, straightforward, elegant, ungimmicky cuisine: bow-tie pasta with fresh ahi and tomato-basil sauce; risotto with osso buco; fresh chipotle fettuccine (with smoked, vine-ripened tomatoes); house-cured salmon with crème fraîche and capers; kiawe-grilled ribs; New York steak; and special touches such as Tuscan mashed potatoes, housemade Cajun-style potato chips, and oven-roasted garlic with goat cheese. A good bet, all the way around.

Yanagi Sushi. 762 Kapiolani Blvd. ☎ **808/597-1525.** Reservations recommended. Main courses $8–$33, complete dinners $11.50–$18.50. AE, CB, DC, DISC, JCB, MC, V. Daily 11am–2pm; Mon–Sat 5:30pm–2am, Sun 5:30–10pm. JAPANESE.

We love the late-night hours, the sushi bar with its fresh ingredients and well-trained chefs, and the extensive choices in the combination lunches and dinners. But we also love the à la carte Japanese menu, which covers everything from *chazuke* (rice with tea, salmon, seaweed, and other condiments; a comfort food) to shabu-shabu and other steaming earthenware-pot dishes. Nosh on noodles or complete dinners with choices of sashimi, shrimp tempura, broiled salmon, New York steak, and many other possibilities. Dine affordably or extravagantly, on $6 noodles or a $30 lobster nabe, or on nearly 20 different types of sashimi. Consistently crisp tempura, affordable combination lunches, and one of the town's finer spicy ahi hand-rolled sushi also make Yanagi worth remembering.

KALIHI/SAND ISLAND

La Mariana Restaurant & Bar. 50 Sand Island Rd. ☎ **808/848-2800.** Reservations recommended, especially on weekends. AE, MC, V. Daily 11:30am–11:30pm: lunch 11:30am–2pm; pupus 3–5pm; dinner Sun–Thurs 5–9pm, Fri–Sat 5–10pm. To find it, turn makai (toward the ocean) on Sand Island Road from Nimitz Highway; immediately after the 1st stoplight on Sand Island, take a right and drive to the ocean; it's not far from the airport. AMERICAN.

Try to find a spot more evocative, more nostalgic than this South Seas oasis at water's edge in the bowels of industrial Honolulu, with carved tikis, glass balls suspended in fishing nets, shell chandeliers, and tables made from koa trees before they became scarce. Owner Annette La Mariana Nahinu, who also runs the La Mariana Sailing Club, is the most spritely octogenarian you could hope to meet, a bon vivant who crossed the South Pacific in a 36-foot sailboat before settling in Hawaii, where she wound up converting a Honolulu junkyard into a lush marina. Enveloped in greenery at water's edge, furnished with 1950s shell chandeliers and furniture from the old Trader Vic's and South Seas restaurants, this unique 42-year-old restaurant is popular for lunch, sunset appetizers, and impromptu Friday and Saturday night sing-alongs at the piano bar. Seared Cajun-style ahi is your best bet as appetizer or entrée, but there are ample seafood choices and salads and sandwiches at lunch.

Sam Choy's Breakfast, Lunch & Crab. 580 Nimitz Hwy., Iwilei (in the Iwilei industrial area near Honolulu Harbor, across the street from Gentry Pacific Center and in the same building as Garakuta-Do Janapese Antiques). ☎ **808/545-7979.** Reservations recommended for lunch and dinner. Main courses $5–$10 at breakfast, $6–$27 at lunch, $19–$35 at dinner. AE, DC, DISC, JCB, MC, V. Mon–Fri 6:30–10am, 10:30am–4pm, 5–10pm; Sat–Sun 6:30–11:30am, 11:30am–4pm, 5–10pm. ISLAND CUISINE/SEAFOOD.

Until Sam Choy's opened in this industrial part of Honolulu, Hawaii diners had long lamented the absence of an informal, roll-up-your-sleeves-and-get-messy kind of restaurant where you could crack crab with mallets and wear plastic bibs with abandon. Voilà! This may be Honolulu's happiest, most carefree eatery, elegance and cholesterol be damned. Chef-restaurateur Sam Choy's long-awaited crabhouse, open since May 1997, features great fun and lots of fabulous food (big meals are, after all, the Choy trademark). Imagine dining in an all-wood sampan (it's the centerpiece of the 11,000-square-foot restaurant) and washing your hands in an oversized wok in the center of the room, under a faucet activated by an automatic sensor (the kind that wreaks havoc in airport bathrooms). That giant wok comes in handy, as the menu assures delightfully messy dining—if not on beef stew, omelets, and fried rice at breakfast or the Hawaiian plate and fresh fish at lunch, then decidedly at dinner, when all thoughts turn to the featured attraction: crab.

A 2,000-gallon live crab tank lines the open kitchen, serving as temporary shelter for the assortment of crabs in season: Kona, Maryland, Samoan, Dungeness, and Florida stone crabs. Clam chowder, seafood gumbos, assorted poke, and an oyster bar and brew pub are also offered at dinner, which, in Choy fashion, comes complete with soup, salad, and entree. The priciest items are the surf-and-turf combinations of lobster or crab with ribs or New York steak—up to $35 and heroic for sure. Children's menus—needed more than ever at Choy's restaurants, where big is the operative word—are an additional family feature.

Yohei Sushi. 1111 Dillingham Blvd., across from Honolulu Community College. ☎ **808/841-3773.** Reservations recommended. Lunch entrees $6–$15; complete dinners $15–$24. DC, JCB, V, MC. Mon–Sat 11am–1:45pm, 5–9:30pm.

Yohei is difficult to find, tucked away in a small, nondescript complex just before Dillingham crosses the bridge into Kalihi, Honolulu's industrial area. But it's well worth the hunt, especially for lovers of authentic Tokyo-style sushi. Duck into the tiny room, find a seat at the sushi bar, and tuck into the sweet shrimp (amaebi), surf clam (akagai), yellowtail tuna (hamachi), butterfly tuna (negi toro temaki), bluefish (kohada gari chiso temaki), and wonderful assortment of seafood, fresh as can be. A friend from Tokyo discovered this restaurant for us and gave it her highest approval for authenticity, freshness, quality, and—surprise!—price. An evening at Yohei is like a trip to a Tokyo sushi bar, where regulars know the chef and even familiar gastronomic territory can be a grand adventure. For the sushi aficionado, a must.

MANOA VALLEY/MOILIILI/MAKIKI
Expensive

✪ **Alan Wong's Restaurant.** 1857 S. King St., 5th Floor. ☎ **808/949-2526.** Reservations recommended. Main courses $15–$20. AE, CB, DC, MC, V. Daily 5–10pm. HAWAII REGIONAL.

A brilliant chef with staying power who has influenced the direction of regional cuisine, Alan Wong owns what is arguably Honolulu's busiest restaurant, a 90-seat room with a glassed-in terrace and open kitchen, accented with stylish and imposing floral arrangements, minimalist avant-garde lighting, and curly-koa wall panels. Vertical cuisine is the trend here: Many of the dishes come in high-rise towers of multiple layers and colors, such as the crab-and-chicken lumpia (a Filipino crepe) with three sauces and his famous ahi cake with layers of grilled eggplant, Maui onion, seared ahi, and Big Island goat cheese with lemongrass sauce. The wild-mushroom risotto with basil oil, grilled vegetables, and salmon coulis also appear in a column. Despite this overworked motif, the flavors shine with Asian lemongrass, sweet-sour, garlic, wasabi, and other assertive ingredients deftly melded with the fresh seafood and produce of the islands. The California roll is a triumph, made with salmon roe, wasabi, and Kona lobster instead of rice, served warm. We love the opihi shooters, day-boat scallops, and fresh-fish preparations. But don't get attached, because the menu changes daily.

Moderate

Chiang Mai. 2239 S. King St. ☎ **808/941-1151.** Reservations suggested for dinner. Main courses $8–$13. AE, DC, DISC, JCB, MC, V. Mon–Fri 11am–2pm; daily 5:30–10pm. THAI.

This was one of Honolulu's early Thai restaurants and has retained a stalwart following despite fierce competition. Recently expanded to accommodate 100, Chiang Mai made sticky rice famous, serving it in bamboo steamers to accompany excellent red, green, and yellow curries; the signature Cornish game hen in lemongrass and spices; and a garlic-infused green papaya salad marinated in tamarind sauce. Spicy shrimp soup, eggplant with basil and tofu, and the vegetarian green curry are some time-honored favorites. The vegetarian menu is superb, and new fresh-fish dishes are a welcome addition.

Contemporary Museum Cafe. In The Contemporary Museum, 2411 Makiki Heights Dr. ☎ **808/523-3362.** Reservations recommended. Main courses $8–$11. MC, V. Tues–Sat 10am–3pm, Sun noon–3pm. PACIFIC RIM/MEDITERRANEAN.

The surroundings are an integral part of the dining experience at this tiny lunchtime cafe, part of an art museum nestled on the slopes of Tantalus amid carefully cultivated Oriental gardens, with a breathtaking view of Diamond Head and priceless contemporary art displayed indoors and outdoors. The cafe's menu is limited to sandwiches, soups, salads, and appetizers, but you won't leave disappointed. Before crowning the meal with flourless chocolate cake, consider the grilled eggplant sandwich, the baked Brie and Indonesian mushrooms, or the oven-roasted turkey breast sandwich. The ubiquitous garden burger is given a taste twist with a homemade barbecue sauce, and the house-smoked mahi-mahi with Caesar dressing and a tower of greens is *the* choice for fish lovers.

Diem. 2633 S. King St. ☎ **808/941-8657.** Reservations recommended for dinner. Main courses $6–$10. AE, DISC, JCB, MC, V. Daily 10am–10pm. VIETNAMESE.

We love Diem for its Royal Seafood noodle soup, its roll-up appetizers (fish, shrimp, beef, seafood); its spicy fried rice, vegetarian or with shrimp or chicken; its eggplant with tofu and basil; and its lemongrass fish, chicken, seafood, and vegetarian dishes. Crisp fish and energetic curries also score high on this menu of simple delights, which caters as much to tofu-loving vegetarians as to beef and pork enthusiasts. The tiny eatery in the university area has earned its following by word of mouth and spreads the taste treats with a thriving catering business.

Maple Garden. 909 Isenberg St. ☎ **808/941-6641.** Main courses $5–$29.50. AE, JCB, MC, V. Daily 11am–2pm and 5:30–10pm. SZECHUAN.

In addition to the Peking duck—which has earned its noble reputation and must be ordered a day in advance—Maple Garden is known for many specialties. The Chinaman's Hat, a version of mu shui pork, is reliably good, and you can order it vegetarian as well. Other hits: braised scallops with Chinese mushrooms, spicy garlic eggplant, diced chicken with chili, prawns in chili sauce, fried chicken in five spices, and crisp string beans. The more subdued can try the vegetarian selections (sautéed spinach is a good bet) or any of the dozens of seafood entrées—everything from sea cucumbers to lobster with black-bean sauce and braised salmon. An ever-expanding visual feast adorns the dining-room walls, covered with noted artist John Young's original drawings, sketches, and murals.

Sushi King. 2700 S. King St. ☎ 808/947-2836. Reservations recommended. Main courses $9.50–$22. AE, JCB, MC, V. Wed–Mon 11:30am–2pm and 5:30pm–2am, Tues 5:30–10pm. JAPANESE.

Brusque service sure doesn't deter diners from arriving in throngs for the lunch specials here, and they're highly recommended. This is the king of excellent jumbo jumbo platters, with soup, pickles, California roll sushi, and your choice of chicken teriyaki, beef teriyaki, shrimp and vegetable tempura, and calamari and vegetable tempura—for an unbelievable $6.95. Other combination lunches offer generous choices: sashimi, tempura, butterfish, fried oysters, soba noodles, udon noodles, and more than a dozen selections. Otherwise, the à la carte menu holds its own with noodles, *donburi* (steamed rice with tempura and other toppings), and sushi from the always-full sushi bar. The lunch specials are continued as early-bird specials daily from 5:30 to 6:30pm. With or without the specials, this is the typical neighborhood restaurant whose stern ways are usually forgiven by diners who appreciate the value and the food quality.

Inexpensive

Andy's Sandwiches & Smoothies. 2904 E. Manoa Rd., opposite Manoa Marketplace. ☎ 808/988-6161. Also at 745 Keeaumoku St. near Ala Moana Center. ☎ 808/946-6161. Most items less than $5. MC, V. Mon–Thurs 7am–6pm, Fri 7am–5pm, Sat 7am–2:30pm. GOURMET HEALTH FOOD.

It started as a health-food restaurant, expanded into a juice bar, and today is a neighborhood fixture for fresh baked bread, healthy breakfasts and lunches (its mango muffins are famous), and homemade vegetarian fare. Andy's is a roadside stop that always carries fresh papayas, sandwiches, and healthy snacks for folks on the run. The ahi deluxe sandwich is tops ($6.50), but the fresh roasted turkey sandwiches are the acclaimed favorite.

India Bazaar. Old Stadium Square, 2320 S. King St. ☎ 808/949-4840. Main courses $5.75–$6.75. No credit cards. Daily 11am–9pm. INDIAN.

Spicy curries, crispy papadams, moist chapatis, and the full range of Indian delicacies are served from a counter where you point and choose. The vegetables are overcooked in the Indian fashion, but the flavors bring redemption. A few tables are scattered about a room filled with the scent of spices; one wall is lined with exotic chutneys and Indian condiments for home-cooking. The vegetarian thalli is a favorite: The spiced Indian rice comes with your choice of three vegetable curries and other choices like lentil, cauliflower, eggplant, tofu/peas, potato, spinach/lentil, garbanzo beans, and okra. Chicken tandoori (with two vegetable curries) and shrimp thalli appeal to non-vegetarians.

⭐ **Jimbo's Restaurant.** 1936 S. King St. ☎ 808/947-2211. Reservations not accepted. Main courses $4.50–$11. CB, JCB, MC, V. Wed–Mon 11am–3pm; Wed–Thurs and Sun–Mon 5–10pm, Fri–Sat 5–11pm. JAPANESE.

Jimbo's is tiny, fewer than a dozen tables, and there's such a demand for its sublime fare that you may have to wait for a seating. It's worth it. A must for any noodle lover, Jimbo's serves homemade udon noodles in a flawless homemade broth, then tops the works with shrimp tempura, chicken, eggs and vegetables, seaweed, roasted mochi, and a variety of accompaniments of your choice. The Zo,uni, with chicken, vegetables, and mochi rice roasted to a toasty flavor, is one of life's great pleasures. Cold noodles, stir-fried noodles, donburi steamed-rice dishes with assorted toppings, Japanese-style curries, and combination dinners served on trays are among the many delights that keep diners returning. The earthenware pot of noodles, shiitake mushrooms, vegetables, and udon, with a platter of tempura on the side, is the top-of-the-line combo, a designer dish at an affordable price.

Kozo Sushi. 2334 S. King St. ☎ **808/973-5666.** Most items under $3.50; party plates $15–$24. No credit cards. Mon–Sat 9am–7pm, Sun 9am–6pm. SUSHI.

Into the pricey, floating world of expensive sushi houses came Kozo—fast, affordable, takeout sushi that isn't Kyoto quality, but is respectable and extremely popular. Kozo's combination platters are ubiquitous at pot-luck functions and large gatherings, but individual sushi can also be ordered: California roll, unagi roll, salmon and shrimp, and dozens of other choices, including the newest addition, the odd hybrid called BLT maki. There are four other locations in Honolulu.

Old Waialae Road Cafe. 2820 S. King St. ☎ **808/951-7779.** Reservations not accepted. Main courses $5–$8. No credit cards. Mon–Fri 11am–9pm, Sat–Sun 8am–9pm. LOCAL/PLATE LUNCH.

The plate lunch, the Rodney Dangerfield of the culinary world, has finally been assigned the respect it deserves, thanks to two enterprising women who have infused the "two scoop rice" concept with new options and a gourmet touch. There are a few tables outdoors, but mostly Old Waialae Road is a gourmet take-out stand that has lost none of its local flavor in its offerings: grilled ahi plate, kimchee burgers, sliced chicken-breast pasta with Molokai sweet potato and Waimanalo gourmet greens, and a familiar list of local favorites such as Korean kal bi and teriyaki beef. There's an excellent Hawaiian plate lunch on Fridays, with specials every weekday. The weekend breakfast is a rage, particularly the huevos rancheros, banana-cinnamon nut French toast, and gourmet tofu scramble.

Well Bento. 2570 S. Beretania St., 2nd Floor. ☎ **808/941-5261.** Mostly take-out. Plate lunches $5.95–$7.50. No credit cards. Mon–Sat 11:30am–5pm. GOURMET HEALTH/ORGANIC PLATE LUNCHES.

We wondered whether such healthy organic food, without the use of eggs, refined sugar, or dairy products, would satisfy. Countless plate lunches later, we can report that Well Bento will make a guiltless gourmet out of even the fussiest palate. Each plate is aesthetically pleasing, wholesome, and tasty. Louisiana tempeh (grilled over lava rocks), salmon grilled over lava rocks or poached with shiitake mushrooms, spicy Cajun-style chicken, and creative vegetarian selections ("plant-based plates") make this Honolulu newcomer worth trying. Bean salad, cabbage and seaweed salads, and organic brown rice accompany each plate and are as decorative as they are delicious. Order ahead if possible; only a few seats are provided.

KAIMUKI/KAPAHULU
Expensive

3660 On the Rise. 3660 Waialae Ave. ☎ **808/737-1177.** Reservations suggested. Main courses $17.50–$24.50. AE, DC, DISC, JCB, MC, V. Tues–Thurs 5:30–9pm, Fri–Sat 5:30–10pm, Sun 5:30–9pm. EUROPEAN/ISLAND.

This is a busy, noisy restaurant with a menu that has retained only tried-and-true favorites, ranging from the basics like roasted chicken and an excellent rack of lamb to exotic touches such as ti-leaf-wrapped seafood in a tomato-butter sauce. Our favorites: the ahi katsu, wrapped in nori and deep-fried rare, an excellent appetizer; Caesar salad; and opakapaka simmered in Chinese black-bean broth. The new New York Steak Alaea (Hawaiian red rock salt) and the award-winning desserts keep 3660 on the rise.

✪ **Ninniku-Ya Garlic Restaurant.** 3196 Waialae Ave. ☎ **808/735-0784.** Reservations recommended. Main dishes $11–$28. AE, DISC, JCB, MC, V. Tues–Sat 5:30–11pm; Sun 5:30–10pm. EURO-ASIAN.

Plain and simple, this is a great garlic restaurant, a paean to the stinking rose. Cozy, in an old home with tables in a split-level dining room and under old trees outdoors, Ninniku-Ya titillates the palate. Seasonal specialties (winter pumpkin in garlic potatoes, opah during winter, beer-colored sauces for Valentine's Day) are fine but not necessary, because the staples are entirely satisfying. Garlic bread comes with a mound of garlic, the three-mushroom pasta is sublime, the hot-stone filet mignon is tender and tasty, and the garlic rice is a meal in itself. Everything contains garlic, but it doesn't overpower, even in the homemade garlic gelato. Yes, that's garlic gelato, and it's good.

✪ **Sam Choy's Diamond Head Restaurant.** 449 Kapahulu Ave. ☎ 808/732-8645. Reservations required. Main courses $19–$30; Sun brunch $24.95 adults, $14.95 children. AE, MC, V. Mon–Thurs 5:30–9:30pm, Fri–Sat 5–9:30pm, Sun 9:30am–2pm and 5–9:30pm. HAWAII REGIONAL.

You'll know you're in the right place if you see a parade of exiting diners clutching their Styrofoam bundles, for leftovers are de rigueur at any Sam Choy's operation, where the servings are gargantuan in the Sam Choy tradition. But the food is as big-bodied and big-hearted as the servings. Choy has won over a sizable chunk of Hawaii's dining population, so successfully that you must often book weeks in advance. It's noisy, informal, and full of hearty diners. The master of poke, Choy serves several of the best versions ever invented, among them a white fish (ono, opakapaka) drizzled with hot oil and topped with chopped herbs and condiments. Heartily recommended are the Brie wontons, the teriyaki-style rib-eye steak, and the no-fat steamed fish with ginger and shiitake mushrooms. His Kapakahi mashed potatoes remain unsurpassed, and the entrées, served with salad and soup, make each meal more than most single diners can consume.

Moderate

Genki Sushi. 900 Kapahulu Ave. ☎ 808/735-8889. Individual sushi $1.20 and up per order; combination platters $7.40–$38.60. AE, DC, DISC, MC, V. Sun–Thurs 11am–9pm, Fri–Sat 11am–10pm, take-out available daily 11am–9pm. SUSHI.

Fun! Crowded! Entertaining! Take your place in line for a seat at one of the U-shaped counters at which conveyor belts parade by with freshly made sushi, usually two pieces per color-coded plate, priced inexpensively. The dizzying variety is full of possibilities: spicy tuna topped with scallions, ahi, scallops with mayonnaise, Canadian roll (like California roll, except with salmon), sea urchin, flavored octopus, sweet shrimp, surf clam, corn, tuna salad, and so on. Genki starts with a Japanese culinary tradition and takes liberties with it, so purists miss out on some fun. By the end of the meal, the piled-high plates are tallied up by color and presto, your bill appears, much smaller than the pleasure. Brilliant combination platters stream across the take-out counter.

Inexpensive

Bueno Nalo. 3045 Monsarrat Ave. ☎ 808/735-8818. Most items less than $9.95. MC, V. Daily 11am–10pm. MEXICAN.

Olé for Bueno Nalo and its sizzling fajitas, hearty combination platters, and famous chimichangas. There are two tables outside, six tables indoors, and a brisk take-out business among those who like its simple Mexican fare and adjoining juice bar. The juice bar serves the best smoothies in town.

Cafe Laufer. 3565 Waialae Ave. ☎ 808/735-7717. Most items less than $7. AE, CB, DC, DISC, JCB, MC, V. Sun–Mon and Wed–Thurs 8am–10pm, Fri–Sat 8am–11pm. COFFEE SHOP.

This small, airy, and cheerful cafe has frilly decor and sublime pastries, from apple scones and linzer tortes to fruit flans, decadent chocolate mousses, and carrot cakes to accompany the latté and espresso. Fans drop in for simple soups and deli sandwiches on fresh-baked breads; biscotti for their coffee break; or a hearty loaf of seven-grain, rye, pumpernickel, or French for breaking bread tomorrow. It's a solid hit for lunch: soup-salad-sandwich specials for a song, Chinese chicken salad for $7.25, gourmet greens with mango-infused honey-mustard dressing—a small but satisfying menu. The special Saturday-night desserts such as the made-to-order soufflés—fresh lemon or strawberry, chocolate, Grand Marnier, and other fantasy flavors—are the real thing.

Hale Vietnam. 1140 12th Ave. ☎ **808/735-7581.** Reservations recommended for groups. Main courses $4.50–$16. AE, DISC, MC, V. Mon–Sat 11am–10pm, Sun 11am–9pm. VIET-NAMESE.

Duck into this house of pho and brave the no-frills service for the steaming noodle soups that are the house specialty. The stock is simmered and skimmed for many hours and is accompanied with noodles, beef, chicken, and a platter of bean sprouts and fresh herbs. Approach the green chiles with caution; it's hard to know if they're the ones that can scorch and disable you. Although we love the chicken soup and shrimp vermicelli, as well as the seafood pho and imperial rolls, caution is advised because this restaurant, like most other Vietnamese eateries, uses MSG.

EAST OF WAIKIKI: KAHALA

Hoku's. In Kahala Mandarin Oriental Hotel, 5000 Kahala Ave. ☎ **808/739-8777.** Reservations recommended. Main courses $18–$32.50. AE, CB, DC, DISC, JCB, MC, V. Daily 11:30am–2:30pm and 5:30–10:30pm. PACIFIC/EUROPEAN.

The fine dining room of the Kahala Mandarin has made a name with its informal yet elegant lunches and dazzling dinners with an Island touch. The ocean view, open kitchen, and astonishing bamboo floor are stellar features. Many proclaim this the finest cuisine they've encountered in years, others say it's overrated. Reflecting its cross-cultural influences, the kitchen is equipped with a *kiawe* grill; an Indian tandoori oven for its chicken and naan bread; and Szechuan woks for the prawn, lobster, tofu, and other stir-fried specialties. The deep-fried whole fresh fish is an occasion; traditionalists can stick to the rack of lamb, roasted chicken, or herb-crusted onaga.

✪ **Kahala Moon Cafe.** 4614 Kilauea Ave. ☎ **808/732-7777.** Reservations recommended. Main courses $15–$24. AE, MC, V. Sun, Tues–Thurs 5:30–9:30pm, Fri–Sat 5:30–10:30pm. HAWAII REGIONAL.

Stylish without being pretentious, with designer flowers in behemoth pots accenting the windowless room, Kahala Moon gets our vote as a standout in Honolulu. Fans were crushed when it closed for lunch, but dinner attracts more music and festivity than ever before. Favorites include sautéed salmon with wild mushroom/lemon herb sauce; pan-seared scallops in orange–black peppercorn glaze; sizzling shrimp in chile garlic oil; and, at the top of the culinary heap, the grilled lamb chops with caramelized onions, roasted potatoes, and sherry-coriander–lemon butter. Save room for the mango bread pudding or lemongrass crème brûlée, ambrosia to the final spoonful.

✪ **Olive Tree Cafe.** 4614 Kilauea Ave., next to Kahala Mall. ☎ **808/737-0303.** Reservations not accepted. Main courses $5–$10. No credit cards. Mon–Fri 5–11pm, Sat–Sun 11am–10pm. GREEK/EASTERN MEDITERRANEAN.

The legions of Olive Tree fans are continually amazed at the delectables streaming out of the tiny open kitchen at bargain prices. With umbrellas over tables on the sidewalk, a few seats indoors, and the best Greek food in Hawaii, this informal cafe is one of the top values in town. The tabouli salad is generously greened with herbs and mint, perfectly balanced in flavor and texture. The falafel, eggplant salad, ceviche, mussels, and taramasalata—a pink caviar spread with pita—are a pleasurable launch to a meal that will only ascend. The superb souvlakis (kebabs in pita bread) range from fresh fish to chicken and lean New Zealand lamb, spruced up with the chef's signature yogurt-dill sauce. You'll order at the counter from a blackboard menu that includes the daily specials: lamb shank in tomato and herbs, lemon chicken, spanakopita, and a stuffed eggplant called *imambayaldi*. Located next door to Kahala Mall (where you can buy your own libations), Olive Tree is BYOB, which means a large group can dine like sultans for a song and take in a movie next door, too.

The Patisserie. 4211 Waialae Ave., Kahala Mall. ☎ **808/735-4402.** Deli sandwiches $3.75–$4.75; complete dinners $13.50–$17.50. MC, V. Dinner service Tues–Sat 5:30–8:30pm; deli service Mon–Sat 7am–9pm, Sun 7am–5pm. GERMAN.

The complete dinners are a pleasant surprise, more elegant than the casual mall surroundings would indicate and kind to the pocketbook, too. In its bakery setting with eight tables and a gleaming deli counter, the Patisserie sells everything from deluxe wedding cakes and European breads to inexpensive deli sandwiches (tuna, egg salad, pastrami, black-forest ham), and 10 types of complete dinners. The Tuesday-through-Saturday dinners include sauerbraten, osso buco, veal ribs, baked pork tenderloin, braised lamb shank, and a particularly memorable sautéed chicken breast in a Marsala mushroom sauce and linguine. A fish dinner is offered every Friday, and the German dinners have built a following among those longing for Wiener schnitzel, rahm schnitzel, pepper schnitzel, and potato pancakes with sour cream and applesauce. Served with garden salad and rolls, the dinners are laudable, a terrific value if you're willing to go for a tasty dinner without the candlelight and roses.

EAST OAHU
NIU VALLEY

⭐ **Cliquo.** 5730 Niu Valley Shopping Center, Kalanianaole Hwy. ☎ **808/377-8854.** Reservations recommended. Main courses $16–$29; prix fixe $27. AE, DC, DISC, JCB, MC, V. Mon–Sat 5:30–9pm. FRENCH.

Chef Yves Menoret has a glowing reputation in Honolulu as the man who established the erstwhile Bagwell's and Bali By the Sea before opening his own 50-seat dining room three years ago. His solid French offerings are prepared with care and Old World meticulousness, particularly the flaky opakapaka with watercress and ginger beurre blanc; seared foie gras with leek and Yukon potato; and vol-au-vent, buttery escargots in clouds of leeks and garlic. The medley of lobster with wild mushrooms and the lobster medallion salad come in two sizes, a plus. On such a spare, selective, and elegant menu, the prix fixe selections soar. (One night, the prix-fixe menu included asparagus with wild mushrooms, tournedos of filet mignon in a light cabernet sauce or fresh opakapaka with a purée of organic pumpkin, and macadamia chocolate mousse or fresh fruit granite—all for an affordable $27.) Menoret's following grows.

Swiss Inn. Niu Valley Shopping Center, 5730 Kalanianaole Hwy. ☎ **808/377-5447.** Reservations recommended. Complete dinners $14–$21. AE, CB, DC, DISC, JCB, MC, V. Wed–Sun 6pm–closing, Sunday brunch 10:30am–1pm. CONTINENTAL.

Martin and Jeanie Wyss have been welcoming families for more than 15 years to their cordial "chalet" in suburban Honolulu. The quintessential neighborhood restaurant, Swiss Inn offers terrific values with no compromise in quality: Wiener schnitzel, $16; New York steak, $21; scallops Madagascar, $19.25; baked chicken, $14. The complete dinners include soup, salad, vegetables, and coffee or tea. Families have always been welcome at Swiss Inn, and when the kids grow up, they bring their friends and families too. It's always full. Specialties include the veal dishes and the fresh fish, usually mahi-mahi or onaga in a lemon-butter-caper sauce, and at Thanksgiving and holidays, the home-cooked turkey dinner, just the way mom made it.

HAWAII KAI

✪ **Roy's Restaurant.** 6600 Kalanianaole Hwy., ☎ **808/396-7697.** Reservations recommended. Main courses $9–$25. AE, JCB, MC, V. Daily 5:30–9:15pm. EUROPEAN/ASIAN.

He built in Hawaii Kai, and diners came—in droves. Roy Yamaguchi's flagship Hawaii restaurant was the first of what now number more than a dozen throughout Hawaii, Asia, and the Pacific—but don't count on that figure, because his dining empire grows faster than we can count. A prolific winner of culinary awards, Yamaguchi devised a winning formula: open kitchen, fresh ingredients, ethnic touches, and a good dose of nostalgia mingling with European techniques. The menu changes nightly, but you can generally count on individual pizzas; a varied appetizer menu (summer rolls, blackened ahi, hibachi-style salmon); a small pasta selection; and entrees such as lemongrass roasted chicken, garlic-mustard short ribs, mustard-crusted lamb shanks, hibachi-style salmon in ponzu sauce, and several types of fresh catch prepared at least five different ways. Roy's is also renowned for its high-decibel style of dining, so full and so noisy you'll have to join in the fracas to be heard. But the food quality, service, impeccable timing, and eclectic, well-priced wine list rarely disappoint.

THE WINDWARD COAST

✪ **Ahi's Restaurant.** 59146 Kamehameha Hwy., Punaluu. ☎ **808/293-5650.** Reservations for 8 or more. Main courses $6–$12. No credit cards. Mon–Sat 11am–9pm. AMERICAN/LOCAL.

There is no place like Ahi's in Hawaii—in a beautiful rural setting, with tasty local fare, and the generous aloha of Ahi Logan and his three-generation family business. Ahi's is a lush roadside oasis with split-level indoor dining and an airy, screened-in room (for larger parties) that's a charming throwback to preresort, premarble, preplastic Hawaii. A rolling green lawn and shade-giving trees surround the wooden structure; from food to ambiance to clientele, it's informal and comfortably rural. The shrimp—the menu highlight—comes plump and served four ways: cocktail, scampi, tempura, and deep fried. The mahi-mahi and fresh-fish specials are always good. On Saturdays, the generous Hawaiian lunch plate ($9.50) offers lau-lau, grilled fish, shrimp, and pipikaula (dried, salted beef), and soon there'll be a "shrimp and beer garden" for noshing under the trees. Come here when you're hungering for the taste of real Hawaii that resorts long ago abandoned.

Assaggio Italian Restaurant. 354 Uluniu St., Kailua. ☎ **808/261-2772.** Reservations recommended. Main courses $9–$18. AE, DC, DISC, MC, V. Mon–Fri 11:30am–2:30pm, daily 5–10pm. ITALIAN.

You may not want to make the half-hour trip over the Pali for dinner here, but it's nice to know about Assaggio if you happen to visit the Windward Coast. Affordable prices, attentive service, and some winning items have won Assaggio loyal fans throughout the years. The best-selling homemade hot antipasto has jumbo shrimp, fresh clams, mussels, and calamari in a sauce of cayenne pepper, white wine, and garlic. You can choose linguine, fettuccine, or ziti with 10 different sauces in small or regular portions, or any of nine chicken pastas (the chicken Assaggio, with garlic, peppers, and mushrooms, is especially flavorful). Especially impressive is the extensive list of seafood pastas, including the plainly wonderful garlic/olive oil sautée.

Brent's Restaurant & Delicatessen. 629-A Kailua Rd. ☎ **808/262-8588.** Most items under $15. MC, V. Tues–Sat 7am–9pm, Sun 7am–8pm. KOSHER DELI.

Finally, a kosher deli with real cheese blintzes, cream-cheese and shrimp omelets, and some spirited cultural digressions, such as pesto poached eggs and an artichoke-laced frittata. And bagels galore, with baked salmon, sturgeon and cream cheese, or any number of accompaniments to compete with the New York–style pastrami and hot corned-beef sandwiches on Bren's abundant menu.

Kimoz. 41-1537 Kalanianaole Hwy., Waimanalo. ☎ **808/259-8800.** AE, MC, V. Mon–Thurs 6:30am–9pm, Fri 6:30am–2am, Sat 8:30am–2am, Sun 8:30am–8pm. LOCAL/KOREAN.

Kimoz is doing a brisk business with its popular plates and generous *kal bi*, the spicy marinated Korean meat. Lovers of local food will find no stone unturned, from generous Portuguese sausage or seafood omelets to plate lunches, grilled mahi-mahi, made-from-scratch mandoo, saimin, and home-style hamburgers, meat loaf, seafood, and Hawaiian plates are among the popular items on a diverse local menu. You'll sit at wooden picnictable–style booths with a view of the jukebox and the bubble-gum machines at the entrance. Karaoke explains the late hours.

THE NORTH SHORE

Cafe Haleiwa. 66-460 Kamehameha Hwy., Haleiwa. ☎ **808/637-5516.** Reservations not accepted. Main courses $5.50–$10.50. AE, MC, V. Daily 7am–2pm, Sun 7am–2pm. MEXICAN/ESPRESSO BAR.

Haleiwa's legendary breakfast joint is a big hit with surfers, urban gentry with weekend country homes, reclusive artists, and anyone who loves mahi-mahi plate lunches and homemade Mexican food. It's one of those wake-up-and-hit-the-beach kind of places serving generous burritos and omelets with names like Off the Wall, Off the Lip, and Breakfast in a Barrel. Surf pictures line the walls, and the ambiance is Formica-style casual. A mahi-mahi plate lunch with home fries, rice, or beans; spicy chicken tacos; fish tacos with grilled mahi, tomatoes, lime, and cilantro; and burritos, tostadas, and combination plates will make it hard for you to stick to a veggie or chicken sandwich. But they serve those, too—tuna salad, mahimahi, burgers, steak sandwiches—made with individual attention and grilled onions on request. Our favorite breakfast is the truly epic huevos rancheros, smothered with cheese and salsa.

Coffee Gallery. In North Shore Marketplace, 66-250 Kamehameha Hwy., Haleiwa. ☎ **808/637-5355.** Reservations not accepted. Most items less than $6. AE, DISC, MC, V. Mon–Fri 6am–9pm, Sat–Sun 7am–9pm. COFFEEHOUSE/VEGETARIAN.

On the other side of town from Kua Aina (see below) and its meat-lover's cuisine, this indoor-outdoor coffeehouse has carved a firm niche in the hearts of Haleiwa's health-conscious diners, vegetarians, and coffee lovers. The lemon squares here are famous (the recipe was printed, by popular request, in the local newspaper), and the granola is made with premium Big Island honey. There are tofu burritos with fresh spinach and roasted garlic tomato sauce, bagels galore, salads and pastas, and a spicy three-bean vegetarian chili served with renetless cheddar cheese. The vegan soup is served with fresh baked whole-wheat French bread. Spinach pesto, vegetarian enchiladas, tempeh and garden burgers, hummus platters, and many pages of healthy enticements make this one of Haleiwa's heavenly stops.

Jameson's By the Sea. 62-540 Kamehameha Hwy., Haleiwa. ☎ **808/637-4336.** Reservations recommended. Main courses $13–$39 in upstairs dining room; downstairs lunch menu $7–$12. AE, DC, DISC, JCB, MC, V. Downstairs, daily 11am–5pm; pub menu Mon–Tues 5–9pm, Sat–Sun 11am–9pm. Upstairs, Wed–Sun 5–9pm. SEAFOOD.

The roadside watering hole across the street from the ocean is a place to duck in for cocktails, sashimi, and salmon pâté, or for other hot and cold appetizers, salads, and sandwiches throughout the day. Jameson's vegetarian and curried chicken salads are also recommended. Eternally popular are the grilled crab and shrimp sandwich (pardon the mayonnaise) on sourdough bread, as well as the fresh fish sandwich of the day, grilled plain and simple. Upstairs, the dining room opens its doors five nights a week for the usual surf-and-turf choices: fresh opakapaka, ulua (Hawaiian jack fish), and mahi-mahi; scallops in lemon butter and capers; and lobster tail, New York steak, and filet mignon. Jameson's is a North Shore standby that has stuck to its generic formulas, without apology, for years.

Kua Aina. 66-214 Kamehameha Hwy., Haleiwa. ☎ **808/637-6067.** Most items less than $6. No credit cards. Daily 11am–8pm. AMERICAN.

"What's the name of the sandwich shop on the North Shore?" We hear that often. Although this North Shore staple has expanded to the Ward Centre area in town, you'd never know it by the lines. It's busy as ever, and because there are never enough tables inside or on the porch, many diners pick up their burgers and head for the beach. Kua Aina's thin and spindly French fries are renowned islandwide and are the perfect accompaniment to its legendary burgers. Fat, moist, and homemade, the burgers can be ordered with avocado, bacon, and many other accompaniments, including ortega chiles and cheese.

North Shore Pizza Company. In North Shore Marketplace, 66-250 Kamehameha Hwy., Haleiwa. ☎ **808/637-2782.** Main courses and pizzas $6–$20. AE, JCB, MC, V. Daily 4–9pm. PIZZA.

The same folks who introduced Portofino and Zorro's Pizza to Hawaii also make and deliver (free) the pizzas, calzones, focaccia sandwiches, and pastas from a small but dynamic menu fashioned by chefs from Milan and Florence. The 16-inch New York–style pizzas are named after North Shore surf spots and are topped with fresh island produce such as Maui onions, North Shore basil, Portuguese sausage, and, for pizza heretics, Hawaiian pineapple. The Kaena Point, with barbecue chicken, Maui onions, fresh tomatoes, and cilantro, is a nontraditional good bet. Healthy eaters will notice the Healthy Italian, a calzone with grilled zucchini, eggplant, peppers, mushrooms, onions, and marinara sauce. A mouthful to be sure, but slightly reassuring. A small pasta selection with Mediterranean touches is a bonus.

Paradise Found Cafe. 66-443 Kamehameha Hwy., Haleiwa. ☎ **808/637-4540.** Most items less than $5. No credit cards. Mon–Sat 9am–6pm, Sun 10am–6pm. VEGETARIAN.

We love Haleiwa for its vegetarian choices, and this is one of them. A tiny cafe behind the Celestial Natural foods, Paradise Found takes looking for, but it's an appropriate way to begin a North Shore sojourn. You can buy a bowl of vegetarian chili and rice for $3, and for a dollar more, a hummus dip with pita and cucumber. It's as good as the baba ganouj, the enchiladas, vegan pateles, veggie burgers (with cheese and avocado, a winner), and any of the fresh fruit smoothies that have fueled many a beach-lover's day. The mix of Mexican favorites (quesadillas with chile and avocado) and Middle-Eastern samplings is a solid success at this tiny corner of the health-food store, barely more than a takeout counter.

Portofino. In North Shore Marketplace, 66-250 Kamehameha Hwy., Haleiwa. ☎ **808/637-7678.** Reservations recommended. Main courses $6.25–$17. AE, JCB, MC, V. Mon–Thurs 10am–10pm, Fri–Sat 10am–11pm, Sun 9am–10pm. NORTHERN ITALIAN.

Terra-cotta tile floors, columns and arches, and hand-painted murals bring a splendid scene of Portofino into the airy room. Although the decibels reverberate off the tile, it's a cordial environment in which to enjoy the aromas and creations emanating from the wood-burning oven and open kitchen. Chefs from Italy have devised a menu of

5 Beaches

by Jeanette Foster

homemade pastas, focaccia, calzones, sandwiches, and 9-inch pizzas, as well as everyday comforts such as rosemary chicken and a classic meat loaf served with roasted-garlic mashed potatoes.

THE WAIKIKI COAST
ALA MOANA BEACH PARK

Quite possibly America's best urban beach, gold-sand Ala Moana ("by the sea"), on sunny Mamala Bay, stretches for more than a mile along Honolulu's coast between downtown and Waikiki. This 76-acre midtown beach park, with spreading lawns shaded by banyans and palms, is one of the island's most popular playgrounds. It has a manmade beach, created in the 1930s by filling a coral reef with Waianae Coast sand, as well as its own lagoon, yacht harbor, tennis courts, music pavilion, bathhouses, picnic tables, and enough wide-open green spaces to accommodate its 4 million visitors a year. The water's calm almost year-round, protected by black lava rocks set offshore. There's a large parking lot as well as metered street parking.

WAIKIKI BEACH

No beach anywhere is so widely known or so universally sought after than this narrow, 1½-mile-long crescent of imported sand (from Molokai) at the foot of a string of highrise hotels. Home to the world's longest-running beach party, Waikiki attracts nearly 5 million visitors a year from every corner of the planet. First-timers are always amazed to discover how small Waikiki Beach actually is, but there's always a place for them under the tropical sun here.

Waikiki is actually a string of beaches that extends between **Sans Souci State Recreational Area** near Diamond Head to the east and **Duke Kahanamoku Beach**, in front of the Hilton Hawaiian Village, to the west. Great stretches along Waikiki include **Kuhio Beach**, next to the Sheraton Moana Surfrider, which provides the quickest access to the Waikiki shoreline; the stretch in front of the Royal Hawaiian Hotel known as **Gray's Beach**, which is canted so it catches the rays perfectly; and **Sans Souci**, the small, popular beach in front of the New Otani Kaimana Beach Hotel that's locally known as "Dig Me" Beach because of all the gorgeous bods who strut their stuff here.

Waikiki is fabulous for swimming, board- and bodysurfing, outrigger canoeing, diving, sailing, snorkeling, and pole fishing. Every imaginable type of marine equipment is available for rent here. The best place to park is at Kapiolani Park, near Sans Souci. Facilities include showers, lifeguards, rest rooms, grills, picnic tables, and pavilions at the **Queen's Surf** end of the beach (at Kapiolani Park, between the zoo and the aquarium).

EAST OAHU
✪ HANAUMA BAY

Oahu's most popular snorkeling spot is this volcanic crater with a broken sea wall; its small, curved, 2,000-foot gold-sand beach is packed elbow-to-elbow with people yearround. The bay's shallow shoreline water and abundant marine life are the main attractions, but this good-looking beach is also popular for sunbathing and peoplewatching. Serious divers shoot "the slot" (a passage through the reef) to gain Witch's Brew, a turbulent cove, then brave strong currents in 70-foot depths at the bay mouth to see coral gardens, turtles, and—that's right—sharks. (Divers: Beware the Molokai Express, a strong current that can put you in Kaunakakai, li'dat!) Snorkelers hug the safe, shallow (10 ft.) inner bay that, depending on when you go, is either like swimming in a fish-feeding frenzy or bathing with 300,000 honeymooners. Since Hanauma Bay is a conservation district, you may look but not touch or take any marine life from the ocean here.

Facilities include parking, rest rooms, a pavilion, grass volleyball court, lifeguard, barbecue, picnic tables, and food concession. Expect to pay $1 per vehicle to park and a $3 per-person entrance fee. If you're driving, take Kalanianaole Highway to Koko Head Regional Park. Avoid the crowds by going early, about 8am, on a weekday morning; once the parking lot's full, you're out of luck. Or take TheBus to escape the parking problem: The Hanauma Bay Shuttle runs from Waikiki to Hanauma Bay every half-hour from 8:45am to 1pm; you can catch it at the Ala Moana Hotel, the Ilikai Hotel, or at any city bus stop. It returns every hour from noon to 4:30pm. Hanauma Bay is closed on Tuesdays so the fish can have a day off.

SANDY BEACH

Sandy Beach is one of the best bodysurfing beaches on Oahu; it's also one of the most dangerous. It's better to just stand and watch the daredevils literally risk their necks at this 1,200-foot-long gold sand beach that's pounded by wild waves and haunted by a dangerous shore break and strong backwash. Weak swimmers and children should definitely stay out of the water here; Sandy Beach's heroic lifeguards make more rescues in a year than those at any other beach. Visitors, easily fooled by experienced bodysurfers who make wave-riding look easy, often fall victim to the bone-crunching waves. Lifeguards post flags to alert beachgoers to the day's surf. Green means safe, yellow caution, and red indicates very dangerous water conditions; always check the flags before you dive in. Facilities include rest rooms and parking. Go weekdays to avoid the crowds, weekends to catch the bodysurfers in action. From Waikiki, drive east on the H-1, which becomes Kalanianaole Highway; proceed past Hawaii Kai, up the hill to Hanauma Bay, past the Halona Blow Hole, and along the coast. The next big, gold, sandy beach you see ahead on the right is Sandy Beach. TheBus no. 22 will also get you there.

MAKAPUU BEACH PARK

Makapuu Beach, the most famous bodysurfing beach in Hawaii, is a beautiful 1,000-foot-long gold-sand beach cupped in the stark black Koolau cliffs on Oahu's easternmost point. Even if you never venture into the water, it's worth a visit just to enjoy the great natural beauty of this classic Hawaiian beach. You've probably already seen it in countless Hollywood TV shows, from *Hawaii Five-O* to *Magnum, P.I.*

In summer, the ocean here is as gentle as a Jacuzzi and swimming and diving are perfect; but come winter, Makapuu is hit with big, pounding waves that are ideal for expert bodysurfers, but too dangerous for regular swimmers. Small boards—3 feet or less with no *skeg* (bottom fin)—are permitted; board surfing is banned by state law. Facilities include rest rooms, lifeguards, barbecue grills, picnic tables, and parking. To get here, follow Kalanianaole Highway toward Waimanalo, or take TheBus no. 57 or 58.

THE WINDWARD COAST
✪ LANIKAI BEACH

One of Hawaii's best spots for swimming, gold-sand Lanikai's crystal-clear lagoon is like a giant saltwater swimming pool that you're lucky enough to be able to share with

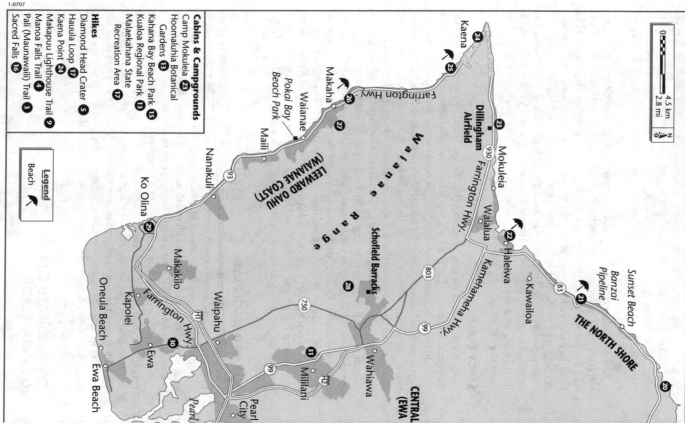

Legend

 Beach

Cabins & Campgrounds

Camp Mokuleia 23
Hoomaluhia Botanical
   Gardens 6
Kahana Bay Beach Park 13
Kualoa Regional Park 13
Malaekahana State
   Recreation Area 17

Hikes

Diamond Head Crater 5
Hauula Loop 17
Kaena Point 24
Makapuu Lighthouse Trail 4
Manoa Falls Trail 9
Pali (Maunawili) Trail 3
Sacred Falls 16

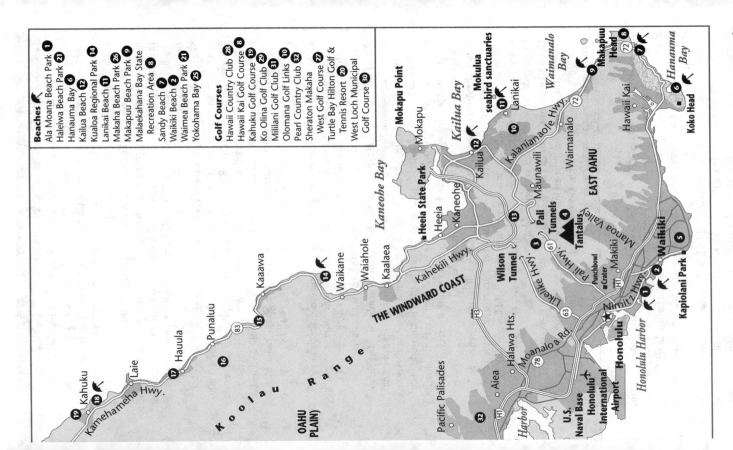

Beaches

- Ala Moana Beach Park ❶
- Haleiwa Beach Park ㉑
- Hanauma Bay ❻
- Kailua Beach ⓬
- Kualoa Regional Park ⓮
- Lanikai Beach ⓫
- Makaha Beach Park ㉕
- Makapuu Beach Park ❾
- Malaekahana Bay State Recreation Area ❽
- Sandy Beach ❼
- Waikiki Beach ❷
- Waimea Beach Park ㉑
- Yokohama Bay ㉕

Golf Courses

- Hawaii Country Club ㉓
- Hawaii Kai Golf Course ❽
- Kahuku Golf Course ⓙ
- Ko Olina Golf Club ㉙
- Mililani Golf Club ㉛
- Olomana Golf Links ❿
- Pearl Country Club ㉜
- Sheraton Makaha West Golf Course ㉗
- Turtle Bay Hilton Golf & Tennis Resort ⓴
- West Loch Municipal Golf Course ㉚

Mokapu Point

Mokulua seabird sanctuaries ⓫

Mokapu

Kailua Bay

Kailua ⓬

Lanikai

Kaneohe Bay

Heeia State Park

Heeia

Kaneohe

THE WINDWARD COAST

Waikane ⓮

Waiahole

Kaalaea

Kaaawa

Punaluu

⓯

Hauula ⓰

Laie

⓱

Kahuku

⓲

⓳

Kamehameha Hwy.

OAHU PLAIN)

K o o l a u   R a n g e

Pacific Palisades

Aiea

Halawa Hts.

ⓜ

Moanalua Rd

Pali Tunnels ❹

Wilson Tunnel

⓭

❸ ㉛

Tantalus

Manoa Valley

Makiki

Punchbowl Crater

Nimitz Hwy.

★ **Honolulu**

U.S. Naval Base

Honolulu International Airport

Harbor

Honolulu Harbor

Waimanalo Bay

Maunawili

Waimanalo

Kalanianaole Hwy.

⓾

EAST OAHU

Hawaii Kai

Makapuu Head ❽

❾

Hanauma Bay ❼

❻

Koko Head

Waikiki ❺

❷

Kapiolani Park

❶

⊙ Frommer's Favorite Oahu Experiences

Get a Suntan on Waikiki Beach. The best place for catching the rays on the world-famous beach is in front of the Royal Hawaiian Hotel (the big, pink one)—the beach here is cantered at the perfect angle for sunning. It's also a great spot for people-watching. Get to the beach early; by midday (when the rays are at their peak) beach towels are corner-to-corner.

Explore Oahu's Rain Forests. In the misty sunbeams, colorful birds flit among giant ferns and hanging vines, and towering tropical trees form a thick canopy that shelters all below in cool shadows. This emerald world is a true Eden. For the full experience, try Manoa Falls Trail, a walk of about a mile that ends at a freshwater pool and waterfall.

Snorkel the Glistening Waters of Hanauma Bay. This underwater park, once a volcanic crater, is teeming with a rainbow of tropical fish. Bordered by a 2,000-foot golden-sand beach, the bay's shallow water (10 feet in places) is the perfect setup for neophyte snorkelers to enjoy the underwater world. Get there early, before it gets crowded—and don't forget that the bay is closed on Wednesday. The closest place to rent snorkeling gear is **Aloha Dive Shop,** Koko Marine Shopping Center (☎ **808/395-5922**). For just $7 a day, you'll be set up with fins, mask, and snorkel.

Hike to the Top of Diamond Head Crater. Everyone can make this easy hike to the top of Hawaii's most famous landmark. The 1.4-mile round-trip goes up to the top of the 750-foot volcanic cone, where you have a 360° view of Oahu. Allow an hour for the trip up and back, and don't forget your camera.

When the Surf's Up, Head to Waimea Bay. From November to March, monstrous waves—some 30 feet tall—roll into Waimea. When the waves break on the shore, the ground actually shakes, an explosive sound fills the air, and everyone on the beach is covered with salt spray mist. The best surfers in the world paddle out to challenge these freight trains. When the surfers catch a ride, it's amazing to see how small they appear in the lip of the giant waves. It's an experience you'll never forget—and it won't cost you a dime for the show.

Watch the Ancient Hawaiian Sport of Canoe Paddling. On weekday evenings and weekend days from February to September, hundreds of canoe paddlers gather at Ala Wai Canal and practice paddling traditional Hawaiian canoes out to sea. Find a comfortable spot at Ala Wai Park, next to the canal, and watch the canoe paddlers re-create this centuries-old sport.

Get a Bargain at the Aloha Flea Market. Just 50¢ will get you into this all-day show at the Aloha Stadium parking lot, where more than 1,000 vendors sell everything from junk to jewels. Go early for the best deals. Open Wednesday, Saturday, and Sunday from 6am to 3pm.

the resident tropical fish and sea turtles. Too gorgeous to be real, this is one of Hawaii's postcard-perfect beaches: It's a mile long and thin in places, but the sand's as soft as talcum powder. Prevailing onshore trade winds make this an excellent beach for sailing and windsurfing. Kayakers often paddle out to the two tiny offshore Mokulua islands, which are seabird sanctuaries.

Because Lanikai is in a residential neighborhood, it's less crowded than other Oahu beaches; it's the perfect place to enjoy a quiet day at the beach. Sun worshipers should arrive in the morning, though, as the Koolau Range blocks the afternoon rays. There

Attend a Hawaiian-Language Church Service. Built in 1842, Kawaiahao Church (957 Punchbowl St., near King Street), is the Westminster Abbey of Hawaii; the vestibule is lined with portraits of the Hawaiian monarchy, many of whom where coronated in this very building. The coral church is a perfect setting to experience an all-Hawaiian service, complete with Hawaiian song. Hawaiian-language services are held every Sunday at 10:30am and admission is free—let your conscience be your guide as to a donation.

Visit the Lei Sellers in Chinatown. There's actually a host of cultural sights and experiences to be had in Honolulu's Chinatown. Wander through this several-square-block area with its jumble of exotic shops offering herbs, Chinese groceries, and acupuncture services. Before you leave, be sure to check out the lei sellers on Maunakea Street (near N. Hotel Street), where Hawaii's finest leis go for as little as $2.50.

Experience a Turning Point in America's History: The Bombing of Pearl Harbor. Standing on the deck of the USS *Arizona* Memorial at Pearl Harbor, with the ship underneath, is an experience you'll never forget. On that fateful day—December 7, 1941—the 608-foot *Arizona* sank in just 9 minutes after being bombed during the Japanese air raid. The 1,177 men on board plunged to a fiery death—and the U.S. went to war. Go early; you'll wait 2 to 3 hours if you wait until midday. You must wear closed-toed shoes, no slippers.

Watch the Sun Sink into the Pacific from a 1,048-Foot Hill Named After a Sweet Potato. Actually, it's more romantic than it sounds. Puu Ualakaa State Park, at the end of Round Hill Drive, translates into "rolling sweet potato hill" (which was how the early Hawaiians harvested the crop). The majestic view of the sunset from here is not to be missed.

Order a Shave Ice in a Tropical Flavor You Can Hardly Pronounce. When you're in Haleiwa, stop at Matsumoto Shave Ice (66-087 Kamehameha Hwy.) for a snow cone with an exotic flavor poured over the top, such as the local favorite, *li hing mui*, or sweet Japanese azuki beans hidden inside. This taste of tropical paradise goes for just $1.

Listen to the Soothing Sounds of Hawaiian Music. You can sit under the huge canopy of the banyan tree at the Sheraton Moana Surfrider's Banyan Veranda in Waikiki, order a cocktail, and sway to the live Hawaiian music any night of the week. Another quintessential sunset oasis is the Halekulani's House Without a Key, a sophisticated oceanfront lounge with wonderful hula and steel-guitar music, a great view of Diamond Head, and the best mai tais on the island.

---

are no facilities, just off-street parking. From Waikiki, take the H-1 to the Pali Highway (Hwy. 61) through the Nuuanu Pali Tunnel to Kailua, where the Pali Highway becomes Kailua Road as it proceeds through town. At Kalaheo Avenue, turn right and follow the coast about 2 miles to Kailua Beach Park; just past it, turn left at the T intersection and drive uphill on Aalapapa Drive, a one-way street that loops back as Mokulua Drive. Park on Mokulua Drive and walk down any of the eight public-access lanes to the shore. Or take TheBus no. 56 or 57 (Kailua), then transfer to the shuttle bus.

✪ KAILUA BEACH

Windward Oahu's premier beach is a 2-mile-long, wide, golden strand with dunes, palm trees, panoramic views, and offshore islets. The swimming is excellent, and the azure waters are usually decorated with bright sails; this is Oahu's premier windsurfing beach. It's also a favorite spot to sail catamarans, bodysurf the gentle waves, or paddle a kayak. Water conditions are quite safe, especially at the mouth of Kaelepulu Stream, where toddlers play in the freshwater shallows at the middle of the beach park. The tiny offshore islands are home to seabirds. The water's usually about 78°F, the views are spectacular, and the setting, at the foot of the sheer, green Koolaus, is idyllic. Best of all, the crowds haven't found it yet.

The 35-acre beach park is intersected by a freshwater stream and watched over by lifeguards. Facilities include picnic tables, barbecues, rest rooms, a volleyball court, a public boat ramp, and free parking; an open-air café is also at hand. Kailua's new bike path weaves through the park, and windsurf and kayak rentals are available. To get here, take Pali Highway (Hwy. 61) to Kailua, drive through town, turn right on Kalaheo Avenue, and go a mile until you see the beach on your left. Or take TheBus no. 56 or 57 into Kailua, then the no. 70 shuttle.

KUALOA REGIONAL PARK

One of Hawaii's most scenic beach parks is this 150-acre coco palm–fringed peninsula on Kaneohe Bay's North Shore, at the foot of the spiky Koolau Ridge. The biggest beach park on the windward side, it has a broad, grassy lawn and a long, narrow, white-sand beach ideal for swimming, walking, beachcombing, kite-flying, or just enjoying the natural beauty of this once-sacred Hawaiian shore, listed on the National Register of Historic Places. The waters are shallow and safe for swimming year-round. Offshore is Mokolii, the picturesque islet otherwise known as Chinaman's Hat. At low tide, you can swim or wade out to the island, which has a small sandy beach and is a bird preserve—so don't spook the red-footed boobies. Lifeguards are on duty. The park is located on Kamehameha Highway (Hwy. 83) in Kualoa; you can get there via TheBus no. 55.

THE NORTH SHORE
✪ MALAEKAHANA BAY STATE RECREATION AREA

This almost mile-long white-sand crescent lives up to just about everyone's image of the perfect Hawaii beach. It's excellent for swimming. On any weekday, you may be the only one here; but should some net fisherman—or kindred soul—intrude upon your delicious privacy, you can swim out to Goat Island (or wade across at low tide) and play Robinson Crusoe. (The islet is a sanctuary for seabirds and turtles, so no chase 'em, brah.) Facilities include rest rooms, barbecue grills, picnic tables, outdoor showers, and parking. To get there, take Kamehameha Highway (Hwy. 83) 2 miles north of the Polynesian Cultural Center; as you enter the main gate, you'll come upon the wooded beach park. Or you can take TheBus no. 52.

WAIMEA BEACH PARK

This deep, sandy bowl has gentle summer waves that are excellent for swimming, snorkeling, and bodysurfing. To one side of the bay is a huge rock that local kids like to climb up and dive off. In this placid scene, the only clue of what's to come in winter are those evacuation whistles on poles beside the road. But what a difference a season makes: Winter waves pound the narrow bay, sometimes rising 50 feet high. When the surf's really up, very strong currents and shore breaks sweep the bay—and it seems like everyone on Oahu drives out to Waimea to get a look at the monster waves and those who ride them. Go on weekdays when this popular beach is less crowded; on the other hand, the weekends are great if you're looking for the surf crowd. *A safety tip:* Don't get too distracted by the waves and forget to pay attention when parking or crossing the road. Facilities include lifeguards, rest rooms, showers, parking, and nearby restaurants and shops in Haleiwa town. The beach is located on Kahekameha Highway (Hwy. 83); from Waikiki, you can take TheBus no. 52.

LEEWARD OAHU/THE WAIANAE COAST
MAKAHA BEACH PARK

When surf's up here, it's spectacular: Monstrous waves pound the beach. This is the original home of Hawaii's big-wave surfing championship; surfers today know it as the home of Buffalo's Big Board Surf Classic, where surfers ride the waves on 10-foot-long wooden boards in the old Hawaiian style of surfing. Nearly a mile-long, this half-moon gold-sand beach is tucked between Lahilahi Point, a 231-foot rock locals call Black Rock, and Kepuhi Point, a toe of the Waianae mountain range. Summer is the best time to hit this beach—the waves are small, the sand abundant, and the water safe for swimming. Children hug the shore on the north side of the beach, near the lifeguard stand, while surfers dodge the rocks and divers seek an offshore channel full of big fish. *A caveat:* This is a "local" beach; you are welcome, of course, but you can expect "stink eye" (mild approbation) if you are not respectful of the beach and the local residents who use the facility all the time. Facilities include rest rooms, lifeguards, and parking. To get here, take the H-1 freeway to the end of the line, where it becomes Hwy. 93 (or Farrington Hwy.), and follow it to the beach; or you can take TheBus no. 51.

YOKOHAMA BAY

Where Farrington Highway (Hwy. 93) ends, the wilderness of Kaena Point State Park begins. It's a remote 853-acre coastline park of empty beaches, sand dunes, cliffs, and deep blue water. This is the last sandy stretch of shore on the northwest coast of Oahu. Sometimes it's known as Keawalua Beach or Puau Beach, but everybody here calls it Yokohama, after the Japanese immigrants who came from that port city to work the cane fields and fished along this shoreline. When the surf's calm—mainly in summer—this is a good area for snorkeling, diving, swimming, shore fishing, and picnicking. When surf's up, board- and bodysurfers are out in droves; don't go in the water then unless you're an expert. There are no lifeguards or facilities, except at the park entrance, where there's a rest room and lifeguard stand. No bus service.

6 Hitting the Water

by Jeanette Foster

For more details on the activities listed below, see "The Active Vacation Planner" in chapter 3.

BOATING

A funny thing happens to people when they come to Hawaii: Maybe it's the salt air, the warm tropical nights, or the blue Hawaiian moonlight, but otherwise rational people who have never set foot on a boat in their life suddenly want to go out to sea. You can go to sea on a "booze cruise" with a thousand loud, rum-soaked strangers, or you can sail on one of these special yachts, all of which will take you our **whale-watching** in season (roughly December to April). For fishing charters, see "Sport-fishing," below.

See the majestic Windward Coast the way it should be seen—from a boat. Captain Bob will take you on a 4-hour, lazy-day sail of Kaneohe Bay aboard his 42-foot catamaran, which skims across the almost-always calm water above the shallow coral reef, lands at Ahu o Laka, a disappearing sandbar, and takes you past two small islands and to snorkel spots full of tropical fish and, sometimes, turtles. The color of the water alone is worth the price. A shuttle will pick you up at your Waikiki hotel between 9 and 9:30am and return you there at about 4pm, which is a lot quicker than taking TheBus (no. 55 or 56).

Captain Bob's Adventure Cruises. ☎ **808/942-5077.** No cruises Sun and holidays. $69 adults, $59 children 13–17, $49 children 12 and under. Prices include all-you-can-eat barbecue lunch.

Dream Cruises. Waianae Small Boat Harbor. ☎ **800/400-7300** or 808/592-5200. $74.95 adults, $44.95 children 2–11. Rates include hotel pick-up and drop-off, plus breakfast.

If you aren't lucky enough to be in Hawaii during humpback-whale season, December to March, you can go **dolphin-watching** instead. Dream Cruises offers year-round dolphin-watching cruises of friendly pods of bottle-nosed and spinner dolphins near Yokahama Bay on the northern end of Oahu aboard their 70-foot catamaran, *Rainbow.* In addition to hotel pick-up, a local-style breakfast of Spam and eggs is included in the price.

Honolulu Sailing Co. Pier 2, Honolulu Harbor (across from Restaurant Row). ☎ **800/829-0114** or 808/239-3900. Fax 808/239-9718. www.duhe.com/wwsail/sailhi. For all-day cruises, park at Restaurant Row, 500 Ala Moana Blvd. (entrance is on Pohukaina St., between South and Punchbowl sts.), for $6 all day; for half-day cruises, park in metered spaces in front of pier 2 (50¢ per hour). Bus: 19, 20, or 47.

From a 2-hour sunset sail to a day-long adventure on the waves, Honolulu Sailing Co. offers a variety of sailing activities, including sailing lessons—picture yourself at the helm! They've been in the business for nearly two decades, providing everything from weddings at sea to honeymoon cruises, sail/snorkel trips, private lessons, and exclusive charters. The fleet ranges from 36- to 70-foot yachts; charters start at $50 per person, and lessons start at $125 per person per day.

Leahi. On the beach in front of the Sheraton Waikiki, 2255 Kalakaua Ave. ☎ **808/922-5665.** 1-hour sightseeing tours sail 5 times daily; $16 adults, $6 children 7–14, Sunset sail (5–6:30pm): $24 adults, including 3 drinks ($20 for passengers who don't drink alcohol), $12 children. Repeat guests receive discounts. Bus: 19 or 20.

You're a sailor and you want the real thing. Come fly aboard the *Leahi,* the green-sailed, aluminum-hulled, 45-foot racing catamaran skippered by George Howland Parsons III, an ex–Pearl Harbor submariner and great-grandson of a New Bedford whaler who called on Lahaina in the late 1700s. Parsons's sleek 48-passenger catamaran is the best choice for authentic experience and price.

Navatek I. Aloha Tower Marketplace, Pier 6, c/o Royal Hawaiian Cruises Ltd. ☎ **800/852-4183** or 808/848-6360. Prices vary depending on cruise. Parking: Validated, so you only pay $3. Bus: 8, 19, 20, 55, 56, or 57; or the Waikiki Trolley to stop no. 7.

You've never been on a boat, you don't want to be on a boat, you are being dragged aboard a boat to see the sunset you can see perfectly well from your hotel lanai. Why are you boarding this weird-looking boat? It guarantees that you'll be "seasick-free," that's why. The 140-foot-long *Navatek I* isn't even called a boat; it's actually a SWATH (Small Waterplane Area Twin Hull) vessel. That means the ship's superstructure—the part you ride on—rests on twin torpedo-like hulls that cut through the water so you don't bob like a cork and spill your mai tai. It's the smoothest ride on Mamala Bay. In fact, *Navatek I* is the only dinner cruise ship to receive U.S. Coast Guard certification to travel beyond Diamond Head.

Sunset dinner cruises leave Pier 6 (across from the Hawaii Maritime Museum) seven nights a week. If you have your heart set on seeing the city lights at night, your best bet is to take the Skyline dinner cruise, which runs nightly from 8:15 to 10:15pm and costs $75 for a three-course gourmet dinner in a romantic, candlelit setting with a great jazz band entertaining. Upstairs is an upscale dinner (four courses for $125). There's an even more expensive dinner cruise at 5pm that lasts until 7:30pm; it's $140 for adults, $115 for kids 2 to 11, and features top local entertainers and gourmet meals. Meals are designed by award-winning Chef George Mavrothalassitis of the Four Seasons Resort Maui at Wailea.

The best deal is the **lunch cruise** (noon–2pm), with a full buffet lunch, live Hawaiian music, and a great view of Oahu offshore for $47 adults, $28.50 kids.

In **whale season** (roughly January to April), whale-watching cruises depart at 8:30am and return at 11am. The cost is $39 adults, $24 kids 2 to 11, and includes a breakfast buffet, Hawaiian entertainment, and commentary by a naturalist.

BODY BOARDING (BOOGIE BOARDING) & BODYSURFING

Good places to learn to body board are in the small waves of **Waikiki Beach** and **Kailua Beach**, and **Bellows Field Beach Park**, off Kalanianole Hwy. (Hwy. 72) in Waimanalo, which is open to the public on weekends (from Friday noon to midnight on Sunday and holidays); to get there, turn toward the ocean on Hughs Road, then right on Tinker Road, which takes you right to the park.

You can rent boogie boards and fins for as little as $10 to $20 a day from **Aloha Beach Service**, at the Sheraton Moana Surfrider Hotel, 2365 Kalakaua Ave., Waikiki (☎ 808/922-3111), **Blue Sky Rentals**, Inn on the Park, 1920 Ala Moana Blvd., Waikiki (☎ 808/947-0101), **Surf & Sea**, 62-595 Kamehameha Hwy., Haleiwa (☎ 808/637-9887; fax 808/637-3008), and at all **Local Motion** locations, including 1714 Kapiolani Blvd., Honolulu (☎ 808/955-7873); Koko Marina Shopping Center, 7192 Kalanianaole Hwy., Hawaii Kai (☎ 808/396-7873); and Windward Mall, Kaneohe (☎ 808/263-7873). Also check out "Shopping A to Z," below.

OCEAN KAYAKING

A wonderful adventure is to rent a kayak, arrive at Lanikai Beach just as the sun is appearing, and paddle across the emerald lagoon to the pyramid-shaped islands off the beach called Mokulua—it's an experience you won't forget. Kayak equipment rental starts at $10 an hour, or $37 for a day; try **Prime Time Sports**, Fort DeRussy Beach, Waikiki (☎ 808/949-8952), or **Karel's Fiberglass**, 789 Kailua Rd., Kailua (☎ 808/261-8424).

First-timers should go to the North Shore's **Kayak Oahu Adventures**, in Waimea Valley and Adventure Park at 59-864 Kamehameha Hwy. (☎ 808/638-8189; e-mail kayak@lava.net), where kayak lessons, including equipment, are $15 per person. The kayaking takes place along the Waimea River; you'll paddle out to the golden sands of Waimea Bay, where you can rest or swim. They also offer a couple of guided tours: down the Waimea Rivers for $35 each and, between June and August, an hour-long guided snorkel trip to Shark's Cove for $25. All equipment and instruction is provided.

SCUBA DIVING

Oahu is a wonderful place to scuba dive, especially for those interested in wreck diving. One of the more famous wrecks in Hawaii is the *Mahi*, a 185-foot former mine sweeper easily accessible just south of Waianae. Abundant marine life makes this a great place to shoot photos—schools of lemon butterfly fish and taape are so comfortable with divers and photographers that they practically pose. Eagle rays, green sea turtles, manta rays, and white-tipped sharks occasionally cruise by, and eels peer from the wreck.

For nonwreck diving, one of the best dive spots in the summer is **Kahuna Canyon.** In Hawaiian, *kahuna* translates as priest, wise man, or sorcerer; this massive amphitheater, located near Mokuleia, is a perfect example of something a sorcerer might conjure up. Walls rising from the ocean floor create the illusion of an underwater Grand Canyon. Inside the amphitheater, crabs, octopi, slippers, and spiny lobsters abound (be aware that taking them in the summer is illegal), and giant trevally, parrot fish, and unicorn fish congregate. Outside the amphitheater, you're likely to see the occasional shark in the distance.

Since Oahu's best dives are offshore, your best bet is to book a two-tank dive from a dive boat. In Waipahu, try **Ocean Concepts Scuba,** 94-547 Ukee St., Waipahu (☎ **808/677-7975**); they'll take you diving in local lava caves, volcanic ledges, and the *Mahi* wreck. A two-tank boat dive costs $85 with your own equipment; add another $16 for complete equipment rental.

Hawaii's oldest and largest dive shop is **Aaron's Dive Shop,** 602 Kailua Rd., Kailua (☎ **808/262-2333**; e-mail aarons@aloha.com). Aaron's offers boat and beach dive excursions off the coast of Oahu. The boat dive is $90 per person, including two tanks and all gear and transportation from the Kailua shop or their Pearl City location. The beach dive off the North Shore in summer and the Waianae Coast in winter is the same price as a boat dive, including all gear and transportation, so Aaron's recommends the boat dive.

SNORKELING

Some of the best snorkeling in Oahu is at the underwater park at **Hanauma Bay:** It's crowded, and sometimes it seems there are more people than fish, but Hanauma has clear, warm, protected waters and an abundance of friendly reef fish—including Moorish idols, scores of butterfly fish, damsel fish, and wrasses. Hanauma Bay has two reefs, an inner and an outer—the first for novices, the other for experts. The inner reef is calm and shallow (less than 10 feet); in some places, you can just wade and put your face in the water. Go early: It's packed by 10am and closed on Wednesdays. For details, see "Beaches," above.

Braver snorkelers may want to head to **Shark's Cove,** on the North Shore just off Kamehameha Highway, between Haleiwa and Pupukea. Sounds risky; we know, but we've never seen nor heard of any sharks in this cove, and in summer this big, lava-edged pool is one of Oahu's best snorkel spots. Waves splash over the natural lava grotto and cascade like waterfalls into the pool full of tropical fish. There are deep-sea caves to explore to the right of the cove.

Snorkel rentals are available at most dive shops and beach activity centers: in Waikiki call **Blue Sky Rentals,** Inn on the Park, 1920 Ala Moana Blvd., (☎ **808/947-0101**); **Aloha Dive Shop,** Koko Marine Shopping Center (☎ **808/ 395-5922**), the closest dive shop to the underwater park at Hanauma Bay; **Snorkel**

Bob's, also on the way to Hanauma Bay at 700 Kapahulu Ave. (at Date Street), Honolulu (☎ **808/735-7944**); and **Haleiwa Surf Center**, 66-167 Haleiwa Rd., Haleiwa (☎ **808/637-5051**), which also teaches snorkeling and offers guided snorkel tours.

SPORTFISHING

Kewalo Basin, located between the Honolulu International Airport and Waikiki, is the main location for charter fishing boats on Oahu. Top sportfishing boats from Kewalo Basin include the *Fish Hawk* (☎ 808/536-7472), *Maggie Joe* (☎ 808/591-8888), and *Mary I Sportfishing* (☎ 808/596-2998). From Waikiki, take Kalakaua Ewa (west) beyond Ala Moana Center; Kewalo Basin is on the left, across from Ward Centre. Look for charter boats all in a row in their slips; on lucky days, the captains display the catch of the day in the afternoon. You can also take TheBus no. 19 or 20 (Airport).

If you aren't interested in bagging a big marlin, but more interested in catching small fish on spinning gear, **Dream Cruises** (☎ **800/400-7300** or **808/592-5200**) has a 3-hour fishing cruise on board the 70-foot Chinese junk, *Lin Wa II*, from Kewalo Basin. As the boat drifts from Waikiki to Diamond Head or out to the airport, preset lines are cast into the water, party-boat style, and glass viewing ports below allow you to watch your fish take the bait underwater. There are two trips a day: afternoon fishing from 1:30 to 4:30pm, accompanied by finger sandwiches and petite desserts, for $49.95 adults, $24.95 children 17 and under and spectators; and a sunset fishing and dinner cruise from 5 to 8pm, which includes dinner (they'll even grill your catch); it's $59.95 adults, $29.95 children (17 and under) and spectators. Prices include round-trip transportation from Waikiki hotels.

SUBMARINE DIVES

Here's your chance to play Jules Verne and experience the underwater world from the comfort of a submarine, which will take you on an adventure below the surface in high-tech comfort. The entire trip is narrated as you watch tropical fish and sunken ships just outside the sub; this is a great way to see Hawaii's spectacular underwater world if swimming's not your thing. Shuttle boats to the sub leave from Hilton Hawaiian Village Pier. The cost is $89 for adults, $39 for kids 12 and younger (children must be at least 36 inches tall); call **Atlantis Submarines** (☎ **800/548-6262** or 808/973-9811; www.goatlantis.com) to reserve. *A word of warning:* The ride is safe for everyone, but skip it if you suffer from severe claustrophobia.

SURFING

In the summertime, when the water's warm and there's a soft breeze in the air, the south swell comes up. It's surf season in Waikiki, the best place to learn how to surf on Oahu. To learn to surf, go early to **Aloha Beach Service**, next to the Sheraton Moana Surfrider, 2365 Kalakaua Ave, Waikiki (☎ 808/922-3111). The beach boys offer surfing lessons for $25 an hour; board rentals are $8 for an hour and $12 for 2 hours. You must know how to swim. Surfboards are also available for rent at **Local Motion**, 1714 Kapiolani Blvd., Honolulu (☎ 808/955-7873); **Planet Surf**, 412 Nahua, Waikiki (☎ 808/926-2060); or **Surf & Sea**, 62-595 Kamehameha Hwy., Haliewa (☎ 808/637-9887). For the best surf shops, where you can soak in the culture as well as pick up gear, also see "Shopping A to Z," below.

More experienced surfers should drop in on any surf shop around Oahu, or call the **Surf News Network Surfline** at ☎ **808/596-SURF** or 808/836-1952 to get the latest surf conditions. A good surfing spot for advanced surfers is **The Cliffs**, at the base of Diamond Head; the 4- to 6-foot waves churn here, allowing high-performance surfing. And the view of Diamond Head is great.

If you're in Hawaii in the winter and want to see the serious surfers catch the really big waves, bring your binoculars and grab a front-row seat on the beach near **Kalalua Point**. To get there from Waikiki, take the H-1 toward the North Shore, veering off at H-2, which becomes Kamehameha Highway (Hwy. 83). Keep going to the funky surf town of Haleiwa and Waimea Bay; the big waves will be on your left, just past Pupukea Beach Park.

WINDSURFING

Windward Oahu's **Kailua Beach** is the home of champion and pioneer windsurfer Robbie Naish; it's also the best place to learn to windsurf. The oldest and most established windsurfing business in Hawaii is **Naish Windsurfing Hawaii**, 155-C Hamakua Dr., Kailua (☎ **808/261-3539**; www.naish.com). The company offers everything: sales, rentals, instruction, repair, and free advice on where to go when the wind and waves are happening. Lessons start at $55 private lesson for one, $75 for two; equipment rental is $25 for a half-day and $30 for a full day. The **Kailua Sailboard Co.**, 130 Kailua Dr., across the street from the Kailua Beach Park (☎ **808/262-2555**), offers 3-hour small group lessons $39 each and also offers rentals.

Windsurfer wannabes on the North Shore can contact **North Shore Windsurf School**, 59-452 Makana Rd. (Kamehameha Hwy.), Haleiwa (☎ **808/638-8198**; fax 808/638-5532). Experts give 2½-hour lessons in a protected area on the North Shore for $35. Some people can get up and sail away in one lesson, but it usually takes about three lessons to be sailing over the waves.

7 Nature Hikes

by Jeanette Foster

Everyone thinks Oahu is just one big urban island, so they're always surprised to discover that the great outdoors is less than an hour away from downtown Honolulu. The island's 33 major trails take you across razor-thin ridge backs and deep into waterfall valleys.

Check out Stuart Ball's *The Hiker's Guide to Oahu* (Honolulu: University of Hawaii Press, 1993) before you go. For a free Oahu recreation map listing all 33 trails, write to the **Department of Land and Natural Resources**, 1151 Punchbowl St., Room 130, Honolulu, HI 96813 (☎ **808/587-0300**). They'll also send you free topographic trail maps on request and issue camping permits. Another good source of information is the *Hiking/Camping Information Packet* from **Hawaii Geographic Maps and Books**, 49 S. Hotel St., Honolulu, HI 96813 (☎ **808/538-3952**), for a cost of $7 (postage included). They also carry a full line of United States Geographic Survey topographic maps very handy for hikers. Also be sure to get a copy of *Hiking on Oahu: The Official Guide*, a hiking safety guide that includes instructions on hiking preparation, safety procedures, emergency phone numbers, and necessary equipment; for a copy of the brochure, contact Erin Lau, Trails and Access Manager, **City and County of Honolulu** (☎ **808/973-9782**); the **Hawaii Nature Center**, 2131 Makiki Heights Dr. (☎ **808/955-0100**); or **The Bike Shop**, 1149 S. King St. (☎ **808/596-0588**).

The **Hawaiian Trail and Mountain Club**, P.O. Box 2238, Honolulu, HI 96804, offers regular hikes on Oahu. You bring your own lunch and drinking water and meet up with the club at the Iolani Palace to join them on a hike. They also have an information packet on hiking and camping in Hawaii, as well as a schedule of all upcoming hikes; send $1.25 plus a legal-sized, self-addressed, stamped envelope to the address above, or check out their site at **www.geocities.com/yosemite/trails/3660.**

The **Sierra Club**, P.O. Box 2577, Honolulu, HI 96803, also offers regularly scheduled hikes on which they welcome visitors. The **Hawaii Nature Center**, 2131 Makiki Heights Dr. (☎ **808/955-0100;** open Monday to Friday 8am to 4:30pm), is another organization that offers organized hikes, as well as "Sunday Adventures" for children.

HONOLULU AREA HIKES
✪ DIAMOND HEAD CRATER

Just about everyone can make this easy but steep walk to the summit of Hawaii's most famous landmark. Kids love the top of the 760-foot volcanic cone, where they have 360° views of Oahu up the leeward coast from Waikiki. The 1.4-mile round trip will take about 1½ hours.

Diamond Head was created by a volcanic explosion about a half-million years ago. The Hawaiians called the crater *Leahi* (meaning the brow of the *ahi*, or tuna, referring to the shape of the crater). Diamond Head was considered a sacred spot; King Kamehameha offered human sacrifices at a *heiau* (temple) on the western slope. It wasn't until the 19th century that Mount Leahi got its current name: A group of sailors found what they thought were diamonds in the crater; it turned out they really only found worthless calcite crystals, but the Diamond Head moniker stuck.

Before you begin your adventure hiking to the top of the crater, put on some decent shoes (rubber-soled tennies are fine) and gather a flashlight (you walk through several dark tunnels), binoculars (for better viewing at the top), water, and your camera. If you don't have a flashlight or your hotel can't lend you one, you can buy a small one for a few dollars as part of a Diamond Head climbers "kit" at the gift shop at the **New Otani Kaimana Beach Hotel,** on the Diamond Head end of Kalakaua Avenue, just past the Waikiki Aquarium and across from Kapiolani Park.

Go early, before the noonday sun starts beating down. Start your hike to the summit of Diamond Head at Monsarrat and 18th avenues on the crater's inland (or mauka) side. To get there, take TheBus no. 58 from the Ala Moana Shopping Center or drive to the intersection of Diamond Head Road and 18th Avenue. Follow the road through the tunnel (which is closed from 6pm to 6am) and park in the lot. The trailhead starts in the parking lot and proceeds along a paved walkway (with handrails) as it climbs up the slope. You'll pass old World War I and II pillboxes, gun emplacements, and tunnels built as part of the Pacific defense network. Several steps take you up to the top observation post on Point Leahi. The views are indescribable.

✪ MANOA FALLS TRAIL

This easy, eight-tenths of a mile (one-way) hike is terrific for families; it takes less than an hour to reach idyllic Manoa Falls. The trailhead, marked by a footbridge, is at the end of Manoa Road, past Lyon Arboretum. The staff at the arboretum prefers that hikers do not park in their lot, so the best place to park is in the residential area below Paradise Park; you can also get to the arboretum via TheBus no. 5. The often-muddy trail follows Waihi Stream and meanders through the forest reserve past guavas, mountain apples, and wild ginger. The forest is moist and humid and is inhabited by giant blood-thirsty mosquitoes, so bring repellent.

EAST OAHU HIKES
MAKAPUU LIGHTHOUSE TRAIL

You've seen this famous old lighthouse on episodes of *Magnum, P.I.* and *Hawaii Five-O.* No longer manned by the Coast Guard (it's fully automated now), the lighthouse is the goal of hikers who challenge a precipitous cliff trail to gain an airy perch over the Windward Coast, Manana (Rabbit) Island, and the azure Pacific. It's about a 45-minute, mile-long hike from Kalanianaole Highway (Hwy. 72), along a paved road that begins across from Hawaii Kai Executive Golf Course and winds around the 646-foot-high sea bluff to the lighthouse lookout.

To get to the trailhead from Waikiki, take Kalanianaole Highway (Hwy. 72) past Hanauma Bay and Sandy Beach to Makapu Head, the southeastern tip of the island; you can also take TheBus no. 57 or 58. Look for a sign that says NO VEHICLES ALLOWED on a gate to the right, a few hundred yards past the entrance to the golf course. The trail isn't marked, but it's fairly obvious: Just follow the abandoned road that leads gradually uphill to a trail that wraps around Makapu Point. It's a little precarious, but anyone in reasonably good shape can handle it.

Blowhole alert: When the south swell is running, usually in the summer, there are a couple of blowholes on the south side of Makapu Head that put the famous Halona blowhole to shame.

WINDWARD OAHU HIKES
HAULA LOOP

For one of the best views of the coast and the ocean, follow the Hauula Loop Trail on the windward side of the island. It's an easy, 2½-mile loop on a well-maintained path that passes through a whispering ironwood forest and a grove of tall Norfolk pines. The trip takes about 3 hours and gains some 600 feet in elevation.

To get to the trail, take TheBus no. 55 or follow Hwy. 83 to Hauula Beach Park. Turn toward the mountains on Hauula Homestead Road; when the road forks to the left at Maakua Road, park on the side of the road. Walk along Maakua Road to the wide, grassy trail that begins the hike into the mountains. The climb is fairly steep for about 300 yards but continues on to easier-on-the-calves switchbacks as you go up the ridge. Look down as you climb: You'll spot wildflowers and mushrooms among the matted needles. The trail continues up, crossing Waipilopilo Gulch, where you'll see several forms of native plant life. Eventually, you reach the top of the ridge, where the views are spectacular.

Camping is permitted along the trail, but it's difficult to find a place to pitch a tent on the steep slopes and in the dense forest growth. There are a few places along the ridge, however, that are wide enough for a tent. Contact the **Division of Forestry and Wildlife**, 1151 Punchbowl St., Honolulu, HI 96813 (☎ 808/587-0166) for information on camping permits.

PALI (MAUNAWILI) TRAIL

For a million-dollar view of the Windward Coast, take this easy 11-mile (one-way) foothill trail. The trailhead is about 6 miles from downtown Honolulu, on the windward side of the Nuuanu Pali Tunnel, at the scenic lookout just beyond the hairpin turn of the Pali Highway (Hwy. 61). Just as you begin the turn, look for the SCENIC OVERLOOK sign, slow down, and pull off the highway into the parking lot (sorry, no bus service available).

The mostly flat, well-marked, easy-to-moderate trail goes through the forest on the lower slopes of the 3,000-foot Koolau Mountain range and ends up in the backyard of the coastal Hawaiian village of Waimanalo. Go halfway to get the view and return to your car, or have someone meet you in 'Nalo.

SACRED FALLS

It's easy to see why this place was given the name "Sacred": Clear, cold water, originating from the top of the Koolau Mountains, descends down the Kaluanui Stream and cascades over Sacred Falls into a deep, boulder-strewn pool. The hike to this awe-inspiring waterfall passes under guava and mountain apple trees and through a fern-filled narrow canyon that parallels the streambed.

A few words of warning before you grab your walking shoes and hiking boots: Do not attempt this hike in wet weather. In fact, the State Parks Division closes the falls if there's a danger of flash floods. This is no idle warning—in 1987, five hikers attempting to reach the falls died in three separate incidents while the normally babbling stream was flooded; in October 1993, a Boy Scout troop had to be rescued by helicopter during a flash flood. And go in a group—there have been a few muggings along the 2.2-mile trail in recent years.

The best time to take this hike is in the morning, when the light is good. Be prepared with rain gear and insect repellent. The easy 4.4-mile round-trip will take about 2 to 3 hours. To get to the trail, drive north on Kamehameha Highway (Hwy. 83) to the turnoff for Sacred Falls State Park, or take TheBus no. 55. The trail begins at the parking lot and heads for the mountains, paralleling the Kaluanui Stream. About a mile into the trail is a grassy area with emergency-warning equipment inside a cyclone fence; the trailhead is to the left of the fence. The beginning is a bit rough—the trail is muddy and passes under tangled branches and through a tunnel of Christmas berry. About a half-mile beyond the trailhead, you'll cross the Kaluanui Stream; if the water is high or muddy, don't cross—you could become trapped in the canyon during a flash flood. As you continue up the trail, the canyon becomes increasingly narrow, with steep walls on either side. Be on the lookout for falling rocks. At the end of the trail are the majestic falls and an extremely cold pool, home to spidery Malaysian prawns.

TO LAND'S END: A LEEWARD OAHU HIKE
KAENA POINT

At the very western tip of Oahu lie the dry, barren lands of Kaena Point State Park, 853 acres consisting of a remote, wild coastline of jagged sea cliffs, deep gulches, sand dunes, endangered plant life, and a wind- and surf-battered coastline. *Kaena* means "red-hot" or "glowing" in Hawaiian; the name refers to the brilliant sunsets visible from the point.

Kaena is steeped in numerous legends. A popular one concerns the demigod Maui: Maui had a famous hook that he used to raise islands from the sea. He decided that he wanted to bring the islands of Oahu and Kauai closer together, so one day he threw his hook across the Kauai Channel and snagged the island of Kauai (which actually is visible from Kaena Point on clear days). Using all his might, Maui was only able to pull loose a huge boulder, which fell into the waters very close to the present lighthouse at Kaena. The rock is still called Pohaku o Kauai (the rock from Kauai). Like Black Rock in Kaanapali on Maui, Kaena is thought of as the point on Oahu from which souls depart.

To hike out to the departing place, take the clearly marked trail from the parking lot of the Makua-Kaena Point State Park. The moderate, 5-mile round-trip hike to the point will take a couple of hours. The trail along the cliff passes tide pools abundant in marine life and rugged protrusions of lava reaching out to the turbulent sea; seabirds circle overhead. There are no sandy beaches, and the water is nearly always turbulent. During the winter months, when a big north swell is running, the waves at Kaena are the biggest in the state, averaging heights of 30 to 40 feet. Even when the water appears calm, offshore currents are powerful, so don't plan to swim. Go early in the morning to see the schools of porpoises that frequent the area just off-shore.

To get to the trailhead from Honolulu or Waikiki, take the H-1 freeway west to its end; continue on Highway 93 past Makaha and follow Highway 930 to the end of the road. There's no bus service.

8 Camping & Wilderness Cabins

by Jeanette Foster

If you don't plan to bring your own camping gear, you can rent or buy it at **Omar the Tent Man,** 650A Kakoi St. (☎ **808/836-8785**), or **The Bike Shop,** at 1149 S. King St. (☎ **808/595-0588**) and Windward City Shopping Center (☎ **808/235-8722**). Also check our "Surf & Sports" under "Shopping A to Z," later in this chapter.

The best places to camp on Oahu are listed below, but remember: You're allowed only one bag, which has to fit under the seat. If you have more gear, you're going to have to drive (or take a cab).

WINDWARD OAHU
HOOMALUHIA BOTANICAL GARDENS

This windward campground, outside Kaneohe, is almost a secret place and a real treasure. It's hard to believe that you're just a half-hour from downtown Honolulu.

Hoomaluhia, or "peace and tranquility," accurately describes this 400-acre botanical garden at the foot of the jagged Koolaus. In this lush, tropical setting, gardens are devoted to the plants specific to tropical America, native Hawaii, Polynesia, India, Sri Lanka, and Africa. A 32-acre lake sits in the middle of the scenic park (no swimming or boating is allowed, though), and there are numerous hiking trails. The visitors center offers free guided walks Saturday 10am and Sunday 1pm.

Facilities for this tent-camp area include rest rooms, cold showers, dishwashing stations, picnic tables, grills, and water. A public phone is available at the visitors center, and shopping and gas are available in Kaneohe, 2 miles away. Permits are free, but stays are limited to three nights (Friday, Saturday, and Sunday only). The gate is locked at 4pm and doesn't open again until 9am, so you're locked in for the night.

Hoomaluhia Botanical Gardens is at 45-680 Luluku Rd. (at Kamehameha Hwy.), Kaneohe (☎ **808/233-7323,** fax 808/247-3199). To get there from Waikiki, take H-1 to the Pali Highway (Hwy. 61); turn left on Kamehameha Hwy. (Hwy. 83); at the fourth light, turn left on Luluku Road. TheBus nos. 55 and 56 stop nearby on Kamehameha Highway; from there, you have to walk 2 miles to the visitors center.

KUALOA REGIONAL PARK

Located on a peninsula on Kaneohe Bay, this park has a spectacular setting. The gold-sand beach is excellent for snorkeling, and fishing can be rewarding (see "Beaches," above, for details). There are two campgrounds: Campground A—in a wooded area with a sandy beach and palm, ironwood, kamani, and monkeypod trees—is mainly used for groups, but it has a few sites for families, except during the summer (June through August), when the Department of Parks and Recreation conducts a children's camping program here. Campground B is on the main beach; it has fewer shade trees but a great view of Mokolii Island. Facilities at both sites include rest rooms, showers, picnic tables, drinking fountains, and a public phone. Campground A also has sinks for dishwashing, a volleyball court, and a kitchen building. Gas and groceries are available in Kaawa, 2½ miles away. The gate hours at Kualoa Regional Park are 7am to 8pm; if you're not back to the park by 8pm, you're locked out for the night.

Permits are free but limited to 5 days (no camping on Wednesday and Thursday). Contact the **Honolulu Department of Parks and Recreation**, 650 S. King St., Honolulu, HI 96713 (☎ **808/523-4525**), for information and permits. Kualoa Regional Park is located in the 49-600 area of Kamehameha Hwy., across from Mokolii Island. To get there, take the Likelike Hwy. (Hwy. 63); after the Wilson Tunnel, get in the right lane and turn off on Kahakili Hwy. (Hwy. 83). Or, you can take TheBus no. 55.

KAHANA BAY BEACH PARK

Under Tahiti-like cliffs, with a beautiful, gold-sand crescent beach framed by pine-needle casuarina trees, Kahana Bay Beach Park is a place of serene beauty. You can swim, bodysurf, fish, hike, and picnic, or just sit and listen to the trade winds whistle through the beach pines.

Tent and vehicle camping only are allowed at this oceanside oasis. Facilities include rest rooms, picnic tables, drinking water, public phones, and a boat-launching ramp. Do note that the rest rooms are located at the north end of the beach, far away from the camping area, and there are no showers. There's no fee for camping, but you must get a permit. Permits are free but limited to 5 nights; you can get one at the **State Parks Division**, P.O. Box 621, Honolulu, HI 96809 (☎ **808/587-0300**).

Kahana Bay Beach Park is located in the 52-222 block of Kamehameha Hwy. (Hwy. 83) in Kahana. To get there from Waikiki, take the H-1 west to the Likelike Highway (Hwy. 63). Continue north on the Likelike, through the Wilson Tunnel, turning left on Highway 83; Kahana Bay is 13 miles down the road on the right. You can also get there via TheBus no. 55.

THE NORTH SHORE
MALAEKAHANA BAY STATE RECREATION AREA

This is one of the most beautiful beach-camping areas in the state, with a mile-long gold-sand beach on Oahu's Windward Coast (see "Beaches," above, for details). There are two areas for tent camping. Facilities include picnic tables, rest rooms, showers, sinks, drinking water, and a phone. Permits are free but limited to five nights and may be obtained at any state parks office, including the **State Parks Division**, P.O. Box 621, Honolulu, HI 96809 (☎ **808/587-0300**).

The recreation area is located on Kamehameha Hwy. (Hwy. 83) between Laie and Kahuku. To get there, take the H-2 Freeway to Highway 99 to Highway 83 (both roads are called Kamehameha Hwy.); continue on Highway 83 just past Kahuku. You can also get there via TheBus no. 55.

For your safety, the park gate is closed between 6:45pm and 7am; vehicles cannot enter or exit during those hours. Groceries and gas are available in Laie and Kahuku, less than a mile away.

CAMP MOKULEIA

A quiet, isolated beach on Oahu's North Shore, 4 miles from Kaena Point, is the centerpiece of a 9-acre campground that's a great getaway. Camping is available on the beach or in a grassy, wooded area. Activities include swimming, surfing, shore fishing, and beachcombing.

Facilities include tent camping, cabins, and lodge accommodations. The tent-camping site has portable chemical toilets, a water spigot, and outdoor showers; there are no picnic tables or barbecue grills, so come prepared. The cabins sleep up to 18 people in bunk beds. The cabins are $125 per night for the 14-bed cabin and $160 per night for the 18-bed cabin. Rooms at the lodge are $45 to $50 for a shared bath and \$55 to \$60 for a private bath. Tent camping is \$5 per person, per night. Many groups use the camp, but there's a real sense of privacy. Reservations are required; contact **Camp Mokuleia**, 68-729 Farrington Hwy., Waialua, HI 96791 (☎ **808/ 637-6241**).

Camp Mokuleia is located on Farrington Hwy., west of Haleiwa. To get there from Waikiki, take the H-1 to the H-2 exit; stay on H-2 until the end. Where the road forks, bear left to Waialua on Highway 803, which turns into Highway 930 to Kaena Point. Look for the green fence on the right, where a small sign at the driveway reads CAMP MOKULEIA, EPISCOPAL CHURCH OF HAWAII.

9 Golf & Other Outdoor Activities

by Jeanette Foster

BICYCLING

Island Triathlon and Bike, 569 Kapahulu Ave. (☎ **808/732-7227**), has mountain-bike rentals—complete with lock, pump, repair kit, and helmet—for \$25 the first day and \$10 for each additional day. They're also in the know about upcoming bicycle events or interesting bike rides you can enjoy on your own. Other bicycle-rental sources include **Diamond Head Rentals**, 2463 Kuhio Ave. (next to Kuhio Village Resort), Waikiki (☎ **808/923-0105**), and **Blue Sky Rentals**, Inn on the Park, 1920 Ala Moana Blvd., Waikiki (☎ **808/947-0101**).

For information on bikeways and maps, contact the **Honolulu City and County Bike Coordinator** (☎ **808/527-5044**).

If you'd like to join in on some club rides, contact the **Hawaii Bicycle League**, P.O. Box 4403, Honolulu, HI 96812 (☎ **808/735-5756**), which offers rides every weekend, as well as several annual events. The league can also provide you with a schedule of upcoming rides, races, and outings.

On Sundays, the **Kualoa Ranch & Activity Club**, 49-560 Kamehameha Hwy., Kaaawa (☎ **800/231-7321** or 808/231-7371; Bus: 55), opens up nearly 1,000 acres of the 4,000-acre ranch lands, including the Kaaawa Valley, where *Jurassic Park* was filmed. Prices range from \$15 to \$30; bring your own bike.

GOLF

Oahu has nearly three dozen golf courses, ranging from bare-bones municipal courses to exclusive country-club courses with membership fees at six figures a year. Below are the best of a great bunch.

As you play Oahu's courses, you'll come to know that the windward courses play much differently than the leeward courses. On the windward side, the prevailing winds blow from the ocean to shore, and the grain direction of the greens tends to run the same way—from the ocean to the mountains. Leeward golf courses have the opposite tendency: the winds usually blow from the mountains to the ocean, with the grain direction of the greens corresponding.

Some hot tips on beating the crowds and saving money: Oahu's golf courses tend to be crowded, so we suggest that you go midweek if you can. Also, most island courses have twilight rates that offer you substantial discounts if you're willing to tee off in the afternoon, usually between 1 and 3pm; we've included them in the listings below where applicable.

Transportation note: TheBus does not allow golf-club bags onboard, so if you want to use TheBus to get to a course, you're going to have to rent clubs at the course.

Travel Tip

For last-minute and discount tee times, call **Stand-by Golf** (☎ **888/645-BOOK** or 808/322-BOOK), which offers discounted tee times for same-day or next-day golfing. Call between 7am and 9pm for a guaranteed tee time at a 10 to 40% discount.

EAST OAHU

Hawaii Kai Golf Course. 8902 Kalanianaole Hwy., Honolulu. ☎ **808/395-2358.** From Waikiki, go east on H-1, past Hawaii Kai; it's immediately past Sandy Beach on the left. Bus: 58.

Actually, this is two golf courses in one. The par-72, 6,222-yard **Hawaii Kai Championship Golf Course** is moderately challenging, with scenic vistas. The course is forgiving to high-handicap golfers, although it does have a few surprises. Greens fees are $100; twilight rates are half off if you're willing to tee off between 1 and 2:30pm weekdays. The par-3 **Hawaii Kai Executive Golf Course** is fun for beginners and those just getting back in the game after a few years. The course has lots of hills and valleys, with no water hazards and only a few sand traps. Rates for this course are a mere $37, with twilight rates (after 4pm) just $6. Lockers are available.

THE WINDWARD COAST

Olomana Golf Links. 41-1801 Kalanianaole Hwy., Waimanalo. ☎ **808/259-7926.** From Waikiki, take H-1 to the Pali Highway (Hwy. 61); turn right on Kalanianaole Hwy.; after 5 miles, it will be on the left. Bus: 57.

Low-handicap golfers may not find this gorgeous course difficult, but the striking views of the craggy Koolau mountain ridge are worth the greens fees alone. The par-72, 6,326-yard course is very popular with local residents and visitors alike. The course starts off a bit hilly on the front nine, but flattens out by the back nine. The back nine have their own special surprises, including tricky water hazards. The first hole, a 384-yard, par-4 that tees downhill and approaches uphill, is definitely a warmup. The next hole is a 160-yard, par-3 that starts from an elevated tee to an elevated green over a severely banked, V-shaped gully. Shoot long here—it's longer than you think—as short shots tend to roll all the way back down the fairway to the base of the gully. This course is very, very green; the rain gods bless it regularly with brief passing showers. You can tell the regular players here—they all carry umbrellas and wait patiently for the squalls to pass, then resume play. Reservations are a must. Fees are $60, including cart; after 2:30pm weekdays, it's $23 with cart, $13 without. Facilities include a driving range, practice greens, club rental, pro shop, and restaurant.

THE NORTH SHORE

Kahuku Golf Course. ☎ **808/293-5842.** From Waikiki, take H-1 west to H-2; follow H-2 through Wahiawa to Kamehameha Hwy. (Hwy. 99, then Hwy. 83); follow it to Kahuku. Bus: 55.

We admit that this nine-hole budget golf course is a bit funky. Except a few pull carts that disappear with the first handful of golfers, there are no facilities: no club rentals, no clubhouse. But playing here, amongst the scenic beauty of this oceanside course and the tranquillity of the North Shore, is quite an experience nonetheless. Duffers will love the ease of this recreational course, and weight watchers will be happy to walk the gently sloping greens. Don't forget to bring your camera for the views (especially at holes 3, 4, 7, and 8, which are right on the ocean). No reservations are taken; tee times are doled out on a first-come, first-served basis—with plenty of retirees happy to sit and wait, the competition is fierce for early tee times. Bring your own clubs and call ahead to check the weather. The cost for this experience? Just $20 for nine holes.

✪ **Turtle Bay Hilton Golf & Tennis Resort. ☎ 808/293-8574.** Take H-1 west past Pearl City; when the freeway splits, take H-1 and follow the signs to Haleiwa; at Haleiwa, take Hwy. 83 to Turtle Bay Resort. Bus: 52 or 55.

This North Shore resort is home to two of Hawaii's top golf courses. The 18-hole **Links at Kuilima** was designed by Arnold Palmer and Ed Seay—*Golf Digest* rated it the fourth-best new resort course in 1994. Turtle Bay used to be labeled a "wind tunnel"; it still is one, but the casuarina (ironwood) trees have matured and dampened the wind somewhat. But Palmer and Seay never meant for golfers to get off too easy; this is a challenging course. The front nine holes, with rolling terrain, only a few trees, and lots of wind, play like a British Isles course. The back nine holes have narrower, tree-lined fairways and water. The course circles Punahoolapa Marsh, a protected wetland for endangered Hawaiian waterfowl. Greens fees are $125 (Turtle Bay guests pay $75).

The budget course is the **George Fazio–designed nine-hole course**—the only one Fazio designed in Hawaii—which can be played twice for a regulation par-71, 6,200-yard course. The course has two sets of tees, one designed for men and one for women, so you can get a slightly different play if you decide to tackle 18 holes. Larry Keil, pro at Turtle Bay, says that people like the Fazio course because it's more of a forgiving resort course, without the water hazards and bunkers of the more challenging Links course. "A lot of visitors like the option to just play nine holes," he says. The sixth hole has two greens so you can play the hole as a par-3 or a par-4. The toughest hole has to be the par-3, 176-yard second hole, where you tee off across a lake with the normal trade winds creating a mean crosswind; you have to clear the lake and land on the green and two putt to make par. The most scenic hole is the seventh, where the ocean is on your left; if you're lucky, you'll see whales cavorting in the winter months. Greens fees are $50 for 18 holes.

Facilities include pro shop, driving range, putting and chipping green, and snack bar. Weekdays are best for tee times. Unfortunately, no twilight rates are available.

CENTRAL OAHU

Mililani Golf Club. 95-176 Kuahelani Ave., Mililani, HI 96789. ☎ **808/623-2222.** From Waikiki, take H-1 west (toward Ewa), past Aloha Stadium; at the split in the freeway, turn off onto H-2. Exit at Mililani (Exit 5-B) onto Meheula Pkwy.; go to the 3rd stoplight (about 2 miles from the exit), and make a right turn on to Kuahelani Ave. Bus: 52.

This par-72, 6,455-yard public course is home to the Sports Shinko Rainbow Open, where Hawaii's top professionals compete. Located between the Koolau and Waianae mountain ranges on the Leilehua Plateau, this is one of Oahu's scenic courses, with views of mountains from every hole. Unfortunately, there are also lots of views of trees, especially eucalyptus, Norfolk pine, and coconut palm; it's a lesson in patience to stay on the fairways and away from the trees. The two signature holes, the par-4 no. 4 (a classic middle hole with water, flowers, and bunkers) and the par-3 no. 12 (a comfortable tee shot over a ravine filled with tropical flowers that jumps to the undulating green with bunkers on each side) are so scenic, you'll forgive the challenges they pose. Greens fees are $89 on weekdays ($65 on weekdays after 11am, $45 after 1pm) and $95 on weekends and holidays.

LEEWARD OAHU

✪ **Ko Olina Golf Club.** 3733 Alii Dr., West Beach, HI 96707. ☎ **808/676-5300.** Men are asked to wear shirts with a collar. From Waikiki, take H-1 until it becomes Hwy. 93 (Farrington Hwy.); turn off at the Ko Olina exit; take the exit road (Alinui Dr.) into Ko Olina Resort; turn left on Alii Dr. No bus service.

Golf Digest named this 6,867-yard, par-72 course one of "America's Top 75 Resort Courses" in 1992. The Ted Robinson–designed course has rolling fairways and elevated tee and water features. The signature hole—the 12th, a par-3—has an elevated tee that sits on a rock garden with a cascading waterfall. Wait until you get to the 18th hole; you'll see and hear water all around you—seven pools begin on the right side of the fairway and slope down to a lake. A waterfall is on your left off the elevated green. You'll have no choice but to play the left and approach the green over the water. Greens fees are $145 ($95 for Ihilani Resort guests); twilight rates after 2:30pm are $65. Book in advance; this course is crowded all the time. Facilities include a driving range, locker rooms, Jacuzzi/steam rooms, and a restaurant/bar. Lessons are available.

Pearl Country Club. 98-535 Kaonohi St., Aiea. ☎ **808/487-3802.** Call for a tee time at least a week in advance. From Waikiki, take H-1 past Pearl Harbor to the Hwy. 78 (Moanalua Freeway) exit; stay in the left lane, where Hwy. 78 becomes Hwy. 99 (Kamehameha Hwy.); turn right on Kaonohi St. Bus: 32 (stops at Pearlridge Shopping Center at Kaonohi and Moanalua sts; you'll have to walk about a 1/2 mile uphill from here).

Looking for a challenge? This popular public course, located just above Pearl City in Aiea, has all the challenges you can imagine. Sure, the 6,230-yard, par-72 looks harmless enough, and the views of Pearl Harbor and the USS *Arizona* Memorial are gorgeous, but around the fifth hole, you'll start to see what you're in for. That par-5, a blind 472-yard hole, doglegs quite seriously to the left (with a small margin of error between the tee and the steep out-of-bounds hillside on the entire left side of the fairway). A water hazard and a forest await your next two shots. Suddenly, this nice public course becomes not so nice. Oahu residents can't get enough it, so don't even try to get a tee time on weekends; stick to weekdays—Mondays are usually the best bet. Greens fees, including cart, are $75 weekdays, $80 weekends. After 4pm, nine holes are $25; on Wednesdays after 3pm, 18 holes are $35. Facilities include a driving range, practice greens, club rental, pro shop, and restaurant.

✪ **Sheraton Makaha Golf Club.** 84-626 Makaha Valley Rd., Waianae. ☎ **800/757-8060** or 808/695-9544. From Waikiki, take H-1 west until it turns into Hwy. 93, which winds through the coastal towns of Nanakuli, Waianae, and Makaha. Turn right on Makaha Valley Rd and follow it to the fork; the course is on the left. Bus: 51. Shuttle: 75.

This challenging course—recently named "The Best Golf Course on Oahu" by *Honolulu* magazine and ranked as one of Hawaii's top 10 by the readers of *Golfweek*—sits some 45 miles west of Honolulu, in Makaha Valley. Designed by William Bell, the par-72, 7,091-yard course meanders toward the ocean before turning and heading into the valley. Sheer volcanic walls tower 1,500 feet above the course, and swaying palm trees and neon bright bougainvillea surround it; an occasional peacock will even strut across the fairways. The beauty of the course might make it difficult to keep your mind on the game if it weren't for the challenges of it: eight water hazards, 107 bunkers, and frequent and brisk winds. This course is packed on weekends, so it's best to try weekdays. For guests of Waikiki's Sheraton resorts (Sheraton Moana Surfrider, Royal Hawaiian, Sheraton Waikiki, and Princess Kaiulani), greens fees are $90 any time of day; for non-Sheraton guests, they're $160 and drop to $90 after noon. Facilities include a pro shop, bag storage, and a snack shop.

West Loch Municipal Golf Course. 91-1126 Olepekepue Loop, Ewa Beach. ☎ **808/296-2000.** Booking a week in advance is recommended. From Waikiki, take H-1 west to the Hwy. 76 exit; stay in the left lane and turn left at West Loch Estates, just opposite St. Francis Medical Center. To park, take two immediate right turns. Bus: 50.

This par-72, 6,615-yard course located just 30 minutes from Waikiki, in Ewa Beach, offers golfers a challenge at bargain rates. The challenges on this municipal course are water (lots of hazards), wind (constant trade winds), and narrow fairways. To help you out, the course features a "water" driving range (with a lake) to practice your drives. After a few practice rounds on the driving range, you'll be ready to take on this unusual course, designed by Robin Nelson and Rodney Wright. The first hole starts in front of the clubhouse; the course then crosses a freeway for the next 10 holes and then goes back across the freeway for holes 12 to 18. In addition to the driving range, West Loch also has practice greens, a pro shop, and a restaurant. Greens fees are $47; if you're willing to tee off between 1 and 3:30pm on weekdays and 1 to 3pm on weekends, you'll pay just $23.50. We suggest booking a week in advance to get the tee time you want.

HORSEBACK RIDING

Up into the valley of kings, riders on horseback go deep into Oahu's interior, which only a lucky few have ever seen. Scenes of *Jurassic Park* were filmed in this natural place of beauty. Take a ride on **Kualoa Ranch & Activity Club,** 49-560 Kamehameha Hwy. (Hwy. 93), Kaaawa (☎ **800/231-7321** or 808/231-7321; Bus: 55), a 4,000-acre working cattle ranch that John Morgan, a scion of a sugar planter, turned into an outdoor playground. The ranch offers a number of different tours through its 4,000-acre property: 45-minute rides go for $25, 1½-hour rides for $40. You're required to wear long pants and closed-toe shoes.

You can gallop on the beach at the **Turtle Bay Hilton Golf and Tennis Resort,** 57-091 Kamehameha Hwy., Kahuku, HI 96731 (☎ **808/293-8811;** Bus: 52 or 55), where 45-minute rides along sandy beaches with spectacular ocean views and through a forest of ironwood trees cost $30 for adults and $20 for children nine to 12 (they must be at least four foot, six inches tall). Romantic evening rides take place on Friday and Saturday from 5 to 6:30pm and cost $60 per person. Advanced riders can sign up for a 40-minute trot-and-canter ride along Kawela Bay for $45.

If you've dreamed of learning how to ride, the **Hilltop Equestrian Center,** 41-430 Waikupanaha St., Waimanalo, HI 96895 (☎ **808/259-8463;** Bus: 57 or 58), will be happy to teach you. They offer lessons in either British or Western style from British Horse Society–accredited instructors for $40 per lesson, minimum of three lessons.

SKYDIVING

Everything you need to leap from a plane and float to earth can be had from **Blue Sky Rentals and Sports Center,** on the ground floor of Inn on the Park, 1920 Ala Moana Blvd. (at Ena Road) in Waikiki (☎ **808/947-0101**), for $225 per jump (including suit, parachute, goggles, plane rental, and lesson). If you want to try skydiving first to see if you like it, call **SkyDive Hawaii,** 68-760 Farrington Hwy., Wahaiwa (☎ **808/637-9700**), which offers a tandem jump (where you're strapped to an expert who wears a chute big enough for the both of you) for $275. There's no doubt about it—this is the thrill of a lifetime.

TENNIS

Oahu has 181 free public tennis courts. To get a complete list of all facilities or information on upcoming tournaments, send a self-addressed, stamped envelope to

Department of Parks and Recreation, Tennis Unit, 650 S. King St., Honolulu 96813 (☎ 808/971-7150). The courts are available on a first-come, first-served basis; playing time is limited to 45 minutes if others are waiting.

If you're staying in Waikiki, the **Ilikai Sports Center** at the Ilikai Hotel, 1777 Ala Moana Blvd., at Hobron Lane (☎ 808/949-3811; Bus: 19 or 20), has six courts, equipment rental, lessons, and repair service. Courts are $7.50 per person per hour; lessons are $44 per hour.

If you're on the North Shore, the **Turtle Bay Hilton Golf and Tennis Resort,** 57-091 Kamehameha Hwy., Kahuku, HI 96731 (☎ 808/293-8811, ext. 24; Bus: 52 or 55), has 10 courts, four of which are lit for night play. You must make reservations for the night courts in advance, as they're very popular. Court rates are $12 for the entire day. *Budget tip:* Book a court between noon and 4pm for half off. Equipment rental and lessons are available.

10 Orientation Tours

by Jeanette Foster

GUIDED SIGHTSEEING TOURS

If your time is limited, you might want to consider a guided tour: They're informative, entertaining, and you'll probably be surprised at how much you'll enjoy yourself. **E Noa Tours,** 1141 Waimanu St., Honolulu, HI 96814 (☎ 800/824-8804 or 808/591-2561; fax 808/591-9065; www.hawaiiguide.com/waiktrol.htm; e-mail enoa@pixi.com), offers a range of tours, from circling the island to exploring historic Honolulu. Their 2-hour narrated tour of Honolulu and Waikiki is aboard an open-air trolley and includes 20 stops from Waikiki to the Bishop Museum. It's a great way to get the lay of the land, with the driver pointing out not only historic sights but also Honolulu's attractions, shopping locations, and restaurants. You can get on and off the trolley as needed (trolleys come along every 15 minutes). An all-day pass (from 8am to 4:30pm) is $17 for adults, $5 for children under 11; a 5-day pass is $30 for adults, $10 for kids. Other E Noa Tours include a Circle Island beach and waterfall tour ($49 adults, $37 children 6 to 12, $31 children under 5), which stops at Diamond Head Crater, the Mormon Temple, Sunset Beach, Waimea Valley (admission is included in the cost), Hanauma Bay, and various beach sites along the way. Shopping excursions, nightlife tours, and a Pearl Harbor historic tour are also available.

Polynesian Adventure Tours, 1049 Kikowaena Pl., Honolulu, HI 96819 (☎ 808/833-3000), also offers a range of guided tours, from Circle Island to shopping excursions. The all-day island tours start at $46 adults, $37 for children 6 to 12, $31 for children 4 to 5, $15 for those 3 and under. The half-day scenic shore and rainforest tour is $23 for adults, $18 for children 3 to 11, while the half-day Arizona Memorial Excursion is $14 adults, $10 children 3 to 11.

WAIKIKI & HONOLULU WALKING TOURS

DOWNTOWN HONOLULU The **Mission Houses Museum,** 553 S. King St., at Kawaiahao St. (☎ 808/531-0481; Bus: 2), offers a walking tour of historic downtown buildings on Thursday and Friday mornings. A guide takes visitors through the capitol district, making stops at sites such as Iolani Place, the Kamehameha Statue, the Royal Tomb, and James Kekela's grave. The tour starts at 9:30am at the museum and last until 12:30pm. The museum also offers a **Women's History Walking Tour** one Saturday a month, which tells the stories of women of the Hawaiian *alii* (royalty). The fee for walking tours is $7 for adults, $4 for college students, $3 for kids 4 to 18, and

Tour of Duty

We are bound for Pearl Harbor in Honolulu's early-morning commute when the radio announcer suddenly interrupts: *"The Japanese have attacked Pearl Harbor."* Even now, a half-century later, the bulletin is arresting.

"Now, hear this," says Jim Wetmore, the lieutenant-looking chap in a World War II pilot's outfit at the wheel of our tour van, as he pops another cassette into the tape deck. *"This is CBS in America, calling Honolulu,"* intones a New York announcer on that fateful day in 1941. *"Come in, Honolulu . . ."*

There's a silence as big as the Pacific as we roll down the highway. We're on a tour of duty, back in Hawaii's khaki past, on a Hawaii military-base tour that's so historically accurate and information-packed that it's almost like being there that Sunday morning. All it takes is a little imagination.

Conducted with a "you are there" flourish by well-informed guides, this new 8-hour tour in 15-passenger vans began operating six days a week in 1996, after Pearl Harbor's 50th anniversary revived national interest. Along the route, you'll see the bullet holes at Hickam Air Field, cruise Pearl Harbor to Battleship Row, pay your respects to the 1,177 men lost aboard the battleship USS *Arizona,* board a heroic World War II submarine credited with 44 enemy "kills," see a B-17 bomber and P-40 Mustang, eat lunch at Schofield Barracks Officers Club, trace the history of Hawaii's 25th Infantry ("Tropic Lightning") Division, and visit graves of "unknown" heroes at the National Memorial Cemetery of the Pacific; all the while, your soundtrack is the Big Band music of the 1940s and such historic sound bites as President Roosevelt's war speech (*"We have suffered a severe setback in Hawaii"*).

"Our biggest surprise is that so many young people go on the tour," says tour director Glen Tomlinson. "We thought it would only attract veterans."

Our two-van group on this journey back in time is no exception. We are a Norman Rockwell portrait of Americans young and old, from coast-to-coast. Two men are veterans of Korea and Vietnam. Ahead of us lie the ghosts of Pearl Harbor.

A melancholy pervades the USS *Arizona* Memorial, which serves as an eternal tomb for the 1,177 sailors and Marines trapped below when the battleship sank in 9 minutes on December 7, 1941. The only sound is the soft whir of video cameras recording names of victims carved in tombstone.

On this gray day, the memorial smells like a gas station. A rivulet of 1941-vintage bunker oil gushes out of the broken battleship's hull, slicking the blue-green water. A steel plate has rusted through, perhaps. On days when oil flows heavily, people say the ship weeps.

A few visitors turn the *Arizona* into a wishing well by tossing pennies over the side. The copper coins tumble, flashing back glints of light before settling on the hull. Strange behavior—but people aren't sure how to behave at this funeral attraction. Nobody talks as we head for shore in the thin drizzle.

On Pearl Harbor's near shore, we pass by the USS *Bowfin* submarine, which offers the only bright ray against the *Arizona's* gloom. Nicknamed the "Pearl Harbor Avenger," this sub got to war a year late—it was launched December 7,

1942—but her valiant crew wasted no time, sinking 44 ships on nine South Pacific patrols.

Aboard the sub, we tiptoe around torpedoes and slip into the gleaming engine room; we squeeze through narrow passageways into crew quarters so squared away that it looks as if all 80 men just went ashore for liberty. We try to imagine ourselves down here, under the sea, and are reminded that 3,505 submariners died aboard 52 U.S. subs in World War II. We scramble up the open hatch, glad to be free, and climb back into the van.

Driving down Freedom Avenue—in 1941 the main runway of Hickam Air Field—we pass a B-17 bomber outside 1940s-era hangars with big blue stars symbolizing the U.S. Army Air Corps. Our destination is Hale Makai Barracks, shot up by Japanese Zero pilots, who killed 35 airmen at breakfast that Sunday. The barracks is a Pacific Air Force headquarters, a base museum, and a National Historic Monument.

"If you walk around the building, you can see bullet holes on all sides," says Air Force Sgt. Gail Ornong, our official escort. Up close, the stucco walls look like Swiss cheese. "We didn't get a plane up that day," Sergeant Ornong says. "Not a plane." Some craters are so big and deep that they can swallow your fist. One commander ordered the holes filled, but veterans protested. These scars will not heal.

Our next stop is Schofield Barracks. In his 1951 best-selling novel, *From Here to Eternity*, James Jones calls this "the most beautiful army post the U.S. has or ever had." With broad, palm-lined boulevards and art-deco buildings, it still is. It looks just as it did in 1941—an enigma to those who believe the Japanese bombed Schofield. Our guide knows better. "Not a single bomb fell here," Jim says over hula burgers at the Schofield Officers Club. But in the film version of the novel—filmed on location, starring Montgomery Clift, Frank Sinatra, Burt Lancaster, and Deborah Kerr—that myth became gospel truth. Other Hollywood embellishments also live on: The World War II P-40 inside Wheeler Field's main gate is a replica built in 1966 for *Tora! Tora! Tora!*

Late in the afternoon, after a few moments of reflection at the National Memorial Cemetery of the Pacific, we are coming down the old volcanic crater called Punchbowl, leaving behind the 35,000 simple graves of American service personnel killed in the Pacific in World War II and the Korean and Vietnam wars. We are coming down the mountain road counterclockwise, spiraling back to real time. As we reenter Honolulu, Jim plays *The Star Spangled Banner*—the jazzy, Whitney Houston version. "I tried to find Kate Smith's version," he says, apologetically. The national anthem ends, and we ride in silence to Waikiki. You could tell the veterans wanted to hear Kate Smith.

The **Home of The Brave Hawaii Military Base Tour** departs from Waikiki Monday through Friday at 6am and returns at 1:30pm. It's $69 for adults, $59 for kids 2 to 11, and includes a stop at Wheeler Army Air Base in addition to those mentioned above; hotel pickup and drop-off are also included. Call ☏ **808/396-8112** to reserve.

includes the regular Mission Houses tour (see "Attractions In & Around Honolulu & Waikiki," below). Reserve a day ahead in person or by phone.

Kapiolani Community College has a unique series of walking tours into Hawaii's past, including visits to Honolulu's famous cemeteries, the almost-vanished "Little Tokyo" neighborhood, and many more fascinating destinations. Tours, which generally cost about $5, are for groups only, but you may be able to tag along. For information and reservations, call ☎ 808/734-9245.

The Hawaii Geographic Society (☎ 808/538-3952) presents numerous interesting and unusual tours, like "A Temple Tour," including Chinese, Japanese, Christian, and Jewish temples, cathedrals, and other houses of worship; an archeology tour in and around downtown Honolulu; and others. Each is guided by an expert from the Hawaii Geographic Society and must have a minimum of three people; the cost is $10 per person. The society's brochure, *Historic Downtown Honolulu Honolulu Walking Tour*, is a fascinating self-guided tour of the 200-year-old city center. If you'd like a copy, send $3 to **Hawaii Geographic Maps and Books**, 49 S. Hotel St. (P.O. Box 1698), Honolulu, HI 96808.

CHINATOWN HISTORIC DISTRICT In addition to the Chinatown walk offered by Honolulu TimeWalks (see above), two 3-hour guided tours of Chinatown are offered Tuesdays at 9:30am by the **Chinese Chamber of Commerce**, 42 N. King St., at Smith Street (☎ 808/533-3181; Bus: 2). The cost is $5 per person; call to reserve.

The **Hawaii Heritage Center** (☎ 808/521-2749) also conducts 2-hour walking tours every Friday at 9:30am that focus on the history, culture, and multicultural aspects of Chinatown. Tours begin at the Ramsay Gallery, 1128 Smith St., at N. King Street (Bus: 2 or 13); the cost is $5 per person.

Also see our very own walking tour of Chinatown, later in this chapter.

BEYOND HONOLULU The **Moanalua Gardens Foundation**, 1352 Pineapple Pl., Honolulu, HI 96819 (☎ 808/839-5334), offers a 4- to 5-hour guided walking tour of Kamananui Valley once a month; it's a great way to see what Hawaii looked like before the introduction of numerous alien plants. The cost is $3.

GUIDED ECOTOURS

A day with Darren Akan is a rare chance to explore the "real" Hawaii. This award-winning guide takes groups of eight or more on guided, active, day-long outings, such as a hike to Manoa Falls for a splash in the waterfall pool, a beach picnic, or snorkeling and boogie boarding at very local Waimanalo Beach. Along the way, Darren discusses island ways and local customs, flora and fauna, history and culture, language and food, and more. The day starts at 7am and usually ends at about 3:30pm. The cost is $75 for adults and $64 for kids, which includes lunch and hotel pickup and return. You should be in fairly good shape and be able to hike at least a half-mile in a rain forest and feel at ease in gentle-to-moderate waves. Reservations are required at least a day in advance; call **Darren Akau's Hideaway Tours** (☎ 808/259-9165).

11 Attractions In & Around Honolulu & Waikiki

by Jeanette Foster

HISTORIC HONOLULU

For just about as long as we can remember, the Eastman Kodak Company has been hosting the **Kodak Hula Show** at the Waikiki Band Shell at Kapiolani Park (Bus: 4, 8, 19, or 20). It's really more '50s nostalgia than ancient culture, but it's a good bit of fun any way you slice it. Shows begin at 10am every Tuesday, Wednesday, and Thursday, and last until 11:15am. Admission is free. The area seats 1,500, and you'll have a good view no matter where you sit; however, if you want to be front and center (the best spot for photo ops), Kodak suggests that you arrive around 9:15am. For more information, call ☎ 808/627-3300.

For a more genuine Hawaiian hula experience, catch the hula *halau* that performs weekdays at 1pm at the **Bishop Museum** (below).

✪ **Bishop Museum.** 1525 Bernice St., just off Kalihi St. (also known as Likelike Hwy.). ☎ **808/847-3511.** Fax 808/841-8968. www.bishop.hawaii.org. Admission $8 adults, $7 children 6–17 and seniors. Daily 9am–5pm. Bus: 2.

This forbidding, four-story Romanesque lava rock structure (it looks like something out of a Charles Addams cartoon) holds safe the world's greatest collection of natural and cultural artifacts from Hawaii and the Pacific. The museum was founded by a Hawaiian princess, Bernice Pauahi, who collected priceless artifacts and in her will instructed her husband, Charles Reed Bishop, to establish a Hawaiian museum "to enrich and delight" the people of Hawaii. It's now world-renowned and home to Dr. Yoshihiko Sinoto, the last in a proud line of adventuring archaeologists who explored more of the Pacific than Captain Cook and traced Hawaii's history and culture through its fish hooks.

The Bishop is jam-packed with more than 20 million acquisitions—there are 12 million insect specimens alone—from ceremonial spears to calabashes to old photos of topless hula dancers. A visit here will give you a good basis for understanding Hawaiian life and culture. You'll see the great feathered capes of kings, the last grass shack in Hawaii, preindustrial Polynesian art, even the skeleton of a 50-foot sperm whale. There are seashells, koa-wood bowls, nose flutes, and Dr. Sinoto's major collection of fish hooks.

A ✪ hula *halau* performs weekdays at 1pm, and various Hawaiian crafts like leimaking, featherworking, and quilting are demonstrated. This daily cultural event is worth making time for.

Hawaii Maritime Center. Pier 7 (near Aloha Tower), Honolulu Harbor. ☎ **808/536-6373.** Admission $7.50 adults, $4.50 children 6–17. Daily 9am–5pm. Bus: 19, 20, 55, 56, or 57.

From the ancient journey of Polynesian voyagers to the nostalgic days of the *Lurline*, which once brought tourists from San Francisco on four-day cruises, the story of Hawaii's rich maritime heritage is told with artifacts and exhibits at the Hawaii Maritime Center's Kalakaua Boat House, patterned after His Majesty King David Kalakaua's own canoe house.

Outside, the *Hokulea*, a double-hulled sailing canoe that in 1976 reenacted the Polynesian voyage of discovery, is moored next to the *Falls of Clyde*, a four-masted schooner that once ran tea from China to the West Coast. Inside, the more than 30 exhibits include Matson cruise ships, which brought the first tourists to Waikiki; flying boats that delivered the mail; and the skeleton of a Pacific humpback whale that beached on Kahoolawe.

Iolani Palace. At S. King and Richards sts. ☎ **808/522-0832.** Admission $8 adults, $3 children 5–13. Guided tours Wed–Sat 9am–2:15pm; call ahead to reserve. You must be booked on a guided tour to enter the palace; children under 5 not permitted. Bus: 2.

This royal palace was built by King David Kalakaua, who spared no expense. The 4-year project, completed in 1882, cost $360,000—and nearly bankrupted the Hawaiian kingdom. The four-story Italian Renaissance palace, complete with Corinthian columns imported from San Francisco, was the first electrified building in

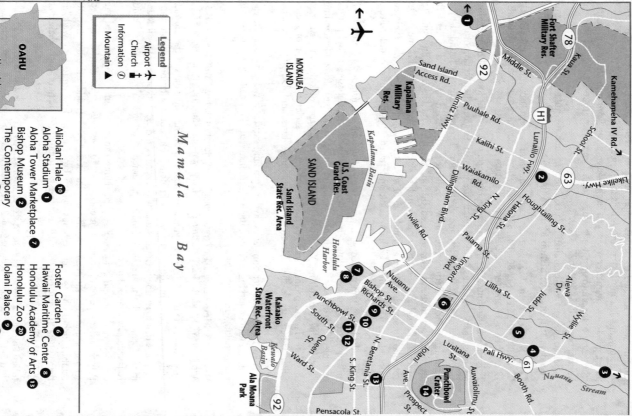

1-0708

Legend

▲ Mountain
① Information
✛ Church
✈ Airport

OAHU

★ Honolulu

Aliiolani Hale ⑩
Aloha Stadium ①
Aloha Tower Marketplace ⑦
Bishop Museum ②
The Contemporary Museum ⑮
Damien Museum ⑲
Diamond Head ㉓

Foster Garden ⑥
Hawaii Maritime Center ⑥
Honolulu Academy of Arts ⑧
Honolulu Zoo ⑳
Iolani Palace ⑨
Kapiolani Park ㉑
Kawaiahao Church ⑪
Kodak Hula Show ㉑

Mamala Bay

MOKAUEA ISLAND

SAND ISLAND

Sand Island State Rec. Area

Sand Island Access Rd.

Kapalama Military Res.

Kapalama Basin

U.S. Coast Guard Res.

Honolulu Harbor

Kakaako Waterfront State Rec. Area

Kewalo Basin

Ala Moana Park

Fort Shafter Military Res.

Kamehameha IV Rd.

Likelike Hwy.

Middle St.

School St.

Kaua St.

78

63

92

H1

Nimitz Hwy.

Puuhale Rd.

Kalihi St.

Waiakamilo Rd.

Dillingham Blvd.

Iwilei Rd.

Nuuanu Ave.

Bishop St.
Richards St.

Punchbowl St.

South St.

Queen St.

Ward St.

Pensacola St.

Lunalilo Fwy.

N. King St.

Halona St.

Palama St.

N. Vineyard Blvd.

Liliha St.

Alewa Dr.

Wyllie St.

Iholu St.

Houghtailing St.

Iolani Ave.

Lusitana St.

Pali Hwy.

Booth Rd.

Nuuanu Ave.

Prospect St.

Auwaiolimu St.

Punchbowl Crater

Nuuanu Stream

N. Beretania St.

S. King St.

92

61

①
②
③
④
⑤
⑥
⑦
⑧
⑨
⑩
⑪
⑫
⑬
⑭

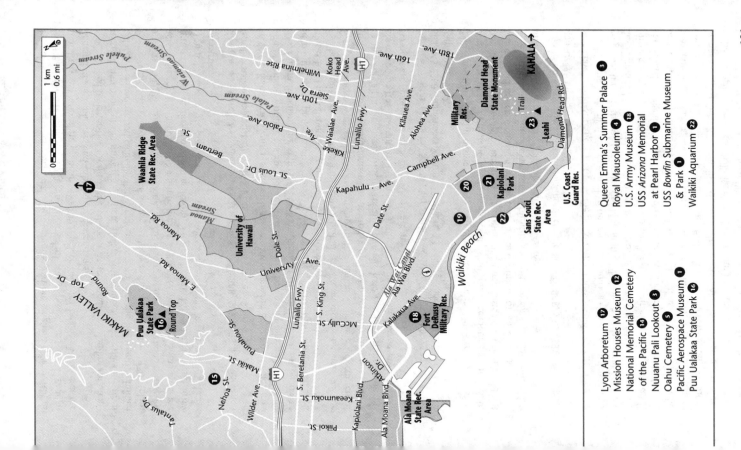

191

Lyon Arboretum ⑰
Mission Houses Museum ⑫
National Memorial Cemetery
of the Pacific ⑭
Nuuanu Pali Lookout ⑤
Oahu Cemetery ⑤
Pacific Aerospace Museum ⑪
Puu Ualakaa State Park ⑯

Queen Emma's Summer Palace ③
Royal Mausoleum ④
U.S. Army Museum ⑱
USS Arizona Memorial
at Pearl Harbor ❶
USS Bowfin Submarine Museum
& Park ❶
Waikiki Aquarium ㉒

Honolulu (it had electricity before the White House and Buckingham Palace). Royals lived here for 11 years, until Queen Liliuokalani was deposed, and the Hawaiian monarchy fell forever, in a January 17, 1893, palace coup led by U.S. Marines at the demand of sugar planters and missionary descendants.

Cherished by latter-day royalists, the 10-room palace stands as a flamboyant architectural statement of the monarchy period. (Iolani, often identified as the only royal palace on American soil, actually shares that distinction with the Big Island's Hulihee Palace, which also served as a royal house.) Open to the public since 1970, Iolani attracts 100,000 visitors a year in groups of 20, who must don denim booties to scoot across the royal floors. The 45-minute tour is well worth your time. Some areas are unfurnished, but the State Dining Room, Throne Room, King's Library, and Privy Council Chamber are complete. The two-story staircase is the largest koa-wood case on earth.

Kawaiahao Church. 957 Punchbowl St. (at King St.). ☎ **808/522-1333.** Free admission (small donations appreciated). Mon–Sat 8am–4pm; Sun services 10:30am. Bus: 2.

In 1842, Kawaiahao Church stood at last, the crowning achievement of missionaries and Hawaiians working together for the first time on a common project. Designed by Rev. Hiram Bingham and supervised by Kamehameha III, who ordered his people to help build it, the project took 5 years. Workers quarried 14,000 thousand-pound coral blocks from the offshore reefs and cut timber in the forests for the beams.

The proud stone church, complete with bell tower and colonial colonnade, was the first permanent Western house of worship in the islands. It became the church of the Hawaiian royalty and remains in use today by Hawaiians who conduct services in the Hawaiian language (which probably sets old Rev. Bingham spinning in his grave). Some fine portraits of Hawaiian royalty hang inside. ✪ **Hawaiian-language services** are conducted on Sundays at 10:30am.

Mission Houses Museum. 553 S. King St. (at Kawaiahao St.). ☎ **808/531-0481.** Fax 808/545-2280. Admission $6 adults, $5 seniors, $3 college students, $2 children. Tues–Sat 9am–4pm. Bus: 2.

This museum tells the dramatic story of cultural change in 19th-century Hawaii. Here, American Protestant missionaries established their headquarters in 1820. Included in the complex are a visitor center and three historic mission buildings restored and refurnished to reflect the daily life and work of the missionaries.

Walking tours of historic downtown buildings are offered on Thursday and Friday mornings; for details, see "Orientation Tours," above.

Oahu Cemetery. 2162 Nuuanu Ave. (north of Judd St.). ☎ **808/538-1538.** Free admission. Daily 7am–6pm. Bus: 4.

Not Hawaii's oldest cemetery or even the biggest, this 150-year-old, 35-acre cemetery is a burying place in America's rural, monumental tradition—more a garden than a golgotha. It holds the earthly remains of Honolulu's Who's Who of days gone by. Here lies Honolulu history: advisors to kings, sugar barons and sea captains, musicians and missionaries, all buried in a reclaimed taro patch on the outskirts of the mud-and-grass-thatch village they helped transform into the city of Honolulu. Under shade trees beside old carriage trails are Damons, Judds, and Thurstons, the missionaries who stayed on in the islands; and patriarchs of Hawaii's first foreign families, whose names now appear on in buildings and street signs: Blaisdell, Dudoit, Farrington, Magoon, Stangewald, Wilder. Here, too, lies Alexander Joy Cartwright, Jr., who some consider to be the real father of baseball: he chaired the committee that adopted the rules of play in 1845 and set base paths at 90 feet, and he umpired in the first official game in

1846. A few grave markers give sketchy details of death: a British sea captain spilled from his horse; a 9-year-old girl drowned off Kauai; a Boston missionary, the victim of consumption; an army private killed while looking for a leper in Kalalau. It's all there, carved in stone, old obituaries and grim reminders of timeless mortality.

Queen Emma Summer Palace. 2913 Pali Hwy. (at Old Pali Rd.). ☎ **808/595-3167.** Admission $5 adults, $4 seniors, $1 children ages 16 and under. Daily 9am–4pm. Bus: 4.

Hanaiakamalama, the name of the country estate of Kamehameha IV and Queen Emma, was once in the secluded uplands of Nuuanu Valley; these days, it's adjacent to a six-lane highway full of speeding cars that sound remarkably—if oddly—like surf as they zip by. This simple, seven-room New England–style house, built in 1848 and restored by the Daughters of Hawaii, holds an interesting blend of Victorian furniture and hallmarks of Hawaiian royalty, including feather cloaks and *kahili*, the feathered standards that mark the presence of *alii* (royalty). Other royal treasures include a canoe-shaped cradle for Queen Emma's baby, Prince Albert, who died at the age of 4. (Kauai's ultra-ritzy Princeville Resort is named for the little prince.)

Royal Mausoleum. 2261 Nuuanu Ave. (between Wyllie and Judd sts). ☎ **808/536-7602.** Free admission. Mon–Fri 8am–4:30pm. Bus: 4.

In the cool uplands of Nuuanu, on a 3.7-acre patch of sacred land dedicated in 1865—and never surrendered to America—stands the Royal Mausoleum, the final resting place of King Kalakaua, Queen Kapiolani, and 16 other Hawaiian royals. Only the Hawaiian flag flies over this grave remnant of kingdom.

JUST BEYOND PEARL HARBOR

Hawaiian Railway. Ewa Station, Ewa Beach. ☎ **808/681-5461.** Fax 808/681-4860. Admission $8 adults, $5 seniors and children 2–12. Sun 12:30pm and 2:30pm. Take H-1 west to exit 5a; drive makai (toward the ocean) 2½ miles on Kunia Rd., which becomes Fort Weaver Rd. Turn right on Renton Rd. (look for the Gas Express on the corner); follow it all the way to the end, about 1½ miles. Bus: 49, 50, 51, 52, 53, or 55 to the State Capitol, then transfer to bus no. 48 (Ewa Mill).

All aboard! This is a genuine train ride back into history. Between 1890 and 1947, the chief means of transportation for Oahu's sugar mills was the Oahu Railway and Land Co.'s narrow-gauge trains. Not only did the line carry equipment, raw sugar, and supplies, but also passengers from one side of the island to the other. You can relive those days every Sunday with a 1½-hour narrated ride through Ko Olina Resort and out to Makaha. As an added attraction, on the second Sunday of the month, they hook up the custom-built parlor-observation car belonging to Benjamin F. Dillingham, founder of the Oahu Railway and Land Co.; fares to ride in this nearly 100-year-old car are $15 (no kids under 13).

Hawaii's Plantation Village. Waipahu Cultural Garden Park, 94-695 Waipahu St. (at Waipahu Depot Rd.), Waipahu. ☎ **808/677-0110.** Fax 808/677-0110. Admission $5 adults, $4 seniors, students, and children 5–17. Mon–Sat 9am–4:30pm. Take H-1 west to Waikele-Waipahu exit (Exit 7); get in the left lane on exit and turn left on Paiwa St.; at the 5th stoplight, turn right on Waipahu St.; after the 2nd light, turn left. Bus: 47.

This symbolic cornerstone of Hawaii's multiethnic society offers a glimpse back in time to when sugar planters from America shaped the land, economy, and culture of territorial Hawaii. From 1852, when the first contract laborers arrived here from China, until 1947, when the plantation era ended, more than 400,000 men, women, and children from China, Japan, Portugal, Puerto Rico, Korea, and the Philippines came to work the sugarcane fields. The village stands as a collective monument to these brave immigrants, who brought their food, culture, language, art, and architecture to Hawaii, making it a cosmopolitan place. The $2.7 million, 50-acre village was developed from old blueprints, photos, and oral histories; it includes 30 faithfully restored Filipino camp houses, Chinese and Japanese temples, the Plantation Store, and even a sumo-wrestling ring.

WARTIME HONOLULU

For a guided tour of WWII Honolulu, see "Tour of Duty," above.

✪ **USS *Arizona* Memorial at Pearl Harbor.** ☎ 808/422-0561. Daily 7:30am–5pm (boat shuttles run 8am–3pm). Free admission. Children under 12 must be accompanied by an adult. Shirts and shoes required; no swimsuits or flip-flops allowed (shorts are okay). Wheelchairs gladly accommodated. Drive west on H-1 past the airport; take the USS *Arizona* Memorial exit, and follow the green-and-white signs; there's ample free parking. Bus: 20 or *Arizona* Memorial Shuttle Bus, which picks up at Waikiki hotels 6:50am–1pm ($6 round-trip); ☎ 808/839-0911.

On December 7, 1941, while moored in Pearl Harbor, the USS *Arizona* was bombed in a Japanese air raid. The 608-foot battleship sank in 9 minutes without firing a shot, taking 1,177 sailors and Marines to a fiery death—and plunging the United States into World War II.

Nobody who visits the memorial will ever forget. The deck of the ship lies 6 feet below the surface of the sea. Oil still oozes slowly up from the *Arizona's* engine room to stain the harbor's calm, blue water; some say the ship still weeps for its lost crew. The memorial is a stark white 184-foot rectangle that spans the sunken hull of the ship; it was designed by the late Alfred Pries, a German architect interned on Sand Island during the war. It contains the ship's bell, recovered from the wreckage, and a shrine room with the names of the dead carved in stone.

Today, free U.S. Navy launches take visitors to the *Arizona*. Try to arrive early at the visitors center, operated jointly by the National Park Service and the U.S. Navy, to avoid the huge crowds; waits of 1 to 3 hours are common. No reservations are taken. While you're waiting for the shuttle to take you out to the ship—you'll be issued a number and time of departure, which you must pick up yourself—you can explore the arresting museum, with personal mementos, photographs, and historic documents. A 20-minute film precedes your trip to the ship. Allow at least 4 hours to visit the memorial. USS Bowfin Submarine Museum & Park. 11 *Arizona* Memorial Dr. (next to the USS *Arizona* Memorial Visitor Center). ☎ 808/423-1342. Fax 808/422-5201. E-mail bowfin@aloha.net. Admission $8 adults, $6 active-duty military, $3 children 4–12. Daily 8am–5pm. See USS *Arizona* Memorial at Pearl Harbor above for driving, bus, and shuttle directions.

The USS *Bowfin* is one of only 15 World War II submarines still in existence today. You can go below deck of this famous submarine—nicknamed the "Pearl Harbor Avenger" for its successful retaliatory attacks on the Japanese—and see how the 80-man crew lived during wartime. The *Bowfin* Museum has an impressive collection of submarine-related artifacts. The Waterfront Memorial honors submariners lost during World War II.

National Cemetery of the Pacific. Punchbowl Crater, 2177 Puowaina Dr. (at the end of the road). ☎ 808/541-1434. Free admission. Daily 8am–5:30pm; Mar–Sept to 6:30pm. Bus: 15.

Go in the morning when the air is still, and listen. Except for the occasional sob of a sad widow, the Punchbowl is silent as a tomb.

The National Cemetery of the Pacific, as it's officially known, is an ash-and-lava tuff cone that exploded about 150,000 years ago—like Diamond Head, only smaller. Early Hawaiians called it Puowaina, or "hill of sacrifice." The old crater is a burial ground for 35,000 victims of three American wars in Asia and the Pacific: World War II, and the Korean and Vietnam wars. Among the graves, you'll find many unmarked ones with the date December 7, 1941 carved in stone. Some forever will be unknown; others are famous, like that of war correspondent Ernie Pyle, killed by a Japanese sniper in April of 1945 on Okinawa; still others buried here are remembered only by family and surviving buddies, now in their mid-'70s. The Cours of The Missing, white stone tablets, bear the names of 28,788 Americans missing in action in World War II.

Survivors come here often to reflect on the meaning of war and remember those, like themselves, who stood in harm's way to win peace a half-century ago. Some fight back tears, remembering lost buddies, lost missions, and the sacrifice of all who died in "the last good war."

FISH, FLORA & FAUNA

Foster Garden. 50 N. Vineyard Blvd. (at Nuuanu Ave.). ☎ **808/522-7060.** Fax 808/522-7050. Admission $5 adults, $1 children 6–12. Daily 9am–4pm; guided tours Mon–Fri at 1pm (reservations recommended). Bus: 2, 4, or 13.

This unique and historic garden is a leafy oasis amid the high-rises of downtown Honolulu. The giant trees that tower over the main terrace were planted in the 1850s by William Hillebrand, a German physician and botanist, on royal land leased from Queen Emma; today, this 14-acre public garden, on the north side of Chinatown, is a living museum of plants, some rare and endangered, collected from the tropical regions of the world. Of special interest are 26 "Exceptional Trees" protected by state law, a large palm collection, a primitive cycad garden, and a hybrid orchid collection.

Honolulu Zoo. 151 Kapahulu Ave. (between Paki and Kalakaua avenues), at entrance to Kapiolani Park. ☎ **808/971-7171.** Fax 808/971-7173. E-mail nordic@aol.com. Admission $6 adults, $1 children 6–12 when accompanied by an adult (children under 6 must be accompanied by an adult). Daily 9am–4:30pm. Bus: 2, 8, 19, 20, or 47.

Nobody comes to Hawaii to see an Indian elephant, or African lions and zebras. Right? Wrong. This 43-acre municipal zoo in Waikiki attracts visitors in droves, who come to see the new African Savannah, a 10-acre wild preserve exhibit with more than 40 uncapped African critters roaming around in the open. The zoo has a rare Hawaiian nene goose, a Hawaiian pig, and mouflon sheep. (Only the goose, an evolved version of the Canadian honker, is considered to be truly Hawaiian; the others are imported from Polynesia, India, and elsewhere.)

For a real treat, take the Zoo by Moonlight tour, which offers you a rare behind-the-scenes look into the lives of the zoo's nocturnal citizens. Tours are offered 2 days before, during, and 2 days after the full moon from 7 to 9pm; the cost is $7 for adults, $5 for children.

Lyon Arboretum. 3860 Manoa Rd. (near the top of the road). ☎ **808/988-7378.** Fax 808/988-4231. $1 donation requested. Mon–Sat 9am–3pm. Bus: 5.

Six-story-tall breadfruit trees . . . yellow orchids no bigger than a bus token . . . ferns with fuzzy buds as big as a human head: Lyon Arboretum is 194 budding acres of botanical wonders. A whole different world opens up to you along the self-guided 20-minute hike through Lyon Arboretum to Inspiration Point. You'll pass more than 5,000 exotic tropical plants full of birdsong in this cultivated rain forest (a University of Hawaii research facility) at the head of Manoa Valley.

Guided tours for serious plant lovers are offered one or two Saturdays a month; call ☎ **808/988-3177** for schedule and reservations.

✪ **Waikiki Aquarium.** 2777 Kalakaua Ave. (across from Kapiolani Park). ☎ **808/923-9741.** Fax 808/923-1771. Admission $6 adults, $4 seniors and students, $2.50 children 13–17. Daily 9am–5pm. Bus: 19 or 20.

Behold the chambered nautilus, nature's submarine and inspiration for Jules Verne's *20,000 Leagues Under the Sea*: You may see this tropical cephalopod mollusk—the only living one born in captivity—with its spiral shell any day of the week at the Waikiki Aquarium. Its natural habitat is the deep waters of Micronesia; but aquarium director Bruce Carlson succeeded not only in trapping the pearly shell in 1,500 feet of water by dangling chunks of raw tuna, but also managed to breed this ancient relative of the octopus. There are plenty of other fish as well in this small but first-class aquarium, located on a live coral reef. After a $3 million upgrade, it now features a Hawaiian reef habitat with sharks, eels, a touch tank, and habitats for the endangered Hawaiian monk seal and green sea turtle. Recently added: a rotating biodiversity exhibit featuring a look at the diversity of sea life, and interactive exhibits focusing on corals and coral reefs.

IN NEARBY EAST OAH

Sea Life Park. 41-202 Kalanianaole Hwy. (at Makapuu Point), Honolulu, ☎ **808/ 259-7933.** Admission $24 adults, $12 children 4-12, children under 4 free. Sat-Thurs 9:30am–5pm, Fri 9:30am–10pm. Parking $3. Shuttle buses from Waikiki $5. Bus: 22 or 58.

This 62-acre ocean theme park is one of Oahu's main attractions. It features whales from Puget Sound, Atlantic bottle-nosed dolphins, California sea lions, and penguins going through their hoops to the delight of kids of all ages. There's a Hawaiian reef tank full of tropical fish, a "touch" pool, where you can touch a real sea cucumber (commonly found in tide pools), and a bird sanctuary, where you can see birds like the red-footed booby and the frigate bird. The chief curiosity, though, is the world's only "wholphin"—a cross between a false killer whale and an Atlantic bottle-nosed dolphin. On site, marine biologists operate a recovery center for endangered marine life; during your visit, you'll be able to see rehabilitated Hawaiian monk seals and seabirds.

OTHER NATURAL WONDERS & SPECTACULAR VIEWS

In addition to the attractions listed below, check out "Diamond Head Crater" under "Nature Hikes," above; almost everybody can handle this hike, and the 360° views from the top are fabulous.

Nuuanu Valley Rain Forest. Take the Old Nuuanu Pali Rd. exit off Pali Hwy. (Hwy. 61).

It's not the same as a peaceful nature walk, but if time is short and hiking isn't your thing, Honolulu has a rain forest you can drive through. It's only a few minutes from downtown Honolulu in verdant Nuuanu Valley, where it rains nearly 300 inches a year. And it's easy to reach: As the Pali Highway leaves residential Nuuanu and begins its climb through the forest, the last stoplight is the Nuuanu Pali Road turnoff; turn right for a jungly detour of about 2 miles under a thick canopy strung with liana vines, past giant, golden bamboo that creaks in the wind, Norfolk pines, and wild shell ginger. The road rises and the vegetation clears as you drive, blinking in the bright light of day, past a small mountain reservoir.

Soon the road rejoins the Pali Highway. Kailua is to the right; Honolulu is to the left—but it can be a hair-raising turn. Instead, turn right, go a half-mile to the Nuuanu Pali Lookout (see below), stop for a panoramic look at Oahu's windward side, and return to the town-bound highway on the other side.

✪ **Nuuanu Pali Lookout.** Near the summit of Pali Hwy. (Hwy. 61); take the Nuuanu Pali Lookout turnoff.

Sometimes, gale-force winds howl through the mountain pass at this 1,186-foot high perch guarded by 3,000-foot peaks, so hold on to your hat—and small children. But if you walk up from the parking lot to the precipice, you'll be rewarded with a view that'll blow you away. At the edge, the dizzying panorama of Oahu's windward side is breathtaking; Clouds low enough to pinch scoot by on trade winds; pinnacles of the *pali* (cliffs), green with ferns, often disappear in the mist. From on high, the tropical palette of green and blue runs down to the sea.

ON THE WAY TO WINDWARD OAHU

✪ **Puu Ualakaa State Park.** At the end of Round Hill Dr. Daily 7am–6:45pm (to 7:45pm in summer). From Waikiki, take Ala Wai Blvd. to McCully St., turn right, and drive *mauka* beyond the H-1 on-ramps to Wilder St.; turn left and go to Makiki St.; turn right, and continue onward and upward about 3 miles.

The best sunset view of Honolulu is from a 1,048-foot-high hill named for sweet potatoes. Actually, the poetic Hawaiian name means "rolling sweet potato hill," which is how early planters used gravity to harvest their crop. The panorama from on high is sweeping and majestic. On a clear day—which is almost always—you can see from Diamond Head to the Waianae Range, almost the length of Oahu. At night, several scenic overlooks provide romantic spots for young lovers who like to smooch under the stars with the city lights at their feet. It's a top-of-the-world experience—the view, that is.

MORE MUSEUMS

For details on Honolulu's two world-class art museums, **The Contemporary Museum** and the **Honolulu Academy of Arts,** see "Oahu's Vibrant Art Scene," below.

Aliiolani Hale. 417 S. King St. (between Bishop and Punchbowl sts). ☎ **808/539-4999.** Fax 808/539-4996. Free admission. Mon–Fri 10am–3pm; reservations for group tours only. Bus: 1, 2, 3, 4, 8, 11, or 12.

Don't be surprised if this place looks familiar; you probably saw it on *Magnum, P.I.* or the made-for-TV movie *Blood and Orchids,* which correctly used it as the courthouse where Clarence Darrow defended the perpetrators in the famed Massie case in 1931. This gingerbread Italianate, designed by Australian Thomas Rowe in Renaissance revival–style, was built in 1874 and originally was intended to be a palace. Instead, Aliiolani Hale ("chief unto heavens") became the Supreme Court and Parliament government office building. Inside there's a **Judiciary History Center** (Monday to Friday 10am to 3pm), which features a multimedia presentation, a restored historic courtroom, and exhibits tracing Hawaii's transition from precontact Hawaiian law to Western law.

Damien Museum. 130 Ohua St. (between Kuhio and Kalakaua aves., behind St. Augustine's Catholic Church). ☎ **808/923-2690.** Donations accepted. Mon–Fri 9am–3pm, Sat 9am–noon. Bus: 8, 19, or 20.

This is a tiny museum about a large subject in Hawaii's history: Father Damien's work with leprosy victims on the island of Molokai. The museum contains prayer books used by Father Damien in his ministry, as well as his personal items. Don't miss the award-winning video on Damien's story.

Pacific Aerospace Museum. In the Central Waiting Lobby, Honolulu International Airport, 300 Rodgers Blvd., Honolulu, HI 96819. ☎ **808/839-0767.** Fax 808/836-3267. Admission $3 adults; $2.50 children 6–12, military, and students; children under 5 free. Daily 9am–6pm. Bus: 19 or 20.

While you're waiting for your flight to depart, check out the history of flight in the Pacific at this $3.8 million shrine to flying. You can trace elapsed time and distance of all direct flights from Honolulu on a 6-foot globe using fiber optics, watch old film clips of NASA astronauts splashing down in Hawaiian waters after landing on the

Oahu's Vibrant Art Scene

Passionate art lovers find solace and serenity in Hawaii's two top cultural resources: the Contemporary Museum and the Honolulu Academy of Arts. The vastly differing collections are housed in two of Hawaii's most memorable settings, both the legacy of one woman, Mrs. Charles Montague Cooke, who built the Alice Cooke Spalding house in 1925 (which now houses the Contemporary Museum) and, 2 years later, founded the Academy, a beacon in the arts to this day. One shudders to think what Hawaii's art world would have been without these two kamaaina legacies.

The **Honolulu Academy of Arts**, 900 S. Beretania St. (☎ **808/532-8701**), claims one of the finest Asian art collections in the country, as well as an acclaimed collection of American and European masters and prehistoric works that include Mayan, Greek, and Hawaiian art. The Moorish structure is a paragon of graciousness, with curved, tiled rooflines, open courtyards and lily ponds, and wide hallways leading to sensitively organized galleries. The Academy's setting, art collections, Garden Cafe, gift shop, and theatre make this a must for any resident or visitor. Open Tuesday through Saturday from 10am to 4:30pm, Sunday from 1 to 5pm. Admission is $5 per adult, with discounts for seniors and military personnel; members free.

Located up on the slopes of Tantalus, one of Honolulu's most prestigious residential communities, the **Contemporary Museum**, 2411 Makiki Heights Dr. (☎ **808/526-0232**), is renowned for several features: its 3½ acres of Oriental gardens with reflecting pools, sun-drenched terraces, views of Diamond Head, and stone benches for quiet contemplation; the Cades Pavilion, housing David Hockney's *L'Enfant et les Sortilèges*, an environmental installation of his sets and costumes for Ravel's 1925 opera; its excellent cafe and gift shop; and six galleries representing significant work and artists of the last four decades. Equally prominent is the presence of contemporary Hawaii artists in the museum's programs and exhibitions. Open Tuesday through Saturday from 10am to 4pm, Sunday from noon to 4pm. A one-day membership for adults is $5; seniors and students, $3; members and children free. The third Thursday of each month is free. Ask about their daily docent-led tours.

GALLERIES Longevity matters in Hawaii's art world. Like restaurants, galleries come and go in Chinatown, where well-meaning efforts to revitalize the area have moved in fits and spurts, especially in recent years. Two exceptions are the **Ramsay Galleries** in Tan Sing Building, 1128 Smith St. (☎ **808/537-2787**), celebrating nearly 200 exhibitions and its 18th year in 1998; and the **Pegge Hopper Gallery**, 1164 Nuuanu Ave. (☎ **808/524-1160**). Both are housed in historic Chinatown buildings that have been renovated and transformed into stunning showplaces for their and other artists' work. Nationally known quill-and-ink artist Ramsay, who has drawn everything from the Plaza in New York to most of Honolulu's historic buildings, maintains a vital monthly show schedule featuring her own work, as well as one-person shows of her fellow Hawaiian artists. The finest names in contemporary crafts and art have appeared here, ranging in media from photography to sculpture to glass, painting, prints, and, yes, computer art. When Ramsay's work is exhibited, each drawing is displayed with a magnifying glass to invite intimate viewing of the rich details. One of Hawaii's most popular artists, Pegge Hopper's widely collected paintings of Hawaiian women with broad, strong features, shown in simple lines and colors in relaxed poses, are displayed in her attractive two-story gallery.

Fans (and there are many) of prominent contemporary artist Roy Venters are paying close attention to his downtown gallery. The **Roy Venters Gallery**, 1160-B Nuuanu Ave. (☎ **808/273-3983**), next door to the Pegge Hopper Gallery, is a showcase and studio for Venters' powerful, unconventional works in two- and three-dimensional art: paintings, sculpture, furniture, interiors, and wearable art. Venters' pieces—avant-garde "shrines," three-dimensional crosses made of sea glass and colored stones, canvases and assemblages taking on taboo subjects—and his sheer brilliance of execution make him the Andy Warhol of Hawaii, a bold and welcome presence among Hawaii's contemporary artists. Next door is Seth Goldstein's **Sisu Gallery**, 1160-A Nuuanu Ave. (☎ **808/537-5880**), offering rotating monthly displays of local art, as well as a labyrinthine, two-story space devoted to retro contemporary design. Wander downstairs among the Herman Miller and other designer furniture, the Tamara de Lempicka charcoals, and the restored new '50s furniture and interior accents, and see if you don't agree that Sisu is a repository for works with a designer flair.

The darling of Hawaii's ceramics world, Gail Bakutis, gathered 11 other artists in varied media and formed **Art à la Carte** in Ward Centre, 1200 Ala Moana Blvd. (☎ **808/597-8034**). The gallery celebrates its 12th anniversary in 1998. What's there: paper, clay, scratchboard, oils, acrylics, watercolors, collages, woodblocks, lithographs, and Bakutis' award-winning raku- and pit-fired ceramics, known throughout Hawaii.

Hawaii's most unusual gallery is perched on the slopes of Punchbowl. It is the **Tennent Art Foundation Gallery**, 203 Prospect St. (☎ **808/531-1987**), devoted to the *oeuvre* of internationally esteemed artist Madge Tennent, whose work hangs in the National Museum of Women with the work of Georgia O'Keeffe. Tennent's much-imitated style depicts Polynesians throughout the 1920s to the 1940s in bold, modernist strokes that left an indelible influence on Hawaii art. The gallery is open only limited hours or by appointment.

In windward Oahu, flush against the lush Koolau Mountains, the garden idyll of **Hart Tagami and Powell Gallery and Gardens** (☎ **808/239-8146**; please call before going) turns out to be the most memorable Oahu stop for many visitors. The gallery, showcasing works by local artists—including Hiroshi Tagami and Michael Powell, both well known for their inspired paintings of Hawaii—is itself a work of art, a place of simple majesty where art and nature converge. The paintings, hand-turned bowls of native woods, ceramics, and sculptures by the best of Hawaii's artists are arranged in a serene environment surrounded by lush gardens. Tagami, an inveterate gardener, planted every tree himself and has introduced several magnificent botanical species to Hawaii.

—*Jocelyn Fujii*

moon, see models of early planes and flying boats (including a life-size replica of the Flight Deck of the space shuttle *Challenger*), and hear the heroic stories of the aviators who pioneered sky routes to the islands and beyond.

U.S. Army Museum. Fort DeRussy Park. ☎ **808/955-9552.** Free admission. Tues–Sun 10am–4:30pm. Bus: 8.

This museum, built in 1909 and used in defense of Honolulu and Pearl Harbor, houses military memorabilia ranging from ancient Hawaiian warfare items to modern-day high-tech munitions. On the upper deck, the Corps of Engineers Pacific Regional Visitors Center shows how the corps work with the civilian community to manage water resources in an island environment.

A STROLL THROUGH HISTORIC CHINATOWN

Chinese laborers from the Guangdong Province first came to work on Hawaii's sugar and pineapple plantations in the 1850s. They quickly figured out that they would never get rich working in the fields; once their plantation contracts were completed, a few of the ambitious ones started up small shops and restaurants in the area around River Street. At the time, the area wasn't much—mainly a handful of dirt streets—but it was well located, close to the docks and the newly developing businesses around Iolani Palace in downtown Honolulu.

Chinatown was twice devastated by fire, once in 1886 and again in 1900. It's the second fire that still intrigues historians: In December 1899, bubonic plague broke out in the area, and the Board of Health immediately quarantined its 7,000 Chinese and Japanese residents. But the plague continued to spread. On January 20, 1900, the Board decided to burn down plague-infected homes, starting at the corner of Beretania Street and Nuuanu Avenue. But the fire department wasn't quite ready; a sudden wind quickly spread the flames from one wooden building to another in the densely built area, and soon Chinatown's entire 40 acres were leveled, all the way to the waterfront. Many historians believe that the "out-of-control" fire may have been purposely set to drive the Chinese merchants—who were becoming economically powerful and controlled prime real estate—out of Honolulu. If this was indeed the case, it didn't work: To everyone's surprise, the determined merchants built a new Chinatown out of the ashes.

Chinatown reached its peak in the 1930s. In the days before air travel to the islands, visitors arrived by cruise ship. Just a block up the street was the pier where they disembarked—and they often headed straight for the shops and restaurants of Chinatown, which mainlanders considered an exotic treat. In the '40s, military personnel on leave flocked to Chinatown looking for different kinds of exotic treats—this time in the form of pool halls, beer parlors, tattoo joints, and houses of ill-repute.

Today, Chinatown is again rising phoenix-like from the ashes. Having deteriorated over the years into a tawdry red-light district of seedy bars and drug dealing, as well as being the favorite squatting area for Honolulu's homeless population, the neighborhood recently underwent extensive urban renewal. There's still just enough sleaze on the fringes (a few peep shows and a couple of topless bars) to keep it from being some theme park–style tourist attraction, but Chinatown is poised to relive its glory days.

Today's Chinatown appeals to the senses, with the pungent aroma of Vietnamese *pho* mingling with the ever-present sweet scent of burning incense; a jumble of streets that come alive every day with bustling residents and visitors from all over the world; a cacophony of sounds in the air, from the high-pitched bleating of vendors in the open market to the lyrical dialects of the retired men "talking story" over a game of mahjong; and brilliant reds, blues, and greens trimming buildings and goods everywhere you look. This isn't quite Hawaii, but it's not really a microcosm of China, either—rather, what you'll find is a mix of Asian cultures, all packed into a small area where tangy spices rule the cuisine, open-air markets have kept out the mini-malls, shrines and temples stand instead of churches, and the way to good health is through acupuncture and herbalists; even the candy is sweeter, the snacks saltier. No trip to Honolulu is complete without a visit to this exotic, historic district—welcome to Chinatown.

GETTING THERE From Waikiki, take Bus no. 2 or 20 toward downtown; get off on North Hotel Street (after Maunakea Street). If you're driving, take Ala Moana Boulevard and turn right on Smith Street; make a left on Beretania Street and a left again at Maunakea Street. The City parking garage (50¢ per hour) is located on the Ewa (west) side of Maunakea Street, between No. Hotel and No. King streets.

Start: No. Hotel and Maunakea streets.
Finish: Same intersection.
Time: Approximately 1 to 2 hours, depending on how much time you spend browsing.
Best Times: Daylight hours.

Start your walk on the Ewa (west) side of Maunakea Street at:

1. **Hotel Street.** During World War II, Hotel Street was synonymous with "good times." Pool halls and beer parlors lined the blocks, and prostitutes were plentiful; but the nefarious establishments have been replaced with small shops, from art galleries to specialty boutiques, and urban professionals and recent immigrants now walk where the sailors once roamed, looking for bargains.

   Once you're done wandering through the shops, head back to the intersection with Maunakea Street. Turn right on Maunakea; proceed to the corner of King Street and the:

2. **Bank of Hawaii.** At King and Maunakea streets sits this very unusual-looking bank: Not the conservative edifice you'd expect, but one guarded by two fire-breathing dragon statues.

   Continue down King Street. As you go, you'll pass the shops of various Chinese herbalists, such as the:

3. **Viet Hoa Chinese Herb Shop,** 162 N. King St. Chinese herbalists act as both doctor and dispenser of herbs. Patients come in and tell the herbalist what ails them; the herbalist then decides which of the myriad herbs he'll mix together. Usually, there's a wall of tiny drawers all labeled in Chinese characters; the herbalist quickly pulls various ground, powdered, and dried things from the drawers that range from dried flowers and ground-up roots to such exotics as mashed antelope antler. The patient then takes the concoction home to brew into a strong tea.

   Another interesting shop on No. King Street is the:

4. **Yat Tung Chow Noodle Factory,** 150 N. King St. The delicious, delicate noodles that star in numerous Asian dishes are made here, ranging from thread-like noodles (literally no thicker than embroidery thread) to fat, wide udon noodles. There aren't any tours of the factory, but you can look through the window, past the white cloud of flour that hangs in the air, and watch as dough is fed into rollers at one end of the noodle machines, and perfectly cut noodles emerge at the other end.

   On the Ewa side of Kekaulike Street, on King Street, lies the most visited part of Chinatown, the open-air market known as:

5. **Oahu Market Place.** If you're interested in Asian cooking, you'll find everything you could possibly want here, including pig's heads, poultry (some still squawking), fresh octopi, salted jellyfish, pungent fish sauce, fresh herbs, and thousand-year-old eggs. The friendly vendors are happy to explain their wares and give instructions on how to prepare these exotic treats. The market is divided into meats, poultry, fish, vegetables, and fruits; past the open market are several grocery stores with fresh produce on display on the sidewalk. You're bound to spot some varieties here that you're not used to seeing at your local supermarket. Follow King down to River Street and turn right toward the mountains and the:

6. **River Street Pedestrian Mall.** A range of inexpensive restaurants lines River Street from King Street to Beretania Street; you can get the best Vietnamese and Filipino food in town in these blocks, but go early—lines for lunch start at 11:15am. At Beretania Street, River Street ends and the pedestrian mall begins with the **statue of Chinese revolutionary leader Sun Yat-Sen.** The wide mall, which borders the Nuuanu Stream, is lined with shade trees, park benches, and tables where senior citizens gather to pay mahjong and checkers. Plenty of take-out restaurants are nearby if you'd like to eat outdoors.

   Along the River Street Mall, extending nearly a block over to Maunakea Street, is the:

7. **Chinatown Cultural Plaza.** This modern complex is filled with shops featuring everything from tailors to calligraphers (most somewhat more expensive than their streetside counterparts), as well as numerous restaurants—a great idea, but in reality, people seem to prefer wandering Chinatown's crowded streets to venturing into a modern mall. The plaza does have one excellent feature, though: In the center is the **Moongate Stage,** the site of many cultural presentations, especially around the Chinese New Year. Continue up the River Street Mall and cross the Nuuanu Stream via the bridge at Kukui Street, which will bring you to:

8. **Izumo Taisha Mission Cultural Hall.** This small, wooden Shinto shrine, built in 1923, houses a male deity (look for the X-shaped crosses on the top). Members of the faith ring the bell out front as an act of purification when they come to pray. Inside the temple is a 100-pound sack of rice, symbolizing good health. During World War II, the shrine was confiscated by the city of Honolulu and wasn't returned to the congregation until 1962.

   If temples are of interest to you, walk one block toward the mountains to Vineyard Boulevard; cross back over Nuuanu Stream, past the entrance of Foster Botanical Gardens, to:

9. **Kuan Yin Temple.** This Buddhist temple, painted in a brilliant red with a green ceramic-tiled roof, is dedicated to Kuan Yin Bodhisatva, the goddess of mercy, whose statue towers in the prayer hall. The piquant aroma of burning incense is your clue that the temple is still a house of worship, not an exhibit, so enter with respect and leave your shoes outside. You may see people burning paper "money," which is for prosperity and good luck, or leaving flowers and fruits at the altar (also gifts to the goddess). A frequent offering is the *pomelo,* a grapefruit-like fruit that's a fertility symbol as well as a gift indicating a request for the blessing of children.

   Continue down Vineyard and then turn left toward the ocean on:

10. **Maunakea Street.** Between Beretania and King streets are numerous lei shops (with lei-makers working away right on the premises) on both sides of the street. The air is heavy with the aroma of flowers being woven into beautiful treasures.

Walking Tour—Historic Chinatown

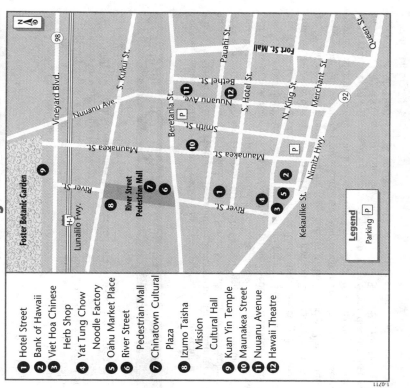

Legend
P Parking

1. Hotel Street
2. Bank of Hawaii
3. Viet Hoa Chinese Herb Shop
4. Yat Tung Chow Noodle Factory
5. Oahu Market Place
6. River Street Pedestrian Mall
7. Chinatown Cultural Plaza
8. Izumo Taisha Mission Cultural Hall
9. Kuan Yin Temple
10. Maunakea Street
11. Nuuanu Avenue
12. Hawaii Theatre

1-0711

Not only is this the best place in all of Hawaii to get a deal on leis, but the size, color, and design of the leis made here are exceptional. Wander through all the shops before you decide which lei you want.

If you have a sweet tooth, stop in at **Shung Chong Yuein**, 1027 Maunakea St. (near Hotel St.), for delicious Asian pastries like moon cakes and almond cookies, all at very reasonable prices. They also have a wide selection of dried and sugared candies (like ginger, pineapple, lotus root) that you can eat as you stroll or give as an exotic gift to friends back home.

Turn up Hotel Street in the Diamond Head direction, and walk to:

11. **Nuuanu Avenue.** You may notice that the sidewalks on Nuuanu Avenue are made of granite blocks; they came from the ballast of ships that brought tea from China to Hawaii in the 1800s. On the corner of Nuuanu Avenue and Hotel Street is the **Chinatown Police Station**, located in the Perry Block building; built in 1888, it looks like something straight out of a film noir.

Across the street from the police station is the **Lai Fong Department Store**, a classic Chinatown store owned by the same family for more than three-quarters of a century. Walking into Lai Fong is like stepping back in time. The old store sells everything from precious antiques to god-awful knickknacks to rare turn-of-the-century Hawaiian postcards—but it has built its reputation on the fabulous selection of Chinese silks, brocades, and custom dresses it carries.

Between Hotel and Pauahi streets is the **Pegge Hooper Gallery**, 1164 Nuuanu Ave., where you can admire Pegge's well-known paintings of beautiful Hawaiian women.

At Pauahi Street, turn toward Diamond Head and walk up to Bethel Street and the:

12. Hawaii Theatre. This restored 1920 art-deco theater is a work of art in itself. It hosts a variety of programs, from the Hawaii International Film Festival to beauty pageants (see "Oahu After Dark," below, for details on how to find out what's on while you're in town).

Walk toward the ocean on Bethel Street and turn right on Hotel Street, which will lead you back to where you started.

12 Beyond Honolulu: Exploring the Island

by Jeanette Foster

The moment always arrives—usually after 2 or 3 days at the beach, snorkeling in the warm, blue-green waters of Hanauma Bay, enjoying sundown mai tais, listening to the mellifluous tones of Sonny Kamahele and the Sunset Serenaders at the Halekulani—when a certain curiosity kicks in in about the rest of Oahu, largely unknown to most visitors. It's time to find the rental car in the hotel garage and set out around the island.

If you don't have a car, you can explore the island via TheBus. There are two buses that "Circle the Island": no. 52, which goes around the island clockwise, and no. 55, which goes around the island counterclockwise. Both run about every 30 minutes. However, be aware that at Turtle Bay Hilton, just outside of Kahuku, the 52 becomes the 55 and returns to Honolulu via the coast, and the 55 becomes the 52 and returns to Honolulu on the inland route. Translation: You have to get off and switch buses to complete your island tour, which takes about 4 hours, not including stops. If there's one specific area you want to go to, there are express buses to certain destinations (i.e., 54 to Pearl City; 46 to Kailua-Kaneohe; and 57 and 58 to Sea Life Park). For more information, call TheBus at ☎ **808/848-5555,** or check out routes and timetables at **www.thebus.org.**

For great places to stop for a bite to eat while you're exploring, see "Dining," above. You also might want to check our "Shopping Around the Island," below.

OAHU'S SOUTHEAST COAST

Some head immediately to the North Shore, but you might want to go south because, believe it or not, you'll get out of town faster. Once you clear suburban Hawaii Kai and the Kalanianaole Highway (Hwy. 72) heads uphill to Hanauma Bay, you're on one of the last unspoiled coasts on Oahu. It's a great little getaway, especially if you spin around the South Coast and loop back to town on the Pali Highway (Hwy. 61).

Around **Koko Head,** Oahu looks like Arizona-by-the-sea: it's an arid moonscape with prickly cacti onshore and, in the winter, spouting whales cavorting in the water. Some call it the South Shore, others Sandy's after the mile-long beach here, but Hawaiians call it **Ka Iwi,** which means "the bone"—no doubt because of all the bone-cracking shore breaks along this popular body-boarding coastline. The beaches here are long, wide, and popular with local daredevils.

This open, scenic coast is the best place on Oahu to watch sea, shore, and even land birds. It's also a good whale-watching spot in season, and the night sky is ideal for amateur astronomers to watch meteors, comets, and stars.

The jagged lava coast itself spouts sea foam at the **Halona Blowhole.** Look out to sea from Halona over Sandy Beach and across the 26-mile gulf to neighboring Molokai and the faint triangular shadow of Lanai on the far horizon. **Sandy Beach** (see "Beaches," above) is Oahu's most dangerous beach; it's the only one with an

Eastern Oahu & The Windward Coast

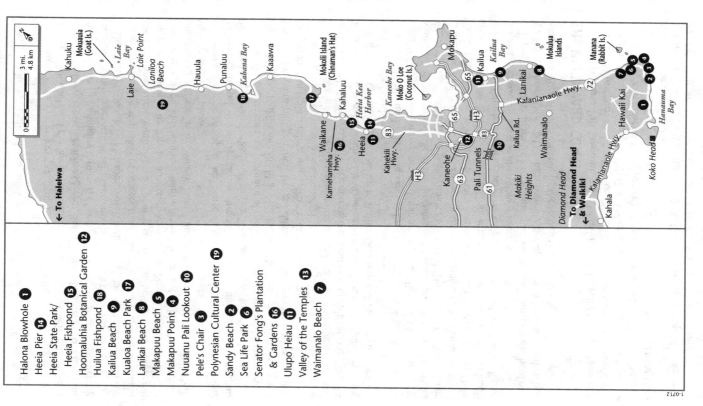

Halona Blowhole **1**
Heeia Pier **14**
Heeia State Park/
Heeia Fishpond **15**
Hoomaluhia Botanical Garden **12**
Huilua Fishpond **18**
Kailua Beach **9**
Kualoa Beach Park **17**
Lanikai Beach **8**
Makapuu Beach **5**
Makapuu Point **4**
Nuuanu Pali Lookout **10**
Pele's Chair **3**
Polynesian Cultural Center **19**
Sandy Beach **2**
Sea Life Park **6**
Senator Fong's Plantation
& Gardens **16**
Ulupo Heiau **11**
Valley of the Temples **13**
Waimanalo Beach **7**

1-0712

ambulance always standing by to whisk injured wave catchers to the hospital. Body boarders just love it.

The coast looks raw and empty along this stretch, but the road weaves past old Hawaiian fishponds and the famous formation known as **Pele's Chair**, just off Kalanianaole Highway (Hwy. 72) above Queen's Beach. From a distance, the lava rock outcropping looks like a mighty throne; it's believed to be the fire goddess's last resting place on Oahu before she flew off to continue her work on other islands.

Ahead lies 647-foot-high **Makapuu Point**, with a lighthouse that once signaled safe passage for arriving steamship passengers from San Francisco. The automated light now brightens Oahu's South Coast for passing tankers, fishing boats, and sailors. You can take a short hike up here for a spectacular vista; see "Nature Hikes," above.

If you're with the kids, you may want to spend the day at **Sea Life Park**, a marine amusement park; see "Fish, Flora & Fauna" under "Attractions In & Around Honolulu & Waikiki," above.

Turn the corner at Makapuu, and you're on Oahu's windward side, where cooling trade winds propel windsurfers across turquoise bays, and the waves at **Makapuu Beach Park** are perfect for bodysurfing (see "Beaches," above, for more details).

Ahead, the coastal vista is a profusion of fluted green mountains and strange peaks, edged by golden beaches and the blue, blue Pacific. The 3,000-foot-high sheer green Koolau Mountains plunge almost straight down, presenting an irresistible jumping-off spot for hang-glider pilots, who catch the thermals on hours-long rides.

Winding up the coast, Kalanianaole Highway (Hwy. 72) leads through rural **Waimanalo**, a country beach town of nurseries and stables, fresh-fruit stands, and some of the island's best conch and triton shell specimens at roadside stands. Nearly 4 miles long, **Waimanalo Beach** is Oahu's longest beach and the most popular for bodysurfing. Take a swim here or head on to **Kailua Beach**, one of Hawaii's best beaches (see "The Windward Coast," below, and "Beaches," above).

If it's still early in the day, you can head up the lush, green Windward Coast by turning right at the Castle Junction, Highway 72, and Highway 61 (which is also Kailua Rd. on the makai side of the junction, and Kalanianaole Hwy. on the mauka side of the junction), and continuing down Kailua Road (Hwy. 61). After Kailua Road crosses the Kaelepulu Stream, the name of the road changes to Kiuulei Road. When Kiuulei Road ends, turn left onto Kalaheo Avenue, which becomes Kaneohe Bay Drive after it crosses the Kawainui Channel. Follow this scenic drive around the peninsula until it crosses Kamehameha Highway (Hwy. 83); turn right and continue on Kamehameha Highway for a scenic drive along the ocean.

If you're in a hurry to get back to Waikiki, turn left at Castle Junction and head over the Pali Highway (Hwy. 61), which becomes Bishop Street in Honolulu and ends at Ala Moana. Turn left for Waikiki; it's the second beach on the right.

THE WINDWARD COAST

From the **Nuuanu Pali Lookout**, near the summit of the Pali Highway (Hwy. 61), you get the first hint of the other side of Oahu, a region so green and lovely that it could be an island sibling of Tahiti or Moorea. With many beaches and bays, the scenic 30-mile Windward Coast parallels the corduroy-ridged, nearly perpendicular cliffs of the Koolau Range, which separates the windward side of the island from Honolulu and the rest of Oahu.

From the Pali Highway, to the right is **Kailua**, Hawaii's biggest beach town, with more than 50,000 residents and two special beaches, **Kailua** and **Lanikai**, begging for visitors (see "Beaches," above, for more details). Funky little Kailua is lined with

⓫ Especially for Kids

Visiting the Honolulu Zoo (see p. 195) Visit Africa in Hawaii at Waikiki's Kapiolani Park. The lions, giraffes, zebras, and elephants delight youngsters and their parents alike. But the great new thrill is the Zoo by Moonlight tour—so kids can see and hear what really goes bump in the dark.

Shopping Aloha Flea Market (see p. 215) Most kids hate to shop. But the Aloha Flea Market, a giant outdoor bazaar at Aloha Stadium on Wednesday, Saturday, and Sunday, is more than shopping: It's an experience akin to a carnival, full of strange food, odd goods, and bold barkers. Nobody ever leaves this place empty-handed—or without having had lots of fun.

Seeing the World's Only Wholphin (see p. 196) It's a freak of nature, a cross between a whale and a dolphin—and you can see it at Sea Life Park. Kids love this marine amusement park, where trained dolphins, whales, and seals do their thing.

Flying a Kite at Kapiolani Park (see p. 190) Great open expanses of green and constant trade winds make this urban park one of Hawaii's prime locations for kite-flying. You can watch the pros fly dragon kites and stake kite-fighting contests, or join in the fun after checking out the convenient kite shop across the street in New Otani's arcade.

Spending a Day at Waimea Valley and Adventure Park (see p. 214) What many think is only a botanical garden tucked away on the North Shore is really a child's garden of delight. There are waterfalls and pools for swimming, cliff divers to watch, and much more to do, like kayaking the Waimea River and taking a three-wheeled ATV through a jungly forest. Kids of all ages find great adventure here.

Eating Shave Ice at Haleiwa (see p. 214) No kid's visit to Hawaii is complete until he or she tastes an authentic shave ice. You can find shave ice in all kinds of tropical flavors throughout the islands, but for some reason, it tastes better in this funky North Shore surf town.

$1 million houses next to tarpaper shacks, antique shops, and bed-and-breakfasts. Although the Pali Highway (Hwy. 61) proceeds directly to the coast, it undergoes two name changes, becoming first Kalanianaole Highway—from the intersection of Kamehameha Highway (Hwy. 83)—and then Kailua Road as it heads into Kailua town—the road remains Highway 61 the whole way. Kailua Road ends at the T-intersection at Kalaheo Drive, which follows the coast in a northerly and southerly direction. Turn right on South Kalaheo Drive to get to Kailua Beach Park and Lanikai Beach. No signs point the way, but you can't miss them.

If you spend a day at the beach here, stick around for sunset, when the sun sinks behind the Koolau Range and tints the clouds pink and orange. After a hard day at the beach, you work up an appetite, and Kailua has several great, inexpensive restaurants (see "Dining," above). And don't forget to stop by the Agnes Portuguese Bake Shop, **A Panaderia**, 35 Kainehe St., Kailua (☎ **808/262-5367**). Don't go snorkeling after eating two or three of these weighty treats, or you'll sink to the bottom.

As you descend on the serpentine Pali Highway beneath often gushing waterfalls, you'll see the nearly 1,000-foot spike of **Olomana**, the bold pinnacle that always reminds us of that mountain in *Close Encounters*, and beyond, the Hawaiian village of

Waimanalo. If you want to skip the beaches this time, turn left on North Kalaheo Drive, which becomes Kaneohe Bay Drive as it skirts Kaneohe Bay and leads back to Kamehameha Highway (Hwy. 83), which then passes through **Kaneohe.** The suburban maze of Kaneohe is one giant strip mall of retail excess that mars one of the Pacific's most picturesque bays. After clearing this obstacle, the place begins to look like Hawaii again.

Incredibly scenic **Kaneohe Bay** is spiked with islets and lined with gold-sand beach parks like **Kualoa,** a favorite picnic spot (see "Beaches," above). The bay has a barrier reef and four tiny islets, one of which is known as Moku o loe, or Coconut Island. Don't be surprised if it looks familiar—it appeared in *Gilligan's Island.*

Little poly-voweled beach towns like **Kaaawa, Hauula, Punaluu,** and **Kahaluu** pop up along the coast, offering passersby shell shops and art galleries to explore. Famed hula photographer Kim Taylor Reece lives on this coast; his gallery at 53-866 Kamehameha Hwy., near Sacred Falls (☎ **808/293-2000**), is open Sunday through Tuesday 10am to 6pm. There are also working cattle ranches, fisherman's wharfs, and roadside fruit and flower stands vending ice-cold coconuts (to drink) and tree-ripened mangoes, papayas, and apple bananas.

At **Heeia State Park** (☎ **808/247-3156**) is **Heeia Fishpond,** which ancient Hawaiians built by enclosing natural bays with rocks to trap fish on the incoming tide. The 88-acre fishpond, which is made of lava rock and had four watchtowers to observe fish movement and several sluice gates along the 5,000-foot long wall, is now in the process of being restored.

Stop by the **Heeia Pier,** which juts onto Kaneohe Bay. You can take a snorkel cruise here, or sail out to a sandbar in the middle of the bay for an incredible view of Oahu that most people, even those who live here, never see. If it's Tuesday through Saturday between 7am and 6pm, stop in and see Ernie Choy at the **Deli on Heeia Kea Pier** (☎ **808/235-2192**). He has served fishermen, sailors, and kayakers the beach town's best omelets and plate lunches at reasonable prices since 1979.

Everyone calls it Chinaman's Hat, but the tiny island off the eastern shore of Kualoa Regional Park is really **Mokolii.** It's a sacred *puu honua,* or place of refuge, like the restored Puu Honua Honaunau on the Big Island of Hawaii. Excavations have unearthed evidence that this area was the home of ancient *alii* (royalty). Early Hawaiians believed that Mokolii (or "fin of the lizard") is all that remains of a *mo'o,* or lizard, slain by Pele's sister, Hiiaka, and hurled into the sea. At low tide, you can swim out to the island, but keep watch on the changing tide, which can sweep you out to sea. The islet has a small, sandy beach and is a bird preserve, so don't spook the red-footed boobies.

Farther along, on the east side Kahana Bay by Kamehameha Highway is **Huilua Fishpond.** This national historic landmark is one of Windward Oahu's most beautiful fishponds and the easiest to see. Once fed by a freshwater spring and refreshed by the ocean, this pond proved ideal for raising mullet and milk fish.

Sugar, once the sole industry of this region, is gone. But **Kahuku,** the former sugarplantation town, has new life as a small aquaculture community with prawn and clam farms that supply island restaurants.

From here, continue along Kamehameha Highway (Hwy. 83) to the North Shore.

ATTRACTIONS ALONG THE WINDWARD COAST

The attractions below are arranged geographically as you drive up the coast from south to north.

Hoomaluhia Botanical Gardens. 45-680 Luluku Rd., Kaneohe. ☎ **808/233-7323.** Fax 808/247-3199. Free admission. Daily 9am–4pm. Guided nature hikes Sat 10am, Sun 1pm.

Take H-1 to the Pali Hwy. (Hwy. 61); turn left on Kamehameha Hwy. (Hwy. 83); at the 4th light, turn left onto Luluku Rd. Bus: 55 or 56 will stop on Kamehameha Hwy.; you'll have a 2-mile walk to the visitors center.

This 400-acre botanical garden at the foot of the steepled Koolau Mountains is the perfect place for a mauka picnic. Its name means "a peaceful refuge"; that's exactly what the Army Corps of Engineers created when they installed a flood-control project here, which resulted in a 32-acre freshwater lake and the garden. Just unfold a beach mat, lay back, and watch the clouds race across the rippled cliffs of the majestic Koolau Range. It's one of the few public places on Oahu that provides a close-up view of the steepled cliffs. The park has hiking trails and—best of all—the island's only free inland campground (see "Camping & Wilderness Cabins," above).

Valley of the Temples. 47-200 Kahekili Hwy. (across the street from Temple Valley Shopping Center), Kaneohe. ☎ **808/239-8811.** Admission $2 adults, $1 children under 12 and seniors 65 and older. Daily 8:30am–4:30pm. From Honolulu, take the H-1 to the Likelike Hwy. (Hwy. 63); after the Wilson Tunnel, get in the right lane and take the Kahekili Hwy. (Hwy. 63); at the 6th traffic light is the entrance to the cemetery (on the left). Bus: 65.

The people of Honolulu bury their pets and their grandparents in this graveyard. Awhile back, Ferdinand Marcos, the exiled Filipino dictator, was also here; he occupied a temporary mausoleum until the Philippines relented and let him be buried in his native land. Marcos may be gone now, but dogs and cats and a lot of local folks remain. In a cleft of the pali, the graveyard is stalked by wild peacocks and about 700 curious people a day who pay to see the 9-foot meditation Buddha, 2 acres of ponds full of more than 10,000 Japanese Koi carp, and a replica of Japan's 900-year-old Byodo-in Temple of Equality. The original, made of wood, stands in Uji, on the outskirts of Kyoto; the Hawaiian version, made of concrete, was erected in 1968 to commemorate the 100th anniversary of the arrival of the first Japanese immigrants to Hawaii. It's not the same as seeing the original, but it's worth a detour. A 3-ton brass temple bell brings good luck to those who can ring it—although the gongs do jar the Zen-like serenity of this little bit of Japan.

Senator Fong's Plantation & Gardens. 47-285 Pulama Rd., Kaneohe. ☎ **808/ 239-6775.** Fax 808/239-6469. Admission $10 adults, $6 children 5–12. 45-minute narrated tram tours daily from 10:30am; last tour 3pm. From Honolulu, take the H-1 to the Likelike Hwy. (Hwy. 63); turn left at Kahekili Hwy. (Hwy. 83); continue on to Kahaluu, and turn left on Pulama Rd. Bus: 55; it's a mile walk uphill from the bus stop.

Senator Hiram Fong, the first Chinese-American elected to the U.S. Senate, served 17 years before retiring to tropical gardening years ago. Now you can ride an open-air tram through five gardens named for the American presidents he served. His 725-acre private estate includes 75 edible nuts and fruits. It's definitely worth an hour—if you haven't already seen enough botanics to last a lifetime.

Kualoa Ranch & Activity Club. 49-560 Kamehameha Hwy., Kaaawa. ☎ **800/237-7321** or 808/237-7321. Daily 9:30am–3:30pm. Various packages $69–$99 adults, $45–$65 children. Reservations required. Take H-1 to the Likelike Hwy. (Hwy. 63); turn left at Kahekili Hwy. (Hwy. 83); continue on to Kaaawa. Bus: 52.

This once-working ranch now has some two dozen activities on its 4,000 acres. Depending on the package you buy, you have a selection of activities, including horseback riding, mountain-bike riding, shooting a rifle or a .22-caliber handgun, hiking, dune cycling, jet skiing, canoeing, kayaking, windsurfing, snorkeling, freshwater fishing, and more. We highly recommend the beach activities, where you'll be shuttled to Molii fishpond's outermost bank, which is decked out like a country club: hammocks on the beach, volleyball courts, horseshoe pits, Ping-Pong tables, and beach pavilions. From there, you can take a 45-foot catamaran to Kaneohe Bay for snorkeling.

Polynesian Cultural Center, 55-370 Kamehameha Hwy., Laie. **☎ 800/367-7060,** 808/293-3333, or 808/923-2911. Fax 808/923-2917; www.polynesia.com. Mon-Sat 12:30-9:30pm. Admission only $27 adults, $16 children 5-11. Admission, buffet, and nightly show $47 adults, $30 children. IMAX, luau, and nightly show $59 adults, $37 children. Ambassador VIP (deluxe) tour $95 adults, $63 children. Take H-1 to Pali Hwy. (Hwy. 61) and turn left on Kamehameha Hwy. (Hwy. 83). Bus: 55. Polynesian Cultural Center coaches $15 round trip; book at numbers above.

If the extent of your travel to Polynesia ends in Hawaii, you can still experience the natural beauty and culture of the vast Pacific in a single day at the Polynesian Cultural Center. Here, you can see first-hand the lifestyles, songs, dance, costumes, and architecture of seven Pacific islands—Fiji, New Zealand, Marquesas, Samoa, Tahiti, Tonga, and Hawaii—in the re-created villages scattered throughout the 42-acre lagoon park.

You "travel" through this kind of living museum of Polynesia by foot or in a canoe on a manmade freshwater lagoon. Each village is "inhabited" by native students from Polynesia, who attend Hawaii's Brigham Young University. Operated by the Mormon Church, the park also features a variety of stage shows celebrating the music, dance, history, and culture of Polynesia. There's also a luau every evening. Since a visit can take up to 8 hours, it's a good idea to arrive before 2pm.

Just beyond the center is the **Hawaii Temple** of The Church of Jesus Christ of Latter-Day Saints, which is built of volcanic rock and concrete in the form of a Greek cross and includes reflecting pools, formal gardens, and royal palms. Completed in 1919, it was the first Mormon temple built outside the continental U.S. An optional tour of the Temple Visitors Center, as well as neighboring Brigham Young University-Hawaii, is included in the package admission prices.

CENTRAL OAHU & THE NORTH SHORE

If you can afford the splurge, rent a bright, shiny convertible—the perfect car for Oahu, since you can tan as you go—and head for the North Shore and Hawaii's surf city: **Haleiwa,** a quaint turn-of-the-century sugar-plantation town designated as a historic site (your Ford Escort will get you there just fine, too). A collection of faded clapboard stores with a picturesque harbor, Haleiwa has evolved into a surfer outpost and major roadside attraction with art galleries, restaurants, and shops that sell hand-decorated clothing, jewelry, and sports gear (see "Shopping A to Z," below).

Getting there is half the fun. You have a choice: cruise up the H-2 through Oahu's broad and fertile central valley, past Pearl Harbor and Schofield Barracks of *From Here to Eternity* fame and on through the red-earthed heart of the island where pineapple and sugarcane fields stretch from the Koolau to the Waianae mountains, until the sea reappears on the horizon. Or meander north along the lush Windward Coast, through country hamlets with roadside stands selling mangos, bright tropical pareaus, fresh corn, and pond-raised prawns (see "The Windward Coast," above).

TAKING THE CENTRAL OAHU ROUTE

If you go the central route, the tough part is getting on and off the H-1 freeway from Waikiki, which is done by way of convoluted routing on neighborhood streets. Try McCully Street off Ala Wai Boulevard, which is always crowded but usually the most direct route.

Once you're on H-1, stay to the right side; the freeway tends to divide abruptly. Keep following the signs for the H-1 (it separates off to Highway 78 at the airport and reunites later on; either way will get you there), then the H-1/H-2. Leave the H-1 where the two "interstates" divide; take the H-2 up the middle of the island, heading

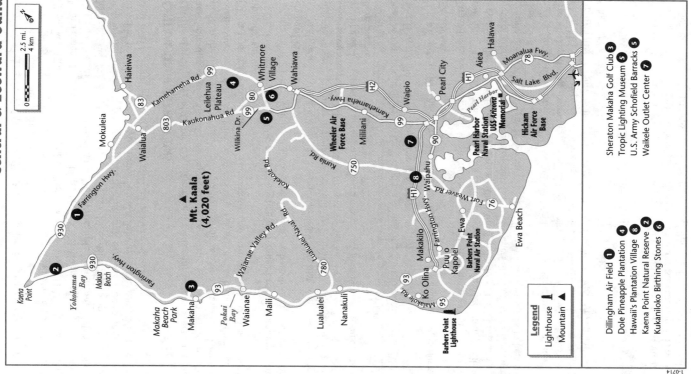

Central & Leeward Oahu

N

2.5 mi.
4 km
0

Legend

⛯ Lighthouse

▲ Mountain

Sheraton Makaha Golf Club **3**
Tropic Lighting Museum **5**
U.S. Army Schofield Barracks **5**
Waikele Outlet Center **7**

Dillingham Air Field **1**
Dole Pineapple Plantation **4**
Hawaii's Plantation Village **8**
Kaena Point Natural Reserve **2**
Kukaniloko Birthing Stones **6**

Mokuleia

Haleiwa

Waialua

83

Kamehameha Rd.

Kaukonahua Rd.

803

99

Leilehua Plateau

Wilikina Dr.

99

Whitmore Village

80

Wahiawa

99

Mt. Kaala
(4,020 feet)

Kolekole Rd.

Kunia Rd.

Waianae Valley Rd.

Lualualei Naval Rd.

Wheeler Air Force Base

Kamehameha Hwy.

Mililani

H2

Waipio

99

Pearl City

Aiea

Halawa

Moanalua Fwy.

78

Salt Lake Blvd.

H1

Pearl Harbor

Pearl Harbor Naval Station

USS Arizona Memorial

Hickam Air Force Base

750

7

90

8

H1

Waipahu

Fort Weaver Rd.

76

Ewa Beach

Ewa

Makakilo

Puu o Kapolei

Ko Olina

Barbers Point Naval Air Station

Makakole Rd.

93

95

Barbers Point Lighthouse

780

Nanakuli

Lualualei

Maili

Waianae

Pokai Bay

93

Makaha

Makaha Beach Park

Makua Beach

Yokohama Bay

930

Kaena Point

2

1

Farrington Hwy.

930

Farrington Hwy.

3

5

6

4

1-0714

north toward the town of Wahiawa. That's what the freeway sign will say—not North Shore or Haleiwa, but Wahiawa.

The H-2 runs out and becomes a two-lane country road about 18 miles out of downtown Honolulu, near Schofield Barracks (see below). The highway becomes Kamehameha Highway (Hwy. 99 and later Hwy. 83) at Wahiawa. Just past Wahiawa, about a half-hour out of Honolulu, the **Dole Pineapple Plantation**, 64-1550 Kamehameha Hwy. (☎ **808/621-8408**; fax 808/621-1926; daily 9am to 6pm), offers a rest stop with pineapples, pineapple history, pineapple trinkets, and pineapple juice (TheBus no. 52 also can get you here). "Kam" Highway, as everyone calls it, will be your road for most of the rest of the trip to Haleiwa.

CENTRAL OAHU ATTRACTIONS

On the central plains of Oahu, tract homes and malls with factory-outlet stores are now spreading across abandoned sugarcane fields, where sandalwood forests once stood at the foot of Mount Kaala, the mighty summit of Oahu. Hawaiian chiefs sent commoners into thick sandalwood forests to cut down trees, which were then sold to China traders for small fortunes. The scantily clad natives caught cold in the cool uplands, and many died.

On those plains in the 1800s, planters began growing sugarcane and pineapple, and a man named James Campbell discovered artesian wells to irrigate the fields that changed Hawaii forever.

On those plains in 1908, the U.S. army pitched a tent that would become a fort that's the biggest and most beautiful in Hawaii. On December 7, 1941, Japanese pilots came screaming through Kolekole Pass to shoot up the art-deco barracks at Schofield, sending soldiers running for cover in their skivvies, and then flew on to sink ships at Pearl Harbor.

On those plains in the 1950s, an out-of-work pop singer named Sinatra made a Hollywood comeback portraying Maggio, a soldier at Schofield on the eve of World War II in the film classic *From Here to Eternity*.

U.S. Army Schofield Barracks. Bus: 52 to Wahiawa; transfer at California Ave. to bus no. 72, Schofield Barracks Shuttle.

James Jones called Schofield Barracks "the most beautiful army post the U.S. has or ever had." The *Honolulu Star Bulletin* called it a country club. More than 1 million soldiers called Schofield Barracks home. With broad, palm-lined boulevards and art-deco buildings, this old army calvary post is still the largest operated by the U.S. Army outside the continental United States. And it's still one of the best places to be a soldier.

The history of Schofield Barracks and the 25th Infantry Division is told in the small **Tropic Lightning Museum**, Schofield Barracks (☎ **808/655-0438**; fax 808/655-8301; e-mail troplight1@juno.com; free admission; Tuesday to Saturday 10am to 4pm). Displays range from a 1917 bunk exhibit to a replica of Vietnam's infamous Cu Chi tunnels.

Kukaniloko Birthing Stones. Off Kamehameha Hwy., between Wahiawa and Haleiwa, opposite the road to Whitmore Village.

Two rows of 18 lava rocks once flanked a central birthing stone, where women of ancient Hawaii gave birth to potential *ali'i* (royalty). The rocks, according to Hawaiian belief, held the power to ease the labor pains of childbirth. Birth rituals involved 48 chiefs who pounded drums to announce the arrival of newborns likely to become chiefs. Children born here were taken to the now destroyed Holonopahu Heiau in the pineapple field, where chiefs ceremoniously cut the umbilical cord.

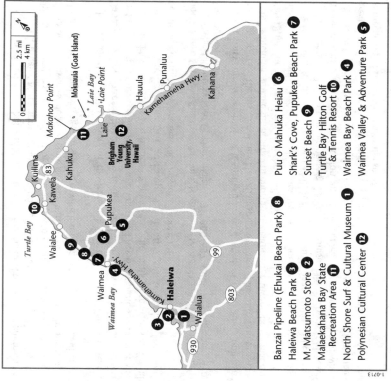

The North Shore

Map legend:

Banzai Pipeline (Ehukai Beach Park) **8**
Haleiwa Beach Park **3**
M. Matsumoto Store **2**
Malaekahana Bay State Recreation Area **11**
North Shore Surf & Cultural Museum **1**
Polynesian Cultural Center **12**

Puu o Mahuka Heiau **6**
Shark's Cove, Pupukea Beach Park **7**
Sunset Beach **9**
Turtle Bay Hilton Golf & Tennis Resort **10**
Waimea Bay Beach Park **4**
Waimea Valley & Adventure Park **5**

1-0713

Used by Oahu's *alii* for generations of births, the *pohaku* (or rocks), many in bowl-like shapes, now lie strewn in a coconut grove in a pineapple field at this, the most sacred site in central Oahu. Some think it also may have served as an ancient astronomy site, sort of a Hawaiian Stonehenge. Petroglyphs of human forms and circles appear on some of the stones.

SURF CITY: HALEIWA

Only 28 miles from Waikiki is Haleiwa, the funky ex-sugar-plantation town that's the world capital of big-wave surfing. This beach town really comes alive in the winter, when waves rise up, light rain falls, and temperatures dip into the 70s; then, it seems, every surfer in the world is here to see and be seen.

Officially designated a historic cultural and scenic district, Haleiwa thrives in a time warp recalling the turn of the century, when it was founded by sugar baron Benjamin Dillingham; he built a 30-mile railroad to link his Honolulu and North Shore plantations in 1899. He opened a Victorian hotel overlooking Kaiaka Bay and named it Haleiwa, or "house of the Iwa," the tropical seabird often seen here. The turn-of-the-century hotel and railroad are gone, but Haleiwa, which was rediscovered in the late 1960s by hippies, resonates with rare rustic charm. Tofu, not taro, is a staple in the local diet. Arts and crafts, boutiques and burger stands line both sides of the town; there's a busy fishing harbor full of charter boats and captains who hunt the Kauai Channel daily for tuna, mahi-mahi, and marlin. The bartenders at ✪ **Jameson's**, 62-540 Kamehameha Hwy., Haleiwa (☎ **808/637-6272**), make the best mai tais on the North Shore; it's the classic, according to the original recipe by Trader Vic Bergeron.

Once in Haleiwa, the hot and thirsty traveler reports directly to the nearest shave-ice stand, usually **Matsumoto Shave Ice**, 66-087 Kamehameha Hwy. For 40 years, this small, humble shop operated by the Matsumoto family has served a popular rendition of the Hawaii-style snow cone flavored with tropical tastes. The cooling treat is also available at neighboring stores, some of which still shave the ice with a hand-crank device.

Just down the road are some of the fabled shrines of surfing—**Waimea Beach, Banzai Pipeline, Sunset Beach**—where the world's largest waves, reaching 20 feet and more, rise up between November and January. They draw professional surfers as well as reckless daredevils and hoards of onlookers, who jump in their cars and head north when word goes out that "surf's up." Don't forget your binoculars. (For more details on North Shore beaches, see "Beaches," above.)

North Shore Surf and Cultural Museum. North Shore Marketplace, 66-250 Kamehameha Hwy. (behind Kentucky Fried Chicken), Haleiwa. ☎ **808/637-8888.** Free admission. Wed, Sat, and Sun 10am–5pm.

Even if you've never set foot on a surfboard, you'll want to visit Oahu's only surf museum to trace the history of this Hawaiian sport of kings. The collection of memorabilia includes vintage surfboards (an enormous weathered, redwood board made in the 1930s for Turkey Love, one of Waikiki's legendary beach boys) next to the modern-day equivalent (a light, sleek, racy foam-and-fiberglass board made for big-wave surfer Mark Foo, who drowned while surfing in California in 1994). Other items include classic 1950s surf-meet posters, 1960s surf music album covers, old beach movie posters starring Frankie Avalon and Sandra Dee, the early black-and-white photos by legendary surf photographer LeRoy Grannis, and trophies won by surfing's greatest. Informal tours by the museum's curator, Lynne Oakley, will give you a real appreciation of the evolution of the sport.

MORE NORTH SHORE ATTRACTIONS

⭐ **Waimea Valley & Adventure Park.** 59-864 Kamehameha Hwy. ☎ **808/638-8511.** Fax 808/638-7900. Admission $24 adults, $12 children 4–12; tram ride $2. Daily 10am–5:30pm. Parking $3. Bus: 52. Shuttle service from some Waikiki hotels $5 round-trip.

If you only have a day to spend on Oahu and want to see an ancient hula, sniff tropical flowers, go kayaking along the shore or hiking to archaeological sites and a waterfall, and play the games of ancient Hawaii (spear-throwing, lawn bowling), there's only one place to be: Waimea Falls Park. This is the perfect family place—it takes a whole family to do everything. You can explore remnants of the old Hawaiian settlements in a scenic 1,800-acre river valley that's full of tropical blooms. Or watch authentic demonstrations of the ancient (*kahiko*) hula by the park's own *halau* (school), and see cliff divers swan-dive into a pool fed by a 45-foot waterfall. Everyone is invited to explore the valley. You can ride a mountain bike, paddle a kayak, or run the Elehaha River on an all-terrain vehicle into the jungle.

Puu o Mahuka Heiau. One mile past Waimea Bay; take Pupukea Rd. mauka off Kamehameha Hwy. at Foodland, and drive .7 of a mile up a switchback road. Bus: 52 and walk up Pupukea Rd.

Go around sundown to feel the mana of this sacred Hawaiian place, the largest sacrificial temple on Oahu, associated with the great kahuna Kaopulupulu, who sought peace between Oahu and Kauai. The prescient *kahuna* predicted that the island would be overrun by strangers from a distant land. In 1794, three of Capt. George

Vancouver's men of the *Daedalus* were sacrificed here. In 1819, the year before New England missionaries landed in Hawaii, King Kamehameha II ordered all idols at the heiau to be destroyed.

A national historic landmark, this 18th-century heiau, known as the "hill of escape," sits on a 5-acre, 300-foot bluff overlooking Waimea Bay and 25 miles of Oahu's wave-lashed North Coast—all the way to Kaena Point, where the Waianae Range ends in a spirit leap to the other world. The heiau appears as a huge rectangle of rocks twice as big as a football field (170 by 575 ft.), with an altar often covered by the flower and fruit offerings left by native Hawaiians.

13 Shopping A to Z

by Jocelyn Fujii

In this land of the alluring outdoors, few people like to admit that shopping is a major temptation. With bodysurfing, hiking on volcanoes, and other invigorating, exotic adventures beckoning, spending time in a shopping mall seems so, well, bourgeois. Truth be known, the proliferation of topnotch made-in-Hawaii products, the vitality of the local crafts scene, and the unquenchable thirst for mementos of the islands lend a new respectability to shopping here. And Oahu (Maui, too) is a haven for mall mavens. From T-shirts to Versace, posh European to down-home local, avant-garde to unspeakably tacky, Oahu's offerings are wide-ranging indeed. But shopping on this island is slightly schizophrenic. You must sometimes wade through oceans of schlock to arrive at the mother lode. Nestled amid the Louis Vuitton, Chanel, and Tiffany boutiques on Waikiki's Kalakaua Avenue are plenty of tacky booths hawking air-brushed T-shirts, gold by the inch, and tasteless aloha shirts.

The section that follows is not about finding cheap souvenirs or tiny items from designer fashion chains; you can find these on your own. Rather, we offer a guide to finding those special treasures that lie somewhere in between.

SHOPPING IN & AROUND HONOLULU & WAIKIKI
ANTIQUES & COLLECTIBLES

For the best in collectible aloha wear, see "Fashion," below.

Aloha Antiques and Collectables. 926 Maunakea St. ☎ 808/536-6187.

You may find rare Japanese plates or a priceless Lalique among the chachkas that fill every square inch of this dizzying shop. But you'll have to look hard, because there are so many items, they literally spill out onto the sidewalk. Upstairs, downstairs, in adjoining rooms, around corners—the place defies inventory. Jewelry, vintage aloha shirts, vases, silver, ephemera, and countless eclectic items make up this mind-boggling collection of junk, treasures, and nostalgia.

Aloha Flea Market. Aloha Stadium. ☎ 808/486-1529. Admission 50¢. Wed, Sat, and Sun 6am–3pm.

Our advice is to go as early as possible, take a hat, and wear sunscreen. It gets very hot in this neck of the woods, and with more than 1,000 vendors sprawling across the stadium floor, it can be exhausting as well. You'll find the more interesting individuals and estates offering vintage treasures interspersed among produce stands and tacky stalls with cheap sunglasses and T-shirts. You never know when that extra-special 1940s tablecloth, Matson liner menu, vintage silkie aloha shirt, or Roseville vase will appear. These elusive treasures are becoming increasingly rare and are snatched up quickly by flea-market habitués, so serious collectors had best go early.

Anchor House Antiques. 471 Kapahulu Ave. ☎ **808/732-3884.**

This highly eclectic collection of Hawaiian, Oriental, and European pieces sprawls over thousands of square feet. You'll find wooden calabashes, camphor chests, paintings, Hawaiian artifacts, and trinkets, priced from $10 to $2,000.

Antique Alley. 1347 Kapiolani Blvd. ☎ **808/941-8551.**

This narrow shop is chockablock with the passionate collections of several vendors. The showcases include estate jewelry, antique silver, Hawaiian bottles, collectible toys, pottery, Depression glass, linens, plantation photos and ephemera, and a wide selection of nostalgic items from Hawaii and across America. At the rear is a small, attractive selection of soiree clothing, made by Julie Lauster out of antique kimonos and obis.

Antique House. Royal Hawaiian Hotel, 2259 Kalakaua Ave. ☎ **808/923-5101.**

Small but tasteful, the low-profile Antique House is hidden below the lobby level of the illustrious Royal Hawaiian Hotel. Come here for small items: Oriental antiques; Chinese and Japanese porcelains; and a stunning selection of snuff bottles, bronzes, vases, and china.

Garakuta-Do. 580 N. Nimitz Hwy., across from Gentry Pacific Center. ☎ **808/524-7755.**

If it's Japanese antiques you're after, it's worth driving to the industrial harbor area to view the late-Edo period (1800s through early 1900s) antiques collected and sold by cheerful owner Wataru Harada. A wide selection of gorgeous tansus, mingei folk art, Japanese screens, scrolls, Imari plates, bronze sculptures, kimonos, obis, and stone objects fill the sprawling space.

✪ **Kilohana Square.** 1016 Kapahulu Ave.

If there is any one destination that we would recommend for antiques, it would be this tiny square in Kapahulu. Kilohana's five antiques shops cover a rich range of Oriental art, Japanese and European antiques, and high-quality collectibles. Many of the shops have loyal clients across the country who know they can find authentic goods, particularly Asian antiques, here. Our favorites include **T. Fujii Japanese Antiques** (☎ **808/732-7860**), a long-standing icon in Hawaii's antiques world and an impeccable source for ukiyoe prints, scrolls, obis, Imari porcelain, tansus, tea-ceremony bowls, and screens, as well as contemporary ceramics from Mashiko and Kasama, with prices from $25 to $18,000; **Miko Oriental Art Gallery** (☎ **808/735-4503**), a large repository of Chinese, Japanese, Korean, and Southeast Asian ceramics, bronzes, and furniture, ranging in price from $50 to $22,000; ✪ **Silk Winds** (☎ **808/735-6599**), a tasteful collection of Asian antiques, everything from beads and jewelry to cricket cages, jade sculptures, furniture, and porcelain; and **Carriage House Antiques** (☎ **808/737-2622**), whose owner is an expert in antique silver and European porcelain. Each shop has its own hours; call to be sure they're open.

✪ **Robyn Buntin.** 848 S. Beretania St. ☎ **808/523-5913.**

The gracious and authoritative Robyn Buntin is an expert in netsuke and a highly esteemed resource in Oriental art. Located not far from the Honolulu Academy of Arts, the 2,500-square-foot space, as much a gallery as an antiques store, radiates a tasteful serenity. The offerings include jade; scholar's table items; Buddhist sculpture; Japanese prints; contemporary Chinese, Japanese, and Korean pictorial (graphic) art; and a large and magnificent collection of Hawaiiana. Some pieces are 5,000 years old, while many others are hot off the press from Tokyo, Seoul, and Beijing. The brilliant selection of netsuke and Japanese carvings is complemented with Hawaiian works by Isami Doi, Avi Kiriaty, Guy Buffet, Mark Kadota, and others. Few people know that John Kelly's legacy includes Oriental works; they're here, along with rare etchings and prints that move swiftly to waiting collectors. Also known for his meticulous craftsmanship and taste in framing, Buntin has a framing operation downtown.

BOOKSTORES

In addition to the local stores below, Honolulu is home to branches of the famous names in bookselling. With more than 150,000 titles, a respectable music department, strong Hawaiiana, fiction, and new-release departments, as well as a popular coffee bar, **Barnes & Noble**, at Kahala Mall, 4211 Waialae Ave. (☎ **808/737-3323**) has become the second home of Honolulu's casual readers and bibliophiles. **Borders Books & Music**, at Ward Centre, 1200 Ala Moana Blvd. (☎ **808/591-8995**), is a beehive of literary activity, with weekly signings, prominent local and mainland musicians at least monthly, and special events almost daily that make this a major Honolulu attraction; there's a second Borders at Waikele Center, 94-821 Lumiaina St. (☎ **808/676-6699**). And **Waldenbooks** still ranks high as a boutique bookseller, with branches at Kahala Mall, 4211 Waialae Ave. (☎ **808/737-9550**); Waikiki Trade Center, 2255 Kuhio Ave. (☎ **808/924-8330**); Waikiki Shopping Plaza, 2270 Kalakaua Ave. (☎ **808/922-4154**); and other Oahu locations.

Book Cellar. 222 Merchant St. ☎ **808/523-3772.**

Located downtown for more than a decade, it's definitely a cellar, spilling over with used and rare books, plus a few new items. This is a good general used-book store, with about 35,000 titles—Hawaiiana, nonfiction, and books of the Pacific are among its stronger categories. Ask for CC (Carl Carroll, the man who knows the inventory).

Honolulu Book Shops. Ala Moana Center, 1450 Ala Moana Blvd. ☎ **808/941-2274.**

Children's books and Hawaiian and local titles are the strong suit of this longtime Honolulu bookstore, much smaller than the other giants mentioned and clearly affected by the competition. Two branches have closed recently, but the Ala Moana store remains, with its 80,000 titles and sizable discounts on *New York Times* best-selling hardcovers and paperbacks and 11% off on the "category of the month."

Pacific Book House. 1249 S. Beretania St. ☎ **808/591-1599.**

Dennis Perron, connoisseur of rare books, has moved his venerable Pacific Book House to a new location; kept and expanded the rare and out-of-print book inventory; and expanded into paintings, antiques, and estate jewelry, even offering appraisals of rare books and paintings and handling restorations others are afraid to touch. Literati still come here for finds in Hawaiiana, rare prints, collectible books, and other out-of-print treasures.

Rainbow Books and Records. 1010 University Ave. ☎ **808/955-7994.**

A little weird but totally lovable, especially among students and eccentrics (and insatiable readers), Rainbow Books is notable for its selection of popular fiction, records, and Hawaii-themed books, secondhand and reduced. Because it's located in the university area, it's always bulging with textbooks, Hawaiiana, and popular music. It's about the size of a large closet, but you'll be surprised at what you'll find.

Tusitala Bookshop. 116 Hekili St., Kailua. ☎ **808/262-6343.**

Named after Robert Louis Stevenson—whose Samoan name, *Tusitala*, means "teller of tales" —this Kailua mainstay has a loyal following among book lovers and collectors.

The quintessential specialty bookstore, it boasts a strong selection of hard-to-find books on Hawaii and the South Pacific. All books are used, rare, and out-of-print; prices range from $10 to $20,000 (for the eight-volume set of *Cook's Voyages* from the 1700s). Nancy Abe knows the inventory and the stories that come with the volumes.

EDIBLES

In addition to the stores listed below, we also recommend **Executive Chef** in the Ward Warehouse and **Islands' Best** in the Ala Moana Center.

Asian Grocery. 1319 S. Beretania St. ☎ **808/593-8440.**

Asian Grocery supplies many of Honolulu's Thai, Vietnamese, Chinese, and Filipino eateries with authentic spices, rices, noodles, produce, sauces, herbs, and adventurous ingredients for their native cookery. Browse among the kaffir lime leaves, tamarind and fish pastes, red and green chiles, curry sauces, chutneys, lotus leaves, gingko nuts, jasmine and basmati rices, and shelf upon shelf of medium to hot chili sauces.

Daiei. 801 Kaheka St. ☎ **808/973-4800.**

Stands offering take-out sushi, Korean kal bi, pizza, Chinese food, flowers, Mrs. Fields cookies, and other items for self and home rim this huge emporium. Inside, you'll find household products, a pharmacy, and inexpensive clothing, but it's the prepared foods and produce that excel. The fresh-seafood section is one of Honolulu's best bets, not far from where regulars line up for the bento lunches and individually wrapped sushi. When Kau navel oranges, macadamia nuts, Kona coffee, Chinese taro, and other Hawaii products are on sale, savvy locals arrive in droves to take advantage of the high quality and good value.

Honolulu Chocolate Co. Ward Centre, 1200 Ala Moana Blvd. ☎ **808/591-2997;** and Restaurant Row, 500 Ala Moana Blvd. ☎ **808/528-4033.**

Life's greatest pleasures are dispensed here with abandon: expensive gourmet chocolates made in Honolulu, chocolate-covered macadamia nuts, Italian and Hawaiian biscotti, boulder-size turtles (caramel and pecans covered with chocolate), truffles, chocolate-covered coffee beans, jumbo apricots in white and dark chocolate. There are tinned biscuits, European candies, and sweets in a million disguises at this Honolulu people-pleaser.

It's Chili in Hawaii. 2080 S. King St., Ste. 105. ☎ **808/945-7070.**

Scoville units (measurements of heat in food) are the topic of the day in this shop lined with thousands of bottles of hot sauces, salsas, and other chile-based food products. Although many of the products are made in Hawaii, owners Ken Martinez and Gary Toyama travel regularly throughout the mainland to scour the finest hot sauces and chile products. Not everything is scorching, however; some products, like Dave's Soyaki and the limu-habañero sauce called Makai, are everyday flavor enhancers that can be used on rice, salads, meats, and pasta. These make great gifts to go. Every Saturday, Martinez and Toyama dish out free samples of green-chile stew to go with their generous hot-sauce tastings.

✪ **Mauna Kea Marketplace Food Court.** 1120 Maunakea St., Chinatown. ☎ **808/524-3409.**

Hungry patrons line up in front of the no-nonsense food booths proffering everything from pizza to plate lunches and many other types of quick, authentic, inexpensive Vietnamese, Thai, Italian, Chinese, Japanese, and Filipino cuisine. The best seafood fried rice comes from the woks of **Malee Thai/Vietnamese Cuisine** at the mauka end of the marketplace—generous, perfectly flavored, endowed with morsels of fish, squid, and shrimp. Walk the few steps down to the produce stalls (pungent odors, fish heads, and chicken feet on counters—not for the squeamish) and join in the spirit of discovery. Fish counters and produce stalls vend everything from fresh ahi and whole snappers to yams and taro, seaweed, and fresh fruits and vegetables of every shape and size.

✪ **Paradise Produce Co.** 84 N. King St., Chinatown. ☎ **808/533-2125.**

Neat rows of mangoes, top-quality papayas, and reasonably priced and very fresh produce make this a paradise for food lovers. When asparagus is plentiful, it will be inexpensive and fresh. When mangoes are in season, you'll find Yee's Orchard Haydens set apart from the less desirable Mexican mangoes and, if you're lucky, a stash of ambrosial Piries that will sell out quickly. Chinese taro, litchis in season, local eggplant, and dozens of fruits and vegetables are offered up fresh, neat, and colorful.

✪ **People's Open Markets.** Various sites around town. ☎ **808/527-5167.** Call the number above to find the open market nearest you.

Truck farmers from all over the island bring their produce to Oahu's neighborhoods in regularly scheduled, city-sponsored open markets. Among the tables of ong choy, choi sum, Okinawan spinach, opal basil, papayas, mangoes, seaweed, and fresh fish, you'll find homemade banana bread, Chinese *pomelo* (like large grapefruit), fresh *fiddleheads* (fern shoots) when available, and colorful, bountiful harvests from land and sea. The offerings change by the week and the season, but you'll always find a satisfying sampling of inexpensive, freshly gathered greens.

✪ **R. Field Wine Co.** Foodland Super Market, 1460 S. Beretania St. ☎ **808/596-9463.**

The big news among foodies is Oenophile, gourmet, and cigar aficionado Richard Field's move from Ward Centre to this new location in Foodland, where a special section has been built to accommodate his expanded inventory. At this writing, big plans are afoot: specialty breads, more wines at better prices, fresh New York bagels, and authentic gourmet products from around the world. He continues to provide hard-to-find vintages; the classic malts of Scotland; organic, vine-ripened tomatoes; salmon mousse; poha and ohelo berry preserves; plum pudding; designer vinegars; Kulana "organic" beef; Langenstein estate Kona coffee; estate-grown, super-luxe Hawaiian Vintage Chocolate; Petrossian caviar; Waimanalo baby greens; gourmet cheeses, and more.

Shirokiya. Ala Moana Center, 1450 Ala Moana Blvd. ☎ **808/973-9111.**

Shirokiya's upstairs food department is well-known throughout Honolulu as *the* marketplace for Japanese treats. Food samples hot off the grill or out of the oven are offered from the counters: fish, mochi, pickled vegetables, and black beans fill the air with briny, smoky scents. A separate take-out food department sells sushi, udon and noodle soups, and many varieties of boxed bento lunches. Tables are available, or you can order the food to go. In the surrounding retail food department, exotic assortments of everything from deluxe dried shiitake mushrooms to Japanese teas call out for your attention.

✪ **Strawberry Connection of Hawaii.** 1931 Kahai St., Kalihi. ☎ **808/842-0278.**

If you love food enough to search for it in the bowels of industrial Honolulu, this place is worth the effort. Epicures swear by this ever-growing showcase of Hawaii and gourmet food products. The new deli was the logical next step: custom picnic baskets, special-diet meals, Cajun cooking by a former chef for Emeril Lagasse, gourmet lunches and dinners for take-out, and more—everything from homemade granola to caviar and macrobiotics. Grab a jacket and venture into the chill boxes for the best portobello or shiitake mushrooms, flawless asparagus spears, plump strawberries, Waimanalo gourmet greens, and stacks of designer produce from all the Hawaiian islands. They will also pack and ship produce to the mainland.

Taniguchi Store. 2065 S. Beretania St. ☎ **808/949-1489.**

Taniguchi Store's prepared foods—rice balls (*musubi*), salmon/rice bentos, fried saimin, chicken salad, tofu salad, Korean chicken, chicken cutlet, and many other easy treats—are much loved in Honolulu. A small produce section proffers fresh chiso, exotic mushrooms, burdocks, and mountain yams, while the seafood counter is lined with several kinds of ahi and tako poke. A new plate-lunch department, Stephie's Kitchen, serves plate lunches for $5 and $6, and the home-baked cookies and sweets, though pricey, are as good as gold.

Bakeries

The **Saint-Germain** bakeries in Shirokiya at Ala Moana Shopping Center (☎ **808/955-1711**) and near Times Supermarket, 1296 S. Beretania St. (☎ **808/593-8711**), are the best in town for French breads, baguettes, country loaves, and oddball delicacies, such as mini mushroom and spinach pizzas in Danish-type shapes and dough; the breads are so good that many of Honolulu's fine restaurants serve their French loaves at candlelit tables. In Ward Warehouse, **Mary Catherine's** (☎ **808/591-8525**), the darling of the gourmet bakeries, still turns out sinful cakes, fruit tarts, and cookies. The best, though, is **Cafe Laufer,** 3565 Waialae Ave. (☎ **808/735-7717;** see "Dining," above), where the baked goods compete with the towering, made-to-order soufflés and inexpensive sandwiches. Nearby, old-timers still line up at **Bea's Pies & Deli,** 1117 12th Ave. (☎ **808/734-4024**), which often runs out of pies (custard-pumpkin is a must) by noon.

Fish Markets

Safeway on Beretania Street (☎ **808/591-8315**) has a seafood counter with fresh choices and a staff that takes pride in its deftness with prepared foods (fresh ahi poke, seaweed salad, shrimp cocktail, marinated crab—if you're curious, don't be shy about asking for a taste). **Foodland** on Beretania Street (☎ **808/946-4654**) also offers good buys on live lobster and Dungeness crab, fresh ahi, and a wide variety of fresh fish and shellfish, including whole snappers and oysters when available.

Good service and the most extensive selection in Honolulu make **Tamashiro Market,** 802 N. King St., Kalihi (☎ **808/841-8047**), the grandfather of fish markets and the ace in the hole for home chefs with bouillabaisse or paella in mind. You'll think you're in a Fellini movie amid the tanks of live lobsters and crabs and the dizzying array of counters glistening with fresh slabs of ahi, opakapaka, onaga, and ehu; point and ask if you don't know what you're looking at, and one of the many fish cutters will explain, then clean and fillet your selection. Also a magnet for shoppers is the separate counter of seaweed salads, prepared poke, Filipino and Puerto Rican ti-wrapped steamed rice, Japanese pickles, and dozens of other ethnic foods.

Neighbor islanders have been known to drive directly from the airport to **Yama's Fish Market,** 2203 Young St., Moiliili (☎ **808/941-9994**), for a plate lunch, one of the best in Honolulu: Robust Hawaiian plates with pork or chicken lau-lau (20 combinations!), baked ahi, chili, beef stew, shoyu chicken, and dozens of other varieties. But Yama's is also known for its inexpensive fresh fish (mahi-mahi is always less expensive here than in the supermarkets), tasty poke, lomi salmon, and many varieties of prepared seafood. Chilled beer, boiled peanuts, and fresh ahi they'll slice into sashimi are popular for local-style gatherings, sunset beach parties, and festive *pau hana* (end of work) celebrations. New standouts include coconut pudding (*haupia*) pie layered with bright-purple Okinawan sweet potato—flying out the door by the dozens every day.

Health Food

In the university district, **Down to Earth**, 2525 S. King St., Moiliili (☎ **808/947-7678**), is a respectable source of organic vegetables and vegetarian bulk foods, with a strong selection and good prices in supplements, herbs, environment-friendly paper and household products, and cosmetics; a vegetarian juice and sandwich bar are among its draws. Nearby **Kokua Market**, 2643 S. King St. (☎ **808/941-1922**), is Honolulu's best source for voluminous, leafy, organic vegetables; an excellent variety of cheeses; pastas and bulk grains; sandwiches, salads, and prepared foods; and a solid selection of organic wines. Ample parking is behind and *makai* (toward the beach) of the store.

Tiny but powerful, with a loyal clientele, **Hou Ola**, 1541 S. Beretania St. (☎ **808/955-6168**), has competitive prices and a wide and user-friendly selection of health-food supplements. No produce, but there are frozen vegetarian foods, bulk grains, and healthy snacks.

In Nuuanu Valley, mauka of downtown Honolulu, **Huckleberry Farms**, 1613 Nuuanu Ave. (☎ **808/524-7960**) has a wide selection of produce, vitamins, cosmetics, books, and prepared vegetarian foods. A few doors down is the beauty and vitamin retail outlet stocked with beauty creams, cosmetics, nutritional supplements, and nonperishable, nongrocery health products.

FASHION

Also see "Shopping Centers" and "Surf & Sports," below.

Aloha Wear

One of Hawaii's lasting afflictions is the penchant tourists have for wearing loud, matching aloha shirts and muumuus. We applaud such visitors' good intentions (to act local), but they are not Hawaiian. No local resident would be caught dead in such a get-up. Muumuus and aloha shirts are wonderful, but the real thing is what island folks wear on Aloha Friday (every Friday), to the Brothers Cazimero Lei Day Concert (every May 1), or to work (where allowed). It's what they wear at home and to special parties where the invitation reads "Aloha Attire."

Aside from the vintage Hawaiian wear (i.e., made from the 1930s through 1950s) that one finds only in collectibles shops and swap meets, our favorite contemporary aloha wear designer is **Avanti**, who makes a stunning line of silk shirts and dresses in authentic 1930s to 1950s fabric patterns. The shirts are the *ne plus ultra* of aloha shirts, with all the qualities of a vintage silkie without the high price or the web-thin fragility of authentic antique shirts. For about $60, you can find a stylish shirt that's wearable long after you leave Hawaii. Women's dresses, pants sets, and many other styles are the epitome of comfort and nostalgic good looks. The line is distributed in better boutiques and department stores throughout Hawaii. In Waikiki, the major retail outlets for the designs are ✪ **Avanti Fashion**, at 2229 Kuhio Ave. (☎ **808/926-6886**), and in Waikiki Shopping Plaza, 2270 Kalakaua Ave. (☎ **808/926-6886**).

Also noteworthy are the aloha shirts and dresses by **Kahala Sportswear**, a well-known local company established in 1936. Kahala has faithfully reproduced, with astounding success, the linoleum-block prints of noted Big Island artist Avi Kiriaty and the designs of other contemporary artists, including surfer John Severson. Kahala designs for women include Mandarin-style dresses, shorts, and tank dresses; distinctive aloha shirts bear scenes of fishing, canoeing, farming, and other idyllic Polynesian pursuits, as well as humorous, spirited images of joyful contemporary pursuits, Kahala is sold in department stores (from Liberty House to Nordstrom), surf shops, and stylish boutiques throughout Hawaii and the mainland.

For the most culturally correct aloha wear, check out the aloha shirts, dresses, and pareus of **Sig Zane Designs** (see "Shops & Galleries" in chapter 6, "Hawaii: The Big Island"), available on Oahu at **Martin & MacArthur** (☎ 808/524-6066) in Aloha Tower Marketplace. Zane, an accomplished hula dancer married to one of Hawaii's most revered hula masters, has an unmistakable visual style and a profound knowledge of Hawaiian culture that bring depth and meaning to his boldly styled renditions of the ti plant, ohia, kukui, koa, kaunaoa, and other prominent Hawaiian flora. Each Sig Zane pareu and aloha shirt, in pure cotton, tells a story. No wonder it's the garb of the cultural connoisseurs, who also buy fabrics by the yard for cushions, curtains, and interior accents that bring the rain forest into their homes.

Another name to watch for is **Tutuvi**, whose T-shirts, dresses, and pareus are distinctive for their brilliant color combinations and witty juxtaposition of design motifs. Tutuvi designs can be found in various shops throughout Hawaii or by appointment at **Tutuvi**, 2850 S. King St. (☎ 808/947-5950).

Reyn's Spooner is another source of attractive aloha shirts and muumuus in traditional and contemporary styles, with stores in Ala Moana Center, Kahala Mall, and the Sheraton Waikiki. The reverse-print aloha shirt—the uniform of downtown boardrooms—was popularized by Reyn's, which has also jumped aboard the vintage-look bandwagon with its old-Hawaii cotton prints, some of them in attractive two-color pareu patterns.

Well-known muumuu labels in Hawaii include **Mamo Howell**, who has a boutique in Ward Warehouse; **Princess Kaiulani** and **Bete** for the dressier muus, sold along with many other lines at Liberty House and other department stores. **Hilo Hattie's** new Ala Moana store (☎ 808/973-3266) is a gold mine of affordable aloha wear. **Hilo Hattie's** (☎ 808/537-2926) also offers daily shuttle service from Waikiki to its sprawling retail outlet on Nimitz Highway, where quality and selection have improved noticeably in recent years. You'll also find macadamia nuts, Hawaii coffees, jewelry, and other Hawaii souvenirs at these Hilo Hattie's stores, as well as live Hawaiian entertainment and free Kona coffee samples.

Vintage Clothing

It costs big bucks to wear old clothes if they're in good shape and have a past—$600 to $1,000, say, for a vintage silkie in perfect condition. Take a peek in **Bailey's Antiques and Aloha Shirts**, 517 Kapahulu Ave. (☎ 808/734-7628), and check out vintage finds from the tatty to the sublime: old lamps, cushions, jewelry, salt and pepper shakers, fur stoles, and a dizzying selection of clothing for both collectors and neophytes. A vintage rayon Chinese-style muu or any vintage schmatte in perfect condition could fetch $600 and up, but you may be able to turn up some cheaper options. Prices begin below $20, and a lucky hunter could find a velvet dress or sarong skirt for less than $50. Also in Kapahulu, **Coconut Bay**, 3114 Monsarrat Ave. (☎ 808/737-2699), is a neighborhood hit with its unique Hawaiian wear and Southeast Asian imports. Its clothing *looks* vintage, and pulls it off with panache. Quilts, clothing, retro Hawaiian wear, and scads of men's shirts have gained this newcomer lots of fans.

FLOWERS & LEIS

For a special-occasion, top-of-the-line, designer bouquet or lei, you can't do better than Michael Miyashiro of **Rain Forest Plantes et Fleurs**, 1550 Rycroft St., near Ala Moana Center (☎ 808/942-1550). He's a nature-loving, ecologically aware, and highly gifted lei-maker—pricey, but worth it. He custom designs the lei for the person and the occasion, and the personalized attention shows.

The other primary sources for flowers and leis are the shops lining the streets of Moilili and Chinatown. Moilili favorites include **Rudy's Flowers,** 2722 S. King St. (☎ **808/944-8844**), a local institution with the best prices on roses, Micronesian ginger lei (they can go as low as $8.50 here while others sell them for $15), and a variety of cut blooms. Nearby, **Flowers by Jr. and Lou,** 2652 S. King St. (☎ **808/941-2022**) has calla lilies, Gerber daisies, a riot of potted orchids, and the full range of cut flowers along with its lei selection. Across the street from Rudy's, **Flowers for a Friend,** 2739 S. King St. (☎ **808/955-4227**), has good prices on cut flowers.

In Chinatown, lei vendors line Beretania and Maunakea streets, and the fragrances of their wares mix with the earthy scents of incense and ethnic foods. Our top picks are **Lita's Leis,** 59 N. Beretania St. (☎ **808/521-9065**), which has fresh puakenikeni, gardenias that last, and a supply of fresh and reasonable leis; **Sweetheart's Leis,** 69 N. Beretania St. (☎ **808/537-3011**), with a worthy selection of the classics at fair prices; **Lin's Lei Shop,** 1017 A Maunakea St. (☎ **808/537-4112**), with creatively-fashioned, unusual leis; and **Cindy's Lei Shoppe,** 1034 Maunakea St. (☎ **808/536-6538**), a household word with terrific sources for unusual leis, such as feather dendrobiums; firecracker combinations; and everyday favorites such as ginger, tuberose, orchid, and pikake. At this and other lei shops, simple leis sell for $3 and up, deluxe leis, $10 and up. Ask Cindy's about their unique "curb service," available with advance phone orders. Give them your car color and model, and you can pick up your lei at curbside—what a convenience, especially on this busy street.

HAWAIIANA & GIFT ITEMS

Our top recommendations are the ✪ **Academy Shop** at the Honolulu Academy of Arts, 900 S. Beretania St. (☎ **808/523-8703**), and the ✪ **Contemporary Museum Gift Shop,** 2411 Makiki Heights Rd. (☎ **808/523-3447**), two of the finest shopping stops on Oahu and worth a special trip whether or not you're in the mood to peruse Hawaii's cultural and artistic treasures. The Academy Shop offers art books, jewelry, basketry, ethnic fabrics and native crafts from all over the world, posters and books, and fiber vessels and accessories. The Contemporary Museum shop focuses on contemporary arts and crafts, such as avant-garde jewelry, cards and stationery, books, home accessories, and gift items made by artists from Hawaii and across the country. We love the new French neon reading glasses that line the counter at the Contemporary, and the glammy selection of jewelry and novelties, such as the twisted-wire wall hangings. (For details on the collections at both museums, see "Oahu's Vibrant Art Scene" earlier in this chapter.)

Other good sources for quality gift items are the **Little Hawaiian Craft Shop** in the Royal Hawaiian Shopping Center, and **Martin and MacArthur,** in the Aloha Tower Marketplace.

✪ **Following Sea,** 4211 Waialae Ave. ☎ **808/734-4425.**

The buyers scour the country for the best representations of fine American craftsmanship in everything from candles and bath products to fine arts and crafts. Hawaii is well represented in the collection, with handsome hand-turned bowls and accessories made of native and introduced woods, jewelry, ceramics, handmade paper and hand-bound books, a notable selection of koa boxes, and Hawaii-inspired jewelry in gold and silver among the offerings of local artists.

Hula Supply Center. 2346 S. King St., Moiliili. ☎ 808/941-5379.

Hawaiiana meets kitsch in this shop's marvelous selection of Day-Glo cellophane skirts, bamboo nose flutes, T-shirts, hula drums, shell leis, feathered rattle gourds, lauhala accessories, fiber mats, and a wide assortment of pareu fabrics. Although hula dancers shop here for their dance accoutrements, it's not all serious shopping. This is fertile ground for finding souvenirs and memorabilia of Hawaii, a selection well-balanced between irreverent humor and cultural integrity.

✪ **Island Provision Co. at Vagabond House.** Ward Centre, 1200 Ala Moana Blvd. ☎ 808/593-0288.

Home accessories, gift items, one-of-a-kind island crafts, and multicultural treasures are collected from the owners' travels and displayed in this attractive 1,700-square-foot space. Gleaming woods, fine porcelain and pottery, children's books, bath products, and Asian and Indonesian imports highlight this shop of wonders. Leave time to browse, because shopping here is more like a journey through an island-style kamaaina home, with unique photo gifts for all occasions.

✪ **Native Books & Beautiful Things.** 222 Merchant St., downtown. ☎ 808/599-5511. Also at the Bishop Museum, 1525 Bernice St.

Come to either location of this *hui* (association) of artists and crafters to be enveloped in a love of things Hawaiian, from musical instruments to calabashes, jewelry, leis, books, and items of woven fibers—beautiful things, indeed. You'll find contemporary and Hawaiian clothing, handmade koa journals, Hawaii-themed home accessories, lauhala handbags and accessories, jams and jellies, and wide-ranging, high-quality gift items. Some of Hawaii's finest artists in all craft media have their works available here on a regular basis, and the Hawaiian-book selection is tops in Hawaii.

✪ **Nohea Gallery.** Ward Warehouse, 1050 Ala Moana Blvd. ☎ 808/596-0074. Also at Kahala Mandarin Oriental Hawaii, 5000 Kahala Ave. ☎ 808/737-8688.

A fine showcase for contemporary Hawaii art, Nohea celebrates the islands with thoughtful, attractive selections in all media, from pit-fired raku and finely turned wood vessels to jewelry, glassware, fabrics (including Hawaiian-quilt cushions), and furniture. Ninety percent of the works are by Hawaii artists. Gleaming koa accessories, from hair sticks to jewelry boxes, are among the items that grace the pleasing showrooms.

Nui Mono. 2745 S. King St., Moiliili. ☎ 808/946-7407.

We love the kimono clothing and accessories and the contemporary clothes made from ethnic fabrics sold in this tiny shop in Moiliili. Handbags made of patchwork vintage fabrics and priceless kimono silks, drapey Asian shapes and ikat fabrics, richly textured vests and skirts, and warm, rich colors are the Nui Mono signature—and it's all moderately priced.

Quilts Hawaii. 2338 S. King St., Moiliili. ☎ 808/942-3195.

Handmade Hawaiian quilts in traditional Hawaiian and contemporary patterns drape this shop from top to bottom. Hawaiian-quilt cushions (much more affordable than full-size quilts, which run, understandably, in the thousands of dollars) and quilt-sewing kits can also be found here. You can custom-order larger works.

Shop Pacifica. Bishop Museum, 1335 Kalihi St. ☎ 808/848-4158.

Local crafts, lauhala and Cook Island woven coconut, Hawaiian music tapes and CDs, pareus, and a vast selection of Hawaii-themed books anchor the museum's gift shop.

Hawaiian quilt cushion kits, jewelry, glassware, seed and Niihau shell leis, cookbooks, and many other gift possibilities will keep you occupied between stargazing in the planetarium and pondering the shells and antiquities of the esteemed historical museum.

SHOPPING CENTERS

Ala Moana Center, 1450 Ala Moana Blvd. ☎ **808/946-2811.** Mon-Sat 9:30am-9pm, Sun 10am-5pm. Bus: 8, 19, or 20. Ala Moana Shuttle Bus runs daily every 15 minutes from 8 spots in Waikiki; Waikiki Trolley also stops at Ala Moana from various Waikiki locales (see "Getting Around," earlier in this chapter).

With Neiman-Marcus poised to open in the fall of 1988, and Nordstrom men's and women's shoe stores firmly ensconced on the mall, Ala Moana Center remains a teeming megalopolis of consumerism. But there are practical touches, too, as in airline ticket counters (in **Sears**), a foreign-exchange service (**Thomas Cook**, street level), a dry cleaners (**Al Phillips**, street level), a U.S. Post Office (street level), several optical companies (including 1-hour service by **LensCrafters**), the **Foodland Supermarket**, a pharmacy, and several services for quick photo processing. Its 200 shops and restaurants sprawl over several blocks, catering to every imaginable need, from over-the-top upscale (**Tiffany, Chanel, Versace**), to mainland chains such as **The Gap, The Body Shop**, and **J.C. Penney**. A perennial favorite, **Banana Republic** continues to weave its spell with huge reductions in its wonderfully minimalist clothing and accessories. Department stores such as **Liberty House** and the endlessly entertaining **Shirokiya** sell fashion and household needs. One of the best stops for gifts is **Islands' Best**, a small, wonderful store that spills over with Hawaiian-made foodstuffs, ceramics, fragrances, and more. **Splash! Hawaii** is a good source for women's swimwear; for men's swimwear, try **Liberty House, Town & Country Surf**, or the terminally hip **Hawaiian Island Creations.** Lovers of Polynesian wear and pareus shouldn't miss **Tahiti Imports.**

Aloha Tower Marketplace. 1 Aloha Tower Dr., on the waterfront between piers 8 and 11, Honolulu Harbor. ☎ **808/528-5700.** Sun-Thurs 9am-9pm, Fri and Sat 9am-10pm. Various Honolulu trolleys stop at the Marketplace, but if you want a direct ride from Waikiki, take the $2 Aloha Tower Marketplace Express, which continues on to Hilo Hattie's in Iwilei.

Despite valet parking and trolley stops, parking is a discouraging aspect of shopping at Aloha Tower. Once you get to the new harborfront complex, however, a sense of nostalgia, of what it must have been like in the "Boat Days" of the 1920s to 1940s, will inevitably take over. Sleek ocean liners still tie up across the harbor, and the refurbished Aloha Tower stands high over the complex, as it did in the days when it was the tallest structure in Honolulu. Dining and shopping prospects abound. Places we love include **Martin & MacArthur,** for its Sig Zane clothing, kupee shell and wiliwili leis, and kamaaina-style accents and furnishings; **Patagonia,** for outdoor enthusiasts; and topnotch fragrance maven **Caswell Massey.** For dining, consider **Gordon Biersch Brewery** (see "Dining," above).

Kahala Mall. 4211 Waialae Ave., Kahala. ☎ **808/732-7736.** Mon-Sat 10am-9pm, Sun 10am-5pm.

Chic, manageable, unfrenzied, Kahala Mall is home to some of Honolulu's best shops. Located east of Waikiki in the posh neighborhood of Kahala, the mall has everything from a small **Liberty House** to chain stores such as **Banana Republic** and **The Gap.** One of the town's more popular coffee counters, **Espresso Bravissimo,** is here, along with some 90 other restaurants and specialty shops. **The Gourmet Express** counter proffers fast, healthy salads, tortilla wraps, and fresh juices and smoothies, and **Big**

Burrito is the place for cheap, tasty Mexican food. Our picks for the mall's best and brightest are **Corner Loft**, ablaze with gorgeous estate jewelry, glass, and dazzling collectibles; **Paradizio**, for home accessories; and **The Following Sea** (see "Hawaiiana/Gift Items" above). Other favorites include **Riches**, a tiny kiosk with a big, bold selection of jewelry; **The Compleat Kitchen**, for culinary needs; and **Eyewear Hawaii**, for sunglasses. Look also for the **Liberty House Men's Store** at the mauka corner of the mall, under a separate roof from the main store.

Royal Hawaiian Shopping Center. 2201 Kalakaua Ave. ☎ 808/922-0588. Daily 9:30am–10pm.

If you let it, this three-block shopping complex in the heart of Waikiki could absorb your entire Hawaii budget. *Upscale* is the operative word here. Although there are drugstores, lei stands, restaurants, and food kiosks, the most conspicuous stores are the European designer boutiques (**Chanel, Cartier, Hermès, Prada, Van Cleef & Arpels,** and more) that cater largely to visitors from Japan. One of our favorite stops is the **Little Hawaiian Craft Shop** (☎ 808/926-2662), which features a distinctive collection of Niihau shell leis, museum replicas of Hawaiian artifacts, and works by Hawaii artists as well as South Pacific crafts. **Bereatnia Florist,** located in the hut under the large banyan tree, will ship cut tropical flowers anywhere in the United States. A favorite fashion stop is **McInerny Galleria,** a cluster of boutiques under one roof, with such big names as **DKNY, Ralph Lauren, Coach,** and **Armani.**

Ward Centre. 1200 Ala Moana Blvd. ☎ 808/591-8411.

Although it has a high turnover and a changeable profile, Ward Centre is a standout for its concentration of restaurants, including coffee bar and health-food haven **Mocha Java** (see "Dining"), **Ryan's Grill** (the happy-hour hangout), **Compadres,** and dining institution **A Pacific Café Oahu** (see "Dining"), as well as gift shops and galleries, including **Tropical Clay** for island-themed ceramics, **Island Provision Co. at Vagabond House** (see "Hawaiiana/Gift Items") for unique home accessories; **Honolulu Chocolate Company** (see "Edibles," above), and the very attractive **Art à la Carte.** And **Borders Books & Music** always bustling with browsers and music lovers.

Ward Warehouse. 1050 Ala Moana Blvd. ☎ 808/591-8411.

Older than its sister property, Ward Centre, and endowed with an endearing patina, Ward Warehouse remains a popular stop for dining and shopping. Recommended stops in the low-rise brown wooden structure include the ever-colorful **C. June Shoes,**

Waikele Center. 94-790 Lumiaina St., Waikele (about 20 miles from Waikiki). ☎ 808/676-5858. Mon–Fri 9am–9pm, Sun 10am–6pm. Take H-1 west toward Waianae and turn off at exit 7. Bus: no. 2 from Waikiki and transfer at King and Beretania sts. to no. 48, which drops you off directly in front of the center. Companies offering shopping tours with Waikiki pickups include **Apple Tour** (☎ 808/395-8557; **E Noa Tours** (☎ 808/591-2561); **Da Shopping Shuttle** (☎ 808/924-8882); and **Polynesian Adventure Tours** (☎ 808/833-3000).

There are two sections to this sprawling shopping mecca: the **Waikele Factory Outlets,** some 51 retailers; and the **Waikele Value Stores** across the street, with another 25 stores. The 64-acre complex has made discount shopping a major activity and a travel pursuit in itself, with shopping tours for visitor groups and carloads of neighbor islanders and Oahu residents making virtual pilgrimages from all corners of the state. They come to hunt down bargains on everything from perfumes, luggage, and hardware to sporting goods, fashions, china, and footwear by names like Geoffrey Beene, Donna Karan, Saks Fifth Ave., Anne Klein, Max Studio, Levi's, Converse, Kenneth Cole, and dozens of other name brands at a fraction of retail. Newcomers Joan and David and the ultra-chic Barneys have added new cachet to this shopping haven.

with flamboyant designer women's shoes and handbags (tony, expensive, but oh so entertaining!); **Executive Chef,** for gourmet Hawaii food items and household accessories; **Pomegranates in the Sun,** for creative, colorful sportswear; **Out of Africa,** for pottery, beads, and interior accents; **East of Sun, West of Moon,** for its sensuous array of fragrances, linens, music, bath products, bedspreads, candles, and accessories for body, home, and spirit; **Kamuela Hat Company; Indo-Pacific Trading Co.,** for clothing and home accessories; **Yes! Perfumes,** with its hundreds of brand-name fragrances; **Mamo Howell,** for distinctive aloha wear; and **Private World,** for delicate sachets, linens, and fragrances. Brilliant newcomers include **Paradise Walking Co.,** with Arche, Mephisto, and all manner of cloud-comfort footwear; and **Interior Flavors,** brimming with tasteful gifts and home accessories. For T-shirts and swimwear, check out the **Town & Country Surf Shop,** and for an excellent selection of sunglasses, knapsacks, and footwear to take you from the beach to the ridgetops, don't miss **Thongs 'N Things.** Another favorite is the **Nohea Gallery** (see "Hawaiiana/Gift Items" above), a fine source for quality Hawaii-made arts and crafts.

SURF & SPORTS

The surf-and-sports shops scattered throughout Honolulu are a highly competitive lot, with each trying to capture your interest (and dollars). The top sources for sports gear and accessories in town are **McCully Bicycle & Sporting Goods,** 2124 S. King St. (☎ **808/955-6329**), with everything from bicycles and fishing gear to athletic shoes and accessories, and a stunning selection of sunglasses; and **The Bike Shop,** 1149 S. King St., near Piikoi St. (☎ **808/596-0588**), excellent for cycling and backpacking equipment for all levels, with major camping lines such as North Face, MSR, and Kelty. **The Sports Authority,** 333 Ward Ave. (☎ **808/596-0166**), and at Waikele Center (☎ **808/677-9933**), is a discount megaoutlet offering clothing, cycles, and equipment.

Surf shops, centers of fashion as well as definers of daring, include **Local Motion,** 1714 Kapiolani Blvd. (☎ **808/955-7873**), and other locations in Waikele, Windward Mall, and Koko Marina; and **Hawaiian Island Creations** at Ala Moana Center (☎ **808/941-4491**). Local Motion is the icon of surfers and skateboarders, both professionals and wannabes; the shop offers surfboards, T-shirts, aloha and casual wear, boogie boards, and every imaginable accessory for life in the sun. Hawaiian Island Creations is another super-cool surf shop offering sunglasses, sun lotions, surfwear, and accessories galore.

SHOPPING AROUND THE ISLAND
WINDWARD OAHU

Kailua

Longs Drugs and **Liberty House** department store, located side-by-side on Kailua Road in the heart of this windward Oahu community, form the shopping nexus of the neighborhood.

Agnes Portuguese Bake Shop, 35 Kainehe St. (☎ **808/262-5367**), is the favorite of the malassada mavens. These sugary Portuguese dumplings—like doughnuts without holes—fly out of the bakery, along with a full variety of pastries, cookies, scones, Portuguese bean and other soups, and local- and European-style breads that infuse the neighborhood with irresistible aromas.

Heritage Antiques & Gifts. 767 Kailua Rd. ☎ **808/261-8700.**

This Kailua landmark is known for its large selection of Tiffany-style lamps ($200 to $2,000), many of which are hand-carted back to the mainland. The mind-boggling selection also includes European, Asian, American, local, and Pacific Island collectibles. It's fun, the people are friendly, and the selection is diverse enough to appeal to the casual as well as serious collector. Glassware, china, and estate, costume, and fine jewelry are among the items of note. Heritage has its own jeweler who custom designs, repairs, and resurrects jewelry, while a stable of wood craftsmen turn out custom-made koa rockers and hutches to complement the antique furniture selection.

Kaneohe

Windward Mall, 46-056 Kamehameha Hwy, (☎ **808/235-1143;** open Monday to Saturday 9:30am to 9pm, Sun 10am to 5pm), is basically a suburban mall serving windwardites. Its more than 100 stores and services include health stores, department stores (**Liberty House, Sears, J.C. Penney**), airline counters, surf shops, **LensCrafters,** and dozens of other retail businesses spread out over windward Oahu's largest shopping complex. The star of the mall is **Kauila Maxwell** (see below). A small food court serves pizza, Chinese food, tacos, and other morsels for the dine-and-dash set.

Kauila Maxwell. 46-056 Kamehameha Hwy. ☎ **808/235-8383.**

The shop specializes in serious, top-quality Hawaiian crafts and gift items and in educating shoppers on their value and cultural significance. Everything is made in Hawaii, from the paddles, adzes, and other reproductions of traditional implements to the extensive selection of calabash bowls in koa, milo, kamani, mango, Norfolk pine, and other gleaming woods. The 1,000-square-foot shop also specializes in Niihau shell leis, made by a couple from Niihau and beautifully displayed in the shop with generous educational literature. Jewelry, locally made tropical perfumes (plumeria, gardenia, orchid), koa jewelry boxes, hula implements, and a few Liliuokalani-style koa rockers round out the selection. Linens, clothing by Nanea Designs, and kitchen and dining accessories are welcome new additions.

SHOPPING THE NORTH SHORE: HALEIWA

Like Hilo, Haleiwa means serious shopping for those who know that the unhurried pace of rural life can also conceal vast material treasures. Ask the legions of townies who drive an hour each way just to stock up on wine and clothes at Haleiwa stores. (Of course, a cooler is de rigueur for perishables.) Here are our Haleiwa highlights.

Art, Gifts & Crafts

Haleiwa's galleries display a combination of marine art, watercolors, sculptures, and a multitude of crafts trying to masquerade (not always successfully) as fine art. This is the town for gifts, fashions, and surf stuff—mostly casual, despite some price tags in the hundreds of thousands of dollars. The **Art Plantation,** 66-521 Kamehameha Hwy. (☎ **808/637-2343**), located in a historic wooden storefront, displays works by more than 70 artists.

The two locations of **Global Creations Interiors,** 66-079 Kamehameha Hwy. (☎ **808/637-1505**), across the street from each other, offer clothing (hemp is cheap, sturdy, and attractive here), shoes, caps, backpacks, and other accessories for top to toe. Also offered are international imports for the home, including Balinese bamboo furniture and lamps, as well as colorful Yucatan hammocks and crafts by local artisans and designers.

At the high end of the gallery scene, the indomitable **Wyland,** a North Shore resident who made a name throughout Hawaii and other locales with his large "whaling walls," has his largest Hawaii gallery at 66-150 Kamehameha Hwy. (☎ **808/ 637-7498**). **Thomas Deir Galleries,** 66-208 Kamehameha Hwy. (☎ **808/**

637-7431), displays the artist's marine paintings and hand-painted tiles, along with the works of more than a dozen other artists: Pottery, oils, acrylics, and sculptures in themes ranging from seascapes to strong Hawaiian women go for $30 to $250,000.

Edibles

Haleiwa is best known for its roadside shave-ice stands: the famous **M. Matsumoto,** with the perennial queue snaking along Kamehameha Highway, and nearby **Aoki's.** Shave ice is the popular island version of a snow cone, a heap of shaved ice topped with your choice of syrups, such as strawberry, rainbow, root beer, vanilla, or passion fruit. Aficionados order it with a scoop of ice cream and sweetened black azuki beans nestled in the middle.

For food-and-wine shopping, our mightiest accolade goes to **Fujioka Super Market,** 66-190 Kamehameha Hwy. (☎ 808/637-4520). Oenophiles and tony wine clubs from town shop here for the best prices on California reds, coveted Italian reds, and a growing selection of cabernets, merlots, and French vintages that are thoughtfully selected and unbelievably priced. Fresh produce and no-cholesterol, vegetarian health foods, in addition to the standards, fill the aisles of this third-generation store.

Tiny, funky **Celestial Natural Foods,** 66-443 Kamehameha Hwy. (☎ 808/637-6729), is the health foodies' Grand Central for everything from wooden spine-massagers to health supplements, produce, cosmetics, and bulk foods.

Fashion

Although Haleiwa used to be an incense-infused surfer outpost in which zoris and tank tops were the regional uniform and the Beach Boys and Ravi Shankar the music of the day, today it's one of the top shopping destinations for those with unconventional tastes. Specialty shops abound here. Top-drawer ✪ **Silver Moon Emporium,** North Shore Marketplace, 66-250 Kamehameha Hwy. (☎ 808/637-7710), is an islandwide phenomenon with the terrific finds of buyer/owner Lucie Talbot-Holu. Exquisite clothing and handbags, reasonably priced footwear, hats straight out of *Vogue,* jewelry, scarves, and a full gamut of other treasures pepper the attractive boutique. Down the road, amid banana trees and picnic tables in the shade of a towering monkeypod tree, Silver Moon's sister store, **Bella Luna,** 66-037 Kamehameha Hwy. (☎ 808/637-5040), still captures our hearts with its Victorian dresses, dropdead-gorgeous French Connection dresses, and affordable Italian footwear. Nearby **Oceania,** 66-218 Kamehameha Hwy. (☎ 808/637-4581), also has some treasures among its racks of casual and leisure wear. Foldable straw hats, diaphanous dresses, dressy T-shirts, friendly service, and good prices are what we've found at Oceania. **Oogenesis Boutique,** at 66-249 Kamehameha Hwy. (☎ 808/637-4580), in the southern part of Haleiwa, features a storefront lined with vintage-looking dresses that flutter prettily in the North Shore breeze.

In addition to Silver Moon, other highlights of the prominent North Shore Marketplace include **Patagonia** (☎ 808/637-1245) for high-quality surf, swim, hiking, kayaking, and all-around adventure wear; and **Jungle Gems** (☎ 808/637-6609), the mother lode of gemstones, crystals, silver, and beadwork.

Among all these Haleiwa newcomers, the perennial favorite remains **H. Miura Store and Tailor Shop,** 66-057 Kamehameha Hwy. (☎ 808/637-4845). You can custom-order swim trunks, an aloha shirt, or a muumuu from the bolts of Polynesian-printed fabrics that line the store, from tapa designs to two-color pareu prints. They will sew, ship, and remember you years later when you return. It's the most versatile tailor shop we've ever seen, with coconut-shell bikini tops, fake hula skirts, aloha shirts, and heaps of cheap and glorious chachkas lining the aisles.

Surf Shops

Haleiwa's ubiquitous surf shops are the best on earth, surfers say. At the top of the heap is **Northshore Boardriders Club**, North Shore Marketplace, 66-250 Kamehameha Hwy. (☎ **808/637-5026**), the mecca of the board-riding elite, with sleek, fast, elegant, and top-of-the-line boards designed by North Shore legends such as longboard shaper Barry Kanaiaupuni, John Carper, Jeff Bushman, and Pat Rawson. This is a Quicksilver "concept store," which means that it's the testing grounds for the newest and hottest trends in surfwear put out by the retail giant. Kanaiaupuni's other store, **B K Ocean Sports,** in the old Haleiwa Post Office at 66-215 Kamehameha Hwy. (☎ **808/637-4966**), is a more casual version, appealing to surfers and watersports enthusiasts of all levels. Across the street, **Hawaii Surf & Sail,** 66-214 Kamehameha Hwy. (☎ **808/637-5373**), offers new and used surfboards and accessories for surfers, bodyboarders, and sailboarders.

Strong Current Surf Design, North Shore Marketplace (☎ **808/637-3406**), is the North Shore's nexus for memorabilia and surf nostalgia because of the passion of its owners, Bonnie and John Moore. Moore, a lifetime collector and surfer since 1963, expanded the commercial surf-shop space to encompass the North Shore Surf and Cultural Museum (see "Exploring the Island," earlier in this chapter). From head level down, Strong Current sells shorts, jewelry, and ocean sportswear; from head level up, the walls and ceilings are lined with vintage boards, posters, and pictures from the '50s and '60s. Although Strong Current is a longboard surf shop, the current popularity of longboarding among all age groups makes this a popular stop. World-famous North Shore shapers Dick Brewer and Mike Diffenderfer are among the big names who design the fiberglass and balsa wood boards.

Also in the North Shore Marketplace, **Barnfield's Raging Isle Sports** (☎ **808/637-7707**) is the surf-and-cycle center of the area, with everything from wet suits and surfboards to surf gear and clothing for men, women, and children. The adjoining surfboard factory puts out custom-built boards of high renown. Cyclists also highail it here because of its large inventory of mountain bikes for rent and sale; Marin, Kona, and Electra are among the name brands in their mountain-bike inventory.

A longtime favorite among old-timers is the newly expanded **Surf & Sea Surf Sail & Dive Shop,** 62-595 Kamehameha Hwy. (☎ **808/637-9887**), a flamboyant roadside structure just over the bridge, with old wood floors, fans blowing, and a tangle of surf and swim wear, T-shirts, surfboards, boogie boards, fins, watches, sunglasses, and countless other miscellany; you can also rent surf and snorkel equipment here. **Tropical Rush,** 62-620-A Kamehameha Hwy. (☎ **808/637-8886**), is a surfer haven with its huge inventory of surf and swim gear, much of it for rent: longboards and Perfect Line surfboards, Reef Brazil shoes and slippers, swimwear for men and women, T-shirts, visors, sunglasses, and scads of cool gear. An added feature is the shop's surf report line for the up-to-the-minute lowdown on wave action (☎ **808/638-7874**), updated daily and quite entertaining, covering surf and weather details for all of Oahu.

14 Oahu After Dark

by Jocelyn Fujii

One of my favorite occasions in life is sunset at Ke Iki Beach, in the thatched, open-sided *hale* of my friend Alice Tracy's vacation rental, Ke Iki Hale (see "Accommodations," earlier in this chapter). The entire day builds up to sunset: shopping for the mai-tai ingredients, checking the angle of the sun, swimming with the knowledge that the big, salty thirst will soon be quenched with a tall, homemade mai tai on the beach

I love most in the world. When the sun is low, we make our mix: fresh lime juice, fresh lemon juice, fresh orange juice, passion-orange-guava juice, and fresh grapefruit juice, if possible. We pour this mix on ice in tall, frosty glasses, then add Meyer's rum, in which Tahitian vanilla beans have been soaking for days. (Add cinnamon if desired, or soak a cinnamon stick with the rum and vanilla beans.) A dash of Angostura bitters, a few drops of Southern Comfort as a float, a sprig of mint, a garnish of fresh lime, and voilà! The homemade Ke Iki mai tai, a cross between planter's punch and the classic Trader Vic's mai tai. As the sun sets, we lift our glasses and savor the moment, the setting, and the first sip—not a bad way to end the day.

In Hawaii, the mai tai is more than a libation. It's a festive, happy ritual that signals holiday, vacation, or a time of play, not work. Computers and mai tais don't mix. Mai tais and hammocks do. Mai tais and sunsets go hand in hand.

IT BEGINS WITH SUNSET . . . .

Nightlife in Hawaii begins at sunset, when all eyes turn westward to see how the day will end, and revelers begin planning their Technicolor venue to launch the evening's festivities. Like seeing the same pod of whales or school of spinner dolphins, sunset viewers seem to bond in the mutual enjoyment of a natural spectacle. People in Hawaii are fortunate to have a benign environment that encourages this cultural ritual.

On Fridays and Saturdays at 6:30pm, as the sun casts its golden glow on the beach and surfers and beachboys paddle in for the day, **Kuhio Beach,** where Kalakaua Avenue intersects with Kaiulani, eases into evening with a torch-lighting ceremony and hula dancing. This is a thoroughly delightful, free weekend offering. Start off earlier with a picnic basket and your favorite libations and walk along the oceanside path fronting Queen's Surf, near the Waikiki Aquarium. (You can park along Kapiolani Park or near the Honolulu Zoo.) There are few more pleasing spots in Waikiki than the benches at the water's edge at this Diamond Head end of Kalakaua Avenue, where lovers and families of all ages stop to peruse the sinking sun. A short walk across the intersection of Kalakaua and Kapahulu avenues, where the seawall and daring boogie boarders attract hordes of spectators, takes you to the Duke Kahanamoku statue on Kuhio Beach. There you can view the torch-lighting and hula and gear up for the strolling musicians who amble down Kalakaua Avenue every Friday evening from 8 to 10pm. The musicians begin at Beachwalk Avenue at the Ewa end of Waikiki and end up at the statue.

BEACHFRONT BARS   Waikiki's beachfront bars also offer many possibilities, from the Royal Hawaiian Hotel's ✪ **Mai Tai Bar** (☎ 808/923-7311) a few feet from the sand, to the unfailingly enchanting ✪ **House Without a Key** at the Halekulani (☎ 808/923-2311), where the breathtaking **Kanoelehua Miller** dances hula to the riffs of Hawaiian steel-pedal guitar under a century-old kiawe tree. With the sunset and ocean glowing behind her and Diamond Head visible in the distance, the scene is straight out of Somerset Maugham—romantic, evocative, nostalgic. It doesn't hurt, either, that the Halekulani happens to make the best mai tais in the world. Halekulani has the after-dinner hours covered, too, with light jazz by the mellifluous **Loretta Ables Trio** and elegant libations at **Lewers Lounge** (see "Jazz," below).

ALOHA TOWER MARKETPLACE   The landmark Aloha Tower at Honolulu Harbor, once Oahu's tallest building, has always occupied Honolulu's prime downtown location—on the water, at a naturally sheltered bay, near the business and civic center of Honolulu. Since the Aloha Tower Marketplace, 1 Aloha Tower Dr., on the waterfront between piers 8 and 11, Honolulu Harbor (☎ 808/528-5700), was constructed, it's gained popularity as an entertainment and nightlife spot, with more than

100 shops and restaurants, including several venues for Honolulu's leading musical groups.

Unlike Waikiki, there are no swaying palm trees at your fingertips at Aloha Tower Marketplace, but you'll see tugboats and cruise ships from the popular open-air **Pier Bar** and various venues throughout the marketplace offering live entertainment during happy hour and beyond. The Pier Bar's main stage, **Gordon Biersch Brewery** (see "Dining," above), and the **Atrium Center Court** feature ongoing programs of foot-stomping good times. Sunday is jazz day at the Pier Bar, Friday Hawaiian music day, and Saturday, the dance music rocks and rolls like the swells of Honolulu Harbor. At Gordon Biersch Brewery and Restaurant, diners swing to jazz, blues, and island riffs with entertainers ranging from **Nueva Vida** to **Mackey Feary, Day Trippers, Loco Spice,** and **Toast and Jam.** Also watch for jazz singer **Azure McCall;** riveting rhythm-and-blues chanteuse **Alisa Randolph; Mojo Hand,** unbeatable blues and dance music for those too hip for the Clyde Pound Orchestra; the versatile **Willie K.,** a virtuoso Hawaiian falsetto who also belts out blues, rock, and ballads; **Henry Kapono,** contemporary Hawaiian music; and **Rolando Sanchez & Salsa Hawaii.**

HAWAIIAN MUSIC

Oahu has several key spots for Hawaiian music. The **Brothers Cazimero** remain one of Hawaii's most gifted duos (Robert on bass, Roland on 12-string guitar), appearing spontaneously at Kahala Moon and special venues throughout the year. Watch the dailies, or ask the hotel concierge if the Brothers Caz, as they're called, are giving a special concert (as they do every May 1 at the Waikiki Shell), or if they've found a new stage.

Impromptu hula and spirited music from the family and friends of the performers are an island tradition at places such as the Hilton Hawaiian Village's ❂ **Paradise Lounge** (☎ 808/949-4321), which (despite its pillars) serves as a large living room for the full-bodied music of **Olomana.** The group plays Friday and Saturday from 8pm to midnight, no cover charge. At ❂ **Duke's Canoe Club** at the Outrigger Waikiki (☎ 808/923-0711), it's always three deep at the beachside bar when the sun is setting and the fabulous **Moe Keale** is playing with his trio. **Del Beazley, Brother Noland, Ledward Kaapana, Henry Kapono,** and other top names in Hawaiian entertainment appear at Duke's, where extra-special entertainment is a given. Usually, the entertainment is from 4 to 6pm on Friday, Saturday, and Sunday evenings, but call to see if there's anything cooking later in the evening. Nearby, the Sheraton Moana Surfrider offers a regular program of Hawaiian music in the **Banyan Veranda** (☎ 800/325-3535), which surrounds an islet-sized canopy of banyan tree and roots where Robert Louis Stevenson loved to linger.

Our best advice for lovers of Hawaiian music is to scan the local dailies or the *Honolulu Weekly* to see if and where the following Hawaiian entertainers are appearing: **Ho'okena,** a symphonic rich quintet featuring **Manu Boyd,** one of the most prolific songwriters and chanters in Hawaii; **Hapa,** an award-winning contemporary Hawaii duo; **Keali'i Reichel,** premier chanter, dancer, and award-winning recording artist, voted "Male Vocalist of the Year" in the 1996 Na Hoku Hanohano Awards; **Robbie Kahakalau,** "Female Vocalist of the Year" in the same awards; **Kapena,** contemporary Hawaiian music; **Na Leo Pilimehana,** a trio of angelic Hawaiian singers; the **Makaha Sons of Niihau,** pioneers in the Hawaiian cultural renaissance; and slack-key guitar master **Raymond Kane.** Consider the gods beneficent if you happen to be here when the hula halau of **Frank Kawaikapuokalani Hewett** is holding its annual fund-raiser in Windward Oahu. It's a rousing, inspired, family effort for a good cause, and it always features the best in ancient and contemporary Hawaiian music. For the best in ancient and modern hula, it's a good idea to check the dailies for halau fund-raisers, which are always authentic, enriching, and local to the core.

Showroom acts that have gained a following are led by the tireless, disarming **Don Ho,** who still sings *Tiny Bubbles* and remains a fixture at the **Waikiki Beachcomber** supper club (☎ **800/622-4646**). He's engaging to the core, attentive to fans as he accommodates their requests and sings nostalgic favorites. He's also very generous in sharing his stage with other Hawaii performers. Across Kalakaua Avenue in the **Outrigger Waikiki on the Beach** (☎ **808/923-0711**), the **Society of Seven's** nightclub act (a blend of skits, Broadway hits, popular music, and costumed musical acts) is into its 28th year—no small feat for performers.

BLUES

The best news for blues fans is the growing network of dyed-in-the-wool blues lovers here who have their own newsletter, blues festivals, club gigs, and the indomitable leadership of Louie Wolfenson of the **Maui Blues Association** (☎ **808/879-6123;** see "Maui After Dark" in chapter 7), the primary source for information on blues activities throughout the state. The blues are alive and well in Hawaii, with quality acts both local and from the mainland drawing enthusiastic crowds in even the funkiest of surroundings. **Junior Wells, Willie & Lobo, War,** and surprise appearances by the likes of **Bonnie Raitt** are among the past successes of this genre of big-time licks. The best-loved Oahu venue is **Anna Bannanas,** 2440 S. Beretania St. (☎ **808/ 946-5190**).

THE CLASSICS

Aloha shirt to Armani is what we call the night scene in Honolulu—mostly casual but with ample opportunity to dress up if you dare to part with your flip-flops.

Audiences have stomped to the big off-Broadway percussion hit, *Stomp, Tap Dogs,* barbershop quartets, and John Ka'imikaua's halau at the ★ **Hawaii Theatre,** 1130 Bethel St., downtown (☎ **808/528-0506**), still basking in its renaissance following a 4-year, $22-million renovation. The neoclassical beaux-arts landmark features a 1922 dome, 1,400 plush seats, a hydraulically elevated organ, a mezzanine lobby with two full bars, Corinthian columns, and gilt galore. Breathtaking murals, including a restored proscenium centerpiece lauded as Lionel Walden's "greatest creation," create an atmosphere that's making the theatre a leading multipurpose center for the performing arts.

The **Honolulu Symphony Orchestra** has booked some of its performances at the new theatre, but it still performs at the Waikiki Shell and the **Neal Blaisdell Concert Hall** (☎ **808/591-2211**). Meanwhile, opera lovers, the highly successful **Hawaii Opera Theatre,** in its 38th season (past hits have included *La Bohème, Carmen, Turandot, Romeo and Juliet, Rigoletto, Aida*), still draws fans to the **Neal Blaisdell Concert Hall,** as do many of the performances of Hawaii's four ballet companies: **Hawaii Ballet Theatre, Ballet Hawaii, Hawaii State Ballet,** and **Honolulu Dance Theatre.** Contemporary performances by **Dances We Dance** and the **Iona Pear Dance Company,** a strikingly creative Butoh group, are worth tracking down if you love the avantgarde.

JAZZ

Jazz Hawaii (☎ **808/737-6554**) has an updated list of who's playing where, including the Jazz Hawaii Big Band that now performs at **Eurasia Nightclub** in the Hawaiian Regent Hotel on Tuesdays. This wonderful organization has brought together Hawaii's best musicians in jazz, blues, Latin, Calypso, and Brazilian music, contributing to a higher level of entertainment since they emerged in 1993. At the gateway to Waikiki, **Coconuts,** Ilikai Hotel Nikko Waikiki, 1777 Ala Moana Blvd. (☎ **808/949-3811**), offers Big Band live jazz on Monday evenings from 7 to 10pm and Latin disco on Wednesday nights.

Tops in taste and ambiance is the perennially alluring **Lewers Lounge** in the Halekulani, 2199 Kalia Rd. (☎ **808/923-2311**), where the **Loretta Ables Trio** attracts a sophisticated audience of music lovers who sip vintage ports and expensive champagnes by the glass. Watch for **Sandy Tsukiyama,** a gifted singer (Brazilian, Latin, jazz) and is one of Honolulu's great assets. Other groups to look for from Hawaii and beyond: **Blue Budda, Son Con Clave, Groove Time, M.O.G.I.**

ALTERNATIVE CLUBS

The club scene is abuzz with rave reviews on **1739 Kalakaua Nightclub Lounge,** 1739 Kalakaua Ave. (☎ **808/949-1739**), near the Hard Rock Café and the Hawaii Convention Center. The music themes differ by the night, but their calendar readings give you an idea: jazzy and hip-hop live music; alternative, new-wave '80s music, cheesy and campy; progressive house music; deejay house music; jungle ambient and trip-hop; wine, women, and song; Nat King Soul; mood music; old school; and more jazz and hip-hop. So, whether you're into hip-hop or trip-hop, there's humor and cult appeal here. The cover charge depends on the group.

Anna Bannanas (see "Blues," above) still packs them in, with bands known to generate the most perspiration on the most enthusiastic dance floor in Honolulu. This indomitable and much loved club is a venue for groups with roots in reggae, blues, world music, and alternative music. Most shows start at 9:30pm, and the cover charge depends on the show.

Near the new convention center is the terminally hip **Hard Rock Cafe,** 1837 Kapiolani Blvd. (☎ **808/955-7383**), the bastion of decibels run amok, offering live entertainment on many, but not all, Friday and Saturday nights from 10:30pm to 12:30am. These no-cover events bring out a hip crowd for the local alternative, reggae, and classic-rock bands.

DISCOS

Nicholas Nickolas, Ala Moana Hotel, 410 Atkinson Dr. (☎ **808/955-4466**), has the best view: From the 36th floor of the hotel (take the express elevator), watch the Honolulu city lights wrap around the room and cha-cha-cha to the vertigo! Live music and dancing nightly, and an appetizer menu nightly from 5pm. Downstairs in the lobby of the same hotel, **Rumours Nightclub** (☎ **808/955-4811**) is the disco of choice for those who remember that Paul McCartney was a *Beatle* before *Wings.* The themes change by the month, but generally, it's the "Big Chill" '60s, '70s, and '80s music on Fridays; the "Little Chill" on Saturdays; ballroom dancing in the earlier hours of Sundays and Wednesdays; country and western on Tuesdays; "after-work office party" 5pm to midnight on Thursdays; and Ladies' Night 9pm to 4am on Thursdays. A spacious dance floor, good sound system, and top-40s music draw a mix of generations.

Across town in Waikiki, **Nick's Fishmarket,** Waikiki Gateway Hotel, 2070 Kalakaua Ave. (☎ **808/955-6333**), keeps winning awards for its seafood, but it's also a sophisticated hotspot with live entertainment nightly in its cozy lounge—mild jazz or top-40 contemporary hits. At Restaurant Row, **Ocean Club,** Restaurant Row, 500 Ala Moana Blvd. (☎ **808/526-9888**; see "Dining," above), is the Row's hottest, hippest, and coolest spot. Good seafood appetizers, attractive happy-hour prices, a fabulous quirky interior, and passionate deejays in alternative garb make up a sizzlingly successful formula. The minimum age is 23, and the dress code calls for "smart-casual"—no T-shirts, slippers, or beach wear.

. . . AND MORE

It's true that Elvis and Marilyn didn't die. They're still wowing fans through their impersonators, having achieved entertainment immortality with skillful makeup and voice coaches. Watch Madonna, Michael Jackson, Roy Orbison, Diana Ross, Janet Jackson, Prince, Whitney Houston, Marilyn Monroe, Elvis, and other entertainment icons at the **Legends in Concert** show at the **Aloha Showroom** of the **Royal Hawaiian Shopping Center** (☎ **808/971-1400**). The recently revamped dinner show has added a magic act, new china and menu items (steak and scampi), and a finely tuned cast of impersonators in a $10-million showroom with laser lights, smoke effects, and high-tech stage and sound systems. At least five personalities are featured at each performance, with Elvis, performed by uncanny look-alike Jonathan Von Brana, and Madonna, performed by Von Brana's real-life wife, Eileen Fairbanks, among the show's staples. Two shows (6:25pm and 9pm) are featured 7 nights a week at $29 for cocktails, $65 for dinner show, and $99 for deluxe dinner show, with reduced children's rates available.

Finally, for late-night schmoozing, with a theater complex nearby, the Restaurant Row's **Row Bar,** 500 Ala Moana Blvd. (☎ **808/528-2345**), always seems to be full, smoky, and somewhat, if impersonally, convivial, except after the theaters have emptied from an Oliver Stone movie.

6

Hawaii: The Big Island

The Big Island of Hawaii—the island that lends its good name to the entire 1,500-mile-long Hawaiian archipelago—is like no other place on earth. Simply put, it's spectacular.

This is where Mother Nature pulled out all stops. The island looks like the inside of a barbecue pit on one side, and a lush jungle on the other. The Big Island has it all: fiery volcanoes and sparkling waterfalls, black-lava deserts and snowcapped mountain peaks, tropical rain forests and alpine meadows, a glacial lake and miles of beaches—with a rainbow of black, green, and golden sands. The Big Island has a diversity of terrain and climate unmatched in any one place. A 50-mile drive will take you from snowy winter to sultry summer, passing through spring or fall along the way.

The island can only be described in superlatives. It's the largest island in the Pacific (4,038 sq. miles), the youngest (800,000 years), and the least populated (with 30 people per sq. mile). It has the nation's wettest city, the southernmost point in the United States, the world's biggest telescope, the ocean's biggest trophy marlin, and America's greatest collection of tropical luxury resorts. It has the highest peaks in the Pacific, the most volcanoes of any Hawaiian island, and the newest land on earth.

Five volcanoes—one still erupting—have created a continental island that's as big as Connecticut, and it's growing bigger daily. At its heart is snowcapped Mauna Kea, the world's tallest sea mountain, complete with its own glacial lake. Mauna Kea's nearest neighbor is Mauna Loa (or "Long Mountain"), creator of one-sixth of the island; it's the largest volcano on earth, rising 30,000 feet out of the ocean floor (of course, you can only see the 13,796 feet that are above sea level). Erupting Kilauea makes the Big Island bigger every day—and, if you're lucky and your timing is good, you can stand just a few feet away and watch it do its work.

Steeped in tradition and shrouded in the primal mist of creation, the Big Island called to the Polynesians across 2,000 miles of open ocean. In fact, ancient Hawaiian chants talk about a great burning in the night skies which guided the sojourners to the land of volcanoes. The Big Island radiates what the Hawaiians call "mana," a sense of spirituality that's still palpable through the acres of petroglyphs etched in the black lava, the numerous *heiaus* (ancient temples), burial caves scattered in the cliffs, sacred shrines both on land and in the sea, and even in the sound the wind makes as it blows across the desolate lava fields.

Factoid

Kilauea volcano can fill a stadium the size of the Houston Astrodome with lava in a week.

The Big Island's beauty, vastness, and grandeur is unsurpassed. It's often misunderstood, however, mostly because it refuses to fit the stereotype of a tropical island. Some tourists are taken aback at the sight of stark fields of lava or black-sand beaches. The Big Island is not for everyone. First of all, remember that it's BIG (expect to do lots of driving). And you may have to go out of your way if it's traditional tropical beauty, such as a quintessential white-sand beach, you seek.

If you're into watersports, this is paradise. The two tall volcanoes mean 350 days of calm water on the leeward side. The underwater landscape of caves, cliffs, and tunnels attracts a stunning array of colorful marine life just waiting to be visited by divers and snorkelers. The island's West Coast is one of the best destinations in the world for big-game fishing. And miles of remote coastline are a kayaker's dream of caves, secluded coves, and crescent-shaped beaches reachable only by sea.

On land, hikers, bikers, and horseback riders can head up and down a volcano, across black-sand beaches, into remote valleys, and through rain forests without seeing another soul. Bird watchers are rewarded with sightings of the rare, rapidly dwindling native birds of Hawaii. Golfers can find nirvana on top championship courses, less-crowded municipal courses, and even some unusual off-the-beaten-track choices.

This is the least-explored island in the Hawaiian chain—but if you're looking to get away from it all and back to nature in its most primal state, that might be the best thing of all about it. Where else can you witness fiery creation and swim with dolphins, ponder the stars from the world's tallest mountain and catch a record blue marlin, downhill ski and surf the waves in a single day? You can do all this, and much more, on only one island in the world—the Big Island of Hawaii. Those who come here find a place unlike any other—and an unequaled world of adventure.

1 Orientation

by Jeanette Foster

Most people arrive on the Big Island at Kona International Airport, on the island's West Coast, and discover there are only two ways to go: clockwise or counterclockwise. Nobody knows why, but most Americans go clockwise, and Europeans go counterclockwise. Whichever way you go, all you need to know is that from Keahole, Kilauea volcano is counterclockwise, and the ritzy Kohala Coast is clockwise. (If you land in Hilo, of course, the volcano is clockwise, and Kohala is counterclockwise.)

If you think you can "do" the Big Island in a day, forget it. You need about 3 days just to do Hawaii Volcanoes National Park justice. Plan on spending a week on the Big Island if you hope to catch more than a glimpse of the island through the window of a speeding rental car.

ARRIVING

The Big Island has two major airports for jet traffic between the islands: **Kona International Airport** and **Hilo International Airport,** on the other side of the island.

The Kona Airport receives direct overseas flights from Japan and Canada, as well as direct mainland flights from Los Angeles and San Francisco. Otherwise, you'll have to pick up an interisland flight in Honolulu. **Aloha Airlines** (☎ **800/367-5250**) and

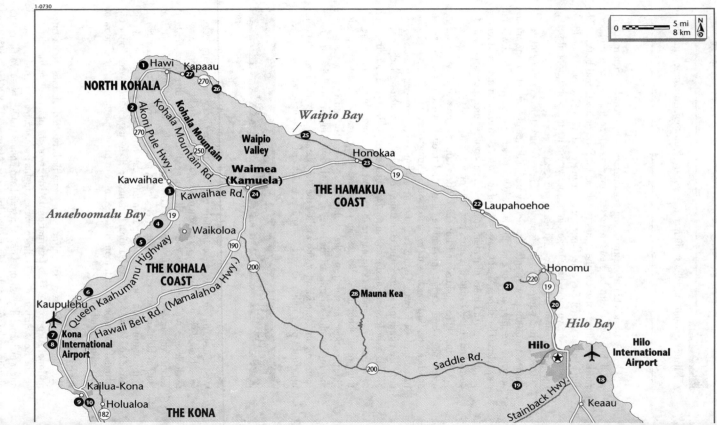

1-0730

0 —■■■■— 5 mi
8 km
N

① Hawi Kapaau
㉗ ㉖
270

NORTH KOHALA

②

Akoni Pule Hwy.
270

Kohala Mountain Rd.

Kohala Mountain

250

Waipio Bay

㉕

Waipio Valley

Honokaa
㉓
19

Waimea (Kamuela)

Kawaihae
③
Kawaihae Rd.
㉔

THE HAMAKUA COAST

㉒ Laupahoehoe

Anaehoomalu Bay

④ 19

○ Waikoloa

⑤

190

Queen Kaahumanu Highway

200

THE KOHALA COAST

Honomu

㉑
220
19

⑥

Kaupulehu

✈

Hawaii Belt Rd. (Mamalahoa Hwy.)

㉘ **Mauna Kea**

⑳

Hilo Bay

⑦ **Kona International Airport**
⑧

Hilo
★

Hilo International Airport
✈

Kailua-Kona

⑨⑩ ○ Holualoa

182

THE KONA

Saddle Rd.

200

⑲

Stainback Hwy.

Keaau

⑱

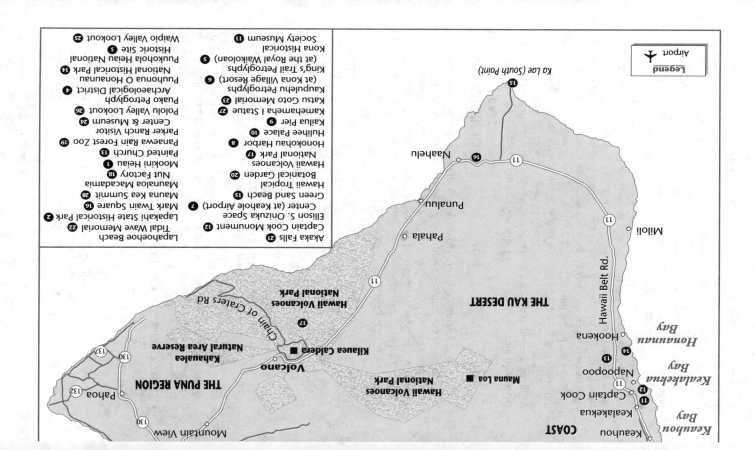

Lapahoehoe Beach
Tidal Wave Memorial **22**
Lapakahi State Historical Park **2**
Mark Twain Square **16**
Mauna Kea Summit **28**
Maunaloa Macadamia
Nut Factory **18**
Mookini Heiau **1**
Painted Church **13**
Panaewa Rain Forest Zoo **19**
Parker Ranch Visitor
Center & Museum **24**
Pololu Valley Lookout **26**
Puako Petroglyph
Archaeological District **4**
Puuhonua O Honaunau
National Historical Park **14**
Puukohola Heiau National
Historic Site **3**
Waipio Valley Lookout **25**

Akaka Falls **21**
Captain Cook Monument **12**
Ellison S. Onizuka Space
Center (at Keahole Airport) **7**
Green Sand Beach **15**
Hawaii Tropical
Botanical Garden **20**
Hawaii Volcanoes
National Park **17**
Honokohau Harbor **8**
Hulihee Palace **10**
Kailua Pier **9**
Kamehameha I Statue **27**
Katsu Goto Memorial **23**
Kaupulehu Petroglyphs
(at Kona Village Resort) **6**
King's Trail Petroglyphs
(at the Royal Waikoloan) **5**
Kona Historical
Society Museum **11**

239

Legend
Airport ✈

Hawaiian Airlines (☎ 800/367-5320) offer jet service to both Big Island airports. All major rental companies have cars available at both airports. See "Getting There & Getting Around" in chapter 3 for more details on interisland travel and car rentals.

VISITOR INFORMATION

The **Big Island Visitors Bureau** has two offices on the Big Island: one at 250 Keawe St., Hilo, HI 96720 (☎ **808/961-5797;** fax 808/961-2126); and on the other side of the island at 75-5719 W. Alii Dr., Kailua-Kona, HI 96740 (☎ **808/329-7787;** fax 808/326-7563). **Hawaii's Big Island Driving Tour** is available, a step-by-step guide that takes you on the Big Island's Circle Island tour, pointing out all the wonders along the way, with legends, facts, and bits of trivia thrown in for fun; stop in and pick one up, or call, and they'll send it to you.

On the west side of the island, there are two additional places to contact for information: the **Kona-Kohala Coast Resort Association,** 69-275 Waikoloa Beach Dr., Kamuela (Waimea) HI 96743 (☎ **800/318-3637** or 808/885-4915; fax 808/885-1044; www.planet-hawaii.com/kohala-coast); and **Destination Kona,** P.O. Box 2850, Kailua-Kona, HI 96745 (☎ **808/322-6809;** fax 808/322-8899). On the east side, you can contact **Destination Hilo,** P.O. Box 1391, Hilo, HI 96721 (☎ **808/935-5294;** fax 808/969-1984).

The Big Island's best free tourist publications are *This Week,* the *Beach and Activity Guide,* and *101 Things to Do on Hawaii The Big Island.* All three offer lots of useful information, as well as discount coupons on a variety of island adventures. Copies are easy to find all around the island.

The *Beach and Activity Guide* is affiliated with the **Activity Connection,** King Kamehameha Mall, Kuakini Hwy. (behind the King Kamehameha Hotel), Kailua-Kona (☎ **808/329-1038;** fax 808/327-9411; e-mail alaka@aloha.net), a discount activity desk offering real discounts (no fees, no timeshares) of up to 15% on activities, including island tours, snorkeling and dive trips, submarine and horseback rides, luaus, and more. Stop by their office; it's open daily from 7:30am to 5:30pm.

THE REGIONS IN BRIEF
THE KONA COAST

One Hawaiian word everyone seems to know is *Kona,* probably because it's synonymous with great coffee and big fish—both of which are found in abundance along this 70-milelong stretch of black lava-covered coast.

Kona is a state of mind more than a distinct place. A collection of tiny communities devoted to farming and fishing along the sunbaked leeward side of the island, the Kona Coast has an amazingly diverse geography and climate for such a compact area.

The oceanfront town of **Kailua-Kona,** a quaint fishing village that now caters more to tourists than boat captains, is its commercial center; sooner or later, everyone meets on Kailua-Kona's Alii Drive, a 2-mile retail strip of shops and restaurants that's fun to cruise on foot or by car, especially on Saturday night. The lands of Kona range from stark, black, dry, coastal desert to cool, cloudy upcountry so fertile that it seems anything could grow there: glossy green coffee, macadamia nuts, tropical fruit, and a riotous profusion of flowers covers the jagged steep slopes. Among the coffee fields, you'll find the funky, artsy village of **Holualoa.** Higher yet in elevation are native forests of giant trees filled with tiny, colorful birds, some periously close to extinction. About 7 miles south of Kailua-Kona, boarding the ocean, is the resort area of **Keauhou,** a suburban-like series of upscale condominiums, several hotels, a shopping center, and homes in the seven-figure range.

Kona means "leeward side" in Hawaiian—and that means full-on summer sun every day of the year. It's an affordable vacation spot: An ample selection of mid-priced condo units, peppered with a few older hotels and B&Bs, line a shoreline that's mostly rocky lava reef, interrupted by an occasional pocket beach. Here, too, stand two world-class resorts: Kona Village, the site of one of the best luaus in the islands, and Hawaii's newest luxury retreat, the Four Seasons at Hualalai.

SOUTH KONA   Away from the bright lights of the town of Kailua lies the rural South Kona Coast, home to coffee farmers, macadamia nut growers, and people escaping to the country. The serrated South Kona Coast is indented with numerous bays, starting with **Kealakekua,** a marine-life preserve that's the island's best diving spot and the place where Capt. James Cook met his demise; down to **Honaunau,** where a national historic park recalls the savage days of old Hawaii. Accommodations in this area are mainly inexpensive B&Bs, everything from the very frugal Japanese Manago Hotel to the very classy McCandless Ranch B&B. This coast is a great place to stay if you want to get away from crowds and experience peaceful country living. You are within driving distance of beaches and the sites of Kailua.

The Kohala Coast

Fringes of palms and flowers, brilliant blankets of emerald green, and an occasional flash of white building are your only clues from the road that this black-lava coast north of Kona is more than bleak and barren. And, oh, is it! Down by the sea, pleasure domes rise like palaces no Hawaiian king ever imagined. This is where the Lear jet set escapes to play in world-class beachfront hotels set like jewels in the golden sand. But you don't have to be a billionaire to visit the Waikoloa, Mauna Lani, and Mauna Kea resorts: The fabulous beaches and abundant historic sites are open to the public, with parking and other facilities provided by the resorts, including restaurants, golf courses, and shopping.

North Kohala

Seven sugar mills once shipped enough sugar to sweeten all the coffee in San Francisco from three harbors on this knob of land at the northernmost reaches of the island. **Hawi,** the region's hub and home to the Kohala Sugar Co., was a flourishing town. It even had its own railroad, a narrow-gauge train that hauled cane down to Mahukona, on North Kohala's lee coast.

Today, Hawi's quaint, three-block-long strip of sun-faded, false-front buildings and 1920s vintage shops lives on as a minor tourist stop in one of Hawaii's most scenic rural regions. The small cosmopolitan community of diverse ethnic groups, including Chinese, Japanese, Puerto Rican, Korean, and Filipino laborers, is slowly shrinking as the old timers die out.

This region is most famous as the birthplace of King Kamehameha the Great; a statue commemorates the royal site. It's also home to the islands' most sacred site, the 1,500-year-old **Mookini Heiau** (see Mookini Luakini; below).

Waimea (Kamuela)

This old upcountry cow town on the northern road between the coasts is lovely country: rolling green pastures, big, wide-open spaces dotted by *puu* (hills), and real Marlboro-smoking cowpokes who ride mammoth **Parker Ranch,** Hawaii's largest working ranch. It's also headquarters for the **Keck Telescope,** the largest and most powerful in the world, bringing world-class, starry-eyed astronomers to town. The nightlife here is far out, in the galactic sense; bring your own telescope. Waimea is home to several affordable B&Bs, and Merriman's Restaurant is a popular foodie outpost at Opelo Plaza.

THE HAMAKUA COAST

This emerald coast, a 52-mile stretch from Honokaa to Hilo on the island's windward northeast side, was once planted with sugar cane; it now blooms with flowers, macadamia nuts, papayas, and marijuana, or *pakalolo* (still Hawaii's number one cash crop). Resort-free and virtually without beaches, the Hamakua Coast's major destinations are spectacular **Waipio Valley**, a picture-perfect valley with impossibly steep sides, taro patches, a green riot of wild plants, and a winding stream leading to a broad, black-sand beach; and the historic plantation town of **Honokaa** (making a comeback as the B&B capital on the coastal trail). Akaka Falls and Laupahoehoe Beach Park are also worth seeking out (see "Seeing the Sights," later in this chapter, for details).

Elsewhere along the coast, communities are reeling in the wake of the sugar-plantation shutdown, and the cane in the fields is going to seed. Valleys draining Mauna Kea's slopes meet the sea every few miles; they're so choked with foliage that they look like Indonesian jungles.

Hilo

When the sun shines in Hilo, it's one of the most beautiful tropical cities in the Pacific. Being here is an entirely different kind of island experience: Hawaii's largest city after Honolulu is a quaint, misty, flower-filled city of Victorian houses overlooking a half-moon bay, with a restored historic downtown and a clear view of Mauna Loa's often snowcapped peak. Hilo catches everyone's eye until it rains—and when it rains in Hilo, it pours.

Hilo is America's wettest town, with 128 inches of rain annually. It's ideal for growing ferns, orchids, and anthuriums, but not for catching a few rays. Yet there's lots to see and do in Hilo, so grab your umbrella. The rain is warm (the temperature seldom dips below 70°F), and there's usually a rainbow afterward.

Hilo's oversized airport and hotels are remnants of a dream: The city wanted to be Hawaii's major port of entry. That didn't happen, but the facilities here are excellent. Hilo is Hawaii's best bargain for budget travelers. It has plenty of hotel rooms—most of the year, that is. Hilo's magic moment comes in spring, the week after Easter, when hula *halau* (schools) arrive for the annual Merrie Monarch Festival hula competition (see "Hawaii Calendar of Events" in chapter 3 for details). This is a full-on Hawaiian spectacle and a wonderful cultural event. Plan ahead if you want to go: Tickets are sold out the first week in January for the post-Easter event, and the hotels within 30 miles are usually booked solid.

Hilo is also the gateway to Hawaii Volcanoes National Park and the greatest show on earth; it's just an hour's drive up-slope.

THE PUNA REGION

Lava, and lots of it, characterizes the Puna Region on the Big Island's remote eastern shore. Black lava covers almost everything, both ancient sites and latter-day villages, with alacrity: In 1963, lava ran down to Cape Kumukahi and oozed around the light-house, which still looks startled; it destroyed the village of Kalapana in 1990. Since it overran Chain of Craters Road in 1988, there's only one way in and out of Puna: Highway 130. Land not buried by lava is planted in red and green anthuriums, golden sunrise papayas, and marijuana. The illegal leaf growers add an edgy element to this remote region. The main town in Puna is **Pahoa**, a town that time forgot, where you might spot residents still dressed like the flower children of the 1960s, complete with peace symbols, dreadlocks, and multicolored VW vans.

HAWAII VOLCANOES NATIONAL PARK & VOLCANO VILLAGE

The sleepy village of Volcano sits in a rain forest on the edge of America's most exciting national park, where a live volcano called Kilauea erupts daily. (If you're lucky, it will be a spectacular sight. At other times, you may not be able see the molten lava at all—but there's still a lot to see and learn.) Ideally, you should plan to spend 3 days at the park, exploring the trails, watching the volcano, visiting the rain forest, and just enjoying this most unusual, spectacular place. But even if you only have a day, get here—it's worth the trip. Bring your sweats or jacket (honest!); it's cooler up here, especially at night.

If you plan to dally in the park—and you should—Volcano has some great places to stay. Several terrifically cozy B&Bs, some with fireplaces, hide under tree ferns in this cool, misty hamlet. The tiny highland (at 4,000 ft.) community, first settled by Japanese immigrants, is now inhabited by artists, soul-searchers, and others who like the crisp air of Hawaii's high country. It has just enough civilization to sustain a good life: a few stores, a gas station, and a golf course.

KA LAE: SOUTH POINT

This is the Plymouth Rock of Hawaii, where the first Polynesians arrived in seagoing canoes, probably from the Marquesas Islands or Tahiti, around A.D. 500. You'll feel like you're at the end of the world on this lonely, windswept place, the southernmost point of the United States (a geographic claim that belonged to Key West, Florida, until 1959, when Hawaii became the 50th state). Hawaii ends in a sharp black-lava point. Bold 500-foot cliffs stand against the blue sea to the west and shelter the old fishing village of Waiahukini, which was born in A.D. 750 and lasted until the 1860s. Ancient canoe moorings, shelter caves, and *heiau* (temples) poke through windblown *pili* grass. The East Coast curves inland to reveal a lonely, green-sand beach, a world-famous anomaly that's accessible only by foot or four-wheel drive. For most, the only reason to venture down to the southern tip is to say you did, or to experience the empty vista of land's end.

Everything in the two wide spots in the road called **Naalehu** and **Waiohinu** that pass for towns at South Point claims to be the southernmost this or that. Except for a monkeypod tree planted by Mark Twain in 1866, there's not much else to crow about. There is, thankfully, a gas station, a couple of eateries and a fruit stand, a picture-postcard 19th-century church, and a B&B. These end-of-the-world towns are just about as far removed from the real world as you can get.

2 Getting Around

by Jeanette Foster

BY CAR You'll really need a rental car on the Big Island; not having one will really limit what you'll be able to see and do. All the major car-rental firms have agencies at both the airports and at the Kohala Coast resorts; for a complete list, as well as tips on insurance and driving rules, see "Car Rentals" under "Getting There & Getting Around" in chapter 3.

There are more than 480 miles of paved road on the Big Island, but only two main highways. The one main highway that circles the island is called the **Hawaii Belt**

Road. On the Kona side of the island, you have two choices: the scenic "upper" road, **Mamalahoa Highway** (Hwy. 190), or the speedier "lower" road, **Queen Kaahumanu Highway** (Hwy. 19). The road that links east to west is called the **Saddle Road** (Hwy. 200), because it crosses the "saddle" between Mauna Kea and Mauna Loa. Saddle Road is the one rental-car agencies ask you to avoid, because it's rough and narrow and the weather conditions can be a handful for motorists.

BY TAXI   Taxis are readily available at both Keahole and Hilo airports. In Hilo, call **Ace-1** (☎ 808/935-8303). In Kailua-Kona, call **Kona Airport Taxi** (☎ 808/329-7779). Taxis will take you wherever you want to go on the Big Island, but it's prohibitively expensive to use them to go long distances.

BY BUS   There is an islandwide bus system, but all it does is take passengers from Kona and Hilo and back. It's the **Hele-On Bus** (☎ 808/961-8744), and it leaves Kailua-Kona from the Lanihau Shopping Center, at Palani Road and Queen Kaahumanu Highway, every morning at 6:45am, getting into Hilo at 9:30am. The afternoon return trip leaves the bus terminal on Kamehameha Avenue at Mamo Street in Hilo at 1:30pm, arriving back in Kailua-Kona at 4:30pm. The fare is $5.25 each way.

FAST FACTS: Big Island

American Express   American Express has an office on the Kohala Coast at the Hilton Waikoloa Village (☎ 808/885-7958). To report lost or stolen traveler's checks, call ☎ 800/221-7282.

Dentists   In an emergency, contact **Dr. Craig C. Kimura** at Kamuela Office Center (☎ 808/885-5947); in Kona, call **Dr. Frank Sayre**, Frame 10 Center, behind Lanihau Shopping Center on Palani Rd. (☎ 808/329-8067); in Hilo, call **Hawaii Smile Center**, Hilo Lagoon Center, 101 Aupuni St. (☎ 808/961-9181).

Doctors   **Hilo Medical Center** is at 1190 Waianuenue Ave., Hilo (☎ 808/974-4700); on the Kona side, call **Hualalai Urgent Care**, 75-1028 Henry St. (across the street from Safeway), ☎ 808/327-HELP).

Emergencies   For ambulance, fire, and rescue services, dial ☎ 911 or call ☎ 808/961-6022. The **Poison Control Center** hotline is ☎ 800/362-3585.

Hospitals   **Hilo Medical Center**, 1190 Waianuenue Ave., Hilo (☎ 808/974-4700); **North Hawaii Community Hospital**, Waimea (☎ 808/885-4444); and **Kona Community Hospital**, on the Kona Coast in Kealakekua (☎ 808/322-9311) all have 24-hour urgent-care facilities.

Police   Dial ☎ 911 or call the **Hawaii Police Department** at ☎ 808/322-5122 or 808/329-1380 in Kona, ☎ 808/959-5881 in Hilo.

Post Office   All calls to the U.S. Post Office can be directed ☎ 800/275-8777. There are local branches in Hilo, at 1299 Kekuanaoa Ave.; in Kailua-Kona, at 74-5577 Palani Rd.; in Waimea, on Lindsey Road.

Weather   For conditions in and around Hilo, call ☎ 808/935-8555; for the rest of the Big Island, call ☎ 808/961-5582. For marine forecasts, call ☎ 808/935-9883.

3 Accommodations

by Jeanette Foster

Before you reach for the phone to book your vacation dream house, refer back to chapter 3 to read up on the types of accommodations available to make sure you book the kind of place you want. Also remember that the Big Island is really big; see "The

Regions in Brief," earlier in this chapter, to make sure that you choose the perfect area in which to base yourself for the kind of vacation you have mapped out.

In the listings below, all rooms have a full private bath (with tub and shower) and free parking unless otherwise noted. Remember to add Hawaii's 10.17% in taxes to your final bill.

RESERVATIONS AGENCIES   To make life easier, you might want to go through a booking agency, which can save you time and money by matching you up with your dream accommodations. We recommend ✪ **Hawaii's Best Bed & Breakfasts,** P.O. Box 563, Kamuela, HI 96743 (☎ **800/262-9912** or 808/885-4550; fax 808/885-0559; e-mail bestbnb@aloha.net). Operated by Barbara Campbell, Hawaii's Best Bed & Breakfasts represents only the crème de la crème of B&Bs across the state.

Knutson & Associates (☎ **800/800-6202** or 808/329-6311; www.planethawaii.com/knutson) is one of Kona's best vacation rental brokers, offering dozens of oceanfront properties (from condos to houses) to fit every budget. Marilyn Knutson has high standards for the properties she chooses to represent. **Sun Quest Vacations** (☎ **800/367-5168** or 808/329-6488; www.sunquest-hawaii.com) handles most of the top condos and homes south of Kailua-Kona in Keauhou, with prices starting at $85 a night.

For luxury condos, townhouses, and estates on the Kohala Coast, contact **South Kohala Management** (☎ **800/822-4252** or 808/883-8500), which also offers rental-car and golf packages.

Brian and Lisha Crawford, owners of Chalet Kilauea (listed below) and a host of other properties near Hawaii Volcanoes National Park, also have a discriminating reservation service that books accommodations priced from $45 double on up: **Volcano Reservations,** P.O. Box 998, Volcano, HI 96785 (☎ **800/736-7140** or 808/967-8216; fax 800/577-1849; e-mail bchawaii@aol.com).

Other services that can hook you up with a great place to stay on the Big Island include **Bed & Breakfast Hawaii,** P.O. Box 449, Kapaa, HI 96746 (☎ **800/733-1632** or 808/822-7771; fax 808/822-2723); and **Three Bears' Hawaii Reservations,** 72-1001 Puukala St., Kailua-Kona, HI 96740 (☎/fax **800/765-0480** or 808/325-7563; e-mail threebears@pobox.com).

THE KONA COAST
IN & AROUND KAILUA-KONA
Very Expensive

✪ **Four Seasons Resort Hualalai at Historic Kaupulehu.** P.O. Box 1119, Kailua-Kona, HI 96745. ☎ **800/334-3443,** 888/340-5662, or 808/325-8000. Fax 808/325-8200. www.fshr.com/locations/Hualalai. 274 units. A/C MINIBAR TV TEL. $450–$600 double, from $725 suite. Extra person $90; children under 18 stay free in parents' room. AE, DC, JCB, MC, V.

This is a great place to relax in the lap of luxury. On arrival, you'll be greeted with an orchid lei, oshibori towels, and tropical juice. You're guaranteed to experience Polynesian paralysis after a few days of lying in a hammock and watching the clouds waft across the sky, though there are plenty of diversions available. Low-rise clusters of oceanfront villas nestle between the sea and the greens of a new golf course. The Four Seasons has no concrete corridors, no massive central building—it looks like a two-story townhouse project, clustered around three seaside swimming pools. The rooms are furnished in Pacific tropical style: beige walls, raffia rugs over clay-colored slate, and Madge Tennent etchings over rattan and bamboo settees. The ground-level rooms have bathrooms with private outdoor gardens (surrounded by black-lava rock), so you can shower naked under the tropic sun or nighttime stars.

The Four Seasons at Hualalai is very different from its cousin, the Four Seasons at Wailea, on Maui. The low-rise bungalows create an entirely different effect than Maui's palatial mansion by the sea. In fact, the staff calls the Maui property "the palace," and the Big Island property "the village."

Dining/Diversions: Pacific Rim cuisine is featured in the main restaurant, Pahu I'a, located right at the ocean's edge. More casual fare is served at the poolside **Beach Tree Bar and Grill.** For reviews on these restaurants, see "Dining," below.

Amenities: Sports club and spa, fabulous 18-hole Jack Nicklaus golf course (reserved for guests and residents; call ☎ **808/325-8480** for tee times), Hawaiian history and cultural interpretive center, daily Kids for All Seasons program, three swimming pools (one carved out of black-lava rock), eight tennis courts, complimentary scuba lessons, open lava-rock amphitheater for special events, 24-hour room service, complimentary valet, same-day laundry, 1-hour pressing, twice-daily maid service, multilingual concierge, free shoeshine and sandal repair, early/late arrival facilities.

✪ **Kona Village Resort.** P.O. Box 1299, Kailua-Kona, HI 96745. ☎ **800/367-5290** or 808/325-5555. Fax 808/325-5124. www.konavillage.com. E-mail kvr@aloha.net. 125 bungalows. $425–$735 double. Extra person $180 adult, $130 children 6–12, kids 5 and under stay free. Rates include all meals, tennis, watersports, walking tours, airport transfers, welcome leis, and a Fri-night luau. Packages available. AE, DC, JCB, MC, V.

In all of Hawaii, there's only one Kona Village. For more than 30 years, those seeking the great escape have crossed the black-lava fields to find refuge at this exclusive haven by the sea, with its wonderful dark-sand beach. A blissful languor settles in as you surrender to the gentle staff and peaceful, low-key atmosphere. Maybe it's the spirit of the ancients who once lived here. Maybe it's the luxe summer-camp setup: thatched-roof island-style bungalows with no air-conditioning and no TVs, a central dining house, and phones only at the office. The resort resembles an eclectic Polynesian village, with proudly tended palms and tropicals, historic sites, and beaches on a secluded cove. Its magic frees children of all ages (except during September, when the resort is reserved for couples only) to relax and play on 82 acres by the sea, behind a lava barrier that keeps the world at bay. The bungalows all have a bedroom, bathroom, and lanai. Standard equipment includes a grind-and-perk coffeemaker, a ceiling fan, and a refrigerator that's replenished daily with free sodas and bottled water. Some units have outdoor hot tubs and an extra anteroom with a single bed.

Dining/Diversions: Breakfast and dinner, served in the communal dining room, feature whatever's fresh in the islands that day. A second restaurant features more formal dining. Lunch is served on the terrace alfresco: a healthy, tempting buffet of veggies and salads, sashimi, burgers, fish, grilled-to-order steaks, and a help-yourself bin of freshly baked oatmeal cookies. The food is terrific. During holidays and the summer, children can eat at an early kids-only dinner, followed by supervised activities. There's some live entertainment most nights, whether it's dancing to a Hawaiian trio at the Bora Bora Bar, a Paniolo Cookout, or the Friday-night luau, the island's best (see "Luaus & Other Local Fun: The Big Island After Dark," below).

Amenities: Watersports, tennis, two pools, petroglyph field.

Moderate

Aston Royal Sea Cliff Resort. 75-6040 Alii Dr., Kailua-Kona, HI 96740. ☎ **800/922-7866** or 808/329-8021. Fax 808/326-1887. www.aston-hotels.com. 148 units. A/C TV TEL. $126–$180 studio double, $139–$230 one-bedroom apt. for 2, $161–$265 two-bedroom apt. for 6, $500–$550 villa for 4. AE, CB, DC, DISC, JCB, MC, V.

Families will love these luxuriously appointed apartments and their affordable rates. The architecturally striking five-story white buildings that make up this resort/condo complex, 2 miles from Kailua-Kona, are stepped back from the ocean for maximum views and privacy. (The downside is that there's no ocean swimming here, but the waves are near enough to lull you to sleep.) Atrium gardens and hanging bougainvillea soften the look. For the price of a moderate hotel room, you'll get a spacious unit furnished in tropical rattan with a large, sunny lanai; a full kitchen, and a washer and dryer. Tennis courts, pools, spas, a sauna, and barbecue facilities are available, as well as services such as voice mail, a small store, and an activities desk.

✪ **Kailua Plantation House.** 75-5948 Alii Dr. (near Lunapule St.), Kailua-Kona, HI 96740. ☎ **808/329-3727.** Fax 808/326-7323. www.konaweb.com/KPH or www.tales.com/KPH. E-mail kphbnb@ilhawaii.net. 5 units. TV TEL. $145–$205 double. Rates include full breakfast. Extra person 20% more. 2-night minimum. AE, MC, V. No children under 12.

The rates here may be high for a B&B—but if you want to stay on the Kona Coast, an oceanfront room at this incredible house right on the water (the patio steps go right into the Pacific Ocean) is a wonderful splurge. The house is immaculately kept and elegantly decorated in island style, with rattan furniture and tile floors, and the views are fabulous. Ocean breezes keep the rooms cool, the romantic setting keeps couples in the mood, and the generous full breakfast keeps everyone happy. Book a couple months in advance—everyone wants to stay here. If you can't get an oceanfront room, stay somewhere else, as the rooms facing Alii Drive are very noisy.

King Kamehameha's Kona Beach Hotel. 75-5660 Palani Rd., Kailua-Kona, HI 96740. ☎ **800/367-6060** or 808/329-2911. Fax 808/922-8061. 462 units. A/C TV TEL. $110–$195 double, from $300 suite. Package of Aloha (including room, car, and breakfast) $125 (subject to availability). AE, CB, DC, DISC, JCB, MC, V.

The best deal at this convenient downtown Kailua-Kona hotel is the Package of Aloha, which comes with a double room, a compact car, and breakfast for two, all for just $125—a price that makes the "King Kam" (as locals call it) attractive to travelers on a budget. It isn't anything fancy—just a standard hotel in need of a little TLC—but it's well located, right in the heart of town, across the street from the pier, where record Pacific blue marlin are weighed in every afternoon. Rooms are ordinary but clean, just like a Holiday Inn, but with views of an ancient banyan tree, the Kona Pier, or sparkling Kailua Bay. There's a Liberty House department store and other shops on the premises, as well as a poolside bar and a snack bar. The hotel's own small, goldsand beach is right out the front door.

Royal Kona Resort. 75-5852 Alii Dr., Kailua-Kona, HI 96740. ☎ **800/919-8333** or 808/329-3111. Fax 808/329-9532. www.royalkona.com. 440 units. A/C MINIBAR TV TEL. $99–$250 double. Children 16 and under stay free in parents' room. Extra person $15. AE, CB, DC, DISC, MC, V. Parking $5.

This sprawling hotel was built in 1968 right on the water's edge. The location is excellent, on a rocky promontory within walking distance of all the shops and restaurants in Kailua-Kona. You'll enter through an open-air lobby, surrounded by the sound of waterfalls and the salt air of the Pacific. The rooms are spread out over three buildings; 70% have an ocean view, and some are just a few feet from the rocky ocean's edge. The design of the building is based on the sloping Hualalai Mountain, so the higher the room, the better the view and the higher the price tag. (Rooms on the lower floors have bigger lanais, but not such spectacular views.) All units have the same layout, with dressing areas, coffeemakers ($3 for coffee), refrigerators, safes ($1.50 a day), two double beds, and a couple of chairs around a small table. All carpeting, bedspreads, and drapes were upgraded in 1997, though we did recently notice some frayed carpets in the hallways and minor maintenance problems.

There's no white-sand beach, so the hotel has created a saltwater lagoon with a man-made sandy beach. In addition, there's a freshwater swimming pool and a children's pool. The Royal Kona Tennis Club is on the property, and two golf courses are just minutes away. There's open-air casual dining right on the ocean's edge at the Tropics Cafe. Monday, Friday, and Saturday nights, there's a luau and Polynesian show. Other perks include room service for breakfast and dinner, an activities desk, four tennis courts (three lit for night play), and a spa.

Inexpensive

Interested in a B&B? Call **Anne's Three Bears' Bed & Breakfast** (☎ **800/765-0480** or 808/325-7563; e-mail three.bears@pobox.com). Rooms at this upcountry retreat start at $65. You could also try the **Hale Maluhia Country Inn** (☎ **800/559-6627** or 808/329-5773; www.hawaii-bnb.com/halemal.html), an eight-bedroom brown-shingle and lava-rock inn where rooms also start at $65.

⭐ **Kona Billfisher.** Alii Dr. (across from the Royal Kona Resort), c/o Kona Hawaii Vacation Rentals, P.O. Box 39, Kailua-Kona, HI 96740. ☎ **800/553-5035** or 808/329-9393. Fax 808/326-4137. www.konahawaii.com. E-mail islander@konahawaii.com. 40 units. A/C TV TEL. High season, $70 one-bedroom condo, $95 two-bedroom condo; low season, $60 one-bedroom condo, $80 two-bedroom condo. 3-night minimum. AE, CB, DC, DISC, JCB, MC, V.

This is our favorite of all the affordable condos on this coast. It's within walking distance of downtown Kailua-Kona, and the big, blue Pacific is just across the street. (Unfortunately, the ocean here is not good for swimming or snorkeling, but there's an on-site swimming pool, and the Kailua Pier, just a mile away, has a good swimming area.) The property is very well maintained, as the management insists on constant renovations; the on-site resident manager keeps everything in tip-top shape. Each unit comes with a full kitchen and a balcony, and all feature brand-new furnishings (from a major renovation in 1997) and king-size beds. The one-bedroom units have sliding glass doors that allow you to close off the living room and make it into another private bedroom, so for the price of a one-bedroom unit, you can have a two-bedroom place—a real deal. Other on-site facilities include a barbecue area and laundry. Book well in advance, as these units fill up fast.

Kona Islander Inn. 75-5776 Kuakini Hwy. (south of Hualalai Rd.), Kailua-Kona. c/o Kona Hawaii Vacation Rentals, P.O. Box 39, Kailua-Kona, HI 96740. ☎ **800/553-5035** or 808/329-9393. Fax 808/326-4137. www.konahawaii.com. E-mail islander@konahawaii.com. 45 studios. A/C TV TEL. $42 double. AE, MC, V.

This isn't the Ritz, but it is the most affordable place to stay in Kailua-Kona. These plantation-style, three-story buildings are surrounded by lush, palm-tree-lined gardens with torch-lit pathways that make it hard to believe you're smack-dab in the middle of downtown. The central location—across the street from the historic Kona Inn Shops—is convenient but can be noisy. Built in 1962, the complex is showing some signs of age, but the units were recently outfitted with new appliances, new bedspreads and curtains, and a coat of fresh paint. The studios are small, but extras like lanais and kitchenettes outfitted with microwaves, mini-fridges, and coffeemakers make up for the lack of space. Facilities include a swimming pool, hot tub, barbecue area, laundry, sundry store, and tour desk.

⭐ **Kona Magic Sands.** 77-6452 Alii Dr. (next to Magic Sands Beach Park). Reservations c/o Kona Hawaii Vacation Rentals, P.O. Box 39, Kailua-Kona, HI 96740. ☎ **800/553-5035** or 808/329-9393. Fax 808/326-4137. www.konahawaii.com. E-mail islander@konahawaii.com. 37 units (with shower only). TV. $75 double. DISC, JCB, MC, V.

Kona Coast Accommodations

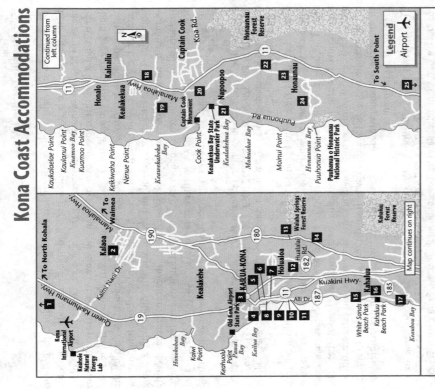

Legend
✈ Airport

Continued from left column

Map continues on right

To North Kohala
To Waimea
To South Point

Kona International Airport
Keahole Natural Energy Lab
Keahole Point
Honokohau Bay
Kaiwi Point
Kailua Bay
Keauhou Bay
Kahaluu Beach Park
White Sands Beach Park
Kahaluu Forest Reserve
Waiaha Springs Forest Reserve
Hualalai Rd.
182 Rd.
Alii Dr.
Kuakini Hwy.
Queen Kaahumanu Hwy.
Mamalahoa Hwy.
Kaloa
Kealakehe
Kealakehe
KAILUA-KONA
Holualoa
Kahaluu
Old Kona Airport State Park
Kaimi Nani Dr.

Kaukalaelae Point
Kaulanui Point
Kuamoo Bay
Kuamoo Point
Kelikwaha Point
Nenue Point
Keawekaheka Bay
Cook Point
Kealakekua Bay
Mokuakae Bay
Moinui Point
Honaunau Bay
Puuhonua Point

Kona International Airport
Honalo
Kalnallu
Kealakekua
Captain Cook
Napoopoo
Honaunau
Captain Cook Monument
Kealakekua Bay State Underwater Park
Kealakekua Bay
Puuhonua Rd.
Puuhonua o Honaunau National Historic Park
Honaunau Forest Reserve
Mamalahoa Hwy.
Koa Rd.

Kona Magic Sands **15**
Kona Seaside Hotel **3**
Kona Sea Spray **16**
Kona Tiki Hotel **9**
Kona Village Resort **1**
Lion's Gate **23**
Manago Hotel **20**
McCandless Ranch Bed & Breakfast **25**
Merryman's Bed & Breakfast **18**
Rainbow Plantation Bed & Breakfast **19**
Rosy's Rest **14**
Royal Kona Resort **8**
Tommy Tinker's Cottage at Kealakekua Bay **21**
Uncle Billy's Kona Bay Hotel **5**

Affordable Hawaii at Pomaikai (Lucky) Farm Bed & Breakfast **22**
Anne's Three Bears' Bed & Breakfast **2**
Aston Royal Sea Cliff Resort **11**
Dragonfly Ranch: Tropical Fantasy Lodging **24**
Four Seasons Resort Hualalai **1**
Hale Maluhia Country Inn **12**
Holualoa Inn **13**
Kailua Plantation House **10**
Kanaloa at Kona **17**
King Kamehameha's Kona Beach Hotel **4**
Kona Billfisher **7**
Kona Islander Inn **6**

249

1-0734

If you want to stay right on the ocean without spending a fortune, this is the place to do it—it's one of the best oceanfront deals you'll find on a Kona condo, and the only one with a beach for swimming and snorkeling right next door. Every unit in this older complex has a lanai that steps out over the ocean and sunset views that you'll dream about long after you return home. These studio units aren't luxurious; they're small (two people max) and cozy, great for people who want to be lulled to sleep by the sound of the waves crashing on the shore. Each studio consists of one long, narrow room with a small kitchen at one end and the lanai at the other, with a living room/dining room/bedroom combo in between. A new management firm has recently upgraded all units in the rental pool, so they all offer full kitchens, new furniture, and new drapes and bedspreads; they're worth every penny. There are laundry facilities on site, and a good Jameson's By the Sea restaurant is just downstairs—what more could you need?

Kona Seaside Hotel. 75-5646 Palani Rd. (at Kuakini Hwy.), Kailua-Kona, HI 96740. ☎ **800/367-7000** or 808/329-2455. Fax 808/922-0052. 225 units. A/C TV TEL. $90–$130 double. Extra person $15; children under 12 stay free in parents' room. Room/car packages available from $130. AE, DC, MC, V.

The package deal here is great: For just a few dollars more than the regular room rate, you can have a rental car thrown in, too, for less than you'd pay to rent one on your own. This budget hotel, located in the heart of Kailua-Kona, stands just steps away from Kailua Bay and Kailua-Kona's shopping, restaurants, and historic sites. The rooms are large and comfy (even if they don't have fancy soaps and extra amenities), but they can be noisy (ask for a room away from the road). You may want to splurge on one of the 14 rooms with kitchenettes. There are two pools, laundry facilities, and a restaurant on the premises.

⭐ **Kona Tiki Hotel.** 75-5968 Alii Dr. (about a mile from downtown Kailua-Kona), Kailua-Kona, HI 96740. ☎ **808/329-1425.** Fax 808/327-9402. 15 units. $58 double, $65 double with kitchenette. Rates include continental breakfast. Extra person $8; children 2–12 $6. 3-night minimum. No credit cards.

It's hard to believe that places like this still exist. Right on the ocean, away from the hustle and bustle of downtown Kailua-Kona, is one of the best budget deals in Hawaii. All of the rooms are tastefully decorated and feature queen beds, ceiling fans, mini-fridges, and private lanais overlooking the ocean. Although it's called a hotel, this small, family-run operation is more like a large B&B, with lots of aloha and plenty of friendly conversation around the pool at the morning breakfast buffet. The staff is helpful in planning activities, and other guests enjoy sharing their experiences. There are no TV or phones in the rooms, but there's a pay phone in the lobby. If a double with a kitchenette is available, grab it—the extra $6 will save you a bundle in food costs. Book way, way, way in advance.

Uncle Billy's Kona Bay Hotel. 75-5739 Alii Dr., Kailua-Kona, HI 96740. ☎ **800/367-5102** or 808/961-5818. Fax 808/935-7903. www.aloha.net/~uncleb. E-mail unclebillys@aloha.net. 139 units. A/C TV TEL. High season, $92–$112 double; low season, $84–$104 double. Extra person $10; children 18 and under stay free in parents' room. Room/car packages, seniors discount, and multiday discounts available. AE, DC, DISC, MC, V.

An institution in Kona, Uncle Billy's is where visitors from the other Hawaiian islands stay when they come to this coast. A thatched roof hangs over the hotel lobby area, and a Polynesian long house restaurant is next door. The rooms are more standard fare, but they're comfortable and come with large lanais; most have mini-fridges (request one at booking if you want one), and 16 are condo-style units with kitchens. It can be noisy at night when big groups book in; avoid Labor Day weekend, when all the canoe paddlers in the state want to stay here and rehash the race into the wee morning hours.

UPCOUNTRY KONA: HOLUALOA

✪ **Holualoa Inn.** P.O. Box 222 (76-5932 Mamalahoa Hwy.), Holualoa, HI 96725. ☎ **800/392-1812** or 808/324-1121. Fax 808/322-2472. www.konaweb.com/HINN. E-mail inn@aloha.net. 6 units (1 with shower only). **$135–$175** double. Rates include full breakfast and sunset pupu platter. Extra person $30. 15% discount for 7 nights or more. AE, MC, V. On Mamalahoa Hwy., just after the Holualoa Post Office, look for Paul's Place General Store; the next driveway is the inn. No children under 13.

The quiet, secluded setting of this B&B—40 pastoral acres just off the main drag of the artsy village of Holualoa, on the slope at 1,350 feet above Kailua-Kona—provides stunning panoramic views of the entire coast. Owned by a *kamaaina* (old-line) family, this contemporary 7,000-square-foot Hawaiian home built of golden woods has six private suites and window-walls that roll back to embrace the gardens and views. Cows graze on the bucolic pastures below the garden Jacuzzi and pool, and the coffee plantation on the property is the source of the morning brew. The inn offers several nice features, like a gas grill for a romantic dinner next to the pool, a telescope for star gazing, and a billiard table to entertain yourself on quiet evenings. It's a 15-minute drive down the hill to busy Kailua-Kona, and about 20 minutes to the beach, but the pool has a stunning view of Kailua-Kona and the sparkling Pacific below.

Rosy's Rest. 76-1012 Mamalahoa Hwy. (north of Hualalai Rd.), Holualoa, HI 96725. ☎ **808/322-REST.** Fax 808/322-7378. E-mail rosyrest@gte.net. 2 apts. (with shower only). **$75–$80** double. Rates include continental breakfast. Extra person $10. 2-night minimum. No credit cards.

Looking for a place to kick back and watch the grass grow? Then head upcountry to Rosy's. Rosy Bartsch has a separate two-story building with two apartment units (one upstairs, one downstairs) in a bucolic setting that's guaranteed to relax even the most stressed-out urbanite. The comfortable apartments (a one-bedroom with full kitchen, and a studio with kitchenette) have such features as ohia-framed queen beds and panoramic views of the Kona coastline. A smiling, congenial hostess, Rosy gives her guests as much or as little attention as they want.

KEAUHOU

Kanaloa at Kona. 78-261 Manukai St., Kailua-Kona, HI 96740. ☎ **800/688-7444** or 808/322-9625. Fax 808/322-3618. 166 units. A/C TV TEL **$175–$210** one-bedroom apt. (sleeps up to 4); **$205–$245** two-bedroom apt. (up to 6); **$245–$265** 3-bedroom apt. (up to 8). AE, CB, DC, DISC, JCB, MC, V.

These big, comfortable, well-managed, and spacious vacation condos border the rocky coast beside Keauhou Bay, 6 miles south of Kailua-Kona. They're exceptional units and ideal for families. They have all the comforts of home, and some that home never had, such as the huge bathrooms with spas, dressing rooms, and bidets. Spacious lanais, tropical decor, and lots of appliances make for free and easy living. Guests get discounted rates at the two 18-hole golf courses at a nearby country club; tennis, watersports, pools, and playgrounds are all at hand. And it's easy to stock up on supplies: There's a supermarket at the new mall just up the hill.

Kona Seaspray. 78-6671 Alii Dr. (P.O. Box 390663), Kailua-Kona, HI 96739. ☎ **808/322-2403.** Fax 808/322-2675. 3 units. TV TEL **$90–$100** one-bedroom apt.; **$125–$150** two-bedroom apt. Extra person $10. 3-night minimum. MC, V.

Great Places to Stay with the Kids

In addition to our favorites below, also consider the **Mauna Kea Resort** and **Mauna Lani Bay Hotel and Bungalows** on the Kohala Coast; **Mountain Meadow Ranch Bed & Breakfast** on the Hamakua Coast; and **Hi'iaka House and Log Cabin** in Volcano.

Note: By state law, hotels can only accept children ages 5 to 12 in supervised activities programs.

Four Seasons at Hualalai *(see p. 245)* This is one of Hawaii's most kid-friendly hotels, offering a complimentary "Kids for All Seasons" program. The activities center features everything from sand-sculpting to kite-flying. The Four Seasons goes above and beyond to make the "keiki" feel welcome, with such amenities as complimentary milk and cookies for kids on arrival, children's menus in all restaurants, complimentary items for infant needs (cribs, strollers, highchairs, playpens, bottles, toys, and car seats), and child safety features. The Four Seasons also offers a game room (Super Nintendo!); a complimentary scuba clinic for ages 12 and older; children's videos; and a host of sailing, snorkeling, and other activities.

Kona Village Resort *(see p. 246)* This is a parent's dream: custom-designed programs to entertain your children—from tots to teenagers—from dawn to well after dusk, all at no charge. There is even a dinner seating for children, at 5:30pm every day, with a special menu, where children can go unescorted so their parents can enjoy an intimate dinner for two later in the evening. The children's activities program is not available in September, when the resort features a month of romance for couples only.

Kona Billfisher *(see p. 248)* This condo complex has completely equipped—and very well priced—one- and two-bedroom units that are great for families. The ocean is just across the street, and there's a great family-style pizza and hamburger joint right next door.

Tommy Tinker's Cottage at Kealakekua Bay *(see p. 255)* Large families—or small families who want a lot of room—will love this two-bedroom, 1½-bath house right on the ocean. The interior is open and airy, and the furnishings can take any punishment the kids can dish out. The house sleeps up to six (there's a sleeper sofa in the living room). Good swimming beaches line the coastline, dolphins swim out front every day, and Puuhonua O Honaunau National Historic Park is just a 5-minute drive away.

The Orchid at Mauna Lani *(see p. 257)* The Keiki Aloha children's program features watersports (from kayaking to snorkeling), Hawaiian cultural activities (storytelling, hula lessons, coconut leaf-weaving, etc.), and just plain fun (face painting, video games, treasure hunts, etc.). Fees are $50 for a full day (includes lunch) and $35 for a half day. The resort also offers family packages—you can book a second room at half price.

Guest House at Volcano *(see p. 263)* If you're bringing the little ones to see the volcano, here's the place to stay. A mother herself, hostess Bonnie Gooddell has childproofed her house ("There's nothing they can ruin," she says), and her guest cottage comes complete with children's toys on the large outside porch and a basketball hoop in the driveway; there's even a swing set. You can take the kids on a hike along the forest trail in the backyard, which cuts through 2 miles of tropical rain forest to the Thurston Lava Tube in Hawaii Volcanoes National Park.

The Kona Seaspray has three things going for it: a great location, a great price, and the wonderful hospitality of the Millers, who own and operate it. It's located just across from the Kahaluu Beach Park, possibly the best snorkeling area in Kona. The prices are a great deal when you consider that the 1-bedroom apartments easily sleep four and the two-bedroom (one-bath) unit can sleep six. This place is not the Ritz (think 1960s décor), but it's spotlessly clean. All the apartments have full kitchens with a microwave and a big refrigerator; you'll also have ceiling fans and cable TV (one unit has a VCR). Laundry facilities are on the property, too. A big swimming pool, surrounded by palm trees, is just outside the front door.

SOUTH KONA
Moderate

⭐ **McCandless Ranch Bed & Breakfast.** P.O. Box 500 (86-4276 Mamalahoa Hwy.), Honaunau, HI 96726. ☎ **808/328-8246.** Fax 808/328-8671. 2 rms in house, 1 cottage (with shower only). $115 double; $150 cottage. Rates include continental breakfast. 2-night minimum. No credit cards. 30 miles south of Kailua-Kona on Hwy. 11, just past mile marker 101. No children under 15.

Far from the crowds and well off the tourist trail—but definitely worth the drive—the McCandless Ranch is a 17,000-acre working cattle spread owned by a prominent old-time Hawaii family, Cynnie and Ray Salley. It's a real ranch, but it's far from rustic. The quiet, serene atmosphere of the high mountain forest, the fabulous views of the Kona coastline far below, and the impeccable ambiance make this pricey B&B well worth the extra bucks. The two rooms in the main house (each with private entrance) are lavishly furnished in monarchy-era (Victorian) style, with lots of rare koa wood. The cottage, next to the 70-foot pool, is a Hawaiian-style residence with kitchen and living room outdoors, under a roof, and a bedroom (inside) featuring an old Hawaiian koa bed frame. The bath, with a huge shower, opens onto a hillside garden.

Inexpensive

Affordable Hawaii at Pomaikai (Lucky) Farm Bed & Breakfast. 83-5465 Mamalahoa Hwy. (south of Kailua-Kona, after mile marker 107), Captain Cook, HI 96704. ☎ **800/325-6427** or **808/328-2112.** Fax 808/328-2255. www.wwte.com/hawaii/pomaikai.htm. E-mail nitab-b@ilhawaii.net. 5 units (4 with private bath). $45–$60 double. Rates include continental breakfast. Rates $10 higher for 1-night stays. Extra person $10, $5 for children under 10. Sixth night free; 10% discount on stays of 7 days or more. No credit cards.

True to its name, Affordable Hawaii offers an affordable perch from which to explore the South Kona Coast. Come share ex-Californian Nita Isherwood's century-old 4-acre farm, which is overflowing with macadamia-nut trees, coffee, tropical fruits, avocados as big as footballs, and even *jaboticaba*, an exotic fruit that makes a zingy jam and local wine. Two small, inexpensive rooms (one with private bath, one with shared bath) are located at the front of the home, on the highway; the recently built wing called The Greenhouse has two rooms with wooden floors, big windows with screens, full private baths, and private entrances. The most unique room is the old coffee barn, updated into a rustic room for two, with a raised queen bed, a fabulous view of the coastline, a private bathroom (with toilet and sink only), and an outdoor shower. There's a common kitchen for guests' use with a refrigerator, microwave, hot plate, sink, and barbecue grill.

Dragonfly Ranch: Tropical Fantasy Lodging. P.O. Box 675 (19 miles south of Kailua-Kona on Hwy. 160), Honaunau, HI 96726. ☎ **800/487-2159** or 808/328-2159. Fax 808/328-9570. E-mail dfly@aloha.net. 5 units (3 with private bath; 1 with shower only). $85 double, $130–$176 suite. Rates include continental breakfast. Extra person $20. Third night half-price, 7th night free. MC, V. From Hwy. 11, turn onto Hwy. 160 (the road to Puuhonua o Honaunau National Historic Park), between mile markers 103 and 104; after 1/2 miles, look for the Dragonfly banner flying in a tree and the sign TROPICAL FANTASY LODGING above the Dragonfly Ranch mailbox.

The Dragonfly Ranch isn't for everyone; some may find it too rustic. But if you want to enjoy Hawaii's tropical outdoors and you're thrilled by the island's most unique architecture—structures that literally bring the outdoors inside—this may be the place for you. The location is ideal, with Puuhonau o Honaunau National Historic Park just down the road and five bays offering great swimming and diving just minutes away. The place itself, with freestanding cabins tucked away on 2 acres of fruit trees and exotic flowers, truly is a tropical fantasy.

Lion's Gate. P.O. Box 761, Honaunau (16 miles south of Kailua-Kona), HI 96726. ☎ **800/ 955-2332** or 808/328-2335. Fax 808/328-2335. www.stayhawaii.com. E-mail liongte@ aloha.net. 3 units (1 with private bath). $65–$80 double. Rates include full breakfast. Extra person $15. 10% discount after 7 nights. MC. V. From Hwy. 11, turn right after the 105 mile marker; follow the driveway for 1/4 mile to the house.

Located on a beautifully landscaped working macadamia-nut and coffee farm, this two-story house features one guest room upstairs (with private bath down the hall), and two that share a bath downstairs. The downstairs rooms have a private entrance and share a large lanai with a hot tub, a common area with TV, refrigerator, microwave, and barbecue. (Guests in the upstairs room have access to these amenities, but we suggest asking for a downstairs room, where the lanai and hot tub are just steps away.) Hosts Bill and Diane Shriner opened their B&B in 1993 as a complement to their 10-acre farm; their secluded country home, well off the main highway, is convenient to beaches and about a 30-minute drive to Kailua-Kona.

Manago Hotel. P.O. Box 145, Captain Cook, HI 96704. ☎ **808/323-2642.** Fax 808/ 323-3451. 64 units (some with shared bath). $25 double without bath, $39–$41 double with private bath; $55 double Japanese room with small furo tub and private bath. DISC, MC, V.

If you're coming to Hawaii for more than just sunshine and sandy beaches—if you want to experience the history and culture of the 50th state—the Manago Hotel may be the place for you. This living relic is still operated by the third generation of the same Japanese family that opened it in 1917. It offers clean accommodations, tasty home cooking, and generous helpings of aloha, all at budget prices. The older rooms (with community baths) are ultra-Spartan—strictly for desperate budget travelers. The rooms with private baths in the new wing are still pretty spare (freshly painted walls with no decoration and no TV), but they're spotlessly clean and surrounded by Japanese gardens with a koi pond. The room price increases as you go up, with the third floor—and most expensive—rooms having the most spectacular views of the Kona coastline. Adventuresome travelers might want to try the Japanese rooms with tatami mats to sleep on and *furo* (deep hot tubs) in each room to soak in. By the end of your stay, you may leave with new friends (it's impossible to meet the Manago family and not become life-long friends), an appreciation of Kona's history from all the stories you've heard, and memories of a few very special days.

⭐ **Merryman's Bed & Breakfast.** P.O. Box 474, Kealakekua, HI 96750. ☎ **800/ 545-4390** or 808/323-2276. Fax 808/323-3749. www.io.com/hawaii/merryman or hawaii-bnb.com/merymn. E-mail merryman@ilhawaii.net. 4 units (2 with private bath). $75–$125 double. Rates include full breakfast. Extra person $15. 10% discount for 7 nights or more. MC, V. From Hwy. 11, make a left at the Goodyear Tire dealer (after mile marker 111) and follow the signs.

Everything about this upcountry B&B is done impeccably: the landscaping, the furnishings, the fresh flowers in every room—even breakfast is served with attention to every detail. This charming cedar home, surrounded by immaculate park-like landscaping, sits above the Captain Cook–Kealakekua area, close to beaches, shopping, and restaurants. Guests enjoy watching the sun sink into the ocean from the large lanai or gazing at the starry sky as they soak in the hot tub. Hosts Don and Penny Merryman make a memorable breakfast, which includes Penny's fresh banana pancakes or Don's famous quiche.

Rainbow Plantation Bed & Breakfast. P.O. Box 122, Captain Cook (7 miles south of Kailua-Kona), HI 96704. ☎ **800/494-2829** or 808/323-2393. Fax 808/323-9445. www.wwte.com/hawaii/rainbow/htm. E-mail konabnb@aloha.net. 2 units, 1 cottage. TV. $65–$75 double, $85 cottage (sleeps up to 4). Rates include full breakfast. Extra person $10. AE, MC, V. From Hwy. 11, turn right between mile markers 110 and 111, just north of Napoopoo Rd. (which leads to the Kealakekua Bay Marine Life Sanctuary).

Sitting upcountry at 1,200 feet, this working coffee farm has two large rooms—each with private entrance—that are rustic but comfortable, with queen beds and hand-painted palm fronds decorating the walls. The cottage, which was formerly used for husking macadamia nuts, has a separate bedroom with a huge two-head shower, a living room, and a front porch. We prefer the bright and airy rooms over the cottage, which was a little dark for our tastes.

For Long-Term Family Stays

Tommy Tinker's Cottage at Kealakekua Bay. P.O. Box 599, Kapaau, HI 96755. ☎ **808/889-5584.** Fax 808/889-05573. E-mail ttinker@aloha.net. 1 cottage. TV. $900–$1,000 per week. MC, V.

For a half-hour beyond Kailua-Kona, the road meanders through coffee country and wild avocado fields, finally arriving at Kealakekua Bay (of "Little Grass Shack" fame), whose underwater sights draw snorkelers on day cruises and dolphin lovers hoping for a swim with a friendly spinner. Good swimming beaches line the coast here and, 4 miles to the south, Puuhounau o Honanunau National Historic Park is a fascinating spot to learn about local history and culture. Perched right on the edge of all this natural wonder is this box-like oceanfront cottage, perfectly located, roomy enough for six, and priced right for families. The interior is open and airy. It's eclectically furnished (lawn furniture seems to be a theme), but the location and amenities—full kitchen, two bedrooms, a sofabed in the living room, and 1½ baths—more than make up for the shortcomings in décor.

THE KOHALA COAST
Very Expensive

Hapuna Beach Prince Hotel. At Mauna Kea. 62-100 Kaunaoa Dr., Kamuela, HI 96743. ☎ **800/882-6060** or 808/880-1111. Fax 808/880-3112. www.hapunabeachprincehotel.com. 386 units. A/C MINIBAR TV TEL. $325–$495 double, from $925 suite. Extra person $45. AE, DC, JCB, MC, V.

This hotel enjoys one of the best locations on the Kohala Coast, adjacent to the magnificent white sands of Hapuna Beach. The Hapuna Beach Prince is a bit more formal than other hotels on the Kohala Coast. Guests, many from Japan, dress up here, some in the latest Tokyo fashions. You won't feel comfortable parading around the lobby and public areas in T-shirt and flip-flops. As you enter the soaring, open-air lobby, the view of Hapuna Beach and the sea beyond is framed like a real-life mural. The building is artistically designed and makes use of fine materials, including natural slate and wood.

The rooms are comfortable, all attuned to that fabulous view and the ocean breezes, though they seem small for a luxury hotel. But the vast lobby area and the sprawling grounds more than make up for it. And the service is friendly and caring, with an unassuming confidence that springs from the Japanese ownership's low-key, hands-on managerial approach. Some complain about the long walk from the lobby to their rooms, but after dinner at Hapuna Court, a short hike is almost a necessity.

Dining/Diversions: The food is uniformly excellent throughout the five restaurants (ranging from Hawaiian Regional Cuisine to Japanese), including the sushi bar (where there's a wide variety of sakes to sample) and oyster bar. In the evening, there's always a local trio singing Hawaiian songs in the open-air, beachfront Reef Lounge.

Amenities: Health and fitness club, 18-hole Arnold Palmer and Ed Seay–designed championship links-style golf course (reserved for guests and residents), tennis pavilion with four Omni courts, pool, Jacuzzis, specialty boutiques, 24-hour room service, valet, spa treatments.

Mauna Kea Beach Hotel. 62-100 Mauna Kea Beach Dr., Kohala Coast, HI 96743. ☎ **800/882-6060** or 808/882-7222. Fax 808/880-3112. www.maunakeabeachhotel.com. 320 units. A/C TV TEL. $325–$550 double, from $555 suite. Extra person $45. AE, DC, JCB, MC, V.

Laurance S. Rockefeller was sailing around Hawaii ("looking for a place to swim," as he tells it) when he spotted a perfect crescent of gold sand and dropped anchor. In 1965, he built the Mauna Kea on it.

After a year-long restorative shutdown, this grande dame is now back in business, with a fresh look after a barely discernible facelift. The swimming's still great, and the food's a whole lot better. But over the years, all the new luxury hotels have eclipsed the Mauna Kea in architectural style (its 1960s New Brutalist style is heavy and dated) and amenities (no TVs—they're available on request, along with a VCR if you're desperate). Still, the beach out front is divine, and the landscaped grounds have a maturity seen no where else on this coast. Also, no other hotel has been able to claim the loyalty of its old-money guests, who keep returning to savor the relaxed clubby ambiance, remote setting, world-class golf course, and old Hawaii ways—the next generation is welcome to find themselves a new and better beach hotel somewhere else. It's the difference between Alan Greenspan and Bill Gates, if you get my drift.

Dining/Diversions: Jackets are required for dinner at The Provençal-inspired Batik Room. Breakfast and more casual Mediterranean/Italian dinners are served at the open-air Pavilion, and lavish lunch buffets at The Terrace (for a complete review, see "Dining," below). All three have live music. Drinks and light fare are served at the beachside Hau Tree Gazebo, which hosts Saturday clambakes. The Tuesday night luau features outstanding Hawaiian music and hula by Nani Lim and her award-winning dancers. There are coffee mugs in your room, so you can trot down to the free coffee-and-pastry bar in the morning.

Amenities: The resort offers fine golf at two top-ranked, award-winning championship courses: Robert Trent Jones, Sr.'s famous Mauna Kea course and the Arnold Palmer–designed Hapuna course. In addition, there's a pool, a spa and fitness center, a 13-court oceanside tennis complex, watersports, horseback riding on Parker Ranch, guided art tours, shops, a beauty salon, free movies, a free children's summer program, concierge, room service, dry cleaning, twice-a-day towel service, and turndown treats.

✪ **Mauna Lani Bay Hotel & Bungalows.** 68-1400 Mauna Lani Dr., Kohala Coast, HI 96743. ☎ **800/367-2323** or 808/885-6622. Fax 808/885-4556. www.maunalani.com. E-mail maunalani@maunalani.com. 350 units. A/C MINIBAR TV TEL. $325–$575 double, $895 suite, $450–$725 villa (3-day minimum), $3,500–$4,400 bungalow. AE, CB, DC, DISC, JCB, MC, V.

Burnt out? Need tranquillity and gorgeous surroundings to restore you back to the human race? Look no further. Sandy beaches and lava tide pools are the focus of this serene seaside resort, where gracious hospitality is dispensed in a setting that's exceptional for its historic features. From the lounge chairs on the pristine beach to the turndown service at night, everything is done to impeccably.

In August 1997, the resort reopened after a three-month and $10 million complete renovation to all the rooms, the lobby, and restaurants. Even the bathrooms were totally remodeled. Louvered doors open onto the guest rooms, which are done in natural tones with teak accents, each with a lanai. They're arranged to capture maximum ocean views, and they surround interior atrium gardens and pools where endangered baby sea turtles are raised for a Fourth of July "Independence Day" release to the sea. The bungalows are posh two-bedroom, 4,000-square-foot enclaves with their own private pool and spa. A shoreline trail leads across the whole 3,200-acre resort, giving you an intimate glimpse into the ancient past, when people lived in lava caves and tended the large complex of spring-fed and tidal fishponds.

Dining: The CanoeHouse is one of the most visually appealing beachside restaurants on the coast, but we found the food and service to be mediocre and the prices astronomical (for a complete review, see "Dining," below). Instead, try the Gallery, at the Francis I'i Brown Golf Course Clubhouse, where island ingredients are prepared with understated excellence.

Amenities: Two celebrated Francis I'i Brown 18-hole championship golf courses, tennis complex, spa, pool, shops, 24-hour room service, nightly turndown, twice-daily towel service.

✪ **The Orchid at Mauna Lani.** 1 N. Kaniku Dr., Kohala Coast, HI 96743. ☎ **800/ 845-9905** or 808/885-2000. Fax 808/885-1064. www.orchid-maunalani.com. 591 units. A/C MINIBAR TV TEL. $350–$595 double, $550–$625 Club level double, from $550 suite. Extra person $50–$80; children 17 and under stay free in parents' room. AE, CB, DC, DISC, JCB, MC, V. Valet parking $5.

Located on 32 acres of oceanfront property, the Orchid is the place for watersports nuts, travelers keen on culture, families with children, or those who just want to lay back and soak up the sun. Born as a Ritz Carlton in 1990, the resort had a dark, European decor that was as out of place on a Hawaiian beach as a fur coat. ITT Sheraton's Luxury Collection took over the hotel in 1996 and remodeled the property into an elegant beach resort, taking advantage of the spectacular ocean views and historical sites on the grounds. The result: readers of *Conde Nast Traveler* magazine gave the Orchid the highest approval rating among Big Island resorts in 1997.

If you want activities, this is the place: The sports facilities are extensive. For cultural buffs, the resort has an excellent Hawaiian program: The "Beach Boys" demonstrate how to do everything from creating drums from the trunks of coconut trees to paddling a Hawaiian canoe or strumming a ukulele.

We recommend spending a few dollars more and booking a room with an ocean view so you can watch that magnificent aqua blue surf roll into the white-sand beach. The spacious rooms feature big lanais (to sit and soak in the view), a sitting area, and marble bathrooms, each with a double vanity and separate shower.

Dining/Diversions: There are three restaurants to choose from (The Grill, the Orchid Court, and Brown's Beach House), all with a casual, relaxed atmosphere (no need to pack your suit jacket). For a complete review of Brown's Beach House, see "Dining," below.

Amenities: Two 18-hole championship golf courses, 10 tennis courts (seven lit for night play), swimming pools and whirlpools, a fine swimming cove, a well-equipped fitness center, excellent beach activities and watersports (including 2-hour complimentary use of equipment), historical sites, walking and jogging trails, 24-hour room service, twice-daily towel service, valet, nightly turndown, activity and car desk, business service center, children's program, and free shuttle within the resort.

Expensive

Hilton Waikoloa Village. 69-425 Waikoloa Beach Dr., Kamuela, HI 96738. ☎ 800/HILTONS or 808/885-1234. Fax 808/885-2900. www.hilton.com/hawaii/waikoloa/index.html. 1,240 units. A/C MINIBAR TV TEL. $260–$460 double, from $650 suite. Extra person $30; children 18 and under stay free in parents' room. AE, DC, DISC, JCB, MC, V.

This is a great place to bring the kids. It's not just another beach hotel (it actually has no real beach)—it's a fantasy world all its own, perfect for families, honeymooners, and everyone who loves Vegas and Disneyland. Its high-rise towers are connected by silver-bullet trams, boats, and museum-like walkways lined with Asian/Pacific reproductions. The kids will love it, but Mom and Dad may get a little weary waiting for the tram or boat to take them to breakfast or walking the 62 acres, which feature tropical gardens, cascading waterfalls, exotic wildlife, exaggerated architecture, a 175-foot waterslide twisting into a 1-acre pool, hidden grottos, and manmade lagoons. The biggest hit—or horror—of all (depending on your point of view) is the dolphin lagoon, where you (if you're lucky enough to be selected by lottery) can pay to swim with real dolphins.

The recently updated, contemporary rooms are spacious and luxurious, with built-in platform beds, lanais, and loads of amenities, from spacious dressing areas with hair dryers and comfy bathrobes to coffeemakers and extensive minibars.

Dining/Diversions: There are plenty of bars and six restaurants to choose from, including Imari, for Japanese cuisine; the award-winning Donatoni's Italian Restaurant; and the Palm Terrace, for a family buffet. For everyday casual dining, try Hang Ten, the open-air café by the dolphin lagoon or the Kamuela Provision Co., out on a prominent point. There's evening entertainment galore, including a Friday-night luau.

Amenities: 24-hour room service, business center, activities and car-rental desk, in-house doctor, American Express Travel desk, and self-service laundry. There's also a 25,000-square-foot spa with cardio machines and weights; three huge swimming pools; eight tennis courts; two championship 18-hole golf courses by Robert Trent Jones, Jr., and Tom Weiskopf; a mini shopping center; a fabulous children's program; and a wide range of activities. You're bound to be entertained here.

Moderate

Elima Lani at Waikoloa Village. 68-3883 Lua Kula St., Waikoloa Village. Reservations c/o The Castle Group, 1150 S. King St., Honolulu, HI 96814. ☎ 800/367-5004 or 808/591-2235. Fax 800/477-2329 or 808/596-0158. www.castle-group.com. 216 units. TV TEL. $99 studio double, $105–$115 one-bedroom suite for 4, $125–$140 two-bedroom suite for 6. AE, CB, DC, MC, V.

Just uphill from the ritzy Kohala resorts is this decade-old two-story condominium complex, located next door to the Waikoloa Village Golf Course (with special rates available for condo guests). The condos all have ceiling fans, lanais, washer/dryers, and full kitchens with dishwashers; also on site are two swimming pools, a sundeck, a hot tub, and barbecues. Shopping is just a walk away, and it's a quick 11-mile drive to world-famous Hapuna Beach. The property is very well-maintained, and the individually owned units are all well decorated with comfortable, practical furniture; some units are even showplaces done by interior designers. The only drawback is that Waikoloa can get very windy; if that doesn't bother you, these units are a real deal.

Royal Waikoloan. 69-275 Waikoloa Beach Rd., Kamuela, HI 96743. ☎ 800/922-5533 or 808/886-6789. Fax 808/886-7852. www.outrigger.com. E-mail reservations@outrigger.com. 555 units. A/C MINIBAR TV TEL. $140–$230 double, $275 Royal Cabana Club double, $365–$765 suite. Extra person $25; children 17 and under stay free in parents' room. All-inclusive rates (including all meals and activities): $389–$449 double, $499 Royal Cabana

Accommodations 259

Club double. All-inclusive rates for children staying with parents in Royal Cabana Club: $104 ages 12–17, $37 ages 5–11, under 4 free. AE, CB, DC, DISC, JCB, MC, V.

Here's the bargain of the Kohala Coast: You can choose an all-inclusive rate, with food, drinks, and activities included, or you can book the room à la carte. Older and more basic than its neighbors, the comfortable Waikoloan has a breathtaking movie-set beach lined with palms and a huge historic fishpond in the backyard, plus a significant petroglyph field and golf course in the front yard. Rooms are small, and some have the lingering odor of smokers, but you can always get fresh air out on the lanai. For larger rooms with more amenities, book the Royal Cabana Club, a two-story structure next to the lagoon. Rooms here have separate living-room areas, oversized tubs, and continental breakfast served in a private lounge. The property also includes a beachfront picnic area suitable for hukilau and other parties.

For dining, choose from the Lava Tube (for poolside burgers), the Royal Terrace (for all-day dining) and Cafe Tiare (for island seafood and pasta, plus vegetarian and low-fat entrées). The open-air Petroglyph Bar is a great sunset-viewing perch. Outstanding golf is available at the adjacent Waikoloa Beach course, designed by Robert Trent Jones, Jr., and the Tom Weiskopf-designed Kings course. Other amenities include six tennis courts, historic petroglyph fields and fishponds, a swimming pool, oceanfront cabanas, a health club, valet, an activities desk, a coin-operated laundry, and concierge.

WAIMEA

Jenny's Country Cottage. Off Mamalahoa Hwy., 2 miles east of Waimea town center. Reservations c/o Hawaii's Best Bed and Breakfasts, P.O. Box 563, Kamuela, HI, 96743 ☎ **800/ 262-9912** or 808/885-4550. Fax 808/885-0559. www.bestbnb.com. E-mail bestbnb@ aloha.net. 1 cottage. TV TEL. $95 double. Rate includes continental breakfast. Extra person $15. 2-night minimum. DISC.

This nearly century-old restored cottage, on a 4-acre farm with goats and a taro patch, has cheerful country appeal with hardwood floors and lace curtains, as well as a four-poster bed (a family heirloom) and other furniture made of rare koa wood; there's also a full kitchen. The host family lives on the property, as it has for generations.

Kamuela Inn. P.O. Box 1994 (Kawaihae Rd.), Kamuela, HI 96743. ☎ **800/555-8968** or 808/885-4243. Fax 808/885-8857. 31 units. $54–$72 double, $83–$185 suite with kitchenette. Rates include continental breakfast. Extra person $10. AE, DC, DISC, MC, V.

The best deals at this rambling inn set high in the hills are the kitchenette suites, which are roomier than the cramped standard units, offer lanais, and come equipped with everything you need to fix basic meals. The clientele generally consists of parents of students at nearby Hawaii Preparatory Academy, a private boarding school.

Kamuela's Mauna Kea View Bed & Breakfast. P.O. Box 6375, Kamuela, HI 96743. ☎ **808/885-8425.** Fax 808/885-6514. www.hawaii-inns.com/bigisle/kohala/maunakea. 1 suite, 1 cottage (with shower only). TV TEL. $55–$65 cottage, $75 suite. Rates include continental breakfast. Extra person $15. 2-night minimum. AE, MC, V. From junction of Hwy. 19 and Hwy. 190, continue east on Hwy. 19 for 3 miles; turn right on Kalake St; it's the last house on the right.

Location, location, location—this B&B has it. Retired Parker Ranch manager Richard Mitchell must've used his ranch connections to get this fabulous property, which borders Parker Ranch's 225,000 acres and looks straight up at 14,000-foot Mauna Kea. The 1,000-square-foot suite features two bedrooms, a full kitchen, a dining area, a living room with a fireplace (handy on chilly winter nights), a covered deck, and a Jacuzzi. The 440-square-foot cottage is a chalet-style studio with a separate, second sleeping area, kitchenette, and deck. Since opening in 1988, Richard has had visitors from 34 countries and 49 states (would someone from North Dakota please stay here and make Richard's life complete?).

Morningstar Meadow, P.O. Box 2396 (3 miles from the center of Waimea, off Hwy. 19), Kamuela, HI 96743. ☎ **808/885-7674.** 3 units. **$85–$95** double. Rates include full breakfast. 2-night minimum or $20 surcharge for 1 night. No credit cards.

Located at 3,000 feet, Dee Dickson's country home has three uniquely decorated rooms—each with special touches that tell a story, which she'll happily tell you as she whips up breakfast. The rooms are comfortable, but it's the food that brings guests back to Morningstar year after year. Dee's breakfasts are gourmet extravaganzas, such as low-fat sausage with fresh sage and pink peppercorns served with polenta slices, topped with pine nuts and basil-grilled green apple slices. Yum!

✪ **Waimea Garden Cottages,** P.O. Box 563 (off Mamalahoa Hwy., 2 miles west of Waimea town center), Kamuela, HI 96743. ☎ **800/262-9912** or 808/885-4550. Fax 808/885-0559. www.bestbnb.com. E-mail bestbnb@aloha.net. 2 cottages. TV TEL. **$135** double. Rates include continental breakfast. $15 extra for 3rd person. 3-night minimum. DISC.

Imagine rolling hills on pastoral ranch land. Then add a babbling stream. Now set two cozy Hawaiian cottages in the scene, and complete the picture with mountain views—and you have Waimea Garden Cottages. One cottage has the feel of an old English country cottage, with oak floors, a fireplace, and French doors opening onto a spacious brick patio. The other is a remodeled century-old Hawaiian wash house, filled with antiques, eucalyptus wooden floors, and a full kitchen. It's the finishing touches that make guests return again and again, like the plush English robes, the sandalwood soaps in the bath, the mints next to the bed, and the fresh flower arrangements throughout. Hosts Barbara and Charlie Campbell live on the 1½-acre property; Barbara also runs Hawaii's premier B&B booking service, Hawaii's Best Bed & Breakfasts, and can set up your accommodations throughout the islands.

THE HAMAKUA COAST

In addition to the B&Bs listed below, other B&Bs in this area are **Waipio Ridge Vacation Rental** (☎ **808/775-0603;** www.e.com/waipio.htm), with studios priced at $85 for two; and **Hale Kukui** (☎ **800/444-7130** or 808/775-7130; www.halekukui. com), with studios to a three-bedroom cottage starting at $95 for two. Both places are in Kukuihaele just minutes from the Waipio Lookout. In Ahualoa, a mountain community a short drive from Waipio, is **Mountain Meadow Ranch Bed & Breakfast** (☎ **808/775-9376**), offering both a private cottage and rooms in a house, starting at $75 a night for two.

Luana Ola B&B Cottages. P.O. Box 430 (45-3474 Kawila St.), Honoka, HI 96727. ☎ **800/357-7727** or 808/775-7727. Fax 808/775-0949. www.island-hawaii.com. E-mail luana@aloha.net. 2 studio cottages (each sleeps up to 4; 1 cottage wheelchair accessible). TV TEL. **$90** double. Rate includes continental breakfast. Extra person **$15;** children $10. 2-night minimum. MC, V. From Honoka's main street, go makai (toward the sea) on Maile St.; take the 2nd left on Kawila St., and go 2 blocks to the cottages on the left.

These cottages are hard to find, but you'll be delighted once you do find them. They're tiny treasures off the tourist trail, at the end of a cul-de-sac in Honoka town. The tin-roofed, plantation-style cottages are newly built in a romantic 1940s style and furnished in rattan and wicker. The 180°-views take in cane fields, the Hamakua coastline, the turquoise waters of the Pacific, the island of Maui across the channel, and some terrific sunsets. Check out the hut housing the laundry facilities—even it has a great view. Your genial hosts, Tim and Jeannie Mann (who live right nearby) provide breakfast every morning. The town, within walking distance, is worth exploring for its Hawaiian craft shopping and genuine, unspoiled old Hawaiian feeling.

Waipio Wayside B&B Inn. P.O. Box 840, Honokaa, HI 96727. ☎ **800/833-8849** or 808/775-0275. Fax 808/775-0275. www.stayhawaii.com/wayside.html. E-mail wayside@ilhawaii.net. 5 units (2 with shared bathroom). $70–$115 double. Rates include full breakfast. Extra person $25. MC, V. On Hwy. 240, 2 miles from the Honokaa Post Office; look on the right for a long white picket fence and sign on the ocean side of the road; the 2nd driveway is the parking lot.

Jackie Horne's restored Hamakua Sugar supervisor's home, built in 1938, sits nestled among fruit trees and surrounded with sweet-smelling ginger, fragile orchids, and blooming birds of paradise. The comfortable house, done in old Hawaii style, abounds with thoughtful touches, such as the help-yourself tea-and-cookies bar with 26 different kinds of tea. A sunny lanai with hammocks overlooks a yard lush with five kinds of banana trees plus lemon, lime, tangerine, and avocado trees; a cliffside gazebo has views of the ocean 600 feet below. There are five vintage rooms to choose from: Our favorite is the master bedroom suite (dubbed the "bird's eye" room) with double doors that open onto the deck; we also love the Library Room, which has an ocean view, hundreds of books, and a skylight in the shower. Jackie's friendly hospitality and excellent breakfasts (such as pesto scrambled eggs with blueberry muffins) really round out the experience.

HILO

Just outside Hilo is a terrific B&B, **Lihi Kai** (☎ **808/935-7865**), a beautifully designed house with mahogany floors. Perched on the edge of a cliff that has a beautiful wide-angle view of Hilo Bay, it offers rooms for just $55 double.

Dolphin Bay Hotel. 333 Iliahi St., Hilo, HI 96720. ☎ **808/935-1466.** Fax 808/935-1523. E-mail johnhilo@gte.net. 18 units. TV TEL. $59–$89 double. Extra person $10. MC, V. From Hwy. 19, turn makai (toward the ocean) on Hwy. 200 (Waianuenue St.), then right on Pueeo St.; go over the bridge, and turn left on Iliahi St.

This two-story motel-like building, on a rise four blocks from downtown, is a clean, family-run property that offers good value in a quiet garden setting: Ripe starfruit hang from the trees, flowers abound, and there's a jungly trail by a stream. The tidy concrete-block apartments are small and often breezeless, but they're equipped with ceiling fans and jalousie windows. Rooms are brightly painted and outfitted with rattan furniture and Hawaiian prints. There are no phones in the rooms, but there's one in the lobby. Children are welcome, and you're welcome to all the papayas and bananas you can eat.

Hawaii Naniloa Hotel. 93 Banyan Dr. (off Hwy. 19), Hilo, HI 96720. ☎ **800/367-5360** or 808/969-3333. Fax 808/969-6622. 325 units. A/C TV TEL. $100–$240 double. Rates include airport shuttle. AE, JCB, MC, V.

This nine-story hotel on Hilo Bay dates from 1929, but it had a major renovation in 1991, and there are ongoing upgrades. Hilo's biggest hotel has nice rooms with lanais and enjoys a quiet, leafy Banyan Drive setting with the ocean just across the road. There are restaurants and lounges, pools, a spa, and shops. Popular with Asian tour groups, it's a generally characterless place to stay but, in terms of comfort and amenities, one of the best that Hilo has to offer.

The rack rates here are on the high side, but it's usually pretty easy to secure one of the cheapest rooms (which have only partial ocean views and no balconies). The general manager told us that getting a $100 room is usually not a problem, except during Merrie Monarch Festival (the week after Easter).

Hilo Hawaiian Hotel. 71 Banyan Dr., Hilo, HI 96720. ☎ **800/367-5004** or 808/935-9361. Fax 808/961-9642. 285 units. A/C TV TEL. **$107-$337** double. Rates include free rental car or 6th night free, with some date restrictions. AE, DISC, MC, V.

Overlooking Coconut Island on picturesque Hilo Bay, this eight-story waterfront crescent, built in 1974, features comfortable rooms (last renovated in 1993). Ask for one with an ocean view. This hotel and its neighbors share a gracious setting on Banyan Drive, which curves away from town into a park and is lined with shady, giant banyan trees planted by visiting celebrities, primarily in the 1930s. There's a pool, as well as shops, a restaurant, and a lounge.

Maureen's Bed and Breakfast. 1896 Kalanianaole Ave. (2.7 miles from Ken's House of Pancakes), Hilo, HI 96720. ☎ **800/935-9018** or 808/935-9018. Fax 808/961-5596. E-mail maureen@ilhawaii.net. 6 units (none with private bath). **$65** double. Rates include full breakfast. 10% discount for 7 nights or more. No credit cards. No children under 7.

The old Saiki mansion, built in 1932 and totally restored by Maureen Goto, is again the grande dame it was always meant to be. Staying here is like taking a trip back in time. The house, constructed of redwood and cedar, features arched windows and doorways and a formal Japanese tea room; large lanais overlook koi ponds and the carefully maintained botanical gardens. Maureen's is comfortable and conveniently located, across the street from good swimming and snorkeling and just 10 minutes from downtown Hilo.

★ **Shipman House Bed and Breakfast.** 131 Kaiulani St., Hilo, HI 96720. ☎ **800/627-8447** or 808/934-8002. Fax 808/935-8002. www.hilo-hawaii.com. E-mail bighouse@bigisland.com. 5 units. **$140-$160** double. Rate includes continental breakfast and afternoon tea. Extra person $25. AE, MC, V. From Hwy. 19, take Waianuenue Ave.; turn right on Kaiulani St. and go 1 block over the wooden bridge; look for the large house on the left.

Built in 1900, the Shipman House is on both the national and state registers of historic places; the nearly century-old Victorian mansion has been totally restored by the great-granddaughter of the original owner and her husband, Barbara and Gary Andersen. Despite the home's historic appearance, Barbara has made sure that its conveniences are strictly 21st century: full baths with all the amenities, ceiling fans, and small refrigerators in each room. (TVs are available on request.) In addition to a large continental breakfast buffet, Barbara serves afternoon tea with nibbles on the enclosed lanai.

Uncle Billy's Hilo Bay Hotel. 87 Banyan Dr. (off Hwy. 19), Hilo, HI 96720. ☎ **800/367-5102** or 808/961-5818. Fax 808/935-7903. Unclebilly.com. E-mail unclebillys@aloha.net. 144 units. A/C TV TEL. High season, **$92-$112** double, **$94-$104** studio with kitchenette; low season, **$84-$104** double, **$92-$112** studio with kitchenette, **$102-$112** studio with kitchenette. Car/room packages and special senior rates available. Extra person $10. Children 18 and under stay free in parents' room. AE, DC, DISC, MC, V.

Uncle Billy's is the least-expensive place to stay along Hilo's hotel row, Banyan Drive. This is an oceanfront budget hotel in a dynamite location, and the car/room package offers an extra incentive to stay here. You enter via a tiny lobby, gussied up in Polynesian style; it's slightly overdone, with sagging fishnets and tapa-covered walls. The rooms are simple: bed, TV, phone, closet, and soap and clean towels in the bathroom—that's about it. The walls seem paper thin, and it can get very noisy at night (you may want to bring ear plugs), but at rates like these, you're still getting more than your money's worth. There's a pool on the property, and kitchenette studios are available.

HAWAII VOLCANOES NATIONAL PARK & VOLCANO VILLAGE

A great B&B on the way to Volcano is **Bed & Breakfast Mt. View** (☎ 808/968-6868; www.bbmtview.com), a 7,000-square-foot home overlooking a 10,000-square-foot fishpond (on a clear day, you can see Mauna Kea's reflection in the pond). Rooms start at $75.

Other excellent choices in Volcano include the ✪ **Guest House at Volcano** (☎ 808/967-7775; fax 808/967-8295; e-mail cmaplan@interpac.net), a terrific cottage that rents for just $60 double. It's an ideal place to stay with the kids: completely childproofed and complete with toys, a basketball hoop, and a swing set. The upstairs bedroom has two twin beds and one queen, and the couch in the living room pulls out into a double bed. The room is outfitted with a full kitchen. There's even a forest trail in the backyard, which goes all the way through 2 miles of tropical rain forest to the Thurston Lava Tube in Hawaii Volcanoes National Park.

Hiiaka House (☎ 800/985-7104 or 808/985-7104) is a two-bedroom, 1930s home that sleeps up to six. It's tucked in the rain forest and rents for $95 double. The **Log Cabin** (☎ 808/262-7249) is a century-old ohia log cabin for the young at heart, starting at $100. And there's the **Volcano Teapot Cottage** (☎ 800/670-8345 or 808/967-7112), a quaint, renovated, 1914, two-bedroom cottage decorated with one-of-a-kind antiques and renting for $105 double.

Expensive

✪ **Chalet Kilauea: The Inn at Volcano.** P.O. Box 998 (off Hwy. 11, ¾ mile up Wright Rd.), Volcano, HI 96785. ☎ **800/937-7786** or 808/967-7786. Fax 800/577-1849 or 808/967-8660. www.volcano-hawaii.com. E-mail reservations@volcano-hawaii.com. 6 units. TV TEL. $125–$395 double. Rates include full gourmet breakfast and afternoon tea. Extra person $15. AE, DC, DISC, JCB, MC, V.

Owner Brian Crawford and his wife, Lisha, may be the Conrad Hiltons of Volcano. Theirs was the first small property to get the prestigious triple Diamond Award from AAA. From the personal service at check-in to the afternoon tea to the rich two-course breakfast served on the finest china and linens, this place is worth the price (though it may be a bit formal for some). Nestled in the forest just a mile from Hawaii Volcanoes National Park, the inn features two rooms, three suites, and a separate elegant mountain cottage. The units are fabulous and filled with the art and furniture the Crawfords have collected during their travels. Most rooms have private hot tubs, but there's also a giant hot tub on the grounds.

In addition to this luxury B&B and two others (see below), Brian and Lisha Crawford also have six vacation homes ranging in price from $125 a night for a two-bedroom cottage to $225 a night for a house that sleeps six. The homes are spacious; nicely furnished; and all have private phones, TV/VCRs, and fully equipped kitchens.

Moderate

✪ **Carson's Volcano Cottage.** P.O. Box 503 (in Mauna Loa Estates, 501 Sixth St., at Jade Ave.), Volcano, HI 96785. ☎ **800/845-5282** or 808/967-7683. Fax 808/967-8094. www.carsonscottage.com. 3 units (with showers only). 3 cottages (1 with shower only). $85–$165 double. Rates include full breakfast. Extra person $15. AE, DISC, MC, V.

In 1988, friends of Tom and Brenda Carson came to visit from Alaska, so the Carsons renovated their 1925 tin-roofed cabin, under giant tree ferns in the rain forest, to accommodate them. That was the beginning of the Carson's B&B business, and today they're quite a success story. They have six units on their 1½ acres in the rain forest: three guest rooms with private entrances and private baths, done in Oriental, 1940s, and 1950s Hawaiiana themes; and three cottages, each with its own décor (Asian, American, and a quaint Victorian English cottage). The property has a hot tub tucked under the ferns for guests' use. Tom and Brenda serve a hearty breakfast in your room and leave you to your own amusement.

Kilauea Lodge. P.O. Box 116 (1 block off Hwy. 11 on Volcano Rd.), Volcano, HI 96785. ☎ **808/967-7366.** Fax 808/967-7367. www.planet-hawaii.com/k-lodge. E-mail k-lodge@aloha.net. 12 units, 1 cottage. $105–$145 double. Rates include full breakfast. Extra person $15. AE, MC, V.

This crowded and popular roadside lodge, built in 1938 as a YMCA camp, sits on 10 acres of wooded and landscaped vistas, has rooms offering heating systems and hot-towel warmers (Volcano Village is located at 3,700 feet), beautiful art on the walls, fresh flowers, and, in some rooms, fireplaces. There's also a 1929 two-bedroom cottage with a fireplace and a full kitchen just a couple of blocks down the street. A full gourmet breakfast is served to guests only at the restaurant, which is open to the public for dinner.

The Lodge at Volcano. P.O. Box 998, Volcano, HI 96785. ☎ **800/736-7140** or 808/967-7244. Fax 800/577-1849 or 808/967-8660. www.volcano-hawaii.com. E-mail reservations@volcano-hawaii.com. 6 units. $85–$125 double. Rates include continental breakfast. Extra person $15. AE, DC, DISC, JCB, MC, V. From Hwy. 11, follow Wright Rd. for 2.2 miles; turn right on Ama Uma U St.; go 1.4 miles, and turn left into the driveway marked HALANA FARMS.

Another property belonging to Brian and Lisha Crawford of Chalet Kilauea (see above), the Lodge at Volcano meets their usual standards of comfortable accommodations and excellent service. The large lodge, located on 30 acres, is geared toward travelers who don't want the expense of a gourmet breakfast, but still desire tasteful, tranquil surroundings. This 4,300-foot ranch-style house has a wraparound covered lanai (with an eight-person Jacuzzi), a big living room with a fireplace, and a separate game room with TV/VCR and video library. The guest rooms range from a queen room to a two-bedroom suite (perfect for families). Brian landscaped 2 acres immediately surrounding the lodge, but he has left the other 28 acres in their natural state as virgin rain forest; they have a myriad of trails for exploring. A continental breakfast buffet is served in the mornings.

Inexpensive

Hale Ohia Cottages. P.O. Box 758 (Hale Ohia Rd., off Hwy. 11), Volcano, HI 96785. ☎ **800/455-3803** or 808/967-7986. Fax 808/967-8610. www.sugarnet.com/haleohia. E-mail haleohia@bigisland.com. 3 units, 3 cottages. $75–$105 double. Rates include continental breakfast. Extra person $15. CB, DC, DISC, MC, V.

Take a step back in time to the 1930s. You have the choice of three suites, all with private entrances, including one located in the main residence. There are also three guest cottages, ranging from one bedroom to three. The surrounding botanical gardens, groomed in the 1930s by a resident Japanese gardener who retained the natural volcanic terrain but gently tamed the flora into soothing shapes and designs, contributes to the overall tranquil ambiance of the estate. The lush grounds are just a mile from Hawaii Volcanoes National Park.

✪ **Volcano Bed & Breakfast.** P.O. Box 998 (on Keonelehua St., off Hwy. 11 on Wright Rd.), Volcano, HI 96785. ☎ **800/736-7140** or 808/967-7779. Fax 800/577-1849 or 808/967-8660. www.volcano-hawaii.com. E-mail reservations@volcano-hawaii.com. 6 units (none with private bath). $45–$65 double. Rates include continental breakfast. Extra person $15. AE, DC, DISC, JCB, MC, V. From Hwy. 11, turn north onto Wright Rd.; go ½ mile; turn left on Keonelehua St.; the B&B is the 5th driveway on the right.

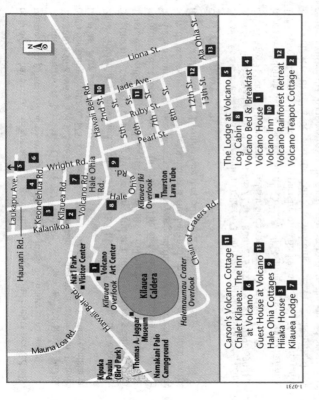

Volcano Area Accommodations

Carson's Volcano Cottage **11**
Chalet Kilauea: The Inn at Volcano **6**
Guest House at Volcano **13**
Hale Ohia Cottages **9**
Hiiaka House **3**
Kilauea Lodge **7**
The Lodge at Volcano **5**
Log Cabin **8**
Volcano Bed & Breakfast **4**
Volcano House **1**
Volcano Inn **10**
Volcano Rainforest Retreat **12**
Volcano Teapot Cottage **2**

It's not as luxurious as Chalet Kilauea (see above), but this B&B (also owned by Brian and Lisha Crawford) is comfortable, clean, quiet, and quite a bargain. Situated on a beautifully landscaped ¾ acre, this restored 1912 historic home is charming. The rooms are small, but Brian and Lisha have made sure that they're clean and inviting; all share bathrooms. The common rooms include a living room with TV (with VCR) and a piano, a reading room, and a sunroom. Hawaii Volcanoes National Park is just 5 minutes away.

Volcano House. P.O. Box 53 (Hawaii Volcanoes National Park), HI 96785. ☎ **808/ 967-7321.** Fax 808/967-8429. 42 units. TEL. $79–$105 double. AE, DC, DISC, JCB, MC, V.

Location, location, location: This old hotel's got it—and that's about all. On the edge of Halemaumau's bubbling crater, this mountain lodge, which evolved out of a grass lean-to in 1865, is Hawaii's oldest visitor accommodation. While its edgy view of the crater is still an awesome sight, the hotel has seen better days. The improved rooms have native koa-wood furniture, but service is inconsistent, and the lobby and public rooms look forlorn. This historic hotel deserves better. A novel treat: Rooms are heated with volcanic steam. Drawbacks: The lodge is a major tour bus lunch stop. The food is edible but forgettable; you might want to stop for ohelo berry pie and coffee (or something stronger) at Uncle George's Lounge and bring it back to enjoy in front of the eerie crater.

Volcano Inn. Jade Ave./2nd St, Volcano. For reservations, write to 200 Kanoelehua Ave., Suite 103-301, Hilo, HI 96720. ☎ **800/628-3876** or 808/967-7773. Fax 808/967-8067. www.commercial-directory.com/volcano. E-mail volcinn@aloha.net. 5 units (2 with shower only), 1 two-bedroom house. $55–$80 double, $95 for 4 in house. MC, V.

Surrounded by trees, the Volcano Inn is the place to go for peace and quiet. All the units have exposed-beam ceilings and large windows overlooking a fern-tree forest. Cooking facilities in the variety of accommodations range from a breakfast bar to fully equipped kitchens. The one-bedroom cottage is perfect for families with children; not only does it have twin beds and a sleeping sofa in the living room, but it's stocked with puzzles and games. Volcano's two grocery stores are just a 5-minute drive away.

Volcano Rainforest Retreat. P.O. Box 957 (12th St., off Jade Ave.), Volcano, HI 96785. ☎ **800/550-8696** or 808/985-8696. E-mail volcanorainforest@naturalhawaii.com. 1 studio (with half bath), 1 cottage. $75 double studio, $95 double cottage. Rates include continental breakfast. Extra person $15. No credit cards.

Peter Golden is a home and land designer, and his wife, Kathleen, is a counselor; together they created a charming guest cottage and an unusual octagon studio on their 1-acre, fern-filled property. The guest cottage has a full kitchen, a sleeping loft, and a bathroom that looks right into the jungle. The eight-sided studio started out as a mediation house, but once guests saw it, they begged the Goldens to rent it out. The only drawback to this unique building is the half-bath, but next door, open to the forest, is a hand-crafted Japanese *furo* (hot tub) with an outdoor shower.

SOUTH POINT

Becky's Bed & Breakfast at Naalehu. P.O. Box 673 (on Hwy. 11 in Naalehu Village, across from the Texaco Station), Naalehu, HI 96772. ☎ **800/235-1233** or 808/929-9690. Fax 808/929-9690. 3 units. TV. $60 double. Rates include continental breakfast. MC, V.

If you're exploring the Big Island's South Coast, your evening respite at this charming 1937 restored doctor's home will be a pleasant one. Becky and Chuck McLinn traded Alaska glaciers for volcanoes and the chance to welcome guests to Naalehu, a sleepy country village that happens to be the southernmost town in the United States. The rooms are fresh and comfy, and the McLinns are friendly country folks. Becky's is 64 miles south of Hilo and 56 miles south of Kailua-Kona on Hwy. 11—a perfect midway point for bicyclists on Circle Island treks.

⭐ **Bougainvillea Bed & Breakfast.** P.O. Box 6045, Ocean View, HI 96737. ☎ **800/688-1763** or 808/929-7089. Fax 808/929-7089. E-mail peaceful@interpac.net. 4 units. $59 double. Rates include full breakfast. Extra person $15. 3% extra for credit cards. AE, CB, DC, DISC, MC, V.

Don and Marie Jean Nitsche bought this 3-acre property in the Hawaiian Rancho subdivision of Ocean View and had a *Field of Dreams* experience: They decided that if they built a bed-and-breakfast, people would come. Where some people just saw lava, the Nitsches saw the ancient Hawaiian path that went from the mountain to the sea. So they built. And out of the lava came gardens—first colorful bougainvillea, then flowers, a pineapple patch, then a fishpond to add to the pool and hot tub. A satellite for TV reception was added. Word got out. Marie's breakfast—her secret-recipe banana-nut pancakes, plus sausage, fruit, and coffee—drew people from all over. Things got so good, they had to add more rooms (all with their own private entrances) and expand the living room (complete with TV/VCR and video library) and dining room (guests usually take their breakfast plates and sit on the lanai to watch the ocean view).

⭐ **South Point Banyan Tree House.** At Hwy. 11 and Piano St., Waiohinu, HI. c/o Hale Kukui, P.O. Box 5044, Honokaa, HI 96727. ☎ **800/444-7130** or 808/775-7130. Fax 808/775-7130. E-mail banyan@halekukui.com. 1 cottage. $95 double, $120 for 4. 2-night minimum stay. MC, V.

Honeymooners (or any romantic couple) looking for an exotic place to nest will find it in this treehouse, which comes complete with see-through roof that lets the outside in and a comfy-just-for-two hot tub on the wraparound deck. Located next door to Kauahaao Church, a classic Missionary-era church (1841) in the quaint little village of Waiohinu, this guest house (completed in 1996) is nestled inside a huge Chinese banyan tree. The designer studio features a clear, corrugated roof that gives it an airy,

4 Dining

by Jocelyn Fujii

open feeling; a queen bed; and a kitchen with microwave, two-burner stove, refrigerator, and coffeemaker. The sweet scent of ginger brings you sweet dreams at night, and the twitter of birds greets you in the morning. This is heaven.

The Big Island's cuisine is anchored in the island's fertile soil and the labors of its tireless farmers and fishermen. The island has produced its share of celebrity chefs, but it's also known for its home-style flair and, especially in Hilo, its abundance of small neighborhood ethnic restaurants. You'll find an extraordinary diversity of dining choices.

Thankfully, the antidote is just outside the door, in the lava fields and rain forests that provide limitless opportunities for exercise. Every time I visit Hawaii, I sing praises to the kitchen gods as I make plans for the next day's hike, a necessary sequel to the typical day's excesses.

Among the star chefs who claim their roots here, or who have cut their teeth on the island, are Peter Merriman (the visionary behind the eponymous Merriman's in Waimea), Sam Choy (the Kona chef who prepares local food with a gourmet twist), and Alan Wong (who put the Mauna Lani's CanoeHouse on the national culinary map before moving to open his own place, now Honolulu's most popular). They are among the hugely talented artists who have honed and shaped Hawaii Regional Cuisine, giving it culinary muscle and credibility.

Big Island dining has become an authentic island attraction rather than an afterthought. Despite the drought conditions brought on by El Niño, the volcanic soil of the island keeps producing fine tomatoes, lettuce, beets, beans, fruit, and basic herbs and vegetables that were at one time hard to find locally. Along with the lamb and beef from Big Island ranches and seafood from local fishermen, the freshness of the produce forms the backbone of ethnic cookery and Hawaii Regional Cuisine.

Kailua-Kona is teeming with restaurants for all pocketbooks; although most of them are touristy and many overpriced, there are some top-notch restaurants along the shoreline. Kona has everything from outstanding Mexican to sublime pizzas to traditional French, and fresh fish is as ubiquitous as the ocean view.

The haute cuisine of the island—and to some degree, the state—is concentrated in the Kohala Coast resorts, where the 2-year-old Hualalai Resort and its tiny Four Seasons Resort at Hualalai; the Mauna Lani Bay Hotel and Bungalows, the Orchid at Mauna Lani; the Mauna Kea Beach Hotel, and the Hapuna Beach Prince Hotel claim their share of the action for deep pockets and special-occasion tastes.

Waimea, also known as Kamuela, is a thriving upcountry hotspot, a haven for yuppies and retirees who know a good place when they see one. Expect bakeries, neighborhood diners, and one tropical-chic restaurant in Hawi, North Kohala. In Hilo, you'll find pockets of trendiness among the precious old Japanese and ethnic restaurants that provide honest, tasty, and affordable meals in unpretentious surroundings.

In the listings below, reservations are not required unless otherwise noted.

THE KONA COAST
IN & AROUND KAILUA-KONA
Expensive

Chart House. Waterfront Row, 75-5770 Alii Dr. ☎ **808/329-2451.** Reservations recommended. Main courses $16.50–$31. Seafood at market price. AE, DC, DISC, MC, V. Mon–Thurs 5–9:30pm, Fri–Sat 5–10pm. STEAK/SEAFOOD.

The Chart House formula—baked potato, salad bar, steak, prime rib, and seafood—endures in this open-air restaurant on Kailua Bay. The view is paramount, and the filet mignon, catch of the day, lobster choices, and familiar surf-and-turf offerings keep this popular chain restaurant among the Kona institutions. The famous mud pie (Kona coffee ice cream, a chocolate wafer crust, fudge, almonds, and whipped cream) is chock full of calories, but no one seems to care.

Edward's at Kanaloa. The Kanaloa at Kona, 78-261 Manukai St., Keauhou. ☎ **808/322-1003.** Reservations recommended. Main courses $16.50–$30. AE, DC, MC, V. Daily 8am–2pm, 5–9pm; bar open 8am–9pm. MEDITERRANEAN.

If you're willing to drive the 10 extra minutes south from Kona to Keauhou, this stellar spot, located on a breathtaking point at the ocean, could very well make your day. Edward's at Kanaloa (the dining room for the Kanaloa condominiums) is an oasis without walls, where you can look for whales and dolphins and take in the ocean breeze over an excellent ragout of mushrooms, or salmon or shrimp with angel-hair pasta and a pomegranate glaze. Edward's is a good choice from morning to evening. The macadamia nut–banana waffle ($7.95 with fresh-squeezed orange juice) is a hit at breakfast. At lunch, the salade Niçoise is a solid choice, a $12 mound of fresh local greens topped with 4 ounces of fresh, grilled ahi. At lunch or dinner, Fray is known for his brilliance with fresh fish, grains, and mushrooms.

Hualalai Club Grille. In the Hualalai Resort, Queen Kaahumanu Hwy., Kaupulehu-Kona. ☎ **808/325-8525.** Reservations recommended. Lunch main courses $10–$14 dinner main courses $18–$32. AE, CB, DC, JCB, MC, V. Daily 11am–3pm, bar menu served 3–9pm, dinner 5–9pm. PACIFIC RIM.

Although a part of the golf clubhouse, the Grille is much more than a clubhouse restaurant. It's a destination in itself, an open-air dining room with an elevated view of the hotel grounds and the ocean. The food is excellent. Start with the shrimp quesadilla or onion flower in Cajun aïoli, a flamboyant presentation and every bit as flavorful. The menu reflects the produce of the island in its salads: seven choices, from steak to shrimp to Caesar. The brick-oven pizzas (you can see them being created in the open kitchen) are gourmet fare, with toppings of Italian sausage, rock shrimp, Kona lobster, and smoked duck. The lighter lunch selections also include sandwiches and pastas, but dinner cranks up a notch. Pan-seared ahi, local lobster, seafood, lamb chops, and other meats, including ostrich, are among the dinnertime possibilities. After dark, a new attraction unfolds—Hawaiian entertainment, with occasional impromptu hula by friends.

✪ **Huggo's.** 75-5828 Kahakai Rd. ☎ **808/329-1493.** Reservations requested. Main courses $7.95–$13.95 at lunch, $19.95–$36.95 at dinner. AE, CB, DC, DISC, JCB, MC, V. Mon–Fri 11:30am–2:30pm and 5:30–10pm, Sat–Sun 5:30–10pm (light menu Mon–Fri 2:30–5:30pm). STEAK/SEAFOOD.

The view—the best in Kailua—keeps this seaside restaurant humming with appreciative diners. The fresh fish is a Huggo's signature, as is the coral-strewn beach with tide pools just beyond the wooden deck. The tables are so close to the water you can see the entire curve of Kailua Bay, and you can hear the crisp chirping of sandpipers and sanderlings over the gentle lapping of the waves. Nosh on Kona Caesar salad with Waimea greens, quesadillas, burgers, pizza, prime-rib sandwiches, hot dogs, and the fresh catch for lunch. The evening's offerings feature specialties such as ono with rock shrimp and garlic-basic aïoli, pan-charred ahi, pasta, and prime rib.

Kona Inn Restaurant. In the Kona Inn Shopping Village, 75-5744 Alii Dr. ☎ **808/329-4455.** Reservations recommended at dinner. Main courses $12.95–$42.95; Cafe Grill

$6.95–$12.95. AE, MC, V. Cafe Grill daily 11:30am–10:30pm; dinner menu served daily 5:30–9:30pm. AMERICAN/SEAFOOD.

In terms of ambiance, the Kona Inn stands out even in a string of waterfront restaurants. Its large, open terrace on the ocean and panoramic view of the Kailua shoreline are its most attractive features, especially for sunset cocktails and appetizers. Touristy as it is (it's impossible not to be in Kona), it delivers solidly good fresh seafood for lunch and dinner, from sandwiches to grilled and sautéed entrées. The ubiquitous seafood, sandwiches, and salads dominate the Cafe Grill menu; the more upscale dinner menu is heavier on pricier fresh catches, chicken, and steaks. Watch for the daily specials on the Cafe Grill menu.

La Bourgogne. Hwy. 11 (3 miles south of Kailua-Kona). ☎ **808/329-6711.** Reservations recommended. Main courses $18.50–$30. AE, CB, DC, DISC, MC, V. Mon–Sat 6–10pm. CLASSIC FRENCH.

Come to this cozy French inn to satisfy your Gallic urgings. An intimate inn of 10 tables, La Bourgogne serves *la cuisine Française* with simple, skillful elegance. Baked Brie in puff pastry ($8.95), a classic onion soup ($4.95), sautéed scallops ($22.50), rack of lamb in rosemary butter ($30), the fresh catch of the day (market price), venison in sherry and pomegranate glaze ($29.95), sweetbreads in Madeira sauce ($23), and a straightforward selection of French offerings give La Bourgogne a special distinction. That La Bourgogne has stuck to its classic French roots is evident in its carefree dessert selection: crème brûlée, chocolate Grand Marnier soufflé, cherries jubilee, baked caramel apple, chocolate mousse, and other pleasures.

Pahu I'a. In the Four Seasons Resort at Hualalai, Queen Kaahumanu Hwy., Kaupulehu-Kona. ☎ **808/325-8000.** Reservations recommended. Breakfast $9–$23.50, dinner main courses $19–$43. AE, CB, DC, JCB, MC, V. Daily 6–11:30am (buffet 7–11:30am) and 5:30–10pm. FRESH ISLAND SEAFOOD/INTERNATIONAL.

A small bridge leads to the oceanfront dining room, where views on three sides expand on the aquatic theme (pahu I'a is Hawaiian for "aquarium," and there is a large one at the entrance). Executive chef Michael Goodman, who can be seen cycling along the hotel's pathways in his toque and crisp white uniform, loves seafood and features the rare *moi* (threadfish, a Hawaiian delicacy), caught fresh daily from aquaculture pools on the premises. Guests begin their day here with the breakfast buffet, a staggering assortment of omelets, meats, and fruit; or the à la carte menu, which includes lobster crepes, chicken chorizo frittata, smoked salmon, and gourmet vegetarian fare. The middle panel of the dinner menu changes daily and always includes several fresh seafood preparations. On the left side of the menu, Asian influences such as curry, moo shui chicken, Szechwan potstickers, crab cakes, and other delicacies are showcased. Those longing for the comforts of home—lobster corn chowder, warm goat cheese and onion tart, thyme-seared salmon, grilled tenderloin, and roasted free-range chicken—need only to peruse the right-hand side of the menu. This is a considerate menu, thoughtful in its inclusiveness, and as wonderfully executed as the view is compelling, with its surfers, Maui silhouettes, and changeable palette of sunsets and waves.

Sam Choy's Restaurant. In the Kaloko Light Industrial Park, 73-5576 Kauhola St. ☎ **808/ 326-1545.** Reservations recommended for dinner. Main courses $4.50–$9 at lunch, $16–$30 at dinner. MC, V. Mon–Sat 6am–2pm, Tues–Sat 5–9pm, Sun 7am–2pm. HAWAII REGIONAL.

An informal atmosphere, humongous servings, and high-volume local food with a gourmet twist: These are Sam Choy's trademarks. His restaurant has turned a nondescript industrial area into a dining mecca that teems with fans who gather for hearty breakfasts and lunchtime favorites such as fried poke, saimin, bentos made to order, and burgers, Choy's legendary dinners include seafood lau-lau, his signature dish of fresh fish with julienned vegetables and seaweed, wrapped and steamed with spinach in a pouch of ti leaves. Choy's other classics include an old-fashioned rib-eye steak with sautéed onions, Chinese-style honey duck, sautéed pork loin, and unforgettable mashed potatoes. Comfort food abounds here, but keep in mind that the servings, invariably too big for mere mortals, can astonish the uninitiated. Thank goodness there's a children's menu.

Moderate

☆ **Beach Tree Bar and Grill.** In the Four Seasons Resort at Hualalai, Queen Kaahu-manu Hwy., Kaupulehu-Kona. ☎ **808/325-8000.** Reservations recommended for dinner. Main courses $9.75–$15. AE, CB, DC, JCB, MC, V. Daily 11am–8pm. CASUAL GOURMET.

Here is an example of outstanding cuisine in a perfect setting—without being fancy, expensive, or fussy. The thatched bar on the sand is a sunset paradise, and the sand-wiches, seafood, and grilled items at the casual outdoor restaurant (a few feet from the bar) are in a class of their own—simple, excellent, prepared with imagination and no shortcuts. The menu, the same for lunch and dinner, features the MLT (wild mush-rooms, lettuce, and tomato sandwich with roasted eggplant and a hint of pesto), a bril-liant vegetarian take on the BLT; an albacore tuna sandwich that merits space on the postcard home; coconut marinated chile prawns; and grilled catch of the day as sand-wich or entrée. You could thrive on the appetizers alone (especially the sampler for two, with spring rolls, prawns, calamari, and sashimi). The Saturday evening Surf & Sand Bar-B-Que ($40 for adults, $19 for children), frequently sold out, has guests lining up at the flaming grills of steak, ribs, fish, and the abundant heaps of oysters and clams. Entertainment from 5 to 8pm nightly is an added attraction, especially when the hula dancer is backlit by the sunset.

Bianelli's Pizza. Pines Plaza, 75-240 Nani Kailua Dr. ☎ **808/326-4800.** Reservations rec-ommended for dinner. Pizzas $8.95–$22.95; main courses $7.95–$22.95. CB, DC, DISC, MC, V. Mon–Fri 11am–10pm, Sat–Sun 5–10pm. PIZZA/ITALIAN.

Local farmers tout Bianelli's as a pioneer in the use of fresh organic herbs and produce, tastefully assembled on handmade crusts with long-simmering sauces from old family recipes. This is Kona's finest pizza, made with wholesome ingredients and cheeses and no sacrifice in flavor. Everything is fresh: the herbs—straight from the farmers—the handmade dough, the homemade pasta, the organic lettuces and produce. The full bar features an international beer selection, including the local Kona Brew. The sensa-tional Ricotta pizza is dripping with garlic, Parmesan, and ricotta, yet it's 40% less fatty than most pizzas. The house specialty is the Buffala, with scads of garlic and buffalo-milk mozzarella. With three pasta specials every day, it isn't easy to choose. Come with an appetite to this warm and lively scene, and you'll leave happy. Bianelli's delivers everything on the menu except alcoholic beverages.

Cassandra's Greek Taverna. 75-5719 Alii Dr. ☎ **808/334-1066.** Main courses $12.95–$28.95. AE, DISC, JCB, MC, V. Mon–Sat 11:30am–2:30pm and 5–10pm, Sun 5–9pm. GREEK.

Saunter over to this indoor-outdoor café for an outstanding Greek salad, melt-in-your-mouth pita bread, and perfectly seasoned spanakopita and stuffed grape leaves. The choices include scallop-stuffed mushroom caps ($7.95) and prawns uvetsi ($17.95), a Mediterranean fantasy baked with fresh tomatoes, spinach, and feta cheese. Whether you're up for moussaka or pasta, comfort-food casseroles or plain old steak and lob-ster, this is a menu of cross-cultural delights.

Kona Galley. In the Kona Seaside Shopping Mall, 75-5663 Palani Rd. (opposite King Kamehameha's Kona Beach Hotel). ☎ **808/329-5550.** Reservations recommended. Main courses $10.95–$34.95. AE, MC, V. Mon–Sat 11:30am–9:30pm, Sun 5–9pm. SEAFOOD.

The Kona Galley's view takes in the lively, upbeat ocean activities that take place day and night offshore from Kailua Pier. The open-air lanai looks out over the picturesque scene of canoe clubs paddling vigorously and ocean liners and boats coming and going, with strings of lights delineating them against the night sky. The restaurant offers everything from pizza (11 different types) to the very popular Chicken Puna, $11.95 at lunch and $14.95 at dinner. The curried chicken breast, presented in papaya with bay shrimp, and rice pilaf will compete with the shrimp in lilikoi-and-basil sauce and the peppercorn chicken. Think big: The restaurant serves up to 300 dinners a night.

Kona Ranch House. Hwy. 11 (at the corner of Kuakini and Palani). ☎ **808/329-7061.** Reservations recommended for dinner. Complete meals $9–$15 in the Paniolo Room, $11–$19 in Plantation Lanai. AE, DC, DISC, MC, V. Daily 6:30am–9pm. AMERICAN.

The Kona Ranch House remains the favorite of locals, who rely on its consistently good quality and high value. The turn-of-the-century plantation-style decor is as comfortable as the cuisine. For 17 years the Kona Ranch House has welcomed families to the Paniolo Room with children's menus and generous platters of steak, shrimp, pork, ribs, and chicken. There's breakfast, too, with hefty favorites that include eggs Benedict and its crab counterpart, with tomatoes and onions, for $8.95. The family-style dining includes stews, spaghetti, and broiled fish for less than $11, plus sandwiches.

In the wicker-accented Plantation Lanai, ranch-house favorites—complete steak, seafood, and prime-rib dinners for less than $20—are big sellers and still a value, especially when accompanied by the cornbread, baked beans, and mashed potatoes that are as comforting as the friendly service.

✪ Oodles of Noodles. In the Crossroads Shopping Center (Suite 102), 75-1027 Henry St. ☎ **808/329-9222.** Noodle dishes $7–$25. DC, JCB, MC, V. Mon–Sat 10am–9pm. NOODLES.

This Kailua magnet proves that noodles are the universal language. If you're looking for the world's best macaroni and cheese, nori pasta with opihi, wok-charred ahi noodles, and fresh mango or mountain-apple shave ice, this is the place. The former executive chef at the Hotel Hana Maui and the former Ritz-Carlton Mauna Lani, Amy Ferguson-Ota, hit upon a concept that has proved to be a resounding winner: creative noodle dishes from all over the world, served informally and affordably. It's always packed. East meets West here, everything from dim sum to saimin to Vietnamese pho, summer rolls, soba, udon, and of course, pasta. Creative sauces, broths, and eclectic presentations in Ota's inimitable style carry the menu—everything tasty and from scratch, and the freshest noodles available. One dessert—the local favorite, shave ice—becomes an exalted delicacy with fresh local fruits, specialty ice creams, and freshly made syrups in flavors known only in Hawaii. Look for Ota's Paradise Spice Company food products as gourmet gifts to go.

Quinn's Almost By the Sea. 75-5655A Palani Rd. ☎ **808/329-3822.** Main courses $7–$19. MC, V. Mon–Sat 11am–2am, Sun 11am–midnight. STEAK/SEAFOOD.

This is a great place to bring friends straight from the airport as part of their decompression process, because it's pleasant without being overwhelming, and the food has been reliable for a decade and a half. The casual alfresco dining is inviting for families or couples, with a garden lanai that takes advantage of the balmy Kona weather. At the northern gateway to town, Quinn's covers all the bases: steak, seafood, and vegetarian fare. From the pier across the street comes fresh fish, prepared several ways and served with salad, vegetables, and potatoes or rice. Fresh ahi sandwiches are among the lunchtime values.

Inexpensive

For an inexpensive meal, also consider the more casual room at the **Kona Inn Restaurant,** the Cafe Grill (see "Expensive," above).

Basil's Pizzeria. 75-5707 Alii Dr. ☎ **808/326-7836.** Individual pizzas $5.95–$9.95; main courses $4.50–$15.95. CB, MC, V. Daily 11am–10pm. PIZZA/ITALIAN.

Two dining rooms seat 100 in a garlic-infused atmosphere where pizza is king; sauces are sizzling, and pasta is cheap. The ocean-view restaurant is redolent with the smells of cheeses, garlic, zesty sauces, and fresh organic herbs (a big plus). Shrimp pesto and the original barbecue-chicken pizzas are long-standing favorites, and so is the artichokes-olive-capers version, a sort of Greek-Italian hybrid.

Ocean View Inn. 75-5683 Alii Dr. ☎ **808/329-9998.** Main courses $7.50–$10.75. No credit cards. Tues–Sun 6:30am–2:45pm and 5:15–9pm. AMERICAN/CHINESE/HAWAIIAN.

The Hawaiian food, rare in Kailua, is reason enough to come here. The local color is another reason, the quality of food less so. But you can't beat the prices, and the Ocean View Inn is as much a Kona fixture as the sunsets that curl around Kailua Pier across the street. Give it a go if you feel like trading your gourmet standards for serviceable food in a casual and endearing atmosphere. Stew and rice, roast pork, a vegetarian selection, and local staples such as shoyu chicken and broiled ahi appear on a menu with dozens of Chinese dishes. A refreshing change, definitely, from the more touristy waterfront eateries, but don't expect epicurean fare.

Sibu Cafe. In Banyan Court, 74-5695 Alii Dr. ☎ **808/329-1112.** Most items less than $12. No credit cards. Daily 11:30am–3pm and 5–9pm. INDONESIAN/SOUTHEAST ASIAN.

An affordable favorite for many years, Sibu offers toothsome curries, homemade condiments, and a very popular grilled Balinese chicken served with peanut sauce, a few of the items that have kept the place humming since its 1982 opening. Equally attractive are the Indonesian decor, courtyard dining, and excellent *satays* (traditional grilled skewers of vegetables, seafood, and meats), a Sibu signature. The daily specials offer a culinary tour of Southeast Asia. The combination plates (vegetarian, beef and chicken, and other combinations, $11.50–$12.25) pamper all palates, while the vegetable curries and stir-fries appeal to vegetarians. Top off your order with the homemade three-jalapeño, red-chile, or spicy coconut condiment (or all three). Wine and beer are available; no white sugar or MSG on the premises.

Thai Rin. 75-5799 Alii Dr. Kona. ☎ **808/329-2929.** Main courses $6.95–$12.95. AE, DC, DISC, JCB, MC, V. Sun–Fri 11am–2:30pm, nightly 5–9pm. THAI.

Kona's most popular Thai eatery offers more than great curries and spicy salads. Because everything is made to order, virtually any item can be prepared for vegetarians. Most popular are the pad Thai noodles, spicy *tom yum kung* (spicy, sweet-sour lemongrass soup with shrimp, curries (red, green, yellow, and panang), and bountiful salads and spring roll appetizers. Stunning sunset and ocean views are a part of the deal. Patchara Suntharo, owner and manager, grows many of her own herbs, including basil, mint, lemongrass, kaffir lime leaves, and the Thai ginger called *kalanga*.

SOUTH KONA

Aloha Cafe. Hwy. 11, Kainaliu. ☎ **808/322-3383.** Reservations recommended for large parties. Most items less than $7 daytime, $6.50–$17.95 evenings. MC, V. Mon–Thurs 8am–3pm, Fri–Sat 8am–9pm, Sun 8am–2pm. ISLAND CUISINE.

There have been changes in the menu, but the Aloha Café's trademarks remain: large portions, the best carrot cake in the area, heroic burgers and sandwiches, and a mix of items for vegetarians and carnivores. Place your order at the counter and grab a seat on the veranda that wraps around the old Aloha Theatre. The view sweeps down the coffee fields to the shoreline, and the air, if it's not a foggy day, is splendidly crisp and gentle. The cheaper daytime staples include omelets, breakfast burritos, tostadas, quesadillas, and home-baked goods. Most of the produce is organic, and fresh-squeezed orange juice and fresh-fruit smoothies are served daily. Sandwiches, from fresh fish to tofu-avocado, are heaped with vegetables on tasty whole-wheat buns, still generous after all these years.

The Coffee Shack. Hwy. 11 (1 mile south of Captain Cook). ☎ **808/328-9555.** Pizzas $3.50, sandwiches $6.50. AE, MC, V. Mon–Sat 6am–5pm. COFFEEHOUSE/DELI.

With great food, crisp air, and a sweeping ocean view, the Coffee Shack is one of South Kona's great finds. It's an informal place, with counter service, pool chairs, and white trellises on the deck framed by ferns, palms, and banana trees. A cheerful assortment of imported beers; excellent sandwiches on home-baked breads; and fresh, hearty salads made with organic lettuces are only a few of the taste treats. Let the kids order peanut-butter-and-jelly or grilled-cheese sandwiches while you head for the smoked Alaskan salmon sandwich (on whole wheat, French, rye bread or focaccia) or the hot corned-beef Reuben with sauerkraut, cheese, and a tangy Russian dressing. The breakfast pizza is inches high and topped with cheese, juicy-fresh mushrooms, olives, ruby-red tomatoes, and artichoke hearts. Not a bad start to the day, especially on the charming wooden deck near a towering old tree that droops with the weight of its avocados. Next door in the gift shop and coffee-tasting room, you can sample some of the many 100% Kona coffees they grow and sell.

✿ **Keei Cafe.** Hwy. 11 (about 25 minutes south of Kailua). ☎ **808/328-8451.** Main courses $9–$16. No credit cards. Tues–Sat 5–9pm. MEDITERRANEAN/LATINO/ISLAND.

The Keei Cafe is the darling of this coastline. It's the restaurant farthest south from Kailua before hitting the South Point area on the main highway, and people drive long distances to get there. A friendly ambiance, great food, and affordable prices are only part of its appeal. After driving the stretch of dark road, whether coming from north or south, it's quite a joy to see the cheerful lights of this intimate roadside restaurant. When you enter the 30-seat dining room, you'll find a country-style setting highlighted by local art. The menu roams the globe, from sashimi from local fishermen to Greek food to Thai spices and pasta specials. The faves and raves: fresh-fish specials; grilled chicken or fish with authentic red Thai curry; vegetarian black bean soup with warm tortilla, salsa, and sour cream; and pan-seared fresh fish with whipped potatoes and caramelized onions. Everything is made from scratch, and virtually everything is grown or harvested in the Honaunau Valley area—meats from the local butcher, fish from down the street, tomatoes grown down the road.

✿ **Manago Hotel Restaurant.** In the H. Manago Hotel, Hwy. 11, Captain Cook. ☎ **808/323-2642.** Reservations recommended for dinner. Main courses $6.50–$11. DISC, MC, V. Mon 7–9am and 11am–2pm; Tues–Sun 7–9am, 11am–2pm, and 5–7:30pm. AMERICAN.

The dining room of the decades-old H. Manago Hotel is a local legend, greatly loved for its unpretentious, tasty food at family prices. At breakfast, $4.50 buys you eggs, bacon, papaya, rice, and coffee. At lunch or dinner, you can dine handsomely on local favorites: a 12-ounce T-bone, fried ahi, opelu, or the house specialty, pork chops, for $10.75 and less. Manago T-shirts announce "the best pork chops in town": the restaurant serves 1,300 pounds monthly. When the akule or opelu are running, count on a

Kona Coffee Mania!

Coffeehouses are booming on the Big Island. Why not? This is, after all, the home of Kona coffee, and it's a wide-open field for the dozens of vendors competing for your loyalty and dollar. Although I often wince at the plethora of T-shirts and mugs that make up the visual merchandising of the coffee world, it seems to come with the turf. Kona coffee co-ops, offering steaming cups of fresh brew or coffee by the bag to go, are simply everywhere.

The real activity, though, is concentrated in the North and South Kona districts, where coffee remains a viable industry. Here are some names to watch for: **Bong Brothers** (☎ **808/328-9289**) thrives with its coffees, roadside fruit stand, and natural-foods deli that sells smoothies and healthy foods featuring local produce. **Rooster Farms** (☎ **808/328-9173**), also in Honaunau, has an excellent reputation for the quality of its coffee beans. The **Kahauloa Coffee Company**, Highway 11 in Captain Cook (☎ **808/328-9555**), sells its own coffee and coffee beans in a gift shop adjoining its wonderful open-air deli; The Coffee Shack. The deli features honest, healthy, affordable food served on a lanai kissed by cool mauka breezes, with a view that sweeps down to Kealakekua Bay. Stop for a final boost before the long drive down and around the south end of the island; although the deli is fairly new, Kahauloa coffees have been around for 24 years. South Kona also has the **Royal Aloha Coffee Mill** (☎ **808/328-9851**), the largest coffee cooperative around, with 300 farmers; both Royal Aloha and Kahauloa are weighty presences in the coffee world. The **Bad Ass Coffee Co.** has franchises in Kainaliu, Kawaihae, Honokaa, Keauhou, and two locations in Kailua-Kona, all selling its 100% Kona as well as coffees from Molokai, Kauai, and other tropical regions.

In Holualoa, upcountry from Kailua-Kona, the **Holualoa Kona Coffee Company** (☎ **808/322-9937**) purveys organic Kona: unsprayed, handpicked,

rush by the regular customers. It's nothing fancy, mind you, and there's a lot of frying going on in the big kitchen, but there would be riots if anything changed after so many years.

Ted's Kona Theater Cafe. Hwy. 11 (across from the Captain Cook Post Office), Captain Cook. ☎ **808/328-2244**. Most items less than $7, dinners $8.50–$14.95. No credit cards. Tues–Sun 7:30am–3:30pm; Fri–Mon 5–9pm. VEGETARIAN/MEDITERRANEAN.

More commonly known as the Kona Theater Cafe, this place is famous for its made-from-scratch garden burger. I vouch for it. It's phenomenal—all vegetables, a sprinkling of dates, and perfectly seasoned, served with banana chutney on homemade bread. The fresh-fish breakfast is served with scrambled eggs, country fries, and toast—a deal at $6.95. The veggie scramble without the fish ($6.25) combines red/green peppers, Kona mushrooms, sundried tomatoes, onions, and roasted sweet peppers—a gourmet concoction. The limited seating makes this largely a takeout place, and some may call it funky, but the Greek salads, Greek chicken sandwich, and fresh fish steamed with ginger-lilikoi sauce have won their share of fans, as have the specialty teas and fresh-fruit drinks. The owner, Ted Georgakis, plans to open the Kona Theater for events soon, so keep your eyes and ears on this place.

Teshima's. Hwy. 11, Honalo. ☎ **808/322-9140**. Reservations recommended for large parties. Complete dinners $14.95 and less. No credit cards. Daily 6:30am–1:45pm and 5–9pm. JAPANESE/AMERICAN.

sundried, and carefully, precisely roasted. They offer free tours of the coffee roasting and processing, and plans are afoot to build a coffee cherry mill to complement the roasting facilities. Not only can you buy premium, unadulterated Kona coffee here, but you can witness the hulling, sorting, roasting, and packaging of beans from 9am to 3pm weekdays. Also in this upcountry village, the **Holuakoa Cafe,** Highway 180 (☎ **808/322-2233**), is famous for its high-octane espresso, made by the owner, Meggi Worbach, who buys green beans, roasts them, grinds them, and makes and serves the coffee. Her caffeine mecca also serves light fare: curried vegetables in puff pastry, spanakopita, and homemade cakes and pastries, all around $3.

In Waimea, the **Waimea Coffee Company,** Parker Square, Highway 19 (☎ **808/885-4472**), a deli/coffeehouse/retail operation, is a whirl of activity and gets top grades from coffee connoisseurs. Coffee is heady stuff here: pure Kona from Rooster Farms, pure organic from Sakamoto Estate, pure water-processed decaf—an impressive selection of the island's best estate-grown coffees. The homemade quiches, sandwiches, and pasta specials are wholesome and affordable, drawing a lively lunchtime crowd. Island-made gourmet foods (pastas, muffin mixes, dipping oils) make great gift baskets, and local Hawaii artists display their work on the walls.

If by the time you reach Hilo, you're still reaching for that mug, a good bet is **Bears' Coffee,** 106 Keawe St. (☎ **808/935-0708**), the quintessential sidewalk coffeehouse. In this world of fleeting pleasures, Bears' is a Hilo stalwart that has weathered storms and sunny days, good times and bad. Regulars of this sidewalk cafe love to start their day here, with coffee and specialties such as souffléed eggs, cooked light and fluffy in the espresso machine and served in a croissant. It's a great lunchtime spot as well.

Shizuko Teshima is still cooking at 90 years old and has a following among those who have made her miso soup and sukiyaki a local staple. The early-morning crowd starts gathering while it's still dark for omelets or Japanese breakfast (soup, rice, and fish). As the day progresses, the orders pour in for shrimp tempura and sukiyaki; and by dinner, Number 3 teishoku trays—miso soup, sashimi, sukiyaki, shrimp, pickles, and other delights—are streaming out of the kitchen; at $12.25, it's a steal. New combinations have appeared on the menu recently, such as steak and shrimp tempura; beef teriyaki and shrimp tempura; and the deep-sea trio of shrimp tempura, fried fish, and sashimi. Original art hangs on the walls of the elongated dining room. This is local style all the way.

Wakefield Gardens & Restaurant. 1 Rodeo Rd., Honaunau. ☎ **808/328-9930.** Main courses $5.95–$6.95. No credit cards. Daily 11:30am–3:30pm. AMERICAN.

Part of a 5-acre garden and macadamia-nut orchard, this restaurant serves basic lunch fare: sandwiches, soups, and mind-altering desserts. Arlene Wakefield prepares home-roasted turkey and home-baked ham, a papaya boat stuffed with fresh-herbed tuna (featured in *Gourmet* magazine), homemade soups, burgers, and salads. They all lead up to dessert, in which macadamia nuts figure prominently. Key-lime pie, coconut cream, triple-chocolate, macadamia-nut mousse, and the "Mystery Macadamia Nut" pie, made without a recipe after Wakefield dreamed about it, compose the glittering finale.

THE KOHALA COAST

☆ **Batik.** In the Mauna Kea Beach Hotel, Kawaihae. ☎ **808/882-7222.** Reservations and jackets required. Prix fixe $65 and $75. AE, DC, JCB, MC, V. Daily 6–10pm. CLASSICAL EUROPEAN/PROVENÇAL.

It's a room of hushed tones and great restraint, with dark-wood ceilings, sedate (and loyal) guests, and sensitive lighting—a shrine to fine dining. Executive chef Goran Streng is doing a first-rate job of showcasing the agricultural products of the island and his finely honed culinary skills. The artichoke salad—a heart cradled in a mandala of petals, with avocados and tomatoes—is the mother lode for artichoke lovers and one of many standouts on the appetizer menu. Other choices: lobster terrine with salmon caviar and watercress sauce, kiawe-smoked salmon, and ahi tartar. Among the sophisticated seafood presentations are mahi-mahi with tomato-seaweed herb sauce, fresh local flounder in an artichoke-herb sauce, and fresh snapper with Kona mushrooms and lobster ragout. The beef classics (rack of lamb, grilled tenderloin, veal chop) are anything but ordinary here.

Brown's Beach House. In The Orchid at Mauna Lani, One North Kaniku Drive. ☎ **808/885-2000.** Reservations recommended for dinner. Main courses $25–$37. AE, DC, DISC, MC, V. Daily 11:30am–5pm, 6:30–10pm. HAWAII REGIONAL.

David Reardon, executive chef of The Orchid at Mauna Lani, quickly turned this new dining room into a household word on the Kohala Coast. Take your pick from lobster-taco appetizers, mango–black bean crab cakes, free-range chicken in kaffir lime, blackened ahi with wasabi mashed potatoes, herb-crusted moonfish, orange-horseradish–crusted salmon, and jumbo sea scallops cradled in Szechwan pepper. Informal, with an open-air room that takes in the ocean view, Brown's takes full advantage of the Kohala Coast sunsets.

☆ **Cafe Pesto.** Kawaihae Shopping Center, at Kawaihae Harbor, Pule Hwy. and Kawaihae Rd. ☎ **808/882-1071.** Main courses $6.95–$16.95. AE, DISC, DC, MC, V. Mon–Thurs 11am–9pm, Fri–Sat 11am–10pm. PIZZA/ITALIAN.

You can always count on Cafe Pesto to serve fresh organic greens, sizzling sauces on great pizza crust, and world-class dressings. Fans drive long miles to this harborside pizza house for gourmet pizzas, calzones, and fresh organic greens grown from Kealakekua to Kamuela. Lobsters from the aquaculture farms on Keahole Point (south on the coastline); shiitake mushrooms from a few miles mauka; and fresh fish, shrimp, and crab adorn the herb-infused Italian pies. Honey-miso crab cakes, Santa Fe chicken pasta, sweet roasted peppers, and herb-garlic Gorgonzola dressing are favorites.

☆ **CanoeHouse.** In the Mauna Lani Bay Hotel and Bungalows. ☎ **808/885-6622.** Reservations recommended. Main courses $27–$48. AE, CB, DC, DISC, JCB, MC, V. Daily 5:30–9:30pm. HAWAII REGIONAL.

Dining at the CanoeHouse is like living in a Don Blanding sketch—sunsets, stars, softly rustling palm fronds, waves lapping a few feet away from the terrace. In the open-air dining room, a koa canoe hangs from the ceiling and evokes thoughts of the Hawaiians of old fishing and canoeing along this coastline. Corked decanters on the table hold soy sauce and chili water, two staples of modern local culture that Alan Wong, who opened CanoeHouse, thrust into gourmet status. Lobster tempura, baby-back ribs, and nori-wrapped ahi remain CanoeHouse staples, but there are always new surprises on the frequently changing menu. Seafood is a good bet here, but if you'd like a change, try the hibachi-grilled chicken in sesame vinegar, a happy, hearty surprise.

Coast Grille. In the Hapuna Beach Prince Hotel. ☎ 808/880-1111. Reservations recommended. Main courses $20-$36. AE, DC, DISC, JCB, MC, V. Daily 6-9pm. STEAK/SEAFOOD/OYSTER BAR.

You'll work up an appetite during the 3-minute walk from the main lobby to the open-air Grille, but you'll enjoy the view all the way. The split-level dining room has banquettes, wicker furniture, and a seafood menu that covers all the bases: buckets of clams, platters of oysters, crab cakes, ono (wahoo) carpaccio spiced up with kim chee, pistachio-crusted opah, aquacultured moi (threadfish), Kona lobster tempura sushi, and the best clam chowder on the coast. Several types of poke and taro chips made from Waipio Valley taro are local touches that shine. The snapper and crab meat lau-lau is garnished with artichokes and shiitake mushrooms—a hit.

✪ **Roy's Waikoloa Bar & Grill.** 250 Waikoloa Beach Dr., Waikoloa Beach Resort. ☎ 808/886-4321. Main courses $7.95-$13.75 at lunch, $21.95-$26.95 at dinner; prix fixe menu $37.95. AE, DC, DISC, JCB, MC, V. Daily 11:30am-2pm, 5:30-9:30pm. PACIFIC RIM/EURO-ASIAN.

Despite its location in a shopping mall, Roy's Waikoloa has several distinctive features: a golf course view, large windows looking out over part of a 10-acre lake, and the east-west cuisine and upbeat service that are the Roy Yamaguchi signatures. This is one of the stellar clones of his Hawaii Kai, Oahu, restaurant, with the signature dishes we have come to love and anticipate wherever a Roy's sign is seen: Szechwan baby back ribs, blackened island ahi, and at least six other types of fresh fish prepared charred, steamed, seared, and topped with exotic sauces of shiitake miso and gingered lime chile butter. Always in demand as well are the roasted wild mushroom polenta gratin and the four-cheese, sun-dried tomato ravioli. Yamaguchi's tireless exploration of local ingredients and traditions from around the world produces food that is itself a cultural phenomenon. Like all Roy's restaurants, this one is always busy, and the food and service of predictably high quality. There are many vegetarian selections, and we think the view and airiness of the dining room give this Roy's an edge.

The Terrace. In the Mauna Kea Beach Hotel, Kawaihae. ☎ 808/882-7222. Reservations recommended. Sunday buffet $29.50. AE, DC, JCB, MC, V. Sun 11am-2pm. BUFFET LUNCH.

The Mauna Kea introduced the concept of the lavish luncheon buffet decades ago and continues the tradition in this most casual of its restaurants. Sunday brunch is still an occasion, with a cornucopia of salads, gourmet breakfast items (eggs Benedict, fresh omelets, Belgian waffles), cheeses, salads, American classics (prime rib, sautéed fresh catch, roast turkey, sautéed chicken), pasta, seafood (sashimi, shrimp cocktail, crab claws), and local favorites (shrimp and vegetable tempura, sushi). In the bay below, you can watch rainbows dance on the water and carefree bodysurfers ride the perfect waves.

NORTH KOHALA

Bamboo. Hwy. 270, Hawi. ☎ 808/889-5555. Reservations recommended. Main courses $7.95-$20.95 (full and half sizes available). DC, MC, V. Tues-Sat 11:30am-2:30pm and 6-9pm, Sun 11am-2:30pm (brunch). PACIFIC RIM.

I heartily approve of the double pricing on the entrees here—full-size and half-size portions. Serving fresh fish and Asian specialties in a turn-of-the-century building, Hawi's self-professed "tropical saloon" is a major attraction on the island's northern coastline. The exotic interior is a tribute to nostalgia, with high, wicker chairs from Waikiki's historic Moana Hotel, works by local artists, and old Matson liner menus accenting the walls. The fare, island favorites in sophisticated presentations, is a match for all this style: imu-smoked pork quesadillas, fish prepared four ways, sesame nori-crusted or tequila-lime shrimp, and herb-roasted leg of lamb. Produce from nearby gardens and fish fresh off the chef's own hook are among the signs of the good life. At Sunday brunch, diners gather for eggs Bamboo (eggs Benedict with a lilikoi-hollandaise sauce) and the famous passion-fruit margaritas. Melodious Hawaiian music wafts through the Bamboo from 7pm to closing on weekends. Next door is a gallery of furniture and arts and crafts, some very good and most locally made.

Don's Family Deli, Kapaau, in front of the King Kamehameha statue. ☎ **808/889-5822.** Most items less than $5. No credit cards. Mon–Fri 8am–6pm, Sat–Sun 9am–5pm. DELI/ITALIAN.

This is a refreshment stop for travelers, nothing fancy—just a deli and corner store-front. Don Rich's quiches, lasagnes, enchiladas, sandwiches, mesquite chicken, and famous fruit smoothies—passion-guava with papaya and frozen banana—are served across the counter, so you can seat yourself at the tables that face the square where the Kamehameha statue stands. Lox and bagels, giant hero sandwiches, eggplant parmesan, and Reuben sandwiches evoke the owner's New York roots, while the super blue-green algae (included by request in smoothies) beckons to the health-conscious.

ICE CREAM

Tropical Dreams and Kohala Coffee Mill, Hwy. 270, Hawi. ☎ **808/889-5577.**

No longer under a single ownership, Tropical Dreams ice creams are spreading out over the island, becoming more accessible, thank goodness, with no sacrifice in quality. The ice creams at Bamboo, Sam Choy's, the Kohala Coast resorts, and most Kohala Coast restaurants are made by Tropical Dreams. Originally established in neighboring Kapaau, this Hawi store, like the others on the island, sells gourmet ice creams still made by founders Louis and Debby Ann Bleier. Flavors include pikake sorbet, poha (gooseberry) sorbet, white-chocolate mango, passion creme, mango cheesecake, Tahitian vanilla, guava, litchi, azuki bean, macadamia nut, raspberry-papaya, and no less than 11 other mouthwatering flavors. They use healthy ingredients, no additives or preservatives. Sandwiches, hot dogs, enchiladas, and espresso are also served here.

If you're not heading for Kapaau, call the factory in Kawaihae (☎ **808/882-1891**) to find out which restaurants and stores around the islands serve Tropical Dreams.

WAIMEA

Aioli's, Opelo Plaza, Hwy. 19. ☎ **808/885-6325.** Lunch main courses $3.95–$8.95, dinner main courses $11.95–$17.95. MC, V. Tues–Thurs 11am–8pm, Fri–Sat 11am–9pm, Sun 8am–2pm. AMERICAN ECLECTIC.

Most of the breads for the sandwiches are homemade, the turkey is roasted in Aioli's own kitchen, the prices are reasonable, and on Saturday mornings, the scent of fresh-baked cinnamon rolls wafts through the neighborhood. Specialty salads, homemade cookies and desserts, and an evening bistro menu (herb-crusted prime rib, herb-marinated grilled shrimp, mahi-mahi en papillote, lemon chicken, and other simple delights, including vegetarian items) are offered.

Edelweiss, Kawaihae Rd. ☎ **808/885-6800.** Lunch $6.50–$10.50; complete dinners $17.50–$46 (most around $21). MC, V. Tues–Sat 11:30am–1:30pm and 5–9pm. CONTI-NENTAL.

Diners with a hankering for Wiener schnitzel, bratwurst, sauerkraut, Black Forest cake, and richly adorned fowl and meats are known to drive all the way from Kona and Hilo for the traditional German offerings at this chalet-like bistro. The upscale ranch burgers and chicken aux champignons may require siesta time after lunch, but they do have a following. In the evening, complete dinners include sautéed veal, rack of lamb, roast pork, roast duck, and other continental classics. Although heavy on the meats and sauces, and certainly not a magnet for vegetarians or folks on a low-fat diet, Edelweiss has anchored itself firmly in the hearts of Hawaii islanders. "We do not believe in all these changes," sniffs chef/owner Hans Peter Hager. "When you enjoy something, you come back for it." The menu has barely changed in his 13 years in Waimea, and the tables are always full, so who's arguing?

The Little Juice Shack. Parker Ranch Shopping Center, Hwy. 19. ☎ **808/885-1686.** Most items less than $5.25. No credit cards. Mon–Fri 7am–6pm, Sat 9am–4pm. JUICE BAR/DELI.

This wonderful smoothie and sandwich shop has wholesome, high standards; the produce is fresh, green, and varied. All juices are made fresh to order: orange, pear, apple, pineapple, carrot, tomato, and many combinations, including vegetable drinks and spirulina powder to order. Smoothies (Bananarama, Nutty Monkey, Hawaii 5-0) are witty, creamy, and healthy, made with low-fat yogurt milk. Bagels and luscious toppings (pesto, smoked salmon, tapénade); vegetarian chili; and hearty soups, salads, and sandwiches (Thai curry vegetable soup, Greek salad, local organic spinach salad, ahituna sandwich) are guiltless and guileless. Tip: When locally grown Ka'u oranges are in season, they're used for the fresh-squeezed orange juice—the best. Unlike many other operations, mainland fruit is an absolute last resort here.

✪ **Maha's Cafe.** Spencer House, Hwy. 19. ☎ **808/885-0693.** Main courses $6–$13.50. MC, V. Wed–Mon 8am–4:30pm. COFFEEHOUSE/SANDWICHES.

The smallest kitchen on the island—the size of a closet, literally—serves the island's best sandwiches in a tiny, wood-floored room of Waimea's first frame house, built in 1852. Harriet-Ann Namahaokalani (Maha) Schutte, who cut her culinary teeth in a large Hawaiian family before making her mark at Mauna Lani Resort's Knickers, dispenses hotcakes and granola for breakfast, delectable sandwiches at lunch, and cookies all day long. The menu reads like a map of the island: smoked-ahi sandwiches with lilikoi salsa, fresh roasted turkey with mushroom stuffing and squaw bread, fresh fish with Waipio taro and Kahua greens, vine-ripened tomatoes with locally made feta cheese and bread made from Waimea sweet corn. Lunch has never been grander, served at cozy wooden tables on lauhala mats and enlivened with a sublime pesto, tangy with a hint of green olive. At the other end of the room is Cook's Discoveries, but that's another story (see "Shops & Galleries," below).

✪ **Merriman's.** Opelu Plaza, Hwy. 19. ☎ **808/885-6822.** Reservations recommended. Lunch main courses $5.95–$14.95, dinner main courses $12.95–$24.95 (market price for ranch lamb or ahi). AE, MC, V. Mon–Fri 11:30am–1:30pm, daily 5:30–9pm. HAWAII REGIONAL.

What a menu. Although he now commutes between the Big Island and Maui, where he runs the Hula Grill, Peter Merriman has maintained the sizzle that made Merriman's a premier Hawaii attraction. Order anything from saimin to poisson cru for lunch, and for dinner, Merriman's signature wok-charred ahi, wok-seared scallops, lamb from nearby Kahua Ranch, and a wonderful selection for vegetarians. Peter's Caesar with sashimi, Pahoa corn, and shrimp fritters, and his sautéed, sesame-crusted fresh catch with spicy lilikoi sauce are among our many favorites. An organic spinach salad (like most things on the menu, grown nearby), Lokelani tomatoes, goat cheese and kalua pig quesadillas, and his famous platters of seafood and meats are among the many reasons Merriman's is THE dining spot in Waimea.

THE HAMAKUA COAST

Cafe II Mondo. Mamane St., Honokaa. ☎ **808/775-7711.** Pizzas $7.50–$17.25; sandwiches $3.95–$4.50; pasta $7.95. No credit cards. Mon–Sat 11am–9pm. PIZZA/ESPRESSO BAR.

A tiny cafe with a big spirit has taken over the Andrade Building in the heart of Honokaa. Tropical watercolors and local art, the irresistible aromas of garlic sauces and pizzas, and a 1924 koa bar meld gracefully in Sergio and Dena Ramirez' tribute to the Old World. A classical and flamenco guitarist, Sergio plays solo guitar regularly in his restaurant and often rehearses with his group, Adaggio Latino, while contented drinkers tuck into the stone oven–baked pizzas. The vegetable pizza, Waipio, is a best seller, but the Sergio—pesto with marinated artichokes and mushrooms—is the one folks remember. Sandwiches come cradled in fresh French, onion, and rosemary buns, all made by local bakeries. Fresh pasta has been added to the menu, and all greens are fresh, local, and organic.

Jolene's Kau Kau Korner. At Mamane St. and Lehua, Honokaa. ☎ **808/775-9498.** Main courses $8–$20. MC, V. Mon–Fri 10am–5pm, Sat 10am–3pm. AMERICAN/LOCAL.

The poi, made from Waipio Valley taro, is reason enough to go to Jolene's. It's homey and friendly, with eight tables and windows that look out into a scene much like an old Western town, but for the cars. The Hawaiian plate—lau-lau, Waipio Valley poi, lomi salmon, and raw fish—has a firm niche in local lunch plans, as does the tempeh sandwich with all the trimmings. Dinner specialties, including the plate lunch–style "mixed plate," could be mahi-mahi, grilled chicken, or Korean-style kal bi. The splurge item of Jolene's, the $20 steak and lobster, is as fancy as you can get here.

Mamane Street Bakery. Mamane St., Honokaa. ☎ **808/775-9478.** Most items less than $3. MC, V. Mon–Sat 7am–5:30pm. BAKERY/CAFE.

Honokaa's gourmet bake shop serves espresso, cappuccino, sandwiches, and snacks, including a legendary focaccia. Most sandwich lovers on the island have tasted their breads, because the Mamane Street Bakery also wholesales breads and pastries, including its well-known burger buns, to the island's most prominent eateries. Portuguese sweet bread and honey-nut muffins are the big sellers in this easygoing, informal coffeehouse with lower-than-coffeehouse prices: Breads sell for $2.25 to $2.95, but most pastries are less than $1.25. Very Honokaa: no marble, wing tips, or pretense, but danishes to die for.

Tex Drive In & Restaurant. Hwy. 19, Honokaa. ☎ **808/775-0598.** Reservations recommended for large parties. Main courses $5.95–$8.25. CB, DC, DISC, MC, V. Daily 6am–8:30pm. AMERICAN/LOCAL ETHNIC.

When Ada Lamme bought the old Tex Drive In, she made significant changes, including improving upon an ages-old recipe for Portuguese *malasadas*, a cake-like doughnut without a hole. Tex sells close to 50,000 of these sugar-rolled morsels a month. The menu has a local flavor and features ethnic specialties: Korean chicken, teriyaki meat, a great Hawaiian plate, kalua pork with cabbage, and Filipino specials. Hamburgers, on buns by Mamane Street Bakery, are a big seller. Many changes are planned for this roadside attraction, including a large new retail store/coffee bar that will carry Hawaiian crafts, local coffees, and, in a nod to her native Holland and Honokaa's large Portuguese community, European chocolates, Dutch wooden shoes, and fine pottery from Portugal.

What's Shakin'. 27-999 Old Mamalahoa Hwy. (on the 4-mile scenic drive), Pepeekeo. ☎ **808/964-3080.** Most items less than $5.95; smoothies $2.95–$3.95. No credit cards. Daily 10am–5:30pm. HEALTH FOOD.

Look for the cheerful plantation-style wooden house in yellow and white, with a green roof, 2 miles north of the Hawaii Tropical Botanical Garden. This is where many of the bananas and papayas from Patsy and Tim Withers' 20-acre farm end up: in fresh-fruit smoothies with names like Papaya Paradise, an ambrosial blend of pineapples, coconuts, papayas, and bananas. If you're in the mood for something more substantial, try the Blue Hawaii blue-corn tamale with homemade salsa, a garden burger, or the teriyaki-ginger tempeh burger (made with the best tempeh in the world, by Lean Green Foods of Hilo). Every plate arrives with fresh fruit and a fresh green salad topped with Patsy's Oriental sesame dressing. Some visitors make the long, beautiful drive to What's Shakin', several times during their stay. You can sit outdoors in the garden, where bunches of bananas hang for the taking and the ocean view is staggering. The gift shop sells preinspected tropical plants ready to be flown home. Patsy is understandably proud of the charming vintage touches: the old Hawaii pictures, porcelain hula girls, and kitschy accents.

HILO
Expensive

Pescatore. 235 Keawe St. ☎ **808/969-9090.** Reservations recommended for dinner. Main courses $6.95–$11.95 at lunch, $15.95–$28.95 at dinner. CB, DC, MC, V. Daily 11am–2pm; Sun–Thurs 5:30–9pm, Fri–Sat 5:30–10pm. SOUTHERN ITALIAN.

This is a special-occasion restaurant, dressier and pricier than the standard neighborhood cafe or mom-and-pop diner. It's ornate, especially for Hilo, with gilded frames on antique paintings, chairs of vintage velvet, koa walls, and a tile floor. The fresh catch is offered five ways, from reduced-cream and Parmesan to capers and wine. The paper-thin ahi carpaccio is garnished with capers, red onion, garlic, lemon, olive oil, and shaved Parmesan, and it is superb. Chicken, veal, and fish Marsala, a rich and garlicky scampi Alfredo, and the Fra Diavolo, a spicy seafood marinara, are the headliners on a long and satisfying menu. At lunch, pasta marinara is simple and satisfying and rivals the chicken Parmesan as one of the values of the day.

Moderate

Harrington's. 135 Kalanianaole. ☎ **808/961-4966.** Reservations recommended. Lunch main courses $6.25–$14.75, dinner main courses $15.50–market price. DISC, MC, V. Mon–Fri 11am–2:30pm; Mon–Sat 5:30–9:30pm, Sun 5:30–9pm. SEAFOOD/STEAK.

The house specialty, thinly sliced Slavic steak swimming in butter and garlic, is part of the old-fashioned steak-and-seafood formula that makes the Harrington's experience a predictable one. The meunière-style fresh catch, sautéed in white wine and topped with a lightly browned lemon-butter sauce, is popular, but it's not for the calorie-conscious. Lobster, scallops in chardonnay sauce, chicken Marsala, and New York peppercorn steak are among the American classics on this conscience-busting menu. The strongest feature of Harrington's is the tranquil beauty of Reeds Pond (also known as Ice Pond), one of Hilo's visual wonders. With the open-air restaurant perched on the pond's shore, the ambiance eclipses the menu.

Naung Mai. 86 Kilauea Ave. ☎ **808/934-7540.** Reservations recommended. Main dishes $4.50–$8.50. No credit cards. Mon–Fri 11am–2pm and 5–8:30pm. THAI.

Owner Alisa Khongno moved her popular Pahoa restaurant (where Sawasdee is now) to Hilo, where she recently opened a tiny eatery (three main booths, two tables) that fills up quickly on the five days a week it's open. In a short time, Naung Mai has gained renown among Hilo residents for its curries and Pad Thai noodles and its use of fresh local ingredients. The seasonings are excellent, the produce is fresh from the

Hilo Farmers Market, and the chef never precooks the food, so it's reliably fresh and appealing. The four curries—green, red, yellow, and Indian-style—go with the jasmine, brown, white, and sticky rice. The Pad Thai rice noodles, served with tofu and fresh vegetables, comes with a choice of chicken, pork, beef, or shrimp, and are sprinkled with fresh peanuts. Khongno can prepare your curry Thai-spicy (incendiary) or American-spicy (moderately hot), but even mild, the flavors are outstanding.

Nihon Restaurant & Cultural Center. Liliuokalani Gardens, 123 Lihiwai St. ☎ **808/969-1133.** Reservations recommended. Main courses $8.95–$19.95. AE, CB, DC, DISC, MC, V. Mon-Sat 11am-1:30pm, 5-8pm. JAPANESE.

The room offers a beautiful view of Hilo Bay on one side and the soothing green sprawl of Liliuokalani Gardens on the other. This is a magnificent part of Hilo that's often overlooked because it's away from the central business district. The reasonably priced menu features steak-and-seafood combination dinners and selections from the sushi bar, including the innovative poke and lomi salmon hand rolls, ranging from $3.95 per order to $30.95 for an array of four dozen pieces. In the "Businessman's Lunch," you make two choices from among butterfish, tempura, sashimi, chicken, and other morsels, and they come with sushi, potato salad, soup, and vegetables, all for $10.95. This isn't inexpensive dining, but the return on your dollar is high, with a presentation that matches the serenity of the room and its stunning view of the bay.

Ocean Sushi Deli. 239 Keawe St. ☎ **808/961-6625.** Sushi boxes $3.75–$19.95; all-you-can-eat sushi lunch $15.95; all-you-can-eat sushi dinner $19.95; sushi family platters $16.95–$43.95. No credit cards. Daily 9am-9pm. SUSHI.

My goodness, it can be busy. We tried three times before we finally got in, but then we returned as soon as we could. Lines down the street announced the popularity of this tiny take-out sushi shop. Hilo's newest sensation. And no wonder. The sushi is good, inexpensive, and imaginative. Local-style specials stretch purist boundaries but are so much fun: lomi salmon, oyster nigiri, opihi nigiri, unagi avocado hand roll, ahi poke roll. For traditionalists, there are ample shrimp, salmon, hamachi, clam, and other sushi delights—a long menu of them, including handy ready-to-cook sukiyaki and shabu-shabu sets at $10 to $12 a person.

Queen's Court Restaurant. Hilo Hawaiian Hotel, 71 Banyan Dr. ☎ **808/935-9361.** Reservations recommended. Wed and Fri Hawaiian lunch buffet 11:15am-1:15pm, $12.50; Mon-Thurs prime rib/crab buffet $21.95; Fri-Sat seafood buffet $24.95; Sun Hawaiian seafood buffet $23.75, Sun brunch 10:30am-1:30pm, $21.95; breakfast buffet 6-9:30am Mon-Sat, Sun 6:30-9am, $9.25. AE, DC, DISC, MC, V. Dinner buffets daily 5:30-9pm. AMERICAN/BUFFET.

Many of those with a "not me" attitude about buffets have been disarmed by the Hilo Hawaiian's generous and well-rounded offerings at budget-friendly prices. À la carte menu items are only offered Monday to Thursday, but the Hawaiian, seafood, and Dungeness-crab/prime-rib buffets throughout the week cover the bases and draw throngs of local families, particularly the seafood buffet. Hawaiian food lovers also come for the Wednesday and Friday Hawaiian lunch buffet, a deal at $12.50. We can't vouch for the breakfast buffet, but we can for the weekend seafood buffets, which are generous.

Restaurant Miwa. In the Hilo Shopping Center, 1261 Kilauea Ave. ☎ **808/961-4454.** Reservations recommended. Main courses $8-$36.50. AE, CB, DC, DISC, MC, V. Mon-Sat 11am-10pm, Sun 5-9pm. JAPANESE.

Duck around a corner of the shopping center and discover sensational seafood in this quintessential neighborhood sushi bar. A self-contained slice of Japan in an otherwise unremarkable shopping mall, it is a pleasant surprise. Shabu-shabu (you cook your own ingredients in a heavy pot), teppankayi, tempura, fresh catch, and a full sushi selection are among the offerings. The top-of-the-line dinner, the $36.50 steak-and-lobster combination, is a splurge you can enjoy without dressing up. Some items, such as the fresh catch, may be ordered American style. The haupia (coconut pudding)—cream-cheese pie is a Miwa signature.

⭐ **Seaside Restaurant.** 1790 Kalanianaole Hwy. ☎ **808/935-8825.** Reservations recommended. Main courses $10.50–$20. DC, MC, V. Tues–Sun 5–8:30pm. AMERICAN/LOCAL.

How fresh are the trout, catfish, mullet, golden perch, and aholehole, the silvery mountain bass devoured passionately by island fish lovers? Fished out of the pond shortly before you arrive, that's how fresh. The restaurant has large windows overlooking the glassy ponds that spawned your dinner, so you can't be sentimental. Colin Nakagawa, whose grandparents opened the restaurant in 1946, maintains the family tradition by raising the fish and cooking them in two unadorned styles: steamed in ti leaves with lemon juice and onions, or fried. Daily specials include steamed opakapaka, onaga, or parrot fish; steak and lobster; paniolo-style prime rib; salmon encrusted with a nori-wasabi sprinkle; New York steak; and shrimp. The fried aholehole, which often sells out, has been known to lure diners on the next plane from Honolulu. You must call ahead, so your order can be fished from the ponds and whisked from kitchen to table. With children's portions at $6.95 to $7.95 for a complete dinner (rice, salad, hot vegetable, and dessert), and free tours of the surrounding aquaculture ponds between 9am and 3pm, this is a terrific stop for families.

Ting Hao. In the Puainako Town Center. ☎ **808/959-6288.** Reservations recommended for dinner. Main courses $7.95–$32. AE, DC, DISC, MC, V. Mon–Fri 10am–2:30pm, daily 4:30–9pm. MANDARIN.

Garlic lovers throughout Hawaii know about Ting Hao's eggplant, skinned and swimming in large chunks of savory garlic. A big plus: no MSG in the hundreds of Cantonese, Mandarin, and Szechwan menu items. Specialties include kung pao shrimp and chicken, shrimp with lobster sauce, kung pao cuttlefish, and light and delicate egg-drop soup. While vegetarians love Ting Hao for its wide-ranging selection (the spicy tofu is superb), nonvegetarians love to tuck into the mu shu pork with fungus and eggs, served rolled up in a crêpe.

Voted the "best Chinese food on the Big Island" by readers of the *Hawaii Tribune-Herald,* Ting Hao has a second restaurant, slightly smaller, in the Naniloa Hotel, 93 Banyan Dr., Hilo (☎ **808/935-8888**), specializing in lobster, crab, and more upscale seafood dishes. It's open Wednesday to Monday from 11am to 2pm and 5 to 9pm, and reservations are required.

Inexpensive

✪ **Cafe Pesto Hilo Bay.** In the S. Hata Building, 308 Kamehameha Ave. ☎ **808/969-6640.** Pizzas $6.95–$17.95. AE, CB, DC, DISC, JCB, MC, V. Mon–Thurs 11am–9pm, Fri–Sat 11am–10pm. PIZZA/PACIFIC RIM.

The Italian brick oven burns many bushels of ohia and kiawe wood to turn out its toothsome pizzas, topped with fresh organic herbs and island-grown produce. The high-ceilinged 1912 room, with windows looking out over Hilo's bayfront, is filled with seductive aromas. It's difficult to resist the wild mushroom–artichoke pizza or the chipotle and tomato-drenched Southwestern, but go with the Four Seasons—dripping with prosciutto, bell peppers, and mushrooms, it won't disappoint. Other personal favorites are the Miloli'i, a crab-shrimp-mushroom sandwich with basil pesto; the smoked salmon mini-pizza appetizer; the chili-grilled shrimp pizza; and the flash-seared poke salad on a bed of spinach. There are many raves on this tried-and-true menu.

Canoes Cafe. In the S. Hata Building, 308 Kamehameha Ave. ☎ **808/935-4070.** Most items less than $6.95. CB, DC, DISC, MC, V. Mon-Sat 7:30am-3pm, Sun 10am-2pm. AMERICAN.

Totally hip and totally Hilo, Canoes does all the right things: it uses fresh organic produce, keeps the food quality up and the prices down, and serves zesty, homemade dressings and bread fresh from the bakery next door. The wrap sandwiches—Thai turkey, chicken breast, kalua pork, pesto chicken, and veggies—are especially popular, served in a garlic-herb-flavored flat bread. You can try any of seven sandwich creations—and they are creations. From roast beef to turkey to vegetarian, the sandwiches are made with homemade mayonnaise, mustard, and dressings (chile vinaigrette salad dressing is a favorite) on rye, sourdough French, focaccia, herbed carrot, or whole-grain bread. Don't be intimidated by the unfamiliar names (Ihoe Wa'akau, Puna Ihoe)—these are American classics, the familiar made new by the uncompromising ingredients. There are only a few tables and a take-out counter, prompting the savvy to take their brown bags across the street, where they can watch fishermen and Hilo Bay from serene bayfront benches.

Fiascos. In Waiakea Square, 200 Kanoelehua Ave. ☎ **808/935-7666.** Reservations recommended for parties of 5 or more. Main courses $6.95-$15.95. AE, DISC, MC, V. Sun-Thurs 11am-10pm, Fri-Sat 11am-11pm. AMERICAN/MEXICAN/ECLECTIC.

All the makings of fantastic fajitas arrive on sizzling cast-iron platters so you can build your own at the table. Although best known for this Mexican dish, Fiascos also offers a huge selection of soups and salads at its $7.50 soup-and-salad bar. There are also four different soups daily, fresh-fish sandwiches, bountiful salads, pastas, burgers, steaks, seafood, fried chicken, smoked chicken breast with sesame dressing—something for everyone. All beef served here, from burgers to prime rib, is raised on the Big Island, and all produce used here is from local growers.

Island Grinds. On Hilo's Bayfront Beach, opposite old Hilo Iron Works (the first right onto the beach after the bridge north of Suisan Fish Market). ☎ **808/895-0625.** Burgers and plate lunches $3.50-$6.95. No credit cards. Mon-Fri 10am-2pm. LUNCH WAGON.

Look for the wooden Island Grinds lunch wagon, as tiny as a closet, under the willowy ironwood trees on Hilo Bay. The plastic table and few chairs are a welcome sight on the sand—it is charming! Paper plates notwithstanding, the dishes that Lisa Werner and Norina Page serve meet all the standards of gourmet fare. The fresh-fish plate ($5.50 regardless of market price—a steal!) comes perfectly sautéed; the turkey is smoky, lean and shredded, the gravies made with a vegetable base, and the grilled lime chicken fork-tender. Fresh island produce appears in such marvels as taro-red potato salad ($1.50), lilikoi-macadamia nut cole slaw ($1), lasagna filled with fresh vegetables and cheese ($5), salads, burritos and rellenos, and submarine sandwiches with an Island twist. The specials change by the day, but the staples—fresh fish plate, Cajun taro burger, imu-style kalua turkey burger, lean all-beef hot dogs, and others—are all served with a smile. With this lunch wagon and its thriving catering business in Hilo, Island Grinds is a local treasure and the consummate find for visitors.

Ken's House of Pancakes. 1730 Kamehameha Ave. ☎ **808/935-8711.** Most items less than $9.50. AE, DC, DISC, MC, V. Daily 24 hours. AMERICAN.

You never know who you'll bump into at Ken's after an important convention, concert, or the Merrie Monarch hula festival. The only 24-hour coffee shop in Hilo, Ken's fulfills basic dining needs with efficiency and simplicity. Omelets, pancakes, sandwiches, tripe stew, oxtail soup—what they call a "poi dog menu"—stream out of the busy kitchen. The affordable selections include fried chicken, steak, grilled fish, and hamburgers with salad and all the accompaniments. Most popular is the Mauna Kea hamburger, which is big as a mountain, topped with pineapple and the works between sweetbread buns—very local, very Hilo.

Kuhio Grille. Prince Kuhio Plaza. ☎ **808/959-2336.** Main courses $4.95–$7.45. MC, V. Mon–Thurs 5am–10pm, Fri 5am–Sun 10pm (24 hours on weekends). AMERICAN/HAWAIIAN.

The "home of the one-pound lau-lau" is quite the local hangout, a coffee/saimin shop with a few tables outdoors and a bustling business indoors. Taro from Waipio Valley is featured in the popular Hawaiian plate ($8.95), but there are other local specialties: saimin, miso-saimin, crab omelets with mushrooms, yakitori, burgers, fried rice (a specialty), and eclectic selections such as nacho salad and chicken yakitori.

⭐ **Miyo's.** At Waiakea Villas, 400 Hualani St. ☎ **808/935-2273.** Lunch main courses $4.50–$8.95, combinations $7.50–$9.25; dinner main courses $4.75–$10.50, combination dinners $8.50–$10.75. No credit cards. Tues–Sat 11am–2pm and 5:30–8:30pm. JAPANESE.

Home-cooked, healthy Japanese food is Miyo's legacy, served in an open-air room on Wailoa Pond, where an idyll of curving footpaths and greenery fills the horizon. Sliding shoji doors bordering the dining area are left open so you can take in the view and gaze at Mauna Kea on a clear day. This is clearly the environment of someone to whom cooking and dining are a meditation. Although sesame chicken (deep-fried and boneless with a spine-tingling sesame sauce) is a bestseller, the entire menu is appealing. For vegetarians, there are constantly changing specials like vegetable tempura, vegetarian shabu-shabu (cooked in a chafing dish at your table, then dipped in a special sauce), and noodle and seaweed dishes. There are also mouth-watering selections of sashimi, beef teriyaki, fried oysters, many different types of tempura, ahi donburi (seasoned and steamed in a bowl of rice), sukiyaki, and generous combination dinners. The daily fresh fish takes many forms, and all dishes are served with rice, soup, and pickled vegetables. With its floating mushrooms and delicate flavor, the miso soup is a wonder, and the ahi tempura plate, at $7.75, is one of Hilo's stellar buys. Special diets (low-sodium, sugarless) are cheerfully accommodated, and no MSG is used. It's no wonder Miyo's won the *Hawaii Tribune-Herald's* 1997 readers' survey as the island's "best Japanese restaurant."

⭐ **Nori's Saimin & Snacks.** 688 Kinoole St. ☎ **808/935-9133.** Most items less than $7.95. MC, V. Sun–Mon 10:30am–9:30pm, Tues–Thurs 10:30am–midnight, Fri–Sat 10:30am–1am. SAIMIN/NOODLE SHOP.

Nori's requires some looking but is worth it. Unmarked on Kinoole Street and not visible from the street, it's located across from the Hilo Lanes bowling alley, down a short driveway into an obscure parking lot. You'll wonder what you're doing here, but stroll into the tiny noodle house with the neon sign of chopsticks and a bowl, plywood booths and Formica tables, and prepare to enjoy the best saimin on the island. Saimin comes fried or in a savory homemade broth—the key to its success—with various embellishments, from seaweed to Chinese dumplings called won ton. Ramen, soba, udon, and a Korean noodle soup, called *mundoo*, are among the 16 varieties of noodle soups, most of them less than $6.95. Barbecued chicken or beef sticks are part of the saimin ritual, smoky and marvelous. Cold noodles, plate lunches (teriyaki beef, ahi, Korean short ribs, all less than $7.95), and sandwiches (an ahi burger for $4.35) give diners ample choices from morning to late night, but noodles are the star. Hilo residents come here after the movies or a game and wouldn't think of leaving without a bag of Nori's famous chocolate mochi cookies or cakes.

Reuben's Mexican Restaurant. 336 Kamehameha Ave. ☎ **808/961-2552.** Most items less than $9.50. MC, V. Mon–Fri 11am–9pm, Sat noon–9pm. MEXICAN.

Reuben's is Hilo's south-of-the-border outpost, with serapes, sombreros, Mexican doilies, and rainbow colors everywhere you look. The juxtaposition of Hilo Bay outside and the dark, funky, margarita-infused atmosphere inside makes for a flamboyantly campy dining experience. The tacos, enchiladas, and hefty combination plates are authentic, as are the award-winning Reuben's margaritas, served in frothy, bountiful pitcherfuls that grease the wheels of conviviality. The free-flowing margaritas are a good match for the moist, tasty tortillas, cilantro-laden salsa, and chile rellenos, a Reuben's specialty. Regulars chuckle over the mustard-orange bathrooms but sing praises over the simple pleasures of rice, beans, and "plain, good old Mexican food."

Royal Siam Thai Restaurant. 70 Mamo St. ☎ **808/961-6100.** Main courses $4.95–$8.95. AE, CB, DC, DISC, MC, V. Mon–Sat 11am–2pm and 5–8:30pm. THAI.

One of Hilo's most popular neighborhood restaurants, the Royal Siam serves consistently good Thai curries in a simple room just off the sidewalk. Fresh herbs and vegetables from the owner's gardens add an extra zip to the platters of noodles, soups, curries, and specialties that pour out of the kitchen in clouds of spicy fragrance. The Buddha Rama, a wildly popular concoction of spinach, chicken, and peanut sauce, is a scene-stealer on a menu of stars. The Thai garlic chicken, in sweet basil with garlic and coconut milk, is equally superb.

Taeng-on Thai Food. 804 Kilauea Ave. ☎ **808/935-0296.** Reservations recommended for dinner. Most items less than $8.95; lunch buffet $3.75–$5.75. Mon–Fri 10:30am–8:30pm, Sat 11am–8pm, Sun 12pm–8:30pm. No credit cards. THAI.

Formerly the Esarn-Thai Kitchen, Taeng-on has kept its best features: a no-fuss, quick-and-easy, inexpensive buffet and spicy, authentic curries redolent with lemongrass, coconut milk, kaffir lime, spices, and fresh vegetables. Takeout lunch plates are a big seller, too; they're a deal at $4.75. Choose from among vegetarian, seafood, and other daily specials; the regional specialty called *larb* (a beef salad fragrant with lemongrass and kaffir lime); noodle soups; and several spicy stir-fries—in all, nearly 100 menu items.

ICE CREAM

Hilo Homemade Ice Cream. 1477 Kalanianaole Ave. (Keaukaha area of Hilo). ☎ **808/959-5959.**

Fresh, creamy, homemade ice cream made in paradise flavors fresh from the island: That's Hilo Homemade. Young Hilo ginger is used for the ginger ice cream, a best-seller; other winners include mango, lilikoi (passion fruit) sherbet, local banana, green tea, Kona coffee, macadamia nut, coconut-crème, banana-poha (gooseberry), and many others. There are takers from the store's 10am opening; some loyalists come daily or several times weekly for the same flavor.

THE PUNA REGION

Huna Ohana Metaphysical Bookstore & Vegetarian Espresso Cafe. In the Akebono Theatre Complex, Old Government Rd., Pahoa. ☎ **808/965-9661.** Breakfast $3.25–$5.60; lunch $3.95–$5.65. MC, V. Mon–Sat 8am–6pm, Sun 9am–1pm. ESPRESSO BAR/SANDWICHES.

The irrepressible Dawn Hurwitz, a retired clothing designer, has turned this corner of Pahoa into quite a cordial center for browsing, noshing, and sipping organic coffee with healthy sandwiches and bagels. Soufflé eggs, tofu scramble, breakfast burritos, and the region's famous Puna papaya are among the breakfast standouts. At lunch, the garden burger is heroic: mushrooms, onions, cheeses, walnuts, bulgur wheat, and other ingredients, topped with cheese, red onion, eggless mayonnaise, and tomatoes. Everything here is vegetarian and healthy; you can even order soy milk in your mocha latte. Bagels, miso soup, black-and-blue nachos (blue corn chips and black beans), and made-on-the-island tempeh are among the wholesome offerings miraculously produced in this tiny kitchen. In the front section of Huna Ohana, browse among the books and retail products.

Luquin's. Old Government Rd., Pahoa. ☎ **808/965-9990.** Main courses $6–$10. AE, DISC, MC, V. Daily 11am–9pm. MEXICAN.

Mexican food lovers frequent Luquin's for the fresh fish, straight off the boat from Pohoiki in easternmost Hawaii. Step off the sidewalk onto its old wooden floors in a room accented with colorful Mexican touches—sombreros, serapes, plates, and pottery. If it's a good fishing day, you'll find ahi tacos or fresh catch with enchiladas, beans, and rice. The 17 different combination plates include steak and shrimp, chile rellenos, beef tacos, and tostadas, all reasonably priced, generously served, and cooked according to family recipes from south of the border. "Real Mexican," say aficionados, who return time and again for the fresh ahi tacos.

Paolo's Bistro. Old Government Rd., Pahoa. ☎ **808/965-7033.** Reservations recommended. Main courses $6.95–$14.95. MC, V. Tues–Sun 5:30–9pm. TUSCAN.

Paolo Bucchioni makes his own melt-in-your-mouth mozzarella, which, when paired with the fresh local organic baby greens, olives, and relishes, makes a handsome lunch salad for $6. He also makes his own pasta, such as black-squid-ink raviolis stuffed with ahi, or black fettuccine with calamari, and composes a culinary symphony every night. The ahi piccata comes in a lemon-caper sauce, and the spinach ricotta, with walnut-Gorgonzola and basil-tomato sauce, is pure gold. A complete dinner of roast-veal lasagna or seafood brochette comes with a side of pasta and vegetable stir-fry, all for $16.95. The bistro banks its reputation on freshness. Bucchioni clearly enjoys his nightly solo performance, and he delivers like a virtuoso.

Sawasdee. Old Government Road. ☎ **808/965-8186.** Reservations recommended. Main courses $4.95–$8.50. DISC, JCB, MC, V. Mon–Sat 11am–9pm. THAI.

Open since August of 1997, Sawasdee is where the Naung Mai was formerly located, with lots of regulars filling its 30 seats. Anything here can be prepared vegetarian; they're very obliging. Green papaya salad, Evil Jungle Prince (vegetables with seafood or chicken in a creamy, intense basil-coconut-lemongrass sauce), and intense curries emit piquant aromas that attract lovers of Thai food. The Pad Thai noodles served with five different curries are popular items on the menu.

VOLCANO VILLAGE & HAWAII VOLCANOES NATIONAL PARK

Kilauea Lodge. Hwy. 11 (Volcano Village exit). ☎ **808/967-7366.** Reservations recommended. Main courses $14.75–$28.50. AE, MC, V. Daily 5:30–9pm. CONTINENTAL.

Kilauea Lodge has loyal fans who travel long distances to drive through its lava-rock pillars lined with hydrangeas and duck from the crisp upland air into the warmth of the high-ceilinged room. The sofa in front of the 1938 fireplace is inviting, especially when the fire is roaring. A cross between chalet-cozy and volcano-rugged, with European cooking by the owner, Albert Jeyte, the lodge is a fine culinary act on the big volcano. Favorites: the fresh catch, hasenpfeffer, potato-leek soup (all flavor and no cream), Alsatian soup. All dinners come with soup, a loaf of warm, freshly baked bread, and salad.

Rainbow Moon Pizza. Delivery only, Volcano area. ☎ **808/967-8617.** Regular pizzas $12.50–$16.50. Wed–Mon 4–9pm. PIZZA.

What a find! "The best pizza we've ever had" is how many describe the roasted garlic pizza with fresh local tomato and the "Big Kahuna," with its generous layers of cheese, roasted garlic, onions, and about 10 other ingredients. You can get regular or thin crust, hand rolled and topped with fresh sauces and a special nine-spice seasoning, and topped with imaginative combinations with names like Rainbow Warrior, Vegetarian Villager, Lava Land, and Mauna Kea. Crater pockets are a unique offering, with smoked sausage, smoked marlin, and other ingredients baked inside the pocket. Rainbow Moon delivers to the Kilauea Lodge and other B&Bs in Volcano. After a full day of hiking, nothing can beat sinking into the sofa in front of a fire and a Rainbow Moon pizza delivered to your door.

Steam Vent Cafe. Haunani Rd. (between mile markers 26 and 27 on Hwy, 11). ☎ **808/985-8744.** Sandwiches $5.95–$6.95, salads $4.95–$8.95. AE, CB, DC, DISC, MC, V. Daily 6:30am–8:30pm. DELI/COFFEE BAR.

Never mind that the Italian Lavazza coffee beans are impressing all of Volcano, or that the self-service espresso and cappuccino machine makes a potent cup of brew in 20 seconds, or that the four gourmet sandwiches, four salads, and delectable pastries are worth a special stop. Those are details. The big news is that the ATM machine was the first to be installed in Volcano Village and is still quite an attraction. Steam Vent is a fount of comforts, from excellent coffees and teas to sweet dessert breads. The tiny deli also carries postcards, gift items, raincoats, polos and tees and, most important, flashlights for lava walks at night or treks through lava tubes by day. Porky's Panic, Tender Bird, vegetarian, Bil-Mar roast beef, and other sandwiches are made with bread by Hilo's O'Keefe & Sons Bakery.

Volcano Golf & Country Club. Hwy. 11 (at mile marker 30). ☎ **808/967-8228.** Reservations recommended for large groups. Breakfast under $6, lunch under $9. AE, DC, MC, V. Daily 7–10am and 10:30am–2pm. Bar open until 4pm. AMERICAN/LOCAL.

This is one of the few places to eat in the Volcano area, so if the Kilauea Lodge is closed, you don't have much choice but to head to this golf course clubhouse—unless you're up for a long drive. Thankfully, the food ranges from okay to good, especially the burgers and tuna sandwiches and many of the inexpensive lunch specials. The room looks out over a fairway, which isn't as clichéd as it sounds, especially when the mists are rolling in and the greens and grays assume an eye-popping intensity. In the typically cool Volcano air, local favorites such as chili, saimin, and Hawaiian stew with rice become especially comforting. Specials include prime rib, teriyaki beef or chicken, stir-fries, and a corned beef and cabbage that's better than it sounds.

SOUTH POINT

Mark Twain Square. Hwy. 11, Waiohinu. ☎ **808/929-7550.** Most items less than $4.95. AE, DC, JCB, MC, V. Mon–Fri 8:30am–8pm, Sat 8:30am–6pm. AMERICAN/LOCAL.

This is a charming stop in a remote village whose most distinctive feature is the row of monkeypod trees that Mark Twain planted. Two of those trees remain, and you can have lunch under one of them. Imagine dining on a turkey sandwich or tuna melt on homemade sweetbread on a shaded veranda in the lap of history. Friendly service and homemade breads (banana, guava, sweetbread), accompanied by Kona coffee and trendy new coffee drinks, add to the appeal. Look for the poi sticks, a Mark Twain Square original. Made with poi and roasted macadamia nuts, they're the best biscotti ever to be dipped into your Kona coffee.

Naalehu Fruit Stand. Hwy. 11, Naalehu. ☎ **808/929-9099.** Most items less than $10. No credit cards. Mon–Thurs 9am–6:30pm, Fri–Sat 9am–7pm, Sun 9am–5pm. AMERICAN/PIZZA.

This little roadside attraction is a bright spot on the long southern route, the liveliest nook in pleasingly sleepy Naalehu. You can buy sandwiches, pizza, fresh salads, and baked goods—its best-loved items—and then nosh away at one of the few tables on the front porch while panting canines from truck beds stare longingly. Big Island macadamia nuts, hefty quiches, fresh local papayas, and Ka'u navel oranges are usually good here, and the pastries are famous, especially the macadamia-nut pie made with whole nuts, like grandma's old-fashioned pecan pie.

South Point Bar & Restaurant. Hwy. 11 (at mile marker 76). ☎ **808/929-9343.** Main courses $5.95–$8.95 at lunch, $9.95–$17.95 at dinner. No credit cards. Mon–Sat noon–3pm, 5–8pm, Sun 8am–2pm. AMERICAN.

This 40-seat diner, the only full-service restaurant between Captain Cook and Volcano, has ocean views from the deck, a surf-and-turf menu, and a separate bar with a piano. Whether it's agony or ecstasy at the ivories, a party mood often prevails, a point made at the outset with the hand-painted parrots and flamingos at the entrance. This is a frontier outpost where area residents know one another and travelers drop by for burgers, enchiladas, Reubens, fresh fish, eggplant lasagne, and vegetarian specials.

5 Beaches

by Jeanette Foster

Too young geologically to have many great beaches, the Big Island instead has an odd collection of unusual ones: brand-new black-sand beaches, green-sand beaches, salt-and-pepper beaches, even a rare white-sand beach.

THE KONA COAST

KEKAHA KAI STATE PARK (KONA COAST STATE PARK)

You'll glimpse this beach as your plane makes its final approach to Kona Airport. It's about 2 miles north of the airport on Queen Kaahumanu Highway; turn left at a sign pointing improbably down a bumpy road. You don't need a four-wheel-drive vehicle to make it down to the beach—just drive slowly and watch out for potholes. What you'll find at the end is 5 miles of shoreline with a half-dozen long, curving beaches and a big cove on Mahaiula Bay, as well as archaeological and historical sites. The series of well-protected coves is excellent for swimming, and there's great snorkeling and diving offshore; the big winter waves attract big-wave surfers. Facilities include rest rooms, picnic tables, and barbecue pits; you'll have to bring your own drinking water. Since it's a state park, the beach is open daily from 8am to 8pm (the closing is strictly enforced, and there's no overnight camping).

WHITE SANDS BEACH

As you cruise Alii Drive, blink and you'll miss White Sands Beach. This small, white-sand pocket beach about 4½ miles south of Kailua-Kona—very unusual on this lava-rock coast—is sometimes called Disappearing Beach because it does just that, especially at high tide or during storms. It vanished completely when Hurricane Iniki hit in 1991, but it's now back in place. (At least it was there the last time we looked.) Locals use the elementary waves here to teach their children how to surf and boogie board. On calm days, the water is perfect for swimming and snorkeling. In winter, the waves swell to expert levels, attracting both surfers and spectators. Facilities include rest rooms, showers, lifeguards, and a small parking lot.

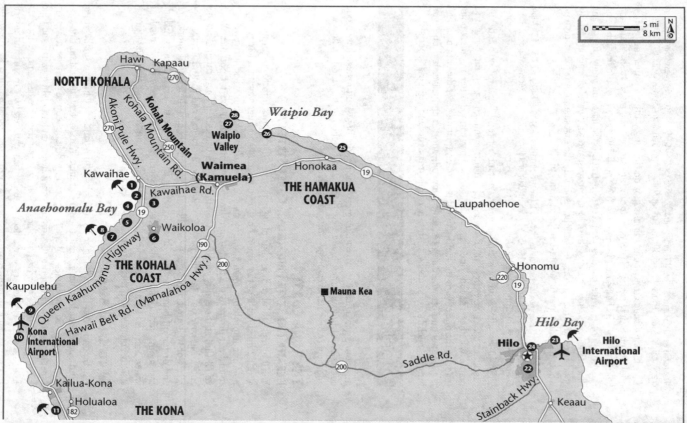

NORTH KOHALA

Hawi

Kapaau

270

Akoni Pule Hwy.

Kohala Mountain Rd.

270

250

Kohala Mountain

Kawaihae

1

2

Kawaihae Rd.

3

4

19

Anaehoomalu Bay

5

8

7

6

Waikoloa

Waipio Valley

27

28

26

Waipio Bay

Waimea (Kamuela)

Honokaa

THE HAMAKUA COAST

19

25

Laupahoehoe

190

200

220

19

Honomu

Queen Kaahumanu Highway

THE KOHALA COAST

Hawaii Belt Rd. (Mamalahoa Hwy.)

Kaupulehu

9

10

Kona International Airport

■ Mauna Kea

200

Saddle Rd.

Hilo

24

23

Hilo Bay

22

Hilo International Airport

Kailua-Kona

Holualoa

11

182

THE KONA

Stainback Hwy.

Keaau

0   5 mi

0   8 km

N

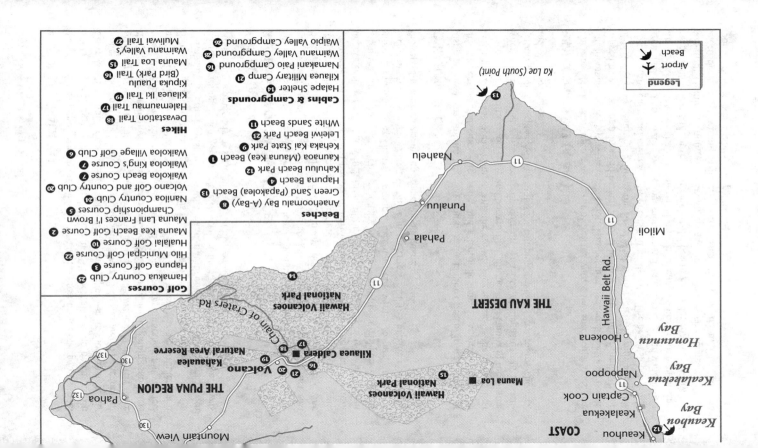

✪ KAHALUU BEACH PARK

This is the most popular beach on the Kona Coast; these reef-protected lagoons attract 1,000 people a day almost year-round. Kahaluu is the best all-around beach on Alii Drive, with coconut trees lining a narrow salt-and-pepper-sand shore that gently slopes to turquoise pools fringed by a protective lava-rock breakwater. The schools of brilliantly colored tropical fish that weave in and out of the well-established reef make this a great place to snorkel. It's also an ideal spot for children and beginning snorkelers to get their fins wet; the water is so shallow that you can literally stand up if you feel uncomfortable. Be careful in winter, though: The placid waters become turbulent, and there's a rip current when high surf rolls in; look for the lifeguard warnings.

Kahaluu isn't the biggest beach on the island, but it's one of the best equipped, with off-road parking, beach-gear rentals, a covered pavilion, and a food concession. It gets crowded, so come early to stake out a beach blanket–sized spot.

THE KOHALA COAST
KAUNAOA BEACH (MAUNA KEA BEACH)

For 25 years, this gold-sand beach at the foot of Mauna Kea Beach Hotel has been the top vacation spot among America's corporate chiefs. Everyone calls it Mauna Kea Beach, but its real name is Hawaiian for "native dodder," a lacy, yellow-orange vine that once thrived on the shore. A coconut grove sweeps around this golden crescent, where the water is calm and protected by two black-lava points. The sandy bottom slopes gently into the bay, which often fills not only with schools of tropical fish but green sea turtles and manta rays, especially at night, when the hotel lights flood the shore. Swimming is excellent year-round, except in rare winter storms. Snorkelers prefer the rocky points, where fish thrive in the surge. Facilities include rest rooms, showers, and ample parking, but there's no lifeguard.

✪ HAPUNA BEACH

Just off Queen Kaahumanu Highway, south of the Hapuna Beach Prince Hotel, lies this crescent of gold sand—big, wide, and a half-mile long. In summer, when the beach is widest, the ocean calmest, and the crowds biggest, this is the island's best beach for swimming, snorkeling, and bodysurfing. But beware Hapuna in the winter, when its thundering waves, strong rip currents, and lack of lifeguards can be dangerous. Facilities include A-frame cabins for camping, pavilions, rest rooms, showers, and plenty of parking.

ANAEHOOMALU BAY (A-BAY)

The Big Island makes up for its dearth of beaches with a few spectacular ones, like Anaehoomalu, or A-Bay, as the locals call it. This popular, peppered, gold-sand beach, fringed by a grove of palms and backed by royal fish ponds still full of mullet, is one of Hawaii's most beautiful. It fronts the Royal Waikoloan Hotel (the only affordable hotel on this coast) and is enjoyed by guests and locals alike. The beach slopes gently from shallow to deep water; swimming, snorkeling, diving, kayaking, and windsurfing are all excellent here. Equipment rental and snorkeling, scuba, and windsurfing instruction are available at the north end of the beach. At the far edge of the bay is a rare-turtle cleaning station, where snorkelers and divers can watch endangered green sea turtles line up, waiting their turn to have small fish clean them. There are rest rooms, showers, picnic tables, and plenty of parking.

HILO
LELEIWI BEACH PARK

Hilo's beaches may be few, but Leleiwi is one of Hawaii's most beautiful. This unusual cove of palm-fringed black-lava tide pools fed by freshwater springs and rippled by gentle waves is a photographer's delight—and the perfect place to take a plunge. In winter, big waves can splash these ponds, but the shallow pools are generally free of currents and ideal for families with children, especially in the protected inlets at the center of the park. Leleiwi often attracts endangered sea turtles seeking safe haven in this natural refuge, making this one of Hawaii's most popular snorkeling spots. The beach is 4 miles out of town on Kalanianaole Avenue; facilities include rest rooms, showers, lifeguards, picnic pavilions, and paved walkways. There's also a marine-life facility here.

SOUTH POINT
GREEN SAND BEACH (PAPAKOLEA BEACH)

Hawaii's famous green-sand beach is located at the base of Puu o Mahana, an old cinder cone spilling into the sea. It's difficult to reach; the open bay is often rough; there are no facilities, no fresh water, no shade from the relentless sun; and howling winds scour the point. Each year, despite the beach's glaring defects, the unusual emerald-green sands attract thousands of oglers, who follow a well-worn four-wheel-drive-only road for 2½ miles to the top of a cliff, which you have to climb down to reach the beach (the south end offers the safest path). Its claim to fame is crushed olivine, a green semiprecious mineral found in eruptive rocks and meteorites. If the surf's up, just check out the beach from the cliff's edge; if the water's calm, it's generally safe to swim and dive.

How to Get to Green Sand Beach: From the boat ramp at South Point, follow the four-wheel-drive trail; even if you have a four-wheel-drive vehicle, you may want to walk, as the trail is very, very bad in parts; it's about 2½ miles and will take you about 45 minutes or an hour to walk. Make sure you have appropriate close-toed footwear: tennis shoes or hiking boots. The trail is relatively flat, but you're usually walking into the wind as you head toward the beach. The beginning of the trail is lava, but after the first 10 to 15 minutes, the lava disappears and the trail begins to cross pasture land. After about 30 to 40 minutes, you'll see an eroded cinder cone by the water; continue to the edge, and there lie the green sands below.

The best way to reach the beach is to go over the edge from the cinder cone. (It looks like walking around the south side of the cone would be easier, but it's not.) From the cinder cone, go over the overhang of the rock, and you'll see a trail.

Going down to the beach is very difficult and treacherous, as you'll be able to see from the top. You'll have to make it over and around big lava boulders, dropping down 4 to 5 feet from boulder to boulder in certain spots. And don't forget that you'll have to climb back up. Look before you start; if you have any hesitation, don't go down (you get a pretty good view from the top, anyway).

Warning: When you get to the beach, watch the waves for about 15 minutes and make sure that they don't break over the entire beach. If you walk on the beach, always keep one eye on the ocean and stick close to the rock wall. There can be strong rip currents here, and it's imperative to avoid them. Allow a minimum of 2 to 3 hours for this entire excursion.

6 Hitting the Water

by Jeanette Foster

For details on the activities listed below, see "The Active Vacation Planner" in chapter 3.

For fishing charters, see "Sportfishing: The Hunt for Granders," below.

BOATING

Body Glove. Kailua Pier. ☎ **800/551-8911** or 808/326-7122. www.bodyglovehawaii.com. $44–$67 adults, $24–$37 children 5-17; $99 for scuba divers.

This 55-foot trimaran runs an adventurous **sail-snorkel-dive cruise** at a reasonable price. The boat carries up to 100 passengers; you'll be greeted with fresh Kona coffee, fruit, and breakfast pastries, then sail north of Kailua to Pawai Bay, a marine preserve where you can snorkel, scuba dive, swim, or just hang out on the deck for a couple of hours. After an all-you-can-eat lunch spread, you might want to take the plunge off the boat's waterslide or diving board before heading back to Kailua Pier. The *Body Glove* departs daily from the Kailua Pier at 9am and returns at 1:30pm. The only thing you need to bring is your towel, as snorkeling equipment (and scuba equipment, if you choose to dive) is provided.

Captain Beans' Cruises. Kailua Pier. ☎ **800/831-5541** or 808/329-2955. $49 per person; you must be 21 to board the boat.

Captain Beans runs Kona's most popular **dinner sails** on its 150-foot catamaran, which can accommodate about 290 passengers. The 2-hour cruise includes dinner, cocktails, dancing, and Hawaiian entertainment.

Captain Dan McSweeney's Year-Round Whale-Watching. Honokohau Harbor. ☎ **888/WHALE6** or 808/322-0028. www.ilovewhales.com. E-mail dmcswwa@interpac.net. $44.50 adults, $29.50 kids under 11.

Hawaii's most impressive visitors—45-foot humpback whales—return to the waters off Kona every winter. Capt. Dan McSweeney, a whale researcher for more than 20 years, is always here to greet them, as well as the other whales who spend the warmer months in Hawaiian waters, like old friends. Since Captain Dan works daily with the whales, he has no problem finding them: he frequently drops an underwater microphone into the water so you can listen to their songs. If the whales aren't singing, he may use his underwater video camera to show you what's going on. In humpback season—roughly December to April—Dan makes two 3½-hour trip a day. The rest of the year, he schedules one morning trip daily to look for pilot, sperm, false killer, melon-headed, pygmy killer, and beaked whales. Capt. Dan guarantees a sighting, or he'll take you out again for free. There are no cruises from May to June, though; that's when he goes whale-watching in Alaska.

Captain Zodiac. From Gentry's Marina, Honokohau Harbor. ☎ **808/329-3199.** www.planet-hawaii.com/zodiac/kona.html. $62 adults, $52 children 2-12.

If you'd prefer to take a **snorkel cruise to Kealakekua Bay** in a small boat, go in Captain Zodiac's 16-passenger, 24-foot inflatable rubber life raft. Pioneered by Jacques Cousteau, the zodiac takes you on a wild ride 14 miles down the Kona Coast to Kealakekua, where you'll spend about an hour snorkeling in the bay. Trips are twice daily, from 8:15am to 12:15pm and from 1 to 5pm. *Warning:* Pregnant women and people with bad backs should avoid this often-bumpy ride.

★ **Fair Wind Snorkeling and Diving Adventures.** ☎ **808/322-2788.** www.fair-wind.com. Prices vary depending on cruise; see below.

One of the best ways to snorkel Kealakekua Bay, the marine life preserve that's one of the best snorkel spots in Hawaii, is on Fair Wind's half-day **sail-and-snorkel cruise to Kealakekua** on their 60-foot catamaran, which holds up to 100 passengers. The morning cruise, which leaves from Keauhou Bay at 9am and returns at 1:30pm, includes breakfast, lunch, snorkeling gear, and lessons; it's $75 for adults, $42 for children ages 6 to 17 (free for those 5 and under). The afternoon cruise is a little shorter and a little cheaper: It leaves at 2pm and returns at 5:30pm and includes snacks, sailing, and snorkeling; it's $48 for adults, $31 for kids 6 to 17.

Fair Wind also has a daily 4-hour **Zodiac snorkel cruise** from Kailua Pier aboard their 28-foot hard-bottom Zodiac boat. The trip includes stops at two snorkel sites (Kealakekua Marine Preserve and Honaunau), snacks, and a historical/cultural tour on the return (including stopping to look in sea caves and lava tubes). They only book 14 people to keep the trip personalized. The cost is $59 per person; you must be 8 years or older to go.

✪ **Hawaiian Ocean Tours.** Honokohau Harbor. ☎ **888/KONA-4-US** or 808/329-HOT1. Fax 808/329-5747. E-mail charter@aloha.net. 3½-hour cruises start at $59.95 adults, half-price for kids 5–15; snacks included.

The Big Island's only jet boat offers the island's best all-around boating experience. The 51½-foot, 900hp jet boat is a high-tech, smooth-riding boat that glides over the water for a fast, comfortable ride. It's certified for 49 passengers, but they limit the number to 30 for a more intimate experience. There are a number of different cruises, from **whale- and dolphin-watching** to **coastal cruises** to **snorkel trips.** The morning cruise features a continental breakfast, which is served as the boat zips along at some 30 knots to pristine bays like Makalawena or Kua, where you can swim and snorkel, listen to a marine naturalist describe the ocean environment, and enjoy a buffet-style lunch. The afternoon trips explore the historic Kona Coast as a historian talks about Kona's past, describes today's environment, and points out places of interest; snacks are served. They guarantee satisfaction or will give you a full refund.

Kamanu. Honokohau Harbor. ☎ **800/348-3091** or 808/329-2021. www.interpac.net/~kamanu. E-mail kamanu@interpac.net. $43 adults, $26 children.

This sleek catamaran offers a laid-back **sail-snorkel cruise** from Honokohau Harbor to Pawai Bay. The 3½-hour trip includes lunch, snorkeling gear, and personalized instruction for first-time snorkelers. The *Kamanu* sails twice daily (weather permitting) at 9am and 1:30pm and can hold up to 24 people.

Nautilus II. Kailua Pier. ☎ **808/326-2003.** 1-hour tours daily at 9:30am, 10:30am, 11:30am, and 12:30pm. $59 adults, $39 children.

People who want to see the underwater world but don't want to get wet might opt for a ride on this semi-submersible 58-foot boat that cruises the waters off the Kona Coast. Claustrophobes and sun worshipers can enjoy the 1-hour trip from the deck, while more adventurous souls can ride below in the air-conditioned cabin, where magnificent sea creatures come to life through oversized windows. A scuba diver is on hand in the water to lure fish, turtles, and other aquatic critters close to the windows.

BODY BOARDING (BOOGIE BOARDING) & BODYSURFING

On the Kona side of the island, the best beaches for body boarding and bodysurfing are **Hapuna Beach**, **White Sands Beach**, and **Kekaha Kai State Park.** On the east side, try **Leleiwi Beach.**

You can rent boogie boards and fins from **Snorkel Bob's**, in the parking lot near Huggo's Restaurant, 75-5831 Kahakai Rd. (off Alii Drive), Kailua-Kona (☎ **800/262-7725** or 808/329-0770; www.snorkelbob.com; e-mail snorkelbob@snorkelbob.

⭐ Frommer's Favorite Big Island Experiences

Creep Up to the Ooze. Hawaii Volcanoes National Park is a work in progress, thanks to Kilauea Volcano, which pours red-hot lava into the sea and adds land to the already big Big Island every day. Since the ongoing eruption began in 1983, Kilauea's been bubbling and oozing in a mild-mannered way that lets you walk right up to the creeping lava flow for an up-close-and-personal encounter.

Go Underwater at Kealakekua Bay. The islands have lots of extraordinary snorkel and dive sites, but none are so easily accessible or have as much to offer as mile-wide Kealakekua Bay, an uncrowded marine preserve on the South Kona Coast. You can swim with dolphins, sea turtles, octopi, and every species of tropical fish that calls Hawaii's waters home.

Gawk at the Day's Catch in Honokohau Harbor. Every afternoon between 4 and 5pm, local fisherman pull into the fuel dock to weigh in their big-game fish. And when we say big, we mean it: We're talking 1,000-pound blue marlins and 200-pound yellowfin tunas, plus plenty of scale-tipping mahi-mahi, ono (also known as wahoo), and other Pacific billfish. Sit in the bleachers and check out these magnificent creatures. Afterward, take some time to walk the docks, inspect the boats, and chat with captains and crew.

Discover Old Hawaii at Puuhonua O Honaunau National Historical Park. Protected by a huge rock wall, this sacred Honaunau site was once a refuge for ancient Hawaiian warriors. Today, you can walk the consecrated grounds and glimpse a former way of life in a partially restored 16th-century village, complete with thatched huts, canoes, forbidding idols, and a temple that holds the bones of 23 Hawaiian chiefs.

Dig Your Toes into Green Sand. No, this isn't some St. Patrick's Day gimmick. Green sand really does exist at the famous Papakolea Beach on the southern tip of the Big Island. The unique emerald color comes from crushed olivine, a semi-precious mineral often found in eruptive rocks and meteorites. The secluded beach is hard to get to—a 12-mile ride on an unpaved road, plus an hour's hike down a steep cliff—but it's worth the trip.

Tour Hilo in a Sampan. There's nothing more fun than cruising around this charming town in an open-air 1940s sedan with a chatty Hawaiian tour guide, who'll take you past Rainbow Falls, under the cool glade of Banyan Tree Drive, and along Hilo's historic waterfront. If you buy a $7 all-day pass, you can jump on and off whenever the fancy strikes you.

Hang Out in Waipio Valley. Pack a picnic and head for this gorgeously lush valley that time forgot. Delve deep into the jungle on foot, comb the black-sand beach, or just laze the day away by a babbling stream, the tail-end of a 1,000-foot waterfall. No matter how you see Waipio Valley, it's an unforgettable experience.

com), for $6.50 a day or $26 a week. No one offers formal boogie-boarding lessons, but the staff at Snorkel Bob's can give you pointers and tell you where waves appropriate for beginners are rolling in. If you're staying on the Kohala Coast, try **Red Sail Sports** (☎ 800/255-6425; www.redsail.com; e-mail info@redsail.com); with locations at Hilton Waikoloa Village (☎ 808/885-2876) and the Hapuna Beach Prince Hotel (☎ 808/880-1111, ext. 3690), they rent body boards for $5 an hour, $10 for a half-day, or $15 for a full day.

Stargaze from Mauna Kea. A jacket, beach mat, and binoculars are all you need to see the Milky Way from here. Every star and planet shines brightly in this ultra-clean atmosphere, where the visibility is so keen that 11 nations have set up telescopes (two of them the biggest in the world), to probe deep space.

Watch Whales. Humpback whales pass through waters off the Kona Coast every winter from December to April. To spot them from shore, head down to the Keahole National Energy Lab, just south of the Kona airport, and keep your eyes peeled as you walk the shoreline. Since humpbacks are so big—up to 45 feet—you can see them for miles when they come out of the water. To reach the Energy Lab, follow Queen Kaahumanu Highway (Hwy. 19) toward the Keahole Airport. About 6 miles outside of town, look for the sign NATURAL ENERGY LAB; turn left. Just after the road takes a sharp turn to the right, there's a small paved parking area with rest rooms and showers. Park in the lot; a beach trail is on the ocean side of the parking lot.

Savor a Cup of Kona Coffee. It's just one of those things you have to do while you're on the Big Island. Most of the coffee craze is centered around the North and South Kona districts, but for a truly authentic cup of java, we suggest that you head upcountry to **Holuakoa Cafe,** on Mamalahoa Highway in Holualoa (☎ **808/322-2233**), where owner Meggi Worbach buys green beans from local farmers, roasts them, grinds them, and then pours you the freshest cup of coffee you've ever had. You may want to invest in one of their famous high-octane espressos ($2.75), guaranteed to keep you going all day long.

Hunt for Petroglyphs. Archaeologists still aren't sure who's responsible for these ancient rock carvings, but the majority of Hawaii's are found in the 233-acre Puako Petroglyph Archaeological District, near Mauna Lani Resort. The best time to go looking for canoes, paddlers, turtles, sails, marchers, dancers, and family groups is either early morning or late afternoon, when it's cool. There are more than 3,000 petroglyphs in this area alone—see how many you can spot!

Chase Rainbows at Akaka Falls. When the light is right, a perfect prism is formed and a rainbow leaps out of this spectacular 442-foot waterfall, located about 11 miles north of Hilo. Take some time to roam through the surrounding tropical rain forest, where you're sure to have close encounters with exotic birds, aromatic plumeria trees, and shocking red-torch ginger.

Shop at the Hilo Farmers Market. For less than $10, you can buy a pound of *rambutan* (a sweet Indonesian fruit), a bouquet of tropical orchids, and a couple of tasty foot-long Hawaiian lau-laus (pork, chicken, or fish steamed in ti leaves). You can spend hours tinkering over baked goods, fresh flowers, exotic fruits, and other local produce. Be sure to arrive early—the market opens at sunrise—as many of the 60 or so vendors quickly sell out of their Big Island specialties.

KAYAKING

OCEAN KAYAKING   Imagine sitting at sea level, eye-to-eye with a turtle, a dolphin, even a whale—it's possible in an oceangoing kayak. Anyone can kayak: Just get in, find your balance, and paddle. After a few minutes of instruction and a little practice in a calm area (like the lagoon in front of the **King Kamehameha's Kona Beach Hotel**), you'll be ready to explore. Beginners can practice their skills in **Kailua** and **Kealakekua bays;** intermediates might try paddling from **Honokohau Harbor** to

Kekaha Kai Beach Park; the **Hamakua Coast** is a challenge for experienced kayakers.

You can rent one- and two-person kayaks, wave-surfing models, and more from **Kona Kai-yaks,** Gentry's Kona Marine, Honokohau Small Boat Harbor (☎ 808/326-2922), starting at $25 a day for a one-person kayak, $50 a day for a two-person kayak.

✪ **FRESHWATER FLUMING** Years ago, the best thing to do on a hot summer day was to grab an old inner tube and go "fluming" down the Kohala Sugar Plantation irrigation system. There were only two problems: You had to trespass to get to the elaborate ditch system, and the water was cold. But the opportunity to float past a pristine rain forest, over ravines, and under waterfalls was worth the risk of getting caught (and worth a numb rear end). You no longer have to worry about either: The **Kohala Mountain Kayak Cruise** (☎ 808/889-6922; fax 808/889-6944; www.kohala.net/kayak) offers access to this North Kohala area (via four-wheel-drive, air-conditioned vans) and guided tours in high-tech, double-hulled, inflatable kayaks, with knowledgeable guides "talking story" about the Hawaiian history, culture, and legends of the area, followed by a swim in a waterfall-fed mountain pool and snacks. Wear a swimsuit or bring a change of clothing, as the kayaks pass under waterfalls and through water pouring in from the intake systems—getting wet is part of the fun, and the whole experience is one you won't forget. The 2½-hour cruises are $75 for adults, $55 for kids 5 to 18. No experience necessary, but children must be at least 5.

PARASAILING

Get a bird's-eye view of Hawaii's pristine waters with **UFO Parasail** (☎ 800/FLY-4UFO or 808/325-5836; www.ufoparasail.com). UFO offers parasail rides daily from 9am to 2pm from Kailua Pier; it's $42 for the standard flight of 7 minutes of air time at 400 feet, $52 for a deluxe 10-minute ride at 800 feet. You can go up alone or with a friend; no experience is necessary.

SCUBA DIVING

The Big Island's leeward coast offers some of the best diving in the world, because the water's calm (protected by the two 13,000-foot volcanoes), warm (75–81°F), and clear (visibility is 100-plus-feet year-round). Want to swim with fast-moving game fish? Try **Ulua Cave** at the north end of the Kohala Coast. How about a dramatic underwater encounter with large, feeding manta rays? **Manta Ray Village,** located outside Keauhou Bay off the Kona Surf Resort, is a proven spot.

There are nearly two dozen dive operators on the west side of the Big Island, plus a couple in Hilo. They offer everything from scuba certification courses (you must be certified to dive, although some operators will offer an "intro" dive), to guided-boat dives. One of Kona's most popular dive operators is **Eco Adventures,** Kona Inn Shopping Center, Alii Drive, Kailua-Kona (☎ 800/949-3483 or 808/329-7116; www.eco-adventure.com). A two-tank dive off either of their 43-foot or 50-foot boats (both with bathrooms and hot showers) costs $90 without gear, including lunch. One-tank shore dives are $60; for two tanks without gear, it's $80. Gear is available for $20 for a two-tank dive or $10 for a one-tank dive. Snorkelers are welcome to ride along for $45, including gear.

Another popular dive operator is **Jack's Diving Locker,** 75-5819 Alii Dr. (☎ 800/345-4807 or 808/329-7585; www.divejdl.com), which offers two-tank morning or sunset dives off either a 24- or 38-foot boat for $85 per person, without gear; rental gear is available for $15. Jack's also offers intro dives for beginners from boat or shore; the cost is $45 per person from shore, plus gear rental.

In Hilo, contact **Nautilus Dive Center,** 382 Kamehameha Ave., between Open Market and the Shell Gas Station (☎ **808/935-6939**). They offer one-tank and two-tank shore dives in Keakeha for $55 and $75, which includes all gear.

HOT LAVA DIVES   Hilo's **Nautilus Dive Center** (☎ **808/935-6939**) also offers a very unusual diving opportunity for advanced divers: diving where the lava flows into the ocean. For $200 each, four divers can dive two tanks where the molten lava pours into the ocean for what owner Bill De Rooy describes as "the dive of a lifetime." "Sometimes you can feel the pressure from the sound waves as the lava explodes," he says. "Sometimes you have perfect visibility to the color show of your life."

✪ **NIGHT DIVING WITH MANTA RAYS**   A little less risky—but still something you'll never forget—is swimming with manta rays on a night dive. These giant, totally harmless creatures, with wingspans that reach up to 14 feet, glide gracefully through the water and flock toward the lights off the Kona Surf Resort in Keauhou Bay to feed on plankton. **Eco Adventures** (☎ **800/949-3483** or 808/329-7116) will take you on a one-tank night dive for $65. **Sandwich Isle Divers,** 75-5729 Alii Dr., in the back of the Kona Market Place (☎ **808/329-9188** or 888/743-3483; www.aloha.net/~sandive), also offers manta dives for $70, including equipment ($60 if you have your own gear).

WEEKLONG DIVES   If you're a serious diver looking for an all-diving vacation, you might think about spending a week on the 80-foot **Kona Aggressor II** (☎ **800/344-5662** or 808/329-8182; www.pac-aggressor.com), a live-aboard dive boat that promises to provide you with unlimited underwater exploration, including day and night dives, along 85 miles of the Big Island's coastline. You may spot harmless 70-foot whale sharks, plus not-so-harmless tiger and hammerhead sharks, dolphins, whales, monk seals, and sea turtles. You'll navigate through caves and lava tubes, glide along huge reefs, and take on the open ocean, too. Ten divers are accommodated in five staterooms. Guided dives are available, but as long as you're certified, just log in with the dive master and you're free to follow the limits of your dive computer. It's $1,795 for 7 days (without gear), which really isn't so bad when you consider that excellent accommodations and all meals are included. Rental gear, from cameras (starting at $100 a week) to dive gear ($120) to computers ($100), is available.

SNORKELING

If you come to Hawaii and don't snorkel, you miss half the fun. The year-round calm waters along the Kona and Kohala coasts are home to spectacular marine life. Some of the best snorkeling areas on the Kona-Kohala Coast include **Hapuna Beach Cove,** at the foot of the Hapuna Beach Prince Hotel, a secret little cove where you can snorkel not only with schools of yellow tangs, needlefish, and green sea turtles, but also, once in a while, with somebody rich and famous. But if you've never snorkeled in your life, **Kahaluu Beach Park** is the best place to start. Just wade in and look down at the schools of fish in the bay's black-lava tide pools. Other great snorkel spots include **White Sands Beach,** as well as **Kekaha Kai State Park,** Hookena, Honaunau, Puako, and Spencer beach parks.

Beach concessions at all the resorts, tour desks, and dive shops offer equipment rentals and snorkel lessons for beginners. Gear rental is about $4.50 to $15 a day, or $10 to $39 a week (including mask, fins, and snorkel); prices go up slightly for prescription masks and high-end snorkels. Dive shops and marine operators who rent gear include **Kona Coast Divers,** 75-5614 Palani Rd., Kailua-Kona (☎ **808/329-8802**). But the best deal on snorkel gear on the Kona Coast is from ✪ **Snorkel Bob's,** in the parking lot of Huggo's Restaurant at 75-5831 Kahakai Rd., at Alii Drive

Snorkeling Kealakekua—& Swimming to England

Flying down the Kona Coast, bow high, the sleek craft skims the water like a flying fish, its twin engines driving us so fast that the coastline goes by in a blur. We laugh in the wind as we go skipping across the big blue sea. Oh, the joy of a fast boat.

Uncle Danny Almonte, our guide, points our historic and cultural landmarks along our 11-mile voyage. Bottle-nose dolphins surface off the bow, and we slow to smile back at them before they take off on a food run. A speed boat (one of those Scarab-looking jobs) comes roaring up full of bluster to check out our boat, to see what it would do. We're neck-and-neck for a while, but soon they disappear in our wake.

We glide into Kealakekua Bay, the Big Island's best dive spot and the last place on earth seen by Capt. James Cook, who stumbled onto the islands in 1778 while looking for the Northwest Passage and claimed them for Great Britain. There it is around the bend: the white obelisk that marks the death site of the great navigator, almost hidden in mangroves on the site of Kaaawaloa, an ancient village gone to dust.

It's 9am on a fine mid-November day, and I'm already in the water, diving with shiny, tropical fish. The water temperature's 76°, the air 80° and climbing. Another perfect day.

From sea level, I scan the rocky, red cliffs trying to imagine what it was like when Capt. Cook returned to the Big Island aboard the *Resolution*, with a broken foremast, to meet his doom on Feb. 14, 1779. There was no god's reception for Cook this time, as there had been a year earlier. The bay ran red with blood that day: Cook, four marines, four Hawaiian chiefs, and 13 warriors were killed. I approach Cook's monument by sea, clamber over slippery rocks, and sit down on the jetty. I look for the brass plaque that's supposed to mark the spot where he fell

☎ 800/262-7725 or **808/329-0770**; snorkelbob.com), where a mask, fins, and snorkel start at just $2.50 a day.

☆ SNORKELING CRUISES TO KEALAKEKUA BAY But probably the best snorkeling for all levels is to be had in **Kealakekua Bay.** The calm waters of this underwater preserve teem with a wealth of marine life. Coral heads, lava tubes, and underwater caves all provide an excellent habitat for Hawaii's vast array of tropical fish, making mile-wide Kealakekua the Big Island's best accessible spot for snorkeling and diving. Without looking very hard, you can see octopi, free-swimming moray eels, parrot fish, and goat fish; once in a while, a pod of spinner dolphins streaks across the bay. Kealakekua is reachable only by boat; check out **Fair Wind** and **Captain Zodiac**, under "Boating," above. If you'd like to kayak out to Kealakekua, see "Kayaking" for rentals.

SNUBA

If you're not quite ready to make the commitment to scuba but you want more time underwater than snorkeling allows, **Big Island Snuba** (**☎ 808/326-7446;** www.hsnhawaii.com/kvp/snuba/bi.html) may be the answer for you. Just like in scuba, the diver wears a regulator and mask; however, rather than the diver wearing their own air tank, the tank floats on the surface on a raft, and it's connected to the diver's reg-

but see only empty black rocks and bright fish. Maybe it's the hot tropic sun, but I decide to do something I've wanted to do for a long time: Take a quick visit to the United Kingdom.

No, I hadn't had too much sun. It's a feat that's possible, thanks to an 1877 land-title transfer. Hawaiian Princess Miriam Likelike and her British consul husband, Archibald Scott Cleghorn, deeded a 5,682-square-foot parcel on the shore of Kealakekua to England for $1, "to keep and maintain" a monument to Capt. Cook. Hawaii was then a kingdom, so you could go from one kingdom to the other by taking a single step over an imaginary line in the sand.

Intrigued ever since I first heard about this geographic delight, I wanted to do it—just to say I did—and now here was my chance. Nobody's looking, so I put one foot in England and leave the other in Hawaii, standing between two islands like a latter-day Colossus of Rhodes. Silly, I know, but a little whimsy amuses me greatly.

While exploring the rest of this England, I notice that the whitewashed monument could use a touchup. Once a year, I'm told, tars in Her Majesty's Service, usually up from Sydney on cadet training missions, stop by to spit-shine the obelisk and its salt-tarnished plaque commemorating Capt. Cook.

I step back into Hawaii, slip into the warm water, and swim through schools of fish to *NavaTrek's* starboard side, where Uncle Danny (that showoff) is playing with a *he'e* caught on a coral head, letting the little gray Hawaiian octopus grip his left arm with eight suction-cup tentacles.

"Where'd you go?" Uncle Danny asks. "Just got back from England," I say. "Over there?" he says, eyebrows raised, hip to the fact there will always be a little bit of England in Hawaii.

—*Rick Carroll*

ulator by a hose that allows the diver to go 20 to 25 feet down. Snuba can actually be easier than snorkeling, because the water is calmer beneath the surface; with just 15 minutes of instruction, neophytes can be down under. It's $65 for a 45-minute dive from the beach, $50 aboard a boat (plus the cost of the boat ride).

✪ SPORTFISHING: THE HUNT FOR GRANDERS

If you want to catch fish, it doesn't get any better than the Kona Coast, known internationally as the marlin capital of the world. Big-game fish, including gigantic blue marlin and other Pacific billfish, tuna, mahi-mahi, sailfish, swordfish, ono (also known as wahoo), and giant trevellies (ulua) roam the waters here. On any given day of the year on any Kona fishing boat, it can be all or nothing, but you seldom come away empty-handed. When anglers here catch marlin that weigh 1,000 pounds or more, they call them *granders*; there's even a "wall of fame" on Kailua-Kona's Waterfront Row honoring 40 anglers who've nailed more than 20 tons of fighting fish.

Nearly 100 charter boats with professional captains and crew offer fishing charters out of **Keauhou, Kawaihae, Honokohau,** and **Kailua Bay harbors.** If you're not an expert angler, the best way to arrange a charter is through a charter boat booking agency; by far the best in Kona is **The Charter Desk at Honokohau Marina** (☎ **888/KONA 4 US** or 808/329-5735; fax 808/329-7960; e-mail charter@aloha. net), the only charter desk at the Fish Dock in the Honokohau Harbor. The Charter

Desk knows the best boats in Honokohau Harbor and can sort through the more than 40 different types of vessels, fishing specialties, and personalities and match you with the right boat—and it's likely to be cheaper than if you book direct. Prices range from $59.95 for a half-day "share charter" (where you share the boat with strangers) to $850 for a full-day exclusive charter aboard a million-dollar yacht. Generally, sportfishing charters run about $325 for a full-day charter on a six-passenger boat.

Serious sportfishers should call the boats direct: **Northern Lights** (☎ 808/329-6522), **Marlin Magic** (☎ 808/325-7138), **Ilaa Nui** (☎ 808/885-4686), or the **Sundowner** (☎ 808/329-7253), which is run by TV personality Capt. Norm Isaacs. If you aren't into hooking a 1,000-pound marlin or 200-pound tuna and just want to go out to catch some smaller fish and have fun, we recommend **Reel Action Light Tackle Sportfishing** (☎ 808/325-6811). Light-tackle anglers and saltwater fly fisherman should contact **Sea Genie** (☎ 808/325-5355), which has helped several anglers to set world records. All of the above outfitters operate out of Honokohau Harbor.

Most big-game charter boats carry six passengers max. Half-day and full-day charters are available, and boats supply all equipment, bait, tackle, and lures. No license is required. Many captains now tag and release marlins and keep other fish for dinner—that's Island style. If you want to eat your catch or have your trophy marlin mounted, tell the captain before you go.

SUBMARINE DIVES

This is the stuff dreams are made up: Venturing 100 feet below the sea in a high-tech, 65-foot submarine. On a 1-hour trip, you'll be able to explore a 25-acre coral reef that's teeming with schools of colorful tropical fish: Look closely, and you may catch glimpses of moray eels—or even a shark—in and around the reef. On selected dives, you'll watch as divers swim among these aquatic creatures, luring them to the viewports for face-to-face observation. Call **Atlantis Submarines**, 75-5669 Alii Dr. (across the street from the Kona Pier, underneath Amigo's Restaurant), Kailua-Kona (☎ 800/548-6262 or 808/329-6626; www.goatlantis.com.) Trips leave daily between 10am and 3pm; it's $79 adults, $39 for children under 12. The best deal is at noon, when prices are discounted $10 for adults. *Note:* The ride is safe for everyone, but skip it if you suffer from severe claustrophobia.

SURFING

Most surfing off the Big Island is for the experienced only; as a general rule, the beaches on the north and west shores of the island get northern swells during the winter, and those on the south and east shores get southern swells in the summer. Experienced surfers should check out the waves at **Pine Trees** (north of Kailua-Kona), **Lyman's** (off Alii Drive in Kailua-Kona), and **Banyan's** (also off Alii Drive); reliable surfing spots on the east side of the island include **Honolii Point** (outside Hilo), **Hilo Bay Front Park,** and **Keaukaha Beach Park.** But there are a few sites where beginners can catch a wave, too: You might want to try the waves at **Kahulua Beach,** where the waves are manageable most of the year, there are other surfers around to give you pointers, and there's a lifeguard on shore.

Ocean Eco Tours (☎ 808/937-0494), owned and operated by veteran surfers Rob Hemshere and Steve Velonza, is the only company on the Big Island that teaches surfing. They offer private lessons for $25 an hour (minimum of 2 hours, including equipment), and 2- to 3-hour group lessons for $75, including lunch and equipment (maximum of four students). Both guys love this ancient Hawaiian sport, and their enthusiasm is contagious; it's a ball to go out with them. The minimum age is 8, and you must be a fairly good swimmer.

Your only Big Island choice for surfboard rentals is **Pacific Vibrations,** 75-5702 Alii Dr., Kailua-Kona (☎ **808/329-4140**), where they're $15 for a 10am to 6pm rental, $20 for 24 hours.

WINDSURFING

Anaehoomalu Bay, on the Kohala Coast, is one of the best beaches for windsurfing, because there are constant 5- to 25-knot winds blowing onshore (toward the beach)— so if you get into trouble, the wind brings you back to shore (instead of taking you out to sea). **Ocean Sports,** at the Royal Waikoloan Hotel (☎ **808/885-5555**), starts beginners on a land simulator to teach them how to handle the sail and "come about" (turn around and come back). Instruction is $45 an hour; after a half-hour or so of instruction on land, you're ready to hit the water. If you're up for more windsurfing after your lesson, get the package deal: a 1-hour lesson, plus an additional hour on the water for $55. Equipment rental is $20 an hour.

Advanced windsurfers should head to **Puako** and **Hilo Bay.**

7 Hiking & Camping

by Jeanette Foster

For information on camping and hiking, contact **Hawaii Volcanoes National Park,** P.O. Box 52, Hawaii National Park, HI 96718 (☎ 808/985-6000); **Puuhonua O Honaunau National Historic Park,** Honaunau, HI 96726 (☎ 808/328-2326); the **State Division of Forestry and Wildlife,** P.O. Box 4849, Hilo, HI 96720 (☎ 808/933-4221); the **State Division of Parks,** P.O. Box 936, Hilo, HI 96721 (☎ 808/974-6200); or **County Department of Parks and Recreation,** 25 Aupuni St., Hilo, HI 96720 (☎ 808/961-8311). For other info sources and general tips on hiking and camping in Hawaii, see "The Active Vacation Planner," in chapter 3.

Camping equipment is available for rent from **Pacific Rent-All,** 1080 Kilauea Ave., Hilo (☎ 808/935-2974). It's for sale at **C&S Cycle and Surf** in Waimea (☎ 808/885-5005); **Gaspro** in Hilo (☎ 808/935-3341), Waimea (☎ 808/885-8636), and Kona (☎ 808/329-7393); and **The Surplus Store** in Hilo (☎ 808/935-6398) and Kona (☎ 808/329-1240).

GUIDED DAY HIKES If you'd like to discover natural Hawaii off the beaten path but don't necessarily want to sleep under a tree to do it, a day hike is your ticket. A long-time resident of Hawaii, Dr. Hugh Montgomery of **Hawaiian Walkways,** P.O. Box 1307, Honokaa, HI 96727 (☎/Fax **800/457-7759** or 808/885-7759; www.21stcenturyhawaii.com/hawaiianwalkways), offers a variety of day hikes, on a scheduled or custom basis, ranging from excursions on shoreline trails with ancient Hawaiian petroglyphs to hikes on volcanic summits reaching over 13,000 feet. Scheduled hikes are $110 for adults, $80 for children under 12; custom trips are $125 adults, $95 children under 12. Prices include transportation to the trailhead, food, beverages, and day-hike equipment.

Naturalist and educator Rob Pacheco of **Hawaii Forest & Trail,** P.O. Box 2975, Kailua-Kona, HI 96745 (☎ **800/464-1993** or 808/322-8881; fax 808/322-8883; e-mail hitrail@aloha.net), will take you out for day trips in his plush four-wheel–drive van to some of the Big Island's most remote, pristine, natural areas, some of which he has exclusive access to. Rob fully narrates his trips, offering extensive natural, geological, and cultural history interpretation (and not just a little humor). Since he only takes a maximum of 10 people, his trips are highly personalized to meet the group's interests and abilities. A day with Rob may just be the highlight of your Big Island experience. He offers waterfall adventures, rain forest discovery hikes, birding tours, and a volcano tour, where he takes you hiking through a pitch-black lava tube and right up to the oozing flow after dark, when the lava is most spectacular—conditions permitting, of course. Each tour has 2 to 4 hours of easy-to-moderate walking, over terrain manageable by anyone in average physical condition. Full-day trips are $130 adult, $95 children ages 5 to 12; children under 5 are free. Price includes pickup and drop-off, continental breakfast, lunch, snacks, water and other beverages, and the use of all the gear you'll need.

Call these outfitters ahead of time (even before you arrive) for a schedule of trips, as they fill up quickly.

HAWAII VOLCANOES NATIONAL PARK

Hawaii Volcanoes National Park is a wilderness wonderland. Miles of trails not only lace the lava, but also cross deserts, rain forests, beaches, and in the winter, snow at 13,650 feet. **Trail maps** are sold at park headquarters and are highly recommended. Check conditions before you head out on a trail. It can be cool and rainy any time of the year; come prepared for hot sun, cold rain, and hard wind. Always wear sunscreen and bring plenty of drinking water.

Warning: If you have heart or respiratory problems, or if you're pregnant, don't attempt any hike in the park; the fumes will get to you.

TRAILS

KILAUEA IKI TRAILS   You'll experience the work of the volcano goddess, Pelé, firsthand on this hike. The 4-mile trail begins at the visitor center, goes down through a forest of ferns into still-fuming Kilauea Iki Crater, and across the crater floor past the vent where a 1959 lava blast shot a fountain of fire 1,900 feet into the air for 36 days. Allow 2 hours for the fair-to-moderate hike.

HALEMAUMAU TRAIL   This moderate 3½-mile hike starts at the visitor center and goes down 500 feet to the floor of Kilauea crater, crosses the crater, and ends at Halemaumau Overlook.

DEVASTATION TRAIL   Up on the rim of Kilauea Iki Crater, you can take a brief walk through and see what an erupting volcano did to a once-flourishing ohia forest; the scorched earth with its ghostly tree skeletons stands in sharp contrast to the rest of the nearby lush forest that escaped the rain of hot molten lava, cinder, and debris. Everyone can—and should—take this half-mile hike on a paved path across the eerie bed of black cinders. The trailhead is on Crater Rim Road at Puu Puai Overlook.

KIPUKA PUAULU (BIRD PARK) TRAIL   This easy 1½-mile, hour-long hike lets you see native Hawaiian flora and fauna in a little oasis of living nature in a field of lava. For some reason (gravity or rate of flow, perhaps), the once red-hot lava skirted—perhaps even surrounded—this miniforest and let it survive. At the trailhead on Mauna Loa Road is a display of plants and birds you'll see on the walk. Go early in the morning or in the evening (or even better, just after a rain) to see native birds like the *apapane* (a small, bright-red bird with black wings and tail that sips the nectar of the red-blossom ohia lehua trees) and the *iiwi* (larger and orange-vermilion colored, with a curved orange bill). Native trees along the trail include giant ohia, koa, soapberry, kolea, and mamani.

MAUNA LOA TRAIL   Probably the most challenging hike in Hawaii, this 7½-mile trail goes from the lookout to a cabin at the Red Hill at 10,035 feet, then 11.6 more miles up to the primitive Mauna Loa summit cabin at 13,250 feet, where the climate is called sub-arctic, whiteouts are common, and overnight temperatures are below freezing year-round; there's often snow in July. This 4-day round-trip requires advance planning, great physical condition, and registration at the visitors center. The park rangers will want to know you're there for your own safety. Call ☎ **808/985-6000** for maps and details. The trailhead begins where Mauna Loa Road ends, 13½ miles north of Highway 11.

CAMPGROUNDS & WILDERNESS CABINS

The only park campground accessible by car is **Namakani Paio,** which has a pavilion with picnic tables and a fireplace, but no wood is provided. Tent camping is free; no reservations are required. Stays are limited to 7 days per year. Backpack camping at hiker shelters and cabins is available on a first-come, sharing basis, but you must register at the visitors center.

Kilauea Military Camp is a rest-and-recreation camp for active and retired military personnel a mile from the visitors center; facilities include 62 one- to four-bedroom cabins, a 100-bunk dorm, a cafeteria, bowling alley, a bar, general store, weight room, and tennis and basketball courts. Rates range from $26 to $73 a night; call ☎ **808/967-8334** for further details and to reserve.

The following cabins and campgrounds are the best of what the park and surrounding area have to offer:

HALAPE SHELTER This backcountry site, about 7 miles from the nearest road, is the place for people who want to get away from it all and enjoy their own private white-sand beach. The small, three-sided stone shelter, with a roof but no floor, can accommodate two people comfortably, but four's a crowd. You could pitch a tent inside, but if the weather is nice, you're better off setting up outside. There's a catchment water tank, but check with rangers on the water situation before hiking in (sometimes they don't have accurate information on the water level; bring extra water just in case). The only other facility is a pit toilet. Go on weekdays if you're really looking to get away from it all. It's free to stay here, but you're limited to 3 nights. Permits are available at the visitors center on a first-come first-served basis no earlier than noon on the day before your trip. For more information, call ☎ **808/985-6000.**

NAMAKANI PAIO CAMPGROUNDS & CABINS Just 5 miles west of the park entrance is a tall eucalyptus forest where you can pitch a tent in an open grassy field. The trail to Kilauea Crater is just a half-mile away. No permit is needed for tent camping, but stays are limited to 7 days. Facilities include pavilions with barbecues and a fireplace, picnic tables, outdoor dishwashing areas, rest rooms, and drinking water. There are 10 cabins that accommodate up to four people each. Each cabin has a covered picnic table at the entrance and a fireplace with a grill. Toilets, sinks, and hot showers are available in a separate building. Groceries and gas are available in the town of Volcano, 4 miles away. Make cabin reservations through **Volcano House,** P.O. Box 53, Hawaii National Park, HI 96718 (☎ **808/967-7321**); the cost is $32 per night for two, $38 for three, $44 for four.

WAIMANU VALLEY'S MULIWAI TRAIL

This difficult 2- to 3-day hiking adventure—only for the hardy—takes you to a hidden valley some call Eden. It probably looks just as it did when Capt. James Cook "discovered" the islands, with virgin waterfalls and pools and spectacular views; it's a chance to merge with the environment that brings hikers back time and time again.

The trail, which goes from sea level to 1,350 feet and down to the sea again, takes more than 9 hours to hike in and more than 10 hours to hike out. Be prepared for clouds of blood-thirsty mosquitoes, and look out for wild pigs. If it's raining, forget it: You'll have 13 streams to cross before you reach the rim of Waimanu Valley, and rain means flash floods.

You must get permission to camp in Waimanu Valley from the **Division of Forestry and Wildlife**, P.O. Box 4849, Hilo, HI 96720-0849 (☎ **808/974-4221;** fax 808/974-4226). Permits to the nine designated campsites are assigned by number. They're free, but you're limited to a seven-day stay. Facilities are limited to two composting pit toilets. The best water in the valley is from the stream on the western wall, a 15-minute walk up a trail from the beach. All water must be treated before drinking. The water from the Waimanu Stream drains from a swamp, so skip it. Be sure to pack out what you take in.

To get to the trailhead, take Highway 19 to the turnoff for Honokaa; drive 9½ miles to the Waipio Valley Lookout. Unless you have four-wheel drive, this is where your hike begins. Walk down the road and wade the Wailoa Stream, cross the beach and go to the northwest wall. The trail starts here and goes up the valley floor, past a swamp, and into a forest before beginning a series of switchbacks that parallel the coastline. These switchbacks go up and down about 14 gulches. At the ninth gulch, about two-thirds of the way along the trail, is a shelter. After the shelter, the trail descends into Waimanu Valley, which looks like a smaller version of Waipio Valley, but without a sign of human intrusion.

WAIPIO VALLEY CAMPING

Camping is permitted on the east side of the Waipio Stream, which is on the ocean side of the mouth of lush Waipio Valley. There's a grove of ironwood trees that provides a nice shady spot. Permits, which are free but limited to 4 days, must be applied for at least 2 weeks in advance from **Kamehameha Schools,** P.O. Box 495, Paauilo, HI 96776 (☎ **808/776-1104;** fax 808/776-1363). Permits are granted on a first-come, first-served basis. There are no facilities in the valley, so you're required to have your own chemical toilet or port-a-john (available at camping supply stores and at Sears, starting at $80). Water is available from the stream, but be sure to treat it before drinking.

8 Golf & Other Outdoor Activities

by Jeanette Foster

The not-for-profit group **Friends for Fitness,** P.O. Box 1671, Kailua-Kona, HI 96745 (☎ **808/325-7602** or 808/322-0033), offers a free brochure on physical activity (from aerobic classes to dancing to yoga) in West Hawaii; they will gladly mail it to you.

BICYCLING & MOUNTAIN BIKING

For mountain-bike and cross-training bike rentals in Kona, see **Dave's Bike and Triathlon Shop,** 75-5669 Alii Dr., across from the Kailua Pier underneath Amigo's Restaurant, behind Atlantis Submarine (☎ **808/329-4522**). Dave rents Specialized, Caloi, and other brand-name mountain bikes for $15 a day or $55 a week (includes helmet and water bottle). If you rent two bikes on a weekly basis, Dave will drop the price to $50 for one and $55 for the other—it's the best deal around. He also rents triathlon road bikes for $25 a day or $110 a week. Feel free to ask Dave for riding advice (such as which roads are closed by lava) and local weather reports. To carry your rented bike around, be sure and get a bike rack for your rental cars ($10 a week), so you can drive and bike as your trip dictates.

If you're a little pickier about the kind of bike you rent, **Hawaiian Pedals,** Kona Inn Shopping Village, Alii Dr., Kailua-Kona (☎ **808/329-2294**), has a huge selection of bikes from mountain bikes and hybrids ($20 a day, $70 a week) to racing bikes and front-suspension mountain bikes ($25 a day, $75 a week) to full-suspension mountain bikes ($30 a day, $80 a week). They also rent bike racks for your rental car at $5 a day and use the honor system for how many days you actually use the bike rack (e.g., if you have it for a week but only use it for two days, they'll just charge you $10). The folks at the shop are friendly and knowledgeable about cycling routes all over the Big Island.

In Waimea, contact **Mauna Kea Mountain Bikes** (☎ **888/MBT-TOUR** or 808/885-2091), Grant Mitchell can set you up with a mountain bike starting at $25 for 5 hours or $30 a day delivered free to your hotel room, helmet, pump, tube, and patch kit included. Mitchell also has guided bike tours (see below).

BIKING AROUND THE BIG ISLAND   When was the last time you bicycled around a tropical island? Jump on a 21-speed mountain bike and do it here; it's a 225-mile Circle Island tour. A novice can do it in 6 days or less; serious bikers do it in two.

Here are a couple of tips if you're going to try to make your way around the island: Plan your trip. Make advance reservations. Get a bike that fits. Go early in the day; just after sunrise is best. Wear lightweight bike togs and a helmet. Take two water bottles and sunscreen. Bring rain gear. Stay on the road, because razor-sharp lava and kiawe thorns cause blowouts. Bring a patch kit, cables, and a lock. But most important, have fun!

GUIDED TOURS   If you want to explore the wilder side of paradise by bike but don't want to head out alone, the best outfitter to ride with is **Chris' Adventures** (☎ **808/326-4600**), which offers a variety of biking and biking-hiking tours. A half-day adventure costs $49 to $69 and includes equipment, transportation, and a snack; a full-day tour (usually 6 to 8 hours) costs from $76 to $110 and includes equipment, breakfast, and lunch. We love the Kohala Mountain Venture; you bike downhill through spectacular volcanic mountains and lush pastures, pass intriguing historic landmarks, and catch phenomenal views from the Pololu Lookout. It's $79 and includes equipment, breakfast, lunch, and snorkeling at a remote beach; it's well worth it.

Another alternative for bike touring, from beginner to advanced, is **Mauna Kea Mountain Bikes, Inc.** (☎ **888/MBT-TOUR** or 808/885-2091), which offers 3-hour downhill cruises in the historic Kohala mountains to advanced rides down monstrous Mauna Kea. Prices range from $45 to $115.

Contact the **Big Island Mountain Bike Association,** P.O. Box 6819, Hilo, HI 96720 (☎ **808/961-4452;** www.ilhinterpac.net/~mtbike), for their free brochure, *Big Island Mountain Biking,* which has useful safety tips on biking as well as great off-road trails for both beginner and advanced riders. Another good contact for bikeway information and maps is Ann Peterson, executive director of PATH (☎ **808/326-9495**).

BIRDING

Native Hawaiian birds are few—and dwindling. Hawaii may be the endangered bird capital of the world, but it still offers extraordinary birding for anyone nimble enough to traverse tough, mucky landscape. And the best birding is on the Big Island; birders the world over come hoping to see three Hawaiian birds in particular: *akiapolaau,* a woodpecker wannabe with a war club–like head; *nukupuu,* an elusive little yellow bird with a curved beak, one of the crown jewels of Hawaiian birding; and *alala,* the critically endangered Hawaiian crow that's now almost impossible to see in the wild.

The best spots for accomplished birders to go on their own are the ohia forests of **Hawaii Volcanoes National Park,** usually at sunrise or sunset, when the little forest birds seem to be most active; you may also see native birds at the entrance to the

Thurston Lava Tube. The Hawaiian nene goose can be spotted at the park's Kipuka Nene Campground, a favorite nesting habitat; geese and pheasants sometimes appear on the Volcano Golf Course in the afternoon. The white-tailed tropic bird often rides the thermals caused by steam inside Halemaumau Crater.

Other spots to see native Hawaiian and other birds include:

HAKALAU FOREST NATIONAL WILDLIFE REFUGE The first national wildlife refuge established solely for forest bird management is on the eastern slope of Mauna Kea above the Hamakua Coast. It's open for birding by permit only on the last weekend of each month and can be reached only by four-wheel-drive vehicle. Contact Refuge Manager Richard Wass, Hakalau Forest, 153 Waianuenue Ave, Room 219, Hilo, HI 96720 (☎ **808/933-6915**).

HILO PONDS Ducks, coots, herons (night and great blue), cattle egrets, even Canadian and snow geese fly into these popular coastal wetlands in Hilo, near the airport. Take Kalanianaole Highway about 3 miles east, past the industrial port facilities to Loko Waka Pond and Waiakea Pond.

THE SADDLE ROAD Check your rental-car agreement to see if you can take your rental car on the 53-mile Saddle Road (Hwy. 200) from Hilo to the Kohala Coast between Mauna Kea and Mauna Loa. It's a beautiful drive—especially at sunset—and one of the best places to see *iao*, the Hawaiian hawk, as it soars over the rolling grasslands. Along the way, you'll see *kipukas* (islands of old forest surrounded by young lava flows), which are natural native-bird preserves. To enter, you must pick your way across razor-sharp lava and then sit and wait for the birds.

BIRDING TOURS

If you don't know an apapane from a nukupuu, go with someone who does. Even rank amateurs can see Hawaii's *rara avis* in the wild. Naturalist Rob Pacheco leads tours with **Hawaii Forest & Trail;** see "Hiking & Camping," above.

The full-day **McCandless Ranch Eco-Tour** (☎ **808/328-8246;** fax 808/328-8671; e-mail hicrow@aloha.net) travels all over the slopes of Mauna Loa through the rain forest, passing by endemic Hawaiian flora and various native birds. The only alala in the world still found in the wild are on the Ranch property, where care is taken to protect them. Tours leave early in the morning to ensure more time for sighting the native birds and stopping for a picnic lunch. Prices start at $400 for two, $150 each for the third and fourth person. You can also book an overnight stay at the ranch's B&B; see "Accommodations," above, for details.

GOLF

For last-minute and discount tee times, call **Stand-by Golf** (☎ **888/645-BOOK** from Hawaii, 808/322-BOOK from the mainland) between 7am and 9pm. Stand-by offers discounted (10 to 40%) guaranteed tee times for same-day or next-day golfing.

In addition to the courses below, we love the fabulous ✪ **Hualalai Golf Course** at Four Seasons Resort Hualalai. Unfortunately, it's only open to resort guests—but for committed duffers, this Jack Nicklaus–designed championship course is reason enough to pay the sky-high rates. For further details, see "Accommodations" earlier in this chapter.

THE KOHALA COAST

✪ **Hapuna Golf Course.** Hapuna Prince Beach Resort, off Hwy. 19 (near mile marker 69). ☎ **808/882-1111.**

Since its opening in 1992, this 18-hole championship course has been named Most Environmentally Sensitive Course and one of the Top 10 New Courses in the Nation by *Golf Magazine*, and Course of the Future by the U.S. Golf Association. Designed by Arnold Palmer and Ed Seay, this 6,027-yard links-style course extends from the shoreline to 700 feet above sea level, with views of the pastoral Kohala Mountains and sweeping vistas of the Kohala coastline. The elevation changes on the course keep it challenging (not to mention the wind at the higher elevations!). There are a few elevated tee boxes and only 40 bunkers. Greens fees are $80 for resort guests, $130 for nonguests; twilight rates (after 3pm) are $45 for guests, $80 for nonguests. Facilities include putting greens, driving ranges, lockers, showers, a pro shop, and restaurants.

✪ **Mauna Kea Beach Golf Course.** Mauna Kea Beach Resort, Hwy. 19 (near mile marker 68). ☎ **808/882-7222.**

This Robert Trent Jones, Jr., championship course is consistently rated one of the top golf courses in the U.S. This par-72, 7,114-yard challenge is breathtakingly beautiful. The signature third hole is 175 yards long (and a shocking par-3), but the Pacific Ocean and shoreline cliffs stand between the tee and the green, giving every golfer, from beginner to pro, a real opportunity to improve their game. Another par-3 that confounds golfers is the 11th hole, which drops 100 feet from tee to green and plays down to the ocean, into the steady trade winds. When the trades are blowing, 181 yards might as well be 1,000 yards. Greens fees are $90 for hotel guests, $150 for nonguests. Facilities include putting greens, driving range, lockers and showers, pro shop, and restaurant. The course is very popular, especially for early weekend tee times, so book ahead.

✪ **Mauna Lani Frances I'i Brown Championship Courses.** Mauna Lani Dr., off Hwy. 19 (20 miles north of Kona Airport). ☎ **808/885-6655.**

The **Mauna Lani South Course**, a 7,029-yard, par-72, has an unforgettable ocean hole: the 221-yard, par-3 7th, which is bordered by the sea, a salt-and-pepper sand dune, and lush kiawe trees. It drops downhill and—depending on the wind—you may need anything from a wood to a wedge to hit the green. The **North Course** may not have the drama of the oceanfront holes, but because it was built on older lava flows, the more extensive indigenous vegetation gives the course a Scottish feel. The hole that's cursed the most is the 140-yard, par-3 17th: It's absolutely beautiful but plays right into the surrounding lava field. On the North Course, greens fees are $85 for resort guests, $160 for nonguests ($50 after 3pm); South Course greens fees are $90 and $170, respectively ($55 after 3pm). Facilities include two driving ranges, a golf shop (with teaching pros), a restaurant, and putting greens.

Waikoloa Beach Course. 1020 Keana Pl. (adjacent to the Royal Waikoloan and Hilton Waikoloa Village), Waikoloa. ☎ **800/552-1422** or 808/885-6060.

This pristine 18-hole, par-70 course certainly reflects designer Robert Trent Jones, Jr.'s motto: "Hard par, easy bogey." Most golfers remember the par-5, 505-yard 12th hole, a sharp dogleg left with bunkers in the corner and an elevated tee surrounded by lava. Greens fees are $85 for resort guests, $120 for nonguests, including cart; twilight rates are $55 after 2pm. Facilities include golf shop, restaurant, and a driving range.

Waikoloa King's Course. 600 Waikoloa Beach Dr., Waikoloa. ☎ **800/552-1422** or 808/885-4647.

This sister course to the Waikoloa Beach Course is about 500 yards longer. Designed by Tom Weiskopf and Jay Morrish, the 18-hole links-style tract features a double green at the third and sixth holes and several carefully placed bunkers that often come into play due to the ever-present trade winds. Greens fees are $85 for resort guests, $120 for nonguests, including cart; rates drop to $55 after 2pm. Facilities include a pro shop and showers. Every Friday, there's a **free golf clinic** at 4pm; call for reservations.

Waikoloa Village Golf Club. Waikoloa Rd., Waikoloa Village, off Hwy. 19 (18 miles north of Kona Airport). ☎ **808/883-9621.** Turn left at the Waikoloa sign; it's about 6 miles up, on your left.

This semiprivate 18-hole course, with a par-72 for each of the three sets of tees, is usually overshadowed by the glamour resort courses along the Kohala Coast. Hidden in the town of Waikoloa, this is not only a beautiful course with great views, but it offers some great golfing. Like most Hawaii courses, wind can play havoc with your game here, so choose your clubs with caution. Robert Trent Jones, Jr., designed this challenging course, inserting his trademark sand traps, slick greens, and great fairways. We're particularly fond of the 18th hole: a par-5, 490-yard thriller that doglegs to the left, and the last 75 yards up to the green are water, water, water—always a great way to end the day. To keep your sense of humor, take time to check out the fabulous views of Mauna Kea and Mauna Loa, and—on a very clear day—Maui's Haleakala in the distance. Green fees are $70 before 1pm, $40 after 1pm.

THE HAMAKUA COAST

Hamakua Country Club. On the ocean side of Hwy. 19 (41 miles from Hilo), Honokaa. ☎ **808/775-7244.**

As you approach the sugar town of Honokaa, you can't miss this funky nine-hole course, built in the 1920s on a very steep hill overlooking the ocean. It's a par-33, 2,520-yard tract that really only had room for about 4½ holes; but somehow, architect Frank Anderson managed to squeeze in nine by crisscrossing holes across fairways—you may never see a layout like this again. The best part about Hamakua, though, is the price: $10 for nine holes. The course is only open to nonmembers on weekdays; you don't need a tee time—you just show up. If no one's around, simply drop your $10 in the box and head right to the first tee. Cars aren't allowed because of the steep hills.

Hilo

Hilo Municipal Golf Course. 340 Haihai St. (between Kinoole and Iwalani sts.), Hilo. ☎ **808/959-7711.** From Hilo, take Hwy. 11 toward Volcano; turn right at Puainako St. (at Prince Kuhio Shopping Center), left on Kinoole, then a right on Haihai St.; the entrance is between Kinoole and Iwalani sts.

This is a great course for the casual golfer; it's flat, it's scenic, and it can be fun. *Warning:* Don't go after a heavy rain storm (especially during the winter months), as the fairways can get really soggy and play can slow way down. The rain does keep the course green and beautiful, though. Wonderful trees (monkeypods, coconuts, eucalyptus, banyans) dot the course, and the views—of Mauna Kea on one side and Hilo Bay on the other—are breathtaking. This is a course where you can challenge yourself. There are four sets of tees, with a par-71 from all; if you carry a medium handicap, go ahead and play from the back (black) tees (6,325 yards of play). The forgiving nature of the course will give you a challenging game. Getting a tee time can be a challenge as well, since lots of golfers in Hilo love this course; weekdays are your best bet. Greens fees are $20 weekdays, $25 Saturday and Sunday, plus cart fee of $14.50.

Naniloa Country Club. 120 Banyan Dr. (at the intersection of Hwy. 11 and Hwy. 19). ☎ **808/935-3000.**

This semiprivate, nine-hole course is a lot more challenging than it looks. At first glance, the course looks pretty flat and short, but once you get beyond the first hole—a wide, pretty straightforward 330-yard, par-4—the challenges come. The tree-lined fairways require the straight drives, and the huge lake on the second and fifth holes is sure to haunt you. This course is very popular with locals and visitors, who can play a quick nine holes in the morning and head off for some sightseeing in the afternoon. On weekdays, green fees are $30 for nine holes, plus $7 for a cart. On weekends, if you can get a tee time, it's $40, plus $9 for the cart. Twilight rates are $5 less after 4pm. Rental clubs are available.

VOLCANO VILLAGE

Volcano Golf and Country Club. Hwy. 11. ☎ **808/967-7331.** On the right side of Hwy. 11, just after the entrance to Hawaii Volcanoes National Park.

While most visitors head up to the national park to see the lava flows, some come for the golf. Located at 4,200 feet, this public course got its start in 1922, when the Black-shear family put in a green, using old tomato cans for the holes. In 1967, the rough patchwork of a traditional Scottish course was redesigned by Arthur Jack Snyder into an 18-hole American course; it now has three sets of tees to choose from, all with a par of 72. The course is unusually landscaped, making use of a few ancient lava flows among the pine and ohia trees. It's considered challenging by locals who frequently play here. *Some tips from the regulars:* Since the course is located at 4,200 feet, the ball travels farther than you're probably used to, so club down. If you hit the ball off the fairway, take the stroke—you don't want to look for your ball in the lava. Also, play a pitch-and-run game, as the greens are slick and your ball just won't stick. Greens fees are $62.50 and include a shared cart.

HORSEBACK RIDING

Kohala Na'alapa, on Kohala Mountain Rd. (Hwy. 250) at mile marker 11 (ask for directions to the stables at the security-guard station; ☎ **808/889-0022**), has unforgettable journeys into the rolling hills of Kahua and Kohala ranches, past ancient Hawaiian ruins, through lush pastures with grazing sheep and cows, and along mountain tops with panoramic coastal views. Their horses and selection of riding areas are suited to a variety of riders, from first-timers to experienced equestrians. There are two trips a day: a 2½-hour tour at 9am for $75 ($65 for children 8–14) and a 1½-hour tour at 1:30pm for $55 (same price for kids). No riders over 230 pounds, no pregnant riders, and no children under 8.

Paniolo Riding Adventure, Kohala Mountain Rd. (Hwy. 250) at mile marker 13 (just past the entrance to Kohala Ranch Estates), Kohala (☎ **808/889-5354**), has a range of different rides on an 11,000-acre working ranch to suit any riding ability. Rides begin with a smoother, more surefooted experience. Rides begin at $85 for a 2½-hour trip that promises stellar views of the Kona and Kohala coasts; a 4-hour tour is $125.

Experienced riders should call **King's Trail Rides, Tack, and Gift Shop,** Hwy. 11 at mile marker 111, Kealakekua (☎ **808/323-2388;** www.interpac.net/~hit/ktr.html), whose rides, which are limited to four people, head down the mountain along Monument Trail to the Captain Cook Monument in Kealakekua Bay, where you'll stop for lunch and snorkeling. The $95 price tag isn't so bad when you consider that it includes both lunch and gear.

To see Waipio Valley on horseback, call **Waipio Na'alapa Trail Rides** (☎ **808/775-0419**). The 2-hour horseback tours of this gorgeous tropical valley depart Monday through Saturday at 9:30am and 1pm (don't forget your camera). The guides are well versed in Hawaiian history and keep a running commentary going as you move through this very historical place. $75 for adults, $65 for children 8 to 14; no kids under 8; no pregnant riders; and no one weighing more than 230 pounds.

RIDING PARKER RANCH   To ride Parker Ranch is to be lost in time and space; it looks familiar and foreign all at once, stretching as it does under the volcano out west of the moon. The land, barren and rolling and dimpled by craters, looks positively lunar, especially when cows jump in the soft chiaroscuro light. You gain a scant clue to the ranch's vast grandeur on a 2-hour trail ride that begins at Mauna Kea Stables in the Old West town of Waimea. Other trail rides are "nose-to-tail," but not on the Parker Ranch—it's too big for that. Here, you can gallop to the horizon across scenic upland pastures dotted with volcanic cinder cones and strewn with bleached white cattle bones. Corrals hold Texas longhorns and lost heifers; the wide-open range even offers a rare glimpse of wild Kona donkeys. Always, the final surprise is that we really are way out West—in Hawaii. **Mauna Kea Riding Stables,** off Hwy. 19 at Punakalani Rd. (look for Ace Hardware Store on the corner; it's down about a half-mile), Waimea (☎/Fax **808/885-4288**), offers guided open-range rides daily except Sundays for beginners to experts; you must be 8 or older and weigh less than 210 pounds. It's $40 for a 1-hour ride, $70 for 2 hours, including instruction and trail guide.

SKIING MAUNA KEA

Downhill skiing in Hawaii sounds like an oxymoron, but there's a season atop Mauna Kea—usually February and March, but it can snow any time of year up here, even in July. When the skiing's good, it's good: The mountain has 100 square miles of virgin powder, 5-mile-long runs, and vertical drops of 2,500 to 4,500 feet per run. **Ski Guides Hawaii** (☎ **808/885-4188;** www.skihawaii.com) will take experienced skiers up for a full day of skiing at $250 a person, including transportation from Waimea, a guide, lunch, and ski gear. Call any time—you never know when it's ski season in Hawaii.

TENNIS

You can play for free at any Hawaii County tennis court; for a detailed list of all the courts on the island, contact **Hawaii County Department of Parks and Recreation,** 25 Apuni St., Hilo, HI 96720 (☎ **808/961-8720**). The best courts are in Hilo at the Hoolulu Tennis Stadium, located next to the Civic Auditorium on Manono Street; in Kona, the best courts are at Old Airport Park.

Most of the resorts in the Kona-Kohala area do not allow nonguests to use their tennis facilities.

by Jeanette Foster

THE KONA COAST

GUIDED WALKS   The **Kona Historical Society** (☎ **808/323-2005**) hosts two historic walking tours in the Kona region. The 90-minute **Kailua Village Walking Tour** is the most comprehensive tour of the Kona Coast. It takes you all around historic Kailua-Kona, from King Kamehameha's last seat of government to the summer palace of the Hawaiian royal family and beyond, with lots of Hawaiian history and colorful lore along the way. Tours leave Tuesday through Thursday and Saturday at 9:30am, Friday at 9:30am and 1:30pm. Tickets are $10 for adults, $5 for children under 12.

There's also a **Preservation in Progress** walking tour of historic Uchida Coffee Farm, which introduces you to life on a coffee farm. Offered Tuesday and Thursday at 9am, it's $15 adults, $7.50 for kids.

All walks must be booked in advance; call for reservations and departure locations.

A SELF-GUIDED DRIVE If you're interested in seeing how your morning cup of joe goes from beans (cherries, really) to brew, get a copy of the **Coffee Country Driving Tour.** This self-guided drive will take you farm by farm through Kona's famous coffee country; it also features a fascinating history of the area, the lowdown on coffeemaking lingo, some inside tips on how to make a great cup, and even a recipe for Kona coffee mac nut chocolate chunk pie (goes great with a cup of java). The free brochure is available at the **Hawaii Visitors and Convention Bureau,** 75-5719 W. Alii Dr., Kailua-Kona (☎ **808/329-7787;** fax 808/326-7563).

IN & AROUND KAILUA-KONA

Ellison S. Onizuka Space Center. At Kona International Airport, Kailua-Kona. ☎ **808/329-3441.** Fax 808/326-9751. Admission $3 adults, $1 children 12 and under. Daily 8:30am–4:30pm. Parking: In Airport lot, $2 per hour.

This small museum has a real moon rock and memorabilia in honor of Big Island–born astronaut Ellison Onizuka, who died in the 1986 *Challenger* space shuttle disaster. Fun displays in the museum include a gravity well, which illustrates orbital motion, and an interactive rocket-propulsion exhibit, where you can launch your own miniature space shuttle.

Hulihee Palace. 75-5718 Alii Dr., Kailua-Kona. ☎ **808/329-1877.** Admission $5 adults, $1 students, 50¢ children under 12. Mon–Fri 9am–4pm, Sat–Sun 10am–4pm. Daily tours held throughout the day (arrive at least an hour before closing).

This two-story New England–style mansion of lava rock and coral mortar, erected in 1838 by the governor of the island of Hawaii, John Adams Kuakini, overlooks the harbor at Kailua-Kona. The largest, most elegant residence on the island when it was erected, Hulihee (it means "turn and flee") was the gracious summer home of Hawaii's royalty, making it the other royal palace in the U.S. (the most famous being Oahu's Iolani Palace). Now run by Daughters of Hawaii, it features many 19th-century mementos and gorgeous koa furniture. You'll get lots of background and royal lore on the guided tour. No photography, please.

The Palace hosts 12 **Hawaii music and hula concerts** a year, each dedicated to a Hawaiian monarch, at 4pm on the last Sunday of the month (except June and December, when the performances are in conjunction with King Kamehameha Day and Christmas).

Across the street is **Mokuaikaua Church** (☎ **808/329-1589**), the oldest Christian church in Hawaii. It's constructed of lava stones, but its architecture is New England–style all the way. The 112-foot steeple is still the tallest manmade structure in Kailua-Kona.

Kamehameha's Compound at Kamakahonu Bay. On the grounds of King Kamehameha's Kona Beach Hotel, 75-5660 Palani Rd., Kailua-Kona. ☎ **808/329-2911.** Free admission. Self-guided tour; guided tours Mon–Fri at 1:30pm. Daily 9am–4pm.

One the oceanside of this hotel is a restored area of deep spiritual meaning to the Hawaiians. This was the spot that King Kamehameha the Great choose to retreat to in 1812 after conquering the Hawaiian islands, and he stayed until his death in 1819. He built a temple, Ahuena Heiau, and used it as a gathering place for his *kahunas* (priests) to counsel him on governing his people in times of peace. It was in this sacred ground in 1820 that Kamehameha's son Liholiho, as king, sat down to eat with his mother, Keopuolani, and Kamehameha's principal queen, Kaahumanu, thus breaking the ancient kapu of eating with women; this act established a new order in the Hawaiian kingdom. Although the temple grounds are now just a third their original size, they're still impressive. You're free to come and wander the grounds, envisioning the days when King Kamehameha appealed to the gods to help him rule with the spirit of humanity's highest nature.

Here you can see some of the finest images in the Hawaiian islands. There are many petroglyphs of sails, canoes, fish, and chiefs in headdresses, plus a burial scene with three stick figures. Kite motifs—rare in rock art—similar to those found in New Zealand are also here.

Kona Brewing Co. 75-5629 Kuakini Hwy. (at Palani Rd.), Kailua-Kona. ☎ **808/334-1133.** E-mail konaale@aloha.net. Free tours and tastings. Mon–Fri 9am–5pm, Sat 10am–4pm. Turn into Firestone's parking lot; the brewery is at the back of the shopping center (behind Zac's Photo)—look for the orange gecko on the door.

This microbrewery is the first of its kind on the Big Island. Spoon and Pops, a father-and-son duo from Oregon, brought their brewing talents here and now produce about 25 barrels (about 124,000 gallons) per year. Drop by at any time during their business hours and take a quick, informal tour of the brewery, after which you get to taste the product.

Kona Pier. On the waterfront, Kailua-Kona.

Outside of Honokohau Harbor, this is action central for water adventures. Fishing charters, snorkel cruises, and party boats all come and go here. Come by around 4pm, when the captains weigh in with the catch of the day, usually huge marlin—the record-setters often come in here. It's also a great place to watch the sunset.

Natural Energy Laboratory of Hawaii Authority. 73-4460 Queen Kaahumanu Hwy. (at mile marker 94), Kailua-Kona. ☎ **808/329-7341.** www.bigisland.com/nelha. Free guided tour Thurs 10am; reservations required.

Technology buffs should consider a visit to NELHA, the only site in the world where the hot, tropical sun, in combination with a complex pumping system that brings 42°F ocean water from 2,000 feet deep up to land, is used to develop innovations in agriculture, aquaculture, and ocean conservation. The interesting 1½-hour tour takes in all areas of the high-tech ocean science and technology park, including the seawater delivery system, the energy-conversion process, and some of its more interesting tenants, from Maine lobsters and giant clams.

UPCOUNTRY KONA: HOLUALOA

On the slope of Hualalai volcano above Kailua-Kona sits the small village of Holualoa, attracting travelers weary of super resorts who are looking for a little art and culture. And shade.

This funky upcountry town, centered around two-lane Mamalaloa Highway, is nestled amid a lush, tropical landscape where avocados grow as big as footballs. Little more than a wide spot in the road, Holualoa is a cluster of brightly painted, tin-roofed plantation shacks enjoying a reprise as B&Bs, art galleries, and quaint shops (see "Shops & Galleries," below, for details). In two blocks, it manages to pack in two first-rate galleries, a frame shop, a potter, a glassworks, a goldsmith, an old-fashioned general store, a vintage 1930s gas station, a tiny post office, a Catholic church, a library that's open 2 days a week, and the **Kona Hotel**, a hot-pink clapboard structure that looks like a Western movie set; you're welcome to peek in, and you should.

Kaupulehu Petroglyphs. At Kona Village Resort, Queen Kaahumanu Hwy. ☎ **808/325-5555.** Free admission. Guided tours three times a week; reservations required. Turn off Hwy. 19 at the sign for Hualalai, then proceed 2.3 miles to the resort. The petroglyphs are reached via a footpath that goes past the luau grounds, but you'll need a reservation to get past the gatehouse.

Kailua-Kona Town

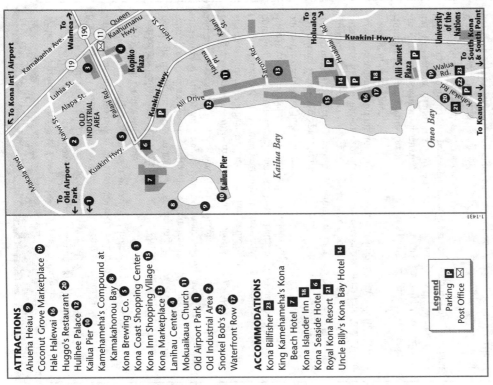

Queen Kaahumanu Hwy.
To Kona Int'l Airport
To Kona Int'l Airport
Kamakaeha Ave. To Waimea →
190
11
19
Kopiko Plaza
Luhia St.
Alapa St.
Kiwi St.
Makala Blvd
OLD INDUSTRIAL AREA
Palani Rd.
Kuakini Hwy.
Kuakini Hwy.
Henry St.
Kaiwi St.
Hanama Pl.
Alii Drive
Sarona Rd.
Kailua Bay
Kailua Pier
Oneo Bay
Kailua Bay
To Old Airport Park →
To Holualoa Rd.
Kuakini Hwy.
Hualalai Rd.
Alii Sunset Plaza
Walua Rd.
Kahakai Rd.
University of the Nations
To South Kona & South Point
To Keauhou →

1-1431

ATTRACTIONS
- Ahuena Heiau **9**
- Coconut Grove Marketplace **19**
- Hale Halewai **16**
- Huggo's Restaurant **12**
- Hulihee Palace **10**
- Kailua Pier **10**
- Kamehameha's Compound at Kamakahonou Bay **8**
- Kona Brewing Co. **5**
- Kona Coast Shopping Center **3**
- Kona Inn Shopping Village **15**
- Kona Marketplace **13**
- Lanihau Center **4**
- Mokuaikaua Church **11**
- Old Airport Park **1**
- Old Industrial Area **2**
- Snorkel Bob's **22**
- Waterfront Row **17**

ACCOMMODATIONS
- Kona Billfisher **23**
- King Kamehameha's Kona Beach Hotel **7**
- Kona Islander Inn **18**
- Kona Seaside Hotel **6**
- Royal Kona Resort **21**
- Uncle Billy's Kona Bay Hotel **14**

Legend
P Parking
☒ Post Office

The cool upslope village is the best place in Hawaii for a coffee break. That's because Holualoa is in the heart of the coffee belt, a 20-mile-long strip at between a 1,000- and 1,400-foot elevation where all the Kona coffee in the world is grown in rich volcanic soil of the cool uplands. Everyone's backyard seems to teem with glossy-green leaves and ruby-red cherries (that's what they call coffee on the vine, because it's a fruit), and the air smells like a San Francisco espresso bar. The **Holuakoa Cafe** is a great place to get a freshly brewed cup.

To reach Holualoa, follow narrow, winding Hualalai Road up the hill from Hwy. 19; it's about a 15-minute drive.

SOUTH KONA

The Painted Church. Hwy. 19, Honaunau. ☎ **808/328-2227.**

Oh, those Belgian priests—what a talented lot. At the turn of the century, Father John Berchman Velghe borrowed a page from Michelangelo and painted biblical scenes inside St. Benedict's Catholic Church so the illiterate Hawaiians could visualize the white man's version of creation.

ⓘ Big Island Highlights for Kids

Walking Through Thurston Lava Tube at Hawaii Volcanoes National Park (*see p. 328*) It's scary, it's spooky, and it's perfect for any kid. You hike downhill through a rain forest full of little chittering native birds to enter this huge, silent black hole full of drips, cobwebs, and tree roots that stretches underground for almost a half-mile to a fork in the tunnel, which leads up a stairway to our world or—or here's the best part—down an unexplored hole that probably goes all the way to China. Double dare you.

Snorkeling Kahalu Beach Park (*see p. 292*) The shallow waters off Kahalu Beach are the perfect place to take kids snorkeling. The waters are shallow and calm, protected by a barrier reef, and the abundance of fish will keep the kids' attention. You might want to pick up a fish identification card at any dive shop and make a game out of seeing how many fish the kids can find.

Riding a Submarine into the Underwater World (*see p. 302*) The huge viewing windows will have the kids enthralled as the high-tech sub leaves the surface and plunges 120 feet down through the mysterious Neptunian waters. The hour-long trip is just enough time to hold their attention as the sub passes through clouds of reef fish and past prehistoric-looking corals. Occasionally, way out in the deep, some lucky divers even spot Jaws!

Launching Your Own Space Shuttle (*see p. 313*) Okay, it's a model of a space shuttle, but it's close enough to the real thing to be a real blast. The Ellison S. Onizuka Space Center has dozens of interactive displays to thrill budding young astronauts, like a hands-on experience with gyroscopic stabilization. Great video clips of astronauts working and living in space may inspire your kids to dream of working in outer space.

Hunting for Petroglyphs (*see p. 318*) There's plenty of space to run around and discover ancient stone carvings at either the Puako Petroglyph Archaeological District, at Mauna Lani Resort, or at the King's Trail by the Royal Waikoloan. And finding the petroglyphs is only part of the game—once you find them, you have to guess what the designs mean.

Watching the Volcano (*see p. 328*) Any kid who doesn't get a kick out of watching a live volcano set the night on fire has been watching too much television. Take hot dogs, bottled water, flashlights, and sturdy shoes and follow the ranger's instructions on where to safely view the lava. You might want to make the trip during daylight so junior can see the Technicolor difference in experiencing a lava flow in the dark.

⭐ **Puuhonua O Honaunau National Historical Park.** Hwy. 160 (off Hwy. 11 at mile marker 104), Honaunau. ☎ **808/328-2288.** Fax 808/328-9485. Admission $2, free for children 15 and under. Visitor center open daily 7:30am–5:30pm; park open Mon–Thurs 6am–8pm, Fri–Sun 6am–11pm. From Hwy. 11, 3½ miles to park entrance.

With its fierce, haunting idols, this sacred site on the black-lava Kona Coast looks forbidding. To ancient Hawaiians, however, it must have been a welcome sight, for Puuhonua O Honaunau served as a 16th-century place of refuge, providing sanctuary for defeated warriors and *kapu* (taboo) violators. A great rock wall—1,000 feet long, 10 feet high, and 17 feet thick—defines the refuge where Hawaiians found safety. On the wall's north end is Hale O Keawe Heiau, which holds the bones of 23 Hawaiian

Impressions

I think the Kona coffee has a richer flavor than any other.

—Mark Twain

chiefs. Other archaeological finds include burial sites, old trails, and a portion of an ancient village. On a self-guided tour of the 180-acre site—restored to its pre-contact state—you can see and learn about reconstructed thatched huts, canoes, and idols and feel the *mana* (power) of old Hawaii.

A cultural festival, usually held in June, invites you to join in games, learn crafts, sample Hawaiian food, see traditional hula, and experience life in the islands before outsiders arrived in the late 1700s. Every Labor Day weekend, one of Hawaii's major outrigger canoe races starts here and ends in Kailua-Kona, 18 miles away. Call for details on both events.

Kona Historical Society Museum. Hwy. 11, between mile markers 111 and 112 (park at Kona Specialty Meats parking lot), Captain Cook. ☎ **808/323-3222** or 808/323-2005. Mon–Fri 9am–3pm; Sat 10am–2pm. Admission $2.

This well-organized pocket museum is housed in the historic Greenwell Store, built in 1875 by Henry Nicholas Greenwell out of native stone and lime mortar made from burnt coral. Inside, antiques, artifacts, and photos tell the story of this fabled coast. Since coffee-growing and cattle-raising were the area's main industries, the museum is filled with items that were common to everyday life in the last century. Serious history buffs should sign up for one of the museum's walking tours; see "Guided Walks," above.

THE KOHALA COAST

ANCIENT HAWAIIAN FISHPONDS   Like their Polynesian forefathers, Hawaiians were among the first aquaculturists on the planet. They had developed ways of using the brackish ponds along the shoreline to stock and harvest fish, which scientists are still marveling at even today. There are actually two different types of ancient fishponds (*loko i'a*): Closed ponds, inshore and closed off from the ocean, were used to raise mullet and milkfish; open ponds were open to the sea, with rock walls as a barrier to the ocean and sluice gates that connected the ponds to the ocean. The gates were woven vines, with just enough room for juvenile fish to swim in at high tide while keeping the bigger, fatter fish from swimming out. Generally, the Hawaiians raised mullet, milkfish, and shrimp in these open ponds; and juvenile manini, papio, eels, and barracuda found their way in during high tides.

The **Kalahuipuaa Fishponds** at Mauna Lani Resort (☎ **808/885-6622**) are great examples of both types of ponds in a lush tropical setting. South of the Mauna Lani Resort are **Kuualii** and **Kahapapa Fishponds** at the Royal Waikoloan Hotel (☎ **808/885-6789**). Both resorts have taken great pains to lovingly restore the ponds to their original states and to preserve them for future generations; call ahead to arrange a free guided tour.

KOHALA COAST PETROGLYPHS   At first glance, the huge slate of pahoehoe looks like any other smooth black slate of lava on the seacoast of the Big Island of Hawaii—until gradually, in slanting rays of the sun, a wonderful cast of characters suddenly leaps to life before your eyes. You see dancers and paddlers, fishermen and chiefs, hundreds of marchers all in a row. Everywhere, there are pictures of the tools of daily life: fish hooks, spears, poi pounders, canoes. Most common are family groups: father, mother, and child. There are post–European contact petroglyphs of ships, anchors, goats, horses, and guns.

The Hawaiian petroglyph is a great enigma of the Pacific. No one knows who made them or why, only that they're here—hard physical evidence that early Hawaiians were gifted illustrators of their life and times. Petroglyphs appear at 135 different sites on six inhabited islands, but most of them are found on the Big Island.

The largest concentration of stone symbols in the Pacific lies within 233-acre **Puako Petroglyph Archaeological District,** near Mauna Lani Resort. Once hard to find, the enigmatic graffiti is now easily reachable. The 1.4-mile **Malama Trail** starts north of Mauna Lani Resort; take Hwy. 19 to the resort turnoff and drive toward the coast on North Kaniku Drive, which ends at a parking lot; the trailhead is marked by a sign and interpretive kiosk. Go in the early morning or late afternoon when it's cool. A total of 3,000 designs have been identified, including paddlers, sails, marchers, dancers, and family groups, as well as dog, chicken, turtle, and deity symbols.

At the **Royal Waikoloan** (☎ 808/885-6789) is the **King's Trail,** an ancient footpath by the sea that leads to a place out by the golf course where the black lava swirls into a flat tablet. The rock art here is especially graphic and easy to see along the well-marked trail. Free, guided, 1-hour tours of the resort's petroglyphs are offered Monday through Friday at 8am; the King's Shops in Waikoloa also offers a free tour of the trail every Saturday at 8:30am, starting in front of the Food Pavilion.

Warning: The petroglyphs are thousands of years old and easily destroyed. Do not walk on them or attempt to take a "rubbing" (there's a special area in the Puako Preserve for doing so). The best way to capture a petroglyph is with a late-afternoon photo, when the shadows are long.

Puukohola Heiau National Historic Site. Hwy. 270, near Kawaihae Harbor. ☎ 808/882-7218. Fax 808/882-7210. Free admission. Daily 7:30am–4pm. The visitor center is on Hwy. 270, and the heiau is a short walk away; the trail is closed when it's too windy, so call ahead if you're in doubt.

This seacoast temple, called "the hill of the whale," is the single most imposing and dramatic structure of the ancient Hawaiians, built by Kamehameha I in 1790–91. The temple stands 224 feet long by 100 feet wide, with three narrow terraces on the seaside and an amphitheater to view canoes. Kamehameha built this temple of sacrifice with mortarless stone after a prophet told him he would conquer and unite the islands if he did; 4 years later, he fulfilled his kingly goal. In addition to the heiau, the site also includes the house of John Young, a trusted advisor of Kamehameha, and offshore, the submerged ruins of Hale O Ka Puni, a shrine dedicated to the shark gods.

NORTH KOHALA
The Original King Kamehameha Statue. Hwy. 270, Kapaau.

King Kamehameha the Great stands, right arm outstretched, left arm holding a spear, as if guarding the senior citizens who have turned a century-old New England–style courthouse into an airy center for their golden years. The center is worth a stop just to meet the town elders, who are quick to point out the sites, hand you a free *Guide to Historic North Kohala,* and give you a brief tour of the courthouse, where a faded photo of FDR looms over the judge's dais and the walls are covered with the faces of innocent-looking local boys killed in World War II, Korea, and Vietnam.

But the statue's the main attraction here. There's one just like it in Honolulu, across the street from Iolani Palace, but this is the original: an 8-foot, 6-inch bronze statue by Thomas R. Gould, a Boston sculptor. It was cast in Europe in 1880 but was lost at sea on its way to Hawaii. A sea captain eventually recovered and delivered it; it was finally put here, near Kamehameha's Kohala birthplace, in 1912.

Kamehameha was born in 1750, became ruler of Hawaii in 1810, and died in Kailua-Kona in 1819. His burial site remains a mystery.

Pololu Valley Lookout. At the end of Hwy. 270, Makapala.

Glimpse the vertical jade-green cliffs of the Hamakua Coast and two islets offshore at this end-of-the-road scenic lookout, which may look familiar once you get here—it often appears on travel posters. Most people race up, jump out, take a snapshot, and turn around and drive off; but it's a beautiful scene, so linger if you can. For the more adventurous, a switchback trail leads to a secluded black-sand beach at the mouth of a wild valley once planted in taro; bring water and bug spray.

Lapakahi State Historical Park. Hwy. 270, Mahukona. ☎ **808/889-5566.** Free admission. Daily 8am–4pm. Guided tours by appointment.

This 14th-century fishing village, on a hot, dry, dusty stretch of coast, offers a glimpse into the lifestyle of the ancients. Lapakahi is the best-preserved fishing village in Hawaii. Take the self-guided, mile-long loop trail past stone platforms, fish shrines, rock shelters, salt pans, and restored *hale* (houses) to a coral-sand beach and the deep blue sea. Wear good hiking shoes or tennies; it's a hearty 45-minute walk. Go early or later in the afternoon, as the sun is hot, shade is at a premium, and water is available (an attendant in a thatch hut, who hands out maps, also keeps a handy cooler of ice water available in case you didn't bring your own).

Mookini Luakini. On the north shore, near Upolu Point Airport.

On the coast where King Kamehameha the Great was born stands Hawaii's oldest, largest, and most sacred religious site, and now a national historical landmark—the 1,500-year-old Mookini Heiau, used by kings to pray and offer human sacrifices. You need a four-wheel–drive to get here, as the road is rough, but it's worth the trip if you can make it. The massive three-story stone temple, dedicated to Ku, the Hawaiian god of war, was erected in A.D. 480; each stone is said to have been passed hand to hand from Pololu Valley, 14 miles away, by 18,000 men who worked from sunset to sunrise. Kamehameha, born nearby under Halley's Comet, sought spiritual guidance here before embarking on his campaign to unite Hawaii. Go in the late afternoon when the setting sun strikes the lava-rock walls and creates a primal mood.

WAIMEA (KAMUELA)

Kamuela Museum. At the junction of Hwy. 19 and Hwy. 250, Waimea. ☎ **808/885-4724.** Admission $5 adults, $2 children under 12. Daily 8am–5pm.

It only takes about an hour to explore tiny Kamuela Museum and its eclectic collection of stuff. An early Hawaiian dogtoothed death cup sits next to a piece of rope used on the *Apollo* mission, which sits near ancient artifacts from the royal family.

PARKER RANCH

Consider the numbers: 225,000 acres, 50,000 head of cattle, 700 miles of fence, 400 working horses, 27 cowboys, producing 80% of the beef marketed in Hawaii. The *paniolo* (cowboy) tradition began here in 1809, when John Parker, a 19-year-old New England sailor, jumped ship and rounded up wild cows for King Kamehameha—and it lives on with a skeleton posse of around 30 to 40 cowboys, each assigned about eight horses to patrol America's third largest ranch, and Hawaii's biggest. There's some evidence that Hawaiian cowboys were the first to be taught by the great Spanish horsemen, the *vaqueros*; they were cowboying 40 years before their counterparts in California, Texas, and the Pacific Northwest.

The **Visitor Center,** located at the Parker Ranch Shopping Center on Hwy. 190 (☎ **808/885-7655),** is open daily from 9am to 5pm and houses the **Parker Ranch Museum,** which displays items that have been used throughout the ranch's history dating back to 1847. The museum also illustrates the six generations of Parker family history. An interesting video takes you inside the ranch and captures the essence of day-to-day life there.

You can also tour two historic homes on the ranch. In 1989, the late Richard Smart—the sixth-generation heir who sought a career on Broadway (and danced with Nanette Fabray in *Bloomer Girl* at the Schubert Theater)—opened his 8,000-square-foot yellow Victorian home, **Puuopelu,** to art lovers, who discovered a French Regency gallery of 100 original works by impressionists including Renoir, Degas, Dufy, Corot, Utrillo, and Pissarro. Next door is **Mana Hale,** built 140 years ago, a little New England saltbox made out of koa wood.

Admission is $10 for both the museum and the tours of both homes; admission to the museum only is $5. If you're buying a dual ticket, the last one is sold at 3pm; if you're visiting the museum only, you can arrive as late as 4pm. Allow about 1½ hours to see everything. See "Horseback Riding," earlier in this chapter, for details on riding tours of Parker Ranch.

MAUNA KEA

Some of us just have to be on top of things. If you do, head for the summit of Mauna Kea, the world's tallest mountain.

Mauna Kea's summit is the best place on earth for astronomical observations, because its mid-Pacific site is near the equator and enjoys clear, pollution-free skies and pitch-black nights with no urban light to interfere with the "seeing." Needless to say, the stargazing from here is fantastic, even with the naked eye. That's why Mauna Kea is home to the world's largest telescope.

SETTING OUT   You need a four-wheel-drive to climb to the peak, **Observatory Hill,** as you'll be climbing from sea level through 10 different climate zones to the alpine heights. A standard car will get you as far as the visitors center, but check your rental agreement before you go; some prohibit you from taking your car on the Saddle Road, which is narrow, rutted, and has a soft shoulder. For four-wheel drives, though, it's no big deal.

SAFETY TIPS   Always check the weather and Mauna Kea Road conditions before you head out (☎ **808/969-3218).** Dress warmly, as the temps drop into the 30s after dark. Other tips for preparing for your drive to the summit: Drink as much liquid as possible, avoiding alcohol and coffee, in the 36 hours surrounding your trip to avoid dehydration. Don't go within 24 hours of scuba diving—you could get the bends. Avoid gas-producing food the day before, like beans, cabbage, onions, soft drinks, or

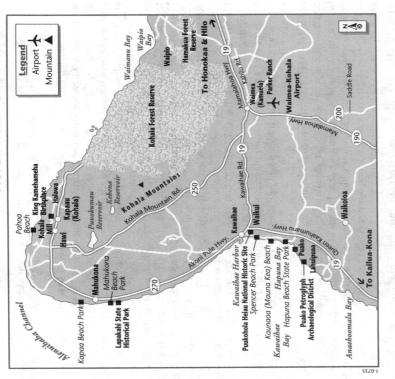

North Kohala & Waimea

Legend
✈ Airport
▲ Mountain

Alenuihaha Channel

Pahoa Beach
Kapaa Beach Park
Kohala Mill
King Kamehameha
Kohala Birthplace
Hawi
Halawa
Kapaau (Kohala)
Puuohumau
Reservoir
Mahukona
Mahukona Beach Park
Lapakahi State Historical Park
Kawaihae Harbor
Puukohola Heiau National Historic Site
Spencer Beach Park
Kawaihae
Kawaihae Bay
Kaunooa (Mauna Kea) Beach
Hapuna Bay
Hapuna Beach State Park
Puako
Puako Petroglyph Archaeological District
Lihuipua
Anaehoomalu Bay
To Kailua-Kona
Queen Kaahumanu Hwy.
Akoni Pule Hwy.
Kawaihae Rd.
Walkui
Kohala Mountains
Kohala Mountain Rd.
Kehena Reservoir
Kohala Forest Reserve
Waimanu Bay
Waipio Bay
Waipio
Hamakua Forest Reserve
To Honokaa & Hilo
Waimea (Kamuela)
Parker Ranch
Waimea-Kohala Airport
Mamalahoa Hwy.
Kahilu Rd.
Saddle Road
Mamalahoa Hwy.
Waikoloa
19
250
270
19
190
200

N

1-0735

starches. If you smoke, take a break for 48 hours before to allow carbon monoxide in your bloodstream to dissipate—you need all the oxygen you can get. Wear dark sunglasses to avoid snow blindness, and use lots of sunscreen and lip balm. Anyone under 16 is advised to stay below; the same caveat holds for pregnant women and anyone with a heart condition or lung ailment. Once you're at the top, don't overexert yourself; it's bad for your heart. Take it easy up there.

ACCESS POINTS & VISITOR CENTERS Before you climb the mountain, you've got to find it. It's about an hour from Hilo and Waimea to the visitors center and another 30 to 45 minutes from there to the summit. Take the Saddle Road (Hwy. 200; also known as the Hawaii Belt Rd.); from Hwy. 190, it's about 19 miles to Mauna Kea State Recreation Area, a good place to stop and stretch your legs. Go another 9 miles to the unmarked Summit Road turnoff, at the 28-mile marker (about 9,300 feet), across from the Hunter's Check-in Station. The higher you go, the more lightheaded you get, sometimes even dizzy; it usually sets in after the 9,600-foot marker (about 6.2 miles up the Summit Road), the last comfort zone and site of the **Onizuka Visitor Center** (☎ **808/961-2180;** open Thursday to Sunday 5:30 to 10pm, Friday 9am to noon and 1 to 4:30pm, Saturday to Sunday 9am to noon and 1 to 2pm), named in memory of Hawaii's fallen astronaut, a native of the Big Island and a victim of the *Challenger* explosion.

TOURS & PROGRAMS If you'd rather not go it alone to the top, you can caravan up as part of a **free summit tour;** the tours, offered Saturday and Sunday at 1pm, start at the visitor center; you must be 16 years or older and have a four-wheel-drive vehicle. The tours explain the development of the facilities on Mauna Kea and include a walking tour of an observatory at 13,796 feet. Call ☎ 808/935-3371 if you'd like to participate.

On Thursday, Friday, Saturday, and Sunday nights from 6:30 to 10pm, you can do some serious **stargazing from the Onizuka Visitor Center.** There's a free lecture at 6:30pm, and you'll have a chance to peer through an 11-inch telescope. Bring your own telescope or binoculars (with a red filter), if you've got 'em, as well as hot drinks and a snack. Dress for 30 to 40°F temperatures, but call for the weather report first (☎ 808/969-3218). Families are welcome.

You can see a model of the world's largest telescope, which sits atop Mauna Kea, at the **Keck Control Center,** 65-1120 Mamalahoa Hwy. (Hwy. 19), across from the North Hawaii Community Hospital, Waimea (☎ 808/885-7887; open Monday to Friday 8am to 4:30pm). Free brochures are available, and there's a 10-minute video explaining the Keck's search for objects in deep space.

If you don't have a four-wheel drive but still want to see the summit, consider **Mauna Kea Summit Tours** (☎ 808/775-7121; fax 808/775-9911), offered Tuesday, Thursday, and Saturday. An experienced local guide will lead you on a 6-hour tour, which includes a stop at one of the observatories. Tours are limited to eight people and leave from the Parker Ranch Shopping Center in Waimea. The cost is $80, including a picnic lunch.

MAKING THE CLIMB If you're heading up on your own, stop at the visitor center for about a half-hour to get acquainted with the altitude, walk around, eat a banana, drink lots of water, and take deep breaths of the crystal-clear air before you press on, upward in low gear, engine whining. It takes about 30 to 45 minutes to get to the top from there. It's a mere 6 miles, but you climb from 9,000 to nearly 14,000 feet.

Up there, 11 nations, including Japan, France, and Canada, have set up peerless infrared telescopes to look into deep space, searching for black holes and far-flung galaxies for signs of life. Among them sits the **Keck Telescope,** the world's largest. Developed by the UC Berkeley and CalTech, it's eight stories high, weighs 150 tons, and has a 33-foot-diameter mirror made of 36 perfectly attuned hexagon mirrors, like a fly's eye, instead of one conventional lens.

Also at the summit, up a narrow footpath, is a **cairn of rocks;** from it, you can see forever across the Pacific Ocean in a 360° view that's beyond words and pictures. When it's socked in (and that can happen while you're standing there), you get a surreal look at the summits of Mauna Loa and Maui's Haleakala poking through the puffy white cumulus clouds beneath your feet.

AT THE SUMMIT

Inside a cinder cone just below the summit is **Lake Waiau,** the only glacial lake in the mid-Pacific and the third highest lake in America (13,020 feet above sea level). The lake never dries up, even though it sits in porous lava where there are no springs and it only rains 15 inches a year. Nobody except "Ripley's Believe It or Not" quite knows what to make of this, although scientists suspect the lake is replenished by snow melt and permafrost from submerged lava tubes. You can't see the lake from Summit Road; you must take a brief, high-altitude hike to see it, but it's easy: On the final approach to the summit area, upon regaining the blacktop road, go about 200 yards to the major switchback, and make a hard right turn. Park on the shoulder of the road (which, if you brought your altimeter, is at 13,200 ft.) No sign points the way, but there's an obvious half-mile trail that goes down to it about 200 feet across the lava. Follow the base of the big cinder cone on your left; you should have the summit of Mauna Loa in view directly ahead as you walk.

THE HAMAKUA COAST
NATURAL WONDERS ALONG THE COAST

Akaka Falls. On Hwy. 19, Honomu (8 miles north of Hilo). Turn left at Honomu and head 3.6 miles inland on Akaka Falls Rd. (Hwy. 220).

One of Hawaii's most scenic waterfalls is an easy, 1-mile paved loop through a rain forest, past bamboo and ginger and down to an observation point, where you'll have a perfect view of 442-foot Akaka and nearby Kahuna Falls, which is a mere 100-footer. Keep your eyes peeled for rainbows.

Hawaii Tropical Botanical Garden. Off Hwy. 19 on the 4-mile Scenic Route, Onomea Bay (8 miles north of Hilo). ☎ **808/964-5233.** E-mail htbg@ilhawaii.net. Admission **$15** adults, **$5** children 6–16, including shuttle to and from Onomea Valley. Daily 8:30am–4:30pm.

More than 1,800 species of tropical plants thrive in this little-known Eden by the sea. The 40-acre garden, nestled between the crashing surf and a thundering waterfall, has the world's largest selection of tropical plants growing in a natural environment, including a torch ginger forest, a banyan canyon, an orchid garden, a banana grove, a bromeliad hill, and a golden bamboo grove, which rattles like a jungle drum in the trade winds. The torch gingers give new meaning to their name, towering as they do on 12-foot stalks. Each spectacular specimen is named by genus and species, and caretakers point out new or rare buds in bloom. Some endangered Hawaiian specimens, like the rare Gardenia remyi, are flourishing in this habitat.

The gardens are seldom crowded; you can wander around by yourself all day, taking pictures, writing in your journal, or just soaking up the peace and quiet.

Laupahoehoe Beach Park. Laupahoehoe Point exit off Hwy. 19.

This idyllic place holds a grim reminder of nature's fury. In 1946, a tidal wave swept across the village that once stood on this lava-leaf (that's what *laupahoehoe* means) peninsula and claimed the lives of 20 students and four teachers. A memorial recalls the tragedy in this pretty little park, where the land ends in black sea stacks that resemble tombstones. It's not a place for swimming, but the views are spectacular.

HONOKAA

Worth a visit to see the remnants of plantation life when sugar was king, Honokaa is a real place that hasn't yet been boutiqued into a shopping mall; it looks as if someone has kept it in a bell jar since 1920. There's a real barber shop, a real Filipino store, some really good shopping (see "Shops & Galleries," below), and a real hotel with creaky floorboards that serves real, hearty food. It also serves as the gateway to spectacular Waipio Valley (below).

Honokaa has no attractions, per se, but you might want to check out the **Katsu Goto Memorial,** next to the library at the Hilo end of town. Katsu Goto, one of the first indentured Japanese immigrants, arrived in Honokaa in the late 1800s to work on the sugar plantations. He learned English, quit the plantation, and aided his fellow immigrants in labor disputes with American planters. On Oct. 23, 1889, he was hanged from a lamppost in Honokaa, a victim of local-style justice. Today, a memorial recalls Goto's heroic human-rights struggle.

THE END OF THE ROAD: WAIPIO VALLEY

Long ago, this lush, tropical place was the valley of kings, who called it the valley of "curving water" (which is what *Waipio* means). From the black-sand bay at its mouth, Waipio sweeps back 6 miles between sheer, cathedral-like walls that reach almost a mile high. Here, 40,000 Hawaiians lived in a garden of Eden etched by streams and waterfalls amid evergreen taro, red bananas, and wild guavas. Only about 50 Hawaiians live in the valley today, tending taro, fishing, and soaking up the ambiance of this old Hawaiian place.

A sacred place, many of the ancient royals are buried in Wapio's hidden crevices; some believe they rise up to become Marchers of the Night, whose chants reverberate through the valley. It's here that the caskets of Hawaiian chiefs Liloa and Lono Ika Makahiki, recently stolen from Bishop Museum, are believed to have been returned by Hawaiians. The valley is steeped in myth and legend, some of which you may hear, usually after dark in the company of Hawaiian elders who sometimes tell about Nenewe the Shark Man, who lives in a pool, and the ghost of the underworld, who periodically rises to the surface through a tunnel by the sea.

To get to Waipio Valley, take Hwy. 19 from Hilo to Honokaa, then Hwy. 240 to

⭐ **Waipio Valley Lookout,** a grassy park on the edge of Waipio Valley's sheer cliffs with splendid views of the wild oasis below. This is a great place for a picnic; you can sit at old redwood picnic tables and watch the white combers race upon the black-sand beach at the mouth of Waipio Valley.

From the lookout, you can hike down into the valley (see "Hiking & Camping," above), or take the **Waipio Valley Shuttle** (☎ **808/775-7121**) on a 90-minute guided tour. The shuttle runs Monday to Saturday from 9am to 4pm; tickets are $35 for adults, $15 for kids 3 to 11. Get your tickets at **Waipio Valley Art Works,** on Hwy. 240, 2 miles from the lookout (☎ **808/775-0958**).

You can also explore the valley on a **Waipio Valley Wagon Tour** (☎ **808/775-9518;** fax 808/775-9318), a mule-drawn surrey that takes you on a narrated 90-minute historical tour of the valley. Tours are offered Monday to Saturday at 9:30am, 11:30am, 1:30pm, and 3:30pm. They're $40 for adults, $20 for children ages 3 to 12; call for reservations.

If you want to spend more than a day in the valley, plan ahead. A few simple B&Bs are situated on the ridge overlooking the valley and require advance reservations (see "Accommodations," above). While it's possible to camp (see "Hiking & Camping," above), it does put a strain on the natural environment here.

HILO

A SELF-GUIDED WALKING TOUR

Program, 252 Kamehameha Ave., Hilo, HI 96720 (☎ **808/935-8850**) for a copy of their very informative self-guided walking tour of 18 historic sites in Hilo, focusing on various sites from the 1870s to the present. Contact or stop by the **Hilo Main Street**

SAMPAN TOURS Here's an ideal way to sightsee: Catch a sampan with **Hilo Sampan History Tours** (☎ **808/959-7864**) and ride around Hilo like everyone did back in the 1930s, in the vintage open-air jitneys that served as the city's main source of public transportation between 1931 and 1940. The history route runs around downtown, taking in the port, the beaches, Banyan Gardens, and some lovely old residential neighborhoods. The sampans leave the Pier every hour on the hour between 9am and 5pm weekdays and stop along Banyan Drive and at about a dozen other locations around town; call for the pickup spot nearest you. The driver delivers an animated running commentary on Hilo's colorful history, and local passengers often contribute historic or personal anecdotes. A one-way ticket is $2, a full-day pass is $7. It's the Big Island's best transit bargain—cheap, friendly, and fun.

ON THE WATERFRONT

Old banyan trees shade **Banyan Drive,** the lane that curves along the waterfront to the Hilo Bay hotels. Most of the trees were planted in the mid-1930s by memorable

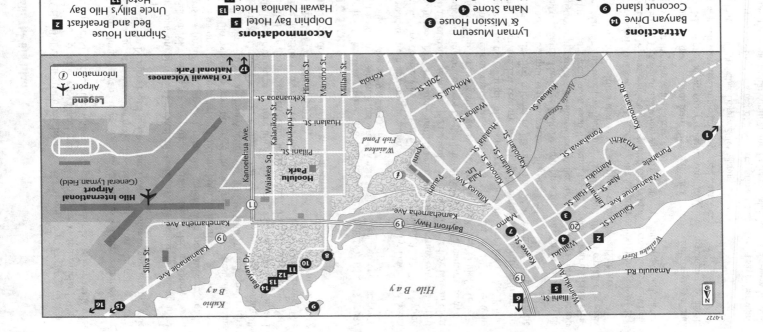

Attractions

14 Banyan Drive
9 Coconut Island
7 Hilo Farmer's Market
15 Leleiwi Beach Park
10 Liliuokalani Gardens
3 Lyman Museum & Mission House
4 Naha Stone
17 Nani Mau Gardens
1 Rainbow Falls
8 Suisan Fish Market & Auction

Accommodations

5 Dolphin Bay Hotel
13 Hawaii Naniloa Hotel
11 Hilo Hawaiian Hotel
6 Lihi Kai
16 Maureen's Bed and Breakfast
2 Shipman House Bed and Breakfast
12 Uncle Billy's Hilo Bay Hotel

Legend

ℹ Information
✈ Airport

To Hawaii Volcanoes National Park

Hilo International Airport (General Lyman Field)

Hilo Bay
Kuhio Bay

1-0727

visitors like Cecil B. DeMille (who was here in 1933 filming *Four Frightened People*), Babe Ruth (in front of Hilo Hawaiian Hotel), King George V, and Amelia Earhart, but many were planted by celebrities whose fleeting fame didn't last as long as the trees themselves.

It's worth a stop along Banyan Drive—especially if the coast is clear and the summit of Mauna Kea is free of clouds—to make the short walk across the concrete-arch bridge in front of the Naniloa Hotel to **Coconut Island**, if only to gain a panoramic sense of the place.

Also along Banyan Drive is **Liliuokalani Gardens**, the largest formal Japanese garden this side of Tokyo. This 30-acre park, named for Hawaii's last monarch, Queen Liliuokalani, is as pretty as a postcard from the Orient with bonsai, carp ponds, pagodas, and a moon gate bridge. Free admission; open 24 hours.

Since 1914, Hilo fishermen have delivered the catch of the day—fresh ahi, mahi-mahi, and opakapaka—to **Suisan Fish Auction** (☎ 808/935-8051), at Kamehameha Avenue and Banyan Drive. The boats return to harbor just at sunrise after fishing all night; the auction is conducted in three lingoes, including Hawaii's own pidgin, and can last an hour if the catch has been good. It begins at 7:30am Monday through Saturday, so arrive at 6:30am to get a good look as the fishers unload the boats. The **Suisan Fish Market** (☎ 808/935-9349; Monday to Friday 8am to 5pm, Saturday 8am to 4pm) is next door if you miss the early-morning action.

OTHER HILO SIGHTS

Lyman Museum & Mission House. 276 Haili St. (at Kapiolani St.), Hilo. ☎ 808/935-5021. E-mail lymanwks@interpac.net. Admission $5 adults, $3 seniors over 60, students, and children under 18. Mon-Sat 9am-4:30pm.

The oldest wood-frame house on the island was built in 1839 by David and Sarah Lyman, a missionary couple who arrived from New England in 1832. This hybrid Cape Cod combined New England– and Hawaiian-style architecture with a pitched thatch roof. Built of hand-hewn koa planks and timbers, it's crowned by Hawaii's first corrugated zinc roof, imported from England in 1856. Here, the Lymans served as the spiritual center of Hilo, receiving such guests as Mark Twain, Robert Louis Stevenson, and Hawaii's own curious monarchs. Opened as a museum in 1931, the well-preserved house is the best example of missionary life and times in Hawaii. You'll find lots of artifacts from the last century, including furniture and clothing from the Lymans and one of the first mirrors in Hawaii. The 21st century has entered the museum with online computers to interactive, high-tech exhibits.

Next door, the **Earth Heritage Gallery** continues the story of the islands with geology and astronomy exhibits, a mineral rock collection that's rated as one of the top 10 in the country, and a section on local flora and fauna. Upstairs is the **Island Heritage Gallery**, featuring native Hawaii cultural displays, including a replica of a grass hut, and those from other cultures that were transplanted on Hawaii's shores.

Maunaloa Macadamia Nut Factory. Macadamia Nut Rd. (8 miles from Hilo, off Hwy. 11), Hilo. ☎ 808/966-8618. Free admission, self-guided factory tours; orchard tours every hour 10am–4pm; $5 adults, $3 children. Daily 9am–4pm. From Hwy. 11, turn on Macadamia Nut Road; go 3 miles down the road to the factory.

Explore this unique factory and learn how Hawaii's favorite nut is grown and processed; the 1-hour guided van tour even takes you through the macadamia orchard. And, of course, you'll want to sample the tasty mac nuts, too.

Naha Stone. In front of Hilo Public Library, 300 Waianuenue Ave.

This 2½-ton stone was used as a test of royal strength: Ancient legend says that whoever could move the stone would conquer and unite the islands. As a 14-year-old boy,

King Kamehameha the Great moved the stone—and fulfilled his destiny. The **Pinao stone**, next to it, once guarded an ancient heiau.

Nani Mau Gardens. 421 Makalika St. (3 miles south of Hilo Airport on Hwy. 11), Hilo. ☎ **808/959-3541.** Fax 808/959-3152. Admission $7.50 adults, $6 seniors, $4.50 children 6–18. Tram tours $5 extra. Reservations required for parties of 5 or more. Daily 8am–5pm.

Just outside Hilo is Nani Mau ("forever beautiful") Gardens, where Makato Nitahara, who turned a 20-acre papaya patch into a tropical garden, claims to have every flowering plant in Hawaii. That's more than 2,000 varieties, from fragile hibiscus, whose boom lasts only a day, to durable red anthuriums imported from South America. There are also Japanese gardens, an orchid walkway, a botanical museum, and two restaurants.

Panaewa Rainforest Zoo. Mamaki Rd. (off Hwy. 11), Hilo. ☎ **808/959-7224.** Admission free. Daily 9am–4pm.

Nestled in the heart of the Panaewa Forest Reserve south of Hilo, this 12-acre zoo is the only outdoor rain forest zoo in the U.S. Some 50 species of animals from rain forests around the globe call Panaewa home—including several endangered Hawaiian birds—and are exhibited in a natural setting. This is one of the few zoos where you can observe Sumatran tigers, Brazilian tapirs, and the rare pygmy hippopotamus, an endangered "mini-hipo" found in Western Africa.

Rainbow Falls. West on Waianuenue Ave., past Kaumana Dr.

Go in the morning, around 9 or 10am, just as the sun comes over the mango trees, to see Rainbow Falls at its best; the 80-foot falls spill into a big round natural pool surrounded by wild ginger. If you like legends, try this: Hina, the mother of Maui, lives in the cave behind the falls. In the old days, before liability suits and lawyers, people swam in the pool, but it's now prohibited.

ON THE ROAD TO THE VOLCANO
VOLCANO VILLAGE: GATEWAY TO HAWAII VOLCANOES NATIONAL PARK

In the 19th century, before tourism became Hawaii's middle name, the islands' singular attraction for world travelers wasn't the beach, but the volcano. From the world over, curious spectators gathered on the rim of Kilauea's Halemaumau crater to see one of the greatest wonders of the globe. Those who came to stand in awe took shelter after sundown in a large grass hut perched on the rim of Kilauea—Hawaii's first tourist hotel, which became **Volcano House.**

Since Kilauea and environs were officially designated Hawaii Volcanoes National Park in 1916, a village has popped up at its front door. Not even a real town, Volcano is just a wide spot in Old Volcano Road: a 10-block area with two general stores, a couple of restaurants, a post office, a coffee shop, a new firehouse (built in one weekend by volunteers), and the only ATM between Keeau and Ocean View. Volcano has no stoplights or jail, not even a church or a cemetery; but there is a winery. There's no baseball diamond either, which is probably just as well, since it rains a lot in Volcano—100 inches a year—which makes everything grow Jack-and-the-Beanstalk style. If Volcano didn't have a real volcano in its backyard, it would probably be called Rain Forest.

Geographically speaking, Volcano isn't actually the gateway to Hawaii Volcanoes National Park; it's really a little off to the side and north. Highway 11, the Hawaii Belt Road, which leads directly to the park, bypasses Volcano village. But if you're going to see the volcano, Volcano is a great place to spend a few days—in fact, it's the only place (see "Accommodations," earlier in this chapter).

Even if you're just visiting the park for the day, it's worth turning off to stop for gas at **Volcano General Store**, on Haunani Road, where kindly clerks give directions and sell fresh orchid sprays, local poha berry jam, and bowls of chili rice, a local favorite.

Volcano Winery, Volcano Golf Course Road, off Hwy. 11 at the 30-mile marker; go all the way to the end (☎ **808/967-7479**), is worth a stop to taste the local wines, pressed from hybrid grapes from California. Lift a glass of Volcano Blush or Passion Star Chablis and toast Madame Pelé at this boutique winery, open daily 10am to 5pm; tastings are free.

APPROACHING THE PARK FROM THE SOUTH: CROSSING THE KAU DESERT

Lava land, hot, scorched, quake-shaken, bubbling-up, new/dead land: This is the great Kau Desert, layer upon layer of lava flows and fine ash and fallout, of which only those in recent history have been recorded—1790, 1880, 1920, 1926, 1950, 1969, 1971, 1974. The dates draw closer in time the farther you go across the desert, crossing the Great Crack and the Southwest Rift Zone, a major fault zone that looks like a giant groove in the earth, onward to Kilauea Volcano, which created all this desert.

⭐ HAWAII VOLCANOES NATIONAL PARK

Yellowstone, Yosemite, and other national parks are spectacular, no doubt about it. But they're all ho-hum compared to this one: Here, nothing less than the miracle of creation is the daily attraction.

Founded in 1916, Hawaii Volcanoes National Park is Hawaii's premier natural attraction. Visiting the park is a yin/yang experience, as it's the only rain forest in the U.S. National Park system—and the only one that's home to an active volcano. Most people drive through the park (it has 50 miles of good roads, some of them often covered by lava flows) and call it a day. But it takes at least 3 days to explore the whole park, including such oddities as **Halemaumau Crater**, a still-fuming pit of steam and sulfur; the intestinal-looking **Thurston Lava Tube**; **Devastation Trail**, a short hike through a desolated area destroyed by lava, right next to an Eden-like rain forest; and finally, the end of **Chain of Craters Road**, where lava regularly spills across the man-made two-lane blacktop to create its own red-hot freeway to the sea. In addition to some of the world's weirdest landscape, the park also has hiking trails, rain forests, campgrounds, a historic old hotel on a crater's rim, and that spectacular, still-erupting volcano.

NOTES ON THE ERUPTING VOLCANO

In Hawaii, volcanoes aren't the violent pyroclastic killers like Mount Pinatubo in the Philippines or even Mt. St. Helens in Oregon. Vulcanologists refer to Hawaii's volcanic eruptions as "quiet" eruptions, since gases escape slowly instead of building up and exploding violently all at once. What that means is slow-moving, oozing lava that provides excellent, safe viewing most of the time. In Hawaii, people run to volcanoes instead of fleeing from them.

Since the current eruption of Kilauea began on January 3, 1983, lava has covered some 16,000 acres of lowland and rain forest, threatening rare hawks, honeycreeper birds, spiders, and bats, while destroying power and telephone lines and eliminating water service possibly forever. Some areas have been mantled repeatedly and are now buried underneath 80 feet of lava.

Even though people haven't had to run fleeing from this flow, it has still caused its share of destruction. At last count in early 1998, the lava flow had destroyed nearly 200 homes and businesses, wiped out Kaimu Black Sand Beach (once Hawaii's most photographed beach) and Queen's Bath, obliterated entire towns and subdivisions (Kalapana, Royal Gardens and Kalapana Gardens subdivisions, and Kapaahu

Hawaii Volcanoes National Park

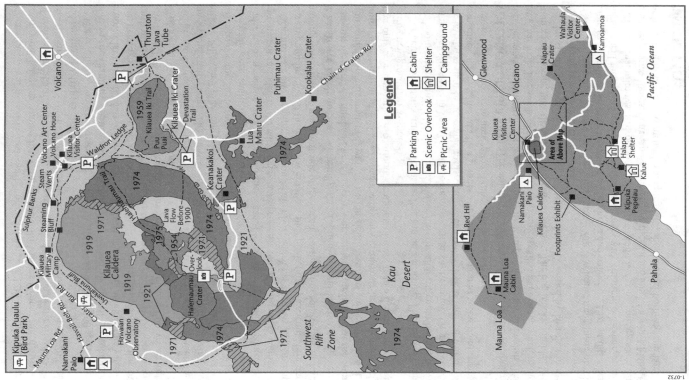

Legend

P Parking	Cabin
Scenic Overlook	Shelter
Picnic Area	Campground

Volcano

Thurston Lava Tube

Volcano Art Center
Volcano House
Kilauea Visitor Center
Waldron Ledge

1959
Puu Puai
Kilauea Iki Trail
Kilauea Iki Crater
Devastation Trail

Puhimau Crater
Kookalau Crater

Chain of Craters Rd.

Lua Manu Crater

1974

Keanakakoi Crater

Steam Vents
Sulphur Banks
Steaming Bluff

Kilauea Military Camp

1971
1974
1919
1921
1975
1954
Lava Flow Before 1900
1971
1974
1921

Kilauea Caldera

1919
Halemaumau Trail
Halemaumau Crater Over-look
1971
1974

Hawaiian Volcano Observatory

Crater Rim Rd.
Hawaii Belt Rd.
Uwekahuna Bluff
Mauna Loa Rd.

Kipuka Puaulu (Bird Park)

Namakani Paio

Southwest Rift Zone

Kau Desert

1971
1974

Glenwood

Volcano

Napau Crater

Wahaula Visitor Center

Kamoamoa

Pacific Ocean

Kilauea Visitors Center

Area of Above Map

Kilauea Caldera
Namakani Paio
Footprints Exhibit

Red Hill

Halape Shelter
Kipuka Pepelau
Kalue

Mauna Loa Cabin

Mauna Loa

1974

Pahala

Homesteads), and buried natural and historic landmarks (a 12th-century heiau, the century-old Kalapana Mauna Kea Church, Wahaula Visitors Center, and thousands of archaeological artifacts and sites). The cost of the destruction of the eruption—so far—is estimated at $100 million. But how do you price the destruction of a 700-year old temple or a 100-year-old church?

The volcano not only has destroyed, it also has added—more than 560 acres of new land to the island by the beginning of 1998. To give you an idea of the volume of erupted lava over the last 1½ decades: It measures nearly two billion cubic yards—that's enough new rock to pave a two-lane highway 1.2 million miles long, circling the earth some 50 times. Or, as a spokesperson for the park puts it: "Every five days, there is enough lava coming out of Kilauea volcano's eruption to place a thin veneer over Washington D.C.—all 63 square miles."

The most prominent vent of the eruption has been Puu Oo, a 760-foot-high cinder-and-spatter cone. The most recent flow—the one you'll be able to see, if you're lucky—follows a 7-mile-long tube from the Puu Oo vent area to the sea. This lava flow has extended the Big Island's shoreline seaward and added some 540 acres of new land along the steep southern slopes. Periodically, the new land proves unstable, falling under its own weight, and slides into the ocean. (These areas of ground gained and lost are not included in the tally of new acreage—only the land that sticks counts.)

Scientists are also keeping an eye on Mauna Loa, which has been swelling since its last eruption in 1983. If there's a new eruption, they predict that there could be a fast-moving flow down the southwest side of the island, possibly into South Kona or Kau.

What You're Likely to See

Hopefully, the eruption will still be continuing when you visit the park. As this book went to press, vulcanologists predicted that the eruption would continue unabated, with no end in sight. Scientists are perplexed by the continuing eruption of Kilauea, as major eruptions in the past have ended abruptly after only several months. A continuous eruption of more than a decade and a half is setting new ground, so to speak.

But neither Mother Nature nor Madame Pelé run on a schedule. The volcano could be shooting fountains of lava hundreds of feet into the air, or it could be shut down on the day you arrive in Volcano—there are no guarantees with nature. On many days, the lava flows right by accessible roads, and you can get as close as the heat will allow; sometimes, however, the lava flow is miles away from the nearest access point, visible only in the distance or in underground tubes where you can't see it.

VOLCANO VOCABULARY

The volcano has its own unique, poetic vocabulary that describes in Hawaiian words what otherwise is impossible to say in English. The lava that looks like swirls of chocolate cake frosting is called **pahoehoe,** which results from a fast-moving flow that curls artistically as it flows. The big, blocky, jumbled lava that looks like a chopped-up parking lot is called **aa;** it's caused by lava that moves slowly, pulling apart as it overruns itself.

You also may hear the words "vog" and "laze." **Vog** is volcanic smog made of volcanic gases and smoke from forests set on fire by aa and pahoehoe. **Laze** results when sulfuric acid hits the water and vaporizes and mixes with chlorine to become, as any chemistry major knows, hydrochloric acid. Both vog and laze sting your eyes and can cause respiratory illness; don't expose yourself to either for too long. Anyone with heart or breathing trouble, or women who are pregnant, should avoid both vog and laze.

JUST THE FACTS

WHEN TO GO

The best time to go is when Kilauea is really pumping. You may be lucky and be in the park when the volcano is really active and fountaining; mostly, the lava runs like a red river downslope into the sea. If you're on another island and hear a TV news bulletin that the volcano is acting up, catch the next flight to Hilo to see the spectacle. You won't be sorry. Your favorite beach will still be there when you get back. Also see "Notes on the Erupting Volcano," above.

ACCESS POINTS   Hawaii Volcanoes National Park is 29 miles from Hilo, on Hawaii Belt Road (Hwy. 11). If you're staying in Kailua-Kona, it's 100 miles, or about a 2½-hour drive, to the park. Admission is $10 per vehicle; you can come and go as often as you want for 7 days. Hikers and bicyclists pay $5; bikes are only allowed on roads and paved trails.

INFORMATION & VISITOR CENTERS   For information before you go, contact **Hawaii Volcanoes National Park,** P.O. Box 52, Hawaii Volcanoes National Park, HI 96718 (☎ **808/985-6000;** www.nps.gov/havo; e-mail hvnpint@aloha.net). **Kilauea Visitor Center** is at the entrance of the park, just off Hwy. 11; it's open daily from 7:45am to 5pm.

For the latest **eruption update** and information on volcanic activity in the park, call the park's 24-hour hotline at ☎ **808/985-6000.** Updates on volcanic activity are also posted daily on the bulletin board at the visitor center.

HIKING & CAMPING IN THE PARK   Hawaii Volcanoes National Park offers a wealth of hiking and camping possibilities. See "Hiking & Camping," earlier in this chapter, for details.

ACCOMMODATIONS IN & AROUND THE PARK   If camping isn't your thing, don't worry. In addition to historic Volcano House, on the rim of Halemaumau Crater, adjacent Volcano Village has plenty of comfortable and convenient places to stay; see "Accommodations," earlier in this chapter.

EMERGENCIES   Call ☎ **911** if you have an emergency in the park.

SEEING THE HIGHLIGHTS

Your first stop should be **Kilauea Visitor Center,** a rustic park-like structure in a shady grove of trees just inside the entrance to the park. Here, you can get up-to-the-minute reports on the volcano's activity, learn how volcanoes work, see a film showing blasts from the past, get information on hiking and camping, and pick up the obligatory postcards, taken by some great photographers who risked their lives on the lava to capture the awesome fury of a live volcano.

Filled with a new understanding of vulcanology and the volcano goddess, Pelé, walk across the street to **Volcano House;** go through the lobby and out the other side, where you can have a good look at **Kilauea Caldera,** a 2½-mile-wide, 500-foot-deep pit, once known as one of "the greatest wonders of the globe." The bubbling pit of fountaining lava is out now, but you can see wisps of steam that could, while you're standing there, turn into something more.

Travel Tip

Remember: Thanks to higher elevation and a windward (rainier) location, it's always colder in this neck of the woods than it is at the beach. If you're coming from the Kona side of the island in the summer, expect it to be at least 10 to 20°F cooler at the volcano, so bring a sweater or light jacket. In the winter months, expect temperatures to be in the 40s or 50s, and dress accordingly. Always have rain gear on hand, especially in winter.

Now get out on the highway and drive by the **Sulphur Banks**, which smell like rotten eggs, and the **Steam Vents**, where trails of smoke, once molten lava, rise from within the inner reaches of the earth. It's one of the few places where you feel that the volcano is really alive. Stop at the **Thomas A. Jaggar Museum** (open daily 8:30am to 5pm; free admission) for a good look at Halemaumau Crater, which is a half-mile across and 1,000 feet deep, and (maybe) Mauna Loa, 20 miles to the west. The museum shows eruption videos, explains the Pelé legend in murals, and monitors earthquakes (a precursor of eruptions) on a seismograph, recording every twitch in the earth.

Once you've seen everything at the museum, drive around the caldera to the other side, park, and take the short walk to Halemaumau Crater's edge, past stinky sulfur banks and steam vents, to stand at the overlook and stare in awe at this once-fuming and bubbling old firepit, which still generates ferocious heat out of vestigial vents.

If you feel the need to cool off now, go to the **Thurston Lava Tube**, the coolest place in the park. You'll hike down into a natural bowl in the earth, a forest preserve the lava didn't touch—full of native bird songs and giant tree ferns. You'll see a black hole in the earth; step in. It's all drippy and cool, with bare roots hanging down. You can either resurface into the bright daylight or, if you have a flashlight, poke on deeper into the tube, which goes for another quarter-mile or so.

If you're still game for a good hike, try **Kilauea Iki Crater**, a 4-mile, 2-hour hike across the floor of the crater, which became a bubbling pool of lava in 1959 and sent fountains of lava 1,900 feet in the air, completely devastating a nearby ohia forest and leaving another popular hike ominously known as **Devastation Trail**. The half-mile walk is a startling look at the powers of a volcanic eruption on the environment. (See pp. 304–306 for details on these and other park hikes.)

For a glimpse of ancient Hawaiian art, the **Puu Loa Petroglyphs** are found around the 15 mile marker on Chain of Craters Road. Look for the stack of rocks on the road to park; a brief, half-mile walk from the road will bring you to a circular boardwalk where you can see the thousands of mysterious Hawaiian petroglyphs carved in stone. This area, Puu Loa, was a sacred place for generations; fathers came here to bury their newborn's umbilical cord in the numerous small holes in the lava, thus ensuring a long life for the child. *A word of warning:* It's very easy to destroy these ancient works of art. Do not leave the boardwalk, and don't walk on or around the petroglyphs. Rubbings of petroglyphs will destroy them; the best way to capture the petroglyphs is via a photo.

THE VOLCANO AFTER DARK If the volcano is still erupting, be sure to see it after dark as it snakes down the side of the mountain and pours into the sea. About an hour before sunset, head back into the park and 23 miles down **Chain of Craters Road.** Get ready to see the red—it's a vivid display you'll never forget. If conditions are good and it's accessible when you're there—sometimes it's too far from the road to hike to, so you'll have to be content with seeing it in the distance—park rangers positioned at the barricades will tell you how to get to the current lava flow. *Be sure to heed the ranger.* In the past, a handful of hikers who ignored these directions died en route; new lava can be unstable and break off without warning. Take water, a flashlight, and your camera, and wear sturdy shoes.

Viewing the Volcano From the Air The best way to see the volcano is from on high, in a helicopter. This bird's-eye view puts the enormity of it all into perspective. No two ways about it—this is an extraordinary way to see the red. The best helicopter firm is ✪ **Blue Hawaiian Helicopter** (☎ 800/745-BLUE or 808/885-1768; www.bluehawaiian.com), the Cadillac of helicopter tour companies. The

Seeing the Red at Hawaii Volcanoes National Park

Just before the hot tropic sun quits for the day, we race down Chain of Craters Road in a nimble Geo Tracker through fields of black lava on a descent to the Big Island's "volcano coast."

We are gong to see the red—that's what I call the live volcano show. At night, it's the greatest show on earth: a spectacular explosion of fire; red rivers of fire flowing just below the surface, visible through the fissures between your feet; Jell-O-like globs of molten lava inching their way down the mountain and pouring into the steaming Pacific, creating the newest land on earth.

I have gone to see the red so many times—and will go again, every chance I get—because each time is different. And once you see it, you can't tear your eyes from it until the sulfur literally drives you away. It's downright addictive.

Usually I go just about an hour before sunset, always in a hurry, alone or with others, it doesn't matter. I pack sandwiches and beer, and a banana and an apple (for later, to rid my mouth of the lingering sulfur taste), plus an extra jug of water because it's hot out there on the lava, even after dark.

We see the telltale plume of smog that rises 1,000 feet in the sky, like a giant exclamation point, and speed on. As I scan downslope, I see ruby rivers of lava running to the sea. We come to a halt: The two-lane blacktop ends under a pile of steaming black plumpy stuff with a silvery sheen—hardened *pahoehoe* lava. It looks like swirls of chocolate frosting. We arrive just as the sun hits the horizon and turns this hellish landscape into God's land, with sunbeams radiating against virgin pink clouds. And the best is still to come.

Tonight, the glow on the mountain is like a distant forest fire. The first step onto the hardened lava is scary. It crunches like crushed glass under the heels of my hiking boots. I can see a red road map of molten lava glowing in the cracks and flowing in fiery rivulets about a foot below the surface. And there's still a nervous mile-long walk ahead, in pitch-black darkness, to the intersection of lava and sea—but it's a walk that I know is worth the trouble.

Silhouettes against the fire, we stand at the edge of the earth like primal natives witnessing the schizophrenic act of creation and destruction. The lava hisses and spits and crackles as it moves, snake-like, in its perpetual flow to the sea, dripping like candle wax into the wavy surf. Fire and water, the very stuff of islands: The lava still burns underwater until the ocean, the vast Pacific, finally douses the fire and transforms it into yet more black-sand beach.

At the turn of the century, folks used to singe postcards and send them home to disbelieving friends. Today, most people, I've noticed, try to douse the lava with bottled water, but it vaporizes instantly—that's what 2,500°F will do. I know a man in Hilo who drops silver dollars in the path of the lava, then retrieves them, lava and all; they cool and harden into paper weights. I like to toast ball-park franks on a long kiawe stick—smokes 'em fast, from the inside out.

professionally run, locally based company has an excellent safety record, the top-of-the-line 'copters are very comfortable, and the pilots are all extremely knowledgeable about everything from vulcanology to Hawaii lore. They fly out of both Hilo and Waikoloa (Hilo is cheaper because it's closer). The **Circle of Fire/Waterfalls**

—*Rick Carroll*

50-minute flight from Hilo takes you to the volcano and past waterfalls, valleys, and remote beaches for $130 per person; the 70-minute **East Island Epic,** a tour of rain forests, waterfalls, and the volcano, is $175 per person. From Waikoloa, there's the **Kohala Coast Adventure,** a 50-minute flight over the Kohala Mountains and remote valleys for $135 per person (volcano not included); or—our favorite—the 2-hour **Big Island Spectacular,** starring the volcano, tropical valleys, Hamakua Coast waterfalls, and the Kohala Mountains—for $290 (worth every penny). Prices include a video of your trip.

If you'd prefer a fixed-wing aircraft, we recommend **Big Island Air** (☎ 808/329-4868), which offers 1¾-hour volcano tours from Kona Airport in their twin-engine, air-conditioned airplane for $169 per person. **Classic Aviation** (☎ 800/695-8100 or 808/329-TOUR) offers flights to the volcano from Hilo Airport in their new edition of a classic 1935 Waco biplane for $99 each. Two passengers, seated side by side in the open cockpit of this propeller plane, get cloth helmets, goggles, and white silk scarves to wear on their classic flight over the volcano ("Curse you, Red Baron!").

SOUTH POINT: LAND'S END

The history of Hawaii is condensed here, at the end of 11 miles of bad road that peters out at Kaulana Bay, in the lee of a jagged, black-lava point—the tail end of the United States. No historic marker marks the spot or gives any clue as to the geographical significance of the place. If you walk out to the very tip, beware of the big waves that lash the shore; the nearest continental landfall is Antarctica, 7,500 miles away.

It's a 2½-mile four-wheel-drive trip and a hike down a cliff from South Point to the anomaly known as **Green Sand Beach** (see "Beaches," above).

Back on the Mamalahoa Highway (Hwy. 11), about 20 miles east is the small town of Pahoa; turn off the highway and travel about 5 miles through this once-thriving sugar plantation and beyond to the **Wood Valley Temple and Retreat Center** (☎ 808/928-8539). Also known as *Nechung Drayang Ling* ("Island of Melodious Sound"), it's an oasis of tranquility tucked into the rain forest. Built by Japanese sugarcane workers, the temple, retreat center, and surrounding gardens were rededicated by the Dalai Lama in 1980 to serve as a spiritual center for Tibetan Buddhism. You can walk the beautiful grounds, attend morning or evening services, and breathe in the quiet mindfulness of this serene area.

10 Shops & Galleries

by Jocelyn Fujii

While chefs and farmers tout this island as fertile ground for crops and food, artists point to its primal, volcanic energy as a boost to their creative endeavors, too. Arts communities and galleries are sprinkled across this gargantuan island, in villages like Holualoa and Volcano, where fine works in pottery, wood-turning, handmade glass, and most two- and three-dimensional media are proffered in serene settings.

Though the visual arts are flourishing on this island, the line between shop and gallery often can be too fine to define, or even to approach. Too many self-proclaimed "galleries" purvey schlock or a mixture of arts, crafts, and tacky souvenirs. (T-shirts and Kona coffee mugs are a souvenir staple in many galleries.) In between is a spate of items for the home, jewelry and accessories, vintage Hawaiiana, and accouterments at various prices and for various tastes; locally made food products like preserves, cookies, flowers, Kona coffee, and macadamia nuts also make great gifts to go.

The galleries and shops below offer a broad mix in many media, but you'll find that bowls made of rare native woods such as koa are especially abundant on this island. This is an area in which politics and art intersect: Although reforestation efforts are underway to plant new koa trees, the decline of old-growth forests is causing many artists to turn to equally beautiful, and more environmentally correct, alternative woods.

THE KONA COAST
IN & AROUND KAILUA-KONA

Kailua-Kona's shopping prospects pour out into the streets in a festival atmosphere of T-shirts, trinkets, and dime-a-dozen souvenirs, with Alii Drive at the center of this activity. **Kona Square,** across from **King Kamehameha's Kona Beach Hotel;** the hotel's shopping mall, with close to two dozen shops, including a Liberty House; and the **Kona Inn Shopping Village** on Alii Drive all include a plethora of shops for vacationers' needs, but be forewarned: The going can be rocky for those with seriously refined tastes. In Kailua-Kona, tacky is king—so set your expectations accordingly.

EDIBLES & EVERYDAY THINGS The Big Island's **greenmarkets** are notable for the quality of produce and the abundance of island specialties at better-than-usual prices. Luck counts here, though, because they usually only occur on weekends. From dawn to noon on Friday, Saturday, and Sunday, look for the (loosely assembled tarps of the **Farmers Market across from Waterfront Row.** (Go as early as possible, because it gets hot as the morning wears on.) Local farmers sell organic produce, unsprayed Waimea corn, anthuriums of every hue, star fruit, breadfruit, papayas, sugarcane, Ka'u oranges, vine-ripened tomatoes, locally made crafts, and macadamia nuts. It's a great way to sample the region's specialties, some of which can also make affordable souvenirs.

Lest you feel deprived, there are also two **Great Pacific** ice cream shops Keauhou Shopping Center (corner of Kam III Highway and Alii Drive) in Keauhow, with an additional store scheduled for a fall opening at the new development in Kailau called Crossroads Center, 75-1027 Henry St., Kailua-Kona, mauka of the Palani-Kaahumanu intersection (where the ever-popular Oodles of Noodles is located). Veteran ice cream maker Larry Neff and his son have been making gourmet ice creams for more than 26 years. Winning flavors include Toasted Coconut, Extreme Ginger, Volcano (fresh banana with strawberry swirl and Oreo cookies), Kealakekua Krunch (Kona coffee ice cream with a coffee swirl and coffee cinnamon brittle), and dozens of others. The classics (mac nut, Kona coffee, sorbets) remain, but there's always something new at Great Pacific. Two dollars for a single can buy a lot of good licks.

For everyday grocery needs, **KTA Stores** (in the Kona Coast Shopping Center, at Palani Road and the Queen Kaahumanu Highway; and in the Keauhou Shopping Village, on Alii Drive) are always my first choice. Through its Mountain Apple brand, KTA sells hundreds of top-notch local products—from Kona smoked marlin and Hilo-grown rainbow trout to cookies, breads, taro chips, and *kulolo,* the decadently dense taro-coconut steamed pudding—by dozens of local vendors. The fresh-fish department is always an adventure; if anything esoteric or rare is running, such as the flashy red aweoweo, it's sure to be on the counters at KTA, along with a large spread of prepared foods for sunset picnics and barbecues. A few doors away in the same shopping center, **Kona Healthways** is the only full-service health-food store for miles, selling bulk grains and cereals, vitamins, snacks, fresh fruit smoothies, and sandwiches and salads from its takeout deli. Organic greens, grown with special cachet in the South Kona area, are a small but strong feature of the organic produce section.

By far the best and busiest place for produce and flowers straight from the farm is the **Farmers Market in Kaiwi Square,** in Kona's old industrial area (follow the sign on the Queen Kaahumanu Highway). Open on Saturday from 7am to 1pm, it teems with dedicated vendors and eager shoppers. You'll find live catfish, taro, organic vine-ripened tomatoes, fresh Kamuela string beans, lettuces, potatoes, and just-picked blooms, such as anthuriums and feathery, sturdy protea, at friendly prices.

Alapaki's Hawaiian Gifts. In the Keauhou Shopping Village, Alii Dr. ☎ **808/322-2007.**

Lovers of Hawaiian crafts will appreciate this attractive selection of gift items, made by more than 120 artists from Hawaii's islands, with about 1% of the inventory from Fiji, Samoa, Marquesas, and other Polynesian islands. Alapaki's includes bookmarks with pressed island flowers, jewelry, kukui nut leis, original paintings, and handblown glass by the noted Holualoa artist Wilfred Yamazawa. The owners clearly make an effort to showcase quality local works and are active in fundraising activities for Big Island hula schools, canoe projects, and other Hawaiian efforts.

Cloud Nine. In Kona Plaza, 75-5719 Alii Dr. ☎ **800/329-9294** or 808/329-9294.

The more than 100 oils and 75 skincare products will literally put you on cloud nine, especially when you see how affordable they are. Cloud Nine makes, custom blends, and sells Hawaiian botanical products that are biodegradable and completely natural, have no animal ingredients, and have not been tested on animals. Many of the products come unscented and can be custom-blended with the fragrance of your choice. The gardenia oil is the best we've encountered and is one of the essential oils, perfumes, and skin-care products Cloud Nine does best.

Honolua Surf Company. In the Kona Inn Shopping Village, Alii Dr. ☎ **808/329-1001.**

This shop targets the surf-and-sun enthusiast with good things for good times: surfboards and accessories, towels, visors, flip-flops, sunglasses, swimsuits, and everything else you need for ocean and shore action—including sunscreens of every stripe, a must in the West Hawaii sun. Quicksilver, Tommy Bahama, and Kahala are among the top menswear labels here, but we also like the quirky, colorful Toes on the Nose. For women, the Beach Club slippers are comfortable and well suited to the island lifestyle.

⭐ **Hula Heaven.** In the Kona Inn Shopping Village, Alii Dr. (next to Hulihee Palace). ☎ **808/329-7885.**

There's no such thing as "dropping in" at Hula Heaven. Neighbor islanders have been known to make special trips to Kona to shop here, because there's no place like it in Hawaii. Gwen and Evan Olins have made their treasure-laden shop the nexus of Hawaiian collectibles for serious and casual collectors, or anyone with an eye for island-style treasures. People find it impossible not to linger among the vintage aloha shirts, nodding hula-girl dolls, out-of-print books, lauhala bags, Mundorff prints, Matson liner menus, vintage ukuleles and guitars, Don Blanding dinnerware, koa perfume bottles, Ming's jewelry (the *ne plus ultra* of vintage jewelry), and accessories made of authentic vintage bark cloth. Gwen's fondness for textiles is reflected in the window displays, which often feature one-of-a-kind 1940s fabrics, and on the racks, where traditional tea-timer tops and muumuus in spirited old prints mingle with new clothing in faithfully reproduced fabrics. What isn't vintage—and 50% of the store is—is vintage-looking, exuding nostalgia, color, and a high-spirited style. Look up when you enter, too: Hanging over the door is a 1930s aloha shirt with the "Aloha" label of the man who invented Hawaii's sartorial staple.

Just Looking

The finest art on the Kona Coast hangs, of all places, in a bank. Award-winning **First Hawaiian Bank**, 74-5593 Palani Rd. (☎ **808/329-2461**), has art lovers making special trips to view Hiroki Morinoue's mural, John Buck's prints, Chiu Leong's ceramic sculpture, Franco Salmoiraghi's photographs, Setsuko Morinoue's abstract fiber wallpiece, and other works that were incorporated as part of the bank's design, rather than added on as an afterthought. Artists Yvonne Cheng and Sharon Carter Smith, whose works are included, assembled this exhibition, which is destined to achieve immortality as a sterling example of corporate sponsorship of the arts.

Island Salsa. In the Kona Inn Shopping Village, Alii Dr. ☎ **808/329-9279.**

There's no food involved here, but the sportswear does sizzle. The tiny boutique is lined with excellent, high-quality sportswear and accessories: slouchy linens by Flax, top-of-the-line City Lights T-shirts, an excellent selection of Tommy Bahama aloha shirts and Jams World rayons, island-made pottery, and the obscure but wonderful Sven Design leather bags. Whether for urban pursuits or the active outdoor life, this is a carefully selected assortment of stylish necessities for work and play. Most of the prices are moderate, and even the higher-end items aren't out of this world.

Kailua Village Artists Gallery. King Kamehameha's Kona Beach Hotel, 75-5660 Palani Rd. ☎ **808/329-6653.**

A co-op of 40 Hawaii island artists, plus a few guest artists, display their works in various media: watercolors, paintings, prints, handblown and blasted glass, and photography. Books, pottery, and an attractive assortment of greeting cards are among the lower-priced items.

Kona Arts & Crafts Gallery. 75-5699 Alii Dr. ☎ **808/329-5590.**

If you cross Alii Drive from the seawall, you'll find a charming selection of goods in this tiny shop: chimes, hula implements, wood carvings, handpainted tiles and Hawaiian dolls, tikis, koa brushes and mirrors, and koa bowls for $30 to $200. Run by senior citizens, the shop highlights Hawaiian craftsmanship by Hawaii artists at realistic prices.

MiddleEarth Bookshoppe. In Kona Plaza, 75-5719 Alii Dr. ☎ **808/329-2123.**

Every square inch is occupied with bestsellers, cookbooks, literary fiction, travel guides, metaphysical books, health books, offbeat titles . . . known and obscure adventures into the world of words. With its strong selection of Hawaii-themed publications and piles of discounted books, MiddleEarth is a staple for residents and a pleasant surprise for visitors, appreciated more for its longevity than for its sometimes unsmiling service.

Once in a Blue Moon. 74-5598 Luhia St. ☎ **808/334-0022.**

Tuck in your elbows and hang on to your backpack, lest you topple a crystal vase or piece of estate china packed into this showroom in Kailua's industrial area. This antiques/secondhand store is chockablock with vintage Hawaiian items, estate jewelry, handwoven throws and linens, and an entire floor of furniture (some koa pieces, which disappear quickly). Among the treasures the day I was there: fine, high-thread-count vintage sheets in excellent condition, mint-condition Japanese dolls, and koa bowls.

Paradise Found. In the Keauhou Shopping Village, Alii Dr. ☎ **808/326-1211.** Paradise Found appeals to women who like retro-style camp shirts with sequins and hula girls, stylish T-shirts, and draping. Harlow-esque dresses that make a grand entrance at parties. With a bold yet solidly stylish selection of clothing and accessories for daytime to evening, it's that rare blend: a resortwear shop that appeals equally to working women and vacationers.

Te-Noe, Inc. Phone orders only. ☎ **808/322-3579.** Noelani Whittington's grandfather planted the coffee trees on their farm when he was 85 years old. He's well past 90 now, but the trees are yielding tasty coffee beans that Noelani and her husband, Rick, sell wholesale and retail in 2-ounce, 3-ounce, and 1-pound bags. The 100% Kona coffee is available by phone order or at various outlets in Kailua-Kona. The beans are hand-roasted only 15 pounds at a time and packed with lots of TLC. You can also order the seasonally available pincushion and miniature king protea, and the dazzling Telopa protea, resembling torch gingers in all red and all white. Protea are sturdy, showy flowers with a long afterlife—they dry beautifully. The selection varies, depending on the time of year, so there are always surprises.

UPCOUNTRY KONA: HOLUALOA

Charming Holualoa, 1,400 feet and 10 minutes above Kailua-Kona at the top of Hualalai Road, is a place for strong espresso, leisurely gallery hopping, and nostalgic explorations across several cultural and time zones. Prominent Holualoa artists include the jewelry maker/sculptor Sam Rosen, who years ago set the pace for found-object art; the ceramist and wood sculptor Gerald Ben; the printmaker Nora Yamanoha; the glass artist Wilfred Yamazawa; the sculptor Cal Hashimoto; and Hiroki and Setsuko Morinoue of Studio 7 gallery. All galleries listed are on the main street, Mamalahoa Highway, and all are within walking distance of each other.

Cinderella Unlimited. Mamalahoa Hwy. ☎ **808/322-2474.** Most of the treasures here are tucked away, so don't be shy about asking the owner, Cindi Nespor, where her prized antique engravings are or her cache of out-of-print naturalists' books with handpainted engravings. Many of the items here come from the estate of a reclusive couture model who retired in Kona and died there, after a prolific career sitting for Picasso, Cecil Beaton, and the world's most prominent photographers. There are engravings of old Hawaii, rare prints and vases, kimono, lamps, and home accessories. The rare books will quicken a book-lover's heart, and the estate jewelry, vintage linens, rattan furniture, and hats will make this a brilliant browse.

Holualoa Gallery. 76-5921 Mamalahoa Hwy. ☎ **808/322-8484.** Owners Matthew and Mary Lovein show their own work as well the work of selected Hawaii artists in this roadside gallery in Holualoa. Sculptures, paintings, koa furniture (the Tai Lake koa furniture is outstanding), fused-glass bowls by the award-winning Patricia Van Asperen-Hume, and creations in paper, bronze, metal, and glass are among the offerings.

Kimura Lauhala Shop. At Mamalahoa Hwy. and Hualalai Rd. ☎ **808/324-0053.** Tsuruyo Kimura, looking 20 years younger than her 90 years, presides over a labor-intensive legacy (lauhala) that's increasingly difficult to maintain. All the better, because everyone loves Kimura's and the fiberworks that spill out of the tiny shop. It's lined with lauhala, from rolled-up mats and wide-brimmed hats to coasters and coin purses. The fragrant, resilient fiber, woven from the spiny leaves of the hala (pandanus) tree, is smooth to the touch and becomes softer with use. Lauhala also varies in color (terra-cotta to beige) according to region and growing conditions. Woven in varying widths, lauhala in its finer weaves is time-consuming and expensive. Although Kimura employs a covey of local weavers who use the renowned hala leaves of Kona, some South Pacific imports bolster the supply.

Kona Arts Center. Mamalahoa Hwy. (P.O. Box 272), Holualoa, HI 96725. No phone.

Because they've never had a phone, anyone interested in the pottery, tie-dye, weaving, painting, and other arts-and-crafts workshops of this not-for-profit center, in a ramshackle tin-roofed former coffee mill, has to write or drop in. Carol Rogers is the director of the program, a mainstay of the local arts community since 1965.

✪ **Studio 7.** Mamalahoa Hwy. ☎ **808/324-1335.**

Some of Hawaii's most respected artists, among them gallery owners Setsuko and Hiroki Morinoue, exhibit their works in this serenely beautiful studio. Smooth pebbles, stark woods, and a garden setting provide the backdrop for Hiroki's paintings and prints and Setsuko's pottery, paper collages, and wallpieces. The Main Gallery houses multimedia art, the Print Gallery houses sculptural pieces and two-dimensional works, and the Ceramic Gallery showcases the works of Clayton Amemiya, Chiu Leong, and Gerald Ben, whose mixed-media sculptures made of ceramic raku with wood continue to be a pleasing attraction. With the Morinoues at the helm of the volunteer-driven **Holualoa Foundation for Culture and the Arts,** this is the hub of the Holualoa art community; activities include workshops, classes, and special events by visiting artists.

SOUTH KONA

EDIBLES In Kealakekua, the **Kamigaki Market** on Highway 11 is a reliable source for food items, especially for specialties of the region, such as macadamia nuts and Kona coffee. In Honaunau, farther south, keep an eye out for the **Bong Brothers Store** on Highway 11 and its eye-catching selections of fresh local fruit—from chirimoya (in season) to star fruit and white Sugarloaf pineapples. The Bongs are known for their Kona coffee and deli items, but I think their black, very hip Bong Brothers T-shirts are the find of the region and season.

Aloha Store. Hwy. 11, Kainaliu. ☎ **808/322-1717.**

The size, selection, and location of this store make it a wonderful stop. Only highquality goods are sold here, whether it's the handmade beeswax candles made on the slopes of Hualalai, the Tommy Bahama duffelbags, the Kahala aloha shirts, or Liz and Jane sportswear, a favorite for island living. You can sail through the day in the Jams dresses and sarongs or the Reyn Spooner retro rayon dresses, and wind up sinking into a luxurious cushion with a unique book, all from the Aloha Store. Stylish vintage-look bark-cloth cushions, home accessories, and books are included in the constantly changing inventory of gift items.

The Grass Shack. Hwy. 11, Kealakekua. ☎ **808/323-2877.**

The new traffic signal out front has made this less of a country road, but it does alert you to the presence of this shop. Grass Shack has been here for 29 years, offering a large selection of local woodcrafts, plus Niihau shell and wiliwili-seed leis, packaged coffee, pahu drums, nose flutes, and lauhala (woven pandanus leaves) in every form. Bowls, boxes, and accessories of Norfolk pine, the rare kou, and other local woods take up a sizable portion of the shop. Lauhala baskets, made of fiber from the region and the Hamakua Coast, are among the Shack's finest, as are the custom ukuleles and feather gourds for hula dancing.

Kimura Store. Hwy. 11, Kainaliu. ☎ **808/322-3771.**

This old-fashioned general store is one of those places you're happy you've found and hope will be there forever, a store with spirit and character plus everything you need and don't need. You'll find Hawaii's finest selection of yardage, enough cookware for a multicourse dinner, aspirin, Shiseido cosmetics, and an eye-popping assortment of buttons, zippers, and quilting materials. Irene Kimura, whose store has been here for 56 years, says she quit counting the fabric bolts at 8,000 but knows she has more than 10,000. Kimura's is the spot for pareu and Hawaiian fabrics, brocades, silks, and off-beat gift items, such as Japanese china and *tabi*, the comfortable cloth footwear.

The Rainbow Path. Hwy. 11, Kainaliu. ☎ **808/322-0651.**

This shop specializes in products for healing and well-being, such as New Age crystals and gems, metaphysical books and accessories, aromatherapy oils, jewelry, flaxseed eye pillows (don't knock 'em till you've tried 'em!), tapes and CDs, candles, cards, art books, and Ayurvedic self-care health products. The made-on-Oahu Paradise essential oils are pure and popular, and when the owner's fruit trees are bearing, he shares the bounty. Adjoining the store is the newly opened **Rainbow Cafe,** serving soups, salads, sandwiches, smoothies, shave ice, and ice cream.

THE KOHALA COAST

Shops on the Kohala Coast are concentrated in the resorts, most notably the **Hilton Waikoloa Village,** where the hotel and the neighboring **King's Shops** offer a long string of possibilities.

HILTON WAIKOLOA VILLAGE　I recommend **Flamingo's** in the main arcade, a must for confident men and women. It's full of bright and beautiful wearables, from aloha wear and contemporary clothing—including Avanti aloha shirts, classic mandarin-style tea-timer tops, and dresses in authentic 1930s to 1950s retro prints, all reproduced on silk—to an occasional vintage handbag. Next door, the **Sandal Tree** carries footwear with style and kick: Italian sandals at non-Italian prices, designer pumps, and footwear to carry you from sailing deck to dance floor.

KING'S SHOPS　A recent find—and a life-saving one!—is **Paradise Walking Company.** This is a striking concept for anyone exploring the harsh lava terrain of this island or the pedestrian culture of Kailua's Alii Drive with its many shops and restaurants. The footwear can be expensive, much of it made in France (Mephisto, Arche), but it's worthwhile for those seeking comfort without sacrificing style. Toward the mauka end is **Noa's Ark** for children, a tot-sized space filled with tropical cottons, pricey but colorful mini-muumuus, pint-sized aloha shirts, and sophisticated linens and jerseys in cradle-to-teen sizes. Its sibling store for adults, **Noa Noa,** is several doors

Just Looking

The Mauna Kea Beach Hotel, 62-100 Mauna Kea Beach Dr. (☎ **808/882-7222**), is home to one of the world's most impressive collections of Asian and Oceanic art. It's displayed unpretentiously, in public and private spaces. Laurance Rockefeller planned his resort so the art would be totally integrated into the environment: indoors, outdoors, in hallways, lounges, and alcoves. The result is a spiritually and aesthetically uplifting view in every direction. A 7th-century granite Buddha is the oldest work in a collection that includes art from China, Japan, India, Southeast Asia, Melanesia, and Polynesia, including Hawaii. The Lloyd Sexton Gallery and John Young paintings throughout the hotel reflect Rockefeller's commitment to the finest.

away, filled with exotic artifacts from Java and Borneo and tropical clothing for easy-going life in the Pacific Rim. **Kunah's** offers Kahala, Kamehameha, and other hip aloha shirts, as well as baseball caps, flip-flops, swim shorts, and colorful tropical-print canvas bags. For snacks, ice, sunscreen, wine, postcards, newspapers, and everyday essentials, there's the **Whalers General Store.**

NORTH KOHALA

Ackerman Gallery. Hwy. 270 (across from the Kamehameha statue; also 3 blocks away, on the opposite side of the street), Kapaau. ☎ **808/889-5971.**

Crafts and fine arts are housed in two separate galleries a few blocks apart. The craft and gift gallery across from the King Kamehameha statue has doubled in size recently, featuring gift ideas in all media and price ranges. Artist Gary Ackerman and his wife, Yesan, display gifts, crafts, and the works of award-winning Big Island artists, including Ackerman's own impressionistic paintings. There are Kelly Dunn's hand-turned Norfolk pine bowls, Jer Houston's heirloom-quality koa-and-ebony desks, and Wilfred Yamazawa's handblown-glass perfume bottles and sculptures. Primitive arti-facts, Asian antiques, and Cal Hashimoto's bamboo sculptures are among the discov-eries here.

Kohala Kollection. In the Kawaihae Shopping Center, Hwy. 270. ☎ **808/882-1510.**

This two-story gallery, the biggest draw next to the Cafe Pesto in this industrial harbor area, features Pegge Hopper originals and prints, Frances Dennis' painted island scenes on canvas and ceramics, bright tropical paintings by the internationally known Zhou Ling, and other works by more than 150 artists, primarily from the Big Island. The range is vast—from jewelry to basketry to heirloom-quality koa furniture by Tai Lake—and the works are tastefully displayed on two floors. Upstairs, you'll find a large selection of fine-art prints; downstairs are bowls, boxes, jewelry, bronze and wood sculptures, ranging from a few dollars to the high prices expected of original fine art.

WAIMEA

Shops here range from the small roadside storefronts lining Highway 19 and Highway 190, which intersect in the middle of town, to complexes such as **Parker Square** and **Waimea Center,** where you'll find the trusty old **KTA Super Store,** the one-stop shop for all your basic necessities, plus a glorious profusion of interesting local foods. At **Parker Ranch Shopping Center** across the street is **Big Island Coffee Co.** and a smattering of shops and casual eateries, including the ever popular **Reyn's,** but gener-ally this complex is unremarkable. The petite but satisfying **Opelo Plaza,** the historic **Spencer House,** and **Parker Square** will likely be your most rewarding stops.

Hilo's wonderful **Dan De Luz Woods** (see below) has a branch at 64-1013 Mamalahoa Hwy., in front of the True-Value hardware store.

FARMER'S MARKETS Small and sublime, with only about five booths, the ✪ **Waimea Farmers Market,** Highway 19, at mile marker 55 on the Hamakua side of Waimea town (on the lawn in front of the Department of Hawaiian Home Lands, West Hawaii office), draws a loyal crowd from 7am to noon on Saturday mornings. Waimea is lei country and the island's breadbasket, so you can imagine the protea, veg-etables, vine-ripened tomatoes, and tuberose stalks you can buy here at reasonable prices. Mainstays include **Honopua Farm** and **Hufford's Farm,** side by side selling flowers and organic vegetables: a dozen different lettuces, three different types of kale, and many other finds you'd never encounter in a supermarket. And the flowers: freesias, irises, heather, stars-of-Bethlehem, Australian teas, and cleomes, all freshly clipped. The colors and fragrances change with the season. You'll find **Marie**

McDonald at the booth, one of Hawaii's premier lei-makers. (If you want one of her designer Waimea leis, you have to order ahead; call ☎ **808/885-4148.**) Also here is **Bernice Berdon,** considered the best maker of akulikuli leis, a Waimea signature that comes in yellows, oranges, and fuchsias. Ask about her bar-face kika, the cigar-flower lei with bar-faced blossoms. If you're here around Christmas, the protea wreaths are phenomenal.

At the other end of Waimea, the **Parker School Farmers Market** is smaller and more subdued, but with choice items as well: Kalopa macadamia nuts and potted greens, and Lokelani Gardens' fabulous herbal vinegars and luxuriant herb topiaries ($15 to $20).

Bentley's Home & Garden Collection. In Parker Square, Hwy. 19. ☎ **808/885-5565.**

To its lavish list of glassware, linens, chenille throws, home fragrances, stuffed animals, and Wild West giftwraps, Bentley's has added casual country clothing in linens and cottons. Dresses, sweaters, raffia hats, top-drawer Western shirts, handbags, woven shoes, and all things Martha Stewart adorn this fragrant, gardenesque shop. This is for people who like to raise flowers and herbs, cook with them, breathe potpourried air, take relaxing baths (with expensive designer soaps), read well, and look good.

✪ **Cook's Discoveries.** At the Historic Spencer House, in front of Waimea Center, Hwy. 190. ☎ **808/885-3633.**

It's a heady mix: Hawaii-themed wearables, fine collectibles, locally made crafts, books, Hawaiian quilts, and ranching memorabilia. You could start with Waipio poi hotcakes at **Maha's Cafe** in one part of the tiny shop (see "Dining," above); then select a lei by Alice Humbert from her veranda flower shop, **Made in a Hawaiian Garden;** and then dive into the nooks and crannies of **Cook's Discoveries.** Treasures you'll find: palaka nightshirts and napkins, kupe'e shell necklaces by Patrick Horimoto, the rare miniature kukui-nut lei, pareus by Tutuvi, lauhala baskets, T-shirts, Doug Tolentino originals and prints, and hundreds of other surprises. The rare ivory and silver Ming jewelry has collectors salivating over the counter, while foodies throng to the Hamakua coffee, mango chutney, and the new line of condiments and seasonings by renowned chef Amy Ferguson Ota. The Cooks' own triple-chocolate-chunk or oat-meal cookies (as deadly as they sound) should claim a fair share of the shopping basket. Another special touch: Alice Humbert sells hand creams, sea salts, and pot-pourris she makes from the harvests of her own garden. The old-fashioned tea cups filled with potted narcisuses and tea roses make superb gifts, as do the Hawaiian lomi lomi massage oil, gardener's hand cream, and made-from-scratch perfumes.

Gallery of Great Things. In Parker Square, Hwy. 19. ☎ **808/885-7706.**

Here's an eye-popping assemblage of local art and Pacific Rim artifacts. Browse under the watchful gaze of a 150-year-old Tongan war club (not for sale) and authentic rhinoceros- and deer-horn blowguns from Borneo among the plethora of treasures from Polynesia, Micronesia, and Indonesia. You'll find jewelry, glassware, photographs, greeting cards (including top-of-the-line Yvonne Cheng designer cards), fiber baskets, and hand-turned bowls of beautifully grained woods. Marian Berger's watercolors of endangered birds are contemporary classics.

Imagination. In Parker Square, Hwy. 19. ☎ **808/885-0430.**

This children's shop is stacked high with upscale toys, dolls, books, games, and other upper-end diversions. The selection is strong in educational toys and European and Asian imports—sure to appeal to the parents who are buying.

Kamuela Hat Company. In Waimea Center, Hwy. 190. ☎ **808/885-8875.**

The requisite hats of the paniolo life appear here in spades. Choose from among Kona lauhala, Stetsons, Panamas, Italian straw, white coconut, and more. You'll find other accoutrements for a life astride: belts, macho buckles, Western jewelry, and oilskin jackets à la J. Peterman, plus cowboy boots at non-Dallas prices. A personal favorite are the slippers made of palaka, the two-color plaid that has come to symbolize the rugged ranching and plantation eras of Hawaii. Styled into thongs, they're a hit.

✪ Silk Road Gallery. In Parker Square, Hwy. 19. ☎ **808/885-7474.**

It's worth a special stop if you love Asian antiques: porcelain tea cups, jade cups, kimono, lacquerware, Buddhas, tansus, bronze bells and chimes, Indonesian woven baskets, and all manner of delights for elevated living. You can part with $15 for a bronze bell, thousands for an antique tansu, or something in between.

Sweet Wind. In Parker Square, Hwy. 19. ☎ **808/885-0562.**

Owner Wendy Gilliam's bias shows: She loves beauty and things that induce harmony. So you'll find chimes, carved dolphins, crystals, geodes, incense, beads, essential oils, and thoughtfully selected books worth more than a casual glance, covering self-help, health, metaphysics, Hawaiian spirituality, yoga, meditation, and other topics for wholesome living.

✪ Upcountry Booksellers. In Opelo Plaza, Hwy. 19. ☎ **808/885-8077.**

You couldn't ask for much more from a bookstore: more than 20,000 titles, readings by local poets and authors, and window benches and chairs in which to peruse your selections. This is a real community bookstore for browsers and hardcore bibliophiles. The broad selection spans children's books to literary fiction to Thomas Mann and *How to Find Your Ideal Country Home*—tailor-made for Waimea. It accepts trades, too: Bring in what you've finished reading for credit, and spend as much time as you want deciding between their other tomes. For connoisseurs, this friendly store also has two dozen book-review subscriptions for leisurely contemplation.

✪ Upcountry Connection. At the Mauna Kea Center, Hwy. 19 and Hwy. 190. ☎ **808/885-0623.**

You may not be looking for a $1,900 koa chest, but it's here, along with a large, antique koa mirror reflecting the Ed Kayton originals on the wall. This warm, gleaming gallery offers an even mix of fine art, antiques, and crafts, all of impeccable taste. One-of-a-kind finds for bountiful budgets include a $1,200 coconut-wood Polynesian drum, Hawaiian musical instruments of feathers and coconut shells, Jerry Kotz's hand-turned Norfolk pine bowls, and Erik Wold's raku-fired ceramic vases for under $100. Other great finds: the original oils, limited prints, cards, and books of Herb Kawainui Kane, a living treasure of Hawaii; and bronzes by Lark Dimond-Cates, whose work greets arrivals at the Kona Airport. It's worth browsing here to see what island artists are up to.

Waimea General Store. In Parker Square, Hwy. 19. ☎ **808/885-4479.**

This charming, unpretentious country store has always offered a superb assortment of Hawaii-themed books, soaps and toiletries, cookbooks and kitchen accessories, candles and linens, greeting cards and dolls, Japanese hapi coats and island teas, rare kiawe honey, preserves, and countless gift items from the practical to the whimsical. Lovers of Crabtree and Evelyn soaps, fragrances, and cookies won't be disappointed.

THE HAMAKUA COAST

Waipio Valley Artworks. Kukuihaele. ☎ **808/775-0958.**

The focus here is strictly local, with a strong emphasis on wood works—one of the largest selections, if not the largest, in the state. A recent expansion has brought more chests and tables and gift items by Big Island artists. Housed in an old wooden building at the end of the road before the Waipio Valley, the gallery/boutique offers treasures for the home: pheasant wood, sandalwood, hau, kamani, avocado, mango, koa, kou, and a rainbow of native and introduced woods. All the luminaries of wood-turning have works here: Jack Straka, Robert Butts, Scott Hare, Kevin Parks. Their bowls, rocking chairs, and jewelry boxes exhibit flawless craftsmanship and richly burnished grains. More affordable are the pens and hair accessories, and the deli sandwiches and Tropical Dreams ice cream served in the expanded café section.

HONOKAA

EDIBLES **Mamane Street Bakery** on the main drag will fill all of your coffee-shop needs. Fresh-baked breads, pies, and pastries (including melt-in-your-mouth danishes) are served with good coffee in a tiny café lined with old photographs. Every Saturday morning from 7am, about a dozen local farmers and vendors set up their wares at the **Honokaa Farmers Market** in front of the Botelho Building. No crafts or arts here—just edibles, good and fresh. Vendors bring their home-baked breads and pastries, bananas, papayas, and bushels of freshly picked garden vegetables—and they're all available at unbeatable prices.

Decorative Arts by Joe Rivera. Mamane St. ☎ **808/775-9090.**

Light and function converge in this studio, where Joe Rivera, one of a hui of eight local artists, makes art of stained glass and gives space to fine work by local high-school students. Their hand-turned wooden bowls and milo bracelets don't bear the scars of apprenticeship, and the larger pieces, such as the mango chest with handmade copper corners, deserve premier placement in a manor. Beautiful, one-of-a-kind lamps of hammered copper, glass-mosaic tile, and pottery by local ceramists are among the works in this pleasing, friendly shop.

Honokaa Market Place. 45-3321 Mamane St. ☎ **808/775-8255.**

New and old, antiques and imports mingle freely in this eclectic selection of Hawaiian, Asian, and Indonesian handicrafts. Open since late 1994, the shop is gaining recognition for its old and new Hawaiiana. There's a large selection of wood bowls (koa, mango, hau, kou, ohia, kamani, Norfolk pine), and the Hawaiian quilts come in several forms and sizes, from wall hangings and pillows to the full-sized quilts. Hawaiian prints and lithographs, a few Oriental antiques, and a profusion of beads attract shoppers, collectors, and jewelry makers who can buy and string on the spot.

Honokaa Trading Company. Mamane St. ☎ **808/775-0808.**

"Rustic, tacky, rare—there's something for everyone," offers owner Grace Walker, who provides a lion's share of the town's local color. Every inch of the labyrinthine, 2,200-square-foot bazaar is occupied by antiques and collectibles, new and used goods, and countless treasures—all of it plantation memorabilia or Hawaiiana. Bark-cloth fabrics from the 1940s, rhinestone jewelry and rattan furniture from the 1930s, vintage ukuleles, Depression glass, dinnerware from Honolulu's landmark Willows restaurant, koa lamps, Francis Oda airbrush paintings—it's an unbelievable conglomeration, and surprises lurk in every corner. Vigilant collectors make regular forays here to scoop up the 1950s ivory jewelry and John Kelly prints.

Kamaaina Woods. Lehua St. (down the hill from the post office). ☎ **808/775-7722.**

The showroom is adjacent to the workshop, so visitors can watch the craftspeople at work on the other side of the glass panel. Local woods are the specialty here, with a strong emphasis on koa and milo bowls. Boxes, carvings, albums, and smaller accessories are also included in the mix, but bowl-turning is clearly the focus. Prices begin at about $10.

S. Hasegawa, Ltd. Mamane St. ☎ **808/775-0668.**

For 70 years, Honokaa residents have known that they could count on Hasegawa Store to provide the necessities of life. Here's a sampling of what you'll find in the narrow aisles of this country store: playing cards, shoes, Shiseido cosmetics, totebags, stuffed animals, dishes, baby dresses, stockings, zippers, and fabrics (pareu fabrics a big plus), plus hardware and cable cord for the industrial-minded.

Seconds to Go. Mamane St. ☎ **808/775-9212.**

Elaine Carlsmith spends a lot of time collecting vintage pottery, glassware, kimono, fabrics, and other treasures, only to release them to eager seekers of nostalgia. In her nearly two decades in this spot, many memories and beautiful things have passed through her doors, including antique koa furniture sets, old maps, music sheets, rare and out-of-print books, and reams of ephemera. The vintage ivory jewelry and Don Blanding dinnerware is grabbed up quickly. The main store is a few doors away from the warehouse, where furniture and larger pieces are displayed.

Starseed. Mamane St. ☎ **808/775-9344.**

Shop here for offbeat holographic bumper stickers, jewelry, beads, incense, and new-age amulets to fuel your day. The selection of beads and crystals is impressive, and the owner has a special camera that purportedly photographs people's auras, or electro-magnetic fields. Find out what your colors are, or look for them in the hundreds of boxes of beads, some of them rare European and Asian imports.

Taro Patch Gifts. In the Andrade Building, Mamane St. ☎ **808/776-1602.**

Taro Patch carries an eclectic assortment of Hawaiian music tapes and CDs, switch-plates printed with Hawaiian labels, Ka'u coffee, local jams and jellies, soaps, and sportswear. The Hawaiian seed lei selection is the best in town, from kamani to blue marble, wiliwili, double sheep eye, betel nut, and other attractive native species with melodious Hawaiian names.

HONOMU

An artists' colony has sprouted in Honomu, near Akaka Falls on the outskirts of Hilo, where artists and entrepreneurs have spruced up old storefronts and breathed new life into the area. Start your jaunt with a lilikoi shave ice, smoked-turkey plate lunch, or an opihi miso soup at **Aloha Akaka**, a local-style diner that's been there since 1936—lots of home-style noodles, wooden school chairs and concrete floors, and an ancient counter with an antique shave-ice machine.

A few doors down, the **Woodshop Gallery/Cafe** and espresso bar sells Island-made crafts and gift items, koa bowls, furniture, pottery, plantation memorabilia, and locally made ice creams by Hilo Homemade and Great Pacific, an up-and-coming Kona ice cream maker whose Toasted Coconut, Extreme Ginger, and Volcano flavors are riding the waves of popularity. Nearby, at the **Akaka Falls Inn and Gift Gallery** (housed in a 1923 building, the old Akita Store), you can nosh on snacks or lunch and browse in the adjoining room among shell and seed leis, koa accessories, books, candles, and lauhala bags for carting them home. Honomu newcomer **Panua Collections** has added imports from Papua New Guinea to the arts and crafts scene.

HILO

Shopping in Hilo is centered around the **Kaiko'o Hilo Mall** at 777 Kilauea Ave., near the state and county buildings; the **Prince Kuhio Shopping Plaza**, at 111 E. Puainako, just off Highway 11 on the road north to Volcano, where you'll find a supermarket, drugstore, Liberty House, and other standards; and the **Bayfront area** downtown, where the hippest new businesses have taken up residence in the historic buildings lining Kamehameha Avenue. For practical needs, there's a **KTA Super Store** at 323 Keawe St. and another at 50 E. Puainako, and a **Sure Save** supermarket at 1990 Kinoole St. Also see "Edibles," below.

For shopping that's more fun than obligatory, here are my Hilo highlights:

Basically Books. 160 Kamehameha Ave. ☎ **808/961-0144.**

We're happy to see our favorite Hilo bookstore in larger, more convenient digs in the bayfront area, next to the historic Kress Building. Affectionately called "the map shop," this is a sanctuary for lovers of books, maps, and the environment, with an engaging selection of printed materials in geology, history, topography, botany, mythology, and more. Get your bearings by browsing among the nautical charts; U.S. Geological Survey maps (the authoritative word in cartography); street maps; raised relief maps; out-of-print books; atlases, compasses, and countless books on travel, cooking; and history. Specializing in Hawaii and the Pacific, this is a bountiful source of information that will enhance any visit. Even the most knowledgeable residents stop by here to keep current and conscious.

Dan De Luz Woods. 760 Kilauea Ave. ☎ **808/935-5587.**

The unstoppable Dan De Luz has been turning bowls for more than 30 years. In his workshop behind the store, he turns koa, milo, mango, kamani, kou, sandalwood, hau, and other island woods, some very rare, into bowls, trays, and accessories of all shapes and sizes. You can find bookmarks, rice and stir-fry paddles, letter openers, and calabashes, priced from $3 to $1,000.

Dragon Mama. 266 Kamehameha Ave. ☎ **808/934-9081.**

For a dreamy stop in Hilo, head for this haven of all-natural comforters, cushions, futons, meditation pillows, hemp yarns and shirts, antique kimono and obi, tatami mats sold by the panel, and all manner of comforts in the elegantly spare Japanese esthetic. The bolts of lavish silks and pure, crisp cottons, sold by the yard, can be used in clothing or interior decorating; Dragon Mama also offers custom sewing, and you know she's good. She sewed the futon and bedding for the Dalai Lama when he visited the island a few years ago.

Ets'ko. 35 Waianuenue Ave. ☎ **808/961-3778.**

Ets'ko Rosendahl's dizzying selection of avant-garde treasures demand focus, or apoplexy will set in. Shop and be entertained by the sumptuous loungewear, Natoma Studio porcelains, Dina Angelwings teapots, Johnny Farrah backpacks, bamboo accessories, and the hundreds of items she finds from the design centers of the world. Futuristic wine racks, minimalist jewelry, handblown-glass pens, Japanese furniture and accessories, and ultra-luxe candles are included in the glittering assortment.

Hana Hou. 164 Kamehameha Ave. ☎ **808/935-4555.**

Michele Zane-Faridi has done a superlative job of assembling, designing, and collecting things of beauty that evoke old and new Hawaii. Last time I visited, she had a museum-quality amber necklace with large, evenly colored, perfectly shaped orbs the size of golf balls—a month's salary to buy, but a once-in-a-lifetime find. Vintage shirts, china, books, furniture, lamps, jewelry, handbags, accessories, and fabrics are displayed in surprising corners. The bark-cloth lampshades and collector's dreams—vintage silver and ivory jewelry by Ming's—disappear quickly from the elegant, evocative selection. Notice the lauhala hats in the vintage styles of the 1930s and 1940s—unspeakably chic, like the ties she has had made out of authentic vintage silkie fabrics. Mundorff prints, 1940s sheet music, and the tour de force, the nicest dressing room on the island (with a mango-wood bench made from the same tree as the desk), are more reasons for a standing ovation.

Hawaiian Force. 140 Kilauea Ave. ☎ **808/934-7171.**

Artist Craig Neff and his wife, Luana, set out their shingle in the original location of Sig Zane Designs (good karma), where they sell bold, wonderful T-shirt dresses, mamaki tea they gather themselves, lauhala fans and trivets, surfwear, aloha shirts, and jewelry made of opihi and Niihau shells. Everything here is Hawaiian, most of it made or designed by the Neffs. Luana's pikake oil is the best we've found, true to the last pheromone.

Mauna Kea Galleries. 276 Keawe St. ☎ **808/969-1184.**

Mark Blackburn, who wrote *Hawaiiana: The Best of Hawaiian Design,* proves that he's solidly grounded in the world of collecting with this gallery of nostalgic treasures. With his wife, Carolyn, he amasses vintage Hawaiiana in mint condition from estate sales and collectors all over the country, then respectfully displays it in their two-story Hilo gallery. Much is hidden here, but what is visible is riveting: large selections of monarchy and Ming jewelry; mint-condition Santa Anita and Don Blanding dinnerware, including very rare pieces; adz-hewn, not lathed, koa- and kou- wood bowls; and vintage photography and menus, all individually stored in plastic sleeves ($10 to $300). Rare books and prints, including hand-colored 1870s lithographs; original Hawaiian fish prints from the early 1900s; and limited-edition, vintage, black-and-white, museum-quality reproductions of hula-girl photos from the 1890s ($12 each!) are among the limitless finds. I love the children's aloha shirts from the 1970s and the paintings by Madge Tennent, Lloyd Sexton, D. Howard Hitchcock, Jules Tavernier—masters of the canvas, all.

The Most Irresistible Shop in Hilo. 110 Keawe St. ☎ **808/935-9644.**

It's not really the most irresistible shop in Hilo, but there aren't many tastes or categories of gift items that are overlooked here, from T-shirts and greeting cards to Tahitian and Balinese pareus, jewelry, glass and ceramic ware, koa cutting boards, plumeria hand lotion, and countless other chachkas.

Plantation Memories. 179 Kilauea St. ☎ **808/935-7100.**

The owner, Billy Perreira, has a particular fondness for plantation memorabilia and the resourcefulness it reflects. In his shop of plantation memories, everything has a story, and he's likely to know most of them: the one-of-a-kind handmade wooden wheelbarrow, made by a man for his young son; the handpainted wooden signs from the neighboring sugar communities of Honomu, Hakalau, and Hilo; plus vintage Hawaiian clothing, toys, china, furniture, lamps, baskets, textiles, and countless other collectibles from the turn of the century through the 1950s.

⭐ **Sig Zane Designs.** 122 Kamehameha Ave. ☎ **808/935-7077.**

My favorite stop in Hilo, Sig Zane Designs, evokes such loyalty that people make special trips from the outer islands for his culturally enlightening, inspired line of authentic Hawaiian wear. The spirit of this place complements the high esthetic level; everyone involved is completely immersed in Hawaiian culture and dance. The partnership of Zane and his wife, the revered hula master Nalani Kanaka'ole, is unrivaled in its creativity, style, and cultural and educational value. One step in the door and you'll see: The shop is awash in gleaming woods, lauhala mats, and clothing and accessories—from handmade house slippers to aloha shirts, pareus, muumuus, dresses, T-shirts, purses, and high-quality, made-in-Hawaii crafts. His fabric prints carry a cultural significance that deepens their visual beauty. New designs appear constantly, yet the classics remain fresh and compelling: ti, koa, kukui, taro, the lehua blossoms of the ohia tree, and many others. Koa books by Jesus Sanchez and intricately carved tapa-beating implements of ohia wood are popular, but the best and the brightest are the Sig Zane bedcovers, cushions, and custom-ordered upholstery, which bring the forest into your room. In a completely enriching experience, Sig and his staff take time to "talk story" and explain the significance of the images, or simply chat about Hilo, hula, and Hawaiian culture. Fabrics, including upholstery fabrics, are sold by the yard, and it's a good thing—it's hard to choose.

A Special Arts Center & Gallery
961-5711.

East Hawaii Cultural Center. 141 Kalakaua St. (across from Kalakaua Park). ☎ 808/

Part gallery, part retail store, and part consortium of the arts, the cultural center is run by volunteers in the visual and performing arts. Keep it in mind for gifts of Hawaii, or if you have any questions regarding the **Hawaii Concert Society, Hilo Community Players, Big Island Dance Council,** and **Big Island Art Guild.** The art gallery and gift shop exhibit locally made cards, jewelry, handmade books, sculptures, and wood objects, as well as museum-quality works, such as sculptures by Patrick Sarsfield and Henry Bianchini.

EDIBLES

Abundant Life Natural Foods. 292 Kamehameha Ave. ☎ **808/935-7411.**

Stock up here on healthy snacks, fresh organic produce, vitamins and supplements, bulk grains, baked goods, and the latest in health foods. There's a sound selection of natural remedies and herbal body, face, and hair products. The takeout deli makes fresh fruit smoothies and sprout- and nutrient-rich sandwiches and salads. Senior citizens get a 10% discount.

⭐ **Big Island Candies.** 500 Kalanianaole Ave. ☎ **808/935-8890.**

Abandon all restraint as you pull in—the smell of butter mixing with chocolate is as thick as honey, and chocolate-dipped shortbread and macadamia nuts, macadamia nut rocky road, and dozens of other dangers will make it very hard to be sensible. Allan Ikawa's vigilance about quality control demands eggs straight from a nearby farm, pure butter, Hawaiian cane sugar, no preservatives, and premium chocolate. Giftboxes are available, and they're carried interisland in staggering volumes. The Hawaiian Da Kine line is irrepressibly local: mochi crunch, fortune cookies, animal crackers, and other crunchy morsels—all dipped in chocolate, of course. By far, the best are the shortbread cookies, dipped in chocolate, peanut butter, and white chocolate.

Doris' Island Delights. In the Hilo Shopping Center, 1221 Kilauea Ave. ☎ **808/935-7113.**

Doris' hibachi seasonings, made with Hawaiian salt, are easily transported and waiting to be paired with chicken, steak, fish, or vegetables at your welcome-home barbecue. Among the flavors: Hilo style (with vinegar), chili pepper–lemon, lemon-herb, and for those on salt-restricted diets, no-salt seasoning with chili pepper and other condiments. The lilikoi and strawberry waiwi (small guava) cream cheeses don't require refrigeration until opening, and the stone cookies, like the sundried, jerky-like strips of ahi, require nothing more than strong jaws and a taste for local specialties. Cookies to love: Donna's shortbread and Hilo Kine's corn-flake, chocolate-chip, and macadamia-nut shortbread.

⭐ **Hilo Farmers Market.** Kamehameha Ave. at Mamo. ☎ **808/969-9114.**

It has grown into the state's best farmers market, embodying what we love most in Hawaii: local color, good soil and weather, the mixing of cultures, and new adventures in taste. More than 60 vendors from around the island bring their flowers, produce, and baked goods to this teeming corner of Hilo every Wednesday and Saturday from sunrise to 4pm. Because many of the vendors sell out early, go as early as you can. Expect to find a rapturous assortment: fresh, homegrown oyster mushrooms from Kona—three or four different colors and sizes—for about $5 a pound; the creamy, sweet, queenly Indonesian fruit called rambutan; moist, warm breads, from focaccia to walnut; an array of flowers; fresh aquacultured seaweed; corn from Pahoa; Waimea strawberries; taro and taro products; foot-long, miso-flavored, and traditional Hawaiian lau-lau; made-from-scratch tamales; and fabulous ethnic vegetables with unpronounceable names. The selection changes by the week, but it's always reasonable, fresh, and appealing, and a good cross-section of the island's specialties.

O'Keefe & Sons. In the S. Hata Building, 308 Kamehameha Ave. ☎ **808/935-0215.**

You can enjoy O'Keefe's fresh breads throughout the island, served in the best delis, coffee shops, and restaurants. But come to the source, this friendly Hilo bakery, for the full selection hot from the oven: Hilo nori bread, black-pepper/cilantro bread, focaccia in many flavors, cracked rye, challah, three types of sourdough, carrot-herb bread, and the classic French country loaf. Ask about their plans to open a coffee shop/pastry bar in the old Hilo Rising Bakery a few blocks away.

Paradise Gourmet. 308 Kamehameha Ave. ☎ **808/969-9146.**

Hilo is the crunchy-snack capital of the world, and the snack center of Hilo is Paradise Gourmet, where fish jerky, beef jerky, Maui onion jelly, taro-chip popcorn, and a sublime macadamia-nut shortbread will clamor for your taste buds. Ohelo-berry jam, from berries said to be the favorite food of the volcano goddess, is one of the big sellers, but my favorites are the silky hot guava sauce, the Maui onion sauce, and the buttery corn-flake cookies. Pure Kona coffee and a variety of tropical teas, from mango to passion fruit to an apple-litchi blend, are also sold here.

There's another Paradise Gourmet in Prince Kuhio Plaza, 111 E. Puainako (☎ **808/959-2339**).

THE PUNA REGION

Keaau Natural Foods. In the Keaau Shopping Center, 16-586 Old Volcano Rd., Keaau. ☎ **808/966-8877.**

This health-food store has grown with the years, with expanded selections in loose herbs, vitamins, cosmetics, fresh organic produce, and prepared foods. Ginger Moon bakery brings in healthy food to go: pizzas, curries, rice-and-vegetable dishes, tofu salad, eggless dishes, and a changing roster of vegetarian specialties. Fresh juices, Ka'u navel oranges, Puna papayas, sandwiches, and snacks have all the makings of a top-notch picnic lunch for your explorations of East Hawaii.

Pahoa Natural Groceries. Government Main Rd., Pahoa. ☎ **808/965-8322.** I never pass through Pahoa without stopping here for sandwiches, salads, and fresh fruit for a picnic at Lava Tree State Park or the ponds of Kapoho. The prolific kitchen makes several kinds of puddings and a dozen different salads and dips a day, as well as stunning sandwiches: artichoke-frittata, shrimp-and-avocado, and garden burgers. Other choices for takeout include Mexican casseroles, spinach lasagne, tofu salad, and everything from pasta to buckwheat noodles. There are always fresh pies, cakes, organic produce, and specialties of the region, such as Kapoho papayas and oranges.

HAWAII VOLCANOES NATIONAL PARK & VOLCANO VILLAGE

⭐ **STUDIO VISITS** Adding to the vitality of the art environment are the studio visits offered by the **Volcano Village Artists Hui,** several respected artists in various media who open their studios to the public by appointment. **Chiu Leong's** (☎ **808/967-7637**) airy, geometric studio/showroom is a mountain idyll that shows off splendidly his raku, pitfire, and porcelain works. His Japanese-style house and studio include a large, 25-foot-high performance room with a glass ceiling, where guest artists dance, play music, and present dramatic performances to widespread community support. Leong and his wife, dancer Eva Lee, built their redwood home from scratch, and it is a marvel, large enough to house his large-format (5 feet high), black-and-white, award-winning, lifesize photographs as well as his ceramic pots. All this is going on in an atmosphere of peaceful hospitality. Other artists in the hui: **Pam Barton** (☎ **808/967-7247**), who transforms vines, leaves, roots, bark, and tree shed-dings into stunning fiber sculptures and vessels, from baskets to handmade paper and books; photographer **Mary Walsh** (☎ **808/985-8520**); ceramist **Zeke Israel** (☎ **808/985-8554**); and **Ira Ono** (☎ **808/967-7261**), an artist in collage mixed-media who makes masks, water containers, fountains, paste-paper journals, garden vessels, and goddesses out of clay and found objects. These artists are tops in their fields and have their work displayed in fine galleries throughout the islands.

Kilauea Creations. Old Volcano Rd. ☎ **808/967-8090.**

Visitors interested in quilting are usually happy to discover that starter kits are avail-able to initiate the needlework into this Hawaiian and American craft. And this is the quilting center of Volcano, a co-op made up of seven crafters who make quilts, jewelry, feather leis, ceramics, baskets, and fiber arts. Gift items made by Volcano artists are sold here, but it's the quilts and quilting materials that make the shop dif-ferent, all offered in a boutique the size of a small living room. A few choice Hawaiian crafts appeal to non-quilters (lauhala mats, Hawaiian seed leis), and the fabulous trop-ical fruit preserves (especially the lilikoi butter spread that was featured in *Sunset* mag-azine) have universal appeal.

⭐ **Volcano Art Center.** Hawaii Volcanoes National Park. ☎ **808/967-8222.**

The Volcano Island's frontier spirit and raw, primal energy have spawned a close-knit community of artists. Although their works appear in galleries and gift shops throughout the island, the Volcano Art Center is the hub of the island's arts activity. Housed in the original 1877 Volcano House, VAC, as it's called, is a not-for-profit art-education center that offers exhibits and shows that change monthly, as well as work-shops and retail space. Marian Berger's watercolors of endangered birds, Dietrich Varez oils and block prints, Avi Kiriaty oils, Kelly Dunn and Jack Straka woods, Brad Lewis photography, and Mike Reily furnishings are among the works you'll see as you wander around those old wooden floors. Of the 300 artists represented, 90% come from Hawaii Island. The fine crafts at VAC include baskets, jewelry, mixed-media pieces, stone and wood carvings, and the journals and wood diaries of Jesus Sanchez, a third-generation Vatican bookbinder who has turned his skills to the island woods.

Volcano Store. At Huanani and Old Volcano Hwy. ☎ **808/967-7210.**

Walk up the wooden steps into a wonderland of flowers and Island specialties. Tangy lilikoi butter (transportable, and worth a special trip) and flamboyant sprays of cymbidiums, tuberoses, dendrobiums, anthuriums, hanging plants, mixed bouquets, and calla lilies (splendid when grown in Volcano), make a breathtaking assemblage in the enclosed front porch. Volcano residents are fortunate to have these blooms at such prices. The flowers can also be shipped (orders are taken by phone); Marie and Ronald Onouye and their staff pack them meticulously. Mainland recipients have gushed about the fresh, carefully wrapped treasures that arrive on time and in good shape. If mainland weather is too humid or frosty for reliable shipping, they'll let you know. Produce, stone cookies (as in hard-as-stone) from Mountain View, Hilo taro chips, cookies, bottled water (a necessity in Volcano), and other food and paper products round out the selection.

11 The Big Island After Dark

by Jocelyn Fujii

Jokes abound about neighbor-island nightlife being an oxymoron, but there are a few pockets of entertainment, largely in the Kailua-Kona and Kohala Coast resorts. Your best bet is to check the local newspapers—*Honolulu Advertiser*, *West Hawaii Today*—for special shows, such as fund-raisers for Punana Leo or local Hawaiian and civic groups, that are occasionally held at venues such as Kona Surf. Other than that, regular entertainment in the local clubs usually consists of mellow Hawaiian music at sunset, small hula groups, or jazz trios.

Some of the island's best events are usually held at **Kahilu Theatre** in Waimea (☎ **808/885-6017**), so be on the lookout for any mention of it during your stay. Hula, the top Hawaiian music groups from all over Hawaii, drama, and all aspects of the performing arts use Kahilu as a favored venue.

HULA   On this and all the islands, word of mouth is your most authentic source for finding and supporting good hula, and the place for that is usually a *halau* (hula school) fund-raiser. Check the local papers, or ask your hotel concierge if any of Hilo's hula halau are having a fundraising concert or backyard luau that's open to the public. (I also find hotel valets enormously helpful with this kind of information.) It's these local, community-based events that offer the greatest authenticity and spirit, often with spontaneous contributions of dance and song by visiting aunts and cousins.

IN & AROUND KAILUA-KONA

King Kamehameha's Kona Beach Hotel (☎ **808/329-2911**) holds a **luau and Polynesian revue** on the beach, next to the Ahuena Heiau, on Tuesday, Wednesday, Thursday, and Sunday. The hotel also offers Hawaiian and contemporary music at its **Billfish Bar** nightly except Monday.

Elsewhere in Kailua-Kona, the activity seems to have moved down an octave since our last edition. **Jolly Roger**, on Waterfront Row (☎ **808/329-1344**), once the spot for live entertainment, now offers only sporadic live entertainment. At the Kona Surf, the **Polynesian Paradise Revue** (☎ 808/322-3411) is a nearly 20-year tradition (more sunset than after dark), offered Tuesday and Friday from 5:30 to 7pm on the Nalu Terrace, a large room on the cliffs above Keauhou Bay; it's free to the public and very popular.

LUAU!

Kona Village Luau. Kona Village Resort. ☎ **808/325-5555.** Part of the Full American Plan for Kona Village guests; for nonguests, $69.75. AE, MC, V. Fridays at 5pm. Reservations required.

The longest continuously running luau on the island is still the best—a combination of an authentic Polynesian venue with a menu that works, impressive entertainment, and the spirit of old Hawaii. The feast begins with a ceremony in a sandy kiawe grove, where the pig is unearthed after a full day of cooking in its rock-heated underground oven. In the open-air dining room, next to prehistoric lagoons and tropical gardens, you'll sample a Polynesian buffet: poisson cru, poi, lau-lau (butterfish, seasoned pork, and taro leaves cooked in ti leaves), lomi salmon, squid luau (cooked taro leaves with steamed octopus and coconut milk), ahi poke, opihi (fresh limpets), coconut pudding, taro chips, sweet potatoes, chicken long rice, steamed breadfruit, and the shredded kalua pig. The generosity is striking. The Polynesian revue, a fast-moving, mesmerizing tour of South Pacific cultures, is far from limited to ancient and modern hula and manages, miraculously, to avoid being cliché or corny.

THE KOHALA COAST RESORTS

Evening entertainment here usually takes the form of a luau or indistinctive lounge music at scenic terrace bars with scintillating sunset views. The **Kona Village Resort's Friday luau** (see above) is the best luau on the island and one of the top three in the state, worth the price of admission. Otherwise, the resort roundup includes the Hilton Waikoloa Village's **Legends of the Pacific** dinner show (☎ **808/885-1234**) on Fridays, the **Royal Waikoloan luau** (☎ **808/886-6789**) on Sundays and Wednesdays near Anaehoomalu Bay, noted for its royal ponds and petroglyph fields; and the **Mauna Kea Beach Hotel's luau** (☎ **808/882-7222**) on Tuesdays.

If you get a chance to hear or see the **Lim Family**, don't miss them. Immensely talented in hula and song, members of the family perform in the intimate setting of the **Atrium Bar at Mauna Lani Bay Resort** (☎ **808/885-6622**) and at the **Hapuna Beach Prince Hotel** (☎ **808/880-1111**), where Nani Lim and Gary Haleamau fill the open-air **Reef Lounge** with their celestial sounds as the sun sets on Hapuna Beach below.

Our favorite night spot on the Kohala Coast is the ✪ **Mauna Lani Bay's Honu Bar** (☎ **808/885-6622**), a sleek, chic place for light supper, live light jazz with dancing, gourmet desserts, fine wines, and after-dinner drinks in an intimate, convivial atmosphere. There's nothing like being able to order toothsome pastas and light suppers with fine wines by the glass when most other restaurants are closing.

HILO

Hilo's most notable events are special or annual occasions such as the **Merrie Monarch Hula Festival,** the state's largest, which continues for a week after Easter Sunday with hula competitions from all over the world, demonstrations and craft fairs, and a staggering spirit of pageantry that takes over the entire town. Tickets are always hard to come by; call ☎ **808/935-9168** well ahead of time, and see the "Calendar of Events" in chapter 3 for further information.

Special concerts are also held at the **Hawaii Naniloa Hotel's Crown Room** (☎ **808/969-3333**), the Hilo venue for name performers when they fly in from Oahu and the outer islands. You can always count on a great act here, whether it's the Brothers Cazimero or Willie K. For dancing and live music on weekends, head for **Fiascos** at Waiakea Square (☎ **808/935-7666**). On Friday and Saturday nights, dancing and live contemporary and Hawaiian music take over the second floor; on Thursday nights, it's line dancing and country music.

Maui, the Valley Isle

Each of us holds a different image of tropical paradise in our mind's eye, but Maui just may fulfill every one: swaying palm trees bordering perfect white-sand coves; free-falling waterfalls etching the faces of mountains; voluptuous jungles bursting with bright color and bird-song; moonlight sparkling on calm, turquoise seas. This island is the one that can meet all the expectations—it's the realization of the dream.

And everybody, it seems, knows it. Next to Waikiki, Maui is Hawaii's most famous destination, welcoming 2½ million people each year to its sunny shores. As soon as you arrive at Kahului Airport, a huge banner will tell you that the readers of *Condé Nast Traveler* voted Maui the best island *in the world*—and they've done so 3 years running.

As the 20th century draws to a close, Maui has become *the* hip travel destination. Indeed, sometimes it feels a little too well-known—especially when you're stuck in bumper-to-bumper traffic around the airport or the wall-to-wall boat jam at Maui's popular snorkeling-diving atoll, Molokini Crater. However, the congestion here pales in comparison to big-city Honolulu; Maui, really, is just a casual collection of small towns. Once you move beyond the resort areas, you'll find a slower, more peaceful way of life, where car horns are used only to greet friends, posted store hours mean nothing if the surf's up, and taking time to watch the sunset is part of the daily routine.

Visitors from other small towns in America and elsewhere find Maui just right: warm and friendly and not too foreign, with a easy-going lifestyle that's perfect for relaxing. But Maui also has an under-lying energy that can nudge devout sunbathers right off the beach. People get inspired to do things they might not do otherwise, like rise before dawn to catch the sunrise over Haleakala Crater, then board a bicycle to coast 37 switchbacked miles back down to sea level; head out to sea on a kayak to look for wintering humpback whales; swim in the clear pool of a waterfall; ride a horse from mauka to makai; or discover a whole new world of exotic flowers and tropical fish.

On a map, Maui doesn't look like much—a tiny apostrophe with an attitude—but it's bigger than you might think. The 727.3-square-mile island has three peaks more than a mile high, thousands of water-falls, 120 miles of shoreline, more than 80 golden-sand beaches (including two more than a mile long), some great seaside hotels, and endless summer weather. The island is the result of a marriage of two shield volcanoes, 10,023-foot-high Haleakala and 5,788-foot-high Puu Kukui, that spilled enough lava between them to create a valley—and inspire the island's nickname. Thanks to this unusual makeup, Maui packs a lot of nature in and around its landscape, and its microclimates offer distinct variations on the tropical-island theme: The island's as lush as an equatorial rain forest in Hana; as dry as the Arizona desert in Makena; as hot as Mexico in Lahaina; and as cool and misty, like Oregon, up in Kula. The shores of Hookipa are ideal for windsurfers, and channel breezes challenge golfers in Kapalua.

Be warned: Once visitors have tasted the magic of Maui, they seem to yearn to return. At the back of their brain, the images flicker: the dapple of the sun's rays on a thundering waterfall; the song of bamboo as it dances in the wind; the power of the ocean waves as they pummel the base of soaring lava-rock cliffs; a Technicolor sun rising over the raw lava and primal ferns of otherworldly Haleakala, a crater so big and so deep that it could swallow the island of Manhattan whole; the double rainbow that brightens the vast sky after a warm summer rain. Maui is a place like no other . . . come and see.

1 Orientation

by Jeanette Foster

ARRIVING

If you think of the island of Maui as the shape of a head and shoulders of a person, you'll probably arrive on its neck, at **Kahului Airport.**

At press time, three airlines fly directly from the mainland to Maui: **United Airlines** (☎ 800/241-6522; www.ual.com) has one nonstop per day from Los Angeles and one from San Francisco; **Hawaiian Airlines** (☎ 800/367-5320; www.hawaiianair.com), has several daily flights from San Francisco and Los Angeles with a stopover in Honolulu, but no plane change, plus direct flights from San Francisco and Seattle; **American Airlines** (☎ 800/433-7300; www.americanair.com) flies direct from Los Angeles; and **Delta Airlines** (☎ 800/221-1212; www.delta-air.com) flies direct from San Francisco and Los Angeles.

The other major carriers fly to Honolulu, where you'll have to pick up an interisland flight to Maui. **Aloha Airlines** (☎ 800/367-5250 or 808/484-1111; www.alohaair.com) and **Hawaiian Airlines** (☎ 800/367-5320 or 808/838-1555; www.hawaiianair.com; e-mail webmaster@hawaiianair.com) both offer jet service from Honolulu and the other neighbor islands.

LANDING AT KAHULUI If there's a long wait at baggage claim, step over to the state-operated **Visitor Information Center** and pick up brochures and the latest issue of *This Week Maui,* which features great regional maps of the islands; ask the person in the booth about island activities. After collecting your bags from the poky, automated carousels, step out, take a deep breath, and proceed to the curbside rental car pickup area (at the ocean end, to your right as you stand with your back to the terminal) and wait for the appropriate rental agency shuttle van to take you a half-mile away to the rental car check-out desk. (All the major rental companies have branches at Kahului; see "Getting There & Getting Around" in chapter 3 for details on renting in Hawaii.)

If you're not renting a car, the cheapest way to get to your hotel is **SpeediShuttle** (☎ 808/875-8070), which can take you between Kahului Airport and all the major resorts between 5am and 9pm daily. Rates vary, but figure on $20 for two to Wailea

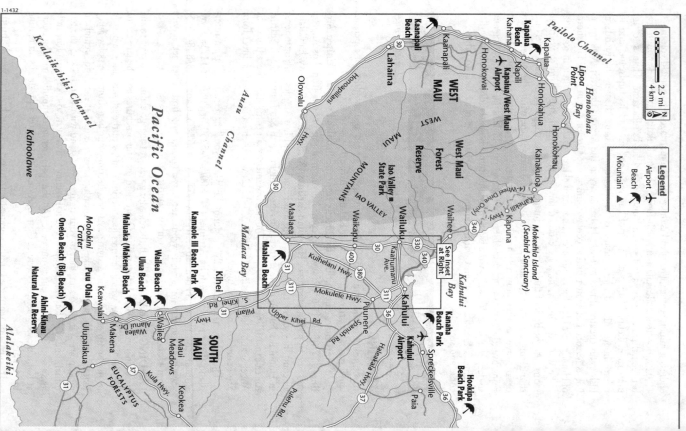

1-1432

Legend

✈ Airport
☂ Beach
▲ Mountain

0 | 2.5 mi
| 4 km
N

Pailolo Channel

Kaanapali Beach ☂
Kapalua Beach ☂
Kahana
Kapalua
Napili
Honokowai
Kapalua/West Maui Airport ✈
Lahaina
Kaanapali

Lipoa Point
Honokohau Bay
Honokohua
Honokahua
Honolua

WEST MAUI

WEST MAUI Forest Reserve

Honoapiilani Hwy.

Kahakuloa
(4-Wheel Drive Only)
Kahekili Hwy.
Kapuna
Mokeehia Island (Seabird Sanctuary)

Kealaikahiki Channel

Kahoolawe

Pacific Ocean

Olowalu

Iao Valley State Park ■
IAO VALLEY

WEST MAUI MOUNTAINS

Waihee
340
Waiehu
Wailuku
Waikapu
330
Kaahumanu Ave.
340
Kahului
See Inset at Right
Kahului Bay

Auau Channel

Maalaea

30
400
380
Kuihelani Hwy.

31 Maalaea Beach ☂

Kamaole III Beach Park ☂
Wailea Beach ☂
Ulua Beach ☂
Maluaka (Makena) Beach ☂

Mokulele Hwy.
Puunene
311
36
Spanish Rd.
Kanaha Beach Park ☂
Kahului Airport ✈
Spreckelsville
36

Maalaea Bay

Kihei
S. Kihei Rd.
311
Piilani Hwy.
31
Upper Kihei Rd.

SOUTH MAUI

Keawalai
Makena
Wailea
Wailea Alanui Dr.
Maui Meadows

Molokini Crater
Puu Olai ▲
Oneloa Beach (Big Beach) ☂
Ahihi-Kinau Natural Area Reserve ☂

Ulupalakua
37
Kula Hwy.
Keokea
EUCALYPTUS FORESTS
31

Haleakala Hwy.
Puleni Rd.
37
Paia
Hoolipa Beach Park ☂
36

Alalakeiki

Central Maui

To → Hana

Kahului Airport

To → Hana

Kahului

Kahului Bay

Amala Rd.

Keolani Pl.

Hana Hwy.

Haleakala Hwy.

36

370

Hansen Rd.

Mokulele Hwy.

311

Alexander & Baldwin Sugar Museum

Maui Marketplace

Dairy Rd.

Puunene

Puuene Ave.

Lono Ave.

350

Kuihelani Hwy.

380

31

To South Maui

Maalaea Beach

Kealia Pond

Kealia Pond National Wildlife Preserve

Maalaea Harbor

Maalaea

To West Maui

30

Honoapiilani Hwy.

Waiale Rd.

Waikapu

Maui Tropical Plantation

Wailuku

Kaahumanu Ave.

32

340

Pacific Ocean

Waipio Bay

Pauwela

Haiku

Huelo

Kailua

Keanae

Nahiku

Hana Hwy.

36

360

365

Makawao Hwy.

Makawao

Olinda

Pukalani

377

Haleakala Hwy.

Pulehu

Kula Hwy.

37

Kula

377

Waiohuli

PINE FORESTS

Crater Rd.

378

Haleakala Crater Rd.

Puu Ulaula

Science City

UPCOUNTRY MAUI

Koolau

Makawao Forest Reserve

Forest

Reserve

Haleakala National Park

EAST MAUI

Hana Airport

Waianapanapa State Park

Hana

Hana Forest Reserve

Hamoa Beach

Hamoa

Kakio

31

Oheo Gulch

Kipahulu

Kipahulu Forest Reserve

Kaupo

Kailo Point

31

Pilani Hwy.

Kula Forest Reserve

Polipoli Springs State Rec. Area

Kahikinui Forest Reserve

Alenuihaha

Channel

Channel

(one way) and $40 for two to Kapalua (one way). Be sure to call before your flight to arrange pickup.

If you are staying in the Lahaina-Kaanapali area, transportation service is available through **Airporter Shuttle** (☎ **800/533-8765** or 808/661-6667), which runs every half-hour from 9am to 4pm; the cost is $26 one way and $56 round trip.

If possible, avoid landing on Maui between 3 and 6pm, when the working stiffs on Maui are "pau work" (finished with work) and a major traffic jam occurs at the first intersection.

AVOIDING KAHULUI You can avoid Kahului Airport altogether by taking an **Island Air** (☎ **800/323-3345**) flight to **Kapalua–West Maui Airport**, which is convenient if you're planning to stay at any of the hotels in Kapalua or at the Kaanapali resorts. If you're staying in Kapalua, it's only a 10- or 15-minute drive to your hotel, and it's 10 or 15 minutes to Kaanapali (as opposed to 35 or 40 minutes from Kahului). Island Air also flies into tiny **Hana Airport,** but you have to make a connection at Kahului to get there.

VISITOR INFORMATION

The **Maui Visitors Bureau** is located at 1727 Wili Pa Loop, Wailuku, Maui, HI 96793 (☎ **800/525-MAUI** or 808/244-3530; fax 808/244-1337; www.visitmaui. com). To get there from the airport, go right on Highway 36 (the Hana Highway) to Kaahumanu Avenue (Hwy. 32); follow it past Maui Community College and Wailuku War Memorial Park onto East Main Street in Wailuku. At North Market Street, turn right, and then turn right again on Mill Street; go left on Kala Street and left again onto Wili Pa Loop.

THE REGIONS IN BRIEF
CENTRAL MAUI

This flat, often windy corridor between Maui's two volcanoes is where you'll most likely arrive—it's where the main airport is. It's also the home of the majority of the island's population. You'll find good shopping and dining bargains here, the heart of the business community and the local government (courts, cops, and county and state government agencies).

Kahului This is "Dream City," home to thousands of former sugarcane workers whose dream in life was to own their own home away from the sugar plantation. There's great shopping here (especially at discount stores), but not a lot of great accommodations for visitors. Three small hotels close to the airport are good for late arrival and early departure, but this is not a place to spend your vacation.

Wailuku With its faded wooden storefronts, old plantation homes, shops straight out of the '50s, and relaxed way of life, Wailuku is like a time capsule. While most people race through the town on their way to see the natural beauty of **Iao Valley,** this quaint little town is worth a brief visit, if only to see a real place where real people actually appear to be working at something other than a suntan. This is the county seat, so you'll see men in neckties and women in dressy suits on important missions in the tropical heat. The town has a spectacular view of Haleakala Crater, great budget restaurants, some interesting bungalow architecture, a Frank Lloyd Wright building on the outskirts of town, a wonderful historic B&B, and the always-endearing Bailey House Museum.

WEST MAUI

This is the fabled Maui you see on postcards. Jagged peaks, green velvet valleys, a wilderness full of native species—the majestic West Maui Mountains are the epitome of earthly paradise. The beaches here are some of the islands' best. And it's no secret: This stretch of coastline along Maui's "forehead," from Kapalua to the historic port of Lahaina, is the island's most bustling resort area (with South Maui close behind).

If you want to book into a resort or a condo on this coast, first consider what community you'd like to base yourself in. Starting at the southern end of West Maui and moving northward, the coastal communities look like this:

Lahaina   This old whaler seaport teems with restaurants, T-shirt shops, and a gallery on nearly every block, but there's still lots of real history to be found amid the gimcrackery. This vintage village is a tame version of its former self, when whalers swaggered ashore in search of women and grog. Lahaina town is a great place to stay: a few old hotels (such as the newly restored 1901 Pioneer Inn on the harbor), quaint bedand-breakfasts, and a handful of oceanfront condos offer a variety of choices in which to base yourself.

Kaanapali   Farther north along the West Maui Coast is Hawaii's first masterplanned family resort. Pricey mid-rise hotels line nearly 3 miles of gold-sand beach; they're linked by a landscaped parkway and a walking path along the sand. Golf greens wrap around the slope between beachfront and hillside properties. **Whalers Village**—a seaside mall with 48 shops and restaurants, including such fancy names as Tiffany and Co. and Louis Vuitton, plus the best little whale museum in Hawaii—and other restaurants are reach on foot along the oceanfront walkway or by resort shuttle, which also serves the small West Maui airport just to the north. Shuttles also go to Lahaina (see above), 3 miles to the south, for shopping, dining, entertainment, and boat tours. Kaanapali is popular with meeting groups and families—especially those with teenagers, who like all the action.

From Honokowai to Napili   In the building binge of the 1970s, condominiums sprouted along this gorgeous coastline like mushrooms after a rain. Today, these older oceanside units offer excellent bargains for astute travelers. The great location—along sandy beaches, within minutes of both the Kapalua and Kaanapali resort areas, and close enough to the goings-on in Lahaina town—makes this area an accommodation heaven for the budget-minded.

Honokowai and **Mahinahina** is the next beachfront area as you travel upcoast from Kaanapali, where you'll find mostly older units that tend to be cheaper; there's not much shopping here (mostly convenience stores), but you'll have easy access to the shops and restaurants of Kaanapali.

Kahana is a little more upscale than Honokowai and Mahinahina. Most of its condos are big high-rise types, more recently built than those immediately to the south. You'll find a nice selection of shops and restaurants (including the Maui branch of Roy's) in the area, and Kapalua West Maui Airport is nearby.

Napili is a much sought-after area for condo seekers: It's quiet; it has great beaches, restaurants, and shops; and it's close to Kapalua. Units are generally more expensive here (although we've found a few hidden gems at affordable prices; see Napili Bay on p. 376).

Kapalua   North beyond Kaanapali and the shopping centers of Napili and Kahana, the road starts to climb and the vista opens up to fields of silver-green pineapple and manicured golf fairways. Turn down the country lane of Pacific pines toward the sea, and you could only be in Kapalua. It's the very exclusive domain of two gracious—and expensive—hotels set on one of Hawaii's best gold-sand beaches, next to two bays that are marine-life preserves (with fabulous surfing in winter).

Even if you don't stay here, you're welcome to come and enjoy Kapalua. Both of the fancy hotels here provide public parking and beach access. The resort champions innovative environmental programs; it also has an art school where you can learn local crafts as well as three favorite golf courses, historic features, a collection of swanky condos and homes (many available for vacation rental at astronomical prices), and wide-open spaces that include a rain-forest preserve—all open to the general public.

SOUTH MAUI

This is the hottest, sunniest, driest, most popular coastline on Maui for sun lovers—Arizona by the sea. Rain rarely falls, and temperatures stick around 85°F year-round. On former scrubland from Maalaea to Makena, where cacti once grew wild and cows grazed, are now four distinctive areas—Maalaea, Kihei, Wailea, and Makena—each appealing to a different crowd.

Maalaea   If West Maui is the island's head, Maalea is just under the chin. This windy, oceanfront village centers around the small boat harbor (with a general store and a couple of restaurants) and the newly opened **Maui Ocean Center,** an aquarium/ocean complex. Visitors staying here should be aware that it's often—like, 350 days a year—very windy (all the wind from the Pacific is funneled between the West Maui Mountains and Haleakala and comes out in Maalaea); you may want to stay a bit farther down the coast in one of the resort areas.

Kihei   Kihei isn't really a town; it's more a nearly continuous series of condos and mini-malls lining South Kihei Road. This is Maui's best vacation bargain: Budget travelers swarm like sun-seeking geckos to lay out on eight sandy beaches along this scalloped, condo-packed, 7-mile stretch of coast. Kihei is neither charming nor quaint; what it lacks in aesthetics, though, it more than makes up for in sunshine, affordability, and convenience. If you want café in the morning, beach in the afternoon, and Hawaii Regional Cuisine in the evening—all at budget prices—head to Kihei.

Wailea   Only 2½ decades ago, this was wall-to-wall scrub kiawe trees, but now Wailea is a manicured oasis of multimillion-dollar resort hotels along 2 miles of palm-fringed gold coast—sort of Beverly Hills by the sea, except California never had it so good: warm, clear water full of tropical fish, year-round golden sunshine and clear blue skies, and hedonistic pleasure palaces on 1,500 acres of black-lava shore indented by five beautiful beaches. Amazing what a billion dollars can do.

This is the playground of the stretch-limo set. The planned resort development—practically a well-heeled town—has a shopping village, three prized golf courses of its own and 3 more in close range, and a tennis complex. A growing number of large homes sprawls over the upper hillside, some offering excellent bed-and-breakfast units at reasonable prices. The resorts along this fantasy coast are spectacular, to say the least: Next door to the Four Seasons, the most elegant, is the Grand Wailea Resort and Spa, a public display of ego by Tokyo mogul Takeshi Sekiguchi, who dropped $600 million in 1991 to create his own minicity. There's nothing like it in Hawaii, maybe even on the planet. Stop in and take a look—it's so gauche you gotta see it.

Nice natural features include the coastal trail, a 3-mile round-trip path along the oceanfront with pleasing views everywhere you look—out to sea and to the neighboring islands, or inland to the broad lawns and gardens of the hotels. The trail's south end borders an extensive native coastal plant garden, as well as ancient lava-rock house ruins juxtaposed with elegant oceanfront condos. But the chief attractions, of course, are those five outstanding beaches (the best is Wailea).

Makena   Suddenly, the road enters raw wilderness. After Wailea's overdone density, the thorny landscape is a welcome relief. Although beautiful, this is an end-of-the-road kind of place: It's a long drive from Makena to anywhere on Maui. If you're looking for an activity-filled vacation, you might want to book somewhere else, or you'll spend your vacation in the car. But if you want a quiet, relaxing vacation where the biggest trip of the day is from your bed to the beach, Makena is your place.

Puu Olai stands like Maui's Diamond Head on the shore, where a sunken crater shelters tropical fish, and empty golden-sand beaches stand at the end of dirt roads. Beyond Makena, you'll discover Haleakala's last lava flow, which ran to the sea in 1790; the bay named for French explorer La Pérouse; and a chunky, *aa* lava trail known as the *King's Highway,* which leads around Maui's empty south shore past ruins and fish camps, turning into a dirt path and eventually dead-ending at private land.

UPCOUNTRY MAUI

After a few days at the beach, you'll probably take notice of the 10,000-foot mountain in the middle of Maui. The slopes of Haleakala ("House of the Sun") are home to cowboys, growers, and other country people who wave back as you drive by. They're all up here enjoying the crisp air, emerald pastures, eucalyptuses, and flower farms of this tropical Olympus; there's even a misty California redwood grove. You can see a thousand tropical sunsets reflected in the windows of houses old and new, strung along a road that runs like a loose hound starting in Makawao, an old-paniolo-turned–New Age village, and wanders up to Kula, where the road leads up to the crater and Haleakala National Park. The rumpled, two-lane blacktop of Highway 37 turns narrow on the other side of Tedeschi Winery, where wine grapes and wild elk flourish on the Ulupalakua Ranch, the biggest on Maui. A stay upcountry is usually affordable and a nice contrast to the sizzling beaches and busy resorts below.

Makawao   Until recently, this small, two-street upcountry town was little more than a post office, a gas station, a feed store, a bakery, and a restaurant/bar serving the cowboys and farmers living in the surrounding community; the hitching posts outside of storefronts were really used to tie up horses. As the population of Maui started expanding in the '70s, a health-food store sprang up, followed by boutiques, a chiropractic clinic, and a host of health-conscious restaurants. The result is an eclectic amalgam of old paniolo Hawaii and transplanted mainland baby-boomer modernism.

Hui No'Eau Visual Arts Center, Hawaii's premier arts collective, is definitely worth a peek. The only accommodations here are reasonably priced bed-and-breakfasts with great views and slightly chilly nights.

Kula   A feeling of pastoral remoteness prevails in this upcountry community of old flower farms, humble cottages, and new suburban ranch houses with million-dollar views that take in the ocean, the isthmus, the West Maui Mountains, more ocean dotted with Lanai and Kahoolawe, and at night, the string of pearls that lights the gold coast from Maalaea to Puu Olai. They flourish at a cool 3,000 feet (bring a jacket), just below the cloud line, along a winding road on the way up to Haleakala National Park. Everyone here grows something—Maui onions, carnations, orchids, and proteas, that strange-looking blossom that looks like a *Star Trek* prop—and B&Bs cater to guests seeking cool tropic nights, panoramic views, and a rural upland escape. This is a destination where you get away to the peace and quiet that only rural farming country can bring—yet you're just 30 or 40 minutes away from the beach, and Lahaina's just an hour's drive away.

EAST MAUI

On the Road to Hana   When old sugar towns die, they usually fade away in rust and red dirt. Not **Paia.** The tangled spaghetti of electrical, phone, and cable wires that hang above the two-street town symbolizes its ability to adapt to the times: It may look messy, but it works. In Paia, trendy restaurants, eclectic boutiques, and high-tech windsurf shops stand next door to a ma-and-pa grocery store, a fish market, and storefronts that have been serving customers since the plantation days. Hippies took over in the '70s; while their macrobiotic restaurants have made way for Hawaii Regional Cuisine, and galleries featuring the works of renowned international artists have taken over for the old-style artists' co-op, Paia still manages to maintain a pleasant vibe of hippiedom. The town's main attraction, though, is **Hookipa Beach Park,** where the wind that roars through the isthmus of Maui brings windsurfers from the world over, who come to fly over the waves on gossamer wings linked to surfboards. There are a few B&Bs just outside Paia in the tiny community of **Kuau.**

Ten minutes down the road from Paia and up the hill from the Hana Highway—the connector road to the entire east side of Maui—is **Haiku.** Once a pineapple-plantation village, complete with working cannery (today a shopping complex), Haiku offers vacation rentals and B&Bs in a quiet, pastoral setting. Haiku is a great base for those who want to get off the beaten path and experience the quieter side of Maui but don't want to feel too removed: the beach is only 10 minutes away.

About 15 to 20 minutes past Haiku is the largely unknown community of **Huelo.** Every day, thousands of cars whiz by on the road to Hana; most barely glance at the double row of mailboxes overseen by a fading Hawaii Visitors Bureau sign. But down the gun-metal road lies a hidden Hawaii: a Hawaii of an earlier time, where Mother Nature is still sensual and wild, where ocean waves pummel soaring lava cliffs, and where an indescribable sense of serenity prevails. Huelo is not for everyone—but for those who don't hunger for the magic of a place still largely untouched by "progress," check into a B&B or vacation rental here.

Hana Set between an emerald rain forest and the forever blue Pacific is a village probably best defined by what it lacks: golf courses, shopping malls, McDonald's; except for a gas station and a bank with an ATM, you'll find little of what passes for progress here. Instead, you'll discover the simple joys of fragrant tropical flowers, the sweet taste of backyard bananas and papayas, and the easy calm and unabashed small-town aloha of Old Hawaii. What saved "Heavenly" Hana from the inevitable march of progress? The 52-mile road that winds around 600 curves and crosses more than 50 one-lane bridges that separates it from Kahului and is known as **Hana Highway.** You can go to Hana for the day—it's a 3-hour drive (and a half-century away)—but 3 days are better. There's a first-class resort here, a handful of great B&Bs, and some spectacular vacation rentals, but be sure to read our warning (see p. 393) on booking agents before you plunk your money down.

2 Getting Around

by Jeanette Foster

The only way to really see Maui is by rental car; while inter-resort trolley service is available (see "Other Transportation Options," below), there's no islandwide public transit.

DRIVING AROUND MAUI

Maui only has a handful of major roads: Two roads follow the coastline around the two volcanoes that form the island, Haleakala and Puu Kukui; one road goes up to Haleakala's summit; one road goes to Hana; one goes to Wailea; and one goes to Lahaina. It sounds simple, right? Well, it isn't, because the names of the few roads change en route. Study the island map on p. 356 before you set out.

TRAFFIC ADVISORY The road from Central Maui to Kihei and Wailea, Mokulele Highway (Hwy. 311), is a dangerous strip that's often the scene of head-on crashes involving intoxicated and speeding drivers; be careful. Also, be alert on the Honoapiilani Highway (Hwy. 30) en route to Lahaina, since drivers who spot whales in the channel between Maui and Lanai often slam on the brakes and cause major tie-ups and accidents.

If you get into trouble on Maui's highways, look for the flashing blue strobe lights on 12-foot poles; at the base are emergency, solar powered call boxes (programmed to dial 911 as soon as you pick up the handset). There are 29 emergency call boxes on the islands busiest highways and remote areas, including along the Hana and Haleakala highways and on the north end of the island in the remote community of Kahakuloa.

Another traffic note: Buckle up your seat belt—Hawaii has stiff fines for noncompliance.

CAR RENTALS   All of the major car-rental firms have agencies on Maui, usually at both Kahului and West Maui airports; for a complete list as well as tips on insurance and driving rules, see "Car Rentals" under "Getting There & Getting Around" in chapter 3. Cars are usually plentiful, except on holiday weekends, which in Hawaii also means King Kamehameha Day, Prince Kuhio Day, and Admission Day (see "When to Go" in chapter 3).

MOPEDS   Mopeds are available for rent from **Rental Warehouse,** 578 Front St. (near Prison Street), Lahaina (☎ **808/661-1970**); and in Azeka Place II, on the mountain side of Kihei Road near Lipoa Street, Kihei (☎ **808/875-4050**), starting at $18.99 a day. Mopeds are little more than motorized bicycles that maybe get up to 35m.p.h. (with a good wind at your back), so we would suggest using them only locally (to get to the beach or to go shopping). Don't take them out on the highway, as they can't keep up with the traffic.

OTHER TRANSPORTATION OPTIONS

TAXIS   **Alii Taxi** (☎ **808/661-3688** or 808/667-2605) offers 24-hour service island-wide. You can also call **Kihei Taxi** (☎ **808/879-3000**), **Wailea Taxi** (☎ **808/874-5000**), and **Yellow Cab of Maui** (☎ **808/877-7000**) if you need a ride.

SHUTTLES   **Maui Trolley,** a San Francisco-style trolley on wheels, offers shuttle-bus service between some 13 hotels in South Maui's Wailea-Kihei area to the Lahaina and Kaanapali commercial centers in West Maui four times a day; the first hotel pickup is at the Maui Makena Prince Hotel at 9am. The cost is $15 from the South Maui hotels to West Maui ($10 for teenagers, $7.50 for children 12 and younger), with unlimited reboarding; it's $5 for the return trip from West Maui to Kihei-Wailea ($3 for teenagers, $2 for children 12 and under); and it's $2 for rides from one hotel to another in the Kihei-Wailea area. For more information, call ☎ **800/824-8804.**

Free shuttle vans operate within the resort areas of Kaanapali, Kapalua, and Wailea.

FAST FACTS: Maui

American Express   In South Maui, at the **Grand Wailea Resort** (☎ **808/875-4526**), and in West Maui at the **Ritz-Carlton Kapalua** (☎ **808/669-6016**) and the **Westin Maui** at Kaanapali Beach (☎ **808/661-7155**).

Dentists   Emergency dental care is available at **Maui Dental Center,** 162 Alamaha St., Kahului (☎ **808/871-6283**).

Doctors   **West Maui Healthcare Center,** Whaler's Village, 2435 Kaanapali Pkwy., Suite H-7 (near Leilani's Restaurant), Kaanapali (☎ **808/667-9721**; fax 808/661-1584), is open 365 days a year until 10pm nightly; no appointment is necessary. In Kihei, call **Kihei Physicians**, 1325 S. Kihei Rd, Suite 103 (at Lipoa Street, across from Star Market), Kihei (☎ **808/879-7781**), which is open daily from 8am to 7pm; doctors are on call 24 hours a day.

Emergencies Call ☎ **911** for police, fire, and ambulance service. District stations are located in Lahaina (☎ **808/661-4441**) and in Hana (☎ **808/248-8311**).

Hospitals **Maui Memorial Hospital**, in Central Maui, is at 221 Mahalani, Wailuku (☎ **808/244-9056**); East Maui's **Hana Medical Center** is on Hana Highway (☎ **808/248-8924**); and **Kula Hospital**, in upcountry Maui, is at 204 Kula Hwy., Kula (☎ **808/878-1221**).

Newspapers The *Maui News* is the island's daily paper.

Poison Control Center In an emergency, call ☎ **800/362-3585**.

Post Office To find the nearest post office branch, call ☎ **800/ASK-USPS**. In Lahaina, there are branches at the Lahaina Shopping Center, 132 Papalaua St.; in Kahului, there's a branch at 138 S. Puunene Ave.; and in Kihei, there's one at 1254 S. Kihei Rd.

Weather Reports For the current weather, call ☎ **808/871-5054**; for Haleakala National Park weather, call ☎ **808/572-9306**; for marine weather and surf and wave conditions, call ☎ **808/877-3477**.

3 Accommodations

by Jeanette Foster

Maui has accommodations to fit every kind of vacation, from deluxe oceanfront resorts to reasonably priced condos to historic bed-and-breakfasts. Before you book, be sure to read "The Regions in Brief," above, which will help you to settle on your ideal location. Also check our "Tips on Accommodations" in chapter 3 for reliable booking agents that can help you plan your trip, and other useful tips.

Remember to add Hawaii's 10.17% accommodation tax to your final bill. Parking is free unless otherwise noted.

For an even wider selection of places to stay, check our *Frommer's Maui*.

CENTRAL MAUI

AT KAHULUI AIRPORT If you're arriving late at night or you have an early-morning flight out, the best choice near the airport is the **Maui Beach Hotel**, 170 Kaahumanu Ave. (Hwy. 32 at Hwy. 340), Kahului, HI 96740 (☎ **800/367-5004** or 808/877-0051). The nondescript, motel-like rooms go for $90 to $110 double (extra person $17) and include free airport shuttle service. Okay for a night, but not a place to spend your vacation.

WAILUKU

✿ **Old Wailuku Inn at Ulupono**, 2199 Kahookele St. (at High St., across from the Wailuku School), Wailuku, HI 96732. ☎ **800/305-4899** or 808/244-5897. Fax 808/242-9600. E-mail Mauibandb@aol.com. 11 units. A/C TV TEL. **$120-$180** double. Rates include gourmet breakfast. Extra person $20. AE, MC, V.

This restored 1924 former plantation manager's home is the place to stay if you are looking for a genuine Old Hawaii experience. Innkeepers Janice and Thomas Fairbanks, both with years of experience in the hospitality and hotel industries, have lovingly restored this home. Inspired by Hawaii's poet laureate, Don Blanding, the theme is Hawaii of the 1920s and '30s, with decor, design, and landscaping to match.

The guest rooms are wide and spacious, reminiscent of a day when land was cheap and building materials were affordable, and gorgeously furnished. Exotic ohia wood covers the floors, high ceilings with slow-moving ceiling fans make the rooms light and airy, and traditional Hawaiian quilts grace the beds. The mammoth bathrooms (some with clawfoot tubs, others with Jacuzzis) have plush towels and "earth-friendly" toiletries on hand. The morning meal is a full gourmet Hawaii-style breakfast served on the enclosed back lanai, or on a tray delivered to your room if you prefer. You'll feel right at home lounging on the generously sized living-room sofa or watching the world go by from an old wicker chair on the lanai.

Located in the old historic area of Wailuku, the inn is just a few minutes' walk from the Maui County Seat Government Building, the courthouse, and a wonderful stretch of antique shops. It's fully equipped to handle business travelers, with automated messaging, modem jacks, and multiple phones in each room; fax and copy services and computers are available for use.

WEST MAUI
LAHAINA
Moderate

✪ **Aston Maui Islander.** 660 Wainee St. (between Dickenson and Prison sts.), Lahaina, HI 96761. ☎ **800/92-ASTON,** 800/367-5226, or 808/667-9766. Fax 808/661-3733. www.aston-hotels.com. 372 units. A/C TV TEL. High season $92 double, $105–$114 studio with kitchenette, $125 one-bedroom with kitchen, $182 two-bedroom with kitchen (sleeps 4); low season $82 double, $95–$104 studio with kitchenette, $115 one-bedroom with kitchen, $172 two-bedroom with kitchen. Extra person $6; kids 17 and younger stay free using existing bedding. AE, CB, DC, DISC, JCB, MC, V.

These units are one of Lahaina's great buys—especially the kitchenette units; the larger ones are great for families on a budget. This wooden complex isn't on the beach, but it is on a quiet side street (a rarity in Lahaina) and within walking distance of restaurants, shops, attractions, and yes, the beach (it's just three blocks away). All of the good-sized rooms, decorated in a tropical-island style, are comfortable and quiet. The entire complex is spread across 10 landscaped acres and includes tennis courts (lit for night play until 10pm), a pool, a sundeck, a barbecue, and a picnic area. The aloha-friendly staff will take the time to answer all of your questions.

Best Western Pioneer Inn. 658 Wharf St. (in front of Lahaina Pier), Lahaina, HI 96761. ☎ **800/457-5457** or 808/661-3636. Fax 808/667-5708. E-mail pioneer@maui.net. 50 units. A/C TV TEL. $99–$159 double. Extra person $15. AE, CB, DC, DISC, MC, V. Parking $4 in lot 2 blocks away.

This historic hotel has come a long way since its origins as a turn-of-the-century whalers' saloon and inn. Until the 1970s, a room at the Pioneer Inn overlooking Lahaina Harbor went for $20 and included a can of Raid insect repellent, and the honky-tonk bar downstairs went until the wee hours of the morning, so no one slept. But those days are long gone—and this venerable waterfront hotel has never looked better. At the end of 1997, it became a Best Western, and the finishing touches of its restoration were completed.

This once-rowdy home away from home for sailors and whalers now seems almost respectable, like visiting your great-grandma's house—old but nice, even charming (a word never before associated with this relic). The hotel is a two-story plantation-style structure with big verandas that overlook the streets of Lahaina and the harbor. All the rooms are totally remodeled with vintage baths and new curtains and carpets; they even have TVs, VCRs, and direct-dial phones now. There's a new outdoor pool, three restaurants, the historic Whalers Saloon (without the honky-tonk music), 20 shops, and the Lahaina Harbor just 50 feet away. The quietest rooms face either the garden courtyard—devoted to refined outdoor dining accompanied by live (but quiet) music—or the square-block-sized banyan tree next door. We recommend room no. 47, over the banyan court, with a view of the ocean and the harbor. If you want a front-row seat for all the Front Street action, book no. 48.

House of Fountains Bed & Breakfast. 1579 Lokia St. (off Fleming Rd., north of Lahaina town), Lahaina, HI 96761. ☎ **800/789-6865** or 808/667-2121. Fax 808/667-2120. www.maui.net/~private/home. E-mail private@maui.net. 6 units (private baths have shower only). A/C TV. **$85–$125** double. Rates include full breakfast. Extra person $15. AE, DISC, MC, V. From Hwy. 30, take the Fleming Rd. exit; turn left on Ainakea; after 2 blocks, turn right on Malanai St.; go 3 blocks, and turn left onto Lokia St.

Talk about escape: A young German couple ran away to Maui for their honeymoon, fell in love with the island, bought a big house above Lahaina, and turned it into one of Lahaina's best B&Bs. Their 7,000-square-foot contemporary home, in a quiet residential subdivision at the north end of town, is popular with visitors from around the world. This place is immaculate (hostess Daniela Clement provides daily maid service). The oversized rooms are fresh and quiet, with white ceramic-tile floors, bright tropical fabrics, and wicker furnishings; the four downstairs rooms all open onto flower-filled private patios. Guests share a pool, a Jacuzzi, a fully equipped guest kitchen, and a barbecue area; you're welcome to curl up on the living-room sofa facing the fireplace (not really needed in Lahaina) with a book from the library. Breakfast is served in the sunny dining room. Self-service laundry facilities are available for $2. The nearest beach is about 10 minutes away.

Lahaina Inn. 127 Lahainaluna Rd. (near Front St.), Lahaina, HI 96761. ☎ **800/669-3444** or 808/661-0577. Fax 808/667-9480. 12 units (most baths have showers only). A/C TEL. **$89–$149** double. Rates include continental breakfast. Children under 14 not accepted. AE, DISC, JCB, MC, V. Next-door parking $5.

If the romance of historic Lahaina catches your fancy, a stay here will really underscore the experience. Built in 1938 as a general store, swept by fire in the mid-1960s, and reopened as a hotel in the '70s, this place deteriorated into a fleabag with an eyesore bar at street level. Then, in 1986, rescue came in a classy way: It was saved from extinction by Rick Ralston, the Waikiki airbrush artist who became the Crazy Shirts mogul—and a one-man historic restoration society. About a million dollars of T-shirt money has brought this place back to life as a charming, antique-filled inn right in the heart of Lahaina.

If you like old hotels that have genuinely historic touches, you'll love this place. As it is with old hotels, some of these Victorian antique-stuffed rooms are small; if that's a problem for you, ask for a larger one. All come with private bathes and lanais. The best room in the house is no. 7 ($99), which overlooks the beach, the town, and the island of Lanai; you can watch the action below or close the door and ignore it. Downstairs is one of Hawaii's finest bistros, David Paul's Lahaina Grill (see "Dining," below).

Lahaina Roads. 1403 Front St. (1 block north of Lahaina Canney Shopping Center). Reservations c/o Kiahani Travel, 505 Front St., Lahaina, HI 96761. ☎ **800/MAUI** or 808/667-2712. Fax 808/661-5875. E-mail robyn@maui.net. 17 units. TV TEL. **$100** one-bedroom (sleeps up to 4), **$180** two-bedroom (up to 6). 3-night minimum. AE, MC, V.

If you dream of an oceanfront condo, but your budget is on the slim side, here's your place. This 17-unit condominium offers small, reasonably priced units in an older building located in the quiet part of Lahaina, away from the noisy, crowded

Lahaina & Kaanapali

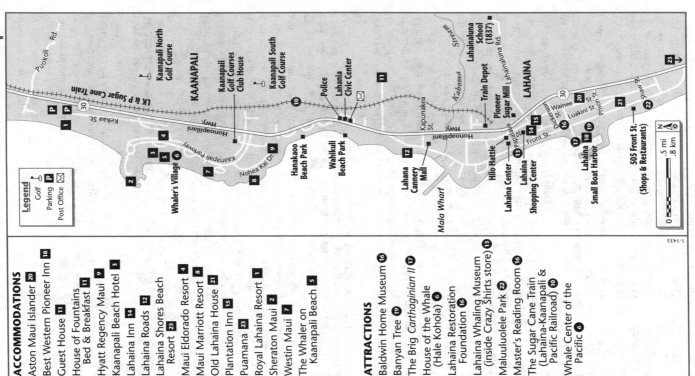

Legend
- Golf
- P Parking
- ⊠ Post Office

KAANAPALI

Kaanapali North Golf Course
Kaanapali Golf Courses Club House
Kaanapali South Golf Course

LK & P Sugar Cane Train

Puukoli Rd.
Kekaa St.
Honoapiilani Hwy.
Kaanapali Parkway
Nohea Kai Dr.
Whaler's Village
Hanakaoo Beach Park
Wahikuli Beach Park

Police
Lahaina Civic Center

Kapunakea St.
Kahoma Stream
Lahainaluna School (1837)
Train Depot
Pioneer Sugar Mill
Lahainaluna Rd.
Honoapiilani Hwy.

LAHAINA

Lahaina Cannery Mall
Mala Wharf
Hilo Hattie
Papalaua St.
Front St.
Lahaina Center
Lahaina Shopping Center
Wainee St.
Dickenson St.
Luakini St.
Prison St.
Shaw St.
Lahaina Small Boat Harbor
505 Front St. (Shops & Restaurants)

N
.5 mi
.8 km
0

1-1433

ACCOMMODATIONS

- Aston Maui Islander **20**
- Best Western Pioneer Inn **18**
- Guest House **11**
- House of Fountains Bed & Breakfast **11**
- Hyatt Regency Maui **9**
- Kaanapali Beach Hotel **3**
- Lahaina Inn **14**
- Lahaina Roads **12**
- Lahaina Shores Beach Resort **23**
- Maui Eldorado Resort **4**
- Maui Marriott Resort **8**
- Old Lahaina House **21**
- Plantation Inn **15**
- Puamana **23**
- Royal Lahaina Resort **1**
- Sheraton Maui **2**
- Westin Maui **7**
- The Whaler on Kaanapali Beach **5**

ATTRACTIONS

- Baldwin Home Museum **16**
- Banyan Tree **19**
- The Brig *Carthaginian II* **17**
- House of the Whale (Hale Kohola) **6**
- Lahaina Restoration Foundation **16**
- Lahaina Whaling Museum (inside Crazy Shirts store) **13**
- Maluuluolele Park **22**
- Master's Reading Room **16**
- The Sugar Cane Train (Lahaina-Kaanapali & Pacific Railroad) **10**
- Whale Center of the Pacific **6**

downtown area, overlooking the boats in the Mala Wharf roadstead (a protected place to anchor near the shore). The units are compact and come with full kitchens, with the bedrooms facing the road and the living rooms and lanais overlooking the ocean and the island of Lanai in the distance. A real plus are the soundproof walls. The building's three decades old, but the units have been well maintained, and the oceanside swimming pool was just completely renovated. The only drawback is that there are no laundry facilities—but for these prices, you won't mind schlepping your dirty clothes to a Laundromat in Lahaina.

Lahaina Shores Beach Resort. 475 Front St. (near Shaw St.), Lahaina, HI 96761. ☎ **800/628-6699** or 808/661-4835. Fax 808/661-4696. 151 units. A/C one-bedroom (sleeps up to 4); low season $120–$145 studio, $155–$215 one-bedroom. AE, MC, V.

Lahaina Shores is affordable and convenient. What's special about this place is its location: right on the beach, just outside the rowdy, trafficky central core of Lahaina. It's a catbird seat for watching whales and ships coming and going, day and night, from Lahaina's busy harbor. Although the beach here isn't the greatest on the coast, it's just a short walk down the street to a good swimming beach. The roomy, individually owned condo units come with full kitchens, VCRs, and ample space, plus daily maid service and a concierge; laundry facilities are available. In general, the bathrooms are small, but they do the job. There's a pool and spa off the newly renovated lobby. Shops and restaurants are right next door at the 505 Front Street complex.

⭐ **Plantation Inn.** 174 Lahainaluna Rd. (between Wainee and Luakini sts., 1 block from Hwy. 30), Lahaina, HI 96761. ☎ **800/433-6815** or 808/667-9225. Fax 808/667-9293. www.maui.net/~inn. E-mail inn@maui.net. 18 units (some with showers only). A/C TV TEL. $135–$215 double. Rates include full breakfast. AE, CB, DC, DISC, JCB, MC, V.

Attention, romance-seeking couples—look no further. This charming inn looks like it's been here 100 years or more, but looks can be deceiving: The Victorian-style hotel is actually of 1990s vintage—an artful deception. The rooms are romantic to the max, tastefully done with period furniture, hardwood floors, stained glass, and ceiling fans; there are four-poster canopy beds and armoires in some rooms, brass beds and wicker in others. All rooms are equipped with soundproofing (a plus in Lahaina), TV, VCRs, fridges, private baths, and lanais; the suites have kitchenettes. The rooms wrap around the large swimming pool and deck. Also on property is a spa, as well as an elegantly decorated pavilion lounge. Also on site is Gerard's, an excellent French restaurant (see "Dining," below); it can be pricey, but hotel guests get a discount on dinner (you'll kick yourself if you don't eat here). Breakfast is served around the pool and in the elegant pavilion lounge; ours featured fresh fruit, followed by a choice of Gerard's French toast or his homemade yogurt and granola.

Puamana. Front St. (at the extreme southern end of Lahaina, a ½-mile from downtown), P.O. Box 11108, Lahaina, HI 96760. ☎ **800/669-6284** or 808/667-2712. Fax 808/661-5875. E-mail robyn@maui.com. 40 units. TV TEL. $100–$175 one-bedroom double, $140–$250 two-bedroom, $300–$350 three-bedroom. 3-night minimum. AE, MC, V.

These 28 acres of townhouses right on the water are the place for people who want to be able to retreat from the crowds and cacophony of downtown Lahaina into the serene quiet of an elegant neighborhood. Private and peaceful are apt descriptions of the complex: Each unit is an individual home, with no one above or below. They're all privately owned (most are exquisitely decorated) with full kitchens, TV, at least two bathrooms, lanais, and barbecues. There are three pools (one for adults only), a tennis court, table-tennis tables, and on-site laundry facilities (some units have washers and dryers as well). Puamana was once a private estate in the 1920s, part of the sugar plantations that dominated Lahaina; the plantation manager's house has been converted into a clubhouse with an oceanfront lanai, library, card room, sauna, and office.

Inexpensive

Also consider value-priced **Old Lahaina House** (☎ 800/847-0761 or 808/667-4663; fax 808/667-5615; www.mauiweb.com/maui/olhouse), which features comfy twin- and king-bedded doubles for $69 to $95.

✪ **Guest House.** 1620 Ainakea Rd. (off Fleming Rd., north of Lahaina town), Lahaina, HI 96761. ☎ **800/621-8942** or 808/661-8085. Fax 808/661-1896. www.ourworld.compuserve.com/homepages/guesthouse. E-mail guesthouse@compuserve. 5 units (1 shares a bath with hosts). A/C TV TEL. $59–$89 double. Rates include full breakfast. Extra person $15. AE, DISC, MC, V. Take Fleming Rd. off Hwy. 30; turn left on Ainakea; it's 2 blocks down.

This is one of Lahaina's great bed-and-breakfast deals: a charming B&B with more amenities than the expensive Kaanapali hotels just down the road a piece. The roomy, architecturally designed home, with parquet floors and floor-to-ceiling windows, has a swimming pool—surrounded by a deck and comfortable lounge chairs—that's larger than some at high-priced condos. Every guest room is air-conditioned and has a ceiling fan, a small fridge, a color TV, and a private phone; four of the rooms each have a quiet lanai and a romantic hot tub. The large kitchen (with every gadget you can imagine) is available for guests' use. The Guest House also operates Trinity Tours and offers discounts on car rentals and just about every island activity.

KAANAPALI
Very Expensive

In addition to those listed below, another option to consider is the **Royal Lahaina Resort** (☎ 800/44-ROYAL or 808/661-3611; fax 800/432-9752 or 808/661-6150). But skip the overpriced hotel rooms; only stay here if you can get one of the 122 cottages tucked among the well-manicured grounds ($295 to $385 double). And the **Maui Marriott Resort** (☎ 800/228-9290 or 808/667-1200; fax 808/667-8181; www.travelweb.com) is wonderful if you love the Marriott style, not so wonderful if you're looking for something a little more Hawaiian. It's a big hit with conventions and incentive groups; usually one or the other is in residence. The 15 beachfront acres are loaded with amenities: three pools (including one for the kids), two whirlpools, tennis courts, a video game room, lots of shops and restaurants, and more. Rates are $280 to $328 double, from $400 suite; ask about packages.

✪ **Sheraton Maui.** 2605 Kaanapali Pkwy., Lahaina, HI 96761. ☎ **800/STAY-ITT** or 808/661-0031. Fax 808/661-9991. www.sheraton-maui.com. 510 units. A/C TV TEL. $290–$465 double, from $575 suite. Extra person $40; children 17 and under stay free using existing bedding. AE, CB, DC, DISC, MC, V. Self-parking $5, valet $8.

Terrific facilities for families and fitness buffs and a premier beach location make this beautiful resort an all-around great place to stay. The first to set up camp in Kaanapali (in 1963), the hoteliers took the best location on the beach: the curving, white-sand cove next to Black Rock (a lava formation that rises 80 feet above the beach), where they built into the side of the cliff. The grande dame of Kaanapali Beach reopened in 1997 after a $160 million, two-year renovation; the resort is virtually new, with six buildings of six stories or less set in well-established tropical gardens. The lobby has been elevated to take advantage of panoramic views, and a new lagoon-like pool features lava-rock waterways, wooden bridges, and an open-air spa.

The new emphasis is on family appeal, with a class of rooms dedicated to those traveling with kids (665-square-feet units with two double beds and a pull-down wall bed), and other kid-friendly amenities. Every room is outfitted with all the comforts—from minifridges and free Kona coffee for the coffeemakers to irons, hair dryers, and even toothbrushes and toothpaste—that make for easy travel. Other plusses include a "no hassle" check-in policy; the valet takes you and your luggage straight to your room—no standing in line at registration.

But not everything has changed, thankfully. Cliff divers still swan-dive off the torch-lit lava-rock headland in a traditional sunset ceremony—a sight to see. And the views of Kaanapali Beach, with Lanai and Molokai in the distance, are some of the best in Kaanapali.

Dining/Diversions: Three restaurants, with cuisine ranging from teppanyaki to steaks and seafood, plus a snack bar and three bars and cocktail lounges to choose from.

Amenities: Nightly cliff-diving show, free summer children's program, in-room dining 6:30am to 10:30pm (guaranteed to be delivered in 30 minutes or less), valet laundry, baby-sitting, express check-out, in-house doctor's office, two pools, three tennis courts, conference facilities, and activities desk. A fitness center, a game center, full beach services, 24-hour coin-op laundry, and hospitality suite for early arrivals or late departures extend the usual list of Kaanapali features: golf, tennis, ocean sports, shopping, and beach.

Westin Maui. 2365 Kaanapali Pkwy., Lahaina, HI 96761. ☎ **800/228-3000** or 808/667-2525. Fax 808/661-5831. 793 units. A/C TV MINIBAR TEL. $265–$495 double, from $800 suite. Wedding/honeymoon and other packages available. Extra person $30 ($50 in Royal Beach Club rooms). AE, DC, DISC, ER, JCB, MC, V. $6 "resort fee" for such amenities as free local phone calls, use of fitness center, complimentary coffee and tea, free parking, and free local paper.

The *aquatic playground*—an 87,000-square-foot pool area with five freeform heated pools joined by swim-through grottos, waterfalls, and a 128-foot-long water slide—sets this resort apart from its peers along Kaanapali Beach. Thanks to mega-hotelier Christopher Hemmeter, who waved his magic wand over the property in the late 1980s, this is the Disney World of waterpark resorts—your kids will be in water-hog heaven.

The fantasy theme extends from the estate-like grounds into the interior's public spaces, which are filled with the shrieks of tropical birds and the splash of waterfalls; the oversized architecture, requisite colonnade, and $2 million art collection make a pleasing backdrop for all the action. Guests seem to love it: The resort has taken top honors in various readers surveys, from *Condé Nast Traveler* to *Travel & Leisure* to *Frequent Flyer* magazine. With lots of indoor and outdoor meeting spaces, it's also a big hit with wedding parties and groups.

The majority of the rooms (refurbished in '95) in the two 11-story towers overlook the aquatic playground, the ocean, and the island of Lanai in the distance; in addition to the standard features, each comes with a safe, an iron and board, a coffeemaker, and its own lanai. The top-floor Royal Beach Club rooms feature a hospitality lounge and special amenities.

Dining/Diversions: Several outdoor restaurants and lounges, ranging from a sushi bar to a seafood buffet, take advantage of the casual mood and balmy weather. The Sound of the Falls features an elegant Sunday brunch amid flamingoes and waterfalls.

Amenities: Twice-daily maid service, nightly turndown, multilingual staff, American Express and Hertz desks, and secretarial services. Guest Services will help you plan sightseeing and activities. Extensive health-club and spa facilities. Extensive supervised kids' program weekdays. Five pools, Jacuzzi, aquacise classes, scuba lessons for beginners and refresher courses, and outdoor guided adventure hikes. Coin-op laundry, ATM, and hospitality suite for early check-ins and late departures. Salon, retail shops, business center, and conference facilities. Golf, tennis, and shopping are all at hand. A wedding coordinator, known as the Director of Romance, can help you throw an unforgettable wedding.

Expensive

Hyatt Regency Maui. 200 Nohea Kai Dr., Lahaina, HI 96761. ☎ **800/233-1234** or 808/661-1234. Fax 808/667-4714. 815 units. A/C TV MINIBAR TEL. $260–$495 double, from $600 suite. Extra person $25 ($45 in Regency Club rooms); children 18 and under stay free with existing bedding. Packages available. AE, DC, DISC, JCB, MC, V. Free self-parking, $8 valet parking.

People either absolutely love this fantasy resort, or they hate it. One of several built by Christopher Hemmeter for Hyatt in the 1980s, this hotel—the southernmost of the Kaanapali properties—has lots of imagination: a collection of exotic species (flaming pink flamingoes, unhappy looking penguins, and an assortment of loud parrots and macaws in the lobby), nine waterfalls, and an eclectic Asian and Pacific art collection. This huge place covers some 40 acres; even if you don't stay here, you might want to walk through the expansive tree-filled atrium and the park-like grounds, with their dense riot of plants and fantasy pools with grottos, slides, and a suspended walking bridge. There's even a manmade beach in case the adjacent public beach is just too crowded.

In a welcome change from the typical beiges, the rooms—spread through three towers—are pleasantly decorated in rich colors, floral prints, and Asian lamps and have separate sitting areas and private lanais. In-room extras include safes, hair dryers, coffeemakers, and irons and boards.

Dining/Diversions: Swan Court is a romantic setting for dinner; its rollaway walls open wide to let in the moonlight, and tables sit beside a waterfall pool where black and white swans cruise for a handout (for a full review, see "Dining," below). Steaks and seafood are served in the open-air Lahaina Provisions Company, while Spats (see "Dining," below) serves Italian fare; The Pavilion is a casual poolside choice. The Drums of the Pacific dinner show keeps things rolling at night. In addition to numerous lounges, the cool pool has a swimup bar for cocktails.

Amenities: Twice-daily maid service, concierge, room service, activity desk, and baby-sitting on request. Two Regency Club floors have a private concierge, complimentary breakfast, sunset cocktails, and snacks. The Camp Hyatt kids' program offers daytime and evening supervised activities for 3- to 12-year-olds. Special programs include a rooftop astronomy program. In addition to the Great Pool, there's a health club with a weight and exercise room, Jacuzzi, sauna, and massage studio; six hard-surface tennis courts; three nearby golf courses; a game room; and a small lending library. Snorkel gear, bicycles, kayaks, boogie boards, and video and underwater cameras are available for rent. *Kiele V,* the Hyatt's 55-foot catamaran, sponsors snorkel trips, whale-watching excursions, and evening cruises.

✪ **Maui Eldorado Resort.** 2661 Kekaa Dr., Lahaina, HI 96761. ☎ **800/688-7444** or 808/661-0021. Fax 808/667-7039. www.outrigger.com. E-mail reservations@ outrigger.com. 98 units. AC TV TEL. High season, $175–$200 studio double, $220–$250 one-bedroom (sleeps up to 4), $285–$325 two-bedroom (up to 6); low season, $150–$175 studio, $185–$210 one-bedroom, $260–$290 two-bedroom. Numerous packages available, including 7th night free, car packages, senior rates, and more. AE, CB, DC, DISC, JCB, MC, V.

These spacious condominium units—all with full kitchens, washer/dryers, and daily maid service—were built at a time when land in Kaanapali was cheap, contractors took pride in their work, and visitors expected large, spacious units with views from every window. You'll find it hard to believe that this was one of Kaanapali's first properties in the late 1960s—this first-class property looks like new. The Outrigger chain has managed to keep prices down to reasonable levels, especially if you come in the spring or fall. This is a great choice for families, with big units, grassy areas that are perfect for running off energy, and beachfront that's usually safe for swimming.

Amenities: Daily maid service. Three swimming pools, beach cabanas, and barbecue areas. Shops, travel desk, fax equipment, laundry facilities, and personal safe.

★ **The Whaler on Kaanapali Beach.** 2481 Kaanapali Pkwy. (next to Whalers Village), Lahaina, HI 96761. ☎ **800/367-7052** or 808/661-4861. Fax 510/939-6644. www. ten-io.com/vri. 360 units; 150 in rental pool. A/C TV TEL. High season, **$195–$205** studio double, $250–$380 one-bedroom (sleeps up to 4), **$415–$495** two-bedroom (up to 6); low season, $195–$205 studio, $230–$350 one-bedroom, $360–$470 two-bedroom. Extra person $15; crib $10. 2-night minimum. Packages available. AE, MC, V.

Location, location, location—in the heart of Kaanapali, right on the world-famous beach, lies this oasis of elegance, privacy, and luxury. The relaxing atmosphere starts at the entry, which is through an open-air lobby where light reflects off the dazzling koi in the meditative lily pond. No expense has been spared, and the units are gorgeous; each has a complete kitchen, washer/dryer, marble bath, 10-foot beamed ceilings, and a blue-tiled lanai—plus daily maid service, an in-room safe, a pool and spa, an exercise room, tennis courts, and a rarity in Kaanapali these days, free parking. The views from every unit are spectacular and include vistas of both Kaanapali's gentle waves and the humpback peaks of the West Maui Mountains.

Dining/Diversions: Next door is Whalers Village, where you'll fine Peter Merriman's terrific Hula Grill (see "Dining," below) and a handful of other restaurant and bar choices.

Amenities: Daily maid service, a pool and spa, an exercise room, and five tennis courts. The Kaanapali Golf Club's 36 holes are across the street, and all the ocean activities Maui has to offer are just out back.

Moderate

Kaanapali Beach Hotel. 2525 Kaanapali Pkwy., Lahaina, HI 96761. ☎ **800/262-8450** or 808/661-0011. Fax 808/667-5978. www.kaanapalibeachhotel.com. 433 units. A/C TV TEL. $150–$235 double; from $210 suite. Extra person $25. Free car, golf, bed-and-breakfast and romance packages available, as well as discount rates for seniors. AE, CB, DC, DISC, JCB, MC, V.

This old beach hotel, set in a garden by the sea, is Maui's most genuinely Hawaiian place to stay. You live aloha here.

This isn't a luxury property, but it's not bad, either. The three low-rise wings are set around a wide, grassy lawn with coco palms and a whale-shaped swimming pool and border a fabulous stretch of beach. The spacious, spotless motel-like rooms are done in wicker and rattan, with Hawaiian-style bedspreads and a lanai that looks toward the courtyard and the beach. The beachfront rooms are separated from the water only by Kaanapali's landscaped walking trail.

It's older and less high-tech than its upscale neighbors, but the Kaanapali has an irresistible local style and real Hawaiian warmth that's absent from many other Maui hotels. Old Hawaii values and customs are always close at hand, and in true aloha style, the service is some of the friendliest around. Tiki torches, hula, and Hawaiian music create a festive atmosphere in the expansive open courtyard every night. As part of the hotel's extensive Hawaiiana program, you can learn to cut pineapple, weave lauhala, even dance the *red* hula; there's also an arts-and-crafts fair three days a week, a morning welcome reception weekdays, and a Hawaiian library.

The hotel's three restaurants feature native Hawaiian dishes as well as modern Hawaiian cuisine; there's also a poolside bar that fixes a mean piña colada. Amenities include a concierge; a coin-op laundry; in-room movies; and ice, drink, and snack machines. You also get baby-sitting services, a United Airlines desk, free scuba and snorkeling lessons, convenience shops and a salon, conference rooms, beach equipment rentals, and access to tennis and Kaanapali golf.

FROM HONOKOWAI TO NAPILI

Very Expensive

Embassy Suites. 104 Kaanapali Shores Pl. (in Honokowai), Lahaina, HI 96761. ☎ **800/669-3155** or 808/661-2000. Fax 808/661-1353. www.maui.net/~embassy. E-mail embassy@maui.net. 413 units. A/C TV TEL. $260–$400 one-bedroom suite (sleeps up to 4), $550 two-bedroom suite (up to 4). Rates include full breakfast and 2-hour cocktail party daily. Extra person $20; children 18 and younger stay free using existing bedding. AE, CB, DC, DISC, MC, V. Parking $5. Take the 1st turn off Hwy. 30 after Kaanapali onto Lower Honoapiilani Rd.; turn left at Kaanapali Shores Place.

This is kid heaven: The all-suite property features a mammoth 1-acre pool with a 24-foot water slide, a great beach for swimming and snorkeling, and complete entertainment centers in every unit that will satisfy the surliest teenager: 35-inch TV (with HBO), VCR (there's a vast video library on site), and stereo system (with dual-cassette player). With roomy condo-like suites (ranging from 820 to 1,100 square feet) that feature hotel-style amenities, all-you-can-eat breakfasts, and free daily cocktail parties included in the price, Mom and Dad will be happy, too.

You can't miss this place; the shockingly pink pyramid-shaped building is visible from the highway. It's composed of three towers, each set around a central atrium and among tropical gardens with interlocking waterfalls and waterways; a huge wooden deck overlooks the koi-filled ponds and streams. Every unit has a full-sized sofa bed, a good-sized lanai, a mini-kitchen (microwave, small fridge with icemaker, wet bar, and coffeemaker with free Kona coffee), two phones, a soaking tub big enough for two in the bathroom, and a second TV in the bedroom.

Dining/Diversions: There are three on-site dining choices: the oceanfront North Beach Grille, the poolside Ohana Bar and Grill, and a sandwich/snack bar, the Deli Planet.

Amenities: 18-hole mini-golf; Kaanapali's shops, golf, tennis, and restaurants are just minutes away. Concierge, laundry facilities and dry cleaning, pool, health club, Jacuzzi, sauna, sundeck, tour desk, and children's program available during holidays and in the summer months.

Expensive

Also consider **Sands of Kahana** (☎ **888/669-0400** or 808/669-1199; www.sands-of-kahana.com), an eight-story condo/timeshare complex that's great for families. The one- to three-bedroom units have small kitchens with dishwasher and microwave, plus a washer/dryer. The property is loaded with kid-friendly extras, including a large children's pool, a playground, and a stretch the beach that's safe for swimming. Rates are $165 to $335 in high season, $145–$305 in low season; there's a 5-night minimum.

★ **Napili Kai Beach Club.** 5900 Honoapiilani Rd. (at the extreme north end of Napili, next to Kapalua), Lahaina, HI 96761. ☎ **800/367-5030** or 808/669-6271. Fax 808/669-0085. E-mail nkbc@maui.net. www.napilikai.com. 162 units. TV TEL. $170–$265 double studio, $270–$550 one-bedroom suite (sleeps up to 4), $270–$550 two-bedroom (up to 6). Packages available. Extra person $10. AE, MC, V.

Just south of The Bay Club restaurant in Kapalua, nestled in a small, white-sand cove, lies this comfortable oceanfront complex of one- and two-story units with double-hipped Hawaii-style roofs that face their very own gold-sand safe-swimming beach. Many units have a view of the Pacific, with Molokai and Lanai in the distance. The older beachfront Lahaina Building units—with ceiling fans only—are a good buy at $215. People who prefer air conditioning should book into the Honolua Building where, for the same price, you'll get a fully air-conditioned room set back from the shore around a grassy, park-like lawn and pool. All units (except eight hotel rooms) have fully stocked kitchenettes with full-sized refrigerator (with ice maker), cooktop, microwave, toaster oven, washer/dryer, and coffeemaker; some have dishwashers.

Dining/Diversions: The Sea House Restaurant serves breakfast, lunch, and dinner, while the Whale Watcher's Bar takes care of cocktails.

Amenities: Daily maid service; dry cleaning; free children's activities at Easter, June 15 to August 31, and at Christmas; complimentary beach chairs, mats, swim masks and snorkels; complimentary tennis rackets and golf putters; activities desk; nearby tennis course; golf just minutes away; two shuffleboard courts; barbecue areas; four pools; and two 18-hole putting greens. Complimentary coffee at the beach pagoda every morning, free tea in the lobby every afternoon, and a free mai tai party weekly.

Moderate

Hale Kai. 3691 Lower Honoapiilani Rd. (in Honokowai), Lahaina, HI 96761. ☎ **800/446-7307** or 808/669-6333. Fax 808/669-7474. www.halekai.com. E-mail halekai@halekai.com. 40 units. TV TEL. High season, $110 one-bedroom double, $140–$145 two-bedroom (sleeps up to 4), $180 three-bedroom (up to 6); low season, $95 one-bedroom double, $125–$130 two-bedroom, $180 three-bedroom. Extra person $10; children 3 and younger stay free. 3-night minimum. MC, V.

This small, two-story, two-building condo complex is ideally located, right on the beach and next door to a county park; shops, restaurants, and ocean activities are all within a 6-mile radius. The units are older but in excellent shape and come with a well-equipped kitchen (with dishwasher, disposal, microwave, even a blender), TV and VCR, and louvered windows that open to the trade winds. Lots of guests clamor for the oceanfront pool units, but we find the park-view units to be cooler, and they still have ocean views (upstairs units also have cathedral ceilings). Book early, as this place fills up fast; repeat guests make up most of the clientele.

⭐ **Kahana Sunset.** 4909 Lower Honoapiilani Rd., at the northern end of Kahana, almost in Napili. c/o P.O. Box 10219 Lahaina, HI 96761. ☎ **800/669-1488** or 808/669-8011. Fax 808/669-9170. E-mail sun2set@maui.net. 49 units; 29 in rental pool. A/C TV TEL. High season, $160–$180 one-bedroom (sleeps up to 6), $165–$265 two-bedroom (up to 6); low season, $120–160 one-bedroom, $140–$200 two-bedroom, 3-night minimum. AE, MC, V. From Hwy. 30, turn makai (toward the ocean) at the Napili Plaza (Napilihau St.), then left on Lower Honoapiilani Rd.

Lying in the crook of a sharp horseshoe curve on Lower Honoapiilani Road is this series of wooden condo units, stair-stepping down the side of a hill to a postcard-perfect white-sand beach. The unique location, nestled between the coastline and road above, makes this a very private place to stay. In the midst of the buildings lies a grassy lawn with a small pool and Jacuzzi; down by the sandy beach are gazebos and picnic areas. The units feature full kitchens with dishwashers, washer/dryers, large lanais with terrific views, and sleeper sofas. This is a great complex for families: The beach here is safe for swimming, the grassy area is away from traffic, and the units are roomy enough to accommodate. The two-bedrooms have parking just outside, making carrying luggage and groceries much easier.

Maui Sands. Maui Resort Management, 3600 Lower Honoapiilani Rd. (in Honokowai), Lahaina, HI 96761. ☎ **800/367-5037** or 808/669-1902. Fax 808/669-8790. www.mauigetaway.com.

E-mail getaway@maui.net. 76 units. A/C TEL. $85–$130 one-bedroom (sleeps up to 3); $115–$160 two-bedroom (up to 5). Extra person $9. 7-night minimum. MC, V.

The Maui Sands was built back in a time when property wasn't as expensive and developers took the time and money to make sure that their condos were surrounded by lush landscaping. It's hard to get a unit with a bad view: They either face the ocean (with views of Lanai and Molokai) or tropical gardens blooming with brilliant heliconia, flowering hibiscus, and sweet-smelling ginger. All units have big lanais, fully equipped kitchens, and lots of space (including plenty of dancing room in the living room). With two big bedrooms plus space for a fifth person (or even a sixth) in the living room, the larger ones are good deals for families. There's a narrow beach out front and a swimming pool and laundry facilities on site. The management agency is just across the street, in case you have any problems or questions.

Mauian on Napili Bay. 5441 Lower Honoapiilani Rd. (in Napili), Lahaina, HI 96761. ☎ 800/367-5034 or 808/669-6205. Fax 808/669-0129. E-mail Mauian@maui.net. 44 units. High season, $145–$175 double; low season, $125–$155 double. Extra 3rd or 4th person $10 each. AE, DISC, MC, V.

The Hawaiian family who built this low-rise hotel in 1961 now own it again, and they've restored the studio units to their original old Hawaiian style. This is a great place to get away from it all: The Mauian is perched above a beautiful half-mile-long white-sand beach with great swimming and snorkeling in the turquoise waters just offshore; there's a pool with chaise lounges, umbrellas, and tables on the sundeck; and the verdant grounds are bursting with tropical color. The renovated rooms feature hardwood floors, Indonesian-style furniture, and big lanais with great views. It's the small touches that have brought return guests back for more than three decades, such as the fresh flowers in rooms upon arrival (plus chilled champagne for guests celebrating a special occasion) and the "Breakfast with the Manager" every Thursday (with freshbaked Hawaiian breads). There are no phones and no TVs in the rooms (this place really is about getting away from it all), but the large Ohana (family) room does have a TV with VCR and an extensive library for those who can't bear the solitude, plus complimentary coffee; phones and fax service are available in the business center. Great restaurants are just a 5-minute walk away, Kapalua Resort is just up the street, and the nightly sunsets off the beach are spectacular.

✪ **Noelani Condominium Resort.** 4095 Lower Honoapiilani Rd. (in Kahana), Lahaina, HI 96761. ☎ **800/367-6030** or 808/669-8374. Fax 808/669-7904. www.noelanicondo-resort.com. E-mail noelani@maui.net. 50 units. TV TEL. $97–$107 studio double, $120 one-bedroom (sleeps up to 3), $167 two-bedroom (up to 4), $197 three-bedroom (up to 6). Rates include continental breakfast 1st morning. Extra person $10; children under 12 stay free. Packages for honeymooners, seniors, and AAA members available. 3-night minimum. AE, MC, V.

This oceanfront condo is a great value all the way around, from the studios to the three-bedrooms (great for large families). This top-notch property is AAA approved and, after extensive exterior and interior renovations, has just been awarded a three-diamond designation. Everything is first class, from the furnishings and the level of building maintenance to the location, on the ocean with a sandy cove next door at the new county park. There's good snorkeling off the cove, which is frequented by spinner dolphins and turtles in summer and humpback whales in winter. The units feature complete kitchens, stereo entertainment centers, and spectacular views. Our favorites are in the Antherium Building, where the one-, two-, and three-bedrooms have oceanfront lanais just 20 feet from the water. There are two freshwater swimming pools (one heated for night swimming) and an oceanfront Jacuzzi. Guests are invited to a continental breakfast orientation on their first day and mai tai parties at night.

Inexpensive

In addition to the choices below, there's also **Hale Maui Apartment Hotel** (☎ 808/669-6312; fax 808/669-1302), a wonderful tiny apartment hotel run by Hans and Eva Zimmerman, whose spirit is 100% aloha. All their one-bedroom suites, which run $65 to $95 double, come with ceiling fans, private lanais, and complete kitchens. There's no pool, but a private path leads to the great swimming beach.

Kalelaloha. 3785 Lower Honoapiilani Rd. (in Honokowai), Lahaina, HI 96761. ☎ 800/222-8688 or 808/669-8197. Fax 808/669-2502. E-mail dwhipple@maui.net. 26 units, TV TEL. $75 studio double; $90–$100 one-bedroom double. Extra person $7.50. 3-night minimum. MC, V.

This condo for the budget-minded has recently been upgraded with new paint, bedspreads, and drapes in each unit. Frugal travelers should book the studios, which face the vast sugarcane fields of West Maui and the mountains. If there are only two of you, save the dough it would cost to upgrade to an ocean-view apartment and plunk down in one of the chairs on the grassy lawn fronting the ocean—the money you'll save will buy you a great dinner in Lahaina. For larger groups, the advantage of the one-bedroom units—besides the ocean view—is the sofa bed in the living room, which allows the apartments to comfortably sleep four (and makes them ultra-affordable). All the island-style units feature fully equipped kitchens, with everything from dishwashers to washers and dryers. The complex has a pool, but there's great ocean swimming just off the rock wall; a protective reef mows waves down and allows even timid swimmers to relax.

✪ **The Napili Bay.** 33 Hui Dr. (off Lower Honoapiilani Hwy., in Napili). c/o Maui Beachfront Rentals, 256 Papalaua St., Lahaina, HI 96767. ☎ 888/661-7200 or 808/661-3500. Fax 808/661-5210. www.involved.com/baldys/napili.htm. E-mail maui-pru@maui.net. 33 units. TV TEL. $58–$75 double. 5-night minimum. MC, V.

One of Maui's best secret bargains is this small, two-story complex right on Napili's beautiful half-mile white-sand beach. Couples looking for a romantic getaway, look no further. The atmosphere here is comfortable and relaxing; the ocean lulls you to sleep at night, and birdsong wakes you in the morning. The beach is one of the best on the coast, with great swimming and snorkeling—in fact, it's so beautiful that people staying at much more expensive resorts down the road frequently haul all their beach paraphernalia here for the day. The compact studio apartments have everything you need to feel at home, from complete kitchens (including microwave, oven, range, coffeemaker, disposal, toaster, blender, and more) to big TVs, comfortable queen beds, and roomy lanais that are great for watching the sun set over the Pacific. Louvered windows and ceiling fans keep the units cool during the day. Our favorite is no. 201, a corner unit with fabulous views and a king bed.

Within walking distance of restaurants and a convenience store, the complex is just a mile from a shopping center, 10 minutes from world-class golf and tennis, and 15 minutes from Lahaina town. A resident on-site manager is an encyclopedia of information on where to go and what to do while you're on Maui. All this for as little as $58 a night—unbelievable! Book early, and tell 'em *Frommer's* sent you.

Napili Sunset. 46 Hui Rd. (in Napili), Lahaina, HI 96761. ☎ 800/447-9229 or 808/669-8083. Fax 808/669-2730. E-mail info@napilisunset.com. www.napilisunset.com. 42 units, TV TEL. High season, $95 studio double, $185 one-bedroom double, $265 two-bedroom; low season, $75 studio, $159 one-bedroom, $219 two-bedroom. Extra person $12; children under 3 stay free. 3-night minimum. MC, V.

Housed in three buildings (two on the ocean and one across the street) and located just down the street from Napili Bay (see above), these clean, older, but well-maintained units offer a good value. At first glance, the plain two-story structures don't look like much, but the location, the bargain prices, and the friendly spirit of the staff are the real hidden treasures here. In addition to daily maid service, the units all have free in-room safes, full kitchens (with dishwashers), ceiling fans, sofabeds in the living room, small dining rooms, and small bedrooms. Laundry facilities are on-site (you provide the quarters, they provide the free laundry soap). The beach—one of Maui's best—can get a little crowded, as the public beach access is through this property (and everyone on Maui seems to want to come here). The studio units are all located in the building off the beach and a few steps up a slight hill; they're good-sized, with complete kitchens and either a sofabed or a queen Murphy bed, and they overlook the small swimming pool and garden. The one- and two-bedrooms are all on the beach (the downstairs units have lanais that step right out onto the sand). The staff makes sure each unit has the basics—paper towels, dishwasher soap, coffee filters, condiments—to get your stay off to a good start.

KAPALUA
Very Expensive

If you're interested in a luxurious condo or townhouse, also consider **Kapalua Villas** (☎ **800/545-0018** or 808/669-8088; www.kapaluavillas.com). These palatial units dotting the oceanfront cliffs and fairways of this idyllic coast are a relative bargain, especially if you're traveling with a group. The one- and two-bedroom condos go for $165 to $375; three-bedroom homes are $700 to $995; a five-bedroom home is $3,000.

Kapalua Bay Hotel & Villas. 1 Bay Dr., Kapalua, HI 96761. ☎ **800/367-8000** or 808/669-5656. Fax 808/669-4694. www.kapaluabayhotel.com. 209 units. A/C TV MINIBAR TEL. $275–$525 double, $400–$550 villa suite, from $800 one- and two-bedroom suites. Extra person $50; children 17 and younger stay free with existing bedding. AE, CB, DC, JCB, MC, V.

When we visited in the fall of 1997, this hotel had just reopened after a year of complete restoration and was still in the "shakedown" phase of operations. We expect to see great things here, as the management consultant is no less than the Halekulani Corporation, of Waikiki's Halekulani, one of Hawaii's finest luxury hotels.

Few Hawaiian resorts have the luxury of open space like this one. It sits seaward of 23,000 acres of green fields lined by spiky Norfolk pine windbreaks. The 1970s-style rectilinear building sits down by the often windy shore, full of angles that frame stunning views of the ocean, mountains, and blue sky. The tastefully designed maze of oversized rooms fronts a palm-fringed gold-sand beach that's one of the best in Hawaii, as well as an excellent Ben Crenshaw golf course. Each guest room has a sitting area with sofa, a king or two double beds, and an entertainment center; plantation-style shutter doors open onto private lanais with views of Molokai across the channel. The renovated bathrooms feature two granite vanities, a large soaking tub, and a glass-enclosed shower.

The one- and two-bedroom villas are on the ocean at the very private Oneloa Bay. Each one has several lanais, full kitchens, washer/dryers, ceiling fans, oversized tubs, and access to three swimming pools with cabanas and barbecue facilities.

Dining/Diversions: The most appealing dining spot is The Bay Club, in its own plantation-style building overlooking the sea, specializing in seafood for lunch and dinner (see "Dining," below). The casual Gardenia Court serves all day.

Amenities: 24-hour room service, twice-daily maid service, ice service every afternoon and on request, resort shuttle, complimentary transfer to Kapalua–West Maui Airport, secretarial services, and baby-sitting services. Two pools, an exercise facility, a famous trio of golf courses (each with its own pro shop), and 10 Plexi-pave tennis courts for day and night play; villa guests have access to two additional tennis courts. Kamp Kapalua is for kids 5 to 12; they'll enjoy activities ranging from snorkeling and surfing to lei-making and cookie-baking. Adults can plan similar activities through the hotel's Beach Activity Center. The Kapalua Shops are within easy walking distance.

⭐ **Ritz-Carlton Kapalua.** 1 Ritz-Carlton Dr., Kapalua, HI 96761. ☎ **800/262-8440** or 808/669-6200. Fax 808/665-0026. www.ritzcarlton.com. 598 units. A/C TV MINIBAR TEL. $260–$595 double, suites from $495. Extra person $40 ($80 in Club Floor rooms). Wedding/honeymoon and other packages available. AE, DC, DISC, MC, V. Valet parking $10 (free self-parking).

Of all the Ritz-Carltons in the world, this is probably the best. It's in the best place (Hawaii), near the best beach (Kapalua), and it's got a friendly staff that goes above and beyond the call of duty to make sure that your vacation is a dream. The Ritz is a complete universe, one of those resorts where you can sit by the pool with a book for two whole weeks. It rises proudly on a knoll, in a singularly spectacular setting between the rain forest and the sea. During construction, hundreds of ancient Hawaiians were discovered buried in the sand, so the hotel was moved inland to avoid disrupting the graves. The setback improved the hotel's outlook, which now has a commanding view of Molokai.

The style is fancy plantation, elegant but not imposing. The public spaces are open, airy, and graceful, with plenty of tropical foliage and landscapes by artist Sarah Supplee that recall the not-so-long-ago agrarian past. Rooms are up to the usual Ritz standard, with marble baths, private lanais, in-room fax capability, and voice mail. Hospitality is the keynote here; you'll find the exemplary service you expect from Ritz-Carlton seasoned with good old-fashioned Hawaiian aloha.

Dining/Diversions: Dining is excellent at the Anuenue Room (also great for elegant Sunday brunch), the outdoor Terrace (for breakfast and dinner), and poolside (for lunch). Whether you have your gourmet fare regular or macrobiotic, it'll be memorable, thanks to Executive Chef Patrick Callarec and crew. It's a small hike to the beach, so fortunately, the Beach House serves daytime drinks and light fare. Cocktails are served in the Lobby Lounge, and it doubles as an espresso bar in the morning. A new pool bar serves drinks by the three pools.

Amenities: 24-hour room service, twice-daily towels, and nightly turndowns; private club floors with concierge, private lounge, and other extras. Airport and golf shuttle, secretarial services, daily kids' programs, lei greetings, and multilingual employees. Three top-rated golf courses, a tennis complex, three pools, a nine-hole putting green, a croquet lawn, beach volleyball, a fitness center and salon, guests-only full-day guided backcountry hikes, and a historic plantation-style wedding chapel.

SOUTH MAUI
KIHEI
Expensive

In addition to the choices below, also consider **Aston at the Maui Banyan** (☎ **800/92-ASTON** or 808/875-0004; www.aston-hotels.com), a very nice condo property across the street from Kamaole Beach Park II. The one- to three-bedroom units are all very nicely done and feature full kitchens (with microwaves), air-conditioning, and washer/dryers, and you'll find a tennis court and a Jacuzzi on site. Rates are $180 to $305 in high season, $145 to $270 in low season; be sure to ask about packages.

Maalaea Surf Resort. 12 S. Kihei Rd. (at S. Kihei Rd. and Hwy. 350), Kihei, HI 96743. ☎ **800/423-7953** or 808/879-1267. Fax 808/874-2884. 34 units in rental pool. A/C TV TEL.

High season, $186 one-bedroom double, $252 two-bedroom (sleeps up to 4); low season, $165 one-bedroom, $217 two-bedroom. Extra person $15. MC, V.

This is the place for people who want a quiet, relaxing vacation on a well-landscaped property, with a beautiful white-sand beach right outside. Located at the quiet end of Kihei Road, this two-story complex sprawls over 5 acres of lush tropical gardens. The large, luxury townhouses all have ocean views, big kitchens, air-conditioning, cable TVs, VCRs, and phones. Maid service (Monday through Saturday) is included in the price.

Amenities: Two swimming pools, two tennis courts, shuffleboard, barbecue grills. Discounts on tee times at nearby golf courses. No restaurants or shops on site, but both are within a 5-minute drive.

⭐ **Maui Hill.** 2881 S. Kihei Rd. (across from Kamaole Park III, between Keonekai St. and Kilohana Dr.), Kihei, HI 96753. ☎ **800/922-7866** or 808/879-6321. Fax 808/879-8945. 140 units. A/C TV TEL. High season $205 one-bedroom, $235 two-bedroom, $315 three-bedroom; low season $170 one-bedroom, $200 two-bedroom, $280 three-bedroom. AE, CB, DC, DISC, JCB, MC, V.

If you can't decide between the privacy of a condominium unit and the conveniences a hotel offers, this place will solve your dilemma. Managed by the respected Aston chain, Maui Hill gives you the best of both. Located on a hill above the heat of Kihei town, this large, Spanish-style resort (with white stucco buildings, red-tile roof, and arched entries) combines all the amenities and activities of a hotel—a large pool, a hot tub, tennis courts, Hawaiiana classes, and more—with large luxury condos that have full kitchens, lots of space, and plenty of privacy. Nearly all units feature ocean views, dishwashers, washer/dryers, queen sofabeds, and big lanais. Beaches are within easy walking distance. The management here goes out of their way to make sure your stay is as perfect as you planned it.

Amenities: Daily maid service. Large pool, hot tub, putting green, tennis courts, classes in lei-making and Hawaiian crafts. Restaurants and shops within walking distance.

Moderate

⭐ **Aston Maui Lu Resort.** 575 S. Kihei Rd. (between Kaonoulu and Ohukai sts.), Kihei, HI 96753. ☎ **800/92-ASTON** or 808/879-5881. Fax 808/879-4627. 120 rms. A/C TV TEL. High season $120–$185; low season $99–$165. Packages available. AE, DC, DISC, JCB, MC, V.

They just don't make them like this anymore. Located at the quieter, northern end of Kihei, the Polynesian-style Maui Lu offers a nostalgic Old Hawaii atmosphere on its 28 green acres by the sea. Ask for a beach unit if you'd like to be right on the sand; the rest of the resort is across the road and up on a rise, around a pool shaped like the island of Maui. The big, airy rooms are outfitted with rattan furniture, ceiling fans, Hawaiian art, two double beds, coffeemakers, and small fridges. Tennis and laundry facilities are available. The Ukulele Grill has an inspired local chef and a reasonably priced continental/Hawaiian gourmet menu.

Haleakala Shores. 2619 S. Kihei Rd. (across from Kamaole Park III, at Keonekai St.), Kihei, HI 96753. ☎ **800/869-1097** or 808/879-1218. Fax 808/879-2219. 144 units; 76 in rental pool. TV TEL. High season $120 two-bedroom (sleeps up to 6); 7-night minimum; low season $90 two-bedroom, 5-night minimum. Extra person $10. MC, V.

This is a great buy for frugal travelers and families on a budget. Each large unit (some 1,200 square feet) has two bedrooms, two baths, a private lanai, a full kitchen with dishwasher, and a washer/dryer. The great location, just across the street from Kamaole Park III, makes it an easy walk to restaurants and shopping. Even the parking situation is ideal: There's a free, covered garage. Okay, now for the bad news: The units were built in 1974, and most still sport '70s-style decor (avocado-green appliances, shag carpets, liberal use of the color gold). Also, they can be noisy, thanks to Kihei Road traffic (ask for a unit inside the complex) and thin walls (you can hear your neighbors' TVs and conversations quite clearly). If you manage to get a quiet unit and can overlook the nostalgic decor, these units are winners.

Kamaole Nalu Resort. 2450 S. Kihei Rd. (between Kanani and Keonekai roads, next to Kamaole Beach Park II), Kihei, HI 96753. ☎ **800/767-1497** or 808/879-1006. Fax 808/879-8693. www.mauigateway.com/~kamaole. E-mail abeach@maui.net. 36 units. TV TEL. High season **$145–$165** double; low season **$90–$110** double. Extra person **$10–$15.** 3-night minimum. MC, V.

Located between two beach parks, Kamaole I and Kamaole II, this six-story condominium boasts fabulous ocean views. The property, right across the street from a shopping complex housing the popular restaurant Radio Cairo, has an oceanside pool and barbecue facilities that are great for a sunset cookout. The units have large living rooms and private lanais; the kitchens are a bit small but come fully equipped. We recommend no. 306 for its wonderful bird's-eye ocean view. Be warned: Since it's right on Kihei Road, the units can be noisy.

Kihei Beach Resort. 36 S. Kihei Rd. (between Uwapo and Ohukai rds, south of Hwy, 31 at the Maalaea end of Kihei), Kihei, HI 96753. ☎ **800/367-6034** or 808/879-2744. Fax 808/875-0306. 36 units. A/C TV TEL. **$110–$125** one-bedroom, **$140–$160** two-bedroom. Extra person **$10**; children 4 and under stay free. 3-night minimum. DISC, MC, V.

The downside of a condominium located on Kihei Road is traffic; it's noisy all day and into the night. The upside is the location, right on the beach. This modern high-rise features spacious, comfortable units with carpeted living/dining areas (with sleeper sofas) and all-electric kitchens. The solar-heated pool is great for dips after sunset or early in the morning, when the management puts out free coffee. A coin-operated laundry is on site.

⭐ **Koa Resort.** 811 S. Kihei Rd. (between Kulanihakoi St. and Namauu Pl.), c/o Bello Realty, P.O. Box 1776, Kihei, HI 96753. ☎ **800/541-3060** or 808/879-3328. Fax 808/875-1483. www.bellowmaui.com. E-mail bello@maui.net. 54 units. TV TEL. High season **$105–$180** double; low season **$85–$160** double. No credit cards.

Located just across the street from the ocean, Koa Resort consists of five two-story wooden buildings on more than 5½ acres of landscaped grounds. The spacious, privately owned one-, two-, and three-bedroom units are decorated with care and come fully equipped. Each kitchen comes complete with fridge (with icemaker,) dishwasher, disposal, microwave, blender, and coffeemaker. The larger units have both showers and tubs, while the smaller units have showers only. All feature large lanais, ceiling fans, and washer/dryers. The property has two tennis courts, a pool, a hot tub, and an 18-hole putting green. For maximum peace and quiet, ask for a unit far from Kihei Road.

Maui Coast Hotel. 2259 S. Kihei Rd. (1 block from Kamaole Beach Park I), Kihei, HI 96753. ☎ **800/895-6284** or 808/874-6284. Fax 808/875-4731. 370 units. A/C TV TEL. **$129–$139** double, **$149–$159** suite, **$169–$179** one-bedroom double, **$240** two-bedroom (sleeps up to 4). Extra person **$10.** Rental-car packages available. AE, DC, DISC, JCB, MC, V.

Built in 1993, this off-beach mid-rise stands out as one of the only moderately priced new hotels in Hawaii. That's big news—especially on Maui, where luxury abounds. For the price of a room (or a one- or two-bedroom apartment), the Maui Coast's Extra Value package gives you a rental car for free—more great news! The chief advantages of this hotel are price and location: about a block from Kamaole Beach Park I, with plenty of bars, restaurants, and shopping within walking distance. Rooms are clean

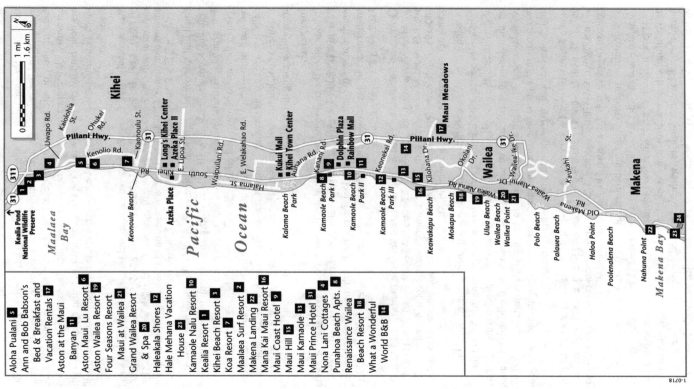

South Maui Coast Accommodations

Kihei

Pi'ilani Hwy.
Uwapo Rd.
Katolohia St.
Ohukai Rd.
Kaonoulu St.
Long's Kihei Center
Azeka Place II
E. Lipoa St.
Kenolio Rd.
Azeka Place
Kihei Rd.
South Kihei Rd.
Waipulani Rd.
E. Welakahao Rd.
Halama St.

Maalaea Bay

Kealia Pond National Wildlife Preserve

Keonoulu Beach

Pacific Ocean

Kalama Beach Park
Kukui Mall
Kihei Town Center
Auhana Rd.
Kanani Rd.
Dolphin Plaza
Rainbow Mall
Kamaole Beach Park I
Kamaole Beach Park II
Keonekai Rd.
Kamaole Beach Park III
Pi'ilani Hwy.
Kilohana Dr.
Keawakapu Beach
Okolani Dr.

Wailea
Wailea Alanui Rd.
Wailea Ike Dr.
Mokapu Beach
Ulua Beach
Wailea Beach
Wailea Point
Polo Beach
Palauea Beach
Haloa Point
Poolenalena Beach

Makena
Kaukahi St.
Old Makena Rd.
Nahuna Point
Makena Bay

Aloha Pualani **5**
Ann and Bob Babson's Bed & Breakfast and Vacation Rentals **17**
Aston at the Maui Banyan **11**
Aston Maui Lu Resort **6**
Aston Wailea Resort **19**
Four Seasons Resort Maui at Wailea **21**
Grand Wailea Resort & Spa **20**
Haleakala Shores **12**
Hale Mehana Vacation House **23**
Kamaole Nalu Resort **10**
Kealia Resort **1**
Kihei Beach Resort **3**
Koa Resort **7**
Maalaea Surf Resort **2**
Makena Landing **22**
Mana Kai Maui Resort **16**
Maui Coast Hotel **9**
Maui Hill **15**
Maui Kamaole **13**
Maui Prince Hotel **31**
Nona Lani Cottages **4**
Punahoa Beach Apts. **8**
Renaissance Wailea Beach Resort **18**
What a Wonderful World B&B **14**

1-0718

and simple; they remind us of college dorms, only with lots of extras: sitting areas, coffeemakers and free coffee, hair dryers, whirlpool tubs, mini-fridges, safes, ceiling fans, and furnished, private lanais. There's a casual restaurant, a sushi bar, and a poolside bar with nightly entertainment. Additional amenities include room service, an activities desk, laundry, two pools (one for the kids), two Jacuzzis, tennis courts, and a gift shop. This ain't the Ritz, but you'll be very comfortable here—and your wallet will thank you.

Maui Kamaole. 2777 S. Kihei Rd. (between Keonekai and Kilohana rds.), at the Wailea end of Kihei), Kihei, HI 96753. ☎ **800/367-5242** or 808/874-5151. Fax 808/879-6900. www.maui.net/~crh/. E-mail crh@maui.net. 210 units. A/C TV TEL. High season $135-$150 one-bedroom double, $170-$190 two-bedroom. Extra person $12. 4-night minimum. No credit cards.

You'll find this complex right across the street from the Kihei Public Boat Ramp and beautiful Kamaole Beach Park III, which is great for swimming, snorkeling, and beachcombing. Each roomy, fully furnished unit comes with a private lanai, two baths (even in the one-bedrooms), washer/dryer, and all-electric kitchen. The one-bedroom, two-bath units—which can comfortably accommodate four—are quite a deal, especially if you're a family traveling in the off season. The grounds are nicely landscaped and offer a pool, hot tub, and barbecues. There's no on-site restaurant, but restaurants are within walking distance.

Inexpensive

In addition to the choices below, also consider the five fully equipped suites at **Aloha Pualani** (☎ **800/PUALANI** or 808/874-9265; www.mauigateway.com/~pualani), which manages to combine the personal service of a B&B with the independent living arrangements of a condo—and the beach is just across the street. Rates are $79 to $109, with a 3-night minimum.

★ **Ann and Bob Babson's Bed & Breakfast and Vacation Rentals.** 3371 Keha Dr. (in Maui Meadows), Kihei, HI 96753. ☎ **800/824-6409** or 808/874-1166. Fax 808/879-7906. www.mauibnb.com. E-mail babson@mauibnb.com. 4 units. TV TEL. $80-$95 double room (including breakfast Mon-Sat), $95 apt. double, $115 cottage double. Extra person $15. 3-night minimum. MC, V.

In addition to the wonderful accommodations on their property, Ann and Bob Babson also operate a B&B booking service, where they go above and beyond the call of duty to find the ideal place for you. But we highly recommend staying right here on their landscaped half-acre, which boasts 180° views of the islands of Lanai, Kahoolawe, and Molokini, and sunsets not to be missed. Accommodations include two rooms in the house (one with panoramic ocean views, skylights, and a whirlpool tub), a one-bedroom apartment, and a two-bedroom cottage.

Kealia Resort. 191 N. Kihei Rd. (north of Hwy. 31, at the Maalaea end of Kihei), Kihei, HI 96753. ☎ **800/265-0686** or 808/879-0952. Fax 808/875-1540. E-mail kealia@uno.com. 51 units. TV TEL. $55-$70 studio double, $75-$110 one-bedroom double, $135-$155 two-bedroom (sleeps up to 4). Extra person $10. 4-night minimum. MC, V.

This oceanfront property at the northern end of Kihei is well-maintained and nicely furnished—and the price is excellent. As tempting as the $55 studio units may sound, don't give in: they face noisy Kihei Road and are near a major junction, so big trucks downshifting can be especially noisy at night. Instead, go for one of the ocean-view units; they all have full kitchens, washer/dryers, and private lanais. The grounds, which abut a 5-mile stretch of beach, feature a recently retiled pool with sundeck. The management goes out of its way to provide opportunities for guests to meet; social gatherings include free coffee-and-doughnut get-togethers every Friday morning and pupu parties on Wednesdays.

Mana Kai Maui Resort. 2960 S. Kihei Rd. (between Kilohana and Keonekai rds., at the Wailea end of Kihei), Kihei, HI 96753. ☎ **800/367-5242** or 808/879-1561. Fax 808/876-5042. www.maui.net/~crh. E-mail crh@maui.net. 132 units. A/C TV TEL. $80–$100 double, $150–$180 one-bedroom (sleeps up to 4), $180–$220 two-bedroom (up to 6). AE, DC, MC, V.

This eight-story complex, situated on a beautiful white-sand cove, is an unusual combination of hotel and condominium. The hotel rooms, which account for half of the total number of units, are small but nicely furnished. The condo units feature full kitchens and open living rooms with sliding-glass doors that lead to small lanais overlooking the sandy beach and ocean. Some units are beginning to show their age in this 20+-year-old building, but they're all clean and comfortable. There are laundry facilities on each floor, an open-air restaurant in the building, a swimming pool on the property, and one of the best snorkeling beaches on the coast just steps away.

Nona Lani Cottages. 455 S. Kihei Rd. (just south of Hwy. 31). P.O. Box 655, Kihei, HI 96753. ☎ **800/733-2688** or 808/879-2491. Fax 808/891-0273. 11 units. TV. $60 double, $60–$80 cottage. Extra person $7–$15. 4-night minimum. No credit cards.

Picture this: Right across the street from a white-sand beach, a grassy expanse dotted with eight small cottages tucked among palm and fruit trees. Built in 1975, the 400-square-foot cottages are tiny but contain everything you'll need: a small but complete kitchen, twin beds that double as couches in the living room, a separate bedroom with queen bed, and a lanai with table and chairs—ideal for watching the ocean waves as you eat your breakfast. The cottages are slightly worn, but the setting and the privacy of your own bungalow make up for it. There are no phones in the cabins (a blessing if you're trying to escape civilization), but there's a public one near the coin-op laundry.

If the cabins are booked, or if you just want a bit more luxury, you might opt for one of the private guest rooms in host David Kong's main house. Each beautiful room features cathedral-like open-beam ceilings, plush carpet, koa bed frames, air-conditioning, and a private entrance.

✪ **Punahoa Beach Apts.** 2142 Iliili Rd. (off S. Kihei Rd., 100 yards from Kamaole Beach I), Kihei, HI 96753. ☎ **800/564-4380** or 808/879-2720. Fax 808/875-3147. E-mail pb6110@aol.com. 12 units. TV TEL. High season $93 studio double, $127 one-bedroom double, $130 two-bedroom double; low season $66 studio double, $85 one-bedroom, $94 two-bedroom. Extra person $12. 5-night minimum. AE, MC, V.

Book this place: We can't put it any more simply than that. The location—off noisy, traffic-ridden Kihei Road, on a quiet side street with ocean frontage—is fabulous; a grassy lawn rolls about 50 feet down to the beach, there's great snorkeling just offshore and a popular surfing spot next door, and shopping and restaurants are all within walking distance. All of the beautifully decorated units in this small, four-story building have lanais with great ocean views and fully equipped kitchens. Rooms go quickly in the winter months, so book early.

✪ **What a Wonderful World B&B.** 2828 Umalu Pl. (off Keonakai St., near Hwy. 31), Kihei, HI 96753. ☎ **808/879-9103.** Fax 808/874-9352. E-mail amauibnb@maui.net. 4 units. A/C TV TEL. $65 double, $75 studio double, $85–$95 one-bedroom apt. Rates include full breakfast. Children 11 and under stay free. AE, DC, DISC, MC, V.

We couldn't believe what we'd discovered here: an impeccably done B&B with thought and care put into every room, a great location, and excellent rates. Then we met hostess Eva Tantillo, who has not only a full-service travel agency, but also a master's degree—along with several years of experience—in hotel management. The result? One of Maui's finest bed-and-breakfasts, centrally located in Kihei (a half-mile to Kamaole II Beach Park, five minutes from Wailea golf courses, and convenient to shopping and restaurants). Choose from one of four units: the master suite (with small fridge, coffeemaker, and barbecue grill on the lanai), studio apartment (with fully equipped kitchen), or two one-bedroom apartments (also with fully equipped kitchens). All come with private bath, phone, and entrance. You're welcome to use the barbecue, laundry facilities, and hot tub. Eva serves a gourmet family-style breakfast (eggs Benedict, Alaskan waffles, skillet eggs with mushroom sauce, fruit blintzes, and more) on her lanai, which has views of white-sand beaches, the West Maui Mountains, and Haleakala.

WAILEA

For a complete selection of condominium units throughout Wailea and Makena, contact **Destination Resorts Hawaii,** 2750 Wailea Alanui Dr., Wailea, HI 96753 (☎ **800/367-5246** or 808/879-1595; fax 808/874-3554; maui.net/~drh). Their luxury units include one-bedroom doubles from $140 to $435; two-bedrooms, which sleep up to 4, from $170 to $510; and three-bedrooms, which sleep up to 6, from $450 to $600. Minimum stays vary by property.

Very Expensive

✪ **Four Seasons Resort Maui at Wailea.** 3900 Wailea Alanui Dr., Wailea, HI 96753. ☎ **800/334-MAUI** or 808/874-8000. Fax 808/874-2222. www.fshr.com/locations/maui. 463 units. A/C MINIBAR TV TEL. **$295–$690** double, from **$545** suite. Packages available. Extra person **$80** (**$140** in Club Floor rooms); children under 18 stay free using existing bedding. AE, DC, JCB, MC, V.

All the luxury hotels in Wailea are fabulous, boasting terrific views and luxurious accommodations. What sets this AAA 5-Diamond award winner apart is its relaxing, casual atmosphere, combined with service so great you hardly notice it. If money's not a factor, this is the place to spend it. And bring the kids, too: there's a complete activities program designed just for them.

It's hard to beat this modern version of a Hawaiian palace by the sea. Although it sits on the beach between two other hotels, you won't feel like you're on chockablock resort row: The Four Seasons inhabits its own separate world, thanks to an open courtyard of pools and gardens. The spacious (about 600 square feet) rooms feature furnished lanais (nearly all with ocean views) that are great for watching whales in winter and sunsets year-round. The grand bathrooms have deep marble tubs, showers for two, and lighted French makeup mirrors. Other amenities include safes, hair dryers, and plush terry robes.

Service is attentive but not cloying. At the pool, guests lounge in casbah-like tents, pampered with special touches like iced Evian and chilled towels. And you'll never see a housekeeping cart in the hall: The cleaning staff works in teams, so they're as unobtrusive as possible and in and out of your room in minutes.

This ritzy neighborhood is home to great restaurants and shopping, the Wailea Tennis Center (known as Wimbledon West), and 6 golf courses—not to mention that great beach, with gentle waves and islands framing the view on either side.

Dining/Diversions: Chef George Mavrothalassitis was lured from Honolulu's Halekulani to Seasons, where his Hawaii Regional Cuisine shines in a memorable setting (see "Dining," below, for a complete review). The Seaside Restaurant offers a casual atmosphere overlooking the Pacific by day; at night, it's transformed into

Ferraro's at Seaside, serving authentic Italian. The poolside Pacific Grill offers lavish breakfast buffets and dinners featuring Pacific Edge cuisine and Chef Mavro's specials (see "Dining," below, for a review).

Amenities: Twice-daily maid service, 24-hour room service, same-day dry cleaning and laundry, free overnight shoe shine or sandal repair, complimentary valet and resort shuttle, airport limousine service, rental cars at concierge desk, 24-hour medical service. Lei greeting and oshibori towel on arrival, early arrival/late departure facility. Special amenities on Club Floors, including breakfast, afternoon tea and snacks, cocktails, pupus, and open bar. Two pools (one for adults only), 41 pool and beach cabanas, two whirlpools (one for adults only), fitness center, tennis courts (two lighted Plexi-courts; rackets and tennis balls provided), putting green. Beach pavilion with watersports gear; one hour free use of snorkel equipment, complimentary use of bicycles; complimentary exercise and tennis attire on loan. Game room, video library, salon, shops. Fabulous year-round kids' program, plus a teen recreation center and a children's video library and toys.

Grand Wailea Resort & Spa. 3850 Wailea Alanui Dr., Wailea, HI 96753. ☎ **800/ 888-6100** or 808/875-1234. Fax 808/879-4077. www.grandwailea.com. 814 units. A/C MINIBAR TV TEL. $380–$580 double, from $1,100 suite. Packages available. Extra person $30 ($50 in Napua Club rms and suites). AE, DC, DISC, JCB, MC, V.

Here's where grand becomes grandiose. The pinnacle of Hawaii's brief fling with fantasy megaresorts, this monument to excess is extremely popular with families, incentive groups, and conventions; it's the grand prize in Hawaii vacation contests and the dream of many honeymooners.

This hotel really is too much. It has a Japanese restaurant decorated with real rocks hewn from the slopes of Mount Fuji; 10,000 tropical plants in the lobby; an intricate pool system with slides, waterfalls, rapids, and a water-powered elevator to take you up to the top; Hawaii's most elaborate spa (not even the Romans had it this good); a restaurant in a manmade tide pool; a floating New England–style wedding chapel; and nothing but ocean-view rooms, outfitted with every amenity you could ask for. And it's all crowned with a $30-million collection of original art, much of it created expressly for the hotel by Hawaii artists and sculptors. There's also a fantastic beach out front.

Dining/Diversions: Six restaurants and 12 bars range from fine-dining Italian and spa cuisine to casual poolside snacks. A nightclub features laser light shows, a hydraulic dance floor, and 20 video monitors. There's also luau grounds for 300.

Amenities: Lei greeting; complimentary valet parking; 24-hour room service; twice-daily towel service; same-day laundry and dry cleaning; multilingual concierge; infant care center; art and hotel tours; Budget Rent-A-Car and American Express tour desks; 100 Napua Club rooms with attendants; complimentary continental breakfast, cocktails, and tea service. Hawaii's largest spa, the 50,000-square-foot Spa Grande, with a blend of European-, Japanese-, and American-style techniques; 2,000-foot-long Action Pool, featuring a 10-minute swim/ride through mountains and grottoes; complimentary dive and windsurf lessons; seaside wedding chapel; conference facilities. Kids enjoy a computer center, video game room, arts and crafts, 60-seat children's theater, and outdoor playground. Five golf courses, including two 18-hole championship courses, nearby.

⭐ **Renaissance Wailea Beach Resort.** 3550 Wailea Alanui Dr., Wailea, HI 96753. ☎ **800/9-WAILEA** or 808/879-4900. Fax 808/874-5370. www.renaissancehotels.com. 345 units. A/C TV TEL. $290–$515 double, from $820 suite. Extra person $40; children 18 and under stay free using existing bedding. AE, CB, DC, DISC, MC, V. Parking $3.

This is the place for visitors in search of Wailea-style luxury, but in a smaller, more intimate setting. Located on 15 acres of rolling lawn and tropical gardens, the Renaissance Wailea has the air of a small boutique hotel. Perhaps it's the resort's U-shaped design, the series of small coves and beaches, or the spaciousness of the rooms—whatever the reason, you just don't feel crowded here.

Each room has a sitting area, a large lanai, a TV and VCR hidden away in the armoire, three phones (with data ports), a fridge, and a safe. The bathrooms include such extras as double vanities (one with lighted make-up mirror) and hapi coats, Bedspreads, drapes, and towels in all rooms have recently been upgraded. Rooms in the Mokapu Beach Club, an exclusive two-story building just steps from a crescent-shaped beach, feature such extras as private check-in, in-room continental breakfast, and access to a private pool and beach cabanas.

Dining/Diversions: The casual, open-air Palm Court offers buffets and oven-baked pizzas. Hana Gion features a sushi bar and teppanyaki grill. Maui Onion is a casual poolside breakfast-and-lunch restaurant surrounded by lush gardens and a cascading waterfall. Every Monday, there's a traditional luau at sunset.

Amenities: Room service (6am to 11pm), lei greeting; concierge; complimentary in-room coffee and daily newspaper; complimentary video library; traditional Hawaiian craft classes; massage therapy; baby-sitting; children's program; Complete fitness center, two freshwater pools, two whirlpools, nearby golf and tennis, shopping arcade, hair salon, basketball court, Ping-Pong, shuffleboard.

Expensive

✪ **Aston Wailea Resort.** 3700 Wailea Alanui Dr., Wailea, HI 96753. ☎ **800/92-ASTON** or 808/879-1922. Fax 808/875-4878. www.aston-hotels.com. 566 units. A/C TV TEL. $219-$309 double, from $499 suite. Packages available. AE, DC, DISC, JCB, MC, V.

This classic, open-air, 1970s-style hotel in a tropical garden by the sea gives you a sense of what Maui was like before the big resort boom. It was the first resort built in Wailea (in 1976), yet it remains the most Hawaiian of them all. Airy and comfortable, with touches of Hawaiian art throughout and a terrific aquarium that stretches forever behind the front desk, it just feels right.

What's truly special about this hotel is how it fits into its environment without overwhelming it. Eight buildings, all low-rise except for an eight-story tower, are spread along 22 gracious acres of lawns and gardens spiked by coco palms, with lots of open space and a half-mile of oceanfront on a point between Wailea and Ulua beaches. The vast, park-like expanses are a luxury on this now-crowded coast.

All the rooms have private lanais and separate dressing and bath areas with marble-topped basins. When Aston took over management in 1996, it did a million dollars' worth of renovations to restore this once grande dame to her former glory.

Dining/Diversions: Hula Moons, a casual indoor/outdoor restaurant, serves pizza, burgers, and cool drinks at lunch and fresh Hawaii seafood specialties at dinner; there's a free hula show nightly. There's also the ocean-view Lanai Terrace for breakfast and dinner, and the Kai Puka Lounge offers cocktails, Hawaiian music, and seasonal pupus along with dramatic ocean views. A luau takes place on Tuesday, Thursday, and Friday and features two-time world-champion fire/knife dancer Efi.

Amenities: Room service (6:30am to 11pm), same-day laundry and valet, multilingual concierge. A comprehensive Hawaiian culture program offers free activities like lei-making and hula lessons; there's also an activities and culture program for the kids. Three pools, gift shop, newsstand, beauty salon, barber shop. Three championship golf courses nearby.

MAKENA

Expensive

✪ **Hale Mehana Vacation House.** 176 Makena Rd. (by the Keawalai Church in South Makena), Kihei, HI 96753. ☎ **808/875-8231.** Fax 808/877-2046. E-mail dugal@maui.net. TV TEL. three-bedroom/2-bath home. $200 double. Extra person $25, maximum 6 people. 5-night minimum. No credit cards.

Located right on the ocean at Makena (with the waves lapping just a few feet from the magnificent deck), Hale Mehana ("warm-hearted house") consists of the entire upstairs floor of a luxury home. Not a penny has been spared to make this property a dream oceanfront accommodation. A huge deck wraps around the house, offering breathtaking views of Molokini and Kahoolawe in the distance and easy access to swimming, snorkeling, and kayaking. The living area has big picture windows, polished wooden floors, a huge sofa, and a complete entertainment center. The kitchen opens onto the living/dining area, taking advantage of those incredible views; it contains every possible appliance a cook could want. The master bedroom is simply fabulous: a huge bay window looks out on the ocean, and the large master bathroom has a Jacuzzi big enough for two. Two smallish bedrooms share a full bath. Makena golf and tennis are just two minutes away, and Wailea restaurants and shopping are a 5-minute drive.

Maui Prince Hotel. 5400 Makena Alanui, Makena, HI 96753. ☎ **800/321-MAUI** or 808/874-1111. Fax 808/879-8763. 304 units. A/C MINIBAR TV TEL. $230–$395 double, $440–$840 suite. Packages available. AE, DC, JCB, MC, V.

If you're looking for a vacation in a beautiful, tranquil spot with a golden-sand beach, here's your place. But if you plan to tour Maui, this is definitely far out of your way: It's at the end of the road, far, far away from anything else on the island.

When you first see the stark white hotel, it looks like a high-rise motel stuck in the woods—from the outside. Inside, you'll discover an atrium garden with a koi-filled waterfall stream, an ocean view from every room, and a simplicity to the furnishings that makes some people feel uncomfortable and others blissfully clutter-free. Rooms are small but come with private lanais with great views.

Dining/Diversions: Japanese cuisine tops the menu at the elegant Hakone, which has a sushi bar (for a full review, see "Dining," below). The Prince Court specializes in Hawaii Regional Cuisine, while the casual Cafe Kiowai offers seasonal and international specialties. There's also a casual spot serving lunch and snacks, and local Hawaiian music nightly in the lounge.

Amenities: Lei greeting, complimentary early-morning coffee and tea, complimentary valet parking, multilingual concierge, same-day dry cleaning and laundry, daily kids' program, early-arrival and late-departure services. Tennis (six Plexi-pave courts, two lit for night play), 36 holes of Robert Trent Jones—designed golf, adults' and children's pools, fitness center, six-station fitness trail, library.

Inexpensive

✪ **Makena Landing.** 5100 Makena Rd. (next to the county beach park), Makena, HI 96753. ☎ **808/879-6286.** 2 units. TV TEL. $95 double. Extra person $10. 3-night minimum. No credit cards.

This has to be the most fabulous location for a bed-and-breakfast: right on the ocean at Makena Landing. Once you settle in, you may not want to leave. The view is incredible; the sunsets are to die for; some of the best swimming, snorkeling, diving, and shoreline fishing are within walking distance; and the hosts are the nicest people you'll ever meet. The property has been in the Lu'uwai family for seven generations; hosts Boogie and Vi are both native Hawaiians, and they're brimming with generosity.

To ensure privacy, the two units are at opposite ends of the two-story cedar house. Both have private entrances, full baths, kitchens, and private balconies that overlook the ocean, with Molokini and Kahoolawe in the distance. The kitchens have everything you can think of, and Vi makes sure you have all the fixings for breakfast. Outside are a barbecue area and a sundeck, a ringside seat to watch whales from December to April.

UPCOUNTRY MAUI

You'll find it cool and peaceful up here; be sure to bring a sweater.

MAKAWAO & OLINDA

Moderate

✪ **Olinda Country Cottage & Inn.** 536 Olinda Rd. (near the top of Olinda Rd., a 15-minute drive from Makawao), Makawao, HI 96768. ☎ **800/932-3435** or 808/572-1453. Fax 808/572-1453. www.maui.net/~bbinn. E-mail bbinn@maui.net. 5 units, TV TEL. $95–$110 double (includes continental breakfast), $125–$140 suite double (includes 1st morning's breakfast in fridge), $110–$120 suite double (sleeps up to 5; includes 1st morning's breakfast in fridge). Extra person $15. 2-night minimum for rooms and suite, 3- to 5-night minimum for cottages. No credit cards.

When Ellen Unterman and Rupa McLaughlin bought this old Tudor mansion, they saw distinct possibilities. The couple lovingly refurbished it; then Ellen, owner of a trendy antique store in Santa Monica, California, shipped almost a warehouseful of antiques and collectibles over to furnish it—and the result is one of the best-decorated country inns in Hawaii.

Set on the slopes of Haleakala in the crisp, clean air of Olinda, this charming B&B is on an 8½-acre protea farm, surrounded by 35,000 acres of ranch lands (with miles of great hiking trails). The 5,000-square-foot country home, outfitted with a professional eye to detail, has large windows with incredible panoramic views of all of Maui. Upstairs are two guest rooms with antique beds, private full baths, and a separate entryway. Connected to the main house but with its own private entrance, the Pineapple Sweet has a full kitchen, an antique-filled living room, a marble-tiled full bath, and a separate bedroom. A separate 1,000-square-foot cottage is the epitome of cozy country luxury, with a fireplace, a bedroom with a queen bed, cushioned window seats (with great sunset views), and open-beam cathedral ceilings. Just added in 1997, the 950-square-foot Hidden Cottage (in a truly secluded spot surrounded by protea flowers) features three decks, 8-foot French glass doors, a full kitchen, washer/dryer, and private tub for two on the deck.

Restaurants are a 15-minute drive away in Makawao, and beaches are another 15 minutes beyond that. Once ensconced, however, you may never want to leave this enchanting inn.

Inexpensive

✪ **Banyan Tree House.** 3265 Baldwin Ave. (next to Veteran's Cemetery, just ⁸⁄₁₀ mile below Makawao), Makawao, HI 96768. ☎ **808/572.9021.** Fax 808/579-8180. www.maui.net/~holter/banyantree.html. E-mail holter@maui.net. 3 units. $45–$65 cottage double, $185 three-bedroom/three-bath house (sleeps up to 6). 2- to 3-night minimum for house. MC, V.

Huge monkeypod trees (complete with swing and hammock) extend their branches over this 2½-acre property like a giant green canopy. The restored 1920s plantation manager's house is decorated with Hawaiian furniture from the 1930s; the large guest rooms have big, comfortable beds and private, marble-tiled bathrooms. A fireplace stands at one end of the huge living room, a large lanai runs the entire length of the house, and the hardwood floors shine throughout. The two guest cottages have been totally renovated and also feature hardwood floors and marble baths. The small cottage has a queen bed, private bathroom, microwave, coffeepot, and access to the fridge in the laundry room. The larger cottage has a queen bed and a twin bed, private bath, small fridge, microwave, coffeepot, toaster, and TV. Guests have use of laundry facilities. The quiet neighborhood and nostalgic Old Hawaii ambiance give this place a comfortable, easygoing atmosphere. Restaurants and shops are just minutes away in Makawao, and the beach is a 15-minute drive—but this place is so relaxing that you may find yourself wanting to do nothing more than lie in the hammock and watch the clouds float by.

Hale Ho'okipa Inn Makawao. 32 Pakani Pl., Makawao, HI 96768. ☎ **808/572-6698.** Fax 808/573-2580. www.maui.net/~mauibnb. E-mail cherie@mauigateway.com. 3 units (2 with shower only). $60–$70 double. Rates include continental breakfast. Extra person $8. No credit cards. From Haleakala Hwy., turn left on Makawao Ave., then right on the 5th street on the right (Pakani Pl.); it's the last house on the right.

Step back in time at this 1924 plantation-style home, rescued by owner Cherie Attix and restored to its original charm. Cherie, who owns an interior-design store, lovingly refurbished the old wooden floors, filled the rooms with period furniture, and hung works by local artists on the walls. The result is a charming, serene place to stay, just a 5-minute walk from Makawao town, 15 minutes from beaches, and a 1½-hour drive from the top of Haleakala. The guest rooms have separate outside entrances and private baths. The house's front and back porches are wonderful for sipping tea and watching the sunset. The living room has a TV and a private phone for guest use.

IN KULA (AT THE BASE OF HALEAKALA NATIONAL PARK)
Moderate

✪ **Silver Cloud Ranch.** Old Thompson Rd. (1.2 miles past Hwy. 37). RR 2, Box 201, Kula, HI 96790. ☎ **800/532-1111** or 808/878-6101. Fax 808/878-2132. www.maui.net/~slvrcld. E-mail slvrcld@maui.net. 12 units. $85–$125 double in main house, $105–$145 double studio in bunkhouse, $150 double cottage. Rates include full breakfast. Extra person $15. AE, DISC, MC, V.

Old Hawaii lives on at Silver Cloud Ranch, founded in 1902 by a sailor who jumped ship when he got to Maui. The former working cattle spread has a commanding view of four islands, the West Maui Mountains, and the valley and beaches below. The Lanai Cottage, a honeymoon favorite nestled in a flower garden, has an ocean-view lanai, clawfoot bathtub, full kitchen, and wood-burning stove to warm chilly nights; a futon is available if you're traveling with a third person. The best rooms in the main house are on the second floor: the King Kamehameha Suite (with king bed) and the Queen Emma Suite (with queen bed). Each has a royal view, though some prefer Emma's. The Paniolo Bunkhouse, once used by real cowboys, is now fully restored and houses five studios, each with private bath, kitchenette, and views of the Pacific or Haleakala (go for the ocean view). All guests are free to use the main house and kitchen.

One-lane Thompson Road makes an ideal morning walk (about 3 miles round-trip), and you can go horseback riding next door at Thompson Ranch. There's a TV available if you feel visually deprived, but after a few Maui sunsets, you won't even remember why you bothered to ask.

Inexpensive

✪ **Kula Cottage.** 206 Puakea Pl. (off Lower Kula Rd.), Kula, HI 96790. ☎ **808/ 878-2043** or 808/871-6230. Fax 808/871-9187. E-mail gilassoc@maui.net. 1 cottage. $85 double. Rate includes continental breakfast. 2-night minimum. No credit cards.

We can't imagine having a less-than-fantastic vacation here. Tucked away on a quiet street amid a half-acre of blooming papaya and banana trees, Cecilia and Larry Gilbert's romantic honeymoon cottage is very private—it even has its own driveway and carport. The 700-square-foot cottage has a full kitchen (complete with dishwasher), washer/dryer, and three huge closets that offer enough storage space for you to move in permanently. An outside lanai has a big gas barbecue and an umbrella table and chairs. Cecilia delivers a continental breakfast daily (visitors rave about her homemade bread in the guest book). If you're an animal lover, Hana, the dog, will be more than happy to be a surrogate pet to you during your vacation; otherwise, Cecilia makes sure that Hana stays out of your way. Groceries and a small take-out lunch counter are within walking distance; it's a 30-minute drive to the beach.

✪ **Nohona Laule'a**, 763-2 Kamehameiki Rd (off Kula Hwy.), Kula, HI 96790. ☎ **808/878-6646.** Fax 808/878-6646. 1 two-bedroom cottage. TV TEL. $85 double. Extra person $10. 3-night minimum. No credit cards.

What a deal—an impeccable two-bedroom cottage for $85 for two! Located on a windy road at about 2,500 feet, Nohona Laule'a (which means "peaceful dwelling") is 4 acres of tropical paradise with the cottage smack-dab in the middle. The 700-square-foot cottage, decorated in Asian style, features open-beam ceilings, skylights, a complete gourmet kitchen, a full bath, a living room, a huge deck, and a washer/dryer. The whole cottage has great island views: one bedroom, with Japanese shoji doors and two twin beds, looks out onto Haleakala; the other, with a double bed, has a big picture window overlooking the garden and the north shore beyond. The living room has a comfortable couch, a wooden rocker, and another huge picture window. Owners Brian and Sue Kanegai are congenial hosts; Sue greets guests with her delicious mango or banana bread. True to its name, this place is indeed peaceful. Kick back in a comfortable chair on the big deck, survey the blooming landscape at your feet, and you'll know what it must have been like to experience Eden.

EAST MAUI: ON THE ROAD TO HANA

KUAU

✪ **Mama's Beachfront Cottages**, 799 Poho Pl, (off the Hana Hwy. in Kuau), Paia, HI 96779. ☎ **800/860-HULA** or 808/579-9764. Fax 808/579-8594. www.maui.net/~mamas. E-mail mamas@maui.net. 6 apts. TV TEL. $90 one-bedroom (sleeps up to 4); $175 two-bedroom (up to 6). 3-night minimum. AE, DC, DISC, MC, V.

The fabulous location (nestled in a coconut grove on secluded Kuau Beach), beautifully decorated interior (with island-style rattan furniture and works by Hawaiian artists), and plenty of extras (Weber gas barbecue, huge 27-inch TVs, and all the beach toys you can think of) make this place a must-stay for people looking for a centrally located vacation rental. It has everything, even Mama's Fish House next door (where guests get a discount of 20% off lunch and dinner). The one-bedrooms are nestled in tropical jungle (red ginger surrounds the garden patio), while the two-bedrooms face the beach. Both have terra-cotta floors, complete kitchens (even dishwashers), pullout sofabeds, and laundry. We love Mama's sense of humor: We opened the closet in one unit and found a grass hula skirt complete with a coconut shell top tacked to the back wall.

HAIKU

Moderate

✪ **Pilialoha B&B Cottage**, 2512 Kaupakalua Rd. (.7-mile from Kokomo intersection), Haiku, HI 96708. ☎ **808/572-1440.** Fax 808/572-4612. www.mauigateway.com/

~heyde. E-mail Heyde@mauigateway.com. 1 cottage. TV TEL. **$100–$110** double. Rates include continental breakfast. 3-night minimum. No credit cards.

The minute you arrive at this split-level country cottage, located on 2 acres of half-century-old eucalyptus trees, you'll see owner Machiko Heyde's artistry at work. Just in front of the cottage is a garden blooming with some 200 varieties of roses; Machiko is an artist who believes that gardening is just another art form. You'll find more of her handiwork inside the quaint cottage, which is great for couples but can sleep up to five: There's a queen bed in the master bedroom, a twin bed in a small adjoining room, and a queen sleeper sofa in the living room. A large lanai extends from the master bedroom. There's a great movie collection for rainy days or cool, country nights, a washer/dryer, beach paraphernalia (including snorkel equipment), and a garage. Machiko delivers breakfast daily; if you plan on an early-morning ride to the top of Haleakala, she'll make sure you go with a thermos of coffee and her homemade bread. *Pilialoha* translates as "friendship," which is how you will feel about your hostess by the time you leave.

Inexpensive

Maui Dream Cottages. 265 W. Kuiaha Rd. (1 block from Pauwela Cafe), Haiku, HI 96708. ☎ **808/575-9079.** Fax **808/575-9477.** E-mail gblue@aloha.net. 2 cottages (with showers only). TV. **$70** for 4. 7-night minimum. MC, V.

Essentially a vacation rental, this 2-acre country estate is located atop a hill overlooking the ocean. The grounds are dotted with fruit trees (bananas, papayas, and avocados, all free for the picking), and the front lawn is comfortably equipped with a double hammock, chaise lounges, and table and chairs. One cottage has two bedrooms, a full kitchen (with microwave and coffeemaker), a washer/dryer, and entertainment center. The other is basically the same, but with only one bedroom (plus a sofabed in the living room). They're both very well maintained, comfortably outfitted with furniture that's not only attractive but also casual enough that you won't have to worry about the kids putting their feet up on it. The Haiku location is quiet and restful and offers the opportunity to see how real islanders live. However, you'll have to drive a good 20 to 25 minutes to restaurants in Makawao or Paia for dinner. Hookipa Beach is about a 20-minute drive, and Baldwin Beach (good swimming) is 25 minutes away.

TWIN FALLS

✪ **Maluhia Hale.** P.O. Box 687 (off Hana Hwy., nearly a mile past Twin Falls bridge), Haiku, HI 96708. ☎ **808/572-2959.** Fax **808/572-2959.** www.maui.net/~djg/index.html. E-mail djg@maui.net. 3 units. TV. **$85** cottage double, **$105** suite double. Rates include continental breakfast on the 1st morning. Extra person **$15.** 2-night minimum. No credit cards.

Diane and Robert Garrett design and build homes that are works of art. Here, they've created a private country cottage that has the feeling of a gracious old Hawaiian plantation home. A sense of peace and orderliness reigns in the cottage: You enter through an open and airy screened veranda, which leads to a glassed-in sitting room, a bed in lacy white linen, and a kitchenette. Hand-selected antiques fill the cottage, and Diane's exquisite flower arrangements add splashes of color. In the main house are two suites: one with a solarium, complete with an old clawfoot tub and separate shower. In the more romantic suite with cherrywood floors, a lacy bedspread, and a view of the lily pond outside. Diane does light housekeeping daily; no matter which accommodation you choose, at the end of the day, you'll return to a softly lit place filled with sweet-smelling tropical flowers. A simply wonderful place.

HUELO

✪ **Huelo Point Flower Farm.** Off Hana Hwy., between mile markers 3 and 4. P.O. Box 1195, Paia, HI 96779. ☎ **808/572-1850.** www.maui.net/~huelopt. E-mail huelopt@ maui.net. 4 units. $110 cottage double, $135 carriage house double, $200 guest house double; rates include continental breakfast. $2,300 per week for main house for 6. Extra person $15. No credit cards.

Here's a little Eden by the sea on a spectacular, remote 300-foot sea cliff near a waterfall stream: a 2-acre estate overlooking Waipio Bay with two guest cottages, a guest house, and a main house available for rent. This is where the celebs (Ann-Margaret, Woody Harrelson, and Roger Clinton, to name a few) stay. The studio-sized Gazebo Cottage has a glass-walled ocean front, a koa-wood captain's bed, TV, stereo, kitchenette, private oceanside patio, private hot tub, and a half-bath with outdoor shower. The new 900-square-foot Carriage House apartment sleeps four and has glass walls facing the mountain and sea, plus a kitchen, den, decks, and a loft bedroom. The two-bedroom main house has an exercise room, fireplace, sunken Roman bath, cathedral ceilings, and other extras. There's a natural pool with a waterfall and an oceanfront hot tub. You're welcome to pick fruit, vegetables, and flowers from the extensive garden. Homemade scones, tree-ripened papayas, and fresh-roasted coffee start your day. Despite its seclusion, off the crooked road to Hana, it's just a half-hour to Kahului, or about 20 minutes to Paia's shops and restaurants.

✪ **Huelo Point Lookout B&B.** Off Hana Hwy., between mile markers 3 and 4. Reservations c/o Hawaii's Best Bed & Breakfasts, P.O. Box 563, Kamuela, HI 96743. ☎ **800/262-9912** or 808/885-4550. Fax 808/885-0559. E-mail bestbnb@aloha.net. 3 cottages. TV TEL. $95–$275 double. Rates include a welcome breakfast. Extra person $20. 3-night minimum. DISC.

About a quarter-mile from the 300-foot cliffs of Waipio Bay is this lovely B&B, situated on 2 acres of tropical jungle with a hot tub, a 40-foot freeform swimming pool, and a view all the way down the coastline to Hana. The main house has pentagonal glass walls that offer sweeping views of the ocean and up the side of Haleakala. It has two private entrances, a large bedroom with a king bed, a kitchenette, a big bath with a tub big enough for two, and a lotus pond and waterfall outside on the private deck. The Honeymoon Cottage is a renovated old fisherman's residence, with an upstairs bedroom, a full kitchen, a sitting room, and a solarium with lots of windows, skylights, and a deck. The bathroom has a Victorian tub and glass all around, with views of Haleakala on one side and the ocean on the other. The Halekala Cottage is smaller but full of amenities, including a full kitchen (with dishwasher), a king bed, and a bathroom that extends outside into the garden so you can actually take a hot shower under the stars, surrounded by white lattice and tropical flowers. The newest cottage, Rainbow, features 25-foot-high glass walls with nothing but views. Other amenities include a private indoor hot tub, a glass-ceiling bathroom, and a work-of-art wooden staircase. The owners, Jeff and Sharyn, also own a video store in Paia, so they can get you the movies of your choice.

AT THE END OF THE ROAD IN EAST MAUI: HANA

Picture Shangri-La, Hawaiian-style: 66 acres rolling down to the sea in a remote Hawaiian village, with a wellness center, two pools, and access to one of the best beaches in Hana. It all adds up to **Hotel Hana-Maui** (☎ **800/321-HANA** or 808/248-8211; fax 808/248-7202, $395 double, $450 to $495 suite, $525 to $795 cottage). However, this gorgeous luxury resort has been suffering from neglect of late. As we went to press, welcome rumors were in the wind that a new management team (of impeccable international stature) was poised to take over. We hope so, as this gem of a property is in need of massive renovation.

In the past, we've recommended a couple of agencies representing vacation rentals in Hana; however, on our most recent site inspections, we found that several properties needed repairs, were way overpriced, or were downright dirty. At this time, we cannot recommend any local agencies, but we'll continue to inspect their properties and let you know in future editions if the necessary improvements have been made.

Moderate

✪ **Ekena.** P.O. Box 728 (off Hana Hwy., above Hana Airport), Hana, HI 96713. ☎ **808/248-7047.** Fax 808/248-7047. www.maui.net/~ekena. E-mail ekena@maui.net. 2 two-bedroom apts. TV TEL. **$150 double, $190–$275 for 4.** Extra person $15. 3-night minimum. No credit cards.

Just one glance at the 360° view, and you can see why hosts Robin and Gaylord gave up their careers on the mainland and moved here. This 8½-acre piece of paradise in rural Hana boasts ocean and rain-forest views; the floor-to-ceiling glass doors in the spacious Hawaiian-style pole house bring the outside in. The elegant two-story home is exquisitely furnished, from the comfortable U-shaped couch that invites you to relax and take in the view to the top-of-the-line mattress on the king bed. The kitchen is fully equipped (guests have made complete holiday meals here) with every high-tech convenience you can imagine. The grounds are impeccably groomed with tropical plants and fruit trees. Hiking trails into the rain forest start right on the property, and beaches and waterfalls are just minutes away. Only one floor (and one two-bedroom unit) is rented at any one time to ensure privacy. Robin places fresh flowers in every room and makes sure you're comfortable; after that, she's available to answer questions about what Hana has to offer, but also respects your privacy and lets you enjoy your vacation in peace.

✪ **Hamoa Bay Bungalow.** P.O. Box 773, Hana, HI 96713. ☎ **808/248-7884.** Fax 808/248-8642. E-mail jody@maui.net. 1 cottage. TV TEL. **$145 double.** Rate includes continental breakfast. 2-night minimum. No credit cards.

Down a country lane guarded by two Balinese statues stands a little bit of Indonesia in Hawaii: a carefully crafted bungalow overlooking Hamoa Bay. Only 2 miles beyond Hasegawa's general store on the way to Kipahulu, this enchanting retreat sits on 4 verdant acres within walking distance of black-sand Hamoa Beach (which James Michener considered one of the most beautiful in the Pacific). The romantic, 600-square-foot Balinese-style cottage is distinctly tropical, with giant Elephant bamboo furniture from Indonesia, batik prints, a king bed, full kitchen, and screened porch with hot tub and shower. Host Jody Baldwin, a lifelong Mauian who lives on the estate, serves a tropical breakfast of fruit, yogurt, and muffins; she'll be happy to share the secrets of Hana, including the great mountain hiking trail nearby.

Hana Hale Malamalama. Reservations c/o Hawaii's Best Bed & Breakfasts, P.O. Box 563, Kamuela, HI 96743. ☎ **800/262-9912** or 808/885-4550. Fax 808/885-0559. E-mail bestbnb@aloha.net. TV TEL. 3 units. **$110–$175 suite double, $150 cottage double.** Extra person $15. 2-night minimum. DISC.

Located on a historic site with ancient fish ponds and a cave mentioned in ancient chants, this place definitely exudes the spirit of Old Hawaii. Host John takes excellent care of the ponds (you're welcome to watch him feed the fish at 5pm daily) and is fiercely protective of the hidden cave ("it's not a tourist attraction, but a sacred spot"). There's access to a nearby rocky beach, which isn't good for swimming but makes a wonderful place to watch the sun set. All accommodations include fully equipped

🏨 Great Places to Stay with the Kids

If you're traveling with the kids, you'll be welcomed with open arms at many of Maui's resorts, condos, vacation rentals, and B&Bs. Our favorite family-friendly accommodations on the island are listed below. In addition to these, you might also consider **Maui Park, Noelani Condominium Resort, Maui Marriott, Koa Resort, Nohona Laulea**, and the **Kaanapali Beach Hotel**, all of which are great for families traveling with kids.

Note that by state law, hotels can only accept children ages 5 to 12 into their supervised activities programs.

Our Favorite: Four Seasons Resort at Wailea (*see p. 384*)   This is the most kid-friendly hotel on Maui. The Four Seasons offers a complimentary Kids for All Seasons program, a year-round activities center featuring a range of activities, from sand-sculpturing to kite-flying. The resort goes out of its way to make the *keikis* feel welcome with such amenities as complimentary milk and cookies on the first day, children's menus in all restaurants (including room service), free infant needs (cribs, strollers, highchairs, playpens, and car seats), and child-safety features (like toilet-seat locks, plug covers, and security gates). The resort can also pre-purchase a range of necessities (such as diapers and baby food) for you before your arrival. Kids and teens have a huge list of activities and equipment to choose from, including a game room (with Super Nintendo, Sony PlayStation, foosball, billiards, and more); a scuba clinic (for ages 12 and older); videos; and a host of activities.

Hyatt Regency Maui (*see p. 371*)   The Camp Hyatt program, for hotel guests only, operates daily from 9am to 3pm and offers a range of activities, from "Olympic Games" to a scavenger hunt. The cost is $65, which includes lunch and

kitchens, baths, bedrooms, living/dining areas, and private lanais. With two duplex suites—one with more than 1,800 square feet of living space—the main house is an architectural masterpiece, built entirely of Philippine mahogany with 4-foot-wide skylights the entire length of the house. The skylights are wonderful at night, but we think they make the house too hot in the summer. Entry is down stone steps, so this is not a place for small children or anyone who has trouble climbing steep steps.

The separate two-level Tree House cottage is nestled between a kamani tree and a coconut palm. Downstairs is the bathroom with a Jacuzzi tub for two, while upstairs is a Balinese bamboo bed, small kitchen/living area, and a small deck. Although the view is wonderful, we weren't too fond of walking up and down the steep steps at night to go to the bathroom.

Ho'onanea Farm. Star Route 165A (10 miles from Hana, next to Oheo Gulch), Hana, HI 96713. ☎ 808/248-7816. Fax 808/248-8648. 2 huts (with shared bath). TEL. **$105** double. Rates include continental breakfast fixings. Extra person **$15**. 2-night minimum or **$15** cleaning fee. No credit cards.

This is an incredibly beautiful place to stay, but it's not for everyone. Located in the rain forest of Kipahulu Valley, within walking distance of the pools at Oheo Gulch in Haleakala National Park, this 6-acre property of exotic fruit trees offers unique accommodations in a series of huts. The main house, built in the round with first-class kitchen appliances and a well-decorated living area, serves as the common area. There are two sleeping *hales*, or houses: one with a queen bed and one with a double bed

snacks. The Camp also has nightly activities (from 6 to 10pm), such as table games, movies, and video games. The cost is $12 per hour, per child, and includes light snacks and refreshments.

Hale Kai (see p. 374) This small condo complex in Honokowai is ideally located for families: right on the beach; next door to a county park; and within a 10-minute drive of Lahaina's shops, restaurants, and attractions. Kids can hang out at the pool, swim in the ocean, or play in the park next door. There's a TV and VCR in every unit, and the well-equipped kitchens (with dishwasher, disposal, microwave, even a blender) allow Mom and Dad to save money on eating out.

Ritz-Carlton Kapalua (see p. 378) The Ritz Kids is a year-round daytime activities center that features both educational activities (from exploring the ecosystems in streams to learning the hula) and sports (from golf to swimming). The cost for the program is $60 for a full day (non–Ritz-Carlton guests pay $75), which includes lunch and a T-shirt, and $40 for a half day (non–Ritz-Carlton guests pay $55).

Mana Kai Maui Resort (see p. 383) This eight-story complex, an unusual combination of hotel and condominium, sits on a beautiful white-sand cove in Kihei that's one of the best snorkeling beaches on Maui's South Coast. Families should consider the condo units, which feature full kitchens and open living rooms; sliding-glass doors lead to small lanais overlooking the sandy beach and ocean.

(best for children or one person). The only catch to this incredible tropical dream: There's just one bathroom, which is in yet another hale, and it's quite a long walk—especially at night, in the dark. If none of this bothers you, though, this could be your Hawaiian fantasy come true.

Papalani. Star Route 27 (3 miles past Hasagawa's General Store, before the bridge at mile marker 48), Hana, HI 96713. ☎ **808/248-7204.** Fax 808/248-7285. 1 apt, 1 cottage. TEL. **$150 double. Extra person $25. No children under 8. 3-night minimum. No credit cards.**

These luxurious, romantic accommodations are hidden from the road, offering privacy and quiet in a gorgeous setting. There is only one tiny drawback: mosquitoes—swarms of them, as a matter of fact. A stream runs through the property next to the apartment and cottage, and although hostess Cybil has done everything possible to eliminate this nuisance (like providing screened-in lanais so you can enjoy the outdoors without experiencing these biting pests), bring your insect repellent.

Otherwise, Papalani lives up to its name, which means "heaven and all the spiritual powers." The apartment and the cottage, both professionally decorated, have white leather couches, wood floors, Berber carpets, and expensive artwork. Everything is first-class, from the appliances in the kitchen to the faucets in the bathroom. The apartment has a kitchenette with mini-fridge, blender, and coffeemaker, while the separate cottage has a full kitchen. Both units have their own laundry facilities and private hot tubs. This is a TV-free environment, so you can really get in touch with nature. The great location means you're just a 5-minute walk to Waioka Stream (where there's good swimming in the pools), a mile from beautiful Hamoa Beach, and 5 minutes from Hana. Cybil asks that guests not smoke on the property and that meat be cooked on a barbecue outside.

Inexpensive

Mrs. Nakamura has been renting her **Aloha Cottages,** P.O. Box 205, Hana, HI 96713 (☎ **808/248-8420**), since the '70s, and she now has five. Located in residential areas near Hana Bay, her budget rentals are simple but adequately furnished, varying in size from a roomy studio with kitchenette to a three-bedroom, two-bath; rates run $60 to $95 double. They're all fully equipped, clean, and fairly well kept. Not all units have TVs and none have phones, but Mrs. N. is happy to take messages.

✪ **Tradewinds Cottage.** 135 Alalele Pl., P.O. Box 385, Hana, HI 96713. ☎ **800/327-8097** or 808/248-8980. Fax 808/248-7735. www.maui.net/~twt/cottage.html. E-mail twt@maui.net. 2 cottages. TV TEL. $95 studio double, $115 two-bedroom double. Extra person $10. 2-night minimum. MC, V.

Nestled among the ginger and heliconias on a 5-acre flower farm are two separate cottages, each with complete kitchen, carport, barbecue, private hot tub, TV, ceiling fans, and sleeper sofa. The studio cottage sleeps up to four; a bamboo shoji blind separates the sleeping area (with queen bed) from the sofabed in the living room. The Tradewinds cottage has two bedrooms (with a queen bed in one room and two twins in the other), one bathroom (with shower only), and a huge front porch. The atmosphere is quiet and relaxing, and hosts Mike and Rebecca Buckley, who have been in business for a decade, welcome families (they have two children, a cat, and a very sweet golden retriever). You can use their laundry facilities at no extra charge.

Waianapanapa State Park Cabins. Off Hana Hwy. c/o State Parks Division, 54 S. High St., Rm. 101, Wailuku, HI 96793. ☎ **808/984-8109.** 12 cabins. $45 for 4 (sleeps up to 6). Extra person $5. 5-night maximum. No credit cards.

These 12 rustic cabins are the best lodging deal on Maui. Everyone knows it, too—so make your reservations early (up to 6 months in advance). The cabins are warm and dry and come complete with kitchen, living room, bedroom, and bathroom with hot shower; furnishings include bedding, linen, towels, dishes, and very basic cooking and eating utensils. Don't expect luxury—this is a step above camping, albeit in a beautiful tropical jungle setting unlike any other in the islands. The key attraction at this 120-acre state beach park is the unusual horseshoe-shaped black-sand beach on Pailoa Bay, popular for shore fishing, snorkeling, and swimming. There's a caretaker on site, along with rest rooms, showers, picnic tables, shoreline hiking trails, and historic sites. But bring mosquito protection—this *is* the jungle.

4 Dining

by Jocelyn Fujii

In the past decade, with the ascension of Hawaii Regional Cuisine into national prominence, and with Maui as Hawaii's visitor-industry success story, the islands' best chefs have opened their Maui doors and turned this island into a culinary nexus. Good food on this island means chefs like David Paul, Beverly Gannon, Eric Leterc (the newly arrived wunderkind at Maui Prince's Prince Court), Steve Amaral at his new Cucina Pacifica, and arrivals from outer islands: Peter Merriman (Big Island), Jean-Marie Josselin (Kauai), Roy Yamaguchi (Oahu), and George Mavrothalassitis, the former Halekulani chef who moved to Maui to become the best thing about the Four Seasons Resort at Wailea.

If there are any doubts in your mind that Maui is a dining mecca, consider the latest in the restaurant scene. Superchef Sam Choy of the hugely successful Sam Choy's restaurant chain has opened a large new eatery in a prime spot at the Kaahumanu Center, with plans to convert the former site of Shark's Tooth Brewery and Grill (in the same shopping center) into a contemporary Chinese restaurant. Peter Merriman, chef extraordinaire and a pioneer of Hawaii Regional Cuisine, plans to open his new restaurant in late 1998, in the new Maui Ocean Center. The new restaurant will offer Hawaii Regional Cuisine, with an emphasis on "shared dining." In Hawaii, where combination platters and family-style ethnic dining are commonplace, Merriman's concept fits like a glove; combined with his imaginative menu and allegiance to seasonal produce and fresh local ingredients, it's sure to succeed. Merriman also oversees Hula Grill in Kaanapali, as well as his own Merriman's restaurant on the Big Island.

You can also dine well at Lahaina's open-air waterfront watering holes. There are budget eateries here, but not many; Maui's old-fashioned, multigenerational mom-and-pop diners are disappearing by attrition, eclipsed by the flashy newcomers, or clinging to the edge of existence in the older neighborhoods of central Maui. Although you'll have to work harder to find them in the resort areas, you won't have to go far to find creative cuisine, pleasing style, and stellar views in Upcountry, South, and West Maui.

In the listings below, reservations are not necessary unless otherwise noted.

CENTRAL MAUI

The **Kaahumanu Center,** the structure that looks like a white *Star Wars* umbrella in the center of Kahului, at 275 Kaahumanu Ave. (5 minutes from Kahului Airport on Hwy. 32), has a very popular food court with concessions that serve, for the most part, excellent food. The **Juiceland** kiosk near the top of the elevator offers vitamin-rich (and delicious!) freshly squeezed beet, celery, wheat-grass, carrot, ginger, and creative combinations of vegetable and fruit juices, as well as smoothies made from the legendary fresh fruits of Maui. And busy shoppers seem more than willing to dispense with fine china and other formalities to enjoy a no-nonsense meal on Styrofoam plates that efficiently refreshes them between spurts of shopping. Among the standouts: **Maui Tacos,** one of the string of palate-pleasing Mexican diners sprinkled throughout Maui (see p. 405). (Watch for them on the mainland; founder/chef Mark Ellman has formed a partnership with Blimpie International to open Maui Tacos outlets nationwide.) The green burritos, painted naturally with spinach, are the best this side of the Rio Grande. **Edo Japan** teppanyaki is a real find, its flat Benihana-like grill dispensing marvelous, flavorful mounds of grilled fresh vegetables and chicken teriyaki for $4.15. **Yummy Korean B-B-Q,** part of a chain well-known on Oahu, proffers soups; sesame bean sprouts; potato salad; and many combinations of vegetables, meats, fish, and ribs infused with the assertive flavors of Korea. **Panda Cuisine** serves tasty Chinese food. One spot that's always abuzz is **The Coffee Store** (see p. 409), a no-nonsense java stop that serves sandwiches, salads, pasta, and nearly two dozen different coffee drinks.

When you leave Kaahumanu Center, take a moment to gaze at the West Maui Mountains to your left from the parking lot. They are one of Maui's wonders, a kaleidoscopic show of clouds, sunlight, textured canyons, and deep greens that reflect the mystical qualities of the old mountains.

Class Act. At Maui Community College, 310 Kaahumanu Ave., Wailuku. ☎ **808/984-3480.** Reservations required. 4-course lunch $13. No credit cards. Wed and Fri 11am–12:15pm (last seating). Cuisine changes weekly.

Part of a program run by the Food Service Department of Maui Community College, this restaurant has quite a following. Student chefs show their stuff with a flourish in their "classroom," where they pull out all the stops as if it were their own place. Linen, china, servers in ties and white shirts, and a four-course lunch make this a four-star value. The appetizer, soup, salad, and dessert are set, but you can choose between the regular entrée and a heart-healthy entrée prepared in the culinary tradition of the week. The filet mignon of French week is popular, and so are the Thai curries; Chinese stir-fries; pastas; and Japanese, Austrian, Moroccan, and other international menus served throughout the months. There's no air-conditioning, but there are fans and balcony seating. Tea and soft drinks are offered—and they can get pretty fancy, with fresh fruit and spritzers—but otherwise it's BYOB.

Hamburger Mary's. 2010 Main St., Wailuku. ☎ **808/244-7776.** Reservations suggested for dinner and Sunday brunch. Most items less than $8; Sun brunch $20. DISC, MC, V. Mon 10am–4pm, Tues–Sat 10am–9pm and bar until 2am; Sun brunch 10am–2pm. AMERICAN.

Hamburger Mary's is famous for its one-third-pound hamburgers and as a gay hangout. It's Wailuku's version of *Cheers*, a place where gays and straights are equally at home enjoying wholesome food in an upbeat atmosphere. Among the specialties: excellent homemade soups (fish chowder, spicy black bean, lentil) and burgers on three different types of bread, heaped high with vegetables and smothered in homemade dressings. Fans rave about the veggie burgers, crowned with grilled onions and homemade Thousand Island dressing. They're made with larger, meatier garden *steaks* (as opposed to garden *burgers*), and you can pile them high with sautéed mushrooms and other toppings for a small extra charge. Only fresh seafood is used, so pay attention to the specials—like the Sunday brunch, they're also très populaire.

Ichiban. In the Kahului Shopping Center, 47 Kaahumanu Ave., Kahului. ☎ **808/871-6977.** Main courses $4.25–$5.25 at breakfast, $4.25 and up at lunch (combination plates $8.50), $4.95–$26.95 at dinner (combination dinner $11.95, dinner specials $8.95 and up). MC, V. Mon–Fri 6:30am–2pm and 5–9pm, Sat 10:30am–2pm and 5–9pm. JAPANESE/SUSHI.

What a find: an informal neighborhood restaurant that serves inexpensive, home-cooked Japanese food *and* good sushi at realistic prices. Local residents consider Ichiban a staple for breakfast, lunch, or dinner and a haven of comforts: egg-white omelets, great saimin, combination plates (teriyaki chicken, teriyaki meat, *tonkatsu* (pork cutlet), rice, and pickled cabbage), chicken yakitori, and sushi—everything from unagi and scallop to California roll. The sushi items may not be inexpensive, but like the specials, such as steamed opakapaka for $18.75, it's a good value. *Tip:* We love the tempura, miso soup, and spicy ahi hand roll.

Marco's Grill & Deli. 444 Hana Hwy., Kahului. ☎ **808/877-4446.** Main courses $12.95–$19.95. AE, CB, DC, DISC, JCB, MC, V. Daily 7:30am–10pm (hot entrées from 10am). ITALIAN.

Located in the elbow of central Maui, where the roads to Upcountry, West, and South Maui converge, Marco's is popular among area residents who like its homemade Italian fare and friendly informality. This is one of those comfortable neighborhood fixtures favored by all generations who stop here for breakfast, lunch, and dinner, before and after movies, on the way to and from baseball games and concerts. The antipasto salad, vegetarian lasagna, and roasted peppers with garlic, provolone cheese, and anchovies are taste treats, but don't ignore the meatballs and Italian sausage; homemade and robust, they're served on French bread with all the trimming.

Maui Bake Shop. 2092 Vineyard St., Wailuku. ☎ **808/242-0064.** Most items under $5. AE, DC, DISC, MC, V. Mon–Fri 6am–5pm, Sat 7am–3pm. BAKERY/DELI.

Sleepy Vineyard Street has seen many a mom-and-pop business come and go, but Maui Bake Shop has come to stay. Maui native Claire Fujii-Krall and her husband, baker José Krall (who was trained in the South of France and throughout Europe), are turning out buttery brioches, healthy nine-grain and two-tone rye breads, focaccia, strudels, sumptuous fresh-fruit gâteaux, puff pastries, and dozens of other baked goods and confections. The breads are baked in one of Maui's oldest brick ovens, installed in 1935: a high-tech European diesel oven handles the rest. The front window displays the more than 100 bakery and deli items, among them salads, a popular eggplant marinara focaccia, homemade quiches, and a moist $3 calzone with chicken/pesto/mushroom/cheese filling. Homemade soups (clam chowder, minestrone, cream of asparagus) team up nicely with sandwiches on freshly baked bread, and they're light enough (well, almost) to justify the Ultimate Dessert: white-chocolate macadamia-nut cheesecake.

Restaurant Matsu. In the Maui Mall, 70 E. Kaahumanu Ave., Kahului. ☎ **808/871-0822.** Most items less than $6. No credit cards. Mon–Thurs 9am–6pm, Fri 9am–9pm, Sat 9am–5:30pm, Sun 10am–4pm. JAPANESE/LOCAL.

Customers have come from Hana (more than 50 miles away) just for Matsu's California rolls, while regulars line up for the cold saimin (julienned cucumber, egg, Chinese-style sweet pork, and red ginger on noodles) and the bento plates, various assemblages of chicken, teriyaki beef, fish, and rice, which make great take-out lunches for working folks and picnickers. The new nigiri sushi items are popular, especially for the don't-dally lunch crowd. The katsu pork and chicken, breaded and deep-fried, are other specialties of this casual Formica-style diner. I love the tempura udon and the saimin, steaming mounds of wide and fine noodles swimming in homemade broths and topped with condiments. The daily specials are a changing lineup of home-cooked classics: ox-tail soup, roast pork with gravy, teriyaki ahi, miso butterfish, and breaded mahi-mahi.

✪ A Saigon Cafe. 1792 Main St., Wailuku. ☎ **808/243-9560.** Main courses $6.50–$16.95. DC, MC, V. Mon–Sat 10am–9:30pm, Sun 10am–8:30pm. VIETNAMESE.

Saigon's feisty flavors find expression in Jennifer Nguyen's authentic Vietnamese cuisine, enjoying a sterling reputation even among picky Maui residents. There's no sign (the Maui grapevine is hyperactive), but it's always busy with regulars. The menu covers the gamut, from a dozen different soups to cold and hot noodles (including the popular beef noodle soup called *pho*) and chicken and shrimp cooked in a clay pot. Wok-cooked Vietnamese specialties—sautéed, with spicy lemongrass and sweet-and-sour sauces—highlight the produce of the season, and the fresh catch (ono, opaka-paka) comes whole and crisp or steamed with ginger and garlic. You can create your own Vietnamese "burritos" from a platter of tofu, noodles, and vegetables that you wrap in rice paper and dip in garlic sauce. Among my favorites are the shrimp lemongrass, piquant and refreshing, and the tofu curry, swimming in herbs and vegetables straight from the garden. The Nhung Dam, the Vietnamese version of fondue—a hearty spread of basil, cucumbers, mint, romaine, bean sprouts, pickled carrots, turnips, and vermicelli; wrapped in rice paper and dipped in a legendary sauce—is cooked at your table.

Sam Choy's Kahului. At Kaahumanu Center, 275 Kaahumanu Ave. (5 min from Kahului Airport on Hwy. 32), Kahului. ☎ **808/893-0366.** Reservations recommended. Breakfast main courses $4.25–$9.50, lunch main courses $4.95–$9.95, dinner main courses $22.95–$29.95. AE, DC, JCB, MC, V. Daily 7am–3pm, Sun–Thurs 5:30–9pm, Fri–Sat 5–9:30pm. LOCAL/HAWAII REGIONAL.

Sam Choy's restaurants have many layers. Maui-style favorites abound at breakfast and lunch, and at dinner, the menu shifts gears into much more sophisticated fare—but it's all tasty and all distinctively Sam Choy. This means gargantuan servings and such local ravishments as baked, stuffed shiitake mushrooms; a seafood sampler of mahimahi, lau-lau, macadamia-nut-crusted ono, and salmon Wellington; vegetarian tofu lasagna; Oriental lamb chops; Brie won ton (a favorite); and Sam's signature kapakahi mashed potatoes, a hit. At breakfast, residents gather for poke omelets, spinach and shiitake mushroom omelets, the morning's fresh catch with shiitake cream, Keanae taro cakes, and other local fantasies. The new dining room, smack in the middle of the shopping-center entrance, is impossible to miss.

Stanton's of Maui. In the Maui Mall, 70 E. Kaahumanu Ave., Kahului. (☎ **808/877-3711.** Most items less than $6.95. AE, DC, DISC, MC, V. Mon–Thurs and Sat 9am–6pm, Fri 9am–9pm. Live music Fri noon–2pm and 6–9pm, and Mon and Wed noon–2pm. COFFEESHOP/DELI.

Local Kaanapali coffee from Maui, Kona coffee from the Big Island, Ethiopian mocha, Haitian Blue French Roast, and many other versions of the bean are sold here in light, dark, decaf, and rotating flavors of the day. To accompany the high-octane libations is a small, attractive menu of soups, sandwiches, and salads (including a great vegetarian sandwich and homemade fishburgers). This being Maui, a growing list of vegetarian items is de rigueur and much appreciated. The lean machines love the tofu burger, piled high with sprouts, tomatoes, cucumbers, and a special dressing. If coffee isn't your cup of tea, there's a full bar.

WEST MAUI
LAHAINA

Maui's branch of the **Hard Rock Café** is in Lahaina at 900 Front St. (☎ **808/667-7400**). You'll find **Planet Hollywood** down the street at 744 Front St. (☎ **808/667-7877**).

Expensive

Avalon. 844 Front St. ☎ **808/667-5559.** Reservations recommended. Main courses $5.95–$15.95 at lunch, $14.95–$26.95 at dinner. AE, CB, DC, DISC, JCB, MC, V. Daily 11am–11pm. HAWAII REGIONAL.

Ten-year-old Avalon is now one of Mark and Judy Ellman's many Maui enterprises, which include six Maui Tacos "healthy Maui Mex" take-out stands. Avalon's signature dishes still tower (as in the salmon-tiki salad) and titillate (as in its signature Caramel Miranda dessert). Order and share appetizers! Crisp flavors from California, Indonesia, Thailand, China, Japan, and Vietnam include summer rolls, sugar snap peas, exotic stir-fries, potstickers, luau-roasted garlic seafood, black beans, and tamarind flavors. The chili-seared salmon tiki style, an edible high-rise of mashed potatoes, eggplants, greens, tomato salsa, and salmon with a plum vinaigrette, is one of the more flamboyant of Ellman's signature dishes. Caramel Miranda, the only dessert, is a heroic mound of macadamia-nut-brittle ice cream, caramel sauce, and exotic local fruit (the best of what's in season).

Chart House. 1450 Front St., at Honoapiilani Hwy. (Hwy. 30). ☎ **808/661-0937.** Also at 100 Wailea Ike Dr. in Wailea (☎ 808/637-8005) and 500 N. Puunene in Kahului (808/877-2476). Main courses $16.95–$44.95. AE, CB, DC, DISC, MC, V. Daily 5–10pm, lounge until 1am. AMERICAN.

Chart House restaurants have a knack for finding terrific locations with ocean views, and Lahaina has one of the best. Location is its strongest suit: Perched at the north end of Front Street, removed from congested Lahaina proper and elevated for optimal view, the restaurant offers a singular look at Lanai, Molokai, the ocean, and the sunset. Otherwise, expect the predictable fare that marks all Chart Houses: prime rib; East-West prawns and garlic steak; and an assortment of fresh fish in teriyaki, garlic-herb, and mayonnaise sauces. Especially indulgent is the mud pie, a weighty dessert of Kona coffee ice cream, Oreo cookie crust, fudge, almonds, and whipped cream.

★ **David Paul's Lahaina Grill.** 127 Lahainaluna Rd. ☎ **808/667-5117.** Reservations required. Main courses $19–$38. AE, CB, DC, DISC, MC, V. Daily 5:30–10pm. Bar, daily 5:30pm–midnight. NEW AMERICAN.

Nationally applauded and a recipient of numerous culinary awards, David Paul's is most people's favorite restaurant on Maui. On an island where excellent dining is as ubiquitous as Haleakala, that's saying a lot. With two restaurants, including a new one on Oahu, he's dividing his attention between two islands yet shows no signs of withering in creativity. His chic Lahaina oasis is located in a historic building next to the faithfully restored Lahaina Inn. Special custom-designed degustation dinners can be arranged with 48 hours' notice for parties of five to eight, but the daily menu is completely satisfying. The Kula salad is a masterpiece (olives, beet tops, feta cheese, Maui onions, a superb vinaigrette), the kalua duck is fork-tender, and there's a roster of other classics that keep diners returning: tequila shrimp with firecracker rice, spicy crab cake in a sesame-Dijon sauce, Kona coffee–roasted rack of lamb, and many other seductions. The bar is the busiest spot in Lahaina, and the ambiance—black-and-white tile floors, pressed tin ceilings, eclectic 1890s decor—is a good match for the cuisine.

Gerard's. Plantation Inn, 174 Lahainaluna Rd. ☎ **808/661-8939.** Reservations recommended. Main courses $26.50–$32.50. AE, DC, JCB, DISC, MC, V. Daily 6–10pm. FRENCH.

Winner of the *Wine Spectator* Award of Excellence for 1994, 1995, and 1997, Gerard's Gallic offerings still score high in this competitive culinary atmosphere. A worthy starter is the oyster and shiitake mushroom appetizer, savory and steaming in puff pastry, or the ahi tartar with taro chips, followed by the roasted Hawaiian snapper in a spicy orange and ginger-butter sauce. Gerard Reversade specializes in fresh seafood, which he buys daily from the fishermen at the harbor, then transforms into haute cuisine. Game lovers also have some sophisticated choices: venison with peppered sauce and poha-berry compote, Ulupalakua lamb and pork cassoulet, and a popular rosemary rack of lamb. His duck confit and filet mignon in mustard sauce are noteworthy as well. Gerard's is very accommodating with vegetarian requests.

Pacific'o Restaurant. 505 Front St. ☎ **808/667-4341.** Reservations recommended. Main courses $9–$14 at lunch, $19–$26 at dinner. AE, DC, MC, V. Daily 11am–4pm, 5:30–10pm. Live jazz Thurs–Sat 9pm–midnight. PACIFIC RIM/CONTEMPORARY PACIFIC.

You can't get closer to the ocean than the tables here, which are literally on the beach. The split-level dining starts at the top, near the entrance, with a long, cordial bar (where you can also order lunch or dinner) and some tables along the railing. Steps lead to the outdoor tables, where the award-winning seafood dishes come to you with the backdrop of Lanai across the channel. The restaurant's many awards include *Wine Spectator's* Award of Excellence for 1996 and '97, and three first-place awards for seafood in the Taste of Lahaina culinary festival in the last several years. You can't go wrong with the shrimp won ton appetizer or the shiso spicy tuna, seared and served over green papaya tomato salad with a miso sauce. The Asian gravlax is another winner, a marriage of house-cured salmon with sweet potato applejack, wasabi sour cream, and caviar. Fresh fish comes grilled, steamed in bamboo, bathed in Indonesian spices and Mandarin fennel sauce, fried tempura style, and coated in crisp coconut–macadamia with a Thai peanut-coconut sauce. Vegetarians love Pacific'o, too, for the marvelous quinoa-lentil-shiitake–Maui onion entrée with roasted tofu steak.

Moderate

Compadres Bar & Grill. In Lahaina Cannery Mall, 1221 Honoapiilani Hwy. ☎ 808/661-7189. Main courses $11.99–$18.50. DC, JCB, MC, V. Daily 8am–11:30pm. MEXICAN.

Despite its concrete floor and high industrial ceilings, Compadres exudes good cheer. And its food is classic Tex-Mex, good any time of the day, beginning with huevos rancheros, egg burritos, hotcakes, and omelets (the $7.99 Acapulco is heroic) and progressing to enchiladas and appetizers for the margarita-happy crowd. Stay spare (vegetable enchilada in fresh spinach tortilla, $9.50) or get hefty (Texas T-bone and enchiladas, $18.50); it's a carefree place with a large capacity for merrymaking.

✪ **Kimo's.** 845 Front St. ☎ 808/661-4811. Reservations recommended for dinner. Lunch $5.95–$10.95; dinner main courses $12.95–$23.95. AE, MC, V. Daily 11am–3pm and 5–10:30pm. STEAK/SEAFOOD.

Kimo's has a loyal following that keeps it from falling into the faceless morass of waterfront restaurants serving surf-and-turf with great sunset views. It's a formula restaurant (sibling to Leilani's and the Hula Grill) that works not only because of its oceanfront patio and upstairs dining room, but because, for the price, there are some satisfying choices. It's always crowded, buzzing with people having fun on a deck that takes in Molokai, Lanai, and Kahoolawe. Burgers and sandwiches are affordable and reliable, and the fresh catch in garlic-lemon and a sweet-basil glaze is a top seller, rivaling the hefty prime rib, complete with salad, carrot muffins, herb rolls, and herb rice. Keep in mind that the waistline-defying hula pie—macadamia-nut ice cream in a chocolate-wafer crust with fudge and whipped cream—originated here.

Lahaina Coolers. 180 Dickensen St. ☎ 808/661-7082. Most items less than $14. AE, MC, V. Daily 7–11:15am and 11:30am–midnight; bar until 2am. AMERICAN.

A huge marlin hangs above the bar, and epic wave shots and wall sconces made of surfboard fins line the walls at this indoor/outdoor restaurant, with open windows on three sides taking advantage of the shade trees to create a cordial, cheerful ambiance. The bar is open until 2am, so you can go from the Surfer Special (a gourmet bean burrito) or fruit pancakes to the famous mango daiquiri at the end of the day. The pasta machine is a special touch for a place that's more Beach Boys than Puccini. Great bites: shrimp pesto linguine, smoked salmon fettuccine in dill-caper–cream sauce, and nightly steak and fish specials at $16 to $18.50, two of Lahaina's terrific deals. The Evil Jungle Pizza, grilled chicken in a spicy Thai peanut sauce, is a novelty and one of several successful "tropic pizzas." A big plus: Everything can be prepared as vegetarian upon request.

Lahaina Fish Company. 831 Front St. ☎ 808/661-3472. Main courses $7.95–$22.95. AE, JCB, MC, V. Daily 11am–midnight. SEAFOOD.

The open-air dining room is literally over the water, with flickering torches after sunset and an affordable menu that covers the seafood-pasta basics. If you have to wait for a table—and many people do—the beach end of Hammerheads Fish Bar, with the draft from the huge refrigerator, is not where you want to be. Between noon and 3pm, head to an oceanside table and order a cheeseburger, chickenburger, fishburger, a generous basket of peel-and-eat shrimp, or sashimi; lingering is highly recommended. From noon to 5pm, mai tais are $2.50—a big attraction to accompany the appetizer-happy menu. Nightly specials range from island fish and chips to several pastas; standard steak-and-seafood combos; and four types of fresh island fish prepared in Asian, American, and European styles.

Inexpensive

Aloha Mixed Plate. 1285 Front St., Lahaina. ☎ **808/661-3322.** Main courses $2.95–$9.95. MC, V. Mon–Wed and Sun 10:30am–10pm, Thurs–Sat 10:30am–1am. PLATE LUNCH/NOODLE HOUSE.

The operators of the Old Lahaina Luau have moved north in a big way. Recently, they opened this eatery in a charming, freestanding, plantation-style building directly across the Lahaina Cannery Mall, to be followed later in 1998 with a move of the luau from its 505 Front St. location to a spot next door. At Aloha Mixed Plate, you can sit on an open deck under umbrellas and tuck into inexpensive mahi-mahi, kalua pig and cabbage, shoyu chicken, teriyaki beef, and other local plate-lunch specials, all less than $5. Garden burgers and hamburgers cost even less. Five ethnic noodle dishes, including Thai noodles, udon, saimin, and chow fun, round out what is a great concept in informal—and mostly pricey—Lahaina.

Cheeseburger in Paradise. 811 Front St. ☎ **808/661-4855.** Main courses $5.95–$9.95. AE, MC, V. Daily 8am–10:15pm. AMERICAN.

Wildly successful, always crowded, highly visible, and very noisy with its live music in the evenings, Cheeseburger is a shrine to the American classic. This is burger country, tropical style, with everything from tofu and garden burgers to the biggest, juiciest beef and chicken burgers, served on whole-wheat and sesame buns baked fresh daily. There are good reasons why the two-story green-and-white building next to the seawall is always packed: good value, good grinds, and a great ocean view. The Cheeseburger in Paradise—a hefty hunk with Jack and Cheddar cheeses, sautéed onions, lettuce, fresh tomatoes, and Thousand Island dressing—is a paean to the basics. You can build your own burger by adding sautéed mushrooms, bacon, grilled ortega chiles, and other condiments for an extra charge. Onion rings, chili-cheese fries, and cold beer complete the carefree fantasy.

Groovy Smoothies. 708 Front St. ☎ **808/661-8219.** Smoothies less than $4.50. No credit cards. Daily 9am–9:30pm. SMOOTHIES.

This closet-size take-out stand makes the best smoothies in Lahaina. But if they're too pure for you, there are always muffins, espresso, and danishes. We love the mango-and-banana smoothie, but others may pine for the piña colada, the Elvis Peachly, or any of the berry delights. Protein powders, bee pollen, and other nutritious ingredients can be blended into these tasty, healthy treats.

Village Pizzeria. 505 Front St. ☎ **808/661-8112.** Salad and pizza $3.95; $6.95–$24.50 for main courses and special pizzas. AE, DC, DISC, MC, V. Daily 11am–9:30pm. PIZZA.

With thin or thick crust, more than a dozen toppings, and the signature clam-and-garlic pizza that you can smell from around the corner, this pizzeria draws a steady stream of diners to its corner cafe at the popular shopping complex called 505 Front. Appetizers, sandwiches (on homemade bread), pasta, and famous tiramisu make this more than a pizza joint.

KAANAPALI

Beachside Grill and Leilani's on the Beach. In Whaler's Village, 2435 Kaanapali Pkwy. ☎ **808/661-4495.** Reservations suggested for dinner. Lunch (Beachside Grill) $5.95–$9.95; dinner (Leilani's) $10.95–$35.95. AE, DC, DISC, MC, V. Beachside Grill, daily 11am–11pm (bar, daily until 12:30am); Leilani's, daily 5–10pm. STEAK/SEAFOOD.

The Beachside Grill is the informal, less-expensive room downstairs on the beach, where folks wander in off the sand for a frothy beer and a beachside burger. Leilani's is the dinner-only room, with more expensive but still not outrageously priced steak and seafood offerings. At Leilani's, spinach, cheese, and mushroom raviolis cost $10.95, while the lobster and steak are at the higher market price. Still, children can order a quarter-pound hamburger for $4.95 or broiled chicken breast for $2 more—a value for sure. Pasta, rack of lamb, a $25.95 filet mignon, and Alaskan king crab at market price are among the temptations in the upstairs room. Although the steak-and-lobster combinations can be a pricey $35.95, the good thing about Leilani's is the strong middle range of entrée prices, with fresh fish for $19.95. I love the informality of both rooms, but the Beachside Grill is geared toward the budget-conscious (seafood chowder is $3.50, and a fillet of ono burger goes for $7.95).

This is a lively spot, with live Hawaiian music every afternoon except Fridays, when the Rock 'n' Roll Aloha Friday set gets those decibels climbing. Free concerts are usually offered on a stage outside the restaurant on the last Sunday of the month. The popular program, Music on the Beach, is always a big draw—and another big reason to love Leilani's. Any way you cut it, the view, food, prices, and location make this a hard-to-beat Kaanapali staple.

⭐ **Hula Grill.** In Whaler's Village, 2435 Kaanapali Pkwy. ☎ **808/667-6636.** Reservations recommended for dinner. Lunch and Barefoot Bar menus $5.95–$11.95; dinner main courses $14.95–$35. AE, MC, V. Barefoot Bar, daily 11am–midnight, dining room, daily 5–9:30pm. HAWAII REGIONAL/SEAFOOD.

Who wouldn't want to be tucking into poisson cru, crab and corn cakes, or ahi poke rolls under a thatched umbrella, with a sand floor and palm trees at arm's length and a view of Lanai across the channel? What a cheerful place this is, a Kaanapali magnet, *the* place to dine while watching swimmers and catamarans bobbing in the sea. Peter Merriman, a culinary guru and one of the originators of Hawaii Regional Cuisine, segued seamlessly from his smallish, Big Island upcountry enclave to this large, high-volume dining room on the beach. He has redefined chain-restaurant cuisine.

Hula Grill is one of those dining rooms with a wide choice in prices and choices; although it can be expensive, it doesn't have to be. The superb menu includes Merriman's signature wok-charred ahi; firecracker mahi-mahi (baked in tomato, chili, and cumin aïoli); scallop and lobster potstickers; crab and corn cakes; and six different fresh-fish preparations, including his famous ahi poke rolls, lightly sautéed rare ahi wrapped in rice paper with Maui onions. Lunchtime burgers are de rigueur, or order gourmet appetizers from the Barefoot Bar menu (macadamia-nut/crab won tons, fresh ono fish and chips, pizza, smoked-turkey sandwiches). There's happy-hour entertainment from 3 to 5pm daily, and Hawaiian music with a hula dancer from 6:30 to 9pm.

Pizza Paradiso. In Whaler's Village, 2435 Kaanapali Pkwy. ☎ **808/667-0333.** Breakfast pizza $3.35–$3.85 (by the slice); 12-inch pizzas $12.99–$18. No credit cards. Daily 7:30am–9:30pm. PIZZA.

From the Nutty Vegan to the Maui Wowie (with ham and pineapple), the Jimmy Hoffa (pepperoni and mozzarella), the Godfather (roasted chicken, artichoke hearts, sundried tomatoes, the works), and the Clam Slam (with juicy clams and tons of garlic), these pizzas are always described in superlatives, even by jaded New Yorkers. It's not *totally* Little Italy (there's even Thai chicken pizza with spicy peanut sauce), but the crust, sauce, and toppings earn high ratings in flavor and quality. Create your own pizza with a long menu of possibilities (roasted eggplants, mushrooms, anchovies, artichoke hearts, MacNut pesto, and more), and enjoy it in this mallish fast-food atmosphere or take it to Kaanapali Beach, just a few steps away.

Spats. In the Hyatt Regency Maui, 200 Nohea Kai Dr. ☎ **808/661-1234.** Reservations recommended. Main courses $20–$30. AE, DISC, MC, V. Daily 6–10pm. ITALIAN.

Spats is all seduction: Descend the stairs to the lavishly Italianate entrance and behold the chandeliers, titian reds, and host of sensory stimuli, including the aroma of garlic and tomato and an Italian aria over the sound system. It used to be a lot more upright than it is today; one female server even wore a visor during dinner. The Spats salad is notable, a celebration of simplicity and freshness. The puttanesca and assorted pastas get appreciative nods, and the service is excellent. For dessert, the tiramisu is lighter and cakier than most, delicious without being frothy.

Swan Court. In the Hyatt Regency Maui, 200 Nohea Kai Dr. ☎ **808/661-1234.** Reservations recommended for dinner. Main courses $28–$36. AE, DC, DISC, JCB, MC, V. Daily 6:30–11:30am, 6–10pm. CONTINENTAL.

Even as a resort restaurant, Swan Court is hard to resist. But come here as a splurge or on a bottomless expense account, and enjoy its continental menu in incomparable surroundings. The combination of waterfalls, ocean view, Japanese gardens, and swans and flamingos serenely gliding by is irresistibly romantic, especially with alfresco dining and appropriately extravagant fare. The menu changes nightly in this tiered dining room. Hunan marinated lamb chops and the island-style bouillabaisse are perennial favorites, but many other seafood and game specials will compete for your attention.

KAHANA/NAPILI

Fish & Games Sports Grill. In Kahana Gateway Shopping Center, 4405 Honoapiilani Hwy. ☎ **808/669-3474.** Reservations recommended for dinner. Main courses $6.95–$10.95 at lunch, $13.95–$25.95 at dinner. AE, CB, DC, DISC, JCB, MC, V. Daily 11am–3pm, happy hour 3–5:30pm, dinner 6–10pm, late-night menu 10:30pm–1am. SEAFOOD.

One of the owners is a major fresh-seafood distributor for Maui, so guess what the specialties are. A recent expansion has added space, a microbrewery, and a new rotisserie oven to the seafood delights in this formerly unremarkable corner of a mall in Kahana. Fish & Games is friendly, busy, and secure in the knowledge that it is well-liked by the Napili crowd. A constant stream of fresh clams, oysters, fish, and mussels flows out of the kitchen. A small retail section sells fresh seafood, and the menu for sitdown covers basic tastes, but covers them well: an oyster bar, soups, salads, and sandwiches for lunch, and seafood pastas and entrées for dinner, with a flame-broiled New York steak (with homemade Cognac-green peppercorn sauce), rack of lamb, and steak/seafood combinations for heftier tastes.

Maui Tacos. In Napili Plaza, 5095 Napili Hau St. ☎ **808/665-0222.** Also in Kaahumanu Center, Kahului (☎ 808/871-7726); Lahaina Square, Lahaina (☎ 808/661-8883); and Kamaole Beach Center, Kihei (☎ 808/665-0222). Most items less than $6.95. No credit cards. Mon–Sat 11am–9pm, Sun 11am–8pm. MEXICAN.

Mark Ellman of Lahaina's Avalon fame put gourmet Mexican on paper plates and on the island's culinary map. Barely more than a take-out counter with a few tables, this and the other three Maui Tacos on the island are the rage of hungry surfers, discerning diners, burrito buffs, and Hollywood glitterati, like Sharon Stone, whose picture adorns a wall or two. The food is worth seeking out: excellent fresh-fish tacos, chimichangas, searing salsas, and mouth-breaking compositions such as the Hookipa, a "surf burrito" of fresh fish, black beans, and salsa. The green-spinach burrito contains four kinds of beans, rice, and potatoes—a knockout.

✪ **Roy's Kahana Bar & Grill/Roy's Nicolina Restaurant.** Kahana Gateway, 4405 Honoapiilani Hwy. ☎ **808/669-6999.** Reservations strongly suggested. Main courses $13–$26. AE, CB, DC, DISC, JCB, MC, V. Roy's Kahana, daily 5:30–10pm; Roy's Nicolina, daily 5:30–9:30pm. EURO-ASIAN.

These two sibling restaurants are next door to each other, have the same menu, and are busy, busy, busy. They bustle with young, hip servers impeccably trained to deliver blackened ahi or perfectly seared lemongrass shutome (broadbill swordfish) hot to your table, in rooms that sizzle with cross-cultural tastings. Both are known for their rack of lamb and fresh seafood (usually eight or nine choices), and for the large, open kitchens that turn out everything from pizza to sake-grilled New York steak and roasted half-chickens in garlic and orange, glistening in cardamom and cabernet sauce. If potstickers are on the menu, don't resist. Large picture windows open up Roy's Kahana but don't quell the noise, another tireless trail long ago established by Roy's Restaurant in Honolulu, the flagship of Roy Yamaguchi's burgeoning empire. Roy's Nicolina now features dining on the lanai.

KAPALUA

The Bay Club. Kapalua Bay Hotel & Villas. ☎ **808/669-5656.** Reservations recommended for dinner. Dress code at dinner: collared shirts and long slacks for men; no jeans, shorts, or T-shirts for women. Main courses $24–$38. AE, CB, JCB, MC, V. Daily 11:30am–2pm, 6–9:30pm. SEAFOOD.

Tried and true, The Bay Club is one of Maui's lasting pleasures. The classic enjoyments—a stellar view, beatific sunsets, attentive service from bow-tied servers—are matched by a seafood menu that has lost none of its luster with the years. The Caesar salad is still tossed tableside, the seafood is fresh, the peppered steak just so, the vegetarian dishes quite elegant. Duck, rack of lamb, bouillabaisse, excellent salads, fresh catches, sandwiches and pasta for lunch, and a host of simple delights can be enjoyed in this open-air dining room with a view that changes as the sun moves south, eventually to set behind Lanai in the winter months.

Jameson's Grill & Bar at Kapalua. 200 Kapalua Dr. (at the 18th hole of the Kapalua Golf Course). ☎ **808/669-5653.** Reservations recommended for dinner. Lunch $5.95–$11.95; main courses $6.95–$12.95 on the cafe menu, $15.95–$39.95 at dinner. AE, DC, DISC, JCB, MC, V. Daily 8am–10pm; breakfast, lunch available 8am–3pm, cafe menu 3–10pm, dinner 5–10pm daily. AMERICAN.

This is the quintessential country-club restaurant, open-air with mountain views—and the familiar Jameson's mix of fresh fish (sautéed, wok-seared, or grilled), stuffed shrimp, prawns, rack of lamb, ahi steak, and other basic surf-and turf selections for dinner. At lunch, for duffers dashing to make tee time, Golf Sandwiches are $5.95 for roast beef, turkey, tuna salad, or a hot dog. Other choices catering to the sports set: fish and chips, patty melt, crab cakes, and an affordable cafe menu with gourmet appetizers (potstickers), Thai summer rolls, seared sashimi, baked artichoke). At dinner, herb-roasted chicken is a favorite for $18.95, pasta for $16.95, and ahi au poivre for $23.95, with many temptations in between.

Plantation House. 200 Plantation Club Dr. (right at Kapalua Plantation Golf Course). ☎ **808/669-6299.** Reservations recommended. Main courses $18–$24. AE, MC, V. Daily 8am–3pm, 5:30–10pm. SEAFOOD/ISLAND REGIONAL.

With its teak tables, fireplace, and open sides, Plantation House gets high marks for ambiance: the 360° view from high among the resort's pine-studded hills takes in Molokai and Lanai (they look close enough to touch), the ocean, the rolling fairways and greens, the northwestern flanks of the West Maui Mountains, and the daily sunset spectacular. Readers of the *Maui News* have deemed this the island's "Best Ambiance"—a big honor on this island of ubiquitous views. Choices include fresh fish prepared seven ways—among them, Mediterranean (seared), Upcountry (sautéed with Maui onions and vegetable stew), Island (pan-seared in sweet sake and chile-sesame sauce), Asian Pacific (charred with Asian mushrooms and sake sauce), and Rich Forest (with roasted wild mushrooms), the top seller. Salads, using fresh Maui produce, are also strong. The menu is bolstered by other seafood, pasta, and meat entrées, such as the rosemary-infused double-cut lamb chops at dinner, also a hit.

Sansei Seafood Restaurant and Sushi Bar. At the Kapalua Shops, 115 Bay Dr. ☎ 808/669-6286. Reservations recommended. Main courses $15–$19.75. AE, DC, DISC, MC, V. Sat–Wed 5:30–10pm, sushi bar until 11pm; Thurs–Fri 5:30pm–1am. SEAFOOD/SUSHI.

People drive from central Maui to dine here, and that's a long drive. Why do they come? Part Japanese fusion, part Hawaii Regional Cuisine, and all parts sushi, Sansei is tirelessly creative, with a menu that manages to please both purists and the adventurous. Nori ravioli of shrimp, opah, and Chinese sausage with shiitake-mushroom sauce. Roasted Japanese eggplant with a sweet miso sauce. Sashimi trio. Ahi carpaccio. Udon and ramen. Lobster tail. Traditional shrimp and vegetable tempura. The Asian rock shrimp cake in ginger-lime chili butter and cilantro pesto is a first-place "Taste of Lahaina" winner, but there is simpler fare as well, such as pastas and wok-tossed upcountry vegetables. Oh—the desserts: tempura fried ice cream with chocolate sauce, crème brûlée, and an autumn phenomenon, persimmon crème brûlée, made with Kula persimmons.

SOUTH MAUI
KIHEI/MAALAEA
Expensive

✪ **A Pacific Cafe Maui.** In Azeka Place II, 1279 S. Kihei Rd. ☎ 808/879-0069. Reservations recommended. Main courses $24.75–$32. AE, DC, CB, MC, V. Daily 5:30–10pm. HAWAII REGIONAL.

This restaurant is busy every night of the week, so make your reservations as early as possible, because it's difficult to get in. You'll dine on rattan chairs at hammered-copper tables, under very high ceilings, in a room bordered with windows overlooking the parking lot (but you'll be so busy enjoying the food, you won't notice the lack of view). From the open kitchen and a menu that changes daily comes a stream of marvels: the signature tiger-eye ahi sushi tempura, light and delectable; garlic-sesame, pan-seared mahi-mahi, a Pacific Café staple; salmon firecracker rolls; pan-seared sea scallops with herb-polenta crust; and many others. Jean-Marie Josselin, chef extraordinaire, recently introduced hormone-free, Hawaii-grown specialty meats, such as lamb, elk, veal, and Kobe beef.

Carelli's on the Beach. 2980 S. Kihei Rd. ☎ 808/875-0001. Reservations recommended. Main courses $22–$38. AE, MC, V. Daily 6–10pm, bar until 11pm. ITALIAN/SEAFOOD.

Kihei's well-tanned, chicly attired trendy come here for pasta, seafood, and the view. It is stupendous: With its prime on-the-sand location at Keawakapu Beach, you can view the sunset in ravishing surroundings over cioppino (the most popular item, at $36), fresh fish, ravioli, carpaccio, and other Italian favorites. The wood-burning brick oven turns out great pizzas, and the food is top-drawer. To sit at a table on the dining floor, though, a $25 minimum order is required.

Steve Amaral's Cucina Pacifica. Upstairs in the Rainbow Mall, 2439 S. Kihei Rd., no. 201A. ☎ 808/875-7831. Reservations recommended. Main courses $15–$28. DC, DISC, MC, V. Daily 5:30pm–closing. MEDITERRANEAN/SEAFOOD.

Kihei is shaping up to be quite a dining destination. Amaral's new restaurant is stirring up excitement with a menu that features the best of Mediterranean culinary traditions *and* a striking way with fresh Maui ingredients, seafood, and vegetables. Maui/Mediterranean, I like to call it. The menu changes seasonally to honor and use fresh seasonal produce. In the winter: Italian winter truffle and potato soup; Tuscan bean soup with pancetta; spicy elk sausage with slow-cooked fagioli in garlic sage; wild-mushroom risotto; spanakopita of pan-seared diver scallops (with spinach, feta, pine nuts, and nine-olive tapenade!); Spanish stew of clams, mussels, shrimp, and scallops; and something as simple as four-cheese manicotti. The remarkable menu and Amaral's irrepressible imagination cater to anyone who loves good food. The vegetarian sampler—a medley of grilled zucchini, wild mushrooms, polenta, couscous, garlic mashed potatoes, and pan-seared tofu—is a triumph.

The Waterfront at Maalaea. Maalaea Harbor, 50 Hauoli St. ☎ **808/244-9028.** Reservations recommended. Main courses $18–$38. AE, DC, DISC, JCB, MC, V. Daily 11:30am–1:30pm, 5:30–8:30pm (last seating). SEAFOOD.

The Waterfront has won awards for wine excellence, service, and seafood, but its biggest boost is word of mouth. Loyal diners rave about the friendly staff and seafood, served in simple surroundings with a bay and harbor view. You have nine choices of preparations for the five to eight varieties of fresh Hawaiian fish, ranging from en papillote (baked in buttered parchment) to Southwestern (smoked chili and cilantro butter) to light cuisine (broiled or poached, then topped with steamed, fresh vegetables). The baked triple-cream Danish appetizer is an excellent starter, but there are so many choices: Kula onion soup, an excellent Caesar salad, lobster chowder. Vegetarians favor the grilled eggplant layered with Maui onions, tomatoes, and spinach, served with red-pepper coulis and Big Island goat cheese.

Moderate

Buzz's Wharf. Maalaea Harbor, 50 Hauoli St. ☎ **808/244-5426.** Reservations suggested. Main courses $10.95–$24.95. AE, CB, DC, DISC, JCB, MC, V. Daily 11am–10pm. AMERICAN.

Buzz's is another formula restaurant that offers a superb view, substantial sandwiches, meaty French fries, and surf-and-turf fare that's satisfying but not sensational. Still, this bright, airy dining room is a fine way station for whale-watching over a cold beer and a fresh mahi-mahi sandwich with fries, or if you're feeling extravagant, the house specialty, Prawns Tahitian ($18.95 at lunch, $24.95 for dinner). Many diners opt for several appetizers (stuffed mushrooms, steamer clams, clam chowder, onion soup) and a salad (there are three different types of Caesar). It's hard to keep the resolve at dessert time: Buzz's prize-winning dessert—Tahitian Baked Papaya, a warm, fragrant melding of fresh papaya with vanilla and coconut—is the pride of the house.

The Greek Bistro. 2511 S. Kihei Rd. ☎ **808/879-9330.** Reservations recommended. Combination and family-style dinners $14.95–$21.95 per person; family-style platter $35 for 2. Children's portions also available for considerably less. AE, DC, CB, JCB, MC, V. Daily 5–10pm. GREEK.

The banana trees, yellow ginger, and hibiscus that surround the tile-floored terrace add immeasurably to the dining experience at this indoor/outdoor bistro, especially in chaotic Kihei. Homemade pita bread, quality feta and spices, classic spanakopita (spinach pie in microthin layers of phyllo dough), and chicken and lamb souvlaki (the Greek version of shish kebab) are some of the authentic and well-received Mediterranean offerings. Popular items include the family-style combination platters, lamb kebabs ($19.95), and the fresh fish of the day ($21.95). Also popular is the Greek lasagna; chopped lamb and beef with cinnamon and cheeses; and the Mediterranean chicken breast, an elaborate platter of mushroom-and-wine-infused organic skinless chicken, served with linguine and vegetables.

Hapa's Brew Haus & Restaurant. In the Lipoa Shopping Center, 41 E. Lipoa St. ☎ **808/879-9001.** Reservations recommended. Main courses $8–$18.95. AE, DISC, JCB, MC, V. Daily 11am–2am. BREW HOUSE/INTERNATIONAL.

Food, beer, and music are the primary offerings here. Besides being a full-service restaurant and a nightclub, it's also a microbrewery with four lagers to accompany the seafood, prime rib, sandwiches, gourmet pizza, and pasta on the menu. The appetizers—blackened ahi ($9.50), potstickers ($7.50), steamer clams ($9.95), baked artichoke ($7.95)—reflect the gregarious, happy-hour nature of the place. Some top happy-hour specials: From 5 to 6pm daily, they serve free pizza and $2 drafts—a happy marriage indeed. Gourmet pizzas come heaped with grilled chicken, pesto shrimp, clams, garlic sauce, vegetables, and any number of combinations, on thin or thick crust. On Sundays from 2 to 6pm, members of the Maui Symphony Swing Band take over the stage and play swing music. It's worth searching out this bistro from among the faceless strip malls of Kihei, because it works hard to keep up the value. (See also "Maui After Dark," p. 475).

Stella Blues Cafe & Deli. In Long's Center, 1215 S. Kihei Rd. ☎ **808/874-3779.** Main courses $9.95–$16.95. DISC, MC, V. Daily 8am–9pm. AMERICAN.

Stella Blues gets going at breakfast and continues through to dinner with something for everyone—vegetarians, children, pasta and sandwich lovers, hefty steak eaters, and sensible diners who'll spring for the $2.50 fresh Kula green salad. Grateful Dead posters line the walls of this corner cafe, and a covey of gleaming motorcycles is invariably parked outside. It's loud and lively, casual and unpretentious. Sandwiches are the highlight, two dozen selections ranging from Tofu Extraordinaire to Mom's egg salad on croissant to garden burgers and grilled chicken. Tofu wraps and the mountain-size Cobb salads are popular, and for the carefree, large coffee shakes with mounds of whipped cream. The Stella Special is a hit—spiced grilled eggplant with roasted garlic and sweet red peppers, feta cheese, and greens with pesto mayonnaise on homemade herb bread. At dinner, selections are geared toward good-value family dining, from affordable full dinners (Thai sweet-chili chicken for $14.95, including rice pilaf or potato, vegetable of the day, fresh Kula greens, and French bread) to pastas and burgers.

Inexpensive

✪ **Alexander's Fish & Chicken & Chips.** 1913 S. Kihei Rd. ☎ **808/874-0788.** Fish and chips $6.75–$9.50. MC, V. Daily 11am–9pm. FISH & CHIPS/SEAFOOD.

Look for the ocean mural in front, Kalama Park across the street, and a marketplace next door: This is Alexander's, a friendly neighborhood take-out stand with patio seating outside and a very busy kitchen. Fresh ono, mahi-mahi, and ahi, broiled or fried, fly out of the kitchen with baskets of French fries or rice. Equally popular are the 13-piece shrimp, chicken, oyster, calamari, rib, or fish baskets for $16.50 to $19.95. Fresh fish, Cajun chicken, teriyaki chicken, barbecued beef, and shrimp sandwiches, along with onion rings, cornbread, chicken wings, and other side orders in a light and tasty batter, make this a budget-friendly family favorite. And they use canola oil!

The Coffee Store. In Azeka's Place II, 1279 Kihei Rd. ☎ **808/875-4244.** All items less than $8.50. AE, CB, DC, DISC, MC, V. Sun–Thurs 6am–10pm, Fri–Sat 6am–11pm. COFFEEHOUSE.

This simple, classic coffeehouse for caffeine connoisseurs serves two dozen different types of coffee and coffee drinks, from mochas, lattés, and frappés to cappuccino, espresso, and toddies. Breakfast items include smoothies, lox and bagels, quiches, granola, and assorted pastries. Pizza, salads, vegetarian lasagne, veggie-and-shrimp quesadillas, and sandwiches (garden burger, tuna, turkey, ham, grilled veggie panini) also move briskly from the take-out counter. The turkey and veggie tortilla-wrapped sandwiches are a hit at $6.50. There are only a few small tables and they fill up fast, often with musicians and artists who spent the previous evening entertaining at the Wailea and Kihei resorts.

Hawaiian Moons Pizza & Deli. 2411 Kihei Rd., Kihei. ☎ **808/875-4356.** Pizzas $15.50-$20.95; sandwiches $5.50-$7.50. Sun–Thurs 11am–7pm, Fri–Sat 11am–9pm (pizzas on Fri–Sat nights only) PIZZA/DELI.

My favorite Kihei health-food store also runs this deli/pizzeria, which serves healthy gourmet salads, sandwiches, and smoothies, always with wholesome ingredients. Among the special touches: It uses unbleached, organically grown wheat for the pizza flour, organically grown herbs and tomatoes, and free-range, antibiotic- and chemical-free turkey and chicken. Although pizzas are baked only on weekends, they are sensational: healthy, Maui style, with gourmet toppings and fresh Maui produce—and loads of flavor. I love the deli sandwiches (tempeh burger, roasted vegetarian, smoked turkey, vegetarian, and other choices) with their fresh vegetables and homemade dressings, but the lasagne and a salad are hard to beat.

Peggy Sue's. In Azeka Place II, 1279 S. Kihei Rd. ☎ **808/875-8944.** Main courses $5.95–$9.25, milkshakes $3.75. DC, MC, V. Sun–Thurs 11am–9pm, Fri–Sat 11am–10pm. AMERICAN.

Just for a moment, forget that diet and take a leap. Peggy Sue's, a fifties-style diner with oodles of charm, is a swell place to spring for a chocolate malt and French fries. You'll find the best chocolate malt on the island here, as well as sodas, milkshakes, floats, and egg creams. Pink, yellow, and green old-fashioned soda-shop stools; an Elvis Presley Boulevard sign; and jukeboxes on every Formica table provide the visuals. Burgers go for $6 to $11, and they're famous—more round than flat, brushed with teriyaki sauce, served with all the goodies. The plate lunches—chicken, steak, mahimahi—sell for $5 to $10, but there are garden burgers for the discreet. We think the Maui-made Roselani ice cream is why the malts are so creamy.

Señor Taco. In the Dolphin Shopping Plaza, 2395 S. Kihei Rd. ☎ **808/875-2910.** Prices $1.90–$6.50. No credit cards. Mon–Sat 10am–9pm. TACOS/MEXICAN.

The smells and menu—beef-tongue tacos, smoked meat with chile sauce, chimichangas, steak burritos, fresh-fish tacos, and many other savory concoctions— exude authenticity. Beef, chicken, steak, and the popular pork burrito (top of the line at $6.25); beef, chicken, and potato chimichangas ($6.50, including rice and beans); and a $5.75 combination plate are tasty and affordable, and nothing less than the real thing. On these as well as the daily specials, Oscar Del Campo, whose mother's secret recipes are featured, makes a promise not to disappoint.

Shaka Sandwich & Pizza. 1295 S. Kihei Rd. ☎ **808/874-0331.** Sandwiches $3.75–$8; pizzas $12.95–$25.95. Daily 10:30am–9pm (deliveries daily 10:30am–9pm) PIZZA.

Award-winning pizzas share the limelight with New York-style hoagies and Philly cheese steaks, and they're all top-drawer. Shaka uses fresh Maui produce, long-simmering homemade sauces, and homemade Italian bread. Choose thin or Sicilian thick crust with gourmet toppings: Maui onions, spinach, anchovies, jalapeño peppers, and a spate of other vegetables. Don't be misled by the whiteness of the white pizza; with the perfectly balanced flavors of olive oil, garlic, and cheese, you won't even miss the tomato sauce. Clam-and-garlic pizza, spinach pizza (with olive oil, spinach, garlic, and mozzarella), and the Shaka Supreme (with at least 11 toppings!) will satisfy even the insatiable.

WAILEA

Joe's Bar & Grill. At the Wailea Tennis Club, 131 Wailea Ike Place. ☎ **808/875-7767.** Reservations recommended. Main items $17–$30. AE, DC, MC, V. Daily 5:30–10:30pm. AMERICAN GRILL.

Beverly Gannon's style of American home-cooking with a regional twist is inspiring and inimitable, with hearty staples you're not likely to forget: mashed potatoes (including Molokai mashed potatoes), perhaps the best you'll have on Maui; grilled applewood salmon, the signature item, smoky and sublime; mixed grill of mushrooms with spinach, tomatoes, toasted walnuts, and crumbled Roquefort; grilled lamb chops; chocolate cake, layered with bittersweet chocolate, with a hint of orange. The 360° view spans the golf course, tennis courts, ocean, and Haleakala. At night, the theater lighting, 43-foot copper bar, high ceilings, plank floors, and Julia Child's familiar nasal voice in the ladies-room sound system ("Here we go! There you are! Some elegant cheese soufflé!") all add up to an enormously pleasing dining experience.

Kea Lani Restaurant. Kea Lani Hotel, 4100 Wailea Alanui Dr. ☎ **808/875-4100.** Reservations preferred for dinner. Main courses $26–$38. AE, DC, JCB, MC, V. Daily 6:30–11am, 5:30–10pm. EURO-PACIFIC.

The organic herb garden still fuels the kitchens of Kea Lani, where the Grand Chefs on Tour series presents culinary explorations on a regular basis. The year-round programs unite renowned chefs from Hawaii and the mainland for tastings, demonstrations, and bountiful dinners. Breakfast in this open-air dining room is a generous buffet with cornucopian carts that spill over with lilikoi, figs, star fruit, avocados, coconuts, mangoes and litchis (in season), herbs, edible flowers, and countless other colorful things from the garden and throughout Maui. From its hollandaise sauce to its home-cured Canadian bacon, the eggs Benedict ($11.50) is perfect. The dining room reopens for fine dining at dinner, when it's transformed into a Mediterranean fantasy: ocean view, candlelight flickering over tile floors, and a menu of Pacific Rim specialties. Diners report favorably on the ginger hoisin hibachi rack of lamb with plum wine sauce and the nori-wrapped ono, prepared à la California, with crab, avocado, and wasabi beurre blanc.

Maui Onion. Renaissance Wailea Beach Resort, 3550 Wailea Alanui Dr. ☎ **808/879-4900.** Most items less than $13.50. AE, DISC, JCB, MC, V. Daily 11am–5:30pm. AMERICAN.

Poolside dining on patio furniture, under a canopy of white alamandra blossoms dripping from vines in the trellises, with an ocean view—that's Maui Onion. I recommend it for the bold souls who love onion rings, French fries, hamburgers, and smoothies. The Maui onion rings are the best in the world: thick, juicy, and crisp, cooked in a miracle batter that seals in moisture and flavor. The fries, Cajun style and thin, are equally commendable. After these successes, a so-so sandwich would be acceptable. Thankfully, the sandwiches, particularly the mahi-mahi with honey-mustard and the tuna melt on sourdough, are also heartily recommended—and, for the more discreet, the Cobb salad with shrimp.

Pacific Grill. Four Seasons Resort Wailea, 3900 Wailea Alanui. ☎ **808/874-8000.** Main courses $9.25–$24.50 at breakfast, $23–$28.50 at dinner. AE, CB, DC, DISC, JCB, MC, V. Daily 6–11:30am, 6–9:30pm. PACIFIC EDGE.

This is a good alternative for those wanting something between very casual and superluxe. Open for lunch only occasionally, Pacific Grill features gourmet breakfasts and smashing dinners, ranging from Oriental-style steamed snapper to lemongrass mahi-mahi baked in parchment paper with shiitake mushrooms and spinach. One could dine happily on the starters alone, from the limu kohu ahi poke with watercress and fried taro (a favorite) to the scallop-and-goat-cheese won tons (another favorite). You don't have to be vegan to love the vegan miso risotto with spinach, mushrooms, and tomatoes; or the Kula tomato salad, a paean to the rich volcanic soil of Maui.

★ **Seasons.** Four Seasons Resort Wailea, 3900 Wailea Alanui. ☎ **808/874-8000.** Reservations recommended. Main courses $36–$46; prix fixe $75–$95. AE, CB, DC, DISC, JCB, MC, V. Tues–Sat 6–9pm. HAWAII REGIONAL/PROVENÇAL.

"Sometimes I get fish in the morning, and it's still alive!" exclaims Senior Executive Chef George Mavrothalassitis, who has found his match in Maui's abundance of fresh produce and seafood. This tony seaside room is a showcase for his mastery of Provençal and Hawaii Regional cuisines. Renowned for his use of local ingredients and the most vaunted traditions of his native Provence, he has invented the pleasures of onaga baked in a Hawaiian salt crust, with an ogo (seaweed) sauce; a whole kumu (goatfish) filled with watercress, garnished with Swiss chard and wild mushrooms; and poached ehu (red snapper) and clams in lemongrass, ginger, and tamarind. Other winners: charbroiled opakapaka with Pacific oyster sauce, Hungarian paprika lamb loin, and star anise–rotisserie duckling. The seared yellowfin tuna is marinated for 48 hours in garlic, basil, Hawaiian chiles, and olive oil, served on organic tomato coulis. In the winter truffle–rotisserie chicken, slivers of fresh truffles are nestled between the meat and skin, and the dish is served with fresh creamed corn, fresh mashed Molokai sweet potatoes, and a hint of French vanilla. With his perfectly balanced flavors (nothing overpowers) and masterful use of spices, Mavrothalassitis has won a loyal following among foodies here and beyond. The room—elegant, understated, and open to the Wailea sea—is a temple of fine dining, and the walnut bread and French cheeses are still the best dessert in the islands.

SeaWatch. 100 Wailea Golf Club Dr. ☎ **808/875-8080.** Reservations required for dinner. Lunch $4.50–$12; dinner main courses $18–$30. AE, DC, MC, V. Daily 8am–3pm, 3–5:30pm (grille menu), and 5:30–10pm. ISLAND CUISINE.

SeaWatch's use of fresh Maui produce, Big Island goat cheese, and island fish in ethnic preparations sets it apart from most other upscale clubhouse restaurants, and it's one of the more affordable stops in tony Wailea. Lunchtime sandwiches, pastas, salads, crab cakes, and soups are moderately priced, and you get pretty, 360° views to go with them. You'll dine on the terrace or in a high-ceilinged room, on a menu that carries the tee-off-to-19th-hole crowd with ease. Pacific crab cakes, Chinese chicken salad, fresh-fish tacos, and the fresh-catch sandwich are some of the lunchtime stars. At dinner, the nightly fresh catch, which can be ordered in one of three preparations, is a SeaWatch staple. Favorites include the Island Breeze, fresh fish seared in a black-bean crab broth; the Makai, bamboo-steamed fresh catch; and the Upcountry, kiawe-grilled fish on garlic mashed potatoes, with oyster mushrooms from Haiku and an herb-tomato-butter sauce.

MAKENA

★ **Hakone.** Maui Prince Hotel, 5400 Makena Alanui. ☎ **808/874-1111.** Reservations recommended. Complete dinners $22–$42; Mon night buffet $38, Sun sushi buffet $45; Kaiseki (24-hour advance notice) $85. AE, JCB, MC, V. Sun 6–9pm, Mon–Sat 6–9:30pm. JAPANESE.

The Prince Hotels know Japanese cuisine and spared no effort to create a slice of Kyoto here, complete with sandalwood walls and pillars that were assembled by Japanese craftsmen and imported. Hakone offers super-luxe Japanese fare, very haute-Kyoto, gorgeously presented, and pricey. The difficulty of choosing has been tempered by the popular Sunday-night sushi buffet and Monday-night Japanese dinner buffet. The Japanese dinner buffet includes sushi, broiled miso butterfish, shrimp tempura, and several appealing salads, as well as pupus, miso soup, and rice. Sashimi, tempura, broiled fish, California roll, and other traditional Japanese delicacies are offered on the regular menu.

Prince Court. Maui Prince Hotel, 5400 Makena Alanui: ☎ **808/874-1111.** Reservations recommended. Main courses $27–29; Sun brunch $34. AE, JCB, MC, V. Sun 9:30am–1pm, Thurs–Mon 6–9:30pm. HAWAII REGIONAL.

Half the Sunday brunch experience is the fabulous view of Makena Beach, the crescent-shaped islet called Molokini, and Kahoolawe island. The other half is the lavish buffet, spread over several tables: pasta, omelets, cheeses, pastries, sashimi, crab legs, smoked salmon, fresh Maui produce, and an eye-popping array of ethnic and continental foods. As for dinner, it is something to write home about. Chef Eric Leterc's guava-glazed, shredded baby-back ribs with ginger and hoisin are brilliant, and his seafood risotto, with Kona lobster, chiso butter sauce, and poi (the master touch) is a great idea that is perfectly executed. The chef's special changes weekly, but if the grilled ono with warm herb salad and musubi fried rice is offered, don't miss it.

UPCOUNTRY MAUI
HALIIMAILE (ON THE WAY TO UPCOUNTRY MAUI)

✿ **Haliimaile General Store.** Haliimaile Rd., Haliimaile. ☎ **808/572-2666.** Reservations recommended. Lunch $6–$14; dinner $14–$28. AE, DC, MC, V. Mon-Fri 11am–2pm, Sun 10am–2:30pm (brunch), and daily 5:30–9:30pm. AMERICAN.

One of the 12 original Hawaii Regional Cuisine chefs, Bev Gannon has proven her staying power. You'll dine at tables set on old wood floors under high ceilings (sound ricochets fiercely here), in a peach-colored room emblazoned with works by local artists. The food, a blend of eclectic American with ethnic touches, manages to avoid the usual pitfalls of Hawaii Regional Cuisine: the same-old, same-old, I'm-bored-with-seared-ahi syndrome. Even the fresh-catch sandwich on the lunch menu is anything but prosaic. The chicken-tortilla soup and salade Niçoise disappear quickly at lunch, when soups, salads, fresh fish, and salads dominate. Dinner splurges include the spicy rack of lamb Hunan style, roasted duck, and paniolo ribs in tangy barbecue sauce.

Upcountry Cafe. In the Andrade Building, 7-2 Aewa Place (just off Haleakala Hwy.), Pukalani. ☎ **808/572-2395.** Lunch $5.95–$8.95; most dinner items less than $14.95. MC, V. Mon 6:30am–3pm, Wed–Thurs 6:30am–3pm and 5:30–8:30pm, Fri-Sat 6:30am–3pm and 5:30–9pm, Sun 6:30am–1pm. AMERICAN/LOCAL.

Pukalani's inexpensive, casual, and very popular cafe features cows everywhere: on the walls, chairs, menus, aprons, even the exterior. But the food is the draw: simple, home-cooked comfort food like meat loaf, roast pork, and humongous hamburgers, plus home-baked bread, oven-fresh muffins, and local faves such as saimin and Chinese chicken salad. Soups and salads (homemade cream of mushroom, Cobb and Caesar salads) and shrimp scampi with bow-tie pasta are among the cafe's other pleasures. The signature dessert is the cow pie, a naughty pile of chocolate cream cheese with macadamia nuts in a cookie crust, shaped like you-know-what.

MAKAWAO

Casanova Italian Restaurant. 1188 Makawao Ave. ☎ **808/572-0220.** Reservations recommended for dinner. Main courses $8–$23; 12-inch pizzas $10 and up. CB, DC, DISC, MC, V. Mon–Sat 11:30am–2pm and 5:30–9pm, Sun 5:30–9pm. Lounge, daily 5:30pm–12:30am or 1am; deli, Mon–Sat 8am–6:30pm, Sun 8:30am–6:30pm. ITALIAN.

Look for the tiny veranda with a few stools, always full, in front of a deli at Makawao's busiest intersection—that's the most visible part of Casanova's restaurant and lounge.

Makawao's center of nightlife consists of a stage and dance floor adjoining a cozy café and bar in the wing next to the deli. Pizza: gnocchi; rosemary lamb chops; and pasta in a dozen shapes, colors, and flavors appear on a menu that has made this a long-lasting Italian star. You can dine simply or lavishly—from a tomato, garlic, and four-cheese pizza to penne with lobster tail and scallops in a tomato-garlic-sherry sauce ($19), or a simple but tasty short pasta with sautéed vegetables and Greek olives, sprinkled with Gorgonzola ($10). The wood-fired Neapolitan pizzas are thin crusted and fabulous, in 10 varieties with dozens of additional toppings.

Makawao Steak House. 3612 Baldwin Ave. ☎ **808/572-8711.** Reservations recommended. Main courses $13.95–$24.95. AE, DC, DISC, MC, V. Mon–Thurs 5–9:30pm, Fri–Sat 5–10pm. STEAK/SEAFOOD.

The new owners (who also owned it in the mid-1970s) redid the kitchen, revised the menu, and put some spit and polish into this old Makawao fixture. Only two weeks old at this writing, the new Makawao Steak House has brought back its popular salad bar and a menu of chicken, fish, shrimp, crab, pork, and steaks—plain old basics and friendly service. The King crab legs are a big seller in this paniolo town, as is the prime rib.

Polli's Mexican Restaurant. 1202 Makawao Ave. ☎ **808/572-7808.** Main courses $6–$15. AE, DC, DISC, MC, V. Daily from about 9am (call to see if they're open) to 10pm. MEXICAN.

This is a democratic restaurant that offers an extensive menu equally considerate of health foodies, vegetarians, and carnivores. There's something for everyone, from baby-back ribs and steak dinners to substitutions of tofu or vegetarian taco mix happily accommodated on all menu items. Sizzling fajitas are the house special, featuring fish, shrimp, chicken, tofu, or steak in a dramatic entrance, on a crackling hot platter with vegetables and spices, six flour tortillas, sour cream, and guacamole—a good group endeavor. Expect the full roster of south-of-the-border favorites, from the usual tamales, tacos, and burritos to cheese-, mushroom-, and Mexi-burgers, laced with jalapeños and pepper jack cheese. Best of all, the menu is lard-free.

KULA (AT THE BASE OF HALEAKALA NATIONAL PARK)

Grandma's Coffee House. At the end of Hwy. 37, Keokea. ☎ **808/878-2140.** Most items less than $8.95. MC, V. Daily 7am–7pm. COFFEEHOUSE/AMERICAN.

Alfred Franco's grandmother started what is now a five-generation coffee business back in 1918, when she was 16 years old. Today, the tiny wooden coffeehouse he named after her, still fueled by homegrown Haleakala coffee beans, is the quintessential roadside oasis. About 6 miles before the Tedeschi Vineyards in Ulupalakua, Grandma's is a gathering place for espresso, hot and cold coffees, home-baked pastries, inexpensive pasta, sandwiches (including sensational avocado and garden burgers), homemade soups, fresh juices, and local plate-lunch specials that change daily. Aside from Grandmother's coffeecake, muffins, cinnamon rolls, and pastries, baked fresh daily, rotating specials include Hawaiian beef stew, ginger chicken, saimin, chicken curry, lentil soup, and sandwiches piled high with Kula vegetables.

Kula Lodge. Haleakala Hwy. (Hwy. 377). ☎ **808/878-2517.** Reservations recommended for dinner. Lunch $7.25–$14; dinner main courses $18–$26. MC, V. Daily 6:30am–9pm. HAWAII REGIONAL/AMERICAN.

Don't let the dinner prices scare you, because the Kula Lodge is equally enjoyable, if not more so, for breakfast and lunch, when the prices are lower and the views through the picture windows have an eye-popping intensity. A new feature is the outdoor dining area with its wood-burning oven, open from 11am daily for as long as the weather permits. The million-dollar view through the large picture windows spans the flanks of Haleakala, rolling 3,200 feet down to central Maui, the ocean, and the West Maui Mountains. If possible, go for sunset cocktails and watch the colors change into deep purples and other end-of-day hues. When darkness descends, a roaring fire and lodge atmosphere turn the attention to the coziness of the room. For breakfast, the lodge is famous for its banana–macadamia nut pancakes. At lunch, choices include smoked-turkey sandwiches, garden and mahi-mahi burgers, soups, salads, seared ahi, and pizza.

Kula Sandalwoods Restaurant. Haleakala Hwy. (Hwy. 377). ☎ **808/878-3523.** Most items less than $8.75. DISC, MC, V. Mon–Sat 6:30–2pm, Sun 6:30am–noon (brunch). AMERICAN.

The chef, Eleanor Loui, a graduate of the Culinary Institute of America, makes hollandaise sauce every morning from fresh upcountry egg yolks, sweet butter, and Myers lemons, which her family grows in the yard above the restaurant. "This is very basic home-cooking, but everything is fresh," says the chef, who works with her husband, sister, and brother in their parents' restaurant. This is Kula cuisine, with produce from the backyard and everything made from scratch: French toast with home-baked Portuguese sweetbread, crab cakes, hotcakes or Belgian waffles with fresh fruit, French baguettes, hamburgers drenched in a special cheese sauce made with grated sharp Cheddar, grilled teriyaki chicken breast, and an outstanding garden veggie burger. The Kula Sandalwoods salad features grilled chicken breast with crimson Kula tomatoes and onions and, when the garden allows, just-picked red-oak, curly-green, and red-leaf lettuces. The Kula Sandalwoods omelet is an open-faced marvel with Cheddar and Jack cheeses, tomatoes, and green onions, served with cottage potatoes—a gourmet treat. You'll dine in one of two separate rooms, in the gazebo, or on the terrace, with dazzling views in all directions, including, in the spring, a yard dusted with lavender jacaranda flowers and a hillside ablaze with fields of orange akulikuli blossoms.

EAST MAUI
PAIA

Impromptu Cafe. 71 Baldwin Ave. ☎ **808/579-8477.** Main courses $9.95–$18.95. AE, DISC, MC, V. Daily 7:30am–11pm. NEW AMERICAN.

The next time you have a yen for curry grilled chicken; grilled vegetable pasta; Caribbean jerk pork tenderloin; coconut-and-ginger lamb kebab with spicy peanut sauce; scallops on weed (nori); grilled pizza; white clam-and-garlic pizza; and fantastic salads with things like feta, shiitakes, pine nuts, Gorgonzola, grilled vegetables, and organic greens, try Impromptu. It's a hit in Paia, with a menu sophisticated enough but not terribly pricey, offered in a chic environment with flowers, windows looking out to Baldwin Avenue, and original works by local artists.

Jacques Bistro. 89 Hana Hwy. ☎ **808/579-6255.** Reservations accepted. Main courses $5–$18 at brunch, $8–$19 at dinner. MC, V. Daily 10:30am–10:30pm. FRENCH/AMERICAN/ISLAND.

Fresh local seafood with a French touch, served in Paia by a chef named Jacques in a room with a 42-foot monkeypod bar and arches, columns, and a garden lanai—that's Paia's newest bistro. New owners with fresh ideas and a likable chef proffer a menu of affordable delights: catch of the day (from Paia fishermen), ahi poke, bouillabaisse, sashimi, seafood curry, and special touches such as seasoned purple potatoes and lightly steamed Kula vegetables. Pasta dishes, starting at $7.50, are a good deal after a day of windsurfing (or even shopping), and the half-roasted chicken ($12.95) is an event. Meat lovers can choose rib-eye steak, baby-back ribs, or rack of lamb. The garden area is lush with palms, bromeliads, and towering banyan trees—a world of serenity in quirky Paia.

Milagros Food Company. Hana Hwy. and Baldwin Ave., Paia. ☎ 808/579-8755. Breakfast about $7; lunch $3–$8; dinner $7–$16. DC, DISC, MC, V. Daily 8am–9:30pm. SOUTHWESTERN/SEAFOOD.

Milagros quickly gained a following with its great food, upbeat atmosphere, and highly touted margaritas. Although there are fabulous fish tacos ($7.25 for a plate of two with beans and rice, flavored with Milagros' secret sauce), this is much more than Mexican food. Regulars anticipate the fresh ahi creation of the evening, a combination of Southwestern and Pacific Rim styles and flavors accompanied by fresh veggies and Kula greens. The $15.95 chile-rellenos plate comes with grilled ahi, beans, rice, and Kula greens—a sensation, and very generous. The daily happy hour features $2.50 margaritas ($12 for a pitcher) from 3 to 6pm.

Paia Fish Market. 110 Hana Hwy. ☎ 808/579-8030. Lunch and dinner plates $6.95–$14.95. AE, DC, MC, V. Daily 11am–9:30pm. SEAFOOD.

This really is a fish market, with fresh fish to take home and cooked seafood, salads, pastas, fajitas, and quesadillas to take out or enjoy at the few picnic tables inside the restaurant. It's an appealing and budget-friendly selection: Cajun-style fresh catch, Mexican food with fresh fish, fresh-fish tacos and quesadillas, and seafood and chicken pastas. You can also order hamburgers, cheeseburgers, and fish and chips (shrimp and chips, too), and wonderful lunch and dinner plates, cheap and tasty. Peppering the walls are photos of the number-one sport here, windsurfing.

Pic-nics. 30 Baldwin Ave. ☎ 808/579-8021. Most items less than $6.95. JCB, MC, V. Daily 7am–7pm. SANDWICHES/PICNIC LUNCHES.

Breakfast is terrific here—omelets, eggs to order, Maui Portuguese sausage, Hawaiian pancakes—and so is lunch. Pic-nics is famous for many things, among them the spinach-nut burger, an ingenious vegetarian blend topped with vegetables and Cheddar cheese. A cold version of the nut burger is topped with vegetables and Pic-nics' own homemade nonfat yogurt dressing. Stop here to fill your picnic basket for the drive to Hana or Upcountry Maui. These are gourmet sandwiches (Kula vegetables, home-baked breast of turkey, Cajun chicken, Cajun fish) worthy of the most idyllic picnic spot. The rosemary herb-roasted chicken can be ordered as a plate lunch (two scoops of rice and Haiku greens) for $7.95 or as part of the Hana Bay picnic ($22.95 for two), which includes sandwiches, meats, Maui-style potato chips, and home-baked cookies and muffins. You can order old-fashioned fish and chips, too, or shrimp and chips, or pastries baked fresh daily. Fresh breads from the Maui Bake Shop add to the appeal, and several coffee drinks made with Maui-blend coffee may give you the jolt you need for the drive ahead.

The Vegan. 115 Baldwin Ave. ☎ 808/579-9144. Main courses $4.95–$8.95. MC, V. Daily 11:30am–9pm. GOURMET VEGETARIAN/VEGAN.

The Vegan proves that "vegan" doesn't have to mean boring. Wholesome foods with ingenious soy substitutes and satisfying flavors appear on a menu that defies deprivation. Garlic noodles, called Pad Thai noodles, are the bestselling item, cooked in a creamy coconut sauce and generously seasoned with garlic and spices. Curries, grilled polenta, pepper steak made of Seitan (a meat substitute), and organic hummus are among the items that draw vegetarians from around the island. Proving that desserts are justly deserved, Vegan offers a carob cake and coconut milk–flavored tapioca pudding that hint of Thailand and don't contain dairy milk.

ON THE HANA ROAD

✪ **Pauwela Cafe.** 375 W. Kuiaha Rd., Haiku. ☎ **808/575-9242.** Most items less than $6. No credit cards. Mon–Sat 7am–3pm, Sun 8am–2pm. INTERNATIONAL.

It's a long drive from anywhere, but the kalua turkey sandwich is reason enough for the journey. Because it's located in an industrial center of sailboard and surfboard manufacturers, you may find a surf legend dining at the next table. For many reasons, the tiny cafe with concrete floors and six tables has a strong local following. Becky Speere, a gifted chef, and her husband, Chris, a food-service instructor at Maui Community College and a former sous chef at the Maui Prince Hotel, infuse every sandwich, salad, and muffin with a high degree of culinary finesse. I never dreamed that I could dine so well with such pleasing informality. The scene-stealing kalua turkey is one success layered on the other: warm, smoky, moist shredded turkey, served with cheese on home-baked French bread and covered with a green-chili and cilantro sauce. It gets my vote as the best sandwich on the island. The black-bean chili bursts with flavor and is served over brown rice with sour cream, cheese, and onions—a hearty, healthy choice. The salads, too, are fresh and uncomplicated, served with homemade dressings. For breakfast, eggs chilaquile are a good starter, with layers of corn tortillas, pinto beans, chiles, cheese, and herbs, topped with egg custard and served hot with salsa and sour cream—the works, for an unbelievable $5.

HANA

The Cafe at Hana Gardenland. Hana Hwy. at Kalo Rd. ☎ **808/248-8975.** Most items less than $8.95. MC, V. Daily 8:30am–5pm. HEALTHY AMERICAN.

Hot sellers at this Hana roadside cafe are the Hana Wraps, rice and vegetables wrapped in the tortilla of your choice. The light, healthy fare and foliage both indoors and out are pure, garden-style Hana, with a touch of the Southwest in the peach and aqua-colored accents. The koi pond, art gallery, and gift shop are accessories to a menu that has won the hearts of diners with its honest simplicity: ahi salad in Hana papaya halves, garlic potato salad, and generously towering sandwiches on whole-wheat Maui Crunch bread. When Hilary Rodham Clinton and her daughter, Chelsea, came to Hana, they dined on steamed eggs with salsa on Maui Crunch bread and waffles topped with fresh mangos. Most of the produce is grown on the Gardenland property, and the Espresso Bar serves teas, Hana-blend coffee, fresh juices, and smoothies made with freshly picked bananas and papayas.

Hana Ranch Restaurant. Hana Hwy. ☎ **808/248-8255.** Reservations recommended for dinner. Main courses $16.95–$34.95. DC, DISC, MC, V. Daily 11am–2:30pm, Fri–Sat 6–8:30pm (buffet, daily 11am–2:30pm; take-out, daily 6:30am–6:30pm). AMERICAN.

Part of the Hotel Hana-Maui operation, the Hana Ranch Restaurant is an informal alternative to the hotel's dining room. Here are some of your dinner choices: New York steak for $22.95, prawns and pasta for $22.95, and a few Pacific Rim options, such as spicy shrimp won tons and the predictable fresh-fish poke. Aside from the weekly, warmly received Wednesday Pizza Night, the luncheon buffet is a more affordable prospect: barbecued ribs, chicken, baked potatoes, beans, and salads for $10.95. There are indoor tables as well as two outdoor pavilions that offer stunning ocean views. At the take-out stand adjoining the restaurant, Saimin, a $6.25 teriyaki plate lunch, a $5.95 chicken Caesar salad, and a mahi-mahi sandwich for $4.25 are reasonable alternatives for the dine-and-dash set.

5 Beaches

by Jeanette Foster

For beach toys and equipment, head to **Rental Warehouse**, 578 Front St. (near Prison St.), Lahaina (☎ **808/661-1970**), which rents beach chairs and coolers (with ice!) for $1.99 a day, and a host of toys (frisbees, volleyballs, and more) for 99¢ a day.

WEST MAUI

KAANAPALI BEACH

Four-mile-long Kaanapali is one of Maui's best beaches, with grainy gold sand as far as the eye can see. The beach parallels the sea channel through most of its length, and a paved beach walk links hotels and condos, open-air restaurants, and the Whalers Village shopping center. Because Kaanapali is so long and most hotels have adjacent swimming pools, the beach is crowded only in pockets—there's plenty of room to find seclusion. Summertime swimming is excellent. The best snorkeling is around Black Rock, in front of the new Sheraton; the water's clear, calm, and populated with clouds of tropical fish. Facilities include outdoor showers; you can use the rest rooms at the hotel pools. Various beach-activity vendors line up in front of the hotels, offering nearly every type of water activity and equipment. Parking is a problem, though. There are two public entrances: at the south end, turn off Honoapiilani Highway into the Kaanapali Resort, and pay for parking there; or continue on Honoapiilani Highway, turn off at the last Kaanapali exit at the stoplight near the Maui Kaanapali Villas, and park next to the beach signs indicating public access.

✪ KAPALUA BEACH

The beach cove that fronts the Kapalua Bay Hotel and Villas is the stuff of dreams: a golden crescent bordered by two palm-studded points. The sandy bottom slopes gently to deep water at the bay mouth; the water's so clear that you can see where the gold sands turn to green and then deep blue. Protected from strong winds and currents by the lava-rock promontories, Kapalua's calm waters are great for snorkelers and swimmers of all ages and abilities, and the bay is big enough to paddle a kayak around without getting into the more challenging channel that separates Maui from Molokai. Waves come in just right for riding, and fish hang out by the rocks, making it great for snorkeling. The beach is accessible from the hotel on one end, which provides sun chairs with shades and a beach-activities center for its guests, and a public access way on the other. It isn't so wide that you burn your feet getting in or out of the water, and the inland side is edged by a shady path and cool lawns. Parking is limited to about 30 spaces in a small lot off Lower Honoapiilani Road, by Napili Kai Beach Club, so arrive early; next door is a nice but pricey oceanfront restaurant, Kapalua's Bay Club (see "Dining," above). Facilities include showers, rest rooms, lifeguards, a rental shack, and plenty of shade.

SOUTH MAUI

Wailea's beaches may seem off-limits, hidden from plain view as they are by an intimidating wall of luxury resorts; but they're all open to the public by law. Look for the SHORELINE ACCESS signs along **Wailea Alanui Drive**, the resort's main boulevard.

KAMAOLE III BEACH PARK

Three beach parks—Kamaole I, II, and III—stand like golden jewels in the front yard of the funky seaside town of Kihei, which all of a sudden is sprawling like suburban blight. The beaches are the best thing about Kihei (if you don't count A Pacific Cafe). All three are popular with local residents and visitors because they're easily accessible. On weekends, they're jam-packed with fishermen, picnickers, swimmers, and snorkelers. The most popular is Kamaole III, or "Kam-3," as locals say. The biggest of the three beaches, with wide pockets of golden sand, it's the only one with a playground for children and a grassy lawn that meets the sand. Swimming is safe here, but scattered lava rocks are toe-stubbers at the water line, and parents should watch to make sure their kids don't venture too far out, as the bottom slopes off quickly. Both the north and south shores are rocky fingers with a surge big enough to attract fish and snorkelers, and the winter waves attract bodysurfers. Kam-3 is also a wonderful place to watch the sunset. Facilities include rest rooms, showers, picnic tables, barbecue grills, and lifeguards. There's plenty of parking on South Kihei Road across from the Maui Parkshore condos.

WAILEA BEACH

Wailea is the best golden-sand crescent on Maui's sunbaked Southwestern Coast. One of five beaches within Wailea Resort, Wailea is big, wide, and protected on both sides by black-lava points. It's the front yard of the Four Seasons Wailea and the Grand Wailea Resort Hotel and Spa, Maui's most elegant and outrageous beach hotels, respectively. From the beach, the view out to sea is magnificent, framed by neighboring Kahoolawe and Lanai and the tiny crescent of Molokini, probably the most popular snorkel spot in these parts. The clear waters tumble to shore in waves just the right size for gentle riding, with or without a board. From shore, you can see Pacific humpback whales in season (December through April) and unreal sunsets nightly. Facilities include rest rooms, outdoor showers, and limited free parking at the blue SHORELINE ACCESS sign, which points toward Wailea Alanui Drive.

ULUA BEACH

One of the most popular beaches in Wailea, Ulua is a long, wide, crescent-shaped gold-sand beach between two rocky points. When the ocean's calm, Ulua offers Wailea's best snorkeling; when it's rough, the waves are excellent for bodysurfers. The ocean bottom is shallow and gently slopes down to deeper waters, making swimming generally safe. The beach is usually occupied by guests of nearby resorts; during the high season (Christmas through March and June through August), it's carpeted with beach towels and packed with sunbathers like sardines in cocoa butter. Facilities include showers and rest rooms. Beach equipment is available for rent at the nearby Wailea Ocean Activity Center. To find Ulua, look for the blue SHORELINE ACCESS sign on South Kihei Road, near Renaissance Wailea Beach Resort. A tiny parking lot is nearby.

MALUAKA BEACH (MAKENA BEACH)

On the southern end of Maui's resort coast, development falls off dramatically, leaving a wild, dry countryside of green kiawe trees. The Maui Prince sits in isolated splendor, sharing Makena Resort's 1,800 acres only with a couple of first-rate golf courses and a necklace of perfect beaches. The strand nearest the hotel is Maluaka Beach, often called Makena, notable for its beauty and its views of Molokini Crater, the offshore islet, and Kahoolawe, the so-called "target" island. It's a short, wide, palm-fringed crescent of golden, grainy sand set between two black-lava points and bounded by big sand dunes topped by a grassy knoll. Swimming in this mostly calm bay is considered the best on Makena Bay, which is bordered on the south by Puu Olai Cinder Cone and historic Keawalai Congregational Church, whose graveyard sits on its own

⭐ **Frommer's Favorite Maui Experiences**

Greet the Rising Sun from atop Haleakala. Bundle up, fill a thermos full of hot java, and drive up the 37 miles from sea level to 10,000 feet to witness the birth of yet another day. The sky turns from inky black to muted charcoal as a small sliver of orange forms on the horizon. There's something about standing up so high, breathing in the rarified air and watching the first rays of light streak across the sky, that makes a Haleakala sunrise a mystical experience of the first magnitude. Of all the memories you will take home, this one will remain vivid even after all the others have faded.

Watch for Whales. No need to head out in a boat—in the winter, you can even watch these majestic mammals breach and spyhop from shore. One of the best places is McGregor Point, the scenic point at mile marker 9 along Honoapiilani Highway, just outside of Maalaea in South Maui. The humpbacks arrive as early as November, but the majority travel through Maui's waters from mid-December to mid-April, with a few stragglers hanging around until May.

Plunge into the Neptunian World of Makena Landing. Makena Bay is one of Hawaii's best places to swim with the fishes. Calm waters and an abundance of marine life make this a great place for snorkelers. Don a mask and snorkel and paddle with turtles, watch clouds of butterfly fish flitter past, and search for tiny damsel fish in the coral.

Take a Dip in the Seven Sacred Pools. There are actually more than seven of these fern-shrouded waterfall pools, and they're all beautiful. They spill seaward at Oheo Gulch, on the rainy eastern flanks of Haleakala. Some try to swim in the pools nearest the sea if you do, keep an eye on the sky overhead so that a sudden cloudburst doesn't send you cascading out to sea.

Venture Back in Time in a Historic Port Town. In the 1800s, when whaling was at its height, seafarers swarmed into Lahaina and missionaries fought to stem the spread of their evil. In was a wild time, and this tiny town was an exciting place. The Lahaina Restoration Society, in the Master's Reading Room on Front and Dickenson streets, will give you a free map that will let you discover those wild whaling days for yourself.

ONELOA BEACH (BIG BEACH)

Oneloa, meaning "long sand" in Hawaiian, is one of the most popular beaches on Maui. Locals call it "Big Beach"—it's 3,300 feet long and more than 100 feet wide. Mauians come here to swim, fish, sunbathe, surf, and enjoy the view of Kahoolawe and Lanai. Snorkeling is good around the north end, at the foot of Puu Olai, a 360-foot cinder cone. During storms, however, big waves lash the shore, and a strong rip current sweeps the sharp drop-off, posing a danger for inexperienced open-ocean swimmers. There's no facilities except for portable toilets, but there's plenty of parking. To get there, drive past the Maui Prince Hotel to the second dirt road, which leads through a kiawe thicket to the beach.

sheltered cove. The waters around Makena Landing, at the north end of the bay, are particularly good for snorkeling. Facilities include rest rooms, showers, a landscaped park, lifeguards, and roadside parking. Along Makena Alanui, look for the SHORE-LINE ACCESS sign near the hotel, turn right, and head down to the shore.

Watch Spellbound as the Windsurfers Ride the Waves at Hookipa. Just off the Hana Highway past Paia is Hookipa Beach, known the world over as a windsurfing mecca. The great waves and consistent wind draw top windsurfers from around the globe. Watch in awe as these colorful sailboarders ride, sail, and pirouette over the waves, turning into the wind and flipping into the air while rotating 360°. It's the best free show in town.

Explore Iao Valley. When the sun strikes Iao Valley in the West Maui Mountains, an almost ethereal light sends rays out in all directions, like a biblical holy picture. This really may be Eden.

Walk the Shoreline Trial at Waianapanapa. A 6-mile trail follows along the shoreline, bordered on one side by lava cliffs and a forest of lauhala trees, by the open ocean on the other. As you go, you'll pass an ancient *heiau* (temple), some fascinating caves, a pretty cool blowhole, jungly native Hawaiian plants, and the everchanging sea.

Head to Kula to Bid the Sun Aloha. Just off Kula Highway, Harold Rice Park is the perfect vantage point for watching the sun set over the entire island: down the side of Haleakala, out across the isthmus, and over to the West Maui Mountains, with the islands of Molokai and Lanai in the distance. As the sun sinks in the sky and daytime turns to dusk, the light subtly shifts from bright yellow to a mellow red. After the sun drops below the horizon, the sky puts on its own Technicolor show in a dazzling array of electric rainbow colors.

Experience Art Night in Lahaina. Every Friday after the sun goes down, most of the town's galleries open their doors, serve pupus and refreshments, and hope you'll wander in. Hawaii is full of talented artists; this is a fun, festive way to see what's going on in Maui's creative community. You may even be able to meet the artists, as many are on hand to talk about their works.

Taste Maui-Made Wine. In the cool upcountry on the slopes of Haleakala is Maui's only winery, Tedeschi Vineyards. You can sample the wine at Tedeschi's free tasting. The grounds are a perfect place for a picnic; spread your lunch out under the sprawling camphor tree, pop the cork on a Blanc du Blanc, and toast your good fortune in being here.

On the other side of Puu Olai is **Little Beach**, a small pocket beach where assorted nudists work on their all-over tans, to the chagrin of uptight authorities who take a dim view of public nudity. You can get a nasty sunburn and a lewd-conduct ticket, too.

EAST MAUI
HOOKIPA BEACH PARK

Two miles past Paia, on the Hana Highway, is one of the most famous windsurfing sites in the world. Due to hard, constant wind and endless waves, Hookipa attracts top windsurfers and wave jumpers from around the globe. Surfers and fishermen also enjoy this small, gold-sand beach at the foot of a grassy cliff, which provides a natural amphitheater for spectators. Except when competitions are being held, weekdays are the best times to watch the daredevils fly over the waves. When waves are flat, snorkelers and divers explore the reef. Facilities include rest rooms, showers, pavilions, picnic tables, barbecues, and parking.

1-1434

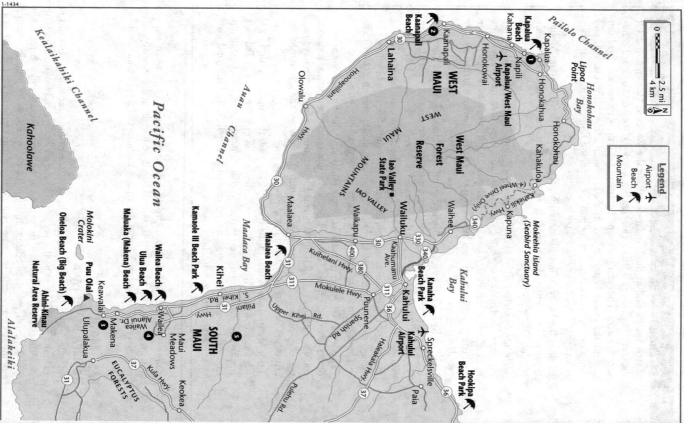

Legend
Airport ✈
Beach ⚓
Mountain ▲

0   2.5 mi
0   4 km
N

Pailolo Channel

Kealaikahiki Channel

Pacific Ocean

Kahoolawe

Alalakeiki Channel

Kapalua Beach
Kaanapali Beach
Kahana
Napili
Honokowai
Kapalua
Lipoa Point
Honokohau Bay
Honokahua
Honokowai
Kahakuloa
Honokohau
Mokeehia Island (Seabird Sanctuary)
Kahakuloa Kapuna
Kahekili Hwy. (Seabird Sanctuary)
Kapalua/West Maui Airport
Lahaina
WEST MAUI
WEST MAUI MOUNTAINS
West Maui Forest Reserve
Iao Valley State Park
IAO VALLEY
Kahakiloa Hwy. (4-Wheel Drive Only)
Olowalu
Honoapiilani Hwy.
Auau Channel
Waihee
Wailuku
Waikapu
Kaahumanu Ave.
Waihee

Maalaea Bay
Maalaea
Maalaea Beach
Kihei
Kuihelani Hwy.
Mokulele Hwy.
Upper Kihei Rd.
S. Kihei Rd.
Piilani Hwy.
Kamaole III Beach Park
Wailea Beach
Ulua Beach
Mokapu (Makena) Beach
Puu Olai
Molokini Crater
Oneloa Beach (Big Beach)
Ahini-Kinau Natural Area Reserve
Keawalai
Makena
Ulupalakua
Wailea
Wailea Alanui Dr.
Maui Meadows
SOUTH MAUI
Keokea
Kula Hwy.
EUCALYPTUS FORESTS
Puunene
Spanish Rd.
Puunene
Kanaha Beach Park
Kahului
Kahului Airport
Spreckelsville
Paia
Hookipa Beach Park
Kahului Bay
Kahana Beach Park
Haleakala Hwy.
Pulehu Rd.

30
340
330
36
340
311
400
380
31
311
37
31

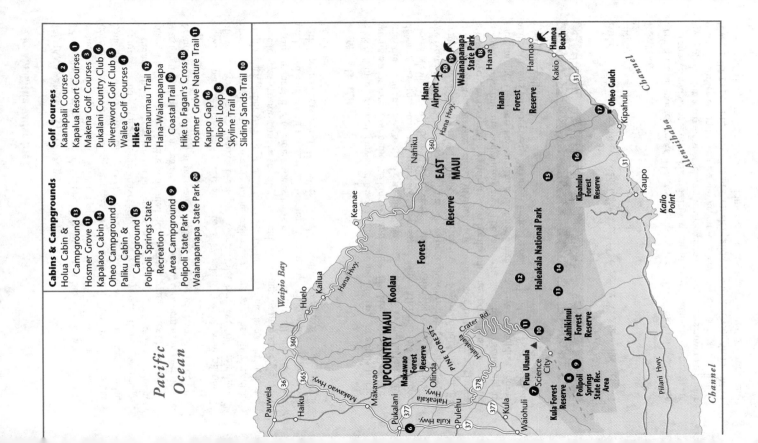

Cabins & Campgrounds

Holua Cabin & Campground **13**
Hosmer Grove **11**
Kapalaoa Cabin **14**
Oheo Campground **17**
Paliku Cabin & Campground **15**
Polipoli Springs State Recreation Area Campground **9**
Polipoli State Park **9**
Waianapanapa State Park **20**

Golf Courses

Kaanapali Courses **2**
Kapalua Resort Courses **1**
Makena Golf Courses **3**
Pukalani Country Club **6**
Silversword Golf Club **5**
Wailea Golf Courses **4**

Hikes

Halemaumau Trail **12**
Hana-Waianapanapa Coastal Trail **19**
Hike to Fagan's Cross **18**
Hosmer Grove Nature Trail **11**
Kaupo Gap **16**
Polipoli Loop **8**
Skyline Trail **7**
Sliding Sands Trail **10**

Pacific Ocean

Channel

Alenuihaha Channel

423

WAIANAPANAPA STATE PARK

Four miles before Hana, off the Hana Highway, is this beach park, which takes its name from the legend of the Waianapanapa Cave, where Chief Kaakea, a jealous and cruel man, suspected his wife, Popoalaea, of having an affair. Popoalaea left her husband and hid herself in a chamber of the Waianapanapa Cave. She and her attendant ventured out only at night for food. Nevertheless, a few days later, Kaakea was passing by the area and saw the shadow of the servant. Knowing he had found his wife's hiding place, Kaakea entered the cave and killed her. During certain times of the year, the water in the tide pool turns red as a tribute to Popoalaea, commemorating her death. Scientists claim, however, that the water turns red due to the presence of small red shrimp.

Waianapanapa State Park's 120 acres have 12 cabins (see "Accommodations," above), a caretaker's residence, a beach park, picnic tables, barbecue grills, rest rooms, showers, a parking lot, a shoreline hiking trail, and a black-sand beach (it's actually small, black pebbles). This is a wonderful area for shoreline hikes (bring insect repellent, as the mosquitoes are plentiful) and picnicking. Swimming is generally unsafe, though, due to strong waves breaking offshore, which roll into the beach unchecked, and strong rip currents. Because Waianapanapa is crowded on weekends with local residents and their families, as well as tourists, weekdays are generally a better bet.

HAMOA BEACH

This half moon–shaped, gray-sand beach (a mix of coral and lava) in a truly tropical setting is a favorite of sunbathers seeking rest and refuge. The Hotel Hana-Maui maintains the beach and tries to act like it's their private beach, but it's not—so just march down the lava-rock steps and grab a spot on the sand. James Michener said of Hamoa: "Paradoxically, the only beach I have ever seen that looks like the South Pacific was in the North Pacific–Hamoa Beach . . . a beach so perfectly formed that I wonder at its comparative obscurity." The 100-foot-wide beach is three football fields long and sits below 30-foot black-lava sea cliffs. An unprotected beach open to the ocean, Hamoa is often swept by powerful rip currents. Surf breaks offshore and rolls ashore, making it a popular surfing and bodysurfing area. The calm left side is best for snorkeling in the summer. The hotel has numerous facilities for guests; there's an outdoor shower and rest rooms for nonguests. Parking is limited. Look for the Hamoa Beach turn-off from Hana Highway.

6 Hitting the Water

by Jeanette Foster

For details on the activities listed below, see "The Active Vacation Planner" in chapter 3.

BOATING

Maui is big on snorkel cruises. The crescent-shaped islet called **Molokini** is one of the best snorkel and scuba spots in Hawaii. Trips to the island of **Lanai** (see chapter 9) are also popular for a day of snorkeling. Always remember to bring a towel and your swimsuit, sunscreen, and a hat on a snorkel cruise; everything else is usually included. If you'd like to go a little deeper than snorkeling allows, consider trying **Snuba**. Most of these snorkel boats offer it for an additional cost; it's usually around $50 for a half-hour or so.

In addition to the choices below, during whale season (mid-December through April), **UFO Parasail** (☎ **800/FLY-4UFO** or 808/661-7UFO; www.ufoparasail. com) converts their 37-foot speedboat into a **whale-watching** machine. Their 1½-hour whale-watching trips are $25 per person.

For fishing charters, see "Sportfishing," below.

America II. Lahaina Harbor, slip 5. ☎ **808/667-2195.** www.galaxymall.com/stores/ americaii. $29.95 adults, $14.95 children 6-12 (free for kids 5 and under).

This U.S. contender in the 1987 America's Cup race is a true racing boat, a 65-foot, 12-meter sailing yacht offering four different 2-hour trips in winter, three in summer: a **morning sail**, an **afternoon sail**, and a **sunset sail**, plus **whale-watching** in winter. These are sailing trips. No snorkeling—just the thrill of racing with the wind. Complimentary bottled water, soda, and chips are available.

Maui Classic Charters. Maalaea Harbor, slip 80. ☎ **800/736-5740** or 808/879-8188. www.maui.net/~charters/MCC.html. Prices vary depending on cruise.

Maui Classic Charters offers **snorkel-sail cruises to Molokini** plus a second location on the 63-foot *Lavengro*. The 6-hour journey costs $59 for adults and $40 for children under 12, including a continental breakfast and deli lunch. They also offer 5-hour sail-snorkel trips to Molokini aboard their new 53-foot glass-bottom catamaran, *Four Winds II*, for $69 for adults and $45 for children 3 to 12 years old; as well as a 3½-hour afternoon trip (with a naturalist onboard during **whale season**) for $39.95 for adults and $29.95 for children. *Four Winds* trips include a continental breakfast; a barbecue lunch; complimentary beer, wine, and soda; and sportfishing along the way.

Navatek II. 162 Lahainaluna Rd., Lahaina; cruises depart from Maalaea Harbor. ☎ **800/ 852-4183** or 808/661-8787. www.maui.net/~navatek. Prices vary depending on cruise.

For all of you who go out on the sea with patches stuck behind your ears, this boat's for you; you couldn't get sick if you tried. The new and unusual 82-foot SWATH (Small Waterplane Area Twin Hull) vessel is designed to operate in heavy seas without spilling your mai tai. The ship's superstructure (the part you ride on) rests on twin torpedo-like hulls that slash the water, creating a remarkably smooth ride. In fact, the comfortable, air-conditioned boat (with spacious outside decks and hot and cold showers) glides through the water so smoothly that out on the water, you'll forget that you're even on a boat.

Cruises to Lanai on *Navatek II* include a 90-minute snorkel off Lanai's rugged West Coast, breakfast, lunch, a sail along Lanai's remote coastline, plus **whale-watching** in season. This 8am to 2pm adventure is $125 for adults, $95 for kids 12 to 17, and $75 for children 5 to 11. In season, they also offer a 2-hour **afternoon whale watch** for $39 for adults and $26.50 for children 2 to 11.

Navatek II offers one of Hawaii's best **sunset dinner cruises.** You can watch porpoises play as the sun sets (and whales in the winter), and then watch the stars come out as you sail to Lahaina. The 2-hour dinner cruise, operating Saturday through Thursday, is $87 for adults and $55 for kids 2 to 11, including Hawaiian entertainment and a full bar.

Ocean Activities Center. 1847 S. Kihei Rd., Kihei. ☎ **800/798-0652** or 808/879-4485.

In season, this activity center runs 2-hour **whale-watching cruises** on its own spacious 65-foot catamaran; trips are $30 for adults and $18 for children 3 to 12. Their best deal to **Molokini** is the 5-hour Maka Kai cruise, which includes a continental breakfast, deli lunch, snorkel gear, and instruction; it's $55 for adults and $35 for children 3 to 12. Trips leave from Maalaea Harbor, slip 62.

Pacific Whale Foundation. 101 N. Kihei Rd., Kihei. ☎ **800/942-5311** or 808/879-8811. www.pacificwhale.org. $19 adults, $17 children.

This not-for-profit foundation supports its whale research by offering **whale-watch cruises and snorkel tours,** some to Molokini and Lanai. They operate a 53-foot motor vessel called *Whale I,* a 50-foot sailing ketch called *Whale II,* a 65-foot power catamaran, *Ocean Spirit,* and a sea kayak. They have 15 daily trips to choose from, and their rates for a 2-hour whale-watch cruise would make Moby Dick smile. Cruises are offered from December through May, out of both Lahaina and Maalaea harbors.

Pride of Maui. Maalaea Harbor. ☎ **808/875-0955.** $76 adults, $69 children 13–17, $49 children 3–12.

For a high-speed, action-packed snorkel-sail experience, consider the *Pride of Maui.* Their 5½-hour **snorkel cruises** take in not only **Molokini,** but also Turtle Bay and Makena for more snorkeling. A continental breakfast, a barbecue lunch, gear, and instruction are included.

⭐ **Trilogy Excursions.** ☎ **800/874-2666,** 888/MAUI-800, or 808/661-4743. www. sailtrilogy.com. Prices and departure points vary with cruise.

Trilogy Excursions offers my favorite **snorkel-sail trips.** Hop aboard Trilogy's 50-foot catamaran for a 90-mile sail from Lahaina Harbor to **Lanai's Hulopoe Beach,** a terrific marine preserve, for a fun-filled day of sailing, snorkeling, swimming, and **whale-watching** (in season, of course). This is the only cruise that offers a personalized ground tour of the island, and the only one with rights to take you to Hulopoe Beach. The full-day trip costs $159 for adults, and $79.50 for children 3 to 12. Ask about overnights to Lanai if you're interested.

Trilogy also offers snorkel/sail trips to **Molokini,** one of Hawaii's best snorkel spots. This half-day trip leaves from Maalaea Harbor and costs $89 for adults, $44.50 for kids 3 to 12, including breakfast and a BBQ lunch. There's also a late-morning half-day **snorkel-sail off Kaanapali Beach** for the same price.

These are the most expensive sail-snorkel cruises on Maui, but they're worth every penny. The crews are fun and knowledgeable, and the boats are comfortable and well-equipped. All trips include breakfast (Mom's homemade cinnamon buns) and a very good barbecue lunch (shipboard on the half-day trip, on land on the Lanai trip). Note, however, that they will require you to wear a floatation device no matter how good your swimming skills are; if this bothers you, go with another outfitter.

World Class Yacht Charters. 107 Kahului Heliport, Kahului; trips leave from Kaanapali Beach. ☎ **800/600-0959** or 808/667-7733. Prices vary depending on cruise; see below.

You can experience the thrill of competition sailing on the *World Class,* a 65-foot custom yacht designed for Maui waters, which takes 24 passengers for a variety of sailing adventures, including 2-hour **whale-watching** tours in season for $25. When the whales aren't here, they offer a 4-hour morning **snorkel sail** for $59, a 1½-hour afternoon **high-performance sail** for $35, and a 2-hour **trade-winds sunset sail** for $45. The 2pm high-performance sail is the most exciting; there's nothing like it, especially when all you have to do is hold on and cheer. Be prepared to get wet: The captain and crews of this cutter-rigged, high-tech yacht are serious about sailing.

Day Cruises to Lanai

In addition to the *Navatek II* and **Trilogy Excursions** (above), these boats specialize in day trips to the island of Lanai.

Club Lanai. Lahaina Harbor, slip 4. ☎ **808/871-1144.** $89 adults, $69 children 13–20, $29 children 4–12. Price includes all-you-can-eat buffet lunch and open bar.

A day with Club Lanai consists of a trimaran trip from Lahaina Harbor at 7:30am to Lanai's eastern shore, where you can spend the day snorkeling, kayaking, bicycling, or just relaxing in a hammock at an 8-acre beachfront estate. Kahalepalaoa Beach is safe for swimming year-round. Bicycles, kayaks, and all other gear is included in the price.

Maui Nui Explorer. Lahaina Harbor. ☎ **808/661-3776.** $65 adults, $45.50 children 5–11.

This 48-foot, 49-passenger adventure craft offers an amazingly smooth, stable, and swift ride. You'll take a 4-hour journey along the coast of Lanai, where you'll be able to swim and snorkel in remote coves and bays. Coffee and juice and a deli-style lunch are included, along with snacks, snorkel gear, and **whale-watching** (in season). There's always a Hawaiian cultural specialist/marine-life expert onboard to answer questions about the islands and their surrounding waters.

Scotch Mist. Lahaina Harbor, slip 9. ☎ **808/661-0386.** $55 adults, $45 children 11–16, $35 children 4–10.

This 50-foot Santa Cruz sailboat offers half-day sail-snorkel cruises to Lanai; you won't actually set foot on Lanai, but you'll swim with the fish in its sparkling offshore waters. The price includes snorkel gear, fruit juice, fresh pineapple spears, Maui chips, beer, wine, and soda.

BODY BOARDING (BOOGIE BOARDING) & BODYSURFING

You can rent boogie boards and fins from **Snorkel Bob's** at three locations: 161 Lahainaluna Rd. (between Front and Wainee streets), Lahaina (☎ **808/661-4421**); Napili Village, 5425-C Lower Honapiilani Hwy., Napili (☎ **808/669-9603**); and Kihei Market Place, 34 Keala St. (just off S. Kihei Rd.), Kihei (☎ **808/879-7449**), for $6.50 a day or $26 a week. All locations are open 8am to 5pm daily. Gear is also available for rent from **West Hawaii Surfing Academy,** 658 Front St. (in front of the Wharf Cinema Center, across the street from the banyan tree), Lahaina ☎ **808/667-5399**), for $5 for 2 hours. The cheapest place to rent from is **Rental Warehouse,** 578 Front St. (near Prison St.), Lahaina (☎ **808/661-1970**); or in Kihei at Azeka Place II, Kihei Rd. near Lipoa St. (☎ **808/875-4050**), where boogie boards go for as little as $1.99 a day.

In the winter, Maui's best bodysurfing spot is **Mokuleia Beach,** known locally as Slaughterhouse because of the cattle slaughterhouse that once stood here, not because of the waves—although these waves are for expert bodysurfers only. Take Honoapiilani Highway just past Kapalua Bay Resort; various hiking trails will take you down to the pocket beach.

Storms from the south bring fair bodysurfing conditions and great boogie boarding to the lee side of Maui: **Oneloa Beach** (or Big Beach) in Makena, **Ulua** and **Kamaole III** in Kihei, and **Kapalua** beaches are all good choices.

OCEAN KAYAKING

Gliding silently over the water, propelled by a paddle, seeing Maui from the sea the way the early Hawaiians did—that's what ocean kayaking is all about. One of Maui's best kayak routes is along the Kihei Coast, where there's easy access to calm water. Mornings are always best, as the wind comes up around 11am, making seas choppy and paddling difficult. Kayak rentals are available for $15 per hour from **West Hawaii Surfing Academy,** 658 Front St. (in front of the Wharf Cinema Center, across the street from the banyan tree), Lahaina ☎ **808/667-5399.** The cheapest kayak rentals are at **Rental Warehouse,** 578 Front St. (near Prison St.), Lahaina (☎ **808/661-1970**); or in Kihei at Azeka Place II, Kihei Rd. at Lipoa St. (☎ **808/875-4050**), where one-person kayaks are $19.99 a day, and two-person kayaks are $39.99 a day.

GUIDED KAYAK TRIPS

For the uninitiated, our favorite kayak tour operator is **Makena Kayak Tours** (☎ **808/879-8426**). Professional guide Dino leads a 2½-hour tour from Makena Landing and loves taking first-time kayakers over the secluded coral reefs and into remote coves. His wonderful tour will be the highlight of your trip; it's $55 per person, including refreshments and snorkel and kayak equipment.

Gordon Godfrey, Suzanne Simmons, and the expert guides of **South Pacific Kayaks**, at 2439 S. Kihei Rd., Kihei (☎ **800/776-2326** or 808/875-4848; fax 808/875-4691; www.maui.net/~kayak), are Maui's oldest kayak tour company. They offer ocean kayak tours that include lessons, a guided tour, and snorkeling. Tours run from 2½ to 5 hours and range in price from $59 to $89. They also offer kayak rentals starting at $20 a day.

In Hana, **Hana Kayak and Snorkel Tours** (☎ **808/248-7711**) runs 4½-hour tours of Hana's coastline on wide, stable "no roll" kayaks for $59 per person. You can also spend a day learning how to kayak-surf with an instructor for $59 for 7 hours, or rent your own kayak for $27.50 per hour.

OCEAN RAFTING

If you're semi-adventurous and looking for a more intimate experience with the sea, try ocean rafting. The inflatable rafts hold six to 24 passengers, and tours usually include snorkeling and coastal cruising. One of the best (and most reasonable) outfitters is **Hawaiian Ocean Raft** (☎ **888/677-RAFT** or 808/667-2191; fax 808/878-3574), which operates out of the Lahaina Harbor. The best deal here is the 5-hour morning tour, including two snorkeling stops, for $69 adults, $49 children 5 to 12 (children under 5 ride free), which travels over to Lanai and goes searching for dolphins. Their all day, eight-snorkel-stops tour is $109 for adults and $79 for children 5 to 12, with lunch.

PARASAILING

Soar high above the crowds (around 400 feet) for a bird's-eye view of Maui. Parasailing tours are offered from mid-May to mid-December. I'd go with **UFO Parasail** (☎ **800/FLY-4UFO** or 808/661-7UFO; www.ufoparasail.com), which picks you up at Kaanapali Beach. It's $42 for a 7-minute ride; you can save $5 with their Early Bird Special (you must arrive at 7am).

SCUBA DIVING

Everyone dives Molokini, a marine-life park and one of Hawaii's top dive spots. This crescent-shaped crater has three tiers of diving: a 35-foot plateau inside the crater basin (used by beginning divers and snorkelers), a wall sloping to 70 feet just beyond the inside plateau, and a sheer wall on the outside and backside of the crater that plunges 350 feet. This underwater park is very popular, thanks to calm, clear, protected waters and an abundance of marine life, from manta rays to clouds of yellow butterfly fish.

For personalized diving, **Ed Robinson's Diving Adventures** (☎ **800/635-1273** or 808/879-3584; fax 808/874-1939; www.mauiscuba.com/erd1.htm) is one of the best on Maui. This widely published underwater photographer offers specialized charters for small groups. Most of his business is repeat customers. Ed offers two-tank dives for $104 ($10 extra for equipment); his dive boats depart from Kihei Boat Ramp.

If Ed is booked, call **Mike Severns Diving** (☎ **808/879-6596**, www.severns.maui.hi.us), for small (maximum 12 people, divided into two groups of six), personal diving tours on his 38-foot Munson/Hammerhead boat with freshwater shower. Mike and his wife, Pauline Fiene-Severns, are both biologists who make diving in Hawaii not only fun but also educational (they have a spectacular underwater photography book, *Molokini Island*). In their 18 years of operation, they have been accident-free. Two-tank dives are $100 without equipment ($109 with equipment).

Maui's largest diving retailer, with everything from rentals to scuba-diving instruction to diveboat charters, is **Maui Dive Shop,** which can be found all over the island: in Kihei at Azeka Place II Shopping Center (☎ **808/879-3388**), Kamaole Shopping Center (☎ **808/879-1533**), and Kihei Town Center (☎ **808/879-1919**); and in Lahaina at Lahaina Cannery Mall (☎ **808/661-5388**) and 626 Front St. (☎ **808/667-0722**). Other locations include Wailea Shopping Village (☎ **808/879-3166**), Whalers Shopping Village, Kaanapali (☎ **808/661-5117**), Kahana Gateway, Kahana (☎ **808/669-3800**), and 444 Hana Hwy, Kahului (☎ **808/871-2111**).

SNORKELING

Snorkel Bob's can rent everything you need at their three Maui locations: 161 Lahainaluna Rd. (between Front and Wainee streets), Lahaina (☎ **808/661-4421**); Napili Village, 5425-C Lower Honapiilani Hwy, Napili (☎ **808/669-9603**); and Kihei Market Place, 34 Keala St. (just off S. Kihei Road), Kihei (☎ **808/879-7449**). Snorkel gear (fins, mask and snorkel) rent for $2.50 to $6.50 a day, or $9 to $39 a week. **Rental Warehouse,** 578 Front St. (near Prison St.), Lahaina (☎ **808/661-1970**), also has everything you need to experience the underwater world. Sets include mask, fins, snorkel, gear bag, a map of great snorkeling areas, no-fog lotion (for your mask), and a fish ID chart—just add water, and you're ready to go.

Snorkeling on Maui is easy, because there are so many great spots where you can just wade in the water with a face mask and look down to see the tropical fish. Mornings are best, because local winds don't kick in until around noon. Maui's best snorkeling beaches include **Kapalua Beach; Black Rock,** at Kaanapali Beach; along the Kihei coastline, especially at **Kamaole Beach Park III;** and along the Wailea coastline, particularly at **Ulua Beach.** For an off-the-beaten track experience, head south to **Makena Beach;** not only is the bay filled with clouds of tropical fish, but on weekdays, the waters are virtually empty.

When the whales aren't around, **Capt. Steve's Rafting Excursions** (☎ **808/667-5565**) offers all-day (7-hour) snorkel trips to the waters around **Lanai** (you don't actually land on the island) for $130 for adults and $95 for children 12 and under; breakfast, lunch, snorkel gear, and wet suits are included.

Two truly terrific snorkel spots are difficult to get to but worth the effort, because they're home to Hawaii's tropical marine life at its best:

✪ **MOLOKINI**   Like a crescent moon fallen from the sky, this sunken crater sits almost midway between Maui and the uninhabited island of Kahoolawe. Tilted so that only the thin rim of its southern side shows above water in a perfect semicircle, Molokini stands like a scoop against the tide and serves, on its concave side, as a natural sanctuary for tropical fish and snorkelers who commute daily in a fleet of dive boats to this marine-life preserve. Molokini is only accessible by boat; see "Boating," above, for outfitters that can take you there.

AHIHI-KINAU NATURAL PRESERVE   You can't miss in Ahihi Bay, a 2,000-acre state natural area reserve in the lee of Cape Kinau, on Maui's rugged South Coast, where Haleakala spilled red-hot lava that ran to the sea in 1790. Fishing is strictly *kapu* here, and the fish know it; they're everywhere in this series of rocky coves and black-lava tide pools. To get here, drive south of Makena past Puu Olai to Ahihi Bay, where the road turns to gravel and sometimes seems like it'll disappear under the waves. At Cape Kinau, three four-wheel–drive trails lead across the lava flow; take the shortest one, nearest La Pérouse Bay. A 4-wheel drive will get you all the way there; if

An Expert Shares His Secrets: Maui's Best Dives

Ed Robinson, of Ed Robinson's Diving Adventures (see above), knows what makes a great dive. Here are five of his favorites on Maui—and he'll be happy to take you to any or all of them:

Hawaiian Reef This area off the Kihei-Wailea Coast is so named because it hosts a good cross-section of topography and marine life typical of Hawaiian waters. Diving to depths of 85 feet, you'll see everything from lava formations and coral reef to sand and rubble, plus a diverse range of both shallow and deep-water creatures. It's clear why this area was so popular with ancient Hawaiian fishermen: large helmet shells, a healthy garden of large antler coral heads, and large schools of snapper are common.

Third Tank Located off Makena Beach at 80 feet, this World War II tank is one of the most picturesque artificial reefs you're likely to see around Maui. It acts like a fish magnet. Because it's the only large solid object in the area, any fish or invertebrates looking for a safe home come here. Surrounding the tank is a cloak of schooling snapper and goatfish just waiting for a photographer with a wide-angle lens. For its small size, the Third Tank is loaded with more marine life per square inch than any site off Maui.

Molokini Crater The backside is always done as a live boat-drift dive. The vertical wall plummets from over 150 feet above sea level to around 250 feet below. Looking down to unseen depths gives you a feeling for the vastness of the open ocean. Pelagic fish and sharks are often sighted, and living coral perches on the wall, which is home to lobsters, crabs, and a number of photogenic black-coral trees at 50 feet.

There are actually two great dive sites around Molokini Crater. Named after common chub or rudderfish, **Enenue Side** gently slopes from the surface to

you have a standard car, drive as far as you can, park, and walk the remainder of the way. Après-snorkel, check out La Pérouse Bay on the south side of Cape Kinau, where the French admiral La Pérouse became the first European to set foot on Maui. A lava-rock pyramid known as Pérouse Monument marks the spot.

SPORTFISHING

Marlin, tuna, onos, and mahi-mahis await the baited hook in Maui's coastal and channel waters. No license is required; just book a sportfishing vessel out of Lahaina or Maalaea Harbor. Most charter boats that troll for big-game fish carry six passengers max. You can walk the docks, inspecting boats and talking to captains and crew, or book through an activities desk or one of the outfits recommended below.

If you want to fish out of Maalaea, call **Rhythm and Blues Sportfishing** (☎ 808/879-7098); Capt. Mike Crawford is an experienced fishermen with top-flight gear and a comfortable 36-foot Pacifica sportfishing boat. Or spend the day with **Capt. Joe Yurkanin** and **Capt. Ermin Fergerstrom** on their 37-foot Tollycraft, the *No Ka Oi III* (☎ 800/798-0652 or 808/879-4485). For other ideas, try the **Maalaea Activities** desk at the harbor (☎ 808/242-6982).

At Lahaina Harbor, go for one of the following charter companies: **Hinata Sportfishing**, slip 27 (☎ 808/667-7548); **Lucky Strike Charters**, slips 50 and 51 (☎ 808/661-4606); or **Aerial Sportfishing Charters**, slip 2 (☎ 808/667-9089).

about 60 feet, then drops rapidly to deeper waters. The shallower area is an easy dive, with lots of tame butterfly fish. It's also the home of Morgan Benajaw, one of our friendliest moray eels. Enenue Side is often done as a live boat-drift dive to extend the range of the tour. Diving depths vary. Divers usually do a 50-foot dive, but on occasion, advanced divers drop to the 130-foot level to visit the rare boarfish and the shark condos.

Almost every kind of fish found in Hawaii can be seen in the crystalline waters of **Reef's End.** It's an extension of the rim of the crater, which runs for about 200 yards underwater, barely breaking the surface. Reef's End is shallow enough for novice snorkelers and exciting enough for experienced divers. The end and outside of this shoal drop off in dramatic terraces to beyond diving range. In deeper waters, there are shark ledges at varying depths and dozens of eels, some of which are tame, including moray, dragon, snowflake, and garden eels. The shallower inner side is home to Garbanzo, one of the largest and first eels to be tamed. The reef is covered with cauliflower coral; in bright sunlight, it's one of the most dramatic underwater scenes in Hawaii.

La Pérouse Pinnacle   In the middle of scenic La Pérouse Bay, site of Haleakala's most recent lava flow, is a pinnacle rising from the 60-foot bottom to about 10 feet below the surface. Getting to the dive site is half the fun: The scenery above water is as exciting as that below the surface. Underwater, you'll enjoy a very diversified dive. Clouds of damselfish and triggerfish will greet you on the surface. There are more porcupine puffers here than anywhere else, as well as schools of goatfish and fields of healthy finger coral. La Pérouse is good for snorkeling and long, shallow second dives.

Or check with **West Maui Charter** (☎ 808/669-6193), offering everything from light- to heavy-tackle fishing.

SUBMARINE DIVES

This is the stuff dreams are made of: Plunging 100 feet below the surface of the sea in a state-of-the-art, high-tech submarine. This is a great way to experience Maui's magnificent underwater world if you're a nonswimmer. **Atlantis Submarines,** 665 Front St., Lahaina (☎ **800/548-6262,** 888/REAL-SUB, or 808/667-7816; www.go atlantis.com), offers trips out of Lahaina Harbor every hour on the hour from 8am to 2pm; tickets are $79 each (you'll save $10 by taking the 8am, 1pm, 2pm, or 3pm tour). Allow 2 hours for your underwater adventure.

SURFING

You say you always wanted to know how to surf but didn't know who to ask? Call the **Nancy Emerson School of Surfing** (☎ **808/244-SURF** or 808/874-1183; fax 808/874-2581; www.maui.net/~ncesurf/ncesurf.html). Nancy has been surfing since 1961, and she has been a stunt performer for various movies, including *Waterworld.* She's pioneered a new instructional technique called "Learn to Surf in One Lesson"—you can, really. It's $50 per person for 1 hour, $65 per person for 2 hours with a group; private 2-hour classes are $110.

Even if you've never seen a surfboard before, Andrea Thomas claims she can teach you the art of riding the waves. She's instructed thousands at **Maui Surfing School** (☎ **808/875-0625;** www.mauisurf.com), including students as young as 3 and as "chronologically gifted" as 70. She backs her classes with a guarantee that she'll get you surfing, or you'll get 110% of your money back. Two-hour lessons are $60; call for an appointment.

Steve and Ava Mcnanie, owners of the **West Maui Surfing Academy,** 658 Front St. (in front of the Wharf Cinema Center, across the street from the banyan tree), Lahaina (☎ **808/667-5399),** teach surfing the Hawaiian way; 2½-hour lessons are $65. You can also rent surfboards here, $10 for 2 hours. Surfboards are also available for rent from **Hunt Hawaii Surf and Sail** in Paia (☎ **808/575-2300),** starting at $20 a day. Surfers on a budget will find the least-expensive rates on rental boards at **Rental Warehouse,** 578 Front St. (near Prison St.), Lahaina (☎ **808/661-1970);** and in Kihei at Azeka Place II, on Kihei Rd. near Lipoa St. (☎ **808/875-4050),** where "goober's" boards rent for $9.99 a day, and "shredder's" boards go for $18.99 a day.

Expert surfers visit Maui in winter when the surf's really up. The best surfing beaches include **Honolua Bay,** north of the Kapalua Resort (the third bay past the Ritz Carlton Kapalua, off the Honoapiilani Highway, or Hwy. 30); **Lahaina Harbor** (in the summer, there'll be waves just off the Lahaina Harbor channel entrance with a south swell); **Maalaea,** just outside the breakwall of the Maalaea Harbor (a clean, world-class left); and **Hookipa Beach,** where surfers get the waves until noon; after that—in a carefully worked-out compromise to share this prized surf spot—the windsurfers take over.

WHALE-WATCHING

The humpback whale is a cottage industry on Maui. No creature on earth is celebrated in so many ways as the whale. Don't waste your money on whale stuff; go see the real thing. You can—the humpback is the star of the annual whale-watching season, which usually begins in December and can last until May.

WHALE-WATCHING FROM SHORE   The best time to whale-watch is between mid-December and April. Just look out to sea. There's no best time of day for whale-watching, but it seems when the sea is glassy and there's no wind, the whales appear. Once you see one, keep watching in the same vicinity; they may stay down 20 minutes. Bring a book. And binoculars, if you can. You can rent a pair for $1.99 a day at **Rental Warehouse,** 578 Front St. (near Prison St.), Lahaina (☎ **808/661-1970);** and in Kihei at Azeka Place II, on S. Kihei Rd. near Lipoa St. (☎ **808/875-4050).** Some good whale-watching points on Maui are:

McGregor Point   On the way to Lahaina, there's a scenic lookout at mile marker 9 (just before you get to the Lahaina Tunnel); it's a good viewpoint for whale-scanning.

Aston Wailea Resort   On the Wailea coastal walk, stop at this resort (formerly the Maui Intercontinental) to look for whales through the telescope installed as a public service by the Hawaii Island Humpback Whale National Marine Sanctuary.

Olowalu Reef   Along the straight part of Honoapiilani Highway, between McGregor Point and Olowalu, you'll see whales leap out of the water. Sometimes, their appearance brings traffic to a screeching halt: People abandon their cars and run down to the sea to watch, causing a major traffic jam. If you stop, pull off the road so others may pass.

Puu Olai   It's a tough climb up this coastal landmark near the Maui Prince Hotel, but you're likely to be well rewarded: This is the island's best spot for offshore whale-watching. On the 360-foot cinder cone overlooking Makena Beach, you'll be at the right elevation to see Pacific humpbacks as they dodge Molokini and cruise up

Alalakeiki Channel between Maui and Kahoolawe. If you don't see one, you'll at least have a whale of a view.

WHALE-WATCHING CRUISES   For a closer look, take a whale-watching cruise. Just about all of Hawaii's snorkel and dive boats become whale-watching boats in season; some of them even carry professional naturalists onboard so you'll know what you're seeing. For the best boats, see "Boating," above.

WHALE-WATCHING BY KAYAK & RAFT   Seeing a humpback whale from an ocean kayak or raft is awesome. **Capt. Steve's Rafting Excursions** (☎ **808/ 667-5565**) offers 2-hour whale-watching excursions out of Lahaina Harbor for $45 for adults, $35 for children 12 and under. Take the early-bird trip at 7:30am and spot some whales for only $35 per person.

Experienced kayakers should call **South Pacific Kayaks and Outfitters** (☎ **800/ 776-2326** or 808/875-4848; www.maui.net/~kayak). They lead small groups on 3-hour trips in the calm waters off both Makena and Lahaina for $59 per person.

WINDSURFING

Maui has Hawaii's best windsurfing beaches. In winter, windsurfers from around the world flock to the town of **Paia** to ride the waves; **Hookipa Beach**, known all over the globe for its brisk winds and excellent waves, is the site of several world-championship contests. **Kanaha**, west of Kahului Airport, also has dependable winds; when conditions are right, it's packed with colorful butterfly-like sails. When the winds turn northerly, **Kihei** is the spot to be; some days, you can spot whales in the distance behind the windsurfers. The northern end of Kihei is best: at **Ohukai Park**, the first beach as you enter South Kihei Road from the northern end, not only are the winds good, but there's parking, a long strip of grass to assemble your gear, and good access to the water. Experienced windsurfers are found in front of the **Maui Sunset** condo, 1032 S. Kihei Rd., near Waipuilani Street (one block north of McDonald's), which has great windsurfing conditions but a very shallow reef (not good for beginners).

Hawaiian Island Surf and Sport, 415 Dairy Rd., Kahului (☎ **800/231-6958** or 808/871-4981; fax 808/871-4624; www.hawaiianisland.com), offers lessons, rentals, and repairs. Other shops featuring rentals and lessons are **Hawaiian Sailboarding Techniques,** 444 Hana Hwy., Kahului (☎ **808/871-5423**); and **Maui Windsurf Co,** 520 Keolani Place, Kahului (☎ **800/872-0999** or 808/877-4816). Complete equipment rental (board, sail, rig harness, and roof rack) is available from $45 a day and $295 a week. Lessons, from beginning to advanced, range from $50 to $75 for a 1- or 2-hour lesson.

For daily reports on wind and surf conditions, call the **Wind and Surf Report** at ☎ **808/877-3611.**

7 Hiking & Camping

by Jeanette Foster

In the past two decades, Maui has grown from a rural island to a fast-paced resort destination, but its natural beauty remains largely inviolate; there are still many places that can be explored only on foot. Those interested in seeing the backcountry—complete with virgin waterfalls, remote wilderness trails, and quiet, meditative settings—should head for Haleakala's upcountry or the tropical Hana Coast.

Camping on Maui can be extreme (inside a volcano) or benign (by the sea in Hana). It can be wet, cold, and rainy; or hot, dry, and windy—often, all on the same day. If you're heading for Haleakala, remember that U.S. astronauts trained for the moon inside the volcano; bring survival gear. Don't forget both your swimsuit and rain gear if you're bound for Waianapanapa, and bring your own equipment, as there's no place to rent gear on Maui yet. If you need to buy equipment, check out **Gaspro**, 365 Hanakai, Kahului (☎ **808/877-0056**); **Maui Expedition**, Kihei Commercial Center, (☎ **808/875-7470**); or **Maui Sporting Goods**, 92 N. Market, Wailuku (☎ **808/244-0011**).

For more information on Maui camping and hiking trails, and to obtain free maps, contact **Haleakala National Park**, P.O. Box 369, Makawao, HI 96768 (☎ **808/572-9306**); and the **State Division of Forestry and Wildlife**, 54 S. High St., Wailuku, HI 96793 (☎ **808/984-8100**). For information on trails, hikes, camping, and permits for state parks, contact the **Hawaii State Department of Land and Natural Resources**, State Parks Division, 54 S. High St., Rm. 101, Wailuku, HI 96793 (☎ **808/984-8109**).

GUIDED HIKES   If you would like a knowledgeable guide to accompany you on a hike, call **Maui Hiking Safaris** (☎ **888/445-3963** or 808/573-0168; fax 808/572-3037; www.maui.net/~mhs). Owner Randy Warner takes visitors on half-day and full-day hikes into valleys, rain forests, and coastal areas. Randy's been hiking around Maui for more than 10 years and is wise in the ways of Hawaiian history, native flora and fauna, and vulcanology. His rates are $49 for a half-day and $89 for a full day (10% off for kids 13 and under), and include day-packs, rain parkas, snacks, water, and on full-day hikes, sandwiches.

Maui's oldest hiking guide company is **Hike Maui** (☎ **808/879-5270**; fax 808/876-0308; www.hikemaui.com), headed by Ken Schmitt, who pioneered guided hikes on the Valley Isle. Hike Maui offers five different hikes a day, ranging from an easy 3½-mile stroll in the rain forest to a waterfall ($70 for adults, $50 for children 15 and under) to a strenuous, full-day rain-forest hike along a mountain ridge ($110 for adults, $85 for children). All prices include equipment and transportation.

All-day hikes to lush rain forests and waterfall pools in the West Maui Mountains are offered Saturdays from 8am to noon by the not-for-profit **Kapalua Nature Society** (☎ **800/KAPALUA** or 808/669-0244). Groups of up to nine can go on guided hiking tours, which include a picnic lunch and transportation to and from the trails. Two exclusive hikes are offered: the easy, 1½-mile **Maunalei Arboretum/Puu Kaeo Nature Walk**, which starts at 1,200 feet and goes to the 1,635-foot summit of Puu Kaeo; and the breathtaking 4-mile **Manienie Ridge Hike**, a more strenuous hike with moderate slope, some uneven footing, and close vegetation. The cost is $59; children must be at least 12. Proceeds go toward the preservation of Puu Kukui rain forest.

Venture into the lush West Maui Mountains with an experienced guide on one of the **Ritz-Carlton Kapalua's Eco-Tours** (☎ **808/669-6200**). After a continental breakfast, you'll hike by streams and waterfalls, through native trees and plants, and on to breathtaking vistas. The tour stops for a picnic lunch, swimming in secluded pools, and memorable photo ops. The 6-hour excursion (offered Tuesday through Friday at 8am) costs $110 for adults, $90 for children 13 to 18; the 4-hour excursion (Saturday through Monday at 8am) is $65. The 2- to 3-mile, 4-hour hike is classified as "easy"; the 4- to 5-mile, 6-hour hike is classified as "easy-moderate." Ritz-Carlton suggests that you wear comfortable walking or hiking shoes and bring a swimsuit, sunscreen, and camera; they supply the meals, a fanny pack with bottled water, and rain gear if necessary. No children under 13 allowed.

About 1,500 years ago, the verdant Kahakuloa Valley was a thriving Hawaiian village. Today, only a few hundred people live in this secluded hamlet, but Old Hawaii still lives on here. Explore the valley with **Ekahi Tours** (☎ **808/877-9775**). Your guide, a Kahakuloa resident and a Hawaiiana expert, walks you through a taro farm, explains the mystical legends of the valley, and provides you with a peek into ancient Hawaii. The 7½-hour Kahakuloa Valley Tour is $60 for adults, $50 for children under 12; snacks, beverages, and hotel pickup are included.

HALEAKALA NATIONAL PARK

For complete coverage of the national park, see "Seeing the Sights," below.

INTO THE WILDERNESS: SLIDING SANDS & HALEMAU TRAILS

Hiking into Maui's dormant volcano is really the way to see it. The terrain inside the wilderness area of the volcano, which ranges from burnt-red cinder cones to ebony-black lava flows, is simply spectacular. There are some 27 miles of hiking trails, two camping sites, and three cabins.

The best route takes in two trails: into the crater along **Sliding Sands Trail**, which begins on the rim at 9,800 feet and descends into the belly of the beast, to the valley floor at 6,600 feet; and back out along **Halemau Trail**. Hardy hikers can consider making the 11.3-mile, one-way descent, which takes 9 hours, and the equally-as-long returning ascent in 1 day. The rest of us will probably have a wonderful time extending this steep hike to two days. The descending and ascending trails aren't loops; the trail-heads are miles (and several thousand feet in elevation) apart, so you'll need to make transportation arrangements in advance. Arrange to stay at least one night in the park; two or three will allow you more time to explore the fascinating interior of the volcano; see below for details on the cabins and campgrounds in the wilderness area of the valley.

Before you set out, stop at park headquarters to get camping and hiking updates. There is no registration for day hikers.

A word of warning about the weather: The weather at nearly 10,000 feet can change suddenly and without warning. Come prepared for cold, high winds, rain, even snow in the winter. Temperatures can range from 77°F down to 26°F (they're even lower when you factor in the wind chill), and high winds are frequent. Rainfall varies from 40 inches a year on the west end of the crater to more than 200 inches on the eastern side. Bring boots, waterproof wear, warm clothes, extra layers, and lots of sunscreen—the sun shines very brightly up here.

The trailhead for Sliding Sands is well-marked and the trail easy to follow over lava flows and cinders. As you descend, look around: The view is breathtaking. In the after-noon, waves of clouds flow into the Kaupo and Koolau gaps. Vegetation is spare to nonexistent at the top, but the closer you get to the valley floor, the more vegetation you'll see: bracken ferns, pili grass, shrubs, even flowers. On the floor, the trail travels across rough lava flows, passing by rare silversword plants, volcanic vents, and multi-colored cinder cones.

The Halemau Trail goes over red and black lava and past vegetation, like evening primrose, as it begins its ascent up the valley wall. Occasionally, riders on horseback use this trail as an entry and exit from the park. The proper etiquette is to step aside and stand quietly next to the trail as the horses pass.

Some Shorter & Easier Options   Take a half-mile walk down the **Hosmer Grove Nature Trail** or start down **Sliding Sands Trail** for a mile or two to get a hint of what lies ahead. Even this short hike is exhausting at the high altitude. A good day hike is **Halemau Trail** to Holua Cabin and back, an 8-mile, half-day trip.

STAYING IN THE WILDERNESS AREA   Most people stay at one of two tent campgrounds, unless they get lucky and win the lottery—the lottery, that is, for one of the three wilderness cabins. For more information, contact **Haleakala National Park,** P.O. Box 369, Makawao, HI 96768 (☎ **808/572-9306**).

The Cabins It can get really cold and windy down in the valley (see above), so try for a cabin. They're warm, protected from the elements, and reasonably priced. Each has 12 padded bunks (but no bedding; bring your own), a table, chairs, cooking utensils, a two-burner propane stove, and a wood-burning stove with firewood (you may also have a few cockroaches). The cabins are spaced so that each one is an easy walk from the other: Holua cabin is on the Halemauu Trail, Kapalaoa cabin on Sliding Sands Trail, and Paliku cabin on the eastern end by the Kaupo Gap. The rates are $40 a night for one to six people, $80 a night for seven to twelve.

The cabins are so popular that the National Park Service has a lottery system for reservations. Requests for cabins must be made 3 months in advance (be sure to request alternate dates). You can request all three cabins at once; you're limited to no more than 2 nights in one cabin and no more than 3 nights within the wilderness per month.

The Campgrounds If you don't win the cabin lottery, all isn't lost, as there are three tent-camping sites that can accommodate you: two in the wilderness and one just outside at Hosmer Grove. There is no charge for tent camping.

Hosmer Grove is located at 6,800 feet; it's a small, open, grassy area surrounded by a forest. Trees protect campers from the winds, but nights still get very cold. Hard to believe, but sometimes there's ice on the ground up here. This is the best place to spend the night in a tent if you want to see the Haleakala sunrise. Come up the day before, enjoy the park, take a day hike, then turn in early. The enclosed-glass summit building opens at sunrise for those who come to greet the dawn—a welcome windbreak. Facilities include a covered pavilion with picnic tables and grills, chemical toilets, and drinking water. No permits are needed at Hosmer Grove, and there's no charge; but you can only stay for 3 nights in 30 days.

The two tent-camping areas inside the volcano are **Holua**, just off Halemauu at 6,920 feet; and **Paliku**, just before the Kaupo Gap at the eastern end of the valley, at 6,380 feet. Facilities at both campgrounds are limited to pit toilets and nonpotable catchment water. Water at Holua is limited, especially in summer. No open fires are allowed inside the volcano, so bring a stove if you plan to cook. Tent camping is restricted to the signed area. No camping is allowed in the horse pasture. The inviting grassy lawn in front of the cabin is *kapu*. Camping is free but limited to two consecutive nights, and no more than three nights a month inside the volcano. Permits are issued daily at Park Headquarters on a first-come, first-served basis. Occupancy is limited to 25 people in each campground.

HIKING & CAMPING AT KIPAHULU (NEAR HANA)

In the East Maui section of Haleakala National Park, you can set up at **Oheo Campground**, a first-come, first-served drive-in campground with tent sites for 100 near the ocean, with a few tables, barbecue grills, and chemical toilets. No permit is required, but there's a 3-night limit. No food or drinking water is available, so bring your own. Bring a tent, because it rains 75 inches a year here. Contact **Kipahulu Ranger Station**, Haleakala National Park, HI 96713 (☎ **808/248-7375**).

HIKING FROM THE SUMMIT If you hike from the crater rim down **Kaupo Gap** to the ocean, more than 20 miles away, you'll pass through climate zones ranging from Arctic to tropical. On a clear day, you can see every island except Kauai on the trip down.

APPROACHING KIPAHULU FROM HANA If you drive to Kipahulu, you'll have to approach it from the Hana Highway, as it's not accessible from the summit. From the ranger station, it's a short hike above the famous **Oheo Gulch** (which was misnamed the Seven Sacred Pools in the 1940s) to two spectacular waterfalls. The first, **Makahiku Falls**, is easily reached from the central parking area: The trailhead begins near the ranger station. Pipiwai Trail leads you up to the road and beyond for a half-mile to the overlook. If you like another 1½ miles up the trail across two bridges and through a bamboo forest, you reach **Waimoku Falls**. It's a good uphill hike, but press on to avoid the pool's crowd. In hard rain, streams swell quickly. Always be aware of your surroundings.

SKYLINE TRAIL, POLIPOLI SPRINGS STATE RECREATION AREA

This is some hike—strenuous but worth every step, if you like to see the big picture. It's 8 miles, all downhill, with a dazzling 100-mile view of the islands dotting the blue Pacific, plus the West Maui Mountains, which seem like a separate island.

The trail is just outside Haleakala National Park at Polipoli Springs National Recreation Area; however, you access it by going through the national park to the summit. It starts just beyond the Puu Ulaula summit building on the south side of Science City and follows the southwest rift zone of Haleakala from its lunar-like cinder cones to a cool redwood grove. The trail drops 3,800 feet on a 4-hour hike to the recreation area in the 12,000-acre Kahikinui Forest Reserve. If you'd rather drive it, you need a four-wheel vehicle to access the trail.

There's a **campground** at the recreation area at 6,300 feet. No fee or reservations are required, but your stay must be limited to 5 nights. Tent camping is free, but you must get a permit. One 10-bunk cabin is available for $45 a night for 1 to 4 guests and $5 for each additional guest; it has no electricity, a cold shower, and a gas stove. There's no drinking water available; you must bring in your own. To reserve, write the **State Parks Division**, 54 High St., Rm 101, Wailuku, HI 96793, or call ☎ **808/ 984-8109** between 8am and 4pm weekdays.

POLIPOLI STATE PARK

One of the most unusual hiking experiences in the state can be found at Polipoli State Park, part of the 21,000-acre Polipoli Springs Forest Reserve on the slope of Haleakala. At Polipoli, it's hard to believe that you're in Hawaii: First of all, it's cold, even in the summer, since the loop's at 5,300 to 6,200 feet; second, this former forest of native koa, ohia, and mamane trees, which was overlogged in the 1800s, was reforested in the 1930s with introduced species: pine, Monterey cypress, ash, sugi, red adler, redwood, and several varieties of eucalyptus. The result is a cool area, with muted sunlight filtered by towering trees.

The **Polipoli Loop** is an easy 5-mile hike that takes about 3 hours; dress warmly for it. To get there, take the Haleakala Highway (Hwy. 37) to Keokea and turn right onto Highway 337; after less than a half-mile, turn on Waipoli Road, which climbs swiftly. After 10 miles, Waipoli Road ends at the Polipoli State Park campgrounds. The well-marked trailhead is next to the parking lot, near a stand of Monterey cypresses; the tree-lined trail offers the best view of the island.

Polipoli Loop is really a network of three trails: Haleakala Ridge, Plum Trail, and Redwood Trail. After a half-mile of meandering through groves of eucalyptus, blackwood, swamp mahogany, and hybrid cypress, you'll join the Haleakala Ridge Trail, which, about a mile into the trail, joins with the Plum Trail (named for the plums that ripen in June and July). It passes through massive redwoods and by an old Conservation Corps bunkhouse and a rundown cabin before joining up with the Redwood Trail, which climbs through Mexican pine, tropical ash, Port Orford cedar, and—of course—redwood.

Camping is allowed with a permit from the **Division of State Parks**, 54 S. High St., Rm 101, Wailuku, HI 96793 (☎ **808/984-8109**). There's one cabin, available by reservation.

WAIANANAPANAPA STATE PARK

Tucked in a tropical jungle, on the outskirts of the little coastal town of Hana, is Waiananapanapa State Park, a black-sand beach set in an emerald forest.

THE HANA-WAIANAPANAPA COAST TRAIL This is an easy 6-mile hike that takes you back in time. Allow four hours to walk along this relatively flat trail, which parallels the sea, along lava cliffs and a forest of lauhala trees. The best time to take the hike is either in the early morning or late evening, when the light on the lava and surf makes for great photos. Midday is the worst time; not only is it hot (lava intensifies the heat), but no shade or potable water is available.

There's no formal trailhead; join the route at any point along the Waianapanapa Campground and go in either direction. Along the trail, you'll see remains of an ancient *heiau* (temple), stands of lauhala trees, caves, a blowhole, and a remarkable plant, *naupaka*, that flourishes along the beach. Upon close inspection, you'll see that the naupaka have only half-blossoms; according to Hawaiian legend, a similar plant living in the mountains has the other half of the blossoms. One ancient explanation is that the two plants represent never-to-be reunited lovers: as the story goes, the two lovers bickered so much that the gods, fed up with their incessant quarreling, banished one lover to the mountain and the other to the sea.

CAMPING Waianapanapa has 12 cabins and a tent campground. Go for the cabins (see "Accommodations," above), as it rains torrentially here, sometimes turning the campground into a mud-wrestling arena. If you opt to tent-camp, it's free but limited to 5 nights in a 30-day period. Permits are available from the **State Parks Division, 54 S. High St., Rm 101, Wailuku, HI 96793 (☎ 808/984-8109)**. Facilities include rest rooms, outdoor showers, drinking water, and picnic tables.

HANA: THE HIKE TO FAGAN'S CROSS

This 3-mile hike to the cross erected in memory of Hana Ranch and Hotel Hana-Maui founder Paul Fagan offers spectacular views of the Hana Coast, particularly at sunset. The uphill trail starts across Hana Highway from the Hotel Hana-Maui. Enter the pastures at your own risk; they're often occupied by glaring bulls with sharp horns and cows with new calves. Avoid the nursing cows, and don't wear red. Watch your step as you ascend this steep hill on a jeep trail across open pastures to the cross and the breathtaking view.

8 Golf & Other Outdoor Activities

by Jeanette Foster

BICYCLING

For bike excursions throughout Maui, call **Chris' Adventures (☎ 800/224-5344** or **808/871-2453)**. Chris offers a variety of bike tours (ranging from $49 to $110); we recommend the Waihee-Kahakuloa Coastal Adventure ($59), where you'll hike the Waihee Valley or Ridge and then bike along the spectacular northwestern coast, which feels like Old Hawaii.

If you want to venture out on your own, cheap rentals—$9.99 a day for cruisers and $19.99 a day for mountain bikes—are available from **Rental Warehouse**, 578 Front St. (near Prison St.), Lahaina (☎ **808/661-1970**); or in Kihei at Azeka Place II, on Kihei Rd. near Lipoa St. (☎ **808/875-4050**).

For information on bikeways and maps, contact the **Mayor's Advisory Committee on Bicycling (☎ 808/871-6886)**.

CRUISING HALEAKALA   It's not even close to dawn, but here you are, rubbing your eyes awake, riding in a van up the long, dark road to the top of Maui's sleeping volcano. It's colder than you ever thought possible for a tropical island. The air is thin. You stomp your chilly feet while you wait, sipping hot coffee. Then comes the sun, exploding over the yawning Haleakala Crater, big enough to swallow Manhattan—a mystic moment you won't soon forget, imprinted on a palette of dawn colors. Now you know why Hawaiians named it the House of the Sun. But there's no time to linger. Decked out in your screaming-yellow parka, you mount your special steed and test its most important feature, the brakes—because you're about to coast 37 miles down a 10,000-foot volcano.

Cruising down Haleakala, from the lunar-like landscape at the top, past flower farms, pineapple fields, and eucalyptus groves, is quite an experience—and just about anybody can do it. This is a safe, no-strain bicycle trip that requires some stamina in the colder, wetter winter months but is fun for everyone from the kids to grandma in the warmer months. You don't have to be an expert cyclist; you just have to be able to ride a bike.

Maui's oldest downhill company is **Maui Downhill** (☎ **800/535-BIKE** or 808/871-2155; e-mail mauidown@gte.net), which has a sunrise safari bike tour, including continental breakfast and brunch, starting at $100; both **Maui Mountain Chasers** (☎ **800/232-6284** or 808/871-6014) and **Mountain Riders Bike Tours** (☎ **808/242-9739**) have Haleakala rides for $120. Trips include hotel pickup, transport to the top, bicycle, safety equipment, and meals. Wear layers of warm clothing, as there may be a 30°F change in temperature from the top of the mountain to the ocean. Generally, the tour groups will not take riders under 12, but younger children can ride along in the van that accompanies the groups. Pregnant women should also ride in the van.

GOLF

If you don't bring your own with you, you can rent clubs from **Rental Warehouse,** 578 Front St. (near Prison St.), Lahaina (☎ **808/661-1970**), where top-quality clubs go for $14.99 a day, not-so-top-quality for $9.99 a day. **Golf Club Rentals** (☎ **808/665-0800**) also has custom-built clubs for men, woman, and juniors in both right- and left-handed. Their rates are just $15 a day, and they deliver islandwide.

For last-minute and discount tee times, call **Stand-by Golf** (☎ **888/645-BOOK** from Hawaii, 808/322-BOOK from the mainland) between 7am and 9pm. Stand-by offers discounted (10 to 40%) guaranteed tee times for same-day or next-day golfing.

WEST MAUI

Kaanapali Courses. Off Hwy. 30, Kaanapali. ☎ **808/661-3691.** At the first stoplight in Kaanapali, turn onto Kaanapali Pkwy.; the first building on your right is the clubhouse.

Both Kaanapali courses offer a challenge to all golfers, from high handicappers to near-pros. The par-72, 6,305-yard **North Course** is a true Robert Trent Jones design: an abundance of wide bunkers; several long, stretched-out tees; and the largest, most contoured greens on Maui. It has a tricky 18th hole (par 4, 435 yards) with a water hazard on the approach to the green.

The par-72, 6,250-yard **South Course** is an Arthur Jack Snyder design; although shorter than the North Course, it does require more accuracy on the narrow, hilly fairways. It also has a water hazard on its final hole, so don't tally up your scorecard until the final putt is sunk.

Facilities include a driving range, putting course, and clubhouse with dining. Greens fees for golfers not staying in Kaanapali are $120, $60 after 2pm ($100 for resort guests, $62 after 2pm); weekday tee times are best.

⊙ **Kapalua Resort Courses.** Off Hwy. 30, Kapalua.

The views from these three championship courses are worth the greens fees alone. The first to open was the **Bay Course** (☎ 808/669-8820), a par-72, 6,761-yard course inaugurated in 1975. Designed by Arnold Palmer and Ed Seay, this course is a bit forgiving with its wide fairways; the greens, however, are difficult to read. The well-photographed 5th overlooks a small ocean cove; even the pros have trouble with this rocky par-3, 205-yard hole.

The par-71, 6,632-yard **Village Course** (☎ 808/669-8830), another Palmer/Seay design, is the most scenic of the three courses; the hole with the best vista definitely is the 6th, which overlooks a lake with the ocean in the distance. But don't get distracted by the view—the tee is between two rows of Cook pines.

The **Plantation Course** (☎ 808/669-8877), scene of the Lincoln/Mercury Kapalua International and the Kirin Cup World Championship of Golf, is Ben Crenshaw/Bill Coore designed. A 6,547-yard, par-73 course on a rolling hillside, this one is excellent for developing your low shots and precise chipping.

Facilities for all three courses include locker rooms, a driving range, and an excellent restaurant. Greens fees are $140 at the Village and Bay courses ($65 after 2pm), $150 at the Plantation Course ($70 after 2pm). Weekdays are your best bet for tee times.

SOUTH MAUI

⊙ **Makena Courses.** On Makena Alanui Dr., just past the Maui Prince Hotel. ☎ 808/879-3344.

Here you'll find 36 holes of "Mr. Hawaii Golf"—Robert Trent Jones, Jr.—at its best. Add to that spectacular views: Molokini islet looms in the background, humpback whales gambol offshore in winter, and the tropical sunsets are spectacular. This is golf not to be missed. The par-72, 6,876-yard **South Course** has a couple of holes you'll never forget. The view from the par-4 15th hole, which shoots from an elevated tee 183 yards downhill to the Pacific, is magnificent. The 16th hole has a two-tiered green that's blind from the tee 383 yards away (that is, if you make it past the gully off the fairway).

The par-72, 6,823-yard **North Course** is more difficult and more spectacular. The 13th hole, located partway up the mountain, has a view that makes most golfers stop and stare. The next hole is even more memorable: a 200-foot drop between tee and green.

Facilities include clubhouse, driving range, two putting greens, pro shop, lockers, and lessons. Beware of crowded conditions on weekends. Greens fees are $100 for Makena Resort guests, $120 for nonguests.

Silversword Golf Club. 1345 Piilani Hwy. (near Lipoa St. turnoff), Kihei. ☎ 808/874-0777.

Sitting in the foothills of Haleakala, just high enough to afford spectacular ocean views from every hole, this is a course for golfers who love the views as much as the fairways and greens. It's very forgiving, especially for duffers and high handicappers. Just one caveat: Go in the morning. Not only is it cooler, but more important, it's less windy. In the afternoon, the winds really pick up, blustering down Haleakala with great gusto. Silversword is a fun course to play, with some challenging holes (the par-5 no.

2 is a virtual minefield of bunkers, and the par-5 no. 8 shoots over a swale and then uphill). Green fees vary with the season; from April 1 to October 31, they're $59, with twilight rates of $42 for 18 holes. The rest of the year, they're $70, with $44 twilight rates. You can play nine holes after 3:30pm year-round for $23.

✪ **Wailea Courses.** Wailea Alanui Dr. (off Wailea Iki Dr.), Wailea. ☎ **808/879-2966** or 808/875-5111.

There are three courses to choose from at Wailea. The **Blue Course,** a par-72, 6,700-yard flat, open course designed by Arthur Jack Snyder and dotted with bunkers and water hazards, is for duffers and pros alike. The wide fairways appeal to beginners, and the undulating terrain makes it a course everyone can enjoy. A little more difficult is the par-72, 7,073-yard championship **Gold Course,** with narrow fairways, several tricky dogleg holes, and the classic Robert Trent Jones, Jr. challenges: natural hazards, like lava-rock walls, and native Hawaiian grasses. The **Orange Course,** originally an Arthur Jack Snyder design, was renovated by Robert Trent Jones, Jr. to a more challenging course.

With 54 holes to play, getting a tee time is slightly easier on weekends than at other resorts, but weekdays are best (the Gold Course is usually the toughest to book). Facilities include a pro shop, restaurant, locker rooms, and a complete golf training facility. Greens fees are $130.

UPCOUNTRY MAUI

Pukalani Country Club. 360 Pukalani St., Pukalani. ☎ **808/572-1314.** Take the Hana Hwy. (Hwy. 36) to Haleakala Hwy. (Hwy. 37) to the Pukalani exit; turn right onto Pukalani St. and go 2 blocks.

This cool course at 1,100 feet offers a break from the resorts' high greens fees, and it's really fun to play. The par-72, 6,962-yard course has 19 greens. There's an extra green because the third hole offers golfers two different options: a tough iron shot from the tee (especially into the wind), across a gully (yuck!) to the green; or a shot down the side of the gully across a second green into sand traps below. (Most people choose to shoot down the side of the gully; it's actually easier than shooting across a ravine.) High handicappers will love this course, and more experienced players can make it more challenging by playing from the back tees. Greens fees, including cart, are $35 for 18 holes; they drop to $30 after noon, and just $15 after 2:30pm. Facilities include club and shoe rentals, practice areas, lockers, a pro shop, and a restaurant.

FLYING HIGH: HELICOPTER RIDES

Pablo Picasso once said that the three greatest inventions of the 20th century were the blues, cubism, and Polish vodka. Had he ever visited Hawaii, he might have added the helicopter.

There's a *huhu* over helicopters in Hawaii—too many are flying too low, sometimes taking too many risks—but only a helicopter can bring you face to face with volcanoes, waterfalls, and remote places like Maui's little-known Wall of Tears, up near the summit of Puu Kukui in the West Maui Mountains.

A helicopter ride on Maui isn't a wild ride; it's more like a gentle gee-whiz zip into a seldom-seen Eden. You'll glide through canyons etched with 1,000-foot waterfalls and over dense rain forests, climb to 10,000 feet—high enough to glimpse the summit of Haleakala—fly by the dramatic vistas at Molokai.

The first chopper pilots in Hawaii were good ole boys on their way back from Vietnam—hard-flying, hard-drinking cowboys who cared more about the ride than the scenery. But not anymore. Today, pilots are an interesting hybrid: part Hawaiian historian, part DJ, part tour guide, and part amusement-ride operator. As you soar through the clouds absorbing Maui's scenic terrain, you'll learn about Hawaii's flora and fauna, its history, and its culture.

There are lots of helicopter tours on Maui, but ★ **Blue Hawaiian Helicopter** (☎ **800/745-BLUE** or 808/871-8844; www.bluehawaiian.com) is the Cadillac of helicopter tour companies. They'll not only take you on the ride of your life, they'll leave you with a memory you'll never forget. Flights vary from 45 minutes to a half-day affair and range from $130 to $220.

If Blue Hawaiian is booked, try **Sunshine Helicopters** (☎ **800/544-2520** or 808/871-0722; www.sunshinehelicopters.com). Sunshine offers a variety of flights, from short hops around the West Maui Mountains to full island tours ($99 to $179).

HORSEBACK RIDING

Maui offers spectacular adventure rides through rugged ranchlands, into tropical forests, and to remote swimming holes. For a 5½-hour tour on horseback—complete with swimming and lunch—call **Adventure on Horseback** (☎ **808/242-7445** or 808/572-6211); the cost is $175 per person. The day begins over coffee and pastries, while owner Frank Levinson matches the horses to the riders, both skill- and personality-wise. Frank leads small groups across pastures, through thick rain forests, along side streams, and up to waterfalls and pools. After a hearty lunch, the group retraces its route back.

If you're out in Hana, **Oheo Stables**, Kipahulu Ranch (1 mile past Oheo Gulch), Kipahulu (☎ **808/667-2222**, e-mail ray@maui.net), has two daily rides through the mountains above Oheo Gulch (Seven Sacred Pools). The best deal is the 10:30am ride ($119), which includes brunch and snacks during the 4-hour adventure (2½ hours in the saddle), into Haleakala National Park, stopping at scenic spots like Pipuwai Lookout, where you can glimpse the 400-foot Waimoku Falls.

If you enjoy your ride, remember to kiss your horse and tip your guide.

HALEAKALA CRATER ON HORSEBACK   If you'd like to ride down into Haleakala Crater, contact **Pony Express Tours** (☎ **808/667-2200** or 808/878-6698; fax 808/878-3581). They offer a variety of half-day and full-day rides down to the crater floor and back up, from $85 to $130 per person; gentler 1- and 2-hour rides are also offered at Haleakala Ranch, located on the beautiful lower slopes of the volcano, for $40 and $65. Pony Express provides well-trained horses and experienced guides, and all riding levels are accommodated. You must be at least 10 years old, weigh no more than 230 pounds, and wear long pants and closed-toe shoes.

WAY OUT WEST ON MAUI: RANCH RIDES   We recommend riding with **Mendes Ranch & Trail Rides**, on Kahekili Highway, 4 miles past Wailuku (☎ **808/871-5222**). The 300-acre Mendes Ranch is a real-life working cowboy ranch that has the essential elements of an earthly paradise—rainbows, waterfalls, palm trees, coral-sand beaches, lagoons, tide pools, a rain forest, and its own more than mile-high volcanic peak. Allan Mendes, a third-generation wrangler, will take you from the edge of the rain forest and out to the sea. On the way, you'll cross tree-studded meadows where Texas longhorns sit in the shade like surreal lawn statues, and past a dusty corral where Allan's father, Ernest, a champion roper, may be breaking in a wild horse. Allan keeps close watch, turning often in his saddle on his pinto, Pride, to make sure everyone is happy. He points out flora and fauna and fields questions, but generally just lets you soak up Maui's natural splendor in golden silence. The morning ride, which lasts 3 hours and ends with a barbecue back at the corral (the perfect ranch-style lunch after a morning in the saddle), is $130; the 2½-hour afternoon ride is $85, including snacks.

Adventures for Kids (& Kids at Heart)

Taking a Submarine Ride   Atlantis Submarines takes you and the kids down into the shallow coastal waters off Lahaina in a real sub, where you'll see plenty of fish (and maybe even a shark). They love it, and you stay dry the entire time.

Riding the Sugarcane Train   Small kids love this ride, as do train buffs of all ages. A steam engine pulls open-passenger cars of the Lahaina/Kaanapali and Pacific Railroad on a 30-minute, 12-mile round trip through sugarcane fields between Lahaina and Kaanapali while the conductor sings and calls out the landmarks. Along the way, you can see the backside of Kaanapali, and the islands of Molokai and Lanai, beyond. Tickets are $13 for grownups, $6.50 for kids; call ☎ 808/661-0089.

Searching for Stars   After sunset, the stars over Kaanapali shine big and bright, because the tropical sky is almost pollutant-free and no big-city lights interfere with the cosmic view. Amateur astronomers can probe the Milky Way, see the rings of Saturn and Jupiter's moons, and scan the Sea of Tranquillity in a 60-minute star search on the world's first recreational computer-driven telescope. This cosmic adventure takes place every night at the **Hyatt Regency Maui,** 200 Nohea Kai Dr. (☎ 808/661-1234), at 8pm, 9pm, and 10pm. It's $12 for adults and $6 for children—a bargain for anyone who's starry-eyed.

In-Line Skating   Bring your own skates and roll, glide, and skid around the brand-new in-line rink at Kalama Park in Kihei. The park is just north of Kamaole Beach Park I, between Kanai Road and Kupuna Street. Occasionally, the **Maui In-Line Hockey Association** has games scheduled here; call ☎ 808/874-4860 to see when the next one's on.

TENNIS

Maui County has excellent tennis courts located all over the island. All are free and available from daylight to sunset; a few are even lit for night play until 10pm. The courts are available on a first-come, first-served basis; when someone's waiting, limit your play to no more than 45 minutes. For a complete list of public courts, contact **Maui County of Parks and Recreation,** 1580-C Kaahumanu Ave., Wailuku, HI 96793 (☎ 808/243-7389).

Private tennis courts are available at most resorts and hotels on the island. The **Kapalua Tennis Garden and Village Tennis Center,** Kapalua Resort (☎ 808/669-5677), is home to the Kapalua Open, featuring the largest purse in the state, on Labor Day weekend, and the Kapalua Betsy Nagelsen Tennis Invitational Pro-Am in November. Court rentals are $10 an hour for resort guests and $15 an hour for nonguests. In Wailea, the **Wailea Tennis Club,** 131 Wailea Iki Place, Wailea (☎ 808/879-1958), has Plexi-paved courts. Per-day court rentals are $25 for resort guests, $30 an hour for players not staying in Wailea.

9 Seeing the Sights

by Jeanette Foster

There's enough to see and do on Maui to keep you busy for years—so squeezing it all into a week can be a real trial. But it's doable; you can even do it in less than a week if you have to. The 1-week itinerary below should serve as a good starting point. If you only have 3 or 4 days to spend on Maui, stay in the old whaling capital of Lahaina to gain a sense of history, then make day trips by car.

A SUGGESTED ITINERARY FOR SEEING MAUI

Day 1 Get up early—while it's still dark—and drive up to the summit of Haleakala to see the sunrise. The first day of your vacation is probably the best day for this activity, since your biological clock may still be tuned into mainland time. It's a Technicolor miracle and worth the early rising time.

After the park, you'll end up in **Kula**, around 3,000 feet, where gardens feature the weird pincushion and feather-duster blooms known as protea (a South African original, living comfortably on Hawaii's slopes). Turn left and keep on going around the high shoulder of the mountain until you reach **Tedeschi Vineyards**; stop for a taste of Maui wine and a picnic under the giant wild avocado trees. Or turn right and spend the afternoon poking around the shops of **Makawao**. Either way, you'll be reminded that Maui's more than just a tropical beach.

Day 2 Head for **Hana**—but go early in the morning before the crooked road becomes crowded with traffic. Wear your swimsuit and plan to stop at roadside waterfall parks for a swim. Go slow and enjoy the natural surroundings. Get out and walk by the taro patch in the botanical gardens, enjoy the peaceful vista of the Keanae Peninsula and the other sights—it's all part of the Hana Road experience. Plan an overnight stay in Hana in a B&B or vacation rental if you can so that you can meander. Otherwise, be sure to turn around a good couple of hours before sunset, as this curving road of one-lane bridges is not fun to drive in the dark.

Day 3 If you've spent the night in Hana, take the morning to explore the little town and surrounding area before heading back down the Hana Highway. You might want to check out the funky shops in **Paia**. After lunch, head to **Wailuku** and **Iao Valley State Park**. Tour buses roll into the valley in the misty hills behind quaint Wailuku town for a quick photo-op: the Iao Needle rock formation. But head out on your own if you can, as there's much more here to see. Go for a hike, or spend time at the park's collection of miniature houses that represent Maui's plantation cultures from an architectural perspective.

On the way back down from the valley, visit the **Bailey House Museum** in Wailuku for all the historic details. Then take the rest of the day off and hit the beach at **Kaanapali**, where you can wiggle your bare feet in the sand and watch the sunset.

Day 4 Now it's time to sail, splash, and snorkel. Take Trilogy's all-day snorkel cruise to Lanai (see "Hitting the Water," above), a two-for-one island experience, which includes a land tour of this private plantation turned luxury enclave. Snorkeling occurs in Lanai's clear waters off Hulopoe Beach, a marine-life preserve.

Day 5 Explore Makena, the natural part of Maui's South Coast resort cluster, or catch a catamaran to **Molokini** for a day of snorkeling or whale-watching in season. Or bump down a dusty road to **La Pérouse Bay** for some extraordinary snorkeling in green pools set amid lava fingers left over from when Haleakala last exploded and sent lava running to the sea in 1790.

Day 6 Collapse at your favorite beach—probably **Kapalua**, one of the finest gold-sand beaches in Hawaii—and work on your tan. (You don't want people back home to think you didn't hit the beach.) Bring a picnic lunch to eat under the shade of the palm trees that line the beach.

Day 7 Head around the wild side of Maui on the narrow coastal highway beyond Kapalua. Your destination is the remote Hawaiian village of **Kahakuloa,** where time has stood still. Or take a kayak cruise around Kapalua Bay and look for endangered sea turtles among the tropical fish. End your perfect week on Maui with a splurge—a sunset dinner at David Paul's in Lahaina, perhaps.

CENTRAL MAUI

Central Maui isn't exactly tourist central; this is where real people live. Most likely, you'll land here and head directly to the beach. However, there are a few sights worth checking out if you feel like a respite from the sun 'n' surf.

KAHULUI

Under the airport flight path, next to Maui's busiest intersection and across from Costco and K-Mart in Kahului's new business park, is the most unlikely place: **Kanaha Wildlife Sanctuary,** Haleakala Highway Extension and Hana Highway (☎ **808/984-8100**). Look for a parking area off Haleakala Highway Extension (behind the mall, across the Hana Hwy. from Cutter Automotive), and you'll find a 50-yard trail that meanders along the shore to a shade shelter and lookout. Look for the sign proclaiming it to be the permanent home of the endangered black-neck Hawaiian stilt, whose population is now down to about 1,000. Naturalists say this is a good place to see endangered Hawaiian Koloa ducks, stilts, coots, and other migrating shorebirds. For a quieter, more natural-looking wildlife preserve, see the **Kealia Pond National Wildlife Preserve** in Kihei (below).

WAILUKU

This historic gateway to Iao Valley is worth a visit for a little antiquing and a visit to the **Bailey House Museum,** 2375-A Main St. (☎ **808/244-3326;** open daily 10am to 4pm). Missionary and sugar planter Edward Bailey's 1833 home—an architectural hybrid of stones laid by Hawaiian craftsmen and timbers joined in a display of Yankee ingenuity—is a treasure trove of Hawaiiana. Inside, you'll find an eclectic collection, from precontact artifacts like scary temple images, dogtooth necklaces, and a rare lei made of tree snail shells to latter-day relics like Duke Kahanamoku's 1919 redwood surfboard and a koa-wood table given to President Ulysses S. Grant, who had to refuse it because he couldn't accept gifts from foreign countries. There's also a gallery devoted to a few of Bailey's landscapes, painted from 1866 to 1896, which capture on canvas a Maui we can only imagine today. Admission is $4 for adults, $3.50 for seniors, and $1 for children 6 to 12.

IN NEARBY WAIKAPU About 3 miles south of Wailuku lies the tiny, one-street village of Waikapu, which has two attractions that are worth a peek. Relive Maui's past by taking a 40-minute narrated tram ride around fields of pineapple, sugarcane, and papaya trees at **Maui Tropical Plantation,** 1670 Honoapiilani Hwy. (☎ **800/ 451-6805** or 808/244-7643; open daily 9am to 5pm), a real working plantation. A shop sells fresh and dried fruit. Admission is free; the tram tour is $8.50 for adults, $3.50 for kids 5 to 12.

Marilyn Monroe and Frank Lloyd Wright meet for dinner every night at one of Maui's most unusual buildings, the **Waikapu Golf and Country Club,** 2500 Honoapiilani Hwy. (☎ **808/244-2011**). Neither actually came to Maui in real life, but these icons of architecture and glamour who traded on the curvilinear live on in this paradise setting. Wright designed this place for a Pennsylvania family in 1949, but it never happened. In 1957, Marilyn and husband Arthur Miller wanted it built for them in Connecticut, but they separated the following year. When Tokyo billionaire Takeshi Sekiguchi went shopping at Taliesen West for a signature building to adorn his 18-hole golf course, he found the blueprints and had Marilyn's Wright house cleverly redesigned as a clubhouse. A horizontal in a vertical landscape, it doesn't quite fit the setting, but it's still the best-looking building on Maui today.

IAO VALLEY

A couple of miles north of Wailuku, past the Bailey House museum where the little plantation houses stop and the road climbs ever higher, Maui's true nature begins to reveal itself. The transition between suburban sprawl and raw nature is so quick that most people who drive up into the valley don't realize that they're suddenly in a rain forest. Walls of the canyon begin to close around them, and a 2,250-foot needle pricks gray clouds scudding across the blue sky. After the hot tropic sun, the air is moist and cool and the shade a welcome comfort. This is Iao Valley, a 6.2-acre state park that's a place of great nature, history, and beauty enjoyed by millions of people from around the world for more than a century.

Iao (literally, "Supreme Light") Valley, 10 miles long and 4,000 acres, is the eroded volcanic caldera of the West Maui Mountains. The head of the Iao Valley is a broad circular amphitheater where four major streams converge into Iao Stream. At the back of the amphitheater is rain-drenched Puu Kukui, the West Maui Mountains' highest point. No other Hawaiian valley lets you go from seacoast to rain forest so easily. This peaceful valley, full of tropical plants, rainbows, waterfalls, swimming holes, and hiking trails, is a place of solitude, reflection, and escape for residents and visitors alike.

Just the Facts

WHEN TO GO   The park is open daily from 7am to 7pm. Go early in the morning or late in the afternoon, when the sun's rays slant into the valley and create a mystical mood. You can bring a picnic and spend the day, but be prepared at any time for a tropical cloudburst, which often soaks the valley and swells both waterfalls and streams.

ACCESS POINTS   From Wailuku, take Main Street to Iao Valley Road to the entrance to the state park.

INFORMATION & VISITOR CENTERS   For information, contact **Iao Valley State Park,** State Parks and Recreation, 54 High St., Rm. 101, Wailuku, HI 96793 (☎ 808/984-8109; fax 808/984-8111).

The **Hawaii Nature Center,** 875 Iao Valley Rd. (☎ 808/244-6500; open daily 10am to 4pm), home to the Iao Valley Nature Center, with hands-on, interactive exhibits and displays relating the story of Hawaiian natural history, is an important stopping point for all who want to explore Iao Valley. Admission is $5 for adults, $3 for children under 12.

Seeing the Highlights

Two paved walkways loop into the massive green amphitheater, across the bridge of Iao Valley Stream, and along the stream itself. The one-third-mile loop on a paved trail is Maui's easiest hike—you can take your grandmother on this one. The leisurely walk will allow you to enjoy lovely views of the Iao Needle and the lush vegetation. Others often proceed beyond the state park border and take two trails deeper into the valley, but the trails enter private land, and NO TRESPASSING signs are posted.

The feature known as **Iao Needle** is an erosional remnant consisting of basalt dikes. The phallic rock juts an impressive 2,250 feet above sea level. Youngsters play in **Iao Stream,** a peaceful brook that belies its bloody history. In 1790, King Kamehameha the Great and his men engaged in the bloody battle of Iao Valley to gain control of Maui. When the battle ended, so many bodies blocked Iao Stream that the battle site was named Kepaniwai, or "damning of the waters." An architectural heritage park of Hawaiian, Japanese, Chinese, Filipino, and New England–style houses stands in harmony by Iao Stream at **Kepaniwai Heritage Garden.** This is a good picnic spot, as there are plenty of picnic tables and benches. You can see ferns, banana trees, and other native and exotic plants in the **Iao Valley Botanic Garden** along the stream.

THE SCENIC ROUTE TO WEST MAUI: THE KAHEKILI HIGHWAY

The usual road to West Maui from Wailuku is the Honoapiilani Highway, which takes you across the isthmus to Maalaea and around to Lahaina, Kaapanali, and Kapalua. But those wanting a back-to-nature driving experience should go the other way, along the **Kahekili Highway** (Hwy. 340). "Highway" is a bit of a euphemism for this paved but somewhat precarious road.

Drive north from Wailuku to Waiehu and onto this road named for King Kahekili, who built houses out of the skulls of his enemies (a practice Maui planners perhaps should have adopted to slow the island's growth). The true wild nature of Maui is on full display. The narrow and winding road weaves for 20 miles along an ancient Hawaiian coastal footpath to Honokohau Bay, at the island's northernmost tip, past blowholes, sea stacks, seabird rookeries, and the imposing 636-foot Kahakaloa headland. On the land side, you'll pass high cliffs, deep valleys dotted with plantation houses, cattle grazing on green plateaus, old wooden churches, taro fields, and houses hung with fishing nets. It's slow going (you can only drive about 10 miles an hour along the road), but it's probably the most beautiful drive in Maui. Your rental-car company might try to deter you, but it's not really a hard drive (don't go if it's been raining), and the views are spectacular. If you lose your heart on Maui, it'll probably be somewhere along this coastal highway.

At Honokohau, pick up Highway 30 and continue on to the West Maui resorts; the first one you'll reach is Kapalua (see below).

WEST MAUI
HISTORIC LAHAINA

When "there was no God west of the Horn," Lahaina was the capital of Hawaii and the Pacific's wildest port. Today, it's a mild, mollified version of its old self—mostly a hustle-bustle of whale art, timeshares, and "Just Got Lei'd" T-shirts. I'm not sure the rowdy whalers would be pleased. But if you look hard, you'll still find the historic port town they loved, filled with the kind of history that inspired James Michener to write his best-selling epic novel, *Hawaii.*

Baldwin Home Museum. 696 Front St. (at Dickenson St.). ☎ **808/661-3262.** Admission $3 adults, $2 seniors, $1 children, $5 family. Daily 10am–4:30pm.

The oldest house in Lahaina, this coral-and-rock structure was built in 1834 by Rev. Dwight Baldwin, a doctor with the fourth company of American missionaries to sail 'round the Horn to Hawaii. Like many missionaries, he came to Hawaii to do good—and did very well for himself. After 17 years of service, Baldwin was granted 2,600 acres for farming and grazing in Kapalua. His ranch manager experimented with what Hawaiians called *hala-kahiki,* or pineapple, on a 4-acre plot; the rest is history. The house looks as if Baldwin just stepped out for a minute to tend a sick neighbor down the street.

Next door is the **Master's Reading Room**, Maui's oldest building. This became visiting sea captains' favorite hangout once the missionaries closed down all of Lahaina's grog shops and banned prostitution; but by 1844, once hotels and bars started reopening, it lost its appeal. It's now the headquarters of the plucky band of historians who try to keep this town alive and antique at the same time, the **Lahaina Restoration Foundation** (☎ 808/661-3262). Stop in and pick up a self-guided walking tour map, which will take you to Lahaina's most historic sites.

Banyan Tree. At the Courthouse Building, 649 Wharf St.

Of all the banyan trees in Hawaii, this is the biggest, most sheltering of all—so big that you can't get it in your camera's viewfinder. It was only 8 feet tall when it was planted in 1873 by Maui Sheriff William O. Smith to mark the 50th anniversary of Lahaina's first Christian mission; the big old banyan from India is now more than 50 feet tall, has 12 major trunks, and shades two-thirds of an acre in Courthouse Square.

The Brig *Carthaginian II.* Lahaina Harbor. ☎ 808/661-8527. Admission $3 adults, $5 family, $2 seniors. Daily 10am–4:30pm.

This authentically restored square-rigged brigantine is an authentic replica of a 19th-century whaling ship, the kind that brought the first missionaries to Hawaii. This floating museum features exhibits on whales and 19th-century whaling life. You won't believe how cramped the living quarters were—they make today's cruise-ship cabins look downright roomy.

Lahaina Whaling Museum. At Crazy Shirts, 865 Front St. (near Papalaua St.), ☎ 808/661-4775. Free admission. Daily 9:30am–9pm.

Yankee whalers came to Lahaina to reprovision ships' stores, get drunk, and raise hell with "the girls of old Mowee." Everything was fine and dandy until 1819, when Congregational missionaries arrived and declared the port town "one of the breathing holes of hell." They tried to curb drinking and prostitution but failed; Lahaina grew ever lawless until the whaling era came to an end with the discovery of oil in Pennsylvania and the birth of the petroleum industry. That rambunctious era is recalled in this small museum full of art and relics from Lahaina's glory days.

Malu'uluolele Park. Front and Shaw sts.

At first glance, this Front Street park appears to be only a hot, dry, dusty softball field. But under home plate is an edge of Mokula, now buried under tons of red dirt and sand, where a royal compound once stood more than 100 years ago. Here, Prince Kauikeaolii, who ascended the throne as King Kamehameha III when he was only 10, lived with the love of his life, his sister Princess Nahienaena. Missionaries took a dim view of incest, which was acceptable to Hawaiian nobles in order to preserve the royal bloodline. Torn between love for her brother and the new Christian morality, Nahienaena grew despondent and died at the age of 21. King Kamehameha III, who reigned for 29 years—longer than any other Hawaiian monarch—presided over Hawaii as it went from kingdom to constitutional monarchy, and absolute power over the islands began to transfer from island nobles to missionaries, merchants, and sugar planters. Kamehameha died in 1854; he was 39. In 1918, his royal compound, containing a mausoleum and artifacts of the kingdom, was demolished and covered with dirt to make a public park. The baseball team from Lahainaluna School, the first American school founded by missionaries west of the Rockies, now plays games on the site of this royal place, still considered sacred to many Hawaiians.

A WHALE OF A PLACE IN KAANAPALI

If you haven't seen a real whale yet, go to **Whalers Village**, 2435 Kaanapali Pkwy., an oceanfront shopping center that has adopted the whale as its mascot. You can't miss it: A huge, almost life-size metal sculpture of a mother whale and two nursing whalelets greets you. A few more steps, and you're met by the looming, bleached-white bony skeleton of a 40-foot sperm whale; it's pretty impressive.

On the second floor of the mall is the **Whale Center of the Pacific** (☎ **808/661-5992**), a museum celebrating the "Golden Era of Whaling" (1825–60) from the whaler's point of view: Harpoons and scrimshaw are on display; the museum has even re-created the cramped quarters of a whaler's seagoing vessel.

Across the way, you'll find the **House of the Whale**, or Hale Kohola (☎ **808/661-6752**), which tells the story from the whale's point of view, as it were. The museum houses exhibits on 70 species of whales and more whale lore than you could hope to absorb during your entire 2-week vacation in Hawaii. Venture into the Bone Room, where volunteers scrape and identify the bones of marine mammals that wash ashore in Hawaiian waters to use in future exhibits.

Both museums are open during mall hours, daily from 9:30am to 10pm. Admission is free. For tips on seeing the real thing, see "Whale-Watching," earlier in this chapter.

KAPALUA

For generations, West Maui meant pineapple. Hawaii's only pineapple canner today, **Maui Pineapple Co.**, (☎ **808/669-8088**), offers tours of its plantation through the Kapalua Resort Activity Center (☎ **808/669-8088**). Real plantation workers lead the 2½-hour tours, which feature the history of West Maui, facts about growing and harvesting pineapple, and lots of trivia about plantation life; you're even able to pick and harvest your own pineapple. The tours, which depart from the Kapalua Shops, next to the Kapalua Bay Hotel, are offered twice daily on weekdays. Fees are $19 per person; children must be at least 12.

SOUTH MAUI
MAALAEA

Maui Ocean Center. Maalaea Harbor Village, at the triangle between Honoapiilani Hwy. and Maalaea Rd. ☎ **808/875-1962**. www.coralworld.com/moc. Admission $17 adults, $12 children 3–12. Daily 9am–5pm.

This brand-new 5-acre facility houses the largest aquarium in Hawaii and features one of Hawaii's largest predators: the tiger shark. Exhibits are all geared toward the residents of Hawaii's ocean waters. As you walk past the three dozen or so tanks and countless exhibits, you'll slowly descend from the "beach" to the deepest part of the ocean without ever getting wet. You'll start at the surge pool, where you'll see shallow-water marine life like spiny urchins and cauliflower coral, then move on to the reef tanks, turtle pool, "touch" pool (with starfish and urchins), and eagle-ray pool before reaching the star of the show: a 100-foot long, 600,000-gallon main tank featuring tiger, gray, and white-tip sharks, as well as tuna, surgeonfish, triggerfish, and numerous other large-scale tropicals. The most phenomenal thing about this tank is that the walkway goes right through it—so you'll be surrounded on three sides by marine creatures. A very cool place, and well worth the time.

KIHEI

Capt. George Vancouver "discovered" Kihei in 1778, when it was only a collection of fishermen's grass shacks on the hot, dry, dusty coast (hard to believe, eh?). A **totem** pole stands today, where he's believed to have landed, across from Aston Maui Lu Resort, 575 S. Kihei Rd. Vancouver sailed on to discover British Columbia, where a great international city and harbor now bears his name.

West of the junction of Piilani Highway (Hwy. 31) and Mokulele Highway (Hwy. 350) is **Kealia Pond National Wildlife Preserve** (☎ **808/875-1582**), a 700-acre U.S. Fish and Wildlife wetland preserve where endangered Hawaiian stilts, coots, and ducks hang out and splash. These ponds work two ways: as bird preserves and as sedimentation basins that keep the coral reefs from silting from runoff. You can take a self-guided tour along a boardwalk dotted with interpretive signs and shade shelters, through sand dunes and around ponds to Maalaea Harbor. The boardwalk starts at the outlet of Kealia Pond on the ocean side of North Kihei Road (near mile marker 2 on Piilani Hwy.). Among the birds seen here are Hawaiian waterbirds like the black-crowned high heron, Hawaiian coot, Hawaiian duck, and Hawaiian stilt. There also are shorebirds like sanderlings, Pacific golden plovers, ruddy turnstones, and wandering tartlers. From July to December, the hawksbill turtle comes ashore here to lay her eggs.

WAILEA

The best way to explore this golden resort coast is to rise with the sun and head for Wailea's 1½-mile **coastal nature trail**, stretching between the Kea Lani Hotel and the kiawe thicker just beyond the Renaissance Wailea. It's a great morning walk, a serpentine path that meanders uphill and down past native plants, Old Hawaiian habitats, and a billion dollars' worth of luxury hotels. You can pick up the trail at any of the resorts or from clearly marked SHORELINE ACCESS points along the coast. The best time to go is when you first wake up; by midmorning, the coastal trail is too often clogged with pushy joggers (somebody should tell them that this is a scenic nature walk, not a fitness loop); and it gets crowded with beachgoers as the day wears on. As the path crosses several bold black-lava points, it affords new vistas of islands and ocean; there are benches so you can pause to contemplate the view across Alalakeiki Channel, which jumps with whales in season. Sunset is another good time to hit the trail; many come down here to watch the glorious end of yet another perfect day in paradise.

MAKENA

A few miles south of Wailea, the manicured coast turns to wilderness; now you're in Makena.

Once cattle were driven down the slope from upland ranches, lashed to rafts, and sent into the water to swim to boats that waited to take them to market. Now, **Makena Landing** is the best place to launch kayaks bound for La Pérouse Bay and Ahihi-Kinau preserve. From the landing, go south on Makena Road; on the right is **Keawali Congregational Church** (☎ **808/879-5557**). Surrounded by ti leaves, which by Hawaiian custom provides protection, and built of coral block cut from the reef in 1831, this Protestant church sits on its own cove with a gold-sand beach and always attracts a Sunday crowd for its Hawaiian-language service.

A little farther south on the coast is **La Pérouse Monument,** a pyramid of lava rocks that marks the spot where French explorer Admiral Comte de la Pérouse set foot on Maui in 1786. The first Westerner to "discover" the island, he described the "burning climate" of the leeward coast, observed several fishing villages near Kihei, and sailed on into oblivion, never to be seen again; some believe he may have been eaten by cannibals in what now is Vanuatu. To get there, drive south past Puu Olai to Ahihi Bay, where the road turns to gravel. Go another 2 miles along the coast to La Pérouse Bay, the monument sits amid a clearing in black lava at the end of the dirt road.

✪ HOUSE OF THE SUN: HALEAKALA NATIONAL PARK

At once forbidding and compelling, Haleakala National Park ("House of the Sun") is Maui's main natural attraction. More than 1.3 million people a year go up the 10,023-foot-high mountain to peer down into the crater of the world's largest dormant volcano. (Haleakala is officially considered to be active but not currently erupting, even though it has not rumbled since 1790.) That hole would hold Manhattan.

But there's more to do than just stare in a big black hole. Just going up the mountain is an experience. This is one of the few places on the planet where you can climb from sea level to 10,000 feet in just 37 miles, or a 2-hour drive, and never leave the ground. The snaky road passes through big, puffy, cumulus clouds to offer magnificent views of the isthmus of Maui, the West Maui Mountains, and the calm, blue Pacific Ocean.

Many drive up to the summit in predawn darkness to watch the ✪ sunrise over Haleakala; others take a trail ride inside the bleak lunar landscape of the wilderness inside the crater (see "Horseback Riding," p. 442), or coast down the 37-mile road from the summit on a bicycle with special brakes (see "Bicycling," p. 438). Hardy adventurers hike and camp inside the crater's wilderness (see "Hiking & Camping," p. 433). Those bound for the interior bring their survival gear, for the terrain is raw, rugged, and punishing—not unlike the moon. However you choose to experience Haleakala, it will prove memorable—guaranteed.

JUST THE FACTS

Haleakala National Park extends from the summit of Mt. Haleakala down the volcano's southeast flank to Maui's eastern coast, beyond Hana. There are actually two separate and distinct destinations within the park: **Haleakala Summit,** and the **Kipahulu Coast** (see "Tropical Haleakla," p. 458). The summit gets all the publicity, but Kipahulu draws crowds too, because it's lush, green, and tropical, and home to Oheo Gulch (also known as Seven Sacred Pools). No road links the summit and the coast; you have to approach them separately, and you need at least a day to see each place.

WHEN TO GO   At the 10,023-foot summit, weather changes fast. With wind chill, temperatures can be freezing any time of year. Summer can be dry and warm, winter can be wet, windy, and cold or the opposite. Always call the park for current weather conditions before you go (☎ **808/572-9306**), or the **National Weather Service** for a recorded forecast at ☎ **808/871-5054.**

From sunrise to noon, the light is weak, but the view is usually free of clouds. The best time for photos is in the afternoon, when the sun lights the crater and clouds are few. Go on full-moon nights for spectacular viewing.

ACCESS POINTS   **Haleakala Summit** is 37 miles, or a 1½- to 2-hour drive, from Kahului. To get there, take Highway 37 to Highway 377 to Highway 378. For details on the drive, see "The Drive to the Summit," below. Pukalani is the last town for water, food, and gas.

The **Kipahulu** section of Haleakala National Park is on Maui's east end near Hana, 60 miles from Kahului on Highway 36 (the Hana Hwy.). Due to traffic and rough road conditions, plan on the drive taking 4 hours, one-way; for complete information, see "Tropical Haleakala: Oheo Gulch at Kipahulu," later in this chapter.

INFORMATION, VISITOR CENTERS & RANGER PROGRAMS   For information before you go, contact **Haleakala National Park,** Box 369, Makawao, HI 96768 (☎ **808/572-9306**).

One mile from the park entrance, at 7,000 feet, is **Haleakala National Park Head-quarters** (☎ **808/572-9306**), open daily from 7am to 4pm. Here, you can pick up

Impressions

There are few enough places in the world that belong entirely to themselves. The human passion to carry all things everywhere, so that every place is home, seems well on its way to homogenizing our planet, save for the odd unreachable corner. Haleakala Crater is one of those corners.

—Barbara Kingsolver, The New York Times

information on park programs and activities, get camping permits, and occasionally, see a Hawaiian nene; one or more are often here to greet visitors. Rest rooms, a pay phone, and drinking water are available.

The **Summit Visitor Center**, open daily from sunrise to 3pm, is near the summit of Mount Haleakala, 11 miles from the park entrance. It offers a panoramic view of the volcanic landscape, with photos identifying the various features, and exhibits that explain the history, ecology, geology, and vulcanology. Park staff members are often handy to answer questions. The only facilities are rest rooms and water.

Rangers offer excellent, informative, and free **naturalist talks** at 9:30, 10:30, and 11:30am daily in the summit building.

HIKING & CAMPING Haleakala National Park offers a number of hiking and camping possibilities, including wilderness cabins and campgrounds. See "Hiking & Camping," earlier in this chapter, for details.

THE DRIVE TO THE SUMMIT

If you look on a Maui map, almost in the middle of the part that resembles a torso, there is a black, wiggly line that looks like this: WWWWW. That's **Highway 378,** also known as **Haleakala Crater Road**—one of the few roads in the world that climb from sea level to 10,000 feet in the short distance of just 37 miles. This grand corniche has at least 33 switchbacks; passes through numerous climate zones; goes under, in, and out of clouds; takes you past rare silversword plants and endangered Hawaiian geese sailing through the clear, thin air; and offers a view that extends for more than 100 miles.

Going to the summit takes 1½ to 2 hours from Kahului. No matter where you start out, you'll follow Highway 37 (Haleakala Hwy.) to Pukalani, where you'll pick up Highway 377 (which also is Haleakala Hwy.), which you'll take to Highway 378. Along the way, expect fog, rain, and wind. You may encounter stray cattle and downhill bicyclists. Fill up your gas tank before you go—the only gas available is 27 miles below the summit at Pukalani. There are no facilities beyond the ranger stations. Bring your own food and water.

Remember, you're entering a high-altitude wilderness area. Some people get dizzy due to the lack of oxygen; you may also suffer lightheadedness, shortness of breath, nausea, or worse: severe headaches, flatulence, and dehydration. People with asthma, pregnant women, heavy smokers, and people with heart conditions should be especially careful in the rarefied air. Bring water and a jacket or a blanket, especially if you go up for sunrise. Or you might want to go up to the summit for sunset, which is also spectacular.

At the **park entrance**, you'll pay an entrance fee of $4 per car (or $2 for a bicycle). About a mile from the entrance is **Park Headquarters**, where an endangered **nene**, or Hawaiian goose, may greet you with its unique call. With its black face, buff cheeks,

Haleakala National Park

Oheo Gulch
Oheo Gulch
Kukui Bay
Oheo Campground
Makahiku Falls
Waimoku Falls Trail
31
To Hana →
Kipahulu Area
Palikea
Kipahulu Valley

Kaupo Trail

Kaupo Gap

Scientific Research Reserve
(Closed to Entry)

Haupaakea Peak ▽
Kapaloa Cabin
Sliding Sands Trail

Puu-Ulaula Overlook

Paliku Cabin & Campground

Hanakauhi ▽

Kalapawili Ridge

Bottomless Pit
Area
Haleakala Crater
Silversword Loop
Halemauu Trail

Information ⓘ
Visitor Center

Kalahaku Overlook

Koolau Gap
Holua Cabin & Campground

Leleiwi Overlook

Hosmer Grove

Park Headquarters
378
To Kahului →

Legend

Hiking Trail		
Point of Interest ■	**Picnic Area** ⊼	**Scientific Research Reserve**
Mountain Peak ▽	**Handicap Access** ♿	**Campground** ▽	**Information** ⓘ
	Shelter Cabin	**Ranger Station**	

Legend

Ranger Station
Shelter Cabin
Campground
Information ⓘ

1-0719

and partially webbed feet, the gray-brown bird looks like a small Canadian goose with zebra stripes; it brays out "nay-nay," telling you its name, doesn't migrate, and prefers lava beds to lakes. The unusual goose clings to a precarious existence on these slopes. More than 25,000 once habited Hawaii, but hunters, pigs, feral cats and dogs, and mongooses preyed on the nene, coupled with habitat destruction, nearly causing its extinction. By 1951, there were only 30 left. Now protected as Hawaii's state bird, the number of wild nene on Haleakala is fewer than 250—and the species remains endangered.

Beyond headquarters are **two scenic overlooks** on the way to the summit; stop at Leleiwi on the way up and Kalahaku on the way back down, if only to get out, stretch, and get accustomed to the heights. Take a deep breath, a good look around, and pop your ears. If you feel dizzy, drowsy, or get a sudden headache, consider turning around and going back down.

Leleiwi Overlook is just beyond mile marker 17. From the parking area, a short trail leads you to a panoramic view of the lunar-like crater. When the clouds are low and the sun is in the right place, usually around sunset, you may experience a phenomenon known as the "Specter of the Brocken"—you can see a reflection of your shadow, ringed by a rainbow, in the clouds below. It's an optical illusion caused by a rare combination of sun, shadow, and fog that occurs on only three places on the planet: Haleakala, Scotland, and Germany.

Two miles farther along is **Kalahaku Overlook**, the best place to see a rare **silversword**. You can only turn into this overlook when you are descending from the top. The silversword is the punker of the plant world, its silvery bayonets displaying tiny, purple bouquets—like a spacey artichoke with an attitude. This botanical wonder proved irresistible to humans, who gathered them in gunnysacks for Chinese potions, British specimen collections, and just for the sheer thrill of having something so rare. Silverswords grow only in Hawaii, take from 4 to 50 years to bloom, then, usually between May and October, send up a 1- to 6-foot stalk with a purple bouquet of sunflower-like blooms. They're now very rare, so don't even think about taking one home.

Continue on, and you'll quickly reach **Haleakala Visitor Center,** which offers spectacular views. You'll feel as if you're at the edge of the earth. But don't turn around here; the actual summit's a little farther on, at **Puu Ulaula Overlook** (also known as Red Hill), the volcano's highest point, where you'll find a mysterious cluster of buildings officially known as Haleakala Observatories, but unofficially called **Science City** (see box below). If you do go up for sunrise, the building at Puu Ulaula Overlook, a triangle of glass that serves as a windbreak, is the best viewing spot. After the daily miracle of sunrise—the sun seems to rise out of the vast ocean (hence the name "the House of the Sun")—you can see all the way across Alenuihaha Channel to the often snowcapped summit of Mauna Kea on the Big Island.

MAKING YOUR DESCENT Put your car in low gear; that way, you won't suddenly see smoke coming from your brakes, and you won't destroy your brakes by riding them the whole way down.

UPCOUNTRY MAUI

Come upcountry and discover a different side of Maui: On the slopes of Haleakala, cowboys, planters, and other country people make their homes in serene, neighborly communities like **Makawao** and **Kula** that are a world away from the bustling beach resorts. Even if you can't spare a day or two in the cool, upcountry air, there are some sights that are worth a look on your way to or from the crater. Shoppers and gallery hoppers might really want to make the effort; see "Shops & Galleries," below.

Haleakala National Park's Very Own "X-File": Science City

Haleakala Crater looks like the surface of the moon; the resemblance is so uncanny, in fact, that astronauts have trained for lunar flights here. There may not be a man in the moon anymore, but the summit still holds a few mysteries: a series of antennaed, white-domed structures that the locals call "Science City." Nobody really knows what goes on there, as these enigmatic structures are strictly off-limits to the public. What's the secret, you ask? We've done some digging, and here's what we've been able to learn through official channels:

Science City can be traced back to 1951, when the 18-acre parcel was set aside for the University of Hawaii to establish a High Altitude Observatory. In 1958, the first tracking telescope was installed as part of a Smithsonian Institute satellite tracking program. The buildings now house a series of powerful telescopes and listening devices that study explosions on the sun, monitor movement of the earth's crust, track satellites circling the globe, and examine distant galaxies and quasars—at least according to "officials."

The tracking of satellites and "other objects in space" from Science City is now under the U.S. Air Force Space Command. The Air Force admits that it maintains the Maui Space Surveillance Site and keeps a 3.7-meter Advanced Electro-Optical System Telescope trained on our spacecraft and satellites. But we all know what they're really looking for up there.

Visitors from Earth, I'm sorry to report, are cordially *not* welcome at this research facility. Hmmm. This may require a Mulder and Scully–style investigation. Because, as we all know, the truth is out there.

Kula Botanical Garden. Hwy. 377 south of Haleakala Crater Rd. (Hwy. 378), ⁷⁄₁₀-mile from Hwy. 37. ☎ **808/878-1715. Admission $4 adults, $1 children 6–12. Daily 9am–4pm.**

You can take a self-guided, informative, leisurely stroll through more than 700 native and exotic plants—including three unique collections of orchids, proteas, and bromiliads—at this 5-acre garden. It offers a good overview of Hawaii's exotic flora in one small, cool place.

Tedeschi Vineyards and Winery. Off Hwy. 37 (Kula Hwy.). ☎ **808/878-6058.** Free tastings. Winery tours daily 9am–5pm.

On the southern shoulder of Haleakala is Ulupalakua Ranch, a 20,000-acre spread once owned by legendary sea captain James Makee, celebrated in the Hawaiian song and dance *Hula O Makee.* Wounded in a Honolulu waterfront brawl in 1843, Captain Makee moved to Maui and bought Ulupalakua. He renamed it Rose Ranch and planted sugar as a cash crop. He grew rich and toasted life until his death in 1879. Still in operation, the ranch is now home to Maui's only winery, established in 1974 by Napa vintner Emil Tedeschi, who began growing California and European grapes here and producing serious still and sparkling wines, plus a silly wine made of pineapple juice. The rustic grounds are the perfect place for a picnic. Pack a basket before you go, but don't BYOB: There's plenty of great wine to enjoy at Tedeschi. So spread your picnic lunch under the sprawling camphor tree, pop the cork on a Blanc du Blanc, and toast your good fortune in being here.

EAST MAUI & HEAVENLY HANA

Hana is Paradise on Earth—or just about as close as you can get to it, anyway. In and around Hana, you'll find a lush tropical rain forest dotted with cascading waterfalls

Travel Tip

If you'd like to know exactly what you're seeing as you head down the road to Hana, we suggest renting a cassette tour. They're available from **Rental Warehouse**, 578 Front St. (near Prison St.), Lahaina (☎ **808/661-1970**), for $9.99 a day.

and sparkling blue pools, skirted by red- and black-sand beaches. This is probably what you came to Maui looking for.

THE ROAD TO HANA

Top down, sunscreen on, radio tuned to a little Hawaiian music on a Maui morning. It's time to head our to Hana along the Hana Highway (Hwy. 36), a wiggle of a road that runs along Maui's northeastern shore. The drive takes at least 3 hours—but take all day. Going to Hana is about the journey, not the destination.

There are wilder roads and steeper roads and even more dangerous roads, but in all of Hawaii, no road is more celebrated than this one. It winds for 50 miles past taro patches, magnificent seascapes, waterfall pools, botanical gardens, and verdant rain forests, and ends at one of Hawaii's most beautiful tropical places.

The outside world discovered the little village of Hana in 1926, when the narrow coastal road, carved by pick-ax wielding convicts, opened with 56 bridges and 600 hairpin switchbacks. The mud-and-gravel road, often subject to landslides and washouts, was paved in 1962, when tourist traffic began to increase; it now exceeds 1,000 cars and dozens of vans a day, according to storekeeper Harry Hasegawa. That figures out to be about 500,000 people a year on this road, which is way too many. Go at the wrong time, and you'll be stuck in a bumper-to-bumper rental-car parade—peak traffic times are midmorning and midafternoon year-round, especially on weekends.

In the rush to "do" Hana in a day, most visitors spin around town in 10 minutes flat and wonder what all the fuss is about. It takes time to take in Hana, to play in the waterfalls, sniff the tropical flowers, hike to bamboo forests, and take in the spectacular scenery; stay overnight if you can, and meander back in a day or two—or three.

If you really must do the Hana Highway in a day, go just before sunrise and return after sunset: On a full-moon night, you'll believe in magic when the sea and the waterfalls glow in soft white light and mysterious shadows appear in the jungle. And you'll have the road almost to yourself on the way back.

Akamai trips: Forget your mainland road manners. Practice aloha: Give way at the one-lane bridges, wave at oncoming motorists, let the big guys in 4x4s with pighunting dogs in the back have the right of way—it's just common sense, brah. If the guy behind you blinks his lights, let him pass. And don't honk your horn—in Hawaii, it's considered rude.

GREAT PLUNGES ALONG THE WAY   A plunge in a waterfall pool is everybody's tropical-island fantasy. The first great place to stop for a plunge is ✪ **Twin Falls**, at mile marker 2. Just before the wide, concrete bridge, pull over on the mountain side and park. Hop over the ladder on the right side of the red gate and walk about 3 to 5 minutes to the waterfall and pool, or continue on another 10 to 15 minutes to the second, larger waterfall and pool. What a way to start the trip to Hana.

Another great waterfall is **Puohokamoa Falls**, a 30-foot falls that spills into an idyllic pool in a fern-filled amphitheater. Naturalist Ken Schmid says that its name, loosely translated, means "valley of the chickens bursting into flight"—which is what hot, sweaty hikers look like as they take the plunge. Park at mile marker 11, clamber over river rocks, scramble up a Tarzan trail through dense jungle and—bingo!—plunge into the ice-cold pool of upper Puohokamoa Falls.

THE GARDEN OF EDEN   Just past mile marker 10 is the **Garden of Eden Arboretum and Botanical Garden** (☎ **808/572-6453;** open daily 9am to 2pm), some 26 acres of nature trails, picnic areas, and more than 500 exotic plants and trees from around the Pacific (including wild ginger, an assortment of ti plants, and an impressive palm collection). The Garden of Eden is the dream of arborist/landscape designer Alan Bradbury; he and his staff have been helping to restore a natural ecosystem and promote Hawaii's native and indigenous species here since 1991. Don't be surprised if this place looks familiar; it's in the opening sequence of *Jurassic Park*. Admission is $3 per person; come early and spend some time.

CAN'T-MISS PHOTO OPS   Just past mile marker 12 is the **Kaumahina** ("moonrise") **State Wayside Park.** Not only is this a good pit stop (rest rooms are available here) and a wonderful place for a picnic under the tall eucalyptus trees (with tables and barbecue area), but it's also a great vista point. The view of the rugged coastline makes an excellent shot—you can see all the way down to the jutting Keanae Peninsula.

Another mile and a couple of bends in the road, and you'll enter the Honomanu Valley ("valley of the bird"), with its beautiful bay. To get to the **Honomanu Bay County Beach Park,** look for the turnoff on your left, just after mile marker 14, as you begin your ascent up the other side of the valley. The rutted dirt-and-cinder road takes you down to the rocky black-sand beach. There are no facilities here, except for a stone fire pit someone has made in the sand. There are strong rip currents offshore, so swimming is best in the stream inland from the ocean. You'll consider the drive down worthwhile as you stand on the beach, well away from the ocean, and turn to look back on the steep cliffs covered with vegetation.

KEANAE PENINSULA & ARBORETUM   Farther along the winding road, about 26½ miles past Paia at mile marker 17, the old Hawaiian village of **Keanae** stands out against the Pacific like a place time forgot. Here, on an old lava flow graced by an 1860 stone church and swaying palms is one of the last coastal enclaves of native Hawaiians. They still grow taro in patches and pound it into poi, the staple of the Old Hawaiian diet; they still pluck *opihi* (shellfish) from tide pools along the jagged coast and cast throw-nets at schools of fish. At nearby **Keanae Arboretum** off the Hana Hwy., Hawaii's botanical world is divided into three parts: native forest; introduced forest; and traditional Hawaiian plants, food, and medicine. You can swim in pools of Piinaau Stream, or press on along a mile-long trail into Keanae Valley, where a lovely tropical rain forest waits at the end. It's open 24 hours a day; there's no admission fee.

WAIANAPANAPA STATE PARK   At mile marker 51, just on the outskirts of Hana, shiny black-sand Waianapanapa Beach appears like a vivid dream, with bright-green jungle foliage on three sides and cobalt blue water lapping at its feet. The 120-acre park on an ancient *aa* lava flow includes sea cliffs, lava tubes, arches, and that beach—plus a dozen rustic beach cabins. If you're interested in staying here, see "Accommodations," earlier in this chapter. Also see "Beaches" and "Hiking & Camping."

HANA

Green, tropical, almost Tahiti-like **Hana,** which some call heavenly, is a destination all its own, a small coastal village in a rain forest inhabited by 2,500 people, many part Hawaiian. Beautiful Hana enjoys more than 90 inches of rain a year—more than enough to keep the scenery lush. Banyans, bamboo, breadfruit trees—everything seems larger than life in this small town. Especially the flowers, like wild ginger and plumeria. Several roadside stands offer exotic blooms for $1 a bunch. Just "put money in box." It's the Hana honor system.

The last unspoiled Hawaiian town on Maui is, oddly enough, the home of Maui's first resort, which opened in 1946. Paul Fagan, owner of the San Francisco Seals baseball team, bought an old inn and turned it into the **Hotel Hana-Maui**, which gave Hana its first and, as it turns out, last taste of tourism. Others have tried to open hotels and golf courses and more resorts, but Hana, which is interested in remaining Hana, always politely refuses. There are a few B&Bs here, though; if you'd like to wallow in this fresh-faced ambiance, see "Accommodations," above.

In a wood-frame 1871 building that served as the old Hana District Police Station is the history of the place in artifacts, memorabilia, and photographs. **Hana Museum Cultural Center,** Uakea Road (☎ **808/248-8622**), has some real treasures, so take a few minutes to see it. You'll also want to stop in at **Hasegawa General Store,** a Maui institution (see "Shops & Galleries," below).

On the green hills above Hana stands a 30-foot-high white cross made of lava rock. The cross was erected by citizens in memory of Paul Fagan, who founded the Hana Ranch as well as the hotel, and helped keep the town alive. The 3-mile hike up to **Fagan's Cross** provides a gorgeous view of the Hana coast, especially at sunset, when Fagan himself liked to climb this hill. See "Hiking & Camping," above, for details.

Most day-trippers to Hana miss the most unusual natural attraction of all: **Red Sand Beach.** Officially named Kaihalulu Beach, which means "roaring sea," everyone here calls it Red Sand Beach. It's easy to see why: The beach is as red as a Ferrari at a five-alarm fire. It's really something to see. The beach is on the ocean side of Kauiki Hill, just south of Hana Bay, in a wild, natural setting in a pocket cove. Kauiki, a 390-foot-high volcanic cinder cone, lost its seaward wall to erosion and spilled red cinders everywhere to create the red sands. The only other red-sand beach in the world is supposed to be in Iceland. Moah bettah you see Maui's.

To get there, walk south on Uakea Road, past the Hotel Hana-Maui to the end of the parking lot for Sea Ranch Cottages. Turn left, cross an open field, past an old Japanese cemetery, and follow a well-worn footpath a short distance down a narrow cliff trail. In this private, romantic setting, some beachgoers shed their clothes, so try not to be offended.

TROPICAL HALEAKALA: OHEO GULCH AT KIPAHULU

If you're thinking about heading out to the so-called Seven Sacred Pools, our past Hana at the Kipahulu end of Haleakala National Park, let's clear this up right now: There are more than seven pools—about 24, actually—and all water in Hawaii is considered sacred. It's all a PR scam that has spun out of control into contemporary myth. Folks here call it by its rightful name, **Oheo Gulch,** and visitors sometimes refer to it as Kipahulu; but Kipahulu is the name of the area where Oheo Gulch is located. No matter what you call it, it's beautiful. This dazzling series of pools and cataracts is so popular that it now has its own roadside parking lot.

ACCESS POINTS Even though it's part of Haleakala National Park, you cannot drive to Oheo Gulch from the summit; you have to continue on the Hana Highway. Oheo is about 30 to 50 minutes beyond Hana town, along Highway 31. The Highway 31 bridge passes over some of the pools near the ocean; the others, plus magnificent 400-foot Waimoku Falls, are uphill, via an often-muddy but rewarding hour-long hike (see "Hiking & Camping," above). Expect showers on the Kipahulu Coast.

VISITOR CENTER **Kipahulu Ranger Station** (☎ **808/248-7375**), is staffed from 9am to 5pm daily. Rest rooms are available, but no drinking water. Rangers offer

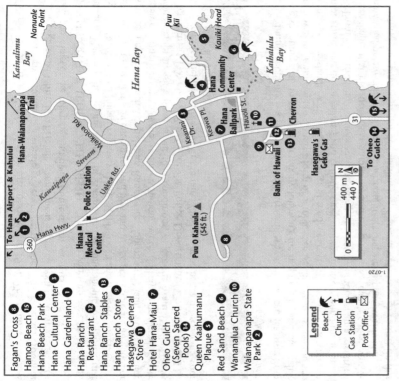

Hana

Legend

🚩 Beach
✝ Church
⛽ Gas Station
✉ Post Office

400 m
440 y

1-0720

Fagan's Cross **8**
Hamoa Beach **15**
Hana Beach Park **4**
Hana Cultural Center **1**
Hana Gardenland **1**
Hana Ranch Restaurant **12**
Hana Ranch Stables **13**
Hana Ranch Store **9**
Hasegawa General Store **11**
Hotel Hana-Maui **7**
Oheo Gulch (Seven Sacred Pools) **14**
Queen Kaahumanu Plaque **5**
Red Sand Beach **6**
Wananalua Church **10**
Waianapanapa State Park **2**

---

park-safety information, exhibits, books, and a variety of walks and hikes year-round; check at the station for current activities.

HIKING & CAMPING

There are a number of hikes in the park, and tent camping is allowed; see "Hiking & Camping" on p. 433 for details.

SEEING THE HIGHLIGHTS

From the ranger station, it's just a short hike above the famous **Oheo Gulch** to two spectacular waterfalls. Check with the Haleakala Park rangers before hiking up to or swimming in the pools, and always keep one eye on the water in the streams; the sky can be sunny near the coast, but flood waters travel 6 miles down from 8,000 acres of Kipahulu Valley and can rise 4 feet in less than 10 minutes. In hard rain, streams swell quickly; always be aware of your surroundings. It's not a good idea to swim in the pools in the winter, when the waters are just too rough; they're much better for swimming in summer, when they become calm as glass.

Makahiku Falls is easily reached from the central parking area: The trailhead begins near the ranger station. **Pipiwai Trail** leads you up to the road and beyond for a half-mile to the overlook. If you hike another 1½ miles up the trail across two bridges and through a bamboo forest, you reach **Waimoku Falls.** It's a good uphill hike, but press on to avoid the pool's crowd.

BEYOND OHEO GULCH

A mile past Oheo Gulch on the ocean side of the road is **Lindbergh's Grave.** First to fly across the Atlantic Ocean, Charles A. Lindbergh (1902–74) found peace in the

Pacific; he settled in Hana, where he died of cancer in 1974. The famous aviator is buried under river stones in a seaside graveyard behind the 1857 **Palapala Hooman Congregational Church**, where his tombstone is engraved with his own words: "If I take the wings of the morning and dwell in the uttermost parts of the sea. . . ."

EVEN FARTHER AROUND THE BEND Those of you who are continuing on around Maui to the fishing village of **Kaupo** and beyond should be warned that Kaupo Road, or Old Piilani Highway (Hwy. 31), is rough and unpaved, often full of potholes and ruts. You may encounter wild pigs and stray cows. There are no goods or services until you reach **Ulupalakua Ranch** (see "Upcountry Maui," above), where there's a winery, a general store, and a gas station, which is likely to be closed. Before you attempt it, ask around about road conditions, or call the **Maui Public Works Department** (☎ 808/248-8254) or the **Police Department** (☎ 808/248-8311). This road frequently washes out in the rain. You'd really be better off retracing your route back through Hana.

10 Shops & Galleries

by Jocelyn Fujii

Like dining, shopping is a major Maui activity. And why not? You can leapfrog from one shopping mall to the next simply by following the main road—and rationalize that walking from store to store is a form of aerobic exercise. But Maui is also the arts center of the islands, with a large number of resident artists who show their works in more than four dozen galleries and countless gift shops scattered around the island.

From Kula to Hana, Maui is also the queen of specialty products, an agricultural cornucopia that produces Kula onions, upcountry protea, Kaanapali coffee, world-renowned potato chips, and many other taste treats that are shipped worldwide.

As with any popular visitor destination, you'll have to wade through bad art (in this case, oceans of trite marine art) and mountains of trinkets, particularly in Lahaina and Kihei, where touristy boutiques line the streets between rare pockets of treasures. If you shop in South or West Maui, expect to pay resort prices, clear down to a bottle of Evian or sunscreen. But Maui's gorgeous finds are particularly rewarding. Residents shop live, and shop for everyday needs in central Maui, and it's home to first-rate boutiques for specialized tastes as well: Wailuku has its own antiques alleys (N. Market and Main streets), and the Kaahumanu Center in neighboring Kahului is becoming more fashionable by the month. Also in Kahului is the $28 million Maui Arts and Cultural Center, a dream venue for the performing and visual arts, with two theaters and a 3,500-square-foot gallery. Upcountry, Makawao's boutiques are worth seeking out, despite some attitude and high prices.

CENTRAL MAUI
KAHULUI

Kahului's best shopping is concentrated in two places. Almost all of the shops listed below are at one of these centers:

Kaahumanu Center, 275 Kaahumanu Ave. (☎ 808/877-3369), a commercial hub only 5 minutes from the Kahului Airport on Highway 32, offers more than 100 shops, restaurants, and theaters. More manageable than Honolulu's Ala Moana, with a thoughtful selection of food and retail shops, Kaahumanu covers all the bases, from the finest arts and crafts to a **Foodland Supermarket**, with everything in between: a thriving food court; the island's best beauty supply, **Lisa's Beauty Supply & Salon** (☎ 808/877-6463), with every imaginable item for a well-groomed life; mall standards like **Sunglass Hut, Radio Shack, Local Motion** (surf and beach wear, including the current fad, women's board shorts, a combination of hot pants and men's surf trunks); department stores **JC Penney, Liberty House,** and **Shirokiya;** and attractive boutique/galleries such as **Ki'i** and **Maui Hands.** From 11:30am to 1:30pm on the last Friday of every month, there are food demonstrations and samplings, fashion shows, and live entertainment in the center's **Queen's Market Food Court.**

Rough around the edges and dramatically eclipsed by the Kaahumanu Center down the street, **Maui Mall,** 70 E. Kaahumanu Ave. (☎ **808/877-7559**), is still a place of everyday good things, from **Longs Drugs,** which anchors the modest mall, to 60-minute photo processing and a **Star Market.**

EDIBLES The **Star Market** in the Maui Mall, **Foodland** in the Kaahumanu Center, and **Safeway** at 170 E. Kamehameha Ave. will satisfy your ordinary grocery needs. On Saturday, you may want to check out the **Maui Swap Meet** (see below). A few sources of local specialties, flowers, health foods, and other mighty morsels are worth checking out:

With a move from Wailuku to Kahului, both the service and the selection have improved at **Down to Earth Natural Foods,** 305 Dairy Rd. (☎ **808/877-2661**). Fresh organic Maui produce, a bountiful salad bar, sandwiches and smoothies, vitamins and supplements, freshly baked goods, chips and snacks, whole grains, and several packed aisles of vegetarian and health foods have made Down to Earth a health-food staple for many years.

Established in 1941, the **Ooka Super Market,** 1870 Main St., Wailuku (☎ **808/244-3931**). Maui's ultimate home-grown supermarket, is a mom-and-pop business that has grown by leaps and bounds but still manages to keep its neighborhood flavor. Ooka sells inexpensive produce (fresh Maui mushrooms for a song), fresh island seafood, certified Angus beef, and Maui specialties such as manju and mochi. Proteas cut the same day, freesias in season, hydrangeas, fresh leis, torch gingers from Hana, upcountry calla lilies in season, and multicolored anthuriums are offered at what is one of Maui's finest and most affordable retail flower selections. Prepared foods are also a hit: bentos and plate lunches, roast chicken and lau-lau, and specialties from all the islands abound. The fish is always fresh, and the seaweed, poi, Kula persimmons in the fall, fresh Haiku mushrooms, and dried marlin from Kona are among the local delicacies that make Ooka a Maui favorite.

Most of the space at **Shirokiya,** in the Kaahumanu Center (☎ **808/877-5551**), is devoted to food, with a well-stocked prepared-foods section, but check out the fresh produce (bananas, papayas), juices, health-food supplements, home appliances, and audio-video equipment as well. The Dee Lite Bakery has a small corner, with its famous haupia cakes and other white-and-bright pastries, but most of the other foods are local or Japanese plate-lunch fare offered in neatly packaged bento boxes or hot from the counter. Specialties such as Maui manju and Maui mochi are also available.

Maui's produce has long been a source of pride for islanders, and **Maui Farmers Market,** Kahului Shopping Center (next to Ah Fook's Super Market; ☎ **808/573-1934**), is where you'll find a fresh, inexpensive selection of Maui-grown fruit, vegetables, flowers, and plants in season. Local color, too. Crafts and gourmet foods add to the event, and the large monkeypod trees provide welcome shade.

Located in the northern section of Wailuku, **Takamiya Market,** 359 N. Market St. (☎ **808/244-3404**), is much loved by local folks and visitors, who often drive all the way from Kihei to stock up on picnic fare and mouth-watering ethnic foods for sunset gatherings and beach parties. This is a highly recommended stop for all those with adventurous palates. Unpretentious home-cooked foods from East and West are prepared daily and served on Styrofoam plates from an ethnic smorgasbord. From the chilled-fish counter come fresh sashimi and poke, and in the renowned assortment of prepared foods are mounds of shoyu chicken, tender fried squid, roast pork, kalua pork, lau-lau, Chinese noodles, fiddlehead ferns, and Western comfort foods, such as cornbread and potato salad. Fresh produce and paper products are also available, but it's the prepared foods that have made Takamiya's a household name in central Maui.

Caswell-Massey. Kaahumanu Center. ☎ **808/877-7761.**

Although part of a worlwide chain, this is a Maui store of distinction. What makes this Caswell-Massey special is the presence of Maui-made soaps and bath products that use tropical fragrances and botanicals. As America's oldest perfume company, established in 1752, Caswell-Massey triple-mills all its soaps (so they last three times longer) scents them with natural oils, and uses old-fashioned, tried-and-true methods and ingredients. You can handpick your selection from hundreds of specialty products, from decadent bath salts with 23k gold flakes to Damask rose shampoo and bath gels, eye creams, body lotions, old Swedish soaps, sachets, candles, perfume bottles, potpourris, room mists, and an array of pamperings. They prepare handsome, custom-designed baskets for no extra charge.

Cost Less Imports. Maui Mall. ☎ **808/877-0300.**

Natural fibers are everywhere in this tiny corner of the mall. Lauhala, bamboo blinds, grassy floor and window coverings, shoji-style lamps, burlap yardage, baskets, tactile Balinese cushions—all Asian, Indonesian, and Polynesian imports, as well as top-of-the-line, made-on-Maui soaps and handicrafts. This is Hawaii's only direct importer of Chinese seagrass-rush mats.

Hoaloha Heirlooms. Kaahumanu Center. ☎ **808/873-0461.**

Lavish ukuleles by Maui Ukulele and leis made of kukui nuts, wiliwili seeds, and Job's tears are part of the Hawaiian offerings at this new Maui gift shop. Paintings, place mats, koa tables, small Hawaiian quilts, children's clothes, muumuus and dresses, hair ornaments, handmade paper, fiber baskets, and hundreds of gift items from Hawaii, Indonesia, and the South Pacific are part of Hoaloha's offerings.

Ki'i Gallery. Kaahumanu Center. ☎ **808/871-4557.**

The eclectic collection includes glass art and black pearls, as well as a wide assortment of made-on-Maui crafts. Chinese porcelains, clay teapots, jewelry, handpainted maple-wood bowls, perfume bottles, and an occasional esoteric item (such as the Viking clay forms from Shanghai) keep regulars coming back. But it's the glass vases that dominate the room with their brilliance and luminosity. All handcrafted, of the highest quality, the glass reflects excellent craftsmanship and design, from Venetian and Czechoslovakian glass to Pizzo from Maui and Vandemark Merritt from New Jersey.

Lightning Bolt Maui Inc. 55 Kaahumanu Ave. ☎ **808/877-3484.**

There's an excellent selection of women's board shorts, aloha shirts, swimwear, sandals and shoes, beach towels, and everything else needed for fun in the sun. Quality labels such as Patagonia and high-tech, state-of-the-art outdoor gear like Polartec sweaters and moccasins attract adventurers heading for the chilly hinterlands as well as the sun-drenched shores.

Maui Hands. Kaahumanu Center. ☎ **808/877-0568.**

Maui hands have made most of the items in this tiny store. The assortment of arts and crafts includes paintings, prints, and things whimsical and serious, from jewelry to glass marbles (chachkas handsomer than they sound). This is an ideal stop for made-on-Maui products and crafts of good quality; 90% of what's sold here was made on the island. There are paintings and prints aplenty, in all price ranges.

The original Maui Hands remains in Makawao at The Courtyard, 3620 Baldwin Ave. (☎ 808/572-5194).

Maui Swap Meet. S. Puunene Ave. (next to the Kahului Post Office). ☎ **808/242-0240.**

Throughout the year, there are more than 100 vendors here, which makes Maui Swap Meet, the pioneer of neighbor-island markets, a large and popular event. After Thanksgiving and throughout December, the number of booths nearly doubles and the activity reaches fever pitch. The colorful assortments of Maui specialties include Kula vegetables, vegetables from Keanae, fresh taro, plants, proteas, crafts, household items, homemade ethnic foods, and baked goods. Every Saturday from early morning to noon, vendors spread out their wares in booths, under tarps, in a festival-like atmosphere that is pure Maui with a touch of kitsch. Admission is 50¢, and if you go before 7am while the vendors are setting up, no one will turn you away.

Summerhouse. In the Dairy Center, 385 Dairy Rd. ☎ **808/871-1320.**

Sleek and chic, tiny Summerhouse is big on style: linens by Russ Berens, FLAX, Kiko, and Christy Allen; hats by Mui Milner and Emi Azeka Preston; unique jewelry; up-to-the-minute evening dresses; and high-quality T-shirts take women from day to evening.

WAILUKU

Just as they love to dine out, Mauians love to shop, and Wailuku, the old part of town, makes it easy for everyone to indulge this passion. Wailuku is the center of antiquing on Maui, and very likely all of Hawaii. There is some junk, but a stroll along Main and Market streets usually turns up a treasure or two. Maui residents LOVE to decorate their homes, and when they're buying or getting rid of things, they're likely to end up in Wailuku. It's a mixed bag, for sure, but thoroughly enjoyable.

✪ **Bailey House Gift Shop.** At the Bailey House Museum, 2375-A Main St. ☎ **808/244-3920.**

If you're shopping for made-in-Hawaii items and have to pick one stop in Wailuku, make it Bailey House. The small space, discriminating taste, and high level of integrity have honed a selection of remarkable gift items, from Hawaiian music albums to exquisite woods, traditional Hawaiian games (konane, checkers, and tik tak toe), pareus, and an impressive selection of books. Koa-framed prints by the legendary Hawaii artist Madge Tennent, lauhala hats hanging in mid-air, handsewn pheasant hatbands (with Ulupalakua feathers, by Diane Masumura), Tutuvi T-shirts, jams and jellies, Maui cookbooks, and an occasional Hawaiian quilt are some of the treasures to be found here. Hawaiian music often wafts in from a neighboring room, where a slack-key guitar class may be in session. This is a thoroughly enjoyable browse through authoritative Hawaiiana, in a museum that's one of the finest examples of missionary architecture, dating back to 1833.

✪ **Bird of Paradise Unique Antiques.** 56 N. Market St. ☎ **808/242-7699.**

The owner, Joe Myhand, loves furniture, old Matson liner menus, blue willow china, kimonos for children, and anything nostalgic that happens to be Hawaiian. The furniture in the strongly Hawaiian collection ranges from 1940s rattan to wicker and old koa—those items tailor-made for informal island living and leisurely moments on the lanai. Myhand also collects bottles and mails his license plates all over the world. The collection ebbs and flows with his finds, keeping buyers waiting in the wings for his Depression glass, California pottery from the 1930s and 1940s (Bauer, Metlox, Vernon, Friscan ware, the occasional precious Roseville), old dinnerware, perfume bottles, vintage aloha shirts, and vintage Hawaiian music on cassettes. Items from the South Pacific are showing a stronger presence in the shop.

★ **Brown-Kobayashi.** 160-A N. Market St. ☎ **808/242-0804.**
From self-adornment to interior design, graceful living is the theme here. Prices range from $2 to $7,000 in this 750-square-foot treasure trove. Asian antiques mingle quietly with old and new French, European, and Hawaiian objects, expressing an eclectic yet cohesive aesthetic. Japanese kimono and obi, Bakelite and Peking glass beads, breathtaking Japanese lacquerware, cricket carriers (from $38 for the woven to $1,400 for the one of antique carved ivory), cloisonné, and a lotus-leaf basket carved of bamboo are among the many treasures here. Exotic and precious Chinese woods (purple sandalwood and huanghuaali) glow discreetly from quiet corners, and an occasional monarchy-style lidded milo bowl comes in and flies out.

Gima Designs. 2058 Main St. ☎ **808/242-1839.**
Elaine Gima creates art to wear with her original silk designs, a blend of traditional forms with a modern eye and a timeless sense of style. Her clothing, accessories, and silk forms, and her collaborations with husband Thomas Calhoun, a fine woodworker, have won top honors at the "Woods of Hawaii" show. Call ahead to make sure she's there; she doesn't keep regular hours.

Memory Lane. 130 N. Market St. ☎ **808/244-4196.**
This 1,500-square-foot showroom is filled with fine art, Hawaiian collectibles, Oriental antiques, kitsch, vintage textiles and aloha shirts, English crystal from the 1700s, Depression glass, antique silver, and furniture "from the very old to the 1950s and Federal," says the owner. Like all shop owners in Wailuku, Joe Ransberger, a painter, finds that old koa furniture is a rarity that flies out of the store to collectors, who must lie in wait. Some things he can't part with, such as the curly-koa chest made in the 1800s, and some of the one-of-a-kind wood-pulp rayon textiles. Prices range from $1 to $30,000, with many pieces over $1,000. It's a treasure hunt from the moment you enter: A man searching for a needle for his antiquated 78-rpm phonograph miraculously found one here.

Traders of the Lost Art. 62 N. Market St. ☎ **808/242-7753.**
It's a mixed bag, and you may have to wade through a dense landscape with musty recesses, but you never know what the store promises: collectibles, kitsch, tribal art, African trade-bead bracelets, carpets from Katmandu, Hawaiian carvings, nautical Oceanic art, vintage koa furniture.

WEST MAUI
LAHAINA

Lahaina's merchants and art galleries go all out from 6:30 to 9pm on Friday night, when **Art Night** evokes an extra measure of hospitality and community spirit. The Art Night openings are usually marked with live entertainment and refreshments and a livelier-than-usual street scene.

If you're in Lahaina on the second or last Thursday of each month, stroll by the front lawn of the **Baldwin Home,** 696 Front St. (at Dickenson Street) for a splendid look at lei-making and an opportunity to meet the gregarious senior citizens of Lahaina. In a program sponsored by the American Association of Retired Persons, they gather from 10am to 4pm to demonstrate lei-making, to sell their floral creations, and equally important, to socialize.

SHOPPING CENTERS Any day of the week, the waterfront shopping/dining complex at the southern end of Lahaina simply known as **505 Front Street** (☎ 808/667-0727) is a place to tuck into pizza (**Village Pizzeria**), shop (**Foreign Intrigue Imports** and **Maui To Go**), attend Maui's best luau (the **Old Lahaina Luau;** see "Maui After Dark," later in this chapter), have a sunset drink or dinner (**Pacific'o Restaurant;** see "Dining," above), buy art-deco posters or rock-star paintings (**New York–Paris**), and ease into Avanti's popular retro silk aloha shirts. It's not a large complex, and it gets mixed reviews, but it does hold some surprises.

What was formerly a big, belching pineapple cannery is now a maze of shops and restaurants at the northern end of Lahaina town known as the **Lahaina Cannery Mall,** 1221 Honoapiilani Hwy. (☎ 808/661-5304). Find your way through the T-shirt and sportswear shops (**Reyn's** has fabulous aloha shirts) to **Lahaina Printsellers,** home of rare maps, antique originals, prints, paintings, and wonderful 18th- to 20th-century cartography representing the largest collection of engravings and antique maps in Hawaii. You can buy a book at **Waldenbooks** and follow the scent of coffee to **Sir Wilfred's Coffee House** a few doors away, where you can unwind with espresso and croissants, or you can head for **Compadres Bar and Grill,** where the margaritas flow freely and the Mexican food is tasty (see "Dining," above). The artist **Guy Buffet** has his gallery here. For film, water, aspirin, groceries, sunscreen, and other things you can't live without, nothing beats **Longs Drugs** and **Safeway,** two old standbys that anchor the cannery.

The **Lahaina Center,** 900 Front St. (☎ 808/667-9216), is north of Lahaina's most congested strip, where Front Street begins. Across the street from the center, the seawall is a much-sought-after front-row seat to the sunset. There's plenty of free validated parking with easy access to more than 30 shops, a hair salon, restaurants, a nightclub, and a four-plex movie theater complex. Among the shopping stops: **Banana Republic,** the **Hilo Hattie Fashion Center** (a dizzying emporium of aloha wear), **McInerny** (wonderfully discounted designer clothes), **Local Motion,** an **ABC Discount Store,** and a dozen other recreational, entertainment, dining, and shopping prospects.

The recent conversion of 10,000 square feet of parking space into the re-creation of a traditional Hawaiian village is a welcome touch of Hawaiiana. With the commercialization of modern Lahaina, it's easy to forget that it was once the capital of the Hawaiian kingdom and a significant historic site. The village, called **Hale Kahiko,** features three main houses, called *hale:* a sleeping house; the men's dining house; and the crafts house, where women pounded lauhala for mats and baskets. Construction of the houses consumed 10,000 feet of ohia wood from the island, 20 tons of pili grass, and more than 4 miles of handwoven coconut sennit for the lashings. Artifacts, weapons, a canoe, and indigenous trees are among the authentic touches in this village, which can be toured privately or with a guide.

David Lee Galleries. 712 Front St. ☎ **808/667-7740.**

The gallery is devoted to the works of David Lee, who uses natural powder colors to paint on silk. The pigments and technique create a luminous, ethereal quality.

Foreign Intrigue Imports. 505 Front St. ☎ **808/667-4004.**

The large selection of interior accents puts a new spin on the often-tired world of Indian and Balinese imports. Gorgeous handpainted wooden trays, gilded Buddhas, car benches, chests and armoires of all sizes, and sturdy hemp pouches and accessories make the collection an intriguing one. Hundreds of functional and nonfunctional accessories line the shop and reflect the mastery of detail that Balinese villagers possess. Although handpainted cabinets, trunks, and household accessories from India are a new hit in the store, there are items in all price ranges—and intrepid shoppers may find some wonderful deals among the vast and colorful selection, including one-of-a-kind, made-on-Maui necklaces of antique beads and jades.

⭐ **Gallery Ltd.** 716 Front St. ☎ **808/661-0696.**

One of the beauties of Lahaina, the recently renovated Gallery is easy to miss among the bright windows of Front Street. You'll need a good chunk of browsing time here; the jade and pearls alone could account for the better part of an afternoon. The Gallery is awash in gorgeous antiquities, from snuff bottles and netsukes to lacquerware, jade carvings, Buddhas, scrolls, screens, and precious jewelry, most of it Chinese and Japanese. Although antiques make up half of the impressive selection, there are also some remarkable contemporary works of Asian art. The Japanese screens and larger porcelains are upstairs. Children whose parents were customers are now looking for their own wedding strands among the Biwa, South Seas black pearls and stunning Japanese strands, which can be lengthened and clasped according to the customer's design.

Lahaina Body & Bath. 713 Front St. ☎ **808/661-1076.**

The new Front Street location is an extension of Lei Spa, and both stores are worth a stop. It's a good sign that 95% of the beauty and bath products sold here are made on Maui, and that includes Hawaiian Botanical Pikake shower gel; kukui and macadamia-nut oils; Hawaiian potpourris; mud masks with Hawaiian seaweed; and a space of rejuvenating, cleansing, skin-soothing potions for hair and skin. Aromatherapy body oils and perfumes are popular, as are the handmade Hawaiian soaps and fragrances of torch ginger, plumeria, coconut, tuberose, and sandalwood. Scented candles in coconut shells, inexpensive and fragrant, make great gifts.

Martin Lawrence Galleries. In the Lahaina Market Place, 126 Lahainaluna Rd. ☎ **808/661-1788.**

The front is garish, with pop art, kinetic sculptures, and bright, carnivalesque glass objects. Toward the back of the gallery, however, there's a sizable inventory of two-dimensional art and some plausible choices for collectors of Keith Haring, Andy Warhol, and other controversial artists. The focus is on pop art and national and international artists; only one artist represented here is from Maui.

Maui to Go. 505 Front St. ☎ **808/667-2292.**

Shop here for high-quality, made-on-Maui products: plump, sundried macadamia nuts (with no cholesterol), upcountry jams in several flavors, Maui coffee, Maui teas and popourris, Maui onion mustards and condiments, cookies, chocolates, and many other island delectables. Throw in a nostalgic aloha shirt while you're at it, in retro prints that were worn by Elvis, Tony Curtis, and President Eisenhower. The owners, Colleen Noah-Marti and her husband, Gerard, make sure their shop is stocked with Maui's finest specialty products. Other items from far-flung islands include fiber handbags, books, ceramics, lauhala mats from the South Pacific, and other accessories for the home.

Miki's. 762 Front St. ☎ **808/661-8991.**

Walk in off the sidewalk onto the bleached-wood floors and see why aloha shirts are so fab. Tiny, busy, and bursting with color, Miki's has a tasteful assortment of aloha wear, from Tommy Bahama shirts and coordinates to Honu Bay T-shirts, jams, surf shorts, and beach slippers.

South Seas Trading Post. 780 Front St. ☎ **808/661-3168.**

Treasures from the South Pacific, from masks to jewelry to wall hangings and puppets, acknowledge the tribal arts of Borneo, Papua New Guinea, Thailand, Kashmir, and the Himalayas. Take a journey through these exotic destinations through the carvings, drums, implements, and arts of their cultures.

Totally Hawaiian. 1221 Honoapiilani Hwy. ☎ **808/667-2558.**

A good browse for its selection of Niihau shell jewelry, excellent Hawaiian CDs, Norfolk pine bowls, and Hawaiian quilt kits. Hawaiian quilt patterns sewn in Thailand (at least they're honest about it) are labor-intensive, less expensive, and attractive, although not totally Hawaiian.

★ **Village Galleries in Lahaina.** 120 and 180 Dickenson St. ☎ **808/661-4402** and **808/661-5559.**

The 27-year-old Village Galleries is the oldest continuously running gallery on Maui, and it's highly esteemed as one of the few galleries with consistently high standards. The recent addition of a contemporary gallery (with colorful gift items and jewelry!) has upped the enjoyment and value of dropping by. The selection of mostly original two- and three-dimensional art offers a good look at the quality of work emanating from the island. Art collectors know the Village Galleries as a respectable showcase for regional artists.

There's another location in the Ritz-Carlton Kapalua, 1 Ritz-Carlton Dr. (☎ **808/669-1800**).

Westside Natural Foods. 193 Lahainaluna Rd. ☎ **808/667-2855.**

A longtime Lahaina staple, Westside is serious about providing tasty food that's healthy and affordable. Its excellent food bar attracts a healthy clientele with vegetarian lasagne, marinated tofu strips, vegetarian pot pie, crisp salads, grains, curries, and gorgeous organic produce.

KAANAPALI

Whalers Village, 2435 Kaanapali Pkwy. (☎ **808/661-4567**), has gone shockingly upscale. Once you've stood under the authentic whale skeleton or squeezed the plastic whale blubber at the **Whale Center of the Pacific** (see "Seeing the Sights," earlier in this chapter), you can blow a bundle at **Tiffany, Prada, Chanel, Ferragamo, Dolce & Gabbana,** and **Sharper Image,** or any of the 70 shops and restaurants that have sprouted up in this beachfront shopping center. The posh Euro trend doesn't bode well; there's next to nothing here that's Hawaiian. Some of the village's mainstream possibilities: the **Body Shop** for the best and most globally conscious products for bath and home; **Hobie Hawaii** for swim and surf things; **Paradise Clothing** for Speedos and bathing suits; and **Canoe** for crisp, tasteful aloha shirts. **The Eyecatcher** has one of the most extensive selections of sunglasses on the island, located just across from the busiest **ABC** store in the state. The most comforting stop of all is the **Maui Yogurt Company,** where Maui-made Roselani ice cream is sold in mouth-watering flavors, including a bracing mint chocolate chip. The Whalers Village is open daily from 9:30am to 10pm.

Rhonda's Quilts. In the Hyatt Regency Maui, 210 Nohea Kai Dr. ☎ **808/667-7660.**

Rhonda's has increased its made-in-Hawaii selection. Some T-shirts, tote bags, mouse pads, and Hawaiian quilt designs are designed in-house, but there are also dolls, children's clothing, locally made tiles in Hawaiian quilt patterns, books, stuffed animals, and other eclectic goods in this cheerful store. The assortment includes a small selection of women's clothing among the antique quilts and Americana. The Hawaiian quilts are made both here and, much less expensively, in the Philippines, and all are of high quality. Quilt pillows, supplies, patterns, and kits are sold here, and quilting classes are offered on Fridays.

☆ **Sandal Tree.** In the Westin Maui. ☎ **808/667-5330.**

It's unusual for a resort shop to draw local customers on a regular basis (add time and parking costs to that pair of sandals), but the Sandal Tree has a flock of footwear fanatics who come here from throughout the islands for their chic kicks. They sell rubber thongs and topsiders, sandals and dressy pumps, athletic shoes and hats, Arche comfort footwear, and much more. Accessories range from fashionable knapsacks to indulgences such as avant-garde geometrical handbags. Prices are realistic, too.

Three of the six Sandal Tree resort shops throughout Hawaii are on Maui. There's another at the Hyatt Regency Maui, 200 Nohea Kai Dr., Kaanapali Beach (☎ **808/661-3495**); and the third is at the Grand Wailea Resort.

KAHANA

Kahana Gateway is an unimpressive mall built to serve the condominium community that has sprawled along the coastline north of Kaanapali, before Kapalua. If you need women's swimsuits, however, **Rainbow Beach Swimwear** is a find, boldly situated near the waistline-challenging dining mecca, Roy's Kahana Bar and Grill, and a stone's throw from the Fish & Games Sports Grill (see "Dining," earlier in this chapter). At Rainbow, you'll find a wide selection of suits for all shapes, at lower-than-resort prices, slashed even further during the frequent (and welcome) sales.

Also in Kahana Gateway, **Hutton's Fine Jewelry** is a breath of fresh air for lovers of fine jewelry. High-end jewelry from designers around the country (a lot of platinum and diamonds) reflect discerning taste for those who can afford it. Tahitian black pearls and jade (some hundreds of years old, all certified) are among Hutton's specialties, but we love the Carleton Kinkade oil paintings hanging on the walls.

KAPALUA

Honolua Store. 502 Office Rd. (next to the Ritz-Carlton Kapalua). ☎ **808/669-6128.**

Walk on the old wood floors peppered with holes from golf shoes and find your everyday essentials: bottled water, stationery, mailing tape, jackets, chips, wine, soft drinks, paper products, fresh fruit and produce, and aisles of notions and necessities. One corner is dedicated to the Kapalua Nature Society, which leads hikes into the West Maui Mountains. With picnic tables on the veranda and a take-out counter offering deli items; 13 types of sandwiches; salads; and a $3.50 breakfast of eggs, biscuits, and gravy, there are always long lines of customers. Golfers and surfers love to come here for the morning paper and coffee.

Kapalua Shops. At the Kapalua Bay Hotel and Villas. ☎ **808/669-1029.**

Shops have come and gone in this small, exclusive, and once-chic shopping center, now much quieter than in days past. Tiny **Mandalay** still sells East-West luxe with its silk clothing and handful of interior accents. Kapalua old-timer **South Seas Trading Post** brims with exotic artifacts such as Balinese beads, tribal masks, jewelry, and stunning coconut-shell bowls with mother-of-pearl inlay. Around the corner is **San Luigi,** an Italian shoetique with a small and not overwhelmingly expensive selection of footwear in all grades of leather, fiber, and even futuristic plastic. At one of its many Maui locations, the sleek **Lahaina Galleries** occupies a corner of the mall with

A Creative Way to Spend the Day

Make a bowl from clay or paint a premade one, then fire it and take it home. Or paint a picture, or learn ballet, or learn to sketch like the masters at the **Art School at Kapalua** (☎ **808/665-0007**). West Maui's only art school, featuring local and visiting instructors, is open daily for people of all ages and skill levels. (A group of students, ages 8 to 10, recently beautified a construction site by painting an oceanic mural at Lahaina Cannery Mall.) Projects, programs, classes, and workshops at this not-for-profit organization highlight creativity in all forms. Classes in using your camera, sketching, painting on silk, throwing at the potter's wheel, and in the performing arts (ballet, creative dramatics, yoga, and the Pilates stretch for muscular development) are offered in a charming 1920s plantation building that was part of an old cannery operation in the heart of the Kapalua resort. Costs range from $7 a class for nonmembers for a children's creative-movement class to $360 for nonmembers for a twice-weekly, 4-week class in potting on the wheel and hand-building ceramics. Call the school to see what's scheduled while you're on Maui.

artworks by Guy Buffet, Macedo, Andrea Smith, and others. **Reyn's** and **McInerny's** purvey clothing for resort life, and **Kapalua Kids** weighs in with equal time (and toys) for kids.

Village Galleries. In the Ritz-Carlton Kapalua, 1 Ritz-Carlton Dr. ☎ **808/669-1800.**

Maui's finest exhibit their works here and in the other two Village Galleries in Lahaina. Take heart, art lovers: There's no clichéd marine art here. Translucent, delicately turned bowls of Norfolk pine gleam in the light, and George Allan, Betty Hay Freeland, Joyce Clark, Diana Lehr, and Pamela Andelin are included in the pantheon of respected artists represented in the tiny gallery. Watercolors, oils, sculptures, hand-blown glass, Niihau shell leis, jewelry, and all media are represented. The Ritz-Carlton's monthly Artist-in-Residence program features Village Gallery artists in demonstrations and special hands-on workshops—free, including materials.

SOUTH MAUI
KIHEI

Kihei is one long strip of strip malls. Most of the shopping to be done here is concentrated in the **Azeka Place Shopping Center** on South Kihei Road. Fast foods abound at Azeka's—Taco Bell, Pizza Hut, Baskin Robbins—as do tourist-oriented clothing shops like **Crazy Shirts** and the overly tropical **Tropical Tantrum.** It also houses several prominent attractions, including the popular restaurant called A Pacific Cafe, **General Nutrition Center,** and a cluster of specialty shops with everything from children's clothes to shoes, sunglasses, beauty services, a nail salon, and swimwear. Also on South Kihei Road is the **Kukui Mall,** with its movie theaters, **Waldenbooks,** and **Whaler's General Store.**

Here are some of the worthy shopping stops in Kihei:

Aloha Books. In the Kamaole Beach Center, 2411 S. Kihei Rd. ☎ **808/874-8070.**

The owner, Tom Holland, has been a collector and dealer in Hawaiian antiques, collectibles, and art, and his new bookstore reflects his passion. The shelves are stocked with books on and about Hawaii, particularly vintage Hawaiiana, and the walls are draped with vintage Hawaiian and Polynesian art. There are new, used, and rare books, and although this isn't a big bookstore, the titles cover a range of tastes, from popular fiction to historic novels and Dick Francis whodunits. If there's an out-of-print Don Blanding or 1940s music sheet to be found in the neighborhood, it's likely to be here.

⭐ **Hawaiian Moons Natural Foods.** In Azeka I, 2411 S. Kihei Rd. ☎ **808/875-4356.**

Hawaiian Moons is a health-food store, and a great one, but it's also a mini-supermarket with one of the best selections of made-on-Maui products I've encountered on the island. Those who love wholesome, unadulterated food that is not boring love Hawaiian Moons. The Mexican tortillas are made on Maui (and good!), and much of the produce here, such as organic vine-ripened tomatoes and organic onions, is grown in the fertile upcountry soil of Kula. There's Ono Farms Organic Coffee grown in Hana, and a spate of Maui teas by the Hawaiian Tea Company in Wailuku. Chocolate-covered macadamia nuts from Captain Cook are aptly named Tropical Temptations, and there are Tropical Gourmet Salsas to follow the Dave's 100% Natural muffins and cakes. Big Island *tempeh* (a sensible soybean meat substitute), eggs from upcountry, Water's Tofu and Volcano Spices (spicy garlic-lemon powdered seasonings) made on Maui, Maui bagels, Maui shiitake mushrooms, organic lemongrass and okra, Maui Crunch bread, free-range Big Island turkeys and chickens (no antibiotics or artificial nasties), and fresh Maui juices are some of the reasons for coming here. The juice bar/deli puts out pizzas and gourmet sandwiches. Cosmetics are also top-of-the-line: sunblocks, fragrant floral oils, healthy kukui-nut oil from Waialua on Oahu, and the Island Essence made-on-Maui mango-coconut and vanilla-papaya skin lotions, the ultimate in body pampering.

Maui Sports & Cycle. In Dolphin Plaza, 2395 S. Kihei Rd. ☎ **808/875-2882.**

South Maui's upbeat watersports retail and rental shop is a hit among beachgoers and watersports enthusiasts. A friendly, knowledgeable staff helps you choose from among the mind-boggling selection of snorkel gear, boogie boards, kayaks, beach umbrellas, coolers, and view boards for "snorkeling lying down." You'll find swimwear and mountain bikes, too, and gear for riding on land or sea. There's good-quality snorkel gear, with a selection so extensive you can tailor your choice to your budget as well as your fit. Prescription masks are available, as are underwater cameras, sunscreens and lotions, jewelry, T-shirts, postcards, and hats and visors by the bushel.

There's a second Maui Sports & Cycle in Longs Center, 1215 S. Kihei Rd. (☎ **808/875-8448**).

Old Daze. In Azeka I, 1280 S. Kihei Rd. ☎ **808/875-7566.**

Nineteenth-century Americana and Hawaiian collectibles are nicely married in this charming shop. Some recent finds: an 1850s German sideboard, a Don Blanding teapot, 1940s head vases, a turn-of-the-century pie safe, antique kimonos, framed vintage music sheets, and Hawaiian silver collectible spoons. The collection features a modest furniture selection, Hawaiian pictures, 1960s ashtrays, Depression glass, old washboards, souvenir plates from county fairs, and an eclectic assortment of items for table and home. Choices range from hokey to rustic to pleasantly nostalgic, with many items for the kitchen.

Tuna Luna. Kihei Kalama Village, 1941 S. Kihei Rd. ☎ **808/874-9482.**

There are treasures to be found in this small cluster of tables and booths where Maui artists display their work. Ceramics, exotic wood photo albums, jewelry, candles and soaps, handmade paper, and fiber accessories are functional and not, and make great gifts to go.

WAILEA

Wailea consists largely of upscale resort shops that sell expensive souvenirs, gift items, clothing, and accessories for an active life or a life of leisure. **Sandal Tree** (see Kaanapali, above), with its affordable-and-up designer wear, raises the footwear banner at the Grand Wailea Resort, while stores like **Mandalay**, in the Grand Wailea Shops and the Four Seasons Resort Maui, specialize in sumptuous Thai silks and Asian imports, from resort wear to the very dressy. More Wailea highlights for your day of splurge shopping:

Coast Gallery Wailea. 3750 Wailea Alanui Dr., in the Wailea Shopping Village. ☎ 808/879-2301.

This venerable Maui gallery recently moved from the Aston Wailea to an attractive space in the Shopping Village, where the same level of service and selection prevails. From its inception in the mid-1980s, the Coast Gallery has maintained a high profile and level of esteem for its well-balanced mix of local, national, and international artists. Wood carvings, feather art, oil paintings, jewelry, bronze sculptures, prints, ceramics, and tasteful marinescapes reflect the discriminating tastes of the gallery owners, who include old masters and new talent in the selected works. This is a powerful and attractive venue for island artists, who are well represented in the collection.

Grand Wailea Shops. At the Grand Wailea Resort, 3850 Wailea Alanui Dr. ☎ 808/875-1234.

The gargantuan Grand Wailea Resort has always been known for its long arcade of shops and galleries tailored to hefty pocketbooks. However, gift items in all price ranges can be found at **Lahaina Printsellers** (the premier store for old maps and prints), **Dolphin Galleries, H. F. Wichman, Sandal Tree,** the blindingly white resort shop called **Cruise,** and the **Napua Gallery,** which houses the private collection of the resort owner. And these are only some of the shops that line the arcade. **Ki'i Gallery** (☎ 808/871-4557) is slightly larger than a corner, but what a corner it is. Sleek and taut, the gallery is luminous with studio glass and the warm glow of exquisitely turned woods. Dale Zarella's naio-wood sculpture on a koa-and-marble base and the Romeo glass vase from Amsterdam are breathtaking.

✪ **Mango Club.** In the Kea Lani Hotel, 4100 Wailea Alanui Dr. ☎ 808/874-1885.

Shop here if you like the hip-retro look, or if you just need a spiffy swimsuit. Treasures await on those racks of aloha shirts, vintage muumuus, 1940s teatimer tops, and contemporary silk aloha shirts in authentic fabric prints from the 1920s to 1940s. Draped on the walls are collectible treasures with collectible prices, such as aloha shirts and Chinese-collared muumuus from the 1940s in vintage rayon. A dress or aloha shirt in good shape could carry a price tag in the hundreds of dollars, but the modern retros by Avanti, Kamehameha, and Reyn Spooner offer the same look at a fraction of the price. Nicole Miller dresses, La Perla and Diva swimwear, Private Eyes sunglasses—we love Mango Club for its spirited tropical chic.

Wailea Shopping Village. 3750 Wailea Alanui Dr.

Wailea's only shopping complex is a mediocre assemblage of usually empty boutiques, a couple of galleries and gift shops, and the ubiquitous **Whalers General Store,** where people shop for macadamia nuts, newspapers, postcards, ice, sunscreen, Hawaiian teas, and wines at inflated prices. Otherwise, the center is filled with great shades in **For Your Eyes Only,** footwear and beachwear, and the rare, luminous pearls of the **Black Pearl Gallery.** Two bright spots in this complex are **The Elephant Walk** gift shop, where you can find quilted palaka house slippers, Lilikoi Gold Passion Fruit Butter, and coconut lidded bowls; and the tiny **Wailea Espresso**, a kiosk near the parking lot where cappuccino and cinnamon rolls move briskly.

UPCOUNTRY MAUI

MAKAWAO

Besides being a shopper's paradise, Makawao is the home of the island's most prominent arts organization, the ✪ **Hui No'eau Visual Arts Center**, 2841 Baldwin Ave. (☎ **808/572-6560**). Designed in 1917 by C. W. Dickey, one of Hawaii's most prominent architects, the two-story, Mediterranean-style stucco home that houses the center is located on a sprawling, manicured, 9-acre estate called Kaluanui. A tree-lined driveway leading here features two of Maui's largest hybrid Cook and Norfolk Island pines. A legacy of Maui's prominent kamaaina, Harry and Ethel Baldwin, the estate became an art center in 1976 and remains a complete aesthetic experience. Visiting artists offer lectures, classes, and demonstrations, all at reasonable prices, in basketry, jewelry-making, ceramics, printmaking, painting, and all conceivable media. Half-day classes on Hawaiian art, culture, and history are available to visitors and residents. The Hui is one of the few facilities available on Maui for independent art study and studios. Call ahead for schedules and details. Hui No'eau's exhibits are drawn from a wide range of disciplines and multicultural sources, and include both contemporary and traditional art from established and emerging artists. Maui artists long to exhibit here, considering it the most prestigious of venues. There's also a unique gift shop worth a special stop, featuring many one-of-a-kind works by local artists and artisans. Hours are Monday to Saturday from 10am to 4pm.

EDIBLES Working folks in Makawao who long to eat in arrive at the **Rodeo General Store**, 3661 Baldwin Ave. (☎ **808/572-7841**), to pick up their spaghetti and lasagne, sandwiches, salads, and changing specials from the deli. Even in their plastic-wrapped paper trays, the pastas are tasty, as if they came from a neighborhood trattoria in Little Italy. You can pick up all the necessary accompaniments here, from fresh produce, wine, and soft drinks to paper products and baked goods.

Down to Earth Natural Foods, 1169 Makawao Ave. (☎ **808/572-1488**), always has fresh salads and sandwiches, a full section of organic produce (Kula onions, strawberry papayas, mangos, and litchis in season), bulk grains, vitamins and supplements, beauty aids, herbs, juices, snacks, condiments, tofu, seaweed, soy products, and aisles of vegetarian and health foods—canned, packaged, prepared, and fresh. Whether it's a smoothie, a Ginger Blast, or a burrito, it's Down to Earth territory.

In the more than six decades that the **T. Komoda Store and Bakery**, 3674 Baldwin Ave. (☎ **808/572-7261**), has spent in this spot, untold numbers have creaked over the wooden floors to pick up Komoda's famous cream puffs. Old-timers know to come early, or they'll be sold out. Then the cinnamon rolls, doughnuts, pies, chocolate cake, and assorted edibles take over, keeping the aromas of fresh baking wafting through the old store. Pastries are just the beginning; poi, macadamia-nut candies and cookies, and small bunches of local fruit keep the customers coming.

✪ **Collections**, 3677 Baldwin Ave. (☎ **808/572-0781**).

Collections is a longtime Makawao attraction that shows renewed vigor after more than two decades on Baldwin Avenue. Its selection of sportswear, soaps, jewelry, candles, and tasteful, marvelous miscellany reflects the buyer's good sense and good style. Dresses, separates, home and bath accessories, sweaters, and a shop full of good things make this a Makawao must.

Holiday & Co. 3681 Baldwin Ave. ☎ **808/572-1470.**

Attractive women's clothing in natural fibers hangs from racks, while jewelry to go with it beckons from the counter. Recent finds include lotus-fiber bags from Bali, unlike any you've seen before, and Ambre bubble bath, expensive and French and worth it. The latest in comfortable clothing and interchangeable styles in easy-care fabrics are the Holiday signature. Classic linen dresses, cotton and chenille sweaters, tasteful T-shirts, and silks in all weaves fill this understated store.

Hurricane. 3639 Baldwin Ave. ☎ **808/572-5076.**

This split-level boutique with gleaming knotty-pine floors and a cache of finds carries clothing that's two steps ahead of the competition. Tommy Bahama silk pique aloha print dresses, Sigrid Olsen's clothing (knitted shells, Tencel jeans and skirts, cardigans, extraordinary silk tank dresses —expensive but wonderful), and hard-to-find, eccentric books and home accessories are part of the Hurricane appeal. Next door is the men's version, **Tropo**, where stylish, sensitive men can shop for the latest in shirts, and the literary tomes to go with them.

✪ **The Mercantile.** 3673 Baldwin Ave. ☎ **808/572-1407.**

The jewelry, home accessories (especially the Tiffany-style glass-and-shell lamps), dinnerware, Provençal soaps, pocketknives, and clothing are tastefully selected, a salute to the good life. Soothing eye pillows filled with flaxseeds, scented neck pillows, and a riveting section of Bopla dinnerware, decorated by different designers and made of durable hotel porcelain, make it hard to stick to the clothing. You'll also find Italian linen clothing for men and women, and designer jewelry by Dana Kellin and Beth Orduna—they're fun to look at, but expensive.

✪ **Ola's.** In the Paniolo Building, 1156 Makawao Ave. ☎ **808/573-1334.**

Doug Britt's scintillating paintings and photographs by his wife, Sharon, line the walls of Makawao's top gift gallery. The Britts own Ola's Hanalei on Kauai and helped set up Makawao's version, under different ownership (sisters Cindy Heacock and Shari O'Brien) but designed around the same concept of handmade, American-made art by more than 100 artists, including Hawaii's best. Ola's is a bright, crisp, uncluttered, and thoughtfully designed space with a beach-glass counter, concrete floors, and objects that look great, feel good, and have varying degrees of utility. There's the koa-maple checkerboard, a masterpiece of detail; the melodious thumb pianos, called *kalimbas*; elegant Lundberg studio glass, including a celestial lamp; jewelry; and exquisite porcelain vases, with Picassoesque anatomical features, by Donna Polseno. Enjoy the chopsticks, silks, glasses, woods, ceramics, bath products, and art, but don't forget Bella's at Ola's, a line of fourth-generation handmade chocolates from Brooklyn, offered in 12 pricey but irresistible varieties.

Viewpoints Gallery. 3620 Baldwin Ave. ☎ **808/572-5979.**

Maui's only fine-arts cooperative showcases the work of dozens of Maui artists in an airy, attractive gallery located in a restored theater with a courtyard, glass-blowing studio, and restaurants. This is a delightful odyssey through the creative atmosphere of Maui. The gallery features two-dimensional art, jewelry, fiber art, stained glass, papermaking, sculpture, and other media. A high degree of professionalism is maintained, because the artists involved have passed a rigorous screening, and all are full-time professionals. A fine example of what can happen in a collectively supportive artistic environment.

FRESH FLOWERS IN KULA (AT THE BASE OF HALEAKALA NATIONAL PARK)

Like anthuriums on the Big Island, proteas are a Maui trademark and an abundant crop on Haleakala's rich volcanic slopes. They also travel well, dry beautifully, and can be shipped worldwide with ease. Among Maui's most prominent sources is **Sunrise Protea** (☎ **808/876-0200**), in Kula. It has a walk-through garden and gift shops and provides friendly service and a larger-than-usual selection. If you want the freshly cut flowers, they arrive from the fields on Tuesday and Friday afternoons. You can order individual blooms, baskets, arrangements, or wreaths for shipping all over the world. (Next door, the Sunrise Country Market proffers fresh local fruits, snacks, and sandwiches, with picnic tables for lingering.) **Proteas of Hawaii** (☎ **808/878-2533**), another reliable source, offers regular walking tours of the University of Hawaii Extension Service gardens across the street in Kula. **Clouds Rest Protea** (☎ **808/878-2544**) has a garden and extensive selection and will ship anywhere in the U.S.

For flower shopping in other parts of Maui, **Ooka Super Market** (see "Edibles" under "Central Maui," above) and the Saturday-morning **Maui Swap Meet** (see "Kahului," above) are among the best and least expensive places for tropical flowers of every stripe.

EAST MAUI ON THE HANA ROAD: PAIA

Katie's Place Gifts & Collectibles. At Baldwin Ave. and Hana Hwy. ☎ **808/579-8660.**

Hula dolls galore! Find the wiggling collectibles here in all price ranges, a good match for the Don Blanding dinnerware (popular and hard to find), Depression glass, salt and pepper shakers, Mason liner menus, music sheets, vintage 1940s bark-cloth curtains, and countless other snippets of the past, with prices ranging from $10 to $60. As with all collectibles shops, there are things for both serious and whimsical collectors, and the selection changes constantly.

Maui Crafts Guild. 43 Hana Hwy. ☎ **808/579-9697.**

The old wooden storefront at the gateway to Paia houses local crafts of high quality and in all price ranges, from pit-fired raku to bowls of Norfolk pine and other Maui woods fashioned by Maui hands. Basketry, scarves, jewelry, bamboo flutes, koa accessories, prints, pressed flowers, and hundreds of items are displayed in the rustic two-story gift gallery. They ship anywhere, and all artists are selectively screened.

EDIBLES ALONG THE ROAD TO HANA

A golden retriever named Mahi holds court with his growing public at the **Maui Grown Market**, 914 Hana Hwy., Paia (☎ **808/572-1693**). As much of an attraction as the Maui produce sold here, Mahi has a gregarious nature that prompts some dogsick visitors to take her to Hana for the day. But the friendly country store holds its own, with avocado trees, a white picket fence, and picnic tables on a deck. Maui produce abounds: fresh bananas, papayas, star fruit, chirimoyas, pineapples, tomatoes, onions, mangoes in season, lettuces, and whatever can be harvested from all corners of the island. Jams made in Makawao and Maui onion mustards are big sellers, as well as the sandwiches drenched in homemade dressings. There are many options for the 54-mile Hana drive, among them the Hana box lunches in coolers loaned for the day for a returnable $5 deposit.

Homegrown aloha is what you'll find at the roadside oasis known as **Uncle Harry's Hawaiian Crafts and Fresh Fruits**, on the Hana Highway, Keanae (☎ **808/248-7019**), about halfway to Hana. Local papayas, bananas, lilikois, coconuts, and other produce from the region are sold at this Keanae landmark, a legacy of the late Uncle Harry Mitchell, a local legend and respected Hawaiian elder who devoted his life to the Hawaiian-rights and nuclear-free movements. You can browse among the wood carvings and Hawaiian crafts and stock up on smoothies, chips, and snacks for the road.

HANA

✪ **Hana Coast Gallery.** Hotel Hana Maui. ☎ **808/248-8636.**

Tucked away in the lush folds of this posh hideaway hotel, the gallery is known for its high level of curatorship and commitment to the cultural art of Hawaii. One section of the 3,000-square-foot gallery is called The Library, containing a small selection of works by European masters, but the rest is a paean to original Island art and the master crafts of Hawaii. Dozens of well-established Hawaiian artists display their sculptures, paintings, prints, feather work, stone work, carvings, and three-dimensional works in displays that are so natural they could well exist in someone's home. The strong presence of native Hawaiian artists lends cultural weight to the aesthetic statement. We recommend that you make this gallery one of your reasons for going to Hana; it's an esthetic and cultural experience that informs as it enlightens.

Hasegawa General Store. Hana Hwy. ☎ **808/248-8231.**

Established in 1910, immortalized in song since 1961, burned to the ground in 1990, and back in business in 1991, this legendary store is indefatigable and more colorful than ever in its third generation in business. The aisles are choked with merchandise: Hana-blend coffee specially roasted and blended for the store, Ono Farms organic dried fruit, fishing equipment, every tape and CD that mentions Hana, the best books on Hana to be found, T-shirts, beach and garden essentials, mugs, baseball caps, film, baby food, napkins, and other necessities for the Hana life.

11 Maui After Dark

by Jocelyn Fujii

The island's most prestigious entertainment venue is the $28 million **Maui Arts and Cultural Center** in Kahului (☎ **808/242-7469**), a first-class center for the visual and performing arts. It is an astonishing success, a Maui star. Bonnie Raitt has performed here, as have Hiroshima, Pearl Jam, Ziggy Marley, and Tony Bennett, not to mention the finest in local and Hawaii talent. It has booked world-class cultural exhibits, rock and reggae, the Lakota Sioux Indian Dance Theatre, the Maui Symphony Orchestra, the stars of the Moscow Ballet, John Mayall, Kenny Loggins, magic shows, top Hawaiian performers, the Hawaii International Film Festival, and many other notable acts. The center is as precious to Maui as the Met is to New York, with a visual arts gallery, an outdoor amphitheater, offices, rehearsal space, a 300-seat theater for experimental performances, and a 1,200-seat main theater. Since its 1994 opening, the state-of-the-art facilities have attracted first-rate performers and sold-out shows. Whether it's hula, the Iona Pear Dance Company, Willie Nelson, or Hawaiian music icon Keali'i Reichel, only the best will appear at the Maui Arts and Cultural Center. The center's activities are well publicized locally, so check the *Maui News* or ask your hotel concierge what's going on during your visit.

HAWAIIAN MUSIC Except for Casanova in Makawao, Hapa's in Kihei, and Tsunami in Wailea, nightlife options on this island are limited. The major hotels generally have lobby lounges offering regular Hawaiian music, soft jazz, or hula shows beginning at sunset. If the duo called **Hapa, Willie K and Amy Gilliom,** and the soloist **Keali'i Reichel** are playing anywhere on their native island, don't miss them; they're a Hawaiian music bonanza, among the finest Hawaiian musicians around today.

JAZZ & BLUES   To find out what's happening in jazz or blues, look in at **Hapa's Brew Haus** (☎ 808/879-9001) in Kihei (see below). It seems to be the nightlife nexus for this genre, with quality music and overflow crowds that linger into the wee hours. The thriving blues scene throughout Hawaii can be credited to the efforts of Louie Wolfenson, his partner Kurt Kangas, and the **Maui Blues Association** (☎ 808/879-6123), which books sold-out events at clubs throughout the state. Check the papers to see what's on while you're on Maui. Their annual Islands Blues Mele, a festival around Memorial Day, grows by the year and has assumed a life of its own.

WEST MAUI: LAHAINA

At **Longhi's** (☎ 808/667-2288), live music spills out into the streets from 9:30pm to midnight on Fridays and Saturdays. Usually it's salsa or jazz, but call ahead to confirm. Other special gigs can be expected if rock 'n' rollers or jazz musicians who are friends of the owner happen to be passing through. It wouldn't hurt to ask what's happening here.

You won't have to ask what's going on at **Cheeseburger in Paradise** (☎ 808/661-4855), the two-story green-and-white building at the corner of Front and Lahainaluna streets. Just go outside and you'll hear it: loud, live, and lively tropical rock blasting into the streets and out to sea daily from 4:30 to 11pm.

SOUTH MAUI

KIHEI   **Hapa's Brew Haus** (☎ 808/879-9001) is the only game in town. And with its fairly recent renovations, tiered seating, state-of-the-art sound and lighting, and 40-seat oval bar, it's quite popular. Happy hours here are generous, with free pizza and $2 drafts from 5 to 6pm daily. Every Tuesday is comedy night, followed by DJ spins. When visiting bands are featured, improvisation and jamming bring a pulsing spontaneity to the scene. Call the hotline, ☎ 808/875-1990, to find out whether jazz, blues, rock, reggae, funk, Jawaiian (a fusion of Jamaican and Hawaiian), or the duo Hapa's slack key will be filling the house.

WAILEA   The Grand Wailea Resort's **Tsunami** (☎ 808/875-1234), Maui's most high-tech club, happens to be South Maui's only nightspot for dancing. But what a club: 10,000 square feet, with marble, laser lights, huge video screens, futuristic decor, and well-dressed revelers. It's all disco, no live music, and is open Thursday, Friday, and Saturday from 9pm to 2am; the rest of the week it's closed for private functions. The DJ plays everything from 1980s hits to Top 40 on weekends. Thursday is ladies' night: no cover charge for women, drink specials, and a flower or other memento for the wily females who turn out to "dress and impress." On Fridays, "Flashback Fever" (music from the '70s and '80s) takes over. Cover charge is $5 on Thursday and Friday and $10 on Saturday; entrance is free the rest of the week. Open Thursday through Saturday from 9pm to 3am, Friday and Saturday from 9pm to 2am.

UPCOUNTRY MAUI

Upcountry in Makawao, the partying never ends at **Casanova** (☎ 808/572-0220), the popular Italian ristorante (see "Dining," earlier in this chapter) where the good

A Night to Remember: Luau, Maui Style

Most of the larger hotels in Maui's major resorts offer luaus and Polynesian entertainment on a regular basis. You'll pay about $60 or more to attend one. To protect yourself from disappointment, don't expect it to be a homegrown affair prepared in the traditional Hawaiian way. The labor-intensive nature of this traditional Hawaiian feast makes it an impossible endeavor for large-scale commercial operations offered on a regular basis. There are, however, commercial luaus that capture the romance and spirit of the affair with quality food and entertainment in outdoor settings.

Maui's best luau is indisputably the nightly **Old Lahaina Luau,** on the beach side of 505 Front St. in Lahaina (☎ **808/667-1998**). At this writing, there are plans to move the luau a few blocks north in Lahaina to a presently vacant 2-acre site just oceanside of the Lahaina Cannery. In the works are thatched buildings, an amphitheater seating, and a price increase of less than 10%, but the phone number will remain the same. This is the consummate luau, with a healthy balance of entertainment, showmanship, good food, educational value, and sheer romantic beauty. It begins at sunset and features Tahitian and Hawaiian entertainment, including ancient hula and an intelligent narrative on its rocky course of survival into modern times. The entertainment is riveting, even for jaded locals, and the food is entirely authentic: imu-roasted kalua pig, lomi salmon, poi, dried fish, poke, breadfruit, sweet potatoes, and for the more cautious, teriyaki steak, barbecued chicken, and mahi-mahi. The cost is $62 plus tax for adults, $30 for children. They're often booked a week in advance, so call ahead.

The **Maui Marriott Luau** (☎ **808/667-1200**) is beachside in Kaanapali and costs $60 for adults and $27 for children, free for those under 5. An open bar, Hawaiian menu, and after-dinner show add up to a pleasing experience, with fire dancers and traditional hula. The luau is offered from 5 to 8pm nightly.

If you'd like to be prepared for your luau, head over to **Wailea Shopping Village,** 3750 Wailea Alanui Dr., where free hula lessons are offered every Wednesday; there's also Polynesian entertainment every Tuesday.

times roll with the pasta. If a big-name mainland band is resting up on Maui following a sold-out concert on Oahu, you may find its members setting up for an impromptu night here. On Maui, word spreads quickly. DJs take over on Wednesday (ladies' night) and Thursday nights. Every other Thursday is a fundraiser for the Maui AIDS Society, and on Friday and Saturday, live entertainment draws fun-lovers from even the most remote reaches of the island. Entertainment starts at 9:45pm and continues to 1:30am. Expect good blues, rock 'n' roll, reggae, jazz, Hawaiian, and the top names in local and visiting entertainment. Elvin Bishop, the local duo Hapa, Los Lobos, and many others have filled Casanova's stage and limelight. The cover charge is usually $5.

8

Molokai, the Most Hawaiian Isle

Born of volcanic eruptions 1½ million years ago, Molokai remains a time capsule on the eve of the 21st century. It has no deluxe resorts, no fancy restaurants, no stoplights, and no buildings taller than a coconut tree. Less is definitely more on this languid island—and, fortunately for adventure travelers, Molokai is the least developed, most "Hawaiian" of all the islands.

The cradle of Hawaiian dance (the hula was born here), the ancient science of aquaculture, and sacred rites, Molokai lives up to its reputation as the most Hawaiian place chiefly through its lineage; there are, in fact, more people here of Hawaiian blood than anywhere else. An aura of ancient mysticism clings to the slipper-shaped island, and the old ways still govern life here. The residents survive by taking fish from the sea and hunting wild pigs and axis deer on the range. Some folks still catch reef fish in throw nets and troll the reef for squid, a traditional Hawaiian delicacy. Families are important, friendship ties are cherished, and the Hawaiian concept of taking care of the land remains a priority. The modern Hawaii of high-rise hotels, shopping centers, and other trappings of tourism hasn't been able to gain a foothold here—one lone low-rise resort, Kaluakoi, built more than 20 years ago, is Molokai's token attempt at contemporary tourism.

The only "new" development since Kaluakoi is the Molokai Ranch's ecotourism project of upscale "camping" in semipermanent tentalows (a combination of a bungalow and a tent) on the 53,000-acre ranch. The focus here is on outdoor recreation and adventure, with a comfortable place to sleep in the wilderness.

The slow-paced, simple life of the people and the absence of contemporary landmarks is what attracts those in search of the "real" Hawaii. But what makes them stand in awe is this little island's diverse natural wonders: Hawaii's highest waterfall and greatest collection of fishponds; the world's tallest sea cliffs; and sand dunes, coral reefs, rain forests, hidden coves—and empty, gloriously empty, beaches.

EXPLORING THE "MOST HAWAIIAN" ISLE   Only 38 miles from end to end and just 10 miles wide, Molokai stands like a big green wedge in the blue Pacific. It has an east side, a west side, a backside, and a topside. Formed by three volcanic eruptions, the long, narrow island is like yin and yang: one side is a flat, austere, arid desert; the other is a lush, green, steepled tropical Eden. But the volcanic gods

Molokai

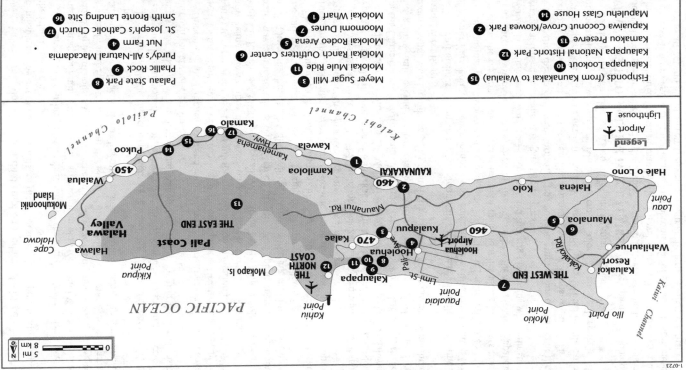

Moomomi Dunes **7**
Molokai Rodeo Arena **5**
Molokai Ranch Outfitters Center **6**
Molokai Mule Ride **11**
Meyer Sugar Mill **3**
Molokai Wharf **1**

Smith Bronte Landing Site **16**
St. Joseph's Catholic Church **17**
Nut Farm **4**
Purdy's All-Natural Macadamia
Phallic Rock **9**
Palaau State Park **8**

Mapulehu Glass House **14**
Kapuaiwa Coconut Grove/Kiowea Park **2**
Kamakou Preserve **13**
Kalaupapa National Historic Park **12**
Kalaupapa Lookout **10**
Fishponds (from Kaunakakai to Waialua) **15**

Legend
↕ Lighthouse
✈ Airport

1-0723

weren't done with Molokai until a third eruption produced the island's "thumb"—a peninsula jutting out of the steep cliffs of the north shore, like a punctuation mark on the island's geological story.

On the red-dirt southern plain, where most of the island's 6,000 residents live, the rustic village of Kaunakakai looks like the set of an old Hollywood Western, with sun-faded clapboard houses and horses tethered in tall grass on the side of the road. At mile-marker 0, in the center of town, the island is divided into East and West so dramatically that an arid cactus desert lies on one side, and a lush coco-palm jungle on the other.

Eastbound, along the coastal highway named for King Kamehameha V, are Gauguin-like, palm-shaded cottages set on small coves or near fishponds; spectacular vistas that take in Maui, Lanai, and Kahoolawe; and a fringing coral reef visible through the crystal-clear waves.

Out on the sun-scorched west end is the island's lone destination resort, Kaluakoi, overlooking a gold-sand beach too big to fit on a postcard with water usually too rough to swim. A few old-timers inhabit the old hilltop plantation town of Maunaloa, now being remade into an upscale version of itself. Cowboys ride the range on Molokai Ranch, a 53,000-acre spread. Adventure travelers and outdoor recreation buffs stay at the tentalows on the ranch property and spend their days mountain biking, kayaking, horseback riding, sailing, hiking, snorkeling, and just vegetating on the endless white-sand beaches (see "Hiking & Camping," below).

Elsewhere around the island, in hamlets like Kualapuu, old farmhouses with pickup trucks in the yards and sleepy dogs under the shade trees stand amid row crops of papaya, coffee, and corn—just like farm towns in Anywhere, USA.

But that's not all there is. The "backside" of Molokai is a rugged wilderness of spectacular beauty. On the outskirts of Kaunakakai, the land rises gradually from sea-level fishponds to cool uplands and the Molokai Forest, long ago stripped of sandalwood for the China trade. All that remains is an indentation in the earth that natives shaped like a ship's hull, a crude matrix that gave them a rough idea of when they'd cut enough sandalwood to fill a ship (it's identified on good maps as Luanamokuiliahi, or Sandalwood Boat).

The land inclines sharply to the lofty mountains and the nearly mile-high summit of Mount Kamakou, then ends abruptly with emerald-green cliffs, which plunge into a lurid aquamarine sea dotted with tiny deserted islets. These breathtaking 3,250-foot sea cliffs, the highest in the world, stretch 14 majestic miles along Molokai's north shore, laced by waterfalls and creased by five Eden-like valleys—Halawa, Papalaua, Wailau, Pelekunu, and Waikolu—once occupied by early Hawaiians who built stone terraces and used waterfalls to irrigate taro patches.

Long after the sea cliffs were formed, a tiny volcano erupted out of the sea at their feet and spread lava into a flat, leaf-like peninsula called Kalaupapa—the infamous 1860s leper exile where Father Damien de Veuster of Belgium devoted his life caring for the afflicted. A few people remain in the remote colony by choice, keeping it tidy for the daily company that arrives on mules and by small planes.

WHAT A VISIT TO MOLOKAI IS *REALLY* LIKE   There's plenty of aloha on Molokai, but the so-called "friendly island" remains ambivalent about vacationers. One of the least visited Hawaiian islands, Molokai welcomes visitors on its own take-it-or-leave-it terms and makes few concessions beyond that of gracious host; it never wants to attract too big of a crowd, anyway. A sign at the airport offers the first clue: SLOW DOWN, YOU ON MOLOKAI NOW—a caveat to heed on this island, where life proceeds at its own pace.

Rugged, red-dirt Molokai isn't for everyone, but those who like to explore remote places and seek their own adventures should love it. The best of the island can only be seen on foot, mule, or horse, or via kayak or sailboat. The sea cliffs are only accessible by sea in the summer, when the Pacific is calm, or via a 10-mile trek through the Wailau Valley—an adventure only a handful of hardy hikers attempt each year. The great Kamakou Preserve is open just once a month, by special arrangement with the Nature Conservancy. Even Moomomi, which holds bony relics of prehistoric flightless birds and other Lost World creatures, requires a guide to divulge the secrets of the dunes.

Those in search of nightlife have come to the wrong place; Molokai shuts down after sunset. The only public diversions are softball games under the lights of Mitchell Pauole Field, movies at Maunaloa, and the few restaurants that stay open after dark, serving everything from local brew to pizza.

The "friendly" island may captivate you—on the other hand, you may leave with your head shaking, never to return. It all depends on how you approach Molokai. Boots or loafers. Either way, take it slow.

1 Orientation

by Jeanette Foster

ARRIVING

BY PLANE Molokai has two airports, but you'll most likely fly into the one at Hoolehua Airport, on a dusty plain about 6 miles from Kaunakakai town, which everyone calls "the Molokai Airport." From Maui, Island Air (☎ 800/323-3345 from the mainland, 800/652-6541 from Maui) offers four direct flights a day. A new Maui-based carrier, Pacific Wings (☎ 888/575-4546 from the mainland, 808/873-0877 from Maui; www.pacificwings.com), has just recently begun offering flights from Kahului to both Molokai airports in eight-passenger, twin-engine Cessna 402-C aircraft.

Molokai Air Shuttle (☎ 808/545-4988) and **Hawaiian Airlines** (☎ 800/367-5320 or 808/553-3644) both have direct daily flights from Honolulu to Molokai.

VISITOR INFORMATION

Look for a sun-faded, yellow building on the main drag, Kamehameha V Highway (Hwy. 460), on the right just past the town's first stop sign, at mile marker 0; it's the **Molokai Visitors Association,** P.O. Box 960 Kaunakakai, HI 96748 (☎ **800/800-6367,** 808/553-3876 from the U.S. mainland and Canada, 800/553-0404 or 808/553-3876 interisland; www.molokai.com). They can give you all the information you need on what to see and do while you're on the friendly isle.

THE REGIONS IN BRIEF

KAUNAKAKAI Dusty cars are parked diagonally along Ala Malama Street. The family car is a pickup truck. It could be any small town, except it's Kaunakakai, Molokai, 96748, where Friendly Isle Realty and Friendly Isle Travel offer islanders dream homes and impossible vacations; Rabang's Filipino Food posts bad checks in the window; antlered deer-head trophies guard the grocery aisles at Misaki's Market; and Kanemitsu's, the town's legendary bakery, churns out fresh loaves of onion-cheese bread daily.

Once an ancient canoe landing, Kaunakakai was the royal summer place of King Kamehameha V. The port town bustled when pineapple and sugar were king, but those days, too, are gone. With Old West–style storefronts laid out in a 3-block grid on a flat, dusty plain, Kaunakakai is a town from the past. Molokai's main settlement may appear rustic, but the spirit of aloha—the generous giving of one's self—still reigns. At the end of Wharf Road is **Molokai Wharf,** a rather picturesque place to fish, photograph, and just hang out.

THE NORTH COAST Upland from Kaunakakai, the land tilts skyward and turns green with scented plumeria in yards and glossy coffee trees all in a row until it blooms into a true forest—then abruptly ends at a great precipice, falling 3,250 feet to the sea. The green cliffs are creased with five V-shaped cliffs so deep that light in the crevices is seldom seen (to paraphrase a Hawaii poet).

The North Coast is the wild coast, a remote, forbidding place with a solitary peninsula—**Kalaupapa**—once the home for exiled lepers (it's now a national historical park). Easy on the eyes, difficult to visit.

THE WEST END This end of the island, home to Molokai Ranch, is miles of stark, minimal desert terrain, bordered by the most beautiful white-sand beaches in Hawaii. The rugged rolling terrain slopes down to Molokai's only destination resort, Kaluakoi, a cul-de-sac of condos clustered around a 20-year-old seafront hotel near 3-mile-long Papohaku, the island's biggest beach. On the way to Kaluakoi—where everyone shows up at least once, if only to wait in line to eat dinner at Ohia Lodge—you'll find Maunaloa, a 1920s-era pineapple plantation town that's in the midst of being transformed into a master-planned community, Maunaloa Village.

THE EAST END The area east of Kaunakakai becomes lush, green, and tropical, with golden pocket beaches and a handful of cottages and condos that are popular with thrifty travelers. Beyond Kaunakakai, the two-lane road curves along the coast past piggeries, palm groves, and a 20-mile string of fishponds as well as an ancient heiau, Damien-built churches, and a few contemporary condos by the sea. It ends in the earthly paradise of **Halawa Valley,** one of Hawaii's most beautiful valleys.

2 Getting Around

by Jeanette Foster

Getting around Molokai isn't easy if you don't have a rental car, and rental cars are often hard to find on Molokai. On holiday weekends—and remember, Hawaii celebrates different holidays than the rest of the United States (see "When to Go" in chapter 3)—car-rental agencies simply run out of cars. Book before you go. There's no municipal transit or shuttle service, but a 24-hour taxi service is available.

CAR-RENTAL AGENCIES Rental cars are available from **Budget** (T 808/567-6877) and **Dollar** (T 808/567-6156); both agencies are located at the Molokai Airport.

TAXI & TOUR SERVICES Regular taxi service and island tours are offered by **Molokai Off-Road Tours & Taxi** (T 808/553-3369). **Kukui Tours & Limousines** (T 808/553-5133) has air-conditioned limos available for tours, airport shuttle, and 24-hour taxi service.

FAST FACTS: Molokai

Molokai, like Lanai, is part of Maui County. For **local emergencies,** call **T 911.** For non-emergencies, call **T** 808/553-5355 for police, **T** 808/553-5601 for fire, and **T** 808/553-5331 for **Molokai General Hospital,** in Kaunakakai. Downtown Kaunakakai also has a **post office** (**T** 808/553-5845) and several banks, including the **Bank of Hawaii** (☎ 808/553-3273), which has a 24-hour ATM.

Rawlins Chevron Service (mile marker 0, Kaunakakai; ☎ **808/553-3214**) is the "last stop to the airport from Kaunakakai"—where you'll rush to fill up your rental car with 87-octane at the self-serve pump. Or wish you had. It's open Monday through Thursday from 6:30am to 8:30pm, Friday and Saturday from 6:30am to 9pm, and on Sunday from 7am to 6pm.

3 Accommodations

by Jeanette Foster

Molokai is Hawaii's most affordable island; in fact, hotel prices here are lower than those on any other island. Plus, because the island's restaurants are few, most hotel rooms and condos come with kitchens, which can save you a bundle on dining costs.

There aren't a ton of accommodations options on Molokai—mostly B&Bs, condos, and a handful of funky hotels that are really more like motels. Camping on Molokai involves two options: the upscale tentalows offered by Molokai Ranch, along with a host of activities; or for hardy souls, camping with your own tent at the beach or in the cool upland forest (see "Hiking & Camping," below). We've listed our top picks below; you may want to contact **Destination Molokai Association** (☎ **800/800-6367**; fax 808/553-5288) for additional options.

Note: Taxes of 10.17% will be added to your hotel bill. Parking is free.

KAUNAKAKAI
Moderate

Molokai Shores Suites. Kamehameha V Hwy. (P.O. Box 1037), Kaunakakai, HI 96748. ☎ **800/535-0085** or 808/553-5954. Fax 808/553-5954. www.marcresorts.com. E-mail marc@marcresorts.com. 100 units. TV. $129 one-bedroom apt. (sleeps up to 4); $159 two-bedroom apt. (up to 6). Discounted rates for weekly and extended stays; plus corporate, military, and senior discounts. AE, DC, JCB, MC, V.

Bright, clean, basic units with kitchens and large lanais face a small gold-sand beach and the ocean beyond in this quiet complex of three-story Polynesian-style buildings, less than a mile from Kaunakakai. Alas, the beach is mostly for show (offshore, it's shallow mud flats underfoot), fishing, or launching kayaks, but the swimming pool comes with an ocean view. Well-tended gardens, spreading lawns, and palms frame a restful view of fishponds, offshore reefs, and neighbor islands. The central location can be a plus, minimizing driving time from the airport or town, and it's convenient to the mule ride, as well as the lush East End countryside.

Inexpensive

Kahale Mala Bed and Breakfast. 7 Kamakana Pl. (P.O. Box 1582), Kaunakakai, HI 96748. ☎/Fax **808/553-9001.** www.Molokai.com/kahalemala. E-mail cpgroup@aloha.net. 1 studio. TV. $60 double. Extra person $15; breakfast $10 for 2. No credit cards.

In a subdivision just outside of town (off Kamehameha V Hwy., before the 5-mile marker), you'll find the home of Jack Pugh and Cheryl Corbell. When they moved here from Western Canada, Jack and Cheryl loved the property but thought it was too big for two. So in 1995, they bought the house and started a one-room B&B. The large unit has a private entrance through the garden, with a Jacuzzi just outside. Inside, the decor consists of white rattan furnishings, including two twin beds, and a full kitchen—Cheryl will happily share her homegrown, organic produce. Although you'll pay less if you make your own breakfast, we recommend Cheryl's: taro pancakes, sourdough waffles, or a vegetable-egg pie, along with fresh fruit, homemade bread, muffins, and cinnamon buns.

Pau Hana Inn. 40 Oki Pl., off Kamehameha V Hwy. (P.O. Box 860), Kaunakakai, HI 96748. ☎ **888/PAU-HANA** or 808/553-5342. Fax 808/553-3928. 40 units. $45 Long House double; $55 double in main hotel; $55–$69 cottage double (sleeps up to 4); $90 oceanfront double (up to 4). Extra person $10. AE, MC, V.

If you want to experience true Molokai living, we recommend this funky seaside hotel. It's not the plushest place on the island—just a quaint collection of cottages, studios, and hotel rooms that's been around for years—but it may be the friendliest. The Inn was somewhat languorous when it was up for sale. At the end of 1997, the property was sold at a public auction, so the new owners may breathe life into this historic hotel. The grounds here remain tropically lush, and the pool is always crystal clear. There's a restaurant (yes, they still serve mahi burgers—see "Dining," below), and the open-air bar attracts quite a crowd, especially on Friday nights, when you might encounter live music, dancing, and plenty of storytelling.

WEST END
Moderate

Also consider **Kaluakoi Villas,** Kaluakoi Resort, 1131 Kaluakoi Rd., Maunaloa, HI 96770 ☎ **800/367-5004** or 808/552-2721; fax 800/477-2329 or 808/552-2201); the aging, Polynesian-style units are comfortable but could definitely use some work ($125 to $150 studio; $150 to $180 one-bedroom apt.; $200 cottage). Another option is the **Kaluakoi Hotel & Golf Club,** Kaluakoi Resort, Kepuhi Beach (P.O. Box 1977), HI 96770 ☎ **888/552-2550** or 808/552-2555; fax 808/552-2821), the only resort hotel on the island, with a faultless location—but we still consider it way overpriced and in need of dire renovations; if you choose to stay here, book a condo with a kitchen ($105 to $130 double; $205 to $275 suite; $155 to $170 studio; $185 to $195 one-bedroom condo; $220 one-bedroom cottage).

And don't forget about the upscale camping at the ✪ **Great Molokai Ranch Trail;** see "Hiking & Camping" below.

Ke Nani Kai Resort. Kaluakoi Resort, Kaluakoi Rd., off Hwy. 460 (P.O. Box 289), Maunaloa, HI 96770. ☎ **800/888-2791** or 808/552-2761. Fax 808/552-0045. www.marcresorts.com. E-mail marc@marcresorts.com. 100 apts. TV TEL. $139–$159 one-bedroom apt. (sleeps up to 4); $169–$199 two-bedroom apt. (up to 4). 2-night minimum; 4-night minimum Dec 15–Jan 4. AE, CB, DISC, DC, JCB, MC, V.

A home away from home, especially for families who'll like the space and quiet. These large apartments are set up for full-time living with real kitchens, washer/dryers, VCRs, attractive furnishings, and breezy lanais. There's a huge pool, a volleyball court, tennis courts, and golf on the neighboring Kaluakoi course. These condos are the farthest from the sea of those at Kaluakoi Resort, but it's just a brief walk down to the hotel facilities and the beach beyond. The two-story buildings are surrounded by parking and garden areas.

✪ **Paniolo Hale.** Next door to Kaluakoi Resort, Lio Place (P.O. Box 190), Maunaloa, HI 96770. ☎ **800/367-2984** or 808/552-2731. Fax 808/552-2288. www.lava.net/paniolo. E-mail paniolo@lava.net. 77 units. TV. $95–$155 double studio; $115–$180 one-bedroom apt. (sleeps up to 4); $145–$215 two-bedroom apt. (up to 6). Extra person $10. 2-night minimum; 1-week minimum Dec. 20–Jan. 5. AE, MC, V.

This is far and away Molokai's most charming lodging, and probably its best value—be sure to ask about discounted weekly rates and special condo/car packages when booking your reservations here. Paniolo Hale's two-story Old Hawaii ranch-house design is airy and homey, with oak floors and walls of folding glass doors that open to huge screened verandas, doubling your living space. The one- and two-bedrooms come with two baths, so they accommodate three or four easily. Some have hot tubs on the lanai. Units are spacious and well equipped, with full kitchens and washer/dryers. They're comfortably furnished by the owners, who run their own rental operation.

The whole place overlooks the Kaluakoi Golf Course, a green barrier that separates these condos from the rest of Kaluakoi Resort. Hotel shops, a restaurant, and a lounge are just across the fairway, as is Kepuhi Beach (these are the closest units to the beach); it's a scenic place to walk and beachcomb, but the seas are too hazardous for most swimmers. A pool, paddle tennis, and barbecue facilities are on the property, which adjoins open grassland countryside.

EAST END
Moderate

Wavecrest Resort. Kamehameha V Hwy. (P.O. Box 1037), Kaunakakai, HI 96748. ☎ **800/535-0085** or 808/558-8103. Fax 808/558-8206 or 800/633-5085. E-mail marc@marcresorts.com. 126 units. TV. $109–$139 one-bedroom apt. (sleeps up to 4); $169 two-bedroom apt. (up to 6). AE, MC, V.

When you want to get away and pull up the drawbridge, this is a good place to go. The condos—some of them newly remodeled, some in need of remodeling—are in three-story tropical structures surrounded by lawns, palms, mountainous inland slopes, and the solitude of the island's lush East End. The units, individually decorated by the owners, come with full kitchens, large lanais, and garden or ocean views. If the complex is full, it can be noisy. Wavecrest is more remote than Molokai Shores—it's about a dozen miles of leisurely driving to Kaunakakai (translation: 30-plus minutes), seven more to the airport, and a substantial drive to West End properties. Fortunately, there's a small store on the property for snacks, drinks, and video rentals, as well as two lighted tennis courts and a pool. The haunting views of the three neighboring islands provide a truly unique sense of place, but the shoreline here isn't Molokai's best for swimming.

Inexpensive

Country Cottage at Puu O Hoku Ranch. Kamehameha V Hwy., at mile marker 25 (HC-01, Box 900), Kaunakakai, HI 96748 ☎ **808/558-8109**. Fax 808/558-8100. 1 two-bedroom cottage (sleeps up to 6). $85 double. Extra person $10. 2-night minimum. No credit cards.

Escape to a working cattle ranch! Ranch manager Jack Spruance welcomes visitors to *Puu o Hoku* ("Star Hill") Ranch, which spreads across the East End of Molokai. The ranch, on 14,000 acres of pasture and forests, is the last place to stay before Halawa Valley—it's at least an hour's drive from Kaunakai along the shoreline. Two acres of tropically landscaped property circle the ranch's rustic cottage, which has breathtaking views of rolling hills and the Pacific ocean. The wooden cottage features comfortable country furniture, a fully equipped kitchen, two bedrooms (one with double bed, one with two twins), two baths, a big living area, and a separate dining room on the enclosed lanai. TVs and VCRs are available on request. We recommend stargazing at night, watching the sunrise in the morning, and playing in the afternoon: croquet, hiking, swimming, or just roaming the grounds.

Honomuni House. Kamehameha V Hwy., just after mile marker 17 (HC01, Box 700), Kaunakakai, HI 96748. ☎ **808/558-8383**. 1 one-bedroom cottage. TV. $80 double. Extra person $10 ($5 child). No credit cards.

ⓘ From Tentalows to Condos: Great Places to Stay with the Kids

Great Molokai Ranch Trail (see p. 498)   The upscale, luxurious "camping" at the Panaolo Camp (on Molokai Ranch property), just outside of Maunaloa, features comfortable bungalow-tents (called *tentalows*) and lots of outdoor activities, including special activities for kids. Prices ($185 each for adults, $75 each for kids) include three all-you-can-eat meals and snacks every day, two activities, transportation (including airport pickup), and daily maid service.

Ke Nani Kai Resort (see p. 484)   Located in Kaluakoi Resort, these one- and two-bedroom condo units offer families lots of space, with complete kitchens, washer/dryers, VCRs, attractive furnishings, and breezy lanais. For active families, there's a huge pool, a volleyball court, tennis courts, and golf at neighboring Kaluakoi.

Molokai Shores (see p. 483)   At this great central location, just outside of Kaunakakai, families can choose from large one- and two-bedroom units in a tropical garden complex with great views of the fishponds, offshore reefs, and neighbor islands. Amenities include a swimming pool and laundry facilities; shopping is nearby.

Puunana/Pauwalu Beachfront Cottages (see p. 487)   Here, you'll find private two-bedroom cottages located on the beach in the lush East End—the perfect spot for a family getaway vacation. Each cottage sits on its own secluded beach and features complete kitchens, washer/dryers, VCRs, large decks, and breathtaking views (great for watching whales in the winter).

Old stonework taro terraces and house foundations testify that Honomuni Valley was popular with early Hawaiians, whose groves of breadfruit, coconut, fruit, ginger, and coffee still flourish in the wilderness. Modern folks can sample this mini-Eden at a remote cottage—17½ miles from Kaunakakai, a mile or more from the nearest public beach area—set in the forest along the foot of the East End upslope. Freshwater prawns and native fish hide out in the stream that carved the valley. Experienced hikers will enjoy exploring upstream, where they'll find pools for swimming and watching (or catching) prawns and, farther up, a waterfall of their very own. The small cottage has a complete kitchen, a separate bedroom, a full bath, and an outside shower for rinsing off the sand from the beach. You're welcome to enjoy the tropical fruits growing right on the premises, which are dominated by a huge monkeypod tree. The cottage does sit right on the road, but there's generally little traffic after dark.

⭐ **Kamalo Plantation Bed & Breakfast.** Kamehameha V Hwy., just past mile marker 10 (HC01, Box 300), Kaunakakai, HI 96748. ☎/Fax **808/558-8236.** 2 units. TV. $75 cottage double (with shower only; sleeps up to 4); $65 double. Rates include continental breakfast. Extra person $10. 2-night minimum in cottage. No credit cards.

Glenn and Akiko Foster's 5-acre spread includes an ancient heiau ruin in the front yard, plus leafy tropical gardens and a working fruit orchard. The genial Fosters have lived and sailed in the islands for many years and are full of island lore. The Eden-like property, which they bought in 1992, is easy to find: it's right across the East End road from Father Damien's historic St. Joseph church. The plantation-style cottage is tucked under flower trees and surrounded by swaying palms and tropical foliage; it has its own lanai, a big living room with a queen-size pull-out couch, and a separate bedroom with a king bed, so it can sleep four comfortably. The kitchen is fully equipped (including spices), and there's a barbecue outside. The room in the home has a separate entrance, private lanai, bathroom, coffeemaker, microwave, and fridge. Guests are provided with beach mats and towels. A breakfast of fruit and freshly baked bread is served every morning.

⭐ **Puunana/Pauwalu Beachfront Cottages.** Kamehameha V Hwy., past mile marker 18. Reservations c/o Sunscapes, 3538 207th SE, Issaquah, WA 98029. ☎ **800/637-0861** or 206/391-8932. Fax 206/391-9121. 2 two-bedroom cottages (each sleeps up to 4). TV. $100 cottage; $600 per week. 3-night minimum. No credit cards.

As clichéd as it sounds, these two five-star cottages by the sea really are the stuff that dreams are made of. Some 18 miles from Kaunakakai, this is one of the most peaceful, comfortable, and elegant properties on Molokai's East End, and the setting is simply stunning. Built in 1996, each of these green-and-white plantation-style cottages sits on its own secluded beach—you'll feel like you're on your own private island. The Puunana Cottage has a king bed and two twins, while Pauwalu has a queen, a double, and a sofabed. Both have full kitchens, VCRs, washer/dryers, ceiling fans, comfortable tropical furniture, large furnished decks, and views of Maui, Lanai, and Kahoolawe across the channel; in the winter, the deck is a perfect place for whale watching. Your hosts, whose family has held this property for generations, live nearby.

4 Dining

by Jocelyn Fujii

A few new eateries have opened up recently on this traditionally slow-moving island. Most of them are fast-food or takeout places, but a few of them have a home-cooked touch.

Even with these new developments, one of the best things about Molokai is its glacial pace of change. Lovers of the fast lane might consider this aspect of the island's personality a con rather than a pro, but they wouldn't choose to come here, anyway. Molokai is for those who want to get away from it all, who consider the lack of highrises and traffic lights a welcome change from the urban chaos that keeps nibbling at the edges of the more popular and populated islands. Sybarites, foodies, and pampered oenophiles had best lower their expectations upon arrival, or turn around and leave the island's natural beauty to nature lovers.

Personally, we like the unpretentiousness of the island; it's an oasis in a state where plastic aloha abounds. Most Molokai residents fish, collect seaweed, grow potatoes and tomatoes, and prepare for backyard luaus; if you happen to be walking past on the beach (as we were on a first trip to the island many years ago), they may invite you in with a broad, generous wave of the arm, hollering, "Come eat, come eat! Got plenty food."

Unlike Lanai (see chapter 9), which is small and rural but offers some of the finest dining in the islands, Molokai provides no such mix of innocence and sophistication. You must meet this island on its own terms: it doesn't pretend to be anything more than a combination of old ways and an informal lifestyle, a lifestyle closer to the land than to a chef's toque.

You'll even find a certain defiant stance against the trappings of modernity. Although some of the best produce in Hawaii is grown on this island, you're not likely to find much of it served in its restaurants, other than in the takeout items at Outpost Natural Foods, or at the Molokai Pizza Cafe, which is one of the most pleasing eateries on the island. (The yet-to-open Village Grill promises to use Molokai vegetables.)

The rest of the time, content yourself with ethnic or diner fare, or fresh fish from the Molokai Ice House—or by cooking for yourself. The many visitors who stay in condos find that it doesn't take long to sniff out the best sources of produce, groceries, and fresh fish to fire up at home when the island's other dining options are exhausted. The "Edibles" sections in "Shopping," later in this chapter, will point you to the shops and markets where you can pick up foodstuffs for your own island-style feast.

All of Molokai's restaurants are inexpensive or moderately priced, and many of them don't accept credit cards. The **Village Grill** (Kamehameha Hwy., Maunaloa, ☎ **808/552-0012**), set to open two weeks from the time of this writing, will be more expensive than diner fare, as is the Ohia Lodge. But you certainly won't have to dress up on Molokai. In most cases, we've listed just the town rather than the street address, because as you'll see, street addresses are as meaningless on this island as fancy cars and sequins.

Reservations are not accepted unless otherwise noted.

KAUNAKAKAI

Codi's Lunch Wagon. 90 Makena Place, Kaunakakai. ☎ **808/553-3443.** $4.25–$5. No credit cards. Mon–Fri 10:30am–1:30pm. LOCAL.

Only days after its opening in March 1998, residents were touting the spare ribs, oxtail soup, and pork adobo served up at this tiny lunch wagon. "A welcome addition to Kaunakakai" is how Codi's is commonly described. The four different plate lunches a day are served with rice, macaroni salad, and kim chee—a good value. The rotating menu includes chicken broccoli, chicken papaya, roast pork, meat loaf, shrimp curry, and other ethnic fare, served with a smile.

Kamoi Snack-N-Go. Kamoi Professional Center. ☎ **808/553-3742.** Ice cream $1.66–$3.38. No credit cards. Mon–Sat 9am–9pm, Sun noon–9pm. ICE CREAM/SNACKS.

Sweets and icy treats are the Kamoi specialty. Ice cream made by Dave's on Oahu comes in flavors like green tea, litchi sherbet, and many other tropical and traditional flavors. Schoolchildren and their parents line up for the ice cream cones, shakes, floats, sundaes, and the popular Icee floats (in four flavors instead of the usual two) served at this tiny snack shop. No tables, but there are aisles of candies.

Kanemitsu's Bakery & Restaurant. 79 Ala Malama St., Kaunakakai. ☎ **808/553-5855.** Most items less than $5.50. No credit cards. Restaurant, Wed–Sat 5:30am–1pm, Sun 5:30–11am; bakery, Wed–Mon 5:30am–6:30pm. BAKERY/DELI.

Morning, noon, and night, this local legend fills the Kaunakakai air with the sweet smells of baking. Taro lavosh is the hot new seller, joining Molokai bread—developed in 1935 in a cast-iron, kiawe-fired oven—as a Kanemitsu signature. Flavors range from apricot-pineapple to mango (in season), but the classics remain the regular white and wheat, cheese, and onion-cheese breads. For those who like their bread warm, the bread mixes (regular, sweet, and macadamia-nut) offer a way to take Molokai home.

In the adjoining coffee shop/deli, all sandwiches come on their own freshly baked buns and breads. The hamburgers, egg-salad sandwiches, mahi burgers, and honey-dipped fried chicken are all popular.

Not many people know about Kanemitsu's other life as a late-night institution for die-hard bread lovers. Those in the know line up at the bakery's back door beginning at 10:30pm, when the bread is whisked hot out of the oven and into waiting hands. You can order your fresh bread with butter, jelly, cinnamon, cream cheese, "whatever," say the bakers, and they'll cut the hot loaves down the middle and slather on the works so it melts in the bread.

Molokai Drive-Inn. Kaunakakai. ☎ **808/553-5655.** Most items less than $6. No credit cards. Mon–Fri 5:30am–10pm, Sat–Sun 6am–10:30pm. AMERICAN/TAKE-OUT.

The $6 plate-lunch prices are a bit steep at this greasy spoon, but it's one of the rare drive-up places with fresh *akule* (mackerel) and ahi (when available); and fried saimin for $2.75. The honey-dipped fried chicken is a favorite among residents, who also come here for the floats, shakes, potstickers, and other artery-clogging choices. But don't expect much in terms of ambiance: This is a fast-food takeout counter with the smells of frying in the surrounding air—and no pretensions otherwise.

Molokai Mango. 93-D Ala Malama St. ☎ **808/553-3981.** MC, V. Mon–Sat 9am–8:30pm, Sun noon–8:30pm. DELI/AMERICAN.

The former owner of JoJo's restaurant in Maunaloa opened this video store and popular sandwich shop in downtown Kaunakakai, where he sells sandwiches and nachos from the takeout counter. Turkey, ham, and roast beef (Angus beef) are served on five different breads, and all are popular. The $2.88 nachos are a big hit, too, for those evenings at home with an old rented movie. Molokai Mango also rents and sells videos, games, and equipment, including TV sets.

⊙ **Molokai Pizza Cafe.** At Kahua Center, on the old Wharf Rd. ☎ **808/553-3288.** Large pizzas $12.70–$22.15. No credit cards. PIZZA.

This place was the talk of the town when it opened—"Molokai has pizza now," locals announced proudly—and its excellent pizzas and sandwiches have made it a Kaunakakai staple as well as our favorite eatery on the island. There are seven different pizzas, each named after a Hawaiian island. (Niihau has yet to arrive in the Kaunakakai pizza pantheon.) The best-selling pizzas: the Molokai (pepperoni and cheese), the Big Island (pepperoni, ham, mushroom, Italian sausage, bacon, and vegetables), and the Molokini (simple, individual cheese slices). Coin-operated cars and a toy airplane follow the children's theme, but adults should feel equally at home with the very popular barbecued baby-back rib plate or the oven-roasted chicken dinner. Children's art and letters in the tiled dining room add an entertaining and charming touch. "Dear Uncle Sean," reads one of them. "Thank you from the bottom of our tummies."

⊙ **Outpost Natural Foods.** 70 Makaena, Kaunakakai. ☎ **808/553-3377.** Most items less than $5. No credit cards. Sun–Fri 10am–3pm. VEGETARIAN.

The healthiest and freshest food on the island is served at the lunch counter of this health-food store, around the corner from the main drag on the makai side of Kaunakakai town. The tiny store abounds in dewy-fresh Molokai papayas, bananas, herbs, potatoes, watermelon, and other produce, complementing its selection of vitamins, cosmetics, and health aids. But the real star is the closet-size lunch counter. The salads, burritos, tempeh sandwiches, tofu-spinach lasagna specials, and mock chicken, turkey, lamb, and meat loaf (made from oats, sprouts, seeds, and seasonings) will likely dispel the notion most folks have about vegetarian food being boring. Not so! Outpost serves hearty, creative lunches using no animal or unwholesome products. The Eastern taco salad, for example, contains brown rice topped with lentil stew and a cashew-pimento cheese poured over the works. Greens, sprouts, and a soy sour cream crown this marvel—invented, like all items on the menu, by the loving hands that prepare it.

Rabang's. Kaunakakai. ☎ **808/553-5841.** Most items less than $4.50; combination plate $6. No credit cards. Daily 7am–9pm. FILIPINO.

Specialties here include sweet-and-sour turkey tail prepared Ilocano style (as opposed to Tagalog) and a Filipino dish called *pinat bet*—a mixture of eggplant, string beans, pumpkin, lima beans, and other vegetables, with a smidgen of pork and some assertive seasonings. The diner is a bit more in the thick of things and more inviting than Oviedo's down the street, but it's still extremely casual, with only a few tables that are always full at lunchtime. The Friday Hawaiian plate ($6.50), barbecued chicken plate, and sweet-and-sour pork are among the Molokai favorites.

Sundown Deli. 145 Puali St. ☎ **808/553-3713.** Sandwiches and salads $3-$5.95. No credit cards. Mon–Fri 10:30am–6pm, Sat 10:30am–2pm. DELI.

Across the street from Veteran's Memorial Park, Sundown is another Molokai new-comer serving sandwiches and food-to-go with a home-cooked flavor. Eight types of sandwiches (like smoked turkey and chicken salad) are served daily, with a soup that changes by the day (it might be clam chowder, Portuguese bean, or cream of broccoli); saimin is $3.50. There are a couple of tables for those who want to eat in.

THE WEST END

Ohia Lodge. Kaluakoi Hotel and Golf Club, Maunaloa. ☎ **808/552-2555.** Reservations recommended at dinner. Main courses $12-$22. AE, DC, DISC, MC, V. CONTINENTAL/HAWAII REGIONAL.

The view of Kepuhi Beach has always been the best thing about this room, well positioned for spectacular sunsets and close enough to hear the waves. On a clear day, diners can even see the Makapuu Lighthouse on Oahu, and whales are in full view during the height of the winter whale season. This is the only full-service restaurant serving the West End.

The food: Well, they try. The Friday-night prime-rib buffet is a popular choice on this paniolo island. Some of the options on the current menu: Molokai baby-back ribs (we've heard good reports on this one); seafood linguine in a creamy basil Alfredo; and fresh fish served broiled (with papaya-pineapple salsa), sautéed (with lemon, butter, capers, and macadamia nuts), and wok-seared (with Asian black-bean buerre blanc). The fresh catch is served with aromatic basmati rice, a plus. Visitors staying on the West End have been starved for an alternative, because until the Village Grill opens, it's a long drive to the next restaurant.

EN ROUTE TO THE NORTH COAST

Kualapuu Cook House. Kualapuu. ☎ **808/567-6185.** Main courses $7.50-$17.95. No credit cards. Mon–Sat 7am–9pm. AMERICAN.

The rusting wagon frame in front of the old plantation house marks this popular diner and breakfast spot where local farmers and cowboys gather to chitchat over coffee and the renowned omelets (humongous), steak and eggs (more humongous!), or other American dishes with a local twist. At lunch and dinner, burgers, chili, fresh fish, and surf-and-turf items are the norm. Thursday is prime-rib night, when you can order a sizable dinner for $14.25. You can dine indoors or out. Unsolicited advice: Save room for the chocolate–macadamia-nut pie.

Fancified Maunaloa has undergone major changes. We miss JoJo's and its wonderful curries. Molokai Ranch has renovated the entire building and aims for a planta-tion/western ambiance in the new, larger, and more expensive **Village Grill,** scheduled to open in mid-April 1998. Plans call for a steakhouse featuring Molokai Ranch–brand beef and island produce (taro, sweet potatoes, green beans, bananas); entrée prices are expected to range from $6 to $22.50, and it is scheduled to be open daily from 7am to 1:30pm and 6 to 9pm. Call the **Molokai Ranch Center** at ☎ **808/552-2791** for the latest.

THE EAST END

Neighborhood Store 'N Counter. Pukoo. ☎ **808/558-8498.** Most items less than $6. No credit cards. Thurs–Tues 8am–6pm. AMERICAN.

The store/lunch counter appears like a mirage near mile marker 16 in the Pukoo area en route to the East End. The food stop serves omelets, Portuguese sausage, and other breakfast specials, then segues into sandwiches, salads, chicken katsu, mahi-mahi plates, and varied over-the-counter lunch offerings. There are daily specials, ethnic dishes, and some vegetarian dishes, such as the new vegetable pita at $4.95. The Neighborhood Store is nothing fancy, but it's most welcome on the long drive to East Molokai. (Also see "Shopping," later in this chapter.)

5 Beaches

by Jeanette Foster

With imposing sea cliffs on one side and lazy fishponds on the other, Molokai has little room for beaches along its 106-mile coast. Still, a big gold-sand beach flourishes on the West End, and you'll find tiny pocket beaches on the East End. The emptiness of Molokai's beaches is both a blessing and a curse: The welcome seclusion means no lifeguards, and nobody to rely on except yourself.

KAUNAKAKAI'S BEACH
ONE ALII BEACH PARK

This thin strip of sand, once reserved for the *alii* (chiefs), is the oldest public beach park on Molokai. You'll find One Alii Beach Park (pronounced *onay*, not *won*) by a coconut grove on the outskirts of Kaunakakai. Safe for swimmers of all ages and abilities, it's often crowded with splashy families on weekends, but it can be all yours on weekdays. Facilities include outdoor showers, rest rooms, and free parking.

WEST END BEACHES
✪ PAPOHAKU BEACH

Nearly 3 miles long and 100 yards wide, gold-sand Papohaku Beach is one of the biggest in Hawaii (17-mile-long Polihale Beach on Kauai is the biggest). The big surf and rip tides make swimming risky except in the summer, when its calm waters make it hospitable. It's great for walking, beachcombing, picnics, and sunset-watching year-round. Go early in the day when the tropic sun is less fierce and the wind calm. The beach is so big that you may never see another soul except at sunset, when a few people gather on the shore to watch the sun sink into the Pacific in hopes of spotting the elusive green flash, a daily natural wonder when the horizon is cloud-free. Facilities include outdoor showers, rest rooms, picnic grounds, and free parking.

KEPUHI BEACH

Duffers see this picturesque golden strand in front of the Kaluakoi Resort and Golf Course as just another sand trap, but sunbathers like the semiprivate grassy dunes; they're seldom, if ever, crowded. Beachcombers often find what they're looking for here, but swimmers won't: They'll have to dodge lava rocks and risk rip tides to survive. Oh, *yes*—look out for errant golf balls. There are no facilities or lifeguards, but cold drinks and rest rooms are handy at the resort.

EAST END BEACHES
SANDY BEACH

Molokai's most popular swimming beach—ideal for families with small kids—is a roadside pocket of gold sand protected by a reef with a great view of Maui and Lanai.

You'll find it off the King Kamehameha V Highway (Hwy. 450) at mile marker 20. There are no facilities—just you, the sun, the sand, and the surf.

MURPHY BEACH PARK (KUMIMI BEACH PARK)

In 1970, the Molokai jaycees wanted to create a sandy beach park with a good swimming area for the children of the East End. They chose a section known as Kumimi Beach, which was owned by the Puu o Hoku Ranch. The beach was a dump, literally. The ranch owner, George Murphy, immediately gave his permission to use the site as a park; the jaycees cleaned it up and built three small pavilions, plus picnic tables and barbecue grills. Officially, the park is called the George Murphy Beach Park (shortened to Murphy Beach Park over the years), but some old-timers still call it Kumimi Beach, and just to make things real confusing, some people call it Jaycees Park.

No matter what you call it, this small park is shaded by ironwood trees that line a white-sand beach. Generally, it's a very safe swimming area. On calm days, snorkeling and diving are great outside the reef. Fishermen are also frequently spotted here looking for papio and other island fish.

HALAWA BEACH PARK

At the foot of scenic Halawa Valley is this beautiful black-sand beach with a palm-fringed lagoon, a wave-lashed island offshore, and a distant view of the West Maui Mountains across the Pailolo Channel. The swimming is safe in the shallows close to shore, but where the waterfall stream meets the sea, the ocean is often murky and unnerving. A winter swell creases the mouth of Halawa Valley on the north side of the bay and attracts a crowd of local surfers. Facilities are minimal; bring your own water. To get there, take King Kamehameha V Highway (Hwy. 450) east to the end.

6 Hitting the Water

by Jeanette Foster

BODY BOARDING (BOOGIE BOARDING) & BODYSURFING

Molokai only has three beaches that offer rideable waves for body boarding and body-surfing: Papohaku, Kepuhi, and Halawa. Even these beaches are only for experienced bodysurfers, due to the strength of the rip currents and undertows. Bring your own boogie boards, as no one rents them on Molokai. However, **Molokai Ranch & Fun Hogs** (☎ 808/552-2791) offers surfing or body-boarding excursions on Monday, Wednesday, Friday, and Sunday afternoons for $60 for 3 hours, including lesson, equipment, and transportation.

OCEAN KAYAKING

During the summer months, when the waters on the north shore are calm, Molokai offers some of the most spectacular kayaking in Hawaii. You can paddle from remote valley to remote valley, spending a week or more exploring the exotic terrain. However, Molokai is for the experienced kayaker only, especially those adept in open ocean swells and through rough waves. Kayak tours are available through **Molokai Ranch & Fun Hogs** (☎ 808/552-2791); during the winter, this is a great way to whale-watch.

Molokai Fish & Dive (☎ 808/553-5926) in Kaunakakai is a mind-boggling store filled with outdoor gear. You can rent snorkeling gear, fishing gear, and even ice chests here. This is also the hotspot for fishing news and tips on what's running where.

For details on the activities listed below, see "The Active Vacation Planner" in chapter 3.

Molokai Beaches & Outdoor Activities

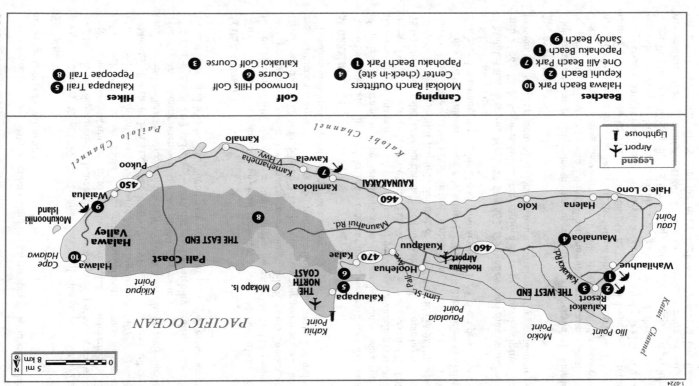

Hikes
- **5** Kalaupapa Trail
- **8** Pepeopae Trail

Golf
- **3** Kaluakoi Golf Course
- **6** Ironwood Hills Golf Course

Camping
- **4** Molokai Ranch Outfitters Center (check-in site) Papohaku Beach Park

Beaches
- **9** Sandy Beach
- **1** Papohaku Beach
- **7** One Alii Beach Park
- **2** Kepuhi Beach
- **10** Halawa Beach Park

Legend
- ✈ Airport
- ⊥ Lighthouse

PACIFIC OCEAN

Pailolo Channel

Kalohi Channel

Kauai Channel

Kamalo
Kaunakakai
Pukoo
Waialua
Mokuhooniki Island
Halawa Valley
Cape Halawa
Kikipua Point
Mokapo Is.
Kahiu Point
Kaweia
Kamiloloa
Kaunakakai
Kalae
Kalaupapa
THE NORTH COAST
Pali Coast
THE EAST END
Kamehameha V Hwy.
Maunahui Rd.
Kualapuu
Hoolehua Airport
Hoolehua
Pali St.
Limi St.
Paualaia Point
Mokio Point
Kaluakoi Resort
THE WEST END
Wahilauhue
Manaloa
Kolo
Halena
Hale o Lono
Ilio Point
Laau Point
Kaluakoi Rd.

450
460
460
470

0 5 mi
0 8 km
N

493

1-0724

The escorted tours cost $60 per person (minimum age 10 years old) and are available on Saturday only from 1 to 4pm.

SAILING

Molokai Charters (☎ 808/553-5852) offers a variety of sailing trips on *Satan's Doll*, a 42-foot sloop: 2-hour sunset sails for $40 per person, a half-day of sailing and whale-watching for $50, and a full-day sail to Lanai with swimming and snorkeling for $90 (which includes lunch, cold drinks, snacks, and all equipment). Owners Richard and Doris Reed have been sailing visitors around Molokai's waters since 1975.

Molokai Ranch & Fun Hogs (☎ 808/552-2791) offers catamaran sailing by expert sailor/diver/kayaker Mike Holmes in his 28-foot boat, *Nanea*, every Tuesday, Thursday, and Saturday afternoon, at a cost of $60 per person. Both the *Satan's Doll* and the *Nanea* offer **whale-watching cruises** from mid-December to mid-March when humpback whales frequent the waters around Molokai.

SCUBA DIVING

Want to see turtles or manta rays up close? How about sharks? Molokai resident Bill Kapuni has been diving the waters around Molokai his entire life; he'll be happy to show you whatever you're brave enough to encounter. **Bill Kapuni's Snorkel and Dive**, Kaunakakai (☎ 808/553-9867), can provide everything you need: gear, boat, even instruction. Two tank dives are $85 in his 22-foot Boston whaler and include Bill's voluminous knowledge of the legends and lore of Hawaii.

SNORKELING

When the waters are calm, Molokai offers excellent snorkeling; you'll see a wide range of butterfly fish, tangs, and angelfish. Good snorkeling can be found—when conditions are right—at many of Molokai's beaches (see box above). Snorkeling gear can be rented for $8.95 a day from **Molokai Fish & Dive** in Kaunakakai (☎ 808/553-5926); they'll also point out that day's best snorkeling spots. Snorkeling tours are available for $45 from **Bill Kapuni's Snorkel & Dive** (☎ 808/553-9867), which also rents snorkeling gear for $25 a day (see "Scuba Diving," above).

Walter Naki of **Molokai Action Adventures** (☎ 808/558-8184) offers snorkeling, diving, and swimming trips in his 21-foot Boston whaler for $75 per person for a 4- to 6-hour custom tour.

Molokai Ranch & Fun Hogs (☎ 808/552-2791) offers snorkeling excursions in their 25-foot hard-bottom inflatable boat (certified for 18 passengers) daily from 9am to noon, for $60 per person, which includes lunch and all snorkeling equipment.

SPORTFISHING

Molokai's waters can provide prime sporting opportunities, whether you're looking for big-game sportfishing or bottom fishing. When customers are scarce, Captain Joe Reich, who has been fishing the waters around Molokai for two decades, goes commercial fishing, so he always knows where the fish are biting. He runs *Alyce C Sportfishing* out of Kaunakakai Harbor (☎ 808/558-8377). A full day of fishing for up to six people is $400, three-quarters of a day is $350, and a half-day is $300. You can persuade him to do a whale-watching cruise during the winter months.

For fly-fishing or light-tackle reef-fish trolling, contact Walter Naki at **Molokai Action Adventures** (☎ 808/558-8184). Walter's been fishing his entire life and loves to share his "secret spots" with visiting fishermen—he knows *the* place for bonefishing on the flats. A half-day trip in his 21-foot Boston whaler is $50 per person (minimum two people), $100 per person for a full day.

Molokai's Best Snorkel Spots

Most Molokai beaches are too dangerous to snorkel in the winter, when big waves and strong currents are generated by storms that sweep down from Alaska. Stick to the Kumimi or Murphy's Beach on the East End in winter. In summer, roughly May to mid-September, when the Pacific Ocean takes a holiday and turns into a flat lake, the whole West Coast of Molokai opens up for snorkeling. "Fun Hog" Mike Holmes's favorite snorkel spots are:

Kawaikiunui, Ilio Point, and Pohaku Moiliili, on the West End: These are all special places seldom seen by even those who live on Molokai. You can reach Kawaikikunui and Pohaku Moiliili on foot after a long, hot, dusty ride in a four-wheel-drive vehicle, but it's much easier and quicker to go by sea.

Kapukahehu or Dixie Maru, on the West End: This is a good, gold-sand family beach, because the cove is well protected and the reef is close and shallow. The name Dixie Maru comes from a 1920s Japanese fishing boat stranded off the rocky shore. One of the Molokai Ranch cowboys hung the wrecked boat's nameplate on a gate by Kapukahehu Beach, and the name Dixie Maru stuck. To get there, take Kaluakoi Road to the end of the pavement, and then take the footpath 100 yards to the beach.

Murphy Beach Park or Kumimi Beach, on the East End. Located between mile markers 20 and 21, off Kamehameha V Highway, the reef here is easily reachable, and the waters are calm year-round.

For light-tackle/deep-sea fishing, **Molokai Ranch & Fun Hogs** (☎ **808/ 552-2791**) has afternoon (from 1 to 4pm) fishing excursions on Tuesdays, Thursdays, and Saturdays on their 25-foot hard-bottom inflatable boat, for $250 for one to four passengers.

7 Hiking & Camping

by Jeanette Foster

HIKING MOLOKAI'S PEPEOPAE TRAIL

Molokai's most awesome hike is the **Pepeopae Trail;** it takes you back a few million years to a time before any human or creature set foot on the island. On the cloud-draped trail (actually a boardwalk across the bog), you'll see mosses, sedges, native violets, knee-high ancient ohias, and lichens that evolved in total isolation over eons. Eerie intermittent mists blowing in and out will give you an idea of this island at its creation.

The narrow boardwalk, built by volunteers, protects the bog and keeps you out of the primal ooze. Don't venture off of it; you could damage this fragile environment or get lost. The 3-mile round-trip takes about 90 minutes to hike—after you drive about 20 miles from Kaunakakai, deep into the Molokai Forest Preserve on a four-wheel-drive road. Plan a full day for this outing. Better yet, go on a guided nature hike with **The Nature Conservancy of Hawaii,** which guards this unusual ecosystem. For information, write The Nature Conservancy of Hawaii, 1116 Smith St, Suite 201, Honolulu, HI 96817. No permit is required for this easy hike. You should call ahead (☎ **808/537-4508** or 808/553-5236 on Molokai) to check on the

✪ Frommer's Favorite Molokai Experiences

Travel Back in Time on the Pepeopae Trail. This awesome hike takes you through the Molokai Forest Reserve and back a few million years to a time before any human or creature set foot on the island. Along the misty trail (actually a boardwalk across the bog), expect close encounters of the wildlife kind: mosses, sedges, violets, lichens, and knee-high ancient ohias.

Stroll the Sands at Papohaku. Go early, when the tropic sun isn't so fierce, and stroll this 3-mile stretch of unspoiled golden sand—it's one of the longest in Hawaii. The big surf and rip tides make swimming somewhat risky, but Papohaku is perfect for walking, beachcombing, and in the evening, sunset-watching.

Soak in the Warm Waters off Sandy Beach. On Molokai's East End, about 20 miles outside of Kaunakakai—just before the road starts to climb to Halawa Valley—lies a small pocket of white sand known as Sandy Beach. Submerging yourself in the warm, calm waters (an outer reef protects the cove) is a sensual experience par excellence—and it's absolutely free.

Snorkel Among Clouds of Butterfly Fish. The calm waters off Kumimi Beach, on the East End, are perfect for snorkelers. Just don your gear and head to the reef, where you'll find lots of exotic tropical fish, including long-nosed butterfly fish, saddle wrasses, and convict tangs.

Venture into the Garden of Eden. Drive the 30 miles of road along Molokai's East End. Take your time. Stop to smell the flowers and pick guavas by the side of the road. Pull over for a swim. Wave at every car you pass and every person you see. At the end of the road, stand on the beach at Halawa Valley and see Hawaii as it must've looked in A.D. 650, when the first people arrived in the islands.

Celebrate the Ancient Hula. Hula is the heartbeat of Hawaiian culture, and Molokai is the birthplace of the hula. While most visitors to Hawaii never get to see the real thing, it's possible to see it here—once a year, on the third Saturday in May, when Molokai celebrates the birth of the hula at its ✪ **Ka Hula Piko'i Festival.** The day-long affair at Papohaku Beach Park includes dance, music, food, and crafts; see "Hawaii Calendar of Events" in chapter 3 for details.

Ride a Mule into Kalaupapa. Don't pass up the opportunity to see this hauntingly beautiful peninsula. It's a once-in-a-lifetime ride for most, and the cliffs are taller than a 300-story skyscraper, but Buzzy Sproat's mules go up and down the 2.9-mile trail (with 26 switchbacks; it can be a bit tricky) to Molokai's famous

condition of the ungraded four-wheel-drive red-dirt road that leads to the trailhead and to let people know that you'll be up there.

To get there, take Highway 460 west from Kaunakakai for 3½ miles and turn right before the Maunawainui Bridge onto the unmarked Molokai Forest Reserve Road (sorry, there aren't any road signs). The pavement ends at the cemetery; continue on the dirt road. After about 2 to 2½ miles, you'll see a sign telling you that you are now in the Molokai Forest Reserve. At the Waikolu Lookout and picnic area, which is just over 9 miles on the Molokai Forest Reserve Road, sign in at the box near the entrance. Continue on the road for another 5 miles to a fork in the road with the sign PUU KOLEKOLE pointing to the right side of the fork. Do not turn right; instead, continue straight at the fork, which will lead to the clearly marked trailhead.

leper colony. The views are breathtaking: You'll see the world's highest sea cliffs and waterfalls plunging thousands of feet into the ocean. If you're afraid of heights, catch the views from the Kalaupapa Lookout.

Kayak Along the North Shore. This is the Hawaii of your dreams: waterfalls thundering down sheer cliffs, remote sand beaches, miles of tropical vegetation, tropical seabirds soaring overhead, and the sounds of the sea splashing on your kayak and the wind whispering in your ear. The best times to go are during the brief window in early spring, around March to April, and during the summer months, especially August to September, when the normally galloping ocean lies down flat.

Sample the Local Brew. Saunter up to the Espresso Bar at the Coffees of Hawaii Plantation Store in Kualapuu for a fresh cup of java made from beans that were grown, processed, and packed on this 450-acre plantation. While you sip, survey the vast collection of native crafts.

Taste Aloha at a Macadamia Nut Farm. It could be the owner, Tuddie Purdy, and his friendly disposition that make the macadamia nuts here taste so good. Or it could be his years of practice in growing, harvesting, and shelling them on his 1½-acre farm. Either way, Purdy produces a perfect crop. You can see how he does it on a short, free tour of Purdy's All Natural Macadamia Nut Farm in Hoolehua, just a nut's throw from the airport.

Talk Story with the Locals. The number-one favorite pastime of most islanders is "talking story," or exchanging experiences and knowledge. It's an old Hawaiian custom that brings people, and generations, closer together. You can probably find residents more than willing to share their wisdom with you while fishing from the wharf at Kaunakakai, hanging out at Molokai Fish & Dive, or having coffee at any of the island's restaurants.

Post a Nut. Why send a picturesque postcard to your friends and family back home when you can send a fresh coconut? The Hoolehua Post Office will supply the free coconuts, if you'll supply the $3 postage fee.

Watch the Sunset from a Coconut Grove. Kapuaiwa Coconut Beach Park, off Maunaloa Highway (Hwy. 460), is a perfect place to watch the sunset: The sky behind the coconut trees fills with a kaleidoscope of colors as the sun sinks into the Pacific. Molokai's tropical sunsets—often red, sometimes orange, always different—are an everyday miracle that stop people in their tracks. Be careful where you sit, though: Falling coconuts could have you seeing stars well before dusk.

HIKING TO KALAUPAPA

This hike is like going down a switchback staircase with what seems like a million steps. You don't always see the breathtaking view, because you're too busy watching your step. It's easier going down—you go from 2,000 feet to sea level in 2½ miles—which takes about an hour, and sometimes takes twice as long on the way up. The trailhead starts on the mauka side of Highway 470, just past the Mule Barn (you can't miss it). Check in there at 7:30am, get a permit, and go before the mule train departs. You must be 16 or older (it's an old state law that kept kids out of the leper colony) and should be in good shape. Wear good hiking boots or sneakers; you won't make it past the first turn in zoris.

If it's action you're looking for, call **Molokai Action Adventures** (☎ 808/558-8184). Island guide Walter Naki will take you skin diving, reef trolling, kayaking, hunting, or hiking into Molokai's remote hidden valleys. Hiking tours are $50 per person for 4 hours, and he limits the number of participants to no more than four. Not only does Walter know Molokai like the back of his hand, but he also loves being outdoors and talking story with visitors; he tells them about the island, the people, the politics, the myths, and anything else his guests want to know.

CAMPING AT THE BEACH

One of the best year-round places to camp on Molokai is **Papohaku Beach Park** on the island's West End, a drive-up seaside site that's a great getaway. The island's largest beach is ideal for rest and relaxation. Facilities include rest rooms, drinking water, outdoor showers, barbecue grills, and picnic tables. Groceries and gas are available in Maunaloa, 6 miles away. Kaluakoi Resort is a mile away. Obtain camping permits by contacting **Maui County Parks Department,** P.O. Box 526, Kaunakakai, HI 96748 (☎ 808/553-3204). Camping is limited to 3 days, but if nobody has applied, the time limit is waived. Cost is $3 a person per night.

IN AN IRONWOOD FOREST

At the end of Highway 470 is the 234-acre piney woods known as **Palaau State Park,** home to the Kalaupapa Lookout (the best vantage point for seeing the historic leper colony if you're not hiking or mule-riding in). It's airy and cool in the park's ironwood forest, where many love to camp at the designated state campground. Camping is free here, but you need a permit from the **State Division of Parks** (☎ 808/567-6618). For more on the park, see "Seeing the Sights," below.

ON MOLOKAI RANCH

For a unique experience, the **Molokai Ranch Outfitters Center,** P.O. Box 259, Maunaloa, HI 96770 (☎ 800/254-8871 or 808/552-2791; www.molokai-ranch.com), offers an eco-adventure called the ✪ **Great Molokai Ranch Trail.** It features upscale, "comfortable" camping in a bungalow/tent called a *tentalow*, plus lots of outdoor activities. Paniolo Camp, the first camp to open in 1997, is located just south of Molokai Ranch headquarters in Maunaloa. The camp is a collection of 40 comfortable tents mounted on wooden platforms. All tents have queen-size beds, ceiling fans, private bathrooms with self-composting toilets, hot-water showers, and solar-powered lights. Each individual campsite is on a footpath that meanders through ironwood trees.

Within the Paniolo Camp is an open-air dining pavilion, a swimming pool, a fire pit, nature trails, mountain-bike paths, ocean activities, and volleyball and horseshoe areas. Rates are $185 per person (double occupancy) and include meals, snacks, transportation (including airport pickup), daily maid service, and 2 major adventures per day (mountain biking, hiking, snorkeling, kayaking, beach and ocean sports, cultural experiences, and children's program). Equestrian and aquatic adventures are available for an additional charge.

The Paniolo Camp is set up for families with children. The newer Kalo Camp, which features 20 *yurts* (circular canvas shelters on platforms) down by the beach, is for adults only. Rates are $215 per person, double occupancy. In either camp, don't miss the mountain-biking adventures, conducted by Bob Ward of Hairbrain Adventures; he offers the best tours on the best mountain-bike trails in the state.

Even if you aren't a "camping" fan, don't miss this fabulous opportunity to experience a comfortable yet adventuresome side of Molokai.

8 Golf & Tennis

by Jeanette Foster

GOLF

Golf is one of Molokai's best-kept secrets; it's challenging and fun, tee times are open, and the rates are lower than your your score will be. Most popular is the par-72, 6,564-yard **Kaluakoi Golf Course,** which designer Ted Robinson calls "the most spectacular and unusual course in the islands." The course is cut along the ocean (six holes are along the shoreline) and through the woods (pheasants, axis deer, and wild turkeys freely roam the fairways); it offers hilly, wooded fairways bisected by ravines, and a grand finish, beginning at the par-3, 16th hole. Called "The Gorge," the 16th hole plays 190 yards over a deep ravine to a two-tiered green. When you finish that, both the 17th and 18th holes are very long par-4s, with greens blind from the tee. Facilities include driving range, putting green, pro shop, and restaurant. It's rarely crowded; greens fees are $40 for Kaluakoi Resort guests and $60 for nonguests, and twilight rates are $40 for nonguests and $32 for guests. Call ☎ **808/552-2739.**

The real find in golf courses is the **Ironwood Hills Golf Course,** off Kalae Highway (☎ **808/567-6000**). It's located just before the Molokai Mule Ride Mule Barn, on the road to the Lookout. One of the oldest golf courses in the state, Ironwood Hills (named after the two predominant features of the course, ironwood trees and hills) was built in 1929 by Del Monte Plantation for its executives. This unusual course, which sits in the cool air at 1,200 feet, delights with its rich foliage, open fairways, and spectacular views of the rest of the island. Surrounded by bushes, the third hole—a par-3, 158-yard shot from the tee over a gully—could qualify as the signature hole. If you play here, use a trick developed by the local residents: After teeing off on the 6th hole, just take whatever clubs you need to finish playing the hole and a driver for the 7th hole, and park your bag under a tree. The climb to the 7th hole is steep—you'll be glad that you're only carrying a few clubs. Greens fees are $10 for nine holes, $14 for 18 holes. Cart fees are $7 for nine holes, $14 for 18. You can also rent a hand cart for just $2.50, and club rentals are $7 for nine holes and $12 for 18.

TENNIS

Maui County has only two tennis courts on Molokai. Both are located at the **Mitchell Pauole Center** in Kaunakakai (☎ **808/553-5141**). Both courts have night lights and are available on a first-come, first-served basis, with at 45-minute time limit if someone is waiting.

9 Seeing the Sights

by Jeanette Foster

IN & AROUND KAUNAKAKAI

Kapuaiwa Coconut Grove/Kiowea Park. Along Maunaloa Highway (Hwy. 460), 2 miles west of Kaunakakai.

This royal grove—a thousand coconut trees on 10 acres planted in 1863 by the island's high chief Kapua'iwa (later, King Kamehameha V)—is a major roadside attraction in

Molokai. The shoreline park, 2 miles west of Kaunakakai, is a favorite subject of sunset photographers and visitors who delight in a hand-lettered sign that warns: DANGER: FALLING COCONUTS. In its backyard, across the highway, stands Church Row: seven churches, each a different denomination, stark evidence of the missionary impact on Hawaii.

Post-A-Nut. Hoolehua Post Office, Puu Peelua Ave., near Maunaloa Highway (Hwy. 460). ☎ **808/567-6144.** Mon-Fri 7:30-11:30am and 12:30-4:30pm.

Postmaster Margaret Keahi-Leary will help you say "Aloha" with a dried Molokai coconut: Write a message on the coconut with a felt-tip pen, and she'll send it via U.S. mail over the sea. Coconuts are free, but postage is $3 for a mainland-bound 2-pound coconut.

Purdy's All-Natural Macadamia Nut Farm. Lihipali St., Hoolehua. ☎ **808/567-6601.** Mon-Fri 9:30am-3:30pm, Sat 10am-2pm, Sun by appointment only. Free admission.

The Purdys have made macadamia nut–buying an entertainment event, offering tours of the 1½-acre homestead and lively demonstrations of nutshell-cracking in the shade of their towering, shade-giving trees. The tour of the 70-year-old nut farm explains the growth, bearing, harvesting, and shelling processes, so that by the time you crunch into the luxurious macadamia nut, you'll have more than a passing knowledge of its entire life cycle.

Tuddie Purdy has invented a rubber holding device that has conquered the otherwise slippery (and hazardous) shelling process. The nuts sold here are grown on Molokai and the Big Island and packaged on the farm—they make great, affordable souvenirs.

THE NORTH COAST

Most people never get a chance to see Hawaii's most dramatic coast in its entirety, but nobody should miss the opportunity to glimpse it from the Kalaupapa Lookout at Palau State Park. On the way, there are a few diversions (arranged here in geographical order).

EN ROUTE TO THE NORTH COAST

Coffees of Hawaii. The Plantation Store, Hwy. 480 (near the junction of Hwy. 470). ☎ **800/709-BEAN** or 808/567-9023. Fax 808/567-9270.

The defunct Del Monte pineapple town of Kualapuu is rising again—only this time, coffee is the catch, not pineapple. Located in the cool foothills, Coffees of Hawaii has planted coffee beans on 600 acres of former pineapple land. The plantation is irrigating the plants with a high-tech, continuous water and fertilizer drip system (using the world's largest rubber-lined reservoir, which holds 1.4 billion gallons of water). Stop by the Espresso Bar for a Mocha Mama (Molokai coffee, ice, chocolate, chocolate ice cream, chocolate syrup, whipped cream, and chocolate shavings on top). It'll keep you going all day, maybe even all night.

Molokai Museum and Cultural Center. Meyer Sugar Mill, Hwy. 470 (just after the turnoff for the Ironwood Hills Golf Course, and 2 miles below Kalaupapa Overlook), Kaunakakai. ☎ **808/567-6436.** Admission $2.50 adults, $1 students. Mon-Sat 10am-2pm.

En route to the California Gold Rush in 1849, Rudolph W. Meyer, a German professor, came to Molokai, married the high chiefess Kalama, and, after planting corn, wheat, and potatoes, began to operate a small sugar plantation near his home. Now on the National Register of Historic Places, the restored 1878 sugar mill, with its century-old steam engine, mule-driven cane crusher, copper clarifiers, and redwood evaporating pans—all in working order—is the last of its kind in Hawaii. The mill

🧒 Especially for Kids

Flying a Kite (*see p. 508*) Not only can you get a guaranteed-to-fly kite at the **Big Wind Kite Factory** (☎ **808/552-2634**) in Maunaloa, but kite designer Jonathan Socher offers free kite-flying classes to kids, who'll learn how to make their kites soar, swoop, and most important, stay in the air for more than 5 minutes.

Spending the Day at Kumimi Beach Park (*see p. 492*) Just beyond Wailua on the East End, Kumimi Beach Park (also known as Murphy Beach Park) is a small wayside park that's perfect for kids. There's safe swimming conditions for children, plenty of shade from the ironwood trees, and useful facilities like small pavilions with picnic tables and barbecue grills.

Riding a Wagon (*see p. 504*) Kids will love being in a wagon drawn by two horses as it traverses a dirt trail through a mango grove bound for an ancient temple of sacrifice. After the ride, the whole family is treated to a beachside lunch and old-fashioned ukulele songfest.

Watching Whales (*see p. 494*) From mid-December to mid-March, whale-watching for kids of all ages on Molokai Charters' 42-foot sloop, *Satan's Doll*, offers a variety of ways to spot these giant leviathans that visit Hawaiian waters in the winter.

Visiting the Past (*see p. 500*) The Molokai Museum and Cultural Center lets kids step into the past and see how sugar was made (with a restored 1878 sugar mill, complete with old steam engine, mule-driven cane crusher, and redwood evaporating pans).

also houses a museum that traces the history of sugar-growing on Molokai and features special events, such as wine tastings every 2 months; taro festivals; an annual music festival; and occasional classes in ukulele making, loom weaving, and sewing. Call for a schedule.

Palaau State Park. At the end of Hwy. 470.

This 234-acre piney-woods park 8 miles out of Kaunakakai is a sleeper. It doesn't look like much until you get out of the car and take a hike, which literally puts you between a rock and a hard place: Go right, and you end up on the edge of Molokai's magnificent sea cliffs, with its panoramic view of the infamous Kalaupapa leper colony; go left, and you come face to face with a stone phallus.

If you have no plans to scale the cliffs on mule or foot (see "Hiking & Camping" and "In an Ironwood Forest," above), the ⭐ **Kalaupapa Lookout** is the only place from which to see the former place of exile. The trail is marked, and there are historic photos and interpretive signs to explain what you're seeing.

It's airy and cool in the ironwood forest, where camping is free at the designated state campground. You'll need a permit from the **State Division of Parks** (☎ **808/567-6618**). Not many people seem to camp here, probably because of the legend associated with the **Phallic Rock.** Six feet high, pointed at an angle that means business, Molokai's famous Phallic Rock is a legendary fertility tool that appears to be working today. According to Hawaiian legend, a woman who wishes to become pregnant need only spend the night near the rock and . . . Voilà! It's probably just a coincidence, of course, but Molokai does have a growing population of young, pregnant women. If you want to avoid pregnancy, it might be wise to avoid camping in the rock's vicinity.

Phallic Rock is at the end of a well-worn uphill path, through an ironwood grove past other rocks that vaguely resemble sexual body parts. No mistaking the big guy, though—it's definitely a giant, erect male penis. Supposedly, it belonged to Nanahoa, a demigod who quarreled with his wife, Kawahuna, over a pretty girl. In the tussle, Kawahuna was thrown over the cliff, and both husband and wife were turned to stone.

Of all the phallic rocks in Hawaii and the Pacific, this is the one to see. It's so famous, it's featured on a postcard with a tiny, awe-struck Japanese woman standing next to it.

THE LEGACY OF FATHER DAMIEN: KALAUPAPA NATIONAL HISTORIC PARK

An old tongue of lava that sticks out to form a peninsula, Kalaupapa became infamous because of man's inhumanity to victims of a formerly incurable contagious disease.

King Kamehameha V sent the first lepers—nine men and three women—into exile on this lonely shore, at the base of ramparts that rise like temples against the unbroken Pacific, on January 6, 1866. More than 11,000 lepers arrived between 1865 and 1874, dispatched to disfigure and die in one of the world's most beautiful—and lonely—places. They called Kalaupapa "The Place of the Living Dead."

One of the world's least-contagious diseases, leprosy is caused by a germ, Mycobacterium leprae, that attacks the nerves, skin, and eyes. It's found mainly, but not exclusively, in tropical regions and is transmitted by direct, repetitive, person-to-person contact over a long period of time. American scientists found a cure for the disease, sulfone, in the 1940s.

Before science intervened, there was Father Damien. Born to wealth in Belgium, Joseph de Veuster traded a life of excess for missionary life, and eventually for exile among lepers; he devoted himself to caring for the afflicted at Kalaupapa. Father Damien, as he became known, volunteered to go out to the Pacific in place of his ailing brother when he was 33. Horrified at the conditions in the leper colony, Father Damien worked at Kalaupapa for 11 years, building houses, schools, and churches, and giving patients hope of redemption. He died on April 15, 1889, in Kalaupapa, of leprosy. He was 49.

A hero nominated for Catholic sainthood, Father Damien is buried not in his tomb next to St. Philomena Church, but in his native Belgium. His hand was recently returned to Molokai, however, and was reinterred at Kalaupapa as a relic of his martyrdom.

This small peninsula is probably the final resting place of more than 11,000 souls. The sand dunes are littered with grave markers, sorted by the religious affiliation—Catholic, Protestant, Lutheran, Buddhist—of those who died here. But so many are buried in unmarked graves that no census of the dead is believed to be either accurate or complete.

Kalaupapa is now a National Historic Park and one of Hawaii's richest archaeological preserves, with sites that date to A.D. 1000. About 60 former patients chose to remain in the tidy village of whitewashed houses with tombstones on the coast and statues of angels in their yards. The original name for their former affliction, "leprosy," was officially banned in Hawaii by the State Legislature in 1981. The politically correct name now is "Hansen's disease," for Dr. Gerhard Hansen of Norway, who discovered the germ in 1873. The few residents of Kalaupapa still call their disease leprosy, although none are too keen on being called lepers.

Kalaupapa welcomes visitors who arrive on foot, by mule, or by small plane. You can visit Father Damien's St. Philomena church, built in 1872. Once off-limits, the quiet village is now open to visitors, who can see it from a yellow school bus driven by resident tour guide Richard Marks, an ex-seaman and sheriff who survived the disease.

You won't be able to roam freely, and you'll only be allowed to enter the museum, the craft shop, and the church.

✪ MULE RIDES TO KALAUPAPA

The first turn's a gasp, and it's all downhill from there. You can close your eyes and hold on for dear life, or slip the reins over the pommel and sit back, letting the mule do the walking down the precipitous path to Kalaupapa National Historic Park, Molokai's famous leper colony.

Even if you have only 1 day to spend on Molokai, spend it on a mule. It's a once-in-a-lifetime ride for most—the cliffs are taller than a 300-story skyscraper—but Buzzy Sproat's mules go up and down the narrow 2.9-mile trail daily, rain or shine, without ever losing a rider or mount on 26 switchbacks. From 1,600 feet on the nearly perpendicular ridge, the surefooted mules step down the muddy trail, pausing often on switchbacks to calculate their next move—and always, it seems to me, veering a little too close to the edge. Each switchback is numbered; by the time you get to number four, you'll catch your breath, put the mule on cruise control, and begin to enjoy Hawaii's most awesome trail ride.

The mule tours are offered once daily starting at 8am, and they last until about 3:30pm. It's $135 per person for the all-day adventure, which includes the round-trip mule ride, a guided tour of the settlement, a visit to Father Damien's church and grave, lunch at Kalawao, and souvenirs. To go, you must be at least 16 years old and physically fit. Contact **Molokai Mule Ride,** 100 Kalae Hwy., Suite 104, on Hwy. 470, 6 miles north of Hwy. 460 (☎ **800/567-7550** or 808/567-6088, or 808/567-6400 between 8 and 10pm; fax 808/567-6244; www.muleride.com; e-mail muleman@ aloha.net). Advance reservations are required.

SEEING KALAUPAPA BY PLANE **Father Damien Tours,** P.O. Box 1, Kalaupapa, HI 96742 (☎/Fax **808/567-6171**) picks you up at the Kalaupapa airport and takes you to some of the area's most scenic spots, including Kalawao, where Father Damien's church still stands; the Kauhako Crater; and the town of Kalaupapa. The $30 fee includes the tour of Kalaupapa and the permit to enter this secluded area. Airfare is additional $49.90 round-trip for the Molokai-Lanai Air Shuttle, from Molokai Airport (in Hoolehua). Island Air round-trip from either Honolulu or Molokai Airport is $86 (AAA members get special fare of $64.75). Paragon Air on Maui offers package deal of airfare from Kahului Airport on Maui to Kalaupapa, plus the 4½-hour tour, with lunch and drinks for $199. Bring your own lunch and drinks and arrange for air transportation to Kalaupapa Airport (contact **Molokai-Lanai Air Shuttle** at ☎ **808/567-6847, Island Air** at ☎ **800/652-6541,** or **Paragon Air** at ☎ **808/ 244-3356**). You must be at least 16 years old.

THE WEST END
MAUNALOA

In the first and only urban renewal on Molokai, the 1920s-era pineapple-plantation town of Maunaloa is being reinvented. Streets are being widened and paved, and curbs and sidewalks are going in to serve a new tract of $125,000 houses. Historic Maunaloa is being transformed into Maunaloa Village, and there's already a triplex movie theater and a Kentucky Fried Chicken.

The only master-planned village on Molokai will have a museum, a bed-and-breakfast lodge, a town park with a playing field, new restaurants, and artisan's studios—uptown stuff for Molokai. For now, only Jonathan Socher's Big Wind Kite Factory (see "Shopping," below), the town's main attraction, remains in place, his kites and books wrapped in cellophane against constant clouds of red dust raised by construction crews. Even the Cooke Island pines of Maunaloa need a bath.

Impressions

In the chronicle of man there is perhaps no more melancholy landing than this . . . .

—Robert Louis Stevenson, on Kalaupapa

Smile. It No Broke Your Face.

—sign at Kalaupapa

Unfortunately, the very popular Molokai Ranch Wildlife Conservation Park, which offered entertaining tours of the collection of exotic African and Indian animals in the wild, has closed. Tours are no longer available.

ON THE NORTHWEST SHORE: MOOMOMI DUNES

Undisturbed for centuries, the Moomomi Dunes, on Molokai's northwest shore, are a unique treasure chest of great scientific value. It may look like just a pile of sand to you as you fly over on the final approach to Hoolehua Airport, but Moomomi Dunes is much more than that. Archaeologists have found adz quarries, ancient Hawaiian burial sites, and shelter caves; botanists have identified five endangered plant species; and marine biologists are finding evidence that endangered green sea turtles are hauling out from the waters once again to lay eggs here. The greatest discovery, however, belongs to Smithsonian Institute ornithologists, who have found bones of prehistoric birds—some of them flightless—that existed nowhere else on earth.

Accessible by jeep trails that thread downhill to the shore, this wild coast is buffeted by strong afternoon breezes. It's hot, dry, and windy, so take water, sunscreen, and a Windbreaker. At Kawaaloa Bay, a 20-minute walk to the west, there's a broad golden beach that you can have all to yourself. Stay on the trails, out of the water, and along the beach.

This 920-acre preserve is open to guided nature tours once a month led by **The Nature Conservancy of Hawaii;** call ☎ **808/553-5236** or 808/524-0779 for an exact schedule and details.

To get to Moomomi Dunes, take Highway 460 (Maunaloa Hwy.) from Kaunakakai; turn right onto Highway 470, and follow it to Kualapuu. At Kualapuu, turn left on Highway 480 and go through Hoolehua Village; it's 3 miles to the bay.

THE EAST END

The East End is a cool and inviting green place that's worth a drive to the end of King Kamehameha V Highway (Hwy. 450), even if one of the island's greatest natural attractions, Halawa Valley, is now essentially off-limits.

AN ADVENTURE FOR EVERYONE: A WAGON RIDE TO ILIILIOPAE HEIAU

In a wagon drawn by two horses, you bump along a dirt trail through an incredible mango grove, bound for an ancient temple of human sacrifice. The temple of doom—right out of *Indiana Jones*—is Iliʻiliʻopae, a huge rectangle of stone made of 90 million rocks, overlooking the once important village of Mapulehu and four ancient fishponds. The wagon glides under the perfumed mangoes, then heads uphill through a kiawe forest filled with Java plums to the heiau, which stands across a dry streambed under cloud-spiked Kaunolu, the 4,970-foot island summit.

Hawaii's most powerful heiau attracted kahunas from all over the islands who came to learn the rules of human sacrifice at this university of sacred rites. Contrary to Hollywood's version, historians say the victims here were always men, not young virgins.

and they were strangled, not thrown into a volcano, while priests sat on lauhala mats watching silently. Spooky, eh?

This is the biggest, oldest, and most famous heiau on Molokai. It's a massive 22-foot-high stone altar, dedicated to Lono, the Hawaiian god of fertility. The heiau resonates with *mana* (power) strong enough to lean on. Legend says Ili'ili'opae was built in a single night by a thousand men who passed rocks hand over hand through the Wailau Valley from the other side of the island; each received a shrimp (*'opae*) in exchange for the rock (*ili'ili*). Others say it was built by *menehunes*, the mythic elves who accomplished Herculean feats.

After the visit to the awesome temple, the horse-drawn wagon takes you back to the mango grove for a beachside lunch and an old-fashioned backyard ukulele songfest. Popular with families, this little adventure may sound too down-home for some, but the search for the "real" Molokai begins here.

Contact **Molokai Wagon Rides**, P.O. Box 1528, King Kamehameha V Highway (Hwy. 450), at the 15-mile marker, Kaunakakai, HI 96748 (☎ **808/558-8132**). The adventure via the wagon ride is $35 per person and includes lunch; it begins daily at 10am and lasts at least a couple of hours, sometimes longer. They also offer a tour to the heiau on horseback for $40 per person (no lunch). The hour-long ride goes up to the heiau, then beyond it to the top of the mountain for those breathtaking views, and finally back down to the beach.

KAMAKOU PRESERVE

It's hard to believe, but close to the nearly mile-high summit, it rains more than 80 inches a year—enough to qualify as a rain forest. The Molokai Forest, as it was historically known, is the source of 60% of Molokai's water. Nearly 3,000 acres from the summit to the lowland forests of eucalyptus and pine are now held in preserve by the Nature Conservancy, which has identified 219 Hawaiian plants that grow here exclusively. The preserve is also the last stand of the endangered Molokai Thrush (*olomao*) and Molokai Creeper (*kawawahie*).

To get to this Nature Conservancy preserve, take the Forest Reserve jeep road from Kaunakakai. It's a 45-minute, four-wheel-drive trip on a dirt trail to Waikolu Lookout Campground; from there, you can venture into the wilderness preserve on foot across a boardwalk on a 1½-hour hike (see "Hiking Molokai's Pepeopae Trail," above). For more information, contact **The Nature Conservancy** at ☎ **808/553-5236.**

EN ROUTE TO HALAWA VALLEY

No visit to Molokai is complete without at least a passing glance at the island's **ancient fishponds,** a singular achievement in Pacific aquaculture. With a hunger for fresh fish and a lack of ice or refrigeration, Hawaiians perfected aquaculture in 1400, before Christopher Columbus "discovered" America. They built gated, U-shaped stone and coral walls on the shore to catch fish on the incoming tide; they would then raise them in captivity. The result: A constant, ready supply of fresh fish.

The ponds stretch for 20 miles along Molokai's south shore and are visible from Kamehameha V Highway (Hwy. 450). Molokai's fishponds offer a clue to the island's ancient population. It took something like a thousand people to tend a single fishpond, and more than 60 ponds once existed on this coast. All of the fishponds are named; a few are privately owned. Some are silted in by red-dirt runoff from South Coast gulches. Others have been revived by folks who raise fish and seaweed.

The largest, 54-acre **Keawa Nui Pond,** is surrounded by a 3-foot-high, 2,000-foot-long stone wall. **Alii Fishpond,** reserved for kings, is visible through the coconut groves at One Alii Beach Park (see "Beaches," above). You can see **Kalokoeli Pond,** 6 miles east of Kaunakakai on the highway, from the road.

Our Lady of Sorrows Catholic Church, one of five built by Father Damien on Molokai and the first outside Kalaupapa, sits across the highway from a fishpond. Park in the church lot (except on Sundays) for a closer look.

St. Joseph's Catholic Church. King Kamehameha V Hwy. (Hwy. 450), just after mile marker 10.

The afternoon sun strikes St. Joseph's Church with such a bold ray of light that it's as if God is about to perform a miracle. The stunning brightness compels you to stop and visit the little 1876 wood-frame church, one of four Father Damien built "topside" on Molokai. Restored in 1971, the church stands beside a seaside cemetery, where feral cats play under the gaze of a Damien statue amid gravestones decorated with flower leis.

Smith Bronte Landing Site. King Kamehameha V Hwy. (Hwy. 450), at mile marker 11, on the *makai* (ocean) side.

In 1927, Charles Lindbergh soloed the Atlantic Ocean in a plane called *The Spirit of St. Louis* and became an American hero. That same year, Ernie Smith and Emory B. Bronte took off from Oakland, California, on July 14 in a single-engine Travelair aircraft named *The City of Oakland*, setting out 2,397 miles across the Pacific Ocean for Honolulu. The next day, after running out of fuel, they crash-landed upside-down in a kiawe thicket on Molokai, but emerged unhurt to become the first civilians to fly to Hawaii from the U.S. mainland. The 25-hour, 2-minute flight landed Smith and Bronte a place in aviation history—and on a roadside marker on Molokai.

10 Shopping

by Jocelyn Fujii

KAUNAKAKAI

Seaside Place, Molokai Surf, Molokai Imports, and **Lourdes** are clothing and gift shops in close proximity to each other in downtown Kaunakakai, where most of the retail shops sell T-shirts, muumuus, surfwear, and informal apparel. For food shopping, there are several good alternatives. Since many visitors to the island stay in condominiums, knowing where the grocery stores are on this island is especially important. Other than that, serious shoppers will be disappointed, unless they love kukies or native wood vessels. The following are Kaunakakai's notables.

Imamura Store. ☎ 808/553-5615.

Wilfred Imamura, whose mother founded the store (she died in 1992 at age 97), recalls the old railroad track that stretched from the pier to a spot across the street. "We brought our household things from the pier on a hand-pumped vehicle," he recalls. His store, appropriately, is a leap into the past, a marvelous amalgam of precious old-fashioned things. Rubber boots, Hawaiian-print tablecloths, Japanese tea plates, ukulele cases, plastic slippers, and even coconut bikini tops line the shelves. But it's not all nostalgia. The Molokai T-shirts, jeans, and palaka shorts are of good quality and inexpensive, and the pareu fabrics are a find.

Molokai Drugs. In the Kamoi Professional Center. **☎ 808/553-5313.**

David Mikami, whose father-in-law founded the pharmacy in 1935, has made this more than a drugstore: It's a gleaming, friendly stop full of life's basic necessities, with generous amenities such as a phone and a rest room for passersby (!). You'll find the best selection of guidebooks, books about Molokai, and maps here, as well as greeting cards, paperbacks, party favors, cassette players, flip-flops, and every imaginable essential.

When Mikami's daughter, Kelly, became a pharmacist in 1995, she was the fourth in the family. The Mikamis are a household name on the island not only because of their pharmacy, but also because the family has shown exceptional kindness to the often economically strapped Molokaians.

Molokai Fish & Dive. ☎ 808/553-5926.

The island's largest selection of T-shirts and souvenirs shares space with fishing, snorkeling, and outdoor gear for rent and sale. Wend your way among the fishnets, boogie boards, diving equipment, bamboo rakes, juices and soft drinks, disposable cameras, and the other miscellany of this chockablock store. One entire wall is lined with T-shirts.

Take's Variety Store. ☎ 808/553-5442.

If you need luggage tags, buzz saws, toys, candy, cloth dolls, canned goods, canteens, camping equipment, hardware, pipe fittings, fishing supplies—whew!—and other products for work and play, this 50-year-old variety store may be your answer. You may suffer from claustrophobia in the crowded, dusty aisles, but Take's carries everything—if you can find it. If you can't, the staff is friendly and helpful.

EDIBLES

Friendly Market Center. ☎ 808/553-5595.

You can't miss this salmon-colored wooden storefront on the main drag of "downtown" Kaunakakai, where multigenerational stores are the norm rather than the exception. It's friendly! We like all the old mom-and-pop stores, but Friendly's has an especially good selection of produce and healthy foods. (Another is Outpost Natural Foods.) Blue-corn tortilla chips, soy milk, and Kumu Farms macadamia-nut pesto, the island's stellar gourmet food, are among the items that surpass standard grocery-store fare. The meats are fresh and of good quality, and the selection is democratic, encompassing everything from prime cuts to fresh fish and sashimi fillets.

Misaki's Grocery and Dry Goods. ☎ 808/553-5505.

Established in 1922, this third-generation local legend is one of Kaunakakai's two grocery stores, as essential as the Molokai air. Some surprises lurk on the shelves, such as chopped garlic from Gilroy, California (the garlic capital of the world), but the stock mostly consists of meats, produce, baking products, and a humongous array of soft drinks. Liquor, stationery, candies, and paper products round out the selection.

Molokai Ice House. At the end of Kaunakakai Wharf Rd. ☎ 808/553-3054.

A fishermen's co-op established in 1988 opened its retail doors as a fish market in 1994—and it's a find. Gathered daily from the fishing boats at the wharf, the seafood comes in all forms—sashimi, poke (the seasoned, raw fish), lomi (mixed, seasoned, and worked with the fingers) salmon and squid, oysters, seaweed, and teriyaki marlin fillets. It can't come any fresher, and it's all skillfully seasoned and reasonably priced. Locals come here for their fresh fish, whole or in fillets. The lomi 'o'io and the lomi ahi (yellowfin tuna) may look like mashed raw fish to the uninitiated, but with perfectly balanced seasonings of green onions, a pungent type of seaweed (limukohu), and roasted kukui nut (inamona), they're delicacies sought by Molokaians and neighbor islanders. Various seasoned shrimp and octopus dishes, and frequent surprise catches that catch the fancy of the chef, make this an ever-changing adventure. Best of all, the Molokai prices are kind and unchanging, even during the winter when fresh-fish prices notoriously skyrocket. The prepared foods are perfect for no-fuss cooking or a quiet lunch at the wharf. This fish market is a find for kamaaina and malihini in terms of quality, freshness, pricing, and heart—and, in true Hawaiian spirit, they sell poi to go with the fish!

Molokai Wines & Spirits. ☎ **808/553-5009.**

This isn't an epicurean's cave, but it's your best bet on the island for a decent bottle of wine. The shop offers 200 labels, including Caymus, Silver Oak, Joseph Phelps, Heitz, and a carefully culled European selection. *Wine Spectator* reviews are tacked to some of the selections, which always helps, and the snack selection shows at least some glimmers of mercy: Cambozola gourmet cheeses, salami, and Carr's biscuits. For those who like the effortless frozen burritos, canned tuna, chips, and prepackaged nibbles, they're on the shelves, too.

EN ROUTE TO THE NORTH COAST

Coffees of Hawaii Plantation Store. Kualapuu. ☎ **808/567-9023.**

This is a fairly slick—for Molokai—combination coffee bar, store, and gallery for more than 30 artists and craftspeople from Molokai, Maui, and the Big Island. Sold here are the Malulani Estate and Muleskinner coffees that are grown, processed, and packed on the 500-acre plantation surrounding the shop. (A tour of the plantation is offered weekdays at 10am and 1pm and, upon special request, Saturdays at 10am; it's $14 for adults and $7 for kids.) You may find better prices on coffee at other retail outlets, but the gift items are worth a look: pikake and plumeria soaps from Kauai; perfumes and pure beeswax candles from Maui; koa bookmarks and hair sticks; and pottery, woods, and baskets.

Molokai Museum Gift Shop. At the old R. W. Meyer Sugar Mill, Kalae. ☎ **808/567-6436.**

The restored 1878 sugar mill sits 1,500 feet above the town of Kualapuu (see "Seeing the Sights," earlier in this chapter). It's a drive from town, definitely, but a good cause for those who'd like to support the museum and the handful of local artisans who sell their crafts, fabrics, cookbooks, quilt sets, and other gift items in its tiny shop. A modest selection of cards, T-shirts, coloring books, and at Christmas, handmade ornaments of lauhala and koa are sprinkled throughout.

EDIBLES

Kualapuu Market. Kualapuu. ☎ **808/567-6243.**

This market, in its third generation, is a stone's throw from the new Coffees of Hawaii Store. It's a scaled-down, one-stop shop with wine, food, and necessities—and a surprisingly presentable, albeit small, assortment of produce, from Molokai sweet potatoes to Kau navel oranges in season. The shelves are filled with canned goods, propane, rope, hoses, paper products, and baking goods, reflecting the uncomplicated, rural lifestyle of the area.

THE WEST END

MAUNALOA

Big Wind Kite Factory & the Plantation Gallery. Maunaloa. ☎ **808/552-2634.**

Jonathan and Daphne Socher, kite designers and inveterate Bali-philes, have combined their interests in a kite factory/import shop that dominates the commercial landscape of Maunaloa, the reconstituted plantation town. Maunaloa's naturally windy conditions make it ideal for kite-flying classes, which are offered free when conditions are right. The adjoining Plantation Gallery features local handicrafts such as milo-wood bowls, locally made T-shirts, Hawaii-themed sandblasted glassware, baskets of lauhala and other fibers, and Hawaiian-music CDs. There are many Balinese handicrafts, from jewelry to clothing and fabrics.

Maunaloa General Store. ☎ 808/552-2346.

Maunaloa's only general store sells everything from paper products to batteries and socks, dairy products, frozen and fresh meats, wine, canned goods, visors, and a cross-section of necessities.

THE EAST END
EDIBLES

The Neighborhood Store 'N Counter. Pukoo. **☎ 808/554-8498.**

With the closing of the Wavecrest, the Neighborhood Store is the only grocery on the East End. In addition to the breakfast and lunch counter, the store sells batteries, film, aspirin, cookies, beer, Molokai produce, candies, paper products, and other sundries for travelers and residents.

11 Molokai After Dark

by Jocelyn Fujii

The big news is that the movies have come to Molokai. **Maunaloa Cinemas** (**☎ 808/552-2707**) is a triplex theater that shows first-run movies in the middle of Maunaloa town—four screenings a day at each of the three theaters, beginning with the matinee. Otherwise, Molokai nightlife is an oxymoron. Aside from the **Ohia Lodge** at the Kaluakoi Resort, which features live entertainment on Friday and Saturday nights, the only other spot for after-dark socializing is the **Pau Hana Inn** in Kaunakakai (**☎ 808/553-5342**). Call the Pau Hana before going over, however. At this writing, its future is uncertain.

9

Lanai: A Different Kind of Paradise

Lanai is not an easy place to get to. There are no direct flights from the mainland, and most air carriers route flights onto the island from Honolulu. It's almost as if this quiet, gentle oasis that's known, paradoxically, for both its small-town feel and celebrity appeal, demands that its visitors go to great lengths to get here to ensure that those who come will appreciate it.

Lanai (pronounced lah nigh ee), Hawaii's sixth largest island and the nation's biggest defunct pineapple patch, now claims to be one of the world's top tropical destinations. It's a bold claim, since so little is here: no stoplights, barely 30 miles of paved road, no fast-food joints, no strip malls, no taxis—in short, none of what you usually find in a vacation destination. Instead, what you have here is something quite rare: an almost virgin island, unspoiled by what passes for progress, except for a tiny 1920s-era plantation village—and, of course, its fancy new neighbors, two first-class luxury hotels where room rates hover around $400 a night.

As soon as you arrive, the blanket of coziness of a small town is felt: people wave to every car, residents stop to "talk story" with their friends, taking time to fish or work in the garden are considered priorities in life, and leaving the keys in your car's ignition is standard practice.

For generations, Lanai was little more than a small village, owned and operated by the pineapple company, surrounded by acres of pineapple fields. The few visitors to the island were either relatives of the mainly Filipino residents or occasional weekend hunters. Life in the 1960s was pretty much the same as in the 1930s.

But all that changed in 1990, when The Lodge at Koele, a 102-room hotel resembling an opulent English Tudor mansion, opened its doors, followed a year later by the 250-room Manele Bay Hotel, a Mediterranean-style luxury resort overlooking Hulopoe Bay. Overnight, the isolated island was transformed: corporate jets streamed into the tiny Lanai Airport, former pineapple plantation workers were retrained in the art of serving gourmet meals, and the population of 2,500 swelled with transient visitors and outsiders coming to work in the island's new hospitality industry. Microsoft millionaire Bill Gates chose the island for his lavish wedding, buying up all its hotel rooms to fend off the press—and uncomplicated Lanai went on the map as a place where the rich and powerful vacation.

Lanai

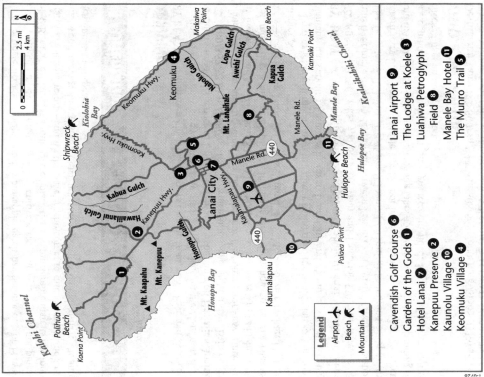

Legend

✈ Airport
⊁ Beach
▲ Mountain

Cavendish Golf Course ⑥
Garden of the Gods ①
Hotel Lanai ⑦
Kanepuu Preserve ②
Kaunolu Village ⑩
Keomuku Village ④

Lanai Airport ⑨
The Lodge at Koele ③
Luahiwa Petroglyph Field ⑧
Manele Bay Hotel ⑪
The Munro Trail ⑤

But it's also a place where people come looking for dramatic beauty, quiet, solitude, and an experience with nature away from the bright lights of Waikiki, the publicity of Maui, and the hoopla surrounding most resorts. The sojourners who find their way to Lanai come seeking the melodramatic views, the tropical fusion of stars at night, and the chance to be alone with the elements.

They also come for the wealth of activities: snorkeling and swimming in the sapphire waters of the marine preserve known as Hulopoe Bay; hiking on a hundred miles of remote trails that canvass the 141-square-mile island; talking story with the friendly locals; and beachcombing and whale-watching along a stretch of otherwise deserted sand. For the adventurous, there's horseback riding in the mist of the forest, scuba diving in caves, playing golf next to scenic ocean views, shooting sporting clays, or renting a four-wheel-drive jeep for the day and discovering wild plains where spotted deer run free and a rich cultural history comes alive in the ruins of a once-vibrant village.

In a single decade, a plain red-dirt pineapple patch has become one of Hawaii's most unusual fantasy destinations. They cultivate vacationers here now, not pineapples. But the real Lanai is a multifaceted place that's so much more than its newfound status as a luxury resort—and it's the traveler who comes to discover the island's natural wonders, local lifestyle, and other inherent joys who's bound to have the most genuine island experience.

1 Orientation

by Jeanette Foster

ARRIVING

BY PLANE No matter which island you're coming from, you'll have to make a connection in Honolulu, where you can easily catch a small plane for the 25-minute flight to Lanai's airport. Jet service to Lanai is now available, but only on **Hawaiian Airlines** (☎ 800/367-5320 or 808/565-6977), which offers one flight a day. Twin-engine planes take longer and are sometimes bumpier, but they offer great views since they fly lower. **IslandAir** (☎ 800/652-6541 or 808/565-6744) offers 9 to 12 flights a day. For more details on these airlines—including details on how to get the cheapest fares—see "Getting There & Getting Around" and "Money-Saving Package Deals" in chapter 3.

Prop or jet, you'll touch down in Puuwai Basin, once the world's largest pineapple plantation; it's about 10 minutes by car to Lanai City and 25 minutes to Manele Bay.

BY BOAT A round-trip on **Expeditions Lahaina/Lanai Passenger Ferry** (☎ 808/661-3756) takes you between Maui and Lanai for $50. The ferry service runs five times a day, 365 days a year, between Lahaina and Lanai's Manele Bay harbor. The ferry leaves Lahaina at 6:45am, 9:15am, 12:45pm, 3:15pm, and 5:45pm; the return ferry from Lanai's Manele Bay Harbor leaves at 8am, 10:30am, 2pm, 4:30pm, and 6:45pm. The 9-mile channel crossing takes 45 minutes to an hour, depending on sea conditions. Reservations are strongly recommended. Baggage is limited to two checked bags and one carryon.

VISITOR INFORMATION

Destination Lanai (☎ 800/947-4774 or 808/565-7600; fax 808/565-9316) and the **Hawaii Visitors and Convention Bureau** (☎ 800/GO-HAWAII or 808/923-1811; www.gohawaii.com) will both provide you with brochures, maps, and island guides. For a free *Road and Site Map* of hikes, archaeological sites, and other sights, contact **The Lanai Company**, P.O. Box 310, Lanai, HI 96763 (☎ 808/565-3812).

THE ISLAND IN BRIEF

Inhabited Lanai is divided into three parts—Lanai City, Koele, and Manele—and two distinct climate zones: hot and dry, and cool and misty.

Lanai City (population 2,800) sits at the heart of the island at 1,645 feet above sea level. This is the only place on the island where you'll find services. Built in 1924, this plantation village is a tidy grid of quaint tin-roofed cottages in bright pastels, with roosters penned in tropical gardens of bananas, lilikois, and papayas. Many of the residents are Filipino immigrants who worked the pineapple fields and imported the art, culture, language, food, and lifestyle of the Philippines. Their clapboard homes, now worth $250,000 or more, are excellent examples of historic preservation; the whole town looks like it's been preserved under a bell jar, or a Guy Buffet painting of an upscale Southern Philippines barangay come to life.

Around Dole Park Square, a charming village square lined with towering Norfolk and Cook Island pines, plantation buildings house general stores with basic necessities: a U.S. post office (where people stop to chat), two banks, and a police station with a jail that consists of three bright blue-and-white wooden outhouse-sized cells with padlocks.

In the nearby cool upland district of **Koele** is The Lodge at Koele, standing by itself on a knoll overlooking pastures and the sea at the edge of a pine forest, like a grand European manor or a British colonial hill station. The other bastion of indulgence, the Manele Bay Hotel, is on the sunny southwestern tip of the island at **Manele**. You'll get more of what you expect from Hawaii here—beaches, swaying palms, mai tais, and the like.

2 Getting Around

by Jeanette Foster

With so few paved roads, you'll need a four-wheel-drive vehicle if you plan on exploring the island's remote shores, its interior, or the summit of Mount Lanaihale. Even if you only have 1 day on Lanai, rent one and see the island. We recommend calling **Red Rover,** P.O. Box 464 (located across the street from the island's only gas station, Lanai City Service), Lanai City, HI 96763 (☎ **808/565-7722;** fax 808/6322). They have a fleet of 10 Land Rover vehicles (which carry from two to nine passengers each), ranging in price from $119 to $159 a day. They will deliver the vehicle to you free anywhere on Lanai. Each vehicle comes equipped with a CB radio and cell phone (in case you get stuck, they'll come and get you), as well as a winch and toolkit. In addition, as part of the rental fee, they'll supply you with all the beach gear you need (masks, fins, snorkels, towels, sunscreen, boogie boards, even fishing rods and reels) and provide a map of the best off-road trips.

A small fleet of rental vehicles is available at the **Dollar Rent-A-Car** desk at **Lanai City Service,** 10-36 Lanai Ave. (☎ **800/800-4000** for Dollar reservations; 808/244-9538 or 808/565-7227 for Lanai City Service). They have both cars and four-wheel-drive vehicles. Expect to pay about $60 a day for the cheapest car available, a Dodge Neon (the rate is 30% cheaper if you rent for a week or more) and $119 a day for a four-wheel-drive jeep (the rate drops 34% if you rent for a week or more).

Be warned: Gas is expensive on Lanai. At press time, it was $2.29 a gallon (versus $1.89 in Kona and $1.55 in Honolulu)—and those jeeps don't get good gas mileage. Since everything in Lanai City is within walking distance, it makes sense to just rent a jeep for the day (or days) that you want to explore the island. (The two big resort hotels run shuttle vans around the island, but you can only use them if you're staying at one of the hotels.) **Lanai City Service** (☎ **808/565-7227**) will provide taxi service from the airport to Lanai City for $5 per person; they'll also transport you from Lanai City to Hulopoe Beach for $10 per person one-way.

Whether or not you rent a car, sooner or later, you'll find yourself at Lanai City Service, the glorified name for the only gas station in town. The all-in-one grocery store, coffee bar, rental-car agency, and souvenir shop serves as the island's Grand Central Station; you can pick up information, directions, maps, and all the local gossip.

FAST FACTS: Lanai

Dentists For emergency dental care, call **Dr. Nick's Family Dentistry** at ☎ 808/565-7801.

Doctors Call **Lanai Family Health Center** at ☎ **808/565-6423** or the Lanai Community Hospital at ☎ **808/565-6411**.

Emergencies Call ☎ **911** for police, fire, and ambulance services. For non-emergencies, call the **Lanai Police** at ☎ **808/565-6428**.

Poison Control Center In an emergency, call ☎ **800/362-3585**.

Weather Reports Call the **National Weather Service** at ☎ **808/565-6033**.

3 Accommodations

by Jeanette Foster

The majority of the accommodations are located "in the village," as residents call Lanai City. Above the village is the luxurious Lodge at Koele, while down the hill at Hulopoe Bay are two options: the luxurious Manele Bay Hotel or tent camping under the stars at the park.

In addition to the choices listed below, also consider the B&B accommodations offered by **Delores Fabrao** (☎ **808/565-6134**), who has two guest rooms in her home: a double with a shared bathroom, and a family room that sleeps up to six ($55 double, $100 for four) with a private bathroom; she doesn't provide breakfast, but you'll have the run of the entire house, including the kitchen. At **Hale Moe** (☎ **808/565-9520**), host and Lanai native Momi Suzuki makes two bedrooms in her Lanai City home available to guests; both have private bathrooms, and guests are welcome to use the entertainment center, large deck, and Momi's two bicycles ($60 to $70 double). For a fully equipped, two-bedroom vacation rental that sleeps up to six, call **Hale O Lanai** in Lanai City (☎ **808/247-3637**); rates range from $95 to $125. Don't forget to add 10.17% in taxes to all accommodation bills. Parking is free.

Very Expensive

⭐ **The Lodge at Koele.** P.O. Box 310, Lanai City, HI 96793. ☎ **800/321-4666** or 808/565-7300. Fax 808/565-3868. 107 units. A/C MINIBAR TV TEL. $325–$485 double, $600–$1,500 suite. AE, CB, DC, MC, V.

This is the place to stay for a quiet, relaxing vacation in the cool mist of the mountains. The atmosphere is informal during the day, more formal after sunset (jackets required in main dining room). The Lodge, as folks here call it, stands in a 21-acre grove of Norfolk Island pines at 1,700 feet above sea level, 8 miles inland from any beach—a locus that flies in the face of conventional wisdom, which dictated for more than a century that the beach was the only place for a Hawaii vacation hotel.

The 102-room resort resembles a grand English country estate. Inside, heavy timbers, beamed ceilings, and the two huge stone fireplaces of the Great Hall complete the look. Oversized furniture sits invitingly around the fireplaces, and all the coffee-table books on Hawaii that you've ever wanted to read are scattered on the tables around you. Richly patterned rugs adorn the floor, while museum-quality art hangs on the walls. Cushioned wicker chairs on the long porches are perfect for a long afternoon with a good book.

The guest rooms continue the English theme with four-poster beds, sitting areas (complete with window seats for reading), flowery wallpaper, formal writing desks, and luxury bathrooms with oversized tubs and just about every amenity imaginable.

There are plenty of activities here and at the sister resort down the hill, Manele Bay, so you'll have the best of both hotels. Most guests who stay at the Lodge are looking for a slightly less frenzied vacation: relaxing out on the porch, reading or watching the turkeys mosey across the manicured lawns; strolling through the Japanese hillside garden; or watching the sun sink into the Pacific and the stars light up at night.

Dining/Diversions: A formal dining room serves dinner (see "Dining," below); a less formal interior terrace is open all day. Both use local island ingredients. Entertainment is limited to quiet, live music; hula; and periodic guest appearances by celebrities who chat informally in a drawing-room setting about their work (see "'Talk Story' with the Greats" under "Lanai After Dark," below).

Amenities: Complimentary shuttle service to the airport, beach, and Manele Bay Hotel. Complimentary coffee and tea in the lobby, and formal tea every afternoon. Twice-daily maid service, turndowns, some rooms with butler service. Golf at the 18-hole championship Greg Norman/Ted Robinson–designed course, the Experience at Koele; croquet lawns; stables; tennis courts; bikes; rental jeeps; an executive putting green; a pool; upcountry hiking trails; extensive lawns; and garden walks. Library, game room, bar, and music room. Guests have access to the Manele Bay facilities as well.

✪ **Manele Bay Hotel.** P.O. Box 310, Lanai City, HI 96793. ☎ **800/321-4666** or 808/565-7700. 250 units. A/C MINIBAR TV TEL. $275–$525 double, $725–$2,000 suite. AE, CB, DC, MC, V.

If you want to stay at the beach, come to this sunwashed southern bluff overlooking Hulopoe Beach, one of Hawaii's best stretches of golden sand. The U-shaped hotel steps down the hillside to the pool and that great beach, then fans out in oceanfront wings separated by gardens with lush flora, manmade waterfalls, lotus ponds, and streams. Bordered on the other side by golf greens on a hillside of dry land scrub, the hotel is a real oasis against the dry Arizona-like heat of Lanai's arid South Coast.

This is a traditional luxury beachfront hotel: open, airy, and situated so that every room has a peek of the big blue Pacific. The lobby is filled with murals depicting scenes from Hawaiian history, sea charts, potted palms, soft camel-hued club chairs, and handwoven kilim rugs. The oversized guest rooms resemble an English country house on the beach: sunny chintz fabrics, mahogany furniture, Audubon prints, huge marble bathrooms, and semiprivate lanais.

This resort is much less formal than the Lodge up the hill. Its proximity to the beach attracts more families, and because it's warmer here, people wander through the lobby in shorts and T-shirts. This is perfect for a beach vacation, with a few forays up to the Lodge and Lanai City to enjoy the mountain activities.

Dining/Diversions: Hulopoe Court features innovative Hawaii Regional Cuisine and ocean views; do not miss Chef Philippe Padovani's creations in the Ihilani, the specialty dining room (see "Dining," below, for a review of both). Entertainment is limited to quiet, live music; hula; and periodic guest-lecture appearances by celebrities (see "'Talk Story' with the Greats" box, below).

Amenities: Complimentary shuttle service to the airport, the Lodge at Koele, and Manele Boat Harbor. Twice-daily maid service; turndown; 13 butlered suites. Jack Nicklaus–designed Challenge at Manele adds 18 more holes to play, a seaside layout in nice contrast to the upland Experience (see "The Lodge at Koele," above). Watersports at the neighboring beach; plus pool, tennis, bicycling, game room, library, spa, historic tours, and jeep tours. Guests can also enjoy the amenities at The Lodge at Koele.

Moderate

✪ **Hotel Lanai.** 828 Lanai Ave. (P.O. Box 520), Lanai City, HI 96763. ☎ **800/795-7211** or 808/565-7211. Fax 808/565-6450. 11 units. $95–$105 double, $135 cottage double. Rates include continental breakfast. Extra person $10. AE, MC, V. Airport shuttle $5 round-trip.

This is the perfect place for families and other vacationers who can't afford to spend $300 to $400 a night for a hotel room but still want to enjoy the atmosphere and activities of Lanai. Just a few years ago, the Hotel Lanai, on a rise overlooking Lanai City, was the only place to stay and eat unless you knew someone who lived on the island. Built in the 1920s for VIP plantation guests, this clapboard plantation-era relic has retained its quaint character and lives on as a country lodge. Soon after the resorts opened, the owners of the Hotel Lanai gave their rustic hotel a $450,000 facelift and repositioned it as a B&B. In August 1996, a well-known chef from Maui, Henry Clay Richardson (formerly of the Kapalua Bay Hotel & Villas, David Paul's Lahaina Grill, and Gerard's Restaurant), became the inn's new owner and executive chef in the dining room (see "Dining," below).

The one-story wooden building is bordered by a verdant lawn, bright flowers, and a stalwart stand of pines. The rooms are small, clean, and newly decorated, plantation style, with Hawaiian quilts, wood furniture, and ceiling fans. The standard hotel rooms are extremely small but have private bathrooms (shower only), a double bed or two twin beds, and little else. The garden rooms, which are the largest, feature king beds and private bathrooms. The most popular are the lanai rooms, which feature a shared lanai with the room next door. They are smaller than the garden rooms and have queen beds, but the lanai is a great spot from which to sit and watch the sunset. The small, one-bedroom cottage on the property is perfect for a family of three or four adults. All rooms have phones, ceiling fans, and bathrooms with shower only. Only the cottage has a TV and bathtub.

The hotel serves as a down-home crossroads where total strangers meet local folks on the lanai to drink iced beer and "talk story" or play the ukulele and sing into the dark, tropic night. Often, a curious visitor in search of an authentic experience will join the party and discover Lanai's very Hawaiian heart. A restaurant is open for continental breakfast for guests only and open to the public for dinner daily.

Inexpensive

⭐ **Dreams Come True.** 547 12th St. (P.O. Box 525), Lanai City, HI 96763. ☎ **800/565-6961** or 808/565-6961. E-mail hunters@aloha.net. 3 units. $75 double. Rates include continental breakfast. Extra person $20. AE, DC, DISC, MC, V.

Your dreams just may come true in this quaint plantation house, tucked away among papaya, banana, lemon, and avocado trees in the heart of Lanai City, at 1,620 feet. Hosts Susan and Michael Hunter have filled their house with Southeast Asian antiques collected on their travels. Both are jewelers, and they operate a working studio on the premises. All three bedrooms have private bathrooms; two feature a four-poster canopied bed, with an additional single bed (perfect for a small family), while the third has just one queen bed. The common area looks out on the garden and is equipped with both TV and VCR. Breakfast usually consists of freshly baked bread with homemade jellies and jams, tropical fruit, juice, and coffee. The Hunters rent a nearby three-bedroom/two-bath house to families for $190 a night.

4 Dining

by Jocelyn Fujii

Dining on Lanai is uncomplicated and extreme. On this island of three hotels, five stores, and fewer than 3,000 residents, you can go from a greasy-spoon breakfast to a five-star dinner in less than a mile and a few hundred feet in altitude. When The Lodge at Koele and The Manele Bay Hotel opened their doors in 1990 and 1991, Lanai went from "Pineapple Island" to luxury resort—and it did so with a vengeance, quickly transforming its agricultural renown into a fine-dining cachet that immediately won top placement in the diner-rated Zagat Hawaii Restaurant Survey.

You can dine like a sultan on this island, but be prepared for high prices. The tony hotel restaurants require deep pockets (or bottomless expense accounts), and there are only a handful of other options.

✪ **Formal Dining Room.** The Lodge at Koele. ☎ **808/565-4580.** Reservations required. Jackets required. Main courses $32–$40. AE, DC, JCB, MC, V. Daily 6–9:30pm. AMERICAN.

Chef Edwin Goto's menu is a stroke of genius in this grand atmosphere of soaring ceilings, splendid fireplaces, and cheek-reddening upcountry chill. What else but American classics would suffice in a hotel with game rooms, pigskin chairs, and the elusive scent of pipe smoke wafting across wide verandas and wainscoted rooms? The octagonal-shaped dining room is elegant yet intimate, with a menu that has earned its rightful place in Hawaii's culinary hierarchy.

Roast rack of lamb and Lanai venison top the list for game lovers, the lamb served with stewed cannellini beans and grilled eggplant and the venison in a sour cherry–red wine reduction, served with grilled sweet potatoes and vegetables. The fish au courant, moi, is also an attraction, served braised with oven-dried tomatoes and crisp pancetta. And in the marinated and grilled quail, the hotel's famous pineapple cider has found its place in American cuisine. The Dining Room is known for its use of fresh herbs, vegetables, and fruit grown on the island, harvested just minutes away, and for its lodge-friendly cuisine—soups both hearty and elegant, and wintry delights of wild mushrooms, buttery squashes, local game, and elegant meats. Although pricey, for most visitors, it remains an unavoidable indulgence. The menu changes seasonally and always features a fresh seafood selection.

Hulopoe Court. Manele Bay Hotel. ☎ **808/565-7700.** Reservations recommended. Collared shirt required. Main courses $26–$32. AE, DC, JCB, MC, V. Daily 6–9:30am, 7–11pm. HAWAII REGIONAL.

Hulopoe is casual compared to the hotel's fine dining room, Ihilani, but formal compared to the Pool Grille, the lunchtime oasis for Manele Bay guests. The 17th-century palanquin in the adjoining lower lobby, the Asian accents, the tropical murals by gifted Lanai artists, and the high vaulted ceilings add up to an eclectic, elegant ambiance, with the view of Hulopoe Bay the crowning glory. There are some stunning entrées: taro-crusted ono (with ginger-chive mashed potatoes); steamed onaga with shiitake mushrooms; guava-glazed chicken breast with Molokai sweet potato; and memorable starters that include shrimp summer rolls, seared ahi, and hearts-of-palm salad.

Ihilani. The Manele Bay Hotel. ☎ **808/565-2290.** Reservations required. Jackets recommended. Main courses $32–$45; set menu $105 without wine, $145 with wine. AE, DC, JCB, MC, V. Daily 6–9:30pm. FRENCH-MEDITERRANEAN.

The Manele Bay's formal dining room sits across the lobby from Hulopoe Court; its lower ceilings (beautifully painted with bird-of-paradise murals) and pleasing design permit an ocean view and a clubby, darker, more intimate ambiance. There are three sections to the split-level dining room: the terrace, overlooking the ocean and pool; the indoor middle area next to the terrace; and the elevated dining area with banquettes and private niches. The inner area, with its rich, warm ambers and mauves and luscious teak gong and Queen Anne console, suits the Mediterranean fare best.

The menu will likely change with the arrival of a new chef (Philippe Padovani has left for Oahu). As of this writing, the choices are every bit as inviting as the ambiance, including pan-fried opakapa; roasted lamb loins in fresh truffle sauce and artichoke mousseline; and a dessert selection that is simply staggering—particularly the Hawaiian Vintage Chocolate desserts and the cheese tray with walnut bread.

The Terrace. The Lodge at Koele. ☎ **808/565-4580.** Reservations recommended. Breakfast main courses $7.25–$14.50, lunch main courses $9.75–$14, dinner main courses $16–$27. AE, DC, JCB, MC, V. Daily 6am–9:30pm. AMERICAN.

Located next to the Formal Dining Room, between the 35-foot-high Great Hall and a wall of glass looking out over prim English gardens, The Terrace is far from your typical hotel dining room. The food is fancy for comfort food, but it does, indeed, comfort. Hearty breakfasts of wild-rice waffles and warm cinnamon-bread pudding, lunches of seared chicken-breast-and-potato sandwiches with red-onion gravy, and grilled artichokes and crisp potatoes with garlic chive aïoli: these are some of the reasons everyone remembers The Terrace. In the evening, seafood; osso bucco; New York steak; barbecued Lanai venison meat loaf; and polenta with eggplant, leeks, porrobello mushrooms, and goat cheese help to satiate the upcountry hunger. In many other places, The Terrace would serve as the fine dining room instead of a full-service restaurant—but here, all standards are broken.

Moderate

Henry Clay's Rotisserie. In the Hotel Lanai, 828 Lanai Ave., Lanai City. ☎ **808/565-4700.** Main courses $8.50–$17.95. JCB, MC, V. Daily 5:30–9pm. AMERICAN.

Henry Clay Richardson, a New Orleans native, has made some considerable changes at what used to be the local hangout for hearty, country-style breakfasts. New additions include a cappuccino machine, sound system, and glass-enclosed viewing kitchen with rotisserie. The menu focuses on American country cuisine: fresh meats, seafood, and local produce. The meats, which could be rabbit, quail, venison, osso bucco, and plain old beef and chicken, are spit-roasted on the rotisserie. Appetizers such as Cajun shrimp and steamed manila clams reflect regional and international influences. From the rotisserie comes herb-marinated half chicken and Louisiana-style pork ribs, while gourmet pizzas and salads occupy the lighter end of the spectrum. The two fireplaces and pine-paneled walls add to the coziness of this old Lanai favorite.

Pool Grille. Manele Bay Hotel. ☎ **808/565-7700.** Main courses $6–$16. AE, DC, JCB, MC, V. Daily 11am–5pm. ECLECTIC.

The sybarite's world you've agreed to enter extends poolside as well as in the formal restaurants. At this, the most casual of the hotel's restaurants, you'll dine on $10 hamburgers (homemade bun, of course) and gourmet salads under beach umbrellas, in weather that can be sweltering during the summer and fall months. The salads ($9 to $16) are perfect for the weather and location—cool, light, and sumptuous, as in marinated grilled vegetables with Big Island goat cheese, spicy chicken-breast salad, poached chicken salad with avocado, tabouleh, Caesar with shrimp, and others. The grilled ahi sandwich and tuna pita are highly recommended.

Inexpensive

Blue Ginger Cafe. 409 Seventh St., Lanai City. ☎ **808/565-7016.** Most items less than $12. No credit cards. Daily 6am–9pm. COFFEE SHOP.

This is a very local, very casual, and moderately priced alternative to Lanai's fancy hotel restaurants. The four tables on the front porch face the cool Norfolk pines of Dole Park and are always filled with locals who "talk story" from morning to night. The tiny café is often jammed from 6 to 7am with construction workers on their way to work. The offerings are solid, no-nonsense, everyday fare: fried saimin (no MSG, a plus), the very popular hamburgers on homemade buns, and the mahi-mahi with capers in a white-wine sauce. Blue Ginger also serves a tasty $1.75 French toast of homemade bread, a vegetable lumpia (the Filipino version of a spring roll), and a homemade omelet for less than $5 that's reportedly luring Lodge guests away from their $20 breakfasts up the hill.

Pele's Other Garden. On Dole Park, 81 Houston St. ☎ **808/565-9628.** Most items less than $6. AE, DISC, MC, V. Mon–Thurs 11am–7pm, Fri–Sat 9am–9pm. DELI/PIZZERIA/JUICE BAR.

Healthy, tasty eats come streaming across the counter at this New York–style deli that breaks all the rules: it's healthy *and* delicious, and it's not expensive. Sandwiches, daily soup and menu specials, salads, pizza, fresh organic produce, fresh juices, and special touches such as top-quality roasted red peppers and free-range turkey are some of the features that make Pele's Other Garden a Lanai City must. Mostly it's take out, but there are a couple of tables on the veranda, facing the tree-shaded square. All menu items are made from natural and organic ingredients.

Tanigawa's. 419 Seventh St., Lanai City. ☎ **808/565-6537.** Reservations not accepted. Main courses less than $7. No credit cards. Sun–Tues, Thurs–Sat 6:30am–1pm. HAMBURGERS.

Formerly S. T. Properties, famous for its hamburgers, Tanigawa's has changed its name but remains the landmark that it's been since the 1920s. In those days, the tiny storefront sold canned goods and cigarettes; the 10 tables, hamburgers, and Filipino food came later. Jerry Tanigawa has kept his hole-in-the-wall a local institution, whose homemade hamburgers and bento lunches (rice with meat or fish, a plantation legacy) have fed two generations of Lanai residents. The fare—saimin, pork teriyaki, beef stew, and omelets—is a nod to sentiment, more greasy spoon than gourmet, and friendliest above all to the pocketbook.

5 Beaches

by Jeanette Foster

If you like big, wide, empty, golden sands and crystal-clear, cobalt-blue water full of bright tropical fish—and who doesn't?—go to Lanai. With 18 miles of sandy shoreline, Lanai has some of Hawaii's least crowded and most interesting beaches. One in particular is perfect for swimming, snorkeling, and watching spinner dolphins play: Hulopoe Beach, Lanai's best.

✪ HULOPOE BEACH

In 1997, Stephen Leatherman, of the University of Maryland, ranked Hulopoe the best beach in the United States. Leatherman, who compiles an annual ranking, considers 50 standards (including sand and waves, water quality, human use, lifeguard protection, noise, etc.) in judging some 650 public beaches every year. It's easy to see why he said this is the best: the bay at the foot of the Manele Bay Hotel is a protected marine preserve, and the schools of colorful fish know it. So do the spinner dolphins who come here to play, and the Pacific Humpback whales who cruise by in winter (that's when the mercury drops below 80°). This palm-fringed, gold-sand beach is bordered by black-lava fingers, protecting swimmers from the serious ocean currents that sweep around Lanai. In summer, Hulopoe is perfect for swimming, snorkeling, or just lolling about; the water temperature is usually in the mid-70s. The protected bay is usually safe, except when swells kick up in the winter. Hulopoe is also Lanai's premier beach park, with a grassy lawn, picnic tables, barbecue grills, rest rooms, showers, and ample parking.

HULOPOE'S TIDE POOLS Some of the best lava-rock tide pools in Hawaii are found along the south shore of Hulopoe Bay. These miniature Sea Worlds are full of strange creatures: asteroids (sea stars) and holothurians (sea cucumbers), not to

⭐ Frommer's Favorite Lanai Experiences

Snorkel Hulopoe Beach. Crystal-clear water teems with brilliant tropical fish off a postcard-perfect beach that's one of Hawaii's best. There are tide pools to explore, waves to play in, and other surprises—like a pod of spinner dolphins that often makes a splashy entrance.

Explore the Garden of the Gods. Eroded by wind, rain, and time, these geologic badlands are worth visiting at sunrise or sunset, when the low light plays tricks on the land—and your mind.

Hike the Munro Trail. The 11-mile Munro Trail is a lofty, rigorous hike along the rim of an old volcano, across a razorback ridge through a cloud forest, that offers big views of the nearby islands. Some hike the ridge to see the rain forest, others take a four-wheel-drive vehicle to spend more time on top of the island, where you might catch a rare five-island view.

Four-Wheel It. Four-wheeling is a way of life on Lanai, since there's only 30 miles of pavement. Plenty of rugged trails lead to deserted beaches, abandoned villages, and wild game-filled valleys. No other island offers off-road adventures like this one.

Camp under the Stars. The campsites at Hulope Beach Park are as about as close to the heavens as you can get. The sound of the crashing surf will lull you to sleep at night, while the sound of chirping birds will wake you in the morning. If you're into roughing it, this is a great way to experience Lanai.

Beachcomb at Shipwreck Beach. This 8-mile stretch along the northeastern shore is a great place to dig up treasures of the sea, or perhaps to pick up a new pair of slippers: You may notice that some Lanai residents wear two different slippers, usually because they've found a perfectly good, though unmatched, pair on a recent beachcombing trip. Occasionally, a glass ball from a Japanese fishing boat will float in—in Hawaii, this is considered the greatest beachcombing treasure you can find.

Watch the Whales at Polihua Beach. Located on the northern coast, this beach—which gets its name from the turtles that nest here—is a great place to spend the day scanning the ocean for whales during the winter months.

mention spaghetti worms, Barber Pole shrimp, and Hawaii's favorite local delicacy, the opihi, a tasty morsel also known as the limpet. Youngsters enjoy swimming in the enlarged tide pool at the eastern edge of the bay.

When you explore tide pools, do it at low tide. Never turn your back on the waves. Wear tennis shoes or reef walkers, as wet rocks are slippery. There's a kapu against collecting specimens in this marine preserve, so don't take any souvenirs home.

SHIPWRECK BEACH

This 8-mile-long windswept strand from Polihua Beach to Kahokunui—named for the rusty ship, *Liberty*, stuck on the coral reef—is a sailor's nightmare and a beachcomber's dream. The strong currents yield all sorts of flotsam, from Japanese handblown-glass fish floats and rare pelagic paper nautilus shells to lots of junk. This is also a great place to spot whales from December to April, when the Pacific humpbacks cruise in from Alaska to winter in the calm offshore waters. The road to the beach is paved most of the way, but you really need a four-wheel drive to get down here.

POLIHUA BEACH

So many sea turtles once hauled themselves out of the water to lay their eggs in the sunbaked sand on Lanai's northwestern shore that Hawaiians named the beach there *Polihua*, or "egg nest." Although Hawaii's endangered green sea turtles are making a comeback, they're seldom seen here now. You're more likely to spot an offshore whale (in season) or the perennial litter that washes up onto this deserted north shore beach, at the end of Polihua Road, a 4-mile jeep trail. There are no facilities except fishermen's huts and driftwood shelters. Bring water and sunscreen. Beware the strong currents, which make the water unsafe for swimming. This strand's really ideal for beach-combing (those little green-glass Japanese fishing-net floats often show up here), fishing, or just being alone.

6   Hitting the Water

by Jeanette Foster

Lanai has Hawaii's best water clarity, because it lacks major development and has low rainfall and runoff, and its coast is washed clean daily by the sea current known as "The Way to Tahiti." But the strong sea currents pose a threat to swimmers, and there are few good surf breaks. Most of the aquatic adventures—swimming, snorkeling, scuba diving—are centered on the somewhat protected south shore, around Hulopoe Bay.

When traveling to Lanai, bring your own snorkel gear (or boogie board or surf-board), as there are no equipment rentals on the island. **Snorkel Bob's** on Maui, Oahu, Kauai, and the Big Island allows you to rent equipment on one island and return it on another. For details on the other activities listed below, see "The Active Vacation Planner" in chapter 3.

BODY BOARDING (BOOGIE BOARDING), BODYSURFING & BOARD SURFING

When the surf's up on Lanai, it's a real treat. Under the right conditions, Hulopoe and Polihua are both great for catching waves. You've got to bring your own board, as the beach shack at Hulopoe Beach has complimentary boogie boards for hotel guests (Manele Bay and The Lodge at Koele) only. Or you can rent a four-wheel Land Rover with **Red Rover**, P.O. Box 464 (located across the street from the island's only gas station, Lanai City Service), Lanai City, HI 96763 (☎ **808/565-7722;** fax 808/565-6322), and they provide free boogie boards with every rental.

SCUBA DIVING

Two of Hawaii's best-known dive spots are found in Lanai's clear waters, just off the south shore: **Cathedrals I and II**, so named because the sun lights up the underwater grotto like a magnificent church. **Trilogy Charters** (☎ **800/TRI-COON** or 808/565-2274; www.maui.net/~trilogy; e-mail trilogy@maui.net) offers sailing, diving, and snorkeling trips on their trimaran. The cost is $85 for snorkelers and $120 for certified scuba divers for a one-tank dive. The trip, from 9am to 1pm, includes continental breakfast, lunch, and all snorkeling and diving equipment.

SNORKELING

Hulopoe is Lanai's best snorkeling spot. Fish are abundant and friendly in the marine-life conservation area. Try the lava-rock points at either end of the beach and around the lava pools. Snorkel gear is free to guests of the two resorts. No snorkel rentals are available, so bring your own if you're not staying at one of the big two resorts, or call

Red Rover (☎ 808/565-7722), which provides free snorkeling gear with each four-wheel Land Rover rental.

SPORTFISHING

Jeff Menze, a Lanai resident, will take you out on the 28-foot Omega boat, *Spinning Dolphin* (☎ 808/565-6613). His 4-hour fishing charters cost $400 for six people, or $600 for six people for 8 hours. He also has exclusive 3-hour whale-watching charters, which are $300 for six passengers.

7 Hiking & Camping

by Jeanette Foster

HIKES
A LEISURELY MORNING HIKE

The 3-hour **Koele Nature Hike** starts by the reflecting pool in the backyard of the Lodge at Koele and takes you on a 5-mile loop trail through a cathedral of Norfolk Island pines, into Hulopoe Valley, past wild ginger, and up to Koloiki Ridge, with its panoramic view of Maunalei Valley and Molokai and Maui in the distance. You're welcome to take the hike even if you're not a guest at the Lodge. The trailhead isn't obvious—just keep going mauka toward the trees—and the path isn't clearly marked, but the concierge will give you a free map.

THE CHALLENGING MUNRO TRAIL

This tough, 11-mile (round-trip) uphill climb through the groves of Norfolk pines is a lung-buster, but you'll get a bonus if you reach the top: that breathtaking view of Molokai, Maui, Kahoolawe, the peaks of the Big Island, and—on a really clear day—Oahu in the distance. Figure on 7 hours. The trail begins at Lanai Cemetery along Keomoku Road (Hwy. 44) and follows Lanai's ancient caldera rim, ending up at the island's highest point, Lanaihale. Go in the morning for the best visibility. After 4 miles, you'll get a view of Lanai City. The weary retrace their steps from there, while those determined to see "the view" go the last 1½ miles to the top. Diehards go down Lanai's steep south-crater rim to join the highway to Manele Bay.

For more details on the Munro Trail—including details on four-wheel-driving it to the top—see "Seeing the Sights," below.

A SELF-GUIDED NATURE TRAIL

In 1997, with the help of some 40 volunteers, Nature Conservancy of Hawaii completed a self-guided nature trail open to the public in the Kanepuu Preserve. The trailhead is clearly marked on the Polihua Road on the way to the Garden of the Gods. The trail is about a 10- to 15-minute walk through eight stations, with interpretive signs explaining the natural or cultural significance of the area. Kanepuu is one of the last remaining examples of the type of forest that once covered the dry lowlands throughout the state. Here, there are some 49 plant species that are found only in Hawaii (such as sandalwood and Hawaiian gardenia, both listed as endangered species). The Nature Conservancy conducts guided hikes every month; call ☎ 808/565-7430.

CAMPING AT HULOPOE BEACH PARK

There is only one place to "legally" camp on Lanai: Hulopoe Beach Park, which is owned by The Lanai Company. To camp in this exquisite beach park, with its crescent-shaped, white-sand beach bordered by kiawe trees, contact the **Lanai**

Company, P.O. Box 310, Lanai City, HI 96763 (☎ **808/565-3982**). There is a $5 registration fee, plus $5 per person, per night. Holupoe has six campsites, each of which can accommodate up to six people. Facilities include rest rooms, running water, showers, barbecue areas, and picnic tables.

Bring your own camping equipment, as there is nowhere to rent gear on Lanai. The Lanai Company recommends a tent (rain can be expected year-round), a cooking stove or hibachi (the number of barbecues are limited), and insect repellent (mosquitoes are plentiful).

8 Golf, Horseback Riding & Tennis

by Jeanette Foster

GOLF

⭐ **The Challenge at Manele.** P.O. Box L, Lanai City, HI 96763. ☎ **808/565-2222.** Located next to the Manele Bay Hotel in Holopoe Bay.

This target-style, desert-links course, designed by Jack Nicklaus, is one of the most "challenging" courses in the state. First of all, check out the local rules: "No retrieving golf balls from the 150-foot cliffs on the ocean holes 12, 13, or 17," and "All whales, axis deer, and other wild animals are considered immovable obstructions." That's just a hint of the uniqueness of this course routed among lava outcroppings, archaeological sites, kiawe groves, and ilima trees. Two of the more challenging holes of this 7,039-yard, par-72 course are the signature 12th hole, where you simply tee off a couple of hundred yards across the Pacific Ocean 150 yards below (bring extra balls); and the par-4 17th, where you tee off on the ocean cliff across a ravine to a sloping, narrow, downhill fairway (shoot long). The five sets of staggered tees give everyone, from the casual golfer to the pro, a challenging game. Rates are $100 for guests of Manele Bay Hotel or Koele Lodge and $150 for nonguests. You can get a rate for play at both this course and The Experience at Koele for $150 for hotel guests and $225 for nonguests, plus $22 for the cart rental for the second round. Facilities include clubhouse, pro shop, rentals, practice area, lockers, and showers.

⭐ **The Experience at Koele.** P.O. Box L, Lanai City, HI 96763. ☎ **808/565-4653.** Located next to the Lodge at Koele in Lanai City.

When this par-72 uplands course opened in 1991, it was voted "Best New Golf Course" by *Fortune* magazine and one of 1991's "Top 10 New Resort Courses" by *Golf* magazine. This traditional course, designed by Greg Norman with fairway architecture by Ted Robinson, has a very different front and back nine holes. You start off on a high plateau at nearly 2,000 feet, where Mother Nature reigns; Cook Island and Norfolk pines, indigenous plants, and water—lots of water, including seven lakes, flowing streams, cascading waterfalls, and one green (the 17th) completely surrounded by a lake. All goes well until you hit the signature hole, number eight, where you tee off from a 250-foot elevated tee to a fairway bordered by a lake on the right and trees and dense shrubs on the left. After you have recovered, the back nine holes drop dramatically through ravines filled with pine, koa, and eucalyptus trees. The grand finale, the 18th, a par five, features a green rimmed by waterfalls which flow into a lake on the left side. To give golfers a break, Norman and Robinson have added four different sets of tees to level the playing field. Rates are $100 for guests of Manele Bay Hotel or Koele Lodge and $150 for nonguests. You can get a rate for play at both this course and The Challenge at Manele for $150 for hotel guests and $225 for nonguests, plus $22 for the cart rental for the second round. Facilities include clubhouse, pro shop, rentals, practice area, lockers, and showers.

Cavendish Golf Course, (no phone) Located next to the Lodge at Koele in Lanai City.

It's a quirky par-36, nine-hole public course with not only no clubhouse or club pros, but also no tee times, scorecards, or club rentals. To play, just show up, put a donation ($5 to $10 would be nice) into the little wooden box next to the first tee, and hit away. The 3,071-yard, E. B. Cavendish-designed course was built by the Dole plantation in 1947 for its employees. The greens are a bit bumpy—nothing will roll straight here—but the views of Lanai are great, and the temperatures are usually quite mild.

HORSEBACK RIDING

A great way to explore Lanai's unique landscape is by horse. You can venture up wooded upland areas that are impossible to get to, even in a four-wheel-drive vehicle. **The Stables at Koele** (☎ 808/565-4424) offer various rides, starting at $35 for a 1-hour trip. We recommend the 2-hour **Paniolo Trail Ride,** where you can escape into the hills surrounding Koele. Meander through guava groves and patches of iron-wood trees, with glimpses of axis deer, quail, wild turkeys, and Santa Gertrudis cattle, and end with panoramic views of Maui and Lanai. The cost is $65. Long pants and shoes are required; safety helmets are provided. Carry a jacket, as the weather is chilly and rain is frequent. Children must be at least 9 years old and 4 feet tall. The maximum weight limit is 250 pounds.

TENNIS

Public courts, lit for night play as well as day, are available in Lanai City at no charge; call ☎ 808/565-6979 for reservations. Guests staying at the Lodge at Koele or the Manele Bay Hotel have complimentary tennis privileges at either the Tennis Center at Manele, with its six Plexi-paved courts, a fully-equipped pro shop, and tournament facilities; or at the courts at Koele. Instruction is available for a fee. For information, call ☎ 808/565-2072.

9 Seeing the Sights

by Jeanette Foster

You'll need a four-wheel-drive vehicle to reach all the sights listed below. Renting a jeep is an expensive proposition on Lanai—about $120 a day—so we suggest that you rent one just for the day (or days) you plan on sightseeing; otherwise, it's easy enough to get to the beach and around Lanai City without your own wheels. For details on how to rent a jeep, see "Getting Around," above.

✪ GARDEN OF THE GODS

A dirt jeep road leads out of Lanai City, through the now uncultivated pineapple fields, and past the Kanepuu Preserve (a dry-land forest preserve teeming with rare plant and animal life) to the so-called Garden of the Gods, out on Lanai's north shore. This place has little to do with gods, Hawaiian or otherwise. It is, however, the ultimate rock garden: a rugged, barren, beautiful place full of rocks strewn by volcanic forces and shaped by the elements into an infinite variety of shapes and colors: brilliant reds, oranges, ochres, and yellows.

Scientists have numerous explanations for how these boulders got here: Some claim it's an "ongoing post-erosional event," while others say they're "plain and simple badlands." However, ancient Hawaiians considered this desolate, windswept place an entirely supernatural phenomenon. Take a four-wheel-drive ride out here and decide for yourself which explanation you accept.

Go early in the morning or just before sunset, when the light casts eerie shadows on the mysterious lava formations that dot the amber- and ocher-colored ground. Drive west from the Lodge on Polihua Road; in about 2 miles, you'll see a handpainted sign that'll point you in the right direction, left down a one-lane, red-dirt road through a kiawe forest and past sisal and scrub to the site.

✪ FIVE ISLANDS AT A SINGLE GLANCE: THE MUNRO TRAIL

In the first golden rays of dawn, when lone owls swoop low over abandoned pineapple fields, hop into your rented Jeep and head out on the two-lane blacktop toward Mt. Lanaihale, the 3,370-foot summit of Lanai. Your destination is the Munro Trail, the narrow, winding ridge trail that runs across Lanai's razorback spine to the summit. From here, hopefully, you will be able to see a rare Hawaii treat: five islands at once. On a clear day, you can see all the main islands in the Hawaiian chain except Kauai.

Lanai's chief arboreal feature isn't the palm tree, the usual tropical icon of Hawaii, but two other interesting Pacific trees: the Norfolk Island and the Cook Island pines, so symmetrical that they look like artificial silk trees made in China. They're everywhere—on ridge lines, in the town square, and on the summit, where they do more than look picturesque: Moisture-laden clouds get snagged on the sharp boughs of the summit trees and shed welcome rain on the island, which receives a precious 37 inches a year. (Oahu's Manoa Valley, by comparison, gets 158 inches a year.) New Zealander George Campbell Munro, who came to Hawaii in 1909 to collect birds, was first to figure out this rainmaking technique, which involves hydraulics far too complex to be explained fully here. He planted the pines on horseback, dropping seeds wherever he went to both promote rain and check erosion. The summit trail is named in his memory.

When it rains, the Munro Trail becomes slick and boggy with major washouts. Rainy-day excursions often end with a rental Jeep on the hook of the island's lone tow truck—and a $150 tow charge. You could even slide off into a major gulch and never be found, so don't try it. But in late August and September, when trade winds stop and the air over the islands stalls in what is called a *kona* condition, Mt. Lanaihale's suddenly visible peak becomes an irresistible attraction.

When you're on Lanai, look to the summit. If it's clear in the morning, get a four-wheel-drive vehicle and take the Munro Trail to the top. Look for a red-dirt road off Manele Road (Hwy. 440), about 5 miles south of Lanai City; turn left and head up the ridge line. No sign marks the peak. Nothing says, "Summit 3,370 feet," so you have to keep an eye out. Look for a wide spot in the road and a clearing that falls sharply to the sea.

The islands stand in order on the flat blue sea, just like a real-life topographic map: Kahoolawe. Maui. The Big Island of Hawaii. Even Molokini's tiny crescent. Even the summits show. You can see the silver domes of Space City on Haleakala; Puu Moaulanui, the tongue-twisting summit of Kahoolawe; and, looming like the mighty sea mountain it is, Mauna Kea peering above the clouds. At another clearing farther along the thickly forested ridge, all of Molokai, including the 4,961-foot summit of Kamakou, and the faint outline of Oahu (more than 30 miles across the sea) are visible. You actually can't see all five in a single glance anymore, because George Munro's thriving pine forest blocks the view. The old forester would have been delighted.

For details on hiking the trail, see "Hiking & Camping," above.

LUAHIWA PETROGLYPH FIELD

With more than 450 known petroglyphs in Hawaii at 23 sites, Lanai is second only to the Big Island in its wealth of prehistoric rock art, but you'll have to search a little to find it. Some of the best examples are on the outskirts of Lanai City, on a hillside site known as Luahiwa Petroglyph Field. The characters you'll see incised on 13 boulders in this grassy 3-acre knoll include a running man, a deer, a turtle, a bird, a goat, and even a rare, curly-tailed Polynesian dog (some latter-day wag has put a leash on him—some joke).

HOW TO FIND LUAHIWA

On the road to Hulopoe Beach, about 2 miles out of Lanai City, look to the left, up on the slopes of the crater, for a cluster of reddish-tan boulders (which ancients believed formed a rain *heiau*, or shrine, where people came up gods Ku and Hina to nourish their crops). A cluster of spiky century plants marks the spot. Take any dirt road that veers across the abandoned pineapple fields to the boulders. Go between 3pm and sunset for ideal viewing and photo ops.

KAUNOLU VILLAGE

Out on Lanai's nearly vertical Gibraltar-like sea cliffs is an old royal compound and fishing village. Now a national historic landmark and one of Hawaii's most treasured ruins, it's believed to have been inhabited by King Kamehameha the Great and hundreds of his closest followers about 200 years ago.

Ruins of 86 house platforms and 35 stone shelters have been identified on both sides of Kaunolu Gulch. The residential complex also includes the Halulu Heiau temple, named after a mythical man-eating bird. His Majesty's royal retreat is thought to have stood on the eastern edge of Kaunolu Gulch, overlooking the rocky shore facing Kahekili's Leap, a 62-foot-high bluff named for the mighty Maui chief who leaped off cliffs as a show of bravado. Nearby are burial caves, a fishing shrine, a lookout tower, and many warrior-like stick figures carved on boulders. Just offshore stands the telltale fin of little Shark Island, a popular dive spot that teems with bright tropical fish and, frequently, sharks.

Excavations are underway to discover more about how ancient Hawaiians lived, worked, and worshiped on Lanai's leeward coast. Who knows? The royal fishing village may yet yield the bones of King Kamehameha. His burial site, according to legend, is known only to the moon and the stars.

It's a hot, dry, dusty, slow-going 3-mile Jeep drive from Lanai City to Kaunolu, but the mini-expedition is worth it. Take plenty of water, don a hat to protect you against the sun, and wear sturdy shoes.

KANEPUU PRESERVE

Don't expect giant sequoias big enough to drive a car through; this ancient forest on the island's western plateau is so fragile, you can only visit once a month. Kanepuu, which has 48 species of plants unique to Hawaii, including the endangered Hawaiian gardenia (*na'u*) and the once-plentiful sandalwood (*iliahi*), survives under the Nature Conservancy's protective wing. Botanists say the 590-acre forest is the last dry lowland forest in Hawaii; the others have all vanished, trashed by axis deer, agriculture, or "progress."

Among the botanical marvels of this dry forest are the remains of *olopua* (native olive), *lama* (native ebony), *mau hau hele* (a native hibiscus) and the rare *'aiea* trees, which were used for canoe parts.

Due to the forest's fragile nature, guided hikes are led only 12 times a year, on a monthly, reservations-only basis. Contact the **Nature Conservancy Oahu Land Preserve** manager at 1116 Smith St., Suite 201, Honolulu, HI 96817 (☎ **808/537-4508**), to reserve.

OFF THE TOURIST TRAIL: KEOMOKU VILLAGE

If you have absolutely nothing better to do, are sunburnt lobster red, have read all the books you brought, and are starting to get island fever, take a little drive to Keomoku Village, on Lanai's East Coast.

You're really off the tourist trail now. All that's in Keomoku, a ghost town since the mid-1950s, is a 1903 clapboard church in disrepair, an overgrown graveyard, an excellent view across the 9-mile Auau Channel to Maui's crowded Kaanapali Beach, and some really empty beaches that are perfect for a picnic or a snorkel. This former ranching and fishing village of 2,000 was the first non-Hawaiian settlement on Lanai, but it dried up after droughts killed off the Maunalei Sugar Company. The village, such as it is, is a great little escape from Lanai City. Follow Keomoku Road for 8 miles to the coast, turn right on the sandy road, and keep going for 5.7 miles.

10 Shopping

by Jocelyn Fujii

Akamai Trading. 408 Eighth St. ☎ 808/565-6587.

Located between Richard's and Pine Isle on Dole Park, Akamai sells newspapers and magazines, cappuccino, soft-serve ice cream, fresh pastries and bagels, Lanai T-shirts, inexpensive Island gifts, and souvenir items. Same-day film processing appeals to visitors.

Gifts with Aloha. On Dole Park, at Eighth and Houston sts. ☎ 808/565-6589.

Phoenix and Kimberly Dupree decided to open a store with their favorite things, and that meant gift items by Hawaii artists, children's books and toys, select jams and jellies, and Hawaiian quilt pillows and kits. And aloha shirts, too. Handmade earrings, raku vessels, gourmet teas, handpoured candles, and aloha wear serve equally well as souvenirs to go or items for life on Lanai.

International Food & Clothing. 833 Ilima Ave. ☎ 808/565-6433.

Old-timers still call it the "Dela Cruz" store, after the family that opened it in 1952. Again, the basics: groceries, a few housewares, T-shirts, hunting and fishing supplies, over-the-counter drugs, paper goods, and hardware.

Lanai Art Program. 339 Seventh St. ☎ 808/565-7503.

This is the retail space for a not-for-profit arts program that supports and showcases Lanai artists and shares their work in classes for adults and children. Located between the Laundromat and the community college office, Lanai Art Program displays and sells jewelry, ceramics, watercolors, woodworks, and other two- and three-dimensional pieces. Fifteen artists, all from this island, participate in the program. Classes are offered in the schools and at this center, where the artists share their skills in a pottery barn, glass shop, and wood shop; and classes in painting, wood crafts, and sculpting.

Lanai Marketplace. Dole Square.

Everyone on Lanai, it seems, is a backyard farmer; from 8am to noon on Saturday, they all throng to the square to sell their dewy-fresh produce, home-baked breads, plate lunches, and handicrafts. This is Lanai's version of the green market: petite in scale, like the island, but charming and unpretentious, especially in the shade of the sky-high pine trees that line the park.

Dolores Fabrao's jams and jellies, under the Fabrao House label (☎ 808/565-6134, if you want to special order), are a big seller at the market and at the resort gift shops where they're sold. The 7 exotic flavors include pineapple-coconut, pineapple-mango, papaya, guaivi (strawberry guava), poha (gooseberry) in season, passion fruit, Surinam cherry, and the very tart karamay jelly. All fruits are grown on the island; gift packs and bags are available.

ⓘ Adventures for Kids (& Kids at Heart)

Explore Hulopoe Tide Pools (*see p. 519*) An entire world of marine life lives in the tide pools on the eastern side of Hulopoe Bay. Not only are there tiny fish swimming around, but everything in the waters is small—kid-size. After examining the wonders of the tide pool, check out the larger swimming holes in the lava rock, perfect for keiki swimming.

Hunt for Petroglyphs (*see p. 525*) The Luahiwa Petroglyphs Field, located just outside Lanai City, is spread out over a 3-acre site. Make it a game: whoever finds the most petroglyphs gets ice cream from the Pine Isle Market.

Listen to Storytelling at the Lanai Library (*see p. 529*) Check with the Lanai Library (Fraser Ave., near Fifth St., Lanai City; ☎ **808/565-6996**) to see if any storytelling or other activities for children are scheduled. The events are usually free and open to everyone.

Run with the Wind (*see p. 512*) Play hide-and-seek or any other game in the town square, Dole Park (bordered by Fraser Avenue, Lanai Avenue, Seventh Street, and Eighth Street), which has plenty of room for active children to run to their heart's content.

Pele's Garden Health Food Store. 811 Houston St. ☎ **808/565-9629.**
Lanai residents have embraced Beverly Zigmond's 500-square-foot store with open arms. Tucked around the corner from Dole Park, it opened in July 1995 with an assortment of vitamins, herbs, homeopathics, and supplements, as well as a complete line of natural and organic groceries, including baby food, natural pet products, nondairy items, free-range chicken, turkey products, and health and beauty aids.

Pine Isle Market. 356 Eighth St. ☎ **808/565-6047.**
A two-generation local landmark, Pine Isle specializes in locally caught fresh fish when it's available. Akule (big-eyed scad), opelu (mackerel scad), onaga (ruby snapper), opakapaka (pink snapper), mahi-mahi (dolphin fish), ahi (tuna), and other fish from local waters make their way to the seafood counter soon after being caught. You can also shop here for fresh herbs and spices from Pete Felipe's garden, fishing gear, canned goods, electronic games, and the basic essentials of work and play.

Richard's Shopping Center. 434 Eighth St.
The Tamashiros' family business has been on the square since 1946, and except for the merchandise, not much has changed. The "shopping center" is, in fact, a general store that sells groceries, paper products, ethnic foods, meats (mostly frozen), a few pieces of clothing, liquor, film, sunscreens and other recreational needs, and sundries. Until recently, you could still unearth some pre–World War II items in the far niches (I still treasure my wooden ginger grater found there years ago), but these days, the merchandise reflects the wants and needs of the island's modern mix—more visitors, and a declining number of plantation workers.

11 Lanai After Dark

by Jocelyn Fujii

Once, when I inquired about nightlife on Lanai, an island woman I had just met raised her eyebrows in mock umbrage. "Oh," she said, "that's personal."

"Talk Story" with the Greats: Lanai's Visiting Artist Program

Not so very long ago, before CNN, e-mail, faxes, and modems, the word spread in person, on the lips of those who chanced by these remote islands, the most distant populated place on earth. Visitors were always welcome, especially if they had a good story to tell. The *tusitala*, or storyteller, was always held in high regard; Hawaii's kings invited them to the grass palace to discuss topics of contemporary life. Maybe you've seen the pictures in history books: King Kalakaua and Robert Louis Stevenson sitting on the beach at Waikiki, the famous author regaling His Majesty with bons mots. Or jaunty Jack London describing the voyage of his Snark to Queen Liliuokalani. In Hawaiian pidgin, it's called "talk story."

Hawaii grew up with this grand tradition of welcoming performing artists from every corner of the globe. Sooner or later, everyone from Kwame Ture to Tab Hunter seems to wash ashore like a note in a bottle. It's amazing, really. You never know who's going to drop in on Hawaii. Islanders may live apart from the continental drift of history, but such brief intense visits illuminate the lives of these insular folks. Joan Didion once remarked that Honolulu without visitors "would be Racine, Wisconsin, Saturday night," a fate presumably worse than death.

It doesn't just happen in Honolulu. When The Lodge at Koele opened, David Murdock invited a few friends over. The "friends" just happened to be the late Henry Mancini, Sidney Sheldon, and Michael York, and they all had a fabulous time in the Great Hall, singing, playing the piano, and reciting poetry. Kurt Matsumoto, general manager at The Lodge, liked what he saw and scheduled more informal gatherings of creative people. "We never had anything like this on this island before," said Matsumoto, born and reared on Lanai, where the only "live" entertainment in plantation days was chicken fights.

In December 1992, the two resorts began the Lanai Visiting Artists Program. To this former black hole of art and culture come the literati of America, in a new version of "talk story." On any given weekend, you may find yourself in the company of poets, musicians, writers, actors, filmmakers, chefs, and other creative types. You can plan your vacation with, say, classical pianist André Watts, humorist Calvin Trillin, author John McPhee, "A Prairie Home Companion" host Garrison Keillor, jazz legend Cleo Laine, chef Larry Forgione (of New York's An American Place), *In the Name of the Father* screenwriter Terry George, award-winning short-story author David Wong Louie, best-selling novelist and screenwriter Susan Isaacs, or who knows which Pulitzer Prize or Academy Award winner, each sharing his or her talent and insights in a casual, living-room atmosphere.

Now, with the Lanai Visiting Artists Program, even this little island is no Racine, Wisconsin.

The program is free and open to everyone, so call **The Lodge at Koele** at ☎ **808/565-7300** to see who's visiting while you're on Lanai.

—*Jeanette Foster*

Except for special programs such as the annual **Pineapple Festival** in May, when some of Hawaii's best musicians arrive to show their support for Lanai (see "Hawaii Calendar of Events" in chapter 3), the only regular nightlife venues are the Lanai Playhouse, at the corner of Seventh and Lanai avenues, and the two resorts, the Lodge at Koele and Manele Bay Hotel.

The **Lanai Playhouse** is a historic 1920s building that has received awards for its renovations. When it opened in 1993, the 150-seat venue stunned residents by offering first-run movies with Dolby sound—quite contemporary for anachronistic Lanai. Except for epics (such as *Titanic*), when only one screening is given, Lanai Playhouse usually shows two movies each evening from Friday to Monday, at 6:30pm and 8:30pm. Tickets are $6 for adults and $3.50 for kids, and five "movie bucks" accumulated on Sundays get you one free ticket. On Tuesday and Wednesday nights, the only show, at 7pm, costs $3.50.

The Hotel Lanai has discontinued its weekend program of live music, while the Lodge at Koele has stepped up its live entertainment. In the **Lodge's Great Hall,** in front of its manorial fireplaces, visiting artists from Oahu or Maui bring contemporary Hawaiian, jazz, Broadway, classical, and other genres to listeners who sip port and fine liqueurs while sinking into plush chairs. The special programs are on weekends, but throughout the week, some form of nightly entertainment takes place in the Great Hall from 7 to 10pm. In the lounge area near the main lobby of the **Manele Bay Hotel,** above Hulani, a pianist plays nightly from 7 to 10pm.

Both the Lodge at Koele and Manele Bay Hotel are known for their Visiting Artist Program (see box above), which brings acclaimed literary and performing artists from across the country to this tiny island. These are scheduled throughout the year, usually on a monthly or bimonthly basis.

Other than that, what happens after dark is really up to you. Dinner becomes leisurely extended entertainment. You can repair to your room with that book you've been meaning to read. You can find an after-dinner crowd in the Tea Room at Koele or a game of billiards at Manele, the local folks out on the veranda of the Hotel Lanai will be happy to welcome you, and there's always a TV set somewhere to remind you of the great world beyond.

10

Kauai, the Garden Isle

On any list of the world's most spectacular islands, Kauai ranks right up there with Bora Bora, Huahine, and Rarotonga. It's full of paradoxes and contradictions. It's a small island, but to adequately see it, you have to take to the air and view it from a helicopter. It gets more than its fair shower of tropical downpours, but that just means it's lush and green—and that there's a profusion of rainbows. Kauai feels remote, but it's just a 30-minute plane ride from the urban bustle of Honolulu.

All the Eden-like elements are here: moody rain forests, majestic cliffs, jagged peaks, emerald valleys, palm trees swaying in the breeze, daily rainbows, and some of the most spectacular golden beaches you'll find anywhere. Soft tropical air, sunrise birdsong, essence of ginger and plumeria, golden sunsets, sparkling waterfalls—you don't just go to Kauai, you absorb it with every sense.

Kauai's great natural beauty derives from its inevitable decline and erosion. Ten million years of wind and rain and epic hurricanes have carved the landscape, shaping now-dormant volcanoes into jagged peaks and reducing giant boulders into miles of soft, white-sand beaches. On September 11, 1992, Hurricane Iniki eroded the island by a century in a single day. Kauai's fabled Na Pali Coast is said to be the fastest-eroding land on earth. Born at the beginning of the archipelago, Kauai is enjoying its last days in the sun— "days" that will last at least a million years or more. Still, the very best time to enjoy Kauai is right now—and nearly a million people do each year.

Essentially a single large shield volcano that rises 3 miles above the sea floor, Kauai lies 90 miles across open ocean from Oahu, but it seems at least a half-century removed in time. The oldest and most remote of the main islands, it's often called "the separate kingdom," because it stood alone and resisted King Kamehameha's efforts to unite Hawaii. It took a royal kidnapping to take the garden isle. After King Kamehameha the Great died, his son, Liholiho, ascended the throne. He gained control of Kauai by luring Kauai's king, Kaumualii, aboard the royal yacht and sailing to Oahu; once there, Kaumualii was forced to marry Kaahumanu, Kamehameha's widow, thereby uniting the islands.

Today, the independent spirit lives on in Kauai, which refuses to surrender its island to wholesale tourism, preferring instead to take care of residents first and visitors second, which it does very well. A Kauai rule of thumb holds that no building may exceed the height of a coconut tree, between three and four stories. That restriction keeps Kauai from becoming another South Florida or Waikiki. As a result, the island itself, not its palatial beach hotels, is still the attention grabber. Its laid-back lifestyle hasn't been altered. There's no real nightlife, no opulent shopping malls. But there's the beauty of the verdant jungle, the endless succession of spectacular beaches, the grandeur of Waimea Canyon, and the drama of the magnificent Na Pali Coast. Even at Princeville, an opulent marble-and-glass luxury hotel does little more than frame the natural glory of Hanalei's spectacular 4,000-foot-high Namolokama mountain range.

Kauai's beauty has won a best-supporting role in more than 40 Hollywood films, from *South Pacific* and *Blue Hawaii* to *Jurassic Park*. But it's not just another pretty face. The island's raw wilderness is daunting, its seas challenging, its canyons forbidding; two-thirds of this island is impenetrable. This is the island for active visitors, with watersports galore; miles of trails for hikers, bicyclists, and horseback riders, winding through rain forests, along ocean cliffs, and across remote beaches; and a range of golf courses, from championship links to funky local courses where chickens roam the greens and balls wind up imbedded in coconut trees.

This great green place remains a sanctuary for native birds and plants and fish and, in a larger sense, even humans. This is the destination for those who need a place to relax and heal jangled nerves. There are miles and miles of sandy beaches, perfect for just sitting and meditating while the waves roll onto the shore. There are quiet spots in the forest to listen to the rain dance on the leaves, and there are laid-back, lazy days that end with the sun sinking into the Pacific amid a blaze of glorious tropical color.

1 Orientation

by Jeanette Foster

ARRIVING

United Airlines (☎ **800/225-5825;** www.ual.com) is the only mainland carrier with direct service to Kauai, with daily flights from Los Angeles. All other carriers land in Honolulu, where you'll have to catch a 20- to 30-minute flight to Kauai's Lihue Airport on an interisland carrier. **Aloha Airlines** (☎ 808/484-1111; www.alohaair.com) and **Hawaiian Airlines** (☎ 800/367-5250, 808/245-3691, or 808/245-1813, or 808/838-1555; www.hawaiianair.com) both offer jet service several times daily to Lihue. The final approach is dramatic, and passengers on the left side of the aircraft are treated to a sneak preview of the island, with an excellent view of the Haupu Ridge, Nawiliwili Bay, and Kilohana Crater.

All the major rental companies have branches at Lihue Airport; see "Getting There & Getting Around" in chapter 3 for details on renting in Hawaii. Rental cars are available at the Lihue Airport. For details, see "Getting Around," below.

If you're not renting a car, call **Al's VIP Limo Taxicab** (☎ **808/742-1390**) or **Kauai Cab Service** (☎ **808/246-9554**) for airport pickup.

VISITOR INFORMATION

The **Kauai Visitors Bureau** is located on the second floor of Lihue Plaza at 3016 Umi St. (at Rice St.), Lihue, HI 96766 (☎ **808/245-3971;** fax 808/246-9235). For a free official *Kauai Vacation Planner* or other information, call ☎ **800/262-1400** or point your web browser to **kauai-hawaii.com.** The **Poipu Beach Resort Association,**

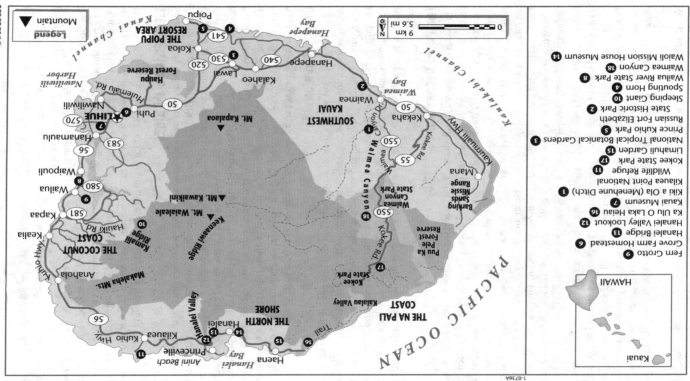

Kauai

Legend
▼ Mountain

0 ___ 5.6 mi
0 ___ 9 km

PACIFIC OCEAN

Kaulakahi Channel

Kauai Channel

1 Kiki a Ola (Menehune Ditch)
2 Russian Fort Elizabeth State Historic Park
3 National Tropical Botanical Gardens
4 Spouting Horn
5 Prince Kuhio Park
6 Grove Farm Homestead
7 Kauai Museum
8 Wailua River State Park
9 Fern Grotto
10 Sleeping Giant
11 Kilauea Point National Wildlife Refuge
12 Hanalei Valley Lookout
13 Hanalei Bridge
14 Waioli Mission House Museum
15 Limahuli Garden
16 Ka Ulu O Laka Heiau
17 Kokee State Park
18 Waimea Canyon

HAWAII
Kauai

P.O. Box 730, Koloa, HI 96756 (☎ 888/744-0888 or 808/742-7444; www. poipu-beach.org), will also send you a free guide to accommodations, activities, shopping, and dining in the Poipu Beach area.

If you'd like to learn more about Kauai before you go, contact the **Kauai Historical Society,** 4396 Rice St., Lihue, HI 96766 (☎ 808/245-3373). The historical society maintains a video-lending library that includes material on a range of topics, including Hawaiian legends, ghost stories, archeology, and travelogues on individual areas around Kauai. Mainland residents can borrow tapes for up to 3 weeks. Rates are $1 for society members; shipping and handling is $5.

THE REGIONS IN BRIEF

Kauai's three main resort areas are quite different in climate, price, architecture, and accommodations; but it's a wide, wonderful range. On the south shore, dry and sunny **Poipu** is anchored by perfect beaches. Here's the place to stay if you like the ocean, watersports, and plenty of sunshine. The **Coconut Coast,** on the East Coast of Kauai, has the most condos, shops, and traffic—this is where all the action is. Up on Kauai's **North Shore,** Hanalei is rainy, lush, and quiet, with spectacular beaches and deep wilderness. Because of its remote location, the North Shore is a great place to get away from it all. But unless you like spending a lot of your vacation time in the car, this is not a great place to use as a home base to explore the other parts of the island.

LIHUE & ENVIRONS

Lihue is where most visitors first set foot on the island. This red-dirt farm town, the county seat, was founded by sugar planters and populated by descendants of Filipino and Japanese cane cutters. It's a plain and simple place with used car lots and mom-and-pop shops. It's also the source of bargains: inexpensive motels and hotels, great deals on meals, and some terrific shopping buys. One of the island's most beautiful beaches, **Kalapaki Beach,** is located just next door at **Nawiliwili,** by the island's main harbor.

THE POIPU RESORT AREA

On Kauai's sun-soaked south shore, Poipu Beach is a pleasant if rather sleepy resort destination of low-rise hotels set on gold-sand pocket beaches fringed by coconut palms. Poipu is Kauai's most popular resort, with the widest variety of accommodations, from luxury hotels to cozy B&Bs to convenient condos. It's a well-done, master-planned resort with 36 holes of golf, 38 tennis courts, and two outstanding restaurants—a branch of Roy's (of Oahu fame) and the Beach House, now under the watch of celebrated Hawaii Regional chef Jean-Marie Josselin. This is a great place for watersports and a good base from which to make excursions and tour the rest of Kauai (although the North Shore is about 1 to 1½ hours away).

Koloa This tiny old town of gaily painted sugar shacks just inland from Poipu Beach is where the Hawaiian sugar industry was born 161 years ago, when Ladd & Co. built a sugar mill and started raising cane. They closed the mill and walked away in July 1996, thereby ending Kauai's plantation era. But this showcase plantation town lives on as a tourist attraction, with delightful shops, an old general store, and a vintage Texaco gas station with a 1930s Model A truck in place, just like the good old days.

Kahaleo/Lawai Just a short 10- to 15-minute drive mauka (or inland) from the beach at Poipu lie the more residential communities of Lawai and Kalaheo. Quiet subdivisions line the streets, restaurants catering to the local population dot the area, and

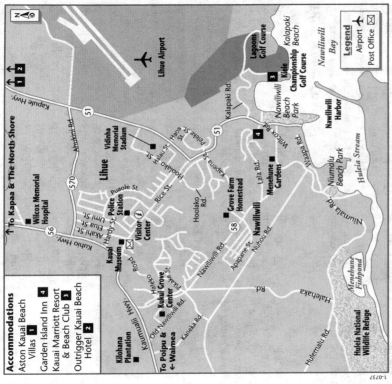

Accommodations

Aston Kauai Beach Villas **1**
Garden Island Inn **4**
Kauai Marriott Resort & Beach Club **3**
Outrigger Kauai Beach Hotel **2**

Legend
✈ Airport
✉ Post Office

life revolves around families and work. Good bargains on bed-and-breakfasts and a handful of good, reasonably priced restaurants can be found here.

SOUTHWEST KAUAI

This region, west of Poipu, is more remote than its eastern neighbor and lacks its terrific beaches. But it is home to one of Hawaii's most spectacular natural wonders, **Waimea Canyon** (the "Grand Canyon of the Pacific") and, farther upland and inland, one of its best parks, **Kokee State Park.**

Hanapepe   For a quick side trip back in time, on your way out to Waimea, turn off Highway 50 at Hanapepe, once one of Kauai's biggest towns. Founded by Chinese rice farmers who harvested the Hanapepe River Valley, today it's such a picturesque old town that Hollywood used it as a backdrop in the Australian epic *The Thornbirds*. A good rest stop on the way to or from Waimea Canyon, Hanapepe has galleries selling antiques as well as art and crafts by local artists, including Georgio's surfboard art and coconut-grams. It also has one of the best restaurants on Kauai, the Hanapepe Bookstore Café & Espresso Bar.

Nearby, at **Salt Pond Beach Park,** Hawaiians since the 17th century have dried a reddish sea salt in shallow, red-clay pans. This is a great place to swim, snorkel, and—maybe—observe ancient industry still in practice.

Waimea   So much happened in Waimea a century or two ago that this little coastal town, the original capital of Kauai, seems to have exhausted itself and quit the march of time. Dogs sleep in the street while old pickups rust in yards on their way to becoming planter boxes. The ambiance is definitely laid back.

On his search for the Northwest Passage in 1778, British explorer Capt. James Cook dropped anchor at Waimea on the southwest coast of Kauai, where the discovered a small, sleepy village of grass shacks on the island's shore. In 1815, the Russians arrived and built a fort here (it's now a national historic landmark), but they didn't last long; Scoundrel George Anton Scheffer tried to claim Kauai for Russia, but he was exposed as an impostor and expelled by King Kamehameha I.

Today, even Waimea's historic relics are spare and simple: a statue of Captain Cook alongside a bas-relief of Cook's ships, *Resolution* and *Discovery*, in the town center; the rubble foundation of the Russian fort; and the remains of an ancient aqueduct unlike any other in the Pacific. Except for an overabundance of churches for a town this size, there's no sign that Waimea was selected as the first landing site of missionaries in 1820. (To see the historic sites, stop at the Waimea Library, at mile marker 23, for a self-guided tour map.)

A stay in Waimea is peaceful and quiet (especially at the Waimea Plantation Cottages, a clutter of restored sugar-plantation cottages on the beach), but the remote location means that this isn't the best base to choose if you want to explore the other regions of Kauai, such as the North Shore, without a lot of driving. But it's a great place to stay to relax and explore the southwest coast, Waimea Canyon, and Kokee State Park.

THE COCONUT COAST

The eastern shore of Kauai north of Lihue is a jumble of commerce and condos strung along the coast road named for Prince Kuhio, with several small beaches beyond. Almost anything you need, and a lot of stuff you can live without, may be found along this condo coast, which is known for its hundreds of coconut trees waving in the breeze. It's popular with budget travelers, with myriad B&Bs and affordable hotels and condos to choose from, and it offers great restaurants and the island's major shopping areas.

Kapaa   The center of East Coast commerce and capital of the Coconut Coast condo and hotel district, this restored plantation town by the sea looks just like an antique. False-front wooden stores line both sides of the highway; it seems as if they've been there forever—until you notice the fresh paint and new roofs and realize that everything has been rebuilt since Hurricane Iniki smacked it flat in 1992. Kapaa has made an amazing comeback without losing its funky charm.

THE NORTH SHORE

Kauai's North Shore may be the most beautiful place in Hawaii. Exotic seabirds, a half-moon bay, jagged peaks soaring into the clouds, and a mighty wilderness lie around the bend from the Coconut Coast, just beyond a series of one-lane bridges traversing the tail ends of waterfalls. This is the land of double rainbows, cascading waterfalls, verdant taro patches, and lush valleys. There's only one road in and out, and two towns, **Hanalei** and **Kilauea**—the former by the sea, the latter on a lighthouse cliff that's home to a bird preserve. Sun seekers may fret about all the rainy days, but Princeville Resort offers elegant shelter and two golf courses where duffers play through rainbows.

Kilauea   The village of Kilauea is home to an antique lighthouse, tropical fruit stands, little stone houses, and Kilauea Point National Wildlife Refuge, a wonderful seabird preserve. The rolling hills and sea cliffs are hideaways for the rich and famous, including Bette Midler and Sylvester Stallone. And the town itself has its charms: the

1892 Kong Lung Company, Kauai's oldest general store, now sells antiques, art, and crafts; you can order a jazzy Billie Holiday Pizza to go at Kilauea Bakery and Pau Hana Pizza, and fuel up at a gas station that's also a souvenir shop.

Anini Beach This little-known residential district on a 2-mile reef (the biggest on Kauai) offers the safest swimming and snorkeling on the island. A great beach park is open to campers and day-trippers, and there's a boat ramp where locals launch sampans to fish for tuna. On Sundays, there's polo in the park and the sizzle of barbecue on the green. Several residents host guests in nearby B&Bs.

Princeville A little overwhelming for Kauai's natural, wild North Shore, Princeville Resort is Kauai's biggest project, an 11,000-acre development set on a high plain overlooking Hanalei Bay. This residential resort community includes a luxury Sheraton hotel with a 180° view of Hanalei Bay, 10 condo complexes, new timeshare units around two championship golf courses, cliffside access to pocket beaches, and one B&B right on the golf course.

Hanalei Picture-postcard Hanalei is the laid-back center of North Shore life and an escapist's dream; it's also the gateway to the wild Na Pali Coast (see below). Hanalei is the last great place on Kauai yet to face the developer's blade of progress; the one-lane bridges that lead to it keep the wolves at bay, and residents regularly veto schemes for marinas, resorts, and timeshare condos. Steepled Bali Ha'i ridges form the backdrop to half-moon **Hanalei Bay,** where sloops anchor and surfers play year-round. The 2-mile-long crescent beach, the biggest indentation on Kauai's coast, sits under towering pinnacles etched by a score of sparkling waterfalls; it's ideal for kids of all ages during the summer months, when the wild winter surf turns placid.

Hanalei still retains the essence of its original sleepy, end-of-the-road charm. On both sides of two-lane Kuhio Highway, you'll find just enough shops and restaurants to sustain you for a week's visit—unless you're a hiker, healer, surfer, sailor, or have some other preoccupation that just might keep you here the rest of your life.

Haena Haena isn't a town or a beach but an ancient Hawaiian district, a place of exceptional natural beauty and the gateway to the Na Pali Coast. Emerald-green Haena is the dream come true, just far enough from real life to keep you in an altered state of relaxation. It's the perfect tropical escape, and everybody knows it: Old house foundations, terraces, and heiau, now covered by jungle, lie in the shadow of the new $1 million beachfront homes (some on stilts to avoid floods) of movie stars and musicians like Jeff Bridges and Graham Nash. This idyllic, 4-mile coast has lagoons, bays, great beaches, spectacular snorkeling, wonderful vistas, a botanical garden, and the only North Shore resort that's right on the sand, the Hanalei Colony Resort.

THE NA PALI COAST

The road comes to an end, and now it begins: the Hawaii you've been dreaming about. The wild North Shore of Kauai rises like a turreted emerald castle. Kauai's Na Pali Coast (*na pali* means "the cliffs" in Hawaiian) is one of Hawaii's greatest natural treasures, a place of extreme beauty and Hawaii's last true wilderness. Its majestic splendor will forever remain unspoiled, because no road will ever traverse it. You can only enter this state park on foot or by sea. Serious hikers tackle the ancient 11-mile-long trail down the forbidding coast to Kalalau Valley, an almost mythical place (see "Hiking & Camping," below). As you hike into this Eden, civilization becomes a distant memory. The lone, thin trail that creases these cliffs isn't for the faint of heart or anyone afraid of heights. Those of us who aren't up to it can explore the wild coast in an inflatable rubber Zodiac, a billowing sailboat, a high-powered catamaran, or a hovering helicopter, which takes you for the ride of your life.

2 Getting Around

by Jeanette Foster

You need a car to see and do everything on Kauai.

DRIVING AROUND KAUAI

Even though no road goes completely around the island, driving on Kauai is easy. There are only two major highways, each beginning in Lihue. From Lihue Airport, turn right, and you'll be on Kapule Highway (Hwy. 51), which eventually merges into Kuhio Highway (Hwy. 56) a mile down the road. This highway will take you to the Coconut Coast and the North Shore. It passes through the plantation town of Kapaa and follows the shoreline to Kilauea, Princeville (where the name of the highway changes to Hwy. 560), Hanalei, and Haena, dead-ending at Ke'e Beach, where the Na Pali Coast begins.

If you turn left from Lihue Airport and follow Kapule Highway (Hwy. 51), you will pass through Lihue and Nawiliwili. Turning on Nawiliwili Road (Hwy. 58) will bring you to the intersection of Kaumualii Highway (Hwy. 50), which will take you to the south and southwest sections of the island. It doesn't follow the coast, however, so if you're heading to Poipu (and most people are), take Maluhia Road (Hwy. 520) south to the coast.

Kaumualii Highway (Hwy. 50) continues through Eleele, Hanapepe, and Waimea, where Captain Cook dropped anchor and "discovered" Kauai; it then dwindles to a secondary road and leads to Polihale State Park, where it dead-ends and the Na Pali Coast begins.

From Waimea, you can take either Waimea Canyon Road (Hwy. 550), which follows the western rim of the canyon and affords spectacular views of it, or Kokee Road (Hwy. 55) up through Waimea Canyon and to Kokee State Park, at more than 4,000 feet; the roads join up about halfway.

CAR RENTALS   All the major rental-car agencies have cars available for rent on Kauai; for a complete list, as well as tips on insurance and driving rules, see "Car Rentals" under "Getting There & Getting Around" in chapter 3. The rental desks are just across the street from Lihue Airport, but you must go by van to collect your car.

For deep discounts on weekly car-rental rates, call **Hookipa Haven Vacation Services,** P.O. Box 108, Paia, HI 96779 (☎ **800/398-6284;** www.hookipa.com; e-mail trolman@maui.net). They discount rates from all the major car-rental agencies.

MOTORCYCLE RENTALS   The best place to find a customized, cherried-out Harley is **Ray's Motorcycle Rentals,** 4558 Kukui St., Kapaa (☎ **808/822-HOGG;** www.renthogg.com). In addition to putting you on a Harley for $100 to $200 a day, they can provide all the accessories, from Harley T-shirts to leathers.

OTHER TRANSPORTATION OPTIONS

Kauai Bus (☎ **808/241-6410**) operates a fleet of 15 buses that serve the entire island. It may be practical for day trips if you know your way around the island, but you can't take anything larger than a shopping bag aboard, and it doesn't stop at any of the resort areas—but it does serve more than a dozen coastal towns between Kekaha, on the southwest shore, all the way to Hanalei. Buses run more or less hourly from 5:30am to 6pm. The fare is $1; 50¢ for seniors, students, and disabled passengers.

Taxi, limousine, and airport shuttle service is available from **Al's VIP Limo Taxicab** (☎ **808/742-1390**) and **Kauai Cab Service** (☎ **808/246-9554**).

FAST FACTS: Kauai

American Express There's no local office on the island, so be sure to conduct your business before you arrive.

Dentists Emergency dental care is available from **Dr. Mark A. Baird**, 4-9768 Kuhio Hwy., Kappa (☎ **808/822-9393**), and **Dr. Michael Furgeson**, 4347 Rice St., Lihue (☎ **808/246-6960**).

Doctors Walk-ins are accepted at **Kauai Medical Group**, 3420-B Kuhio Hwy., Suite B, Lihue (☎ **808/245-1500**), and the **North Shore Clinic**, Kilauea and Oka roads, Kilauea (☎ **808/828-1418**). You can contact **Physicians on Call** 24 hours a day at ☎ **808/245-1831**.

Emergencies Dial ☎ **911** for police, fire, and ambulance service.

Hospitals Wilcox Memorial Hospital, 3420 Kuhio Hwy., Lihue (☎ **808/245-1100**), has emergency services available around the clock.

Newspapers The local papers are the *Garden Island* and *Kauai Times*.

Poison Control Center In an emergency, call ☎ **800/362-3585**.

Police Dial ☎ **911** for emergencies, ☎ **808/245-9711** for other matters.

Post Office The main post office is at 4441 Rice St., Lihue (☎ **808/ 245-4994**). There are also satellite post offices all around the island; to find the branch nearest you, call ☎ **800/ASK-USPS**.

Weather Information For **current weather**, call ☎ **808/245-6001**. For **marine conditions**, call ☎ 808/245-3564.

3 Accommodations

by Jeanette Foster

Kauai is a small island, but you don't want to be stuck with long drives every day to see the highlights, so be sure to review "The Regions in Brief," earlier in this chapter, to choose the location that best fits your vacation. I also suggest that you refer back to "Tips on Accommodations" in chapter 3, so you'll know what to expect from each type of choice.

The rates listed below are rack rates, but you can usually do better, particularly at the big hotels, which can often be booked as part of a money-saving package deal (see chapter 3). Hawaii adds 10.17% in taxes to all hotel bills. Parking is free unless otherwise noted.

LIHUE & ENVIRONS

If you need to stay overnight near the airport, try the **Garden Island Inn** (see below) or the **Kauai Inn** (☎ **808/245-9000**), both just 5 minutes from the airport terminal. To locate the following hotels, see the map on p. 535.

Very Expensive

✪ **Kauai Marriott Resort & Beach Club.** Kalapaki Beach, Lihue, HI 96766. ☎ **800/228-9290** or 808/245-5050. Fax 808/245-5049. www.marriott.com/marriott/ LIHHI. 367 units. A/C TV TEL. $259–$369 double, from $599 suite. Extra person $25. AE, DC, DISC, JCB, MC, V. Valet parking $10.

Once upon a time, this was a glitzy megaresort (the Westin Kauai) with ostentatious fantasy architecture, but then a hurricane and new owners toned it down. The result is grand enough to be memorable, but it's now grounded in reality—it looks like a Hawaiian hotel now instead of a European palace. To check in, you walk through spacious manicured grounds and take the escalators down to the marble lobby, where a full-sized koa canoe sits. Water is everywhere throughout the resort: lagoons, waterfalls, fountains, a 5-acre circular swimming pool (at 26,000 feet, the largest on the island), and a terrific stretch of beach. The lagoons are home to six islands that serve as an exotic minizoo, which still lends an air of fantasy to the place.

The rooms are comfortable, with fabulous views of the golden sands of Kalapaki Beach, verdant gardens, palm trees, and those circular swimming pools. In December 1997, they were renovated with new carpets. They now come with nice extras such as hair dryers, coffeemakers, and dual phone lines with data ports.

There's great golf nearby, and the location allows for easy arrival and departure, since Lihue Airport is only a mile away. (Unfortunately, that means you can hear the takeoff and landing of every jet. Fortunately, air traffic stops by 9pm, but it begins bright and early in the morning.)

Dining/Diversions: The hotel has a wide variety of options, all casual and low-key, from the poolside Kalapaki Grill to the beachfront bar/restaurant Duke's Canoe Club (for a full review, see "Dining," below). Other restaurants, lounges, and shops are a short walk away, off the resort's grounds at the opposite end of Kalapaki Beach.

Amenities: Room service (6am–10pm), concierge, valet service, coin-op laundry, and free airport shuttle. Huge pool with waterfalls, children's pool, 36-hole highly ranked Jack Nicklaus golf course, extensive watersports, horseback riding, health club, hair salon, boutiques, laundry/valet, children's program, and activities desk.

Moderate

Aston Kauai Beach Villas. 4330 Kauai Beach Dr., Lihue, HI 96766. ☎ **800/245-7711.** Fax 808/245-5550. www.aston-hotels.com. E-mail reservations@aston-hotels. 150 units. A/C TV TEL. **$124–$200** one-bedroom for 4. **$176–$315** two-bedroom for 6. AE, CB, DC, DISC, JCB, MC, V.

These beachfront condos are a good option for families and others seeking more space and privacy than they'd get at the neighboring Outrigger or another hotel. All units come with light, tropical decor and bamboo-style furniture; fully equipped kitchen; washers/dryers; and large lanai big enough for two lounge chairs, a table, and four chairs. The two-bedroom units have a lanai off each bedroom, too. Immaculately landscaped grounds contain swimming pools, a spa, tennis courts, barbecue areas, and a volleyball court; the Wailua Municipal golf course is next door. The only caveats are the unsafe swimming conditions on the beautiful but windy white-sand beach.

Outrigger Kauai Beach Hotel. 4331 Kauai Beach Dr., Lihue, HI 96766. ☎ **800/688-7444** or 808/245-1955. Fax 808/246-9085. www.outrigger.com. 341 units. A/C TV TEL. **$150–$195** double, **$250** Voyagers Club double, **$395** suite. Numerous packages available, including 7th night free, car packages, senior rates, and more. AE, DC, DISC, JCB, MC, V.

Out in the cane fields four miles north of Lihue Airport, the Outrigger (formerly the Kauai Hilton) commands a beachfront setting next door to a top-ranked municipal golf course. A fantasy pool with a grotto will keep the kids happy, and the property is home to a restaurant, lounges, tennis courts, shops, and a night club. The location is good, about equidistant from both north- and south-shore activities, and also close to the Wailua River and its kayaking, water-skiing, Wailua river tours, historic sites, and drive-by waterfalls. The setting and location are the draws here. The rooms (refurbished in 1996) are up to Outrigger's usual high standards: They're of medium size, with small refrigerators, coffeemakers, and in-room safes (at a $2.50 charge per day); price differences depend strictly on view. The only problems are the windy conditions and the lack of safe swimming on the beautiful white-sand beach.

ⓘ Great Places to Stay with the Kids

In addition to these, you might also consider the **Embassy Vacation Resort at Poipu Point** and the **Princeville Resort Kauai**, both of which are great for families traveling with kids.

Note that, by state law, hotels can only accept children ages 5 to 12 into their supervised activities programs.

Kauai Marriott Resort & Beach Club (*see p.539*) In addition to the new children's pool, this place also has Hawaii's largest swimming pool (26,000 square feet)—but that's just the beginning. Picture freshwater lagoons with six islands that serve as a minizoo, with kangaroos, monkeys, llamas, flamingoes, and other exotic creatures; draft horses leading carriages through the tropical gardens; and a high-energy beach beside Nawiliwili Harbor, Kauai's port of call. Then add in all the activities of the informal children's program, Kalapaki Kids (ages 5 to 12), which range from boogie boarding to treasure hunting (fees are $45 for the day, which includes lunch, or $25 for a half-day).

Hyatt Regency Kauai Resort & Spa (*see p. 542*) It's the collection of swimming pools—freshwater and salt, with slides, waterfalls, and secret lagoons—that makes this oceanfront Hyatt a real kids' paradise. Camp Hyatt (ages 3 to 12) offers arts and crafts, scavenger hunts, and other special activities for $45 for a full day, including lunch and a T-shirt. Baby-sitting services and kids' activities on weekend evenings (6–10pm) give Mom and Dad some much-needed free time. During the summer months and holiday season, there's Rock Hyatt, a cool activity room for teens to gather and play electronic games. The Hyatt also offers Family Fun Theatre Nights during the summer, usually showing 1 of the more than 400 movies filmed on Kauai.

Waimea Plantation Cottages (*see p. 550*) Among groves of towering coco palms are clusters of meticulously restored turn-of-the-century sugar plantation cottages that offer families the opportunity to relax off the beaten track. Some people may find Waimea a little too out of the way (it's a 1½-hour drive to the North Shore), but it is close to Waimea Canyon and Kokee State Park. The re-created plantation village allows kids plenty of room to wander and play away from traffic and crowds; there's also a pool and tennis courts for them to enjoy.

Holiday Inn SunSpree (*see p. 550*) Here, you'll get moderate rates, lots of free activities, and the quality you've come to expect from this famous name. And it's right next to Lydgate Beach Park and Kamalani Playground.

Kauai Coconut Beach Resort (*see p. 551*) Not only do children 17 and under stay free, but children 11 and younger also eat free when dining with an adult. Situated on 10½ acres in front of Waipouli Beach, the resort offers kids plenty of room to play, and it throws a wonderful luau every night.

Hanalei Colony Resort (*see p. 557*) These spacious two-bedroom condos (with complete kitchens) don't have TVs or stereos, so your kids will get out and enjoy the large swimming pool and the fabulous white-sand beach. Management also has badminton and croquet sets on hand for the whole family, as well as children's toys, puzzles, and games.

Inexpensive

Garden Island Inn. 3445 Wilcox Rd. (across the street from Kalapaki Beach, near Nawiliwili Harbor), Lihue, HI 96766. ☎ **800/648-0154** or 808/245-7227. Fax 808/245-7603.

www.planet-hawaii.com/~g-i-inn. E-mail garden@aloha.net. 21 units (private baths have shower only). TV, $59-$95 double. Extra person $15. MC, V.

Located across the street from the Kalapaki Beach and within hailing distance of the upscale Kauai Marriott, the Garden Isle Inn offers a great location and modest accommodations for travelers on a budget. The spacious rooms at the Garden Island Inn are decorated in island-style furniture and have bright prints on the wall and fresh tropical flowers (grown right on the grounds) in vases throughout. Each room features a refrigerator, a microwave, a wet bar, TV, a coffeemaker, and ocean views; some have private lanais, and the suites have sitting areas. The grounds are filled with flowers and banana and papaya trees (there's always a pile of fruit at the front desk that you're free to take from). Owners Steve and Susan Layne offer friendly service; lots of advice on activities (they'll be happy to use their connections to get you discounts); and even have complimentary beach gear, golf clubs, and coolers that you're welcome to use. Located 2 miles from the airport, 1 mile from Lihue, and within walking distance of shops and restaurants, this is a bargain hunter's delight.

THE POIPU RESORT AREA

Looking for a B&B? See the reviews below for **Marjorie's Kauai Inn, Classic Vacation Cottages**, or **Victoria Place**. Or call **Pua Hale Poipu** (☎ **800/745-7414** or 808/742-1700) to reserve an intimate cottage within walking distance of the beach for $100 for two people. **South Shore Vista** (☎ **808/322-9339**) offers a centrally located one-bedroom apartment for just $59 double. And at the **Garden Isle Cottages** (☎ **800/742-6711** or 808/742-6717), you'll overlook Koloa Landing and Waikomo Stream in a studio apartment starting at $88.

Very Expensive

Embassy Vacation Resort. 1613 Pe'e Rd., Koloa, HI 96756. ☎ **800/535-0085** or 808/922-9700. Fax 808/633-5085 or 808/922-2421. www.marcresorts.com. E-mail marc@aloha.net. 219 units. A/C TV TEL. $275-$440 one-bedroom apt. (sleeps up to 4); $330-$1,000 two-bedroom apt. (up to 6). Rates include continental breakfast and nightly cocktail party. AE, CB, DC, DISC, JCB, MC, V.

Nestled in the sand-dune cliffs on the Poipu Coast and overlooking a rocky shore is this 22-acre complex of 10 two- to four-story buildings, done in an architectural style that echoes the nearby Hyatt's retro look. And it has a new twist: It's a part timeshare, part condo/hotel operation (all with daily maid service). This is a great family spot, filled with happy kids splashing in the lagoon-style pool and poking around the sea cliffs. A coastal footpath takes you to Makawehi Point and the cliffs overlooking Keoniloa Bay to see sea turtles, whales, and occasionally, an endangered monk seal.

The spacious, nicely furnished luxury apartments come with large lanais, full kitchens, and laundry facilities. The best units are the two-bedroom corner suites with views of the Haupu Mountain Range, Shipwreck Beach, and the Hyatt.

The staff is filled with the aloha spirit. New general manager Lyle Otsuka says that if a guest requests something, the staff will go out and buy it. At Thanksgiving, several guests requested disposable turkey pans. No problem—the resort delivered them the next day. And if something is wrong with your condo, not only will the staff fix it immediately, but they'll leave a note with some cookies apologizing for the problem and letting you know it has been taken care of.

Amenities: Concierge, fitness center with sauna and steam room, a lagoon pool bordered by manmade sand beaches, barbecue and picnic areas.

☆ **Hyatt Regency Kauai Resort & Spa.** 1571 Poipu Rd., Koloa, HI 96756. ☎ **800/233-1234** or 808/742-1234. Fax 808/742-1557. www.hyatt.com. 641 units.

A/C MINIBAR TV TEL. $295–$495 double, from $650 suite. Packages available. Extra person $25, Regency Club room extra person $45; children 18 and under stay free in parents' room. AE, CB, DC, DISC, JCB, MC, V. Valet parking $5.

This is one of Hawaii's best luxury hotels and one of the top-ranked tropical resorts in *Conde Nast Traveler's* annual readers poll. The four-story resort, built into the oceanside bluffs, spreads over 50 acres that overlook Shipwreck Beach at the end of the road in Poipu. The $250-million Hyatt uses the island architecture of the mid-1920s to recapture the Old Hawaii of the "blue blazer" Matson Line steamship era.

The atmosphere replicates the casual elegance of a grand plantation overlooking the sea; everything is airy. Instead of being ostentatious, the result is a comfortable vacation home where you can bring the kids and grandma, and everyone feels welcome. The most distant quarters are a good 5-minute hike from the lobby—but upon arrival, you'll find oversized rooms (nearly 600 sq. ft.) elegantly outfitted with rattan and earth tones. All have marble baths with double sinks and spacious private lanais; most have ocean views. Club floors have their own concierge and a lounge serving continental breakfast, drinks, and snacks to club guests.

Dining/Diversions: Dondero's, which features the regional cuisine of Italy, was voted the Best Kauai Hotel Restaurant by the readers of *Honolulu Magazine* in 1997. Romantic spots like Tidepools Restaurant, a series of open-air thatched huts serving seafood, add to the Hyatt's honeymoon appeal. Stevenson's Library is a book-lined, partially open-air watering hole where you can relax and enjoy tropical drinks like a tai chi (the rum-and-juice special) while admiring the ocean view. Kuhio's ups the energy level with dancing on Thursday, Friday, and Saturday nights.

Amenities: Since Shipwreck Beach is too rough for most swimmers, there's an elaborate freshwater fantasy pool complex, plus two more pools and 5 acres of saltwater swimming lagoons with islands and a manmade beach. One of the best reasons to stay here is the ANARA Spa, 25,000 square feet of pampering and revitalizing facilities, such as two whirlpools in a courtyard setting, lava-rock shower gardens, a 10-headed Swedish shower, and indoor-outdoor treatment rooms offering everything from lomi lomi Hawaiian massage to seaweed body wraps. Tennis courts, bicycles, golf at Poipu Bay Resort Course (see below), watersports, horseback riding nearby, twice-daily towel changes and turndowns, an extensive Camp Hyatt kids' program, and a guest-activity program offering everything from dune walks with a naturalist and horse rides in Waimea Canyon to free evening performances of Hawaiian music and hula.

Expensive

Coastline Cottages. Lawai Beach Rd. (just before the small boat harbor), Poipu Beach. c/o P.O. Box 287, Kalaheo, HI 96741. ☎ **808/332-9688.** Fax 808/332-7620. www.hshawaii.com/kvp/coastline. E-mail jds@aloha.net. 5 units. TEL. $175 studio double, $250 one-bedroom cottage for 4, $360 two-bedroom cottage for 6, $500 three-bedroom cottage for 8. 3-night minimum. AE, MC, V.

Location, location, location—these cottages have it: They sit right on their own private beach. This two-building complex can convert into five separate units: two 800-square-foot studios, one 1,600-square-foot one-bedroom/two-bath unit, and an 1,800-square-foot two-bedroom/two-bath unit. Or you can rent the whole extravagant enchilada as a 3,200-square-foot three-bedroom/four-bath house. The best deal here is for two couples to rent the 1,600-square-foot unit at $250 a night for four; a pull-down Murphy bed in the living room makes this into a two-bedroom, two-bath unit with private oceanfront lanais, comfortable window seats, two huge bathrooms with whirlpool tubs, a full kitchen, and washer and dryer. All the units are impeccably decorated in Hawaiian art-deco style, with original artwork, teak floors, and bamboo

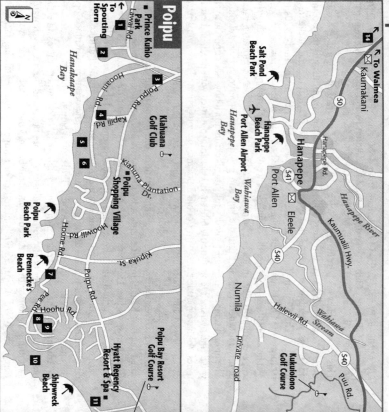

Poipu Resort Area Accommodations

and rattan furniture. Barbecues are outside on the lanais, and lawn furniture dots the grass lawn that leads down to the sea. The only downside is that there's no sandy beach—just the soft, gentle waves lapping against a rock seawall.

⭐ **Gloria's Sporting Horn Bed & Breakfast.** 4464 Lawai Beach Rd. (just before Spouting Horn Park), Koloa, HI 96756. ☎/Fax **808/742-6995.** www.best.com/~travel/gloria. E-mail glorbb@hotmail.com. 3 units. TV TEL. $175 double. Rates include full breakfast and afternoon drinks and pupus. Extra person $35. 3-night minimum. No credit cards.

The price is a little high, but this place is worth every penny. This could be the highlight of your trip. Gloria has been in business since 1986, but the 1992 hurricane flattened her former B&B. She and her husband, Bob, designed the new B&B of their dreams (with reinforced steel to make sure that this one will never blow away). They also added a new solar-heated swimming pool right at the ocean's edge. All three spacious guest rooms are oceanfront, with huge lanais overlooking the secluded beach, and none share any common walls. Our favorite is the Punana Aloha ("love nest") Room, furnished in willow, including a romantic queen bed with a woven willow canopy above. All of the private bathrooms feature Japanese-style deep soaking tubs and separate shower, and each unit comes with a VCR, wet bar, refrigerator, microwave, toaster, blender, and coffeemaker.

Breakfasts are elaborate affairs served on linen, crystal, silver, and English china in the dining room, or for lovers who'd rather stay in bed, on a tray with flowers. The food is five-star quality, and the ambiance is nothing if not romantic. At sunset, Gloria

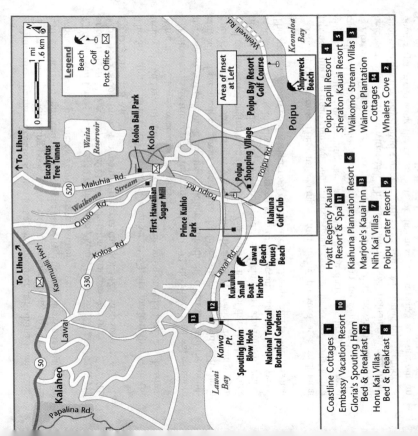

Legend
Beach · Golf · Post Office

Coastline Cottages **1**
Embassy Vacation Resort **10**
Gloria's Spouting Horn Bed & Breakfast **12**
Honu Kai Villas **13**
Hyatt Regency Kauai Resort & Spa **11**
Kiahuna Plantation Resort **6**
Marjorie's Kauai Inn **13**
Nihi Kai Villas **7**
Poipu Crater Resort **9**
Poipu Kapili Resort **4**
Sheraton Kauai Resort **5**
Waikomo Stream Villas **3**
Waimea Plantation Cottages **14**
Whalers Cove **2**

---

offers an open bar and pupus, while Bob plays classical music on his guitar. As one guest put it, "Staying here makes you want to get married again!"

Kiahuna Plantation Resort. 2253 Poipu Rd, Koloa, HI 96756. 333 units. Managed by 2 different management groups: Outrigger: ☎ **800/OUTRIGGER** or 808/742-6411. Fax 808/742-1689. www.outrigger.com. E-mail reservations@outrigger.com. TV TEL. $175–$400 one-bedroom apt. (sleeps up to 4); $315–$450 two-bedroom apt. (sleeps up to 6). Packages available, including 7th night free, car packages, senior rates, and more. AE, CB, DC, DISC, JCB, MC, V. Castle Resorts & Hotels: ☎ **800/367-5004** or 808/742-2200. Fax 800/477-2329 or 808/742-1047. castle-group.com. $170–$400 one-bedroom apt.; $315–$595 two-bedroom apt. 5th night free, or a free car with a 5-night stay. AE, CB, DC, DISC, JCB, MC, V.

This resort consists of a cluster of gracious two- and three-story white plantation-style buildings, loaded with Hawaiian style and sprinkled throughout a 35-acre garden setting with lagoons, green lawns, and a gold-sand beach. And it's all relatively new, totally rebuilt in 1994 after Hurricane Iniki. Golf, shopping, and restaurants are within easy walking distance.

The owners of the condos have chosen two different management companies to handle the rental pool. Outrigger oversees about two-thirds of the units, Castle the remaining one-third. Both companies are excellent and have numerous package deals to fit your budget. All condo units are spacious, with full kitchens, daily maid service, and lanais.

Dining: Piatti Italian Restaurant is housed in an old plantation home; see "Dining," below, for a complete review.

Amenities: Tennis is free and located just across the street at Kiahuna Tennis Club. There's also a big swimming pool, a sundeck with lounge chairs, and barbecue areas with picnic tables sprinkled throughout the property. The individual units do not have washers and dryers, but there's a coin-operated laundry on site.

⭐ **Sheraton Kauai Resort.** 2440 Hoonani Rd., Koloa, HI 96756. ☎ **800/STAY-ITT** or 808/742-1661. Fax 808/923-2023. www.sheraton-kauai.com. 413 units. A/C TV TEL. $250–$390 double (max. 4 in room at no extra charge); $425–$850 suite for 4–5. AE, CB, DC, DISC, JCB, MC, V.

The Sheraton is brand new (opened December 1997), it's modern (but with the feeling of Old Hawaii), and it has a dynamite location on one of Kauai's best beaches. What more can we say besides "Stay here!"

Following its destruction by Hurricane Iniki in 1992, the entire hotel was rebuilt to the tune of $40 million. It features buildings on both the ocean side and the mountain side of the road; all guests check into the lobby on the ocean side. The open horseshoe-shaped lobby features wooden, open-beamed Polynesian buildings with shell chandeliers dangling from the ceilings. You have a choice of three buildings; one nestled in tropical gardens with koi-filled ponds; one facing the palm-fringed, white-sand beach; and one looking across green grass to the ocean with great sunset views. The spacious rooms offer refrigerators, coffeemakers, make-up mirrors, and personal safes.

Dining/Diversions: The cuisine ranges from dishes prepared at a traditional Japanese inn to Friday-night seafood buffets. Appetizers and drinks are available at a glass-walled lounge overlooking the ocean (even if you don't stay here, come for a cocktail and take in that view); it offers Hawaiian music in the evenings.

Amenities: Room service (7 to 11am and 6 to 10pm), daily newspaper, concierge, beach-activities center, activities desk. Three swimming pools, including an oceanfront pool with a water playground complete with slides and a whirlpool, plus a children's pool; a spa overlooking the ocean (one of the most scenic places to work out on Kauai); three tennis courts (two lit for night play); massage; golf; free children's program in summer.

Whalers Cove. 2640 Puuholo Rd., Koloa, HI 96756. ☎ **800/225-2683** or 808/742-7571. Fax 808/742-1185. 39 units. TV TEL. $225–$390 one-bedroom apt.; $275–$455 two-bedroom apt. (sleeps up to 6); $595–$625 suite (up to 4). Rollaway bed $15, crib $5. AE, MC, V.

Hidden at the end of the road on a secluded promontory overlooking the Pacific is this luxurious complex. As you enter, over a flowing manmade stream into an indoor-outdoor slate-floored reception area, you'll immediately see the attention to detail and elegant atmosphere. All the units are oversized (the two-bedroom units are 2,600 square feet) and feature sweeping ocean views plus fully equipped kitchens; large, private lanais; washer/dryers; and ceiling fans. Most have Jacuzzi tubs in the master bathroom. Maid service is provided daily. Also on the property is a heated oceanfront pool with a spa and an adjoining barbecue area. There is no sandy beach here, just a rocky shoreline with concrete steps down to Whalers Cove, one of the best snorkeling and scuba-diving spots on the island.

Moderate

⭐ **Honu Kai Villas Bed & Breakfast.** 1871 Pe'e Rd., Koloa, HI 96756. ☎ **800/ 854-8363** or 808/742-9511. Fax 808/742-7940. www.planet-hawaii.com/honukai. E-mail rjr@aloha.net. 7 units. TV TEL. $110–$175 double (including continental breakfast); $220–$300 two-bedroom apt. 3-night minimum for rooms; 5-night minimum for apts. MC, V.

Just a few minutes' walk from popular Poipu Beach Park and Brennecke's Beach, the Honu Kai is a series of four houses. Owners Robert and Patty Rolland, who live on the property, offer guests two options: either a room with breakfast in their luxury oceanfront B&B or a stay in their two-bedroom, two-and-a-half bathroom villas. Everything here is first-class, from the construction of the building to the gourmet coffee ground for breakfast. All units share a pool and Jacuzzi. The B&B rooms all have private baths, king or queen beds, and ceiling fans, plus the use of the common kitchen and living area. The two-bedroom condos feature complete kitchens with top-notch appliances, a huge living room/dining room area, half bath downstairs, and two bedrooms and two bathrooms upstairs. Ocean views everywhere.

✪ **Nihi Kai Villas.** 1870 Hoone Rd., c/o Grantham Resorts, P.O. Box 983, Koloa, HI 96756. ☎ **800/325-5701** or 808/742-2000. Fax 808/742-9093. www.grantham-resorts.com. 70 units. TV TEL. $161–$211 one-bedroom for 4; $174–$313 two-bedroom for 6; 3-night minimum. If you stay 5 or more nights, rates drop by 25%. $99 "Value Property" two-bedroom for 6; 7-night minimum. AE, CB, DC, DISC, MC, V. From Poipu Rd., turn toward the ocean on Hoowili Rd., then left on Hoone Rd; Nihi Kai Villas is just past Nalo Rd. on Hoone Rd.

Nancy Grantham (see box above) is a marketing genius. She has taken her large, two-bedroom units—which are fabulous, if not "A-plus" units, like what you get at the full price—and is offering the deal of the decade on them: The price for these big, well-furnished, well-equipped, perfectly wonderful apartments is an unbelievable $99 a night. You may not be getting the new carpet, new furniture, new drapes, and prime beachfront location you'll get at the rack rates, but you *are* getting a clean, well-cared-for unit with a full kitchen, washer/dryer, TV, and phone at a bargain price. The sofabed in the living room allows the units to comfortably sleep six. The property is just 200 yards from world-famous Brennecke's Beach (great for body surfing) and just one block from Poipu Beach Park. On-site amenities include an oceanfront swimming pool, tennis and paddle courts, and a barbecue and picnic area. Within a five-minute drive are two great golf courses, several restaurants, and loads of shopping. At these prices—even at the rack rates, for that matter—you simply can't go wrong here.

✪ **Poipu Kapili Resort.** 2221 Kapili Rd., Koloa, HI 96756. ☎ **800/443-7714** or 808/742-6449. Fax 808/742-9162. www.poipukapili.com. E-mail aloha@poipukapili.com. 62 units. TV. $155–$219 one-bedroom apt. (sleeps up to 4); $205–$375 two-bedroom apt. (up to 6). 3-night minimum. Discounts for longer stays; package rates available. MC, V.

This quiet, upscale oceanfront cluster of condos is outstanding in every area but one: The nearest sandy beach is a block away, though the Pacific is right out your window. I like the home-away-from-home amenities and comforts of Poipu Kapili and its special touches: There's a video library, a book-lending library, a spacious pool, several barbecues, tennis courts lit for night play, and an herb garden (you're welcome to take samples if you're cooking). The units are large (one-bedrooms are 1,150 square feet, with two bathrooms; two-bedrooms are 1,820 square feet, with three bathrooms) and have fully equipped kitchens, tropical furnishings, ceiling fans, private lanais, and free continental breakfast by the pool on Fridays. The oceanfront two-story townhouses are my favorites, because they catch the trade winds. The two-bedroom units also have washers and dryers (common laundry facilities are available on the property for the one-bedroom units).

Inexpensive

Classic Vacation Cottages. P.O. Box 901 (2687 Onu Pl.), Kalaheo, HI 96741. ☎ **800/685-7194, ext. 3160,** or 808/332-9201. Fax 808/332-7645. E-mail clascot@hawaiian.net. 5 units. TV. $68–$70 double. Continental breakfast available for an additional $7.50. Extra person $10. 2-night minimum stay. No credit cards. From Hwy. 50, turn toward the mountain at Slim's Appliance on Puuwai Rd., then left on Onu Pl.

The Queen of Condos

One of the easiest ways to find accommodations in the Poipu Beach area is to call **Grantham Resorts**, P.O. Box 983, Koloa, HI 96756 (☎ **800/325-5701** or 808/742-2000; fax 808/742-9093; www.grantham-resorts.com). They handle some 150 rental units for nine different condo developments, plus more than a dozen vacation homes. Owner Nancy Grantham has high standards for her rental units and offers extremely fair prices. When you rent a Grantham unit, you know you're getting a good value at a good price.

Grantham offers a range of accommodations to fit every pocketbook. Their condos all have a 3-day minimum stay and range in price from $110 a night for one-bedroom units to $288 for three-bedroom, deluxe oceanfront units. The vacation homes have a 5-night minimum stay and start at $181 a night for two bedrooms and go up to $350 a night for four bedrooms.

If you plan to stay on Kauai for 7 days, ask Grantham about their *Frommer's* Special: large one- and two-bedroom condos, well-furnished and well-equipped (full kitchen, washer/dryer, wet bar, TV, phone), starting as low as $79 a night for one-bedrooms and $89–$99 for two-bedrooms (see Nihi Kai Villas, Poipu Crater Resort, and Waikomo Stream Villas, below). There's not a better deal on Kauai; kudos to Nancy for these fabulous vacation deals.

What a deal! Wynnis Grow swore a decade ago that she would keep her accommodations affordable—and she has kept that promise. Her exquisitely decorated units (hardwood floors, stained-glass windows) are a real bargain. Each has a well-equipped kitchen and a private lanai and comes outfitted with its own snorkeling equipment, boogie boards, and beach towels. Also on the property is a large Jacuzzi. The peaceful location, in the cool hills of Kalaheo, is great: It's a 7-minute drive to Poipu beaches, 5 minutes to Kukuiolono Golf Course, and 20 minutes to Waimea Canyon. There are hiking trails right down the driveway.

Marjorie's Kauai Inn. P.O. Box 866 (off Hailima Rd., adjacent to the National Tropical Botanical Garden), Lawai, HI 96765. ☎ **800/717-8838** or 808/332-8838. Fax 808/332-8838. E-mail ketcher@aloha.net. 3 units. TV TEL. $55–$75 double. Rates include continental breakfast on 1st day. Extra person $10. 2-night minimum stay. No credit cards.

This quiet, 1.2-acre property is located just 10 minutes from Poipu Beach and 5 minutes from Old Koloa Town. Perched on the side of a hill, Marjorie's offers stunning views from a large lanai over the rolling pastures and the beach at Lawai Valley. The two larger units have mini-kitchens (with microwave, toaster oven, refrigerator, and coffeemaker); the budget units (best for a single) are smaller versions of the large units. As if the great view, the huge, open-air hot tub perched on the hillside, and the comfortable rooms weren't enough, the biggest reason to stay here is Marjorie Ketcher herself. "Do more than one fun thing a day," is Marjorie's motto, and she makes sure that her guests are out diving, snorkeling, sightseeing, hiking, dining, dancing, or doing one of the hundreds of other things she can recommend.

✪ **Poipu Crater Resort.** 2330 Hoohu Rd., Poipu, c/o Grantham Resorts, P.O. Box 983, Koloa, HI 96756. ☎ **800/325-5701** or 808/742-2000. Fax 808/742-9093. www.grantham-resorts.com. 30 units. TV TEL. $111–$125 two-bedroom for 6; 3-night minimum. If you stay 5 or more nights, rates drop by 25%. $89 "Value Property" two-bedroom; 7-night minimum. AE, CB, DC, DISC, MC, V. From Poipu Rd., turn toward the ocean on Hoowili Rd; turn left on Hoone Rd.; continue on Hoone Rd. past the bends, where the road is now called Pee Rd; turn left off Pee Rd. onto Hoohu Rd.

Another Nancy Grantham marketing coup (see above)! Two bedrooms for as little as $89! This exclusive resort consists of 30 very private condo units in a tropical garden setting. Each one has a full kitchen (with microwave), washer/dryer, and VCR. The complex has a swimming pool, tennis and paddleball courts, sauna, Ping-Pong tables, and barbecues. Poipu Beach is about a 10-minute walk away, and the entire Poipu Beach resort area (offering everything from restaurants to golf courses) is within a 5-minute drive. Pick up the phone right now and reserve a unit before the rest of the world beats you to it.

Victoria Place. 3459 Lawai Loa Lane (off Koloa Rd./Hwy. 530), Koloa. c/o P.O. Box 930, Lawai, HI 96765. ☎ **808/332-9300.** Fax 808/332-9465. www.hshawaii.com/kvp/victoria. E-mail victoria@hshawaii.com. 4 units. $60–$80 double, $100 studio apt. Rates include breakfast. Extra person $15. No credit cards. No children under 15.

The reason to stay here? Two words: Edee Seymour. It's easy to see why this gregarious former Michigan resident won the Kauai Chamber of Commerce's Aloha Spirit Award—she lavishes her guests with attention and aloha. Her spacious, skylit, U-shaped house wraps around the swimming pool and garden. Three bedrooms, located in one wing of the home, open onto the pool area, which is surrounded by flowering walls of bougainvillea, hibiscus, gardenia, and ginger. Edee also has an apartment (dubbed "Victoria's Other Secret"); a private path leads to a secluded studio with king bed, bath with shower, kitchen, and TV. Edee's breakfasts are a really big deal: at least five different tropical fruits, then a course of something from the oven, such as homemade bread, scones, or muffins. Most of her guests are returnees. As a couple from Germany told us, "Once you stay with Edee, every place else is cold and indifferent. When we think of Kauai, we think of Edee."

⭐ **Waikomo Stream Villas.** 3176 Poipu Rd., Suite 1 (just after entry to Poipu, on ocean side of Poipu Rd.), Poipu. c/o Grantham Resorts, P.O. Box 983, Koloa, HI 96756. ☎ **800/325-5701** or 808/742-2000. Fax 808/742-9093. www.grantham-resorts.com. 60 units. TV TEL. $124–$137 one-bedroom for 4; $136–$162 two-bedroom for 6; 3-night minimum. If you stay 5 or more nights, rates drop by 25%. $79 "Value Property" one-bedroom, $89 "Value Property" two-bedroom; 7-night minimum. AE, CB, DC, DISC, MC, V.

Nancy Grantham has one more fabulous trick up her sleeve: these 800- to 900-square-foot one-bedroom apartments, which comfortably sleep four, and larger two-bedroom units, which sleep six. Tucked into a lush tropical garden setting, these large, well-decorated units have everything you could possibly need on your vacation: fully-equipped kitchen, VCR, washer/dryer, and private lanai. The complex—which has both adults' and a children's swimming pools, tennis courts, and a barbecue area—is adjacent to the Kiahuna Golf Club and just a 5-minute walk from restaurants, shopping, and Poipu's beaches.

SOUTHWEST KAUAI

Kokee Lodge. P.O. Box 819, Waimea, HI 96796. ☎ **808/335-6061.** 12 cabins. $35 studio, $45 two-bedroom. 5-night maximum. MC, V.

This is an excellent choice, especially if you want to do some hiking in Waimea Canyon and Kokee State Park. There are two types of cabins: The older ones have dormitory-style sleeping arrangements, while the new ones each have two separate bedrooms. Both styles sleep six and come with cooking and eating utensils, bedding, and linens. We recommend the newer units, which have wooden floors, cedar walls, and more modern kitchen facilities (some are wheelchair-accessible). You can purchase firewood for the cabin stove at Kokee Lodge, where there's also a restaurant that's open for continental breakfast and lunch every day. There's also a cocktail lounge, a general store, and a gift shop.

★ **Waimea Plantation Cottages**, 9400 Kaumualii Hwy. (P.O. Box 367), Waimea, HI 96796. ☎ **800/992-7866** or 808/338-1625. Fax 808/338-2338. www.aston-hotels.com. 48 cottages. TV. **$128-$220** one-bedroom, **$165-$280** two-bedroom, **$195-$310** three-bedroom, **$310-$330** four-bedroom, **$470-$490** five-bedroom. AE, DC, DISC, JCB, MC, V.

This beachfront vacation retreat is like no other in the islands: Among groves of towering coco palms are clusters of restored sugar-plantation cottages, dating from the 1880s to the 1930s and bearing the names of their original plantation-worker dwellers. The lovely cottages have been transformed into cozy, comfortable guest units with period rattan and wicker furniture and fabrics from the 1930s, sugar's heyday on Kauai; each has a furnished porch lanai and a fully-equipped modern kitchen and bath. Some units are oceanfront. The larger homes include the Manager's Estate, a five-bedroom home built in 1900 with an ocean view, large living and dining areas, and a lanai—perfect digs for a small family reunion. There's an oceanfront pool, tennis courts, and laundry facilities. The only downsides are the black-sand beach, which is lovely but not conducive to swimming (the water is often murky at the Waimea River mouth), and the location; its remoteness, at the foot of Waimea Canyon Drive, can be very appealing, but the North Shore is an hour and a half away. Still, a fabulous retro retreat—and a perfect place to get away from it all.

THE COCONUT COAST

This is the land of B&Bs and inexpensive vacation rentals. In addition to the B&Bs reviewed below, we also recommend **Kakalina's B&B** (☎ **800/718-1018;** www.kekotix.com/kakalina.html), a 3-acre flower farm and B&B nestled in the foothills of Mt. Waialeale, offering rates from $85 a night. **Royal Drive Cottages** (☎ **808/822-2321;** www.planet-hawaii.com/~royal) features romantic, private cottages in an Eden-like setting for $80 for two. **Surf & Ski Cottage** (☎ **800/344-7915** or 808/822-3574) is the place for watersports; it's an intimate cottage right on the Wailua River ($60 a night for two), owned by the people who run Kauai Water Ski & Surf Co. (they'll give you 20% off on rental of all water toys). And one of the very best deals on Kauai is **Hibiscus Hollow** (☎ **808/823-0925;** www.hawaiian-net/~hollow), a private cottage for two for just $45 a night.

Expensive

Holiday Inn SunSpree Resort. 3-5920 Kuhio Hwy., Kapaa, HI 96746 ☎ **888/823-5111** or 808/246-6976. Fax 808/823-6666. 216 units. A/C TV TEL. $150-$175 room for up to 4; $190-$225 suite for up to 4. Rollaway beds/cribs $10. Special opening rate: $135 for 4, including car rental (expires 12/19/98). AE, CB, DC, DISC, JCB, MC, V.

In 1997, Holiday Inn took over the former Kauai Resort and gutted the property, totally redoing the entry, lobby, restaurants, and even the koi pond and pool. The rooms, which had just been renovated some 8 months earlier, all got new tile, furniture, blackout drapes, and wallpaper. SunSpree Resorts, a division of Holiday Inn, emphasizes moderate rates and lots of free activities for families. The result is a family-friendly choice located right next door to Lydgate Beach Park (with Kamalani Playground for children) and convenient to nearby golf. We toured the property while it was still under construction. Every room features a refrigerator, iron/ironing board, hair dryer, and coffeemaker.

Dining/Diversions: Three restaurants to choose from: the Pacific Room for breakfast and dinner, the Pikake Terrace for snacks and cocktails, and the Marketessen for deli items and espresso.

Amenities: Two swimming pools, spa, tennis court, shuffleboard, volleyball, fitness room, self-service laundry, complimentary snorkeling gear, children's program, room service, dry cleaning/laundry, activities desk.

Lae Nani. 410 Papaloa Rd., Kapaa, HI 96746. ☎ **800/367-7052** or 808/822-4938. Fax 808/822-1022. www.lae-nani.com. 70 units. TV TEL. $165–$225 one-bedroom for 4; $220–$295 two-bedroom for 6. Rollaway bed/crib $10. 2-night minimum. AE, MC, V.

Located right on the beach, the Lae Nani ("beautiful promontory point") offers a quiet, relaxing setting. On the point is the Kukui Heiau, where an ancient temple once stood. Next door is the Coconut Marketplace, with shops, restaurants, and nightlife. The one- and two-bedroom units are roomy, with large living rooms, separate dining rooms, complete kitchens, and generous lanais. The two-bedroom/two-bathroom units can easily fit a family of six without being crowded. Maid service is provided daily.

Amenities: Swimming pool, lava rock–protected swimming area, barbecue facilities, tennis courts, and centrally located self-service Laundromat.

Moderate

Aston Kauai Beachboy Hotel. 4-484 Kuhio Hwy., Kapaa, HI 96746. ☎ **800/92-ASTON** or 808/822-3441. Fax 808/822-0843. www.aston-hotels.com. 233 units (all with shower only). A/C TV TEL. $90–$155 double, $139–$195 one-bedroom with kitchenette for 4. Extra person $18; children under 18 stay free in parents' room. AE, CB, DC, DISC, JCB, MC, V.

On the ocean, behind the Coconut Marketplace, this low-rise, horseshoe-shaped property offers affordable accommodations in a central location. The large rooms were renovated in 1997. All have private lanais that look out over garden or ocean views, and all have at least a mini-refrigerator. The one-bedroom rooms have kitchenettes with coffeemakers, microwaves, toasters, and large refrigerators. A self-service laundry is on the property. Hawaiian games, arts, and crafts are highlighted, and there's an extensive library with books on Hawaiian history, legends, and culture. Other facilities include two oceanfront pools, a tennis court, volleyball, and shuffleboard. Golf and additional tennis facilities are nearby, and there's shopping, dining, and nightlife at the Coconut Marketplace next door.

Islander on the Beach. 484 Kuhio Hwy., Kapaa, HI 96746. ☎ **800/847-7417** or 808/822-7417. Fax 808/822-1947. www.islander-kauai.com. www.islander@aloha.net. 196 units. A/C TV TEL. $102–$135 double, $175 junior suite with kitchen. Breakfast included in high season (Aug and late Dec–Mar); rental car available for $20 more. Low-season rates (Apr–July and early Sept–Dec 23) include rental car and breakfast or the 4th night free. Extra person $20; children 17 and under stay free in parents' room. AE, DISC, JCB, MC, V.

Located on the beach side of Coconut Marketplace, this Hawaiian plantation-style hotel offers families a terrific deal, throwing in a great rate on a rental car. The medium-sized rooms all have coffeemakers, safes, refrigerators, and wet bars. The oceanfront rooms have microwaves; junior suites have full kitchens. On the well-manicured grounds, the hotel has an oceanside pool with a spa, a volleyball court, an activities desk, a restaurant and lounge, barbecue facilities with picnic tables, and a guest Laundromat. Tennis courts are next door.

✪ **Kauai Coconut Beach Resort.** P.O. Box 830, Kapaa, HI 96746. ☎ **800/22-ALOHA** or 808/822-3455. Fax 808/822-1830. www.kcb.com. E-mail reservation@kcb.com. 311 units. A/C TV TEL. $150–$200 double, $250–$500 suite. Extra person $15; children 17 and under stay free in parents' room. AE, CB, DC, DISC, JCB, MC, V.

The only full-service oceanfront resort on this stretch of the coast, the Kauai Coconut Beach Resort has an excellent deal for families: Not only do children 17 and under stay free, but children 11 and younger also eat free when dining with an adult. This well-landscaped resort sits on 10.5 acres in front of the Waipouli Beach next door to the Coconut Marketplace. It's centrally located for shops, restaurants, and great golf, and it's 10 minutes from Lihue Airport. The oversized rooms all feature lanais, refrigerators, safes, and coffeemakers. The ocean-view and ocean-front rooms are decorated in custom-designed, handcarved furniture from Indonesia. Built in 1978 and renovated in 1995, the property offers a range of activities, from a jogging path to free tennis; there's also a nightly torch-lighting ceremony and frequent Hawaiian demonstrations.

In addition to theme buffets at the Flying Lobster Restaurant, there's a wonderful nightly luau (the Hawaii Visitors and Convention Bureau named it the "most authentic luau" in the state). Amenities include a swimming pool, whirlpool, three tennis courts, a pro shop, a jogging path, coin-operated laundry, shuffleboard, a children's program in summer, room service (6:30am–10am, 11am–1:30pm, and 6pm–9pm), an activities desk, and a car-rental desk.

⭐ **Mahina Kai.** 4933 Aliomanu Rd. (off Kuhio Hwy., at mile marker 14). c/o P.O. Box 699, Anahola, HI 96703. ☎ **800/337-1134** or 808/822-9451. Fax 808/822-9451. 5 units. TV. $125 double, $150 double apt, $175 triple apt, $200 apt. for 4–6. Rates include continental breakfast. Extra person $10. 3-night minimum. No credit cards.

Mahina Kai ("moon over the water") is an exquisite Japanese villa (complete with teahouse next door) on two landscaped acres just across the road from one of the most picturesque white-sand beaches on Kauai. Dr. Trudy Comba, an educator who fell in love with Kauai, has filled the house with carefully selected Japanese antiques, kimonos, and fascinating art objects. She offers three rooms in the main house that come complete with shoji screen doors, private baths and lanais, and use of the gorgeous living room, library, and kitchenette with microwave, toaster oven, refrigerator, and coffeemaker. The view from each room—either ocean or garden—is spectacular. The living room features a fish pond, bamboo plants, antique Asian furniture, and views of the lush Japanese gardens and white sands of Aliomanu Beach. Trudy also has two two-bedroom apartments (each of which can sleep up to six people) with private entrances, mini-kitchens, and VCRs. Landscaped into the gardens are a lagoon-style pool and a hot tub. Sitting in the hot tub, listening to the surf across the street, and watching the stars move slowly across the sky is pretty darn close to heaven on earth.

Inexpensive

⭐ **Alohilani Bed & Breakfast.** 1470 Wanaao Rd., Kapaa, HI 96746. ☎ **800/533-9316** or 808/823-0128. Fax 808/823-0128. www.hawaiian.net/~alohila. E-mail alohila@hawaiian.net. 3 units. TV. $89 double suite, $99 double cottage. Rates include continental breakfast. Extra person $10. 3-night minimum stay. MC, V. From Kuhio Highway (Hwy. 56), turn left onto Kawaihau Road; go about 4 miles, then turn left again on Wanaao Road.

Owner Sharon Mitchell has furnished her B&B, on 6 peaceful acres at the very end of a country road, with antiques and other beautiful pieces. Her separate cottage is a large room decorated in country charm with a complete kitchen, sleeper sofa, and an adorable antique bed with its own teddy bear. Our favorite suite is the open, airy Sunshine Atrium, with its floor-to-ceiling windows and arched French glass doors opening onto a lanai that overlooks the entire valley. The white-tiled room has a queen bed, a sleeper sofa, a small fridge, and microwave.

Hotel Coral Reef. 1516 Kuhio Hwy. (at the northern end of Kapaa, between mile markers 8 and 9), Kapaa, HI 96746. ☎ **800/843-4659** or 808/822-4481. Fax 808/822-7705. 24 units.

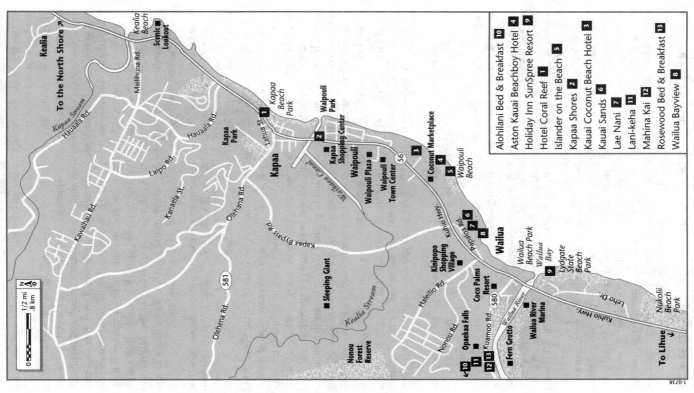

Coconut Coast Accommodations

Legend:
- Alohilani Bed & Breakfast **10**
- Aston Kauai Beachboy Hotel **4**
- Holiday Inn SunSpree Resort **9**
- Hotel Coral Reef **1**
- Islander on the Beach **5**
- Kapaa Shores **2**
- Kauai Coconut Beach Hotel **3**
- Kauai Sands **6**
- Lae Nani **7**
- Lani-keha **11**
- Mahina Kai **12**
- Rosewood Bed & Breakfast **13**
- Wailua Bayview **8**

Map labels:
- Kealia
- To the North Shore ↗
- Kealia Beach
- Scenic Lookout
- Malilihuna Rd.
- Hauaala Rd.
- Kapaa Stream
- Kapaa Beach Park
- Kapaa Park
- Lehua St.
- Waipouli Park
- Kapaa Shopping Center
- Waipouli
- Waipouli Plaza
- Waipouli Town Center
- Coconut Marketplace
- Waipouli Beach
- Kapaa
- Hauaala Rd.
- Laipo Rd.
- Kanaela St.
- Olehena Rd.
- Waikaea Canal
- Kawaihau Rd.
- Kapaa Bypass Rd.
- Kuhio Hwy.
- 56
- 581
- Sleeping Giant
- Kealia Stream
- Papaloa Rd.
- Wailua
- Wailua Beach Park
- Wailua Bay
- Lydgate State Beach Park
- Kinipopo Shopping Village
- Haleilio Rd.
- Coco Palms Resort
- 580
- Nonou Rd.
- Opaekaa Falls
- Nonou Forest Reserve
- Kuamoo Rd.
- Fern Grotto
- Wailua River
- Wailua River Marina
- Kuhio Hwy.
- Leho Dr.
- Nukolii Beach Park
- To Lihue
- Olehena Rd.

N

1/2 mi
.8 km
0

1-07038

553

TV **$59–$89** double. Rates include continental breakfast. Extra person **$10**; children 12 and under stay free in parents' room. MC, V.

Here's a budget choice that's right on the beach! This small, unpretentious hotel facing a grassy lawn, coconut trees, and a white-sand beach offers economical rooms and friendly service in an ideal location. Within walking distance to shops and restaurants, and just 50 yards away from good swimming and snorkeling. There's even an 8-mile bike path that starts right on the grounds. Of the two wings in the hotel, we prefer the oceanfront building, which has big rooms that overlook the beach through sliding-glass doors that lead out onto lanais. The two-room units ($79 double) have a separate bedroom and a living room with a hide-a-bed—perfect for families. Michael and Linda Warriner, owners and operators of this quaint hotel, are always happy to give you pointers on how to stretch your budget and still have a good time.

Kapaa Shores. 900 Kuhio Hwy. (between mile markers 7 and 8), Kapaa, HI 96746. ☎ **800/827-3922** or 808/822-3055. Fax 808/822-1457. 81 units. TV TEL. High season **$90–$150** one-bedroom, **$110–$170** two-bedroom; low season **$75–$135** one-bedroom, **$95–$155** two-bedroom. 3-night minimum. No credit cards.

These apartments are located right on the beach in the heart of Kapaa; the sound of waves breaking will lull you to sleep at night. The budget units have views of the gardens, but ocean views are available for a bit more money. The one-bedrooms can comfortably sleep four, and the two-bedroom units can sleep as many as six (the queen-size sofa in each unit pulls out into a bed). All of the units are in excellent shape and come with fully-equipped modern kitchens and large lanais that are big enough for a patio table and chairs, where you can enjoy a sunrise breakfast or sunset cocktails. On-site amenities include a large swimming pool, a tennis court, a family-size hot tub, a shuffleboard court, laundry facilities, and barbecues.

Kauai Sands. 420 Papaloa Rd., Kapaa, HI 96746. ☎ **800/560-5553** or 808/922-1228. 200 units. A/C TV TEL. **$54–$64** double, **$69** double with kitchenette. Packages including room, car, and breakfast for two from **$75**; seniors get an upgrade and free breakfast for two. MC, V.

These modest motel-style accommodations will do just fine for budget travelers who want a basic, clean room with a central location. Right on the ocean, next door to the Coconut Marketplace, the Kauai Sands has a swimming pool and restaurant on the property. The small rooms have modest furniture (two doubles or a twin bed), ceiling fans, and small refrigerators; most have tiny lanais.

Lani-keha. 848 Kamalu Rd. (Hwy. 581), Kapaa, HI 96746. ☎ **808/822-1605.** Fax 808/823-6308. 4 units. TEL. **$65** double, **$80** suite. Rates include continental breakfast. Extra person **$15**. 2-night minimum. No credit cards. From Kuhio Hwy. (Hi. 56), turn left at the stoplight at Coco Palms onto Hi. 580 (Kuamoo Rd.); go 3 miles; turn right at Hi. 581 (Kamalu Rd.) and go 1½ miles.

Step back in time to the 1940s, when old Hawaiian families lived in open, airy, rambling homes on large plots of land lush with fruit trees and sweet-smelling flowers. This gracious age is still alive and well in Lani-keha, an old *kamaaina (old-line)* home with a large, open living/game/writing/dining room with oversized picture windows to take in the views, and bedrooms with private baths. The house is elegant-casual, with old-style rattan furniture—practicality and comfort outweigh design aesthetics. The large kitchen has everything a cook could possibly want, even a dishwasher.

Rosewood Bed & Breakfast. 872 Kamalu Rd., Kapaa, HI 96746. ☎ **808/822-5216.** Fax 808/822-5478. www.rosewoodkauai.com. E-mail rosewood@aloha.net. 6 units (3 with shared bath). TV TEL. **$65** double in main house (includes continental breakfast); **$40–$50** double in bunkhouse; $85–$115 cottage double (sleeps up to 4). Extra person $10. No credit cards. From Kuhio Hwy. (Hwy. 56), turn left at the stoplight at Coco Palms onto Hi. 580 (Kuamoo Rd.); go 3 miles; at junction of Hi. 581 (Kamalu Rd.), turn right; go 1¾ miles and look for the yellow house on the right with the long picket fence in front.

This lovingly restored century-old plantation home, set on an acre of tropical flowers, lily ponds, and waterfalls, has accommodations to suit everyone. There's a Laura Ashley-style room in the main house and two private cottages: one is a miniature of the main house, with oak floors and the same Laura Ashley-style decor, and the other is a little grass shack set in a tropical garden, with an authentic thatched roof and an outside shower. There's also a bunkhouse with three separate small rooms with a shared shower and toilet.

★ **Wailua Bayview.** 320 Papaloa Rd., Kapaa, HI 96746. ☎ **800/882-9007** or 808/823-0112. Fax 425/391-9121. TV TEL. 45 units. $75–$93 double. 7th night free Apr 15–Dec 15. MC, V.

Located right on the ocean, these spacious one-bedroom apartments offer an excellent value for the price. All units have ceiling fans; some have air conditioning. They all have complete kitchens (including microwaves and dishwashers), washer/dryers, and large lanais. The bedrooms are roomy, and there are also sofabeds in the living room, so each unit sleeps up to four people. Facilities on the property include a swimming pool and barbecue area. Some of the $75 garden units are close to the road and can be noisy; ask for one with air conditioning, and generally, it drowns out the street sounds. The oceanview units are more expensive but still a great deal.

THE NORTH SHORE

Want to rent a rock star's tree house? How about coochy-coochy entertainer Charo's beachfront estate? **Hanalei North Shore Properties** (☎ **800/488-3336** or 808/826-9622; fax 808/826-1188; www.planet-hawaii.com/visit-kauai) handles all kinds of weekly rentals—from beachfront cottages and condos to romantic hideaways and ranch houses—all along the North Shore. Renting a home is a great way to enjoy the area's awesome nature, especially for travelers who like to get away from resorts and fend for themselves. Shopping, restaurants, and nightlife are abundant in nearby Hanalei; several of the rentals are even located around its scenic bay. No credit cards.

In addition to the B&Bs reviewed below, we suggest **Kai Mana** (☎ **808/837-1782** or 808/828-1280), a 5-acre estate overlooking the Kilauea Lighthouse and the ocean. The plantation-style house offers B&B rooms with their own private entrance (starting at $95 a night for two) and a separate eight-sided, mushroom-shaped private cottage on the property ($150 a night for two). **Kalihiwai Jungle Home** (☎ **808/828-1626**) is a luxury one-bedroom apartment hidden in a half-acre tropical forest just minutes from the beach for $125 for two. **North Country Farms** (☎ **808/828-1513**) is a private, handcrafted, redwood cottage on a 4-acre organic farm. It's a great place for families ($85 for two; children under 15 stay free with their parents).

To locate the following accommodations, see the map on p. 608.

Very Expensive

★ **Princeville Resort Kauai.** P.O. Box 3040 (5520 Kahaku Rd.), Princeville, HI 96722-3069. ☎ **800/782-9488** or 808/826-9592. www.princeville.com. E-mail info@princeville.com. 252 units. A/C TV MINIBAR TEL. $350–$495 double, from $575 suite. Extra person $50; children under 18 stay free in parents' room. AE, DC, DISC, JCB, MC, V.

This jewel in the Sheraton crown, a palace full of marble and chandeliers, enjoys one of the world's finest settings, between Hanalei Bay and Kauai's steepled, Bali Ha'i-like mountains. The panoramic view from the lobby has to be the most dramatic vista from any hotel in the state. This resort is Kauai's most popular setting for weddings; more than 300 a year are performed outdoors by the pool. The hotel is located near the shore for snorkeling.

Full of the drama, theatrics, and European-inspired touches that recall Hawaii's decadent monarchy period, this grand hotel steppes down a cliff. The entrance is actually on the ninth floor; you take elevators down to your room and the beach. Each opulent room has such over-the-top extras as a door chime, dimmer switches, lighted closets, bedside control panels, safes, original oil paintings, oversized bathtubs, and a "magic" bathroom window: a liquid-crystal shower window that you can switch in an instant from clear to opaque. There are no lanais, but oversized windows allow you to admire the awesome view from your bed.

Dining/Diversions: One of the most romantic places to dine at sunset is Cafe Hanalei, on a stone terrace overlooking Hanalei Bay; if only the overpriced food and lackadaisical service could match the view. La Cascata features Mediterranean cuisine at dinner (see complete review under "Dining," below), and the Beach Restaurant and Bar serves lunch and snacks.

Amenities: 24-hour room service, twice-daily towels, turndowns on request, free daily newspapers, complimentary resort shuttle, and a comprehensive Hawaiian cultural program. There's outstanding golf on two top-ranked courses designed by Robert Trent Jones, Jr., plus 25 tennis courts, a swimming pool, three outdoor whirlpools (including one really palatial one), shopping center, business center, riding stables, in-house cinema. There's also a first-rate health club and spa, with whirlpools, a 25-meter lap pool, and steam baths (an unneeded amenity in usually humid Hanalei), plus your choice of a seaweed wrap or a Hawaiian salt glow (where you're packed in salt until cured).

Expensive

Hanalei Bay Resort & Suites. P.O. Box 220 (5380 Honoiki St.), Princeville, HI 96722. ☎ 800/367-5004 or 808/826-6522. Fax 808/826-6680. 236 units. A/C TV TEL. $160–$230 double, $170–$240 studio with kitchenette, $290–$500 one-bedroom apt, $380–$750 two-bedroom apt, $690–$1,000 three-bedroom apt. Apts. include full breakfast and 2 afternoon cocktails. AE, DC, DISC, MC, V.

This 22-acre resort is just up the street from ritzy Princeville Resort (see above), overlooking the fabled Bali Ha'i cliffs and Hanalei Bay. It has the same majestic view, but for as little as half the price. The Hanalei Bay took a hit during Hurricane Iniki but is now fully recovered after a $10 million renovation that recaptured the spirit of Old Hawaii, especially in the three-story stucco units that angle down the hill to the gold-sand, palm-fringed beach it shares with its neighbor. Rooms are decorated in island style, in blues and greens with rattan furnishings, with lanais overlooking Hanalei Bay, the lush grounds, and the distant mountains.

Dining/Diversions: Inspired by Michener's *Tales of the South Pacific* (which became the play and film *South Pacific*), the Happy Talk Lounge is one of my favorite places on Kauai to sip a sunset cocktail. While the open-air restaurant may not serve memorable food, it delivers an unforgettable view.

Amenities: Hanalei Bay has focused on outdoor activities rather than traditional in-house amenities (no room service, no concierge, no array of shops). Two inviting freshwater pools, a sundeck, Jacuzzi, a white-sand beach that's great for swimming, eight tennis courts, pro shop, and tennis school, and two world-class golf courses nearby (with complimentary shuttle service). Valet and coin-op laundry (the suites have their own washer/dryers), travel desk, salon, gift shop, baby-sitting.

Moderate

✪ **Hanalei Colony Resort.** 5-7130 Kuhio Hwy. c/o P.O. Box 206, Hanalei, HI 96714. ☎ **800/628-3004** or 808/826-6235. Fax 808/826-9893. www.hcr.com. E-mail hcr@aloha.net. 48 units. High season $145–$235 apt. for 4; low season $125–$210 apt. for 4. Rates includes continental breakfast twice a week. Extra person $15. AE, MC, V.

Picture this: The perfect white-sand beach is just steps from your door; lush tropical gardens, jagged mountain peaks, and fertile jungle serve as your backdrop. Welcome to Haena, Kauai's northernmost town, gateway to the famous Na Pali Coast, with miles of hiking trails, fabulous sunset views, and great beaches. This 5-acre resort of 13 two-story buildings is the place to stay if you're looking to experience the magic of the enchanting North Shore. Upon arrival, you'll get a hearty "aloha" greeting from the front desk before you proceed to your two-bedroom unit, where you'll find fresh flowers awaiting you. The units are unbelievably spacious—six people could sleep comfortably. Each has a private lanai (the less-expensive budget units face the garden), a complete kitchen, a dining area, a big living room, and ceiling fans (the area is blessed with cooling trade winds, so A/C isn't necessary). The atmosphere is quiet and relaxing; no TVs, stereos, or phones. The only sounds are tropical birdsong and waves caressing the sand. The grounds feature a large swimming pool, spa, laundry facilities, and a barbecue and picnic area. Guests also have access to complimentary beach mats and beach towels; a lending library; and children's toys, puzzles, and games (plus badminton and croquet for the entire family).

Inexpensive

Bed, Breakfast & Beach at Hanalei Bay. P.O. Box 748, Hanalei, HI 96714. ☎ **808/826-6111.** Fax 808/826-6111. E-mail hanaleibay@aol.com. 5 units. TV TEL. $65–$115 double room (includes full breakfast); extra person $15. $110 cottage for 2; extra person $10. 2- to 3-night minimum for rooms, 7-night minimum in cottage. No credit cards.

On a quiet street in a residential area just 150 yards from Hanalei Bay lies one of the best deals on the North Shore. Carolyn Barnes has been welcoming visitors for nearly a decade. The four guest rooms in her three-story house range from a 700-square-foot suite with a 360° view to a mini-apartment on the ground floor with a kitchenette and an outdoor shower. The location couldn't be better (some guests don't even bother to rent a car). It's a 4-minute walk to Hanalei Bay's 2-mile-long beach and a 10-minute walk to the shops and restaurants of Hanalei. For families, Carolyn also has a cozy two-bedroom, one-bath house a couple of blocks away.

Hale 'Aha. P.O. Box 3370 (3875 Kamehameha Dr., the 3rd street on the right past the entrance to Princeville), Princeville, HI 96722. ☎ **800/826-6733** or 808/826-6733. Fax 808/826-9052. www.hawaiian.net/~aloha/oceandream!/kauai/hale_aha. E-mail kauai@pixi.com. 4 units. TV TEL. $85–$90 double, $150–$210 suite. Rates include continental breakfast. Extra person $15. 3-night minimum. MC, V.

Golfers take note: This large home, which looks like something out of *Architectural Digest*, fronts 480 feet of the fairway and the 6th hole of the Makai Golf Course at Princeville. In addition to discounts on greens fees at both the Prince and the Makai courses, Hale 'Aha ("house of gathering") offers luxury accommodations in a beautiful setting. The B&B is the dream of Herb and Ruth Bockleman. They've thought out every detail, even designing their guest rooms so that none have adjoining walls, thereby ensuring that all their visitors have peace and privacy. The 4 units range from the Bali Ha'i Room (with an ocean view, private entrance, full bath, refrigerator, and TV) to the Penthouse Suite, a 1,000-square-foot suite with a whirlpool bath, a private lanai, its own washer and dryer, and 360° panoramic views of the golf course, mountains, and ocean.

Hale Ho'o Maha. P.O. Box 422 (on Kaliihiwai Rd., off Kuhio Hwy., at mile marker 24) Kilauea, HI 96754. ☎ **800/851-0291** or 808/828-1341. Fax 808/828-2046. www.aloha.net/ ~hoomaha. E-mail hoomaha@aloha.net. 4 units (2 with shared bathroom). TV TEL. $55–$80 double. Rates include continental breakfast. Extra person $10. AE, DC, JCB, MC, V.

Kirby Guyer and her husband, Toby, have a spacious four-bedroom, three-bath home on 5 acres. It's filled with Hawaiian and South Pacific artifacts and features a fireplace, a library, and a 150-gallon saltwater aquarium (it's more entertaining than TV). The rooms are uniquely decorated and priced with budget travelers in mind: We recommend the Pineapple Room, with its 7-foot round bed (with custom-quilted pineapple spread and matching handmade area rug) and an ocean view from the large picture window. The landscaped grounds feature a stream and a pond, and there's a waterfall across the street. Kirby has everything you need, from beach chairs to surfboards; you'll also have full access to a complete kitchen. Within spitting distance are two remarkable white-sand beaches; also close by are golf courses, riding stables, restaurants, and markets.

Historic Bed and Breakfast. 5-5067 Kuhio Hwy. (on mountain side of road as you enter Hanalei). c/o P.O. Box 1662, Hanalei, HI 96714. ☎ **808/826-4622.** www.planethawaii.com/ ~bubba/B&B/for.html. E-mail jbshepd@aloha.net. 3 units (with shared bath). **$68 double.** Rates include full breakfast. Extra person $10. 2-night minimum. MC, V.

This building used to house Kauai's oldest Buddhist temple (built in 1901) and served the Japanese Buddhist community for 85 years. In 1986, slated for demolition, the wooden structure was given a last-minute reprieve and moved from Lihue to Hanalei. The temple was totally restored, and today it's a three-room B&B. Eight and a half decades of prayer and mediation have rubbed off on this place; you can practically still smell the incense burning. Highly polished wooden floors run throughout the building, and owner Jeff Sheperd's original art decorates the walls. Two of the rooms feature four-poster bamboo queen beds (with antique Hawaiian quilts), and one room has two antique twin beds. All three rooms share one bathroom, with an additional shower outside. Jeff, a professional chef, whips out gourmet breakfasts that include items such as mac-nut pancakes and lilikoi sourdough bread. The location is great, right in the middle of Hanalei, an easy walk from shops, restaurants, and Hanalei Bay. In keeping with the quiet atmosphere, there's no TV, but Jeff has some extra guitars around for plucking, a stereo (for listening to serene music), and a lending library to occupy you on rainy days.

4 Dining

by Jocelyn Fujii

After several lean years following Hurricane Iniki, Kauai is finally buzzing again. Instead of a string of restaurant closures, we've found some hot new eateries and restaurants that have expanded. Hanalei, especially, is thriving, with plans for new food and cabaret-style blues. The owners of the popular Zelo's have big plans for this summer opening of Zelo's Sushi & Blues, a sushi bar with nontraditional Japanese newly installed windows allow views of the eye-popping Hanalei waterfalls and mountains. Kapaa's popular Sukhothai restaurant has opened a second Thai palace in Hanalei, while in Wailua, on the Coconut Coast, the chic new Caffé Coco has opened its doors at the edge of a canefield, under mango and litchi trees. Kauai's unstoppable Jean-Marie Josselin has added another big bang to his expanding galaxy. His Pacific Cafe in Kapaa and the Beach House Restaurant in Poipu have a new sibling, the Pacific Bakery & Grill in Lihue—casual, less expensive, and very busy. In Poipu, Roy's Restaurant continues its romance with happy diners from all over the island and from points afar. The reception there can be chilly, but the food is always sublime. Roy's Restaurant and Josselin's East- and South-Shore hotspots are Kauai's temples of Hawaii Regional Cuisine.

On your jaunt across the island, you'll find moderately priced choices in every town, from hamburger joints to saimin stands to busy neighborhood diners. As long as you don't expect filet mignon on a fish-and-chips budget, it should be pretty easy to please both your palate and your pocketbook. But if you do expect lobster, rack of lamb, or risotto to write home about, you'll find these pleasures, too.

For condominium dwellers who are preparing their own meals, I've featured a variety of markets and shops around Kauai—including some wonderful green markets and fruit stands—where you can pick up the island's best foodstuffs. These are listed in "Shops & Galleries," below. If you're looking for fresh island fruit, also see the box called "Fruity Smoothies & Other Exotic Treats" on p. 612.

In the listings below, reservations are not required unless otherwise noted.

LIHUE & ENVIRONS

Expensive

Gaylord's. Kilohana Square, 3-2087 Kaumualii Hwy., Lihue. ☎ **808/245-9593.** Reservations recommended. Main courses $7.95–11.95 at lunch, $16.95–$27.95 at dinner. AE, MC, V. Mon-Sat 11am–3pm and 5–9pm; Sun brunch 9:30am–3pm, dinner 5–9pm. CONTINENTAL/PACIFIC RIM.

One of Kauai's most splendid examples of kamaaina architecture, Gaylord's is the anchor of a 1930s plantation manager's estate on a 1,700-acre sugar plantation. You'll drive past horse-drawn carriages and enter a complex of shops, galleries, and a living room of Hawaiian artifacts and period furniture. The private dining room has a lavish table, always elegantly set, as if Queen Liliuokalani were expected at any minute. Next door, winding around a flagstone courtyard overlooking rolling lawns and purple mountains, the main dining room serves American classics (rack of lamb, filet mignon, prime rib), along with a few pastas, fresh seafood, and lavish desserts (home-made banana-cream pie, linzertorte, and Kilohana mud pie—layers of mocha and chocolate ice creams with fudge and peanut butter on an Oreo crust). The ambiance, historic surroundings, and soothing views from the terrace make Gaylord's a special spot for lunch, when salads, soups, fish and chips, Oliver Shagnasty's signature baby-back ribs, burgers, sandwiches, and lighter fare predominate and are friendlier to your pocketbook. Vegetarians are pretty much limited to appetizers, soups, and salads, but the selection is honorable: honey-baked Brie, garlic Brie, French-onion soup, and spinach-parmesan salad.

JJ's Broiler. 3416 Rice St., Nawiliwili. ☎ **808/246-4422.** Reservations recommended for dinner. Lunch sandwiches $7.75–$9.95; dinner main courses $15.95–$42.95. DISC, MC, V. Daily 11am–9:30pm. AMERICAN.

Famous for its Slavonic steak (tenderloin in butter, wine, and garlic), herb-crusted ahi, and the lazy Susan of salad greens that's brought to your table, JJ's is the liveliest spot on Kalapaki Bay, with open-air dining and a menu that covers more than the usual surf and turf with a few ethnic touches. The service is friendly, the mood upbeat, and the food quality consistent. The coconut shrimp is a big seller, and the Mauna Kea scallops (looking like the mountain on a heap of rice with nori) is an imaginative twist on seafood. Lunchtime appetizers include potato skins, calamari rings, quesadillas, and won tons—the United Nations of pupus! The nautically designed room and

Culinary Adventures for the Dine-&-Dash Set

If you haven't yet come face to face with the local phenom called *plate lunch*, Kauai is a good place to start. This is the island of paper-plate palaces that relieve the time (and budget) constraints of diners on the run.

Like saimin, the plate lunch is more than a gastronomic experience—it's a part of the local culture, as much a slice of island life as a shave ice or a green-flash sunset. Lihue is peppered with affordable plate-lunch counters and tiny diners that serve two scoops of rice; potato or macaroni salad; and a beef, chicken, fish, or pork entrée—all on a single plate. Although heavy gravies are de rigueur on some plates, some of the less traditional purveyors have streamlined their offerings to include healthier touches, such as lean grilled fresh fish, vegetable salad, and sensible sauces. Pork cutlets and chicken or beef soaked in teriyaki sauce, however, remain staples. Most of the time, "fried" is the operative word in plate-lunch culture, and frequently it's heavy and cholesterol-laden, too. That's why it's best to be ravenously hungry when you approach a plate lunch, or it can over-power you. At its best, a plate lunch can be a marvel of flavors, an appetite pleaser, a saving grace after a long hike or an afternoon of surfing.

The best plate-lunch counters on the island are Koloa Fish Market in Koloa, Fish Express in Lihue, and Pono Market in Kapaa. As fish markets, they always have fresh fish, and they prepare their dishes simply yet creatively. How fortunate for us that they are judiciously located on the south, southeastern, and eastern sections of the island! In southern Kauai, the **Koloa Fish Market,** 5482 Koloa Rd. (☎ **808/742-6199**), is on Koloa's main street. A tiny corner stand with plate lunches, prepared foods, and two stools on a closet-sized veranda, it sells excellent fresh fish poke (several kinds), Hawaiian-food specials, and seared ahi to go—peppered, perfectly seared, and sliced. It's gourmet fare masquerading as takeout. Daily specials may include sautéed ahi or fresh opakapaka with capers, and regular treats include crisp-on-the-outside, chewy-on-the-inside poi dumplings (when poi is available), one of life's consummate pleasures. For a picnic or outing on the South Shore, this is a good place to start.

On the Hanamaulu side of Lihue, across the street from Wal-Mart and the Wilcox Memorial Hospital, look for the prim, freestanding gray building that reads **Fish Express,** 3343 Kuhio Hwy. (☎ **808/245-9918**). It's astonishing what you'll find for $7.95 and less: Cajun-style grilled ahi; seafood stir-fry; stuffed seafood; mahi-mahi Provençale; opakapaka with guava sauce; and many other delectables, all served with rice, salad, and vegetables, and always with fresh fish. The chilled counter purveys freshly sliced sashimi and many styles of poke, from scallop, ahi, and octopus to exotic marinated crab, seaweed salads, and lomi salmon. This is a potluck bonanza! Game newcomers just point and order, while regulars pick up sweeping assortments of seafood appetizers on large platters, all

Moderate

Barbecue Inn. 2982 Kress St. (near Rice St.), Lihue. ☎ **808/245-2921.** Main courses $6.95–$10.95 at lunch, $7.95–$21.95 at dinner. No credit cards or personal checks. sandwiches, and burgers or the fancier dinner fare.

ocean view are inviting day or night, whether you're noshing on lunchtime salads,

fresh and at good prices, especially for Friday afternoon *pau hana* (after work) parties.

In east Kauai's Kapaa town, the indispensable **Pono Market**, 4-1300 Kuhio Hwy. (☎ **808/822-4581**), has similarly enticing counters of sashimi, poke, Hawaiian food, sushi, and a diverse assortment of takeout and appetizer fare. It's known for its flaky *manju* (sweet potato and other fillings in baked crust), apple turnovers, sandwiches, excellent boiled peanuts, pork and chicken lau-lau, and plate lunches—shoyu chicken, sweet-and-sour spareribs, pineapple-glazed chicken, teriyaki fish, kalua turkey or pork, and so on. Pono Market is as good as they come. If you're lucky, they'll have Taro Ko taro chips: made in Hanapepe, hard to find, and worth hand-carrying home.

Lihue, the island's county and business seat, is full of dine-and-dash ethnic eateries serving inexpensive plate-lunch cuisine, everything from bento (rice with beef, chicken, or fish, with condiments, arranged in a lidded box) to Hawaiian, Korean, and Chinese food. **Po's Kitchen**, 4100 Rice St. (☎ **808/246-8617**), offers Japanese specials: cone sushi, chicken cutlet (called *katsu*), teriyaki beef plates, and bentos. Lunch plates include the deluxe bento special (shrimp tempura with fried chicken, rice balls, salad, and a choice of a side dish). One block away, **Garden Island BBQ**, 4252-A Rice St. (☎ **808/245-8868**), is the place for Chinese plate lunches and local staples such as barbecued or lemon chicken and teriyaki steak, as well as soups and tofu dishes.

On the other side of Lihue town, the main drag, Kuhio Highway, is lined with fast-food institutions such as McDonald's and Pizza Hut. Sprinkled in between those familiar signs are places like the **Bento House**, 3122 Kuhio Hwy. (☎ **808/246-9444**). The familiar teriyaki beef and fried chicken are standards, and the kalua-turkey special, when offered, is a bestseller. A stone's throw away is **Oki Bento**, 3125 Kuhio Hwy. (☎ **808/245-5899**), open 24 hours on weekends and all hours except 3 to 5pm weekdays. As with all plate-lunch places, there's zero ambiance, but the bento plates are popular, and the pumpkin-crunch pie is a round-the-clock hit.

In the Kukui Grove Center, at Kaumualii Highway (Hwy. 50) and Old Nawiliwili Road, **Joni-Hana** (☎ **808/245-5213**) is famous for its specials—nearly 20 a day! The tiny counter serves fried noodles, lemon-shoyu ono (wahoo), teriyaki everything, and many other local dishes. It's arguably the busiest place on the mall.

Kunja's, 4-939 Kuhio Hwy., Unit A (next to Taco Bell; ☎ **808/821-2088**), specializes in Korean-style barbecued kal bi ribs ($6.95), served with rice, kim chee, and salad. The 11-table cubicle does a brisk takeout business at lunch among locals who also like the barbecued chicken, pork cutlet, and mun doo (Korean dumplings), all for less than $7.25.

Mon–Thurs 7:30–10:30am, 11am–1:30pm, and 5–8:30pm; Fri–Sat 7:30–10:30am, 11am–1:30pm, and 4:30–8:45pm. AMERICAN/JAPANESE/PACIFIC RIM.

Watch for the specials at this 62-year-old family restaurant, located on a small side street, where everything from soup to dessert is made in the Sasakis's kitchen. While you can still get a $3.50 hamburger for lunch, a new chef has introduced more specials to an already wide-ranging menu that includes complete dinners for $8.95 to $17.95 and Pacific Rim entrées that include deep-fried coconut shrimp ($15.95) and mahi-mahi crusted in macadamia nuts, served with coconut cream-spinach sauce ($15.95). The familiar favorites remain (oxtail soup, Japanese-style dinners, baby-back ribs). Sandwiches come on homemade bread, the tuna salad is made with fresh ahi when available, and several-course dinner combinations of Japanese and American favorites draw long lines. This is a long-time favorite, with many menu choices, ranging from potstickers to fresh-hooked akule (big-eyed scad) to miso-marinated sea bass. At lunch and dinner, pay attention to the combination specials—they're a value, especially the steamed mahi-mahi lau-lau for $9.95.

Cafe Portofino. In Pacific Ocean Plaza, 3501 Rice St., Lihue. ☎ **808/245-2121.** Reservations recommended. Main courses $6.50–$10.25 at lunch, $13.50–$23 at dinner. AE, DC, DISC, JCB, MC, V. Mon–Fri 11am–2pm and 5–10pm, Sat–Sun 5–10pm. NORTHERN ITALIAN.

Fans come to Portofino for the romantic ambiance, a feature that counts in the competitive Nawiliwili dining scene. Draws include alfresco dining and candlelit tables with views of Kalapaki Bay and Nawiliwili Harbor and, during the day, of coconut-laden trees and the mountains beyond Nawiliwili. The beveled-glass sash windows on three sides add light and cheer at lunch, but most diners choose the deck, where the view of the mountain range behind Nawiliwili is up close and personal, beyond the coconut-laden palm trees. The realistically priced menu covers four veal preparations, vegetable lasagne, bistecca (New York steak), and an abundance of pasta choices. The Caesar salad is garlicky and wonderful, and fans rave about the house specialty, osso bucco.

★ **Duke's Canoe Club.** At the Kauai Marriott & Beach Club, 3610 Rice St., Nawiliwili. ☎ **808/246-9599.** Reservations recommended for dinner. Lunch $3.95–$9.95; dinner $7.95–$19.95; Taco Tuesdays 4–6pm, with $2 fish tacos and $2 draft beer. AE, DC, DISC, MC, V. Barefoot Bar, daily 11:30am–11:30pm; main dining room, daily 5–10pm. STEAK/SEAFOOD.

Part of a highly successful restaurant chain (Duke's Canoe Club in Waikiki, Hula Grill and Leilani's in Kaanapali, Kimo's in Lahaina), this oceanfront oasis is the hippest spot in town, with the winning combination of great view, affordable menu, attractive salad bar, popular music, and a very happy happy hour. It's hard to go wrong at Duke's. The noontime bestseller is the stir-fry cashew chicken ($8.95), but the fresh mahi burger ($7.95) and the grilled chicken quesadilla ($5.95) are front-runners, too. On Tuesdays, the $2 fish tacos are a major attraction. Most people go for the five or six varieties of fresh catch a night, served in five different preparations—a great value at $19.95. The biggest appetites lunge for the prime-rib dinner, $16.95 for the 12- to 14-ounce size and $23.95 for the 25- to 30-ounce size, served with garlic mashed potatoes and the salad bar. Hawaiian musicians, the Apana Sisters, serenade diners nightly, while downstairs in the Barefoot Bar, Hawaiian and contemporary Hawaiian music adds to the ambiance. Fridays from 4 to 6pm and 8:30 to 11pm. A tip for happy-hour revelers: Tropical Fridays, from 4 to 6pm, when live Hawaiian music lifts the spirit and tropical drinks cost $3, accompanied by food specials—very popular among the *pau hana* (after work) crowd.

Inexpensive

Dani's Restaurant. 4201 Rice St., Lihue. ☎ **808/245-4991.** Main courses $4.95–$6. No credit cards. Mon–Fri 5am–1:30pm, Sat 5am–1pm. AMERICAN/HAWAIIAN.

Formica all the way, and always packed for breakfast, Dani's is the pancake palace of Lihue: banana, pineapple, papaya, and buttermilk, plus sweetbread French toast and kalua-pig omelets. Regulars know that fried rice is offered on Thursday only, and that the papaya hotcakes are a deal at less than $4. At lunch, Hawaiian specials—lau-lau, kalua pig, lomi salmon, and beef stew in various combinations—dominate the otherwise standard American menu of fried foods (pork chops, liver, scallops, chicken, and more) and sandwiches. Antigourmet to the end.

✪ Hamura's Saimin Stand. 2956 Kress St., Lihue. ☎ **808/245-3271.** Most items less than $4.50. No credit cards. Mon–Thurs 10am–11pm, Fri–Sat 10am–1am, Sun 10am–10pm. SAIMIN.

Hamura's is a cultural experience, a world-renowned saimin stand where fans line up to take their place over steaming bowls of this island specialty at a few U-shaped counters. Hamura's saimin and teriyaki barbecue sticks attract an all-day, late-night, pre- and postmovie crowd that acknowledges saimin as the prevailing cultural ritual, the burgers and fries of Hawaii. The kitchen is a blur of steam and mounds of noodles, which come heaped with vegetables, won tons, hard-boiled eggs, sweetened pork, vegetables, and several condiment combinations. I adore the rubber-slipper casualness of Hamura's and the simple pleasures it unfailingly delivers, with the ever-humorous touch on the wall menu: a sign exhorting diners not to stick gum under the counters.

Hanamaulu Restaurant. 3-4291 Kuhio Hwy., Hanamaulu. ☎ **808/245-2511.** Reservations recommended. Main courses $5.50–$15. MC, V. Tues–Fri 10am–1pm and 4:30–8:30pm, Sat–Sun 4:30–8:30pm. CHINESE/JAPANESE.

When passing this place, you'd never know that serene Japanese gardens with stone pathways and tatami-floored teahouses are hidden within. You can dine at the sushi bar, American style, or in the teahouses for lunch or dinner, but you must call ahead for teahouse dining. At lunch, enter a world of chop suey, won tons, teriyaki chicken, and sukiyaki (less verve than value), with many other choices in Japanese and Chinese plate lunches, $5.75 to $7.50. (The deluxe Chinese plate lunch, with soup, fried chicken, fried shrimp, chop suey, crisp won tons, sweet-and-sour spareribs, and sweetened pork, goes for an astonishing $7.50.) Special Japanese and Chinese menus can be planned ahead for groups of up to 60 people, who can dine at low tables on tatami floors in a Japanese garden setting. Old-timers love this place, and those who came here in diapers are now stopping in for after-golf pupus and beer. Tip for vegetarians: Stir-fried veggies, vegetable tempura, and tofu tempura specials go for $4.50 to $7, and a teishoku vegetarian platter is $13.75. The inexpensive noodle dishes—soft, crisp, saimin, won-ton mein, and others—are always affordable at $3.25 to $6.

Kauai Chop Suey. In Pacific Ocean Plaza, 3501 Rice St., Nawiliwili. ☎ **808/245-8790.** Most dishes $6–$9. No credit cards. Tues–Sat 11am–2pm and 4:30–9pm, Sun 4:30–9pm. CANTONESE.

The large, unremarkable dining room and so-so service can mean only that the legions of loyal diners are coming for one thing: good food at low prices. Local folks who work in the area come for lunch, and those who don't work nearby bring their families in the evenings. The huge menu has something for everyone. Chow mein; Cantonese shrimp; roast duck; lemon chicken; and hundreds of choices of Cantonese noodles, soups, sweet-and-sours, foo-yongs, and stir-fries stream across the dining room to the chopsticks of expectant diners.

La Bamba. 4261 Rice St., Lihue. ☎ **808/245-5972.** Main courses $5.95–$22. MC, V. Daily 11am–10pm. MEXICAN.

Everything comes big here except the room: 10 tables, a friendly atmosphere, and huge platters of fajitas, chile rellenos, and tamales (the three bestsellers). At dinner, the burrito and enchilada combination plates ($11.95) are winners, served, like everything else, with Mexican rice and refried beans. The food is home-style and good, and so are the prices; some house specials are priced as low as $6.95, and the servings are usually too big for one.

Pacific Bakery & Grill. 4479 Rice St. ☎ **808/246-0999.** Main courses **$7.25–$10.50,** specials less than **$12.** MC, V. Mon–Sat 7:30–10:30am and 11:30am–8pm, Sun 7am–3pm. CASUAL HAWAII REGIONAL CUISINE.

What a cheerful change from the musty Eggbert's, which occupied this space in pre-Iniki days. Renowned chef and restaurateur Jean-Marie Josselin picked Don Gusman as executive chef for his new casual eatery with its bright-yellow ceiling, marbled orange walls, and brightly embellished concrete floors. The 115-seat restaurant is located in the middle of Lihue, halfway between Poipu and Kapaa, where Josselin's two other fancier restaurants have built their own large followings. It's a full-service restaurant, bar, and bakery center, but don't fill up on the Danishes and palm-leaf pastries. There are many good things here: for breakfast, huevos rancheros with black Thai rice and avocado salsa, or kalua-turkey omelets with lomi-salmon salsa. For lunch, the half-rotisserie chicken with lemon butter is served with garlic mashed potatoes, an American classic. But the biggest hit (and one that won't require a siesta) is the grilled ahi sandwich on a fresh Kaiser roll, served with avocado pesto, grilled eggplant, and roasted garlic—manna at $8.75. Be sure to inquire about the soup of the day—it's usually an event. The lunch and dinner menus are the same, and they offer bountiful choices for vegetarians, too: grilled eggplant salad with creamy garlic dressing, four-cheese pizza, crisp onion rings with tamarind ketchup, and green papaya salad with rice noodles.

Restaurant Kiibo. 299 Umi St., Lihue. ☎ **808/245-2650.** Main courses **$5–$19.** JCB, MC, V. Mon–Fri 11am–1:30pm, Mon–Sat 5:30–9pm. JAPANESE.

Neither a sleek sushi bar nor a plate-lunch canteen, Kiibo is a neighborhood staple with inexpensive, unpretentious, tasty, home-style Japanese food served in a pleasant room accented with Japanese folk art. At a tiny counter or at tables, dine on sushi, ramen, sukiyaki, tempura, teriyaki, and the steamed egg-rice-vegetable marvel called *oyako donburi.* For $6, you'll get a satisfying lunch special; $15.95 will buy a combination plate with dessert, more than satisfying and more elegant than the folksy surroundings. In between is the $9 teishoku special of mackerel, salmon, soup, dessert, and other condiments. Caveat: The noodle soups can be a bit salty for some careful diners.

THE POIPU RESORT AREA
Expensive

✪ **The Beach House.** 5022 Lawai Rd., Poipu. ☎ **808/742-1424.** Reservations recommended. Appetizers **$7.95–$9.95;** main courses **$20–$24.** AE, DC, DISC, MC, V. Daily 5:30–9:30pm. HAWAII REGIONAL/MEDITERRANEAN.

This is the South Shore's premier spot for sunset drinks and appetizers—a treat for all the senses. Graze on Jean-Marie Josselin's sumptuous creations made from local products, fresh as can be. Ever the discerning businessman, Jean-Marie Josselin has chosen the best view on the South Shore to accompany his culinary creations. Walk through an alcove of paintings by local artists into a large room on the ocean accented with oversize floral bouquets and sliding glass doors that open or close the room, but never the view. Come for cocktails or early dinner, when you can still see the sunsets and perhaps a turtle or two bobbing in the waves. Menus are printed daily, but look for Josselin's signature touches: wok-charred mahi-mahi, sizzling clams, tiger-eye ahi sushi tempura, tenderloin steak, and premium poultry and fresh-fish fantasies. Potatoes in any form (warm potato salad, au gratin, mashed, in warm seafood salad, in saffron-fennel potato broth) catapult the spud to new levels of respect. With or without the sunset, this is one of the top culinary experiences on Kauai.

✪ **Roy's Poipu Bar & Grill.** In the Poipu Shopping Village, 2360 Kiahuna Plantation Dr. ☎ **808/742-5000.** Reservations recommended. Main courses $12.95–$26.95. AE, CB, DC, DISC, MC, V. Daily 5:30–9:30pm. EURO-ASIAN.

Another temptation impossible to resist: Roy's in Poipu. Because appetizers are a major part of the menu (which changes daily), you can sample the legendary fare of Roy Yamaguchi without breaking the bank. This is a loud, lively room with ceiling fans, marble tables, art by local artists, and a menu tailor-made for foodies. Yamaguchi's (of Roy's restaurants on Oahu, Maui, Tokyo, and Guam) signature touches are abundantly present: an excellent, progressive, and affordable wine selection; fresh, local ingredients prepared with a nod to Europe, Asia, and the Pacific; and service so efficient it can be overbearing. You can dine all evening on the appetizers alone: nori-seared ahi with black-bean sauce, spinach-shiitake ravioli, and seafood potstickers in Thai coconut-milk sauce. The three dozen nightly specials invariably include six to eight fresh fish a night, prepared at least five or six different ways. The blackened ahi in soy-mustard-butter sauce ($24.95) is likely to impress.

Moderate

Brennecke's Beach Broiler. 2100 Hoone Rd. (across from Poipu Beach Park). ☎ **808/742-7588.** Main courses $6.95–$29.95. AE, CB, DC, DISC, MC, V. Daily 11am–10pm (street-side deli takeout, daily 8am–9pm). AMERICAN/SEAFOOD.

Window boxes and views of Poipu Beach are pleasing touches at this seafood-burger house, a longtime favorite. Of course, it helps that the best hamburgers on the South Shore are served here, as well as vegetarian selections that are winning fans among even the heartiest carnivores. It's so casual that you can drop in before or after the beach and dine on nachos and peppers, a won-ton/eggroll pupu platter, fresh fish sandwiches, kiawe-broiled fish and kebabs, prime rib, pasta, and a salad bar, as well as build-your-own gourmet burgers. Look for their early-dinner and happy-hour specials daily.

Kalaheo Steak House. 4444 Papalina Rd., Kalaheo (inland from Poipu). ☎ **808/332-9780.** Main courses $12.95–$24.95. DISC, MC, V. Mid-Oct to mid-Mar, daily 5:30–9:30pm; mid-Mar to mid-Oct, daily 6–10pm. STEAKS.

There are booths and tables, a bar area, potted plants, and great salads, baked potatoes, and sautéed mushrooms to go with the surf-and-turf fare. It's informal—no linen tablecloths—so you can wear jeans and feel comfortable, Kalaheo style. Prime rib is the bestseller at this local institution: 12 ounces for $16.95 and double that for $22.95, served with salad, rice or potato, and rolls. The fresh grilled seafood at market price is a close second for hefty appetites, and the sautéed mushrooms a winner.

Keoki's Paradise. In the Poipu Shopping Village, 2360 Kiahuna Plantation Dr. ☎ **808/742-7534.** Reservations recommended. Main courses $6.95–$10.95 at lunch, $10.95–$28.95 at dinner. AE, DC, MC, V. Daily 11am–10pm. (Bar, daily until midnight.) STEAK/SEAFOOD.

It's large and lively and has improved with the years, with lunch favorites that include a fresh ahi sandwich, fresh-fish tacos, and chicken Caesar salad—all good and affordable. In the evenings, regulars tout the fresh fish crusted in lemongrass, basil, and breadcrumbs, a savory entrée among the fresh local seafood, poultry, and meats served in a South Seas atmosphere of waterfalls and abundant foliage. On the dinner menu, the fresh catch is offered in six to eight preparations, such as baked in lemon, sautéed in citrus shoyu, grilled in teriyaki sauce, or broiled butterless. For dessert, the original Hula pie from Kimo's in Lahaina is something to be reckoned with. The café in the bar area serves lighter fare and is open from 11am to 11pm daily, with live Hawaiian music on weekends.

Piatti Italian Restaurant. At the Kiahuna Plantation Resort, Poipu. ☎ **808/742-2216.** Reservations recommended for dinner. Main courses $5.95–$10.95 at lunch, $10.95–$22.95 at dinner. AE, DC, MC, V. Daily 3pm–10pm. NORTHERN ITALIAN.

Poipu's darling attracts diners from all corners of the island and from the mainland, where the Piatti chain has legions of fans. Piatti delights all senses with its plantation-style wood-accented room, wraparound veranda, and Italian fare as lush as its gardens. Dine indoors or on the bistro patio on lasagna, Caesar salad, pizzas, and a fine selection of pasta and grill items. The roasted half chicken is rubbed with 11 spices, cooked over kiawe, and served with garlic mashed potatoes and its own roasting juices—a feast sublime ($16.95). Light eaters are drawn to the Okinawan spinach salad, fresh from the garden, with citrus vinaigrette, shaved parmigiana, orange fillets, and edible flowers. The lamb is popular among carnivores, and fish lovers swear by the pan-seared, taro-crusted ono. The general manager's wife tends a garden of herbs, as well as many of the greens used in the salads and pasta, including the hundreds of basil plants needed for those savory pestos and sauces.

Pomodoro. In the Rainbow Plaza, Kaumualii Hwy. (Hwy. 50), Kalaheo (inland from Poipu). ☎ **808/332-5945.** Reservations recommended. Main courses $9.50–$17.95. MC, V. Daily 8am–10pm. ITALIAN.

Pomodoro is the Italian magnet of the west side, a small, casual, and intimate second-floor dining room with a bar, potted plants, soft lighting, and Italian music softly wafting through the room. Occasionally, you'll see grandma knitting on the porch as you enter, which adds to the family feeling. The European flavor suits the cuisine; homemade mozzarella, fresh steamed clams, penne arrabiatta, chicken saltimbocca, homemade pasta that makes great lasagne, cannelloni, manicotti, and casseroles. Veal, chicken, scampi, calamari, organic green salads, and other Italian attractions round out the menu of homemade delights. You can request heaps of garlic in your scampi; the servings are generous and the flavors are big.

Inexpensive

Brick Oven Pizza. 2-2555 Kaumualii Hwy. (Hwy. 50), Kalaheo (inland from Poipu). ☎ **808/332-8561.** Sandwiches less than $6.70; pizzas $9.25–$25.60. Tues–Sun 11am–10pm. PIZZA.

A Kalaheo fixture for 22 years, Brick Oven is the quintessential mom-and-pop business, serving pizza cooked directly on the brick hearth, brushed with garlic butter and topped with real cheeses and long-simmering sauces. You have your choice of whole-wheat or white crust, plus 16 toppings: Italian sausage, Portuguese sausage, bay shrimp, vegetarian, anchovies, smoked ham, and several weighty combinations. The result is a very popular pizza, particularly when topped with fresh garlic and served with Gordon Biersch beer. The stellar seafood-style pizza-bread sandwiches are big at lunch.

Kalaheo Coffee Co. & Café. 2-2436 Kaumualii Hwy. (Hwy. 50), Kalaheo (inland from Poipu). ☎ **808/332-5858.** Most items less than $6.95. MC, V. Mon–Sat 6:30am–4pm, Sun 7am–2pm. COFFEEHOUSE.

John Ferguson, who made quite a name for himself at the Stouffer Waiohai Beach Resort before it got wiped out by Iniki, has long been one of our favorite Kauai chefs.

He and his wife, Kris, operate a cafe that's a coffee lover's fantasy: Kauai Estate Peaberry, Kona dark roast, Maui's Kaanapali Estate, Molokai Estate, Guatemalan French roast, Colombian, Costa Rican, Sumatran, and African coffees—you can visit the world on a coffee bean! Located at a major intersection in Kalaheo, the coffeehouse serves masterful breakfasts and sandwiches: Bonzo Breakfast Burritos (sautéed ham, peppers, mushrooms, onions, and olives scrambled with cheese, served with salsa and sour cream), veggie omelets with sundried tomatoes and mushrooms, Belgian waffles and bagels. At lunch, the fabulous grilled-turkey burgers (heaped with grilled onions and mushrooms on a sourdough bun) are headliners on a list of winners: grilled Cajun tofu and eggplant, grilled fresh vegetables on homemade focaccia, grilled herbed chicken breast, hot pastrami, and others. Fresh-from-the-garden salads brighten up the day. The soup changes daily, and it's tasty and inexpensive. The cinnamon "knuckles" baked fresh daily, the lilikoi cheesecake, fresh apple pie and carrot cake, and the "killer" chocolate ganache cake are more reasons to stop by.

Koloa Broiler. 5412 Old Koloa Rd., Koloa. ☎ **808/742-9122.** Main courses $6.50–$14.95. AE, DC, JCB, MC, V. Daily 11am–10pm. STEAK/SEAFOOD.

Wood is the visual theme here: creaky steps on a wooden deck in Koloa town, leading up to the rustic dining room with ceiling fans and wooden trellises—a lot like the set for *Gunsmoke*, minus the swinging doors. The food as well is aimed at cowboy tastes. This is broil-your-own dining: top sirloin, mahi-mahi, baby-back pork ribs, beef kebabs, barbecued chicken, and fresh fish (when available). The best feature of this broiler is the locally caught fresh fish and Kauai-grown vegetables and fruits.

La Griglia. In the Poipu Shopping Village, 2360 Kiahuna Plantation Dr. ☎ **808/742-2147.** Main courses $10.95–$11.95. DC, DISC, MC, V. Daily 8am–10pm. ITALIAN.

It's a great place for breakfast, with homemade breads and pastries served in an outdoor cafe with cappuccino and all the rest. The bakery here bakes the bread with which the popular *panini*—sandwiches heaped with meats, vegetables, cheeses, and condiments—are made. It's nice to have an informal outdoor cafe in this sterile shopping plaza, where you can drop in for espresso and a generously liqueured tiramisù, served under umbrellas in a small courtyard. The menu also features burgers (Cajun blackened, meatball, eggplant-parmigiana, and other choices) and affordable dinner entrées of chicken parmigiana, spinach lasagne, and eggplant parmigiana.

La Griglia recently opened two pizzerias, one in Nawiliwili's Anchor Cove Shopping Center (☎ **808/742-8811**) and the other in Old Koloa Town (☎ **808/245-8811**). Spicy shrimp, vegetarian, and puttanesca (with olives, capers, blackened chicken, and spicy red sauce, topped with cheese) are among the pizza selections, delivered free. The biggest, headiest hit is the sundae topped with homemade, espresso-laced hot fudge—wow!

Tomkats Grille. 5404 Koloa Rd., Old Koloa Town. ☎ **808/742-8887.** Main courses $5.75–$16.95. DC, MC, V. Daily 11am–10pm. (Bar, daily until midnight.) AMERICAN/GRILL.

Fried appetizers, inexpensive New York steak ($14.95), rotisserie chicken ($8.50 for a half), seafood salad with fresh catch, and sandwiches and burgers for all tastes are among the offerings at the Grille, in a serene garden setting in Old Koloa Town. Old-fashioned nonmicrobrewed beer is big here—everything from Watney's to Samuel Adams to Guinness Stout plus two dozen others, all the better to wash down the spicy jalapeños stuffed with cream cheese. For the reckless: the Cats' Combo, a basket of jumbo onion rings, mozzarella sticks, zucchini, and mushrooms, all crisply fried. Vegetarians need not feel left out; there are always some choices for them.

SOUTHWEST KAUAI

Moderate

Green Garden. Hwy. 50, Hanapepe. ☎ **808/335-5422.** Reservations recommended for dinner. Sandwiches and plate lunches $6.50; dinner main courses $14.50–$28. AE, MC, V. Mon, Wed–Fri 8:30am–2pm, Wed–Mon 5–9pm. AMERICAN/ISLAND.

This Hanapepe landmark continues a decades-old tradition of offering local fare amid layers of foliage inside and out. A riot of fishing balls suspended in nets, plants everywhere, and a labyrinthine dining room make this a unique environment. The Green Garden is known for its inexpensive fresh-fish sandwiches and lilikoi-cream pies and, at dinner, the kiawe-grilled fresh-fish specials (onaga, opakapaka, and ehu, $14.50) that come with soup and salad.

⭐ **Hanapepe Cafe & Espresso Bar.** 3830 Hanapepe Rd., Hanapepe. ☎ **808/335-5011.** Reservations recommended for dinner. Main courses $15.95–$18.95. DISC, MC, V. Tues–Sat 8am–2pm, Wed–Sat 6–9pm. GOURMET VEGETARIAN.

They really got it right here: excellent slack-key guitar music on the sound system and delectable, wholesome food in a casual, winning ambiance. The low-fat or no-fat vegan specials and creative gourmet vegetarian cuisine have won this cafe a loyal following islandwide. The espresso, pancakes (multigrain with bananas, multigrain with apple-spice, and so on), and homemade sourdough French toast served with fresh bananas and real maple syrup are a major morning attraction, as are the Hanapepe-grown taro home fries. Sliced and sautéed with garlic and fresh herbs, the taro is a creative coup. Pasta, a zesty Caesar salad with homemade croutons, and the best grilled-vegetable sandwich in Hawaii are served at the U-shaped tile bar or at Formica tables under high ceilings. The seven varieties of garden burger elevate this modest staple to gourmet status. At dinner, don't resist the mushroom/wild rice/garlic bread stuffing in puff pastry. Main courses (spinach and Gorgonzola potatoes, sautéed portobellos with Hanapepe taro relish and saffron-butter sauce, seared artichoke hearts, and more) are priced from $15.95 to $18.95, but appetizer portions are available for less. Thursday to Saturday evenings, you can savor all this and listen to the finest guitarists on the island play live. All in all, a sublime experience.

Omoide. 5164 Kaumualii Hwy. (Hwy. 50), Hanapepe. ☎ **808/335-5291.** Lunch plates $4.50–$5.50; dinner main courses $5–$24. MC, V. Deli, Mon 6:30am–3pm, Tues–Sun 8am–9pm; dining room, daily 5–9pm. CHINESE/STEAKHOUSE.

Although there's a lot more competition of late, Omoide's lilikoi-chiffon pie still lives up to its reputation. Pie lovers should make this a priority; if you're getting takeout from the adjoining deli, they sell it by the slice, too. Otherwise, the choices are Cantonese, with a small sampling at the takeout counter, where the Chinese noodles and oyster chicken taste better than they look. The dinner-only dining room offers a wider range of choices, including the bestselling steamed sea bass ($7.85 for half a fish), crisp gau gee mein ($5.75), the popular oyster chicken ($6), and Wong's famous cake noodles ($5.75). The top-of-the-line entrée is the $23 lobster tail, but otherwise, the menu is reasonable.

Toi's Thai Kitchen. In the Eleele Shopping Center, Eleele. ☎ **808/335-3111.** Main courses $8.95–$15.95. CB, DC, MC, V. Mon–Sat 10:30am–2:30pm and 5:30–9:30pm, Sun 5:30–9:30pm. THAI/AMERICAN.

Toi's is a sensible dining choice—informal, affordable, and authentic, using fresh herbs and local ingredients. The house specialty, Toi's Temptation (homegrown herbs, coconut milk, lemongrass, and your choice of seafood, meat, or tofu), has a following, but so do the vegetable curries, shrimp sate, and ginger-sauce nua: your choice of seafood, meat, or tofu in a toothsome fresh ginger stir-fry. Most of the rice, noodle, soup, curry, and main-course selections allow you to choose pork, chicken, seafood, beef, vegetarian, or tofu as the main ingredient. Buttered garlic nua, peanut-rich sates, and stir-fried Basil Delight are among Toi's many tasty preparations. All dishes come with green-papaya salad, dessert, and a choice of jasmine, sticky, or brown rice.

Wrangler's Steakhouse. 9852 Kaumualii Hwy., Waimea. ☎ **808/338-1218.** Main courses $9.95–$19. AE, MC, V. Mon–Thurs 11am–8:30pm, Fri 11am–9pm, Sat 5–9pm, Sun 9am–2pm (brunch). STEAKS.

Waimea's popular dining spot has expanded its offerings by adding a pizza parlor, Pacific Pizza & Deli. Good service and pleasant veranda seating are among the pluses of this family-run operation. Western touches abound: a wagon in the loft, log-framed booths with gas lanterns, and lauhala paniolo hats in the made-in-Hawaii gift shop. A combination of cowboy, plantation, and island traditions, Wrangler's serves everything from shrimp tempura with sashimi to beef teriyaki; imu-style roast pork with cabbage, and grilled mahi-mahi sandwiches, smoky and tender. Families like Wrangler's for its multicourse dinners that won't break the bank, and the pizza adds to the value.

Inexpensive

✪ **Jo-Jo's Clubhouse.** 9734 Kaumualii Hwy. (Hwy. 50; next to the Waimea Library), Waimea. ☎ **808/338-0056.** Most items less than $4. No credit cards. Daily 10am–6pm. SNACK SHOP.

Barely more than a tiny cottage with a large shave-ice sign, Jo-Jo's is the snack central of the neighborhood, an after-school magnet for school kids who converge here for the shave ice, popcorn, nachos, hotdogs, and other dinner-defying temptations. There are 52 choices of shave ice, including the new homemade haupia (coconut custard), lilikoi, mango, and other toothsome tropical flavors. The halo halo is an icy treat with shredded coconut, jack fruit, and azuki beans—$3 worth of exotic refreshment. When the kids aren't lining up for the rainbow shave ice with macadamia-nut ice cream, a treat for $1.50, they're clamoring for the *li hing mui* sprinkles—a tart, salty-sour plum flavor that has made its way into the mainstream, in everything from gummi bears to candies to popcorn and dried mango.

Yumi's. 9691 Kaumualii Hwy., Waimea. ☎ **808/338-1731.** Most items less than $5.25. No credit cards. Mon–Fri 5:30am–3pm, Sat 6am–3pm. LOCAL/PLATE LUNCH.

Yumi's serves hearty egg, sausage, and bacon breakfasts, rolled sushi that flies out the door, and coconut and apple turnovers that are the rage of West Kauai. Flaky, buttery, and substantial without being weighty, the turnovers are straight out of grandmother's kitchen, all lightness and flavor. "I don't know whether I come here for the $3 breakfast or to feel really local," notes a new Kekaha resident. I go there to buy the turnovers, and I cart them off the island when I can. Caveat: Don't take the nononsense service personally.

THE COCONUT COAST
Expensive

✪ **A Pacific Cafe Kauai.** In the Kauai Shopping Village, 4-831 Kuhio Hwy., Kapaa. ☎ **808/822-0013.** Reservations recommended. Main courses $20–$24. AE, DC, DISC, MC, V. Daily 5:30–9:30pm. HAWAII REGIONAL/MEDITERRANEAN.

This is still my favorite of Jean-Marie Josselin's five Hawaii restaurants, and it was his first. This is the hub of dining on the island, a casually chic spot that's always crowded and buzzing with energy. And who can resist the light-as-air, deep-fried tiger-eye sushi with wasabi beurre blanc; the wok-charred mahi-mahi with garlic-sesame crust and lime-ginger-butter sauce; the mushroom-eggplant-tomato-shrimp risotto; or any of the fresh grilled fishes in sauces of coriander, fennel seeds, white truffle, and peppercorns? Josselin has a marvelous way with clams, rice, fish, sauces, meats, and the marvelous Kauai produce he goes out of his way to grow or gather. The menu changes every day, and there are ample appetizers in all price ranges, making this a restaurant that can be expensive but doesn't have to be.

Moderate

The Bull Shed. 796 Kuhio Ave., Waipouli. ☎ **808/822-3791.** Reservations recommended for parties of 6 or more. Main courses $10.95–$28.95. AE, DC, DISC, MC, V. Daily 5:30–10pm. STEAK/SEAFOOD.

The informality and oceanfront location are big pluses, but they're only part of the package. This time-tested steakhouse on a hidden beach in Waipouli serves steaks and chops—prime rib, Australian rack of lamb, a garlic tenderloin—that have been pleasing meat lovers for years; Bull Shed has some very loyal customers from around the island. The fresh catch, grilled to order, is part of a respectable seafood selection that includes broiled shrimp, Alaskan king crab, and Parmesan-drenched scallops. The entrées include rice and the salad bar, and combination dinners aim for the ambivalent, with chicken, steak, seafood, and lobster pairings. The salad bar alone costs $6.95, and the entrées are so big they're often shared.

Buzz's Steak & Lobster. In Coconut Marketplace, 484 Kuhio Hwy., Kapaa. ☎ **808/822-0041.** Reservations recommended for dinner. Main courses $7.50 and less at lunch, $7.95–$38.95 at dinner. AE, DC, DISC, JCB, MC, V. Daily 11am–2:30pm and 4:30–10:30pm. (Bar, daily until 11:30pm; happy hour daily 2–5pm.) STEAK/SEAFOOD.

For years an anchor of the Coconut Marketplace, Buzz's buzzes with happy-hour celebrants who gather for the $3.75 exotic drinks (as opposed to $5) and vegetable crudités or whatever appetizers the chef pulls out of his toque. Soup and salad, and a fresh ahi sandwich, are lunchtime staples in this steak-and-seafood restaurant. But it's popular for dinner, too, when choices range from an early-bird dinner special for $7.95 to a $29.95 lobster tail to steak and lobster for $33.95. With the hotdogs recently added to the lunch menu and the $6.95 salad bar there are options for all budgets.

Kapaa Fish & Chowder House. 4-1639 Kuhio Hwy., Kapaa. ☎ **808/822-7488.** Reservations recommended. Main courses $12.95–$24.95. AE, DISC, MC, V. Daily happy hour 4–6pm, dinner daily 5:30–9:30pm. AMERICAN.

The passion-fruit margaritas (pioneered and perfected here), the garden setting, and the crisp, moist coconut shrimp served with mango-churney sauce make this a pleasant stop at the north end of Kapaa town. The outdoor garden patio is ideal for appetizers and a cold beer or margarita. The choices: steamer clams ($14.95 for a 2-pound bucket), oysters on the half shell, deep-fried calamari ($6.95), a mound of iced shrimp ($10.95, $7.95 for half a dozen), or escargots (half a dozen for $7.95). For dinner, the conventional choices include fresh catch with papaya salsa, sautéed calamari, and a crackly, spicy New York pepper steak.

Mema Thai Cuisine. In the Wailua Shopping Plaza, 4-361 Kuhio Hwy., Wailua. ☎ **808/823-0899.** Main courses $7.95–$17.95. AE, DC, DISC, MC, V. Mon–Fri 11am–2:30pm, daily 5–9:30pm. THAI.

A relative newcomer to Kauai, Thai cookery has introduced a conspiracy of curry to the island, and Mema is one of the instigators. From soup (spicy lemongrass, Thai ginger-coconut) to cool papaya salads and hot curries with complex flavors, Mema's menu appeals to many tastes, including vegetarians. Shrimp rolls, a Thai staple, come with an extra touch: black mushrooms and water chestnuts, rolled up tight in long rice, fresh mint, and cucumber. The Pad Thai noodles ($7.95 with chicken, $9.95 with shrimp) are a satisfying classic. The multicolored curries come mild, medium, or hot, and with your choice of meat, chicken, or seafood. Mema's Curry, with kaffir-lime leaves, lemongrass, garlic, coconut milk, and other rich flavorings, is a house specialty, as is the panang-style Siam curry.

Wailua Marina Restaurant. 5971 Kuhio Hwy., Wailua. ☎ **808/822-4311.** Reservations recommended. Main courses $9–$28. AE, MC, V. Tues–Sun 10:30am–2pm and 5–9pm. AMERICAN.

I recommend the open-air seating along the Wailua River, where you can watch the riverboats heading for the Fern Grotto over sandwiches (mahi-mahi is a favorite) and salads. The interior is cavernous, with a high ceiling and stuffed fish adorning the upper walls—unremarkable bordering on weird, but I love the Marina anyway. The new salad bar makes the Marina friendlier to dieters and vegetarians, but otherwise, there are famous baked stuffed pork chops, hot lobster salad, steamed mullet, stuffed prawns, teriyaki spareribs, and some 40 other down-home items that are unapologetic in their use of heavy sauces and gravies. The menu includes prime rib, filet mignon, boneless teriyaki chicken breast, and on the lighter side, a Chinese oxtail soup with fresh ginger and mustard cabbage, a deal at $9. Except for lobster and a few steaks in the $18-to-$26 range, most of the dinners are $10 to $17, including a fresh catch for $15.50 (salad bar and mashed potatoes included). This is a strange but lovable place, anti-nouvelle to the end. Although the open salad bar ($6.95) is a meal in itself, the more reckless diner can try the mayo-laden mini–lobster salad appetizer ($7.25) or the baked stuffed island chicken ($11.50).

Inexpensive

Aloha Diner. 971-F Kuhio Hwy., Waipouli. ☎ **808/822-3851.** Most items less than $10.75. No credit cards. Tues–Sat 10:30am–3pm and 5:30–9pm. HAWAIIAN.

It's funky and quirky and claims legions of fans who take out or line up for the authentic Hawaiian plates. Lunch and dinner specials offer samplings of the kalua pig, lau-lau, lomi salmon, and other Hawaiian dishes. (Poi, the taro paste that's a Hawaiian staple, is meant to be eaten with the salty dishes.) Saimin and won-ton min are the other favorites at this tiny diner, where electric fans whir over Formica tables. Although the Aloha may intimidate the uninitiated, it's pure comfort for lovers of Hawaiian food, who come here for the fried whole akule (big-eyed scad), lau-lau, lomi salmon, kalua pig, squid luau (octopus and taro greens in coconut milk), and other Hawaiian favorites.

✪ **Bubba Burgers.** 4-1421 Kuhio Hwy., Kapaa. ☎ **808/823-0069.** Most items less than $5.75. MC, V. Daily 10:30am–8pm. AMERICAN.

Bubba's has gone uptown in tiny Kapaa, from its roadside cubicle to a bona-fide free-standing building across from the Kapaa softball field. Here at the house of Bubba, they dish out humor, great T-shirts, and for vegetarians, tempeh burgers, too. Grilled fresh-fish sandwiches cater to the sensible, fish and chips don't, and fish burgers are for the undecided. But old-fashioned hamburgers are still their raison d'être: 88% fat-free, freshly ground Kauai beef, served on a toasted bun with all the appropriate condiments and diced onions. You can order it open-faced (the Slopper), as the half-pound Big Bubba (three patties), the Hubba Bubba (with rice, hotdog, and chili—a Bubba's plate lunch), and in other versions. Chicken burgers, Bubba's famous Budweiser chili, and other American standards are served up at Bubba's, where the burger is king, attitude reigns, and lettuce and tomato cost extra.

Caffé Coco. 4-369 Kuhio Hwy., Wailua. ☎ **808/822-7990.** Reservations recommended for dinner. Main courses $5.25–$7.50; specials usually less than $11. MC, V. Mon 8am–3pm, Tues–Wed 8am–8pm, Thurs–Fri 8am–9pm, Sat 9am–9pm, Sun brunch 9am–3pm. GOURMET BISTRO.

This gets our vote for the most charming ambiance on Kauai. Caffé Coco appears just off the main road at the edge of a canefield in Wailua, its backyard shaded by pomelo, avocado, mango, tangerine, litchi, and banana trees, with a view of the Sleeping Giant Mountain. The trees provide many of the ingredients for the muffins, chutneys, salsas, and fresh-squeezed juices that Ginger Carlson serves in her charming restaurant, done up with colorful, eclectic touches: broken-plate tiles (a technique called *pique assiette*), lauhala, rattan, mosaic, slate, marble, and a concrete floor. Seats are indoors or on the gravel-floored back courtyard, where tiki torches flicker at night. From interior design to cooking, this is clearly a showcase for Carlson's creativity. The food is wonderful: everything is homemade, from the chutneys to the tamales, with delights such as Thai pumpkin-coconut soups, turkey-sausage omelets, roast veggie omelets or sandwiches, spiced ahi sandwiches on focaccia, and great salads and flour tortilla wraps. The specials could be Tuscan roast chicken with salad and veggies; spiced tofu with shiitake gravy, rice, and salad; vegetarian quiche with roast potatoes and salad; or coconut-curry vegetables. Service can be, to say the least, "laid back," but we're hoping that was due to the restaurant's newness. Next door, Carlson's sister runs Bambulei, a vintage shop of treasures (for a review, see "Shops & Galleries," below).

FreeBorn Music Center. 1387 Kuhio Hwy., Kapaa. ☎ **808/822-0400.** Pastry items less than $3, sandwich wraps $3.95–$4.95. MC, V. Mon–Tues 7am–6pm, Wed–Fri 7am–10pm, Sun 8am–noon; check for special Sat shows. COFFEEHOUSE.

FreeBorn is a hybrid—a combination coffeehouse, pastry shop, music store, and recording studio that also makes fresh-fruit smoothies and Italian sodas. The new sandwich wraps—about a dozen different varieties—are a hit with the lunchtime crowd, who dine at the few tables indoors or make a beeline for the tables in the garden, secluded and shaded by a large fruit tree. Wholesome and raucous, traditional and avant-garde, FreeBorn is the brainchild of Casey and Mary Kay Havens, who have turned this corner of Kapaa into music central. The full-service music store repairs instruments, sells pastries, serves excellent Lavazza espresso, and dispenses the best chocolate-chip cookies on the island. (See also "Kauai After Dark," p. 617.)

Jungle Java & Books, Inc. In Kauai Village, 4-831 Kuhio Hwy., Kapaa. ☎ **808/821-2665.** Most items less than $6.50. MC, V. Daily 8am–4pm. COFFEEHOUSE/BOOKSTORE.

Many claim that this is the best coffee on the island, and the owners say it's because the beans come freshly roasted. Habitués gather for espresso-based drinks and Hawaiian (Kauai, Kona, and Maui estate beans) and international private-label coffees that are roasted on demand for the shop in 30-pound increments and sold in 8- and 16-ounce packages. Have a great cup of java on tables inside or out, over inexpensive quiches, sandwiches, and homemade soups (clam chowder and split pea are standouts). The metaphysical book selection spans used and new books; candles, incense, and aromatherapy gift items are also sold here. All in all, a friendly, inviting spot that makes one want to linger.

The King and I. In Waipouli Plaza, 4-901 Kuhio Hwy. ☎ **808/822-1642.** Reservations recommended for dinner. Main courses $5.75–$7.25 at lunch, $5.25–$10.95 at dinner. AE, DC, DISC, MC, V. Mon–Fri 11am–2pm, daily 4:30–9:30pm. THAI.

This medium-size restaurant in an easy-to-miss (small and nondescript) roadside complex recently began lunch service, and it's trying hard. One Thai entrée on a plate lunch costs $5.75, and daily specials can add to the value. At dinner, the game hen marinated in Thai spices is a popular accompaniment to the red, green, and yellow curries, ordered mild, medium, or hot. But most diners come back for the Evil Jungle Prince in its sumptuous sauce of coconut milk, spices, and kaffir-lime leaves. If that doesn't sate the hunger, the sambal usually does. It's the house specialty with a choice of tofu, shrimp, pork, or chicken, for $8.25 to $9.95. A vegetarian menu keeps the balance.

Kountry Kitchen. 1485 Kuhio Hwy., Kapaa. ☎ **808/822-3511.** Main courses less than $6 at lunch, $7.95–$15.95 at dinner. MC, V. Daily 6am–2pm, Wed–Mon 5–9pm. AMERICAN.

Forget counting calories when you sit down to the heavy, buttery omelets that are the Kountry Kitchen trademark. You can choose your own fillings from the mix-and-match possibilities, among them a kimchee (garlicky, spicy Korean pickles) omelet with cream cheese and several vegetable, meat, and cheese combinations. Sandwiches and American dinners (steak, fish, and chicken) are standard coffeehouse fare, but there can be fresh-fish specials that stand out. Caveat: Sit as far away from the grill as possible, because the smell of grease travels—and clings to your clothes.

Norberto's El Cafe. 4-1373 Kuhio Hwy., Kapaa. ☎ **808/822-3362.** Reservations recommended for parties of 6 or more. Main courses $3.25–$8.45; complete dinners $12–$15.45. MC, V. Mon–Sat 5:30–9pm. MEXICAN.

The lard-free, home-style Mexican fare here includes top-notch chili rellenos with homemade everything, vegetarian selections by request, and if you're lucky, fresh-fish enchiladas on those days when the chef's brother has snared his share of ahi, aku, or ono. All the sauces are made from scratch (enchiladas and chili rellenos are especially popular), and the salsa comes red-hot with homegrown chili peppers fresh from the chef's garden. Norberto's signature is the spinachy Hawaiian taro-leaf enchiladas, a Mexican version of lau-lau, served with cheese and taro, or with chicken. At $13.45 with beans, rice, and soup, it's a deal.

Ono Family Restaurant. 4-1292 Kuhio Hwy., Kapaa. ☎ **808/822-1710.** Most items less than $8. AE, DC, DISC, MC, V. Daily 7am–3pm. AMERICAN.

The Garden Patch, a dollop of fried rice topped with fresh steamed vegetables, scrambled eggs, and hollandaise sauce, is a real conscience-buster. Breakfast is a big deal here, with eggs Florentine leading the pack (two poached eggs, blanched spinach, hollandaise sauce), and eggs Canterbury (much like eggs Benedict, but with more ingredients) following close behind. Steak and eggs; banana, coconut, and macadamia-nut pancakes; and dozens of omelet choices attract throngs of loyalists to Ono for the first stop of the day. Lunch is no slouch either, with scads of fish, veggie, steak, tuna, and turkey sandwiches to choose from, and Ono beef or buffalo burgers with various toppings (chili, mushroom, bacon, onion rings) highlighting the menu. The gourmet hamburger with fries and soup demands an after-lunch siesta.

Sukhothai Restaurant. In the Kapaa Shopping Center, 4-1105 Kuhio Hwy., Kapaa. ☎ **808/821-1224.** Main courses $5.95–$16.95. AE, MC, V. Daily 11am–9:30pm. THAI/VIETNAMESE/CHINESE.

Curries, saimin, Chinese soups, satays, Vietnamese pho, and a substantial vegetarian menu are a few of the features of this unobtrusive but extremely popular—Thai restaurant next to Kapaa's Big Save Market. Menu items appeal to many tastes and include 85 Vietnamese, Chinese, and Thai choices, along with much-loved curries and the bestselling Pad Thai noodles. The coconut/lemongrass/kaffir lime soups (eight choices) are the Sukhothai highlights, along with the red and green curries. So popular is Sukhothai that a new Hanalei dining room has opened, where Tahiti Nui is located.

Waipouli Deli & Restaurant. In the Waipouli Town Center, Waipouli. ☎ **808/822-9311.** Most items less than $7. No credit cards. Daily 7am–3pm and 5–9pm. AMERICAN/JAPANESE.

Modest home-style cooking at low, low prices attracts throngs of local folks who love the saimin, pancakes, and $3 "rice bowls" with chili, teriyaki beef, chicken katsu, or "anything," says the owner. The saimin is great here, especially the miso saimin special (but hold the Spam, please!), a hefty bowl of steaming noodles with tofu, vegetables, and a boiled egg. There are always inexpensive dinner specials, ranging from sukiyaki to roast chicken; it's crowded from breakfast to closing.

EN ROUTE TO THE NORTH SHORE

Duane's Ono-Char Burger. Kuhio Hwy., Anahola. ☎ **808/822-9181.** Hamburgers $3.90–$6.20. No credit cards. Mon–Sat 10am–6pm, Sun 11am–6pm. HAMBURGER STAND.

One cannot imagine Anahola without this roadside burger stand; it's been serving up hefty, all-beef burgers for generations. The teriyaki sauce and bleu cheese are only part of the secret; the burgers are beefy and smoky and legendary. New to the menu are the broiled ono sandwich (fish lovers, rejoice—another marvel of the seasoned old grill) and the marionberry ice-cream shake, a three-berry combo that flies over the counter for $2.95.

THE NORTH SHORE
Expensive

La Cascata. In the Princeville Resort, 5520 Ka Haku Rd. ☎ **808/826-9644.** Reservations recommended for dinner. Main courses $24.95–$31.95; 3-course prix-fixe dinner $43.95. AE, CB, DC, DISC, MC, V. Daily 6–9pm. MEDITERRANEAN/SOUTHERN ITALIAN.

The North Shore's special-occasion restaurant is sumptuous—a Silician spree in Eden. If you're there before dark, the view of Bali Ha'i and the waterfalls of Waialeale will reward you before the menu arrives. Click your heels on the terra-cotta floors, train your eyes through the concertina windows, and pretend you're being served on a terrazzo in Sicily. Chef Anthony Layton-Matthews has created a menu that dazzles quietly: appetizers of potato-crusted crab cake on black olive-and-artichoke salad; paper-thin tuna-and-salmon carpaccio; and arugula with pears, Gorgonzola, and walnut vinaigrette. The rack of lamb ($28.95) is a standout among the entrées, served on porcini mushrooms with polenta, charred peppers, and caramelized onions. It will be difficult to decide, however; there's also roasted red snapper on citrus risotto ($27.95), Kona salmon on white-bean ragout, and grilled fresh tuna on spinach gnocchi ($28.95). There are many other entrées and appetizers, too, each one as tempting as the next. The organic Kauai vegetables are fresh and colorful, as in the yellow- and red-tomato napoleon with grilled eggplant and fresh mozzarella. Without doubt, the North Shore's most lavish dining room, La Cascata is worth a splurge, down to that last bite of tiramisú or Kauai macadamia nut pie.

Moderate

Café Luna. In the Hanalei Center, Kuhio Hwy., Hanalei. ☎ **808/826-1177.** Reservations recommended for dinner. Pizzas $8–$14; dinner main courses $13–$22. AE, DC, DISC, JCB, MC, V. Daily 11am–10pm. NORTHERN ITALIAN.

Café Luna offers patio dining on an open-air garden terrace in a chic Hanalei shopping complex, with a brick pizza oven for its gourmet pizzas and a substantial appetizer menu to complement its pastas and entrées. Warm polenta in basil-cream sauce with tomatoes ($8), stuffed artichokes ($9.50), and sautéed mushrooms ($7) are among the appetizers. Café Luna serves continuously, and its not-always-fabulous cuisine is bolstered by the breathtaking view of the Hanalei waterfalls from the open-air lanai.

✪ **Casa di Amici.** 2484 Keneke St., Kilauea. ☎ **808/828-1555.** Reservations recommended. Main courses $5.95–$13 at lunch, $12–$27 at dinner. MC, V. Daily 11:30am–2:30pm and 6–9pm. ITALIAN/MEDITERRANEAN.

Now this is great Italian, especially the porcini-crusted chicken with sundried cherry-and–port mushroom sauce, served with parmesan-basil polenta points. Veranda seating, trellises, and greenery everywhere you look, including large vases dripping with heliconias and banana stalks, are part of the cordial, comfortable atmosphere in which the chef, Randall Yates, presents his brawny Italian cookery. At night, the trees bordering the restaurant glitter with fairy lights, and seductive aromas of garlic and basil emanate from a room warmed by the riffs of Puccini and Verdi. Serious half-pound burgers ($5.95) are for the noontime Ameriphiles, but at dinner, expect a nod to classic and cross-cultural Italian: risotto Milanese or with chipotle chili salsa, polenta with Gorgonzola, pesto linguine with homemade Italian sausage, and an impressive linguine Alfredo. Yates has made this a major North Shore attraction, bolstered with live piano music Thursday to Saturday nights.

Hanalei Dolphin Restaurant & Fish Market. 5-5016 Kuhio Hwy., Hanalei. ☎ **808/826-6113.** Reservations not accepted. Main courses $10 and up; lobster dinner $75 for 2. MC, V. Daily 11am–3:30pm, pupu menu 3:30–5:30pm, dinner 5:30–10pm. (Fish market, daily 11am–7pm.) SEAFOOD.

Hidden behind a gallery called Ola's on the Hanalei River are this fish market (where you can stock up for your barbecue with fresh fish and fresh mainland beef cut to order) and the adjoining restaurant, which features a seafood menu served on the banks of the Hanalei River. Particularly inviting are the fresh-fish sandwiches, served under umbrellas at river's edge. Most appealing (besides the river view) are the appetizers: artichokes steamed simply, buttery stuffed mushrooms, and ceviche fresh from the fish market.

Hanalei Gourmet. In the Old Hanalei Schoolhouse, 5-5161 Kuhio Hwy., Hanalei. ☎ **808/826-2524.** Main courses $10.95–$14.95. Ask about the nightly dinner specials, served 5:30–9pm. DISC, MC, V. Sun–Thurs 8am–10:30pm, Fri–Sat 8am–11:30pm. AMERICAN.

The wood floors, wooden benches, and blackboards of the old Hanalei School, built in 1926, are a haven for Hanalei hipsters noshing on the Tu Tu Tuna (far-from-prosaic tuna salad with green beans, potatoes, Niçoise olives, and hard-boiled eggs); fresh grilled ahi sandwiches; roasted eggplant sandwiches (a personal favorite, with red peppers, onions, cheese, and other goodies); chicken-salad boats (in papaya or avocado, with macadamia nuts and sans mayonnaise); and more sandwiches, salads, and other selections. They've added a new hot kitchen that sends out stuffed salmon with champagne dill, fresh catch, pan-fried crab cakes, and other fancier-than-sandwich-shop entrées. Pastries and huevos Santa Cruz (eggs, chilis, and salsa baked on a flour tortilla, with nacho-like condiments, $7.50) are breakfast headliners, but there's plenty to carry you through the rest of the day. The TV set over the bar competes with the breathtaking view of the Hanalei mountains and waterfalls, and the wooden floors keep the noise level high; but when you relax with a crusty baguette and a serving of unpeeled shrimp in Old Bay broth, all the interference fades, and Hanalei Gourmet is king.

✪ **Postcards Cafe.** In the old Hanalei Museum, Kuhio Hwy. (at the entrance to Hanalei town). ☎ **808/826-1191.** Reservations recommended for dinner. Main courses $8.95–$23.95. AE, DC, MC, V. Daily 8–11am and 6–9:30pm. GOURMET NATURAL FOODS/SEAFOOD.

Bring your own wine to go with the taro fritters, Thai summer rolls, sautéed prawns, and the ever-popular lau-lau–style fish tacos. Or order the tacos with fresh grilled ahi;

you can't lose. Postcards is known for its fresh fish, prepared in macadamia-nut butter, honey Dijon, or peppered-pineapple sage; and for its imaginative use of local ingredients, as in the taro fritters served with pineapple salsa. Omelets, bagels, eggs Florentine, Hanalei hotcakes, and muffins are some of the day's starters, and it only gets better. The dining room is inside what used to be the quaint Hanalei Museum. In the front yard, an immense, mossy, hollowed-out stone serves as a freestanding lily pond and roadside landmark.

Zelo's Beach House. Kuhio Hwy./Aku Rd., Hanalei. ☎ **808/826-9700.** Reservations recommended for parties of 6 or more. Main courses $6.95–$11.95 at lunch, $7.95–$24.95 at dinner. MC, V. Winter, Mon–Thurs 7:30am–9:30pm, Fri–Sun 7:30am–10pm; summer, Mon–Thurs 7am–10pm, Fri–Sun 7am–11pm. STEAK/SEAFOOD/MEXICAN.

Zelo's is the hippest, most popular spot in Hanalei, a "beach house" with good food, sliding doors all around, windows and cozy decks for lanai seating, and a large, congenial bar area with a tin roof and ironwood poles. This is a happy, happening place. Burgers, seafood, pastas, steaks, 50 different microbrewed beers, and 30 different tropical drinks add up to a room that's always crowded. Zelo's is always packed, and when happy hour rolls around (from 3:30 to 5:30pm), the $2 tap beers and $2 tacos start flowing. Some 24 tables, a children's menu, and appetizers and entrées in all price ranges, including the new Martini Madness menu, make this a Hanalei must.

Scheduled for an early summer opening is **Zelo's Sushi & Blues,** featuring a glass-block sushi bar, stir-fry dishes, and a gorgeous view over sushi, in the Ching Young Village.

Inexpensive

Bubba Burgers. Across from the Ching Young Center, Hanalei. ☎ **808/826-7839.** Most items less than $5.75. MC, V. Daily 10:30am–6pm. AMERICAN.

Outdoor seating in a festive green structure smack-dab in Hanalei town draws the kind of attention that Bubba likes. But the burgers are the main attraction. The North Shore version of the Kapaa fixture (see above) has the same menu, same attitude, same ownership, and same high-quality, all-beef, 88%-fat-free burgers that made the original stand such a smashing success.

Hanalei Wake-Up Cafe. 148 Aku Rd. (at the Kuhio Hwy.). ☎ **808/826-5551.** Most items less than $7.95. No credit cards. Daily 6am–3pm. AMERICAN.

What began as a surfers' pre-cowabunga breakfast call has turned into a morning-to-evening center of plate-lunch chic and enchilada heaven. Dawn patrol begins with pancakes; omelets; quesadillas; killer fresh-fruit smoothies; the Hang Ten Special (eggs and toast with bacon or Portuguese sausage); veggie tofu sautée; and the legendary Over the Falls, a custardy French toast topped with pineapple, coconut, and whipped cream—worth every penny. The informal cafe is lined with historic photos of the town from the 1900s, and the crowd is decidedly laid-back and briny. Ahi and veggie burgers; plate-lunch specials (teriyaki chicken, ahi steak); the ever-popular kiawe-smoked chicken, served with Spanish rice and organic salad; and ahi tacos, enchiladas, burritos, and other Mexican favorites are a few of the afternoon and evening attractions.

⭐ **Kilauea Bakery & Pau Hana Pizza.** In the Kong Lung Center, Kilauea Rd. (off Hwy. 56 on the way to the Kilauea Lighthouse), Kilauea. ☎ **808/828-2020.** Pizzas $10.95–$25.75. MC, V. Mon–Sat 6:30am–9pm. PIZZA/BAKERY.

When owner, baker, and avid diver Tom Pickett spears an ono and smokes it himself, his catch appears on the Billie Holiday pizza, guaranteed to obliterate the blues with its brilliant notes of Swiss chard, roasted onions, Gorgonzola-rosemary sauce, and mozzarella cheese. And the much-loved bakery continues to put out guava sourdough, Hanalei poi sourdough, fresh chive-goat-cheese-and-sundried-tomato bread, and other fine baked products that are great gifts from Kauai. The breads go well with the new soups and hot lunch specials. We also love the open-faced vegetarian abrezone, fresh vegetables in olive oil and herbs, baked in a baguette ($3.95); olive tapénade; bialys with Gorgonzola and artichokes or olives; and smoked salmon and other spreads to go. And pizzas, too: basil-pesto Provençale, the Great Gonzo (with roasted eggplant, red onions, goat cheese, and roasted garlic), the classic scampi (with tiger prawns, capers, lemon, cheese, and roasted garlic), and many others, all made with organically grown olive oil, whole-milk mozzarella, whole-wheat or traditional crust, and hearty, homemade sauces. The ingredients are the real thing; chipotle peppers, roasted onions and garlic, kalamata olives, roasted red peppers, basil pesto, and a dozen other far-from-traditional toppings. No wonder everyone loves this place.

Roadrunner Bakery & Cafe. 2430 Oka St., Kilauea. ☎ **808/828-8226.** MC, V. Main courses $5–$13.95. V, MC. Mon–Sat 7am–9pm, Sun 8am–2pm. MEXICAN/SOUTHWESTERN.

Denis and Dawn Johnston use only organic vegetables grown in Kilauea, fresh fish from nearby waters, pork from a Waimea piggery, and free-range chicken from the island. They cook with integrity, and people have responded. Some 30 types of chiles, more than 600 pounds of tomatoes, and more than 200 pounds of sweet butter go into the pastries and fresh sauces for their popular Southwestern menu each week. The locally grown Anaheim chiles mean excellent chile rellenos, topped with red and green sauces and teamed with a fresh-fish taco—$12.95 for the combination. The fresh ahi salad with fresh lime vinaigrette comes with red onions, jicama, and Kilauea greens and is a hit for a mere $8.95. There are hamburgers and tempeh burgers, burritos and fish burgers, all with made-from-scratch sauces and lean ingredients. It's a small restaurant, with a 45-person capacity, with murals of tall palms, ferns, and ficus trees that took Johnston and his cohorts more than 400 hours to paint.

5 Beaches

by Jeanette Foster

Ancient Kauai is what geologists call *post-erosional*—which means that eons of wind and rain have created a geological masterpiece with some fabulous beaches, like Hanalei, Kee, and Kalapaki. All are accessible to the public, as provided by Hawaii law, and many have facilities. Below are our favorites.

For beach toys and equipment, head to the **Rental Warehouse,** 788 Kuhio Hwy. (across from McDonald's), Kapaa (☎ **808/822-4000**); or **Chris The Fun Lady,** 4-746 Kuhio Hwy. (across the street from Waipouli Town Center), Kapaa (☎ **808/822-7447**).

LIHUE'S BEST BEACH
KALAPAKI BEACH

Any town would pay a fortune to have a beach like Kalapaki, one of Kauai's best, in its backyard. But little Lihue turns its back on Kalapaki; there's not even a sign pointing the way through the trafficky labyrinth to this graceful half-moon of golden sand at the foot of the Marriott Resort & Beach Club. Fifty yards wide and a quarter-mile long, Kalapaki is protected by a jetty and patrolled by lifeguards, making it very safe for swimmers. The waves are good for surfing when there's a winter swell, and the view from the sand—of the steepled, 2,200-foot peaks of the majestic Haupu Ridge that shield Nawiliwili Bay—is awesome. Kalapaki is the best beach not only in Lihue, but on the whole East Coast. From Lihue Airport, turn left onto Kapule Highway (Hwy. 51) to Rice Street, turn left, and go to the entrance of the Marriott; go past the hotel's porte-cochère, and turn right at the SHORELINE ACCESS sign. Facilities include lifeguards, free parking, rest rooms, and showers; food and drink are available nearby at JJ's Broiler.

THE POIPU RESORT AREA
✪ MAHAULEPU BEACH

Mahaulepu is the best-looking unspoiled beach on Kauai, and possibly in the whole state. Its 2 miles of reddish-gold, grainy sand line the southeastern shore at the foot of 1,500-foot-high Haupu Ridge, just beyond the Hyatt Regency Poipu and McBryde sugarcane fields, which end in sand dunes and a forest of casuarina trees. Almost untouched by modern life, Mahaulepu is a great escape from the real world. It's ideal for beachcombing, shell-hunting, or just watching endless waves. Swimming can be risky, except in the reef-sheltered shallows 200 yards west of the sandy parking lot. There's no lifeguard, no facilities—just great natural beauty everywhere you look. (This beach is where George C. Scott portrayed Ernest Hemingway in the movie *Islands in the Stream*.) While you're here, see if you can find the Hawaiian petroglyph of a voyaging canoe carved in the beach rock.

To get to Mahaulepu, drive past the Hyatt Regency Poipu 3 miles east on a red-dirt road, past the golf course and the stables. Turn right at the T intersection; stop and register at the security-guard hut, drive 1 mile to the big sand dune, turn left, and drive a half-mile to a small lot under the trees.

POIPU BEACH PARK

Beaten up by Hurricane Iniki (one wrecked hotel that fronts this beach still has not reopened), big, wide Poipu Beach has made a phoenix-like comeback on the sunny South Shore. Much of its sand was blown out to sea in 1992; it was restored by a parade of dump trucks hauling sand from Polihale.

Poipu is actually two beaches in one; it's divided by a sandbar called a *tombolo*. On the left, a lava-rock jetty protects a sandy-bottom pool that's perfect for small children; on the right, the open bay attracts swimmers, snorkelers, and surfers. And everyone likes to picnic on the grassy lawn graced by coconut trees. The swimming is excellent, with small tide pools for exploring and great reefs for snorkeling and diving, good fishing, nice waves for surfers, and a steady wind for windsurfers. Poipu attracts a daily crowd of visitors and local residents, but the density seldom approaches Waikiki levels, except on holidays. There are rest rooms, showers, picnic facilities, a nearby restaurant and snack bar (Brennecke's Beach Broiler; see "Dining," above), and plenty of free parking in the red-dirt lot. To get to Poipu, turn on Poipu Beach Road, and then turn right at Hoowili Road.

SOUTHWEST KAUAI
SALT POND BEACH PARK

Hawaii's only salt ponds still in production are at Salt Pond Beach, just outside Hanapepe. Generations of locals have come here to swim, fish, and collect salt crystals from the sea that are dried in sunbeds. The tangy salt is used to cure fish, to season food, and for health purposes. The curved reddish-gold beach lies between two rocky points and features a protected reef, tide pools, and gentle waves. Swimming is excellent for children and anyone with a fear of water (a lifeguard looks over this beach); it's also good for scuba diving, windsurfing, and fishing. Facilities include showers, rest

Beaches & Outdoor Activities on Kauai

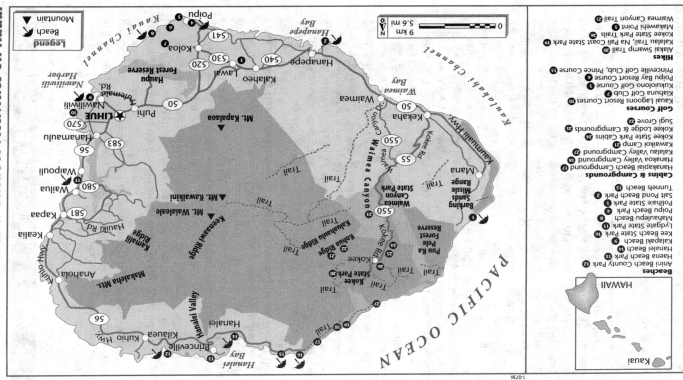

Legend

▲ Mountain

⚓ Beach

Beaches
Anini Beach County Park 12
Haena Beach Park 15
Hanalei Beach 14
Kalapaki Beach 9
Kee Beach State Park 16
Lydgate State Park 11
Mahaulepu Beach 8
Poipu Beach Park 4
Polihale State Park 1
Salt Pond Beach Park 2
Tunnels Beach 15

Cabins & Campgrounds
Hanakapiai Beach Campground 17
Hanakoa Valley Campground 18
Kalalau Valley Campground 27
Kawaikoi Camp 21
Kokee State Park Cabins 24
Kokee Lodge & Campgrounds 25
Sugi Grove 22

Golf Courses
Kauai Lagoons Resort Courses 10
Kiahuna Golf Club 7
Kukuiolono Golf Course 3
Poipu Bay Resort Course 6
Princeville Golf Club, Prince Course 13

Hikes
Alakai Swamp Trail 20
Kalalau Trail, Na Pali Coast State Park 19
Kokee State Park Trails 26
Makaweli Point 5
Waimea Canyon Trail 23

579

★ Frommer's Favorite Kauai Experiences

Snorkel Kee Beach. Rent a mask, fins, and snorkel and enter a magical underwater world. Face down, you'll float like a leaf on a pond, watching brilliant fish dart here and there across coral in water clear as day; a slow-moving turtle may even stop by to check you out. Face up, you'll contemplate green-velvet cathedral-like cliffs under a hopelessly blue sky, with long-tailed tropical birds riding the trade winds. Palms rustle, a wave breaks. You can only smile and think, *if this isn't paradise, what is?*

Hike Waimea Canyon, the Grand Canyon of the Pacific. Ansel Adams would have loved this ageless desert canyon, carved by an ancient river. Sunlight plays against its rustic red cliffs, burnt-orange pinnacles, and blue-green valleys. There's nothing else like it in the islands.

Wander Around a High Mountain Forest. Kokee State Park, through Waimea Canyon at the end of Highway 550, is a combination rain forest and bog up around 4,000 feet. The park's 45 miles of trails offer everything from casual nature strolls to hardy camping and hiking adventures among the redwoods.

Stroll Through Hawaiian History. Old Waimea town looks so unassuming that you'd never guess it stood witness to a great many key events in Hawaii's history. This is the place where Capt. James Cook "discovered" the Hawaiian islands, where Russians once occupied and actually built a fort, and where New England missionaries arrived in 1820 to save the heathens. A three-page self-guided walking tour guide of historic Waimea is available at **Waimea Public Library,** Kaumualii Highway (☎ **808/338-6848**), where the hour-long tour starts.

Watch for Whales from Land. Mahaulepu Beach, in the Poipu area, offers excellent viewing conditions to spot whales that cruise by from December through April. You can spot these mighty mammals spy-hopping, breaching, and generally having a good ol' time in the warm Kauai waters.

Discover the Legendary Little People. According to ancient Hawaiian legend, among Kauai's earliest settlers were the Menehune, a race of small people who worked at night to accomplish magnificent feats. Above Nawiliwili Harbor, the Menehune Fishpond—which at one time extended 25 miles—is said to have been built in just one night, with two rows of thousands of Menehune passing stones hand to hand. The Menehune were promised that no one would watch them work, but one person did; when they discovered the spy, they stopped working immediately, leaving two gaps in the wall. From Nawiliwili Harbor, take Hulemalu Road above Huleia Stream; look for the HAWAII CONVENTION AND VISITORS BUREAU marker at a turnoff in the road, which leads to the legendary fishpond. Kayakers can paddle up Huleia Stream to see it up close.

Take a Long Walk on a Short (but Historic) Pier. First built in 1910, Hanalei's Pier was once a major shipping port for local farmers. Today, the rebuilt pier

POLIHALE STATE PARK

This mini-Sahara on the western end of the island is Hawaii's biggest beach; it's as wide as three football fields and 17 miles long. It's a wonderful place to get away from it all; but always wear rubber slippers—the midday sand is hotter than a griddle. The rooms, camping area, picnic area, pavilion, and parking lot. To get there, take Highway 50 past Hanapepe, and turn on Lokokai Road.

makes a great platform for swimming, fishing, and diving. The pier is located at the end of Hanalei known as Black Pot Beach, where, in the olden days, local families would camp on the beach all summer and always had something cooking in a "black pot" on the shore. Black Pot—and all of Hanalei Beach—is great for swimming, snorkeling, and surfing,

Journey into Eden. For a glimpse of the spectacularly remote Na Pali Coast, all you need to do is hike the first 2 miles along the well-maintained Kalalau Trail into the first tropical valley, Hanakapiai. Hardier hikers may want to venture up into the valley another 2 miles to the Hanakapiai waterfalls and pools. Beware: Na Pali's natural beauty is so enticing that you may want to keep going—but for every mile you hike in, you have to hike out again, unless you contact the State Division of Parks and obtain a permit to camp along the Kalalau Trail.

Catch a Poipu Wave. Vividly turquoise, curling and totally tubular, big enough to hang ten yet small enough to bodysurf, the waves at Poipu are endless in their attraction and timeless in their hold on all who take them on. Grab a boogie board—rentable for just a few dollars a day—or just jump in and go with the flow.

Watch the Hula. The Coconut Marketplace, on Kuhio Highway (Hwy. 56) between mile markers 6 and 7, hosts free hula shows every Monday, Wednesday, Friday, and Saturday at 5pm. Get there early to get a good seat for the hour-long performances of both *kahiko* (ancient) and *auwana* (modern) hula. The real show-stoppers are the *keiki* (children) who perform. Don't forget your camera!

Bid the Sun Aloha. Polihale State Park hugs Kauai's western shore for some 17 miles. It's a great place to bring a picnic dinner, stretch out on the sand, and toast the sun as it sinks into the Pacific, illuminating the island of Niihau in the distance. Queen's Pond has facilities for camping as well as rest rooms, showers, picnic tables, and pavilions.

Gaze at the Stars. Any Kauai beach is great for stargazing almost any night of the year. Once a month, on the Saturday nearest the new moon, when the skies are the blackest, the **Kauai Educational Association for the Study of Astronomy** sponsors a star watch at their observatory on the grounds of the Barking Sands Airfield, outside Mana (turn into the gate at the 30-mile marker on Kaumualii Hwy. and ask the guard for directions to the observatory). Families are welcome to view stars, planets, and even nebulas from the 14-inch computerized telescope (stools are provided for kids who can't reach the scopes on their own). For information on the next star watch, call ☎ **808/245-8250** or write KEASA, P.O. Box 161, Waimea, HI 96796. The two-hour stargazing starts at 7pm in winter and 8pm in summer.

golden sands wrap around Kauai's northwestern shore from Kekaha plantation town, just beyond Waimea, to where the ridgebacks of the Na Pali Coast begin. The state park includes ancient Hawaiian heiau and burial sites, a view of the "forbidden" island of Niihau, and the famed **Barking Sands Beach**, where footfalls sound like a barking dog. (The scientific explanation is simple: The grains of sand are perforated with tiny echo chambers, which emit a "barking" sound when they rub together.) Polihale also takes in the Pacific Missile Range Facility, a U.S. surveillance center that snooped on

Russian subs during the Cold War, and Nohili Dune, which is nearly 3 miles long and 100 feet high in some places.

Be careful in the winter, when high surf and rip currents make swimming dangerous. The safest place to swim is **Queen's Pond**, a small, shallow, sandy-bottom inlet protected from waves and shore currents. There are facilities for camping, as well as rest rooms, showers, picnic tables, and pavilions. To get there, take Highway 50 past Barking Sands Missile Range and follow the signs through the sugarcane fields to Polihale. Local kids like to burgle rental cars out here, so don't leave tempting valuables in your car.

THE COCONUT COAST
LYDGATE STATE PARK

This seacoast park has a rock-wall fishpond that blunts the open ocean waves and provides the only safe swimming and the best snorkeling on the eastern shore. The 1-acre beach park, near the mouth of the Wailua River, is named for the Rev. J. M. Lydgate (1854–1922), founder and first pastor of Lihue English Union Church, who likely would be shocked at the public display of flesh here. This is a great place for a picnic, kite-flying on the green, or just a lazy day at the shore. This popular beach park is 5 miles north of Lihue on Kuhio Highway (Hwy. 56); look for the turnoff just before the Kauai Resort Hotel. Facilities include a pavilion, rest rooms, outdoor showers, picnic tables, barbecue grills, lifeguards, and parking.

THE NORTH SHORE
ANINI BEACH COUNTY PARK

Shielded from the open ocean by the longest, widest fringing reef in Hawaii, Anini is Kauai's safest beach for swimming and windsurfing. It's also one of the island's most beautiful: Three miles long, with golden sand, it sits on a blue lagoon at the foot of emerald cliffs, looking more like Tahiti than almost any other strand in the islands. With shallow water, 4 to 5 feet deep, it's also the very best snorkel spot on Kauai, even for beginners; and on the northwest side, a channel in the reef runs out to the deep blue water with a 60-foot drop that attracts scuba divers. Beachcombers love it, too: seashells, cowries, and sometimes even rare Niihau shells can be found on this great beach. Anini has a park, a campground, picnic and barbecue facilities, and a boat-launch ramp; several B&Bs and vacation rentals are right nearby. Follow Kuhio Highway (Hwy. 56) to Kilauea; take the second exit called Kalihiwai Road (the first dead-ends at Kalihiwai Beach), and drive a half-mile toward the sea; turn left on Anini Beach Road.

HANALEI BEACH

Gentle waves roll across the face of half-moon Hanalei Bay, running up to the wide, golden sand; sheer volcanic ridges laced by waterfalls rise to 4,000 feet on the other side, 3 miles inland. Is there a beach anywhere better sited than Hanalei? Celebrated in song and hula and featured on travel posters, this beach owes its natural beauty to its age—it's an ancient sunken valley with post-erosional cliffs. Hanalei Bay indents the coast a full 1 mile inland and runs 2 miles point to point, with coral reefs on either side and a patch of coral in the middle—plus a sunken ship that belonged to a king, so divers love it. Swimming is excellent year-round, especially in summer, when Hanalei Bay becomes a big, placid lake. The aquamarine water's also great for body boarding, surfing, fishing, windsurfing, canoe paddling, kayaking, and boating (there's a boat ramp on the west bank of the Hanalei River). The area known as Black Pot, near the pier, is particularly great for swimming, snorkeling, and surfing.

Facilities include a pavilion, rest rooms, picnic tables, and parking. This beach is always packed with both local residents and visitors, but you can usually find your own place in the sun by strolling down the shore; the bay is big enough for everyone to enjoy.

To reach Hanalei Beach, take Kuhio Highway (Hwy. 56), which becomes Highway 560 after Princeville. In Hanalei town, make a right turn on Aku Road just after Tahiti Nui, then turn right again on Weke Road, which dead-ends at the parking lot for the Black Pot Beach section of the beach; the easiest beach access is on your left.

✪ TUNNELS BEACH & HAENA BEACH PARK

Postcard-perfect, gold-sand **Tunnels Beach** is one of Hawaii's most beautiful. When the sun sinks into the Pacific along the fabled peaks of Bali Ha'i, there's no better-looking beach in the islands: You're bathed in golden rays that butter-up the blue sky, bounce off the steepled ridges, and tint the pale clouds hot pink. Catch the sunset from the pebbly sand beach or while swimming in the emerald-green waters, but do catch it. Tunnels is excellent for swimming nearly year-round and safe for snorkeling, since it's protected by a fringing coral reef (the waters can get rough in the winter, though). The long, curvy beach is sheltered by a forest of ironwoods that provide welcome shade from the tropic heat.

Around the corner is **Haena Beach Park**, which offers grainy, golden sand and excellent swimming in the summer, with great snorkeling in crystal-clear waters amid clouds of tropical fish. An excellent place to relax. But stay out of the water in the winter; these North Shore waters get fierce, and the big waves are dangerous.

To get here, take Kuhio Highway (Hwy. 56), which becomes Highway 560 after Princeville. Tunnels is about 6 miles past Hanalei town, after the 8-mile marker on the highway (look for the alley with the big double wood gate at the end), and Haena is just down the road. Tunnels has no facilities, but Haena has rest rooms, outdoor showers, barbecue grills, picnic tables, a grassy park for camping, and free parking (no lifeguard, though).

KEE BEACH STATE PARK

Where the road ends on the North Shore, you'll find a dandy little reddish-gold beach almost too beautiful to be real. Don't be surprised if it looks familiar; it was featured in *The Thornbirds*. Kee (*KEE-ee*) is on a reef-protected cove at the foot of fluted volcanic cliffs. Swimming and snorkeling are safe inside the reef but dangerous outside; those North Shore waves and currents can be killers. The beach park has rest rooms, showers, and parking, but no lifeguard. To get there, take Kuhio Highway (Hwy. 56), which becomes Highway 560 after Princeville; Kee is about 7½ miles past Hanalei.

6 Hitting the Water

by Jeanette Foster

For more on the activities listed below, see "The Active Vacation Planner" in chapter 3.

BODY BOARDING (BOOGIE BOARDING) & BODYSURFING

The best beaches for bodysurfing and boogie boarding are **Kalapaki Beach** and **Poipu Beach.**

One of the most inexpensive places to rent boogie boards is **Rental Warehouse,** 788 Kuhio Hwy. (across from McDonald's), Kapaa (☎ **808/822-4000**), where boogie boards rent for $1.99 to $5.99 a day. For boogie boards and fins, you can also

Several outfitters on Kauai not only offer equipment rentals and tours, but also expert advice on weather forecasts, sea and trail conditions, and other important information for hikers, kayakers, sailors, and other backcountry adventurers. For any and all watersports questions, contact **Kayak Kauai Outbound,** 1 mile past Hanalei Bridge on Highway 560, in Hanalei (☎ 800/437-3507 or 808/826-9844; fax 808/822-0577; www.planet-hawaii.com/outbound). They also have their own private dock (the only one on Kauai) for launching kayaks and canoes. Kayak Kauai Outbound has a second location at 1340 Kuhio Hwy., (☎ 808/822-9179, across the street from the Sunny Side Farmer's Market, near Kauwila St.) in Kapaa. Also in Kapaa is **Kauai Water Ski & Surf Co.,** Kinipopo Shopping Village, 4-356 Kuhio Hwy. (on the ocean side of the highway), Kapaa (☎ 808/822-3574). In the Lihue and Poipu areas, go with **Snorkel Bob's** (www.snorkelbob.com), at 4-734 Kuhio Hwy. (just north of Coconut Plantation Marketplace), Kapaa (☎ 808/823-9433), and in Koloa at 3236 Poipu Rd. (just south of Poipu Shopping Village), near Poipu Beach (☎ 808/742-2206).

try **Snorkel Bob's** in Kapaa and Poipu (see below); boards go for $6.50 a day or $26 a week. In Kapaa, boogie boards are also available at **Kauai Water Ski & Surf Co.,** for $5 a day or $20 a week, and on the North Shore at **Kayak Kauai Outbound** (see below for exact locations).

BOATING

One of Hawaii's most spectacular natural attractions is Kauai's Na Pali Coast. Unless you're willing to make the arduous hike in, there are only two ways to see it: by helicopter (see "Golf, Helicopter Rides & Other Outdoor Activities," below) or by boat. Picture yourself cruising the rugged Na Pali coastline in a big 42-foot ketch-rigged yacht under full sail, watching the sunset as you enjoy a tropical cocktail, or speeding through the aquamarine water in a 40-foot trimaran as porpoises play off the bow. Or even more exciting: cruising just above the water in a fast, low-slung rubber Zodiac, just like Jacques Cousteau.

When the Pacific humpback whales make their annual visit to Hawaii from Alaska from December to March, they swim right by Kauai. In season, most boats on Kauai—including sailboats and zodiacs—combine whale-watching with their regular adventures.

For sportfishing charters, see "Fishing," below. For tours of the Fern Grotto, see "Seeing the Sights," later in this chapter.

INDEPENDENT BOAT RENTALS   Kauai has many freshwater areas that are accessible only by boat, including the Fern Grotto, Wailua State Park, Huleia and Hanalei National Wildlife refuges, Menehune Fish Pond, and numerous waterfalls. If you want to strike out on your own on one of these boats, **Paradise Outdoor Adventures,** Kapaa (☎ 800/66-BOATS or 808/822-1112; www.kayakers.com; e-mail mickey@aloha.net or kayaks@aloha.net), has 40 different kinds of rental boats to choose from, like the popular Boston whaler (six-person capacity) for $245 a day, plus kayaks and sea cycles. Included are all the amenities, such as safety equipment, coolers, dry bags (for cameras, wallets, towels), and a comprehensive orientation on where to go. They'll even deliver the boat to the Wailua River at no extra charge. You also can rent a range of water toys, from snorkel equipment to boogie boards.

Bluewater Sailing. ☎ 808/828-1142. www.sail-kauai.com. Prices and departure points vary.

Bluewater runs half-day **sail-snorkel** charters daily from 11am to 3pm on their 42-foot Pierson ketch-rigged sailboat, the *Lady Leanne II* (maximum capacity: 15 passengers). The cost, which includes lunch, is $85 for adults and $75 for children 5 to 12. They also have a 2-hour **sunset cruise,** which includes pupus and drinks; it's $50 for adults, $45 for children. In the summer months (May to October), they sail out of Hanalei Bay on the North Shore; in the winter (October to May), they sail out of Port Allen on the South Shore.

Captain Andy's Sailing Adventures. Kikiaola Small Boat Harbor, Waimea. ☎ **808/822-7833** or 808/335-6833. www.sailing-hawaii.com. Prices vary depending on the cruise.

Capt. Andy operates a 55-foot, 49-passenger catamaran out of Waimea on the South Shore. There's a **snorkel/picnic cruise** daily from 8am until noon; it's $75 for adults, $60 for children 5 to 12, including a deli-style lunch, snorkeling at a few different sites, and drinks. There's also an afternoon version of this cruise on Tuesday, Thursday, and Saturday from 1:30 to 5:30pm, with lunch and afternoon snacks. Two-hour **sunset cruises** set sail five days a week at 4:45pm; they're $45 for adults, $30 for children 5 to 12, with drinks and pupus included.

Capt. Sundown's Catamaran Sailing. Hanalei Beach (trips leave from the right side of the Hanalei River mouth). ☎ **808/826-5585.** www.wp.com/sundown.

A variety of cruises is available on the 40-foot sailing catamaran Ku'uipo, which carries 15 passengers. In the winter, they offer two **sailing/whale-watching trips** daily: a 3-hour sunset trip for $65 for adults, $55 for children 5 to 12; and a 4-hour day sail that's $85 for adults, $65 for children. In summer, there's a 6-hour **Na Pali Coast cruise,** which includes stops for snorkeling, all the gear you'll need, plus lunch and drinks for $95 for adults, $75 for children ages 5 to 12.

✪ **Captain Zodiac Raft Expeditions.** Ching Young Village, Kuhio Hwy., Hanalei. ☎ **800/422-7824** or 808/826-9371. Fax 808/825-7704. www.planet-hawaii.com/zodiac. $68–$120 adults, $53–$100 children 4–12.

For an up-close-and-personal tour of the **Na Pali Coast,** book with Captain Zodiac. Clancy Greff, otherwise known as Captain Zodiac, was the first person to initiate the now-famous sea tours of the Na Pali coastline. The tours take place on 23-foot inflatable boats (zodiacs) that allow you to get close to the incredible shoreline because they have a very shallow draft. You're just inches from the water in the quick-moving rubber craft, which gives you a feeling of intimacy with the marine world below.

The tours, always dependent on the weather and sea conditions, consist of 3-hour **sunrise snorkel** tours; 4-hour **morning and afternoon snorkel tours; 2-hour sunset cruises** (no snorkeling); and 5-hour tours that include landing on the normally inaccessible **Nualolo Kai Beach** for snorkeling, hiking, and lunch. From May 15 to September 15, they're authorized by the State Parks Department as a backpacker and hiker shuttle service, which means that they can drop you off at one of the Na Pali Coast's remote beaches and pick you up again at a later, prearranged time.

The best time of year to take a Zodiac cruise is during the summer months, when the ocean is calmer and the captain can maneuver the boat into caves and up to hidden waterfalls. From October to March, the weather can be rough, and trips may be canceled; but if the weather's good in these months, you might get the added bonus of seeing **whales.** If you're on a trip that features snorkeling, bring your own gear if you have it; your gear will fit you better than that provided by the boat. (Nothing is worse than a leaky mask while you're snorkeling.) And bring your camera; they provide a sealing plastic bag to protect it from salt spray and water. Once on board, try to get a seat on the starboard side (the right side as you face the front of the boat). Most of the sightseeing is on the way out; you'll have a perfect view.

A word of caution: Captain Zodiac recommends that pregnant women, anyone with back problems, and small children skip this trip; they won't be comfortable in the shadeless, bouncing boat (it's sort of like riding on Jell-O).

Liko Kauai Cruises. ☎ **888/SEA-LIKO** or 808/338-0333; fax 808/338-1182. www.extreme-hawaii.com/activities/liko. $85 adults, $65 children 4–14.

Liko offers more than just a typical whale-watching cruise; instead, it's a 4½-hour combination **Na Pali Coast tour–deep-sea fishing–historical lecture–whale-watching** extravaganza with lunch. It all happens on a 38-foot cabin cruiser (with padded seating.) In addition to viewing the whales, you'll glimpse sea caves, waterfalls, lush valleys, and miles of white-sand beaches; you'll also make stops along the way for snorkeling. The 8:30am cruise departs from Kekaha and returns by 1pm; occupancy is limited to 24 people.

FISHING

DEEP-SEA FISHING
Kauai's fishing fleet is smaller and less well-recognized than others in the islands, but the fish are still out there. All you need to bring is your lunch and your luck. Charter boats start at $90 a person for a half-day, during which you'll share the boat with other anglers, and go up to $850 for a full-day exclusive charter. Call **Gent-Lee Fishing,** out of Nawiliwili Harbor (☎ **808/245-7504**), or **Sport Fishing Kauai,** out of Port Allen (☎ **808/742-7013**).

FRESH-WATER FISHING
Freshwater fishing is big on Kauai, thanks to its dozens of "lakes," which are really manmade reservoirs. Regardless, they're full of large-mouth bass, small-mouth bass, and peacock bass (also known as *tucunare*); the **Puu Lua Reservoir** in Kokee State Park also has rainbow trout and is stocked by the state every year.

Before you rush out and get a fishing pole, you have to have a **Hawaii Fresh Water Fishing License,** available through the **State Department of Land and Natural Resources,** Division of Aquatic Resources, P.O. Box 1671, Lihue, HI 96766 (☎ **808/241-3400**), or through any fishing-supply store like **Lihue Fishing Supply,** 2985 Kalena St., Lihue (☎ **808/245-4930**); **Stan's Fishing & Liquor Supplies,** Hanapepe (☎ **808/335-5213**), which also rents fishing equipment; and **Waipouli Variety,** 4-901 Kuhio Hwy., Kapaa (☎ **808/822-1014**). A 1-month license costs $3.75; a 1-year license is $7.50. When you get your license, pick up a copy of the booklet *State of Hawaii Fresh Water Fishing Regulations,* which outlines the dos and don'ts of island freshwater fishing.

Fishing for rainbow trout in Kokee's Puu Lou Reservoir has a limited season: It begins on the first Saturday in August and lasts for 16 days, after which you can only fish on weekends and holidays through the last Sunday in September.

KAYAKING
Kauai is made for kayaking. You can take the Huleia River into Huleia National Wildlife Refuge, the last strand of Kauai's endangered birds—it's the only way the nature refuge can be explored. For the adventurous, there's the Na Pali Coast, featuring majestic cliffs, empty beaches, open-ocean conditions, and monster waves. Or, you can just go out and paddle around Hanalei Bay.

Kayak Kauai Outbound, 1 mile past Hanalei Bridge on Highway 560 in Hanalei (☎ **800/437-3507** or 808/826-9844; fax 808/822-0577; www.kayakkauai.com), has a range of tours for independent souls. The shop's experts will be happy to tell you where to go on your own or to take you on a guided kayaking trip. Equipment rental for a two-person kayak is around $50 a day. Kayak lessons and tours (some including snacks) range from $55 to $125.

Rick Haviland, who gained fame after he was mentioned in Paul Theroux's book *The Happy Isles of Oceania*, is the owner of **Outfitters Kauai,** 2827A Poipu Rd. (look for the small five-shop mall before the road forks to Poipu/Spouting Horn), Poipu (☎ **808/742-9667**), which has a bunch of different kayaking tours, including a half-day trip that takes you from Spouting Horn to hidden Lawaiiki Beach. It's $65, including snacks and drinks. Another good one is the Kipu Kai full-day tour, which runs in the winter (mid-September to mid-May). Participants meet at the Poipu shop, where they take a bus to Nawiliwili Harbor; here, they launch and paddle 11 miles to a secluded beach accessible only by boat. After a picnic at the beach, the kayakers paddle back to Poipu via the ocean. The cost is $115 per person. In the summer (mid-May to mid-September), you can take a full-day trip along the entire **Na Pali Coast;** it's $130 per person and includes a guide, lunch, drinks, and equipment. Outfitters Kauai also rents kayaks by the day ($30 for a single, $45 for a double).

The cheapest place to rent kayaks is **Rental Warehouse,** 788 Kuhio Hwy. (across from McDonald's), Kapaa (☎ **808/822-4000**), where a one-person kayak goes for $19.99 a day and a two-person kayak is $39.99. You can also rent from **Chris The Fun Lady,** 4-746 Kuhio Hwy. (across from Waipouli Town Center), Kapaa (☎ **808/882-7447**); **Kauai Water Ski & Surf Co.,** Kinipopo Shopping Village, 4-356 Kuhio Hwy. (on the ocean side), Kapaa (☎ **808/822-3574**); the cost is $20 per day for a single, $40 for a double. Or try **Pedal 'n Paddle,** Ching Young Village Shopping Center, Hanalei (☎ **808/826-9069**).

In addition to kayak rentals (singles $25 to $35 per day; doubles $50 to $60), **Paradise River Outdoor Adventures,** Kapaa (☎ **800/66-BOATS** or 808/822-1112; www.kayakers.com), also offers introductory kayak classes: $40 for a 90-minute lesson, which includes all equipment. If you just want to try kayaking to see if you like it, they will rent you a kayak for one hour ($10 to $15), and you can paddle around in the ocean behind the store. They also offer a range of Jungle River Safari kayak tours ($45 to $65).

PADDLING INTO HULEIA NATIONAL WILDLIFE REFUGE Ride the Huleia River through Kauai's 240-acre Huleia National Wildlife Refuge, the last stand of Kauai's endangered birds, in a 12-foot-long, virtually unsinkable, canoe-shaped pirogue with **Island Adventures,** Nawiliwili Harbor (☎ **808/245-9662**). You paddle up the picturesque Huleia (which appeared *in Raiders of the Lost Ark* and the remake of *King Kong*) under sheer pinnacles that open into valleys full of lush tropical plants, bright flowers, and hanging vines, where great blue herons and Hawaiian gallinules take wing. The 3-hour voyage, which starts at Nawiliwili Harbor, is ideal for all—especially movie buffs, birders, and great adventurers under 12. Wear a swimsuit, T-shirt, and boat shoes. It's $50 for adults, $25 for children 4–12; lunch is included.

SCUBA DIVING

Diving on Kauai is dictated by the weather. During the winter, when heavy swells and high winds hit the island, it's generally limited to the more protected South Shore. Probably the best-known site along the South Shore is **Caverns.** Located off the Poipu Beach resort area, this dive site consists of a series of lava tubes interconnected by a chain of archways. A constant parade of fish streams by (even shy lionfish are often spotted lurking in crevices); brightly hued Hawaiian lobsters hide in the lava's tiny holes, and turtles soar past.

In the summer, when the North Pacific storms subside, the magnificent North Shore opens up, and you can take a boat dive locally known as the **Oceanarium,** northwest of Hanalei Bay, where you'll find a kaleidoscopic marine world in this horseshoe-shaped cove. From the rare (long-handed spiny lobsters) to the more

ⓘ Ready, Set, Go! Adventures for Kids of All Ages

Surfing with an Expert (see p. 590) If seven-time world champ Margo Oberg, a member of the Surfing Hall of Fame, can't get your kid—or you—up on a surfboard riding a wave, nobody can. She promises same-day results even for a klutz.

Taking a Zodiac Down the Na Pali Coast (see p. 585) Go flying down Kauai's most spectacular coast on a 23-foot rubber life raft. Captain Zodiac has been taking people to Na Pali's jagged cliffs, remote beaches, and hidden sea caves for more than a decade. This is Jacques Cousteau–style adventuring at its best.

Paddling up the Huleia River (see p. 587) Indiana Jones ran for his life up this river to his seaplane in *Raiders of the Lost Ark*. Now you and the kids can venture down it yourself, in a 12-foot-long, virtually unsinkable, canoe-shaped pirogue. The picturesque Huleia winds through tropically lush Huleia National Wildlife Refuge, where endangered species like great blue herons and Hawaiian gallinules take wing. Ideal for everyone.

Climbing the Wooden Jungle Gyms at Kamalani Playground (see p. 607) Located in Lydgate Beach Park in Wailua, this unique playground has a maze of jungle gyms that children of all ages will love. Kids can whip down slides, explore caves, hang from bars, and just climb all over the place. This is a great place for a family to spend the afternoon.

Cooling Off with a Shave Ice (see p. 565) On a hot, hot day, stop by **Brennecke's Beach Broiler**, across the street from the Poipu Beach Park (☎ 808/742-1582), and order a traditional Hawaiian shave ice. Like a snow cone, this local treat consists of crushed ice stuffed into a paper cone and topped with a tropical flavored syrup. If your keiki can't decide on a flavor, go for the "rainbow"—three different flavors in one cone. Be sure to pick up plenty of napkins—this can get sticky.

Exploring a Miniature Marine World (see p. 577) At Lydgate Park (in Wailua), Anini Beach (on the North Shore), and Salt Pond Beach (outside of Hanapepe), kids can safely explore the aquatic action of tide pools, which are situated away from the surf and therefore perfect for small children. They'll discover edible seaweed, round sea slugs, spiny sea urchins, and tiny fish—all harmless critters. Make sure the little ones are wearing tennis shoes, reef walkers, tabis, or some type of sandal (which you can purchase at fishing stores or sports shops) so they don't cut themselves on sharp coral or jagged lava rocks.

Since the best dives on Kauai are offshore, I recommend booking a two-tank dive off a dive boat. **Bubbles Below Scuba Charters**, 6251 Hauaala Rd., Kapaa (☎ 808/822-3483; www.aloha.net/~kaimanu), specializes in highly personalized, small group dives, with an emphasis on marine biology. The 35-foot boat, *Kaimanu*, is a custom-built Radon dive boat that comes complete with a hot shower. They offer two-tank boat dives for $100 and night dives for $85; if you need rental equipment, they have a complete package for an extra $25. In summer (June to October), Bubbles Below offers a three-tank trip for experienced divers only to the "forbidden" island of Niihau, 90 minutes by boat from Kauai. You should be comfortable on vertical

common (taape, conger eels, and nudibranches), the resident population is one of the more diverse on the island. The topography (pinnacles, ridges, and archways) is covered with cup corals, black-coral trees, and nooks and crannies enough for a dozen dives.

drop-offs, in huge underwater caverns, in possibly choppy surface conditions, and in significant currents. You should also be willing to share water space with the resident sharks. The all-day trip is $235, including tanks, weights, dive computer, lunch, drinks, and a marine guide.

On the south side, call **Fathom Five Adventures**, 3450 Poipu Rd. (next to the Chevron Station), Koloa (☎ **808/742-6991**).

GREAT SHORE DIVES FROM KAUAI
You can also rent your own equipment for shore dives; it will probably cost around $25 to $40 a day. Shops that rent equipment include **Aquatic Adventures**, 4-1380 Kuhio Hwy., Kapaa (☎ **808/822-1434**); **Dive Kauai**, 976 Kuhio Hwy., Kapaa (☎ **808/882-0452**); and **Fathom Five Adventures**, 3450 Poipu Rd. (next to the Chevron Station), Koloa (☎ **808/742-6991**).

Here's a list of some spectacular shoreline dive sites:

North Shore Not only is **Kee Beach/Haena Beach Park** (where the road ends on the North Shore) one of the most picturesque beaches on the island, it's also one of the best spots to do some shoreline diving. On a calm summer day, the drop-off near the reef begs for underwater exploration. Another good bet is **Tunnels Beach**, also known as Makua Beach. It's located off Highway 560, just past the 8-mile marker; look for the short dirt road (less than a half-mile) to the beach. The wide reef here makes for some fabulous snorkeling and diving, but again, only during the calm summer months. **Cannons Beach**, east of Haena Beach Park (use the parking for Haena, located across the street from the Dry Cave near the 9-mile marker on Hwy. 560), has lots of vibrant marine life in its sloping offshore reef.

South Shore Head to **Tortugas** (located directly in front of Poipu Beach Park) if you want to catch a glimpse of sea turtles. **Koloa Landing** has a horseshoe-shaped reef that's teeming with tropical fish. **Sheraton Caverns** (located off the Sheraton Kauai) is also popular, due to its three large underwater lava tubes, which are usually filled with marine life.

SNORKELING

Kauai has lots of inshore reefs to make snorkelers happy. **Snorkel Bob's**, 4-734 Kuhio Hwy. (just north of Coconut Plantation Marketplace), Kapaa (☎ **808/823-9433**), and at 3236 Poipu Rd. (just south of Poipu Shopping Village), near Poipu Beach (☎ **808/742-2206**), has complete snorkel sets starting at $9 a day or $39 a week.

HOT SNORKEL SPOTS
For great shoreline snorkeling, try the reef off **Kee Beach/Haena State Park**, located at the end of Highway 560. It's a virtual Disneyland of marine life. **Tunnels Beach**, located about a mile before the end of Highway 560 in Haena, has a wide reef that's great for poking around in search of tropical reef fish. Be sure to check ocean conditions—don't go if the surf is up or if there is a strong current. **Anini Beach**, located off the northern Kalihiwai Rd. (between the 25- and 26-mile markers on Kuhio Hwy., or Hwy. 56), just before the Princeville Airport, has a safe, shallow area with excellent snorkeling opportunities. **Poipu Beach Park** has some good snorkeling to the right side of Nukumoi Point—the tombolo area, where the narrow strip of sand divides the ocean, is best. If this spot is too crowded, wander down the beach in front of the old Waiohai resort; if there are no waves, this place is also hopping with marine life. **Salt Pond Beach Park**, located off Highway 50 near Hanapepe, has good snorkeling around the two rocky points, home to hundreds of tropical fish.

SURFING

Hanalei Bay's winter surf is the most popular on the island, but it's for experts only. **Poipu Beach** is an excellent spot to learn how to surf; the waves are small and—best of all—nobody laughs at you when you wipe out. Check with the local surf shops or phone the **Surfline** (☎ 808/245-3564) to find out where surf's up.

Surf lessons are available for $50 for a 1½-hour lesson plus all-day use of the equipment (board, wet suit top, and carrying rack for your car) from **Windsurf Kauai,** in Hanalei (☎ 808/828-6838). Poipu is also the site of numerous surfing schools; the oldest and best is probably **Margo Oberg's School of Surfing,** at the Nuku Moi Surf Shop, across from Brennecke's Beach, Poipu (☎ 808/742-8019). Margo charges $45 for 60 minutes of instruction (offered daily at noon and 2pm), which includes surfboard, boots, and leash; she guarantees that by the end of the lesson, you'll be standing and catching a wave.

Equipment is available for rent (ranging from $5 an hour or $20 a day for "soft" beginner boards to $7.50 an hour or $25 a day for hard boards) from **Nuku Moi Surf Shop,** across from Brennecke's Beach, Poipu (☎ 808/742-8019); **Hanalei Surf Co.,** 5-5161 Kuhio Hwy. (across from Zelo's Beach House Restaurant in Hanalei Center), Hanalei (☎ 808/826-9000); and **Pedal & Paddle,** Ching Young Village Shopping Center, Hanalei (☎ 808/826-9069). The cheapest place to rent a board is **Rental Warehouse,** 788 Kuhio Hwy. (across from McDonald's), Kapaa (☎ 808/822-4000), where boards start at $9.99 a day.

WATER-SKIING

Hawaii's only freshwater water-skiing is on the Wailua River. Ski boats launch from the boat ramp in Wailua River State Park, directly across the marina. **Kauai Water Ski & Surf Co.,** Kinipopo Shopping Village, 4-356 Kuhio Hwy., Kapaa (☎ 808/822-3574), rents equipment and offers lessons and guided tours; it's $45 for a half-hour trip and $85 for an hour.

WINDSURFING

Anini Beach is one of the safest beaches for beginners to learn windsurfing. Lessons and equipment rental are available at **Windsurf Kauai** in Hanalei (☎ 808/828-6838). It's $75 for a 3-hour lesson, including equipment; rentals are $25 an hour or $65 for a full day. Serious windsurfers should head to **Hanalei Bay** or **Tunnels Beach** on the North Shore.

7 Hiking & Camping

by Jeanette Foster

Kauai is an adventurer's delight. Its very nature calls to those who eschew resort life and head for the great outdoors. The island's greatest tropical beauty isn't easily reachable; you've got to head out on foot and find it.

For more information on Kauai's hiking trails, contact the **State Division of Parks, and Wildlife,** P.O. Box 1671, Lihue, HI 96766 (☎ 808/274-3446); the **State Division of Forestry and Recreation,** P.O. Box 1671, Lihue, HI 96766 (☎ 808/245-4444); **Kauai County Parks and Recreation,** 4193 Hardy St., Lihue, HI 96766 (☎ 808/241-6660 or 808/245-1881); and the **Kokee Lodge Manager,** P.O. Box 819, Waimea, HI 96796 (☎ 808/335-6061).

Despite its name, **Kayak Kauai Outbound,** 1 mile past Hanalei Bridge on Highway 560 in Hanalei (☎ 800/437-3507 or 808/826-9844; fax 808/822-0577), is the premier all-around outfitter's center on the island. It's staffed by local experts who keep track of weather forecasts, sea and trail conditions, and other pertinent information that hikers, campers, and other backcountry adventurers need to know. If you don't plan to bring your own gear, you can rent it there or at **Pedal & Paddle** in Hanalei (☎ 808/826-9069). If you want to buy camping equipment on Kauai, head for **Gaspro**, 3990-C Rice St., Lihue (☎ 808/245-6766); **Village Variety**, Ching Young Village Shopping Center, Hanalei (☎ 808/826-6077); **Waipouli Variety**, 4-901 Kuhio Hwy., Kapaa (☎ 808/822-1014); **Wal-mart**, 3-3300 Kuhio Hwy., Lihue (☎ 808/246-1599); or **K-Mart**, 4303 Nawiliwili Rd, Lihue (☎ 808/245-7742).

A Few Words of Warning about Flash Floods: When it rains on Kauai, the waterfalls rage and rivers and streams overflow and cause flash floods on roads and trails. If you're hiking, avoid dry streambeds, which flood quickly and wash out to sea. Check the weather forecast (☎ **808/245-6001**) before going hiking, camping, or sailing, especially in the rainy season (November to March).

GUIDED HIKES You can set out on your own to explore Kauai or join a guided hike with the **Sierra Club Hawaii Chapter**, P.O. Box 3412, Lihue, HI 96766 (www.hi.sierraclub.org/Kauai/kauai.html). The Kauai chapter of the Hawaii Sierra Club is very active, offering two to three different hikes every month, varying from an easy family beach hike by moonlight to a moderate 4-mile hike up some 1,100 feet in the hills to 8-plus-mile hikes for serious hikers only. Among their offerings are guided hikes of Kokee State Park (see below), usually on weekends. The club has no staffed office, so the best way to contact them is to check their Web site; they generally list their outings three to six months in advance (they also have camp-outs), with complete descriptions of the hike, the hike leader's phone number, and what to wear and bring. You can also check the daily newspaper, the *Garden Island*, for a list of their hikes in the Community Calendar section. Generally, the club asks for a donation of $3 per person per hike for nonmembers, and $1 for members (the fees go to keep their first-aid kits supplied and to constantly retrain their leaders in first aid). They also do service work (clearing trails, picking up trash) on their hikes, so you may spend an hour doing service work, then 2 to 3 hours hiking. Last year, the club took three service-work trips along the Na Pali Coast trail to help maintain it.

Hawaiian Wildlife Tours (☎ **808/639-2968**) are environmental education in action. Biologist Dr. Carl Berg will take you and up to three other friends out into the woods and down to the shoreline to see Kauai's native and vanishing species, from forest birds and flora to hoary bats, monk seals, and green sea turtles. His personalized tours last from 2 hours to a week and are tailored to meet the season and weather, your physical abilities, and what you want to see. He leads tours to Hanalei taro fields to see wetland birds, to Crater Hill to see nene geese, to Mahaulepu to see wildflowers in the sand dunes, to Kilauea Lighthouse to see oceanic birds, and much more. Rates are $45 per couple for the first hour, $25 for each additional hour.

THE POIPU RESORT AREA
✪ A GOOD MORNING HIKE: MAKAWEHI POINT

Bold as a ship's prow, Makawehi Point juts out to sea on the east side of Keoneloa Beach, the beach in front of the Hyatt Regency Poipu, known locally as Shipwreck Beach because of an old marine mishap. This 50-foot-high sand-dune bluff attracts a variety of people: pole fishers, whale-watchers, people who just like the panoramic views of the Pacific, and daredevils who test their courage by leaping off the cliff into the waves that wrap the point (don't try it).

The trailhead begins on the east end of Shipwreck Beach, past the Hyatt. It's an easy 10-minute walk up to Makawehi Point; after you take in the big picture, keep going uphill along the ridge of the sand dunes (said to contain ancient Hawaiian burial sites), past the coves frequented by green sea turtles and endangered Hawaiian monk seals, through the coastal pine forest, and past World War II coastal bunkers to the very top. Now you can see Haupu Ridge and its 2,297-foot peak, the famously craggy ridgeline that eerily resembles Queen Victoria's profile, and in the distance, Mahaulepu Beach, one of the best-looking in Hawaii. Inland, three red craters dimple the green fields; the one in the middle, the biggest one, Pu'u Huni Huni, is said to have been the last to erupt on Kauai—but it was so long ago that nobody here can remember when.

SOUTHWEST KAUAI
WAIMEA CANYON TRAILS

On a wet island like Kauai, a dry hike is hard to find. But in the desert-dry gulch of Waimea Canyon, known as the Grand Canyon of the Pacific, you're not likely to slip and slide in the muck as you go.

CANYON TRAIL You want to hike Hawaii's Grand Canyon, but you only have so much time. Well, then, take the Canyon Trail to the east rim for a breathtaking view into the 3,000-foot-deep canyon. Park your car at the top of Halemaun Valley Road (located between the 14- and 15-mile markers on Waimea Canyon Road, about a mile down from the museum). Walk down the not-very-clearly marked trail on the 3.6-mile round trip, which takes about 2 to 3 hours and leads to Waipoo Falls (as does the hike below) and back. We suggest going in the afternoon when the light in the Canyon is the best.

✪ HIKE TO WAIPOO FALLS The 3-hour round-trip family hike to Waipoo Falls is one of Kauai's best hikes; the two-tiered, 800-foot waterfall that splashes into a natural pool is worth every step it takes to get there. To get to the trail, drive up Kokee Road (Hwy. 550) to the Puu Hina Hina Outlook; a quarter-mile past the lookout, near a NASA satellite tracking station on the right, a two-lane dirt road leads to the Waipoo Falls trailhead. From there, the trail winds gently through a green jungle dotted with wild yellow orchids and flame-red torch ginger before it leads you out on a descending ridgeback that juts deep into the canyon. At the end of the promontory, take a left and push on through the jungle to the falls; once you're there, reward yourself with a refreshing splash in the pool.

KOKEE STATE PARK

At the end of Highway 550, which leads you through Waimea Canyon to its summit, lies a 4,640-acre state park of high-mountain forest wilderness (3,600 to 4,000 ft. above sea level). The rain forest, bogs, and breathtaking views of the Na Pali coastline and Waimea Canyon are the draw at Kokee. This is the place for hiking—among the 45 miles of maintained trails are some of the best hikes in Hawaii. We've described our favorites in detail below. Official trail maps of all the park's trails are for sale for 50¢ at the **Kokee Natural History Museum** (☎ 808/335-9975).

A few words about hiking Kokee: Always check current trail conditions; up-to-date trail information is available on a bulletin board at the Kokee Natural History Museum. Stay on established trails; it's easy to get lost here. Get off the trail well before dark. Carry water and rain gear—even if it's perfectly sunny when you set out—and wear sunscreen.

Trails

Awaawapuhi Trail This 3 1/4-mile hike (6 1/2 miles round trip) takes about 3 hours and is considered strenuous by most, but offers a million-dollar view. Look for the trailhead at the left of the parking lot, at the 17-mile marker between the museum and Kalalau Lookout. The well-marked and maintained trail now sports quarter-mile markers, and you can pick up a free plant guide for it at the museum. The trail drops about 1,600 feet through native forests to a thin precipice right at the very edge of the Na Pali cliffs for a dramatic and dizzying view of the tropical valleys and blue Pacific 2,500 feet below. Not recommended to anyone with vertigo (although a railing will keep you from a major slip and fall). Go early, before clouds obscure the view, or late in the day; the chiaroscuro sunsets are something to behold.

This trail connects to the **Nualolo Trail** (3¾ miles), which provides awesome views and loops back almost to park headquarters, if you have the time.

HALEMANU-KOKEE TRAIL   This trail takes you on a pleasant, easy-to-moderate 2.4-mile round-trip walk through a native koa and ohia forest inhabited by native birds. The trailhead is near the 15-mile marker; pick up the Faye Trail, which leads to this one. The trail links Kokee Valley to Halemanu Valley (hence the name); along the way, you'll see a plum orchard, valleys, and ridges.

PIHEA TRAIL   This is the park's flattest trail, but it's still a pretty strenuous 7.4-mile round-trip hike. A new boardwalk on a third of the trail makes it easier, especially when it's wet. The trail begins at the end of Highway 550 at Puu o Kila Lookout, which overlooks Kalalau Valley; it goes down at first, then flattens out as it traces the back ridge of the valley. Once it enters the rain forest, you'll see native plants and trees, such as maile, ohia lehua, mokihana, and tree ferns. It intersects with the **Alakai Swamp Trail** (below), which is now an easy stroll, mostly on a boardwalk through a fragile bog. If you combine both trails, figure on about 4 hours in and out.

ALAKAI SWAMP TRAIL   This 7-mile hike used to take 5 hours to slosh through the bog, with mud up to your knees. Now a boardwalk has taken out the shoe-grabbing mud, but be prepared for rain. If you want to see the "real" Hawaii, this is it—a big swamp in the heart of Kauai that's home to rare birds and plants. The trail allows a rare glimpse into a wet, cloud-covered wilderness preserve where 460 inches of rain a year is common. Come prepared for the worst, and you might get a ray of sunshine. (The only silver lining is that there are no mosquitoes above 3,000 feet.)

The trailhead is just off Mohihi (Camp 10) Road, just beyond the Forest Reserve entrance sign and the Alakai Shelter picnic area. From the parking lot, the trail follows an old World War II four-wheel-drive road. Stick to the boardwalk, as this is a fragile eco-area (not to mention the mud). At the end of the 3½-mile slog, if you're lucky and the clouds part, you'll have a lovely view of Wainiha Valley and Hanalei from Kilohana Lookout.

Campgrounds & Wilderness Cabins
CABINS & TENT CAMPGROUNDS
Camping facilities include state campgrounds (one next to Kokee Lodge, and four more primitive backcountry sites), one private tent area, and the **Kokee Lodge,** which has 12 cabins for rent at very reasonable rates. At 4,000 feet, the nights are cold, particularly in the winter; since no open fires are permitted at Kokee, the best deal is the cabins; see p. 555 on renting one. The **Kokee Lodge Restaurant** is open from 9am to 3:30pm for continental breakfast and lunch every day. Groceries and gas aren't available in Kokee, so stock up in advance, or you'll have to make the long trip down the mountain.

The **state campground at Kokee** allows tent camping only. Permits for this site can be obtained from a state parks office on any island; on Kauai, it's at 3060 Eiwa St., Room 306, Lihue, HI 96766 (☎ 808/274-3444). The permits are free, and the time limit is 5 nights in a single 30-day period. The facilities include showers, drinking water, picnic tables, a pavilion with tables, rest rooms, barbecue, sinks for dishwashing, and electric lights.

Tent camping at **Camp Sloggett,** owned by the Kauai YWCA, 3094 Elua St., Lihue, HI 96766 (☎ **808/245-5959**; e-mail kauaiyw@pixi.com), is available for $10 per person per night (children under 5 are free). Tent camping is on 1½ acres of open field, with a covered fire pit for fires, a barbecue area, plus volleyball and badminton nets. There's also the **Sloggett Lodge,** which sleeps 9 ($20 per person per night), and the **Weinburg Bunkhouse,** with bunk beds, separate toilets, showers, and kitchenettes ($20 per person per night). To get here, continue on the highway past park head-quarters and take the first right after the Kokee Lodge. Follow the dirt road and look for the wooden CAMP SLOGGETT sign; turn right and follow the bumpy road past the state cabins into a large clearing.

BACKCOUNTRY CAMPING   The more primitive backcountry campgrounds include **Sugi Grove** and **Kawaikoi,** located about 4 miles from Park Headquarters on the Camp 10 Road, an often muddy and steep four-wheel–drive jeep road. Sugi Grove is located across the Kawaikoi Stream from the Kawaikoi campsite. The area is named for the sugi pines which were planted in 1937 by the Civilian Conservation Corps. This is a shady campsite with a single picnic shelter, a pit toilet, a stream, and space for several tents. The Kawaikoi campsite is a 3-acre open grass field, surrounded by Kokee plum trees and forests of koa and ohia. Facilities include two picnic shelters, a composting toilet, and a stream that flows next to the camping area. **There is no potable water**—bring in your own, or treat the stream water.

Permits are available from the **State Forestry and Wildlife Division,** 3060 Eiwa St., Room 306, Lihue, HI 96766 (☎ **808/274-3433**). There's no fee for the permits, but camping is limited to 3 nights. You can also get a Kauai Recreation Map (with illustrations of all roads; trails; and picnic, hunting, and camping areas) by mail from them; send a self-addressed 10-by-13-inch manila envelope with $1.01 postage on it.

BEACH CAMPING AT POLIHALE STATE PARK

Polihale holds the distinction of being the westernmost beach in the U.S. The beach is spectacular—some 300 feet wide in the summer, with rolling sand dunes (some as high as 100 feet) and the islands of Niihau and Lehua just offshore. Bordered by a cur-tain of Na Pali Coast cliffs on the north, razor-sharp ridges and steep valleys to the east, and the blue Pacific on the south and west, it's also one of the most dramatic campgrounds in the state. Expect Technicolor sunsets and brilliant stars against the black night sky.

The campgrounds for tent camping are located at the south end of the beach, affording privacy from the daytime beach activities. There's great swimming in the summer (even then, be on the lookout for waves and rip currents, as there are no life-guards), some surfing (the rides are usually short), and fishing. The camping is on sand, although there are some kiawe trees for shade. (*Warning:* Kiawe trees drop long thorns that can easily pierce slippers, so make sure you have protective footwear.) Facil-ities include rest rooms, showers, picnic tables, barbecues, and a spigot for drinking water. You can purchase supplies about 15 miles away in Waimea.

Permits, which are free, are available through the **State Parks Office,** 3060 Eiwa St., Lihue, HI 96766 (☎ **808/241-3444**). You're limited to five nights in any 30-day period. To reach the park from Lihue, take Highway 50 west to Barking Sands Pacific Missile Range. Bear right onto the paved road, which heads *mauka* (toward the moun-tains). There will be small signs directing you to Polihale; the second sign will direct you to turn left onto a dirt road. Follow this for about 5 miles; at the fork in the road, the campgrounds are to the left and the beach park is to the right.

THE COCONUT COAST
SLEEPING GIANT

This easy family hike takes you up the fabled mountain known as Sleeping Giant (which really does look like a giant resting on his back) to a fabulous view. To get to the trailhead, turn mauka (toward the mountain) off Kuhio Highway (Hwy. 56) onto Haleilio Road (between Wailua and Kapaa, just past the 6-mile marker); follow Haleilio Road for 1.2 miles to the parking area at telephone pole number 38. From there, signs posted by the State of Hawaii Division of Forestry and Wildlife lead you over the 1¾-mile trail, which ends at a picnic table and shelter. The panoramic view is breathtaking. Be sure to bring water—and a picnic, if you like.

THE NORTH SHORE
NA PALI COAST STATE PARK

Simply put, the Na Pali Coast is the most beautiful part of the Hawaiian Islands. Hanging valleys open like green-velvet accordions, and waterfalls tumble to the sea from the 4,120-foot-high cliffs; the spatial experience is exhilarating and humbling. Whether you hike in, fly over, or take a Zodiac cruise past, be sure to see this park.

Established in 1984, Na Pali Coast State Park takes in a 22-mile stretch of fluted cliffs that wrap around the northwest shore of Kauai between Kee Beach and Polihale State Park. Volcanic in origin, carved by wind and sea, "the cliffs" (*na pali* in Hawaiian), which heaved out of the ocean floor 200 million years ago, stand as constant reminders of majesty and endurance. Four major valleys—Kalalau, Honopu, Awaawapuhi, and Nualolo—crease the cliffs.

Unless you fly or boat in (see "Boating," above, or "Golf, Helicopter Rides & Other Outdoor Activities," below), the park is only accessible on foot—and it's not easy. An ancient footpath, the **Kalalau Trail**, winds through this remote, spectacular 6,500-acre park, ultimately leading to Kalalau Valley. Of all the green valleys in Hawaii, and there are many, only Kalalau Valley is a true wilderness, probably the last wild valley in the islands. No road goes there, and none ever will. The remote valley is home to long-plumed tropic birds, golden monarch butterflies, and many of Kauai's 120 rare and endangered species of plants. The hike into the Kalalau Valley is grueling and takes most people 6 to 8 hours one way.

Despite its inaccessibility, this journey into Hawaii's wilderness has become increasingly popular since the 1970s. Overrun with hikers, helicopters, and boaters, the Kalalau Valley was in grave danger of being loved to death. The Hawaii State Department of Land and Natural Resources closed the park for 6 months in 1996 due to unsafe, hazardous conditions as a result of erosion of the trail. Since then, strict rules about access were adopted. The park is open to hikers and campers only on a limited basis, and you must have a permit (you can hike the first 2 miles, to **Hanakapiai Beach**, without a permit). Permits are free and are issued in person at the **Kauai State Parks Office**, 3060 Eiwa St., Room 306, Lihue, HI 96766 (☎ 808/274-3445 or 808/274-3346). You can also request one by writing **Kauai Division of State Parks** at the address listed above.

For more information, contact **Hawaii State Department of Land and Natural Resources**, 1151 Punchbowl St., Room 130, Honolulu, HI 96813 (☎ 808/587-0320).

Hiking the Kalalau Trail

The trailhead is at Kee Beach, at the end of Highway 560. Even if you only go as far as Hanakapiai, bring water.

THE FIRST 2 MILES: TO HANAKAPIAI BEACH It's only 2 miles in to Hanakapiai Beach, but the first mile's all uphill. The tough trail takes about 2 hours one way and dissuades many, but everyone should attempt the first initial stretch, a good hint of the startling beauty that lies ahead. Day hikers love this initial stretch, so it's usually crowded. The island of Niihau and Lehua Rock are often visible on the horizon. At the 1-mile marker, you'll have climbed from sea level to 400 feet; now it's all downhill to Hanakapiai Beach. Sandy in summer, the beach becomes bouldery when winter waves scour the coast. There are strong currents and no lifeguards, so swim at your own risk. You can also hike another 2 miles inland from the beach to **Hanakapiai Falls,** a 120-foot cascade. Allow 3 hours for that stretch.

THE REST OF THE WAY Hiking the Kalalau is the most difficult and challenging hike in Hawaii, and one you'll never forget. Even the Sierra Club rates the 22-mile round trip into Kalalau Valley and back as "strenuous." Follow the footsteps of ancient Hawaiians along a cliffside path that's a mere 10 inches wide in some places, with sheer 1,000-foot drops to the sea. One misstep, and it's *limu* ("seaweed") time. Even the hardy and fit should allow at least 2 days to hike in and out (see below for camping information). Although the trail is usually in good shape, go in summer when it's dry; parts of the trail vanish in winter. When it rains, the trail's super slippery, and flash floods can sweep you away.

A park ranger is now on site full time at Kalalau Beach to greet visitors, provide information, oversee campsites, and keep trails and campgrounds in order.

Camping in Kalalau Valley & Along the Na Pali Coast
You must obtain a camping permit; see above for details on obtaining one. The camping season runs roughly from May or June to September (depending on the site). All campsites are booked almost a year in advance, so call or write well ahead of time. Stays are limited to 5 nights.

Camping areas along the Kalalau Trail include **Hanakapiai Beach** (facilities are pit toilets, and water is from the stream); **Hanakoa Valley** (no facilities, water from the stream); **Miloli** (no facilities, water from the stream), and **Kalalau Valley** (composting toilets, several pit toilets, and water from the stream). Keep your camping permit with you at all times.

---

by Jeanette Foster

BICYCLING

There are a couple of great areas on Kauai for two-wheeling: the **Poipu area,** which has wide, flat roads and several dirt-cane roads (especially around Mahaulepu); and the cane road between **Kealia Beach** and **Anahola,** north of Kapaa. For information on bikeways and maps, contact Ann Leighton, chair of the **Garden Island Resource, Conservation and Development Infrastructure Committee** (☎ 808/639-3249).

The following places rent mountain bikes, usually for $20 to $35 a day (with big discounts for multiple-day rentals): **Rental Warehouse,** 788 Kuhio Hwy. (across from McDonald's), Kapaa (☎ 808/822-4000); **Ray's Rentals & Activities,** 4-1345 Kuhio Hwy., Kapaa (☎ 808/822-5700); **Outfitters Kauai,** 2827A Poipu Rd. (look for the small five-shop mall before the road forks to Poipu/Spouting Horn), Poipu (☎ 808/742-9667); or **Bicycle Kauai,** 1379 Kuhio Hwy., Kapaa (☎ 808/822-3315). For a great selection in high-quality mountain bikes at reasonable prices, it's worth the drive to Hanalei to rent a bike at **Pedal 'n Paddle** (☎ 808/826-9069).

Not only do they have high-grade Kona mountain bikes with Shimano components, but they also have bikes with front-end suspension systems. Rentals start at $20 a day or $80 per week and include helmet, bike lock, and car rack. They even have kids' 20-inch BMX bikes. The knowledgeable folks there are more than happy to provide you with free maps and tell you the best biking spots on the island.

GUIDED BIKE TOURS   **Outfitters Kauai** (☎ 808/742-9667) offers a fabulous downhill bike ride from Waimea Canyon to the ocean. The 12-mile trip (mostly coasting) begins at 6am, when the van leaves the shop in Poipu and heads up to the Waimea Canyon. By the time you've scarfed down their fresh-baked muffins and coffee, you're at the top of the canyon just as the sun is rising over the rim—it's a remarkable moment. The tour makes a couple of stops on the way down for short, scenic nature hikes. You'll be back at the shop around 11am. The cost is $65 per person; children must be 11 or older. If they're booked, try **Kauai Coasters** (☎ 808/639-2412) or **Bicycle Downhill** (☎ 808/742-7421), both of which offer similar canyon-to-coast rides.

BIRDING

Kauai provides some of Hawaii's last sanctuaries for endangered native birds and oceanic birds, such as the albatross. If you didn't bring your binoculars, you can rent some at **Rental Warehouse,** 788 Kuhio Hwy. (across from McDonald's), Kapaa (☎ 808/822-4000), where rentals start at $1.99 a day.

David Kuhn leads custom hikes, pointing out Hawaii's rarest birds in the wild on his **Terran Tours,** P.O. Box 1018, Waimea, HI 96796 (☎ 808/335-3313). He offers custom tours, ranging from a half-day to 3 days, that take you to see endemic and endangered species in the forests of Kauai. If you're thinking of making a journey into **Alakai Swamp,** call David—he's been leading tours through it for a more than 10 years and knows where to find Hawaii's elusive rare birds.

SOUTHWEST KAUAI   At **Kokee State Park,** a 4,345-acre wilderness forest at the end of Highway 550 in Southwest Kauai, you have an excellent chance of seeing some of Hawaii's endangered native birds. You may spot the apapane, a red bird with black wings and a curved black bill; and the iwi, a red bird with black wings, orange legs, and a salmon-colored bill. Other frequently seen native birds are the honeycreeper, which sings like a canary; the amakihi, a plain, olive-green bird with a long, straight bill; and the anianiau, a tiny, yellow bird with a thin, slightly curved bill. Also often visible here is the elepaio, a small, active, gray flycatcher with an orange breast that perches with its tail up. The most common native bird at Kokee is the moa, or red jungle fowl, brought as domestic stock by ancient Polynesians. Ordinarily shy, they're actually quite tame in this environment.

THE NORTH SHORE   ✪ **Kilauea Point National Wildlife Refuge,** 1 mile north of Kilauea on the North Shore (☎ 808/828-1413), is a 200-acre headland habitat that juts 200 feet above the surf and includes cliffs, two rocky wavelashed bays, and a tiny islet that serves as a jumping-off spot for sea birds. Here, you can easily snoop on red-footed boobies, which nest in trees, and wedge-tailed shearwaters, which burrow in nests along the cliffs. You may also see the great frigate bird, the Laysan albatross, the white-tailed tropic bird, and the endangered nene. Native plants and the Kilauea Point Lighthouse are also highlights to see here. The sanctuary is open from 10am to 4pm daily (closed on federal holidays); admission is $2, free for kids under 16. To get here, turn right off Kuhio Highway (Hwy. 56) at Kilauea, just after the 23-mile marker on the highway; follow Kilauea Road to the ocean.

The Kilauea Point National Wildlife Refuge also offers 1-hour **guided hikes** up to the 568-foot summit of Crater Hill, which affords spectacular views. You can join a hike Monday through Friday (the only fee is the $2 admission to the refuge); but you must make a reservation; call ☎ **808/828-0168**.

Peaceful Hanalei Valley is home to Hawaii's endangered Koloa duck, gallinule, coot, and stilt. The **Hanalei National Wildlife Refuge** (☎ **808/828-1413**) also provides a safe habitat for migratory shorebirds and waterfowl. It's not open to the public, but an interpretive overlook along the highway affords a spectacular view. Along Ohiki Road, which begins at the west end of the Hanalei River Bridge, you'll often see white cattle egrets hunting crayfish in streams.

GOLF

If you don't bring your own with you, you can rent clubs from **Rental Warehouse**, 788 Kuhio Hwy. (across from McDonald's), Kapaa (☎ **808/822-4000**), where top-quality clubs go for $14.99 a day, not-so-top-quality for $9.99 a day.

For last-minute and discount tee times, call **Stand-by Golf** (☎ **888/645-BOOK** from Hawaii, 808/322-BOOK from the mainland) between 7am and 9pm. Stand-by offers discounted (10 to 40%) guaranteed tee times for same-day or next-day golfing.

In the listings below, the cart fee is included in the greens fees unless otherwise noted.

LIHUE & ENVIRONS

Kauai Lagoons Golf Courses. Kalapaki Beach, Lihue (less than a mile from Lihue Airport). ☎ **800/634-6400** or 808/246-5061. From the airport, make a left on Kapule Highway (Hwy. 51) and look for the sign on your left.

Choose between two excellent Jack Nicklaus–designed courses: the **Lagoons Course**, with 18 holes for the recreational golfer, or the **Kauai Kiele Championship Course**, for the low handicapper. The 6,942-yard, par-72 Lagoons Course is a links-style course with a bunker that's a little less severe than Kiele; emphasis is on the shore game. The Kiele Course is a mixture of tournament-quality challenge and high-traffic playability; it winds up with one of Hawaii's most difficult holes, a 431-yard, par-4 played straightaway to an island green.

Facilities include a driving range, lockers, showers, a restaurant, a snack bar, a pro shop, practice greens, a golf clubhouse, and golf club and shoe rental; transportation from the airport is provided. For the Lagoons Course, greens fees are $100 for the general public, $80 for guests of major hotels and condos, and $70 for guests of the Kauai Marriott; for the Kiele Course, they're $145 for the general public, $120 for guests of major hotels and condos, and $110 for Kauai Marriott guests.

THE POIPU RESORT AREA

Kiahuna Golf Club. 2545 Kiahuna Plantation Dr. (adjacent to Poipu Resort area), Koloa. ☎ **808/742-9595**. Take Hi. 50 to Hi. 520; bear left into Poipu at the fork in the road, and turn left onto Kiahuna Plantation Dr.

This par-70, 6,353-yard Robert Trent Jones, Jr.–designed course plays around four large archaeological sites, ranging from an ancient Hawaiian temple to the remains of a Portuguese home and crypt built in the early 1800s. This Scottish-style links course has rolling terrain, undulating greens, 70 sand bunkers, and near-constant winds. The 3rd hole, a par-3, 185-yarder, goes over Waikomo Stream. At any given time, just about half the players on the course are Kauai residents, the other half visitors. Facilities include driving range, practice greens, and snack bar. Greens fees are $60 for guests staying in the Poipu area, $65 for everybody else. Twilight rates are $50 after 11am, $37 after 1pm.

Kukuiolono Golf Course. Kukuiolono Park, Kalaheo. ☎ **808/332-9151.** Take Hi. 50 into the town of Kalaheo; turn left on Papaluna Rd., drive up the hill for nearly a mile, and watch for the sign on your right; the entrance has huge iron gates and stone pillars—you can't miss it.

This is a fun 9-hole golf course in a spectacular location with scenic views of the entire South Coast. You can't beat the price—$7 for the day, whether you play nine holes, 18 holes, or however many holes you feel like playing. The course is in Kukuiolono Park, a beautiful wooded area donated by the family of Walter McBryde, a sugar-grower whose family has had a powerful impact on Kauai for more than 100 years. In fact, you will see McBryde's grave on the course, along with some other usual oddities, like wild chickens, ancient Hawaiian rock structures, and Japanese gardens. Of course, there are plenty of trees in this wooded area to keep you on your game: When you get to the second tee box, check out the coconut tree dotted with yellow, pink, orange, and white golf balls that have been driven into the bark. Don't laugh—your next shot might add to the decor! This course shouldn't give you many problems—it's an excellently maintained, relatively straightforward course with few fairway hazards. Facilities include a driving range, practice greens, golf-club rental, a snack bar, and a clubhouse. Greens fees are $7 for the day; optional cart rental is $6 for nine holes, $12 for 18.

✪ Poipu Bay Resort Golf Course. 2250 Ainako St. (across the street from the Hyatt Regency Kauai), Koloa. ☎ **808/742-8711.** Take Hi. 50 to Hi. 520; bear left into Poipu at the fork in the road; turn right on Ainako St.

This 6,959-yard, par-72 course with a links-style layout was designed by Robert Trent Jones, Jr. Fairways and greens are undulating, and water hazards are located on eight holes. The par-4 16th hole must have been designed after Pebble Beach. The 501-yard hole has the coastline weaving along the entire left side. You can take the safe route to the right and maybe make par (but more than likely bogey), or you can try to take it tight against the ocean and possibly make it in two. The most striking (and the most disrespectful of Hawaiian heritage) hole is the 201-yard, par-3 on the 17th, which has a tee built on an ancient Hawaiian stone formation. Facilities include restaurant, locker room, pro shop, driving range, and putting greens. Greens fees are $140; they drop to $95 after noon, $45 after 3pm.

THE NORTH SHORE

✪ Princeville Golf Club, Prince Course. Princeville. ☎ **800/826-1105** or 808/826-2726. Take Hi. 56 to mile marker 27; the course is on your right.

Here's your chance to play one of the best golf courses in Hawaii. This Robert Trent Jones, Jr.–designed devil of a course sits on 390 acres molded to create ocean views from every hole. Some holes have a waterfall backdrop to the greens, others shoot into the hillside, and the famous par-4 12th hole has a long tee shot off a cliff to a narrow, jungle-lined fairway 100 feet below. This is the most challenging course on Kauai; accuracy is key here. Most of the time, if you miss the fairway, your ball's in the drink. "The average vacation golfer may find the Prince Course intimidating, but they don't mind, because it's so beautiful," Jones says. "You get the grandeur, the majesty of Kauai." Facilities include a restaurant, health club and spa, locker, clubhouse, golf shop, and driving range. Greens fees are $120 for Princeville guests, $150 for everyone else. The matinée special is $99; you must arrive between noon and 1pm.

HANG GLIDING

What steers like a shopping cart, soars like an eagle, and comes with a rocket-launched parachute? It's the *Airborne Edge Ultralight* (AEU), reputedly one of the most reliable, stable, quiet, and fun ultralight aircrafts in the world. On days when the air is still, pilot Gerry Charlebois—who has been flying for 20 years and has taken some 4,000 people up with a 100% safety record—can take you up into the wild blue yonder in his tandem power glider for a bird's-eye view of Kauai. You can hang out with this veteran airman on a low-speed reconnaissance flight at 2,000 feet above the island's flute cliffs and valleys. This is a hands-on instructional tour in an open cockpit; you can even fly the hang glider (well, for a few minutes anyway). A boom-mounted camera records the flight as you swoop over the rain forest and soar by jagged volcanic peaks. Chicken hearts will be glad to know that this bird comes with a rocket-launched parachute—just in case. Intro flights are $90 for a half-hour, $110 for an hour. Call **Birds in Paradise** (☎ 808/822-5309; www.birdsinparadise.com). Gerry operates out of the Hanapee Air Strip at Port Allen.

✪ HELICOPTER RIDES OVER WAIMEA CANYON & THE NA PALI COAST

Don't leave Kauai without seeing it from a helicopter. It's expensive but worth the splurge. You can take home memories of the thrilling ride up and over the Kalalau Valley on Kauai's wild North Shore and into the 5,200-foot vertical temple of Mt. Waialeale, the most sacred place on the island and the wettest spot on earth (and in some cases, you can even take a video of your ride home). All flights leave from Lihue Airport.

✪ **Island Helicopters.** ☎ 800/829-5999 or 808/245-6258. www.planet-hawaii. com/island. E-mail island@aloha.net. 1-hour island tour $166, including complimentary video of flight.

Curt Lofstedt has been flying helicopter tours of Kauai for some 25 years. He personally selects and trains professional pilots with an eye not only to their flying skills but also their to ability to share Kauai. All flights are in either the 4-passenger Bell Jet Ranger III or the six-passenger Aerospatiale ASTAR with extra-large windows and stereo headsets to hear the pilot's personal narration. You'll be able to relive your memories of the Na Pali Coast and Nualolo Aina (the Valley of the lost Tribes) with a complimentary video of your trip.

Jack Harter. 4500 Ahukini Rd., Lihue. ☎ 888/245-2001 or 808/245-3774. www. helicopters-kauai.com. E-mail jharter@aloha.net. 1-hour tour $149; 90-minute tour $209.

The pioneer of helicopter flights on Kauai, Jack was the guy who started the sightseeing-via-helicopter trend. He flies a Bell Jet Ranger Model 204, which holds four passengers. The 90-minute tour hovers over the sights a bit longer than the 1-hour flight, so you can get a good look, but we found that the 60-minute tour pretty much covered the island, without whizzing by the big attractions in a blur.

Ohana Helicopter Tours. Anchor Cove Shopping Center, 3416 Rice St., Lihue. ☎ 800/222-6989 or 808/245-3996. 50- to 55-minute tour $140; 65- to 70-minute tour $180. Rates include complimentary video.

Hawaiian-born pilot Bogart Kealoha delights in showing his island his way: aboard one of his four passenger Bell "Jet Rangers" or his six-passenger Aerospatiale "A-Star" helicopters. Passengers are linked to a customized audio entertainment system through individual headsets with narration as you swoop over and through 12-mile-long Waimea Canyon on a memorable sightseeing flight that also includes the valleys and waterfalls of the Na Pali Coast.

Will Squyres Helicopter Tours. 3222 Kuhio Hwy., Lihue. ☎ 888/245-HELI or 808/245-8881. www.helicopters-hawaii.com. E-mail squyres@aloha.net. 50-minute Circle the Island tour $129; 60-minute Grand Tour of Kauai $149. Personalized video $25.

The 1-hour flight starrs in Lihue and takes you through Waimea Canyon, along the Na Pali Coast, and over Waialeale Crater and the two sets of waterfalls that appeared in *Fantasy Island*. Will flies Bell206B four-passenger helicopters, because they have the best safety record—the first priority in choosing a copter tour company. He also maintains a meticulous maintenance record in the salty environs of an island where rust never sleeps. His A-star six-passenger copter has side-by-side seats (nobody sits backward and everybody gets a window seat) and enlarged windows. A veteran pilot, Squyres has flown several thousand hours over Kauai since 1984 and knows the island, its everchanging weather conditions, and his copters.

HORSEBACK RIDING

CJM Country Stables, 1731 Kelaukia St. (1.8 miles beyond the Hyatt Regency Kauai), Koloa (☎ **808/742-6096**), offers both 2- and 3-hour escorted Hidden Valley beach rides. You'll trot over Hidden Valley ranch land, past secluded beaches and bays, along the Haupu Ridge, across sugarcane fields, and to Mahaulepu Beach; it's worth your time and money just to get out to this seldom seen part of Kauai. The Secret Beach and Breakfast Ride (Mon–Sat, 8:30–11:30am) costs $71 and includes breakfast. The 2-hour Hidden Beach Ride, offered Monday through Saturday at 10am and 2pm, is $56.

Only in Kauai can you ride a horse across the wide-open pastures of a working ranch under volcanic peaks and rein up near a waterfall pool. No wonder Kauai's paniolos smile and sing so much. **Princeville Ranch Stables,** Hwy. 56 (just after the Princeville Airport), Hanalei (☎ **808/826-7473;** www.kauai.net/~kwc4), has a variety of outings: the 2½-hour Hanalei Mountain and Valley trip takes you across the Princeville Ranch and up into the mountains to vistas of Hanalei Valley's taro fields, Bali Ha'i, and Hanalei Bay for $55. The 3-hour Adventure to Anini Beach meanders along the bluffs of the North Shore to Anini Beach for $100, including snacks. The 4-hour Waterfall Picnic Ride crosses ranch land, takes you on a short (but steep) hike to swimming pools at the base of waterfalls, and then a picnic lunch for $110. Riders must be in good physical shape. Don't forget to put your swimsuit on under your jeans.

TENNIS

The **Kauai County Parks and Recreation Department,** 4444 Rice St., Suite 150, Lihue (☎ **808/241-6670;** fax 808/241-6807), has a list of the 9 county tennis courts around the island, all of which are free and open to the public.

Private courts that are open to the public include the **Princeville Tennis Club,** Princeville Hotel (☎ **808/826-3620**), which has six courts available for rent for $10 per person for 90 minutes. On the east side, call the **Kauai Lagoons Racquet Club,** Kauai Lagoons Resort, Lihue (☎ **808/246-2414**), which has eight courts to choose from for $20 a day. On the south side, call **Hyatt Regency Resort and Spa,** Poipu Resort (☎ **808/742-1234**), which has four courts, available for $25 an hour; and **Kiahuna Tennis Club,** Poipu Rd. (just past the Poipu Shopping Village on the left), Poipu Resort (☎ **808/742-9533**), which has 10 courts renting for $10 per hour, per person.

9 Seeing the Sights

by Jeanette Foster

No matter how much time you have on Kauai, make it a priority to see the North Shore (see p. 607). No doubt about it—this is Hawaii at its best.

LIHUE & ENVIRONS

Grove Farm Homestead Museum. 4050 Nawiliwili Rd. (Hwy. 58) at Pikaka St. (2 miles from Waapa Rd.), Lihue. ☎ **808/245-3202.** Admission $3, $2 children under 12. Tours offered at 10am and 1pm Mon, Wed, and Thurs. Reserve a week in advance.

You can experience a day in the life of an 1860s sugar planter on a visit to Grove Farm Homestead, which shows how good life was (for some, anyway) when sugar was king. This is Hawaii's best remaining example of a sugar-plantation homestead. Founded in 1864 by George N. Wilcox, a Hanalei missionary's son, Grove Farm was one of the earliest of Hawaii's 86 sugar plantations. A self-made millionaire, Wilcox died a bachelor in 1933 at age 94. His estate looks much like it did when he lived there, complete with period furniture, plantation artifacts, and Hawaiiana.

⭐ **Kauai Museum.** 4428 Rice St., Lihue. ☎ **808/245-6931.** Admission $5, seniors $4, students 13–17 $3, children 6–12 $1. Mon–Fri 9am–4pm, Sat 10am–4pm.

The history of Kauai is kept safe in an imposing Greco-Roman building that once served as the town library. This great little museum is worth a stop before you set out to explore Kauai. It contains a wealth of historical artifacts and information tracing the island's history from the beginning of time through contact (when Capt. James Cook "discovered" Kauai in 1778), the monarchy period, the plantation era, and the present. You'll hear tales of the *menehune* (the mythical elf-like people who built massive stoneworks in a single night) and see old poi pounders and idols, relics of sugar planters and paniolos, a nice sea-shell collection, old Hawaiian quilts, feather leis, a replica of a plantation worker's home, and much more—even a model of Cook's ship, the HMS *Resolution*, riding anchor in Waimea Bay. Vintage photographs by W. J. Senda, a Japanese immigrant of 1906, show Old Kauai, while a contemporary video, shot from a helicopter, captures the island's natural beauty.

Wings Over Hawaii. Kilohana Plantation, 3-2087 Kaumualii Hwy., Puhi. ☎ **808/245-8838.** Free admission. Daily 9:30am–6pm.

You can sit under a tent-like cloth structure and watch thousands of butterflies (familiar orange and black monarchs, yellow- and black-wing citrus swallowtails, silver-dotted lilikoi, and plain cabbage whites) flutter and feed amid a flowering garden. This is the first and only commercial butterfly farm in Hawaii; the adult butterflies are sold to be released at weddings, birthday parties, grand openings, and other celebrations. If you sit quietly and watch carefully, you can see a female butterfly deposit her eggs on some leaves and tiny caterpillars munch on others. The larger monarch caterpillars are picked off the leaves and taken to a 10-acre farm, where they form chrysalis and metamorphose into adult butterflies.

THE POIPU RESORT AREA

No Hawaii resort has a better entry: On Maluhia Road, eucalyptus trees planted in 1911 as a wind break for sugarcane fields now form a monumental **tree tunnel.** The leafy green and cool tunnel starts at Kaumualii Highway; you'll emerge at the beach, golden-red with perfect aquamarine waves rolling ashore.

Prince Kuhio Park. Lawai Rd., Koloa. Just after the 4-mile marker on Poipu Rd., veer to the right of the fork in the road; the park is on the right side.

This small roadside park is the birthplace of Prince Jonah Kuhio Kalanianaole, the "People's Prince," whose March 26 birthday is a holiday in Hawaii. He opened the beaches of Waikiki to the public in 1918 and served as Hawaii's second territorial delegate to the U.S. Congress. What remains here are the foundations of the family home, a royal fishpond, and a shrine where tributes are still paid in flowers.

Spouting Horn. At Kukuiula Bay, beyond Kuhio Park (see above).

This natural phenomenon is second only to Yosimite's Old Faithful. It's quite a sight—big waves hit Kauai's South Shore with enough force to send a spout of funneled salt water about 10 feet or more up in the air; in the winter, it can get as high as 6 stories.

Spouting Horn is different from other blowholes in Hawaii, in that this one has an additional hole which blows air which sounds like a loud moaning. According to Hawaiian legend, this coastline was once guarded by a giant female lizard; she would gobble up anyone who came into her area. Then one day, along came Liko, who wanted to fish in this area. Moo rushed out to eat Liko. Quickly, Liko threw a spear right into the giant lizard's mouth. Moo chased Liko into a lava tube. Liko escaped, but legend says Moo is still in the tube, and the moaning sound at Spouting Horn is her cry for help.

⭐ **National Tropical Botanical Gardens.** Visitor's Center, Lawai Rd. (across the street from Spouting Horn), Poipu. ☎ **808/742-2623.** www.ntbg.org. Admission **$25** for each garden, by guided tour only; at press time, only Allerton Gardens were open to view. 2½-hour guided tours by reservation only, Tues–Sat at 9am, 10am, 1pm, and 2pm. Reserve a week in advance in peak months of July, Aug, and Sept. No children under 5 allowed.

Discover an extraordinary collection of tropical fruit and spice trees, rare Hawaiian plants, and hundreds of varieties of flowers at the 186-acre preserve known as **Lawai Gardens,** said to be the largest collection of rare and endangered plants in the world. Adjacent **Allerton Gardens,** a royal home site of Queen Emma in the 1860s, is known for its formal gardens in the tropics, a delicious kind of colonial decadence. It's set amid fountains, streams, waterfalls, and European statuary where endangered green sea turtles are finally making a big comeback after Iniki. The tours are excellent and fascinating for green thumbs and novices alike.

Also see **Limahuli Garden,** which also falls under the National Tropical Botanical Gardens, in "Paradise Found: The North Shore," below.

SOUTHWEST KAUAI
WAIMEA TOWN

If you'd like to take a self-guided tour of this historic town, stop at the **Waimea Library,** at the 23-mile marker on Highway 50, to pick up a map and guide to the sites.

Kiki a Ola (Menehune Ditch). From Hi. 50, go mauka on Menehune Road; a plaque marks the spot about 1½ miles up.

Hawaiians were expert rock builders. They formed long lines and passed small stones hand over hand, and lifted stones weighing tons with ropes made from native plants; elaborate edifices were built using no mortar. Their mythic feats gave rise to fantastic tales of *menehunes,* elf-like people retained by Hawaiian kings to create massive stoneworks in a single night—reputedly for a payment of a single shrimp. An excellent example is Kiki a Ola, the so-called Menehune Ditch, with cut and dressed stones that form an ancient aqueduct that still directs water to irrigate taro ponds. Historians credit the work to ancient Hawaiian engineers who applied their knowledge of hydraulics to accomplish flood control and irrigation. Only a 2-foot-high portion of the wall can be seen today; the rest of the marvelous stonework is buried under the roadbed.

Russian Fort Elizabeth State Historical Park. Hi. 50 (on the ocean side, just after mile marker 22), east of Waimea.

To the list of all who tried to conquer Hawaii, add the Russians. It didn't work out, though, despite a brief occupation. In 1815, a German doctor tried to claim Kauai for Russia and supervised the construction of a fort in Waimea; but he and his handful of Russian compatriots were expelled by Kamehameha I a couple of years later.

Now a state historic landmark, the Russian Fort Elizabeth (named for the wife of Russia's Czar Alexander I) is on the eastern headlands overlooking the harbor, across from Lucy Kapahu Aukai Wright Beach Park. The fort, built Hawaiian-style with stacked lava rocks in the shape of a star, once bristled with cannons; it's now mostly in ruins. You can take a free, self-guided tour of the site, which affords a keen view of the west bank of the Waimea River, where Captain Cook landed, and the island of Niihau across the channel.

THE GRAND CANYON OF THE PACIFIC: WAIMEA CANYON

The great gaping gulch known as Waimea Canyon is quite a sight; no other island has anything else like it. This valley, known for its reddish lava beds, reminds everyone who sees it of Arizona's Grand Canyon. Kauai's version is bursting with everchanging color, just like its namesake. But it's smaller—only a mile wide, 3,567 feet deep, and 12 miles long.

All this grandeur was caused by a massive earthquake, which sent all the streams flowing into a single river, which then carved this picturesque canyon—quite an astonishing bit of erosion. Today, the Waimea River, a silver thread of water in the gorge, sometimes a trickle, often a torrent, but always there, cuts the canyon deeper, makes it wider, and nobody knows or can say what the final result will be 100 million years from now.

You can stop by the road and look at it, hike down in it, or swoop through it in a helicopter. For information on hiking through the canyon, see "Hiking & Camping," above; also see "Horseback Riding" and "Golf, Helicopter Rides & Other Outdoor Activities," earlier in this chapter.

The Drive Through Waimea Canyon & Up to Kokee

There are two ways to visit Waimea Canyon and reach Kokee State Park, 20 miles up from Waimea, by car. From the coastal road (Hwy. 50), you can turn up Waimea Canyon Drive (Hwy. 550) at Waimea town; or you can pass through Waimea and turn up Kokee Road (Hwy. 55) at Kekaha. The climb is very steep from Kekaha, but Waimea Canyon Drive, the rim road, is narrower and rougher. A few miles up, the roads merge into Kokee Road.

The first good vantage point is **Waimea Canyon Lookout**, located between the 10- and 11-mile markers on Waimea Canyon Road. Take a peek at this gem and see why Mark Twain took one look and coined it the "Grand Canyon of the Pacific." From here, it's another 6 miles to Kokee. There are a few more lookout points along the way that offer spectacular views, such **Puu Hina Hina Lookout**, located between the 13- and 14-mile markers, at 3,336 feet; be sure to pull over and spend a few minutes pondering this natural wonder. (The giant white object that looks like a golf ball and defaces the natural landscape is a radar station left over from the Cold War when we snooped on the Soviets.)

KOKEE STATE PARK

It's only 16 miles from Waimea to Kokee, but it's a whole different world, because the park is 4,345 acres of rain forest. You enter a new climate zone, where the breeze has a bite and trees look quite continental. You're in a cloud forest on the edge of an upland bog known as the Alakai Swamp, the largest bog in Hawaii, on the summit plateau of Kauai. Days are cool, wet, and mild, with intermittent bright sunshine, not unlike Seattle on a good day. You'll be glad you brought your sweater, and be sure you know how to light a fire if you're staying over; overnight lows dip into the 40s. Such is the tropical paradox of Kauai.

The forest is full of native plants, such as maile vine, mokihana berry, the ohia lehua tree, the iliau (similar to Maui's silversword), and imports like Australia's eucalyptus and even California's redwood. Pigs, goats, and black-tailed deer thrive in the forest, but the moa, or Polynesian jungle fowl (*Gallus gallus*), is the cock of the walk.

There's lots to see and do up here: Anglers fly-fish for rainbow trout, and hikers tackle the 45 trails that lace the Alakai Swamp (see "Hitting the Water" and "Hiking & Camping," above). That's a lot of ground to cover, so you might want to plan on staying over. If pitching a tent is a little too rustic for you, there are some wonderful rustic cabins set in a grove of California redwoods; they're one of the best accommodations bargains in the islands (see "Accommodations" for details). There's also a restaurant at **Kokee Lodge** that's open for continental breakfast and lunch every day from 9am to 3:30pm.

Just the Facts

WHEN TO GO   The park is open daily year-round. The best time to go is early in the morning, to see the panoramic view of Kalalau Valley from the lookout at 4,000 feet, before clouds obscure the valley and peaks.

ACCESS POINTS   See "The Drive Through Waimea Canyon & Up to Kokee," above.

INFORMATION & VISITOR CENTER   For information, contact the **State Division of Parks**, P.O. Box 1671, Lihue, HI 96766 (☎ **808/274-3446**); and the **Kokee Lodge Manager**, P.O. Box 819, Waimea, HI 96796 (☎ **808/335-6061**).

Right next to Kokee Lodge is the ✪ **Kokee Natural History Museum** (☎ **808/ 335-9975**; open daily 10am–4pm; free admission). This small, vital museum is the best place to learn about the forest and Alakai Swamp before you set off hiking in the wild. The museum shop has great trail information and local books and maps, including the official park trail map (50¢).

Seeing the Highlights

A **nature walk** with 35 native plants and trees is the best mini-intro to this rain forest; it starts behind the museum at the rare Hawaiian koa tree (which, you'll learn, has hard, red wood, lemon-yellow flowers, and lives only on the Hawaiian Islands and in Australia). This easy, self-guided walk of about one-tenth of a mile takes about 20 minutes if you stop and look at all the plants; they're all identified along the way.

For details on hiking Kokee's 45 miles of trails on your own or on a guided hike, see "Hiking & Camping," above.

Two miles above Kokee Lodge is ✪ **Kalalau Lookout**, the spectacular climax of your drive through Waimea Canyon and Kokee. When you stand at the lookout, below you is a work in progress that began at least 5 million years ago. It's hard to stop looking; the view is breathtaking, especially when light and cloud shadows play across the red-and-orange cliffs.

THE COCONUT COAST

Fern Grotto. Wailua Marina, at the mouth of the Wailua River; turn off Kuhio Hwy. (Hwy. 56) into Wailua Marine State Park. Daily 9am–3:30pm. $15 adults, $7.50 children 2–12; reservations are recommended.

This is one of Kauai's oldest ("since 1947") and most popular tourist attractions. Several times a day, every day, **Smith's Motor Boats** (☎ **808/821-6892**) and **Waialeale**

Hollywood Loves Kauai

More than 50 major Hollywood productions have been shot on Kauai ever since Hollywood discovered the island's spectacular natural beauty. Here are just a few:

- Manawaiopu Falls, Mt. Waialeale, and other scenic areas around the island doubled for *Jurassic Park*.

- Kauai's lush rain forests formed a fantastic backdrop for Harrison Ford in both *Raiders of the Lost Ark* and *Indiana Jones and the Temple of Doom*, as well as the recent romantic comedy *6 Days/7 Nights*, co-starring Anne Heche.

- Mitzi Gaynor sang "I'm Gonna Wash That Man Right Outra My Hair" on Lumahai Beach in *South Pacific*.

- Ricky Nelson and Jack Lemmon sailed *The Wackiest Ship in the Army* (1960) up the Wailua River.

- Jessica Lange, Jeff Bridges, and Charles Grodin tangled with Hollywood's most famous gorilla in Honopu Valley in their remake of *King Kong* (1976).

- Elvis Presley married costar Joan Blackman near the Wailua River in *Blue Hawaii* (1961).

- Kauai's lush jungle doubled as a Vietnam war zone in the 1983 film *Uncommon Valor*, starring Gene Hackman.

- Beautiful Kee Beach, on the North Shore, masqueraded as Australia in the landmark miniseries *The Thornbirds*, starring Richard Chamberlain and Rachel Ward.

- Dustin Hoffman starred in *Outbreak*, the 1994 thriller filmed on Kauai about the spread of a deadly virus on a remote tropical island. He also appeared with Robin Williams and Julia Roberts in *Hook* (1991), in which Kauai appeared as Never-Never Land.

- James Caan, Nicholas Cage, Sarah Jessica Parker, and Pat Morita shared laughs on Kauai (which appeared as itself) in *Honeymoon in Vegas*.

Now you can visit these and other Kauai locations that made it to the silver screen, plus famous locations from such TV classics as *Fantasy Island* and *Gilligan's Island*, with **Hawaii Movie Tours**, Kinipopo Shopping Village (across the street from Sizzler Restaurant), 356 Kuhio Hwy., Kapaa (☎ **800/628-8432** or 808/822-1192; fax 808/822-1608; www.hawaiimovietour.com). The commentary and sightseeing stops are supplemented by video clips of the location shots (complete with surround sound), and a tour guide leads sing-alongs of movie and TV themes as you move from locale to locale in their 15-passenger van. All in all, there's a whole lot of fun to be had, especially for families. You'll see more of Kauai on this tour (including private estates not open to the public) than you would if you toured the island yourself for a whole week. Tours are offered daily from 9am to 2pm. Tickets are $85 for adults, $63.75 for children 11 and under; lunch is included in the price.

Boat Tours (☎ **808/822-4908**) take 150 people up and down the river on a 90-minute, 2½-mile, motorized river trip to a natural amphitheater filled with ferns. It's the source of many Hawaiian legends and a popular site for weddings.

WAILUA RIVER STATE PARK

Ancients called the Wailua River "the river of the great sacred spirit." Seven sacred temples once stood along this 20-mile river, fed by 5,148-foot Mt. Waialeale, the wettest spot on earth—with 40 feet of rain a year, it's the source of Kauai's waterfalls, rivers, and lush, tropical look.

You can go up Hawaii's biggest navigable river by boat or kayak (see "Boating" and "Kayaking" in "Hitting the Water," above), or drive Kuamoo Road (Hwy. 580; sometimes called the King's Highway), which goes inland along the north-side river from Kuhio Highway (Hwy. 56)—from the northbound lane, turn left at the stoplight just before the ruins of Coco Palms Resort—and past the heiau and historical sites to Opaekaa Falls and Keahua Arboretum, a State Division of Forestry attempt to reforest the watershed with native plants.

The entire district from the river mouth to the summit of Waialeale was once royal land. This sacred, historical site was believed to be founded by Puna, a Tahitian priest who, according to legend, arrived in one of the first double-hulled voyaging canoes to arrive in Hawaii, established a beachhead, declared Kauai his kingdom, and put everything in his sight under a kapu. All of Kauai's *alii* (royalty) are believed to be descended from Puna. Here, in this royal settlement, are remains of the seven temples, including a sacrificial *heiau*, a planetarium (a simple array of rocks in a celestial pattern), the royal birthing stones, and a stone bell to announce a royal birth. (You can still ring the bell—many people have—but make sure you have an announcement to make when it stops ringing.)

There's a nice overlook view of 40-foot ✪ **Opaekaa Falls** 1½ miles up Highway 580. This is probably the best-looking drive-up waterfalls on Kauai. With the scenic peaks of Makaleha mountains in the background and a restored Hawaiian village on the river banks, this waterfall is what the tourist bureau folks call an "eye-popping" photo op.

Near Opaekaa Falls overlook is **Poliahu Heiau,** the large black lava-rock temple of Kauai's last king, Kaumualii, who died on Oahu in 1824 after being abducted by King Kamehameha II. If you stop here, you'll notice two signs: One, an official 1928 bronze territorial plaque, which says that the royal heiau was built by menehunes, which it explains parenthetically as "Hawaiian dwarves or brownies." A more recent, hand-painted sign warns visitors not to climb on the rocks, which are sacred to the Hawaiian people.

SLEEPING GIANT

If you squint your eyes just so when you're passing the 1,241-foot-high Nounou Ridge, which forms a dramatic backdrop to the coastal villages of Wailua and Waipouli, you may see the fabled Sleeping Giant. On Kuhio Highway, just after the 7-mile marker, around the mini-mall complex, Waipouli Town Center, look *mauka* and you may see what appears to be the legendary giant named Puni, who, as the story goes, fell asleep after a great feast. If you don't see it at first, visualize it this way: His head is Wailua and his feet are Kapaa.

For details on an easy hike, suitable for the entire family, to the top of the Sleeping Giant, see "Hiking & Camping," above.

PARADISE FOUND: THE NORTH SHORE ON THE ROAD TO HANALEI

The first place everyone should go on Kauai is Hanalei. The drive along **Kuhio Highway** (Hwy. 56, which becomes Hwy. 560 after Princeville to the end of the road), displays Kauai's grandeur at its absolute best. Just before Kilauea, the air and the

The North Shore: Princeville & Hanalei

sea change, the light falls in a different way, and the last signs of development are behind you. Now there are roadside fruit stands, a little stone church in Kilauea, two roadside waterfalls, and a long, stilt-like bridge over the Kalihiwai Stream and its green river valley.

If you don't know a guava from a mango, stop off in Kilauea for a break at the cool, shady **Guava Kai Plantation**, at the end of Kuawa Road (☎ **808/828-6121;** open daily 9am–5pm), for a refreshing, free treat. After you take a walk through the orchards and see what a guava looks like on the tree, you can sample the juice of this exotic pink tropical fruit (which also makes a great jam or jelly—sold here, too). For other sweet treats along the way, be sure to check out the box called "Fruity Smoothies & Other Exotic Treats," later in this chapter.

Birders might want to stop off at **Kilauea Point National Wildlife Refuge**, 1 mile north of Kilauea, and the **Hanalei National Wildlife Refuge**, along Ohiki Road, at the west end of the Hanalei River Bridge. (For details, see "Birding," above.) In the Hanalei Refuge, along a dirt road on a levee, you can see the **Hariguchi Rice Mill**, now a historic treasure.

Now the coastal highway heads due west and the showy ridgelines of Mount Namahana create a grand amphitheater. The two-lane coastal highway rolls over pastures of grazing cattle, past a tiny airport where helicopters buzz in and out, and past the luxurious Princeville Hotel.

Five miles past Kilauea, just past the Princeville Shopping Center, is **Hanalei Valley Lookout.** Big enough for a dozen cars, this lookout attracts crowds of people who peer

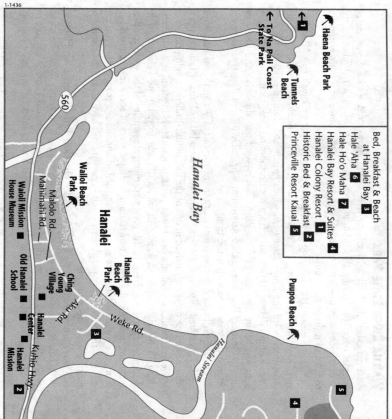

1-1436

Bed, Breakfast & Beach at Hanalei Bay **3**
Hale 'Aha **6**
Hale Ho'o Maha **7**
Hanalei Bay Resort & Suites **1**
Hanalei Colony Resort **4**
Historic Bed & Breakfast **2**
Princeville Resort Kauai **5**

Legend
Beach

Anini Beach →↗

Kaweonui Beach
Princeville Resort
Kamehameha
6
Kenomene Beach
Kahaku Rd.
Edward Rd.
Albert Rd.
Kaweonui Rd.
Kaui Road
Pepelani Loop
Princeville
Honoiki Rd.
Liholino
Golf
Course
Le'o Papa Rd.
Princeville Center
Hanalei Plantation Rd.
Hanalei Valley Lookout
Hanalei Bridge
Hanalei National Wildlife Refuge
To Princeville Airport & Kilauea →
56
560
7 →

over the edge into the 917-acre Hanalei River Valley. Green, green, green, so many shades of green: rice green, taro green, and green streams lace a patchwork of green ponds that back up to green-velvet Bali Ha'i cliffs. Pause to catch the first sight of taro growing in irrigated ponds, and maybe you'll see an endangered Hawaiian black-necked stilt. Don't be put off by the crowds; this is definitely worth a look.

Farther along, a hairpin turn offers another scenic look at Hanalei town; then you cross the **Hanalei Bridge.** The Pratt truss steel bridge, prefabbed in New York City, was erected in 1912; it's now on the National Registry of Historic Landmarks. If it ever goes out, the nature of Hanalei will change forever; currently, this rusty, one-lane bridge (which must violate all kinds of Department of Transportation safety regulations) isn't big enough for a tour bus to cross.

You'll drive slowly past the Hanalei River banks and Bill Mowry's **Hanalei Buffalo Ranch,** where 200 American bison roam in the tropic sun; you may even see buffaloes grazing the pastures on your right. The herd is often thinned to make all-beef buffalo patties. (You wondered why there was a Buffalo Burger on the Ono Family Restaurant menu, didn't you?)

Just past Tahiti Nui, turn right on Aku Road before Ching Young Village, then take a right on Weke Road; **Hanalei Beach Park,** one of Hawaii's most gorgeous, is a half-block ahead on your left. Swimming is excellent here year-round, especially in the summer, when Hanalei Bay becomes a big, placid lake; for more details, see "Beaches," earlier in this chapter.

If this exquisite 2-mile-long beach doesn't meet your expectations, head down the highway, where the next 7 miles of coast yield some of Kauai's other spectacular beaches, including **Lumahai Beach**, of *South Pacific* movie fame; **Tunnels Beach**, where the 1960s puka-shell necklace craze began; and **Haena Beach Park**, a fabulous place to kick back and enjoy the waves, particularly in the summer (see "Beaches," above). Once you've found your Bali Ha'i beach, stick around until sundown, then head back to one of the North Shore's restaurants for a mai tai and a fresh seafood dinner (see "Dining," above). Another perfect day in paradise, pal.

ATTRACTIONS ALONG THE WAY

Waioli Mission House Museum. Kuhio Hwy. (Hwy. 560), just behind the green Waioli Huia Church, Hanalei. ☎ **808/245-3202.** Free admission (donations gratefully accepted). Tues, Thurs, Sat 9am–3pm. Guided tours available at no charge.

If you're lucky and time your visit just right, you can visit this 150-year-old mission house, which serves today as a living museum. It's a real treasure. Others in Honolulu are easier to see, but the Waioli Mission House retains its sense of place and most of its furnishings, so you can really get a clear picture of what life was like for the New England missionaries who came to Kauai to convert the heathens to Christianity.

Most mission houses are small, dark Boston cottages that violate the tropical sense of place. This two-story wood-frame house, built in 1836 by Abner and Lucy Wilcox of New Bedford, Massachusetts, is an excellent example of hybrid architecture. The house features a lanai on both stories, with a cookhouse in a separate building. It has a lava-rock chimney, ohia-wood floors, and Hawaiian koa furniture.

Ka Ulu O Laka Heiau. From the west side of Kee Beach, take the footpath across the big rocks almost to the point, then climb up the steep grassy hill.

On a knoll above the boulders of Kee Beach (see "Beaches," above) stands a sacred altar of rocks, often draped with flower leis and ti-leaf offerings, dedicated to Laka, the goddess of hula. It may seem like a primal relic from the days of idols, but it's very much in use today. Often, dancers (men and women) of Hawaii's hula *halau* (schools) climb the cliff, bearing small gifts of flowers. In Hawaiian myths, Lohiau, a handsome chief, danced here before the fire goddess Pele; their passion became *Haena*, which means "the heat." Sometimes, in a revival of the Old Hawaiian ways (once banned by missionaries), a mother of a newborn will deposit the umbilical cord of her infant at this sacred shrine. The site is filled with what Hawaiians call *mana*, or power. If you climb the cliff to visit this altar, you'll discover that you don't have to be Hawaiian to experience mana.

⭐ **Limahuli Garden.** Kuhio Hwy. (Hwy. 560), Haena. ☎ **808/826-1053.** Admission $10 self-guided, $15 guided. Offers 2½-hour tours Tues–Fri, Sun. Advance reservations required for guided tours. During peak seasons of July, Aug, and Sept, book at least a week in advance.

Out on Kauai's far North Shore, beyond Hanalei and the last wooden bridge, there's a mighty cleft in the coastal range where ancestral Hawaiians lived in what can only be called paradise. Carved by a waterfall stream known as Limahuli, the valley is a lush tropical Eden at the foot of steepled cliffs that Hollywood portrayed as Bali Ha'i in the film classic *South Pacific*. This small, almost secret garden is ecotourism at its best. It appeals not just to green thumbs, but to all who love Hawaii's great outdoors.

That such a place still exists in a Hawaii so full of progress is a wonder. The 17-acre garden is at the heart of a 1,000-acre preserve that began in 1967 when gardener Juliet Rice Wichman drove out wild cattle, fenced in plants, and set out to save Kauai's endangered species in the remnant native forest. She and her grandson donated the property to the National Tropical Botanical Gardens (see above), where botanists hope to save Kauai's endangered native plants. (And Limahuli's stream is sanctuary to the last five species of Hawaiian freshwater fish.) Plants are identified in Hawaiian, English, and by genus and species, family and origin. From taro to sugarcane, the mostly Polynesian imports tell the story of the people who cultivated the plants for food, medicine, clothing, shelter, and decoration.

THE END OF THE ROAD

The real Hawaii always begins where the road stops. While this axiom isn't fail-safe, it's especially true on Kauai—for at the end of Highway 56, the spectacular **Na Pali Coast** begins. To explore it, you have to set out on foot, by boat, or by helicopter. For details on exploring this region, see "Hiking & Camping," p. 590), "Boating," p. 584), and "Helicopter Rides over Waimea Canyon & the Na Pali Coast," p. 600).

10 Shops & Galleries

by Jocelyn Fujii

Kapaa is taking on a new and upbeat flavor, and Hanalei is booming. My favorite shops are in Hanalei, and there are marvels in Kapaa, too—but in general, it's safe to say that your credit cards will probably remain cooler here than on any other island except for Molokai. What's here? A few art galleries and boutiques and a few shopping centers—not much to distract you from an afternoon of hiking or snorkeling. The gift items and treasures you'll find in East and North Kauai, however, may be among your best Hawaiian finds.

GREEN MARKETS & FRUIT STANDS The county of Kauai sponsors regular weekly **Sunshine Markets** throughout the island, featuring fresh Kauai Sunrise papayas (sweeter and redder than most), herbs and vegetables used in ethnic cuisines, exotic fruit such as rambutan and atemoya, and the most exciting development in pineapple agriculture, the low-acid white pineapple called Sugarloaf. Featuring grown-on-Kauai products, these Sunshine Markets, selling the full range of fresh produce and flowers at rock-bottom prices, present the perfect opportunity to see what's best and what's in season. Farmers sell their bounty from the backs of trucks or at tables set up under tarps. Mangoes during the summer, lettuces all year, fleshy bananas and juicy papayas, the full range of Filipino vegetables (wing beans, long beans, exotic squashes, and melons), and an everchanging rainbow of edibles are sold at this movable market. The biggest market is at **Kapaa New Town Park** in the middle of Kapaa town, on Wednesday at 3pm. **Lihue's** Sunshine Market, held on Friday at 3pm at the Vidhina Stadium Parking Lot, is close in size and extremely popular. The schedule for the other markets: **Koloa Ball Park,** Mondays at noon; **Kalaheo Neighborhood Center,** Tuesdays at 3:30pm; **Kilauea Neighborhood Center,** Thursdays at 4:30pm; and **Kekaha Neighborhood Center,** Saturdays at 9am. For more information on **Sunshine Markets,** call ☎ **808/241-6300** or 808/241-6390. Especially at the Koloa Market, which draws hundreds of shoppers, go early and shop briskly.

Those who miss the Sunshine Markets can shop instead at the privately run **Sunny Side Farmers Market,** on Kuhio Highway in the middle of Kapaa, open 8am to 8pm daily. You'll find several varieties of papayas, mangoes, passion fruits, Hawaiian Sugarloaf pineapples, locally grown organic lettuces, Maui onions, purple Molokai sweet potatoes, Molokai watermelons, and exotic fruits, such as soursop and rambutan in season. Fruit preserves, gourmet breads, Taro Ko chips, and Kauai macadamia-nut

Fruity Smoothies & Other Exotic Treats

Fruit stands have sprouted on this island, and smoothies are gaining ground as the milkshake of the millennium. New crops of exotic trees imported from southeast Asia are nearing maturation on Kauai, creating anticipation among residents and fruitful ideas for the smoothie world. "Everyone's waiting for the mangosteens and durians," comments Joe Halasey, who, with his wife, Cynthia, runs **Banana Joe's (☎ 808/828-1092)**, the granddaddy of Kauai's roadside fruit-and-smoothie stands. "They take about 12 years to start bearing, so there are a lot of mature trees. We're all waiting for the fruit. Rambutans (with a hairy, red exterior and a translucent, litchi-like flesh) are good for the farmers here, because they're available, and they are a winter fruit. In the summer, mangoes and litchis are always in high demand." Banana Joe's has been a Kilauea landmark since it opened in 1986 at 52719 Kuhio Hwy., between mile markers 23 and 24 heading north, on the mauka (mountain) side of the street.

Mangosteen, reputedly the favorite fruit of Queen Victoria, has a creamy, custardy flesh of ambrosial sweetness. Ever since I tasted it in Bali, it has gone to the top of my fruit list, up there with white pirie mangoes. When mangosteen starts appearing at Hawaii fruit stands, it will no doubt be in high demand, like mangoes and litchis during their summer season. In the meantime, Banana Joe has a hit on his hands with Sugarloaf, the white, non-acidic, ultra-sweet, organically grown pineapple popularized on the Big Island. Made into smoothies; frostees (frozen fruit put through the Champion juicer); or sold plain, fresh, and whole, the Sugarloaf is pineapple at its best. For litchi lovers, who must wait for their summer appearance, new varieties such as Kaimana and Brewster are adding to the pleasures of the season. In addition to fresh fruit, fruit smoothies, and frostees ($2.50 to $3), Banana Joe's sells organic greens, tropical fruit salsas, jams and cookies are among the made-on-Kauai products. They do a brisk business shipping all over the United States.

On the North Shore, Kilauea is the agricultural heart of the island, with two weekly green markets: the county-sponsored **Sunshine Market** at 4:30pm Thursdays in the Kilauea Gym parking lot, and the **Farmers Market** from 9am Saturdays across from the Kilauea Post Office. Farming activity and enterprises are growing by leaps and bounds in Kilauea; most of the organic vegetables you'll see on the island have been grown here.

Also on the North Shore, about a quarter mile past Hanalei in an area called Waipa, the **Hawaiian Farmers of Hanalei**—anywhere from a dozen to 25 farmers—gather along the main road with their budget-friendly, just-picked produce. The farmers market is held every Tuesday at 2pm. You'll find unbelievably priced papayas (in some seasons, several for a dollar, ready to eat), organic vegetables, inexpensive tropical flowers, avocados and mangoes in season, and when possible, fresh seafood.

LIHUE & ENVIRONS

DOWNTOWN LIHUE   In downtown Lihue, the gift shop of the **Kauai Museum**, 4428 Rice St., (☎ 808/245-6931), is your best bet for made-on-Kauai arts and crafts, from Niihau-shell leis to woodworks, lauhala and coconut products, and more.

About a mile north of the Lihue Airport, on Highway 56 (Kuhio Hwy.) **Kauai Fruit and Flowers** is a great stop for flowers, including the rare Kauai maile, coconut jellies, drinking coconuts (young coconuts containing delicious drinking water), gift items, and baked goods such as papaya-banana bread. It sells only island produce, most of it from Kauai, and its top-selling smoothies are papaya, banana, and pineapple.

Mango Mama's, 4660 Hookui St. (☎ 808/828-1020) is another favorite on the Kilauea roadside. Smoothies, fresh-squeezed juices, sandwiches, coffee, coffee smoothies, and fresh fruit are dispensed from a cheerful stand where the blender is always whirring. The Kauai Breeze (fresh mango, pineapple, passion fruit, and guava, $3.75–$4.50) is the big winner at Mango Mama's.

At the north end of Kapaa town, the new **Killer Juice Bar**, 4-1586 Kuhio Hwy. (☎ 808/821-1905), is a sight for sore eyes after a drive through commercial Kapaa. Smoothies are $4, and fresh juices are $2.50 to $4, and they are good! A small selection of fresh fruit for sale is displayed in the front. Queen of the smoothies is the Amazing Mango Memory, made with fresh local mangoes in season and, when they're not available, fresh mangoes from Mexico.

On the Coconut Coast, just before you reach the center of Kapaa town heading north on Kuhio Highway, keep an eye out to the left for **Sunny Side Market**, 4-1345 Kuhio Hwy. (☎ 808/822-4494 or 808/822-1154). You can always find realistically priced Sunrise papayas, pineapples, local bananas, tomatoes, and other Kauai produce. You won't find smoothies here—it's strictly a fruit-and-gift stand, but when you find local retirees shopping for their produce here, you know it's a good value. They sell preinspected Sunrise papayas for travel out of state, local apple bananas, coconuts, mangoes in season, and pineapples from Maui and Kauai.

drums the owner makes himself, Hawaiian gourds (called *ipu*), cut flowers for shipping, and Kauai fruit, such as papayas and pineapples.

The **Kukui Grove Center**, at Kaumualii Highway (Hwy. 50) and Old Nawiliwili Road, alas, is another story. At one time the commercial center of the island, it staggers under the weight of change. There are many empty spaces, and traffic is far from what it used to be. **Longs Drugs** provides for basic needs, and the affordable **Dan's Sports Shop** meets just about all sporting needs. At the **Indo-Pacific Trading Company**, you'll find Indonesian imports and artifacts—jewelry, textiles, carvings, temple bells, pareus, and accessories. Not to be missed is the **Kauai Products Store** (☎ 808/246-3939 for a list of available Kauai-made products), a respectable showcase of made-on-the-island products, from soaps to paintings to clothing, Kauai coffee, Kukui guava jams, fabrics, and Niihau-shell leis. Across the mall is the **Deli and Bread Connection**, selling soups, sandwiches, and deli items among the pots, china, coffeemakers, and hundreds of kitchen gadgets that crowd the aisles of this popular shop.

IN NEARBY NAWILIWILI Down the road from Lihue in Nawiliwili, on the road between Nawiliwili and Kukui Grove, at a complex called Anchor Cove on Kalapaki Bay, **The Amber Door**, at 3416 Rice St., is chockablock with salt and pepper shakers, Depression glass, collectible linens, and assorted vintage treasures from Hawaii and the rest of America.

KILOHANA PLANTATION

Kilohana, the 35-acre Tudor-style estate that sprawls across the landscape in Puhi, on Highway 50 between Lihue and Poipu, is an architectural marvel that houses a sprinkling of galleries and shops. At the **Country Store** on the ground level, you'll find island and American crafts of decent quality, koa accessories, pottery, home accessories, and Hawaiian-themed gift items. On the other side of Gaylord's, the **Kilohana and Kahn galleries** offer a mix of crafts and two-dimensional art, from originals to affordable prints, at all levels of taste.

THE POIPU RESORT AREA

Expect mostly touristy shops in Poipu, the island's resort mecca; you'll find T-shirts, souvenirs, black pearls, jewelry, and the usual quota of tired marine art and trite hand-painted silks.

The formerly characterless **Poipu Shopping Village**, at 2360 Kiahuna Plantation Dr., is shaping up to be a serious shopping stop, with the tiny **Bamboo Lace** boutique luring the fashionistas, and upbeat aloha shirt and women's sportswear boutiques interspersed between the Italian and Thai cafes.

At the **Hyatt Regency Kauai**, the shopping is surprisingly good, with the footwear mecca, **Sandal Tree**, **Water Wear** for swim stuff, **Reyn's** for top-drawer aloha shirts, and **Kauai Kids** for the under-age.

In neighboring **Old Koloa Town**, you'll find everything from **Lapper's Ice Cream** to **Crazy Shirts** and **Sueoka Store** on Koloa's main drag, Koloa Road. Just walk the long block for gifts, souvenirs, sunwear, groceries, and everyday necessities, but don't expect dazzling temptations.

On Poipu Road between Koloa and Poipu, the **Kukuiula Store** is a way stop for everything from produce and sushi to go, to paper products, sunscreen, beverages, and groceries. Occasionally, when the fishermen drop by, they offer fresh sliced sashimi and poke, popular for sunset picnickers and nearby condo residents.

SOUTHWEST KAUAI

HANAPEPE

This West Kauai hamlet is becoming a haven for artists, but finding them requires some vigilance. The center of town is off Highway 50; turn right on Hanapepe Road just after Eleele if you're driving from Lihue. First, you'll smell the **Taro Ko** chips cooking in a tiny, modest kitchen at the east end of town, where these sumptuous lavender chips, dusted with nothing more than garlic salt, are handmade by the farmers who grow the taro in a nearby valley. Past Taro Ko chips (which, despite their breakable nature, make great gifts to go), Hanapepe Road is lined with gift shops and galleries, among them the cherubic **Aloha Angels** adjoining the Hanapepe Café. As the name indicates, everything is angel-themed or angel-related—corny, for sure, but harmless. The **Kauai Village Gallery**, housed in a building that was a set on the original *The Thornbirds*, offers Kauai art, and nearby **Kauai Fine Arts** offers an odd mix that works: antique maps and prints of Hawaii, authentic Polynesian tapa, rare wiliwili-seed leis, old Matson Liner menus, and a few pieces of contemporary island art. Down the street, in the Shimonishi Orchids building—a recommended stop for orchid lovers—the well-known impressionistic painter, **James Hoyle**, has set up his gallery, surrounded by flowers and the colors that inspire him.

Taking a cue from Maui's Lahaina, where every Friday night is Art Night, Hanapepe's gallery owners and artists recently instituted the **Friday Night Art Walk** every Friday from 6 to 9pm. The event signifies the debut of Hanapepe town as the island's emerging art center. Gallery owners take turns in hosting this informal event along Hanapepe Road, where nearly a dozen galleries display paintings, pottery, prints, sculpture, wood, and works by Kauai artists in all media. The host gallery provides hors d'oeuvres and beverages (or coffee and doughnuts). Some galleries, such as Lew Shortridge's **Kauai Village Gallery,** offer a 20% discount on originals on the nights they host the art night. Other galleries along the short stretch of Hanapepe Road include **Ralph Adamson's Lele Aka Gallery,** featuring his airbrushed and painted works and his son's handcrafted drums; the new **Kim Starr Gallery; The Koa Craftsman,** featuring the hand-turned and carved woods of Al Lopez and other Kauai crafters; the **Arius Hopman Studio,** next to the Hanapepe Café; and the **Dawn Traina Gallery,** featuring her powerful portraits of Hawaiian people.

WAIMEA Neighboring Waimea town is filled more with edibles than with art, with Kauai's favorite native supermarket, **Big Save,** serving as the one-stop shop for area residents and passerby heading for the uplands of Kokee State Park, some 4,000 feet above this sea-level village. A cheerful distraction for lovers of Hawaiian collectibles is **Collectibles and Fine Junque,** on Highway 50, where you'll discover what it's like to be the proverbial bull in a china shop (even a knapsack makes it hard to get through the aisles). Heaps of vintage linens, racks of choice aloha shirts and muumuus, rare glassware (and junque, too), books, ceramics, authentic 1950s cotton chenille bedspreads, and a back room full of bargain-priced secondhand goodies always capture my attention. This is my favorite stop in Waimea.

Up in Kokee State Park, the gift shop of the **Kokee Museum** (☎ **808/335-9975**) is the spot for botanical, geographical, historical, and nature-related books and gifts.

THE COCONUT COAST

As you make your way from Lihue to the North Shore, you'll pass **Bambulei,** next to the canefield in Wailua next to Caffe Coco (☎ **808/823-8641;** watch for the sign just past the Wailua intersection, home of Sizzler). Bambulei houses a charming collection of 1930s and 1940s treasures that owner Diane Blaize has amassed on her travels—everything from Peking lacquerware to exquisite vintage aloha shirts to lamps, quilts, jewelry, parrot figurines, and zany salt and pepper shakers. (Dresses go for $20 to $2,000.)

Wood turner ✪ **Robert Hamada** works in his studio at the foot of the Sleeping Giant, quietly producing museum-quality works with unique textures and grains. His skill, his lathe, and more than 60 years of experience bring luminous life to the kou, milo, kauila, camphor, mango, and native woods he logs himself.

KAPAA Moving toward Kapaa on Highway 56 (Kuhio Hwy.), don't get your hopes up; until you hit Kappa town, quality goods are slim in this neck of the woods. The **Coconut Marketplace** features the ubiquitous **Elephant Walk** gift shop, **Gifts of Kauai,** and various other underwhelming souvenir and clothing shops sprinkled among the ice cream, noodle, and sunglasses huts. My favorite shop in the marketplace is the unassuming **Overboard,** a small but tasteful menswear boutique with great aloha shirts by Kahala, Tommy Bahama, Duke Kahanamoku, and other top labels. Adjoining the menswear shop is a boutique with tropical leisurewear for women. One of the more attractive stops in the marketplace is the burnished, amberwashed **Indo-Pacific Trading Company,** sibling store to the one in Kukui Grove.

Nearby, set back from the main road across from **Foodland** supermarket, **Marta's Boat** is one of the island's more appealing boutiques for children and women. The shop is a tangle of accessories, toys, chic clothing with out-of-the-ordinary labels, and unusual gift items. Next door, **Ambrose's Kapuna Natural Foods** sells fresh Kauai fruit, nut butters, vitamins, and a small selection of healthy foods.

On the opposite side of Highway 56, in the **Waipouli Shopping Plaza** where Foodland and Blockbuster are located, the **Kia Gallery** (☎ **808/821-2672**) is *the* place for Hawaii-made crafts and gift items. The shop is full of Hawaiian soul and handmade crafts that reflect the island lifestyle. Included in the selection are an extensive collection of lauhala mats and accessories, clothing, wiliwili and other seed leis, Sig Zane designs, ukuleles, koa accessories, and sumptuous local woods.

In the green-and-white wooden storefronts of nearby **Kauai Village,** you'll find everything from **Wyland Galleries'** marine art to yin chiao Chinese cold pills and organic produce at **Papayas Natural Foods.** Although its prepared foods and is your only choice priced, Papayas carries the full range of health-food products and is your only choice in the area for vitamins, prepared health foods to go, health-conscious cosmetics, and bulk food items. **ABC, Longs Drugs,** and **Safeway** are the familiar anchors for groceries and staples, with sales that are well-known among savvy local shoppers. There's always a terrific sale on one brand or another of bottled water at ABC.

Less than a mile away on the main road, the **Waipouli Variety Store** is Kapaa's version of Maui's fabled Hasegawa General Store—a tangle of fishing supplies, T-shirts and thongs, beach towels, and souvenirs. Fishermen love this store as much as cookie lovers swear by nearby **Popo's Cookies,** the ne plus ultra of store-bought cookies on the island. Popo's chocolate-chip, macadamia-nut, and other varieties of butter-rich cookies are among the most sought-after food items to leave the island.

And Kapaa town is full of surprises. The biggest and best is **Kela's Glass Gallery** (☎ 808/822-4527), a gallery of handmade glass. It's actually a museum of glassworks in all sizes, shapes, and prices, a heady showcase for top-quality contemporary art in this medium, with the best selection in Hawaii. **Earth Beads,** on the main drag (Hwy. 56), sells beads, jewelry, gemstones, and crafts materials, along with a small selection of accessories for self and home. Across the street is the town's stellar fashion stop, **Island Hemp & Cotton,** where Hawaii's most stylish selection of this miracle fabric is sold: gorgeous silk-hemp dresses, linen-hemp sportswear, and cheap, comfortable clothing and accessories that have shed the hippie image. It's a great gift store with quality items, from Balinese leather goods to jewelry, luxury soaps and natural-fiber clothing for men and women. A few doors to the north, **Orchid Alley** gets my vote for most adorable nursery on the island. A narrow alcove opens into a greenhouse of phalaenopsis, oncidiums, lady's slippers, dendrobiums, and dozens of brilliant orchid varieties for shipping or hand-carrying. Farther north on this short block, **FreeBorn Music Center** is odd and wonderful, a cave of a store with island-made ukuleles, guitars, and other musical instruments, an espresso bar, and the best chocolate-chip cookies in town. When owners Casey and Mary Kay Havens aren't recording in the FreeBorn studio, there's live music in the evenings, often in the form of spontaneous jam sessions and impromptu performances (a Kapaa first). For more on FreeBorn, see "Dining," earlier in this chapter, and "Kauai After Dark," below.

THE NORTH SHORE

Like Haleiwa on Oahu, Kauai's North Shore has emerged as the premier shopping destination on the island. Chic galleries and sophisticated shops, such as ★ **Kong Lung** in Kilauea, in a 1942 stone building (the last to be built in the Kilauea Plantation) off Highway 56 on Kilauea Road (☎ 808/828-1822), and Ola's and Yellowfish Trading Company in Hanalei (see below) have launched these former hippie villages as must-stop shopping spots. Although Hanalei is toward the end of the road for those coming from Poipu and West Kauai, my advice is to save time, energy, and some discretionary funds for this end of the island, because the few shops that are here speak volumes about quality over quantity. Kong Lung, through all its changes, including pricier merchandise in every category, remains a showcase of design, style, and quality items, from top-of-the-line bath products to aloha shirts, jewelry, ceramics, women's wear, china, stationery, and personal and home accessories. It's expensive, but there's no other store like it on the island.

In Hanalei, at ✪ **Ola's,** by the Hanalei River on the Kuhio Highway (Hwy. 560) after the bridge (before the main part of Hanalei town; ☎ **808/826-6937**), Sharon and Doug Britt have amassed a head-turning assortment of American and island crafts, including Doug Britt's paintings and the one-of-a-kind furniture that he makes out of found objects, driftwood, and used materials. Britt's works—armoires, desks, tables, lamps, bookshelves—often serve as the display surfaces for others' work, so look carefully. Lundberg Studio handblown glass, exquisite jewelry, handpainted glass candlesticks, intricately wrought pewter switchplates, and many other fine works fill this tasteful, seductive shop.

Next door to Ola's, **Kai Kane** is a great source of aloha wear for men and women. Briny, brawny wave riders head straight for the second floor, where surfboards made by the up-and-coming North Shore shapers are sold to hard-core Hanalei Bay habitues. On the ground floor, Kahala shirts and dresses, slouchy linen separates, casual dresses, hats, and an ample selection of tropical wear offer great choices for the island lifestyle.

From health foods to groceries to Bakelite jewelry, the **Ching Young Village Shopping Center** in the heart of Hanalei covers a lot of bases. People are never in a rush here, and there are always clusters of people lingering at the few tables outdoors, where tables of Kauai papayas beckon from the entrance of the **Hanalei Health and Natural Foods** store. Next door, **Hot Rocket** is ablaze with surfwear, aloha shirts, jams sportswear, flamingo china, and for collectors, the finest array of Bakelite accessories on the island.

Across the street in the **Hanalei Center**, the standout boutique is the ✪ **Yellowfish Trading Company** (☎ **808/826-1227**), where owner Gritt Benton's impeccable eye and zeal for collecting are reflected in the 1920s to 1940s collectibles: menus, hula-girl nodders, hula lamps, rattan and koa furniture, vases, bark-cloth upholstery, handpainted silk lampshades, must-have vintage textiles, and wonderful finds in books and aloha shirts.

Our Kapaa favorite, **Island Hemp & Cotton Co.,** has joined the Hanalei brigade with a new shop, about the same size as its Kapaa store, at 4489 Aku Rd.

11 Kauai After Dark

by Jocelyn Fujii

Suffice it to say that one does not come to Kauai to trip the night fantastic. For that, you go to Maui or Oahu, but not Kauai. This is the island for winding down—from New York, Houston, even the hiking trails of Kokee or the Na Pali Coast.

But—surprise!—if you'd rather wind up than down, the usually sedate Kapaa town has a new entertainment center. **FreeBorn Music Center,** 1387 Kuhio Hwy, Kapaa (☎ **808/822-0400**), is hot to trot with live music on Wednesday through Saturday evenings. (See also "Dining," p. 558). Owner Casey Havens, a bass player, and his wife, Mary, a baker extraordinaire, combine their talents in this multifaceted music store-café-recording-studio-stage. Hawaiian music, recordings, jam sessions, band rehearsals, rock, jazz, country—it's a musical mother lode here.

There are two dance clubs on the island: **Gilligan's Disco,** at the Outrigger Kauai Beach Hotel, 4331 Kauai Beach Dr., Lihue (☎ **808/245-1955**); and Kuhio's (see below). Gilligan's is open for country line dancing on Thursday nights, line dancing and karaoke (ugh) on Friday evenings, and dancing to a deejay on Saturdays from 9pm to 1am, with a $5 cover charge. In the Outrigger's **Mele Lounge,** there's contemporary Hawaiian music nightly.

On the other side of the island, chic **Kuhio's**, at the Hyatt Regency Kauai Resort & Spa, 1571 Poipu Rd. (☎ **808/742-1234**), is the entertainment and dance center of the South Shore, open on Fridays and Saturdays from 9pm to 1:30am. The art-nouveau room features state-of-the-art technolgy (14 TV monitors, a sleek dance floor) to highlight its contemporary top-40 music selection. The $5 cover charge is waived for hotel guests. The Hyatt's **Stevenson's Library** revs up with live jazz nightly from 8 to 11pm.

Index

Page numbers in italics refer to maps. Note: The following abbreviations have been used in this index: BI = Big Island; H = Honolulu; K = Kauai; Ma = Maui; Mo = Molokai; O = Oahu.

FROMMER'S® COMPLETE TRAVEL GUIDES

(Comprehensive guides with selections in all price ranges—from deluxe to budget)

Alaska
Amsterdam
Arizona
Atlanta
Australia
Austria
Bahamas
Barcelona, Madrid & Seville
Belgium, Holland &
  Luxembourg
Bermuda
Boston
Budapest & the Best of
  Hungary
California
Canada
Cancún, Cozumel & the
  Yucatán
Cape Cod, Nantucket &
  Martha's Vineyard
Caribbean
Caribbean Cruises &
  Ports of Call
Caribbean Ports of Call
Carolinas & Georgia
Chicago
China
Colorado
Costa Rica
Denver, Boulder &
  Colorado Springs
England
Europe
Florida

France
Germany
Greece
Hawaii
Hong Kong
Honolulu, Waikiki & Oahu
Ireland
Israel
Italy
Jamaica & Barbados
Japan
Las Vegas
London
Los Angeles
Maryland & Delaware
Maui
Mexico
Miami & the Keys
Montana & Wyoming
Montréal & Québec City
Munich & the Bavarian Alps
Nashville & Memphis
Nepal
New England
New Mexico
New Orleans
New York City
Nova Scotia, New
  Brunswick &
  Prince Edward Island
Oregon
Paris
Philadelphia & the Amish
  Country

Portugal
Prague & the Best of the
  Czech Republic
Provence & the Riviera
Puerto Rico
Rome
San Antonio & Austin
San Diego
San Francisco
Santa Fe, Taos &
  Albuquerque
Scandinavia
Scotland
Seattle & Portland
Singapore & Malaysia
South Pacific
Spain
Switzerland
Thailand
Tokyo
Toronto
Tuscany & Umbria
USA
Utah
Vancouver & Victoria
Vermont, New Hampshire &
  Maine
Vienna & the Danube Valley
Virginia
Virgin Islands
Walt Disney World &
  Orlando
Washington, D.C.
Washington State

FROMMER'S® DOLLAR-A-DAY GUIDES

(The ultimate guides to comfortable low-cost travel)

Australia from $50 a Day
California from $60 a Day
Caribbean from $60 a Day
England from $60 a Day
Europe from $50 a Day
Florida from $60 a Day
Greece from $50 a Day
Hawaii from $60 a Day
Ireland from $50 a Day

Israel from $45 a Day
Italy from $50 a Day
London from $70 a Day
New York from $75 a Day
New Zealand from $50 a Day
Paris from $70 a Day
San Francisco from $60 a Day
Washington, D.C., from
  $60 a Day

FROMMER'S® MEMORABLE WALKS

Chicago
London

New York
Paris

San Francisco

FROMMER'S® PORTABLE GUIDES

Acapulco, Ixtapa/
  Zihuatanejo
Bahamas
California Wine
  Country
Charleston & Savannah
Chicago
Dublin
Las Vegas
London
Maine Coast
New Orleans
New York City
Paris
Puerto Vallarta, Manzanillo
  & Guadalajara
San Francisco
Sydney
Tampa Bay & St. Petersburg
Venice
Washington, D.C.

FROMMER'S® NATIONAL PARK GUIDES

Grand Canyon
National Parks of the American West
Yellowstone & Grand Teton
Yosemite & Sequoia/
  Kings Canyon
Zion & Bryce Canyon

THE COMPLETE IDIOT'S TRAVEL GUIDES

(The ultimate user-friendly trip planners)

Cruise Vacations
Planning Your Trip to Europe
Hawaii
Las Vegas
Mexico's Beach Resorts
New Orleans
New York City
San Francisco
Walt Disney World

SPECIAL-INTEREST TITLES

The Civil War Trust's Official Guide to
  the Civil War Discovery Trail
Frommer's Caribbean Hideaways
Israel Past & Present
New York City with Kids
New York Times Weekends
Outside Magazine's Adventure Guide
  to New England
Outside Magazine's Adventure Guide
  to Northern California
Outside Magazine's Adventure Guide
  to the Pacific Northwest
Outside Magazine's Guide to Family Vacations
Places Rated Almanac
Retirement Places Rated
Washington, D.C., with Kids
Wonderful Weekends from Boston
Wonderful Weekends from New York City
Wonderful Weekends from San Francisco
Wonderful Weekends from Los Angeles

THE UNOFFICIAL GUIDES®

(Get the unbiased truth from these candid, value-conscious guides)

Atlanta
Branson, Missouri
Chicago
Cruises
Disneyland
Florida with Kids
The Great Smoky
  & Blue Ridge
  Mountains
Las Vegas
Miami & the Keys
Mini-Mickey
New Orleans
New York City
San Francisco
Skiing in the West
Walt Disney World
Walt Disney World
  Companion
Washington, D.C.

FROMMER'S® IRREVERENT GUIDES

(Wickedly honest guides for sophisticated travelers)

Amsterdam
Boston
Chicago
London
Manhattan
New Orleans
Paris
San Francisco
Walt Disney World
Washington, D.C.

FROMMER'S® DRIVING TOURS

America
Britain
California
Florida
France
Germany
Ireland
Italy
New England
Scotland
Spain
Western Europe

WHEREVER YOU TRAVEL, HELP IS NEVER FAR AWAY.

From planning your trip to providing travel assistance along the way, American Express® Travel Service Offices are always there to help you do more.

Hawaii

OAHU

American Express Travel Service
Hilton Hawaiian Village
2005 Kalia Road
Honolulu
808-947-2607

American Express Travel Service
Hyatt Regency Waikiki
2424 Kalakaua Avenue
Honolulu
808-926-5441

American Express Travel Service
Commerce Tower, Suite 104
1440 Kapiolani Blvd.
Honolulu
808-946-7741

MAUI

American Express Travel Service
Westin Maui Hotel, Shop #101
2365 Kaanapali Pkwy
Lahaina
808-661-7155

American Express Travel Service
Ritz Carlton Kapalua
1 Ritz Carlton Drive
Lahaina
808-669-6200

American Express Travel Service
Grand Wailea Resort & Spa
3850 Wailea Alanui Drive
Wailea
808-875-4526

do more

AMERICAN EXPRESS ® Travel

http://www.americanexpress.com/travel
American Express Travel Service Offices are found in central locations throughout Hawaii.